The Continuing Case

© Getty Images

Greensburg, Kansas, had been struggling for years. Located along highway 54, a major trucking route, the town was merely a pit stop for people on their way somewhere else. It did have a few tourist attractions: the Big Well, the world's largest hand-dug well, and a 1,000-pound meteorite that fell from the sky in 2006.

Lonnie McCollum, the town's mayor, had been looking into ways to breathe new life into the town. McCollum wanted to add a little vintage charm to its quaint Main Street but could not raise the money. And he had launched a campaign to put the "green" back in Greensburg by promoting green building technology. But the idea, which many residents associated with hippies and tree-huggers, did not go over well.

Then everything changed. "My town is gone," announced Town Administrator Steve Hewitt on May 5, 2007, after surveying the damage caused by a devastating tornado. "I believe 95 percent of the homes are gone. Downtown buildings are gone, my home is gone." With a clean slate and 700 homes to replace, Hewitt vowed to rebuild Greensburg using sustainable materials. He believed the town had a unique opportunity to control its environmental impact and reduce operating costs through increased energy efficiency.

"What if we turned this tragedy into something beautiful?" asked resident Daniel Wallach in a new business plan he wrote shortly after the disaster. Wallach and his wife had long been interested in sustainable green living. Using their experience in developing nonprofits, the two launched Greensburg GreenTown, an organization designed to support Greensburg's green building efforts through education, fund-raising, and public relations management.

Through a series of brief video clips, students are exposed to several key aspects of the Greensburg rebuilding project. They will see Greensburg residents work through issues such as:

• Building Business in a Global Economy
• Starting and Growing a Business
• Management
• Marketing
• Technology and Information
• Finance

In addition to the video segments, at the end of each part in the textbook, students will find brief discussions highlighting the major issue discussed in that video segment along with three to four discussion questions. These questions are designed to be exercises in critical thinking—promoting discussion and interaction in the classroom. Suggested answers to the questions can be found in the Instructor's Manual, as can a complete video synopsis, list of text concepts covered in the videos, and additional critical-thinking exercises.

ALL THE HELP, RESOURCES, AND PERSONAL SUPPORT YOU AND YOUR STUDENTS NEED!

2-Minute Tutorials and all of the resources you & your students need to get started
www.wileyplus.com/firstday

Student support from an experienced student user Ask your local representative for details!

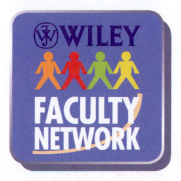

Collaborate with your colleagues, find a mentor, attend virtual and live events, and view resources
www.WhereFacultyConnect.com

Pre-loaded, ready-to-use assignments and presentations
www.wiley.com/college/quickstart

Technical Support 24/7 FAQs, online chat, and phone support
www.wileyplus.com/support

Your *WileyPLUS* Account Manager Training and implementation support
www.wileyplus.com/accountmanager

www.wileyplus.com

MAKE IT YOURS!

Contemporary BUSINESS

**13th Edition
2010 Update**

David L. Kurtz
Distinguished Professor and
R.A. and Vivian Young Chair of
Business Administration
University of Arkansas

John Wiley & Sons, Inc.
WILEY

The 13th edition 2010 Update of *Contemporary Business* is dedicated
to my new colleagues at John Wiley & Sons, Inc.

VP & EXECUTIVE PUBLISHER	*George Hoffman*
EXECUTIVE EDITOR	*Lise Johnson*
SENIOR EDITOR	*Franny Kelly*
DIRECTOR OF DEVELOPMENT	*Barbara Heaney*
PRODUCTION MANAGER	*Dorothy Sinclair*
SENIOR PRODUCTION EDITOR	*Valerie A. Vargas*
MARKETING MANAGER	*Diane Mars*
CREATIVE DIRECTOR	*Harry Nolan*
SENIOR DESIGNER	*Madelyn Lesure*
PRODUCTION MANAGEMENT SERVICES	*Elm Street Publishing Services*
SENIOR ILLUSTRATION EDITOR	*Anna Melhorn*
PHOTO DEPARTMENT MANAGER	*Hilary Newman*
PHOTO RESEARCHER	*Rose Alcorn*
ASSISTANT EDITOR	*Maria Guarascio*
EDITORIAL ASSISTANT	*Emily McGee*
EXECUTIVE MEDIA EDITOR	*Allison Morris*
ASSOCIATE MEDIA EDITOR	*Elena Santa Maria*
MARKETING ASSISTANT	*Laura Finley*
COVER PHOTO CREDIT	*Santokh Kochar/Photodisc/Getty Images*

This book was set in Times New Roman by Integra Software Services Pvt. Ltd. and printed and bound by R.R. Donnelley-JC. The cover was printed by R. R. Donnelley-JC.

ISBN-13   978-0-470-49674-9
ISBN-13   978-0-470-50343-0 (BRV ISBN)
Printed in the United States of America

10 9 8 7 6 5 4 3 2 1

About the Author

During Dave Kurtz's high school days, no one in Salisbury, Maryland, would have mistaken him for a scholar. In fact, he was a mediocre student, so bad that his father steered him toward higher education by finding him a succession of backbreaking summer jobs. Thankfully, most of them have been erased from his memory, but a few linger, including picking peaches, loading watermelons on trucks headed for market, and working as a pipefitter's helper. Unfortunately, these jobs had zero impact on his academic standing. Worse yet for Dave's ego, he was no better than average as a high school athlete in football and track.

But four years at Davis & Elkins College in Elkins, West Virginia, turned him around. Excellent instructors helped get Dave on a sound academic footing. His grade point average soared—enough to get him accepted by the graduate business school at the University of Arkansas, where he met Gene Boone. Gene and Dave became longtime co-authors; together they produced more than 50 books. In addition to writing, Dave and Gene were involved in several entrepreneurial ventures.

This long-term partnership ended with Gene's death in 2005. But, this book will always be Boone & Kurtz's *Contemporary Business*.

Today, Dave is back teaching at the University of Arkansas, after tours of duty in Ypsilanti, Michigan; Seattle, Washington; and Melbourne, Australia. He is the proud grandfather of five "perfect" kids and a sportsman with a golf handicap too high to mention. Dave, his wife, Diane, and four demanding canine companions (Daisy, Lucy, Molly, and Sally) live in Rogers, Arkansas. Dave holds a distinguished professorship at the Sam M. Walton College of Business in nearby Fayetteville, home of the Arkansas Razorbacks.

Dear Student,

Why this course? Remember your biology course in high school? Did you have one of those "invisible man" models (or maybe something more high-tech than that) that gave you the opportunity to look "inside" the human body? This introduction to business course offers something similar: to understand a business, you have to understand the components that make up that business.

This course will give you the perspective you need to understand how a business works, whether you are looking at a large multinational company like Microsoft or Starbucks or a single-owner software consulting business or coffee shop. As an employee, a manager, an investor, a business owner, or a manager of your own personal household—any of which roles you will have at some point in your life—you will be much the wiser for having taken this course.

Why this book? More than 2 million students have used this textbook. Your instructor has chosen it for you because of its trusted reputation. The authors have worked hard to keep the book fresh, timely, and accurate.

How to succeed? We've asked many students and many instructors whether there is a secret to success in this course. The nearly unanimous answer turns out to be not much of a secret:

Engage, engage, engage. The more you come to class, participate, study using the wealth of materials available with the book and in WileyPLUS—videos, flashcards, the various pedagogical features that this book provides—the more likely you are to learn the essential concepts, techniques, and methods of business.

The book contains features to help you learn best, whatever your learning style. To understand what your learning style is, spend about ten minutes to take the learning style quiz and see how you can apply an understanding of your learning style to this course.

Good luck in this course. We hope you enjoy the experience and that you put to good use throughout a lifetime of success the lessons you learn about business! We are sure you will not be disappointed.

What Are Learning Styles?

Have you ever repeated something to yourself over and over to help remember it? Or does your best friend ask you to draw a map to someplace where the two of you are planning to meet, rather than just tell her the directions? If so, then you already have an intuitive sense that people learn in different ways, Researchers in learning theory have developed various categories of learning styles. Some people, for example, learn best by reading or writing. Others learn best by using various senses— seeing, hearing, feeling, tasting, or even smelling. When you understand how you learn best, you can make use of learning strategies that will optimize the time you spend studying. To find out what your particular learning style is, www.wiley.com/college/boone and take the learning styles quiz you find there. The quiz will help you determine your primary learning style:

Visual Learner	Auditory Learner	Haptic Learner	Olfactory Learner
Print Learner	Interactive Learner	Kinesthetic Learner	

Then, consult the information below and on the following pages for study tips for each learning style. This information will help you better understand your learning style and how to apply it to the study of business.

Study Tips for Visual Learners

If you are a Visual Learner, you prefer to work with images and diagrams. It is important that you see information.

Visual Learning
- Draw charts/diagrams during lecture.
- Examine textbook figures and graphs.
- Look at images and videos on WileyPLUS and other Web sites.
- Pay close attention to charts, drawings, and handouts your instructor uses.
- Underline; use different colors.
- Use symbols, flowcharts, graphs, different arrangements on the page, white spaces.

Visual Reinforcement
- Make flashcards by drawing tables/charts on one side and definition or description on the other side.
- Use art-based worksheets; cover labels on images in text and then rewrite the labels.
- Use colored pencils/markers and colored paper to organize information into types.
- Convert your lecture notes into "page pictures." To do this:
  - Use the visual learning strategies outlined above.

– Reconstruct images in different ways.
– Redraw pages from memory.
– Replace words with symbols and initials.
– Draw diagrams where appropriate.
– Practice turning your visuals back into words.

If visual learning is your weakness: If you are not a Visual Learner but want to improve your visual learning, try re-keying tables/charts from the textbook.

Study Tips for Print Learners

If you are a Print Learner, reading will be important but writing will be much more important.

Print Learning
- Write text lecture notes during lecture.
- Read relevant topics in textbook, especially textbook tables.
- Look at text descriptions in animations and Web sites.
- Use lists and headings.
- Use dictionaries, glossaries, and definitions.
- Read handouts, textbooks, and supplementary library readings.
- Use lecture notes.

Print Reinforcement
- Rewrite your notes from class, and copy classroom handouts in your own handwriting.
- Make your own flashcards.
- Write out essays summarizing lecture notes or textbook topics.
- Develop mnemonics.
- Identify word relationships.
- Create tables with information extracted from textbook or lecture notes.
- Use text-based worksheets or crossword puzzles.
- Write out words again and again.
- Reread notes silently.

- Rewrite ideas and principles into other words.
- Turn charts, diagrams, and other illustrations into statements.
- Practice writing exam answers.
- Practice with multiple choice questions.
- Write paragraphs, especially beginnings and endings.
- Write your lists in outline form.
- Arrange your words into hierarchies and points.

If print learning is your weakness: If you are not a Print Learner but want to improve your print learning, try covering labels of figures from the textbook and writing in the labels.

Study Tips for Auditory Learners

If you are an Auditory Learner, then you prefer listening as a way to learn information. Hearing will be very important, and sound helps you focus.

Auditory Learning
- Make audio recordings during lecture.
- Do not skip class; hearing the lecture is essential to understanding.

- Play audio files provided by instructor and textbook.
- Listen to narration of animations.
- Attend lecture and tutorials.

- Discuss topics with students and instructors.
- Explain new ideas to other people.

Study Tips for Auditory Learners (Continued)

- Leave spaces in your lecture notes for later recall.
- Describe overheads, pictures, and visuals to somebody who was not in class.

Auditory Reinforcement
- Record yourself reading the notes and listen to the recording.
- Write out transcripts of the audio files.

- Summarize information that you have read, speaking out loud.
- Use a recorder to create self-tests.
- Compose "songs" about information.
- Play music during studying to help focus.
- Expand your notes by talking with others and with information from your textbook.
- Read summarized notes out loud.
- Explain your notes to another auditory learner.

- Talk with the instructor.
- Spend time in quiet places recalling the ideas.
- Say your answers out loud.

If auditory learning is your weakness: If you are not an Auditory Learner but want to improve your auditory learning, try writing out the scripts from pre-recorded lectures.

Study Tips for Interactive Learners

If you are an Interactive Learner, you will want to share your information. A study group will be important.

Interactive Learning
- Ask a lot of questions during lecture or TA review sessions.
- Contact other students, via e-mail or discussion forums, and ask them to explain what they learned.

Interactive Reinforcement
- "Teach" the content to a group of other students.
- Talking to an empty room may seem odd, but it will be effective for you.
- Discuss information with others, making sure that you both ask and answer questions.

- Work in small group discussions, making a verbal and written discussion of what others say.

If interactive learning is your weakness: If you are not an Interactive Learner but want to improve your interactive learning, try asking your study partner questions and then repeating them to the instructor.

Study Tips for Haptic Learners

If you are a Haptic Learner, you prefer to work with your hands. It is important to physically manipulate material.

Haptic Learning
- Take blank paper to lecture to draw charts/tables/diagrams.
- Using the textbook, run your fingers along the figures and graphs to get a "feel" for shapes and relationships.

Haptic Reinforcement
- Trace words and pictures on flashcards.
- Perform electronic exercises that involve drag-and-drop activities.
- Alternate between speaking and writing information.
- Observe someone performing a task that you would like to learn.

- Make sure you have freedom of movement while studying.

If haptic learning is your weakness: If you are not a Haptic Learner but want to improve your haptic learning, try spending more time in class working with graphs and tables while speaking or writing down information.

Study Tips for Kinesthetic Learners

If you are a Kinesthetic Learner, it will be important that you involve your body during studying.

Kinesthetic Learning
- Ask permission to get up and move during lecture.
- Participate in role-playing activities in the classroom.
- Use all your senses.
- Go to labs; take field trips.
- Listen to real-life examples.
- Pay attention to applications.
- Use trial-and-error methods.
- Use hands-on approaches.

Kinesthetic Reinforcement
- Make flashcards; place them on the floor, and move your body around them.
- Move while you are teaching the material to others.
- Put examples in your summaries.
- Use case studies and applications to help with principles and abstract concepts.
- Talk about your notes with another Kinesthetic person.

- Use pictures and photographs that illustrate an idea.
- Write practice answers.
- Role-play the exam situation.

If kinesthetic learning is your weakness: If you are not a Kinesthetic Learner but want to improve your kinesthetic learning, try moving flash cards to reconstruct graphs and tables, etc.

Study Tips for Olfactory Learners

If you are an Olfactory Learner, you will prefer to use the senses of smell and taste to reinforce learning. This is a rare learning modality.

Olfactory Learning
- During lecture, use different scented markers to identify different types of information.

Olfactory Reinforcement
- Rewrite notes with scented markers.

- If possible, go back to the computer lab to do your studying.
- Burn aromatic candles while studying.
- Try to associate the material that you're studying with a pleasant taste or smell.

If olfactory learning is your weakness: If you are not an Olfactory Learner but want to improve your olfactory learning, try burning an aromatic candle or incense while you study, or eating cookies during study sessions.

LEARNING STYLES SURVEY CHART

Resources	Visual	Print	Auditory	Interactive	Haptic	Kinesthetic
Hit & Miss	✔	✔		✔		
Launching Your Career	✔	✔		✔		
Learning Goals	✔	✔		✔		
They Said It	✔	✔				
Business Etiquette	✔	✔		✔		
Solving an Ethical Controversy	✔	✔				
Assessment Checks	✔	✔		✔		
Review Questions	✔	✔		✔		
Cases	✔	✔		✔		
Project/Teamwork Applications	✔	✔		✔		
Flashcards	✔	✔		✔	✔	✔
Business Terms	✔	✔		✔		
Interactive Quizzes	✔	✔		✔		
Student PowerPoints	✔	✔		✔	✔	
Audio Summary (English/Spanish)	✔	✔	✔	✔	✔	
Animated Figures	✔	✔	✔	✔	✔	
Case Study Animations	✔	✔	✔	✔	✔	✔
E-lectures	✔	✔	✔	✔	✔	
Greensburg, KS Continuing Case	✔	✔	✔	✔	✔	✔
End-of-Chapter Videos	✔	✔	✔	✔	✔	✔
Final Exam Questions	✔	✔		✔		
Quiz Questions	✔	✔		✔		
Pre-lecture Questions	✔	✔		✔		
Post-lecture Questions	✔	✔		✔		
Video Questions	✔	✔	✔	✔		✔
Drop-box Questions	✔	✔		✔		

Instructor and Student Resources

Contemporary Business features a full line of teaching and learning resources that were developed under the close review of the authors. Driven by the same basic beliefs as the textbook, these supplements provide a consistent and well-integrated learning system. This hands-on package guides *instructors* through the process of active learning and provides them with the tools to create an interactive learning environment. With its emphasis on activities, exercises, and the Internet, the package encourages *students* to take an active role in the course and prepares them for decision-making in a real-world context.

INSTRUCTOR'S ACTIVE TEACHING AIDS

WILEYPLUS is an online suite of resources that contains online homework, drill and practice activities with access to an online version of the text. *WileyPLUS* gives you the technology to create an environment where students reach their full potential and experience academic success. Instructor resources include a wealth of presentation and preparation tools, easy-to-navigate assignment and assessment tools, and a complete system to administer and manage your course exactly as you wish.

WileyPLUS is built around the activities you regularly perform:

PREPARE AND PRESENT CLASS PRESENTATIONS using relevant Wiley resources such as PowerPoint slides, image galleries (including all of the exhibits from the book), animations, and other *Wiley-PLUS* materials. You can also upload your own resources or Web pages to use in conjunction with Wiley materials.

CREATE ASSIGNMENTS by choosing from end-of-chapter questions, problems, and test bank questions organized by chapter, level of difficulty, and source—or add your own questions. *WileyPLUS* automatically grades students' homework and quizzes and records the results in your gradebook.

OFFER CONTEXT-SENSITIVE HELP TO STUDENTS, 24/7. When you assign homework or quizzes, you decide if and when students get access to hints, solutions, or answers (where appropriate), or students can be linked to relevant sections of their complete, online text for additional help whenever and wherever they need it most.

TRACK STUDENT PROGRESS. You can analyze students' results and assess their level of understanding on an individual and class level using the *WileyPLUS* gradebook, and you can export data to your own personal gradebook.

WEBCT, BLACKBOARD, D2L, OR ANGEL. Seamlessly integrate all of the rich *WileyPLUS* content and resource with the power and convenience of your WebCT, Angel, Blackboard, and D2L course—with a single sign-on.

BOOK COMPANION SITE—An extensive support package, including print and technology tools, helps you maximize your teaching effectiveness. We offer useful supplements for instructors with varying levels of experience and different instructional circumstances.

INSTRUCTOR'S COMPANION WEBSITE Password protected website **www.wiley.com/college/boone** offers instructors a complete package of teaching resources including:

TEST BANK Contains more than 4,000 questions. Each chapter of the test bank is organized by chapter objective and categorized by difficulty level, type of question, and text page reference.

BASIC AND ENHANCED POWERPOINT PRESENTATIONS WITH VIDEO CLIPS Basic PowerPoints provide an outline of the chapter, Web links, figures and tables from the chapter, as well as teaching notes for the instructor. Expanded PowerPoints provide a complete chapter overview, figures and tables, as well as video clips to enhance lecture material and give you more tools and interesting ways to present chapter concepts in class.

INSTRUCTOR'S RESOURCE CD The IRCD includes electronic versions of all of the instructor supplements: Instructor's Manual, Media Guide, Test Bank, and Diploma Testing Files and Software.

THE GREENSBURG, KS Continuing Video Cases Boone/Kurtz chose the *Greensburg, KS* rebuilding story to show how business works in the real world. Throughout the text, the new video cases combine the entrepreneurial and creative spirit with which *Greensburg* is being rebuilt. In these videos you will visit the town devastated by a horrific tornado, and the people who are rebuilding their lives and their town with a little business ingenuity and a lot of persistence.

CHAPTER VIDEO CASES ON DVD End-of-chapter video cases for every chapter of the text focus on successful real companies' processes, strategies, and procedures. Real employees explain real business situations with which they have been faced, bringing key concepts from the chapter to life.

PRE- AND POST-LECTURE QUESTIONS Brief quizzes designed to assess students' understanding of the material before and after class.

INSTRUCTOR'S MANUAL WITH COLLABORATIVE LEARNING EXERCISES AND MEDIA GUIDE This valuable tool completely integrates the various supplements and the text. A detailed lecture outline provides guidance about how to teach the chapter concepts. Collaborative learning exercises are included for each chapter, which give students a completely different way to apply chapter concepts to their own lives. References to the PowerPoint slides are included in the chapter outline. You'll also find answers to all of the end-of-chapter materials and various critical-thinking exercises.

WEBCT, BLACKBOARD, D2L, AND ANGEL offer an integrated set of course management tools that enable instructors to easily design, develop, and manage web-based and web-enhanced courses.

STUDENT ACTIVE LEARNING AIDS

The *WileyPLUS* course for *Contemporary Business* offers students several tools designed to help them grasp key business concepts discussed in the text. **"Read, Study, and Practice"** resources include the entire online textbook, with animation and interactive case studies. Additional resources include video clips and other problem-solving resources.

AUDIO CHAPTER REVIEWS ON CD Included with every purchase of a new copy of the 13th edition are the ever-popular audio chapter review CDs. Available in English and Spanish, these reviews give students a quick overview of the main chapter concepts, allowing them to review in the car, on foot, at the gym—anywhere! These audio chapter reviews will also be available for download within *WileyPLUS*.

AUDIO CHAPTER REVIEWS A comprehensive review of the chapter that is available for listening online or downloading.

KEY TERMS with definitions are provided online.

INTERACTIVE STUDENT QUIZZES are available for each chapter.

FLASHCARDS Using the end-of-chapter glossary terms, students will be able to review and practice the key terms by chapter.

STUDENT ELECTURES Narrated student PowerPoints.

CHAPTER VIDEO CASES AND GREENSBURG, KS VIDEOS Real world video cases with accompanying critical-thinking questions in the textbook.

Preface

Moving Business Forward... *Faster*

A part of every business is change; now more than ever, business moves at a pace that is unparalleled. Just like the ever-changing business world, so are there changes in the process of writing a textbook. Containing the most important introductory business topics, this 2010 Update of *Contemporary Business* includes the most current information available and the best supplementary package in the business. You'll find that this new edition gets your students excited about the world of business, helps them improve their critical-thinking skills, and will not only move your COURSE FORWARD FASTER but also move your STUDENTS FORWARD FASTER into the new business era.

MOVING INSTRUCTORS FORWARD...FASTER. Consistent with recent editions of *Contemporary Business,* the supplement package is designed to propel the instructor into the classroom with all the materials needed to engage students and help them understand text concepts. All the major teaching materials have been combined into one resource—the Instructor's Manual. While this might not sound revolutionary, good businesses know that the heart of the business is in its ability to keep track of all of its units. In the same way, our new Instructor's Manual combines all of the most important teaching materials into one stellar item. We've included collaborative learning exercises directly in the lecture outlines, so you'll know best where to use them. We've also included references to the PowerPoint slides throughout the lecture notes for your convenience. Greensburg, KS—our brand-new continuing case—is highlighted in all-new part videos, while chapter videos showcase a stellar list of companies, including standard-bearers such as Boeing and companies doing business with a brand new set of ideals such as Herman Miller. We've heard your appreciation for our PowerPoint presentations and have gone one step further: the PowerPoint presentations for this edition are tailored to meet the needs of all instructors, offering both a Basic and Expanded set. In addition, our new certified test bank, verified separately by two different sources, gives instructors that extra edge needed to drive home key concepts and ignite critical thinking, as well as confidence and assurance when creating and issuing tests.

MOVING STUDENTS FORWARD...FASTER. With *contemporary* being the operative word, we've showcased a new, exciting continuing case, the Greensburg, Kansas, rebuilding project. As always, every chapter is loaded with up-to-the-minute business issues and examples to enliven classroom discussion and debate, such as how "social entrepreneurs" are making their mark on emerging businesses. Processes, strategies, and procedures are brought to life through videos highlighting real companies and employees, an inventive business model, and collaborative learning exercises. And to further enhance the student learning process, we've developed an Introduction to Business–focused technology product, *WileyPLUS,* that integrates personalized learning along with a wealth of student and instructor resources.

How Boone & Kurtz Became the Leading Brand in the Market

For more than three decades, *Contemporary Business* has provided the latest in content and pedagogy. Our *current* editions have long been the model for our competitors' *next* editions. Consider Boone & Kurtz's proven record of providing instructors and students with pedagogical firsts:

- *Contemporary Business* was the first introductory business text written specifically for the student—rather than the instructor—featuring a motivational style students readily understood and enjoyed.
- *Contemporary Business* has always been based on marketing research, written the way instructors actually teach the course.
- *Contemporary Business* was the first text to integrate computer applications—and later, Internet assignments—into each chapter.
- *Contemporary Business* was the first business text to offer end-of-chapter video cases as well as end-of-part cases filmed by professional producers.
- *Contemporary Business* was the first to use multimedia technology to integrate all components of the Introduction to Business ancillary program, videos, and PowerPoint CD-ROMs for both instructors and students—enabling instructors to custom-create lively lecture presentations.

Wiley is proud to be publishing a book that has represented the needs of students and instructors so effectively and for so many years. The 2010 Update will continue this excellent tradition and will continue to move students and instructors FORWARD FASTER with new firsts.

Pedagogy

Contemporary Business has always employed extensive pedagogy—such as opening vignettes and boxed features—to breathe life into the exciting concepts and issues facing contemporary business. The 2010 Update is packed with updates and revisions to key pedagogical features, including:

- Business Etiquette
- Assessment Checks
- Teamwork Exercises
- Self-Quizzes
- Hit & Miss
- Solving an Ethical Controversy

Continuing to Build the Boone & Kurtz Brand

Because the business world is constantly MOVING FORWARD FASTER, the Introduction to Business course must keep pace. Trends, strategies, and practices are constantly changing, and students must understand how to perform business in today's world.

You've come to trust *Contemporary Business* to cover every aspect of the business world with a critical but fair eye. Let's face it: there are best business practices and those we'd never want to repeat. However, both provide learning opportunities, and we've always chosen to take a critical look at the way business is being done in the world and help students understand what they need to know in order to have a long and illustrious business career. Keeping this in mind, here are just a few of the important business trends and practices we've focused on for this new edition to help move students forward into a great business career.

What's New in the 2010 Update

THROUGHOUT THE TEXTBOOK the authors have made several global updates, including current Web site links and new chapter opening vignettes. Specific chapter updates are discussed below:

CHAPTER 5 This chapter includes a new table (Table 5.2) on the "Top Ten Franchises."

CHAPTER 6 This chapter includes significant updates to the section on "Categories of Entrepreneurs," as well as new coverage of business incubators and expanded coverage of equity loans and credit cards in the financing section. A new term, *social entrepreneur*, is discussed, along with a new table (Table 6.2) on "How Entrepreneurs Raise Startup Capital."

CHAPTER 7 This chapter was thoroughly revised and updated. Current trends in e-business are identified and discussed.

CHAPTER 9 This chapter includes new coverage of several topics, including Herzberg; hygiene and motivator factors; expectancy theory (with new Figure 9.5); new coverage of equity theory (new Figure 9.6); new coverage of MBO; new key term and discussion of job rotation; new coverage of affirmative action; new discussion of union versus nonunion benefits to members (new Table 9.1).

CHAPTER 10 This chapter includes expanded coverage of team diversity; open communication and the grapevine; new Figure 10.1 on "Formal and Informal Communication."

CHAPTER 11 This chapter includes expanded coverage of advantages of CIM; facility location decisions; disadvantages of outsourcing; new PERT diagram (Figure 11.7).

CHAPTER 15 This chapter was updated to reflect current trends in information systems. Changes include reduced coverage of computer hardware and software discussion; increased coverage of information systems and how businesspeople use them; additional discussion of information systems applications.

CHAPTER 16 This chapter saw significant enhancements to coverage of double-entry bookkeeping, along with more numerical examples; enhanced coverage of financial ratio analysis and budgeting; substantial increase in coverage of international accounting, including the trend toward the adoption of a single set of accounting rules and public reporting requirements for all global companies.

CHAPTER 17 The finance chapters (Chapters 17 and 18) were totally reorganized for this edition in response to user comments and suggestions. Chapter 17 focuses on the financial system: financial markets (such as the New York Stock Exchange), financial instruments (such as stocks and bonds), and financial institutions (such as commercial banks and the Federal Reserve). Chapter 18 covers financial management. In prior editions, these topics were split between Chapter 17 and 18. This new organizational structure is more logical and is consistent with the way in which introductory finance is typically taught.

CHAPTER 18 Chapter 18 in this edition focuses on financial management, the finance function, and the role of the financial manager in the organization. Updates include expanded coverage of sources of long- and short-term financing; enhanced coverage of asset management, including new sections on capital investment analysis and mergers.

Addressing the 2008 Credit Crisis

We have taken extraordinary measures to reflect the impact of the financial market crisis of summer and fall 2008. Changes have been made throughout the book, particularly in Chapter 17, to make sure we are as up to date as possible. Specific changes include:

- Updated Table 1.3, Fortune's Top Ten Most Admired Companies.
- Updated Table 4.4, The World's Leading Companies.
- Inclusion of IFRS discussion in Chapter 16.
- Updates to Chapter17 include the discussions of:
  - Subprime mortgages and the Office of Financial Stability.
  - The volatility of stock prices during the 2008 credit crisis.
  - The Morgan Stanley video case.
  - The Fed's role in the credit crisis and the bailout of AIG.

End-of-Chapter Video Cases

In addition to a fantastic new continuing video case, we've also produced a new set of video cases for each and every chapter, designed to exceed your every expectation. Students need to know the basics about life in the real world of business and how businesses succeed and grow, but they don't need a bunch of talking heads putting them to sleep. So while we admit that will indeed see a few talking heads—they're just there because they really do know what they're talking about—they have something important for students to hear. But do trust us ... the videos we've created for this new edition of *Contemporary Business* contain so much more!

A complete set of written cases accompanies these chapter videos and can be found in the end-of-book video case appendix chapter material. The written segments contain discussion questions. As with the Greensburg, KS continuing case, answers to the questions can be found in the Instructor's Manual, as can a complete video synopsis, a list of text concepts covered in the videos, and even more critical-thinking exercises. The video cases are as follows:

Video Case Chapter 1	Cannondale Keeps Satisfied Customers Rolling
Video Case Chapter 2	Timberland Walks the Walk
Video Case Chapter 3	Burton Snowboards Takes Demand for a Ride
Video Case Chapter 4	ESPN Broadcasts Sports around the World
Video Case Chapter 5	The UL Mark of Approval
Video Case Chapter 6	The Geek Squad to the Rescue!
Video Case Chapter 7	Manifest Digital: Putting the User First
Video Case Chapter 8	Made in the USA: American Apparel
Video Case Chapter 9	Replacements Ltd.: Dogs in the Workplace
Video Case Chapter 10	Meet the People of BP
Video Case Chapter 11	Washburn Guitars: Sound Since 1883
Video Case Chapter 12	WBRU Listens to Its Customers
Video Case Chapter 13	Monopoly: America's Love of Rags-to-Riches Games Is Timeless
Video Case Chapter 14	FUBU: For Us, By Us
Video Case Chapter 15	Peet's Coffee & Tea: Just What the Customer Ordered
Video Case Chapter 16	Taking Account: The Little Guys
Video Case Chapter 17	Morgan Stanley Likes Educated Customers
Video Case Chapter 18	Southwest Bucks Airline Industry Headwinds

Acknowledgments

Contemporary Business has long benefited from the instructors who have offered their time as reviewers. Comprehensive reviews of the 13th edition and ancillary materials were provided by the following colleagues:

Brenda Anthony
Tallahassee Community College

Lorraine P. Bassette
Prince George's Community College

Nathaniel R. Calloway
University of Maryland University College

Barbara Ching
Los Angeles City College

Rachna Condos
American River College

Susan J. Cremins
Westchester Community College

Tamara Davis
Davenport University

Colleen Dunn
Bucks County Community College

Joyce Ezrow
Anne Arundel Community College

Janice Feldbauer
Austin Community College

Chuck Foley
Columbus State Community College

Kathleen K. Ghahramani
Johnson County Community College

Connie Golden
Lakeland Community College

Susan Greer
Horry-Georgetown Technical College

Karen Halpern
South Puget Sound Community College

James V. Isherwood
Community College of Rhode Island

Mary Beth Klinger
College of Southern Maryland

Gary Cohen
University of Maryland

Claudia Levi
Edmonds Community College

Kathy Lorencz
Oakland Community College

Jayre Reaves
Rutgers University

Levi Richard
Citrus College

Jenny C. Rink
Community College of Philadelphia

Susan Roach
Georgia Southern University

Sandra Robertson
Thomas Nelson Community College

Barbara Rosenthal
Miami Dade College, Kendall Campus

JoDee Salisbury
Baker College

Rieann Spence-Gale
Northern Virginia Community College

Bob Urell
Irvine Valley College

Colette Wolfson
Ivy Tech Community College South Bend

In addition, the 13th edition benefited from respondents to an online survey. These colleagues include:

Ed Becker
Housatonic Community College

Cathleen Behan
North Virginia Community College

Vicki Bjerke
Northeast Iowa Community College

Robert Brinkmeyer
University of Cincinnati

Ronald Cereola
James Madison University

Leo Chiantelli
Shasta College

John Cicero
Shasta College

Robert M. Clark
Horry-Georgetown Technical College.

Douglas Crowe
Bradley University

Charles R. Fenner
State University of New York- Canton

Susan Greer
Horry-Georgetown Technical College

William Harvey
Henry Ford Community College

David Hollomon
Victor Valley College

Clark Lambert
Farmingdale State College

James R. Lashley
Bowie State University

Victor Lipe
Trident Technical College

Michael Mandel
Housatonic Community College

Gina McConoughey
Illinois Central College

Dennis R. Murphy
Horry-Georgetown Technical College

John Muzzo
Harold Washington University

Jack Partlow
Northern Virginia Community College

W.J. Patterson
Sullivan University

Michael Quinn
James Madison Univeristy

Rama Ramaswamy
Minneapolis Community and Technical College

JoAnn Rawley
Reading Area Community College

Donna Scarlett
Iowa Western Community College— Clarinda

Charles Smith
Horry-Georgetown Technical College

Michael Thomas
Henry Ford Community College

LaVena Wilkin
Sullivan University

I really appreciate the efforts and thoughts that went into these reviews and survey responses. Your comments have made *Contemporary Business* a better book.

Hundreds of people have contributed their suggestions over the years. I am most appreciative of their efforts and thoughts. Previous reviewers have included the following people:

Jamil Ahmad
Los Angeles Trade—Technical College

Sylvia Allen
Los Angeles Valley College

Kenneth F. Anderson
Borough of Manhattan Community College

Andrea Bailey
Moraine Valley Community College

Norman E. Burns
Bergen Community College

Diana Carmel
Golden West College

Barbara Ching
Los Angeles City College

Ron Colley
South Suburban College

Scott Colvin
Naugatuck Community College

Peter Dawson
Collin County Community College

Dr. Richard L. Drury
Northern Virginia Community College

John A. Fawcett
Norwalk Community College

Dr. Barry Freeman
Bergen Community College

Richard Ghidella
Fullerton College

Ross Gittell
University of New Hampshire

Clark Hallpike
Elgin Community College

Carnella Hardin

Glendale College—Arizona

Britt Hastey
Los Angeles City College

Dave Hickman
Frederick Community College

Nathan Himelstein
Essex County College

Scott Homan
Purdue—West Lafayette

Howard L. Irby, Jr.
Bronx Community College

Robert Ironside
North Lake College

Charlotte Jacobsen
Montgomery College

Bruce Johnson
College of the Desert

Judith Jones
Norwalk Community College

Marce Kelly
Santa Monica College

Gregory Kishel
Cypress College—Santa Ana College

Patricia Kishel
Cypress College

Andy Klein
DeVry University

Mary Beth Klinger
College of Southern Maryland

John S. Leahy
Palomar College

Delores Linton
Tarrant County College–Northwest Campus

Stacy Martin
Southwestern Illinois College

Theresa Mastrianni
Kingsborough Community College

Bob Matthews
Oakton Community College

Hugh McCabe
Westchester Community College

Tricia McConville
Northeastern University

Rebecca Miles
Delaware Tech

Linda Morable
Richland College

Linda Mosley

Tarrant County College

Carol Murphy
Quinsigamond Community College

Andrew Nelson
Montgomery College

Greg Nesty
Humboldt College

Linda Newell
Saddleback College

Emmanuel Nkwenti
Pennsylvania College of Technology

Paul Okello
Tarrant County College

Lynn D. Pape
Northern Virginia Community College—Alexandria Campus

Charles Pedersen
Quinsigamond Community College

John Pharr
Cedar Valley—Dallas County Community College District

Jeff Podoshen
DeVry University

Sally Proffitt
Tarrant County College Northeast

Jude A. Rathburn
University of Wisconsin—Milwaukee

Levi Richard
Citrus College

Joe Ryan
Valley College

Althea Seaborn
Norwalk Community College

John Seilo
Orange Coast Community College

Pat Setlik
Harper College

Richard Sherer
Los Angeles Trade—Technical College

Gerald Silver
Purdue University—Calumet

Leon Singleton
Santa Monica College

Malcolm Skeeter
Norwalk Community College

Robert Smolin
Citrus College

Darrell Thompson
Mountain View College

Sandra Toy
Orange Coast College

Phil Vardiman
Abilene Christian University

Sal Veas
Santa Monica College

Gina Vega
Merrimack College

Michelle Vybiral
Joliet Junior College

Rick Weidmann
Prince George's Community College

S. Martin Welc
Saddleback College

Steve Wong
Rock Valley College

A number of other colleagues at colleges and universities throughout the United States participated in focus group sessions. They provided invaluable recommendations for this new edition. They include the following people:

Greg Akins
Lansing Community College

Ken Anderson
Borough of Manhattan Community College

Nancy Bailey
Middlesex Community College

Mary Barnum
Grand Rapids Community College

Sherry Bell
Ferris State University

Ellen Benowitz
Mercer Community College

Mike Bento
Owens Community College

Pat Bernson
County College of Morris

Trudy Borst
Ferris State University

David Braun
Pierce College

David England
John A. Logan College

Barry Freeman
Bergen Community College

Eric Glohr
Lansing Community College

Karen Hawkins
Miami Dade Community College

Nate Himelstein
Essex Community College

Kim Hurns
Washtenaw Community College

Dmitriy Kalyagin
Chabot College

Elias Konwufine
Keiser College

Carl Kovelowski
Mercer Community College

Pierre Laguerre
Bergen Community College

Stacy Martin
Southwestern Illinois College

Duane Miller
Utah Valley State College

Ed Mitchell
Hillsborough Community College

Frank Novakowski
Davenport University

Tom Passero
Owens Community College

Tom Perkins
Lansing Community College

Robert Reck
Western Michigan University

Paul Ricker
Broward Community College

Jenny Rink
Community College of Philadelphia

Susan Roach
Georgia Southern University

Edith Strickland
Tallahassee Community College

Keith Taylor
Lansing Community College

Joyce Thompson
Lehigh-Carbon Community College

Bob Urell
Irvine Valley College

Richard Warner
Lehigh-Carbon Community College

David Woolgar
Santa Ana College

Chuck Zellerbach
Orange Coast College

Thanks also to all of our colleagues who have assisted us in previous edi-

tions in our continuing efforts to make the best business text even better. The new edition continues to reflect so many of their recommendations. Among the hundreds of reviewers and focus group participants who contributed to the book during previous editions, we acknowledge the special contributions of the following people:

Alison Adderly-Pitman
Brevard Community College

David Alexander
Angelo State University

Kenneth Anderson
Mott Community College

Charles Armstrong
Kansas City Kansas Community College

Donald B. Armstrong
Mesa College

Nathaniel Barber
Winthrop University

Alan Bardwick
Community College of Aurora

Keith Batman
Cayuga Community College

Robb Bay
Community College of Southern Nevada

Charles Beem
Bucks County Community College

Carol Bibly
Triton College

Daniel Biddlecom
Erie Community College—North Campus

Joseph Billingere
Oxnard College

Larry Blenke
Sacramento City College

Paula E. Bobrowski
SUNY Oswego

Charlane Bomrad Held
Onandaga Community College

Brenda Bradford
Missouri Baptist College

Steven E. Bradley
Austin Community College

Willie Caldwell
Houston Community College

Barney Carlson
Yuba College

Bonnie Chavez
Santa Barbara City College

Felipe Chia
Harrisburg Area Community College

Rowland Chidomere
Winston-Salem State University

Marie Comstock
Allan Hancock College

Ronald C. Cooley
South Suburban College

Suzanne Counte
Jefferson College

Robert Cox
Salt Lake Community College

Pam Crader
Jefferson College

Norman B. Cregger
Central Michigan University

Dana D'Angelo
Drexel University

Dean Danielson
San Joaquin College

Kathy Daruty
Los Angeles Pierce College

David DeCook
Arapahoe Community College

Richard L. Drury
Northern Virginia Area Community College—Annandale

Linda Durkin
Delaware County Community College

Lance J. Edwards
Otero Junior College

William Ewald
Concordia University

Carol Fasso
Jamestown Community College

Jodson Faurer
Metropolitan State College at Denver

Jan Feldbauer
Austin Community College

Sandie Ferriter
Harford Community College

Steven H. Floyd
Manatee Community College

Nancy M. Fortunato
Bryant and Stratton

John G. Foster Jr.
Montgomery College—Rockville

William D. Foster
Fontbonne College

Blane Franckowiak
Tarrant County Community College

Edward Friese
Okaloosa-Walton Community College

Atlen Gastineau
Valencia Community College—West Campus

Milton Glisson
North Carolina A&T State University

Bob Googins
Shasta Community College

Robert Gora
Catawba Valley Community College

Don Gordon
Illinois Central College

Gary Greene
Manatee Community College

Blaine Greenfield
Bucks County Community College

Stephen W. Griffin
Tarrant County Community College

Maria Carmen Guerrero-Caldero
Oxnard College

Annette L. Halpin
Beaver College

Michael Hamberger
Northern Virginia Area Community College—Annandale

Neal Hannon
Bryant College

Douglas Heeter
Ferris State University

Paul Hegele
Elgin Community College

Chuck Henry
Coastline Community College

Thomas Herbek
Monroe Community College

Tom Heslin
Indiana University, Bloomington

Joseph Ho
College of Alameda

Alice J. Holt
Benedict College

Vince Howe
University of North Carolina, Wilmington

Eva M. Hyatt
Appalachian State University

Kathy Irwin
Catawba Valley Community College

Gloria M. Jackson
San Antonio College

Ralph Jagodka
Mount San Antonio College

Chris Jelepis
Drexel University

Steven R. Jennings
Highland Community College

Geraldine Jolly
Barton College

Dave Jones
LaSalle University

Don Kelley
Francis Marion University

Bill Kindsfather
Tarrant County Community College

Charles C. Kitzmiller
Indian River Community College

B. J. Kohlin
Pasadena City College

Carl Kovelowski
Mercer Community College

Ken Lafave
Mount San Jacinto College

Rex Lambrecht
Northeastern Junior College

Fay D. Lamphear
San Antonio College

Bruce Leppine
Delta College

Thomas Lloyd
Westmoreland County Community College

Jim Locke
Northern Virginia Area Community College—Annandale

Paul Londrigan
Mott Community College

Kathleen J. Lorencz
Oakland County Community College

John Mack
Salem State College

Paul Martin
Aims College

Lori Martynowicz
Bryant and Stratton

Michael Matukonis
SUNY Oneonta

Virginia Mayes
Montgomery College—Germantown

Joseph E. McAloon
Fitchburg State College

James McKee
Champlain College

Michael McLane
University of Texas, San Antonio

Ina Midkiff
Austin Community College

Rebecca Mihelcic
Howard Community College

Richard Miller
Harford Community College

Joseph Mislivec
Central Michigan University

Kimberly K. Montney
Kellogg Community College

Gail Moran
Harper College

Linda S. Munilla
Georgia Southern University

Kenneth R. Nail
Pasco-Hernando Community College

Joe Newton
Buffalo State College

Janet Nichols
Northeastern University

Frank Nickels
Pasco-Hernando Community College

Sharon Nickels
St. Petersburg Junior College

Nnamdi I. Osakwe
Livingstone College

Tibor Osatreicher
Baltimore City Community College

George Otto
Truman College

Thomas Paczkowski
Cayuga Community College

Alton Parish
Tarrant County Community College

Jack Partlow
Northern Virginia Area Community College—Annandale

Jeff Penley
Catawba Valley Community College

Robert Pollero
Anne Arundel Community College

Alton J. Purdy
Solano Community College

Surat P. Puri
Barber Scottia College

Angela Rabatin
Prince George's Community College

Linda Reynolds
Sacramento City College

Brenda Rhodes
Northeastern Junior College

Merle Rhodes
Morgan Community College

Pollis Robertson
Kellogg Community College

Robert Ross
Drexel University

Benjamin Sackmary
Buffalo State College

Catherina A. Sanders
San Antonio College

Lewis Schlossinger
Community College of Aurora

Gene Schneider
Austin Community College

Raymond Shea
Monroe Community College

Nora Jo Sherman
Houston Community College

Leon J. Singleton
Santa Monica College

Jeff Slater
North Shore Community College

Candy Smith
Folsom Lakes College

Solomon A. Solomon
Community College of Rhode Island

R. Southall
Laney College

Martin St. John
Westmoreland County Community College

E. George Stook
Anne Arundel Community College

James B. Stull
San Jose State University

Bill Syverstein
Fresno City College

Thomas Szezurek
Delaware County Community College

Daryl Taylor
Pasadena City College

John H. Teter
St. Petersburg Junior College

Gary Thomas
Anne Arundel Community College

Michael Thomas
Henry Ford Community College

Frank Titlow
St. Petersburg Junior College

Roland Tollefson
Anne Arundel Community College

Sheb True
Loyola Marymount University

Robert Ulbrich
Parkland College

Ariah Ullman
SUNY Binghamton

Sal Veas
Santa Monica College

Steven Wade
Santa Clara University

Dennis Wahler
San Jacinto Evergreen Community College District

W. J. Walters
Central Piedmont Community College

Timothy Weaver
Moorpark College

Richard Wertz
Concordia University

Darcelle D. White
Eastern Michigan University

Jean G. Wicks
Bornie State University

Tom Wiener
Iowa Central Community College

Dave Wiley
Anne Arundel Community College

Richard J. Williams
Santa Clara University

Joyce Wood
Northern Virginia Community College

Gregory Worosz
Schoolcraft College

Martha Zennis
Jamestown Community College

In Conclusion

I would like to thank Heather Johnson, Karen Hill, and the staff at Elm Street Publishing Services. Their unending efforts on behalf of *Contemporary Business* were truly extraordinary. I would also like to thank Gary Cohen at the University of Maryland for his valuable feedback.

Let me conclude by noting that this new edition would never have become a reality without the outstanding efforts of the Wiley editorial, production, and marketing teams. Special thanks to George Hoffman, Lise Johnson, Amy Scholz, and Franny Kelly.

Dave Kurtz

Dave Kurtz

Brief Contents

Contents

Part 1   Business in a Global Environment   1

chapter 1   The Changing Face of Business   2

Part 2   Starting and Growing Your Business   139

chapter 5   **Options for Organizing Small and Large Businesses**   **140**

chapter 6

Starting Your Own Business: The Entrepreneurship Alternative   **180**

Part 3   Management: Empowering People to Achieve Business Objectives   251

chapter 8   Management, Leadership, and the Internal Organization   252

chapter 12 — Customer-Driven Marketing

Part 5 — Managing Technology and Information — 495

chapter 15 — Using Technology to Manage Information — 496

chapter 16   Understanding Accounting and Financial Statements   **522**

Opening Vignette
Mark-to-Market
Accounting: Who Takes
the Hit? 523

Hit & Miss
Forensic Accountants:
Calculating "Who Done
It" 527

Business Etiquette
Auditing Etiquette 529

**Solving an Ethical
Controversy**
The Burden of
Sarbanes-Oxley on
Small Business 530

Hit & Miss
Accounting Is Booming in
Vietnam 545

appendixes

Contemporary BUSINESS

Part 1

Business in a Global Environment

© Masterfile

chapter

1

The Changing Face of Business

Ugg Sales Have Traction

What brand of footwear is clunky, lacks support for arches and ankles, is no longer new, isn't even waterproof, but is wildly popular? If you guessed Ugg, you're right. The plain sheepskin boots, originally from Australia, have yet to wear out their welcome among fashion-conscious buyers in the United States despite several years of intense popularity. You might even be wearing a pair of Uggs right now. In fact, Uggs, once expected to be a short-lived fad, have grown into a beloved wardrobe staple for millions, in spite of the fact that their very name comes from the word "ugly." They continue to fly off the shelves even as an economic recession slows consumer spending on a wide range of goods and services. They are a highly sought item on eBay as well. According to AMG, which imports Uggs to the United Kingdom, sales of Uggs in UK stores increased 140 percent in a recent six-month period and show no signs of slowing down.

Uggs got their start in Australia, where the boots were first worn by sheepshearers. The footwear soon caught on with Australian surfers, who appreciated the warmth of their woolly lining. Three decades ago, Brian Smith founded his own company to import Uggs into California, reasoning that U.S. surfers would like them, too. But their popularity began to climb when Deckers Outdoor Corporation bought Ugg Australia from Smith in 1995. Deckers saw the boots as a high-end fashion item to sell in limited quantities. The strategy worked: the boots soon attracted the attention of celebrities like Oprah Winfrey. Winfrey purchased Uggs for her entire staff—350 pairs at a cost of more than $50,000—and then put Uggs on her famous list of favorite things for several years. Upscale department store chain Nordstrom agreed to carry them in its shoe departments across the United States. Stars such as Pamela Anderson, Jennifer Aniston, and Kate Hudson were soon photographed wearing Uggs, and the boots turned up at movie sets and film festivals around the country. When Sarah Jessica Parker wore a pair of custom red Uggs on the television show "Sex and the City," a limited-edition replica quickly sold out in retail shops. Uggs became a genuine fashion hit.

Despite their high price, cheaper imitators, and detractors who found them clunky, the boots became a must-have for women, kids, and teens. Deckers ramped up production and began selling Uggs in a range of fashionable colors and styles, and U.S. sales quickly rose, recently topping $400 million annually. But "we didn't want to be known for just one item," says the president of the California firm. So the company expanded into related products—lines of slippers, sandals, clogs, flip-flops, hats, coats, handbags, and even pillows and rugs have brought the Ugg name even more attention and helped establish it internationally.

How have Uggs not only survived but prospered in difficult economic times? "We hate the word 'trendy,'" says a brand spokesperson. "We would want to stay away from that word." While trendiness certainly helped the boots get their start, it doesn't account for their long-lasting popularity. Nor does cold weather; Uggs are still popular in sunny California, and even where winters are cold, some fans wear their boots year-round. The company's award-winning online store, its many retail partners around the world, and a solid distribution system make Uggs easy to obtain in the sizes and colors consumers want. To keep the line fresh, new looks are introduced every season. But availability and innovation aren't the only reasons this trend became a standard as reliable as a white T-shirt or denim jeans. Warmth and comfort from the natural qualities of sheepskin have certainly had something to do with it. Another contributor to success is the boots' instantly recognizable, if slightly quirky, appearance. Says Mohamed Ibrahim, who writes a blog with photos of famous people wearing Uggs (www.igotuggs.com), "It's the way they look. They have this special appeal."

The company isn't resting on its heels. Uggs's next act is a push to get men to adopt the style. "It's a feel-good brand," says the president of Ugg Australia. "We're all about comfort and luxury. And at a time when people might not be able to remodel their house or buy a new car, they can buy a pair of boots." The company is being patient with men, who it recognizes aren't often fashion-conscious. On the other hand, Uggs have already been spotted on the feet of a whole team of English soccer players and on Brad Pitt, Justin Timberlake, Harvey Keitel, and Ronnie Wood.

In the meantime, the only section of Chicago's Nordstrom store that was busy on a recent weekday was the Ugg section of the shoe department, where every seat was filled with women happily trying on floppy sheepskin boots.[1]

Business is the nation's engine for growth. A growing economy—one that produces more goods and services with fewer resources over time—yields income for business owners, their employees, and stockholders. So a country depends on the wealth its businesses generate, from large enterprises like the Walt Disney Company to tiny ones like online jewelry retailer www.thatspretty.com, and from venerable firms like 150-year-old jeans maker Levi Strauss & Company to new powerhouses like Google. What all these companies and many others share is a creative approach to meeting society's needs and wants.

Businesses solve our transportation problems by marketing cars, tires, gasoline, and airline tickets. They bring food to our tables by growing, harvesting, processing, packaging, and shipping everything from spring water to cake mix and frozen shrimp. Restaurants buy, prepare, and serve food, and some even deliver. Construction companies build our schools, homes, and hospitals, while real estate firms bring property buyers and sellers together. Clothing manufacturers design, create, import, and deliver our jeans, sports shoes, work uniforms, and party wear. Entertainment for our leisure hours comes from hundreds of firms that create, produce, and distribute films, television shows, video-games, books, and music CDs and downloads.

To succeed, business firms must know what their customers want so that they can supply it quickly and efficiently. That means they often reflect changes in consumer tastes, such as the growing preference for sports drinks and vitamin-fortified water. But firms can also *lead* in advancing technology and other changes. They have the resources, the human know-how, and the financial incentive to bring about real innovations, such as the iPhone, new cancer treatments, and alternative energy sources like wind power. Thus, when businesses succeed, everybody wins.

You'll see throughout this book that businesses require physical inputs like auto parts, chemicals, sugar, thread, and electricity, as well as the accumulated knowledge and experience of their managers and employees. Yet they also rely heavily on their own ability to change with the times and with the marketplace. Flexibility is a key to long-term success—and to growth.

In short, business is at the forefront of our economy—and *Contemporary Business* is right there with it. This book explores the strategies that allow companies to grow and compete in today's interactive marketplace, along with the skills that you will need to turn ideas into action for your own success in business. This chapter sets the stage for the entire text by defining business and revealing its role in society. The chapter's discussion illustrates how the private enterprise system encourages competition and innovation while preserving business ethics.

What Is Business?

business all profit-seeking activities and enterprises that provide goods and services necessary to an economic system.

What comes to mind when you hear the word *business?* Do you think of big corporations like General Electric or Microsoft? Or does the local bakery or shoe store pop into your mind? Maybe you recall your first summer job. The term *business* is a broad, all-inclusive term that can be applied to many kinds of enterprises. Businesses provide the bulk of employment opportunities, as well as the products that people enjoy.

Business consists of all profit-seeking activities and enterprises that provide goods and services necessary to an economic system. Some businesses produce tangible goods, such as automobiles, breakfast cereals, and digital music players; others provide services such as insurance, hair styling, and entertainment ranging from Six Flags theme parks and sports events to concerts.

Business drives the economic pulse of a nation. It provides the means through which its citizens' standard of living improves. At the heart of every business endeavor is an exchange between a buyer and a seller. A buyer recognizes a need for a good or service and trades money with a seller to obtain that product. The seller participates in the process in hopes of gaining profits—a main ingredient in accomplishing the goals necessary for continuous improvement in the standard of living.

Profits represent rewards for businesspeople who take the risks involved in blending people, technology, and information to create and market want-satisfying goods and services. In contrast, accountants think of profits as the difference between a firm's revenues and the expenses it incurs in generating these revenues. More generally, however, profits serve as incentives for people to start companies, expand them, and provide consistently high-quality competitive goods and services. Fuel refiners, for instance, are adding more ethanol to their gasoline products than the government has so far mandated, because when the price of crude oil rises, it squeezes their profits. According to the senior vice president of one energy company, refiners' decision to increase the blend of ethanol "was primarily driven by economics in the marketplace. It was not driven by mandates, either at the state level or federal level. That really is what is carrying the day for us today as we see the growth in the ethanol supply." But the search for and production of alternative fuels such as ethanol can provide more alternatives for customers and society in the future.[2]

The quest for profits is a central focus of business because without profits, a company could not survive. But businesspeople also recognize their social and ethical responsibilities. To succeed in the long run, companies must deal responsibly with employees, customers, suppliers, competitors, government, and the general public.

Not-for-Profit Organizations

What do Ohio State's athletic department, the U.S. Postal Service, the American Heart Association, and your local library have in common? They are all classified as **not-for-profit organizations,** businesslike establishments that have primary objectives other than returning profits to their owners. These organizations play important roles in society by placing public service above profits, although it is important to understand that these organizations need to raise money so that they can operate and achieve their social goals. Not-for-profit organizations operate in both the private and public sectors. Private-sector not-for-profits include museums, libraries, trade associations, and charitable and religious organizations. Government agencies, political parties, and labor unions, all of which are part of the public sector, are also classified as not-for-profit organizations.

Not-for-profit organizations are a substantial part of the U.S. economy. Currently, 1.5 million nonprofit organizations are registered with the Internal Revenue Service in the United States, in categories ranging from arts and culture to science and technology.[3] These organizations control more than $2 trillion in assets and employ more people than the federal government and all 50 state governments combined.[4] In addition, millions of volunteers work for them in unpaid positions. Not-for-profits secure funding from both private sources, including donations, and government sources. They are commonly exempt from federal, state, and local taxes.

Although they focus on goals other than generating profits, managers of not-for-profit organizations face many of the same challenges as executives of profit-seeking businesses. Without funding, they cannot do research, obtain raw materials, or provide services. St. Jude Children's Research Hospital is the third-largest U.S. healthcare charity. Its pediatric treatment

profits rewards for businesspeople who take the risks involved to offer goods and services to customers.

St. Jude patient Yasmine with her mother

Honor a friend...
Remember a loved one

Honor the accomplishments of a friend or remember a loved one by making a donation in their name to St. Jude Children's Research Hospital®, the world's premier pediatric cancer research center.

Your gift of life to children around the world.

Memorial & Honor Department
501 St. Jude Place
Memphis, TN 38105
1.800.873.6983
www.stjude.org/tribute

St. Jude Children's Research Hospital
ALSAC • Danny Thomas, Founder

Finding cures. Saving children.

Managers of not-for-profit organizations face many of the same challenges as managers of profit-making organizations. To fund research and care for seriously ill children regardless of their parent's means, St. Jude Children's Research Hospital relies on charitable contributions and research grants.

© 2009 St. Jude Children's Research Hospital, a not-for-profit, section

factors of production four basic inputs for effective operation: natural resources, capital, human resources, and entrepreneurship.

and research facility in Memphis treats nearly 5,000 children a year for catastrophic diseases, mainly cancer, immune system problems, and infectious and genetic disorders. Patients come from all over the world and are accepted without regard to the family's ability to pay. To provide top-quality care and to support its research in gene therapy, chemotherapy, bone marrow transplantation, and the psychological effects of illness, among many other critical areas, St. Jude relies on contributions, with some assistance from federal grants and investments.[5] Other not-for-profits mobilize their resources to respond to emergencies, as the Red Cross did following the ice storms that devastated areas of Oklahoma, Missouri, Arkansas, Illinois, Indiana, Ohio, Tennesee, and Kentucky. Thousands of residents fled power outages for warmth and meals in 75 shelters while utility companies worked to repair the damage from snapped tree limbs and downed transmission lines.[6]

Some not-for-profits sell merchandise or set up profit-generating arms to provide goods and services for which people are willing and able to pay. College bookstores sell everything from sweatshirts to coffee mugs with school logos imprinted on them, while the Sierra Club and the Appalachian Mountain Club both have full-fledged publishing programs. The Lance Armstrong Foundation has sold more than 40 million yellow Live Strong wristbands as well as sports gear and accessories for men, women, and children in the United States and abroad, with the money earmarked to fight cancer and support patients and families.[7] Handling merchandising programs like these, as well as launching other fund-raising campaigns, requires managers of not-for-profit organizations to develop effective business skills and experience. Consequently, many of the concepts discussed in this book apply to not-for-profit organizations as well as to profit-oriented firms.

Factors of Production

An economic system requires certain inputs for successful operation. Economists use the term **factors of production** to refer to the four basic inputs: natural resources, capital, human resources, and entrepreneurship. Table 1.1 identifies each of these inputs and the type of payment received by firms and individuals who supply them.

Natural resources include all production inputs that are useful in their natural states, including agricultural land, building sites, forests, and mineral deposits. The sawmill operated by Willamette Industries in the little town of Dallas, Oregon, takes 2,500-pound second-growth logs from Oregon's hillsides and cuts them into boards. Other companies use natural resources after they have been processed by companies like Willamette. Natural resources are the basic inputs required in any economic system.

Capital, another key resource, includes technology, tools, information, and physical facilities. *Technology* is a broad term that refers to such machinery and equipment as computers and software, telecommunications, and inventions designed to improve production. Information, frequently improved by technological innovations, is another critical factor because both managers and operating employees require accurate, timely information for effective performance of their

Table 1.1	Factors of Production and Their Factor Payments
Factor of Production	**Corresponding Factor Payment**
Natural resources	Rent
Capital	Interest
Human resources	Wages
Entrepreneurship	Profit

assigned tasks. Technology plays an important role in the success of many businesses. Sometimes technology results in a new product, such as hybrid autos that run on a combination of gasoline and electricity. Most of the major car companies have introduced hybrid versions of their best-sellers in recent years.

Sometimes technology helps a company improve a product. Amazon.com's new wireless reading device, the Kindle, uses Sprint's high-speed wireless network to free e-book readers from the need to download books via computer. It's also small and comfortable enough to be held in your hands. Weighing in at considerably less than a pound, the Kindle reflects light for ease of reading and generates little heat. "You kind of understand why it has been three years in development because it offers so much in an uncomplicated way," said the chief executive of a book company.[8]

And sometimes technology helps a company operate more smoothly by tracking deliveries, providing more efficient communication, analyzing data, or training employees. The U.S. Postal Service, for example, is cutting costs by expanding the electronic side of its business. Although its attempts to provide electronic bill payment proved unsuccessful, the USPS lets customers order stamps and shipping supplies online and offers merchants like L.L. Bean and eBay the means to buy postage online and create merchandise shipping and return tickets. Automation, bar coding, and electronic kiosks are replacing many tasks postal clerks used to perform.[9]

To remain competitive, a firm's capital needs to be continually acquired, maintained, and upgraded, so businesses need money for that purpose. A company's funds may come from investments by its owners, profits plowed back into the business, or loans extended by others. Money then goes to work building factories; purchasing raw materials and component parts; and hiring, training, and compensating workers. People and firms that supply capital receive factor payments in the form of interest.

Human resources represent another critical input in every economic system. Human resources include anyone who works, from the chief executive officer (CEO) of a huge corporation to a self-employed auto mechanic. This category encompasses both the physical labor and

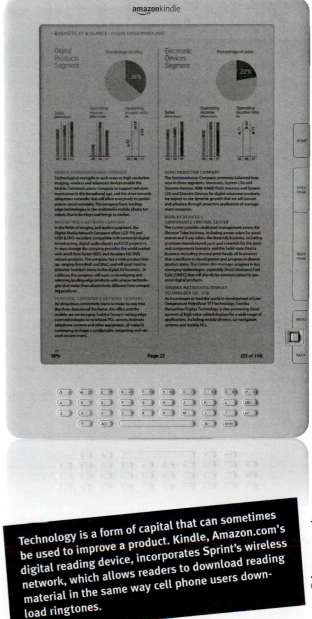

© Amazon.com, Inc.

Technology is a form of capital that can sometimes be used to improve a product. Kindle, Amazon.com's digital reading device, incorporates Sprint's wireless network, which allows readers to download reading material in the same way cell phone users download ringtones.

the intellectual inputs contributed by workers. Companies rely on their employees as a valued source of ideas and innovation, as well as physical effort. Some companies solicit employee ideas through traditional means, such as an online "suggestion box" or in staff meetings. Others encourage creative thinking during company-sponsored hiking or rafting trips or during social gatherings. Effective, well-trained human resources provide a significant competitive edge because competitors cannot easily match another company's talented, motivated employees in the way they can buy the same computer system or purchase the same grade of natural resources.

Hiring the right people matters. Google looks for those who learn fast, learn on the job, and think creatively. It encourages its self-motivated innovators by allowing its engineers to allocate a third of their day between "innovation, creativity, and freedom to think" and personal development time. Google has been rewarded with employees who can each produce an average of more than $1 million in annual revenue for the firm. That productivity level has enabled its stock price to appreciate quickly after the company went public.[10]

Entrepreneurship is the willingness to take risks to create and operate a business. An entrepreneur is someone who sees a potentially profitable opportunity and then devises a plan to achieve success in the marketplace and earn those profits. "I wanted a shot at ownership," says Lisa Daley, who gave up a time-consuming job as managing attorney of a large law firm to start the bakery business she had long dreamed of. "I'd be gone all day and all night at the office," she says, "and all I wanted to do was make cookies." Daley's venture, The Bakery at Four Corners, is so new she has yet to turn a profit, but she is paying off her start-up loans and growing her business by putting out a monthly newsletter with recipes, marketing to schools and churches, and turning her store into a comfortable gathering place for her Pelham Manor, New York, community. Despite the fact that she still works long hours, Daley enjoys being her own boss. "You can work very hard and still not have something turn out," she says. "Now people ask me a million questions because I represent the person who can do it if you want to."[11]

U.S. businesses operate within an economic system called the *private enterprise system*. The next section looks at the private enterprise system, including competition, private property, and the entrepreneurship alternative.

The Private Enterprise System

No business operates in a vacuum. All operate within a larger economic system that determines how goods and services are produced, distributed, and consumed in a society. The type of economic system employed in a society also determines patterns of resource use. Some economic systems, such as communism, feature strict controls on business ownership, profits, and resources to accomplish government goals.

private enterprise system economic system that rewards firms for their ability to identify and serve the needs and demands of customers.

In the United States, businesses function within the **private enterprise system,** an economic system that rewards firms for their ability to perceive and serve the needs and demands of consumers. The private enterprise system minimizes government interference in economic activity. Businesses that are adept at satisfying customers gain access to necessary factors of production and earn profits.

Another name for the private enterprise system is **capitalism.** Adam Smith, often identified as the father of capitalism, first described the concept in his book *The Wealth of Nations,*

Hit & Miss

Nintendo Wiinning the Videogame Wars

A few years ago, irate customers were forced to wait for their Wii system because Nintendo didn't produce enough sets. But the firm bounced back with expanded inventory in time for holiday shopping the next year. The $250 system then sold more than 2 million units that November alone, selling twice as many as the same month the year before. Total sales rose to well over 15 million units. Nintendo leaped to the top spot in the videogame market, outselling Sony's PlayStation 3 and Microsoft's Xbox 360—and it hasn't looked back.

The $16 billion videogame market is on track to set a U.S. sales record in spite of the drop-off in consumer spending elsewhere. Still, the Wii's success "is mind-boggling," said one industry watcher.

Why the popularity? "Consumers ... are looking for the most value," says a Nintendo spokesperson. "With Nintendo products, they know they can get a system that is supported by hundreds of games and many, many hours of game play." The company's president agrees. "That the Wii and the DS [handheld device] represent the best entertainment value in the marketplace explains why these strong sales are happening," he says. The Wii is also easy to learn and relatively inexpensive, and its game applications tap directly into consumers' lifestyles.

With more than 40 million copies sold, *Wii Sports* ranks as "the most successful videogame of all time," according to *VGChartz*. Next is *Wii Play* with nearly 21 million copies.

The innovative *Wii Fit* is third with about 14 million; it has already attracted companion games like Electronic Arts' *EA Sports Active,* developed for the Wii with help from Oprah Winfrey's personal trainer. *Wii Music*, Nintendo's latest entry, is aimed at the fast-growing market dominated by *Guitar Hero. Wii Music* simulates performance on more than 60 different musical instruments. Nintendo hopes it will be at least as successful as *Wii Fit*, which is almost as popular with seniors and physical rehab patients as it is with game geeks and fitness enthusiasts.

Questions for Critical Thinking

1. What do you think Nintendo has identified as its basis for competitive differentiation?
2. How would you expect Sony and Microsoft to react as the three companies fight for dominance in the game market?

Sources: Stephen Kamizuru, "Wii Sports Becomes Most Successful Videogame of All Time," *DailyTech*, February 2, 2009, http://www.dailytech.com; Mike Snider, "Nintendo Wii Sales Hint Video Games Still Play Well," *USA Today*, December 12, 2008, http://www.usatoday.com; Yi-Wyn Yen, "Nintendo Wii Officially Recession-Proof," *Fortune Techland*, December 11, 2008, http://techland.blogs.fortune.cnn.com; "Nintendo Profit Soars on Success of Its Wii Game Console," *International Herald Tribune*, July 30, 2008, http://www.iht.com; "EA Coming Out with Fitness Game for Wii," *Business Journal*, November 14, 2008, http://www.bizjournals.com; Mike Snider, " 'Sports Active' Takes Wii the Extra Mile," *USA Today*, November 13, 2008, http://www.usatoday.com.

---

published in 1776. Smith believed that an economy is best regulated by the "invisible hand" of **competition,** the battle among businesses for consumer acceptance. Smith thought that competition among firms would lead to consumers' receiving the best possible products and prices because less efficient producers would gradually be driven from the marketplace.

The "invisible hand" concept is a basic premise of the private enterprise system. In the United States, competition regulates much of economic life. To compete successfully, each firm must find a basis for **competitive differentiation,** the unique combination of organizational abilities, products, and approaches that sets a company apart from competitors in the minds of consumers. Businesses operating in a private enterprise system face a critical task of keeping up with changing marketplace conditions. Firms that fail to adjust to shifts in consumer preferences or ignore the actions of competitors leave themselves open to failure. Microsoft is hoping to head off a new threat from Google's Documents and Spreadsheets, a set of free Web-based software tools that Google hopes also to make available offline. That capability would make Google's office productivity programs a direct challenge to Microsoft's Word and Excel programs, for which users usually pay hundreds of dollars. So Microsoft is setting up tests of a new online tool called Office Live Workspace, which will let users view, share, and store Microsoft Office documents online.[12] Nintendo is challenging Microsoft on another front—the videogame industry. The Wii console and its interactive games have been best-sellers for consumers of all ages, as the "Hit & Miss" feature describes.

competition battle among businesses for consumer acceptance.

"They Said It"

"I believe the sale of Babe Ruth will ultimately strengthen the team."

—**Harry Frazee** (1881–1929) Boston Red Sox owner, announcing the sale of "The Babe" in January 1920 to the New York Yankees for $125,000 in cash plus a $310,000 loan

In a private enterprise system, companies must stay abreast of competitors' actions if they are going to remain successful. Microsoft developed its new Office Live Workspace, which allows users to view, share, and store Office documents online, to counter a competitive threat from Google.

Throughout this book, our discussion focuses on the tools and methods that 21st-century businesses apply to compete and differentiate their goods and services. We also discuss many of the ways in which market changes will affect business and the private enterprise system in the years ahead.

Basic Rights in the Private Enterprise System

For capitalism to operate effectively, the citizens of a private enterprise economy must have certain rights. As shown in Figure 1.1, these include the rights to private property, profits, freedom of choice, and competition.

The right to **private property** is the most basic freedom under the private enterprise system. Every participant has the right to own, use, buy, sell, and bequeath most forms of property, including land, buildings, machinery, equipment, patents on inventions, individual possessions, and intangible properties.

The private enterprise system also guarantees business owners the right to all profits—after taxes—they earn through their activities. Although a business is not assured of earning a profit, its owner is legally and ethically entitled to any income it generates in excess of costs.

Freedom of choice means that a private enterprise system relies on the potential for citizens to choose their own employment, purchases, and investments. They can change jobs, negotiate wages, join labor unions, and choose among many different brands of goods and services. People living in the capitalist nations of North America, Europe, and other parts of the world are so accustomed to this freedom of choice that they sometimes forget its importance. A private enterprise economy maximizes individual prosperity by providing alternatives. Other economic systems sometimes limit freedom of choice to accomplish government goals, such as increasing industrial production of certain items or military strength.

The private enterprise system also permits fair competition by allowing the public to set rules for competitive activity. For this reason, the U.S. government has passed laws to prohibit "cutthroat" competition—excessively aggressive competitive practices designed to eliminate competition. It also has established ground rules that outlaw price discrimination, fraud in financial markets, and deceptive advertising and packaging. The Federal Communications Commission (FCC) recently considered rules that would force big cable companies like Time Warner Cable and Comcast that lease cable access to smaller companies

Figure 1.1

Basic Rights within a Private Enterprise System

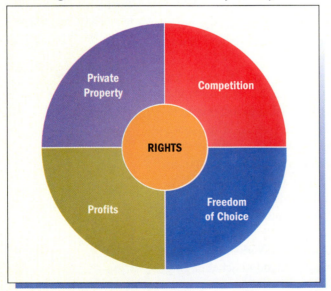

to cut their prices, allowing cable viewers access to a wider variety of programming. The FCC may also consider capping ownership nationally so that no company could sign up more than 30 percent of all cable viewers.[13]

The Entrepreneurship Alternative

The entrepreneurial spirit beats at the heart of private enterprise. An **entrepreneur** is a risk taker in the private enterprise system. You hear about entrepreneurs all the time—two college students starting a software business in their dorm room or a mom who invents a better baby carrier. Many times their success is modest, but once in a while, the risk pays off in huge profits. Individuals who recognize marketplace opportunities are free to use their capital, time, and talents to pursue those opportunities for profit. The willingness of individuals to start new ventures drives economic growth and keeps pressure on existing companies to continue to satisfy customers. If no one were willing to take economic risks, the private enterprise system wouldn't exist.

By almost any measure, the entrepreneurial spirit fuels growth in the U.S. economy. Of all the businesses operating in the United States, about one in seven firms started operations during the past year. These newly formed businesses are also the source of many of the nation's new jobs. Every year, they create more than one of every five new jobs in the economy. Most measures of entrepreneurship count the smallest or youngest businesses on the assumption that they are the enterprises in which entrepreneurship is most significant. These companies are a significant source of employment or self-employment. Of the nearly 27 million U.S. small businesses currently in operation, more than 20 million are self-employed people without any employees. More than 21 million U.S. employees currently work for a business with fewer than 20 employees.[14] Does starting a business require higher education? Not necessarily, although it can help. Figure 1.2 presents the results of a survey of small-business owners, which shows that about 24 percent of all respondents had graduated from college, and 19 percent had postgraduate degrees.

Besides creating jobs and selling products, entrepreneurship provides the benefits of innovation. In contrast to more established firms, start-up companies tend to innovate most in fields of technology that are new and uncrowded with competitors, making new products available to businesses and consumers. Because small companies are more flexible, they can make changes to products and processes more quickly than larger corporations. Entrepreneurs often find new ways to use natural resources, technology, and other factors of production. Often, they do this because they have to—they may not have enough money to build an expensive prototype or launch a nationwide ad campaign. Sometimes an entrepreneur may innovate by simply tweaking an existing idea. At Chipotle Mexican Grill, a hip and successful chain of Mexican "fast casual" restaurants, founder and CEO Steve Ells added a new twist to the idea that less is more. From the time when it opened its first store near the University of Denver to a dozen years later, when it added salads, Chipotle offered only two basic menu items—burritos and tacos. It

entrepreneur person who seeks a profitable opportunity and takes the necessary risks to set up and operate a business.

Figure 1.2

Education Levels of Small-Business Owners

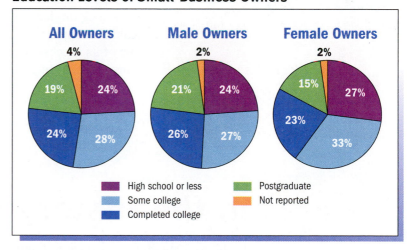

Note: Numbers may not total to 100 percent due to rounding.
Source: Data from "Survey of Business Owners (SBO): Owner's Education Levels at Start-Up, Purchase, or Acquisition of the Business," U.S. Census Bureau, accessed February 17, 2009, http://www.census.gov/csd/sbo/edu.html.

Entrepreneurs must often do more with less. For the first 12 years, Chipotle Mexican Grill offered only two basic menu items, burritos and tacos. "Focus on just a few things and do them better than anybody else," advises CEO Steve Ells.

© Matt York/AP/Wide World Photos

still sells only those three categories of entrées, although its search for the best ingredients and tastiest recipes is never-ending. "Focus on just a few things," says Ells, "and do them better than anybody else. We've had 10 years of double digit [growth] in a row, and we've done that without cookies. So why start now? I see only the downside to adding cookies."[15]

Entrepreneurship is also important to existing companies in a private enterprise system. More and more, large firms are recognizing the value of entrepreneurial thinking among their employees, hoping to benefit from enhanced flexibility, improved innovation, and new market opportunities. Jim Throneburg runs his family's North Carolina sock-manufacturing firm, Thorlo. The company has been around for a long time, and Throneburg makes certain it continually innovates and changes. A few decades ago, he noticed that American consumers had begun buying different athletic shoes for different sports. "If the shoe changed for function, I figured I needed to design a sock that complemented the shoe," he recalls. His figuring resulted in a thick-soled hiking sock and later a padded sock for the military. Since then, Thorlo has created more than 25 varieties of sport socks. Throneburg invests heavily in research—in search of new markets and new technologies. Research helped the firm identify what it calls the "7 Elements of Comfort" for footwear and then develop its Comfort Science program. Thorlo has spent millions on developing new yarns and designs and has responded to requests from its customers for new products. Throneburg likes to differentiate his firm from its competitors. "I determined at the outset that we are not a fashion-driven company," he says. "We are function-driven. We will only make sock products that contribute to foot protection, foot comfort, and foot health."[16] Apple is another company that continually creates new products. One of its successes—the iPhone—has become a platform for other entrepreneurs, as the "Hit & Miss" feature describes.

As the next section explains, entrepreneurs have played a vital role in the history of U.S. business. They have helped create new industries, developed successful new business methods, and improved U.S. standing in global competition.

Assessment Check ✔

1. What is an alternative term for *private enterprise system*?
2. What is the most basic freedom under the private enterprise system?
3. What is an entrepreneur?

Six Eras in the History of Business

In the roughly 400 years since the first European settlements appeared on the North American continent, amazing changes have occurred in the size, focus, and goals of U.S. businesses. As Figure 1.3 indicates, U.S. business history is divided into six distinct time periods: (1) the Colonial period, (2) the Industrial Revolution, (3) the age of industrial entrepreneurs, (4) the production era, (5) the marketing era, and (6) the relationship era. The next sections describe how events in each of these time periods have influenced U.S. business practices.

Hit & Miss

iPhone Apps Give Entrepreneurs an Outlet

When Apple designed the iPhone so it could be customized with downloadable applications, it deliberately left the door open for software entrepreneurs to add to the smartphone's capabilities. And add they did.

- Andrew Erlichson changed his Phanfare photo-sharing service into an iPhone app. "The iPhone represents the beginning of what we believe will be a convergence between smartphones and point-and-shoot cameras," Erlichson told his online customers.
- Ethan Nicholas's iShoot combat game became a runaway iPhone success when he found time from his day job at Sun Microsystems to upgrade it. Ten days later it was being downloaded at the rate of 17,000 times a day. "I've given my two-week notice at Sun Microsystems," said Nicholas. "I'm gonna do this full time now."
- Pandora, an online radio service, was available from the App Store from the first day and is now the number-one music application for the iPhone. It's also brought 3 million new listeners from the phone to Pandora's Web site.
- Jason Boehle and Brian Killen's Grocery IQ app, a provider of digital shopping coupons, reigns as the iPhone's most popular lifestyle application. Its creators recently sold it to Coupons Inc. for "maybe five times more than what we ever dreamed," said Killen.

While most users of Nokia and Motorola phones haven't downloaded applications, the typical iPhone user has downloaded 15 or more from the 15,000 available at the App Store, most of them for free or only 99 cents. As part of iTunes, the App Store attracts millions of users. Few developers charge enough to turn a profit directly from the downloads, but they find other ways to make money. Some apps attract paying advertisers; other developers charge for premium versions of their products. Ameritrade's app earns money from stock trading commissions. Developers keep 70 percent of what users pay for downloads; Apple keeps the other 30 percent and provides all the marketing and bandwidth needed. "The iPhone is the platform of the moment," says one observer. "Apple has sucked all the oxygen out of the room, and developers want to be where the action is."

Entrepreneurs are attracted not only by the iPhone's huge customer base but also by Apple's reputation as a technology innovator. "Our objective," says Apple's chief operating officer, "is not to be the unit-share leader in the cellphone industry; it's to build the world's best phone."

In the short term the proliferation of iPhone applications may benefit Apple more than it does developers, but in the long run the iPhone is expected to grow dramatically, perhaps even taking a commanding 20 percent of the cellphone market. And that can only be good for software entrepreneurs.

Questions for Critical Thinking

1. How have entrepreneurs contributed to the iPhone's success? How might they in the future?
2. For what other kinds of goods or services do you think Apple's add-on strategy for applications and utilities could succeed?

Sources: Peter Burrows, "The Real Potential of Apple's iPhone," *BusinessWeek*, February 2, 2009, pp. 74, 76; Mike Belt, "Lawrence Software Developers Create a Hit with iPhone Grocery App," *Lawrence Journal World*, January 30, 2009, http://www2.ljworld.com; Josh Quittner, "Apple Stock Surges on Upbeat Earnings Report," *Time*, January 22, 2009, http://www.time.com; Jefferson Graham, "Applications Developers See iPhone as Way to Get Noticed," *USA Today*, January 20, 2009, http://www.usatoday.com; "iPhone Developer Quits Day Job as 'iShoot' Hits #1 in Apple's iTunes App Store," *MacDailyNews*, January 14, 2009, http://macdailynews.com.

The Colonial Period

Before the U.S. Declaration of Independence from England in 1776, Colonial society emphasized rural and agricultural production. Colonial towns were small compared with European cities, and they functioned as marketplaces for farmers and craftspeople. The economic focus of the nation centered on rural areas, because prosperity depended on the output of farms and plantations. The success or failure of crops influenced every aspect of the economy.

Colonists depended on England for manufactured items as well as financial backing for their infant industries. Even after the Revolutionary War (1776–1783), the United States maintained close economic ties with England. British investors continued to provide much of the financing for developing the U.S. business system, and this financial influence continued well into the 19th century.

Figure 1.3   **Six Eras in Business History**

Era	Main Characteristics	Time Period
Colonial	Primarily agricultural	Prior to 1776
Industrial Revolution	Mass production by semiskilled workers, aided by machines	1760–1850
Industrial entrepreneurs	Advances in technology and increased demand for manufactured goods, leading to enormous entrepreneurial opportunities	Late 1800s
Production	Emphasis on producing more goods faster, leading to production innovations such as assembly lines	Through the 1920s
Marketing	Consumer orientation, seeking to understand and satisfy needs and preferences of customer groups	Since 1950s
Relationship	Benefits derived from deep, ongoing links with individual customers, employees, suppliers, and other businesses	Began in 1990s

The Industrial Revolution

The Industrial Revolution began in England around 1750. It moved business operations from an emphasis on independent, skilled workers who specialized in building products one by one to a factory system that mass-produced items by bringing together large numbers of semiskilled workers. The factories profited from the savings created by large-scale production, bolstered by increasing support from machines over time. As businesses grew, they could often purchase raw materials more cheaply in larger lots than before. Specialization of labor, limiting each worker to a few specific tasks in the production process, also improved production efficiency.

Influenced by these events in England, business in the United States began a time of rapid industrialization. Agriculture became mechanized, and factories sprang up in cities. During the mid-1800s, the pace of the revolution was increased as newly built railroad systems provided fast, economical transportation. In California, for example, the combination of railroad construction and the gold rush fueled a tremendous demand for construction.

The Age of Industrial Entrepreneurs

Building on the opportunities created by the Industrial Revolution, entrepreneurship increased in the United States. In 1900, Arthur R. Wilson and several partners paid $10,000 in gold coins for a 27-acre parcel of granite-rich land in California. This natural resource was the basis for the

Granite Rock Co., which provided the material for roads and buildings in California's booming economy. The company, now called Graniterock, evolved in response to technological, competitive, and marketplace demands and continues to survive in the 21st century. Today the firm, which has stores throughout California, offers consumer products such as granite countertops as well as many "green" products made from recycled materials.[17]

Inventors created a virtually endless array of commercially useful products and new production methods. Many of them are famous today:

- Eli Whitney introduced the concept of interchangeable parts, an idea that would later facilitate mass production on a previously impossible scale.

- Robert McCormick designed a horse-drawn reaper that reduced the labor involved in harvesting wheat. His son, Cyrus McCormick, saw the commercial potential of the reaper and launched a business to build and sell the machine. By 1902, the company was producing 35 percent of the nation's farm machinery.

- Cornelius Vanderbilt (railroads), J. P. Morgan (banking), and Andrew Carnegie (steel), among others, took advantage of the enormous opportunities waiting for anyone willing to take the risk of starting a new business.

The entrepreneurial spirit of this golden age in business did much to advance the U.S. business system and raise the overall standard of living of its citizens. That market transformation, in turn, created new demand for manufactured goods.

The Production Era

As demand for manufactured goods continued to increase through the 1920s, businesses focused even greater attention on the activities involved in producing those goods. Work became increasingly specialized, and huge, labor-intensive factories dominated U.S. business. Assembly lines, introduced by Henry Ford, became commonplace in major industries. Business owners turned over their responsibilities to a new class of managers trained in operating established companies. Their activities emphasized efforts to produce even more goods through quicker methods.

During the production era, business focused attention on internal processes rather than external influences. Marketing was almost an afterthought, designed solely to distribute items generated by production activities. Little attention was paid to consumer wants or needs. Instead, businesses tended to make decisions about what the market would get. If you wanted to buy a Ford Model T automobile, your color choice was black—the only color produced by the company.

The Marketing Era

The Great Depression of the early 1930s changed the shape of U.S. business yet again. As incomes nose-dived, businesses could no longer automatically count on selling everything they produced. Managers began to pay more attention to the markets for their goods and services, and sales and advertising took on new importance. During this period, selling was often synonymous with marketing.

Demand for all kinds of consumer goods exploded after World War II. After nearly five years of doing without new automobiles, appliances, and other items to contribute to the war effort, consumers were buying again. At the same time, however, competition also heated up. Soon businesses began to think of marketing as more than just selling; they envisioned a process of determining what consumers wanted and needed and then designing products to satisfy those needs. In short, they developed a **consumer orientation.**

Branding creates an identity for a good, service, or company. Costco brought branding to discount retailing by offering superior customer service along with the bargains consumers were seeking.

Businesses began to analyze consumer desires before beginning actual production. Consumer choices skyrocketed. Automobiles came in a wide variety of colors and styles, and car buyers could choose among them. Companies also discovered the need to distinguish their goods and services from those of competitors. **Branding,** the process of creating an identity in consumers' minds for a good, service, or company, is an important marketing tool. A **brand** can be a name, term, sign, symbol, design, or some combination that identifies the products of one firm and differentiates them from competitors' offerings.

Jim Sinegal, cofounder and CEO of Costco, brought branding to an unlikely market—discount retailing. Costco has nearly 500 warehouse-style stores and boasts sales over $52 million a year by appealing to people who can afford to pay full price, as well as those who value its bargains for economy-size packages of items such as juice and paper goods. What makes the Costco brand valuable is superior customer service, which results from the company's policy of treating its employees well. This reduces turnover and creates a knowledgeable and enthusiastic sales staff. The company also has a generous policy that allows returns of any item for any reason. Costco further nurtures its brand by regularly offering "treasure hunt" designer items like Coach handbags and Fila jackets at low prices for limited time periods. "The attitude is that if you see it, you have got to buy it because it may not be there next time," says Sinegal. "We purposely try to merchandise to that type of mind-set."[18]

The marketing era has had a tremendous effect on the way business is conducted today. Even the smallest business owners recognize the importance of understanding what customers want and the reasons they buy.

brand name, term, sign, symbol, design, or some combination that identifies the products of one firm and differentiates them from competitors' offerings.

The Relationship Era

As business continues in the 21st century, a significant change is taking place in the ways companies interact with customers. Since the Industrial Revolution, most businesses have concentrated on building and promoting products in the hope that enough customers will buy them to cover costs and earn acceptable profits, an approach called **transaction management.**

In contrast, in the **relationship era,** businesses are taking a different, longer-term approach to their interactions with customers. Firms now seek ways to actively nurture customer loyalty by carefully managing every interaction. They earn enormous paybacks for their efforts. A company that retains customers over the long haul reduces its advertising and sales costs. Because customer spending tends to accelerate over time, revenues also grow. Companies with long-term customers often can avoid costly reliance on price discounts to attract new business, and they find that many new customers come from loyal customer referrals.

Business owners gain several advantages by developing ongoing relationships with customers. Because it is much less expensive to serve existing customers than to find new ones, businesses that develop long-term customer relationships can reduce their overall costs. Long-term relationships with customers enable businesses to improve their understanding of what customers want and prefer from the company. As a result, businesses enhance their chances of sustaining real advantages through competitive differentiation.

The relationship era is an age of connections—between businesses and customers, employers and employees, technology and manufacturing, and even separate companies. The world economy is increasingly interconnected, as businesses expand beyond their national boundaries. In this new environment, techniques for managing networks of people, businesses, information, and technology are critically important to contemporary business success. As you begin your own career, you will soon see how important relationships are, beginning with your first job interview. Business meals are another important relationship builder; see the "Business Etiquette" feature for suggestions on being a successful host.

Managing Relationships through Technology

Increasingly, businesses focus on **relationship management,** the collection of activities that build and maintain ongoing, mutually beneficial ties with customers and other parties. At its core, relationship management involves gathering knowledge of customer needs and preferences and applying that understanding to get as close to the customer as possible. Many of these activities are based on **technology,** or the business application of knowledge based on scientific discoveries, inventions, and innovations. In managing relationships with customers, technology most often takes the form of communication, via the Internet and cell phone.

Blogs are growing more influential as a link between companies and their customers, and more companies are beginning to take advantage of their directness. Dell was heavily criticized for providing low-cost but generally poor customer service. "It was a real mess," says the company's head of customer service. "In order to become very efficient, I think we became ineffective." One journalist who vented his frustrations with a new Dell laptop in his blog invited Dell to "join the conversation your customers are having without you." A few months later, Dell technicians were chatting with bloggers and working to solve their problems, and shortly after, the company started its own blog, Direct2Dell.

Business Etiquette

DINING DO'S AND DON'TS

The goal of a business meal, if you are the host, is not just to eat. Business plans or prospective partnerships are often discussed. But a meal is also an opportunity to make your guests feel comfortable with you and strengthen your relationship with them. Here are some tips for getting through breakfast, lunch, or dinner with business partners and employees.

1. If you are in a position to hire, take potential employees out to eat. "I can tell a lot about people by the way they act toward the food server," says Julia Stewart, IHOP's chief executive. "If you have a complete conversation with me and you never acknowledge the food server, you are being disrespectful and will never work for me."
2. Check your guests' food preferences ahead of time and make a reservation at an appropriate restaurant. If any special accommodations need to be made, such as for someone with a handicap or food allergy, make tactful preparations with the restaurant ahead of time.
3. If possible, choose a few reliable restaurants to become familiar with, to avoid unpleasant surprises and to allow you to cultivate business relationships with the servers and the manager.
4. Remember that a business meal has a business purpose. Treat it like a meeting in a conference room and always arrive on time. If you are the host, be early to welcome your guests.
5. If there is a coat check, offer to check your guests' hats, coats, umbrellas, and the like, and tip the attendant yourself when your party retrieves belongings after the meal.
6. Keep cell phones, glasses, and bags and briefcases off the table.
7. Unless you expect an emergency to interrupt the meal, turn your cell phone off. If you must answer, keep your conversation brief and quiet.
8. Suggest your group order their meals before beginning any business discussion. This will help you conclude the meal in a reasonable time period.
9. If you have questions about items on the menu, ask before you order. It's better to know what you are getting than to be served something you can't or don't want to eat.
10. The meal begins only after everyone at the table has been served and the host has taken his or her napkin from the table.

Sources: "Business Dining Etiquette," Career Services Center, University of Delaware, http://www.udel.edu, accessed February 17, 2009; "The Etiquette of Formal & Business Dining," *Etiquette Bag,* January 28, 2008, http://www.etiquettebag.com; "The Pancake Pusher," *Fortune,* October 15, 2007, p. 48; Kimberly Palmer, "Etiquette Course," *U.S. News & World Report,* May 28, 2007, p. EE12.

relationship management collection of activities that build and maintain ongoing, mutually beneficial ties between a business and its customers and other parties.

More recently, CEO Michael Dell used IdeaStorm.com to invite customers to rate the company's products and offer advice and suggestions. The company often follows some of the recommendations. "These conversations [about a company] are going to occur whether you like it or not, OK?" says Michael Dell of customer blogs. "Well, do you want to be part of that or not? My argument is you absolutely do. You can learn from that. You can improve your reaction time. And you can be a better company by listening and being involved in that conversation."[19]

Strategic Alliances and Partnerships

Businesses are also finding that they must form partnerships with other organizations to take full advantage of available opportunities. A **partnership** is an affiliation of two or more companies that help each other achieve common goals. One such form of partnership between organizations is a **strategic alliance,** a partnership formed to create a competitive advantage for the businesses involved.

E-business has created a whole new type of strategic alliance. A firm whose entire business is conducted online, such as eBay or Amazon, may team up with traditional retailers that contribute their expertise in buying the right amount of the right merchandise, as well as their knowledge of distribution. Amazon, for instance, now partners with enough third-party retailers to earn more profit from sales of their products than it does from its own inventory of books. It sells billions of dollars of media content such as music, and it is now offering Amazon Web Services to sell storage, computing, and data center services to online start-up firms, allowing them to focus on developing their business innovations without worrying about their technology setup. "I don't need to have a systems administrator or a network administrator," says the CEO of MileMeter, a start-up auto insurer that recently moved its applications to Amazon. "I don't have to worry about hardware becoming irrelevant."[20]

The Green Advantage

Another way of building relationships is to operate responsibly and incorporate issues that your customers care about into your business. As environmental concerns continue to influence consumers' choices of everything from yogurt to clothing to cars and light bulbs, many observers say the question about "going green" is no longer whether, but how. The need to develop environmentally friendly products and processes is becoming a major new force in business today. Companies in every industry are researching ways to save energy, cut emissions and pollution, reduce waste, and, not incidentally, save money and increase profits as well. "It's what survival will be about in the 21st century," says an executive of The Coca-Cola Company's water conservation plans.[21]

Stonyfield Farms has long been in the forefront of the push for sustainability in business operations. Nearly a decade ago, it became one of the first firms to achieve carbon-neutral operations, its dairy products are 100 percent organic, and it donates one-tenth of its profits to other organizations, such as Climate Counts, that are dedicated to protecting and restoring the environment.[22] Nokia has also taken the green advantage to heart: it unveiled a prototype cell phone made entirely of renewable and recycled parts and is working to make that design an operational phone in its product lineup.[23] Such small changes count, as do creative solutions to pollution problems. Enterprise Rent-a-Car, for instance, will now allow customers to do what only large companies could do before—purchase carbon offsets for the pollution created by their rented cars. The firm will match those purchases dollar for dollar.[24]

Energy is among the biggest costs for most firms, and carbon-based fuels such as coal are responsible for most of the additional carbon dioxide in the atmosphere. Ford Motor Company is upgrading lighting fixtures in its manufacturing facilities, replacing old inefficient equipment with fluorescent lighting that saves energy and money and including motion detectors that reduce energy use during periods of low activity.[25] Clean solar energy is coming into its own and may soon be more viable and more widely available. SolarCity, a California installer of rooftop solar cells, is having trouble keeping up with growing demand. "It is hard to find installers," says the company's CEO. "We're at the stage where if we continue to grow at this pace, we won't be able to sustain the growth."[26]

Some "green" initiatives can themselves be costly for firms. General Electric, however, with its Ecomagination line of environmentally friendly products, is among those that have realized thinking "green" can satisfy not only consumers' environmental concerns but also those of shareholders by saving money and earning profits. "We've sold out in eco-certified products for [a year in advance]," says Bob Corcoran, the company's vice president for corporate citizenship, and energy-saving wind turbines are back-ordered for two years. Once criticized for its pollution of New York's Hudson River, the firm has helped form the U.S. Climate Action Partnership to push for a cap on carbon emissions in the United States. GE believes it is doing what its shareholders expect it to do. "No good business can call itself a good corporate citizen if it fritters away shareholder money," Corcoran says.[27]

Each new era in U.S. business history has forced managers to reexamine the tools and techniques they formerly used to compete. Tomorrow's managers will need creativity and vision to stay on top of rapidly changing technology and to manage complex relationships in the global business world of the fast-paced 21st century. As green operations become more cost-effective, and consumers and shareholders demand more responsive management, few firms will choose to be left behind.

RENEWABLE ENERGY. WATER DESALINATION. FUEL CONSERVATION. IT'S NOT A VISION OF THE FUTURE. IT'S ECOMAGINATION RIGHT NOW.

ecomagination.com

imagination at work

© General Electric Co.

Going green doesn't have to be expensive. General Electric's Ecomagination line has shown that green products can save money and earn profits as well as respond to consumers' environmental concerns.

Assessment Check ✔

1. What was the Industrial Revolution?
2. During which era was the idea of branding developed?
3. What is the difference between transaction management and relationship management?

Today's Business Workforce

A skilled and knowledgeable workforce is an essential resource for keeping pace with the accelerating rate of change in today's business world. Employers need reliable workers who are dedicated to fostering strong ties with customers and partners. They must build workforces capable of efficient, high-quality production needed to compete in global markets. Savvy business leaders also realize that the brainpower of employees plays a vital role in a firm's ability to stay on top of new technologies and innovations. In short, a first-class workforce can be the foundation of a firm's competitive differentiation, providing important advantages over competing businesses.

Changes in the Workforce

Companies now face several trends that challenge their skills for managing and developing human resources. Those challenges include aging of the population and a shrinking labor pool, growing diversity of the workforce, the changing nature of work, the need for flexibility and mobility, and the use of collaboration to innovate.

AGING OF THE POPULATION AND SHRINKING LABOR POOL By 2030, the number of U.S. workers 65 or older will reach 72 million—double what it is today—and many of them will be retiring from the workforce, taking their experience and expertise with them. As Table 1.2 shows, the U.S. population as a whole is trending older. Yet today, many members of the Baby Boom generation, the huge number of people born between 1946 and 1964, are still hitting the peaks of their careers. At the same time, members of so-called Generation X (born from 1965 to 1981) and Generation Y (born from 1982 to 2005) are launching and building their careers, so employers are finding more generations in the workforce simultaneously than ever before.[28] This broad age diversity brings management challenges with it, such as accommodating a variety of work-life styles, changing expectations of work, and varying levels of technological expertise.[29] Says one young Gen Y worker, "I need to be connected to be happy. And that means connected in all areas of my life, work and play, not that I think there's much difference between them."[30] Still, despite the widening age spectrum of the workforce, some economists predict the U.S. labor pool could soon fall short by as many as 10 million people as the Baby Boomers retire.

More sophisticated technology has intensified the hiring challenge by requiring workers to have ever more advanced skills. Although the number of college-educated workers has doubled in the last 20 years, the demand is still greater than the supply of these individuals. Because of these changes, companies are increasingly seeking—and finding—talent at the extreme ends of the working-age spectrum. Teenagers are entering the workforce sooner, and some seniors are staying longer—or seeking new careers after retiring from their primary careers. Many older workers work part-time or flexible hours. Dick Chevrette worked for 38 years as a manager at Massachusetts General Hospital. When he hit 62, he wanted to scale back his hours but still be mentally challenged and active. "Reducing my hours gave me a chance to try part-time retirement and see how it works," he says.[31] Meanwhile, for those older employees who do retire, employers must administer a variety of retirement planning and disability programs, retraining, and insurance benefits.

> "They Said It"
>
> "The trick is to make sure you don't die waiting for prosperity to come."
>
> —Lee Iacocca (b. 1924) American executive ("Thoughts on the Business of Life," *Forbes*, December 8, 2008, p. 188.)

Table 1.2	Aging of the U.S. Population		
Age	**2010**	**2020**	**2025**
16–64	203 million	214 million	218 million
	66% of total	63% of total	61% of total
65 and older	40 million	55 million	64 million
	13% of total	16% of total	18% of total
Median	37 years	38 years	38.5 years

Source: U.S. Census Bureau, "Resident Population Projections by Sex and Age: 2010 to 2050," *Statistical Abstract of the United States: 2009,* http://www.census.gov.

INCREASINGLY DIVERSE WORKFORCE The U.S. workforce is growing more diverse, in age and in every other way as well. The two fastest-growing ethnic populations in the United States are Hispanics and people of Asian origin. Currently, Hispanics represent about 16 percent of the United States population and Asians represent about 5 percent.[32] Considering that minority groups now make up more than one-third of the U.S. population, managers must learn to work effectively with diverse ethnic groups, cultures, and lifestyles to develop and retain a superior workforce for their company.

Diversity, blending individuals of different genders, ethnic backgrounds, cultures, religions, ages, and physical and mental abilities, can enhance a firm's chances of success. Several studies have shown that diverse employee teams and workforces tend to perform tasks more effectively and develop better solutions to business problems than homogeneous employee groups. This result is due in part to the varied perspectives and experiences that foster innovation and creativity in multicultural teams.

Practical managers also know that attention to diversity issues can help them avoid damaging legal battles. Losing a discrimination lawsuit can be very costly, yet in a recent survey, a majority of executives from racial and cultural minorities said they had seen discrimination in work assignments.

OUTSOURCING AND THE CHANGING NATURE OF WORK Not only is the U.S. workforce changing, but so is the very nature of work. Manufacturing used to account for most of U.S. annual output, but the scale has now shifted to services such as financial management and communications. This means that firms must rely heavily on well-trained service workers with knowledge, technical skills, the ability to communicate and deal with people, and a talent for creative thinking. The Internet has made possible another business tool for staffing flexibility—**outsourcing,** using outside vendors to produce goods or fulfill services and functions that were previously handled in-house or in-country. For example, if you dial a call center for assistance, your call may be answered by someone in India. In the best situation, outsourcing allows a firm to reduce costs and concentrate its resources on the things it does best while gaining access to expertise it may not have. But outsourcing also creates its own challenges, such as differences in language or culture.

Offshoring is the relocation of business processes to lower-cost locations overseas. This can include both production and services. In recent years, China has emerged as a dominant location for production offshoring for many firms, while India has become the key player in offshoring services. Some U.S. companies are now structured so that entire divisions or functions are developed and staffed overseas—the jobs were never in the United States to start with. Another trend in some industries is **nearshoring,** outsourcing production or services to locations near a firm's home base. For example, western European companies have discovered a talented labor pool in the eastern European countries of Bulgaria and Romania.

FLEXIBILITY AND MOBILITY Younger workers in particular are looking for something other than the work-comes-first lifestyle exemplified by the Baby Boom generation. But workers of all ages are exploring different work arrangements, such as telecommuting from remote locations and sharing jobs with two or more employees. Employers are also hiring growing numbers of temporary and part-time employees, some of whom are less interested in advancing up the career ladder and more interested in using and developing their skills. While the cubicle-filled office will likely never become obsolete, technology makes productive networking and virtual team efforts possible by allowing people to work where they choose and easily share knowledge, a sense of purpose or mission, and a free flow of ideas across any geographical distance or time zone.[33]

Managers of such far-flung workforces need to build and earn their trust, in order to retain valued employees and to ensure that all members are acting ethically and contributing their share without the day-to-day supervision of a more conventional work environment. These managers, and their employees, need to be flexible and responsive to change while work, technology, and the relationships between them continue to evolve.[34]

outsourcing using outside vendors to produce goods or fulfill services and functions that were previously handled in-house or in-country.

INNOVATION THROUGH COLLABORATION Some observers also see a trend toward more collaborative work in the future, as opposed to individuals working alone. Businesses using teamwork hope to build a creative environment where all members contribute their knowledge and skills to solve problems or seize opportunities.

The old relationship between employers and employees was pretty simple: workers arrived at a certain hour, did their jobs, and went home every day at the same time. Companies rarely laid off workers, and employees rarely left for a job at another firm. But all that—and more—has changed. Employees are no longer likely to remain with a single company throughout their entire careers and do not necessarily expect lifetime loyalty from the companies they work for. They do not expect to give that loyalty either. Instead, they build their own careers however and wherever they can.

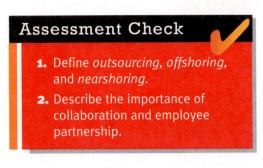

Assessment Check ✔

1. Define *outsourcing, offshoring,* and *nearshoring.*
2. Describe the importance of collaboration and employee partnership.

These changes mean that many firms now recognize the value of a partnership with employees that encourages creative thinking and problem solving and that rewards risk taking and innovation.[35] At Walt Disney Imagineering, which designs the company's theme parks, executive vice president Marty Sklar gathers employees aged 20-something to 80-something for "gab sessions" to elicit ideas. Suggestions of all kinds are welcomed, and none are rejected out of hand. "It's about listening and bringing out the best in people," Sklar says. One result of such a session? Epcot Center's spacecraft simulator.[36]

The 21st–Century Manager

Today's companies look for managers who are intelligent, highly motivated people with the ability to create and sustain a vision of how an organization can succeed. The 21st-century manager must also apply critical-thinking skills and creativity to business challenges and lead change.

Importance of Vision

To thrive in the 21st century, businesspeople need **vision,** the ability to perceive marketplace needs and what an organization must do to satisfy them. Andrea Jung brought a new vision to Avon Products and its 5.5 million people. As CEO, she cut eight levels of management in the company and saved $300 million, entering new markets and expanding advertising to boost growth. In two short years, sales were growing by more than 10 percent and the stock price had increased 40 percent. But improving the company's financial position wasn't Jung's only concern. Her vision of the 100-year-old firm as "The Company for Women" took it beyond its old role as a cosmetics maker and transformed it into a way for its millions of independent sales representatives to become economically self-sufficient. "We elevate women in the community and create commerce that can better their families' lives," says Jung. "There is purpose in my work: enabling women to be self-empowered, to learn to run their own businesses and achieve the economic means to provide education." Jung backs up her commitment to women with loans that allow sales reps to create their start-up inventory and has launched a campaign against domestic violence, as well as donating $450 million to breast cancer education and research.[37]

Importance of Critical Thinking and Creativity

Critical thinking and creativity are essential characteristics of the 21st-century workforce. Today's businesspeople need to look at a wide variety of situations, draw connections between disparate information, and develop future-oriented solutions. This need applies not only to top executives, but to midlevel managers and entry-level workers as well.

Critical thinking is the ability to analyze and assess information to pinpoint problems or opportunities. The critical-thinking process includes activities such as determining the authenticity, accuracy, and worth of information, knowledge, and arguments. It involves looking beneath the surface for deeper meaning and connections that can help identify critical issues and solutions. Without critical thinking, a firm may encounter serious problems.

Creativity is the capacity to develop novel solutions to perceived organizational problems. Although most people think of it in relation to writers, artists, musicians, and inventors, that is a very limited definition. In business, creativity refers to the ability to see better and different ways of doing business. A computer engineer who solves a glitch in a software program is executing a creative act; so is a shipping clerk who finds a way to speed delivery of the company's overnight packages. Sometimes a crisis calls for creative leadership. Airplane Captain Chesley Sullenberger, who guided US Airways Flight 1549 to a safe landing in New York's Hudson River, had to make immediate and critical decisions when both his engines quit after hitting birds upon takeoff. His passengers' and crew members' lives—and those on the ground—depended on his quick thinking and years of training. "Losing thrust on both engines, at low speed, at a low altitude, over one of the most densely populated areas on the planet. Yes, I knew it was a very challenging situation," he said. Losing altitude, Sullenberger ruled out returning to La Guardia Airport or attempting to land at a nearby New Jersey airport, opting instead to splash down in the river close to a ferry terminal. "I needed to touch down with the wings exactly level, … the nose slightly up, … [and] just above our minimum flying speed, but not below it." He accomplished those seemingly impossible feats and saved all 155 people on board.[38]

Some practice and mental exercise can cultivate your own ability to think creatively. Here are some exercises and guidelines:

- In a group, brainstorm by listing ideas as they come to mind. Build on other people's ideas, but don't criticize them. Wait until later to evaluate and organize the ideas.

- Think about how to make familiar concepts unfamiliar. A glue that doesn't stick very well? That's the basis for 3M's popular Post-it notes.

- Plan ways to rearrange your thinking with simple questions such as, "What features can we leave out?" or by imagining what it feels like to be the customer.

- Cultivate curiosity, openness, risk, and energy as you meet people and encounter new situations. View these encounters as opportunities to learn.

- Treat failures as additional opportunities to learn.

- Get regular physical exercise. When you work out, your brain releases endorphins, and these chemicals stimulate creative thinking.

- Pay attention to your dreams and daydreams. You might find that you already know the answer to a problem.

Creativity and critical thinking must go beyond generating new ideas, however. They must lead to action. In addition to creating an environment in which employees can nurture ideas, managers must give them opportunities to take risks and try new solutions.

Ability to Lead Change

Today's business leaders must guide their employees and organizations through the changes brought about by technology, marketplace demands, and global competition. Managers must be skilled at recognizing employee strengths and motivating people to move toward common goals as members of a team. Throughout this book, real-world examples demonstrate how companies have initiated sweeping change initiatives. Most, if not all, have been led by managers comfortable with the tough decisions that today's fluctuating conditions require.

"They Said It"

"My success, part of it certainly, is that I have focused in on a few things."

—Bill Gates (b. 1955)
Chairman, Microsoft

Assessment Check

1. Why is vision an important managerial quality?
2. What is the difference between
   creativity and critical thinking?

Factors that require organizational change can come from both external and internal sources; successful managers must be aware of both. External forces might include feedback from customers, developments in the international marketplace, economic trends, and new technologies. Internal factors might arise from new company goals, emerging employee needs, labor union demands, or production problems.

What Makes a Company Admired?

Who is your hero? Is it someone who has achieved great feats in sports, government, entertainment, or business? Why do you admire the person—does he or she run a company, earn a lot of money, or give back to the community and society? Every year, business magazines and organizations publish lists of companies that they consider to be "most admired." Companies, like individuals, may be admired for many reasons. Most people would mention solid profits, stable growth, a safe and challenging work environment, high-quality goods and services, and business ethics and social responsibility. *Business ethics* refers to the standards of conduct and moral values involving decisions made in the work environment. *Social responsibility* is a management philosophy that includes contributing resources to the community, preserving the natural environment, and developing or participating in nonprofit programs designed to promote the well-being of the general public. You'll find business ethics and social responsibility examples throughout this book, as well as a deeper exploration of these topics in Chapter 2. For businesses to behave ethically and responsibly, their employees need to have strong moral compasses that guide them. The "Solving an Ethical Controversy" feature debates the responsibility that watchdogs have when they fail to perform their duties.

As you read this text, you'll be able to make up your own mind about why companies should—or should not—be admired. *Fortune* publishes two lists of most-admired companies each year, one for U.S.-based firms and one for the world. The list is compiled from surveys and other research conducted by the Hay Group, a global human resources and organizational consulting firm. Criteria for making the list include innovation, people management, use of corporate assets, social responsibility, quality of management, and quality of products and services.[39] Table 1.3 lists the top ten "Most Admired Companies" for a recent year.

Assessment Check

1. Define *business ethics* and *social
   responsibility*.
2. Identify three criteria used to
   judge whether a company might
   be considered admirable.

Table 1.3	*Fortune*'s Top Ten Most Admired Companies	
1. Apple		6. Procter & Gamble
2. Berkshire Hathaway		7. FedEx
3. Toyota Motor		8. Southwest Airlines
4. Google		9. General Electric
5. Johnson & Johnson		10. Microsoft

Source: "World's Most Admired Companies: 2009," *Fortune*, http://money.cnn.com, accessed March 9, 2009.

SEC LAX ON OVERSIGHT?

The Securities and Exchange Commission (SEC) was created by Congress in 1934 to protect investors by monitoring the securities industry. According to the SEC's Web site, "The laws and rules that govern the securities industry in the United States derive from a simple and straightforward concept: all investors, whether large institutions or private individuals, should have access to certain basic facts about an investment prior to buying it, and so long as they hold it. To achieve this, the SEC requires public companies to disclose meaningful financial and other information to the public."

Recently, however, a whopping $50 billion securities fraud came to light when the investment company run by Bernard Madoff turned out to be the biggest Ponzi scheme of all time. Madoff used new investors' funds to pay off the older ones, which can never be sustained indefinitely. All the investment profits Madoff claimed were an illusion. Independent investigator Harry Markopolos told Congress he had been warning the SEC about Madoff's activities for years. "I gift-wrapped and delivered the largest Ponzi scheme in history to them and somehow they couldn't be bothered to conduct a thorough and proper investigation because they were too busy on matters of higher priority," Markopolos testified. Thousands of individual and institutional investors faced financial ruin as Madoff's scheme evaporated.

Does the SEC bear part of the blame for investor losses if it is not doing its job?

PRO

1. A $50 billion fraud could flourish only under a flawed regulatory system. "Our current fragmented regulatory system can allow bad actors to engage in misconduct outside the view and reach of some regulators," said an officer of the securities industry's watchdog organization. "It is undeniable that … the system failed to protect investors."
2. "The SEC is … captive to the industry it regulates, and it is afraid of bringing big cases against the largest, most powerful firms," said Markopolos. "Clearly the SEC was afraid of Mr. Madoff."

CON

1. The SEC's director of enforcement told a Senate committee, "We don't turn a blind eye to fraud. If we see it and we suspect it, we pursue it. We don't want fraudsters out there."
2. The director also said the SEC doesn't have enough resources to pursue all the tip-offs of potential fraud that come before it: "If we had more resources we could clearly do more." Other regulators blamed lack of coordination among government agencies for the lapses in oversight that allowed Madoff to operate.

Summary

Madoff pled guilty to charges of felony securities fraud. The SEC is conducting an internal investigation to discover why it failed to act on information about him that Markopolos and others provided over the years.

Sources: SEC Web site, http://www.sec.gov/about/whatwedo.shtml, accessed February 13, 2009; Linda Sandler, "Madoff Said Only Brother Could Do Audit, Witness Tells Congress," *Bloomberg News*, February 5, 2009, http://www.bloomberg.com; Allan Chernoff, "Madoff Whistleblower Blasts SEC," *CNNMoney*, February 4, 2009, http://www.cnnmoney.com; Dana B. Henriques, "Witness on Madoff Tells of Fear for Safety," *The New York Times*, February 4, 2009, http://www.nytimes.com; Julian Cummings, "Madoff: SEC Defends Its Role," *CNNMoney*, January 28, 2009, http://www.cnnmoney.com; Liz Moyer, "How Regulators Missed Madoff," *Forbes*, January 27, 2009, http://www.forbes.com.

Solving an ETHICAL controversy

What's Ahead

As business speeds along in the 21st century, new technologies, population shifts, and shrinking global barriers are altering the world at a frantic pace. Businesspeople are catalysts for many of these changes, creating new opportunities for individuals who are prepared to take action. Studying contemporary business will help you prepare for the future.

Throughout this book, you'll be exposed to the real-life stories of many businesspeople. You'll learn about the range of business careers available and the daily decisions, tasks, and challenges that they face. By the end of the course, you'll understand how marketing, accounting, finance, and management work together to provide competitive advantages for firms. This knowledge can help you become a more capable employee and enhance your career potential.

Now that this chapter has introduced some basic terms and issues in the business world of the 21st century, Chapter 2 takes a detailed look at the ethical and social responsibility issues facing contemporary business. Chapter 3 deals with economic challenges, and Chapter 4 focuses on the difficulties and opportunities faced by firms competing in world markets.

Summary of Learning Goals

1 Distinguish between business and not-for-profit organizations.

Business consists of all profit-seeking activities that provide goods and services necessary to an economic system. Not-for-profit organizations are business-like establishments whose primary objectives involve social, political, governmental, educational, or similar functions—instead of profits.

Assessment Check Answers

1.1 What activity lies at the heart of every business endeavor? At the heart of every business endeavor is an exchange between a buyer and a seller.

1.2 What are the primary objectives of a not-for-profit organization? Not-for-profit organizations place public service above profits, although they need to raise money in order to operate and achieve their social goals.

2 Identify and describe the factors of production.

The factors of production consist of four basic inputs: natural resources, capital, human resources, and entrepreneurship. Natural resources include all productive inputs that are useful in their natural states. Capital includes technology, tools, information, and physical facilities. Human resources include anyone who works for the firm. Entrepreneurship is the willingness to take risks to create and operate a business.

Assessment Check Answers

2.1 Identify the four basic inputs to an economic system. The four basic inputs are natural resources, capital, human resources, and entrepreneurship.

2.2 List four types of capital. Four types of capital are technology, tools, information, and physical facilities.

3 Describe the private enterprise system, including basic rights and entrepreneurship.

The private enterprise system is an economic system that rewards firms for their ability to perceive and serve the needs and demands of consumers. Competition in the private enterprise system ensures success for firms that satisfy consumer demands. Citizens in a private enterprise economy enjoy the rights to private property, profits, freedom of choice, and competition. Entrepreneurship drives economic growth.

Assessment Check Answers

3.1 What is an alternative term for *private enterprise system*? *Capitalism* is an alternative word for *private enterprise system*.

3.2 What is the most basic freedom under the private enterprise system? The most basic freedom is the right to private property.

3.3 What is an entrepreneur? An entrepreneur is a risk taker who is willing to start, own, and operate a business.

4 Identify the six eras of business, and explain how the relationship era—including alliances, technology, and environmental concerns—influences contemporary business.

The six historical eras are the Colonial period, the Industrial Revolution, the age of industrial entrepreneurs, the production era, the marketing era, and the relationship era. In the Colonial period, businesses were small and rural, emphasizing agricultural production. The Industrial Revolution brought factories and mass production to business. The age of industrial entrepreneurs built on the Industrial Revolution through an expansion in the number and size of firms. The production era focused on the growth of factory operations through assembly lines and other efficient internal processes. During and following the Great Depression, businesses concentrated on finding markets for their products through advertising and selling, giving rise to the marketing era. In the relationship era, businesspeople focus on developing and sustaining long-term relationships with customers and other businesses. Technology promotes innovation and communication, while alliances create a competitive advantage through partnerships. Concern for the environment also helps build strong relationship with customers.

Assessment Check Answers

4.1 What was the Industrial Revolution? The Industrial Revolution began around 1750 in England and moved business operations from an emphasis on independent, skilled workers to a factory system that mass-produced items.

4.2 During which era was the idea of branding developed? The idea of branding began in the marketing era.

4.3 What is the difference between transaction management and relationship management? Transaction management is an approach that focuses on building, promoting, and selling enough products to cover costs and earn profits. Relationship management is the collection of activities that build and maintain ongoing ties with customers and other parties.

5 Explain how today's business workforce is changing.
The workforce is changing in several significant ways: (1) it is aging and the labor pool is shrinking and (2) it is becoming increasingly diverse.

Assessment Check Answers

5.1 How does the aging workforce affect business? An aging workforce requires businesses to hire workers at both extreme ends of the working-age spectrum.

5.2 How can businesses benefit from a diverse workforce? A diverse workforce can enrich a company's chances of success because diverse groups tend to perform tasks more effectively and develop better solutions. They also tend to foster greater innovation.

6 Describe how the nature of work itself is changing.
The nature of work has shifted toward services and a focus on information. More firms now rely on outsourcing, offshoring, and nearshoring to produce goods or fulfill services and functions that were previously handled in-house or in-country. In addition, today's workplaces are becoming increasingly flexible, allowing employees to work from different locations and through different relationships. And companies are fostering innovation through teamwork and collaboration.

Assessment Check Answers

6.1 Define *outsourcing, offshoring,* and *nearshoring*. Outsourcing involves using outside vendors to produce goods or fulfill services and functions that were once handled in-house or in-country. Offshoring is the relocation of business processes to lower-cost locations overseas. Nearshoring is the outsourcing of production or services to locations near a firm's home base.

6.2 Describe the importance of collaboration and employee partnership. Businesses are increasingly focusing on collaboration, rather than on individuals working alone. No longer do employees just put in their time at a job they hold their entire career. The new employer–employee partnership encourages teamwork and creative thinking, problem solving, and innovation. Managers are trained to listen to and respect employees.

7 Identify the skills and attributes that managers need to lead businesses in the 21st century.
Today's managers need vision, the ability to perceive marketplace needs and the way their firm can satisfy them. Critical-thinking skills and creativity allow managers to pinpoint problems and opportunities and plan novel solutions. Finally, managers are dealing with rapid change, and they need skills to help lead their organizations through shifts in external and internal conditions.

Assessment Check Answers

7.1 Why is vision an important managerial quality? Managerial vision allows a firm to innovate and adapt to meet changes in the marketplace.

7.2 What is the difference between creativity and critical thinking? Critical thinking is the ability to analyze and assess information to pinpoint problems or opportunities. Creativity is the capacity to develop novel solutions to perceived organizational problems.

8 Outline the characteristics that make a company admired by the business community.
A company is usually admired for its solid profits, stable growth, a safe and challenging work environment, high-quality goods and services, and business ethics and social responsibility.

Assessment Check Answers

8.1 Define *business ethics* and *social responsibility*. Business ethics refers to the standards of conduct and moral values involving decisions made in the work environment. Social responsibility is a management philosophy that includes contributing resources to the community, preserving the natural environment, and developing or participating in nonprofit programs designed to promote the well-being of the general public.

8.2 Identify three criteria used to judge whether a company might be considered admirable. Criteria in judging whether companies are admirable include three of the following: solid profits, stable growth, a safe and challenging work environment, high-quality goods and services, and business ethics and social responsibility.

Business Terms You Need to Know

business 4

profits 5

factors of production 6

private enterprise system 8

competition 9

entrepreneur 11

brand 16

relationship management 17

outsourcing 21

Other Important Business Terms

not-for-profit
    organizations 5
natural resources 6
capital 6
human resources 7
entrepreneurship 8

capitalism 8
competitive
    differentiation 9
private property 10
consumer orientation 15
branding 16

transaction management 16
relationship era 16
technology 17
partnership 18
strategic alliance 18
diversity 21

offshoring 21
nearshoring 21
vision 22
critical thinking 23
creativity 23

Review Questions

1. Why is business so important to a country's economy?

2. In what ways are not-for-profit organizations a substantial part of the U.S. economy? What challenges do not-for-profits face?

3. Identify and describe the four basic inputs that make up factors of production. Give an example of each factor of production that an auto manufacturer might use.

4. What is a private enterprise system? What are the four rights that are critical to the operation of capitalism? Why would capitalism have difficulty functioning in a society that does not assure these rights for its citizens?

5. In what ways is entrepreneurship vital to the private enterprise system?

6. Identify the six eras of business in the United States. How were businesses changed during each era?

7. Describe the focus of the most recent era of U.S. business. How is this different from previous eras?

8. How might a supermarket chain use technology to assist in its relationship management?

9. Define *partnership* and *strategic alliance.* How might a motorcycle dealer and a local radio station benefit from an alliance?

10. Identify the major changes in the workforce that will affect the way managers build a world-class workforce in the 21st century. Why is brainpower so important?

11. Identify four qualities that the "new" managers of the 21st century must have. Why are these qualities important in a competitive business environment?

Projects and Teamwork Applications

1. The entrepreneurial spirit fuels growth in the U.S. economy. Choose a company that interests you—one you have worked for or dealt with as a customer—and read about the company in the library or visit its Web site. Learn what you can about the company's early history: Who founded it and why? Is the founder still with the organization? Do you think the founder's original vision is still embraced by the company? If not, how has the vision changed?

2. Brands distinguish one company's goods or services from its competitors. Each company you purchase from hopes that you will become loyal to its brand. Some well-known brands are McDonald's, Coca-Cola, Hilton, and Old Navy. Choose a type of good or service you use regularly and identify the major brands associated with it. Are you loyal to a particular brand? Why or why not?

3. More and more businesses are forming strategic alliances to become more competitive. Sometimes, businesses pair up with not-for-profit organizations in a relationship that

is beneficial to both. Choose a company whose goods or services interest you, such as Timberland, FedEx, General Mills, or Target. On your own or with a classmate, research the firm on the Internet to learn about its alliances with not-for-profit organizations. Then describe one of the alliances, including goals and benefits to both parties. Create a presentation for class.

4. This chapter describes how the nature of the workforce is changing: the population is aging, the labor pool is shrinking, the workforce is becoming more diverse, the nature of work is changing, the workplace is becoming more flexible and mobile, and employers are fostering innovation and collaboration among their employees. Form teams of two to three students. Select a company and research how that company is responding to changes in the workforce. When you have completed your research, be prepared to present it to your class. Choose one of the following companies or select your own: State Farm Insurance, Archer Daniels Midland, 3M, Marriott, or Dell Inc.

Web Assignments

1. **Web terminology.** To help Web surfers better understand the Internet, several sites have glossaries of Internet terms. Visit the site listed here and define the following terms:

bookmark   FTP
cache   RSS
cookie   spiders

http://www.lib.berkeley.edu/TeachingLib/Guides/Internet/Glossary.html

2. **Sources of information.** One of the popular news and information sources on the Web is Google News (http://news.google.com). Visit Google News and click on "Business." Choose a key term from the chapter as a search term and see how many articles you find. Now use the name of a company mentioned in the chapter and conduct a search. Write a brief report on your experience.

3. **Organization Web sites.** Virtually all companies and not-for-profit organizations maintain Web sites. Choose two companies and a not-for-profit, and visit each's Web site. What is the main purpose of the Web sites? What information was available? How was each site organized? Which site do you think was most effective?

Note: Internet Web addresses change frequently. If you don't find the exact sites listed, you may need to access the organization's home page and search from there.

Herman Miller Has Designs on the Future   Case 1.1

Michigan-based Herman Miller is best known as the world's second-largest office furniture maker. But did you know it also focuses on "green" production and design? The company produces a programmable energy and data management system for office buildings, publishes a magazine about future trends, and supports environmental initiatives—like the U.S. Green Building Council. It is also involved in recycling its waste and using resources from renewable supply sources. The firm's broader focus is helping it establish new relationships with customers—and prosper.

Herman Miller's employees participate in the management and ownership of their firm. All full-time employees with one month of service are entitled to own stock in the company. With a real stake in the success of their firm, the staff focuses on quality and customer satisfaction.

Herman Miller sees its mission as solving people's problems. According to CEO Brian Walker, "We rarely start off saying, 'We just want a chair in this price point.' More often, we say, 'Here's a problem area that we see for folks. How do we solve it?' ... If you begin by trying to solve the problem, you get a different outcome than [by] saying, 'We need to go do a chair that's $200.'" This problem-solving approach applies to all the firm's activities.

The company also tries to think creatively by engaging it what it calls "global scenario planning." In that effort, staff members think beyond their day-to-day activities and try to imagine what changes may happen in the world a few years down the road. Then they try to devise strategies to meet that vision. Because of the looming presence of the Chinese market, Herman Miller executives and a team of designers visited the country to assess its challenges and opportunities. Of that trip, Walker says it "became clear that we were going to have to create some designs very specific to that marketplace and we would have to hire local people, both on the design and management side, to really understand the Chinese culture and be sensitive to it."

Design innovation comes easily to Herman Miller, but it doesn't necessarily come from within. The company outsources its creative work to a network of award-winning independent designers for what Walker calls "a fresh perspective on existing or emerging problems." He doesn't limit design to internal staff because that would limit the ideas considered. He wants instead to draw from fresh eyes and talent to create truly innovative designs. That strategy is working: more than 50 Herman Miller designs are in the permanent collections of major museums, such as New York's Museum of Modern Art, the Whitney Museum of American Art, the Smithsonian, and other institutions worldwide.

Here the company demonstrates its flexibility: "The central thing that we've learned," says Walker, "is a willingness to follow and give ourselves over to these designers ... following them to places that we may question in the beginning." The bottom line is that creative problem solving drives all the firm's efforts. The goal is to create great designs that solve real problems and creates commercial value. That combination is a winning formula for the company and its customers.[40]

Questions for Critical Thinking

1. Explain how innovation, creativity, and flexibility have played a role in Herman Miller's success.
2. What kind of relationships does Herman Miller seem to have with its employees? With its customers? With its outside designers?

Case 1.2   Facebook's Continuing Makeover

Facebook, the Internet phenomenon created by 23-year-old college dropout Mark Zuckerberg, may not be earning very much money right now. But it is a business, and a highly valuable one: Microsoft recently bought a 1.6 percent share in the company for $240 million, and rumors that Facebook might offer its stock to the public surface regularly. Zuckerberg claims he isn't yet ready to sell stock in his creation, but he does plan to keep reinventing it with new features for its exploding roster of users.

The site was originally built to connect students at Harvard, where Zuckerberg was a student. Then he and two classmates expanded it to include 40 other campuses. Soon they included all U.S. colleges, then high schools. Now anyone can sign up. Facebook's growth has been so rapid that any statistics cited are soon dated. Current projections put Facebook users at 200 million. A Spanish-language version of the site also opened for the nearly 3 million Spanish-speaking users, and sites in German, French, and other languages are opening soon.

Zuckerberg may be a young entrepreneur, but he has already made decisions few managers twice his age would relish. He has built an ever-expanding organization of 400 people and faced a pending lawsuit by former classmates who claim he stole their idea. He has chosen to keep the company private and turned down an offer from Yahoo! to buy Facebook for $1 billion in cash. He has gone from college student to celebrity in California's high-tech Silicon Valley. His every move is watched by the technology industry, competitors, Wall Street, and the press. With all that attention and pressure, however, he says he lives in a one-bedroom apartment with a mattress on the floor.

Facebook has weathered several storms. Although its turndown of Yahoo's offer was controversial, perhaps even more challenging to Zuckerberg was the crisis over Beacon, an information-tracking feature Facebook introduced. The application automatically notified users' friends of all purchases they made at over 40 Web sites. That feature created a firestorm of protest over privacy issues, along with unflattering press coverage.

Zuckerberg may have reacted too slowly to users' concerns, although he did revise the program and now allows users to opt out of it. In the end, Facebook recovered quickly. The site's latest innovation allows any user to create new software applications, charge users for them, and keep the proceeds. The response has been highly positive so far. One application Zuckerberg likes himself is Facebook Scrabble.

But the site needs a way to actually earn money. Zuckerberg is experimenting with advertising applications. As the Beacon crisis showed, however, he will need to consider users' desires and allow them to avoid features they don't like. Users at social-networking sites have different wants and needs from those accessing commercial or news sites. In the latest twist, some users discovered, for instance, that they can't entirely delete their pages if they want to leave the site. Through it all, Zuckerberg remains committed to producing a positive experience. "I'm here to build something for the long term," he says. "Anything else is just a distraction."[41]

Questions for Critical Thinking

1. How does Mark Zuckerberg typify an entrepreneur? In what ways do you think his experience or background as an entrepreneur is unusual?

2. How well do you think Facebook manages its relationships with its users? If it needs to start showing a profit, how do you think this may change that relationship?

VIDEO   Case 1.3   Cannondale Keeps Satisfied Customers Rolling

You'll never forget your first real bicycle. Maybe it had stickers on the fenders, streamers from the handlebars, and maybe even a bell or horn. The important point was that it didn't have training wheels—and it wasn't a tricycle. It was a bona fide bike. The people at Cannondale share your passion for that first bike, and they want you to enjoy cycling as an adult, preferably on one of their models.

The Connecticut-based company stresses quality and customer satisfaction from the ground up, from tires to seats to handlebars. Company management also understands that cyclists come in a variety of types, from recreational to racer. And satisfying the needs of a variety of cyclists means that Cannondale offers a broad product line made up of diverse models—including high-performance road bikes, sport road bikes, cross-country racing models, pack touring cycles, triathlon bikes, mountain bikes, "comfort" bikes, tandems, and even a recumbent cycle with a soft seat and backrest. For the truly persnickety customer, the bike maker also offers customized bike frames. And for cyclists who want to look and feel cool while they are riding, Cannondale can outfit riders with cycling apparel in high-tech fabrics. If that's not enough for the cycling enthusiast, there are hats, socks, shoes, seat and handlebar bags, and more.

It takes teamwork to produce Cannondale products, which are considered by both the cycling industry and their loyal customers to be of superior quality. If you could sit in on a research and development meeting for a particular model, you'd get a good sense of how dedicated Cannondale designers, engineers, and product managers are to their customers. Steve Metz, director of product management, oversees everything from decisions about how to meet customers' needs to selecting components for a bike and making sure the final product is manufactured to quality specifications and delivered promptly to customers. John Horton leads a team of project engineers who develop new models and improve currently popular models like the Jekyll. Designers and engineers meet frequently—and often informally—to discuss ways to add value by installing stronger or lighter components and increasing speed without driving up the price. They test different innovations, communicate with the manufacturing plant, and test them again. Once they have a prototype, they ride the bike. And to continually focus on customers, Cannondale designers use inputs from current and potential customers to guide every phase of the development process. After all, the world's highest quality bike is still a failure if it remains unsold in retail stores.

Technology also plays an important role in creating the lightweight, high-performance bikes for which Cannondale is so well-known. The company isn't hesitant to develop working relationships with outside firms capable of supplying technology not available in house. Years ago, Cannondale reached an agreement with Genosys Technology Management under which Genosys would supply expertise in monitoring quality control and providing improved communication throughout the company. Cannondale has also pioneered such innovations as the electronic shock lockout system for mountain bikes. A traditional mountain bike is equipped with shock absorbers that reduce the amount of shock to a rider's

leg, but the same mechanism also makes it harder to pedal uphill or make the most of sprints during a race. If a rider wants to "lock out" the shock absorber, he or she needs to remove one hand from the handlebar, a cumbersome maneuver for a cyclist on the move. The electronic Cannondale system works with the push of a button. One touch activates the lockout, and a second touch deactivates it. Riders love it. But the new system didn't come easily; Cannondale engineers tested and discarded several designs and prototypes before they had one that worked. The new system made its worldwide debut at the Sydney Olympics, where Swiss rider Christoph Sauser won a bronze medal.

The pursuit of quality requires that a firm must make ethical business decisions, even if that means admitting mistakes. Despite every effort to produce the best components, one year Cannondale discovered that the stems—part of the steering systems—on some of its $3,400 to $5,000 bicycles were breaking. The company responded quickly. After four reported instances and one minor injury, Cannondale issued a recall for the defective parts. Although a recall may have caused initial unwanted publicity, in the long run dealers and cyclists knew they could trust Cannondale to make the right decision. That's the mark of a company whose passion is perfection on wheels.

Like every business, Cannondale execs have made a few mistakes along the way. Their expansion into motorsports proved a failure. Worse yet, it ate up hordes of company funds and, coupled with the economic slowdown, forced founder Joe Montgomery to seek bankruptcy protection. In 2003, the firm was purchased by Pegasus Partners, which provided new funds for the cash-starved company and promised to make Cannondale even better. Pegasus representative David Uri voiced strong support for the company: "The fact that the bike division has remained profitable despite the … costs of its now closed motorsports business clearly demonstrates the strength of the brand. Our job now is to let Cannondale concentrate on what Cannondale does best—designing, manufacturing, and marketing lightweight, high-performance bicycles for the specialty retail market."[42]

Questions for Critical Thinking

1. Identify some of the types of capital that Cannondale uses in producing its bicycles.
2. In what ways do human resources at Cannondale contribute to value and customer satisfaction?
3. Describe how Cannondale can use relationship management to thrive and grow as a company.
4. Cannondale relies on teamwork to produce its bicycles. In what ways does this reflect the changing nature of today's workplace?

chapter **2**

Business Ethics and Social Responsibility

© Masterfile

Entropy Surfboards Ride the Green Wave

Pioneers in many fields have changed our world. Creative businesspeople are a force for positive change, especially when it comes to protecting and preserving the natural environment. Santa Monica, California–based Entropy Surfboards was started by two surfing brothers—Desi and Rey Banatao—who had a different idea about how their products could be manufactured.

Despite their reputation for being free spirits, surfers tend to be traditionalists when it comes to performance. They want their boards to meet strict standards to carve the waves efficiently. Surfboards have long been made from toxic petroleum-based chemicals that also require large amounts of energy. Because of their light weight and durability, polyurethane and fiberglass are the most common construction materials. Yet both are environmental toxins. And when a surfer is ready to toss out an old board, it ends up in a landfill.

Entropy is trying to change that. Convinced that a surfboard can be as green as the ocean itself, Desi and Rey Banatao put their technology education to work on the sport they love. "Our dad gave us the idea to start the company, to make use of our tech degrees," recalls Rey. Their entry into the market was well timed because of the interest in environmentally friendly products. Also, a void occurred in the industry when the major supplier of low-cost surfboard cores was shut down. The Environmental Protection Agency had investigated the company because of the toxic gases that were emitted during production. The Banataos quickly went to work on their own alternative, researching the chemical and mechanical behavior of bio-composites and completing their first bio-boards just two years later. "For us, [the new board] means optimizing the balance between choice of materials, techniques, and performance," notes Rey.

The core, also called a *blank*, of an Entropy surfboard is made with a foam derived from sugar-beet oil instead of polyurethane. The beet polymer, developed by partner firm Ice-Nine, is nearly identical to polyurethane but is processed using fewer toxic chemicals. The blank is then wrapped in hemp and bamboo cloth and coated with a material derived from pine instead of a traditional epoxy resin. Where plastic is necessary, Entropy uses a bio-based

material. The overall result, claims the company, is a 75 percent reduction in the use of petroleum-based materials. The Banataos refer to their construction process as an ecosystem. "Just like an actual ecosystem, all the different components work together and depend on each other to improve the whole thing," observes Rey.

Surfboards are generally produced by small workshops, and Entropy's are no exception. The surfboard shapers, as they are called, must outfit their shops and learn new manufacturing techniques. But these alternative processes benefit the shapers because the toxins and fumes are greatly reduced, creating fewer health hazards for workers.

Building boards with environmentally sustainable materials and processes is fine, but the boards have to perform. Surfers must be convinced that these boards can stand up to the stresses of monster waves. Entropy promises that its boards meet the highest standards. They are lightweight and durable, and each model matches features in its traditional counterparts. The Pocket Rocket is highly maneuverable, offering easy paddling and wave catching. The Kampachi has a raised deck for paddling power and narrow rails for quick turns. Finally comes the important issue of price. Of necessity, the new technologies are cost competitive; otherwise, the boards won't sell.

Now that the manufacture of their bio-boards is under way, Rey and Desi are looking further into the future. What happens to boards that have outlived their useful life? The brothers are researching ways to reuse worn out boards in their ecosystem of production so that the materials can be recycled into the next generation of boards. Although they have not quite solved that problem yet, the Banataos are confident that surfboard recycling represents the wave of the future. "At the end of the day, innovation is our only way to compete with the rest of the world," predicts Rey. "Whether it's innovation in shape, materials, or construction, we've got to keep progressing."[1]

Entropy Surfboards's efforts to create sustainable operations are not unique in the world of business—they just occur on a smaller scale than those of many other firms. Many companies are concerned about the environment and their societies. Sometimes that means growing more slowly than they might or reducing short-term profits for longer, sustained benefits. In Entropy's case, it means not only changing its own operations to help the environment but also persuading consumers that they should change their view of a sport they love.

Although most organizations strive to combine ethical behavior with profitable operation, some have struggled to overcome major ethical lapses in recent years. Ethical failures in a number of large or well-known firms led to lawsuits, indictments, and judgments against firms. The image of the CEO—and of business in general—suffered as the evening news carried reports of executives pocketing millions of dollars in compensation while their companies floundered.

But sometimes bad news is a prelude to good news. In the wake of such stories, both the government and companies have renewed their efforts to conduct themselves in an ethical manner and one that reflects a responsibility to society, to consumers, and to the environment. In 2004 the Federal Sentencing Commission strengthened its guidelines for ethics compliance programs, and more and more firms began to pay attention to formulating more explicit standards and procedures for ethical behavior. Companies also began to recognize the enormous impact of setting a good example rather than a bad one. Today you are likely to hear about the goodwill that companies such as Target Corporation, Ford Motor Company, and Starbucks generate when they give back to their communities through youth reading programs, undertake recycling or energy-conservation programs, or seek to pay fair prices to suppliers.

As we discussed in Chapter 1, the underlying aim of business is to serve customers at a profit. But most companies today try to do more than that, looking for ways to give back to customers, society, and the environment. Sometimes they face difficult questions in the process. When does a company's self-interest conflict with society's and customers' well-being? And must the goal of seeking profits conflict with upholding high principles of right and wrong? In response to the second question, a growing number of businesses of all sizes are answering no.

Concern for Ethical and Societal Issues

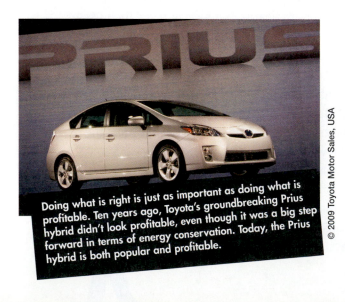

Doing what is right is just as important as doing what is profitable. Ten years ago, Toyota's groundbreaking Prius hybrid didn't look profitable, even though it was a big step forward in terms of energy conservation. Today, the Prius hybrid is both popular and profitable.

© 2009 Toyota Motor Sales, USA

An organization that wants to prosper over the long term is well advised to consider **business ethics,** the standards of conduct and moral values governing actions and decisions in the work environment. Businesses also must take into account a wide range of social issues, including how a decision will affect the environment, employees, and customers. These issues are at the heart of social responsibility, whose primary objective is the enhancement of society's welfare through philosophies, policies, procedures, and actions. In short, businesses must find the delicate balance between doing what is right and doing what is profitable. When Toyota launched its Prius hybrid a decade ago, critics laughed and predicted it would fail. Today, the Prius is so popular that Toyota has expanded its hybrid line to include the Highlander SUV and the Camry. Through its "Ecomagination" initiative, General Electric hopes to double its revenue from environmentally clean technologies. These products include fuel-efficient jets, wind turbine generators, compact fluorescent light bulbs, and water purification systems.[2]

In business, as in life, deciding what is right or wrong in a given situation does not always involve a clear-cut choice. Firms have many responsibilities—to customers, to employees, to investors, and to society as a whole. Sometimes conflicts arise in trying to serve the different needs of these separate constituencies. The ethical values of executives and individual employees at all levels can influence the decisions and actions a business takes. Throughout your own career, you will encounter many situations in which you will need to weigh right and wrong before making a decision or taking action. So we begin our discussion of business ethics by focusing on individual ethics.

Business ethics are also shaped by the ethical climate within an organization. Codes of conduct and ethical standards play increasingly significant roles in businesses in which doing the right thing is both supported and applauded. This chapter demonstrates how a firm can create a framework to encourage—and even demand—high standards of ethical behavior and social responsibility from its employees. The chapter also considers the complex question of what business owes to society and how societal forces mold the actions of businesses. Finally, it examines the influence of business ethics and social responsibility on global business.

business ethics standards of conduct and moral values involving right and wrong actions arising in the work environment.

Assessment Check ✓

1. To whom do businesses have responsibilities?

2. If a firm is meeting all its responsibilities to others, why do ethical conflicts arise?

The Contemporary Ethical Environment

Business ethics are now in the spotlight as never before. Companies realize that they have to work harder to earn the trust of the general public, and many have taken on the challenge as if their very survival depends on it. According to one survey, 95 percent of CEOs replied that society now has greater expectations of business than it did five years ago.[3] This movement toward *corporate social responsibility* should benefit all—consumers, the environment, and the companies themselves.

Most business owners and managers have built and maintained enduring companies without breaking the rules. One example of a firm with a longstanding commitment to ethical practice is Johnson & Johnson, the giant multinational manufacturer of healthcare products. The most admired pharmaceutical maker and the ninth-most-admired company in the world, according to *Fortune,* Johnson & Johnson has abided by the same basic code of ethics, its well-known Credo, for more than 50 years. The Credo, reproduced in Figure 2.1, remains the ethical standard against which the company's employees periodically evaluate how well their firm is performing. Management is pledged to address any lapses that are reported.[4]

Many CEOs personify the best in management practices and are highly respected for their integrity, honesty, and business ethics. Retailer Target has spent millions of dollars to adopt alternative energy sources in selected stores, with the goal of expanding the program nationwide. "Part of Target's DNA is our commitment to the community, and certainly that ties into the environment as well," says company spokesperson Amy von Walter. "We're known as being an ethical company, and we are very sensitive to meeting green standards as we do business whenever possible." In addition to installing solar energy systems, the company partners with suppliers to offer eco-friendly products and recycle packaging, and even designs its gift cards from biodegradable materials.[5]

"They Said It"

"I believe that those who have been successful are obligated to give back to those who have been less successful."

—John Chambers (b. 1950) CEO, Cisco Systems

Figure 2.1   **Johnson & Johnson Credo**

Our Credo

We believe our first responsibility is to the doctors, nurses and patients, to mothers and fathers and all others who use our products and services. In meeting their needs everything we do must be of high quality. We must constantly strive to reduce our costs in order to maintain reasonable prices. Customers' orders must be serviced promptly and accurately. Our suppliers and distributors must have an opportunity to make a fair profit.

We are responsible to our employees, the men and women who work with us throughout the world. Everyone must be considered as an individual. We must respect their dignity and recognize their merit. They must have a sense of security in their jobs. Compensation must be fair and adequate, and working conditions clean, orderly and safe. We must be mindful of ways to help our employees fulfill their family responsibilities. Employees must feel free to make suggestions and complaints. There must be equal opportunity for employment, development and advancement for those qualified. We must provide competent management, and their actions must be just and ethical.

We are responsible to the communities in which we live and work and to the world community as well. We must be good citizens—support good works and charities and bear our fair share of taxes. We must encourage civic improvements and better health and education. We must maintain in good order the property we are privileged to use, protecting the environment and natural resources.

Our final responsibility is to our stockholders. Business must make a sound profit. We must experiment with new ideas. Research must be carried on, innovative programs developed and mistakes paid for. New equipment must be purchased, new facilities provided and new products launched. Reserves must be created to provide for adverse times. When we operate according to these principles, the stockholders should realize a fair return.

Source: "Our Company: Our Credo," Johnson & Johnson Web site, accessed February 19, 2009, http://www.jnj.com. © Johnson & Johnson.

However, not all companies set and meet high ethical standards. The National Business Ethics Survey, conducted by the Ethics Resource Center, found that more than one-half of employees surveyed "witnessed an act of misconduct in their company within the past year." Worse, the survey found that employees often did not report misconduct because they were afraid of retribution or they did not feel they could make an impact. However, the center found that companies with strong ethics cultures experienced a dramatic reduction in the likelihood of misconduct, as shown in Figure 2.2.[6]

With passage of the **Sarbanes-Oxley Act of 2002,** which establishes new rules and regulations for securities trading and accounting practices, a company is also required to publish its code of ethics, if it has one, and inform the public of any changes made to it. The new law may actually motivate even more firms to develop written codes and guidelines for ethical business behavior. The federal government also created the U.S. Sentencing Commission to institutionalize ethics compliance programs that would establish high ethical standards and end corporate misconduct. The requirements for such programs are shown in Table 2.1.

The current ethical environment of business also includes the appointment of new corporate officers specifically charged with deterring wrongdoing and ensuring that ethical standards are met. Ethics compliance officers, whose numbers are rapidly rising, are responsible for conducting employee training programs that help spot potential fraud and abuse within the firm, investigating sexual harassment and discrimination charges, and monitoring any potential conflicts of interest. But practicing corporate social responsibility is more than just monitoring behavior. Many companies now adopt a three-pronged approach to ethics and social responsibility:

1. engaging in traditional corporate philanthropy, which involves giving to worthy causes
2. anticipating and managing risks
3. identifying opportunities to create value by doing the right thing.[7]

Individuals Make a Difference

In today's business environment, individuals can make the difference in ethical expectations and behavior. As executives, managers, and employees demonstrate their personal ethical principles—or lack of ethical principles—the expectations and actions of those who work for and with them can change.

What is the current status of individual business ethics in the United States? Although ethical behavior can be difficult to track or define in all circumstances, evidence suggests that unfortunately some individuals act unethically or illegally on the job. The National Business Ethics Survey identifies such behaviors as putting one's own interests ahead of the organization, lying to employees, misreporting hours worked, Internet abuse, and safety violations, among others.[8]

Technology seems to have expanded the range and impact of unethical behavior. For example, anyone with computer access to data has the potential to steal or manipulate the data or to shut down the system, even from a remote location. During a recent year, more than 75 tech companies admitted to ethical violations or were investigated for their handling of certain issues.[9] While some might shrug these allegations away, in fact they have an impact on how investors, customers, and the general public view a firm. It is difficult to rebuild a tarnished image, and long-term customers may be lost.

Nearly every employee, at every level, wrestles with ethical questions at some point or another. Some

Figure 2.2

Companies with Strong Ethics Cultures Reduce the Risk of Unethical Behavior

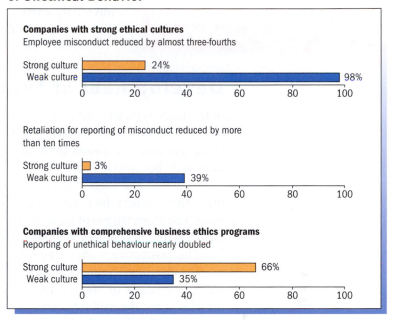

Source: "National Business Ethics Survey," *Ethics Resource Center,* November 2007, accessed February 19, 2009.

Table 2.1	Minimum Requirements for Ethics Compliance Programs

- **Compliance standards and procedures.** Establish standards and procedures, such as codes of ethics and identification of areas of risk, capable of reducing misconduct or criminal activities.

- **High-level personnel responsibility.** Assign high-level personnel, such as boards of directors and top executives, the overall responsibility to actively lead and oversee ethics compliance programs.

- **Due care in assignments.** Avoid delegating authority to individuals with a propensity for misconduct or illegal activities.

- **Communication of standards and procedures.** Communicate ethical requirements to high-level officials and other employees through ethics training programs or publications that explain in practical terms what is required.

- **Establishment of monitoring and auditing systems and reporting system.** Monitor and review ethical compliance systems, and establish a reporting system employees can use to notify the organization of misconduct without fear of retribution.

- **Enforcement of standards through appropriate mechanisms.** Consistently enforce ethical codes, including employee discipline.

- **Appropriate responses to the offense.** Take reasonable steps to respond to the offense and to prevent and detect further violations.

- **Self-reporting.** Report misconduct to the appropriate government agency.

- **Applicable industry practice or standards.** Follow government regulations and industry standards.

Sources: "An Overview of the United States Sentencing Commission and the Federal Sentencing Guidelines," U.S. Sentencing Commission, http://www.epic-online.net; "The Relationship between Law and Ethics, and the Significance of the Federal Sentencing Guidelines for Organizations," Ethics and Policy Integration Center, http://www.ethicaledge.com; U.S. Sentencing Commission, "Sentencing Commission Toughens Requirements for Corporate Compliance and Ethics Programs," USSC news release, http://www.ussc.gov.

Assessment Check ✓

1. What role can an ethics compliance officer play in a firm?
2. What factors influence the ethical environment of a business?

rationalize questionable behavior by saying, "Everybody's doing it." Others act unethically because they feel pressured in their jobs or have to meet performance quotas. Yet some avoid unethical acts that don't mesh with their personal values and morals. To help you understand the differences in the ways individuals arrive at ethical choices, the next section focuses on how personal ethics and morals develop.

Development of Individual Ethics

Individuals typically develop ethical standards in the three stages shown in Figure 2.3: the preconventional, conventional, and postconventional stages. In the preconventional stage, individuals primarily consider their own needs and desires in making decisions. They obey external rules only because they are afraid of punishment or hope to receive rewards if they comply.

In the second stage, the conventional stage, individuals are aware of and act in response to their duty to others, including their obligations to their family members, coworkers, and organizations. The expectations of these groups influence how they choose between what is acceptable and unacceptable in certain situations. Self-interest, however, continues to play a role in decisions.

The postconventional stage, the final stage, represents the highest level of ethical and moral behavior. The individual is able to move beyond mere self-interest and duty and take the larger needs of society into account as well. He or she has developed personal ethical principles for determining what is right and can apply those principles in a wide variety of situations. One issue that you may face at work is the request to make donations to charitable causes; the "Business Etiquette" feature lists some tips to consider before you donate.

An individual's stage in moral and ethical development is determined by a huge number of factors. Experiences help shape responses to different situations. A person's family, educational, cultural, and religious backgrounds can also play a role, as can the environment within the firm. Individuals can also have different styles of deciding ethical dilemmas, no matter what their stage of moral development.

To help you understand and prepare for the ethical dilemmas you may confront in your career, let's take a closer look at some of the factors involved in solving ethical questions on the job.

On-the-Job Ethical Dilemmas

In the fast-paced world of business, you will sometimes be called on to weigh the ethics of decisions that can affect not just your own future but possibly the futures of your fellow workers, your company, and its customers. As already noted, it's not always easy to distinguish between what is right and wrong in many business situations, especially when the needs and concerns of various parties conflict. In the recent past some CEOs (or their companies) who were accused of wrongdoing simply claimed that they had no idea crimes were being committed, but today's top executives are making a greater effort to be informed of all activities taking place in their firms.

Many manufacturers that use factories overseas to produce their goods have faced criticism at home over the poor working conditions found there. Instead of pulling their business back to the United States, however, some companies have focused on efforts to improve the conditions

Figure 2.3

Stages of Moral and Ethical Development

Stage 1: Preconventional

Individual is mainly looking out for his or her own interests. Rules are followed only out of fear of punishment or hope of reward.

↓

Stage 2: Conventional

Individual considers the interests and expectations of others in making decisions. Rules are followed because it is a part of belonging to the group.

↓

Stage 3: Postconventional

Individual follows personal principles for resolving ethical dilemmas. He or she considers personal, group, and societal interests.

abroad. When a newspaper reported that one of Gap Inc.'s factories in India used children who were being forced to work 16 hours a day in abusive conditions, hand-sewing clothing without pay, the firm immediately took action. Gap discovered that the sweatshop was actually a subcontractor that had been hired illegally by one of Gap's vendors. Gap immediately met with all of its suppliers in India to learn the extent of the problem and to reinforce its policies. "We appreciate that the media identified this subcontractor, and we acted swiftly in this situation," said a Gap spokesperson. "Under no circumstances is it acceptable for children to produce or work on garments."[10]

Businesses may sometimes refuse to offer goods or services from a particular country because of civil rights abuses by the government of that country. Recently, some of the world's largest and most prestigious jewelers, including Cartier and Tiffany, announced that they would not purchase jade and other gems from Myanmar (formerly Burma) because of the government's crackdown on protests by students and monks, as well as other civil rights violations. In addition, the 27 countries of the European Union agreed to ban the import of gems from Myanmar. "If the U.S. and European Union were to cease buying all Burmese gemstones, I think it would take a huge chunk out of the regime's pocket," noted one Chicago jeweler.[11]

Solving ethical dilemmas is not easy. In many cases, each possible decision can have both unpleasant consequences and positive benefits that must be evaluated. The ethical issues that confront manufacturers with overseas suppliers are just one example of many different types of ethical questions encountered in the workplace. Figure 2.4 identifies four of the most common ethical challenges that businesspeople

Assessment Check

1. What is the preconventional stage in the development of ethical standards?
2. What is the difference between the conventional and the post-conventional stages?

Business Etiquette

HOW TO HANDLE DONATIONS AT WORK

Wherever you work, at some point you will be asked to donate to a good cause, whether it involves assisting a coworker in need or contributing to a charitable organization. Instead of being caught off guard, be prepared with an appropriate response that coincides with your personal ethics and approach to social responsibility.

When to Say "Yes"

- Agree to contribute if you agree with the cause. If you aren't sure about the organization, ask the person who is doing the soliciting for more information before writing a check.
- If you can't donate money but want to help out, offer your time or skills. These can be just as important and effective as cash.

How Much Is Right?

- No contribution is too small. Donate what you can afford or feel comfortable with. In the case of a major charitable organization, contributions are generally placed in an envelope so even the person collecting donations does not know the amounts.
- If you aren't sure how much to give, ask one or two coworkers who are at the same employment level as you are for an opinion. Then make your own decision.
- If you don't want to order six boxes of Girl Scout cookies or four hockey calendars from the person in the next cubicle, but you're happy to support his or her child's team or activity, donate a few dollars. Every bit helps.
- If people are collecting money toward a gift or party for a person at the company, they may suggest an amount. Of course, you can always chip in more. But if you feel the amount is too high, give what you can afford—or offer to pick up paper goods or a small flower arrangement for the party instead.
- Offer to pool your resources with other coworkers in order to make a larger single donation.

When to Say "No"

- Politely decline an opportunity to contribute if you do not agree with the cause. No one else can decide for you which charitable organizations or efforts you should support.
- Decline if you simply cannot afford it at this time. You may thank the person for asking and note that you might be able to help out in the future.
- If you already support other charitable organizations or causes, you may decline the request and explain that you need to keep your previous commitments.

Regardless of whether you decline or decide to donate this time around, be gracious to the person who is asking for your contribution. Remember that roles may be reversed in the future.

Sources: Bronwyn Harris, "How to Give Gifts at Work," *How To Do Things.com*, http://www.howtodothings.com, accessed February 20, 2009; "Isn't It Wrong to Decline a Charity Donation?" *Yahoo! Answers*, January 31, 2008, http://answers.yahoo.com; Sophie Charalambous, "Corporate Gift Etiquette," *Articles base*, March 13, 2007, http://www.articlesbase.com.

Figure 2.4

Common Business Ethical Challenges

Conflict of Interest

Honesty and Integrity

Ethical Challenges

Whistle-Blowing

Loyalty versus Truth

HOW FAR
WOULD YOU GO FOR
l0ve

Cartier

© Cartier/PRNewsFoto/NewsCom

Ethical conflicts are common in business, especially in today's global business environment. Recently, some of the world's largest and most prestigious jewelers, including Cartier, announced that they would not purchase jade and other gems from Myanmar because of the government's human rights violations.

face: conflict of interest, honesty and integrity, loyalty versus truth, and whistle-blowing.

CONFLICT OF INTEREST A conflict of interest exists when a businessperson is faced with a situation in which an action benefiting one person or group has the potential to harm another. Conflicts of interest may pose ethical challenges when they involve the businessperson's own interests and those of someone to whom he or she has a duty or when they involve two parties to whom the businessperson has a duty. Lawyers, business consultants, or advertising agencies would face a conflict of interest if they represented two competing companies: a strategy that would most benefit one of the client companies might harm the other client. Similarly, a real estate agent would face an ethical conflict by representing both the buyer and seller in a transaction. Handling the situation responsibly would be possible, but it would also be difficult. A conflict may also exist between someone's personal interests and those of an organization or its customers. An offer of gifts or bribes for special treatment creates a situation in which the buyer, but not necessarily the company, may benefit personally.

Physicians have come under fire recently for their ties to pharmaceutical companies. In addition to receiving free meals or drug samples from company representatives, doctors are sometimes paid fees to serve as "consultants" to their colleagues about certain products. One New York physician was on a speakers' bureau for pharmaceutical companies and spoke to large gatherings of doctors or participated in smaller private all-expenses-paid meals with other doctors and drug representatives. For this work, the physician received $30,000. He initially saw his role as a service to his colleagues in giving them information on new drug offerings. But as he reconsidered his substantial fee, the doctor's conscience began bothering him. So he quit. "My role was really simply to be a part of their marketing machinery and that was the value I had for them," he said.[12]

Ethical ways to handle conflicts of interest include (1) avoiding them and (2) disclosing them. Some companies have policies against taking on clients who are competitors of existing clients. Most businesses and government agencies have written policies prohibiting employees from accepting gifts or specifying a maximum gift value. Or a member of a board of directors or committee might abstain from voting on a decision in which he or she has a personal interest. In other situations, people state their potential conflict of interest so that the people affected can decide whether to get information or help they need from another source instead.

HONESTY AND INTEGRITY Employers highly value honesty and integrity. An employee who is honest can be counted on to tell the truth. An employee with **integrity** goes beyond truthfulness. Having integrity means adhering to deeply felt ethical principles in business situations. It includes doing what you say you will do and accepting responsibility for mistakes. Behaving with honesty and integrity inspires trust, and as a result, it can help build long-term relationships with customers, employers, suppliers, and the public. Employees, in turn, want their managers and the company as a whole to treat them honestly and with integrity.

Unfortunately, violations of honesty and integrity are all too common. Some people misrepresent their academic credentials and previous work experience on their résumés or job applications. Although it may seem tempting to embellish a résumé in a competitive job market, the act shows a lack of honesty and integrity—and eventually it will catch up with you. A former dean of admissions at the Massachusetts Institute of Technology (MIT), first padded her qualifications when she applied for a junior position at the school. When she was promoted, she "did not have the courage" to correct her résumé. Many years later, her deception was caught—and she resigned amid public criticism.[13]

Others steal from their employers by taking home supplies or products without permission or by carrying out personal business during the time they are being paid to work. For example, Internet misuse during the work day is increasing. Employees use the Internet during work hours for personal e-mail, shopping, gaming, and visiting chat rooms or such sites as Facebook and YouTube. The use of laptops, cell phones, and other wireless devices makes all of this misconduct easier to hide.[14] While the occurrence of such activity varies widely—and employers may feel more strongly about

Ethical conflicts affect all employees, not just managers. For example, surfing the Internet during working hours is a misuse of company time. Students must deal with this ethical conflict, too: this student is texting during class.

© iStockphoto

cracking down on some activities than others—most agree that Internet misuse is a problem. Some have resorted to electronic monitoring and surveillance. Compliance with laws regarding the privacy and security of client information is another major reason given for the continuing increase in such monitoring.

LOYALTY VERSUS TRUTH Businesspeople expect their employees to be loyal and to act in the best interests of the company. But when the truth about a company is not favorable, an ethical conflict can arise. Individuals may have to decide between loyalty to the company and truthfulness in business relationships. People resolve such dilemmas in various ways. Some place the highest value on loyalty, even at the expense of truth. Others avoid volunteering negative information but answer truthfully if someone asks them a specific question. People may emphasize truthfulness and actively disclose negative information, especially if the cost of silence is high, as in the case of operating a malfunctioning aircraft or selling tainted medicine.

WHISTLE-BLOWING When an individual encounters unethical or illegal actions at work, the person must decide what action to take. Sometimes it is possible to resolve the problem by working through channels within the organization. If that fails, the person should weigh the potential damages to the greater public good. If the damage is significant, a person may conclude that the only solution is to blow the whistle. **Whistle-blowing** is an employee's disclosure to company officials, government authorities, or the media of illegal, immoral, or unethical practices.

A whistle-blower must weigh a number of issues in deciding whether to come forward. Resolving an ethical problem within the organization can be more effective, assuming higher-level managers cooperate. A company that values ethics will try to correct a problem, and staying at a company that does not value ethics may not be worthwhile. In some cases, however, people resort to whistle-blowing because they believe the unethical behavior is causing significant damage that outweighs the risk that the company will retaliate against the whistle-blower. Those risks have been real in some cases. State and federal laws protect whistle-blowers in certain situations, such as reports of discrimination,

conflict of interest situation in which an employee must make a decision about a business's welfare versus personal gain.

whistle-blowing employee's disclosure to company officials, government authorities, or the media of illegal, immoral, or unethical practices committed by an organization.

and the Sarbanes-Oxley Act of 2002 now requires that firms in the private sector provide procedures for anonymous reporting of accusations of fraud. Under the act, anyone who retaliates against an employee for taking concerns of unlawful conduct to a public official can be prosecuted. In addition, whistle-blowers can seek protection under the False Claims Act, a law that was passed in the 1800s, under which they can file a lawsuit on behalf of the government if they believe that a company has somehow defrauded the government. Healthcare companies that are charged with fraudulent billing for Medicare or Medicaid are good examples of this type of lawsuit.[15]

Despite these protections, whistle-blowing still has its risks. Robert Rester was a long-term employee at McWane pipe in Birmingham Alabama, a firm that manufactures sewer and water pipes. Over a seven-year period, the firm had more than 4,600 injuries to workers on the job, most of which were unreported. In addition, the firm was dumping toxic metals and other substances into local streams and lakes—while submitting samples of local tap water for environmental inspection. Rester blew the whistle on McWane and ultimately became a key witness for the Environmental Protection Agency. McWane fired him, and without employment, he was forced to file for bankruptcy. "I lost it all," he says. Rester lost his home, his horses, his land, and many of his possessions. Today he drives a garbage truck in a town near two McWane plants. The company itself has been forced to reform both its safety and environmental practices.[16]

Obviously, whistle-blowing and other ethical issues arise relatively infrequently in firms with strong organizational climates of ethical behavior. The next section examines how a business can develop an environment that discourages unethical behavior among individuals.

Assessment Check ✓

1. What are honesty and integrity, and how do they differ?
2. How can loyalty and truth come into conflict for an employee?

How Organizations Shape Ethical Conduct

No individual makes decisions in a vacuum. Choices are strongly influenced by the standards of conduct established within the organizations where people work. Most ethical lapses in business reflect the values of the firms' corporate cultures.

As shown in Figure 2.5, development of a corporate culture to support business ethics happens on four levels: ethical awareness, ethical reasoning, ethical action, and ethical leadership. If any of these four factors is missing, the ethical climate in an organization will weaken.

Ethical Awareness

The foundation of an ethical climate is ethical awareness. As we have already seen, ethical dilemmas occur frequently in the workplace. So employees need help in identifying ethical problems when they occur. Workers also need guidance about how the firm expects them to respond.

code of conduct formal statement that defines how the organization expects employees to resolve ethical issues.

One way for a firm to provide this support is to develop a **code of conduct,** a formal statement that defines how the organization expects employees to resolve ethical questions. Johnson & Johnson's Credo, presented earlier, is such a code. At the most basic level, a code of conduct may simply specify ground rules for acceptable behavior, such as identifying the laws and regulations that employees must obey. Other companies use their codes of conduct to identify key corporate values and provide frameworks that guide employees as they resolve moral and ethical dilemmas.

Canada-based Nortel Networks, an international telecommunications giant with customers in 150 countries, uses a code of conduct to define its values and help employees put them into practice. The code of conduct defines seven core values that Nortel requires. The code also defines standards for conduct among employees, directors, and officers and between employees and the company's shareholders, customers, suppliers, and communities. Everyone at every level in the company is expected to treat others with respect, including respect for individual and cultural differences; protect the company's assets; and fulfill whatever commitments they make. Managers have the additional responsibility of creating an atmosphere in the workplace that promotes ethical behavior and encourages employees to ask questions or raise concerns about any activities. The code of conduct also states that each employee is responsible for behaving consistently with its standards and for reporting possible violations of the code. Nortel provides each employee with a copy of this code of conduct and also posts it on its Web site.[17]

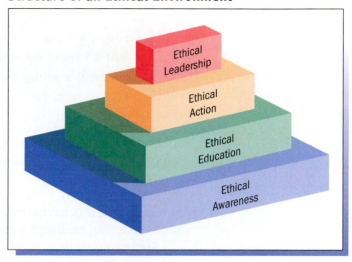

Figure 2.5

Structure of an Ethical Environment

Other firms incorporate similar codes in their policy manuals or mission statements; some issue a code of conduct or statement of values in the form of a small card that employees and managers can carry with them. Harley-Davidson has developed a brief code of ethics that employees can apply both at work and in their personal lives. It reads: "Tell the truth, keep your promises, be fair, respect the individual and encourage intellectual curiosity."

Ethical Education

Although a code of conduct can provide an overall framework, it cannot detail a solution for every ethical situation. Some ethical questions have black-and-white answers, but others do not. Businesses must provide the tools employees need to evaluate the options and arrive at suitable decisions.

Many firms have instituted ethics training programs. Lockheed Martin has developed a training program in the form of interactive lessons that employees can access online. The sessions include cases performed by actors, plus tests in the form of multiple-choice questions. They cover a variety of business-related topics, from security to sexual harassment. The company also tracks which employees have completed which training sessions. In addition, the firm provides a Leaders' Guide training program for managers.[18]

Many authorities debate whether ethics can actually be taught, but training can give employees an opportunity to practice applying ethical values to hypothetical situations as a prelude to applying the same standards to real-world situations. Similar strategies are being used in many business school ethics programs, where case studies and practical scenarios work best. Convicted white-collar criminal Walter Pavlo, a former employee at telecommunications firm MCI, now speaks at colleges and universities about his experiences in the firm and prison. Pavlo, who along with other MCI associates stashed $6 million in offshore accounts, in addition to participating in accounting misreporting, speaks about his actions in an effort to warn students of the consequences of cheating.

Ethical Action

Codes of conduct and ethics training help employees recognize and reason through ethical problems. In addition, firms must also provide structures and approaches that allow decisions to be turned into ethical actions. Texas Instruments gives its employees a reference card to help them make ethical decisions on the job. The size of a standard business card, it lists the following guidelines:

- Does it comply with our values?
- If you do it, will you feel bad as a result?
- How will it look in the newspaper?
- If you know it's wrong, don't do it!
- If you're not sure, ask.
- Keep asking until you get an answer.

Goals set for the business as a whole and for individual departments and employees can affect ethical behavior. A firm whose managers set unrealistic goals for employee performance may find an increase in cheating, lying, and other misdeeds, as employees attempt to protect themselves. In today's Internet economy, the high value placed on speed can create a climate in which ethical behavior is sometimes challenged. Ethical decisions often require careful and quiet thought, a challenging task in today's fast-paced business world.

Some companies encourage ethical action by providing support for employees faced with dilemmas. One common tool is an employee hotline, a telephone number that employees can call, often anonymously, for advice or to report unethical behavior they have witnessed. Ethics compliance officers at some firms, as mentioned previously, guide employees through ethical minefields.

Ethical Leadership

stakeholders the customers, investors, employees, and public affected by or with an interest in a company.

Executives must not only talk about ethical behavior but also demonstrate it in their actions. This principle requires employees to be personally committed to the company's core values and be willing to base their actions on them. One important way for business leaders to model ethical behavior is to admit when they are wrong and correct their organization's mistakes and problems. When it became apparent that electronics firm Dell had engaged in accounting irregularities, founder Michel Dell took responsibility for his firm's actions, while noting that he was not personally aware of the activities while they were occurring. He apologized publicly for the misconduct and promised to take steps to make certain it would not happen again.[19]

However, ethical leadership should also go one step further and charge each employee at every level with the responsibility to be an ethical leader. Everyone should be aware of problems and be willing to defend the organization's standards.

Unfortunately, not all organizations are able to build a solid framework of business ethics. Because the damage from ethical misconduct can powerfully affect a firm's **stakeholders**—customers, investors, employees, and the public—pressure is exerted on businesses to act in acceptable ways. But when businesses fail, the law must step in to enforce good business practices. Many of the laws that affect specific industries or individuals are described in other chapters in this book. For example, legislation affecting international business operations is discussed in Chapter 4. Laws designed to assist small businesses are examined in Chapter 5. Laws related to labor unions are described in Chapter 9. Legislation related to banking and the securities markets is discussed in Chapters 17 and 18. Finally, for an examination of the legal and governmental forces designed to safeguard society's interests when businesses fail at self-regulation, see Appendix A, "Business Law."

Assessment Check ✓

1. What is a code of conduct?
2. How does ethical leadership contribute to ethical standards throughout a company?

Acting Responsibly to Satisfy Society

A second major issue affecting business is the question of social responsibility. In a general sense, **social responsibility** is management's acceptance of the obligation to consider profit, consumer satisfaction, and societal well-being of equal value in evaluating the firm's performance. It is the recognition that business must be concerned with the qualitative dimensions of consumer, employee, and societal benefits, as well as the quantitative measures of sales and profits, by which business performance is traditionally measured. Businesses may exercise social responsibility because such behavior is required by law, because it enhances the company's image, or because management believes it is the ethical course of action.

Historically, a company's social performance has been measured by its contribution to the overall economy and the employment opportunities it provides. Variables such as total wages paid often indicate social performance. Although profits and employment remain important, today many factors contribute to an assessment of a firm's social performance, including providing equal employment opportunities; respecting the cultural diversity of employees; responding to environmental concerns; providing a safe, healthy workplace; and producing high-quality products that are safe to use.

A business is also judged by its interactions with the community. To demonstrate their social responsibility, many corporations highlight charitable contributions and community service in their annual reports and on their Web sites. At the Web site for New Hampshire–based Nobis Engineering, visitors can learn that the firm designates up to 5 percent of its annual profits to organizations devoted to hunger relief, education and youth development, health and social services, and affordable housing. "Our focus is to help create strong and vibrant communities," says the site.[20] Through its Box Tops for Education program, General Mills has helped more than 30,000 grade and middle schools across the nation to raise funds for everything from books to food service. According to the program's Web site, more than $200 million has been raised by consumers who cut out and submitted to participating schools "box top" coupons from General Mills's products such as Progresso soups, Green Giant vegetables, and cereals like Cheerios.[21]

Some firms measure social performance by conducting **social audits,** formal procedures that identify and evaluate all company activities that relate to social issues such as conservation, employment practices, environmental protection, and philanthropy. The social audit informs management about how well the company is performing in these areas. Based on this information, management may revise current programs or develop new ones.

Outside groups may conduct their own evaluations of businesses. Various environmental, religious, and public-interest groups have created standards of corporate performance. Reports on many of these evaluations are available to the general public. The New York–based Council on Economic Priorities is one such group. Other groups publicize their evaluations and include critiques of the social responsibility performance of firms. The Center for Science in the Public Interest evaluates the healthfulness of various foods. As part of this program, the CSPI also works to remove junk foods from school vending machines and cafeterias, remove artery-clogging partially hydrogenated oils from the food supply, and reduce sodium in processed and restaurant foods.[22]

As Figure 2.6 shows, the social responsibilities of business can be classified according to its relationships to the general public, customers, employees, and investors and other members of the financial community. Many of these relationships extend beyond national borders.

social responsibility
business's consideration of society's well-being and consumer satisfaction, in addition to profits.

"They Said It"

"Businesses have the power to do good."

—Anita Roddick
(1942–2007) Founder, The Body Shop

Assessment Check ✔

1. What is meant by social responsibility, and why do firms exercise it?
2. What is a social audit?

Figure 2.6

Business's Social Responsibilities

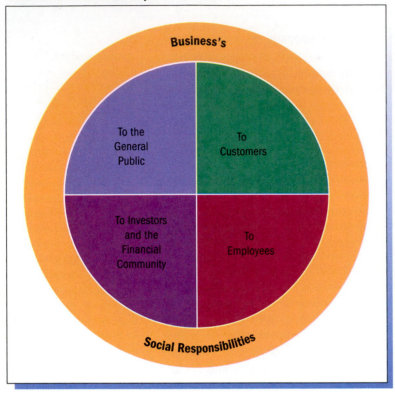

Responsibilities to the General Public

The responsibilities of business to the general public include dealing with public health issues, protecting the environment, and developing the quality of the workforce. Many would argue that businesses also have responsibilities to support charitable and social causes and organizations that work toward the greater public good. In other words, they should give back to the communities in which they earn profits. Such efforts are called *corporate philanthropy*.

PUBLIC-HEALTH ISSUES One of the most complex issues facing business as it addresses its ethical and social responsibilities to the general public is public health. Central to the public-health debate is the question of what businesses should do about dangerous products such as tobacco and alcohol. Tobacco products represent a major health risk, contributing to heart disease, stroke, and cancer among smokers. Families and coworkers of smokers share this danger as well, as their exposure to secondhand smoke increases their risks for cancer, asthma, and respiratory infections. Many cities have not only banned smoking in public places, but also commercial businesses such as restaurants.

Heart disease, diabetes, and obesity have become major public health issues as the rates of these three conditions have been rising. As a result, some firms have tried to take the lead in eliminating ingredients or menu items that might contribute to these health risks. After 18 months of research and testing, to the tune of millions of dollars, KFC was the first major fast-food chain to remove trans fats from its cooking oils, using a blend of soy and corn oils. Other restaurants across the country have converted to soy and other blends in order to eliminate trans fats from their cooking processes. While so far these actions have been voluntary, some municipalities have begun to ban the use of trans fats in restaurants. "If the industry doesn't get smart on this and start policing themselves, big brother will," predicts the owner of a restaurant consulting firm.[23]

Substance abuse is another serious public health problem worldwide. The recent revelations of the use of illegal steroids by many athletes, particularly in professional baseball, highlights the difficulty of devising accurate tests for performance-enhancing and muscle-building drugs and fairly evaluating the results. Many of the drugs in question are so similar to compounds naturally present in the body that identification is extremely difficult. With regard to drug testing, athletes' individual rights to privacy have been questioned, particularly due to their widespread influence on youthful fans. Steroid use is on the rise among high school athletes, despite the publicity about the dangers of such drugs. Tougher penalties for professional players who fail drug tests are being formulated, but some leagues, especially Major League Baseball, appear to be reluctant to act, perhaps because fans continue to buy tickets to games. However, Congress has turned the spotlight on America's favorite pastime, and several prominent players have been suspected of lying to a federal grand jury about the use of steroids.[24] The "Solving an Ethical Controversy" feature explores a related issue of whether businesses also have a responsibility to alert the public about the health of key executives.

WHAT DOES THE PUBLIC HAVE A RIGHT TO KNOW—AND WHEN?

Some companies are linked forever to their founders. A century after Henry Ford rolled his first automobiles off the assembly line, Ford Motor Company is still associated with its founding father. Bill Gates and Paul Allen are the men behind Microsoft. The legacy of their rival, Steve Jobs, is Apple.

When the face of a person also becomes the face of a firm, the company can benefit from the good publicity that a personal image provides. But a founder's fate can dramatically affect the health of the firm as well. When Steve Jobs announced that he would be taking a medical leave from his responsibilities as CEO of Apple due to a hormone imbalance, the media pounced. Why was he really stepping down? How long would he be gone? Shouldn't shareholders and customers be fully informed of his condition? Would Apple's performance suffer in his absence? Shortly thereafter, Jobs announced a leave of absence for "more complex" health issues.

Does the public have the right to be fully informed when a key executive takes a medical leave?

PRO

1. If the CEO or another vital executive of a publicly held firm must step down due to a serious medical condition, shareholders should be informed because their investment in the company could be affected by the outcome of the person's illness. Withholding this type of information could become the basis of legal action, in which the company could be charged with actually deceiving shareholders. "There are people I talk to about Apple and they thank me for the information, but then tell me they're afraid to invest one way or another in the stock because of [this]," noted one observer.

2. Not revealing such information could raise questions about the credibility of other aspects of a firm's reporting, affecting the public's trust and confidence in the firm itself and its products. "That's where the uncertainty is," commented a risk expert on the Apple situation. "No one can predict health issues, but [investors are] looking for some level of assurance that the board [has] a plan in place."

CON

1. According to the health care privacy rule known as HIPAA, which is overseen by the federal Office for Civil Rights, all patients are assured of protection from the revelation of individually identifiable health information. This rule applies to Steve Jobs as well as to any other Apple employee. He should not be forced to discuss his health.

2. Negative publicity concerning a key executive's health could cause unnecessary panic among investors and customers, with a resulting drop in stock prices or orders for products. The worry would then become a self-fulfilling prophecy.

Summary

Apple has always been a secretive company due to its industry. Although Steve Jobs had undergone cancer treatment about five years prior to the announcement of his leave, that outcome was downplayed as Jobs returned to work. When significant weight loss became apparent, the press and medical researchers speculated on Jobs's health, and information was released in a slow trickle. The U.S. government and securities lawyers reportedly are examining the situation to determine whether Apple's shareholders were deceived. Although it can be argued that one person doesn't make an entire company, in the case of Jobs and others like him, one leading figure can influence the public's perception of the company's strength. If a key leader departs, many believe, the public has a right to know why.

Sources: "HIPAA Privacy Rule," Office for Civil Rights, http://www.hhs.gov, accessed February 11, 2009; Adam Lashinsky, "Steve's Leave," *Fortune,* February 2, 2009, pp. 97–102; Rebecca Buckman, "What Steve Jobs Knew about His Health," *Forbes,* January 26, 2009, http://www.forbes.com; Tom Krazit, "Apple Faces Credibility Crisis over Jobs' Health," *CNET News,* January 15, 2009, http://news.cnet.com.

Solving an ETHICAL controversy

PROTECTING THE ENVIRONMENT Businesses consume huge amounts of energy, which increases the use of fossil fuels such as coal and oil for energy production. This activity introduces carbon dioxide and sulfur into the earth's atmosphere. Meanwhile, the sulfur from fossil fuels combines with water vapor in the air to form sulfuric acid. The acid rain that results can travel across continents, killing fish and trees and polluting groundwater. Although acid rain has been tracked for many decades now, companies are still being cited and punished for violations. East Kentucky Power Cooperative was recently fined $11.4 million for violating the Clean Air Act's acid rain program.[25]

Other production and manufacturing methods leave behind large quantities of waste materials that can further pollute the environment and fill already bulging landfills. Some products themselves, particularly electronics that contain toxins such as lead and mercury, are difficult to reuse or recycle. Few manufacturers are really equipped to deal with recycled materials; some refurbish junked products and sell them abroad—where later recycling is even less likely. Hewlett-Packard, however, is making its scanners with a combination of new and recycled plastics, and lead, mercury, and cadmium will soon be banned from new equipment manufactured in Europe. Some firms have actually created a business out of collecting, handling, and recycling many of these items. Advanced Recovery is one such service. The firm contracts with towns to remove electronic equipment that town officials or volunteers collect at a single location on a single day. One town official noted recently that dealing with Advanced Recovery is a bargain—$300 for the removal of electronics, as opposed to $1,650 to incinerate the items, which would create more pollution.[26]

For many managers, finding ways to minimize **pollution** and other environmental damage caused by their products or operating processes has become an important economic, legal, and social issue. The solutions can be difficult—and expensive. But Toyota committed itself to producing hybrid cars early because it saw them as the wave of the future. Hybrid cars use a combination of gas and electricity to power their engines and promise much better fuel efficiency than conventional autos. As gasoline prices soared, sales of U.S. hybrids followed. Toyota sold 277,750 hybrid vehicles during a recent year; its Prius model is the best-selling hybrid in the United States.[27]

Despite the difficulty, however, companies are finding that they can be environmentally friendly and profitable, too. Another solution to the problems of pollutants is **recycling**—reprocessing used materials for reuse. Recycling can sometimes provide much of the raw material that manufacturers need, thereby conserving the world's natural resources and reducing the need for landfills. The "Hit & Miss" feature describes a company with a creative twist on recycling, using shipping containers to construct economical, attractive new housing. Commercial flooring company Tandus has established itself as a leader in the concept of the "product lifecycle," an approach to manufacturing, using, and recycling all its products. The firm even encourages people to recycle competitors' products. In addition to using "green" manufacturing processes, Tandus provides a written guarantee that all vinyl-backed carpet reclaimed for recycling will be recycled into new floor coverings instead of being tossed into incinerators or landfills.[28]

According to the Environmental Protection Agency, discarded electronic items now make up as much as 40 percent of the lead in landfills in the United States, and the International Association of

recycling reprocessing of used materials for reuse.

Recycling programs help keep pollutants out of the environment. Here volunteers sort and collect various items to be recycled.

© Coeur d'Alene Press, Jerome A. Pollos/AP/Wide World Photos

SG Blocks Builds Recycled Homes

When you see a stack of shipping containers lying idle near a shipyard, what do you envision? David Cross, founder of SG Blocks, sees houses. His company transports shipping containers to its facilities and modifies them to be used in home construction. The containers are the building blocks of multifamily, multistory houses—all at a lower cost than traditional homes. The container homes are also completed more quickly, with less energy and fewer new materials.

Shipping containers are the right shape, size, and strength for home construction. "These are built to take a dynamic, moving life aboard ships, and then we take them and put them in a stable environment on a foundation," explains Cross. A typical house might be made up of four to eight containers. A builder or homeowner can add other recycled or environmentally friendly materials—solar panels, a green roof, radiant heating, concrete floors, and recycled cotton insulation. Of course, all the amenities of home—such as energy-efficient appliances—can be added as well.

Architects and homebuilders see many benefits to using shipping containers as a basic construction medium. The containers are less expensive—costing between $2,000 and $3,000 each—than comparable traditional materials. They are durable and require less labor, and they create a new use for products that already exist. "We are utilizing a resource that right now is sitting unused and wasted," notes Kent Pipes, president of Affordable Homes Group, a not-for-profit organization. "We don't just take something and recycle it, we recycle it up in the waste stream so that it becomes better than its alternative use." SG Blocks refers to the process of transforming the containers into homes as Value-Cycling and has even trademarked the name. According to the company, Value-Cycling takes recycling a step farther because it finds a new use for an existing product without spending "significant new energy and resources to convert it."

Shipping containers supplied by SG Blocks are also ideal temporary housing solutions for events such as the Olympics or for communities displaced by natural disasters such as fires or hurricanes. They can be transported, set up, and dismantled quickly. In fact, SG Blocks built and furnished one showcase home for a recent West Coast Green home show in just 13 days and 5 hours. SG Blocks is also working with the U.S. military to build stylish barracks for its personnel. The market for this innovative new product illustrates that environmental practices can be profitable.

Questions for Critical Thinking

1. Describe how SG Blocks might market its products—to consumers and to other businesses or organizations. How could it expand and grow in the future?
2. How does SG Blocks fulfill its responsibilities to the general public?

Sources: Company Web site, http://www.sgblocks.com, accessed February 5, 2009; Michael Kanellos, "Startup Converts Old Shipping Containers into Homes," Greentechmedia, September 25, 2008, http://greenlight.greentechmedia.com; Paul Kilduff, "Shipping Container Prefab at West Coast Green," *San Francisco Chronicle,* September 24, 2008, http://www.sfgate.com; Jaymi Heimbuch, "Sneak Peek Photos of the West Coast Green 2008 Showcase," *Tree Hugger,* September 24, 2008, http://www.treehugger.com.

Electronics Recyclers estimates that consumers and businesses will be disposing of 400 million such items by 2010. Manufacturers and federal agencies are struggling to devise a viable system for managing the problem; one possibility is a surcharge consumers would pay on each electronics purchase. In the meantime, Staples accepts all gadgets for recycling no matter where they were purchased, and Hewlett-Packard and Dell have agreed not to send waste materials overseas. Cisco Systems is building a green-technology center in China as part of its long-term investment in that country. This will be a huge challenge because China's pollution problem exceeds that of the United States. During one recent year, China produced 6,200 million tons of carbon dioxide pollution, compared with 5,800 million tons from the United States. But Cisco is committed to collaborating with China on its new technologies.[29]

Many consumers have favorable impressions of environmentally conscious businesses. To target these customers, companies often use **green marketing,** a marketing strategy that promotes environmentally safe products and production methods. A business cannot simply claim that its goods or services are environmentally friendly, however. The Federal Trade Commission (FTC)

EVERY PLASTIC BOTTLE YOU RECYCLE SAVES ENOUGH ENERGY TO POWER A LIGHT BULB FOR 6 HOURS

recycle
westernriverside.org.uk

Courtesy Waste Watch

Because consumers tend to be friendly toward environmentally conscious businesses, companies use green marketing strategies to promote their environmentally sound products and procedures.

Figure 2.7

FTC Guidelines for Environmental Claims in Green Marketing

If a business says a product is...	The product or package must . . .
Biodegradable	break down and return to nature in a reasonably short period of time.
Recyclable	be entirely reusable as new materials in the manufacture or assembly of a new product or package.
Refillable	be included in a system for the collection and return of the package for refill. If consumers have to find a way to refill it themselves, it is not **refillable**.
Ozone Safe/Ozone Friendly	must not contain any ozone-depleting ingredient.

has issued guidelines for businesses to follow in making environmental claims. A firm must be able to prove that any environmental claim made about a product has been substantiated with reliable scientific evidence. In addition, as shown in Figure 2.7, the FTC has given specific directions about how various environmental terms may be used in advertising and marketing.

Other environmental issues—such as finding renewable sources of clean energy and developing sustainable agriculture—are the focus of many firms' efforts. Vinod Khosla, founder of Sun Microsystems, is now working with a group of high-powered entrepreneurs and investors in the Silicon Valley to develop a new generation of energy. "Change has to come from somewhere, and our business is about to change," he predicts.[30] Solar energy, geothermal energy, biodiesel, and wind power are just a few of the renewable sources of energy being developed by entrepreneurs, large energy firms, and small engineering companies.

In conjunction with several international organizations, Nestlé is working to develop more sustainable cocoa growing around the world. Currently, Nestlé is funding a three-year project with three cocoa cooperatives of about 3,000 farmers along the coast of West Africa. Goals of the project include improving agricultural practices to protect the environment, battle child labor, and improve local farmers' incomes.[31]

DEVELOPING THE QUALITY OF THE WORKFORCE In the past, a nation's wealth has often been based on its money, production equipment, and natural resources. A country's true wealth, however, lies in its people. An educated, skilled workforce provides the intellectual know-how required to develop new technology, improve productivity, and compete in the global marketplace. It is becoming increasingly clear that to remain competitive, U.S. business must assume more responsibility for enhancing the quality of its workforce, including encouraging diversity of all kinds.

In developed economies like that of the United States, many new jobs require college-educated workers. With demand high for workers with advanced skills, the difference between the highest-paid and lowest-paid workers has been increasing. Education plays an important role in earnings, despite success stories of those who dropped out of college or high school to start businesses. Workers with professional degrees earn an average of $1,471 a week, while those with some high school but no diploma earn about $519.[32] Businesses must encourage students to stay in school, continue their education, and sharpen their skills. Target supports Reach Out and Read, a national program designed to encourage young children to read by distributing books through local children's health clinics, and also contributes funds to hundreds of students each year through partnerships with the Hispanic Scholarship Fund and the United Negro College Fund.[33] Companies must also encourage employees to learn new skills and remain competitive. Felix Storch owns a small firm that customizes refrigerators. Despite the higher cost of U.S. workers, Storch refuses to outsource the work to another country. Instead, his workers are taught math skills along with technical skills in order to do the job in New York, where his company and most of his customers are located. Why? It makes good business sense. "We prefer to do [the work] here because we can offer two-day delivery versus two weeks," Storch explains. "If I outsource, you may not buy from me."[34]

Organizations also face enormous responsibilities for helping women, members of various cultural groups, and those who are physically challenged to contribute fully to the economy. Failure to do so is not only a waste of more than half the nation's workforce but also devastating to a firm's public image. Some socially responsible firms also encourage diversity in their business suppliers. Retail giant JCPenney's Partnership Program is designed to foster relationships with minority- and women-owned businesses—an effort the company has worked at for more than 30 years.

Through a commitment to developing employee diversity, The Coca-Cola Company strives to create an inclusive atmosphere, offers diversity training for employees and managers, and encourages regular dialogue among colleagues, suppliers, customers, and stakeholders. "By building an inclusive workplace environment, The Coca-Cola Company seeks to leverage its worldwide team, which is rich in diverse people, talent, and ideas," says the company Web site.[35] For a global organization to function competitively, diversity is vital.

CORPORATE PHILANTHROPY As Chapter 1 pointed out, not-for-profit organizations play an important role in society by serving the public good. They provide the human resources that enhance the quality of life in communities around the world. To fulfill this mission, many not-for-profit organizations rely on financial contributions from the business community. Firms respond by donating billions of dollars each year to not-for-profit organizations. This ==corporate philanthropy== includes cash contributions, donations of equipment and products, and supporting the volunteer efforts of company employees. Recipients include cultural organizations, adopt-a-school programs, community development agencies, and housing and job training programs.

Corporate philanthropy can have many positive benefits beyond the purely "feel-good" rewards of giving, such as higher employee morale, enhanced company image, and improved customer relationships. General Mills, for instance, is a major contributor to the Susan G. Komen Breast Cancer Foundation, through its line of yogurt products marketed under the Yoplait brand name. Yoplait's target market is health-conscious women, the same group most likely to know of or become involved with the Komen Foundation's fund-raising efforts. The firm also sponsors its My Hometown Helper program, a nationwide initiative that provides grants to communities, not-for-profit groups, and public schools for community improvement projects.[36]

Companies often seek to align their marketing efforts with their charitable giving. Many contribute to the Olympics and create advertising that features

corporate philanthropy act of an organization making a contribution to the communities in which it earns profits.

Corporate philanthropy can enhance a company's customer relationships. Through sales of its Yoplait yogurt line, General Mills contributes to the Susan G. Komen Breast Cancer Foundation, a charity that is important to the health-conscious consumers who buy Yoplait.

© Yoplait/General Mills/NewsCom

the company's sponsorship. This is known as *cause-related marketing*. In a recent survey, nearly nine out of ten young people said they believed companies had a duty to support social causes, and nearly seven in eight said they would switch brands in order to reward a company that did so. Consumers are often willing to pay even more for a product, such as Newman's Own salad dressings and salsa, because they know the proceeds are going to a good cause. British supermarket chain Sainsbury's sells Fair Trade bananas, meaning that farmers where the bananas are grown are paid a better price for their crops, so their living conditions are improved. The bananas might cost a bit more, but consumers realize they are supporting a good cause by paying extra.[37]

Another form of corporate philanthropy is volunteerism. In their roles as corporate citizens, thousands of businesses encourage their employees to contribute their efforts to projects as diverse as the Salvation Army, the Red Cross, and Save the Children. In addition to making tangible contributions to the well-being of fellow citizens, such programs generate considerable public support and goodwill for the companies and their employees. In some cases, the volunteer efforts occur mostly during off-hours for employees. In other instances, the firm permits its workforce to volunteer during regular working hours. Boot and clothing manufacturer Timberland is well known for promoting volunteerism among its employees.

Responsibilities to Customers

consumerism public demand that a business consider the wants and needs of its customers in making decisions.

Businesspeople share a social and ethical responsibility to treat their customers fairly and act in a manner that is not harmful to them. **Consumerism**—the public demand that a business consider the wants and needs of its customers in making decisions—has gained widespread acceptance. Consumerism is based on the belief that consumers have certain rights. A frequently quoted statement of consumer rights was made by President John F. Kennedy in 1962. Figure 2.8 summarizes these consumer rights. Numerous state and federal laws have been implemented since then to protect these rights.

THE RIGHT TO BE SAFE Contemporary businesspeople must recognize obligations, both moral and legal, to ensure the safe operation of their products. Consumers should feel assured that the products they purchase will not cause injuries in normal use. **Product liability** refers to the responsibility of manufacturers for injuries and damages caused by their products. Items that lead to injuries, either directly or indirectly, can have disastrous consequences for their makers.

Many companies put their products through rigorous testing to avoid safety problems. Still, testing alone cannot foresee every eventuality. Companies must try to consider all possibilities and provide adequate warning of potential dangers. When a product does pose a threat to customer safety, a responsible manufacturer responds quickly to either correct the problem or recall the dangerous product. Although we take for granted that our food supply is safe, sometimes contamination leaks in, causing illness or even death among some consumers. Contaminated products from the Peanut Corporation of America sickened hundreds of people nationwide and even caused some deaths. After federal health officials traced the source of the problem to its Georgia plant, the firm recalled more than 2,000 of its products. Company executives allegedly knew about the tainted products but shipped them anyway. The firm declared bankruptcy as lawsuits mounted.[38]

Figure 2.8

Consumer Rights as Proposed by President Kennedy

Consumer Rights

Right to Be Heard

Right to Be Safe

Right to Choose

Right to Be Informed

THE RIGHT TO BE INFORMED Consumers should have access to enough education and product information to make responsible buying decisions. In their efforts to promote and sell their goods and services, companies can easily neglect consumers' right to be fully informed. False or misleading advertising is a violation of the Wheeler-Lea Act, a federal law enacted in 1938. The FTC and other federal and state agencies have established rules and regulations that govern advertising truthfulness. These rules prohibit businesses from making unsubstantiated claims about the performance or superiority of their goods or services. They also require businesses to avoid misleading consumers. Businesses that fail to comply face scrutiny from the FTC and consumer protection organizations. In one case, the FTC responded to complaints by filing charges against Star Publishing Group, which under the name National Consumer Services placed want ads promising as much as $800 per week for starting a home-based business. Consumers who called the toll-free number in the ad reached a recording selling a guide to start a business that the recording falsely implied would involve government work.

The Food and Drug Administration (FDA), which sets standards for advertising conducted by drug manufacturers, eased restrictions for prescription drug advertising on television. In print ads, drug makers are required to spell out potential side effects and the proper uses of prescription drugs. Because of the requirement to disclose this information, prescription drug television advertising was limited. Now, however, the FDA says drug ads on radio and television can directly promote a prescription drug's benefits if they provide a quick way for consumers to learn about side-effects, such as displaying a toll-free number or Internet address.

The FDA also monitors "dietary supplements," including vitamins and herbs. These products may make claims about their general effect on health but may not claim to cure a disease, unless the company has presented the FDA with research and received the agency's approval. For instance, a product may say it helps the body maintain a healthy immune system but not that it fights colds. The makers of Airborne recently agreed to pay more than $23 million to settle a class-action lawsuit over false advertising because the herbal formula was touted as a "miracle cold buster." While the formula contains vitamins A, C, and E, magnesium, zinc, selenium, and herbs—all of which are good for the immune system—there are no data to support its claim of curing the common cold. Airborne, which was invented by a former schoolteacher, has been a popular remedy for the past decade, with sales surpassing $100 million. But when an investigation revealed that Airborne's "clinical trial" was conducted by two people without a clinic or scientists, the lawsuit was filed. Since then, the firm has scaled back on its claims, and the word *cold* no longer appears on its packaging. Consumers who still have their receipts are eligible for refunds.[39]

The responsibility of business to preserve consumers' right to be informed extends beyond avoiding misleading advertising. All communications with customers—from salespeople's comments to warranties and invoices—must be controlled to clearly and accurately inform customers. Most packaged-goods firms, personal-computer makers, and other makers of products bought for personal use by consumers include toll-free customer service numbers on their product labels so that consumers can get answers to questions about a product.

To protect their customers and avoid claims of insufficient disclosure, businesses often include warnings on products. As Figure 2.9 shows, sometimes these warnings go far beyond what a reasonable consumer would expect. Others are downright funny.

THE RIGHT TO CHOOSE Consumers should have the right to choose which goods and services they need and want to purchase. Socially responsible firms attempt to preserve this right, even if they reduce their own sales and profits in the process. Brand-name drug makers have recently gone on the defensive in a battle being waged by state governments, insurance companies, consumer groups, unions, and major employers such as General Motors and Verizon. These groups want to force down the rising price of prescription drugs by ensuring that consumers have the right and the opportunity to select cheaper generic brands.

THE RIGHT TO BE HEARD Consumers should be able to express legitimate complaints to appropriate parties. Many companies expend considerable effort to ensure full hearings for consumer

Figure 2.9   **Wacky Warning Labels**

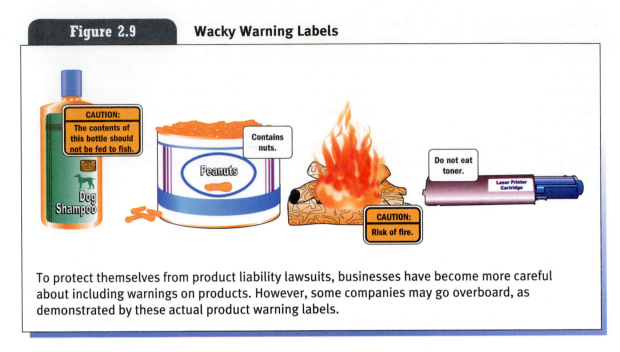

To protect themselves from product liability lawsuits, businesses have become more careful about including warnings on products. However, some companies may go overboard, as demonstrated by these actual product warning labels.

complaints. The eBay auction Web site assists buyers and sellers who believe they were victimized in transactions conducted through the site. It deploys a 200-employee team to work with users and law enforcement agencies to combat fraud. The company has strict guidelines for buyers and sellers and rules for leaving feedback about a buyer or seller. For example, buyers must operate within a list of acceptable goods for sale and may not offer such items as alcohol, pornography, drugs, counterfeit currency, or artifacts from cave formations, graves, or Native American sites. The protection of copyrights is also an important part of eBay's policy.40

Responsibilities to Employees

Companies that can attract skilled and knowledgeable employees are better able to meet the challenges of competing globally. In return, businesses have wide-ranging responsibilities to their employees, both here and abroad. These include workplace safety, quality-of-life issues, ensuring equal opportunity on the job, avoiding age discrimination, and preventing sexual harassment and sexism.

WORKPLACE SAFETY A century ago, few businesses paid much attention to the safety of their workers. In fact, most business owners viewed employees as mere cogs in the production process. Workers—many of whom were young children—toiled in frequently dangerous conditions. In 1911, a fire at the Triangle Shirtwaist Factory in New York City killed 146 people, mostly young girls. Contributing to the massive loss of life were the sweatshop working conditions at the factory, including overcrowding, blocked exits, and a lack of fire escapes. The horrifying tragedy forced businesses to begin to recognize their responsibility for their workers' safety.

The safety and health of workers on the job is now an important business responsibility. The Occupational Safety and Health Administration (OSHA) is the main federal regulatory force in setting workplace safety and health standards. These mandates range from broad guidelines on storing hazardous materials to specific standards for worker safety in industries such as construction, manufacturing, and mining. OSHA tracks and investigates workplace accidents and has the authority to fine employers who are found liable for injuries and deaths that occur on the job.

Although businesses sometimes complain about having to comply with too many OSHA regulations, ultimately management must set standards and implement programs to ensure that employees are safe in the workplace. One unsettling fact is that about 70 teens die every year in the United States as a result of work injuries. Most of these fatalities occur because of unsafe equipment, inadequate safety training, and dangerous work that is illegal or inappropriate for youth. OSHA is taking steps to educate employers and teen workers about safety, health, and a positive work environment. The OSHA Web site has a special section for teens with the answers to most frequently asked questions about such issues as wages, labor standards, harassment issues, and safety at work. In addition, the U.S. Department of Labor has rolled out a new initiative called YouthRules!, a project designed to further educate and empower young workers. The YouthRules! Web page offers information and activities for teens, parents, educators, and employers.[41] Another issue that firms face is the rising cost of health care, as described in the "Hit & Miss" feature.

QUALITY-OF-LIFE ISSUES Balancing work and family is becoming harder for many employees. They find themselves squeezed between working long hours and handling child-care problems, caring for elderly parents, and solving other family crises. A *sandwich generation* of households, those caring for two generations—their children and their aging parents—has arisen. As the population ages, the share of American households providing some type of care to a relative or friend age 50 or older has grown dramatically in the early years of the 21st century. At the same time, as married women spend more time working outside the home, they have fewer hours per week to spend on family. The employees juggling work with life's other demands aren't just working mothers. Childless couples, single people, and men all express frustration with the pressures of balancing work with family and personal needs. To help with the work–life balance, some employers are offering flexible work schedules so that parents can meet the needs of their children (or aging parents) as well as their jobs. But so far, only about 3 percent of companies are offering plans that allow employees to work part of the week at home. According to one survey, 60 percent of mothers say that they would prefer to work-part time, while 21 percent say they prefer full-time employment and 19 percent would opt to stay at home. Increasingly, women are starting their own businesses so they can set their own hours and goals.42

Some companies have come up with truly innovative ways to deal with work schedules, including paid time off for vacation or illness. At some of its locations, IBM has done away with prescribed vacation time altogether—the focus is on results. Employees have an informal agreement with their supervisors about when they will be out of the office, based on their ability to complete their work on schedule. The number of days they take off is not tracked; instead vacation time is considered open ended. But the catch is, the work has to be done. Perhaps surprisingly, the firm found that employees put in just as many hours, if not more, under the new program. "Although you had this wonderful freedom to take days when you want, you really couldn't," admits one worker who has since retired. "IBM tends to be a group of workaholics."43

Another solution has been to offer **family leave** to employees who need to deal with family matters. Under the Family and Medical Leave Act of 1993, businesses with 50 or more employees must provide unpaid leave annually for any employee who wants time off for the birth or adoption of a child, to become a foster parent, or to care for a seriously ill relative or spouse. The law requires employers to grant up to 12 weeks of leave each year, and leave may be taken intermittently as medical conditions make necessary. This unpaid leave also applies to an employee who has a serious illness. Workers must meet certain eligibility requirements. Employers must continue to provide health benefits during the leave and guarantee that employees will return to equivalent jobs. The issue of who is entitled to health benefits can also create a dilemma as companies struggle to balance the needs of their employees against the staggering costs of health care.

ENSURING EQUAL OPPORTUNITY ON THE JOB Businesspeople face many challenges managing an increasingly diverse workforce in the 21st century. Technological advances are expanding the ways people with physical disabilities can contribute in the workplace. Businesses also need to find ways to responsibly recruit and manage older workers and workers with varying

"They Said It"

"When people have stereotypes of what you can't do, show them what you can do. When they have stereotypes of what you won't do, show them what you will do."

—Carly Fiorina (b. 1954)
Former CEO, Hewlett-Packard

Hit & Miss

Businesses Battle the High Cost of Health Care

Business owners often feel they are under siege, battling the costs of everything from supplies to wages. The rising cost of health care has forced companies to find new ways to pay for their employees' coverage without jeopardizing the health of their own bottom line.

Some firms now require employees to contribute more. During a recent year, nearly 60 percent of U.S. companies reported that they planned to increase employees' deductibles, co-pays, or out-of-pocket expenses. Health care costs have been increasing at about 6 percent a year. While that is less than in previous decades, the costs are now so high that even a small increase represents a big bite out of earnings.

Other firms are setting up onsite health clinics, which they claim can save thousands of dollars per employee. Hurst Boiler hired Worksite Rx to open and run a clinic for its 220 employees and their families. Within two years, the company's health care costs had decreased by 32 percent per employee. In addition, the number of sick days workers took decreased significantly. Of course, the firm had to make the initial investment in its health clinic, but the savings outweighed the costs.

Many firms—large and small—are paying much closer attention to the concept of wellness among employees. The idea is not only to prevent costly illnesses but to promote good health. Some firms have adopted incentive programs to entice employees to participate; others simply require participation as a condition of employment.

Firms have long offered health benefits that included gym memberships and healthful food offerings at the company cafeteria. Now they are getting more creative. Ottawa Dental Laboratory has a program called Vitality Bucks, through which employees earn redeemable "bucks" for reaching specific health goals. Those bucks translate to some impressive prizes, ranging from outdoor grills to big-screen TVs. Participating employees enroll in particular health programs and submit to regular testing to receive their bucks. The firm says that 98 percent of employees participate, and it reports an 8 percent reduction in overall health care costs.

Insurance companies have also jumped on the rewards bandwagon. Humana insurance now offers a program that awards points to its members for such activities as signing up for a weight-loss coach and logging daily steps taken. Employees can track their points online and redeem them for everything from movie tickets to golf clubs. Employers pay less for health care and experience a rise in productivity when their employees are healthy, report insurance industry experts.

Questions for Critical Thinking

1. Do you agree that employees should be required to contribute more to the cost of their health care? Why or why not?
2. Describe what you see as the benefits and drawbacks of health "rewards" programs. Brainstorm some creative ideas to help solve the health care crisis.

Sources: Jennifer Brown, "Insurance Plans Reward Good Health with Gifts," *The Atlanta-Journal Constitution,* January 26, 2009, http://www.ajc.com; Brian Klepper, "Work-site Clinics Control Health Care Costs," *Jacksonville Business Journal,* November 7, 2008, http://jacksonville.bizjournals.com; "U.S. Workers Face Higher Health Care Costs," *U.S. News & World Report,* September 4, 2008, http://health.usnews.com; Michael A. Fletcher, "Rising Health Costs Cut into Wages," *Washington Post,* March 24, 2008, http://www.washingtonpost.com; Adrienne Selko, "Prescription for Survival: How to Control Healthcare Costs," *Industry Week,* January 1, 2008, http://www.industryweek.com.

---

lifestyles. In addition, beginning with Lotus Development in 1982, companies have begun to extend benefits equally to employees, regardless of sexual orientation. In particular, that means the company offers benefits such as health insurance to unmarried domestic partners if it offers them to spouses of married couples. Companies that now offer these gender-neutral benefits include Boeing, Citigroup, Disney, General Mills, and Prudential.

To a great extent, efforts at managing diversity are regulated by law. The Civil Rights Act (1964) outlawed many kinds of discriminatory practices, and Title VII of the act specifically prohibits **discrimination** —biased treatment of a job candidate or employee—in the workplace. As shown in Table 2.2, other nondiscrimination laws include the Equal Pay Act (1963), the Age Discrimination in Employment Act (1967), the Equal Employment Opportunity Act (1972), the Pregnancy Discrimination Act (1978), the Civil Rights Act of 1991, and numerous executive orders. The Americans with Disabilities Act (1990) protects the rights of physically challenged people. The Vietnam Era Veterans Readjustment Act (1974) protects the employment of veterans of the Vietnam War.

discrimination biased treatment of a job candidate or employee.

| Table 2.2 | Laws Designed to Ensure Equal Opportunity |

Law	Key Provisions
Title VII of the Civil Rights Act of 1964 (as amended by the Equal Employment Opportunity Act of 1972)	Prohibits discrimination in hiring, promotion, compensation, training, or dismissal on the basis of race, color, religion, sex, or national origin.
Age Discrimination in Employment Act of 1967 (as amended)	Prohibits discrimination in employment against anyone age 40 or older in hiring, promotion, compensation, training, or dismissal.
Equal Pay Act of 1963	Requires equal pay for men and women working for the same firm in jobs that require equal skill, effort, and responsibility.
Vocational Rehabilitation Act of 1973	Requires government contractors and subcontractors to take affirmative action to employ and promote qualified disabled workers. Coverage now extends to all federal employees. Coverage has been broadened by the passage of similar laws in more than 20 states and, through court rulings, to include people with communicable diseases, including AIDS.
Vietnam Era Veterans Readjustment Act of 1974	Requires government contractors and subcontractors to take affirmative action to employ and retain disabled veterans. Coverage now extends to all federal employees and has been broadened by the passage of similar laws in more than 20 states.
Pregnancy Discrimination Act of 1978	Requires employers to treat pregnant women and new mothers the same as other employees for all employment-related purposes, including receipt of benefits under company benefit programs.
Americans with Disabilities Act of 1990	Makes discrimination against the disabled illegal in public accommodations, transportation, and telecommunications; stiffens employer penalties for intentional discrimination on the basis of an employee's disability.
Civil Rights Act of 1991	Makes it easier for workers to sue their employers for alleged discrimination. Enables victims of sexual discrimination to collect punitive damages; includes employment decisions and on-the-job issues such as sexual harassment, unfair promotions, and unfair dismissal. The employer must prove that it did not engage in discrimination.
Family and Medical Leave Act of 1993	Requires all businesses with 50 or more employees to provide up to twelve weeks of unpaid leave annually to employees who have had a child or are adopting a child, are becoming foster parents, are caring for a seriously ill relative or spouse, or are themselves seriously ill. Workers must meet certain eligibility requirements.
Uniformed Services Employment and Reemployment Rights Act of 1994	Prohibits employers from denying employment benefits on the basis of employees' membership in or obligation to serve in the uniformed services and protects the rights of veterans, reservists, and National Guard members to reclaim their jobs after being absent due to military service or training.

The **Equal Employment Opportunity Commission (EEOC)** was created to increase job opportunities for women and minorities and to help end discrimination based on race, color, religion, disability, gender, or national origin in any personnel action. To enforce fair-employment laws, it investigates charges of discrimination and harassment and files suit against violators. The EEOC can also help employers set up programs to increase job opportunities for women, minorities, people with disabilities, and people in other protected categories.

Fair treatment of employees is more than a matter of complying with EEOC regulations, however. All employees want to be treated with respect. A minority employee who misses out on a plum assignment may miss out on the big raise that goes with it. As the employee's salary grows more slowly, managers may eventually begin to use the size of the salary as an indicator that the employee contributes less to the organization. While in the past the EEOC has focused on this type of individual situation, currently it is addressing what it terms "systemic discrimination," which it defines as "a pattern or practice, policy, and/or class in which the alleged discrimination has a far-reaching impact on an industry, profession, company, or geographic location." A systemic discrimination charge usually becomes a class-action suit, which costs considerably more to defend than an individual lawsuit. So firms are examining their employment practices carefully to make sure they are not open to discrimination charges.[44] Chapter 9 takes a closer look at diversity and employment discrimination issues as part of a discussion of human resource management.

AGE DISCRIMINATION With the average age of U.S. workers steadily rising, more than half the workforce is projected to be age 40 or older in a few years. Yet some employers find it less expensive to hire and retain younger workers, who generally have lower medical bills as well as lower salary and benefits packages. At the same time, many older workers have training and skills that younger workers have yet to acquire. The Age Discrimination in Employment Act of 1967 (ADEA) protects individuals who are age 40 or older, prohibiting discrimination on the basis of age and denial of benefits to older employees.

Ruling in a recent lawsuit brought under the ADEA, the Supreme Court determined that employers can be held liable for age discrimination against older workers even if they intended no harm. At the same time, the court allowed employers to use "reasonable" factors such as cost cutting to defend business practices that might have more severe impacts on older than on younger workers.

Legal issues aside, employers might do well to consider not only the experience that older workers bring to the workplace but also their enthusiasm. "Job satisfaction is especially high among those 65 and over because most people working at that age are not forced to still work, due to financial reasons, but choose to do so because they like their jobs," points out the leader of a study conducted by researchers at the University of Chicago. Nearly 75 percent of those over 65 who were interviewed said they were very happy with their jobs.[45]

In all cases, employers need to plan ahead for the aging of the workforce, finding ways to retain accumulated business wisdom, prepare for the demand for health services, and be ready for growth in the industries that serve seniors. The 55 to 64 age group will increase by some 30 million people over the next few years, while the 35 to 44 age group will decrease by nearly 6 percent. These numbers signify a coming shift in the workforce, as well as the goods and services needed.[46]

SEXUAL HARASSMENT AND SEXISM Every employer has a responsibility to ensure that all workers are treated fairly and are safe from sexual harassment. **Sexual harassment** refers to unwelcome and inappropriate actions of a sexual nature in the workplace. It is a form of sex discrimination that violates the Civil Rights Act of 1964, which gives both men and women the right to file lawsuits for intentional sexual harassment. More than 12,000 sexual harassment complaints are filed with the EEOC each year, of which about 15 percent are filed by men.[47] Thousands of other cases are either handled internally by companies or never reported.

Two types of sexual harassment exist. The first type occurs when an employee is pressured to comply with unwelcome advances and requests for sexual favors in return for job security, promotions, and raises. The second type results from a hostile work environment in which an employee feels hassled or degraded because of unwelcome flirting, lewd comments, or obscene jokes. The courts have ruled that allowing sexually oriented materials in the workplace can create a hostile atmosphere that interferes with an employee's ability to do the job. Employers are also legally responsible to protect employees from sexual harassment by customers and clients. The EEOC's Web site informs employers and employees of criteria for identifying sexual harassment and how it should be handled in the workplace.

sexual harassment
unwelcome and inappropriate actions of a sexual nature in the workplace.

Preventing sexual harassment can be difficult because it involves regulating the conduct of individual employees. Sometimes victims, especially young employees, are intimidated or unaware of their rights, but the EEOC has set up a Youth@Work program (http://youth.eeoc.gov) to ensure that young workers can learn about the various types of discrimination and ways to avoid them.

The cost in settlements or fines can be enormous. Morgan Stanley paid $54 million to 340 current or former employees to settle a lawsuit alleging that the women were subjected to lewd behavior by male employees. Another firm paid $100 million to more than 900 women for similar charges. Mitsubishi found itself in the same situation, paying $34 million to 400 female employees. So in addition to ethical and legal reasons, it makes good business sense for firms to prevent this kind of behavior from happening.[48]

To avoid sexual harassment problems, many firms have established policies and employee education programs aimed at preventing such violations. An effective harassment prevention program should include the following measures:

- Issue a specific policy statement prohibiting sexual harassment.

- Develop a complaint procedure for employees to follow.

- Create a work atmosphere that encourages sexually harassed staffers to come forward.

- Investigate and resolve complaints quickly and take disciplinary action against harassers.

Unless all these components are supported by top management, sexual harassment is difficult to eliminate.

Sexual harassment is often part of the broader problem of **sexism**—discrimination against members of either sex, but primarily affecting women. One important sexism issue is equal pay for equal work. On average, women make only 80 percent of the salaries that their male counterparts do one year out of college. Ten years later the gap has widened. A study conducted by the American Association of University Women Educational Foundation revealed that ten years after college, women earn only 69 percent of what their male peers earn. Education, occupation, work hours, and other factors don't seem to affect the gap, which remains unexplained other than the penalty of gender.[49] In some extreme cases, differences in pay and advancement can become the basis for sex discrimination suits, which, like sexual harassment suits, can be costly and time consuming to settle. As in all business practices, it is better to act legally and ethically in the first place.

Assessment Check

1. What is green marketing?
2. What is corporate philanthropy?
3. What are the four main consumer rights?

Responsibilities to Investors and the Financial Community

Although a fundamental goal of any business is to make a profit for its shareholders, investors and the financial community demand that businesses behave ethically as well as legally. When firms fail in this responsibility, thousands of investors and consumers can suffer.

State and federal government agencies are responsible for protecting investors from financial misdeeds. At the federal level, the Securities and Exchange Commission (SEC) investigates suspicions of unethical or illegal behavior by publicly traded firms. It investigates accusations that a business is using faulty accounting practices to inaccurately portray its financial resources and profits to investors. Regulation FD ("Fair Disclosure") is an SEC rule that requires publicly traded companies to announce major information to the general public, rather than first disclosing the information to selected major investors. The agency also operates an Office of Internet Enforcement to target fraud in online trading and online sales of stock by unlicensed sellers. Recall that the Sarbanes-Oxley Act of 2002 also protects investors from unethical accounting practices. Chapter 18 discusses securities trading practices further.

Assessment Check

1. Why do firms need to do more than just earn a profit?
2. What is the role of the Securities and Exchange Commission?

What's Ahead

The decisions and actions of businesspeople are often influenced by outside forces such as the legal environment and society's expectations about business responsibility. Firms also are affected by the economic environments in which they operate. The next chapter discusses the broad economic issues that influence businesses around the world. Our discussion will focus on how factors such as supply and demand, unemployment, inflation, and government monetary policies pose both challenges and opportunities for firms seeking to compete in the global marketplace.

Summary of Learning Goals

1 Explain the concepts of business ethics and social responsibility.

Business ethics refers to the standards of conduct and moral values that govern actions and decisions in the workplace. Businesspeople must take a wide range of social issues into account when making decisions. Social responsibility refers to management's acceptance of the obligation to consider profit, consumer satisfaction, and societal well-being of equal value in evaluating the firm's performance.

Assessment Check Answers

1.1 To whom do businesses have responsibilities? Businesses are responsible to customers, employees, investors, and society.

1.2 If a firm is meeting all its responsibilities to others, why do ethical conflicts arise? Ethical conflicts arise because business must balance doing what is right and doing what is profitable.

2 Describe the factors that influence business ethics.

Among the many factors shaping individual ethics are personal experience, peer pressure, and organizational culture. Individual ethics are also influenced by family, cultural, and religious standards. Additionally, the culture of the organization where a person works can be a factor.

Assessment Check Answers

2.1 What role can an ethics compliance officer play in a firm? Ethics compliance officers are charged with deterring wrongdoing and ensuring that ethical standards are met.

2.2 What factors influence the ethical environment of a business? Individual ethics and technology influence the ethical environment of a business.

3 List the stages in the development of ethical standards.

In the preconventional stage, individuals primarily consider their own needs and desires in making decisions. They obey external rules only from fear of punishment or hope of reward. In the conventional stage, individuals are aware of and respond to their duty to others. Expectations of groups,

as well as self-interest, influence behavior. In the final, postconventional stage, the individual can move beyond self-interest and duty to include consideration of the needs of society. A person in this stage can apply personal ethical principles in a variety of situations.

Assessment Check Answers

3.1 What is the preconventional stage in the development of ethical standards? In the preconventional stage, the individual looks out for his or her own interests and follows rules out of fear of punishment or hope of reward.

3.2 What is the difference between the conventional and the postconventional stages? In the conventional stage, the person considers the interests and expectations of others, and in the postconventional stage, he or she considers personal, group, and societal interests.

4 Identify common ethical dilemmas in the workplace.

Conflicts of interest exist when a businessperson is faced with a situation in which an action benefiting one person has the potential to harm another, as when the person's own interests conflict with those of a customer. Honesty and integrity are valued qualities that engender trust, but a person's immediate self-interest may seem to require violating these principles. Loyalty to an employer sometimes conflicts with truthfulness. Whistle-blowing is a possible response to misconduct in the workplace, but the personal costs of doing so may be high.

Assessment Check Answers

4.1 What are honesty and integrity, and how do they differ? Honesty is the trait of telling the truth; integrity goes beyond truthfulness and means adhering to deeply felt ethical principles.

4.2 How can loyalty and truth come into conflict for an employee? Truth and loyalty can come into conflict when the truth about a company or situation is unfavorable.

5 Discuss how organizations shape ethical behavior.

Employees are strongly influenced by the standards of conduct established and supported within the organizations where they work. Businesses can help shape ethical behavior by developing codes of conduct that define their expectations. Organizations can also use this training to develop employees' ethics awareness and reasoning. They can foster ethical action through decision-making tools, goals consistent with ethical behavior, and advice hotlines. Executives must also demonstrate ethical behavior in their decisions and actions to provide ethical leadership.

Assessment Check Answers

5.1 What is a code of conduct? A code of conduct is a formal statement defining the way the organization expects and requires employees to resolve ethical questions that arise at work.

5.2 How does ethical leadership contribute to ethical standards throughout a company? Employees more readily commit to the company's core values when they see that leaders and managers behave ethically and when the ethics program is not seen as a way to protect top executives from being blamed for wrongdoing.

6 Describe how businesses' social responsibility is measured.

Today's businesses are expected to weigh their qualitative impact on consumers and society, in addition to their quantitative economic contributions such as sales, employment levels, and profits. One measure is their compliance with labor and consumer protection laws and their charitable contributions. Another measure some businesses take is to conduct social audits. Public-interest groups also create standards and measure companies' performance relative to those standards. Consumers may boycott groups that fall short of social standards.

Assessment Check Answers

6.1 What is meant by social responsibility, and why do firms exercise it? Social responsibility is management's acceptance of its obligation to consider profit, consumer satisfaction, and societal well-being to be of equal value when evaluating the firm's performance. Businesses exercise it because it is required by law, because it enhances the company's image, or because management believes it is the right thing to do.

6.2 What is a social audit? A social audit is a formal procedure to identify and evaluate all company activities that relate to social issues such as conservation, employment practices, environmental protection, and philanthropy.

7 Summarize the responsibilities of business to the general public, customers, and employees.

The responsibilities of business to the general public include protecting the public health and the environment and developing the quality of the workforce. Additionally, many would argue that businesses have a social responsibility to support charitable and social causes in the communities in which they earn profits. Business also must treat customers fairly and protect consumers, upholding their rights to be safe, to be informed, to choose, and to be heard. Businesses have wide-ranging responsibilities to their workers. They should make sure that the workplace is safe, address quality-of-life issues, ensure equal opportunity, and prevent sexual harassment or discrimination.

Assessment Check Answers

7.1 What is green marketing? Green marketing is a marketing strategy that promotes environmentally safe products and production methods.

7.2 What is corporate philanthropy? Corporate philanthropy includes cash contributions, donations of equipment and products, and support for the volunteer efforts of company employees.

7.3 What are the four main consumer rights? The four main consumer rights are the right to be safe, to be informed, to choose, and to be heard.

8 Explain why investors and the financial community are concerned with business ethics and social responsibility.

Investors and the financial community demand that businesses behave ethically as well as legally in handling their financial transactions. Businesses must be honest in reporting their profits and financial performance to avoid misleading investors. The Securities and Exchange Commission is the federal agency responsible for investigating suspicions that publicly traded firms have engaged in unethical or illegal financial behavior.

Assessment Check Answers

8.1 Why do firms need to do more than just earn a profit? Firms need to do more than just earn a profit because the law requires them to behave in a legal and ethical manner and because investors and shareholders demand such behavior.

8.2 What is the role of the Securities and Exchange Commission? Among other functions the Securities and Exchange Commission investigates suspicions of unethical or illegal behavior by publicly traded firms.

Business Terms You Need to Know

business ethics 34

conflict of interest 40

whistle-blowing 41

code of conduct 42

stakeholders 44

social responsibility 45

recycling 48

corporate philanthropy 51

consumerism 52

discrimination 56

sexual harassment 58

Other Important Business Terms

Sarbanes-Oxley
 Act 36
integrity 40
social audits 45

pollution 48
green marketing 49
product liability 52
family leave 55

Equal Employment
 Opportunity
 Commission (EEOC) 57
sexism 59

Review Questions

1. What do the terms *business ethics* and *social responsibility* mean? Why are they important components of a firm's overall philosophy toward conducting business?

2. In what ways do individuals make a difference in a firm's commitment to ethics? Describe the three stages in which an individual develops ethical standards.

3. What type of ethical dilemma does each of the following illustrate? (A situation might involve more than one dilemma.)

   a. An attorney agrees to represent both husband and wife in their divorce proceeding.
   b. A newly hired employee learns that the office manager is ordering extra office supplies to take home.
   c. A doctor prescribes a test for a patient, using expensive medical equipment that his or her practice owns.
   d. An employee discovers documents that implicate his or her firm in widespread pollution.
   e. A company spokesperson agrees to give a press conference that puts a positive spin on his or her firm's distribution of defective products.

4. Describe how ethical leadership contributes to the development of each of the other levels of ethical standards in a corporation.

5. How do organizational goals affect ethical behavior? Give an example.

6. In what ways do firms demonstrate their social responsibility?

7. What are the four major areas in which businesses have responsibilities to the general public? In what ways can meeting these responsibilities give a firm a competitive edge?

8. Identify and describe the four basic rights that consumerism tries to protect. How has consumerism improved the contemporary business environment? What challenges has it created for businesses?

9. What are the five major areas in which companies have responsibilities to their employees? What types of changes in society are now affecting these responsibilities?

10. Identify which Equal Opportunity law (or laws) protects workers in the following categories:

    a. parents who are adopting a child and need time off
    b. a National Guard member who is returning from deployment overseas
    c. a job applicant who requires the use of a wheelchair
    d. a person whose heritage is Native American
    e. a woman who is pregnant
    f. a woman who has been sexually harassed on the job

11. How does a company demonstrate its responsibility to investors and the financial community?

Projects and Teamwork Applications

1. Write your own personal code of ethics. Create standards for your behavior at school, in personal relationships, and on the job. Then assess how well you meet your own standards.

2. On your own or with a classmate, visit the Web site of one of the following firms, or choose another that interests you. Based on what you can learn about the company from the site, construct a chart or figure that illustrates examples of the firm's ethical awareness, ethical education, ethical actions, and ethical leadership. Present your findings to class.

   a. Starbucks
   b. NFL, NHL, NBA, MLB (or any major professional sports league)

   c. Kraft Foods
   d. Florida Power & Light
   e. Irving Oil
   f. Whole Foods Market
   g. Ikea

3. Now take the company you studied for question 2 (or choose another one) and conduct a social audit on your firm. Do your findings match with the firm's culture of ethics? If there are any differences, what are they and why might they occur?

4. On your own or with a classmate, go online, flip through a magazine, or surf television channels to identify a firm that is engaged in green marketing. If you see a commercial on television, go to the firm's Web site to learn

more about the product or process advertised. Does the firm make claims that comply with the FTC guidelines? Present your findings in class.

5. As a consumer, you have come to expect a certain level of responsibility toward you on the part of companies that are marketing their goods and services to you. Describe a situation in which you felt that a company did not recognize your rights as a consumer. How did you handle the situation? How did the company handle it? What was the final outcome?

Web Assignments

1. **Ethical standards.** Visit the Web site listed here. It summarizes the ethical standards for all employees of the Walt Disney Company. Review the standards, and then prepare a report relating Disney's ethical standards to the material on corporate ethics discussed in the chapter. http://corporate.disney.go.com/corporate/conduct_standards2.html.

2. **Best places to work.** Each year *Working Mother* magazine compiles a list of the best places to work for working mothers. Go to the magazine's Web site (http://www.workingmother.com) and click on "Best Companies." Which employers made the top ten? What criteria does the magazine use when preparing its list?

3. **Climate change.** Companies throughout the world are adopting new policies and changing existing ones to deal with the issue of climate change. Visit the Web site of a company you believe is committed to responding to climate change, or access the sites listed here. Write a report on that firm's efforts to protect the environment.

http://www.jpmorganchase.com/cm/cs?pagename=Chase/Href&urlname=jpmc/community/env/policy/clim
http://www.alcoa.com/global/en/environment/position_papers/**climate_change**.asp
http://www.astrazeneca.com/article/511607.aspx.

Note: Internet Web addresses change frequently. If you do not find the exact sites listed, you may need to access the organization's or company's home page and search from there.

Honda's FCX Clarity: A Clearer View of the Future

Case 2.1

Hybrids have already hit the road. Diesel-fueled vehicles have been driven for decades. Both are positive steps to reduce pollution, as well as cutting down on the consumption of fossil fuels. But Honda has decided to take off in another direction: producing cars powered by hydrogen fuel cells. The new Honda FCX Clarity runs on electricity generated by its oxygen and compressed hydrogen fuel cell. And while gasoline–electric battery hybrids and diesel-fueled vehicles run cleaner and produce fewer emissions than traditional cars and trucks, the Clarity's only exhaust is water vapor.

Honda is committed to what it believes is the car of the future. The firm plans to be building nearly half a million of these cars by the year 2020. "It is a matter of when, not if, fuel cell cars come to the U.K.," predicts one Honda spokesman there. "We have experimented with other technologies including hybrid cars, and that only convinced us that ultimately hydrogen fuel cells are the long-term solution."

Introducing an entirely new way of fueling a car is not a simple matter. Hybrids have now been through several generations, and only recently has diesel fuel become truly widely available. So the challenge for Honda is to find people who are willing to drive the experimental car and figure out how to fuel it conveniently. Currently, only about 31 hydrogen fueling stations exist nationwide, 23 of which are located in California. Honda is offering a limited number of leases to customers who want to try the Clarity for several months and provide feedback to Honda about its features and performance. At $600 per month, the lease is not inexpensive, but Honda marketers believe that customers who pay to drive the car will provide more honest, accurate feedback than those who might test it out for free. Meanwhile, as Honda gears up for greater production of the Clarity, the firm is considering offering to sell customers their own Home Energy Stations, which will extract hydrogen from natural gas and pressurize it for use in their vehicles.

Some critics point out that the Clarity is not entirely pollution-free; the creation of hydrogen fuel actually requires burning natural gas. But Honda is already experimenting with producing hydrogen fuel through solar- and wind-powered means. If the automaker achieves this, the Clarity may be the first car to signal a whole new era of motor vehicle production.[50]

Questions for Critical Thinking

1. Describe ways in which Honda carries out its responsibilities to the general public.

2. How does consumerism come into play in the production and marketing of a new type of vehicle?

As you browse the produce section of your grocery store, do you know where the tomatoes and cucumbers come from? How about the blueberries and strawberries? Depending on where you live and the season in which you are shopping, the fruits and vegetables you buy may have been picked as much as a week earlier and traveled more than 1,500 miles to reach the shelves of your supermarket. And that's just if they've been grown in the United States. If your salad fixings come from Mexico, Asia, Canada, or South America, they were picked longer ago and traveled even farther. This doesn't necessarily mean they are bad for you—in fact, produce sold in the United States passes high quality standards. But the fuel and refrigeration required during transport of these goods is ultimately harmful to the environment, not to mention the potential risk of contamination that can work its way into a food source that travels many miles. Until now, consumers have enjoyed produce from far-flung regions because the price of fuel has been low, but that is changing, along with the awareness of environmental issues.

Just as small farms producing local foods were disappearing—often swallowed up by huge agribusiness conglomerates—consumers and consumer advocacy groups began to demand more local produce. "It often means getting fresher food," explains Urvashi Rangan, a scientist with the not-for-profit organization Consumers Union. "But there are even more advantages to local food production. It saves on gasoline and reduces pollution from transporting food … and in many cases it supports smaller-scale farmers." Supporting local farms helps bolster local economies. Consumers might pay more for a locally grown lettuce, but the cost goes to the producer. Advocates also point out that a decentralized food system is less susceptible to spreading a virus or other contamination widely.

The term *local* may be defined as the farm at the edge of town—or it may mean anything grown within a 100-mile radius. "You might be able to get eggs raised just five miles down the road, but cheese from the state next to yours," explains Erin Barnett, director of LocalHarvest. org. "Both choices take the food's geographical origins

into account, and that is the decision-making tool at the heart of eating locally grown." She observes that consumers who are willing to vary their diets somewhat seasonally can always find something good to eat. "Certainly it is easier to buy fresh local produce in areas of the country with long growing seasons," says Barnett. "But even in your region's off-season, you may find an excellent variety of pasture-raised meats, or milk from family-owned dairies, or honey, or particular nuts."

In addition, some crops may be stored or even grown in winter. Yet consumers need to proceed with caution. A head of lettuce that is grown in Vermont or New Hampshire probably has less energy impact that one grown in Chile and shipped north from there. But if the lettuce is grown in October or November in a heated greenhouse, the energy impact may be significantly higher. "All things being equal, it's better if food only travels 10 miles," says Peter Tyedmers, an ecological economist at Dalhousie University in Nova Scotia. "Sometimes all things are equal; many times they aren't."

Still, supermarkets have begun to respond to consumer demand for local goods. Regional chains now have special programs to bring local foods into their stores, whether it's Maine blueberries or Washington cheese. Whole Foods, which has built its business on local foods, is committed to offering the freshest local goods possible. "It's pretty territorial," says Jeff Turnas, vice president of purchasing for New York, New Jersey, and Connecticut. "If they live in Connecticut, they want to see products from Connecticut. If they're from New York, they want to see products from New York." Despite the challenges, these markets are delivering the local goods.[51]

Questions for Critical Thinking

1. What responsibilities do food growers and supermarkets have toward their customers when offering locally grown produce?

2. Describe a situation in which there might be a conflict of interest for a supermarket buyer in charge of purchasing produce.

We all know people who talk the talk of volunteerism and service. But do they walk the walk as well? Timberland is an extraordinary example of an entire company based on walking the walk of social responsibility—in its own boots. The Stratham, New Hampshire–based company has been making high-quality, durable work boots for decades under the name of Timberland, and prior to that under the name of the Abington Shoe Co., which Timberland's founder Nathan Swartz purchased in the 1950s. The firm is probably best known for its waterproof leather boots, but it has added new lines of footwear that include casual fashion shoes, boat shoes, and hiking boots, as well as clothing and outerwear. While continuing to build its reputation as a brand that stands for durability, ruggedness, and the American outdoors, Timberland has been constructing a reputation for integrity and commitment to the community as well.

Ken Freitas, Timberland's vice president of social enterprise, loves to talk about the ways that his company has been able to build social responsibility right into its brand. "Doing good and doing well are not separate things," he says. "We're a business … part of our profits get put back into the community. Business and community should be joined together, and you have a more powerful enterprise and community."

Timberland implements this commitment through a series of programs in which its employees—including top managers—and corporate dollars participate. Through its Path of Service Program, employees receive up to 40 hours of paid time per year to participate in community service projects at local schools, day-care centers, the Society for the Prevention of Cruelty to Animals (SPCA), food banks, and the like. They might clean up a nearby beach or help build a park. Years ago, Timberland established its Service Sabbatical Program, in which three- to six-month sabbaticals are awarded to as many as four employees who wish to use their professional skills in assisting local nonprofit organizations full-time. Then there's the Global Serv-A-Palooza, the annual worldwide, companywide celebration during which 2,000 employees, vendors, and community partners participate in a day of service.

Timberland's organized approach to community service began in 1989 following a phone call from a new volunteer program called City Year, which was based in Boston. As part of City Year, graduating high school students from diverse backgrounds would take a year off before starting work or college to participate in community service. Because many of the volunteer jobs involved outdoor work, City Year asked Timberland to donate 50 pairs of its work boots to the cause. Timberland agreed, and the next year City Year requested 70 pairs. A relationship was born during which both City Year and Timberland have grown nationwide. To date, Timberland has invested more than $10 million in the program and now outfits every City Year volunteer in boots, pants, shirts, jackets, and rain gear. "Yes, Timberland is helping to build City Year," notes Ken Freitas. "But City Year is helping to build Timberland."

How does Timberland measure the success of its community service programs? "One of the key challenges in a social responsibility program is measurement," admits Freitas. "How do you know if it is successful?" One way Timberland has been able to keep track of this is through joint marketing efforts with City Year. When a retailer in Philadelphia asked Timberland to make red boots to satisfy its younger customers (instead of the traditional tan work boots), Timberland balked at first. But then managers realized that red was the official color of City Year—and red boots might become the signature footwear of City Year volunteers. So Timberland made the boots and supplied them to the Philadelphia retailer as well as City Year participants—and all three organizations experienced growth in the Philadelphia area. This type of growth is reflected in Timberland's revenues, which currently reach more than $1 billion each year. But Freitas cautions against overdoing measurement. "What brings people to a brand isn't necessarily measurable," he explains. So Timberland adopts a "management and magic" philosophy that incorporates tangible results while leaving room for the unexpected or unexplainable.

At Timberland, social responsibility starts at the top. "Our company has a strong set of values that form the resolve for all that we do in the community —humanity, humility, integrity, and excellence," writes Jeff Swartz, president and CEO. "We strive to lead as responsible corporate citizens and to invest our resources, skills, ingenuity, and dedication to create positive change." If you happen to attend a Timberland national sales meeting, you'd better leave your golf clubs and swimsuit at home and wear your work boots instead. You might spend the day building a playground.[52]

Questions for Critical Thinking

1. In what ways does Timberland fulfill its responsibilities to consumers, employees, investors, and society as a whole?

2. In addition to a climate of social responsibility, do you think Timberland is likely to foster a climate of ethical awareness throughout its organization? Explain your answer.

3. In what ways does Timberland's Path of Service Program help develop the quality of its workforce?

4. Think of a small or large company in your hometown or in the town where you go to school. In what ways does the company serve its community? If it does not, describe ways in which it could.

Economic Challenges Facing Contemporary Business

Ryan McVay/Photodisc/Getty Images

Obamanomics: Stimulus to Help the Economy

As Barack Obama took his historic oath of office, the U.S. economy was faltering. Daily news headlined the worst downturn since the Great Depression. All eyes turned to Washington, D.C., for help getting cash and credit flowing into the financial system again. Opinions remained deeply divided about the new president's $787 billion economic stimulus plan, with some wanting less government spending and more tax cuts, but most people believed that the government had to do *something*.

Reeling from a huge burden of bad debt left over from the bursting of the housing bubble, banks and other lending institutions had essentially withdrawn from the economic playing field, with too little cash or confidence to continue lending. Businesses that depended on short-term loans from these lenders were left without the funds they needed to conduct their everyday operations or expand for the future. As already debt-laden consumers grew wary of spending in an uncertain economy, sales slumped in industries across the board, inventories of unsold goods piled up, and companies like 3M, Home Depot, Starbucks, Microsoft, Nokia, and dozens more announced layoffs of thousands of workers in the wake of unprecedented financial losses. Unemployment was soaring, dampening consumer spending even further. Stock prices fell, sales of new homes—a major indicator of the economy's health—plunged, cars sat on dealers' lots, and retailers reported the worst holiday selling season in decades. The United States cut imports of foreign-made products like televisions and computers. Foreign manufacturers cut back production, and with less money to spend, overseas businesses trimmed demand for U.S. products as well, forcing the country's exports down. Bad news spread worldwide.

In an ominous sign, the U.S. economy began to shrink. An economist at JPMorgan Chase noted, "The fact that you're not seeing any evidence that things are turning for the better has added quite a bit to the urgency to get things done and do something substantial."

After much debate, Congress adopted President Obama's plan to put government money into the economy, although it was certain to be only a partial solution. What was clear, however, was that only the government had both the funds to commit to such a huge economic rescue plan and the power to direct the money broadly to various projects that would create jobs across the nation. Jobs would generate income, increase confidence, and spur a recovery.

In fact, President Obama hoped building projects in transportation and housing would quickly save or create at least 3.5 million jobs. The plan set aside almost $18 billion for investments in high-speed rail and mass transit projects and $48 billion for transportation improvements such as bridge and highway repair to kick-start that job creation. The rest of the $506 billion was divided among social programs that included roughly $87 billion for state Medicaid health insurance plans for lower- and middle-class families and over $82 billion for various education and job training programs. Cash payments to seniors and disabled veterans, financing to repair and modernize public housing, support for local law enforcement, and budgets to increase energy efficiency in government and military facilities, improve public parks, and modernize the nation's electric grid were among many other spending lines.

The stimulus also provided tax relief to businesses that are trying to make payroll and create jobs and to individuals and families. Among the $281 billion in tax breaks were some that rewarded consumers for new home and car purchases and others for businesses to help improve their short-term finances. For instance, business tax incentives for renewable energy facilities added up to more than $14 billion, with millions more for hiring disadvantaged workers and expanding industrial development.

The government's goal was to inject money into the economy for both the short and long term so that businesses could continue to function, new jobs could put the unemployed back to work, and consumers could return money to the economy by picking up their spending on household goods, cars, and appliances, as well as on luxuries like restaurant meals and

© Chuck Kennedy/Bloomberg News/Landov

vacations. It will take time for parts of the plan to be implemented and for the nation to know how well it has worked. Adjustments will be needed along the way. But businesses and individuals were willing to work with the government to get the country back on its feet again. That will be a big step toward a global economic recovery.[1]

When we examine the exchanges that companies and societies make as a whole, we are focusing on the *economic systems* operating in different nations. These systems reflect the combination of policies and choices a nation makes to allocate resources among its citizens. Countries vary in the ways they allocate scarce resources.

Economics, which analyzes the choices people and governments make in allocating scarce resources, affects each of us, because everyone is involved in producing, distributing, or simply consuming goods and services. In fact, your life is affected by economics every day. When you decide what goods to buy, what services to use, or what activities to fit into your schedule, you are making economic choices. Understanding how the activities of one industry affect those of other industries, and how they relate in the overall picture of a country, is an important part of understanding economics.

The choices you make actually may be international in scope. If you are in the market for a new car, you might visit several dealers in a row on the same street—Ford, Chrysler, Honda, Toyota, and General Motors. You might decide on Toyota—a Japanese firm—but your car might very well be manufactured in the United States, using parts from all over the world. Although firms sometimes emphasize the American origin of their goods and services in order to appeal to consumers' desire to support the U.S. economy, many products are made of components from a variety of nations.

Businesses and not-for-profit organizations also make economic decisions when they choose how to use human and natural resources; invest in equipment, machinery, and buildings; and form partnerships with other firms. Economists refer to the study of small economic units, such as individual consumers, families, and businesses, as **microeconomics.**

On a broader level, government decisions about the operation of the country's economy also affect you, your job, and your financial future. A few years ago, in an effort to improve the U.S. economy, the White House and Congress agreed on a package to stimulate markets through tax rebates for families and incentives for businesses. The plan also included elements designed to boost the housing market and provide relief to homeowners facing foreclosure.[2] The study of a country's overall economic issues is called **macroeconomics** (*macro* means "large"). Macroeconomics addresses such issues as how an economy uses its resources and how government policies affect people's standards of living. The substitution of ethanol for gasoline has macroeconomic consequences—affecting many parts of the U.S. economy and suppliers around the world. Macroeconomics examines not just the economic policies of individual nations but the ways in which those individual policies affect the overall world economy. Because so much business is conducted around the world, a law enacted in one country can easily affect a transaction that takes place in another country. Although macroeconomic issues have a broad scope, they help shape the decisions that individuals, families, and businesses make every day.

This chapter introduces economic theory and the economic challenges facing individuals, businesses, and governments in the global marketplace. We begin with the microeconomic concepts of supply and demand and their effect on the prices people pay for goods and services. Next we explain the various types of economic systems, along with tools for comparing and evaluating their performance. Then we examine the ways in which governments seek to manage economies to create stable business environments in their countries. The final section in the chapter looks at some of the driving economic forces currently affecting people's lives.

---

economics social science that analyzes the choices people and governments make in allocating scarce resources.

microeconomics study of small economic units, such as individual consumers, families, and businesses.

macroeconomics study of a nation's overall economic issues, such as how an economy maintains and allocates resources and how a government's policies affect the standards of living of its citizens.

Microeconomics: The Forces of Demand and Supply

Think about your own economic activities. You shop for groceries, you subscribe to a cell phone service, you pay college tuition, you fill your car's tank with gas. Now think about your family's economic activities. When you were growing up, your parents might have owned a home or rented an apartment. You might have taken a summer family vacation. Your parents may have shopped at discount clubs or at local stores. Each of these choices relates to the study of microeconomics. They also help determine both the prices of goods and services and the amounts sold. Information about these activities is vital to companies because their survival and ability to grow depends on selling enough products priced high enough to cover costs and earn profits. The same information is important to consumers who must make purchase decisions based on prices and the availability of the goods and services they need.

At the heart of every business endeavor is an exchange between a buyer and a seller. The buyer recognizes that he or she needs or wants a particular good or service—whether it's a hamburger or a haircut—and is willing to pay a seller for it. The seller requires the exchange in order to earn a profit and stay in business. So the exchange process involves both demand and supply. **Demand** refers to the willingness and ability of buyers to purchase goods and services at different prices. The other side of the exchange process is **supply,** the amount of goods and services for sale at different prices. Understanding the factors that determine demand and supply, as well as how the two interact, can help you understand many actions and decisions of individuals, businesses, and government. This section takes a closer look at these concepts.

Assessment Check ✓

1. Define *microeconomics*.
2. Define *macroeconomics*.

demand willingness and ability of buyers to purchase goods and services.

supply willingness and ability of sellers to provide goods and services.

Factors Driving Demand

For most of us, economics amounts to a balance between what we want and what we can afford. Because of this dilemma, each person must choose how much money to save and how much to spend. We must also decide among all the goods and services competing for our attention. Suppose you wanted to purchase a cell phone. You'd have to choose from a variety of brands and models. You'd also have to decide where you wanted to go to buy one. After shopping around, you might decide you didn't want a cell phone at all. Instead, you might purchase something else, or save your money.

Demand is driven by a number of factors that influence how people decide to spend their money, including price. It may also be driven by outside circumstances or larger economic events. And it can be driven by consumer preferences. Despite a downturn in consumer spending during a recent year, videogames experienced a strong increase in sales of 43 percent above the previous year. Earlier increases were the result of shoppers buying new hardware—Nintendo and Wii were the big hardware winners. But the recent growth represented consumers' desire for new games to play on the systems, leading to strong sales of software.[3]

Demand can also increase the availability of certain types of Web sites and services. Recognizing the enormous popularity of Google's YouTube, and believing the demand would grow, networks NBC and Fox teamed up to launch an advertising-supported online video site, which provides programming from different entertainment companies. The site, called Hulu. com, offers free viewing of full-length movies and television shows. It also hosts programming from NBC and Fox and shows from Sony and Metro-Goldwyn-Mayer. "Consumers identify with shows and films [instead of networks]," explained the site's chief executive, Jason Kilar. "When you aggregate great content together, it makes things easier for the user."[4]

"They Said It"

"Please send me a one-armed economist so we will not always hear 'On the other hand...'"

—Herbert Hoover (1874–1964) 31st president of the United States

Demand is driven by consumer tastes and preferences as well as by economic conditions. Consumers tend to fill up their gas tanks more frequently when the per-gallon price is low.

© Eric Shelton/AP/Wide World Photos

In general, as the price of a good or service goes up, people buy smaller amounts. In other words, as price rises, the quantity demanded declines. At lower prices, consumers are generally willing to buy more of a good. A **demand curve** is a graph of the amount of a product that buyers will purchase at different prices. Demand curves typically slope downward, meaning that lower and lower prices attract larger and larger purchases.

Gasoline provides a classic example of how demand curves work. The left side of Figure 3.1 shows a possible demand curve for the total amount of gasoline that people will purchase at different prices. The prices shown may not reflect the actual price in your location at this particular time, but they still demonstrate the concept. When gasoline is priced at $2.99 a gallon, drivers may fill up their tanks once or twice a week. At $3.39 a gallon, many of them start economizing. They may combine errands or carpool to work. So the quantity of gasoline demanded at $3.39 a gallon is lower than the amount demanded at $2.99 a gallon.

The opposite happens at $2.59 a gallon. More gasoline is sold at $2.59 a gallon than at $2.99 a gallon, as people opt to run more errands or take a weekend trip. However, as mentioned earlier, other factors may cause consumers to accept higher prices anyway. They may have made vacation plans in advance and do not want to cancel them. Or they may be required to drive to work every day.

Economists make a clear distinction between changes in the quantity demanded at various prices and changes in overall demand. A change in quantity demanded, such as the change that occurs at different gasoline prices, is simply movement along the demand curve. A change in overall demand, on the other hand, results in an entirely new demand curve. Businesses are

Figure 3.1   Demand Curves for Gasoline

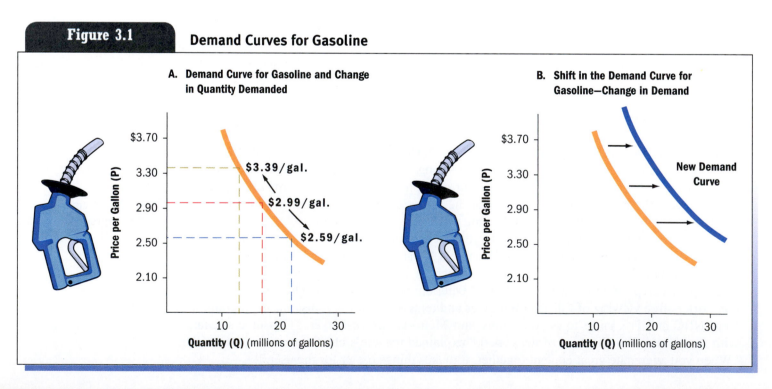

A. Demand Curve for Gasoline and Change in Quantity Demanded

B. Shift in the Demand Curve for Gasoline—Change in Demand

New Demand Curve

constantly trying to make predictions about both kinds of demand, and a miscalculation can cause problems. In the case of gasoline, which is derived from crude oil, many factors come into play. One factor that is beginning to make a major impact is the investment in and development of alternative fuels such as biodiesel, wind, and solar power. If alternatives are developed and readily available, then demand for oil may decrease. Another issue is the U.S. economy. When a downturn occurs, so does the demand for oil and other goods. "If we are slowing down, we will not be buying as much goods from China and services from India," notes Addison Armstrong, director for marketing research at energy broker Tradition Energy. But disruptions in energy sources have the opposite effect; political unrest in oil-rich nations such as Nigeria or extreme weather that takes refineries offline increase the demand for the oil that is available. Also, industrial growth in developing countries such as China and India increase the overall worldwide demand for oil.[5]

We can illustrate how the increased demand for gasoline worldwide has created a new demand curve, as shown in Figure 3.1. The new demand curve shifts to the right of the old demand curve, indicating that overall demand has increased at every price. A demand curve can also shift to the left when the demand for a good or service drops. However, the demand curve still has the same shape.

Although price is the underlying cause of movement along a demand curve, many factors can combine to determine the overall demand for a product—that is, the shape and position of the demand curve. These influences include customer preferences and incomes, the prices of substitute and complementary items, the number of buyers in a market, and the strength of their optimism regarding the future. Changes in any of these factors produce a new demand curve. Although U.S. consumers still love their cup of coffee every morning, makers of supermarket brands like Maxwell House and Folgers are experiencing a decrease in demand for their products. Instead, demand for coffee to go is on the rise. Starbucks, Dunkin' Donuts, and McDonald's (which now serves Newman's Own) recently reported a combined growth of 15 percent.[6] Perhaps the increase is because consumers prefer premium brands, or perhaps they like the convenience of these shops. Still, Starbucks is attempting to ward off competition from its less-expensive rivals by offering smaller cups of drip coffee for $1 with free refills.[7]

Changes in household income also change demand. As consumers have more money to spend, firms can sell more products at every price. This means the demand curve has shifted to the right. When income shrinks, nearly everyone suffers, and the demand curve shifts to the left. High-end retailers like Nordstrom, Saks, and Neiman Marcus experienced a decrease in demand for their luxury goods, as consumers thought twice about buying designer handbags, shoes, and clothing. "Everyone's shopping for the bare necessities, and people have stopped treating themselves," explained one retail consultant. Meanwhile, discount retailers such as JCPenney and Wal-Mart experienced an increase in sales, so their demand curve shifted a bit to the right.[8] Table 3.1 describes how a demand curve is likely to respond to each of these changes.

Table 3.1	Expected Shifts in Demand Curves	
	Demand Curve Shifts	
Factor	**to the Right** *if:*	**to the Left** *if:*
Customer preferences	increase	decrease
Number of buyers	increases	decreases
Buyers' incomes	increase	decrease
Prices of substitute goods	increase	decrease
Prices of complementary goods	decrease	increase
Future expectations become more	optimistic	pessimistic

For a business to succeed, management must carefully monitor the factors that may affect demand for the goods and services it hopes to sell. In setting prices, firms often try to predict how the chosen levels will influence the amounts they sell. The Coca-Cola Company experimented with smart vending machines, adjusting prices to such variables as the weather. If the temperature was hot outside, the machines could automatically raise the price. If the vending machine contained too many cans of root beer and restocking was five days away, the machine could lower the price of root beer. Organizations also try to influence overall demand through advertising, free samples and presentations at retail stores, sales calls, product enhancements, and other marketing techniques.

Factors Driving Supply

Important economic factors also affect supply, the willingness and ability of firms to provide goods and services at different prices. Just as consumers must decide about how to spend their money, businesses must decide what products to sell, and how.

Sellers would prefer to charge higher prices for their products. A **supply curve** shows the relationship between different prices and the quantities that sellers will offer for sale, regardless of demand. Movement along the supply curve is the opposite of movement along the demand curve. So as price rises, the quantity that sellers are willing to supply also rises. At progressively lower prices, the quantity supplied decreases. In Figure 3.2, a possible supply curve for gasoline shows that increasing prices for gasoline should bring increasing supplies to market.

Businesses need certain inputs to operate effectively in producing their output. As discussed in Chapter 1, these *factors of production* include natural resources, capital, human resources, and entrepreneurship. Natural resources include land, building sites, forests, and mineral deposits. Capital refers to resources such as technology, tools, information, physical facilities, and financial capabilities. Human resources include the physical labor and intellectual inputs contributed by employees. Entrepreneurship is the willingness to take risks to create and operate a business.

Factors of production play a central role in determining the overall supply of goods and services.

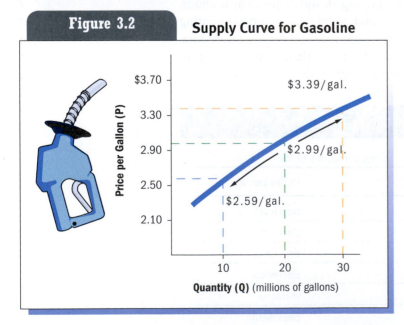

Demand for soft drinks is affected by the weather: on hot days, vendors sell more soft drinks than on cold days. This smart vending machine monitors the outdoor temperature and adjusts the price of the soft drinks it holds accordingly. If the weather is hot, the machine automatically increases the price.

© John Bazemore/AP/Wide World Photos

Figure 3.2   **Supply Curve for Gasoline**

Price per Gallon (P): $3.70, 3.30, 2.90, 2.50, 2.10

$3.39/gal.
$2.99/gal.
$2.59/gal.

Quantity (Q) (millions of gallons): 10, 20, 30

A change in the cost or availability of any of these inputs can shift the entire supply curve, either increasing or decreasing the amount available at every price. If the cost of land increases, a firm might not be able to purchase the site for a more efficient manufacturing plant, which would lower production levels, shifting the supply curve to the left. But if the company finds a way to speed up the production process anyway, allowing it to turn out more products with less labor, the change reduces the overall cost of the finished products, which shifts the supply curve to the right. Table 3.2 summarizes how changes in various factors can affect the supply curve. Sometimes forces of nature can affect the supply curve. During a record-breaking freeze one recent January, nearly 75 percent of California's citrus crop, including oranges and lemons, was severely damaged. Because they could not be harvested and shipped, supply dropped significantly. Agriculture officials estimated that growers lost more than $1.2 billion in crops. As a result, wholesale prices spiked for a short period and then settled in at about one and a half times the regular price. Florida fruit growers filled part of the gap in supply, because they did not experience the freeze.[9]

The agriculture industry has often experienced such shifts in the supply curve. As consumers increase their demand for organic products, more and more dairy farmers are rushing to fill the supply. Organic Valley, a Wisconsin-based cooperative, added 269 dairy farmers to its roster and is processing nearly twice as much milk as it did a year before. Horizon Organic, the largest U.S. organic dairy company, added 64 organic dairy farmers in one year. However, some industry experts caution that an oversupply of organic milk is about to hit the market. While this would normally drive prices down, dairy companies and retailers say they will not lower their prices, which are typically double that of regular milk.[10]

An increase in the demand for a product shifts the supply curve, causing producers to provide more of the product. Because of a recent increase in the demand for organic products, Organic Valley is processing nearly twice as much milk now as it did in the past.

© 2008 Organic Valley Family of Farms

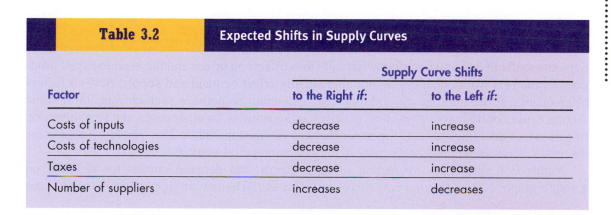

Table 3.2	Expected Shifts in Supply Curves	
	Supply Curve Shifts	
Factor	**to the Right** *if*:	**to the Left** *if*:
Costs of inputs	decrease	increase
Costs of technologies	decrease	increase
Taxes	decrease	increase
Number of suppliers	increases	decreases

Hit & Miss

Supply, Demand, and Swings in Oil Prices

Low crude oil prices are a boon for U.S. consumers, who depend on oil as an ingredient in everything from nonstick cookware to gasoline and home heating fuel. OPEC, the group of oil-producing nations that supplies the bulk of the world's crude oil, is usually able to control the price of crude, and ultimately of gasoline, by controlling the supply. If OPEC's members agree to reduce their output, for example, oil supplies in industrialized nations grow tight, and prices at the pump and factories generally rise. When OPEC starts producing again, supplies rise, and prices are forced down. But everything doesn't always go according to plan.

Following the global financial crisis, oil consumption fell as factories closed and consumer demand slowed, especially in the United States, the world's largest oil consumer. Rising unemployment and a weak economy drastically cut the number of vehicles on the road. Demand for oil fell almost 8 percent and was expected to continue dropping. The price of crude crashed after hitting a high of $145 only a few months before.

OPEC gradually slowed supply, hoping to prop the price up to its preferred level of at least $70 a barrel by reducing output by about 5 percent worldwide. But as much as oil producers want to keep prices up, in part to help meet rising production costs, many observers think any significant increase in the price of this critical factor of production will add more pain to the global economy.

Can the price be too low? From oil consumers' viewpoint, "politically it is better to say we need the lowest possible oil prices," says the director of a Swiss energy research firm. "But there are economic implications to low prices, and not just for OPEC producers." As long as oil is cheap, some fear that industrialized nations will continue to rely on it instead of investing in cheaper, cleaner, and ecologically renewable energy alternatives.

Meanwhile, the drastic swings in oil prices left oil producers shaken. "Our sector is no stranger to cycles," said the CEO of an Italian oil company. "But the turbulence we are currently experiencing—with oil doubling in ... nine months ... and then losing two-thirds of its value in the following six months—is unprecedented."

Further complicating the price picture are oil traders, who buy at low prices, wait for prices to rise, then sell at a profit. The International Monetary Fund reported that such speculation "has played a significant role in the run-up of oil prices" and contributed to a rapid glut of what one observer calls "historic proportions."

While producers are cutting back production to keep prices from falling further, one thing is certain. As an economic recovery gets under way in earnest, global demand will rise again, and so will the price.

Questions for Critical Thinking

1. What roles do supply and demand play in the economics of oil production?
2. What have you observed at your local gas station that suggests the fluctuation of oil supply and oil demand?

Sources: "Crude Oil Falls as Recession Batters U.S.," *MSNBC*, February 6, 2009, http://www.msnbc.com; Jad Mouawad, "OPEC Achieves Cut in Output, Halting Price Slide," *The New York Times*, January 26, 2009, http://www.nytimes.com; Donna Abu-Nasr, "CEO of Eni Says Oil Price Bumps Unprecedented," Associated Press, January 26, 2009, http://www.google.com/hostednews/ap/; Greg Flakus, "Oil Storage at Record Levels as Speculators Await Higher Prices," *VOA News,* January 23, 2009, http://www.voanews.com.

How Demand and Supply Interact

Separate shifts in demand and supply have obvious effects on prices and the availability of products. In the real world, changes do not alternatively affect demand and supply. Several factors often change at the same time—and they keep changing. Sometimes such changes in multiple factors cause contradictory pressures on prices and quantities. In other cases, the final direction of prices and quantities reflects the factor that has changed the most. The "Hit & Miss" feature discusses issues of demand and supply in the international oil market.

Figure 3.3 shows the interaction of both supply and demand curves for gasoline on a single graph. Notice that the two curves intersect at *P.* The law of supply and demand states that prices (*P*) are set by the intersection of the supply and demand curves. The point where the two curves meet identifies the **equilibrium price,** the prevailing market price at which you can buy an item.

If the actual market price differs from the equilibrium price, buyers and sellers tend to make economic choices that restore the equilibrium level. When the price of gold hit $900 an ounce, consumers could expect to pay more for gold jewelry. Also, investors always seem to return to gold as a safe standard, according to economists, and consumers who are intent on buying jewelry most likely will do so, but they may buy fewer pieces.[11]

In other situations, suppliers react to market forces by reducing prices. Chain restaurants such as Church's Chicken and Sonic recently added and began promoting everyday value menus to attract consumers. "Sonic now offers guests more affordable options than ever before," said a Sonic spokesperson. Wendy's and McDonald's have long offered value-priced items and have seen their popularity rise during tough economic times.[12]

As pointed out earlier, the forces of demand and supply can be affected by a variety of factors. One important variable is the larger economic environment. The next section explains how macroeconomics and economic systems influence market forces and, ultimately, demand, supply, and prices.

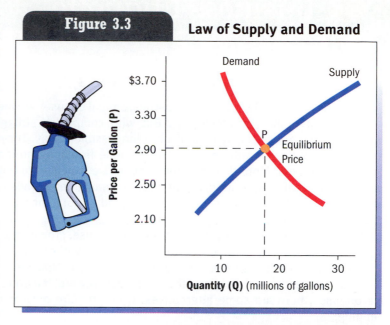

Figure 3.3 **Law of Supply and Demand**

Assessment Check

1. What is a demand curve?
2. What is a supply curve?
3. How do factors of production influence the overall supply of goods and services?

Macroeconomics: Issues for the Entire Economy

Every country faces decisions about how to best use the four basic factors of production. Each nation's policies and choices help determine its economic system. But the political, social, and legal environments differ in every country. So no two countries have exactly the same economic system. In general, however, these systems can be classified into three categories: private enterprise systems; planned economies; or combinations of the two, referred to as mixed economies. As business becomes an increasingly global undertaking, it is important to understand the primary features of the various economic systems operating around the world.

Capitalism: The Private Enterprise System and Competition

Most industrialized nations operate economies based on the *private enterprise system,* also known as *capitalism* or a *market economy.* A private enterprise system rewards businesses for meeting the needs and demands of consumers. Government tends to favor a hands-off attitude toward controlling business ownership, profits, and resource allocations. Instead, competition regulates economic life, creating opportunities and challenges that businesspeople must handle

Business Etiquette

ALTERNATIVES TO BONUSES

Long a way of life in certain industries, annual bonuses are meant to reward and retain key employees. But with companies struggling financially, cash bonuses may be difficult or impossible to pay. They are increasingly unpopular with shareholders in some firms and no longer affordable in others. More than one company in five expected to reduce the dollar value of long-term incentives in the coming year, while even more are looking for alternatives that reward good performance in ways other than financial.

A Canadian Chrysler employee with a working spouse, grown children, and good benefits offered to be laid off so that her coworker with young kids and a laid-off spouse could keep his job instead. That generous offer spurred the idea that helping others is its own reward. If a firm can't give bonuses, here are some alternatives, which require only modest spending:

- Help employees give without spending their own money. Kansas-based Zillner Marketing Communications gave each of its 57 employees $50 to be used to help those less fortunate.
- Give employees extra time off with pay during the holidays when they want to get together with friends and families.
- Set up a time and place to conduct a gift barter, where employees can trade unwanted but new items like clothes, books, tools, or small appliances with one another. Everyone wins by saving time, money, and gas instead of going shopping.
- Barter as a firm, asking clients or suppliers to trade a valuable service your employees can use, like car tune-ups or dry cleaning services, in exchange for one your firm can provide, like computer trouble-shooting or limousine service.
- Use your company's size as a bargaining chip to win year-long discounts for your employees to indulge in pampering services at local gyms and spas.
- Save employees money on their commute by organizing a carpool system. Better yet, let the boss be the designated driver who picks everyone up.
- Provide catered holiday meals to be delivered to everyone in the firm. Offer thoughtful menu choices for those with religious or dietary restrictions and a selection of delivery dates, and everyone will be pleased.
- Offer to pay one monthly bill for each employee—excluding mortgages!

Sources: Sarah Boesveld, "Taking a Bullet for the Team," *The Globe and Mail*, January 26, 2009, http://www.theglobeandmail.com; Linda Cruse, "Employees of Johnson County Firm Use Bonuses to 'Pay It Forward,'" *The Kansas City Star*, January 2, 2009, http://www.kansascity.com; "Recession Forcing Companies to Cut Executive Bonuses, Watson Wyatt Survey Finds," *Washington Business Journal*, December 11, 2008, http://www.bizjournals.com; Scott Allen, "Top 10 Recession-Proof Holiday Bonus Ideas," *About.com*, December 3, 2008, http://entrepreneurs.about.com.

to succeed. One area of business that you will probably encounter in the private enterprise system is employee bonuses, so it is important to know some of the alternatives. Read the "Business Etiquette" feature for some tips.

The relative competitiveness of a particular industry is an important consideration for every firm because it determines the ease and cost of doing business within that industry. Four basic types of competition take shape in a private enterprise system: pure competition, monopolistic competition, oligopoly, and monopoly. Table 3.3 highlights the main differences among these types of competition.

Pure competition is a market structure, like that of small-scale agriculture or fishing, in which large numbers of buyers and sellers exchange homogeneous products and no single participant has a significant influence on price. Instead, prices are set by the market itself as the forces of supply and demand interact. Firms can easily enter or leave a purely competitive market because no single company dominates. Also, in pure competition, buyers see little difference between the goods and services offered by competitors.

Fishing and agriculture are good examples of pure competition. The wheat grown and sold by one farmer in the Midwest is virtually identical to that sold by others. As rainfall and temperatures affect the crop growth, the price for this commodity rises or falls according to the law of supply and demand. The same concept applies to the fishing industry gathering clams and mussels off the coast of New England. The region's notorious "red tide" of algae sometimes contaminates part of the season's supply of shellfish just when summer tourists want them the most—and prices skyrocket. The production of alternative fuels such as ethanol may shift toward pure competition.

Monopolistic competition is a market structure, like that for retailing, in which large numbers of buyers and sellers exchange differentiated (heterogeneous) products, so each participant has some control over price. Sellers can differentiate their products from competing offerings on the basis of price, quality, or other features. In an industry that features monopolistic competition, it is relatively easy for a firm to begin or stop selling a good or service. The success of one seller often

Table 3.3   **Types of Competition**

Characteristics	Types of Competition			
	Pure Competition	**Monopolistic Competition**	**Oligopoly**	**Monopoly**
Number of competitors	Many	Few to many	Few	No direct competition
Ease of entry into industry by new firms	Easy	Somewhat difficult	Difficult	Regulated by government
Similarity of goods or services offered by competing firms	Similar	Different	Similar or different	No directly competing products
Control over price by individual firms	None	Some	Some	Considerable in a pure monopoly; little in a regulated monopoly
Examples	Small-scale farmer in Indiana	Local fitness center	Boeing Aircraft	Rawlings Sporting Goods, exclusive supplier of major-league baseballs

attracts new competitors to such a market. Individual firms also have some control over how their goods and services are priced. Pawnshops are one example of monopolistic competition, as discussed in the "Hit & Miss" feature.

Another example of monopolistic competition is the market for pet food. Consumers can choose from private-label (store brands) and brand-name products in bags, boxes, and cans. Producers of pet food and the stores that sell it have wide latitude in setting prices. Consumers can choose the store or brand with the lowest prices, or sellers can convince them that a more expensive offering is worth more because it offers better nutrition, more convenience, more information, or other benefits.

An **oligopoly** is a market situation in which relatively few sellers compete and high start-up costs form barriers to keep out new competitors. In some oligopolistic industries, such as paper and steel, competitors offer similar products. In others, such as aircraft and automobiles, they sell different models and features. The huge investment required to enter an oligopoly market tends to discourage new competitors. The limited number of sellers also enhances the control these firms exercise over price. Competing products in an oligopoly usually sell for very similar prices because substantial price competition would reduce profits for all firms in the industry. So a price cut by one firm in an oligopoly will typically be met by

Fishing is a good example of pure competition. Because clams gathered by one fisherman are virtually identical to those gathered by others, the price rises and falls with changes in supply and demand. Whenever a poisonous "red tide" of algae infests the clam beds off the coast of New England, the supply of fresh clams plummets and the price skyrockets.

Paul Poplis/Food Pix/Jupiter Images Corp

Hit & Miss

Pawnshops Prosper

Pawnshops lend customers quick cash in exchange for merchandise they leave behind, from jewelry and designer handbags to tools and DVD players. The shops don't run credit checks but can sell the goods—usually for about half of retail—if customers can't repay the loan plus a fee of 10 to 20 percent. Typically about 3 in 10 customers fail to retrieve their pawned items.

Once seen as a sad refuge of the desperate, pawnshops now find their business booming. Financial woes and tightened credit markets have forced more people to try to capitalize on the value of the family silver, a guitar, a digital camera, even a vacuum cleaner, driving the number of first-time customers up 10 percent. "Our door swings all day long," said one pawnshop owner who is president of the Kentucky Pawnbrokers Association. "We are a safety net for so many citizens in our communities."

Customers are changing, too. In the past most had household incomes under $30,000; now many are middle- and upper-middle-class workers struggling with unexpected job losses and diminished savings. In wealthier neighborhoods, transactions involving furs and diamonds are up as much as 40 percent. Cash America, a pawnshop chain, has seen earnings rise dramatically, and a four-shop business in Maine reported lending one-third more cash than the year before. "The banking industry is not giving out any money right now," the owner said, "so people are relying on second-tier lending institutions."

"A pawnshop is a small bank," agrees Charlie Bell, a South Carolina pawnbroker. "We just loan money to people."

Pawnshops do feel the economic pinch in at least one way, however. The rate at which customers pay back their loans and retrieve their collateral has dropped by about 10 percent, which means shops are left with more goods to sell. One young engineer recently tried to pawn his $2,500 Movado watch to make a mortgage payment after being laid off. "I want to help," said the Philadelphia pawnbroker he visited. But no market existed in his neighborhood for such an expensive timepiece, and unsold items become a liability for shop owners. The customer left with the watch in his pocket.

Questions for Critical Thinking

1. In what ways do pawnshops meet the criteria for monopolistic competition?
2. What factors into a pawnbroker's decision about which loans to make?

Sources: Marti Covington, "Pawn Shops among Few Businesses That Get Busier During a Recession," *Beaufort Gazette,* February 7, 2009, http://www.beaufortgazette.com; Kevin Eigelbach, "Some Local Pawn Shops See More People in Need of Short-Term Loans," *Business First of Louisville,* February 6, 2009, http://www.bizjournals.com; Aili McConnon, "For Pawnshops, the Recession Is a Golden Egg," *BusinessWeek,* February 4, 2009, http://www.businessweek.com; Gary Fields, "People Pulling Up to Pawnshops Today Are Driving Cadillacs and BMWs," *The Wall Street Journal,* December 30, 2008, http://www.online.wsj.com; Judy Keen, "Pawnshops Doing Brisk Business," *USA Today,* November 10, 2008, p. 3A.

---

its competitors. However, prices can vary from one market to another, as from one country to another.

Cement is another product for which an oligopoly exists. Mexican-based Cemex SA is the third-largest cement manufacturer in the world and the largest seller of cement in both the United States and Mexico. It holds 60 percent of the market share in Mexico. Cement is usually sold in bulk in the United States, like a commodity. However, it is sold as a branded product in Mexico. Cemex is also Mexico's largest seller of concrete, which is made with cement. Because Cemex has little or no competition in Mexico, individuals and builders often end up paying a higher price for its products. But such dominance can have pitfalls. After it acquired Australian cement company Rinker, Cemex came under scrutiny by the U.S. Department of Justice as a potential monopoly, discussed next.[13]

The final type of market structure is a **monopoly,** in which a single seller dominates trade in a good or service for which buyers can find no close substitutes. A pure monopoly occurs when a firm possesses unique characteristics so important to competition in its industry that they serve as barriers to prevent entry by would-be competitors. After presiding over what many called a monopoly in several areas, Microsoft is facing hefty competition from Google. In addition to its strength in Internet search and online advertising, Google is offering online products aimed at Microsoft's core business: computing tools such as word processing and spreadsheet applications. Google is focusing on Web access to these tools through wired and wireless devices. Ultimately, the competition should benefit consumers.[14]

Many firms create short-term monopolies when research breakthroughs permit them to receive exclusive patents on new products. In the pharmaceuticals industry, drug giants such as Merck and Pfizer invest billions in research and development programs. When the research leads to successful new drugs, the companies can enjoy the benefits of their patents: the ability to set prices without fear of competitors undercutting them. Once the patent expires, generic substitutes enter the market, driving down prices.

Because a monopoly market lacks the benefits of competition, many governments regulate monopolies. Besides issuing patents and limiting their life, the government prohibits most pure monopolies through antitrust legislation such as the Sherman Act and the Clayton Act. The U.S. government has applied these laws against monopoly behavior by Microsoft and by disallowing proposed mergers of large companies in some industries. In other cases, the government permits certain monopolies in exchange for regulating their activities.

With *regulated monopolies,* a local, state, or federal government grants exclusive rights in a certain market to a single firm. Pricing decisions—particularly rate-increase requests—are subject to control by regulatory authorities such as state public service commissions. An example is the delivery of first-class mail, a monopoly held by the U.S. Postal Service. The USPS is a self-supporting corporation wholly owned by the federal government. Although it is no longer run by Congress, postal rates are set by a Postal Commission and approved by a Board of Governors.

During the 1980s and 1990s, the U.S. government trended away from regulated monopolies and toward **deregulation.** Regulated monopolies that have been deregulated include long-distance and local telephone service, cable television, cell phones, and electric utilities. The idea is to improve customer service and reduce prices for customers through increased competition. The Federal Communications Commission recently adopted a rule that bans cable operators from entering into exclusive agreements with owners of apartment buildings. This change will have an impact on the 30 percent of Americans

My immune system is so strong, when I say jump, it asks how high?

I am more than just a dog.

I am an Iams dog

Iams Healthy Naturals with powerful antioxidants to support immunity 100% complete and balanced nutrition combining four food groups. Wholesome chicken, multigrains, leafy greens and fruit. Plus vitamin E and antioxidants for a strong immune system. No fillers or artificial preservatives. And, as always, Iams is veterinarian recommended. Satisfaction guaranteed or your money back.

Life's Better on Iams.

The market for pet food is an example of monopolistic competition. Consumers can choose from assorted bags, boxes, and cans of low-priced store-brand food and high-priced brand-name food. Because pet food is differentiated in these ways, the producers of pet food and the stores that sell it have a great deal of flexibility in setting prices.

Assessment Check ✔

1. What is the difference between pure competition and monopolistic competition?

2. Distinguish between oligopoly and monopoly.

who live in multiple-unit dwellings such as apartments, duplexes, and condominiums. Instead of being forced into a contract with one cable provider, residents of each apartment will have competitive choices. Phone companies such as AT&T and Verizon, which also offer cable service, are included in the rule.[15]

Planned Economies: Socialism and Communism

In a **planned economy,** government controls determine business ownership, profits, and resource allocation to accomplish government goals rather than those set by individual firms. Two forms of planned economies are communism and socialism.

One type of planned economy is socialism. **Socialism** is characterized by government ownership and operation of major industries such as health care and communications. Socialists assert that major industries are too important to a society to be left in private hands and that government-owned businesses can serve the public's interest better than can private firms. However, socialism allows private ownership in industries considered less crucial to social welfare, such as retail shops, restaurants, and certain types of manufacturing facilities. Scandinavian countries such as Denmark, Sweden, and Finland have socialist features in their societies, as do some African nations and India.

The writings of Karl Marx in the mid-1800s formed the basis of communist theory. Marx believed that private enterprise economies created unfair conditions and led to worker exploitation because business owners controlled most of society's resources and reaped most of the economy's rewards. Instead, he suggested an economic system called **communism,** in which all property would be shared equally by the people of a community under the direction of a strong central government. Marx believed that elimination of private ownership of property and businesses would ensure the emergence of a classless society that would benefit all. Each individual would contribute to the nation's overall economic success, and resources would be distributed according to each person's needs. Under communism, the central government owns the means of production, and the people work for state-owned enterprises. The government determines what people can buy because it dictates what is produced in the nation's factories and farms.

A number of nations adopted communist-like economic systems during the early 20th century in an effort to correct abuses they believed existed in their previous systems. In practice, however, these new governments typically gave less freedom of choice in regard to jobs and purchases. These governments might be best described as totalitarian socialism. These nations often made mistakes in allocating resources to compete in the growing global marketplace. Government-owned monopolies often suffer from inefficiency.

Consider the former Soviet Union, where large government bureaucracies controlled nearly every aspect of daily life. Shortages became chronic because producers had little or no incentive to satisfy customers. The quality of goods and services also suffered for the same reason. When Mikhail Gorbachev became the last president of the dying Soviet Union, he tried to improve the quality of Soviet-made products. Effectively shut out of trading in the global marketplace and caught up in a treasury-depleting arms race with the United States, the Soviet Union faced severe financial problems. Eventually, these events led to the collapse of Soviet communism and the breakup of the Soviet Union itself.

Today, communist-like systems exist in just a few countries, such as North Korea. By contrast, the formerly communist People's Republic of China has shifted toward a more market-oriented economy. The national government has given local government and individual plant managers more say in business decisions and has permitted some private businesses. Households now have more control over agriculture, in contrast to the collectivized farms introduced during an earlier era. In addition, Western products such as McDonald's restaurants and Coca-Cola soft drinks are now part of Chinese consumers' lives, and Chinese workers manufacture products for export to other countries.

Mixed Market Economies

Private enterprise systems and planned economies adopt basically opposite approaches to operating economies. In reality, though, many countries operate **mixed market economies,** economic systems that draw from both types of economies, to different degrees. In nations generally considered to have a private enterprise economy, government-owned firms frequently operate alongside private enterprises. In the United States, programs like Medicare are government run.

Privatization, or the conversion of government-owned companies into private enterprises, often lowers costs and increases efficiency. Air Canada, once a state-owned enterprise, went private 20 years ago. The company, which is now the world's tenth-largest international air carrier, is a successful competitor in the global marketplace.

© Jeff McIntosh/AP/Wide World Photos

France has blended socialist and free enterprise policies for hundreds of years. The nation's energy production, public transportation, and defense industries are run as nationalized industries, controlled by the government. Meanwhile, a market economy flourishes in other industries. Over the past two decades, the French government has loosened its reins on state-owned companies, inviting both competition and private investment into industries previously operated as government monopolies. Some former colonies, such as Somalia in Africa, struggle to form working economies, as the "Solving an Ethical Controversy" feature describes.

The proportions of private and public enterprise can vary widely in mixed economies, and the mix frequently changes. Dozens of countries have converted government-owned and -operated companies into privately held businesses in a trend known as **privatization.** Even the United States has seen proposals to privatize everything from the postal service to Social Security. Governments may privatize state-owned enterprises in an effort to raise funds and improve their economies. The objective is to cut costs and run the operation more efficiently. For most of its existence, Air Canada was a state-owned airline. But in 1989 the airline became fully privatized, and in 2000 the firm acquired Canadian Airlines International, becoming the world's tenth-largest international air carrier. Air Canada now maintains an extensive global network, with destinations in the United States, Europe, the Middle East, Asia, Australia, the Caribbean, Mexico, and South America. It offers such amenities as à la carte pricing, personal entertainment systems in seat backs, and fold-flat beds for transatlantic flights.[16]

Table 3.4 compares the alternative economic systems on the basis of ownership and management of enterprises, rights to profits, employee rights, and worker incentives.

Assessment Check ✓

1. On which economic system is the U.S. economy based?

2. What are the two types of planned economies?

3. What is privatization?

HIJACKING ON THE HIGH SEAS

Regardless of their economic systems, some developing countries face the problem of piracy. Today's seafaring pirates are mainly Somalis, supporting various warlords in their leaderless country on the east coast of Africa. In a recent year they attacked over 100 ships in the heavily trafficked shipping lanes of the Gulf of Aden and Indian Ocean. Holding ships, crews, and cargos for ransom, sometimes for months, they have taken in many millions of dollars in ransom money. Foreign governments fear those payments finance more weapons to continue the war and regional conflicts.

The hijackings that began as a desperate bid for economic survival have now become a sophisticated and profitable criminal enterprise. Pirates use high-tech GPS mapping systems, fleets of stolen ships, and heavy weaponry. Corrupt port officials provide safe havens for pirates and their captured ships and crews. Despite international efforts by the United States, Great Britain, Russia, Egypt, France, Germany, China, Yemen, Saudi Arabia, Sudan, Jordan, India, and others, no one can guarantee the safety of commercial ships in the 1.1 million square miles threatened by the pirates and their mother ships. "Unless you have a warship in the immediate area, and crucially, with a helicopter," says an observer in South Africa, "you've got no chance of stopping them."

Should foreign governments pay ransom to pirates on the high seas?

PRO

1. Their willingness to hold hundreds of captives hostage indefinitely gives pirates the upper hand. They will wait, months if necessary, for foreign governments to ransom their cargos and crew.
2. An unending series of attacks have established a business-as-usual pattern for the pirates, particularly when dealing with countries like Britain, in which paying ransom is not illegal. One hijacker of a Ukrainian weapons freighter, accepting $3.2 million in return for leaving the cargo behind, said his group would continue "hunting ships" because "that's our business."

CON

1. "The major problem is that piracy has given some groups the chance to lay their hands on money," says a Somalia expert at the University of South Africa. Since cash is the primary motive, cutting off its flow could help reduce the incentive for pirates to continue their attacks.
2. Some who have dealt with the Somali pirates cite a link with terrorists. If that is the case, governments that pay ransom money could be helping fund violent groups opposed to their own interests.

Summary

India recently sank a pirate vessel, and patrolling U.S. and Russian warship crews have arrested dozens of pirates off the Somali coast. A new international group representing 24 different countries is looking at more ways to prevent piracy and investigate the pirates' link to terrorists. But even as the problem grows, a new threat has appeared: rival pirate groups that try to intercept the ransom payments as they are ferried to captive ships.

Sources: Elizabeth A. Kennedy, "FBI Joins Effort in Hostage Standoff with Pirates," *Associated Press,* April 9, 2009, http://news.yahoo.com; Maria Danilova, "Ukrainian Crew Back Home after Pirates Free Ship," *Associated Press,* February 13, 2009, http://www.google.com/hostednews/; Andrew Njuguna, "Somali Pirates Release Japanese Ship," *Associated Press,* February 13, 2009, http://www.google.com/hostednews; Jeffrey Gettleman and Mohammed Ibrahim, "Somali Pirates Get Ransom and Leave Arms Freighter," *The New York Times,* February 5, 2009, http://www.nytimes.com; "Who Do Pirates Call to Get Their Cash?" *BBC News,* January 29, 2009, http://news-vote.bbc.co.uk/; Scott Baldauf, "Who Are Somalia's Pirates?" *The Christian Science Monitor,* November 21, 2008, http://www.csmonitor.com.

Solving an ETHICAL controversy

		Planned Economies		
System Features	Capitalism (Private Enterprise)	Communism	Socialism	Mixed Economy
Ownership of enterprises	Businesses are owned privately, often by large numbers of people. Minimal government ownership leaves production in private hands.	Government owns the means of production with few exceptions, such as small plots of land.	Government owns basic industries, but private owners operate some small enterprises.	A strong private sector blends with public enterprises.
Management of enterprises	Enterprises are managed by owners or their representatives, with minimal government interference.	Centralized management controls all state enterprises in line with three- to five-year plans. Planning now is being decentralized.	Significant government planning pervades socialist nations. State enterprises are managed directly by government bureaucrats.	Management of the private sector resembles that under capitalism. Professionals may also manage state enterprises.
Rights to profits	Entrepreneurs and investors are entitled to all profits (minus taxes) that their firms earn.	Profits are not allowed under communism.	Only the private sector of a socialist economy generates profits.	Entrepreneurs and investors are entitled to private-sector profits, although they often must pay high taxes. State enterprises are also expected to produce returns.
Rights of employees	The rights to choose one's occupation and to join a labor union have long been recognized.	Employee rights are limited in exchange for promised protection against unemployment.	Workers may choose their occupations and join labor unions, but the government influences career decisions for many people.	Workers may choose jobs and labor union membership. Unions often become quite strong.
Worker incentives	Considerable incentives motivate people to perform at their highest levels.	Incentives are emerging in communist countries.	Incentives usually are limited in state enterprises but do motivate workers in the private sector.	Capitalist-style incentives operate in the private sector. More limited incentives influence public-sector activities.

Table 3.4 Comparison of Alternative Economic Systems

Evaluating Economic Performance

Ideally, an economic system should provide two important benefits for its citizens: a stable business environment and sustained growth. In a stable business environment, the overall supply of needed goods and services is aligned with the overall demand for those goods and services. No wild fluctuations in price or availability complicate economic decisions. Consumers and businesses not only have access to ample supplies of desired products at affordable prices but also have money to buy the items they demand.

Growth is another important economic goal. An ideal economy incorporates steady change directed toward continually expanding the amount of goods and services produced from the nation's resources. Growth leads to expanded job opportunities, improved wages, and a rising standard of living.

Flattening the Business Cycle

A nation's economy tends to flow through various stages of a business cycle: prosperity, recession, depression, and recovery. No true economic depressions have occurred in the United States since the 1930s, and most economists believe that society is capable of preventing future depressions through effective economic policies. Consequently, they expect a recession to give way to a period of economic recovery.

Both business decisions and consumer buying patterns differ at each stage of the business cycle. In periods of economic prosperity, unemployment remains low, consumer confidence about the future leads to more purchases, and businesses expand—by hiring more employees, investing in new technology, and making similar purchases—to take advantage of new opportunities.

As recent events show, during a **recession**—a cyclical economic contraction that lasts for six months or longer—consumers frequently postpone major purchases and shift buying patterns toward basic, functional products carrying low prices. Businesses mirror these changes in the marketplace by slowing production, postponing expansion plans, reducing inventories, and often cutting the size of their workforces. During recessions, people facing layoffs and depletions of household savings become much more conservative in their spending, postponing luxury purchases and vacations. Sometimes they even postpone services like haircuts and dental cleanings. They often turn to lower-priced retailers like Target, Kohl's, and JCPenney for the goods they need. And they have sold cars, jewelry, and stocks to make ends meet. During one recession, they did this as well but with a twist: they turned to eBay. There, they sold everything from old books to art work to kitchenware, contributing to their own success as well as that of eBay.

If an economic slowdown continues in a downward spiral over an extended period of time, the economy falls into depression. Many Americans have grown up hearing stories about their great-grandparents who lived through the Great Depression of the 1930s, when food and other basic necessities were scarce and jobs were rare and precious.

In the *recovery stage* of the business cycle, the economy emerges from recession and consumer spending picks up steam. Even though businesses often continue to rely on part-time and other temporary workers during the early stages of a recovery, unemployment begins to decline as business activity accelerates and firms seek additional workers to meet growing production demands. Gradually, the concerns of recession begin to disappear, and consumers start eating out at restaurants, booking vacations, and purchasing new cars.

recession cyclical economic contraction that lasts for six months or longer.

"They Said It"

"It's a recession when your neighbor loses his job; it's a depression when you lose your own."

—Harry S. Truman
(1884–1972) 33rd president of the United States

Assessment Check ✔

1. Which stages of the business cycle indicate a downturn in the economy?
2. Which stages point to an upswing?

Productivity and the Nation's Gross Domestic Product

An important concern for every economy is **productivity,** the relationship between the goods and services produced in a nation each year and the inputs needed to produce them. In general, as productivity rises, so does an economy's growth and the wealth of its citizens. In a recession, productivity stalls or even declines.

Productivity describes the relationship between the number of units produced and the number of human and other production inputs necessary to produce them. So productivity is a ratio of output to input. When a constant amount of inputs generates increased outputs, an increase in productivity occurs.

Total productivity considers all inputs necessary to produce a specific amount of outputs. Stated in equation form, it can be written as follows:

productivity relationship between the number of units produced and the number of human and other production inputs necessary to produce them.

Total productivity =

$$\frac{\text{Output (goods or services produced)}}{\text{Input (human/natural resources, capital)}}$$

Many productivity ratios focus on only one of the inputs in the equation: labor productivity or output per labor-hour. An increase in labor productivity means that the same amount of work produces more goods and services than before. Many of the gains in U.S. productivity are attributed to technology, and in recent years the United States alone appears to be enjoying the fruits of technology and productivity. No other industrial nation experienced the rapid growth of the United States, which leads the world in worker productivity. Ireland is second. In addition, the productivity gap between the United States and the rest of the world continues to widen, even in the manufacturing sector.[17]

Productivity is a widely recognized measure of a company's efficiency. In turn, the total productivity of a nation's businesses has become a measure of its economic strength and standard of living. Economists refer to this measure as a country's ==gross domestic product (GDP)==—the sum of all goods and services produced within its boundaries. The GDP is based on the per-capita output of a country—in other words, total national output divided by the number of citizens. As Figure 3.4 shows, the U.S. GDP remains the highest in the world. Japan comes in a distant second.

In the United States, GDP is tracked by the Bureau of Economic Analysis (BEA), a division of the U.S. Department of Commerce. Current updates and historical data on the GDP are available at the BEA's Web site (http://www.bea.gov).

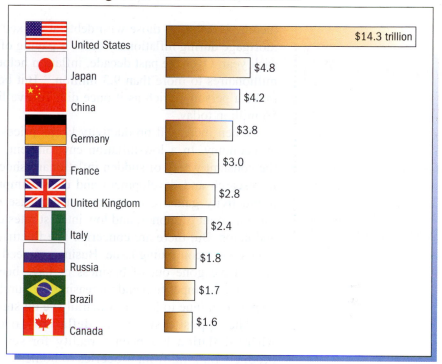

Figure 3.4

Nations with Highest Gross Domestic Products

United States	$14.3 trillion
Japan	$4.8
China	$4.2
Germany	$3.8
France	$3.0
United Kingdom	$2.8
Italy	$2.4
Russia	$1.8
Brazil	$1.7
Canada	$1.6

Source: Central Intelligence Agency, "Field Listing—GDP (Official Exchange Rate)," *The World Factbook,* accessed February 24, 2009, https://www.cia.gov.

gross domestic product (GDP) sum of all goods and services produced within a country's boundaries during a specific time period, such as a year.

Price-Level Changes

Another important indicator of an economy's stability is the general level of prices. For the last 100 years, economic decision makers concerned themselves with ==inflation,== rising prices caused by a combination of excess consumer demand and increases in the costs of raw materials, component parts, human resources, and other factors of production. The **core inflation rate** is the inflation rate of an economy after energy and food prices are removed. This measure is often an accurate prediction of the inflation rate that consumers, businesses, and other organizations can expect to experience during the near future.

Excess consumer demand generates what is known as *demand-pull inflation;* increases in the costs of factors of production generates *cost-push inflation.* America's most severe inflationary period during the last half of the 20th century peaked in 1980, when general price levels jumped almost 14 percent in a single year. In extreme cases, an economy may experience *hyperinflation*—an economic situation characterized by soaring prices. This situation has occurred in South America, as well as in countries that once formed the Soviet Union.

inflation rising prices caused by a combination of excess consumer demand and increases in the costs of raw materials, component parts, human resources, and other factors of production.

Inflation devalues money as persistent price increases reduce the amount of goods and services people can purchase with a given amount of money. This is bad news for people whose earnings do not keep up with inflation, who live on fixed incomes, or who have most of their wealth in investments paying a fixed rate of interest. Inflation can be good news to people whose income is rising or those with debts at a fixed rate of interest. A homeowner with a fixed-rate mortgage during inflationary times is paying off that debt with money that is worth less and less each year. Over the past decade, inflation helped a strong stock market drive up the number of millionaires to more than 9.3 million.[18] But because of inflation, being a millionaire does not make a person as rich as it once did. To live like a 1960s millionaire, you would need almost $6 million today.

When increased productivity keeps prices steady, it can have a major positive impact on an economy. In a low-inflation environment, businesses can make long-range plans without the constant worry of sudden inflationary shocks. Low interest rates encourage firms to invest in research and development and capital improvements, both of which are likely to produce productivity gains. Consumers can purchase growing stocks of goods and services with the same amount of money, and low interest rates encourage major acquisitions such as new homes and autos. But there are concerns. The fluctuating cost of oil—which is used to produce many goods—is a continuing issue. Businesses need to raise prices to cover their costs. Also, smaller firms have gone out of business or have been merged with larger companies, reducing the amount of competition and increasing the purchasing power of the larger corporations. Business owners continue to keep a watchful eye on signs of inflation.

The opposite situation—**deflation**—occurs when prices continue to fall. In Japan, where deflation has been a reality for several years, shoppers pay less for a variety of products ranging from groceries to homes. While this situation may sound ideal to consumers, it can weaken the economy. For instance, industries such as housing and auto manufacturing need to maintain strong prices in order to support all the related businesses that depend on them.

Laid-off workers fill out claims at a local unemployment office. A nation's unemployment rate is often an indicator of its overall economic health.

© Nati Harnik/AP/Wide World Photos

MEASURING PRICE LEVEL CHANGES In the United States, the government tracks changes in price levels with the **Consumer Price Index (CPI),** which measures the monthly average change in prices of goods and services. The federal Bureau of Labor Statistics (BLS) calculates the CPI monthly based on prices of a "market basket," a compilation of the goods and services most commonly purchased by urban consumers. Figure 3.5 shows the categories included in the CPI market basket. Each month, BLS representatives visit thousands of stores, service establishments, rental units, and doctors' offices all over the United States to price the multitude of items in the CPI market basket. They compile the data to create the CPI. Thus, the CPI provides a running measurement of changes in consumer prices.

EMPLOYMENT LEVELS People need money to buy the goods and services produced in an economy. Because most consumers earn that money by working, the number of people in a nation who currently have jobs is an important indicator of how well the economy is doing. In general, employment has been on the rise in the United States the past

Figure 3.5 Contents of the CPI Market Basket

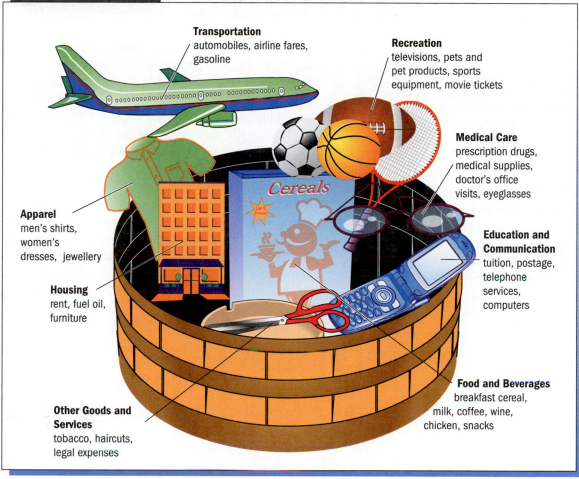

Transportation
automobiles, airline fares, gasoline

Recreation
televisions, pets and pet products, sports equipment, movie tickets

Medical Care
prescription drugs, medical supplies, doctor's office visits, eyeglasses

Apparel
men's shirts, women's dresses, jewellery

Education and Communication
tuition, postage, telephone services, computers

Housing
rent, fuel oil, furniture

Other Goods and Services
tobacco, haircuts, legal expenses

Food and Beverages
breakfast cereal, milk, coffee, wine, chicken, snacks

Source: Information from Bureau of Labor Statistics, "Consumer Price Indexes: Frequently Asked Questions," accessed February 24, 2009, http://www.bls.gov/cpi.

few years, although there have been some dips. Areas that have seen gains include professional and technical services, as well as healthcare and food services.[19]

Economists refer to a nation's **unemployment rate** as an indicator of its economic health. The unemployment rate is usually expressed as a percentage of the total workforce who are actively seeking work but are currently unemployed. The total labor force includes all people who are willing and available to work at the going market wage, whether they currently have jobs or are seeking work. The U.S. Department of Labor, which tracks unemployment rates, also measures so-called discouraged workers. These individuals want to work but have given up looking for jobs, for various reasons. Unemployment can be grouped into the four categories shown in Figure 3.6: frictional, seasonal, cyclical, and structural.

Frictional unemployment applies to members of the workforce who are temporarily not working but are looking for jobs. This pool of potential workers includes new graduates, people who have left jobs for any reason and are looking for other employment, and former workers who have decided to return to the labor force. *Seasonal unemployment* is the joblessness of workers in a seasonal industry. Construction workers, farm laborers,

Assessment Check

1. What is productivity?

2. How does the U.S. government track changes in price levels?

3. Identify the four categories of unemployment.

Figure 3.6   **Four Types of Unemployment**

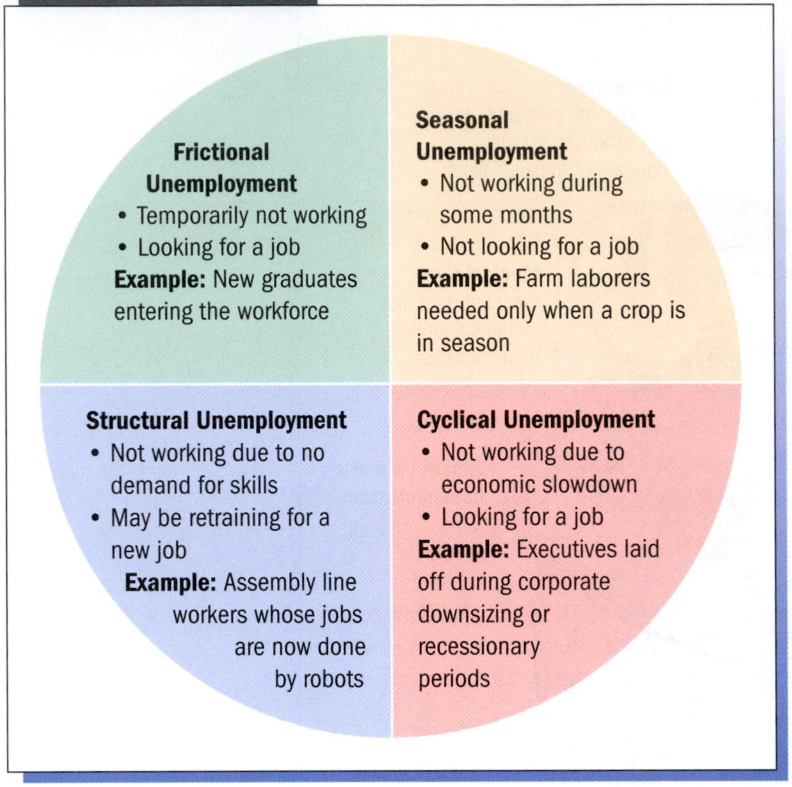

Frictional Unemployment
- Temporarily not working
- Looking for a job

Example: New graduates entering the workforce

Seasonal Unemployment
- Not working during some months
- Not looking for a job

Example: Farm laborers needed only when a crop is in season

Structural Unemployment
- Not working due to no demand for skills
- May be retraining for a new job

Example: Assembly line workers whose jobs are now done by robots

Cyclical Unemployment
- Not working due to economic slowdown
- Looking for a job

Example: Executives laid off during corporate downsizing or recessionary periods

fishing boat operators, and landscape employees may contend with bouts of seasonal unemployment when wintry conditions make work unavailable.

Cyclical unemployment includes people who are out of work because of a cyclical contraction in the economy. During periods of economic expansion, overall employment is likely to rise, but as growth slows and a recession begins, unemployment levels commonly rise. At such times, even workers with good job skills may face temporary unemployment. Workers in high-tech industries, air travel, and manufacturing have all faced unemployment during economic contraction.

Structural unemployment applies to people who remain unemployed for long periods of time, often with little hope of finding new jobs like their old ones. This situation may arise because these workers lack the necessary skills for available jobs or because the skills they have are no longer in demand. For instance, technological developments have increased the demand for people with computer-related skills but have created structural unemployment among many types of manual laborers. Or workers may have been injured and unable to return to work in their original jobs.

Managing the Economy's Performance

As recent years have vividly demonstrated, a national government can use both monetary policy and fiscal policy in its efforts to fight unemployment, increase business and consumer spending, and reduce the length and severity of economic recessions. The Federal Reserve System can increase or reduce interest rates, and the federal government can enact tax cuts and rebates, or propose other reforms.

Monetary Policy

monetary policy
government actions to increase or decrease the money supply and change banking requirements and interest rates to influence bankers' willingness to make loans.

A common method of influencing economic activity is **monetary policy,** government actions to increase or decrease the money supply and change banking requirements and interest rates to influence spending by altering bankers' willingness to make loans. An *expansionary monetary policy* increases the money supply in an effort to cut the cost of borrowing, which encourages business decision makers to make new investments, in turn stimulating employment and economic growth. By contrast, a *restrictive monetary policy* reduces the money supply to curb rising prices, overexpansion, and concerns about overly rapid economic growth.

In the United States, the Federal Reserve System ("the Fed") is responsible for formulating and implementing the nation's monetary policy. It is headed by a chairman and board of governors, all of whom are nominated by the president. The current chairman is Ben Bernanke, who also serves as chairman of the Federal Open Market Committee, the Fed's main agency for monetary policymaking. All national banks must be members of this system and keep some percentage of their checking and savings funds on deposit at the Fed.

The Fed's board of governors uses a number of tools to regulate the economy. By changing the required percentage of checking and savings accounts that banks must deposit with the Fed, the governors can expand or shrink funds available to lend. The Fed also lends money to member banks, which in turn make loans at higher interest rates to business and individual borrowers. By changing the interest rates charged to commercial banks, the Fed affects the interest rates charged to borrowers and, consequently, their willingness to borrow. These rate changes can sometimes help jump-start an economy that may be sliding into recession.

Fiscal Policy

Governments also influence economic activities by making decisions about taxes and spending. Through revenues and expenses, the government implements **fiscal policy.** This is the second technique that officials use to control inflation, reduce unemployment, improve the general standard of living, and encourage economic growth. Increased taxes may restrict economic activities, while lower taxes and increased government spending usually boost spending and profits, cut unemployment rates, and fuel economic expansion. On some occasions, the U.S. federal government has issued tax rebates to its citizens and businesses in an effort to stimulate investment and spending.

fiscal policy government spending and taxation decisions designed to control inflation, reduce unemployment, improve the general welfare of citizens, and encourage economic growth.

INTERNATIONAL FISCAL POLICY Nations in the industrial world, including the United States, are currently struggling to find ways to help developing nations modernize their economies. One proposal is to "forgive" the debts of some of these countries, particularly those in Africa, to stimulate their economies to grow. But not all fiscal experts agree with this idea. They suggest that any debt forgiveness should come with certain conditions so that these countries can build their own fiscal policies. Countries should encourage and allow citizens to own property, lower their tax rates, avoid devaluing their currencies, lay a path for new businesses to start up, and reduce trade barriers. In addition, they must improve agriculture, education, and health care so their citizens can begin to set and reach financial goals. "Hunger and malnutrition is not only an effect of poverty, it also causes poverty," says Robert Zoellick, president of the World Bank. The World Bank is an organization that offers such programs as low-interest loans and interest-free credit and grants to developing countries.[20]

THE FEDERAL BUDGET Each year, the president proposes a **budget** for the federal government, a plan for how it will raise and spend money during the coming year, and presents it to Congress for approval. A typical federal budget proposal undergoes months of deliberation and many modifications before receiving approval. The federal budget includes a number of different spending categories, ranging from defense and Social Security to interest payments on the national debt. The decisions about what to include in the budget have a direct effect on various sectors of the economy. During a recession, the federal government may approve increased spending on interstate highway repairs to improve transportation and increase employment in the construction industry. During prosperity, the government may allocate more money for scientific research toward medical breakthroughs or alternative fuels. Or it may approve funding for job training or arts programs.

budget organization's plan for how it will raise and spend money during a given period of time.

The primary sources of government funds to cover the costs of the annual budget are taxes, fees, and borrowing. Both the overall amount of these funds and their specific combination have major effects on the economic well-being of the nation. One way governments raise money is to impose taxes on sales and income. But increasing taxes leaves people and businesses with less money to spend. This might reduce inflation, but overly high taxes can also slow economic growth. Governments then try to balance taxes to give people necessary services without slowing economic growth.

Taxes don't always generate enough funds to cover every spending project the government hopes to undertake. When the government spends more than the amount of money it raises through taxes, it creates a **budget deficit,** which currently stands at more than $569 billion.[21] To cover the deficit, the U.S. government borrows money by selling Treasury bills, Treasury notes, and Treasury bonds to investors. All of this borrowing makes up the **national debt.** The U.S. Treasury Department estimates that the national debt is $10.9 trillion.[22] One of the factors contributing to the budget deficit has been the war in Iraq and related military operations. If the government takes in more money than it spends, it is said to have a **budget surplus.** A **balanced budget** means total revenues raised by taxes equal the total proposed spending for the year.

Achieving a balanced budget—or even a budget surplus—does not erase the national debt. U.S. legislators continually debate how fast the nation should use revenues to reduce its debt. Most families want to wipe out debt—from credit cards, automobile purchases, and college. To put the national debt into personal perspective, with a little over 306 million U.S. citizens, each one owes about $35,000 as his or her share. But for the federal government, the decision is more complex. When the government raises money by selling Treasury bills, it makes safe investments available to investors worldwide. If foreign investors cannot buy Treasury notes, they might turn to other countries, reducing the amount of money flowing into the United States. U.S. government debt has also been used as a basis for pricing riskier investments. If the government issues less debt, the interest rates it commands are higher, raising the overall cost of debt to private borrowers. In addition, the government uses the funds from borrowing, at least in part, to invest in such public services as education and scientific research. As a society, if we decide our economy needs these services, debt reduction may not always be the best use of government funds. However, it can also be argued that paying down the national debt will free up more money to be invested by individuals and businesses.

Assessment Check

1. What is the difference between an expansionary monetary policy and a restrictive monetary policy?

2. What are the three primary sources of government funds?

3. Does a balanced budget erase the federal debt?

Global Economic Challenges of the 21st Century

Businesses face a number of important economic challenges in the 21st century. As the economies of countries around the globe become increasingly interconnected, governments and businesses must compete throughout the world. Although no one can predict the future, both governments and businesses will likely need to meet several challenges to maintain their global competitiveness. Table 3.5 identifies five key challenges: (1) the economic impact of the continuing threat of international terrorism, (2) the shift to a global information economy, (3) the aging of the world's population, (4) the growth of China and India, and (5) efforts to enhance the competitiveness of every country's workforce.

No country is an economic island in today's global economy. Not only is an ever-increasing stream of goods and services crossing national borders, but a growing number of businesses

Table 3.5	Global Economic Challenges

Challenge	Facts and Examples
International terrorism	Assistance in locating and detaining known terrorists by dozens of nations.
	Cooperation in modifying banking laws in most nations in an effort to cut off funds to terrorist organizations.
	Concerns over the safety of mass-transit systems following bombings in London and elsewhere.
Shift to a global information economy	Half of all American workers hold jobs in information technology or in industries that intensively use information technology, goods, and services.
	Software industry in India is growing more than 50 percent each year.
	Internet users in Asia and western Europe have more than doubled in five years.
Aging of the world's population	Median age of the U.S. population is 36 plus, and by 2025, more than 64 million Americans will be age 65 or older—nearly double today's number. This will increase demands for health care, retirement benefits, and other support services, putting budgetary pressure on governments.
	As Baby Boomers, now reaching their early 60s, begin to retire, businesses around the globe will need to find ways to replace their workplace skills.
Growth of India and China straining commodity prices	China and India now make up more than one-third of the world's population. China's economic growth has been in the industrial sector, and India's focused more in services. Both countries are now consumers of oil and other commodities, affecting prices.
Enhancing competitiveness of every country's workforce	Leaner organizations (with fewer supervisors) require employees with the skills to control, combine, and supervise work operations.

have become true multinational firms, operating manufacturing plants and other facilities around the world. As global trade and investments grow, events in one nation can reverberate around the globe.

Despite the risks of world trade, global expansion can offer huge opportunities to U.S. firms. With U.S. residents accounting for less than 1 in every 20 of the world's nearly 7 billion people, growth-oriented American companies cannot afford to ignore the world market.[23] U.S. businesses also benefit from the lower labor costs in other parts of the world, and some are finding successful niches importing goods and even services provided by foreign firms. Still, it is extremely important for U.S. firms to keep track of the foreign firms that supply their products. When it became apparent that some plastic toys supplied to U.S. toymakers by Chinese manufacturers contained lead paint that could be harmful to children, the U.S. firms issued massive recalls of these toys. Fisher-Price alone recalled 83 types, which amounted to nearly 1 million toys, including its popular Big Bird, Elmo, Dora, and Diego characters. The firm, which is owned by Mattel, urged parents to take toys away from their children if they suspected the toys fell into the recall category and to contact the company. In addition, Fisher-Price quarantined suspect toys before they even made it to store shelves.[24]

U.S. firms must also develop strategies for competing with each other overseas. In the huge but fragmented beverage industry, Coca-Cola still edges out Pepsi as the top-selling cola worldwide. Industry experts predict that China will be the next great battleground for the two soda giants. Coca-Cola still maintains better name recognition, but Pepsi is closing in.[25]

Assessment Check

1. Why is virtually no country an economic island these days?
2. Describe two ways in which global expansion can benefit a U.S. firm.

What's Ahead

Global competition is a key factor in today's economy. In Chapter 4, we focus on the global dimensions of business. We cover basic concepts of doing business internationally and examine how nations can position themselves to benefit from the global economy. Then we describe the specific methods used by individual businesses to expand beyond their national borders and compete successfully in the global marketplace.

Summary of Learning Goals

1 **Distinguish between microeconomics and macroeconomics.**

Microeconomics is the study of economic behavior among individual consumers, families, and businesses whose collective behavior in the marketplace determines the quantity of goods and services demanded and supplied at different prices. Macroeconomics is the study of the broader economic picture and how an economic system maintains and allocates its resources; it focuses on how a government's monetary and fiscal policies affect the overall operation of an economic system.

Assessment Check Answers

1.1 Define *microeconomics*. Microeconomics is the study of economic behavior among individual consumers, families, and businesses whose collective behavior in the marketplace determines the quantity of goods and services demanded and supplied at different prices.

1.2 Define *macroeconomics*. Macroeconomics is the study of the broader economic picture and how an economic system maintains and allocates its resources.

2 **Explain the factors that drive demand and supply.**

Demand is the willingness and ability of buyers to purchase goods and services at different prices. Factors that drive demand for a good or service include customer preferences, the number of buyers and their incomes, the prices of substitute goods, the prices of complementary goods, and consumer expectations about the future. Supply is the willingness and ability of businesses to offer products for sale at different prices. Supply is determined by the cost of inputs and technology resources, taxes, and the number of suppliers operating in the market.

Assessment Check Answers

2.1 What is a demand curve? A demand curve is a graph of the amount of a product that buyers will purchase at different prices.

2.2 What is a supply curve? A supply curve shows the relationship between different prices and the quantities that sellers will offer for sale, regardless of demand.

2.3 How do factors of production influence the overall supply of goods and services? A change in the cost or availability of any of the inputs considered to be factors of production can shift the entire supply curve, either increasing or decreasing the amount available at every price.

3 **Describe each of the four different types of market structures in a private enterprise system.**

Four basic models characterize competition in a private enterprise system: pure competition, monopolistic competition, oligopoly, and monopoly. Pure competition is a market structure, like that in small-scale agriculture, in which large numbers of buyers and sellers exchange homogeneous products and no single participant has a significant influence on price. Monopolistic competition is a market structure, like that of retailing, in which large numbers of buyers and sellers exchange differentiated products, so each participant has some control over price. Oligopolies are market situations, like those in the steel and airline industries, in which relatively few sellers compete and high start-up costs form barriers to keep out new competitors. In a monopoly, one seller dominates trade in a good or service, for which buyers can find no close substitutes. Privately held local water utilities and firms that hold exclusive patent rights on significant product inventions are examples.

Assessment Check Answers

3.1 What is the difference between pure competition and monopolistic competition? Pure competition is a market structure in which large numbers of buyers and sellers exchange homogeneous products. Monopolistic competition is a market structure in which large numbers of buyers and sellers exchange differentiated products.

3.2 Distinguish between oligopoly and monopoly. An oligopoly is a market structure in which relatively few sellers compete, and high start-up costs form barriers to new competitors. In a monopoly, one seller dominates trade in a good or service.

4 Compare the three major types of economic systems.

The major economic systems are private enterprise economy, planned economy (such as communism or socialism), and mixed market economy. In a private enterprise system, individuals and private businesses pursue their own interests—including investment decisions and profits—without undue governmental restriction. In a planned economy, the government exerts stronger control over business ownership, profits, and resources to accomplish governmental and societal—rather than individual—goals. Socialism, one type of planned economic system, is characterized by government ownership and operation of all major industries. Communism is an economic system without private property; goods are owned in common, and factors of production and production decisions are controlled by the state. A mixed market economy blends government ownership and private enterprise, combining characteristics of both planned and private enterprise economies.

Assessment Check Answers

4.1 On which economic system is the U.S. economy based? The U.S. economy is based on the private enterprise system.

4.2 What are the two types of planned economies? The two types of planned economies are socialism and communism.

4.3 What is privatization? Privatization is the conversion of government-owned and -operated agencies into privately held businesses.

5 Identify and describe the four stages of the business cycle.

The four stages are prosperity, recession, depression, and recovery. Prosperity is characterized by low unemployment and strong consumer confidence. In a recession, consumers often postpone major purchases, layoffs may occur, and household savings may be depleted. A depression occurs when an economic slowdown continues in a downward spiral over a long period of time. During recovery, consumer spending begins to increase and business activity accelerates, leading to an increased number of jobs.

Assessment Check Answers

5.1 Which stages of the business cycle indicate a downturn in the economy? Recession and depression indicate a downturn.

5.2 Which stages point to an upswing? Prosperity and recovery point to an upswing.

6 Explain how productivity, price level changes, and employment levels affect the stability of a nation's economy.

As productivity rises, so do an economy's growth and the wealth of its citizens. In a recession, productivity stalls or possibly declines. Changes in general price levels—inflation or deflation—are important indicators of an economy's general stability. The U.S. government measures price-level changes by the Consumer Price Index. A nation's unemployment rate is an indicator of both overall stability and growth. The unemployment rate shows the number of people actively seeking employment who are unable to find jobs as a percentage of the total labor force.

Assessment Check Answers

6.1 What is productivity? Productivity is the relationship between the goods and services produced in a nation each year and the inputs that produce them.

6.2 How does the U.S. government track changes in price levels? The U.S. government tracks changes in price levels with the Consumer Price Index (CPI), which measures the monthly average change in prices of goods and services.

6.3 Identify the four categories of unemployment. The four categories of unemployment are frictional, seasonal, cyclical, and structural.

7 Discuss how monetary policy and fiscal policy are used to manage an economy's performance.

Monetary policy encompasses a government's efforts to control the size of the nation's money supply. Various methods of increasing or decreasing the overall money supply affect interest rates and therefore affect borrowing and investment decisions. By changing the size of the money supply, government can encourage growth or control inflation. Fiscal policy involves decisions regarding government revenues and expenditures. Changes in government spending affect economic growth and employment levels in the private sector. However, a government must also raise money, through taxes or borrowing, to finance its expenditures. Because tax payments represent funds that might otherwise have been spent by individuals and businesses, any taxation changes also affect the overall economy.

Assessment Check Answers

7.1 What is the difference between an expansionary monetary policy and a restrictive monetary policy? An expansionary monetary policy increases the money supply in an effort to cut the cost of borrowing. A restrictive monetary policy reduces the money supply to curb rising prices, overexpansion, and concerns about overly rapid economic growth.

7.2 What are the three primary sources of government funds? The U.S. government acquires funds through taxes, fees, and borrowing.

7.3 Does a balanced budget erase the federal debt? No, a balanced budget does not erase the national debt; it just doesn't increase it.

8 Describe the major global economic challenges of the 21st century.

Businesses face five key challenges in the 21st century: (1) the threat of international terrorism; (2) the shift to a global information economy; (3) the aging of the world's population; (4) the growth of India and China, which compete for resources; and (5) efforts to enhance the competitiveness of every country's workforce.

Assessment Check Answers

8.1 Why is virtually no country an economic island these days? No business or country is an economic island because many goods and services travel across national borders. Companies now are becoming multinational firms.

8.2 Describe two ways in which global expansion can benefit a U.S. firm. A firm can benefit from global expansion by attracting more customers and using less expensive labor and production to produce goods and services.

Business Terms You Need to Know

economics 68
microeconomics 68
macroeconomics 68
demand 69

supply 69
recession 84
productivity 84

gross domestic product (GDP) 85
inflation 85

monetary policy 88
fiscal policy 89
budget 89

Other Important Business Terms

demand curve 70
supply curve 72
equilibrium price 75
pure competition 76
monopolistic competition 76
oligopoly 77

monopoly 78
deregulation 79
planned economy 80
socialism 80
communism 80
mixed market economy 81

privatization 81
core inflation rate 85
deflation 86
Consumer Price Index (CPI) 86
unemployment rate 87

budget deficit 90
national debt 90
budget surplus 90
balanced budget 90

Review Questions

1. How does microeconomics affect business? How does macroeconomics affect business? Why is it important for businesspeople to understand the fundamentals of each?

2. Draw supply and demand graphs that estimate what will happen to demand, supply, and the equilibrium price of pizza if these events occur:
   a. A widely reported medical report suggests that eating cheese supplies a significant amount of the calcium needed in a person's daily diet.
   b. The price of flour increases.
   c. The state imposes a new tax on restaurant meals.
   d. The biggest competitor leaves the area.

3. Describe the four different types of competition in the private enterprise system. In which type of competition would each of the following businesses be likely to engage?
   a. small manufacturer of ice cream
   b. Stop & Shop supermarkets
   c. American Airlines

   d. large farm whose major crop is corn
   e. Google

4. Distinguish between the two types of planned economies. What factors do you think keep them from flourishing in today's environment?

5. What are the four stages of the business cycle? In which stage do you believe the U.S. economy is now? Why?

6. What is the gross domestic product? What is its relationship to productivity?

7. What are the effects of inflation on an economy? What is deflation? How does the Consumer Price Index work?

8. What does a nation's unemployment rate indicate? Describe what type of unemployment you think each of the following illustrates:
   a. recent college graduate interviewing for a job
   b. flight attendants who have been laid off due to a reduction in flights
   c. manufacturing employees whose company has automated most production jobs

d. ski lift attendant

e. retail worker who has quit one job and is looking for another

9. Explain the difference between monetary policy and fiscal policy. How does the government raise funds to cover the costs of its annual budget?

10. What is the difference between the budget deficit and the national debt? What are the benefits of paying down the national debt? What might be the negative effects?

Projects and Teamwork Applications

1. Describe a situation in which you have had to make an economic choice in an attempt to balance your wants with limited means. What factors influenced your decision?

2. Choose one of the following products and describe the different factors that you think might affect its supply and demand.

   a. Crocs sandals
   b. iPhone
   c. Chase Freedom credit card
   d. Glaceau Smartwater
   e. Caribbean cruise

3. Go online to research one of the following agencies—its responsibilities, its budget, and the like. Then make the case for privatizing it:

   a. U.S. Army Corps of Engineers
   b. U.S. Postal Service
   c. Internal Revenue Service
   d. Transportation and Security Administration
   e. Social Security

4. Some businesses automatically experience seasonal unemployment. Increasingly however, owners of these businesses are making efforts to increase demand—and employment—during the off-season. Choose a classmate to be your business partner, and together select one of the following businesses. Create a plan for developing business and keeping employees for a season during which your business does not customarily operate:

   a. surf shop
   b. landscaping business
   c. inn located near a ski resort
   d. house painting service
   e. greenhouse

5. On your own or with a classmate, go online to research the economies of one of the following countries. Learn what you can about the type of economy the country has, its major industries, and its competitive issues. (Note which industries or services are privatized and which are government owned.) Take notes on unemployment rates, monetary policies, and fiscal policies. Present your findings to the class.

   a. China
   b. Japan
   c. India
   d. France
   e. Mexico
   f. United Kingdom
   g. Brazil

Web Assignments

1. **Inflation.** In the United States, the Bureau of Labor Statistics (BLS) compiles and publishes the most widely followed measure of inflation, the Consumer Price Index (CPI). Visit the BLS Web site (http://www.bls.gov) and click on "Inflation & Consumer Spending." Answer the following questions:

   a. What is the current rate of inflation as measured by the CPI?

   b. Which components of the CPI have risen the most over the past year? Which components have risen the least?

   c. What is the difference between the rate of inflation and the so-called *core rate of inflation?*

2. **World economic outlook.** The International Monetary Fund (IMF) publishes several reports each year on the outlook for the world economy. Visit the IMF Web site (http://www.imf.org). Click on the "Publications" link and access the most recent report you can find. Review the report and identify one major policy issue facing the global economy and the economic outlook for one region or country—other than the United States.

3. **Truth in lending regulations.** The Federal Reserve is considering several changes to "truth in lending" regulations. Specifically, the proposed changes deal with unfair and deceptive home mortgage lending practices. Visit the Federal Reserve Web site (http://www.federalreserve.gov)

and click on "News & Events." Then look for news on the proposed rule change to amend the home mortgage regulation (Regulation Z). Prepare a brief report for your class answering the following questions:

a. What did the Federal Reserve change?

b. Whom did these regulatory changes affect?

c. Why did the Federal Reserve make these changes?

Note: Internet Web addresses change frequently. If you do not find the exact sites listed, you may need to access the organization's or company's home page and search from there.

An Economic Windfall: The Rise of Wind Energy

Texas is well known for big things—its size, its houses, its ranches, its dreams. So it's no surprise that the state is going big for wind energy, as the search for clean, renewable energy sources becomes urgent. Currently, Texas is leading the nation in harnessing wind power, partly because its location and topography create the perfect conditions for wind. West Texas, in particular, experiences a near-constant wind speed of 17 miles per hour over wide-open terrain. It also has landowners who are ready and willing to invest in a new business. In addition, state lawmakers passed legislation requiring utilities to buy renewable power, and federal tax credits await those who invest in wind power. Finally, Texas is on its own power grid, separate from the rest of the country. All of this points toward economic opportunity for small towns that have seen a downturn.

Roscoe is one of these towns. The train doesn't stop there anymore, and the Dairy Queen closed. Stores don't have a lot to sell, and the 1,300 people who live there aren't shopping anyway—at least they weren't until recently. Together with Airtricity, an energy firm based in the United Kingdom, the town of Roscoe has built one of the biggest wind farms in the world. The Roscoe Wind Farm generates 209 megawatts of electricity—enough to power about 60,000 homes and save about 375,000 tons per year in greenhouse gas emissions. The wind power is sold through TXU Wholesale under a five-year contract. In addition, the landowners, on whose property the farm is built, will eventually receive royalties on the electricity sales. "We used to cuss the wind," recalls Cliff Etheredge, a local cotton farmer who helped originate the project with Airtricity. "Now, we love the wind." Etheredge also proudly cites the economic rejuvenation of Roscoe: two new restaurants and other businesses that are opening or expanding. "Hopefully, we'll see Roscoe reborn here."

The wind energy industry in Texas has much broader implications than for a single small town, as companies bid for the rights to develop wind farms off the state's coast in the Gulf of Mexico. "The future of the nation's offshore wind industry is off the coast of Texas," asserts the state's Land Office commissioner. The Land Office has jurisdiction over the waters up to 10 miles offshore. "There's international interest in these tracts, and this will be the first time the market will be able to place a value on what I think is a very valuable asset."

Across the nation in upstate New York, an environmental engineering firm named Tetra Tech is working on the Maple Ridge Wind Energy Program as part of the state's initiative to reduce its traditional energy use by the year 2015. The firm is working toward the goal of helping to ensure that one-fourth of New York's energy is produced by renewable sources by 2013. New York officials believe that wind is the most economical resource compared with traditional sources, but wind turbines must be built to certain specifications in order to maximize their output and minimize their impact. Still, wind power is showing great promise.[26]

Questions for Critical Thinking

1. What factors do you think will affect the supply and demand curve for wind energy?

2. Describe what type of competition you predict will arise in the wind energy industry.

Music and Money: Breaking Record-Labels' Stranglehold on Artists

You probably have access to digital downloads of your favorite tunes—whether it's for an iPod, MP3 player, laptop or desktop computer, or other device. You might have discovered the next big hit by watching YouTube or MySpace. The music industry has finally recognized the influence of new technologies on their business. The big record labels have acknowledged that they no longer have as much control over music creation or its distribution as they once did. Whereas a decade ago musicians earned 60 percent of their income through record labels from prerecorded music and the rest from concerts, endorsements, and merchandise, today those percentages are reversed. Concert ticket sales have nearly tripled, and the record labels don't profit from them. As these companies are trying to stop the flood of music and dollars out their own doors, they are also rethinking their business models in an attempt to find new ways of attracting talent and distributing their music.

Some labels such as EMI are revising their contracts with artists. Called multiple-rights or all-rights contracts, these new agreements encompass live music, merchandise, and endorsements, instead of a simple cut of CD sales. Although artists are not enthusiastic about the new agreements, record executives insist that they are necessary. "It's a discussion you have with every new artist now," says Jeanne Meyer of EMI.

Some musicians have said no to the new arrangement, preferring to launch on their own or teaming up with smaller, start-up firms like Musicane, Indie911, Fuzz, Snocap, and TuneCore. Nine Inch Nails, Radiohead, Oasis, and Madonna are just a few of the increasing number of such groups. Trent Reznor of Nine Inch Nails left EMI and went to Musicane, where he dictated his own requirements for Web design, pricing, and other aspects of his music. He also helped the company's programmers, administrators, and designers produce albums for other artists. Reznor is an example of the new musician who is savvy about both technology and business. "Trent is well-informed, articulate and is very knowledgeable about technology," notes Musicane CEO Dushin Shahani.

But the big labels aren't through yet. One of the new business models being adopted by larger firms involves bundling music subscriptions with the price of Internet access so that the music downloads appear to be free. Nokia Corp. is launching a service called Comes With Music, which allows users of certain cell phones a year of unlimited access to music without extra charges. In addition, the music labels are planning to license songs for ad-supported Web sites, where users watch videos or listen to full-length tracks posted by other users for free. Finally, four of the world's largest recording companies—Sony BMG, Vivendi SA's Universal Music Group, Warner Music Group, and EMI—agreed to license music for sale online as unprotected MP3 files, which mean they can be played on multiple devices. "It seems clear there's an accelerated pace of change that comes hand in glove with accelerated decline in traditional business," observes Eric Garland, CEO of a firm that tracks online entertainment.

The big companies are a bit grudging about the changes, acknowledging their necessity if somewhat unenthusiastically. "There's no denying that Warner Music Group and the industry as a whole have been struggling for almost a decade now with the challenges and opportunities that the digital space presents," admits Edgar Bronfman, chairman and CEO. "The recent trend of dramatic changes in the recorded music market will continue … And, though it's a cliché, it's a cliché because it's true: technology will also provide us with new opportunities."[27]

Questions for Critical Thinking

1. How has the rapid development of technology affected competition in the music industry?

2. How does this technology affect supply and demand in the music industry?

Companies build demand for their goods and services in a variety of ways. Automaker Kia attracts buyers with current styling and low prices. Sony increases the demand for its PlayStation games by limiting the supply, making the computer games harder to get—and more popular. A ski resort like New York's Lake Placid builds demand by hosting a variety of competitions and activities for tourists and athletes year round—from horse shows to figure skating tournaments. Jake Burton built demand by creating a sport.

Burton, founder and owner of Burton Snowboards, won't take credit for inventing snowboarding, which he says has actually been around since the 1920s. But when he was a teenager, Burton started sliding down hills on a wooden board with a rope attached to it called a "Snurfer." The Snurfer was primitive and didn't offer much control to the rider, but Burton was hooked. "From that time on, I felt like it could be a sport, but it wasn't a sport for the company that was manufacturing it. They were selling (the Snurfer) like it was a hula hoop or something," he recalls. Burton thought he could improve on the design—and the sport.

In 1977, Burton moved from New York to Vermont to start Burton Snowboards. "I was blindly optimistic," he says. In addition to all of the struggles associated with developing a new product, Burton had to build awareness of and interest in the new sport itself. "I became more concerned with hyping the sport to make sure it happened so that I was right," Burton recalls. One major hurdle was the fact that at the time, ski resorts didn't allow snowboarding on their slopes, so snowboarders had to climb hills, carrying their snowboards, in order to ride down. Burton knew he had to change that situation, or his sport—and company—would never get off the ground. He had to build demand not only among consumers but among the ski resorts that attracted those consumers, convincing them that snowboarders would eventually become an important market. He got his first break when Vermont's Stratton Mountain Resort agreed to allow snowboards on its slopes.

Gradually, interest in the sport and in Burton Snowboards spread. Then Burton began to get inquiries from European dealers and distributors, which opened up a whole new market for him. Fifteen years later, demand had increased so much that snowboarding debuted as an Olympic sport at the Nagano Winter Olympics in 1998—proof positive that the sport had arrived. Today, Burton Snowboards conducts business in more than 30 countries, with 3,000 dealers worldwide.

Still, the company hasn't stopped looking for new ways to build demand by attracting new recruits to the sport. Recognizing that snowboarding has been taught and learned haphazardly—which worries adult riders and parents of young riders—Burton Snowboards has established a systematic method of teaching called the Learn-To-Ride (LTR) program. The program includes lessons taught by certified American Association of Snowboard Instructors, as well as specially manufactured Burton boards, boots, and bindings designed for beginners. Stowe Mountain Resort, in Stowe, Vermont, was one of the first resorts to host the LTR program. "For over a decade, Stowe has been the frontier for learning to snowboard," notes Jeff Wise, director of the Stowe Snowboard School. "Learning from the industry's leading professionals has been made even better with the addition of LTR equipment."

In addition, in 1995 Burton Snowboards started a nonprofit, after-school learning program for underprivileged and at-risk children in the Burlington, Vermont, area where the company is based. The program, called "Chill," has since expanded to Boston, Los Angeles, New York, and Seattle. "Chill" takes schoolchildren snowboarding once a week for seven weeks, providing everything they need, from equipment to lift passes to instruction. Why do this? "There are so many companies out there doing things for the environment, but we decided to address the people side of things," says Burton. "Chill" not only takes kids off the streets but puts them on the slopes—creating a whole new generation and economic class of snowboarders.

During the rush to grow business quickly, when it seemed that companies couldn't go public fast enough, Jake Burton says he'd rather not. He likes the control that ownership of the company gives him, and the flexibility. "I'm first and foremost a snowboarder," he says, "and I use the fact that I don't have to be [in my office] every day like I used to as an opportunity to get more immersed in the sport." Such enthusiastic words from a man who took a sport from its infancy to its debut at the Olympics—and brought a whole new category of athletes along for the ride.[28]

Questions for Critical Thinking

1. In addition to the materials discussed in the case, what other factors might affect demand for Burton Snowboards?
2. What factors might affect supply of the snowboards?
3. What type of competition would you consider the snowboard industry to be at this time?
4. What challenges might Burton Snowboards face when doing business abroad?

chapter 4

Competing in World Markets

Lululemon Athletica Stretches Its Global Reach

Yoga has been around for centuries but has not always been well understood in Western cultures. Today, yoga is gaining ground in the United States. More and more people are trying a variety of styles and levels of yoga and discovering its physical and mental benefits. As its popularity has increased, so has the business of yoga—from classes to related gear and specially designed apparel.

Gone are bulky cotton sweatpants, nylon running shorts, and old gym mats. Instead, you'll see gently form-fitting, stretchy pants and tops made from high-tech fabrics and soft, dense mats that pad the joints and hug the floor. Many of these articles are made by Canada-based Lululemon Athletica, which is dedicated to offering the highest quality yoga apparel and gear to students and their instructors. Founder Chip Wilson created the company after taking a yoga class in Vancouver, where he was living. He loved the class but hated the clothes. So he started a design studio to make innovative yoga clothes and gave them to local instructors in return for their honest feedback.

The clothes were a hit, and the first Lululemon retail store opened in the beach area of Vancouver two years later. Wilson's vision was to make the store more than just a retail outlet for clothing and gear. He wanted it to be a hub for people interested in learning more about yoga, healthy eating, and positive thinking. Salespeople were trained as educators so that "they could in fact positively influence their families, communities, and the people walking into our stores." Each Lululemon store contains a community bulletin board where shoppers can get information about what classes are scheduled, including yoga, Pilates, children's classes, and organized runs; where to find a local nutritionist; or how to recycle an old yoga mat.

Because of this local approach, Lululemon quickly developed a devoted following. Wilson and his team realized that one store wasn't enough and began expanding. Currently, the firm operates 43 stores in Canada, 44 in the United States, and 7 in Australia. The company is planning to add about 35 more stores in North America. Although the firm attempted to enter the Japanese market, it decided to close those stores because they contributed less than 1.5 percent in sales and required intensive management.

Lululemon manufactures its products around the world—in Canada, China, India, Indonesia, Israel, Taiwan, and the United States. The firm chooses factories worldwide based on their commitment to quality and ethical work practices. Lululemon evaluates the conditions at each overseas factory before entering into a working relationship and follows the health and safety standards of the International Labour Organization, a United Nations agency. The company's own Workplace Code of Conduct sets labor standards related to wages and overtime, health and safety, nondiscrimination, prohibition of child or forced labor, and environmental practices. Teams make regular visits to the overseas facilities to evaluate working conditions and product quality. But Lululemon also retains a significant manufacturing base in Vancouver so that new designs can be brought to market quickly and help dodge the threat of cheap knock-offs.

Lululemon recently appointed a new CEO, Christine Day, a former executive at Starbucks Asia-Pacific division. Chip Wilson continues as chairman of the board and chief product designer. Day plans to find ways to grow the company while remaining true to its core values of education and health. "Lululemon has an extraordinary brand with a loyal and growing following around the globe who have embraced our yoga inspired apparel and unique store experience," notes Day.

One new area the firm is exploring is an expanded online presence. The company has an informational Web site containing descriptions of products ranging from tank tops to yoga mats, store locators, and general information about yoga. But Lululemon resisted selling its clothing online, instead relying on the personal experience its in-store educators offered. The firm is now changing course and developing an e-business Web site. The firm is retaining control of key product decisions and customer service functions while using partners for technical support and product distribution. The goal? Allowing yoga aficionados who don't happen to live close to a Lululemon store to enjoy its products while expanding Lululemon's reach.[1]

Consider for a moment how many products you used today that came from outside the United States. Maybe you drank Brazilian coffee with your breakfast, wore clothes manufactured in Honduras or Malaysia, drove to class in a German or Japanese car fueled by gasoline refined from Venezuelan crude oil, and watched a movie on a television set assembled in Mexico for a Japanese company such as Sony. A fellow student in Germany may be wearing Levi's jeans, using a Dell computer, and drinking Coca-Cola.

U.S. and foreign companies alike recognize the importance of international trade to their future success. Economic interdependence is increasing throughout the world as companies seek additional markets for their goods and services and the most cost-effective locations for production facilities. No longer can businesses rely only on domestic sales. Today, foreign sales are essential to U.S. manufacturing, agricultural, and service firms as sources of new markets and profit opportunities. Foreign companies also frequently look to the United States when they seek new markets.

Thousands of products cross national borders every day. The computers that U.S. manufacturers sell in Canada are **exports,** domestically produced goods and services sold in markets in other countries. **Imports** are foreign-made products and services purchased by domestic consumers. Together, U.S. exports and imports make up about a quarter of the U.S. gross domestic product (GDP). U.S. exports recently set a record high of roughly $1.1 trillion, and annual imports hit another new high of nearly $2 trillion. That total amount is more than double the nation's imports and exports from just a decade ago.[2]

Transactions that cross national boundaries may expose a company to an additional set of environmental factors such as new social and cultural practices, economic and political environments, and legal restrictions. Before venturing into world markets, companies must adapt their domestic business strategies and plans to accommodate these differences.

This chapter travels through the world of international business to see how both large and small companies approach globalization. First, we consider the reasons nations trade, the importance and characteristics of the global marketplace, and the ways nations measure international trade. Then we examine barriers to international trade that arise from cultural and environmental differences. To reduce these barriers, countries turn to organizations that promote global business. Finally, we look at the strategies firms implement for entering foreign markets and the way they develop international business strategies.

Why Nations Trade

As domestic markets mature and sales growth slows, companies in every industry recognize the increasing importance of efforts to develop business in other countries. Wal-Mart operates stores in Mexico, Boeing sells jetliners in Asia, and soccer fans in Britain watch their teams being bought by U.S. billionaires. These are only a few of the thousands of U.S. companies taking advantage of large populations, substantial resources, and rising standards of living abroad that boost foreign interest in their goods and services. Likewise, the U.S. market, with the world's highest purchasing power, attracts thousands of foreign companies to its shores.

exports domestically produced goods and services sold in other countries.

imports foreign goods and services purchased by domestic customers.

International trade is vital to a nation and its businesses because it boosts economic growth by providing a market for its products and access to needed resources. Companies can expand their markets, seek growth opportunities in other nations, and make their production and distribution systems more efficient. They also reduce their dependence on the economies of their home nations.

International Sources of Factors of Production

Business decisions to operate abroad depend on the availability, price, and quality of labor, natural resources, capital, and entrepreneurship—the basic factors of production—in the foreign country. Indian colleges and universities produce thousands of highly qualified computer scientists and engineers each year. To take advantage of this talent, many U.S. computer software and hardware firms have set up operations in India, and many others are outsourcing information technology and customer service jobs there.

Trading with other countries also allows a company to spread risk because different nations may be at different stages of the business cycle or in different phases of development. If demand falls off in one country, the company may still enjoy strong demand in other nations. Companies such as Toyota and Sony have long used international sales to offset lower domestic demand.

"They Said It"

"No nation was ever ruined by trade."

—Benjamin Franklin (1706–1790) American statesman and philosopher

Size of the International Marketplace

In addition to human and natural resources, entrepreneurship, and capital, companies are attracted to international business by the sheer size of the global marketplace. Only one in five of the world's nearly 7 billion people lives in a relatively well-developed country. The share of the world's population in the less developed countries will increase over the coming years because more developed nations have lower birthrates. But the U.S. Census Bureau says the global birthrate is slowing overall, and the average woman in today's world bears half as many children as her counterpart did 35 years ago.[3]

As developing nations expand their involvement in global business, the potential for reaching new groups of customers dramatically increases. Firms looking for new revenue are inevitably attracted to giant markets such as China and India, with respective populations of about 1.3 billion and 1.1 billion each. However, people alone are not enough to create a market. Consumer demand also requires purchasing power. As Table 4.1 shows, population size is no

Table 4.1	The World's Top Ten Nations Based on Population and Wealth		
Country	**Population (in Millions)**	**Country**	**Per-Capita GDP (in U.S. dollars)**
China	1,330	Luxembourg	$87,955
India	1,148	Norway	$72,306
United States	304	Qatar	$62,914
Indonesia	238	Iceland	$54,858
Brazil	196	Ireland	$52,440
Pakistan	173	Switzerland	$51,771
Bangladesh	154	Denmark	$50,965
Nigeria	146	United States	$44,190
Russia	141	Sweden	$42,383
Japan	127	Netherlands	$40,571

Sources: U.S. Census Bureau, International Database, "Countries and Areas Ranked by Population: 2008," http://www.census.gov, accessed February 26, 2009; International Monetary Fund, *World Economic Outlook Database,* April 2007, accessed at http://www.answers.com, February 26, 2009.

Economic growth is strong in the developing world, enticing corporations to go global. From China to Brazil, Wal-Mart has opened dozens of new stores in developing countries.

© Elizabeth Dalziel/AP/Wide World Photos

Figure 4.1

Top Ten Trading Partners with the United States

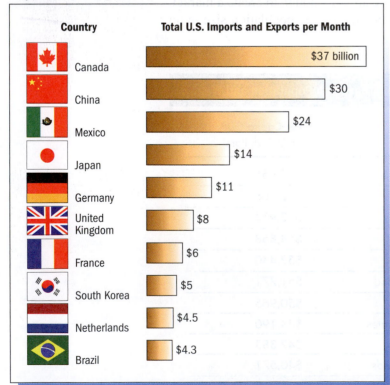

Country	Total U.S. Imports and Exports per Month
Canada	$37 billion
China	$30
Mexico	$24
Japan	$14
Germany	$11
United Kingdom	$8
France	$6
South Korea	$5
Netherlands	$4.5
Brazil	$4.3

Source: Data from U.S. Census Bureau, "Top Ten Countries with which the U.S. Trades," accessed February 26, 2009, http://www.census.gov/foreign-trade/top/dst/current/balance.html.

guarantee of economic prosperity. Of the ten most populous countries, only the United States appears on the list of those with the highest per-capita GDPs.

Although people in the developing nations have lower per-capita incomes than those in the highly developed economies of North America and western Europe, their huge populations do represent lucrative markets. Even when the higher-income segments are only a small percentage of the entire country's population, their sheer numbers may still represent significant and growing markets.

Also, many developing countries have posted high growth rates of annual GDP. For instance, over the past few years, U.S. GDP has grown at an annual rate of about 4.4 percent. By contrast, GDP growth in less developed countries is much greater—China's GDP growth rate was 11.1 percent, and India's was 9.4 percent.[4] These markets represent opportunities for global businesses, even though their per-capita incomes lag behind those in more developed countries. Many firms are establishing operations in these and other developing countries to position themselves to benefit from local sales driven by expanding economies and rising standards of living. Wal-Mart Stores is one of those companies. The retail giant has opened dozens of new stores in developing countries from China to Brazil. It recently opened its 3,000th store outside the United States—in São Paulo, Brazil—and plans to expand more rapidly internationally than domestically over the next few years.[5]

The United States trades with many other nations. As Figure 4.1 shows, the top five are Canada, China, Mexico, Japan, and the Federal Republic of Germany. With the United Kingdom, France, South Korea, the Netherlands, and Brazil, they represent nearly two-thirds of U.S. imports and exports every year.[6] Foreign trade is such an important part of the U.S. economy that it makes up a large portion of the business activity in many of the country's individual states as well. Texas exports more than $151 billion of goods annually, and California exports more than $128 billion. Other big exporting states include Florida, Illinois, New York, Ohio, and Washington.[7]

Absolute and Comparative Advantage

Few countries can produce all the goods and services their people need. For centuries, trading has been the way that countries can meet the demand. If a country focuses on producing what it does best, it can export surplus domestic output and buy foreign products that it lacks or cannot efficiently produce. The potential for foreign sales of a particular item depends largely on whether the country has an absolute advantage or a comparative advantage.

A country has an *absolute advantage* in making a product for which it can maintain a monopoly or that it can produce at a lower cost than any competitor. For centuries, China enjoyed an absolute advantage in silk production. The fabric was woven from fibers recovered from silkworm cocoons, making it a prized raw material in high-quality clothing. Demand among Europeans for silk led to establishment of the famous Silk Road, a 5,000-mile link between Rome and the ancient Chinese capital city of Xian.

Assessment Check

1. Why do nations trade?
2. Cite some measure of the size of the international marketplace.

Absolute advantages are rare these days. But some countries manage to approximate absolute advantages in some products. Climate differences can give some nations or regions an advantage in growing certain plants. Saffron, perhaps the world's most expensive spice at around $40 per ounce, is the stigma of a flowering plant in the crocus family. It is native to the Mediterranean, Asia Minor, and India. Today, however, saffron is cultivated primarily in Spain, where the plant thrives in its soil and climate. Attempts to grow saffron in other parts of the world have generally been unsuccessful.[8]

Saffron, possible the world's most expensive spice, is extracted from crocus flowers. Because the plants grow well in very few places outside Spain, that country enjoys a near absolute advantage in saffron production.

Dinodia Photo Library/Brand X/Jupiter Images Corp

A nation can develop a *comparative advantage* in a product if it can supply it more efficiently and at a lower price than it can supply other goods, compared with the outputs of other countries. China is profiting from its comparative advantage in producing textiles. On the other hand, ensuring that its people are well educated is another way a nation can develop a comparative advantage in skilled human resources. India, for example, has acquired a comparative advantage in software development with its highly educated workforce and low wage scale. As a result, several companies have moved part or all of their software development to India.

Canon has adopted a strategy for research and development based on various nations' comparative advantage in engineering knowledge. Rather than basing all of its research at its Tokyo headquarters, the company operates regional headquarters in Europe and the Americas, each focused on a different area of expertise. In the United States, engineers concentrate on digital and networking technology, whereas Canon engineers in France focus on telecommunications.

Assessment Check

1. Define *absolute advantage*.
2. How does a nation acquire a comparative advantage?

Measuring Trade between Nations

Clearly, engaging in international trade provides tremendous competitive advantages to both the countries and individual companies involved. But how do we measure global business activity? To understand what the trade inflows and outflows mean for a country, we need to examine the concepts of balance of trade and balance of payments. Another important factor is currency exchange rates for each country.

balance of trade difference between a nation's exports and imports.

balance of payments overall money flows into and out of a country.

A nation's **balance of trade** is the difference between its exports and imports. If a country exports more than it imports, it achieves a positive balance of trade, called a *trade surplus*. If it imports more than it exports, it produces a negative balance of trade, called a *trade deficit*. The United States has run a trade deficit every year since 1976. Despite being the world's top exporter, the U.S. has an even greater appetite for foreign-made goods, which creates a trade deficit.

A nation's balance of trade plays a central role in determining its **balance of payments**— the overall flow of money into or out of a country. Other factors also affect the balance of payments, including overseas loans and borrowing, international investments, profits from such investments, and foreign aid payments. To calculate a nation's balance of payments, subtract the monetary outflows from the monetary inflows. A positive balance of payments, or a *balance-of-payments surplus,* means more money has moved into a country than out of it. A negative balance of payments, or *balance-of-payments deficit,* means more money has gone out of the country than entered it.

Major U.S. Exports and Imports

The United States, with combined exports and imports of about $3 trillion, leads the world in the international trade of goods and services. As listed in Table 4.2, the leading categories of goods exchanged by U.S. exporters and importers range from machinery and vehicles to crude oil and chemicals. Strong U.S. demand for imported goods is partly a reflection of the nation's prosperity and diversity.

Although the United States imports more goods than it exports, the opposite is true for services. U.S. exporters sell more than $423 billion in services annually. Much of that money comes from travel and tourism—money spent by foreign nationals visiting the United States.[9] The increase in that figure is especially significant because the dollar has not been worth as much in terms of foreign currencies in recent years. U.S. service exports also include business and technical services such as engineering, financial services, computing, legal services, and entertainment, as well as royalties and licensing fees. Major service exporters include Citibank, Walt Disney, Allstate Insurance, and Federal Express, as well as retailers such as McDonald's and Starbucks.

Table 4.2		Top Ten U.S. Merchandise Exports and Imports	
Exports	**Amount (in Billions)**	**Imports**	**Amount (in Billions)**
Motor vehicles	$95.2	Crude oil	$245.8
Agricultural commodities	89.9	Motor vehicles	210.4
Electrical machinery	81.5	Specialized industrial machinery	129.8
Airplanes	51.9	Electrical machinery	113.6
Power generating machinery	49.9	Office equipment	101.6
Specialized industrial machinery	48.4	Chemicals—plastics	81.2
General industrial machinery	46.6	Petroleum preparations	74.1
Scientific instruments	42.3	Agricultural commodities	72.1
Chemicals—plastics	37.1	General industrial machinery	63.9
Chemicals—organic	33.9	Chemicals—inorganic	53.8

Source: U.S. Census Bureau, "U.S. Exports and General Imports by Selected SITC Commodity Groups," *Statistical Abstract of the United States: 2009,* http://www.census.gov.

Businesses in many foreign countries want the expertise of U.S. financial and business professionals. Accountants are in high demand in Russia, China, the Netherlands, and Australia—Sydney has become one of Asia's biggest financial centers. Dean Gardner, a partner with Tatum LLC and chief financial officer of International Garden Products, says his years of working abroad helped him learn much more quickly and provided him with the ability to conduct business and manage in multicultural environments.[10] Entertainment is another major growth area for U.S. service exports. Following in the footsteps of The Walt Disney Company, which has long had theme parks in Europe and Asia, SeaWorld is planning an overseas resort in the Middle East. The Worlds of Discovery complex will be built on a manmade island shaped like a killer whale in Dubai, United Arab Emirates.[11]

With annual imports reaching nearly $2 trillion, the United States is by far the world's leading importer. American tastes for foreign-made goods for everything from clothing to consumer electronics show up as huge trade deficits with the consumer-goods-exporting nations of China and Japan.

Exchange Rates

A nation's **exchange rate** is the rate at which its currency can be exchanged for the currencies of other nations. It is important to learn how foreign exchange works because we live in a global community and the value of currency is an important economic thermometer for every country. Each currency's exchange rate is usually quoted in terms of another currency, such as the number of Mexican pesos needed to purchase one U.S. dollar. Roughly 11 pesos are needed to exchange for a dollar. A Canadian dollar can be exchanged for approximately $1 in the United States. The euro, the currency used in most of the European Union (EU) member countries, has made considerable moves in exchange value during its few years in circulation—ranging from less than 90 cents when it was first issued to around $1.28 in U.S. currency in more recent years. European consumers and businesses now use the euro to pay bills by check, credit card, or bank transfer. Euro coins and notes are also used in many EU-member countries.

Foreign exchange rates are influenced by a number of factors, including domestic economic and political conditions, central bank intervention, balance-of-payments position, and speculation over future currency values. Currency values fluctuate, or "float," depending on the supply and demand for each currency in the international market. In this system of *floating exchange rates*, currency traders create a market for the world's currencies based on each country's relative trade and investment prospects. In theory, this market permits exchange rates to vary freely according to supply and demand. In practice, exchange rates do not float in total freedom. National governments often intervene in currency markets to adjust their exchange rates.

Nations influence exchange rates in other ways as well. They may form currency blocs by linking their exchange rates to each other. Many governments practice protectionist policies that seek to guard their economies against trade imbalances. For instance, nation sometimes take deliberate action to devalue their currencies as a way to increase exports and stimulate foreign investment. **Devaluation** describes a drop in a currency's value relative to other currencies or to a fixed standard. In Brazil, a currency devaluation made investing in that country relatively cheap, so the devaluation was followed by a flood of foreign investment. Pillsbury bought Brazil's Brisco, which makes a local staple, *pao de queijo,* a cheese bread formed into rolls and served with morning coffee. Other foreign companies invested in Brazil's construction, tourism, banking, communications, and other industries.

For an individual business, the impact of currency devaluation depends on where that business buys its materials and where it sells its products. China's Guanshen Auto, a parts supplier, took advantage of the dollar's decline to purchase 85 percent of Powerline, a South Carolina parts refurbisher that was suffering under the strain of foreign competition. Nearly

exchange rate value of one nation's currency relative to the currencies of other countries.

"They Said It"

"Don't overlook the importance of worldwide thinking. A company that keeps its eye on Tom, Dick, and Harry is going to miss Pierre, Hans, and Yoshio."

—Al Ries (b. 1929)
U.S. advertising executive

one in five manufacturing employees in the state already work for foreign firms, and the parts supplier and its employees were glad to receive the influx of cash. Yu Dan, who represents the state of Pennsylvania in China, says, "The U.S. dollar is getting weaker and weaker, and many medium to small U.S. companies are in economic crisis. So they need investments from China. It is very good timing."[12]

Business transactions are usually conducted in the currency of the particular region in which they take place. When business is conducted in Japan, transactions are likely to be in yen. In the United Kingdom, transactions are in pounds. With the adoption of the euro in the EU, the number of currencies in that region has been reduced. At present, the EU-member countries using the euro include Austria, Belgium, Finland, France, Germany, Greece, Ireland, Italy, Luxembourg, the Netherlands, Portugal, Slovenia, and Spain. Other countries' currencies include the British pound, Australian dollar, the Indian rupee, the Brazilian real, the Mexican peso, the Taiwanese dollar, and the South African rand.

Exchange rate changes can quickly create—or wipe out—a competitive advantage, so they are important factors in decisions about whether to invest abroad. In Europe, a declining dollar means that a price of ten euros is worth more, so companies are pressured to lower prices. At the same time, the falling dollar makes European vacations less affordable for U.S. tourists because their dollars are worth less relative to the euro.

On the Internet you can find currency converters such as those located at http://beginnersinvest.about.com/od/currencycalc/Currency_Calculator.htm, which can help in your dollar-for-dollar conversions. It also helps you understand how much spending power a U.S. dollar has in other countries.

Currencies that owners can easily convert into other currencies are called *hard currencies*. Examples include the euro, the U.S. dollar, and the Japanese yen. The Russian ruble and many central European currencies are considered soft currencies because they cannot be readily converted. Exporters trading with these countries often prefer to barter, accepting payment in oil, timber, or other commodities that they can resell for hard-currency payments.

The foreign currency market is the largest financial market in the world, with a daily volume in excess of 3 trillion U.S. dollars.[13] This is about ten times the size of all the world's stock markets combined, so the foreign exchange market is the most liquid and efficient financial market in the world.

Assessment Check

1. Compare balance of trade and balance of payments.
2. Explain the function of an exchange rate.
3. What happens when a currency is devalued?

Barriers to International Trade

All businesses encounter barriers in their operations, whether they sell only to local customers or trade in international markets. Countries such as Australia and New Zealand regulate the hours and days retailers may be open. Besides complying with a variety of laws and exchanging currencies, international companies may also have to reformulate their products to accommodate different tastes in new locations. Frito-Lay exports cheeseless Cheetos to Asia, and Domino's Pizza offers pickled-ginger pizzas at its Indian fast-food restaurants. Hershey has teamed with a local Chinese partner to introduce green-tea flavored Hershey Kisses in China as part of an aggressive expansion plan.[14]

In addition to social and cultural differences, companies engaged in international business face economic barriers as well as legal and political ones. Some of the hurdles shown in Figure 4.2 are easily breached, but others require major changes in a company's business strategy. To successfully compete in global markets, companies and their managers must understand not only how these barriers affect international trade but also how to overcome them.

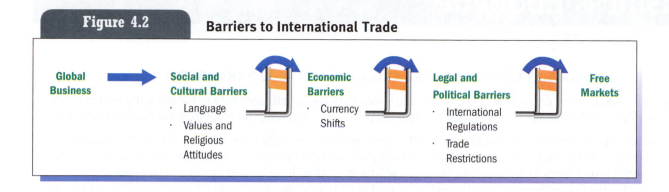

Figure 4.2   Barriers to International Trade

Global Business → Social and Cultural Barriers
· Language
· Values and Religious Attitudes

Economic Barriers
· Currency Shifts

Legal and Political Barriers
· International Regulations
· Trade Restrictions

Free Markets

Social and Cultural Differences

The social and cultural differences among nations range from language and customs to educational background and religious holidays. Understanding and respecting these differences are critical to pave the way for international business success. Businesspeople with knowledge of host countries' cultures, languages, social values, and religious attitudes and practices are well equipped for the marketplace and the negotiating table. Sensitivity to such elements as local attitudes, forms of address, and expectations regarding dress, body language, and timeliness also helps them win customers and achieve their business objectives. It is not only U.S. executives who are adapting to the global business environment. Considering the number of transactions that are sealed on the golf links, Chinese students at Xiamen University must learn golf, as well as business and law, and Peking University is building a practice green. The "Business Etiquette" feature offers suggestions for managing a diverse team of far-flung employees in the new global marketplace.

LANGUAGE English is the second most widely spoken language in the world, followed by Hindustani, Spanish, Russian, and Arabic. Only Mandarin Chinese is more commonly used. It is not uncommon for students abroad for whom English is not their first language to spend eight years of elementary and high school in English language classes. Understanding a business colleague's primary language may prove to be the difference between closing an international business transaction and losing the sale to someone else. Company representatives operating in foreign markets must not only choose correct and appropriate words but also translate words correctly to convey the intended meanings. Firms may also need to rename products or rewrite slogans for foreign markets.

Potential communication barriers include more than mistranslation. Companies may present messages through inappropriate media, overlook local customs and regulations, or ignore differences in taste. Robert Burns, who owns CC Bloom's Hotel in Phuket, Thailand, recalls his inadvertent early mistakes. "I quickly figured out that I was creating problems by talking business before eating lunch and by initiating the talks," he says.[15] Cultural sensitivity is especially critical in cyberspace. Web site developers must be aware that visitors to a site may come from anywhere in the world. Some icons that seem friendly to U.S. Internet users may shock people from other countries. A person making a high-five hand gesture would be insulting people in Greece; the same is true of making a circle with the thumb and index finger in Brazil, a thumbs-up sign in Egypt, and a two-fingered peace sign with the back of the hand facing out in Great Britain.

Gift-giving traditions employ the language of symbolism. For example, in Latin America, knives and scissors should not be given as gifts because they represent the severing of friendship. Flowers are generally acceptable, but Mexicans use yellow flowers in their Day of the Dead festivities, so they are associated with death.

> ## "They Said It"
>
> "If you speak three languages, you are trilingual. If you speak two languages, you are bilingual. If you speak one language, you are American."
>
> —Anonymous

Business Etiquette

Tips for Getting the Most from a Global Workforce

Language barriers, cultural differences, time zones, and sheer distance can all contribute to the difficulty of managing a global workforce. Here are some guidelines managers should keep in mind for getting the most from far-flung employees.

- Know the worldwide labor market for your industry. Hire the right people in the right areas, or transfer the right people to the places where they're needed and can be effective in their jobs. Be alert to your upcoming labor needs and cultivate a network of potential future hires in the country where you will be operating; local knowledge can be priceless.
- Be aware of work–life issues in different countries and cultures. For instance, parents abroad may want to align vacations with local school schedules and avoid having conference calls on local holidays. Some religions have daily observances, so be sure to accommodate foreign employees' needs.
- Know the skills people need to perform in your industry, such as the ability to communicate and ask the right questions, to listen well, to network, to make presentations, or to maintain a high level of technical expertise. Provide regular training to keep employees' skills sharp.
- Remember that workers in remote locations need to feel like part of a team. Cultivate a spirit of teamwork and reward those who demonstrate respect for others and cooperativeness.
- Work at managing your relationships with your team, and help foster good relationships between team members. Communication styles vary in different countries, so you may need to adjust your style to be more subtle or forthright. Try to arrange in-person contacts between members whenever possible.
- Some people need more contact with their manager than others; these needs vary more across cultures but also within them. Get to know your team as individuals, and avoid the "one size fits all" approach to management.
- Understand what motivates each person on the team, whether it's tangible rewards like salary and perks, praise for good teamwork, the opportunity for career advancement, or the chance to transfer to a new and different location. Different cultures value different rewards.
- Offer a broad menu of benefits that team members can tailor to their own needs in their specific location, such as affordable housing on overseas assignments, family medical benefits, or longer vacations.
- Know what your company expects of you as an employee and a role model, and keep in mind that the best way to retain valued employees is to ensure your firm is a well-respected place to work with a good reputation.

Sources: Al Blumenberg, "Global Workforce Mobility: Challenges and Opportunities," *HRM Report,* http://www.hrmreport.com, accessed February 26, 2009; "Winning Strategies for a Global Workforce," Towers Perrin Global Workforce Study, http://www.towersperrin.com, accessed February 26, 2009; "The New Global Workforce," Mercer Human Resource Consulting, http://www.mmc.com, accessed February 26, 2009; Lindsay Clark, "How to Manage a Globalised IT Workforce," *Computer Weekly,* January 14, 2008, http://www.computerweekly.com; "Largest Ever Study of Global Workforce Finds Senior Management Holds Trigger to Unleash Talent Potential," Towers Perrin press release, October 22, 2007; Paul B. Brown, "It's about 'Team,'" *CFO,* July 5, 2007, http://www.cfo.com; Eric Lesser, Tim Ringo, and Andrea Blumberg, "Transforming the Workforce," IBM Institute for Business Value study, May 29, 2007, http://www-935.ibm.com.

VALUES AND RELIGIOUS ATTITUDES Even though today's world is shrinking in many ways, people in different countries do not necessarily share the same values or religious attitudes. Marked differences remain in workers' attitudes from country to country, for instance.

U.S. society places a higher value on business efficiency and low unemployment than European society, where employee benefits are more valued. The U.S. government does not regulate vacation time, and employees typically receive no paid vacation during their first year of employment, then two weeks' vacation, and eventually up to three or four weeks if they stay with the same employer for many years. In contrast, the EU mandates a minimum paid vacation of four weeks per year, and most Europeans get five or six weeks. In these countries, a U.S. company that opens a manufacturing plant would not be able to hire any local employees without offering vacations in line with a nation's business practices.

U.S. culture values national unity, with tolerance of regional differences. The United States is viewed as a national market with a single economy. European countries that are part of the 27-member EU are trying to create a similar marketplace. However, many resist the idea of being European citizens first and British, Danish, or Dutch citizens second. British consumers differ from Italians in important ways, and U.S. companies that fail to recognize this variation will run into problems with brand acceptance.

Religion plays an important role in every society, so businesspeople must also cultivate sensitivity to the dominant religions in countries where they operate. Understanding religious cycles and the timing of major holidays can help prevent embarrassing moments when scheduling meetings, trade shows, conferences, or events such as the opening of a new manufacturing plant. People doing business in Saudi Arabia must take into account Islam's month-long observance of Ramadan, when work ends at noon. Friday is the Muslim Sabbath, so the Saudi workweek runs from Saturday through Thursday. Also, Muslims abstain from alcohol and consider pork unclean, so gifts of pigskin or liquor would be offensive. Westerners should be careful not to make blanket assumptions, however.

Some devout Muslims have raised concerns about interest-bearing loans in their nations, such as car loans or home mortgages, which they fear should be considered usury by the standards of the Koran. However, such reservations are slowly being overcome with the help of arguments by Muslim scholars showing that ordinary loans don't take unfair advantage of the borrower and can help increase the value of the borrowers' assets or property as well as distribute wealth more widely. A rapidly growing tool of international finance is the *sukuk*, a type of bond that meets Islamic guidelines. As much as $500 billion worldwide is now invested in these and similarly acceptable forms of Islamic finance.[16]

Economic Differences

Business opportunities are flourishing in densely populated countries such as China and India, as local consumers eagerly buy Western products. Although such prospects might tempt American firms, managers must first consider the economic factors involved in doing business in these markets. A country's size, per-capita income, and stage of economic development are among the economic factors to consider when evaluating it as a candidate for an international business venture. Making a wrong move—or moving too late—can spell disaster for a firm, as the "Hit & Miss" feature describes.

INFRASTRUCTURE Along with other economic measures, businesses should consider a country's **infrastructure.** Infrastructure refers to basic systems of communication (telecommunications, television, radio, and print media), transportation (roads and highways, railroads, and airports), and energy facilities (power plants and gas and electric utilities). The Internet and technology use can also be considered part of infrastructure.

The widespread availability of telecommunications technology creates fertile soil for Internet and other businesses that use wireless communication. The cell phone market in Africa has doubled every year for several years and now exceeds 200 million users. But there is plenty of room for more growth. "We're halfway, as I see it," says telecom firm Ericsson's managing director of East Africa. "What we have done in the last 30 years we will do in the next four." And in densely populated Rwanda, fiber-optic lines are being laid to connect even the most remote village schools to the Internet via high-speed broadband connections. "In another two years, we should be there," says the country's minister of state for energy and communications. Although Africa faces many problems, including transportation, security, and power supplies, "there is a lot of potential in areas that seem to be poor," says one industry watcher. "People have a desperate need for communication."[17]

Hit & Miss

Waterford Wedgwood Cracks under Economic Pressure

When the giant crystal ball descended into New York City's Times Square at midnight one recent New Year's Eve, it forecast the end of an era. The ball is made of Waterford crystal, whose company—Waterford Wedgwood—went into the British equivalent of bankruptcy shortly afterward. To many in Ireland and England, where the company has its roots, it was like the death of an old friend. Waterford was founded in Ireland in 1783, and Wedgwood was established in England in 1759. For more than 200 years, Waterford crystal and Wedgwood china have graced the tables of royalty and celebrities. Families treasured their pieces, handing them down from generation to generation. About 20 years ago, the two companies were joined, becoming Waterford Wedgwood.

The rich history of Waterford Wedgwood may provide a clue to its downfall. Although pieces of crystal or china might be given to world leaders or to couples as wedding gifts, fewer and fewer families sit down for formal dinners. They don't need or use entire settings of fine china to the extent that families did a few generations ago. "Young people are so happy to have TV dinners," observes an older owner of a china shop that itself is struggling. "They're far more practical than my age group, where I always had a best set." Even if younger families do not consume TV dinners, they still may not need or want the expensive, formal styles offered by Waterford Wedgwood. The company tried to respond to changing tastes by offering more casual and simpler designs but was not successful enough to sustain the business.

Even under normal economic circumstances, plunking down $85 or more for a single wine goblet that needs to be washed by hand can be hard to justify. But in tough times, consumers concentrate on basics and forgo luxuries. A crystal goblet or fine china seems out of reach for many consumers as they worry about their job security and homes.

Some experts also point to Waterford Wedgwood's delay in moving some of its manufacturing operations overseas, where labor is cheaper. The firm does in fact employ several thousand workers at foreign facilities, including 1,500 people at a plant in Jarkarta, Indonesia, which produces many Wedgwood ceramics. However, the move seems to have come too late to make a difference. And Waterford crystal is still made at the same Irish factory where it has been produced for generations. The mayor of Waterford announced that it would be a "national disaster" if production were halted.

Questions for Critical Thinking

1. What steps do you think Waterford Wedgwood might have taken to prevent bankruptcy?
2. Do you think it is worth trying to save a firm like Waterford Wedgwood? Why or why not?

Sources: Company Web site, http://www.waterfordwedgwood.com, accessed February 18, 2009; "Waterford Gets Takeover Bids," *CNNMoney*, February 1, 2009, http://money.cnn.com; "Famous Crystal Company Goes Bust," *CBS News*, January 6, 2009, http://www.cbsnews.com; Julia Werdigier, "Waterford Wedgwood Is in Receivership," *The New York Times*, January 6, 2009, http://www.nytimes.com; "Waterford Wedgwood in Bankruptcy," *Chicago Tribune*, January 6, 2009, http://archives.chicagotribune.com; Graeme Wearden and Henry McDonald, "After 250 Years, Waterford Wedgwood Falls into Administration," *The Guardian*, January 5, 2009, http://www.guardian.co.uk; Jane Wardell, "Crystal, China Maker Waterford Wedgwood Collapses," Associated Press, January 5, 2009, http://news.yahoo.com.

Financial systems also provide a type of infrastructure for businesses. In the United States, buyers have widespread access to checks, credit cards, and debit cards, as well as electronic systems for processing these forms of payment. In many African countries, such as Ethiopia, local businesses do not accept credit cards, so travelers to the capital city, Addis Ababa, are warned to bring plenty of cash and traveler's checks.

CURRENCY CONVERSION AND SHIFTS Despite growing similarities in infrastructure, businesses crossing national borders encounter basic economic differences: national currencies.

Foreign currency fluctuations may present added problems for global businesses. As explained earlier in the chapter, the values of the world's major currencies fluctuate—sometimes drastically—in relation to each other. Rapid and unexpected currency shifts can make pricing in local currencies difficult. Shifts in exchange rates can also influence the attractiveness of various business decisions. A devalued currency may make a nation less desirable as an export destination because of reduced demand in that market. However, devaluation can make the nation desirable as an investment opportunity because investments there will be a bargain in terms of the investor's currency.

Political and Legal Differences

Like social, cultural, and economic differences, legal and political differences in host countries can pose barriers to international trade. Government oversight of Internet use in China is so strict that the Central Propaganda Department employs 30,000 people to monitor electronic communications.[18] Such actions pose threats to those considering doing business there.

To compete in today's world marketplace, managers involved in international business must be well versed in legislation that affects their industries. Some countries impose general trade restrictions. Others have established detailed rules that regulate how foreign companies can operate. A common thread among all countries is the striking lack of consistent laws and regulations governing the conduct of business.

POLITICAL CLIMATE An important factor in any international business investment is the stability of the political climate. The political structures of many nations promote stability similar to that in the United States. Other nations, such as Indonesia, Congo, and Bosnia, feature quite different—and frequently changing—structures. Host nations often pass laws designed to protect their own interests, sometimes at the expense of foreign businesses. One political issue that surfaced recently concerned the rights of U.S. citizens versus those of legal foreign workers when companies lay off employees. The "Solving an Ethical Controversy" feature debates that issue.

In recent years, the political structures of Russia, Turkey, the former Yugoslavia, Hong Kong, and several central European countries, including the Czech Republic and Poland, have seen dramatic changes. Such political changes almost always bring changes in the legal environment. Hong Kong's status as part of China makes it an economy where political developments produced changes in the legal and cultural environments. Since the collapse of the Soviet Union, Russia has struggled to develop a new market structure and political processes.

LEGAL ENVIRONMENT When conducting business internationally, managers must be familiar with three dimensions of the legal environment: U.S. law, international regulations, and the laws of the countries in which they plan to trade. Some laws protect the rights of foreign companies to compete in the United States. Others dictate actions allowed for U.S. companies doing business in foreign countries.

The *Foreign Corrupt Practices Act* forbids U.S. companies from bribing foreign officials, political candidates, or government representatives. This act prescribes fines and jail time for U.S. managers who are aware of illegal payoffs. Until recently, many countries, including France and Germany, not only accepted the practice of bribing foreign officials in countries where such practices were customary but allowed tax deductions for these expenses. The United States, United Kingdom, France, Germany, and 37 other countries have signed the Organization for Economic Cooperation and Development Anti-Bribery Convention. This agreement makes offering or paying bribes a criminal offense and ends the deductibility of bribes.[19]

TOUGH ECONOMIC TIMES FORCE TOUGHER EMPLOYMENT CHOICES

No employer wants to lay off workers. Doing so is a last resort to keep a company alive. But in a significant recession, thousands of firms are forced to lay off hundreds of thousands of employees. Individual business owners must ask themselves: Who goes first? Recently, this issue created a furor when firms in the tech industry began to lay off certain skilled employees, choosing to retain others. Firms that employed foreign workers holding H-1B visas, which allow them to work legally at their U.S. jobs, created controversy as they decided whether to lay off foreign or domestic employees. Microsoft was specifically targeted because of its large pool of H-1B guest workers.

Should U.S. companies be forced to keep domestic workers over foreign workers during layoffs?

PRO

1. In extreme circumstances such as a widespread economic downturn, U.S. firms should favor U.S. workers with comparable skills. "I firmly believe that companies going through layoffs that employ H-1B visas have a moral obligation to protect American workers by putting them first during these difficult times," argued one U.S. senator.
2. Guest worker visa programs were not intended to allow U.S. firms to hire foreign employees over equally qualified American workers; they were formulated to address shortages of skilled workers.

CON

1. If firms are forced to lay off H-1B workers first, they could be put at a disadvantage in the marketplace. They would not have access to the "top-flight global talent who can help create jobs for U.S. workers," according to the American Immigration Lawyers Association.
2. A legal requirement would force artificial decisions. "In a globalized world, corporate decisions should be based on economic realities rather than on political considerations," states one high-tech company.

Summary

While some make a strong argument that U.S. workers should be given employment preference, others point out that antidiscrimination laws might prohibit firms from categorically laying off guest workers. As the debate continues, when unemployment climbs, both businesses and workers share the pain.

Sources: Patrick Thibodeau, "Bill Would Bar H-1B Hiring at Firms Receiving Bailout Money," *InfoWorld*, February 6, 2009, http://www.infoworld; Robert X. Cringely, "Should Foreign Workers Be the First to Get Canned?" *InfoWorld*, February 6, 2009, http://weblog.info-world.com; Frank Bass and Rita Beamish, "Senate Approves Restriction on Foreign Hires," *Associated Press*, February 6, 2009, http://www.google.com; "Deep Corporate Staff Cuts Heat up H-1B Visa Debate," *Workforce Magazine*, February 5, 2009, http://www.workforce.com; Patrick Thibodeau, "Microsoft Told H-1B Workers Should Be Cut Rather than Staff in Layoffs," *CIO*, January 23, 2009, http://www.cio.com.

Solving an ETHICAL controversy

Still, corruption continues to be an international problem. Its pervasiveness, combined with U.S. prohibitions, creates a difficult obstacle for U.S. businesspeople who want to do business in many foreign countries. Chinese pay *huilu,* and Russians rely on *vzyatka.* In the Middle East, palms are greased with *baksheesh.* Figure 4.3 compares 179 countries based on surveys of perceived corruption. This Corruption Perceptions Index is computed by Transparency International, a Berlin-based organization that rates the degree of corruption observed by businesspeople and the general public.

Figure 4.3   **Corruption in Business and Government**

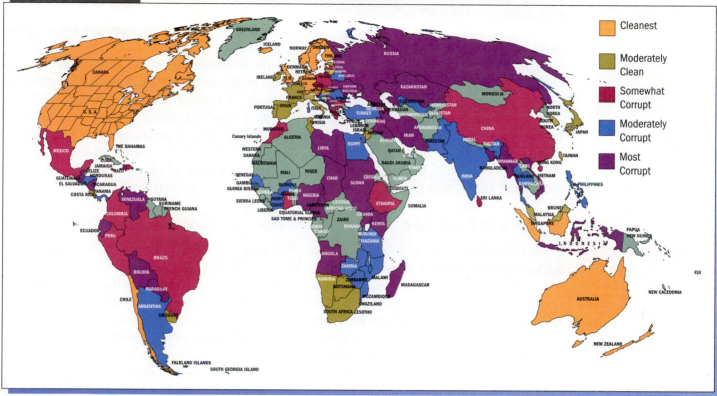

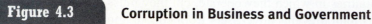

Source: Data from Transparency International, "Annual Corruption Perceptions Index," http://www.transparency.org, accessed February 26, 2009.

The growth of online business has introduced new elements to the legal climate of international business. Patents, brand names, trademarks, copyrights, and other intellectual property are difficult to police, given the availability of information on the Internet. However, some countries are adopting laws to protect information obtained by electronic contacts. Malaysia imposes stiff fines and long jail terms on those convicted of illegally accessing computers and using information that passes through them.

INTERNATIONAL REGULATIONS To regulate international commerce, the United States and many other countries have ratified treaties and signed agreements that dictate the conduct of international business and protect some of its activities. The United States has entered into many *friendship, commerce, and navigation treaties* with other nations. Such treaties address many aspects of international business relations, including the right to conduct business in the treaty partner's domestic market. Other international business agreements involve product standards, patents, trademarks, reciprocal tax policies, export controls, international air travel, and international communications.

When Congress granted China full trade relations with the United States, China agreed to lower trade barriers, including subsidies that held down the prices of food exports, restrictions on where foreign law firms can open offices, and taxes charged on imported goods. In exchange for China's promise to halve these taxes, called *tariffs,* the United States granted Chinese businesses equal access to U.S. markets enjoyed by most other countries.

Many types of regulations affect the actions of managers doing business in international markets. Not only must worldwide producers and marketers maintain required minimum quality levels for all the countries in which they operate, but they must comply with numerous specific local regulations. Britain prevents advertisers from encouraging children to engage in such unhealthy behavior as overeating or replacing regular meals with candy and snack foods. Malaysia's Censorship Board prohibits nudity and profanity on TV. Germany and France allow publishers to set prices that retailers charge for their books.

A lack of international regulations or difficulty in enforcement can generate its own set of problems. Software piracy offers an example, particularly in Asia. About 82 percent of software packages in use in China are pirated, about 71 percent in India, and almost 90 percent in Vietnam—compared with 21 percent for the United States and 34 percent for western Europe. High rates of piracy also cut into the profitability of related businesses such as installation and service. In fact, despite China's and India's efforts to reduce piracy and Vietnam's adoption of an intellectual property code, growth in ownership of personal computers and in broadband access recently drove revenue losses from piracy in Asia up 44 percent.[20]

Types of Trade Restrictions

Trade restrictions such as taxes on imports and complicated administrative procedures create additional barriers to international business. They may limit consumer choices while increasing the costs of foreign-made products. Trade restrictions are also imposed to protect citizens' security, health, and jobs. A government may limit exports of strategic and defense-related goods to unfriendly countries to protect its security, ban imports of insecticide-contaminated farm products to protect health, and restrict imports to protect domestic jobs in the importing country.

Other restrictions are imposed to promote trade with certain countries. Still others protect countries from unfair competition. Regardless of the political reasons for trade restrictions, most take the form of tariffs. In addition to tariffs, governments impose a number of nontariff—or administrative—barriers. These include quotas, embargoes, and exchange controls.

tariff tax imposed on imported goods.

TARIFFS Taxes, surcharges, or duties on foreign products are referred to as **tariffs.** Governments assess two types of tariffs—revenue and protective tariffs—both of which make imports more expensive for domestic buyers. Revenue tariffs generate income for the government. Upon returning home, U.S. leisure travelers who are out of the country more than 48 hours and who bring back goods purchased abroad must pay import taxes on their value in excess of $200 to $1,600, depending on the country of origin. This duty goes directly to the U.S. Treasury. The sole purpose of a protective tariff is to raise the retail price of imported products to match or exceed the prices of similar products manufactured in the home country. In other words, protective tariffs seek to limit imports and level the playing field for local competitors.

Of course, tariffs create a disadvantage to companies that want to export to the countries imposing the tariffs. In addition, governments do not always agree on the reasons behind protective tariffs. So they do not always have the desired effect. The United States imposes a tariff on foreign competitors accused of selling products at lower prices in the United States than U.S. manufacturers charge. The government passed a bill giving the money from these tariffs directly to U.S. plaintiff companies, instead of to the Treasury as in the past. The European Union imposes tariffs on some electronics products, which the United States says violates the 1997 Information Technology Agreement (ITA) calling for the elimination of tariffs on such items as computers and computer parts.[21]

NONTARIFF BARRIERS Nontariff, or administrative, trade barriers restrict imports in more subtle ways than tariffs. These measures may take such forms as quotas on imports, restrictive standards for imports, and export subsidies. Because many countries have recently substantially reduced tariffs or eliminated them entirely, they increasingly use nontariff barriers to control flows of imported products.

Quotas limit the amounts of particular products that countries can import during specified time periods. Limits may be set as quantities, such as number of cars or bushels of wheat, or as values, such as dollars' worth of cigarettes. Governments regularly set quotas for agricultural products and sometimes for imported automobiles. The United States, for example, sets a quota on imports of sugar. Imports under the quota amount are subject to a lower tariff than shipments above the quota. Sugar and related products imported at the higher rate may enter the country in unlimited quantities, however.[22]

Quotas help prevent **dumping.** In one form of dumping, a company sells products abroad at prices below its cost of production. In another, a company exports a large quantity of a product at a lower price than the same product in the home market and drives down the price of the domestic product. Dumping benefits domestic consumers in the importing market, but it hurts domestic producers. It also allows companies to gain quick entry to foreign markets.

More severe than a quota, an **embargo** imposes a total ban on importing a specified product or even a total halt to trading with a particular country. Embargo durations can vary to accommodate changes in foreign policy, but the United States has a longstanding trade embargo with Cuba.

Another form of administrative trade restriction is **exchange controls.** Imposed through a central bank or government agency, exchange controls affect both exporters and importers. Firms that gain foreign currencies through exporting are required to sell them to the central bank or another agency. Importers must buy foreign currencies to pay for their purchases from the same agency. The exchange control authority can then allocate, expand, or restrict foreign exchange in accordance with national policy.

International trade restrictions include *quotas*, or limits on the amount of a product that can be imported into a country. In the United States, sugar is subject to import quotas.

© iStockphoto

Assessment Check

1. How might values and attitudes form a barrier to trade, and how can they be overcome?

2. What is a tariff? What is its purpose?

3. Why is dumping a problem for companies marketing goods internationally?

Reducing Barriers to International Trade

Although tariffs and administrative barriers still restrict trade, overall the world is moving toward free trade. Several types of organizations ease barriers to international trade, including groups that monitor trade policies and practices and institutions that offer monetary assistance. Another type of federation designed to ease trade barriers is the multinational economic community, such as the European Union. This section looks at the roles these organizations play.

Organizations Promoting International Trade

For the 60-plus years of its existence, the **General Agreement on Tariffs and Trade (GATT),** an international trade accord, sponsored a series of negotiations, called rounds, that substantially reduced worldwide tariffs and other barriers. Major industrialized nations founded the multinational organization in 1947 to work toward reducing tariffs and relaxing import quotas. The last set of completed negotiations—the Uruguay Round—cut average tariffs by one-third, in excess of $700 billion; reduced farm subsidies; and improved protection for copyright and patent holders. In addition, international trading rules now apply to various service industries. Finally, the new agreement established the <mark>World Trade Organization (WTO)</mark> to succeed GATT. This organization includes representatives from 151 countries.

World Trade Organization (WTO) 151-member international institution that monitors GATT agreements and mediates international trade disputes.

WORLD TRADE ORGANIZATION Since 1995, the WTO has monitored GATT agreements among the member nations, mediated disputes, and continued the effort to reduce trade barriers throughout the world. Unlike provisions in GATT, the WTO's decisions are binding on parties involved in disputes.

The WTO has grown more controversial in recent years as it issues decisions that have implications for working conditions and the environment in member nations. Concerns have been expressed that the WTO's focus on lowering trade barriers encourages businesses to keep costs down through practices that may increase pollution and human rights abuses. Particularly worrisome is the fact that the organization's member countries must agree on policies, and developing countries tend not to be eager to lose their low-cost advantage by enacting stricter labor and environmental laws. Other critics claim that if well-funded U.S. firms such as fast-food chains, entertainment companies, and Internet retailers can freely enter foreign markets, they will wipe out smaller foreign businesses serving the distinct tastes and practices of other countries' cultures.

Trade unions in developed nations complain that the WTO's support of free trade makes it easier to export manufacturing jobs to low-wage countries. According to the U.S. Department of Commerce, about a million U.S. jobs are lost each year as a result of imports or movement of work to other countries, and the pace of the migration has increased in the past few years. Some economists are beginning to warn that 30 to 40 million U.S. jobs in service industries could be lost abroad in the next decade.[23] But many small and midsize firms have benefited from the WTO's reduction of trade barriers and lowering of the cost of trade. They currently make up 97 percent of all firms that export goods and services, according to the Department of Commerce.

The most recent round of WTO talks was called the *Doha Round* after the city in Qatar where it began. After several years of heated disputes and collapsed negotiations, the eight leading industrial nations recommitted themselves to successful conclusion of the talks. Under discussion were ways to improve global agricultural trade and trade among developing countries. The leaders worked to reduce domestic price supports, eliminate export subsidies, and improve market access for goods. Such changes could help farmers in developing countries compete in the global marketplace.[24]

Although free trade can indeed contribute to economic growth and change, including the creation of new jobs, concerns about WTO policy have led to protest demonstrations—sometimes violent—beginning with the WTO meeting in Seattle several years ago.

WORLD BANK Shortly after the end of World War II, industrialized nations formed an organization to lend money to less developed and developing countries. The **World Bank** primarily funds projects that build or expand nations' infrastructure such as transportation, education, and medical systems and facilities. The World Bank and other development banks provide the largest source of advice and assistance to developing nations. Often, in exchange for granting loans, the World Bank imposes requirements intended to build the economies of borrower nations.

The World Bank has been criticized for making loans with conditions that ultimately hurt the borrower nations. When developing nations are required to balance government budgets, they are sometimes forced to cut vital social programs. Critics also say that the World Bank should consider the impact of its loans on the environment and working conditions.

INTERNATIONAL MONETARY FUND Established a year after the World Bank, the **International Monetary Fund (IMF)** was created to promote trade through financial cooperation and, in the process, eliminate barriers. The IMF makes short-term loans to member nations that are unable to meet their expenses. It operates as a lender of last resort for troubled nations. In exchange for these emergency loans, IMF lenders frequently require significant commitments from the borrowing nations to address the problems that led to the crises. These steps may include curtailing imports or even devaluing currencies. Throughout its existence, the IMF has worked to prevent financial crises by warning the international business community when countries encounter problems meeting their financial obligations. Often, the IMF lends to countries to keep them from defaulting on prior debts and to prevent economic crises in particular countries from spreading to other nations.

However, some countries owe far more money than they can ever hope to repay, and the debt payments make it impossible for their governments to deliver desperately needed services to their citizens. The nations of sub-Saharan Africa are hard-pressed to deal with the ravages of AIDS, yet their debt exceeds their GDP and is three times as high as their total annual exports. The so-called Group of Eight (G8) economic powers—Canada, France, Germany, Italy, Japan, Russia, United Kingdom, and the United States—recently agreed to offer full debt relief to African countries that are working toward government reforms on behalf of education and welfare, but the World Bank and development groups say other aid has been too slow to arrive.[25]

International Economic Communities

International economic communities reduce trade barriers and promote regional economic integration. In the simplest approach, countries may establish a *free-trade area* in which they trade freely among themselves without tariffs or trade restrictions. Each maintains its own tariffs for trade outside this area. A *customs union* sets up a free-trade area and specifies a uniform tariff structure for members' trade with nonmember nations. In a *common market,* or economic union, members go beyond a customs union and try to bring all of their trade rules into agreement.

One example of a free-trade area is the **North American Free Trade Agreement (NAFTA)** enacted by the United States, Canada, and Mexico. Other examples of regional trading blocs include the MERCOSUR customs union (joining Brazil, Argentina, Paraguay, Uruguay, Chile, and Bolivia) and the ten-country Association of South East Asian Nations (ASEAN).

NAFTA

NAFTA became effective in 1994, creating the world's largest free-trade zone with the United States, Canada, and Mexico. With a combined population of more than 450 million and a total GDP of more than $15 trillion, North America represents one of the world's most attractive markets. The United States—the single largest market and one of the world's most stable economies—dominates North America's business environment. Although fewer than 1 person in 20 lives in the United States, the nation's more than $14 trillion GDP represents about one-fifth of total world output.[26]

Canada is far less densely populated but has achieved a similar level of economic development. In fact, Canada's economy has been growing at a faster rate than the U.S. economy in recent years. More than two-thirds of Canada's GDP is generated in the services sector,

North American Free Trade Agreement (NAFTA) agreement among the United States, Canada, and Mexico to break down tariffs and trade restrictions.

and three of every four Canadian workers are engaged in service occupations. The country's per-capita GDP places Canada among the top nations in terms of its people's spending power. Canada's economy is fueled by trade with the United States, and its home markets are strong as well. The United States and Canada are each other's biggest trading partners. About 80 percent of Canada's exports and about 54 percent of its imports are to or from the United States.[27] U.S. business is also attracted by Canada's human resources. For instance, all major U.S. automakers have large production facilities in Canada.

Mexico is moving from developing nation to industrial nation status, thanks largely to NAFTA. Mexico's trade with the United States and Canada has tripled since the signing of NAFTA, although 18 percent of the country's 110 million people live below the poverty line and per-capita income is about a quarter that of the United States.[28] But Mexico's border with the United States is busy with a nearly endless stream of traffic transporting goods from Mexican factories into the United States. The United States is Mexico's largest trading partner by far, accounting for about 82 percent of total exports and 50 percent of all Mexico's imports.

By eliminating all trade barriers and investment restrictions among the United States, Canada, and Mexico over a 15-year period, NAFTA opened more doors for free trade. The agreement also eased regulations governing services, such as banking, and established uniform legal requirements for protection of intellectual property. The three nations can now trade with one another without tariffs or other trade barriers, simplifying shipments of goods across the partners' borders. Standardized customs and uniform labeling regulations create economic efficiencies and smooth import and export procedures. Trade among the partners has increased steadily, more than doubling since NAFTA took effect.

CAFTA-DR

The **Central America–Dominican Republic Free Trade Agreement (CAFTA-DR)** created a free-trade area among the United States, Costa Rica, the Dominican Republic (the DR of the title), El Salvador, Guatemala, Honduras, and Nicaragua. The agreement ends most tariffs on nearly $33 billion in products traded between the United States and its Latin American neighbors. Agricultural producers such as corn, soybean, and dairy farmers stand to gain under the relaxed trade rules. U.S. sugar producers, which were supported by subsidies keeping their prices higher than the rest of the world's, fought against CAFTA-DR's passage. And labor unions complained that the agreement would lower labor standards and export millions more jobs to lower-wage countries. But overall, CAFTA-DR's effects should be positive, increasing both exports and imports substantially, much as NAFTA did.

European Union

Perhaps the best-known example of a common market is the **European Union (EU).** The EU combines 27 countries, nearly 500 million people, and a total GDP of roughly $15 trillion to form a huge common market.[29] As Figure 4.4 shows, 12 countries—Cyprus, Malta, Estonia, Latvia, Lithuania, Hungary, Poland, the Czech Republic, Slovakia,

Central America–Dominican Republic Free Trade Agreement (CAFTA-DR) agreement among the United States, Costa Rica, the Dominican Republic, El Salvador, Guatemala, Honduras, and Nicaragua to reduce tariffs and trade restrictions.

European Union (EU) 27-nation European economic alliance.

Figure 4.4

The 27 Nations of the European Union

Germany, United Kingdom, Netherlands, Ireland, Belgium, Luxembourg, France, Austria, Portugal, Sweden, Denmark, Finland, Estonia, Latvia, Lithuania, Poland, Czech Republic, Slovakia, Hungary, Romania, Slovenia, Bulgaria, Spain, Malta, Italy, Greece, Cyprus

Slovenia, Bulgaria, and Romania—are the latest EU members. Some observers think the EU's efforts to unite Europe suffered a setback after two countries, France and the Netherlands, voted against the proposed constitution intended to make the organization run more smoothly after its recent enlargement from 15 to 27 states. All 27 must ratify the constitution before it can take effect.

The EU's goals include promoting economic and social progress, introducing European citizenship as a complement to national citizenship, and giving the EU a significant role in international affairs. To achieve its goal of a borderless Europe, the EU is removing barriers to free trade among its members. This highly complex process involves standardizing business regulations and requirements, standardizing import duties and taxes, and eliminating customs checks so that companies can transport goods from England to Italy or Poland as easily as from New York to Boston.

Unifying standards and laws can contribute to economic growth. But just as NAFTA sparked fears in the United States about free trade with Mexico, some people in western Europe worried that opening trade with such countries as Poland, Hungary, and the Czech Republic would cause jobs to flow eastward to lower-wage economies.

The EU also introduced the euro to replace currencies such as the French franc and Italian lira. For the 13 member states that have already adopted the euro, potential benefits include eliminating the economic costs of currency exchange and simplifying price comparisons. Businesses and their customers now make check and credit card transactions in euros and use euro notes and coins in making cash purchases.

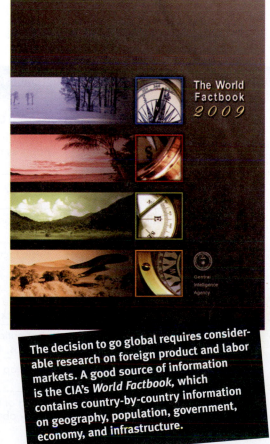

The decision to go global requires considerable research on foreign product and labor markets. A good source of information is the CIA's *World Factbook*, which contains country-by-country information on geography, population, government, economy, and infrastructure.

Central Intelligence Agency/U.S. Government

Assessment Check

1. What international trade organization succeeded GATT, and what is its goal?

2. Compare and contrast the goals of the World Bank and the International Monetary Fund.

3. Identify the members of NAFTA, and briefly explain how it works.

4. What are the goals of the European Union, and how do they promote international trade?

Going Global

While expanding into overseas markets can increase profits and marketing opportunities, it also introduces new complexities to a firm's business operations. Before deciding to go global, a company faces a number of key decisions, beginning with the following:

• determining which foreign market(s) to enter

• analyzing the expenditures required to enter a new market

• deciding the best way to organize the overseas operations.

These issues vary in importance depending on the level of involvement a company chooses. Education and employee training in the host country would be much more important for an electronics manufacturer building an Asian factory than for a firm that is simply planning to export American-made products.

The choice of which markets to enter usually follows extensive research focusing on local demand for the firm's products, availability of needed resources, and ability of the local workforce to produce world-class quality. Other factors include existing and potential competition, tariff rates, currency stability, and investment barriers. A variety of government and other sources are available to facilitate this research process. A good starting place is the CIA's *World Factbook,* which contains country-by-country information on geography, population, government, economy, and infrastructure.

U.S. Department of Commerce counselors at the agency's district offices offer a full range of international business advice, including computerized market data and names of business and government contacts in dozens of countries. As Table 4.3 shows, the Internet provides access to many resources for international trade information.

Levels of Involvement

After a firm has completed its research and decided to do business overseas, it can choose one or more strategies:

- exporting or importing

- entering into contractual agreements such as franchising, licensing, and subcontracting deals

- direct investment in the foreign market through acquisitions, joint ventures, or establishment of an overseas division.

Although the company's risk increases with the level of its involvement, so does its overall control of all aspects of producing and selling its goods or services.

Companies frequently combine more than one of these strategies. Google, for instance, has purchased a small stake in one Chinese music- and video-downloading company that will share Google's search capabilities, and it has partnered with another to provide mobile Internet searching to some of China's 130 million Internet users.[30] Waiting to develop expertise before moving overseas is risky for online businesses, because Web sites are so easy for competitors to copy. Alando, an auction Web site based in Germany, looked remarkably like eBay. Rather than fight the company, eBay entered Germany by acquiring Alando.

Table 4.3	International Trade Research Resources on the Internet
Web Site and Address	**General Description**
Asia Inc. http://www.asia-inc.com	Business news in Asia, featuring articles on Asian countries from India to Japan
Europages http://www.europages.com	Directory of and links to Europe's top 500,000 companies in 33 European countries
World Trade Organization http://www.wto.int	Details on the trade policies of various governments
CIA *World Factbook* https://www.cia.gov/cia/library/publications/the-world-factbook	Basic facts about the world's nations, from geography to economic conditions
STAT-USA http://www.stat-usa.gov	Extensive trade and economic data, information about trends, daily intelligence reports, and background data (access requires paid subscription to the service)
U.S. Commercial Service http://trade.gov/cs	Information about Commerce Department counseling services, trade events, and U.S. export regulations
U.S. Business Advisor http://www.business.gov	One-stop access to a range of federal government information, services, and transactions
U.S. State Department http://www.travel.state.gov/travel/cis_pa_tw/tw/tw_1764.html	Listing of the State Department's latest travel warnings about conditions that may affect safety abroad, supplemented by the list of consulate addresses and country information

IMPORTERS AND EXPORTERS When a firm brings in goods produced abroad to sell domestically, it is an importer. Conversely, companies are exporters when they produce—or purchase—goods at home and sell them in overseas markets. An importing or exporting strategy provides the most basic level of international involvement, with the least risk and control.

Roots, a Canadian clothing manufacturer, has used its success as the chosen outfitter of the U.S. and Canadian Olympic teams to expand its apparel and sportswear brands into the United States and Asia. The company already has more than 175 stores in Canada, Asia, and the United States. Roots earns about $280 million in annual sales and now sells eyewear, watches, and fragrance as well.[31]

Exports are frequently handled by special intermediaries called export trading companies. These firms search out competitively priced local merchandise and then resell it abroad at prices high enough to cover expenses and earn profits. When a retail chain such as Dallas-based Pier 1 Imports wants to purchase West African products for its store shelves, it may contact an export trading company operating in a country such as Ghana. The local firm is responsible for monitoring quality, packaging the order for transatlantic shipment, arranging transportation, and arranging for completion of customs paperwork and other steps required to move the product from Ghana to the United States.

Firms engage in exporting of two types: indirect and direct. A company engages in *indirect exporting* when it manufactures a product, such as an electronic component, that becomes part of another product sold in foreign markets. The second method, *direct exporting,* occurs when a company seeks to sell its products in markets outside its own country. Often the first step for companies entering foreign markets, direct exporting is the most common form of international business. Firms that succeed at this may then move to other strategies. Crops are imported and exported globally. The "Hit & Miss" feature discusses Ocean Spray's expansion into global markets.

In addition to reaching foreign markets by dealing with export trading companies, exporters may choose two other alternatives: export management companies and offset agreements. Rather than simply relying on an export trading company to assist in foreign markets, an exporting firm may turn to an *export management company* for advice and expertise. These international specialists help the exporter complete paperwork, make contacts with local buyers, and comply with local laws governing labeling, product safety, and performance testing. At the same time, the exporting firm retains much more control than would be possible with an export trading company.

An *offset agreement* matches a small business with a major international firm. It basically makes the small firm a subcontractor to the larger one. Such an entry strategy helps a new exporter by allowing it to share in the larger company's international expertise. The small firm also benefits in such important areas

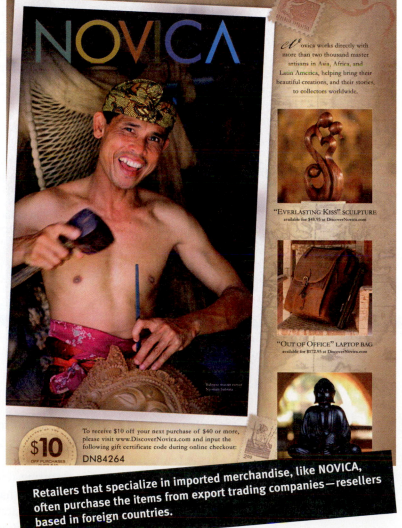

Retailers that specialize in imported merchandise, like NOVICA, often purchase the items from export trading companies—resellers based in foreign countries.

Hit & Miss

Ocean Spray's Global Expansion Bears Fruit

When Americans sit down for a traditional Thanksgiving turkey dinner, they probably add a dab of Ocean Spray cranberry sauce to their plate. Bottles of Ocean Spray cranberry juice sit in U.S. refrigerators. And dark red Craisins—dried sweetened cranberries—often are scattered on top of salads.

Ocean Spray is a Massachusetts-based farmers' organization owned by more than 650 cranberry growers. The firm supplies nearly 70 percent of the world's cranberries. To achieve this impressive status, the company created a strategy that focused on education, health benefits, and heritage.

Cranberry sauce, cranberry juice, and Craisins are familiar household items in the United States. But suppose you had grown up in Asia or the Middle East—and had never heard of a cranberry, let alone seen or eaten one. To attract the attention of consumers in other parts of the world, Ocean Spray had to educate them about cranberries. "The starting point is that you have to explain to consumers in other countries what the heck a cranberry is," notes Stewart Gallagher, president of Ocean Spray International. So Ocean Spray teamed up with businesspeople in the food industry—bakers, heads of supermarkets, and restaurant owners—to spread the word. In China, Ocean Spray partnered with baker ChiaTe to add sweetened dried cranberries to its popular line of pineapple cakes. In Europe, Ocean Spray allied with Boden Spies, a global fruit and nut ingredient firm, to introduce cranberries and cranberry juice into other products.

Cranberries, it turns out, are one of the healthiest foods on the planet. Filled with antioxidants and vitamins that benefit health, they can help prevent heart disease, relieve stomach ulcers, reduce inflammation from gum disease, and guard against food poisoning. So, part of Ocean Spray's global consumer education focused on health benefits. Although the U.S. medical community declines to endorse specific foods, the French government put its stamp of approval on the cranberry.

The cranberry harvest has its own rituals. Most of it takes place on Cape Cod. Every fall, the bright red bogs are harvested much the way they were a century ago. Tourists and school groups come to watch, and Ocean Spray invites the international media and representatives of the food industry from around the world. Not stopping there, Ocean Spray marketers recently decided to transport cranberry "bogs" overseas to Kew Gardens in London so that consumers there could witness the process. "They are the market leader," notes one food industry observer about Ocean Spray. "Nobody's coming close."

Questions for Critical Thinking

1. About one-fourth of the U.S.-grown cranberry crop is now exported overseas. If this percentage grows, how might it affect the market for cranberries in the United States?

2. In addition to those already described, what kinds of contractual agreements might Ocean Spray enter into with foreign firms?

Sources: Company Web site, http://www.oceanspray.com, accessed February 13, 2009; Shane Sterling, "Ocean Spray Builds European Presence," *Nutraingredients.com*, December 22, 2008, http://www.nutraingredients.com; Elisabeth A. Sullivan, "Unlocking the Cranberry Mystique," *Marketing News*, November 15, 2008, pp. 10–11; Sarah Hills, "Demand for Cranberries Close to Outstripping Supply," *Beverage Daily*, September 29, 2008, http://www.beveragedaily.com; Charlotte Eyre, "Ocean Spray Goes for Asian Bakery Market," *Bakeryandsnacks.com*, April 4, 2008, http://www.bakeryandsnacks.com.

---

as international transaction documents and financing, while the larger company benefits from the local expertise and capabilities of its smaller partner.

COUNTERTRADE A sizable share of international trade involves payments made in the form of local products, not currency. This system of international bartering agreements is called **countertrade.**

A common reason for resorting to international barter is inadequate access to needed foreign currency. To complete an international sales agreement, the seller may agree to accept part or all of the purchase cost in merchandise rather than currency. Because the seller may decide to locate a buyer for the bartered goods before completing the transaction, a number of international buyers and sellers frequently join together in a single agreement.

Countertrade may often be a firm's only opportunity to enter a particular market. Many developing countries simply cannot obtain enough credit or financial assistance to afford the imports that their people want. Countries with heavy debt burdens also resort to countertrade. Russian buyers, whose currency is often less acceptable to foreign traders than the stronger currencies of countries such as the United States, Great Britain, Japan, and EU countries, may resort to trading local products ranging from crude oil to diamonds to vodka as payments for purchases from foreign companies unwilling to accept Russian rubles. Still other countries, such as China, may restrict imports. Under such circumstances, countertrade may be the only practical way to win government approval to import needed products.

CONTRACTUAL AGREEMENTS Once a company, large or small, gains some experience in international sales, it may decide to enter into contractual agreements with local parties. These arrangements can include franchising, foreign licensing, and subcontracting.

FRANCHISING Common among U.S. companies, franchising can work well for companies seeking to expand into international markets, too. A **franchise,** as described in detail in Chapter 5, is a contractual agreement in which a wholesaler or retailer (the franchisee) gains the right to sell the franchisor's products under that company's brand name if it agrees to the related operating requirements. The franchisee can also receive marketing, management, and business services from the franchisor. While these arrangements are common among leading fast-food brands such as McDonald's and KFC, other kinds of service providers also often look to franchising as an international marketplace option.

Domino's Pizza has expanded to more than 8,000 stores in more than 55 countries around the world. Its largest international market is in Mexico, but wherever it operates, the company fine-tunes its menus to meet local tastes with such specialties as barbecued chicken in the Bahamas, black bean sauce in Guatemala, squid in Japan, and chorizo in Mexico.[32]

FOREIGN LICENSING In a **foreign licensing agreement,** one firm allows another to produce or sell its product, or use its trademark, patent, or manufacturing processes, in a specific geographical area. In return, the firm gets a royalty or other compensation.

Licensing can be advantageous for a small manufacturer eager to launch a well-known product overseas. Not only does it get a proven product from another market, but little or no investment is required to begin operating. The arrangement can also allow entry into a market otherwise closed to imports due to government restrictions. Godiva, the 80-year-old Belgian chocolate company, began licensing its brand name in 1992 in an agreement with Seagram's to

Godiva, a Belgian chocolate company, now licenses its well-known brand name to manufacturers around the globe. Licensing, franchising, and subcontracting are all tried and true strategies for doing business abroad.

© R. Alcorn, photographed for John Wiley & Sons

produce Godiva Liqueur, but in the last two years its licensing program has grown considerably. "Our company now has a formal mission that includes leveraging external resources and enabling consumers to interact more broadly with the Godiva brand," says the company's vice president of global business development and licensing. Newly licensed products include Cheesecake Factory flavors, Godiva Ice Cream, and Godiva Belgian Blends.Other products outside the food and beverage category may soon be in the chocolatier's future.[33]

SUBCONTRACTING The third type of contractual agreement, **subcontracting,** involves hiring local companies to produce, distribute, or sell goods or services. This move allows a foreign firm to take advantage of the subcontractor's expertise in local culture, contacts, and regulations. Subcontracting works equally well for mail-order companies, which can farm out order fulfillment and customer service functions to local businesses. Manufacturers practice subcontracting to save money on import duties and labor costs, and businesses go this route to market products best sold by locals in a given country. Some firms, such as Maryland-based Pacific Bridge Medical, help medical manufacturers find reliable subcontractors and parts suppliers in Asia.

A key disadvantage of subcontracting is that companies cannot always control their subcontractors' business practices. Several major U.S. companies have been embarrassed by reports that their subcontractors used child labor to manufacture clothing.

OFFSHORING While it is not generally considered a way of initiating business internationally, *offshoring,* or the relocation of business processes to a lower-cost location overseas, has become a widespread practice. China has emerged as the preferred destination for production offshoring and India for services offshoring. Many business leaders argue, in favor of offshoring, that global firms must keep their costs as low as possible to remain competitive. But the apparent link between jobs sent overseas and jobs lost at home has made the practice controversial. Legislatures of various states have tried to slow the tide of offshoring through new laws, but many observers believe the real goal should be to improve corporate research and development efforts in the United States.

Offshoring shows no signs of slowing down, but it is changing. Many firms continue to send work or jobs to India, as does the Chicago-based legal firm Mindcrest. The firm grew from 40 to 400 lawyers in a single year and says it couldn't exist without its employees in Mumbai and Pune, India.[34] But India itself faces competition. GE Money staffs its call centers with workers in Barbados and Puerto Rico, while Delta Air Lines uses Jamaican employees to handle calls.[35] And Valerie King-Bailey, who lost her own engineering job to offshoring, founded OnShore Technology Group specifically to hire U.S. engineers and IT professionals. "I'm reverse offshoring," she says of her 140 client companies, some of whom are overseas. "I'm bringing companies from other countries into the U.S."[36] Meanwhile, in India, the giant of offshoring, Infosys Technologies, is hiring U.S. college graduates as fast as it can, training them in its Mysore headquarters, and sending them back to the United States to work in the company's U.S. offices.[37]

INTERNATIONAL DIRECT INVESTMENT Investing directly in production and marketing operations in a foreign country is the ultimate level of global involvement. Over time, a firm may become successful at conducting business in other countries through exporting and contractual agreements. Its managers may then decide to establish manufacturing facilities in those countries, open branch offices, or buy ownership interests in local companies.

In an *acquisition,* a company purchases another existing firm in the host country. An acquisition permits a largely domestic business operation to gain an international presence very

"They Said It"

"Outsourcing is just a new way of doing international trade."

—N. Gregory Mankiw (b. 1958) Former chairman, Council of Economic Advisers

quickly. Acer, a leading PC brand based in Taiwan, acquired Gateway, the fourth-largest PC maker in the United States, and General Motors, Fiat, Nissan, Honda, and Hyundai have all invested in India's growing auto market.[38]

Joint ventures allow companies to share risks, costs, profits, and management responsibilities with one or more host country nationals. Arkansas-based Tyson Foods expanded its operations into Argentina and China through joint ventures, and it continues to look to international markets for further growth.[39]

By setting up an *overseas division,* a company can conduct a significant amount of its business overseas. This strategy differs from that of a multinational company in that a firm with overseas divisions remains primarily a domestic organization with international operations. Matsushita established Panasonic Automotive Systems Asia Pacific to develop and sell new technology products in India, Thailand, Indonesia, Malaysia, the Philippines, and Vietnam.

From Multinational Corporation to Global Business

A **multinational corporation (MNC)** is an organization with significant foreign operations. As Table 4.4 shows, firms headquartered in the United States make up half the list of the world's largest multinationals. The Netherlands and the United Kingdom each have two companies on the list, and Japan rounds out the top ten, with one company on the list.

Many U.S. multinationals, including Nike and Wal-Mart, have expanded their overseas operations because they believe that domestic markets are peaking and foreign markets offer greater sales and profit potential. Other MNCs are making substantial investments in developing countries in part because these countries provide low-cost labor compared with the United States and western Europe. In addition, many MNCs are locating high-tech facilities in countries with large numbers of technical school graduates, such as India.

multinational corporation (MNC) firm with significant operations and marketing activities outside its home country.

Assessment Check ✔

1. Name three possible strategies for beginning overseas operations.
2. What is countertrade?
3. Compare and contrast licensing and subcontracting.
4. Describe joint ventures.

Table 4.4	The World's Leading Companies (Based on a Combined Ranking for Sales, Profits, Assets, and Market Value)		
Rank	**Company**	**Business**	**Country of Origin**
1	HSBC Holdings	Banking	United Kingdom
2	General Electric	Conglomerate	United States
3	Bank of America	Banking	United States
4	JPMorgan Chase	Banking	United States
5	ExxonMobil	Oil and gas operations	United States
6	Royal Dutch/Shell	Oil and gas operations	Netherlands
7	BP	Oil and gas operations	United Kingdom
8	Toyota Motor	Consumer durables	Japan
9	ING Group	Insurance	Netherlands
10	Berkshire Hathaway	Diversified financials	United States

Source: "The Global 2000," *Forbes,* http://www.forbes.com, accessed February 26, 2009.

Developing a Strategy for International Business

global business strategy offering a standardized, worldwide product and selling it in essentially the same manner throughout a firm's domestic and foreign markets.

In developing a framework in which to conduct international business, managers must first evaluate their corporate objectives, organizational strengths and weaknesses, and strategies for product development and marketing. They can choose to combine these elements in either a global strategy or a multidomestic strategy.

Global Business Strategies

In a **global business** (or *standardization*) **strategy,** a firm sells the same product in essentially the same manner throughout the world. Many companies simply modify their domestic business strategies by translating promotional brochures and product-use instructions into the languages of the host nations.

A global marketing perspective can be appropriate for some goods and services and certain market segments that are common to many nations. The approach works for products with nearly universal appeal and for luxury items such as jewelry. But food retailers such as McDonald's, PepsiCo, and KFC have discovered how much they must adapt their products to consumer tastes in China, for instance. Spinach, egg, and tomato soup is on KFC's menu in China, as are red-bean sundaes at McDonald's. Pizza Hut and Domino's compete in India, where bread, tomatoes, and sauces are already popular, by serving the same food products as in the United States, but the condiments on the table are likely to be chili flakes and ketchup instead of salt and pepper.[40] Scientific equipment, on the other hand, is not bound by geographical differences.

The Colonel welcomes customers at the door to a KFC restaurant in Bangkok, Thailand. Food retailers like KFC have discovered that they must adapt their products to foreign consumers' tastes when they open new locations abroad.

Bonnie Kamin/PhotoEdit

multidomestic business strategy developing and marketing products to serve different needs and tastes of separate national markets.

Multidomestic Business Strategies

Under a **multidomestic business** (or *adaptation*) **strategy,** the firm treats each national market in a different way. It develops products and marketing strategies that appeal to the customs, tastes, and buying habits of particular national markets. Companies that neglect the global nature of the Internet can unwittingly cause problems for potential customers by failing to adapt their strategy. European consumers, for instance, were at first hesitant to adopt online ordering of products ranging from books to railroad tickets. But in recent years, Internet use in western Europe has grown dramatically. Companies as diverse as the European divisions of Amazon.com; Egg PLC of London, an online financial services company; and the French national railroad have seen the numbers of visitors to their Web sites climbing, along with Internet revenues.

Assessment Check

1. What is a global business strategy? What are its advantages?
2. What is a multidomestic business strategy? What are its advantages?

What's Ahead

Examples in this chapter indicate that both large and small businesses are relying on world trade, not just major corporations. Chapter 5 examines the special advantages and challenges that small-business owners encounter. In addition, a critical decision facing any new business is the choice of the most appropriate form of business ownership. Chapter 5 also examines the major ownership structures—sole proprietorship, partnership, and corporation—and assesses the pros and cons of each. The chapter closes with a discussion of recent trends affecting business ownership, such as the growing impact of franchising and business consolidations through mergers and acquisitions.

Summary of Learning Goals

1 **Explain the importance of international business and the primary reasons nations trade.**

The United States is both the world's largest importer and the largest exporter, although less than 5 percent of the world's population lives within its borders. With the increasing globalization of the world's economies, the international marketplace offers tremendous opportunities for U.S. and foreign businesses to expand into new markets for their goods and services. Doing business globally provides new sources of materials and labor. Trading with other countries also reduces a company's dependence on economic conditions in its home market. Countries that encourage international trade enjoy higher levels of economic activity, employment, and wages than those that restrict it.

Assessment Check Answers

1.1 Why do nations trade? Nations trade because trading boosts economic growth by providing a market for products and access to needed resources. This makes production and distribution systems more efficient and reduces dependence on the economy of the domestic market.

1.2 Cite some measure of the size of the international marketplace. Although developing countries have lower per-capita incomes than developed nations in North America and western Europe, their populations are large and growing. China's population is about 1.3 billion and India's is roughly 1.1 billion.

2 **Discuss the concepts of absolute and comparative advantage in international trade.**

Nations usually benefit if they specialize in producing certain goods or services. A country has an absolute advantage if it holds a monopoly or produces a good or service at a lower cost than other nations. It has a comparative advantage if it can supply a particular product more efficiently or at a lower cost than it can produce other items.

Assessment Check Answers

2.1 Define *absolute advantage*. Absolute advantage means a country can maintain a monopoly in or produce a product at lower cost than any other competitor.

2.2 How does a nation acquire a comparative advantage? Comparative advantage exists when a nation can supply a product more efficiently and at a lower price than it can supply other goods, compared with the outputs of other countries.

3 **Describe how nations measure international trade and the significance of exchange rates.**

Countries measure the level of international trade by comparing exports and imports and then calculating whether a trade surplus or a deficit exists. This is the balance of trade, which represents the difference between exports and imports. The term *balance of payments* refers to the overall flow of money into or out of a country, including overseas loans and borrowing, international investments, and profits from such investments. An exchange rate is the value of a nation's currency relative to the currency of another nation. Currency values typically fluctuate, or "float," relative to the supply and demand for specific currencies in the world market. When the value of the dollar falls compared with other currencies, the cost paid by foreign businesses and households for U.S. products declines, and demand for exports may rise. An increase in the value of the dollar raises the prices of U.S. products sold abroad, but it reduces the prices of foreign products sold in the United States.

Assessment Check Answers

3.1 Compare balance of trade and balance of payments. Balance of trade is the difference between exports and imports; balance of payments is the overall flow of money into or out of a country.

3.2 Explain the function of an exchange rate. A nation's exchange rate is the rate at which its currency can be exchanged for the currencies of other nations to make it easier for them to trade with one another.

3.3 What happens when a currency is devalued? Devaluation describes a fall in a currency's value relative to other currencies or to a fixed standard.

4 Identify the major barriers that confront global businesses.

Businesses face several obstacles in the global marketplace. Companies must be sensitive to social and cultural differences, such as languages, values, and religions, when operating in other countries. Economic differences include standard-of-living variations and levels of infrastructure development. Legal and political barriers are among the most difficult to judge. Each country sets its own laws regulating business practices. Trade restrictions such as tariffs and administrative barriers also present obstacles to international business.

Assessment Check Answers

4.1 How might values and attitudes form a barrier to trade, and how can they be overcome? Marked differences in values and attitudes, such as religious attitudes, can form barriers between traditionally capitalist countries and those adapting new capitalist systems. Many of these can be overcome by learning about and respecting such differences.

4.2 What is a tariff? What is its purpose? A tariff is a surcharge or duty charged on foreign products. Its purpose is to protect domestic producers of those items.

4.3 Why is dumping a problem for companies marketing goods internationally? Dumping is selling products abroad at prices below the cost of production or exporting products at a lower price than charged in the home market. It drives the cost of products sharply down in the market where the they are dumped, but it can also hurt the domestic producers of those products.

5 Explain how international trade organizations and economic communities reduce barriers to international trade.

Many international organizations seek to promote international trade by reducing barriers among nations. Examples include the World Trade Organization, the World Bank, and the International Monetary Fund. Multinational economic communities create partnerships to remove barriers to flows of goods, capital, and people across the borders of members. Three such economic agreements are the North American Free Trade Agreement, CAFTA-DR, and the European Union.

Assessment Check Answers

5.1 What international trade organization succeeded GATT, and what is its goal? The World Trade Organization (WTO) succeeded GATT with the goal of monitoring GATT agreements, mediating disputes, and continuing the effort to reduce trade barriers throughout the world.

5.2 Compare and contrast the goals of the World Bank and the International Monetary Fund. The World Bank funds projects that build or expand nations' infrastructure such as transportation, education, and health systems and facilities. The International Monetary Fund makes short-term loans to member nations that are unable to meet their budgets. The fund operates as a lender of last resort.

5.3 Identify the members of NAFTA, and briefly explain how it works. NAFTA created a free-trade zone among the United States, Canada, and Mexico by eliminating trade barriers and investment restrictions among them, as well as easing regulations on services such as banking and establishing uniform rules for protection of intellectual property.

5.4 What are the goals of the European Union, and how do they promote international trade? The European Union's goals include promoting economic and social progress, introducing European citizenship as a complement to national citizenship, and giving the EU a significant role in international affairs. Unifying standards and laws is expected to contribute to international trade and economic growth.

6 Compare the different levels of involvement used by businesses when entering global markets.

Exporting and importing, the first level of involvement in international business, involves the lowest degree of both risk and control. Companies may rely on export trading or management companies to help distribute their products. Contractual agreements such as franchising, foreign licensing, and subcontracting offer additional, flexible options. Franchising and licensing are especially appropriate for services. Companies may also choose local subcontractors to produce goods for local sales. International direct investment in production and marketing facilities provides the highest degree of control but also the greatest risk. Firms make direct investments by acquiring foreign companies or facilities, forming joint ventures with local firms, and setting up their own overseas divisions.

Assessment Check Answers

6.1 Name three possible strategies for beginning overseas business operations. Strategies are exporting or importing; contractual agreements such as franchising, licensing, or subcontracting; and making direct investments in foreign markets through acquisition, joint venture, or establishment of an overseas division.

6.2 What is countertrade? Countertrade consists of payments made in the form of local products, not currency.

6.3 Compare and contrast licensing and subcontracting. In a foreign licensing agreement, one firm allows another to produce or sell its product or use its trademark, patent, or manufacturing process in a specific geographical area in return for royalty payments or other compensations. In subcontracting a firm hires local companies abroad to produce, distribute, or sell its goods and services.

6.4 Describe joint ventures. Joint ventures allow companies to share risks, costs, profits, and management responsibilities with one or more host-country nationals.

---

7 **Distinguish between a global business strategy and a multidomestic business strategy.**

A company that adopts a global (or standardization) strategy develops a single, standardized product and marketing strategy for implementation throughout the world. The firm sells the same product in essentially the same manner in all countries in which it operates. Under a multidomestic (or adaptation) strategy, the firm develops a different treatment for each foreign market. It develops products and marketing strategies that appeal to the customs, tastes, and buying habits of particular nations.

Assessment Check Answers

7.1 What is a global business strategy? What are its advantages? A global business strategy specifies a standardized competitive strategy in which the firm sells the same product in essentially the same manner throughout the world. It works well for goods and services that are common to many nations and allows the firm to market them without making significant changes.

7.2 What is a multidomestic business strategy? What are its advantages? A multidomestic business strategy allows the firm to treat each foreign market in a different way to appeal to the customs, tastes, and buying habits of particular national markets. It allows the firm to customize its marketing appeals for individual cultures or areas.

Business Terms You Need to Know

exports 102
imports 102
balance of trade 106
balance of payments 106
exchange rate 107

tariff 116
World Trade Organization (WTO) 118
North American Free Trade Agreement (NAFTA) 119

Central America–Dominican Republic Free Trade Agreement (CAFTA-DR) 120
European Union (EU) 120

multinational corporation (MNC) 127
global business strategy 128
multidomestic business strategy 128

Other Important Business Terms

devaluation 107
infrastructure 111
quotas 117
dumping 117
embargo 117

exchange control 117
General Agreement on Tariffs and Trade (GATT) 117
World Bank 118

International Monetary Fund (IMF) 119
countertrade 124
franchise 125

foreign licensing agreement 125
subcontracting 126
joint ventures 127

Review Questions

1. How does a business decide whether to trade with a foreign country? What are the key factors for participating in the information economy on a global basis?

2. Why are developing countries such as China and India becoming important international markets?

3. What is the difference between absolute advantage and comparative advantage? Give an example of each.

4. Can a nation have a favorable balance of trade and an unfavorable balance of payments? Why or why not?

5. Identify several potential barriers to communication when a company attempts to conduct business in another country. How might these be overcome?

6. Identify and describe briefly the three dimensions of the legal environment for global business.

7. What are the major nontariff restrictions affecting international business? Describe the difference between tariff and nontariff restrictions.

8. What is NAFTA? How does it work?

9. How has the EU helped trade among European businesses?

10. What are the key choices a company must make before reaching the final decision to go global?

Projects and Teamwork Applications

1. When Britain transferred Hong Kong to China in 1997, China agreed to grant Hong Kong a high degree of autonomy as a capitalist economy for 50 years. Do you think this agreement is holding up? Why or why not? Consider China's economy, population, infrastructure, and other factors in your answer.

2. The tremendous growth of online business has introduced new elements to the legal climate of international business. Patents, brand names, copyrights, and trademarks are difficult to monitor because of the boundary-less nature of the Internet. What steps could businesses take to protect their trademarks and brands in this environment? Come up with at least five suggestions, and compare your list with your classmates'.

3. The WTO monitors GATT agreements, mediates disputes, and continues the effort to reduce trade barriers throughout the world. However, widespread concerns have been expressed that the WTO's focus on lowering trade barriers may encourage businesses to keep costs down through practices that may lead to pollution and human rights abuses. Others argue that human rights should not be linked to international business. Do you think environmental and human rights issues should be linked to trade? Why or why not?

4. The IMF makes short-term loans to developing countries that may not be able to repay them. Do you agree that the IMF should forgive these debts in some cases? Why or why not?

5. Describe briefly the EU and its goals. What are the pros and cons of the EU? Do you predict that the European alliance will hold up over the next 20 years? Why or why not?

6. Use the most recent edition of "The Fortune Global 500," which is published in *Fortune* magazine normally in late July or early August, or go to *Fortune*'s online version at http://money.cnn.com/magazines/fortune/global500, to answer the following questions.

   a. On what is the Global 500 ranking based (e.g., profits, number of employees, revenues)?
   b. Among the world's ten largest corporations, list the countries in which they are based.
   c. Identify the top-ranked company, along with its Global 500 ranking and country, for the following industry classifications: Food and Drug Stores; Industrial and Farm Equipment; Petroleum Refining; Utilities: Gas and Electric; Telecommunications; Pharmaceuticals.

Web Assignments

1. **IMF and World Bank.** Visit the Web sites of the International Monetary Fund (http://www.imf.org) and World Bank (http://www.worldbank.org). The Web sites describe the function, organization, and history of each organization. After reviewing the material, prepare a brief report on both organizations. Be sure you answer the following questions:

   a. When were they created?
   b. Why were they created?
   c. How is each governed and financed?
   d. How do the World Bank and IMF differ from one another?

2. **U.S. trade data.** Visit the Census Bureau's Web site (http://www.census.gov) and click on the "Foreign Trade" link under "Business & Industry." Access the most recent report you can find on U.S. trade statistics and answer the following questions:

   a. Comparing your report with the data shown in Figure 4.1, has the order of major U.S. trading partners changed? By how much has trade increased between the United States and each country shown in Figure 4.1?
   b. Of the top ten U.S. trading partners, with how many does the United States run trade surpluses? Trade deficits?
   c. Comparing the most recent trade report with one a year earlier, by how much have U.S. exports and imports increased? Have exports increased by more than imports or vice versa?

3. **Export assistance.** Assume you own a small business and would like to begin selling your products internationally. Visit the International Trade Administration's Web site (http://trade.gov/index.asp). Click on "Get export counseling." Write a brief report on the types of assistance and advice offered by the ITA.

Note: Internet Web addresses change frequently. If you do not find the exact sites listed, you may need to access the organization's or company's home page and search from there.

McDonald's Delivers for Foreign Markets

To stimulate profit growth in a slowing market, McDonald's now encourages owners of its tightly run franchises around the world to do something a little different—experiment. Some owners in China serve corn instead of fries, and some French and Australian stores have coffee lounges. But the most profitable and most widely adopted idea so far originated in Egypt, where the owner suggested offering a delivery service to compete with other chains and restaurants in the area. Today nearly all McDonald's in the Cairo area deliver.

Delivery proved so profitable that McDonald's now brings food to customers in 25 cities worldwide; most are congested hubs like Manila, Taipei, Beirut, Riyadh, São Paolo, Montevideo, New Delhi, and Mumbai. They charge a small fee, between 50 cents and $1, which more than pays for processing the orders and operating fleets of speedy scooters and motorbikes. As the company's president of operations outside the Americas and Europe notes, "We don't even have to clean up a table. It's incremental profit for us."

Deliveries make up 27 percent of McDonald's revenue in Egypt and were expected to pass $110 million, growing 20 to 30 percent each year, or more than three times the company's overall rate of growth. McDonald's is investing heavily to promote its delivery business in India, adopting another idea that made the Egyptian launch so successful—one toll-free number for all neighborhoods.

Observers approve of the innovations. "Management is looking beyond Oak Brook [headquarters] for inspiration," said one industry expert. "They're becoming better at sharing the best ideas around the globe." Meanwhile, in the United Kingdom, McDonald's plans to collect and recycle the cooking oil from all its stores to supply 85 percent of the fuel mix needed by its delivery fleet of 155 vehicles. Could this be the next idea heard round the world?[41]

Questions for Critical Thinking

1. How do you think "sharing the best ideas around the globe" can benefit McDonald's?
2. Fast-food chains like McDonald's cultivate customer loyalty by offering similar experiences at all their stores. How much do you think McDonald's can let franchise owners in international locations experiment before it risks losing the consistency it relies on for its competitive advantage?

Lego Builds Creatively for Half a Century

Fifty years old and still going strong, Lego is the Danish maker of those unforgettable plastic building blocks beloved around the world. More than 400 million people of all ages play each year with what *Fortune* magazine called "toy of the century," and enough blocks are produced each year to circle the Earth five times. One of the characteristics that account for Lego's enduring attraction is the blocks' ability to foster the imagination. Because of their unique stud-and-hole design, a set as small as six blocks offers 915 million different combinations. "The Lego brick doesn't age with time and continues to fascinate because it allows children, and others, to develop their creativity, imagination and curiosity and let it wander free," said a Lego spokesperson at its headquarters in Billund.

The family-owned company has been through some difficult times, however, and barely escaped disaster between 1998 and 2004, when it lost millions of dollars in each of several years. In the 1960s it introduced Duplos, larger blocks designed for younger children, and opened theme parks in Denmark, England, the United States, and Germany. Duplos were a hit, and the parks drew millions of visitors and launched Lego-brand clothing, watches, books, and multimedia games. But competition from electronic toys and computer games was devastating. As one toy researcher said, "Lego bricks belong to the industrial era when children liked to build things, playing wannabe engineers. Nowadays, the most popular toys are inspired by the virtual world."

Sales declined until finally the company was forced to post a loss for the first time in its history. After several more difficult years, the company's owner invested $158 million of his own fortune in the company, but it took new leadership to turn Lego around. Joergen Vig Knudstorp, the new CEO, laid off hundreds of employees; cut costs; sold the theme parks; and outsourced distribution, packaging, and production to Mexico and eastern Europe. With a new focus on core operations and fewer production sites to operate, the company began to bounce back. A tie-in with the *Star Wars* franchise that spawned a Lego Star Wars videogame proved profitable too, and a few years ago Lego, whose name is based on the Danish words for "play well," posted sales of $1.5 billion in 130 countries with a $281 million profit.[42]

Questions for Critical Thinking

1. One expert attributed Lego's rebound to its ability to "stay relevant" to product tie-ins including *Star Wars* and SpongeBob SquarePants. Why do you think these U.S. character franchises were important to Lego's worldwide profitability?

2. Lego was recently voted number one among 600 companies worldwide by the Reputation Institute, a U.S. research firm. What kind of reputation do you think the Lego brand has among parents and children around the world? How does it achieve and enhance it, and how might the brand's international reputation have contributed to the company's return to profitability?

VIDEO Case 4.3 — ESPN Broadcasts Sports around the World

Bill Rasmussen made a big mistake in 1979. He had decided to launch a Connecticut-based cable TV station to broadcast local sports. So he and his partners leased a building and bought some satellite time. After they signed the agreement, they discovered that their satellite coverage was national, not local—and the idea for a regional cable sports station began to grow. New England, they thought, would be the perfect sports market for the new Entertainment and Sports Programming Network. Later, when business really got rolling, Rasmussen and his partners shortened the name to ESPN—and it stuck.

ESPN long ago leaped its New England borders into national coverage and ultimately extended its reach to covering sports and broadcasting them globally, although the company's headquarters remained in Bristol, Connecticut, where the original building was leased and where they still operate today. Headquarters now includes several buildings, 28 satellite dishes, and 3,200 employees. ESPN operates 6 networks in the U.S. and 25 international networks, reaching between 150 and 155 million households globally. The company also produces ESPN Radio, ESPN Wireless, several Web sites including ESPN.com and ESPNSoccernet. com, magazines, and books, and it is exploring emerging technologies like video on demand and interactive TV. Spanish-speaking viewers can watch ESPN Deportes 24 hours a day. ESPN fans can eat at the ESPN Zone restaurant and buy merchandise at TeamStore@ESPN. Collectively, the ESPN media outlets offer coverage of local sporting events as well as major tournaments like the PGA Championship and the British Open for golf and the America's Cup sailing races—not to mention games of the NFL, NHL, MLB, WNBA, and various college sports. In addition to the game coverage, it offers sports news and analysis; information on scores, statistics, standings, and schedules; and just about any other sports-related content the enthusiast could want.

Reaching out for the global market was something that ESPN founders did "on gut feeling," says Willy Burkhardt, managing director of ESPN International. Because cable television was still new when ESPN was born, not much data existed on who was watching what around the world. But ESPNs executives had the idea that sports, like music and major news stories, had universal appeal. So they decided to try broadcasting American sports events in South America. Today, South and Central America—particularly Argentina, Brazil, and Mexico—represent 40 percent of ESPN's total business. And although the firm continues to broadcast American sports overseas, it now places much greater emphasis on local and regional programming based on the tastes and preferences of the host cultures. For example, says Burkhardt, in India "cricket is a total culture." While few Americans are familiar with the sport, millions of Indians are glued to the TV for cricket matches. In Argentina, rugby and polo occupy prime-time coverage. Major markets such as Argentina and India command their own ESPN offices and on-air announcing teams. In addition to South America and Asia, ESPN has a presence in Europe,

Canada, Australia, and New Zealand—and even a station in Antarctica.

ESPN has used a variety of methods to enter international markets. In Europe, ESPN has had a longstanding partnership with EuroSport, which means that, although many European consumers watch sports on cable television, they are not necessarily aware of the ESPN name. However, recently ESPN did launch ESPN Classic Sport, a network dedicated to the greatest moments of European sporting history. ESPN operates in Canada through partnerships, as well. These arrangements are partly due to varying regulations in different countries and regions. But in Asia, ESPN has a large operation of its own, broadcasting to about 25 countries on the continent, including India, which is one of the firm's most important markets.

ESPN continues to grow in international markets because its managers believe they can bring "a new century of sport" to viewers around the world. "You learn by doing," says Burkhardt. ESPN wants viewers worldwide to watch what it is doing.[43]

Questions for Critical Thinking

1. Describe three barriers to ESPN as it expands in the global marketplace.
2. How might NAFTA and the European Union affect ESPN in those areas?
3. Describe the levels of involvement ESPN uses in its different international markets.
4. Does ESPN adopt a global business strategy or a multidomestic business strategy? Explain your answer.

KANSAS

Greensburg KS.

© Getty Images

New Ways to Be a Better Town

Greensburg, Kansas, had been struggling for years. Located along highway 54, a major trucking route, the town was merely a pit stop for people on their way somewhere else. It did have a few tourist attractions: the Big Well, the world's largest hand-dug well, and a 1,000-pound meteorite that fell from the sky in 2006.

Lonnie McCollum, the town's mayor, had been looking into ways to breathe new life into the town. McCollum wanted to add a little vintage charm to its quaint Main Street, but could not raise the money. And he had launched a campaign to put the "green" back in Greensburg by promoting green building technology. But the idea, which many residents associated with hippies and tree-huggers, did not go over well.

Then everything changed. "My town is gone," announced Town Administrator Steve Hewitt on May 5, 2007, after surveying the damage caused by a devastating tornado. "I believe 95 percent of the homes are gone. Downtown buildings are gone, my home is gone." With a clean slate and 700 homes to replace, Hewitt vowed to rebuild Greensburg using sustainable materials. He believed the town had a unique opportunity to control its environmental impact and reduce operating costs through increased energy efficiency.

"What if we turned this tragedy into something beautiful?" asked resident Dan Wallach in a new business plan he wrote shortly after the disaster. Wallach and his wife had long been interested in sustainable Green living. Using their experience in developing nonprofits, the two launched Greensburg GreenTown, an organization designed to support Greensburg's green building efforts through education, fund-raising, and public relations management.

One of Wallach's favorite new projects was BTI Greensburg, the local John Deere dealership. Owners Kelly and Mike Estes had decided to replace their ruined building with an energy-efficient, technologically state-of-the-art showroom featuring radiant heat, solar energy, passive cooling, and wind power. With corporate support from John Deere, BTI Greensburg would become a flagship green dealership.

Long-term plans for Greensburg include a business incubator, to help displaced businesses get back on their feet and bring new businesses to town; a green industrial park, green museum, and green school system; green building codes and zoning restrictions; and a community of green homes and businesses.

Questions

After viewing the video, answer the following questions:

1. In what ways is the town of Greensburg like any other business?
2. In what ways is the town of Greensburg a socially responsible organization?
3. What might be the effects of the town's new green building guidelines on residents and businesses? On the regional economy?
4. What kind of business is Greensburg GreenTown? How does its structure differ from John Deere's?

Launching Your Global Business and Economics Career

In Part 1, "Business in a Global Environment," you learned about the background and current issues driving contemporary business. The part includes four chapters covering such issues as the changing face of business, business ethics and social responsibility, economic challenges facing contemporary business, and competing in world markets. Business has always been an exciting career field, whether you choose to start your own company, work at a local business, or set your sights on a position with a multinational corporation. But today's environment is especially attractive because businesses are expanding their horizons to compete in a global economy—and they need dedicated and talented people to help them accomplish their goals. In fact, professional and business service jobs are found in some of the fastest-growing industries in the U.S. economy and are projected to grow by more than 23 percent over a decade.[1] So now is the time to explore several different career options that can lead you to your dream job. Each part in this text profiles the many opportunities available in business. Here are a few related to Chapters 1 through 4.

If you're good at number crunching and are interested in how societies and companies function, then maybe a career as an *economist* is in your future. Economists study how resources are allocated, conduct research by collecting and analyzing data, monitor economic trends, and develop forecasts. They look into such vital areas as the cost of energy, foreign trade and exchange between countries, the effect of taxes, and employment levels—both from a big-picture national or global viewpoint and from the perspective of individual businesses. Economists work for corporations to help them run more efficiently, for consulting firms to offer special expertise, or for government agencies to oversee economic decision making. Typically, advanced degrees are needed to climb to top-level positions. Economists usually earn about $77,010 per year.[2]

Or perhaps you are interested in global business. Companies increasingly search the world for the best employees, supplies, and markets. So you could work in the United States for a foreign-based firm such as Nokia or Toyota; abroad in Australia, Asia, Europe, or Latin America for a U.S.-based firm such as Microsoft; or with overseas coworkers via computer networks to develop new products for a firm such as General Electric. With technology and telecommunications, distance is no longer a barrier to conducting business. Global business careers exist in all the areas you'll be reading about in this text—business ownership, management, marketing, technology, and finance.

Global business leaders are not born but made—so how can you start on that career path? Here are the three areas that businesses consider when selecting employees for overseas assignment:

- *competence*—including technical knowledge, language skills, leadership ability, experience, and past performance.
- *adaptability*—including interest in overseas work, communication and other personal skills, empathy for other cultures, and appreciation for varied management styles and work environments.
- *personal characteristics*—level of education, experience, and social compatibility with the host country.[3]

Solid experience in your field or company ranks at the top of the list of needed skills. Firms want to send employees who have expertise in their business and loyalty to the firm to represent them overseas. Those who obtain their master's of business administration (MBA) degree are reaping rewards financially: in a recent year, the average salary for MBA graduates a few years out of school reached $126,000.[4] Companies are reluctant to send new graduates abroad immediately. Instead, they invest in training to orient employees to the new assignment.

Knowledge of and interest in other languages and cultures

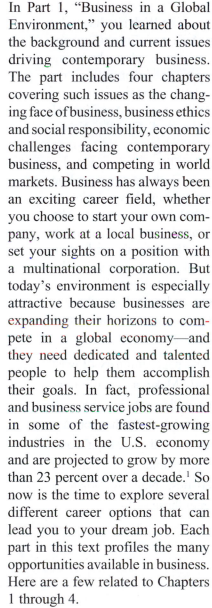

is the second-highest priority. Businesspeople need to function smoothly in another society, so they are selected based on their familiarity with other languages and cultures. Because China is a business hotspot, some people have become fluent in Mandarin Chinese to boost their career prospects. Also, some school systems are offering Chinese language classes in addition to their standard offerings of Spanish, French, German, and Russian.

Finally, employees are evaluated on their personal characteristics to be certain that they will fit well in their new country. A person's talent is still foremost in making assignments, but executives with cross-cultural skills are in high demand.[5]

Career Assessment Exercises in Economics and Global Business

1. With the ups and downs in the U.S. economy, economists have been highlighted in the news. The head of the Federal Reserve, Benjamin Bernanke, has been managing the country's general financial condition. Bernanke has a background in economics. To get an idea of the role economists play in a federal government agency, research Bernanke's background, qualifications, and abilities. Assess how he is performing at the Fed. Now make a list of your own skills. Where is there a match? What do you need to change?

2. To see the effect of the global economy in your community, go to a major retailer. Look at the number of different countries represented in the products on the shelves. Compare your list with those of your classmates to see who found the most countries and what goods those countries provided. Go online to research the career opportunities at the retailer's Web site.

3. To learn more about other countries, do research online for a country in which you are interested. Here are some sources that may be useful:

   • *The World Factbook*, published by the Central Intelligence Agency, https://www.cia.gov/library/publications/the-world-factbook/. This publication, updated yearly, contains a wealth of information about countries—geography and climate, population statistics, cultural and political information, transportation and communications methods, and economic data.

   • *BusinessWeek* magazine, http://www.businessweek.com. The Web site has links to Asia and Europe, where you can explore breaking news or information on global companies.

   • Online news sites Yahoo! News and Google News, http://news.yahoo.com and http://news.google.com. Both of these online news sites have links to global business news. The Yahoo! site has a link for "Business" and then "Global Economy." The Google site has a "Business" link and then lists sites for many countries and many languages.

Write a one-page summary of what you found. Make a list of abilities you would need to function well as a businessperson in that country. Concentrate on the areas of competence, adaptability, and personal characteristics. Now formulate a plan to gain those skills.

Part 2

Starting and Growing Your Business

© Masterfile

Goals

1 Distinguish between small and large businesses, and identify the industries in which most small firms are established.

2 Discuss the economic and social contributions of small business.

3 Describe the reasons that small businesses fail.

4 Describe how the Small Business Administration assists small-business owners.

5 Explain how franchising can provide opportunities for both franchisors and franchisees.

6 Summarize the three basic forms of business ownership and the advantages and disadvantages of each form.

7 Identify the levels of corporate management.

8 Describe recent trends in mergers and acquisitions.

9 Differentiate among private ownership, public ownership, and collective ownership (cooperatives).

chapter

5

Options for Organizing Small and Large Businesses

Digital Vision/Getty Images

Nokia: From Trees to Telecommunications

Success brings staying power in business. Many of today's well-run companies have been in existence for a long time, some for generations. Over the years, most have undergone many changes in organization, size, and direction, branching into new areas to take advantage of opportunities and abandoning old ones to cut losses. Probably very few, however, can rival the dramatic transformations of a small Finnish paper mill as it became one of the world's top cell phone makers.

Almost 150 years ago, Nokia was a wood-pulp mill on the banks of the Nokia River in southern Finland. With several mergers and a move to become a corporation along the way, Nokia is now an international communications technology giant, with over 68,000 employees in 15 manufacturing facilities around the globe and operating profits in excess of 5 billion euros. Nokia is a public company incorporated in Finland and listed on the stock exchanges of Helsinki, Frankfurt, and New York. Its history is one of slow but steady growth and change.

Some years after the Nokia paper mill's founding back in the mid-19th century, another prosperous Finnish firm began to grow—this one specializing in rubber products. Then early in the 20th century a third company, called Finnish Cable Works, was founded; by the 1960s this firm had established an electronics department to operate and sell computers and other devices. In 1967, all three companies formally merged to create Nokia Incorporated, which was by then ideally positioned to take a leading role in the evolution of mobile communications in Europe. Its first joint venture was a radio telephone company launched with a Finnish television manufacturer. By 1984, Nokia had produced its first portable phone, the Mobira Talkman, with more innovations in handheld technologies to follow.

Then came the most influential strategic decision in the company's history, when Jorma Ollila became president and CEO in 1992. Ollila set Nokia on a promising new course, focusing on global telecommunications. Only two years later, the world's first satellite call was placed using a Nokia handset. A phone-based videogame was the next big first for the firm, and soon Nokia had become the world leader in the design and manufacture of mobile phones. The firm sold its milestone one billionth cell phone in Nigeria in 2005. For at least the last decade, Nokia has been the top firm in the highly competitive cell phone market and is considered one of the most valuable brands in the world. Nokia continues to innovate under new president and CEO Olli-Pekka Kallasvuo, who came on staff in 2006, with Ollila serving as chairman of the board. In 2007, the company became the first phone manufacturer to build into its cell phones an energy-saving alert to unplug the charger when it is finished.

Meanwhile, Nokia was not done transforming itself. In 2008 it completely revamped its corporate structure, which formerly had three business groups working on mobile devices with a set of shared support groups. Now the firm consists of three major areas: Services & Software, which specializes in Internet services and software; Devices, which develops new products and their components; and Markets, which manages the company's supply chains, sales channels, and brand and marketing functions. NAVTEQ is a smaller division that provides digital data for mapping and satellite GPS systems for business and government; its focus is on making maps and voice-guided navigation systems available for portable devices. Finally, Nokia Siemens Networks is a separate joint venture with German electronics and engineering powerhouse Siemens that manages the company's technology infrastructure and related services. All these business units are supported by a corporate headquarters and overseen by the executive board of directors.

Nokia hopes its new structure will help it fend off attacks by Korean mobile phone makers Samsung and LG, which have passed U.S. firm Motorola in sales and are mounting a challenge to the market leader. LG's Chocolate cell phone was a smash hit, and Samsung plans to market no fewer than 20 smart phones to follow its success in Great Britain and the United States.

Nokia recently released a compact new camera phone and a smart phone that receives Web-based e-mail. It is also partnering with Facebook and MySpace to open an online software and media store, following the shift to software development started by Apple's applications-rich iPhone.

With a global economic recession, cell phone makers face a contracting market. But the past has taught a valuable lesson: The future will be won by companies that are structured for quick and nimble responses to market changes. When it comes to transformation, Nokia has more experience than most.[1]

If you have ever thought of operating your own business, you are not alone. In fact, on any given day in the United States, more people are trying to start new businesses than are getting married or having children. However, before entering the world of contemporary business, an entrepreneur needs to understand its framework and choose the form the business will take. Nokia started as a small paper mill but underwent several transformations to become a leader in telecommunications. The firm recently reorganized to compete more effectively and began an online service for software downloads.

Several variables affect the choice of the best way to organize your business:

- How easily can you set up the type of firm?
- How much financial liability can you afford to accept?
- What financial resources do you have?

- What strengths and weaknesses do you see in other businesses in the industry?
- What are your own strengths and weaknesses?

This chapter begins by focusing on small-business ownership, including the advantages and disadvantages of small-business ventures, the contributions of small business to the economy, and the reasons small businesses succeed and fail. We also look at the services provided by the U.S. government's Small Business Administration. The role of women and minorities in small business is discussed in detail, as well as franchising and global opportunities for small-business owners. We then provide an overview of the three forms of private business ownership—sole proprietorships, partnerships, and corporations. Next, the structures and operations typical of larger companies are explored, followed by a review of mergers, acquisitions, and joint ventures. The chapter concludes with an explanation of public and collective ownership.

Most Businesses Are Small Businesses

Although many people associate the term *business* with corporate goliaths such as ExxonMobil, Ford, PepsiCo, Pfizer, Microsoft, and Wal-Mart, 90 percent of firms with employees have fewer than 20 people on staff, and 98 percent have fewer than 100 employees.[2] Many U.S. businesses have no payroll at all: more than 20 million people in the United States earn business income without any employees.[3] Almost half the sales in the United States are made by small businesses.[4] In addition, small firms have generated 60 to 80 percent of new jobs over the last decade.[5]

Small business is also the launching pad for entrepreneurs from every sector of the diverse U.S. economy. Of the nation's 26 million small businesses, 40 percent are owned by women.[6] Hispanic-owned businesses account for 6.6 percent of all U.S. businesses; African Americans own another 5 percent and Asian Americans own 4.6 percent.[7]

What Is a Small Business?

How do you distinguish a small business from a large one? Are sales the key indicator? What about market share or number of employees? The Small Business Administration (SBA), the federal agency most directly involved with this sector of the economy, considers a <mark>small business</mark> to be a firm that is independently owned and operated and is not dominant in its field. The SBA also considers annual sales and number of employees to identify small businesses for specific industries.

- Most manufacturing businesses are considered small if they employ fewer than 500 workers.
- To be considered small, wholesalers must employ no more than 100 workers.
- Most kinds of retailers and other services can generate up to $6 million in annual sales and still be considered a small business.
- An agricultural business is generally considered small if its sales are no more than $750,000 a year.[8]

The SBA has established size standards for specific industries. These standards, which range from $500,000 to $25 million in sales and from 100 to 1,500 for employees, are available at the SBA's "Size Regulations" Web page, http://www.sba.gov.

An excellent example of a small business is Happy Green Bee, a Raleigh, North Carolina–based producer of organic cotton clothes for infants and toddlers. The company was founded by Roxanne Quimby, who earlier started Burt's Bees with $400 and had grown it into a $60-million maker of all-natural lotions, lip balm, and other personal-care products before selling it. Happy Green Bee got off to a good start, with sales around $100,000 of brightly colored organic kids' clothes in its first few months. Because grown cotton is traditionally one of the most pesticide-laden crops on the planet, Happy Green Bee also scores points for eco-consciousness. Will the company ever reach the size of Burt's Bees? Quimby says she would be surprised, but for now she likes to manage a company of a dozen people.[9]

Because government agencies offer benefits designed to help small businesses compete with larger firms, small-business owners want to determine whether their companies meet the standards for small-business designation. If it qualifies, a company may be eligible for government loans or for government purchasing programs that encourage proposals from smaller suppliers.

small business firm that is independently owned and operated, is not dominant in its field, and meets industry-specific size standards for income or number of employees.

A pleased toddler models one of Happy Green Bee's organic cotton dresses. The company started small, with sales of around $100,000.

© Happy Green Bee

Typical Small-Business Ventures

For decades, small businesses have competed against some of the world's largest organizations, as well as multitudes of other small companies. For example, City Beans, a coffee shop with two stores in northern New Jersey, found Starbucks at its doorstep. First the coffee giant tried to lease City Beans's space in an office building when its lease came due, but owner Brian Kelly had already agreed to a new lease. Then Starbucks moved into an empty space on the other side of the building. To compete, Kelly capitalized on his strengths as a small company, building customer relations, serving locally supplied coffee roasted fresh every day, and ramping up his catering business to take advantage of local contacts. When Starbucks opened, Kelly did see a drop in sales, but smaller than he expected, and the additional catering business made up the difference. Kelly is working on more ideas like new signage for City Beans and further expanding his catering business, but he doesn't feel sorry for Starbucks quite yet.[10] The "Hit & Miss" feature discusses another small business, a pizza parlor started in South Brooklyn by a former real estate agent who wanted a career change and saw an opportunity in an old building in his neighborhood.

"They Said It"

"I'm a worker. I was not raised in a wealthy family, and I don't know how to act that way ... At the end of the day, it's the work you do that's racking up your purpose in life."

—*Roxanne Quimby* (b. 1951) *Founder and owner, Happy Green Bee*

Hit & Miss

South Brooklyn Pizza Finds the Right Recipe

The word on the street is that few new businesses are successful and new restaurants have the highest failure rate of all. Firms that focus on only a couple of products can also face risks from their decision not to diversify. And it might seem like just plain common sense that if you really *want* to open a brand-new restaurant with a limited menu, you should make sure you have a lot of experience to help you survive. But if you don't, and you insist on breaking all those rules, at least you shouldn't do it in the middle of a recession, right?

Try telling that to Jim McGown, a former math major who recently left a 10-year career in real estate to become the *piazzaiolo* (pizza maker) and owner of South Brooklyn Pizza in New York. McGown is making his business profitable in hard economic times—and without even advertising.

His experience in real estate might have told McGown that the chance to buy an old Irish pub he used to visit was an opportunity he should pass by. The dining area was dark, and the facility needed about $200,000 in renovations. But it had a 19th century brick oven that could be made usable again, and the neighborhood, a largely Italian area called Carroll Gardens, held a number of Old World pizza makers who knew everything there was to know about making pizza. McGown bought the building, poured the money in, and convinced the retired piazzaiolos to share their secrets with him. "It's like golf," McGown says of pizza making. "You take to it immediately and then spend a lifetime learning—about the dough, ambient temperature during rising, all these little things."

Shortly after opening, South Brooklyn Pizza drew rave reviews and recommendations from around the neighborhood. Staff from *The New York Times* came to sample the pizza and liked it. Its positive write-up and other favorable publicity attracted customers from Manhattan, New Jersey, and Connecticut. McGown decided the first night not to try to remember what each table had ordered: It was simpler if everyone got the same thing. For some time that meant he served only classic margherita pizza, oval in shape, with a medley of cheeses, a drizzle of extra-virgin olive oil, and a medium-thick crust. McGown did distinguish his product by serving it on oak boards—from Home Depot. He's since added two other types featuring clams and spinach salad, as well as chocolate cookies for dessert. But he still doesn't offer takeout, individual slices, or delivery.

Yet McGown seems to have hit on a recipe for success by focusing on the basics. "I decided to make what I do really well," he admits. "People talk about pizza. They will go three times a week. In New York, if they hear about good pizza, they will go across town. ... We could do arugula salad, but we make the best pizza and cookies." He estimated earning $300,000 to $400,000 in his first year and now owns another old place that also serves pizza. Not discouraged by a recession, he plans to open still more restaurants soon. "When people walk out, I want them to say, 'That was the best pizza and chocolate-chip cookie I ever had.'"

Questions for Critical Thinking

1. What accounts for the way South Brooklyn Pizza seems to have beaten the odds against small-business success?
2. If you were starting a small restaurant business, what lessons would you take from McGown's experience, and what would you do differently?

Sources: Lisa Lee King, "The Family that Eats Together," *Encore Magazine*, http://encoremag.com, accessed February 17, 2009; Stacy Perman, "From Real Estate Developer to Pizza Man," *BusinessWeek*, July 16, 2008, http://www.businessweek.com; "South Brooklyn Pizza and Artisanal," *The New York Times*, June 18, 2008, http://www.nytimes.com; Robin Raisfeld and Rob Patronite, "Pizza, New-Brooklyn Style," *New York Magazine*, June 8, 2008, http://nymag.com.

The past 15 years have seen a steady erosion of small businesses in many industries as larger firms have bought out small independent businesses and replaced them with larger operations. For example, the number of independent bookstores and hardware stores has fallen dramatically as Barnes & Noble, Home Depot, and Lowe's have dramatically increased their stores over the last decade. But as Table 5.1 reveals, the businesses least likely to be gobbled up and consolidated into larger firms are those that sell services, not things; rely on consumer trust and proximity; and keep their overhead costs low.

Table 5.1	David vs. Goliath: Business Sectors Most Dominated and Least Dominated by Small Firms

Most Likely to Be a Small Firm	Fewer Than 20 Workers
Home builders	97%
Florists	97%
Hair salons	96%
Auto repair	96%
Funeral homes	94%

Least Likely to Be a Small Firm	Fewer Than 20 Workers
Hospitals	14%
Nursing homes	23%
Paper mills	33%
Electric utilities	38%
Oil pipelines	38%

Source: U.S. Census Bureau, "Number of Firms, Number of Establishments, Employment, and Annual Payroll by Employment Size of the Enterprise for the United States, All Industries," accessed March 3, 2009, http://www.census.gov.

For centuries, most nonfarming small businesses have been concentrated in retailing and the service industries. Recently many entrepreneurs have started successful businesses by providing time-starved homeowners with customized services such as housekeeping, lawn care, and home and computer repair. The small size of such a business allows it to cater to customers in ways that big companies find impossible.

As Figure 5.1 indicates, small businesses provide most jobs in the construction, agricultural services, wholesale trade, services, and retail trade industries. Retailing is another important industry for today's small businessperson. Merchandising giants such as Target and Wal-Mart may be the best-known retailing firms, but small, privately owned retail stores far outnumber them. Small-business retailing includes stores that sell shoes, jewelry, office supplies and stationery, clothing, flowers, drugs, convenience foods, and thousands of other products. People wishing to form their own business have always been attracted to retailing because of the ability to start a firm with limited funds, rent a store rather than build a facility, create a Web site, and use family members to staff the new business.

After working many years in the restaurant industry and producing Key Lime pies, Randy Essig decided the

Figure 5.1

Major Industries Dominated by Small Businesses

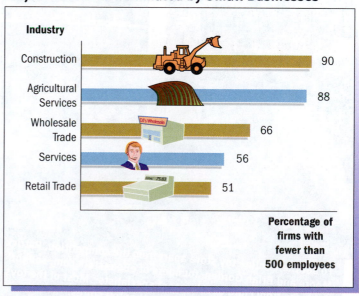

Industry

Construction	90
Agricultural Services	88
Wholesale Trade	66
Services	56
Retail Trade	51

Percentage of firms with fewer than 500 employees

Source: Office of Advocacy, U.S. Small Business Administration, "Small Business Profile: United States," accessed March 3, 2009, http://www.sba.gov/advo.

time was right for a relaxed, casual seafood restaurant and retail fish market, so he opened Randy's Fish Market Restaurant in Naples, Florida. Beside generous portions of fresh seafood, the restaurant features a counter where customers can buy fresh fish, shellfish, and many other dishes. The dessert feature is Randy's famous Key Lime Pie. Customers can purchase whole pies at the restaurant, and pies are also shipped throughout the continental United States. Randy's may not be the largest seafood retailer in Naples, let alone Florida, but many argue it is the best.[11]

Small business also plays a significant role in agriculture. Although most farm acreage is in the hands of large corporate farms, most U.S. farms are owned by individual farmers or families, not partners or shareholders.[12] The family farm is a classic example of a small-business operation. It is independently owned and operated, with relatively few employees, relying instead on the labor of family members. Today's small farmers must combine savvy business and marketing techniques to thrive, like the King family in Rankin County, Mississippi. Chuck King, along with brother Tony and their father Bernard, once owned the only cotton gin in the county, and the family's only crop was cotton. Barely breaking even, they began experimenting with corn. Now the Kings are out of cotton altogether and do all the work themselves on their 1,200-acre corn crop. With the biofuel boom, the decision is being replicated by other farmers across much of the south.[13]

Almost half of small businesses in the United States are **home-based businesses**—firms operated from the residence of the business owner.[14] Between 1960 and 1980, fewer people worked at home, largely because the number of farmers, doctors, and lawyers in home-based practices was declining. But since then, the number of people working at home has more than doubled. A recent study by research firm Access Markets International (AMI) Partners reported that the number of home-based businesses in the United States has grown to an all-time high of 16.5 million. The two major factors accounting for this growth were the freedom to run their own business and the desire to have more control over their personal time.[15] Another factor in this growth is the increased availability of personal computers with access to the Internet and other communications devices such as fax machines and cell phones.

To set their online toy store apart from the competition, Patrick Moore and Brian Gordon, founders of eBeanstalk.com, sought guidance from child development specialists. Most of the toys their Web site carries can't be found in other toy stores.

© eBeanstalk

Lower costs are another reason that the number of home-based businesses is growing so quickly. Financing a small business is a difficult challenge. Home-based business owners who can avoid leasing or maintaining separate office or warehouse space can pour precious funds into the business itself. When Andrew Morrison's direct-mail marketing company NIA Direct hit a snag a few years ago, he scaled back his business and went to work at home. The Brooklyn, New York, native had been featured on *The Oprah Winfrey Show,* in *The Wall Street Journal,* and in *Black Enterprise.* Starting out with less than $1,000 for equipment and office supplies, Morrison leveraged his experience by pursuing work as a direct marketing consultant to some of his former clients, such as Jazz at Lincoln Center, Grolier Books, and Columbia House Music. He says, "As soon as I started working at home, I realized a quality of life increase."[16]

Other benefits of a home-based business include greater flexibility and freedom from the time and expense of commuting. Drawbacks include isolation and less visibility to customers—except, of course, if your customers visit you online. In that case, they don't care where your office is located.

Many small-business start-ups are more competitive because of the Internet. An estimated three of every five small businesses have an online presence. But the Internet does not automatically guarantee success, as illustrated by the thousands of dot-com failures during the early years of e-business. Still, setting up a Web site can be relatively inexpensive and enables a business to reach a huge marketplace.

Norwalk, Connecticut–based eBeanstalk.com is an online toy store. Because a host of online toy sellers had gone broke in the 1990s, the odds of success did not favor founders Patrick Moore and Brian Gordon. To set their business apart from the competition, they sought help from a panel of child development specialists to select toys for their educational value. The toys they sell face the toughest test, a panel of 700 moms called the MotherBoard who receive free toys and test them for a year. The result is about 500 toys chosen from 10,000 original entries; 90 percent of them can't be found at retail stores. Gordon says his nine-person firm has seen its Web site traffic triple and should see revenues of $2 million for a year.[17]

American business history is filled with inspirational stories of great inventors who launched companies in barns, garages, warehouses, and attics. For young visionaries such as Apple Computer founders Steve Jobs and Steve Wozniak, the logical option for transforming their technical idea into a commercial reality was to begin work in a family garage. The impact of today's entrepreneurs, including home-based businesses, is discussed in more depth in Chapter 6.

Assessment Check ✓

1. What characteristics does the SBA use to determine whether a business is a small business?
2. Identify three industries in which small businesses are common.

Contributions of Small Business to the Economy

Small businesses form the core of the U.S. economy. Businesses with fewer than 500 employees generate more than half the nation's gross domestic product. Small firms represent 99.7 percent of all employer firms and pay more than 45 percent of the total U.S. private payroll. Over half of small firms are home-based, while 2 percent are franchises. In addition, small businesses employ almost half of the nation's private nonfarm workforce.[18]

Creating New Jobs

Small businesses make tremendous contributions to the U.S. economy and to society as a whole. One impressive contribution is the number of new jobs created each year by small businesses. While it varies from year to year, on average three of every four new jobs are created by companies with fewer than 500 employees.[19] A significant share of these jobs was created by the smallest companies, those with four or fewer employees. Small firms are dominant factors in many of the industries that have added the most jobs: construction trade contractors, wholesale trade, amusement and recreation, service businesses, restaurants, and engineering and management services.[20]

Even if you never plan to start your own business, you will probably work for a small business at some point in your career. Not only do small firms employ about half of all U.S. workers, but they are more likely than large firms to employ the youngest (and oldest) workers. In addition, as detailed in a later section of this chapter, small businesses offer significant opportunities to women and minorities.

"They Said It"

"You may not think you're going to make it. You may want to quit. But if you keep your eye on the ball, you can accomplish anything."

—*Hank Aaron* (b. 1934)
American baseball legend

Hit & Miss

Turning Technologies Creates High-Tech Jobs

Young companies that grow and add jobs to boost their local economies make a lot of people happy about their success. That's why so many people are smiling in Youngstown, Ohio, since a new technology company came to town.

Helped along by a business organization that provides start-up tech firms with free rent and utilities, Turning Technologies was founded in Youngstown a few years ago. Its breathtaking growth brought dozens of new jobs to a city with 18 percent unemployment that is haunted by the decline of its old steel mills. Turning pays corporate income taxes on more than $30 million annual revenue, and it has already been called the fastest growing privately held software company in the United States—ranked at 18th overall. The firm boasts more than 6,500 clients, and over a million people use its audience-response products.

Audience-response systems are the wireless keypads you've probably seen spectators using on TV game shows to register their opinions or answers to questions. Thanks to Turning's affordable hardware and the availability of both its free and licensed software programs, teachers from kindergarten through college are now enjoying the benefits of audience-response technology. Instructors can ask questions in class using other programs like PowerPoint, Blackboard, and WebCT; have students key in answers—anonymously or not—using their remotes; and instantly collate the responses to see how many students answered correctly. Government agencies and not-for-profit organizations also use the systems for their training programs.

"Audience involvement boosts focus and comprehension levels," says Turning's CEO Mike Broderick, and instructors agree. "It gives you the opportunity to reteach if you need to and then move on if you don't," says one middle-school teacher. Adds a school principal about applications of the Turning program, "We have some teachers that are working hard to find the many avenues they can go beyond. You're really only limited by your creativity."

And it gets better. "Not only can we identify how each student is responding," says Turning's vice president for education sales, but "we can compile that data by classroom, by building, and by district and tag the data to specific standards." Among the impressive results already confirmed is "an increase of 15 points in test scores when our technology is used frequently and effectively."

Most of Turning's 120 employees are young Ohioans who enjoy some of the same benefits as their Silicon Valley counterparts, such as in-house foosball and air hockey for work breaks. The firm takes pride in being the kind of success story people have long thought "doesn't happen here." It has had double- or triple-digit growth since its launch and anticipates 10 to 20 percent more growth in the next year. "I would not be surprised to see Turning Technologies at 2,000 workers in three to four years," says the CEO of the organization that helped the company get its start. That's music to Youngstown's ears. The bottom line? Good products that are affordable, easy to use, and well marketed can help small companies become engines of growth and job creators.

Questions for Critical Thinking

1. Why might a company such as Turning Technologies locate outside the high-tech hotspots where most firms are? List some possible advantages and disadvantages to that strategy.
2. What should a company like Turning Technologies do if, as it grows, it needs to hire people with technical experience or skills that are hard to find in a depressed area?

Sources: Company Web site, http://www.turningtechnologies.com, accessed February 18, 2009; "In Ohio, You Can Maintain Your Balance No Matter How Fast You Grow," *Ohio Means Business,* http://www.ohiomeansbusiness.com, accessed February 17, 2009; "Upside/Downside: Youngstown Business Incubator a Bright Spot in Region," *WCPN Ideastream* transcript, February 12, 2009, http://www.wcpn.org; Matt Sanctis, "Champaign Students Learning by Remote Control," *Springfield News-Sun,* February 8, 2009, http://www.springfieldnewssun.com; Angie Schmitt, "Turning Technologies Unveils New K–12 Programs and Services," *TMCNet,* January 23, 2009, http://www.tmcnet.com; "Hope Amid Gloom Tech Success," *Vindicator (Youngstown, OH),* February 12, 2008, http://www.vindy.com.

Small businesses also contribute to the economy by hiring workers who traditionally have had difficulty finding jobs at larger firms. Compared with large companies, small businesses are more likely to hire former welfare recipients.[21] Driven in part by their limited budgets, small businesses may be more open to locating in economically depressed areas, where they contribute to rehabilitating neighborhoods and reducing unemployment. For example, Turning Technologies in Youngstown, Ohio, a former steel mill city, hires local residents and attracts young, skilled workers, as discussed in the "Hit & Miss" feature.

Creating New Industries

The small-business sector also gives entrepreneurs an outlet for developing their ideas and perhaps for creating entirely new industries. Many of today's successful high-tech firms—Microsoft, Cisco Systems, Yahoo!, and Google—began as small businesses. The growth of new businesses and new industries not only provides new goods and services but also fuels local economies. New industries are sometimes created when small businesses adapt to provide needed services to the larger corporate community. Corporate downsizing has created a demand for other businesses to perform activities previously handled by company employees. For example, every time an iPhone owner activates service online at AT&T, Stephen Waldis gets a slice of the pie, about $8. His small New Jersey company, Synchronoss, sells the software that AT&T (iPhone's exclusive carrier) uses to register and activate the phone. Even better for Waldis, Apple mandated that the only way to activate the iPhone is through the Web.[22] Outsourcing such activities as security, maintenance, employee benefits management, and transportation services creates opportunities that are often filled by small businesses.

Finally, new industries can be created when small businesses adapt to shifts in consumer interests and preferences. Over the last few years, the explosion of wireless Internet access in schools, restaurants, airports, hotels, and cities—some of which are installing wireless access to be used by their residents—has created tremendous growth opportunities. Lifestyle changes can also lead to new opportunities. Many small businesses are offering personal assistant or "concierge" services to professionals, executives, working parents, and others who feel too busy or stressed to do errands or other time-consuming tasks easily done by someone else. Several Houston, Texas, firms, including Leigh Williams Lifestyle Management, Six Stars Club, All for You Concierge, and Pour Vous, will buy and deliver groceries or gifts, wait for the cable guy, run errands, make travel arrangements, buy tickets for sports events, and plan birthday parties.[23]

Innovation

Small businesses are much better than large businesses at developing new and better goods and services. Although the DVD rental market was dominated by Blockbuster Video, Reed Hastings knew that there just had to be a better way. Perhaps it was that $40 late fee he had to pay Blockbuster when he forgot to return *Apollo 13*, but Hastings recalls asking himself, "How come movie rentals don't work like a health club, where whether you use it a lot or a little, you get the same charge?" And from that question, Netflix.com, the first successful online DVD rental service, was born.

Today, after less than a decade in business, the Californian heads a company with more than 8.8 million subscribers, a DVD library of 90,000 titles, and revenue of more than $1.2 billion. DVDs are mailed to subscribers and returned in prepaid postage envelopes provided by Netflix. Because they can rent several movies at a time without late fees, Netflix customers rent twice as many movies per month. Netflix is so successful that Wal-Mart discontinued its DVD rental business, choosing instead to offer Netflix DVD rentals at Wal-Mart.com. Adams Media Research projects that the total market will have more than 20 million online subscribers in the next four to six years. Rated number one in online retail customer satisfaction and with 90 percent of surveyed customers saying they would recommend the service to a friend, Netflix has a bright future.[24]

Small businesses are often fertile ground in which to plant innovative ideas for new goods and services. While designing spacecraft for NASA and world-class mountain bikes for Santa Cruz and Mountain Cycle, Neal Saiki honed his engineering skills. He put them to use developing the world's highest-performing electric motorcycle, the Zero X. The result is 130 pounds of ultra-thin, precision-welded aluminum that can generate 17,000 watts of instant power and hit 60 miles per hour in about four seconds. If electric vehicles ever move into the mainstream, industry experts believe it will begin with motorcycles. Saiki's company, Zero Motorcycles, has sold out the first production run of the Zero X, priced at $7,500.[25]

"They Said It"

"When big businesses want to innovate, what do they do? They take a bunch of guys, throw them out, and let them create a small business."

—*Zach Nelson* (b. 1971) *President and CEO, NetSuite*

In a typical year, small firms develop twice as many product innovations per employee as larger firms. They also produce 13 times more patents per employee than large patenting firms. In addition, the fact that small firms are a richer source of innovations is even more evident than these statistics show because large firms are more likely to patent their discoveries.[26] Key 20th-century innovations that were developed by small businesses include the airplane, the audiotape recorder, double-knit fabrics, the optical scanner, the personal computer, soft contact lenses, and the zipper. One area of innovation that is occupying small businesses during the 21st century is security—whether it's the protection of information or people.

Why Small Businesses Fail

While small businesses benefit the economy by creating new jobs, new industries, and various innovations, small businesses are much more likely to fail than large businesses, especially during economic downturns. Why? Because of management shortcomings, inadequate financing, and difficulty dealing with government regulations. These issues—quality and depth of management, availability of financing, and ability to wade through government rules and requirements—are so important that small businesses with major deficiencies in one or more of these areas may find themselves in bankruptcy proceedings.

As Figure 5.2 shows, almost one new business in three will permanently close within two years of opening, half will close within four years, and 62 percent will fail within the first six years of operation. By the tenth year, 82 of every 100 businesses will have failed. Although highly motivated and well-trained business owner–managers can overcome these potential problems, they should thoroughly analyze whether one or more of these problems may threaten the business before deciding to launch the new company.

Management Shortcomings

Among the most common causes of a small-business failure is inadequate management. Business founders often possess great strengths in specific areas such as marketing or interpersonal relations, but they may suffer from hopeless deficiencies in others such as finance or order fulfillment. Large firms recruit specialists trained to manage individual functions; small businesses frequently rely on small staffs who must be adept at a variety of skills. Owners of small service businesses find that they must concentrate on their most profitable customers and even "fire" customers

Figure 5.2   **Rate of Business Failures**

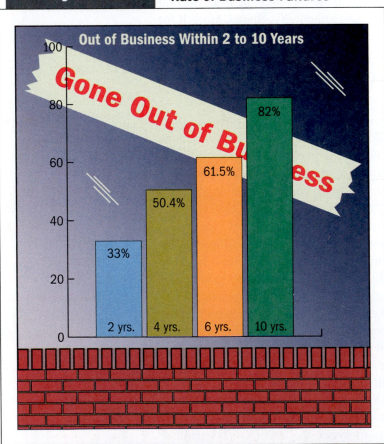

Out of Business Within 2 to 10 Years

Gone Out of Business

33%	50.4%	61.5%	82%
2 yrs.	4 yrs.	6 yrs.	10 yrs.

Source: Office of Advocacy, U.S. Small Business Administration, "Frequently Asked Questions: Advocacy Small Business Statistics and Research," accessed March 2009, http://app1.sba.gov/ faqs.

who don't contribute to the bottom line, as the "Business Etiquette" feature discusses.

An even worse result occurs when people go into business with little, if any, business training. Some new businesses are begun almost entirely on the basis of what seems like a great idea for a new product. Managers assume that they will acquire needed business expertise on the job. All too often, the result is business bankruptcy.

If you are contemplating starting a new business, consider the following warnings. First, learn the basics of business. Second, recognize your own limitations. Although most small-business owners recognize the need to seek out the specialized skills of accountants and attorneys for financial and legal assistance, they often hesitate to turn to consultants and advisors for assistance in areas such as marketing, where they may lack knowledge or experience.

Founders of new businesses are typically excited about the potential of newly designed products, so they may neglect important details such as marketing research to determine whether potential customers share their excitement. Individuals considering launching a new business should first determine whether the proposed product meets the needs of a large enough market and whether they can convince the public of its superiority over competing offerings.

Inadequate Financing

Another leading cause of small-business problems is inadequate financing. First-time business owners often assume that their firms will generate enough funds from the first month's sales to finance continuing operations. Building a business takes time, though. Employees must be trained, equipment purchased, deposits paid for rent and utilities, and marketing dollars spent to inform potential customers about the new firm and its product offerings. Even a one-person, home-based business has start-up expenses—such as a new computer or additional phone lines. Unless the owner has set aside enough funds to cover cash shortfalls during the first several months while the business is being established, the venture may collapse at an early stage.

After surviving the cash crunch that often accompanies the first months of operation, a business must confront another major financial problem: uneven cash flows. For most small and large businesses, cash inflows and outflows fluctuate greatly at different times of the year.

Business Etiquette

WHEN AND HOW TO TELL A CLIENT, "YOU'RE FIRED!"

When starting out, small business owners offering accounting and tax preparation, investment management, advertising, public relations, Internet strategy, and other services usually take any and all customers they can get. Clients are valuable for their both their business and their referrals. Once established, however, small companies need to evaluate their customers regularly to see who is worth keeping. Clients can reduce a small company's profits and make owners crazy when they continually monopolize employee time, pay their bills late, make unreasonable demands, or treat employees with disrespect. Here are some tips for when the customer is *not* right.

1. Be objective in assessing clients. Do the math to figure out what each client contributes to the bottom line. Don't rush to dump a profitable client just because you don't like them. And don't let a client go if it will hurt your business.

2. When a client is not adding to profits, first try to improve the situation. Would clearer communication with the client help? Does the client need to pay more for the number of hours needed to serve the account? Does the client need to be better organized, provide more information, meet deadlines, pay sooner? Write new guidelines for the account, with additional fees for late payments or extra time, work or materials, then meet with the client to present the plan.

3. Let the client go if you cannot agree on new terms for the account. Suggest another company that may be better suited for this customer and provide contact information.

4. If personality conflict is clouding the relationship with the client, try assigning a different employee to be the main contact with this client.

5. Fire a client who is unreasonable, demeaning, or abusive to you or your employees. Have a candid, face-to-face meeting. Practice what you will say beforehand. Tell your client you can see that your services are no longer meeting his needs. Stay calm and professional. Dealing with undesirable clients can be difficult and emotional. Even if you deliver the message in a diplomatic way, the client may become angry. Don't be surprised if the client says he fires you!

Sources: "Letting Customers Go," National Federation of Independent Business, September 12, 2007, http://www.nfib.com, accessed March 3, 2009; Mark Koziel, "Letting Go: Evaluating and Firing Clients," *Journal of Accountancy*, January 2008, pp. 54–58; Amy Barrett, "When, Why, and How to Fire That Customer," *BusinessWeek SmallBiz*, October/November 2007, pp. 42–48.

Small retail outlets generate much of their annual sales revenues during the December holiday period. Florists make most of their deliveries during two holidays: Valentine's Day and Mother's Day. Large firms may build sufficient cash reserves to weather periods of below-average sales, or they can turn to banks and other lenders for short-term loans. By contrast, small business start-ups often lack both cash reserves and access to sources of additional funds.

Another reason that small businesses are inadequately financed is that they rely less on debt for financing than large businesses do; 47 percent of small businesses have no outstanding loans at all, and another 25 percent have just one loan to pay off.[27] But when small firms need loans, the most frequent source of funding, as shown in Figure 5.3, is trade credit, that is, buying goods and agreeing to pay for them later, usually within 30 to 60 days. The next most commonly used sources of financing are personal credit cards, loans from commercial banks, business credit cards, lines of credit from a bank, motor vehicle loans, owner loans in which the owner lends the business money, and then mortgage loans. Figure 5.3 shows that despite their relatively high interest rates, credit cards are an important source of financing for small businesses. The heaviest users of credit cards for business financing are tiny firms with fewer than ten employees.

Figure 5.3 — Sources of Small-Business Financing

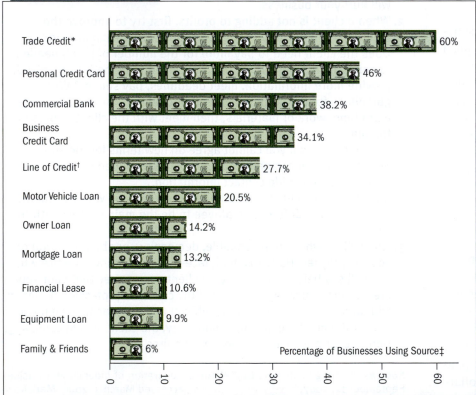

Source	Percentage
Trade Credit*	60%
Personal Credit Card	46%
Commercial Bank	38.2%
Business Credit Card	34.1%
Line of Credit†	27.7%
Motor Vehicle Loan	20.5%
Owner Loan	14.2%
Mortgage Loan	13.2%
Financial Lease	10.6%
Equipment Loan	9.9%
Family & Friends	6%

Percentage of Businesses Using Source‡

*Trade credit is purchasing goods or equipment from a supplier who finances the purchase by delaying the date of payment for those goods.

†A line of credit is an agreement between a bank and a borrower, indicating the maximum amount of credit the bank will extend to the borrower.

Note: Total exceeds 100 percent because businesses typically use more than one source of financing.

Source: Small Business Administration, Office of Advocacy, "Financing Patterns of Small Firms," accessed March 3, 2009, http://www.sba.gov/advo; Susan Coleman, "Free and Costly Trade Credit: A Comparison of Small Firms," Academy of Entrepreneurial Finance, February 2008, www.google.com, accessed March 3, 2009.

Inadequate financing can compound management shortcomings by making it more difficult for small businesses to attract and keep talented people. Typically, a big company can offer a more attractive benefits package and a higher salary. During the wave of dot-com start-ups, many people decided to take a chance and work for these companies, which often offered stock options—the right to buy stock in a firm at a lower price—in place of higher salaries or better benefits. If a company succeeded, its employees could become rich. If it failed, its workers were left not only without profits but often without jobs.

With less money to spend on employees, successful small companies need to be more creative. When J. C. Converse drew up plans for a Laguna Niguel, California, restaurant that would be built of recycled materials and serve quail tacos, buffalo meat, and other organic food, he needed money. Converse, who spent 35 years in the restaurant business, put up $250,000 of his own money and had about $200,000 in home equity to use as collateral. Nonetheless, four banks turned down his request for a $500,000 Small Business Administration loan. According to a survey by Discover Small Business Watch, about 30 percent of small business owners have used a home equity loan, line of credit, or second mortgage to help finance their business.[28]

Government Regulation

Small-business owners often complain bitterly about excessive government regulation and red tape. Paperwork costs alone account for billions of small-business dollars each year. A large company can better cope with requirements for forms and reports. Larger firms often find that it makes economic sense to hire or contract with specialists in specific types of regulation, such as employment law and workplace safety regulations. By contrast, small businesses often struggle to absorb the costs of government paperwork because of their more limited staff and budgets. Some small firms close for this reason alone. Other regulations also result in increased costs that small businesses find more burdensome than larger entities do. When cities ban the use of disposable plastic shopping bags to benefit the environment, for example, it means higher costs for stores, as the "Solving an Ethical Controversy" feature discusses.

Recognizing the burden of regulation on small businesses, Congress sometimes exempts the smallest companies from certain regulations. For example, small businesses with 49 or fewer employees are exempt from the Family and Medical Leave Act, which gives employees up to 12 weeks of unpaid leave each year to take care of a newborn child, adopt a child, or care for a family member who has serious health problems.[29] Most small-business owners comply with employment and other laws, believing that such compliance is ethically correct and fosters better employee relations than trying to determine which regulations don't apply to a small business. To help small businesses obey employment laws, the U.S. Department of Labor provides forms and guidelines at its "elaws Advisors" Web page (http://www. dol.gov/elaws/). Employers can also file these forms online.

Taxes arc another burdensome expense for a small business. In addition to local, state, and federal income taxes, employers must pay taxes covering workers' compensation insurance, Social Security payments, and unemployment benefits. Although large companies have similar expenses, they generally have more resources to cover them.

Assessment Check ✔

1. What percentage of small businesses will still be in business two, four, six, and ten years after starting?
2. How do management shortcomings, inadequate financing, and government regulation make small businesses more likely to fail?

Increasing the Likelihood of Small-Business Success

In spite of the challenges just discussed, many small businesses do succeed. How can a prospective owner gain the many advantages of running a smaller firm while also overcoming the disadvantages? Most successful entrepreneurs believe that two recommendations are critical:

- Develop a business plan.
- Use the resources provided by such agencies as the Small Business Administration, local business incubators, and other sources for advice, funding, and networking opportunities.

Creating a Business Plan

Perhaps the most important task a would-be business owner faces is creating a business plan. An effective business plan can mean the difference between a company that succeeds and one that fails. A **business plan** is a written document that provides an orderly statement of a company's

business plan written document that provides an orderly statement of a company's goals, the methods by which it intends to achieve those goals, and the standards by which it will measure achievements.

PAPER, NOT PLASTIC?

Buying groceries, clothes, books, take-out food, snacks, and many other items usually means leaving the store with one or several plastic bags. While they're inexpensive and convenient for both stores and customers, plastic bags carry their own baggage—environmental harm.

Shoppers like plastic bags because they're lightweight, durable, sanitary, and easy to carry. Store owners like the convenience and the price—two or three cents per bag compared with five for paper. The bags are made from fossil fuel-based polymers, with about 430,000 gallons of oil needed to produce 100 million bags, and are virtually indestructible. Environmentalists estimate that from 4 to 5 trillion nondegradable plastic bags are used worldwide each year. Some are reused or recycled, but many litter roadsides, get into waterways and endanger animals, or end up in landfills.

Some large grocery chains have voluntarily stopped using plastic bags. Small independent groceries, restaurants, and other stores, however, find it harder to pay the higher costs. Several U.S. cities and towns have adopted or are considering bans on disposable plastic bags or fees for their use. San Francisco, the first U.S. city to ban the bags, requires grocery stores with $2 million or more in annual sales to provide reusable cloth or thick plastic bags, recyclable paper bags, or biodegradable cornstarch bags, which all cost more than thin plastic ones. Such bans may be extended to all businesses.

Should laws require small businesses to stop using plastic shopping bags, regardless of added cost or inconvenience?

PRO

1. Eliminating thin plastic bags reduces waste disposal costs for small businesses, slows the need for new landfills, decreases litter and pollution, and reduces petroleum needs.
2. Businesses are developing feasible alternatives to disposable bags; consumers will adapt to buying and reusing bags.

CON

1. Banning plastic bags decreases recycling efforts and increases costs for consumers and retailers, costs that small business owners cannot easily absorb.
2. The environment will be harmed more by using more paper bags. Production and transportation requires more trees, electricity, and water and causes increased air emissions and water pollution.

Summary

The plastic industry and numerous retail groups say they want customers to have the choice of paper, plastic, and reusable bags. Consumers often reuse plastic bags for household jobs such as lining trash cans or picking up after pets. Many grocers say the majority of their shoppers ask for plastic. "Plastic bags are very convenient, and we think folks do like the ease of them and the size," said a spokesman for a retailers association of 3,000 pharmacies, convenience stores, and independent grocers. Some business groups view plastic bag bans as misdirected efforts that detract from greater environmental issues. Grocers and other small businesses often share the public's concern about litter; many have recycling programs, use paper bags and containers, and sell canvas or recycled plastic bags, which they encourage shoppers to use.

Sources: David Gorn, "San Francisco Plastic Bag Ban Interests Other Cities," National Public Radio, March 27, 2008, http://www.npr.org, accessed March 3, 2009; "Bans Turning 'Paper or Plastic' into a Debate," MSNBC, January 22, 2008, http://msnbc.msn.com, accessed March 3, 2009; Paul Eakins, "Plastic, Styrofoam Could Be on Their Way Out in L.B.," October 30, 2007, accessed October 1, 2008, at www.google.com; Matt Viser, "Plastic Bags May Be Banned in Boston," *The Boston Globe,* April 26, 2007, http://www.boston.com, accessed October 1, 2008.

Solving an ETHICAL controversy

goals, the methods by which it intends to achieve these goals, and the standards by which it will measure achievements.

Business plans give the organization a sense of purpose. They provide guidance, influence, and leadership, as well as communicate ideas about goals and the means of achieving them to associates, employees, lenders, and others. In addition, they set standards against which achievements can be measured. Although no single format best suits all situations, a good small-business plan includes the methods and time frames for achieving specific goals (sales, profits, or changes in market share), as well as cash flow projections (both income received by the business and funds disbursed to pay expenses). Because business plans are essential tools for securing funding, the financial section should be thorough, professional, and based on sound assumptions. A business plan also includes the following components:

- an *executive summary* that briefly answers the who, what, why, when, where, and how questions for the business

- an *introduction* that includes a general statement of the concept, purpose, and objectives of the proposed business

- separate *financial* and *marketing sections* that describe the firm's target market and marketing plan as well as detailed financial forecasts of the need for funds and when the firm is expected to break even—the level of sales at which revenues equal costs

- *résumés of principals*—especially in plans written to obtain financing.

Business plans are discussed in more detail in Appendix D, "Developing a Business Plan."

Small Business Administration

Small businesses can benefit from using the resources provided by the ==Small Business Administration (SBA).== The SBA is the principal government agency concerned with helping small U.S. firms, and it is the advocate for small businesses within the federal government. More than 2,100 employees staff the SBA's Washington headquarters and its regional and field offices.[30] The primary operating functions of the SBA include providing financial assistance, aiding in government procurement matters, and providing management training and consulting. The agency is rewriting standard operating procedures for the loan program to improve customer service. Says the SBA administrator, "We're a service organization; employees are the most important component of delivering that service."[31]

FINANCIAL ASSISTANCE FROM THE SBA
Contrary to popular belief, the SBA seldom provides direct business loans. Its major financing contributions are the guarantees it provides for small-business loans made by private lenders, including banks and other institutions. Direct SBA loans are available in only a few special situations, such as natural disaster recovery and energy conservation or development programs. For example, the SBA has offered small businesses disaster loans up to $1.5 million to repair or replace damaged buildings, equipment, inventory, and supplies as rebuilding continues in New Orleans and the coastal regions of Louisiana, Mississippi, and Alabama following Hurricane Katrina.[32] Even in these special instances, a business applicant must contribute a portion of the proposed project's total cost in cash, home equity, or stocks to qualify.

Small Business Administration (SBA) federal agency that aids small businesses by providing management training and consulting, financial assistance, and support in securing government contracts.

A resident walks next to a house damaged by Hurricane Ike in Galveston, Texas. To assist homeowners and businesses, the Small Business Administration offers disaster loans.

© Carlos Barria/Landov LLC.

The SBA also guarantees **microloans** of up to $35,000 to start-ups and other very small firms. The average loan is $13,000 with a maximum term of six years.[33] Microloans may be used to buy equipment or operate a business but not to buy real estate or pay off other loans. These loans are available from nonprofit organizations located in most states. Other sources of microloans include the federal Economic Development Administration, some state governments, and certain private lenders, such as credit unions and community development groups. The most frequent suppliers of credit to small firms are banks.[34]

Small-business loans are also available through SBA-licensed organizations called **Small Business Investment Companies (SBICs),** which are run by experienced venture capitalists. SBICs use their own capital, supplemented with government loans, to invest in small businesses. Like banks, SBICs are profit-making enterprises, but they are likely to be more flexible than banks in their lending decisions. Well-known companies that used SBIC financing when they were start-ups include Apple, Callaway Golf, America Online, Federal Express, Intel, Staples, and Outback Steakhouse.

Another financial resource underwritten by the SBA is *Active Capital,* which matches entrepreneurs looking for start-up capital with potential investors willing to exchange their money and advice for partial ownership of the company. Entrepreneurs post information about their businesses on the Active Capital Web site, where potential investors can review it. Interested parties contact the firms. The goal is to help businesses seeking smaller amounts of capital than those typically handled by bigger investment firms. Small businesses can raise up to $5 million via Active Capital; amounts over $1 million, however, require filing with the Securities and Exchange Commission (SEC). Why use Active Capital? Because, as a nonprofit organization sanctioned by the SBA, Active Capital only charges $199 for a six-month membership, but no commissions, which makes it a cheap, safe, and secure way for entrepreneurs and investors to exchange information and do business.[35]

OTHER SPECIALIZED ASSISTANCE Although government purchases represent a huge market, small companies have difficulty competing for this business with giant firms, which employ specialists to handle the volumes of paperwork involved in preparing proposals and completing bid applications. Today, many government procurement programs set aside portions of government spending for small companies; an additional SBA role is to help small firms secure these contracts. With **set-aside programs** for small businesses, up to 23 percent of certain government contracts are designated for small businesses—with 5 percent to women-owned businesses, 3 percent to service disabled veterans, and 5 percent to small disadvantaged businesses.[36] Every federal agency with buying authority must maintain an Office of Small and Disadvantaged Business Utilization to ensure that small businesses receive a reasonable portion of government procurement contracts. To help connect small businesses with government agencies, the SBA's Web site offers Central Contractor Registration, which includes a search engine for finding business opportunities as well as a chance for small businesses to provide information about themselves.[37] Set-aside programs are also common in the private sector, particularly among major corporations.

In addition to help with financing and government procurement, the SBA delivers a variety of other services to small businesses. It provides information and advice through toll-free telephone numbers and its Web site, http://www.sba.gov, where you can find detailed information about starting, financing, and managing a small business, along with further information about business opportunities and disaster recovery. Finally, through its Small Business Training Network, the SBA offers free online courses; sponsors inexpensive training courses on topics such as taxes, networking, and start-ups in cities and small towns throughout the country; and provides a free online library of more than 200 SBA publications and additional business resources.

Business Incubators

Some local community agencies interested in encouraging business development have implemented a concept called a **business incubator** to provide low-cost shared business facilities to small start-up ventures. A typical incubator might section off space in an abandoned plant and rent it to various small firms. Tenants often share clerical staff, computers, and other business services. The objective is that, after a few months or years, the fledgling business will be ready to move out and operate on its own.

Over a thousand business incubator programs operate nationwide. The vast majority, 94 percent, are run by not-for-profit organizations focused on economic development. More than half of these programs are operated in urban areas, while about 20 percent of them are sponsored by academic institutions.[38] The University of Tennessee, for example, has opened a $2.5 million 15,000-square-foot business incubator to support high-tech companies throughout the Knoxville–Oak Ridge Innovation Valley. The incubator is part of a movement throughout the 16-county area to commercialize new ideas from the University of Tennessee and Oak Ridge National Laboratory, as well as many spin-off companies.[39] These facilities offer management support services and valuable management advice from in-house mentors. Operating in an incubator gives entrepreneurs easy access to such basic needs as telephones and human resource experts. They also can trade ideas with one another.

> **business incubator**
> organization that provides temporary low-cost, shared facilities to small start-up ventures.

Small-Business Opportunities for Women and Minorities

The thousands of new business start-ups each year include growing numbers of women-owned firms as well as new businesses launched by African Americans, Hispanics, and members of other minority groups. The numbers of women-owned and minority-owned businesses are growing much faster than the overall growth in U.S. businesses. The people who start these companies see small-business ownership and operation as an attractive and lucrative alternative to working for someone else.

WOMEN-OWNED BUSINESSES In the United States today, about 10.4 million woman-owned firms provide jobs for 12.8 million people and generate $1.9 trillion in sales. More than 50 percent of U.S. businesses are owned by women; about one of every four of these businesses is owned by a minority woman. Firms owned by women of color are growing at five times the rate of all U.S. firms.[40]

Women, like men, have a variety of reasons for starting their own companies. Some have a unique business idea that they want to bring to life. Others decide to strike out on their own when they lose their jobs or become frustrated with the bureaucracies in large companies. In other cases, women leave large corporations when they feel blocked from opportunities for advancement. Sometimes this occurs because they hit the so-called glass ceiling. Because women are more likely than men to be the primary caregivers in their families, some may seek self-employment as a way to achieve flexible working hours so they can spend more time with their families.

An elite group of corporate achievers, like African American business woman Myrtle Potter, leave corporate America simply to do it their way. That means starting a company and running it the way they want to run a company. Potter, former president of commercial operations at Genentech, cofounded San Jose, California–based Chapman Development Group, a 20-person company that provides high-quality, affordable housing. The firm handles nearly all

> ## "They Said It"
> "Whatever women do, they must do twice as well as men to be thought half as good. Luckily, this is not difficult."
> —*Charlotte Whitton (1896–1975) Mayor of Ottawa*

aspects of the business such as purchasing land, managing construction, and even providing mortgage brokerage services. Potter joins a growing group of high-powered women leaving corporate America to start their own business.[41]

The fastest growth among women-owned firms is occurring in wholesale trade; health-care and social assistance; arts, entertainment, and recreation; and professional, scientific, and technical services.[42] One woman who has chartered her own course is Margaret Wallace, a luminary in the videogame industry. She co-founded Skunk Studios, developer of videogames with no violent scenes. Gutterball2, a cartoon bowling game with alleys set in jungles in the Arctic is the most popular title. She is most recently the co-founder and CEO of Rebel Monkey, a company that hopes to pioneer virtual concepts, carrying casual videogames into the future.[43]

As the number of female small-business owners has grown, they have also been able to establish powerful support networks in a relatively short time. Many nationwide business assistance programs serve women exclusively. Among the programs offered by the Small Business Administration are the Contract Assistance for Women Business Owners program, which teaches women how to market to the federal government; the Women's Network for Entrepreneurial Training, which matches experienced female entrepreneurs with women trying to get started; and dozens of Women's Business Centers, which offer training and counseling in operating a business.

Springboard Enterprise is a nonprofit organization based in Washington, D.C., dedicated to accelerating women's access to capital. The organization's target market is women entrepreneurs who lead high-growth-potential enterprises. Springboard produces programs that educate and support women as they seek capital and grow their companies.[44] In addition, women can find encouragement, advice, and mentors by joining organizations such as Women Entrepreneurs and the Forum for Women Entrepreneurs and Executives, both of which support women who want to start high-growth companies.

MINORITY-OWNED BUSINESSES Business ownership is also an important opportunity for America's racial and ethnic minorities. In recent years, the growth in the number of businesses owned by African Americans, Hispanics, and Asian Americans has far outpaced the growth in the number of U.S. businesses overall. Figure 5.4 shows the percentages of minority ownership in major industries. The relatively strong presence of minorities in the services and retail industries is especially significant because these industries contain the greatest number of businesses.

Hispanics are the nation's largest group of minority business owners, followed by African American, Asian American, and Native American owners.[45] Hispanic firms are growing at three times the national average for all businesses in the United States, fueled by the energy, influence, and entrepreneurial spirit of the Hispanic business community.[46] Even more growth lies ahead for Hispanic-owned businesses during this decade, especially as trade between the United States and Latin America increases under NAFTA and CAFTA-DR (see Chapter 4 for more information on NAFTA and CAFTA-DR).

Despite their progress, minority business owners still face considerable obstacles. Minority entrepreneurs tend to start businesses on a smaller scale and have more difficulty finding investors than other entrepreneurs. They rely less on bank credit than do other business owners, possibly because they have a harder time getting loans from banks. According to Frank Robinson, vice president of the $52 billion Union Bank of California, "Access to capital is the number one issue facing minority-owned businesses." Some banks have begun reaching out to the minority business community. Lynn Ozer is in charge of government lending at Susquehanna Patriot Bank, headquartered in Mt. Laurel, New Jersey. He has built a relationship with the Enterprise Center, an organization devoted to business formulation and entrepreneurial development for

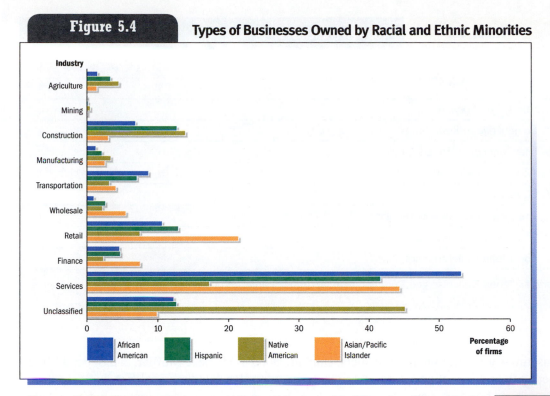

Figure 5.4 Types of Businesses Owned by Racial and Ethnic Minorities

Industry: Agriculture, Mining, Construction, Manufacturing, Transportation, Wholesale, Retail, Finance, Services, Unclassified

Percentage of firms

African American | Hispanic | Native American | Asian/Pacific Islander

Source: Data from Office of Advocacy, U.S. Small Business Administration, "Minorities in Business," accessed March 3, 2009, http://www.sba.gov/advo.

Assessment Check ✔

1. What components should be part of a good business plan?
2. What are the various ways and methods by which the SBA helps small businesses with financing and getting government contracts?

minorities. Five banks in and around Philadelphia are trying to reduce the disparities in minority lending by forging relationships between the banking community and the minority business community. Many other banks throughout the United States are taking similar actions to increase lending and outreach to minority-owned business.[47]

The Franchising Alternative

Franchising is a major factor in the growth of small businesses. **Franchising** is a contractual business arrangement between a manufacturer or another supplier and a dealer. The contract specifies the methods by which the dealer markets the good or service of the supplier. Franchises can involve both goods and services; the top ten franchises are shown in Table 5.2.

Starting a small, independent company can be a risky, time-consuming endeavor, but franchising can reduce the amount of time and effort needed to expand. The franchisor has already developed and tested the concept, and the brand may already be familiar to prospective customers.

franchising contractual agreement that specifies the methods by which a dealer can produce and market a supplier's good or service.

The Franchising Sector

Franchising started just after the U.S. Civil War, when the Singer Company decided to build its business by franchising retail sewing machine outlets. The concept became increasingly popular after 1900 in the automobile industry. Automobile travel led to demand for local auto sales and service outlets, as well as gasoline, oil, and tire retailers. Auto manufacturers created systems of franchised distributors and then set up local retailers in each retail location—auto dealers, gas

Table 5.2	Top Ten Franchises
1. Subway	
2. McDonald's	
3. Liberty Tax Service	
4. Sonic Drive In Restaurants	
5. InterContinental Hotels Group	
6. Ace Hardware Corp.	
7. Pizza Hut	
8. The UPS Store/Mail Boxes, Etc.	
9. Circle K convenience stores	
10. Papa John's International, Inc.	

Source: "2009 Franchise 500," *Entrepreneur,* accessed March 3, 2009, http://www.entrepreneur com.

stations, tire stores, and auto parts retailers. Dunkin' Donuts, Meineke Muffler, and Super 8 Motels also set up their distribution systems through a network of local and regional franchises.

Franchised businesses are a large part of the U.S. economy, accounting for nearly 50 percent of all retail sales. The International Franchise Association reported that franchising is responsible for 760,000 businesses, 18 million jobs, and more than $500 billion in payroll. Total sales by franchises continue to grow and approach $2 trillion. A new franchise is opened every eight minutes every business day; 1 out of 12 businesses in America is a franchise.[48] Jacques Lapointe founded Jan-Pro in 1991 in Providence, Rhode Island, and started franchising the following year. Jan-Pro is a commercial cleaning franchise operating throughout the United States and Canada. With 6,409 U.S. franchises and 609 Canadian franchises, Jan-Pro tops the *Entrepreneur* list of fastest-growing franchises.[49] The top franchise sectors for the next two decades are projected to be home senior care and home healthcare supplies, health food, home improvement, Internet technology, and restaurants.[50]

Franchising overseas is also a growing trend for franchisors and franchisees who want to expand into foreign markets. It seems that anywhere you go in the world, you can get a McDonald's burger. But other international franchises, such as Best Western, Pak Mail, Pizza Hut, KFC, Subway, and 7-Eleven, are almost as common.

Some people get into franchising because they can operate their business from home, another continuing trend. Examples of these franchises include ServiceMaster Clean, Chem-Dry Carpet Drapery & Upholstery Cleaning, Snap-On Tools, and Lawn Doctor.

Franchising Agreements

The two principals in a franchising agreement are the franchisee and the franchisor. The individual or business firm purchasing the franchise is called the **franchisee,** while the small-business owner who contracts to sell the good or service of the supplier is called the **franchisor.** In exchange for some payment (usually a fee plus a percentage of franchise sales) from the franchisee, the franchisor typically provides building plans, site selection help, managerial and accounting systems, and other services to assist the franchisee. Franchisees' total costs can vary over a wide range. The initial fee paid by a franchisee to McDonald's for a new McDonald's franchise is $45,000, but the total start-up costs can run anywhere from $506,000 to $1.6 million. In contrast, the initial fee for a Subway franchise is $15,000, while the total start-up costs range from $76,100 to $227,800.[51] The franchisor also provides name recognition for the small-business owner who becomes a franchisee. This public image is created by their familiarity with the franchise in other geographical areas and by advertising campaigns—all or part of which is paid for by contributions by the franchisees.

Franchise agreements often specify that the franchisee will receive materials, equipment, and training from the franchisor. Gail and Dave Liniger founded RE/MAX Intl Inc. in Denver in 1973 to give real estate agents higher commissions. Today RE/MAX is not only a global network of more than 116,000 real estate agents and one of the top ten franchises, it is the lowest-cost franchise. The franchise fee ranges from $12,500 to $25,000, while the total investment is $35,000 to $191,100. In spite of the low cost, RE/MAX provides training and support to franchisors, including five days of training at headquarters, semiannual conventions, a newsletter, toll-free phone line, Internet, grand-opening assistance, and field operations support. Marketing support includes national media, regional advertising, and brochures and videos.[52]

Benefits and Problems of Franchising

As with any other business, a franchise purchaser bears the responsibility for researching what he or she is buying. Poorly financed or poorly managed franchise systems offer opportunities no better than those in poorly financed or poorly managed independent businesses. Although franchises are more likely than independent businesses to succeed, many franchises do go out of business. The franchising concept does not eliminate the risks of a potential small-business investment; it simply adds alternatives.

Advantages of franchises include a prior performance record, a recognizable company name, a business model that has proven successful in other locations, a tested management program, and business training for the franchisee. An existing franchise has posted a performance record on which the prospective buyer can base comparisons and judgments. Earlier results can indicate the likelihood of success in a proposed venture. In addition, a widely recognized name gives the franchisee a tremendous advantage; auto dealers, for instance, know that their brand-name products will attract particular segments of the market. For example, a person owning a Super 8 franchise will benefit greatly from the relationship Roseanne Zusman, vice president of marketing, has established with NASCAR. The franchise sponsors the Petty Enterprises race team, hosts a Web site aimed at the race car crowd, runs print ads in *NASCAR Scene* and *NASCAR Illustrated,* and displays the Super 8 logo prominently near the race car door. And because 36 percent of Super 8 customers consider themselves NASCAR fans, the NASCAR audience is a great target. Franchisee Amit Govindji says, "It absolutely makes a difference. NASCAR fans are very loyal to their brands and their drivers and their logos on those cars.... They connect with Super 8 as a sponsor of the cars."[53]

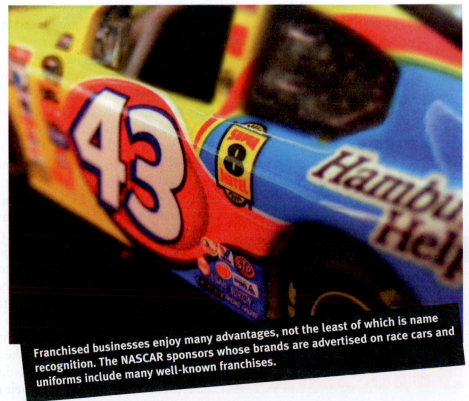

Franchised businesses enjoy many advantages, not the least of which is name recognition. The NASCAR sponsors whose brands are advertised on race cars and uniforms include many well-known franchises.

© R. Alcorn, photographed for John Wiley & Sons

A tested management program usually allows the prospective franchisee to avoid worrying about setting up an accounting system, establishing quality-control standards, or designing employment application forms. In addition, most franchisors offer valuable business training. McDonald's teaches the basics of operating a franchise at its Hamburger University, an 80-acre campus at its headquarters in Oak Brook, Illinois. Franchise operators quickly learn to meet customer expectations by following strict guidelines for how many seconds to cook the french fries and what words to use when serving customers. By following the franchisor's standards and building on an existing brand name, franchise operators typically can generate profits faster than an independent business owner.[54]

Ernie Lederer purchased a PIP Printing Document Services franchise after spending two decades in corporate America. The telecommunications executive had no printing experience but liked the idea of owning a ten-employee shop. At the advice of the franchisor, Lederer hired a new salesperson and added a digital printer to boost color power and data capabilities. Within the first four months, the new printer was running full time, attracting new business, and revenues exceeded Lederer's expectations.[55]

On the negative side, franchise fees and future payments can be very expensive. As with any business, a franchise may well be unprofitable during its first months and at times thereafter. Payments to the franchisor can add to the burden of keeping the business afloat until the owner begins to earn a profit.

Another potential drawback stems from the fact that the franchisee is linked to the reputation and management of the franchise. If customers are unhappy with their experience at one franchised sandwich shop, they might avoid stopping at another one several miles away, even if the second one is owned and operated by someone else. Thus, a strong, effective program of managerial control is essential to maintain a franchise brand's effectiveness. Before signing on with a franchisor, potential franchisees should carefully study its financial performance and reputation and talk with current franchise owners. Sources of information include the franchisor as well as state consumer protection agencies, the Better Business Bureau, and the Federal Trade Commission. The FTC's Web site includes advice for franchisees and reports of complaints against franchisors. Potential franchisees also should study the franchise agreement carefully to make sure they can succeed within the limitations of the agreement. In some instances, franchisors pursue additional sales by establishing new distribution outlets, which may compete directly with established franchisees. In today's online business environment, it is important to ask whether the franchisor retains the right to sell the same products online that the franchisee is trying to sell through a local outlet.

Some franchisees have found the franchising agreement to be overly restrictive. As the saying goes, you can't add a tuna salad sandwich to the menu at McDonald's no matter how many stores you own. The agreements are usually fairly strict, and that generally helps to maintain the integrity of the brand. Toward this end, some franchise companies control promotional activities, select the site location, or even become involved in hiring decisions. This may seem overly restrictive to some franchisees, especially those seeking independence and autonomy. That is why Wings Over restaurants throughout the country are allowed to incorporate the city or region into the name—Wings Over Washington, D.C.—and stay open later when located in a college town. According to Mark Simonds, president of the Agawam, Massachusetts–based franchise, it's all part of a strategy to give franchisees the flexibility to compete against independent businesses.[56] The concept is also attractive to potential franchisees who have many businesses to choose from.

Finally, some people are more suited to the demands of operating a franchise than others. Any person who is considering buying a franchise must think first about whether he or she has the right personality for the endeavor. Chapter 6 features an in-depth discussion of the basic characteristics that entrepreneurs should bring to their new endeavors.

Assessment Check ✔

1. Distinguish between a franchisor and a franchisee.
2. Name some of the largest franchises.
3. What are the benefits and problems of franchising?

Alternatives for Organizing a Business

Whether small or large, every business fits one of three categories of legal ownership: sole proprietorships, partnerships, and corporations. As Figure 5.5 shows, sole proprietorships are the most common form of business ownership. Although a much smaller percentage of firms are organized as corporations, corporate revenues are 19 times as large as the revenues earned by all sole proprietorships. After all, a corporate giant such as Wal-Mart, with annual sales of more than $350 billion, has a huge impact on the nation's economy.

Each form offers unique advantages and disadvantages, as outlined in Table 5.3. To overcome certain limitations of the traditional ownership structures, owners may also use three specialized organizational forms: S corporations, limited-liability partnerships, and limited-liability companies. Along with the basic forms, this section also briefly examines each of these alternatives.

Sole Proprietorships

The most common form of business ownership, the **sole proprietorship** is also the oldest and the simplest because no legal distinction separates the sole proprietor's status as an individual from his or her status as a business owner. Although sole proprietorships are common in a variety of industries, they are concentrated primarily among small businesses such as repair shops, small retail outlets, and service providers, such as painters, plumbers, and lawn care operations.

Sole proprietorships offer advantages that other business entities cannot. For one, they are easy to form and dissolve. (Partnerships are also easy to form, but difficult to dissolve.) A sole proprietorship offers management flexibility for the owner, along with the right to retain all profits after payment of personal income taxes. Retention of all profits and responsibility for all losses give sole proprietors the incentive to maximize efficiency in their operations.

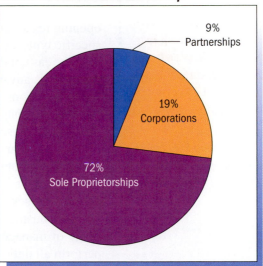

Figure 5.5

Forms of Business Ownership

- 9% Partnerships
- 19% Corporations
- 72% Sole Proprietorships

Source: Data from U.S. Census Bureau, "2009 Statistical Abstract," accessed March 3, 2009, http://www.census.gov.

sole proprietorship form of business ownership in which the company is owned and operated by one person.

Table 5.3		Comparing the Three Major Forms of Private Ownership		
Form of Ownership	**Number of Owners**	**Liability**	**Advantages**	**Disadvantages**
Sole proprietorship	One owner	Unlimited personal liability for business debt	1. Owner retains all profits 2. Easy to form and dissolve 3. Owner has flexibility	1. Unlimited financial liability 2. Financing limitations 3. Management deficiencies 4. Lack of continuity
Partnership	Two or more owners	Personal assets of any operating partner at risk from business creditors	1. Easy to form 2. Can benefit from complementary management skills 3. Expanded financial capacity	1. Unlimited financial liability 2. Interpersonal conflicts 3. Lack of continuity 4. Difficult to dissolve
Corporation	Unlimited number of shareholders; up to 100 shareholders for S corporations	Limited	1. Limited financial liability 2. Specialized management skills 3. Expanded financial capacity 4. Economies of large-scale operations	1. Difficult and costly to form and dissolve 2. Tax disadvantages 3. Legal restrictions

Minimal legal requirements simplify entering and exiting a sole proprietorship. Usually, the owner must meet only a few legal requirements for starting one, including registering the business or trade name—to guarantee that two firms do not use the same name—and taking out any necessary licenses. Local governments require that certain kinds of licenses be obtained before opening restaurants, motels, and retail stores. Some occupational licenses require firms to carry specific types of insurance, such as liability coverage.

The ease of dissolving a sole proprietorship is an attractive feature for certain types of enterprises. This advantage is particularly important for temporary businesses set up to handle just a few transactions. Ownership flexibility is another advantage of a sole proprietorship. The owner can make management decisions without consulting others, take prompt action when needed, and keep trade secrets. You've probably heard people say, "I like being my own boss." This flexibility leads many business owners to prefer the sole proprietorship format.

A disadvantage of the sole proprietorship form is the owner's personal financial liability for all debts of the business. Also, the business must operate with financial resources limited to the owner's personal funds and money that he or she can borrow. Such financing limitations can keep the business from expanding. Another disadvantage is that the owner must handle a wide range of management and operational tasks; as the firm grows, the owner may not be able to perform all duties with equal effectiveness. In addition, taxpayers who file a Schedule C, which is used to report profits and losses from a sole proprietorship, face a higher chance of being audited. Internal Revenue Service research shows the largest compliance problems are typically found among this group.[57] Finally, a sole proprietorship lacks long-term continuity, because death, bankruptcy, retirement, or a change in personal interests can terminate it.

Partnerships

partnership form of business ownership in which the company is operated by two or more people who are co-owners by voluntary legal agreement.

Another option for organizing a business is to form a partnership. The Uniform Partnership Act, which regulates this ownership form in most states, defines a **partnership** as an association of two or more persons who operate a business as co-owners by voluntary legal agreement. The partnership was the traditional form of ownership for professionals offering services, such as physicians, lawyers, and dentists. Today, most of these service providers have switched to other organizational forms to limit personal liability.

Like sole proprietorships, partnerships are easy to form. The legal requirements consist of registering the business name and taking out the necessary licenses. Partnerships also offer expanded financial capabilities when each partner invests money. They also usually increase access to borrowed funds compared with sole proprietorships. Another advantage is the opportunity for professionals to combine complementary skills and knowledge. For example, one partner may have an extensive financial background, while another partner has expertise in marketing.

Like sole proprietorships, most partnerships have the disadvantage of unlimited financial liability. Each partner bears full responsibility for the debts of the firm, and each is legally liable for the actions of the other partners. Partners must pay the partnership's debts from their personal funds if it ceases operations and its debts exceed its assets. Breaking up a partnership is also a much more complicated undertaking than dissolving a sole proprietorship. Rather than simply withdrawing funds from the bank, the partner who wants out may need to find someone to buy his or her interest in the firm.

In many states, partners can minimize some of these risks by organizing as a limited-liability partnership. In many respects, such a partnership resembles a general partnership, but laws limit the liability of the partners to the value of their investments in the company.

The death of a partner also threatens the survival of a partnership. A new partnership must be formed, and the estate of the deceased is entitled to a share of the firm's value. To ease the financial strains of such events, business planners recommend life insurance coverage for each partner, combined with a buy-sell agreement. The insurance proceeds can be used to repay the deceased partner's heirs and allow the surviving partner to retain control of the business.

Because partnerships are vulnerable to personal conflicts that can quickly escalate into business battles, you should carefully choose your business partners. According to Mark Stevens, a business consultant and president of MSCO, a marketing firm in Rye Brook, New York, "Today always looks good" when a partnership begins. But you have to plan for "tomorrow and the day after" to make it work. Communication is critical. Alicia Rockmore and Sara Welch had worked together for about eight years before cofounding Buttoned Up, a company that offers products to help people become more organized; items range from document organizers to moving kits. Both women respect the other's business judgment, and Rockmore's background in brand management and new-product development compliments Welch's experience in advertising and consulting, and vice versa.[58]

Corporations

A **corporation** is a legal organization with assets and liabilities separate from those of its owner(s). Although even the smallest business can choose the corporate form of organization, most people think of large companies when they hear the term *corporation*. In truth, many corporations are extremely large businesses.

Recently, Wal-Mart, whose annual worldwide sales exceed $350 billion, passed ExxonMobil to become the largest U.S.-based corporation in terms of sales. However, ExxonMobil places ahead of Chevron, General Motors, and ConocoPhillips. The list of the ten largest U.S. corporations contains another manufacturer, General Electric, as well as Ford Motor Company and banking firms Citigroup and Bank of America Corporation. Telecommunications giant AT&T came in as number ten on the list. Given the recent market volatility, the list is sure to change again next year.[59]

The corporate ownership form offers considerable advantages. First, because a corporation acquires the status of a separate legal entity, its stockholders have only limited financial risk. If the firm fails, they lose only the money they have invested. Protection also applies to legal risk. Class-action suits filed against automakers, cigarette makers, and drug manufacturers are filed against the companies, not the owners of those companies. The limited risk of corporate ownership is clearly reflected in corporate names throughout the world. While many U.S. and Canadian corporations include the designation *Inc.* in their names, British firms use the abbreviation *Ltd.* to identify their limited liability. In Australia, the abbreviation for *proprietary limited*—Pty. Ltd.—is frequently included in corporate names.

Corporations offer other advantages. They can draw on the specialized skills of many employees, unlike the typical sole proprietorship or partnership, for which managerial skills are usually confined to the abilities of their owners and a small number of employees. Corporations gain access to expanded financial capabilities based on the opportunity to offer direct outside investments such as stock sales.

The large-scale operation permitted by corporate ownership also results in a number of advantages for this legal form of organization. Employees can specialize in their most effective tasks. A large firm can generate internal financing for many projects by transferring money from one part of the corporation to another. Long manufacturing runs usually promote efficient production and allow the firm to charge highly competitive prices that attract customers.

One major disadvantage for a corporation is the double taxation of corporate earnings. After a corporation pays federal, state, and local income taxes on its profits, its owners (stockholders) also pay personal taxes on any distributions of those profits they receive from the corporation in the form of dividends. Corporate ownership also involves some legal issues that sole proprietorships and partnerships do not encounter. The number of laws and regulations that affect corporations has increased dramatically in recent years.

corporation business that stands as a legal entity with assets and liabilities separate from those of its owner(s).

To avoid double taxation of business income while achieving or retaining limited financial liability for their owners, some firms have modified the traditional corporate and partnership structures. Businesses that meet certain size requirements, including ownership by no more than 100 shareholders, may organize as **S corporations,** also called *subchapter S corporations.* These firms can elect to pay federal income taxes as partnerships while retaining the liability limitations typical of corporations. The tax advantage of S corporations over typical corporations, which incur double taxation, is that S corporations are only taxed once. Unlike regular corporations, S corporations do not pay corporate taxes on their profits. Instead, the untaxed profits of S corporations are paid directly as dividends to shareholders, who then pay the individual tax rate. This tax advantage has induced a fivefold increase in the number of S corporations. Consequently, the IRS is closely auditing S corporations for abuse because some businesses don't meet the legal requirements form S corporations.[60]

Business owners may also form **limited liability companies (LLCs)** to secure the corporate advantage of limited liability while avoiding the double taxation characteristic of corporations. An LLC is a business structure that combines the pass-through taxation of a partnership or sole proprietorship with the limited ability of a corporation. Only a few types of businesses cannot be LLCs, such as banks and nonprofit organizations.[61] An LLC is governed by an operating agreement that resembles a partnership agreement, except that it reduces each partner's liability for the actions of the other owners. Corporations of professionals, such as lawyers, accountants, and physicians, use a similar approach, with the abbreviation *PC* shown at the end of the business name. LLCs appear to be a way of the future. About 10 minutes after the first LLC law was passed, nearly all national CPA (certified public accountant) firms in the United States converted to LLC status.[62]

Changing Legal Structures to Meet Changing Needs

Before deciding on an appropriate legal form, someone planning to launch a new business must consider dozens of factors, such as these:

- personal financial situations and the need for additional funds for the business's start-up and continued operation
  - management skills and limitations
  - management styles and capabilities of working with partners and other members of top management
  - concerns about exposure to personal liability.

Although the legal form of organization is a major decision, new business owners need not treat it as a permanent decision. Over time, changing conditions such as business growth may prompt the owner of a sole proprietorship or a group of partners to switch to a more appropriate form. For example, if you have a successful business organized as a limited-liability company, but you want to give your children or other family members partial ownership, you can give them shares of the company by switching to a corporation.

Assessment Check ✔

1. What are the key differences among sole proprietorships, partnerships, and corporations?
2. What are the advantages and disadvantages of sole proprietorships, partnerships, and corporations?

Organizing and Operating a Corporation

One of the first decisions in forming a corporation is determining where to locate its headquarters and where it will do business. This section describes the various types of corporations and considers the options and procedures involved in incorporating a business.

Types of Corporations

Corporations fall into three categories: domestic, foreign, or alien. A firm is considered a **domestic corporation** in the state where it is incorporated. When a company does business in states other than the one where it has filed incorporation papers, it is registered as a **foreign corporation** in each of those states. A firm incorporated in one nation that operates in another is known as an **alien corporation** where it operates. Some firms—particularly large corporations with operations scattered around the world—may operate under all three of these designations.

The Incorporation Process

Suppose that you decide to start a business, and you believe that the corporate form offers the best way to organize it. Where should you set up shop? How do you establish a corporate charter? The following paragraphs discuss the procedures for creating a new corporation.

WHERE TO INCORPORATE Location is one of the most important considerations for any small-business owner. Although most small and medium-sized businesses are incorporated in the states in which they do most of their business, a U.S. firm can actually incorporate in any state it chooses. The founders of large corporations, or of those that will do business nationwide, often compare the benefits provided in various states' laws to firms in various industries.

The favorable legal climate in Delaware and the speed and simplicity of incorporating there have prompted more than half of the companies in *Fortune* magazine's list of the top 500 companies to set up operations there. Because of this popularity, incorporation has become a $400 million government-run industry in Delaware.

stockholder person or organization who owns shares of stock in a corporation.

THE CORPORATE CHARTER Each state mandates a specific procedure for incorporating a business. Most states require at least three *incorporators*—the individuals who create the corporation—which opens incorporation possibilities to small businesses. Another requirement demands that a new corporation adopt a name dissimilar from those of other businesses; most states require that the name must end with the word *Company, Corporation, Incorporated,* or *Limited* to show that the owners have limited liability. Figure 5.6 lists ten elements of the articles of incorporation that most states require for chartering a corporation.

The information provided in the articles of incorporation forms the basis on which a state grants a **corporate charter,** a legal document that formally establishes a corporation. After securing the charter, the owners prepare the company's bylaws, which describe the rules and procedures for its operation.

Corporate Management

Depending on its size, a corporation has some or all of the ownership and management levels illustrated in Figure 5.7. At the top of the figure are **stockholders.** They acquire shares of stock in the corporation and so become part owners of it. Some companies, such as family businesses, are owned by relatively few stockholders, and the stock is generally unavailable to outsiders. In such a firm, known as a *closed* or *closely held corporation,* the stockholders also control and manage all activities. In contrast, an open corporation,

Figure 5.6

Traditional Articles of Incorporation

- Name and Address of the Corporation
- Corporate Objectives
- Type and Amount of Stock to Issue
- Expected Life of the Corporation
- Financial Capital at the Time of Incorporation
- Provisions for Transferring Shares of Stock among Owners
- Provisions for Regulating Internal Corporate Affairs
- Address of the Business Office Registered with the State of Incorporation
- Names and Addresses of the Initial Board of Directors
- Names and Addresses of the Incorporators

Figure 5.7

Levels of Management in a Corporation

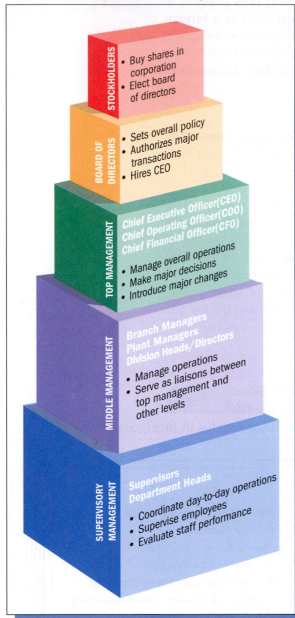

sometimes called a *publicly held corporation,* sells stock to the general public, establishing diversified ownership and often leading to larger operations than those of a closed corporation.

STOCK OWNERSHIP AND STOCKHOLDER RIGHTS Publicly held corporations usually hold annual stockholders' meetings. During these meetings, managers report on corporate activities, and stockholders vote on any decisions that require their approval, including elections of officers. Wal-Mart holds the nation's largest stockholder meeting at the University of Arkansas Bud Walton Arena. Approximately 16,000 people attend. In addition to standard shareholder business, the Wal-Mart meeting has featured celebrities and entertainers such as Sinbad, Tim McGraw, Jimmy Buffett, and Will Smith.[63]

Stockholders' role in the corporation depends on the class of stock they own. Shares are usually classified as common or preferred stock. Although owners of **preferred stock** have limited voting rights, they are entitled to receive dividends before holders of common stock. If the corporation is dissolved, they have first claims on assets, once debtors are repaid. Owners of **common stock** have voting rights but only residual claims on the firm's assets, which means they are last to receive any income distributions. Because one share is typically worth only one vote, small stockholders generally have little influence on corporate management actions.

BOARD OF DIRECTORS Stockholders elect a **board of directors**—the governing body of a corporation. The board sets overall policy, authorizes major transactions involving the corporation, and hires the chief executive officer (CEO). Most boards include both inside directors (corporate executives) and outside directors—people who are not employed by the organization. Sometimes the corporation's top executive also chairs the board. Generally, outside directors are also stockholders.

CORPORATE OFFICERS AND MANAGERS The CEO and other members of top management, such as the chief operating officer (COO) and chief financial officer (CFO), make most major corporate decisions. Managers at the next level down the hierarchy, middle management, handle the ongoing operational functions of the company. At the first tier of management, supervisory personnel coordinate day-to-day operations, assign specific tasks to employees, and evaluate job per-

board of directors
elected governing body
of a corporation.

formance. The activities and responsibilities of managers at various levels in the organization are described in detail in Chapter 8.

In the past, top managers of corporations have had nearly free rein to guide their companies. The firm's CEO has traditionally played a major role in nominating candidates for board membership and often served jointly as board chairperson and CEO. Some recent corporate and accounting scandals were traced to a lack of business ethics, coupled with illegal acts of members of top management and failure of the corporate boards to fulfill their obligations to the firm's investors in providing adequate oversight. These failings prompted Congress to pass the Sarbanes-Oxley Act, which tightened requirements of corporate boards and required CEOs and CFOs of major corporations to certify in writing the accuracy of the firm's financial statements. New criminal penalties were established for corporate wrong-doers. This far-reaching legislation, which focuses on improving corporate governance and increasing the accountability of corporate boards, top executives, and accounting firms, was introduced in Chapter 2. Its impact on business will be also be discussed in the management, accounting, and finance chapters later in the text.

Employee-Owned Corporations

Another alternative in creating a corporation is **employee ownership,** in which workers buy shares of stock in the company that employs them. The corporate organization stays the same, but most stockholders are also employees.

The popularity of this form of corporation is growing. Today about 20 percent of all employees of for-profit companies report owning stock in their companies; approximately 25 million Americans own employer stock through *employee stock ownership plans (ESOPs),* options, stock purchase plans, 401(k) plans, and other plans. The number of employee owner-ship plans has grown dramatically and breaks down as follows: 9,650 ESOPs (10.5 million participants); 2,200 401(k) plans invested in company stock (4 million participants); 4,000 stock option plans (10 million participants); and 4,000 stock purchase plans (12 million participants).[64] Several trends underlie the growth in employee ownership. One is that employ-ees want to share in whatever wealth their company earns. Another is that managers want employees to care deeply about the company's success so that they will contribute their best effort. Because human resources are so essential to the success of a modern business, employ-ers want to build their employees' commitment to the organization. Some of the country's most successful public corporations, including Procter & Gamble, Lowe's, and Southwest Airlines, have embraced employee ownership and watched their stock values hold up better than other companies; sales of employee-owned companies are 2.3 to 2.4 percent larger than non-employee-owned firms.[65]

Not-for-Profit Corporations

The same business concepts that apply to organizations whose objectives include earning profits also apply to **not-for-profit corporations**—firms pursuing objectives other than returning profits to owners. About 1.5 million not-for-profits oper-ate in the United States, including chari-table groups, social-welfare organizations, and religious congregations. This sector includes museums, libraries, religious and human service organizations, private sec-ondary schools, healthcare facilities, sym-phony orchestras, zoos, and thousands of other groups such as government agencies, political parties, and labor unions.

A good example of a not-for-profit corporation is the San Francisco Ballet, which has been at the forefront of dance in America since its founding in 1933 as

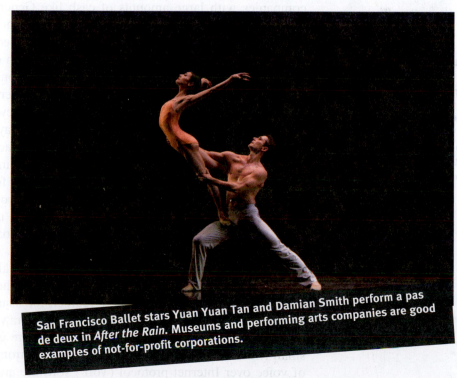

San Francisco Ballet stars Yuan Yuan Tan and Damian Smith perform a pas de deux in *After the Rain.* Museums and performing arts companies are good examples of not-for-profit corporations.

San Francisco Ballet /NewsCom

Assessment Check ✔

1. What is the role of stockholders, the board of directors, and corporate officers and management?
2. Identify the various levels of corporate management.

America's first professional ballet company. It is widely regarded as one of the premier ballet companies in the nation. Visitors to its Web site, http://www.sfballet.org, can learn about upcoming performances, purchase tickets, buy gift certificates, and shop online at the gift shop.[66]

Most states set out separate legal provisions for organizational structures and operations of not-for-profit corporations. These organizations do not issue stock certificates, because they pay no dividends to owners, and ownership rarely changes. They are also exempt from paying income taxes.

When Businesses Join Forces

Today's corporate world features many complex relationships between companies, not always in the same industry or even in the same country. Many well-known firms have changed owners, become parts of other corporations, split into smaller units, or experienced financial bankruptcy. Current trends in corporate ownership include mergers and acquisitions and joint ventures.

Mergers and Acquisitions (M&A)

In recent years, merger mania has hit U.S. corporations. Today, business textbooks are published primarily by one of three large companies; dozens of publishers once competed in the market. The airline industry has witnessed an increase in the number of mergers, as has the technology and telecommunications industries. Since 2004, Microsoft has acquired 27 companies; Google, 33.[67] Some mergers work very well; others don't. After Daimler purchased Chrysler, the integration of the two very different automakers was never successful, and Daimler sold Chrysler to Cerberus Capital. Conversely, Wells Fargo focused on employees when it bought rival bank Norwest, and profits have more than quadrupled.[68] Announced mergers recently set an annual record, exceeding $4.5 trillion globally.[69] With the recent flux in credit markets, companies with large amounts of cash like General Electric ($7.7 billion cash reserve) and Microsoft ($21.6 billion) are likely candidates to acquire other firms.[70]

merger combination of two or more firms to form one company.

acquisition procedure in which one firm purchases the property and assumes the obligations of another.

The terms *merger* and *acquisition* are often used interchangeably, but their meanings differ. In a **merger,** two or more firms combine to form one company; in an **acquisition,** one firm purchases the property and assumes the obligations of another. Acquisitions also occur when one firm buys a division or subsidiary from another firm. Many mergers and acquisitions cross national borders, as managers attempt to enter new markets and improve global competitiveness for their companies. In some cases, this may involve bringing two disparate corporate cultures together. That's what CEO Bill Amelio faced when obscure Chinese computer maker Lenovo purchased ThinkPad, icon IBM's struggling PC division, for $1.75 billion. The first challenge was selecting a corporate headquarters for the merged firm; Lenovo was headquartered in Beijing, ThinkPad in Raleigh, North Carolina. Amelio decided that the best solution was no headquarters at all—top executives meet in a different location each month. Lenovo shares are at an all-time high, and Amelio's approach, which he calls *worldsourcing,* appears to be effective.[71]

Mergers can be classified as vertical, horizontal, or conglomerate. A **vertical merger** combines firms operating at different levels in the production and marketing process—the combination of a manufacturer and a large retailer, for instance. A vertical merger pursues one of two primary goals: (1) to ensure adequate flows of raw materials and supplies needed for a firm's products or (2) to increase distribution. Software giant Microsoft is well known for acquiring small firms that have developed products with strong market potential, such as Teleo, a provider of voice over Internet protocol (VoIP) software and services that can be used to make phone calls via the Internet. Likewise, large petroleum companies often try to reduce the uncertainty of their future petroleum supplies by acquiring successful oil and gas exploration firms.

A **horizontal merger** joins firms in the same industry that wish to diversify, increase their customer bases, cut costs, or offer expanded product lines. India-based automaker Tata Motors bought Ford Motor Co.'s Jaguar and Land Rover division for around $2.3 billion. The agreement called for Ford to continue supplying powertrains, stampings, and other vehicle components for some time. Ford also will provide engineering support, including research and development, plus information technology, accounting, and other services.[72]

A **conglomerate merger** combines unrelated firms. The most common reasons for a conglomerate merger are to diversify, spur sales growth, or spend a cash surplus that might otherwise make the firm a tempting target for a takeover effort. Conglomerate mergers may join firms in totally unrelated industries. A company well known for its conglomerate mergers is General Electric, which owns television broadcaster NBC and cable programmers CNBC and MSNBC, along with its manufacturing businesses such as aircraft engines and industrial products. Experts debate whether conglomerate mergers are beneficial. The usual argument in favor of such mergers is that a company can use its management expertise to succeed in a variety of industries. However, the stock of an acquiring company often falls in price when it makes an acquisition, suggesting that investors doubt the value of this strategy.

Joint Ventures: Specialized Partnerships

A **joint venture** is a partnership between companies formed for a specific undertaking. Sometimes a company enters into a joint venture with a local firm, sharing the operation's costs, risks, management, and profits with its local partner. A joint venture also may enable companies to solve a mutual problem. A study conducted by IBM Institute for Business Value and the Economist Intelligence Unit reported that banks will enter into more joint ventures with rivals to help them survive in an increasingly global financial world. The research projects that the global financial system will quadruple by 2025. More than 80 percent of the banks in the study expect to use joint ventures to compete in a more globally networked economy; over half expect ventures with nonbank financial institutions like insurance companies.[73] As discussed in the previous chapter, joint ventures also offer particularly attractive ways for small firms to conduct international business, because they bring substantial benefits from partners already operating inside the host countries.

Public and Collective Ownership

Most business organizations are owned privately by individuals or groups of people, but municipal, state, and national governments own some firms. In addition, groups of people collectively own some companies. Public ownership is common in many industries, both in the United States and abroad. In the United States, more than 350 municipalities offer Internet or cable TV services, competing with private firms that offer those same services.[74]

Public Ownership

One alternative to private ownership is some form of **public ownership,** in which a unit or agency of government owns and operates an organization. In the United States, local governments often own parking structures and water systems. The Pennsylvania Turnpike Authority operates a vital highway link across the Keystone State. The federal government operates Hoover Dam in Nevada to provide electricity over a large region.

Government-Owned Corporations

Sometimes public ownership results when private investors are unwilling to invest in a high-risk project. This situation occurred with the rural electrification programs of the 1930s, which expanded utility lines in sparsely populated areas. At other times, public ownership has replaced private ownership of failed organizations. Certain functions, such as municipal water systems, are considered so important to public welfare that government often implements public ownership to protect its citizens from problems. Finally, some nations use public business ownership to foster competition by operating public companies as competitive business enterprises. In Bogota, Colombia, the government runs a TV and radio network, Instituto Nacional de Radio & Television, that broadcasts both educational and commercial programs. Public ownership remains common abroad, despite a general trend toward privatization.

Customer-Owned Businesses: Cooperatives

Another alternative to traditional private business ownership is collective ownership of a production, storage, transportation, or marketing organization. Such collective ownership establishes an organization referred to as a **cooperative** (or **co-op**), whose owners join forces to operate all or part of the functions in their industry.

Cooperatives allow small businesses to obtain quantity discounts on purchases, reducing costs and enabling the co-op to pass on the savings to its members. Marketing and advertising expenses are shared among members, and the co-op's facilities can also serve as a distribution center.

Cooperatives are frequently found in small farming communities, but they also serve large growers of specific crops. For instance, Blue Diamond Growers is a cooperative that represents California almond growers. Retailers have also established co-ops, such as IGA (Independent Grocers Alliance), a network of independent supermarkets throughout the United States and abroad. Financial co-ops, such as credit unions, offer members higher interest rates on deposits and lower interest rates on loans than other profit-seeking institutions could provide.

Assessment Check ✔

1. What is private ownership? What is public ownership? What is collective ownership?

2. Where are cooperatives typically found, and what benefits do they provide small businesses?

What's Ahead

The next chapter shifts the book's focus to the driving forces behind new-business formation: entrepreneurs. It examines the differences between a small-business owner and an entrepreneur and identifies certain personality traits typical of entrepreneurs. The chapter also details the process of launching a new venture, including identifying opportunities, locating needed financing, and turning good ideas into successful businesses. Finally, the chapter explores a method for infusing the entrepreneurial spirit into established businesses—intrapreneurship.

Summary of Learning Goals

1 **Distinguish between small and large businesses, and identify the industries in which most small firms are established.**

Small businesses can adopt many profiles, from part-time, home-based businesses to firms with several hundred employees. A small business is a firm that is independently owned and operated, is not dominant in its field, and meets industry-specific size standards for income or number of employees. Small businesses operate in every industry, but retailing, services, and construction feature the highest proportions of small enterprises.

Assessment Check Answers

1.1 What characteristics does the SBA use to determine whether a business is a small business? The SBA looks at the number of employees, annual sales, and whether a firm is independently owned and not dominant in its field.

1.2 Identify three industries in which small businesses are common. Construction, wholesale, retail, and service industries are common for small businesses.

2 **Discuss the economic and social contributions of small business.**

During the past decade, small firms have created 60 to 80 percent of the new jobs in the U.S. economy, and they employ half of U.S. workers. They provide valuable outlets for entrepreneurial activity and often contribute to the creation of new industries or development of new business processes. Women, minorities, and immigrants find small-business ownership to be an attractive alternative to working in large firms and are starting new companies at a much faster rate than the overall growth in U.S. businesses. Small firms may also offer enhanced lifestyle flexibility and opportunities to gain personal satisfaction.

Assessment Check Answers

2.1 To what extent do small businesses help create new jobs? On average, three of four new jobs are created by small businesses.

2.2 In what ways do small businesses contribute to the economy? Small businesses create new jobs, new industries, and innovation goods and services.

3 **Describe the reasons that small businesses fail.**

Because of management shortcomings, inadequate financing, and difficulty dealing with government regulations, small businesses are much more likely to fail than large businesses, especially during economic downturns.

Assessment Check Answers

3.1 What percentage of small businesses will still be in business two, four, six, and ten years after starting? One-third, 50 percent, 62 percent, and 82 percent of small businesses will have failed within two, four, six, and ten years, respectively.

3.2 How do management shortcomings, inadequate financing, and government regulation make small businesses more likely to fail? Founders of new businesses often lack the business expertise and experience needed to grow a small business. Inadequate financing prevents small businesses from handling the inevitable cash shortfalls they face and from attracting and keeping talented people. Government regulation burdens small businesses that have limited staff and budgets with expensive, time-consuming red tape and paperwork.

4 **Describe how the Small Business Administration assists small-business owners.**

The U.S. Small Business Administration helps small-business owners obtain financing through programs that guarantee repayment of their bank loans or match small-business owners with potential investors. The SBA also helps women and minority business owners obtain government purchasing contracts. It offers training and information resources, so business owners can improve their odds of success. Finally, the SBA advocates small-business interests within the federal government.

Assessment Check Answers

4.1 What components should be part of a good business plan? A good business plan contains an executive summary, an introduction, separate financial and marketing sections, and the résumés of the principals.

4.2 What are the various ways and methods by which the SBA helps small businesses with financing and getting government contracts? The SBA guarantees business loans; helps small businesses compete for government set-aside programs; and provides business information, advice, and training.

5 **Explain how franchising can provide opportunities for both franchisors and franchisees.**

A franchisor is a company that sells the rights to use its brand name, operating procedures, and other intellectual property to franchisees. Franchising helps business owners expand their companies' operations with limited financial investments. Franchisees, the individuals who buy the right to operate a business using the franchisor's ideas, gain a proven business system, brand recognition, and training and other support from the franchisor.

Assessment Check Answers

5.1 Distinguish between a franchisor and a franchisee. Franchisors permit franchisees to use their business name and to sell their business's goods and services. Franchisors also provide franchisees a variety of marketing, management, and other services in return for various fees and a percentage of the franchisee's sales.

5.2 Name some of the largest franchises. Subway, McDonald's, Liberty Tax Service, Sonic Drive In Restaurants, InterContinental

Hotels Group, Ace Hardware Corp., Pizza Hut, The UPS Store/ Mail Boxes, Etc., Circle K convenience stores, and Papa John's International, Inc., are some of the largest franchises.

5.3 What are the benefits and problems of franchising? Advantages include a prior performance record, a recognizable company name, a business model that has proven successful in other locations, a tested management program, and business training for the franchisee. On the negative side, franchise fee payments can be very expensive, the franchisee is linked to the reputation and management of the franchise, and new franchise outlets may compete directly with established franchises.

6 Summarize the three basic forms of business ownership and the advantages and disadvantages of each form.

A sole proprietorship is owned and operated by one person. While sole proprietorships are easy to set up and offer great operating flexibility, the owner remains personally liable for all of the firm's debts and legal settlements. In a partnership, two or more individuals share responsibility for owning and running the business. Partnerships are relatively easy to set up, but they do not offer protection from liability. Also, partnerships may experience problems by the death of a partner or when partners fail to communicate or establish effective working relationships. When a business is set up as a corporation, it becomes a separate legal entity. Investors receive shares of stock in the firm. Owners have no legal and financial liability beyond their individual investments.

Assessment Check Answers

6.1 What are the key differences among sole proprietorships, partnerships, and corporations? Sole proprietorships and partnerships expose their owners to unlimited financial liability from their businesses. Corporations shield business owners from financial liability by separating an organization's assets and liabilities from its business owners' assets and liabilities.

6.2 What are the advantages and disadvantages of sole proprietorships, partnerships, and corporations? Sole proprietorships are easy to form and dissolve, and they allow owners to retain all business profits. But they lack long-term continuity, and their owners are personally liable for all business debts and must be capable of handling a wide range of business tasks. Partnerships are easy to form and offer expanded financial capabilities and complementary skills and knowledge. But they are difficult to dissolve, are vulnerable to personal conflicts, and make their owners personally liable for all business debts. Corporations shield owners from financial and legal risks, draw on specialized skills of employees, and can expand financial capabilities by selling stock. However, corporations are more difficult to establish, face double taxation of corporate earnings, and are subject to numerous state and federal laws and regulations.

7 Identify the levels of corporate management.

Stockholders, or shareholders, own a corporation. In return for their financial investments, they receive shares of stock in the company. The number of stockholders in a firm can vary widely, depending on whether the firm is privately owned or makes its stock available to the public. Shareholders elect the firm's board of directors, the individuals responsible for overall corporate management. The board has legal authority to change or create the firm's policies. A company's officers are the top managers who oversee its operating decisions.

Assessment Check Answers

7.1 What is the role of stockholders, the board of directors, and corporate officers and management? Stockholders acquire shares of stock and become corporate owners. At the annual stockholders' meeting, managers report on corporate activities and stockholders vote on any decisions that require their approval. The board of directors sets overall policy, authorizes major transactions involving the corporation, and hires the chief executive officer (CEO). The CEO and other members of top management make most major corporate decisions and are accountable to the board and shareholders.

7.2 Identify the various levels of corporate management. The levels of corporate management include top management, middle management, and supervisory management.

8 Describe recent trends in mergers and acquisitions.

Many industries have experienced an increase in the number of mergers. These business combinations occur worldwide, and companies often merge with or acquire other companies to aid their operations across national boundaries. Global merger activity has hit a record high. Vertical mergers help a firm ensure access to adequate raw materials and supplies for production or improve its distribution outlets. Horizontal mergers occur when firms in the same industry join to diversify or offer expanded product lines. Conglomerate mergers combine unrelated firms, often to help spend cash surpluses that might otherwise make a firm a takeover target.

Assessment Check Answers

8.1 Distinguish between a merger and an acquisition. In a merger, two or more firms combine to form one company. In an acquisition, one firm purchases the property and assumes the obligations of another. Acquisitions also occur when one firm buys a division or subsidiary from another firm.

8.2 What are the different kinds of mergers? Mergers can be classified as vertical, horizontal, or conglome rate.

8.3 What is a joint venture? A joint venture is a partnership between companies formed for a specific undertaking.

9 Differentiate among private ownership, public ownership, and collective ownership (cooperatives).

Managers or a group of major stockholders sometimes buy all of a firm's stock. The firm then becomes a privately owned company, and its stock is no longer publicly traded. Some firms allow workers to buy large blocks of stock, so the employees gain ownership stakes. Municipal, state, and national governments also own and operate some businesses. Public business ownership has declined, however, through a recent trend toward privatization of publicly run organizations. In a cooperative, individuals or companies band together to collectively operate all or part of an industry's functions. The cooperative's owners control its activities by electing a board of directors from its members. Cooperatives are usually set up to provide for collective ownership of a production, storage, transportation, or marketing organization that is important to an industry.

Assessment Check Answers

9.1 What is private ownership? What is public ownership? What is collective ownership? Most business organizations are owned privately by individuals or groups of people. Public ownership occurs when a government unit or agency owns and operates an organization. In a cooperative, individuals or companies band together to collectively operate all or part of an industry's functions. The cooperative's owners control its activities by electing a board of directors from their members.

9.2 Where are cooperatives typically found, and what benefits do they provide small businesses? Cooperatives are usually set up to provide for collective ownership of a production, storage, transportation, or marketing organization that is important to an industry.

Business Terms You Need to Know

small business 143
business plan 153
Small Business
   Administration (SBA) 155

business incubator 157
franchising 159
sole proprietorship 163

partnership 164
corporation 165
stockholder 167

board of directors 168
merger 170
acquisition 170

Other Important Business Terms

home-based business 146
microloans 156
Small Business Investment
   Company (SBIC) 156
set-aside program 156
franchisee 160

franchisor 160
S corporation 166
limited-liability company
   (LLC) 166
domestic corporation 167
foreign corporation 167

alien corporation 167
corporate charter 167
preferred stock 168
common stock 168
employee ownership 169
not-for-profit corporation 169

vertical merger 170
horizontal merger 171
conglomerate merger 171
joint venture 171
public ownership 171
cooperative (co-op) 172

Review Questions

1. What is meant by the term *small business?* What business sectors are most and least likely to be dominated by small firms?

2. What are the most common industries for small businesses? What opportunities do home-based companies and the Internet provide for small business? How do small businesses contribute to a nation's economy in terms of job creation and new industries and innovation?

3. What percentage of small businesses is likely to fail two, four, six, and ten years after starting? Why are small businesses more likely to fail? Explain how poor management, inadequate financing, and government regulations put small businesses at a disadvantage.

4. What are the benefits of a good business plan? Identify the major components of a business plan.

5. What is the Small Business Administration? How does it assist small companies, financially and in other specialized ways?

6. To what extent are small businesses creating opportunities for women today? Why have Hispanics become the nation's largest group of minority business owners? To what extent are other minority groups, including immigrants, taking advantage of opportunities to start and run their own businesses?

7. What are the top franchises and the latest trends in franchising? Describe a typical franchising agreement. What are the advantages and disadvantages of a franchising agreement?

8. What are a sole proprietorship, a partnership, and a corporation? How are they different? What are the advantages and disadvantages of each organizational form?

9. What are the three categories of corporations? What are the steps for creating a new corporation? Why does location matter? What is a corporate charter?

10. What are the levels of management in a corporation? What is the difference between employee-owned and not-for-profit corporations?

11. How are mergers and acquisitions different? What are the three kinds of mergers? What is a joint venture?

12. Distinguish among public ownership, government-owned corporations, and customer-owned businesses (cooperatives).

Projects and Teamwork Applications

1. Go to Entrepreneur.com and look for information on home-based business franchises. Choose three that interest you. Compare their company backgrounds, the costs and fees of becoming a franchisee, the training and support provided by the franchisor, and Entrepreneur.com's ratings for each franchisor. Also, visit the franchisors' Web sites. Which of the three home-based business franchises would represent the best opportunity for you? Why?

2. Read the business page of your local newspaper and choose a small business that has been profiled or mentioned in the paper. What do you think makes this business successful?

3. Propose an idea for a business incubator in an industry that interests you. Describe where the incubator would be located, how it would function, and what it is intended to accomplish.

4. Livewire International (http://www.livewirekiosk.com), a York, Pennsylvania, firm that provides electronic kiosks for ski lift tickets, has made alliances with businesses such as ski resorts and sports retailers. Describe another type of company that Livewire might make an alliance with. How might this alliance benefit Livewire? What precautions should Livewire take in entering into the alliance?

5. Do you think that consumers benefit from public ownership of such functions as municipal water systems and the postal service? Why or why not?

Web Assignments

1. **Small-business successes.** Visit the Web site listed here (http://www.businessweek.com/smallbiz/successstories/). Scroll through the titles of success stories and choose one that interests you. Read the feature and prepare a brief report answering these questions:

   a. What does the firm do?
   b. Where did the idea originate?
   c. What expertise does the owner have?
   d. How did the business begin?
   e. Who are its competitors?

2. **Great small workplaces.** Visit the Web site listed for Winning Workplaces (http://www.winningworkplaces.org/topsmallbiz/2007winners/index.php). Winning Workplaces, in conjunction with *The Wall Street Journal,* selects Top Small Workplaces. Read about three to five award winners. List them, what kind of business each is, and what makes it a stand out among small workplaces.

3. **The value of culture in small business.** Visit the following Web site, http://www.bnet.com/2422–13724 23–191097.html, and watch the video, "Why Is Everyone Smiling?" Paul Spiegelman explains how a positive corporate culture has meant big rewards for his small business, Beryl, a healthcare service provider he established with his brothers. What are some steps these business owners have taken to build a culture that inspires and motivates employees? What benefits have resulted from the Beryl culture?

Note: Internet Web addresses change frequently. If you do not find the exact sites listed, you may need to access the organization's or company's home page and search from there.

For Robbie Doughty, running a Little Caesars pizza store seems easy—at least compared with other challenges he's had in his life. A former Army staff sergeant, Doughty joined the military for adventure and a career. He served on a peacekeeping mission in Haiti in 1994, worked as an Army recruiter, then went to Iraq in May 2004 as a special operations intelligence soldier. On July 8, 2004, Doughty's convoy was ambushed, and his Humvee hit by a mortar round. Doughty lost both legs.

At Walter Reed Army Medical Center, Doughty was determined to recover as soon as possible. He stood again only two months after the ambush and left the center after a six-month stay, much quicker than the typical two years needed for rehabilitation. Fitted with high-tech prosthetic legs, Doughty headed home to Paducah, Kentucky, to figure out what his new life would be.

The Little Caesars connection began when Michael Ilitch, the chain's owner who also owns the Detroit Tigers and the Detroit Red Wings, read a *USA Today* article about Doughty as he recuperated at Walter Reed. Ilitch was so moved that he called Doughty to thank him for serving his country. But he wanted to do more than offer appreciation. After several conversations, Ilitch was impressed by Doughty's courage and determination and offered him a Little Caesars franchise—free, complete with building, equipment, and a special chair for Doughty behind the counter. The veteran accepted the offer and followed Ilitch's suggestion to partner with someone he could trust. The natural choice was Lloyd Allard, his friend and former colleague in Iraq who had just retired from the service.

Working with Doughty and Allard inspired Little Caesars to launch a veterans' program that gives qualified, honorably discharged veterans a $5,000 reduction on the franchise fee, financing benefits, and a $5,000 credit on their store's first equipment order. The company waives the entire $20,000 franchise fee for service-disabled veterans like Doughty and provides them more financing benefits, a $10,000 credit for equipment, and help with grand-opening marketing.

A year after they opened their first Little Caesars in Paducah, the team opened a second in Allard's home-town of Clarksville, Tennessee. Allard planned to run it with help from his family. Doughty says the company's ongoing support helped them expand. The pizza chain provides six weeks of training—required for franchisees—and in-store instruction on the operating system. Little Caesars also helps with real estate and site selection.

Little Caesars is one of the largest pizza brands, with more than 1,000 outlets on five continents. The chain's recent strategy has been to expand in markets like St. Louis, Minneapolis, Denver, Atlanta, and the East Coast, while competitors have been increasing the number of units abroad. New franchisees are helping the long-established company reemerge as a force in the restaurant industry.

Franchisors like Little Caesars consider military veterans excellent franchise candidates because they are disciplined team players who show dedication and leadership skills. "They were trained by one of the greatest systems in the world—the U.S. military," says Terry Hill, a spokesman for the International Franchise Association. "The franchise community is looking for people who know how to fit into a system, how to follow processes, and how to make things happen on schedule." The association's veteran transition program, called VetFran, encourages franchisors to offer financial incentives to veterans wishing to become business owners. Hundreds of companies in many industries—The UPS Store, Handyman Connection, Learning Express, Fantastic Sam's, and Little Caesars, to name a few—have joined VetFran. Nearly 700 veterans in 48 states have acquired franchises through the program. The Web site, http://www.franchise.org, provides details about the program and participating companies.

Veterans agree that they fit well with franchising. Patricia Evans, owner of a Little Caesars in Valdosta, Georgia, expects the skills she learned in the military, including a focus on teamwork, dedication, and a familiarity with processes, to help her become an effective franchisee.[75]

Questions for Critical Thinking

1. What motivates franchisors to give initiatives to military veterans to become business owners in their communities?

2. What personal qualities are important for success as a franchisee? Why are such qualities so important?

Cooperative Helps Furniture Stores Compete

Small furniture stores are struggling as online shopping, competition from large chains, and international product sourcing change the industry. One route to survival is through a purchasing cooperative like Furniture First, which enables members to make volume purchases like large chain stores while remaining independent, local stores with their own brand identity.

About 130 members/stockholders representing 300 stores with $1.3 million in buying power make up Furniture First, which was begun in 1994 in Harrisburg, Pennsylvania. The co-op provides benefits that few independent dealers could afford on their own. It negotiates volume discounts on merchandise, including specialty product packages, and offers financing options. A co-op consultant trains managers and salespeople at member stores to increase their average sales. With products coming increasingly from countries like Canada, China, or Vietnam, Furniture First does whatever it can—from teaching global business practices to sharing shipping containers—to help members compete.

Members also receive the advantage of networking in person and online. At a recent Furniture First trade show, for example, members discussed the advertising that works best for them. The co-op's password-protected Web site contains information on the group's suppliers, including best-selling products, prices, and the best sales representatives. The online bulletin board lets members talk with other dealers. The co-op's public Web site features consumer education—furniture buying tips and interior design—and is available for individual members to put on their own sites, a good move, because most furniture buyers do research online before they buy.

Furniture First, with 16 employees, is governed by elected officers and board members and financed by members' dues and supplier discounts. Members invest in its stock and must buy 30 percent of their inventory through the co-op within their first two years. Furniture First works best for dealers with at least $2 million in yearly revenues in a full-line furniture store, according to president Bill Hartman. "Our average member store has been in business for over 40 years and is family-owned and operated," Hartman says. With Furniture First, stores with names like Riley's Furniture in Monroe, Ohio, and Mike's Furniture in Joliet, Illinois, may increase the chance of being in business 40 years from now.[76]

Questions for Critical Thinking

1. Which of Furniture First's service would be most valuable to an independent furniture-store owner? Which other services could Furniture First offer to increase its membership value?

2. How might co-op membership affect the independence prized by most small business owners?

VIDEO Case 5.3

The UL Mark of Approval

You've seen the little UL mark of approval on countless products. Maybe you've never paid attention to it, or maybe you've wondered briefly what the "UL" stood for. In fact, "UL" represents Underwriters Laboratories, a not-for-profit organization that has existed for more than a century. Founded by Chicago electrical inspector William Merrill in 1894—in response to the constant fires in the Palace of Electricity at the Chicago World's Fair—Underwriters Laboratories has been devoted to inspecting and testing billions of products for safety and quality assurance ever since. UL conducts more than 100,000 product evaluations each year, and only those that pass the organization's rigorous examination get the coveted UL mark. UL tests everything, including computers, electric blankets, and commercial ice cream makers. Currently, 20 billion products from more than 71,000 manufacturers bear the UL mark.

UL started out small. In the first few years, two experts joined Merrill in his enterprise, and they performed 75 tests on a $3,000 budget. By the tenth year, UL's budget had increased to $300,000, with 7,500 test reports issued. UL inspectors had spread out over 67 cities, conducting evaluations and helping set safety standards. In 1916, a team was dispatched to London to monitor England's exports to the United States. By 1958, UL testing centers had spread across Europe. Years later, UL opened facilities in Asia.

Underwriters Laboratories has grown like many other small businesses into a huge international organization. With 5,000 scientists, engineers, and safety specialists, the firm faces daily challenges. Yet UL has not lost sight of William Merrill's original mission—to provide product safety assurance to consumers. And UL continues to develop new standards for the products it tests. So the coffeepot you click on in the morning, the air conditioner that cools your bedroom, and the hair dryer that blows just the right amount of heated air were most likely tested by UL specialists before they ever reached the store shelves—or your home.

Here is how the process works. A firm submits a product to be tested, ideally sometime during its development. UL assigns the product to the correct testing division, where engineers and other specialists will see it through the evaluation. As part of the submission, the firm answers all kinds of questions about the product—what it is, how and when it will be used and by whom, what materials will be used in manufacturing it, and how the product is wired (with diagrams, if applicable). Then UL plans a testing program, tests the product for safety and reliability, and returns a formal report to the manufacturer. The standards for testing are developed by experts from UL, as well as by people from the industry and the public. For instance, standards for testing a fire extinguisher might be developed by UL specialists, members of the manufacturing industry, and firefighting personnel. If a product passes the tests, it gets the UL mark. If it doesn't, a manufacturer can modify the design and resubmit it or appeal the decision.

UL is not the only product-testing organization in existence; it has international competitors such as SGS, Intertek, and Bureau Veritas. Because of this rivalry, UL must remain innovative and current, constantly finding new ways to serve its clients and the general public.

The UL program helps retailers by giving them a standard by which to evaluate the products they want to sell to consumers. And, although not *every* manufactured product must be tested, many states and towns do have ordinances or codes requiring a UL listing for certain items such as smoke alarms and electrical wiring. The certification program helps consumers identify the safest products on the market. The organization's Web site, which is easy for manufacturers, retailers, and consumers to use, also helps UL remain competitive by adding instant and easy access to information. In addition to providing safety standards on products, the UL Web site offers safety tips for a whole range of everyday situations at home, in the office, and elsewhere. Consumers can visit the site to learn more about child safety, college dorm safety, smoke alarms, ladders, lawn mowers, and Christmas lights. The next time you plug in the toaster oven or heat up your dinner in the microwave, check for the UL mark on your appliance—chances are, it's there.[77]

Questions for Critical Thinking

1. How might the Underwriters Laboratories team up with a business incubator? What might be the benefits to both?

2. UL is a not-for-profit organization. Describe its objectives, as well as the business concepts it shares with for-profit companies.

3. Look around your dorm room or apartment, and make a list of all the products with the UL mark on them. Also list those that don't have it, if any. How do you think the UL testing process affects the way manufacturing businesses operate?

4. Think of yourself as an entrepreneur starting a business. Imagine a product that you would like to make or sell. Then visit the UL Web site to learn the procedure for testing your product. Create a plan for your business that includes the way you would organize your business—such as sole proprietorship or partnership—and include a strategy to develop your product and have it tested.

chapter 6

Starting Your Own Business: The Entrepreneurship Alternative

Corbis/Jupiter Images Corp

Revolution Foods Serves Kids a Tasty Lunch

School lunches—who can forget them? Cafeteria lines offered deep-fried chicken, French fries, mystery meatloaf, cakes, and cookies. Most of these foods contained fats, preservatives, and a lot of sugar. Recently, some schools have tried to serve more healthful choices to students, offering salads and carrot sticks, apples and honey. But given the choice, many kids opt for the bad stuff—soft drinks instead of water, a bag of chips instead of a handful of almonds. But two California entrepreneurs are trying to change that by rewriting the menu.

Kirsten Tobey and Kristin Groos Richmond founded Revolution Foods in an effort to produce fresh, nutritious, great-tasting lunches for schoolchildren. Both women have backgrounds in education, so they understood the type of food that children were served at school. And they wanted to start their own business. To gain greater knowledge about the needs of their local school communities, Tobey and Richmond interviewed teachers, students, families, and administrators. Then they searched for financing. They drummed up $4.5 million in capital from angel investors—wealthy individuals who wanted to be involved—and socially responsible investment firms. Tobey and Richmond set up shop in an abandoned McDonald's restaurant. They removed the flash fryers and replaced the cast-iron sewer pipes that were corroded from thrown-out soft drinks. They outfitted the restaurant with new equipment and stocked the refrigerator with fresh produce, lean meats, and hormone-free milk.

In addition to their initial financing, Tobey and Richmond secured a vital partnership with Whole Foods, which gave them a $75,000 low-interest loan and the opportunity to purchase a variety of goods at wholesale prices. In turn, Whole Foods would make some of Revolution's organic branded food items—such as peanut butter and applesauce—available in its stores. With chef Amy Klein, who is also a business partner, Tobey and Richmond hired production workers to cook, pack, and ship the lunches. The team signed agreements with several California school districts and began serving a whole new style of school lunch.

Today, Revolution Foods employs 70 workers and produces roughly 20,000 nutritious breakfasts, lunches, and snacks each day for students in 150 California schools and after-school programs. Most students come from low-income families, so the meals are critical for their nutrition and learning. A typical breakfast might include cereal, yogurt, organic cheese, and fresh fruit. Lunch often includes Revolution's own organic peanut butter and concord grape jelly sandwiches or the more exotic chicken teriyaki with fresh vegetables and organic brown rice. A favorite among students is fresh quesadillas and tamales. Snacks include yogurt, whole-grain crackers and chips, and fruit and nut snack bars. The kids often come back for more.

Although Revolution expects to see revenues of $10 million in the coming year, it may be a bit longer before the company turns profitable. New start-ups take time, and investors know they are betting on two savvy businesswomen who are fulfilling a growing need. Currently, Revolution charges $3 to $3.25 for student meals and $5 for the meals it sells to teachers. Public schools are reimbursed for a portion of the cost through the National School Lunch Program. Revolution plans to expand into more school districts to grow revenues.

The firm also offers its branded lunchbox foods to parents who pack their children's meals at home. Kids can enjoy Pop Alongs organic whole-grain chips or Jammy Sammy snack bars. A box of five Jammy Sammy peanut-butter-and-jelly snack bars sells for $4 at Whole Foods, and a bag of the chips is about $3. The prices aren't cheap, but parents know that the food is good. In addition to expanding its product line, Revolution keeps its costs down by buying ingredients in bulk from local companies and through its wholesale purchases from Whole Foods.

As their business grows, Tobey and Richmond are determined to remain true to their original vision. "We believe that all children deserve healthy, fresh food every day. Our goal is to serve as many students as we possibly can," says Tobey. Richmond echoes her partner's view. "A well-balanced diet can be challenging for kids. We believe that healthy food choices are key drivers of wellness, education, and the future productivity of our youth."[1]

Like millions of people, you'd probably love to start and run your own company. Perhaps, like Revolution Foods founders, you've spent time trying to devise a concept for a business you could launch. If you've been bitten by the entrepreneurial bug, you're not alone. More than ever, people like you, your classmates, and your friends are choosing the path of entrepreneurship.

How do you become an entrepreneur? Experts advise aspiring entrepreneurs to learn as much as possible about business by completing academic programs such as the one in which you are currently enrolled and by gaining practical experience by working part- or full-time for businesses. In addition, you can obtain invaluable insights about the pleasures and pitfalls of entrepreneurship by reading newspaper and magazine articles and biographies of successful entrepreneurs. These sources will help you learn how entrepreneurs handle the challenges of starting their businesses. For advice on how to launch and grow a new venture, turn to magazines such as *Entrepreneur, Success, Black Enterprise, Hispanic,* and *Inc.* Entrepreneurship associations such as the Association of African-American Women Business Owners and the Entrepreneurs' Organization also provide invaluable assistance. Finally, any aspiring entrepreneur should visit these Web sites:

- U.S. Chamber of Commerce (http://www.uschamber.com)
- Entrepreneur.com (http://www.entrepreneur.com)
- Kauffman eVenturing (http://www.kauffman.org/eventuring)
- The Small Business Administration (http://www.sba.gov)
- *The Wall Street Journal* Small Business (http://online.wsj.com/small-business)

In this chapter, we focus on pathways for entering the world of entrepreneurship, describing the activities of entrepreneurs, the different kinds of entrepreneurs, and the reason a growing number of people choose to be entrepreneurs. It discusses the business environment in which entrepreneurs work, the characteristics that help entrepreneurs succeed, and the ways they start new ventures. The chapter ends with a discussion of methods by which large companies try to incorporate the entrepreneurial spirit.

What Is an Entrepreneur?

entrepreneur person who seeks a profitable opportunity and takes the necessary risks to set up and operate a business.

"They Said It"

"It's just paper. All I own is a pickup truck and a little Wal-Mart stock."

—*Sam Walton (1918–1992) American entrepreneur*

You learned in Chapter 1 that an **entrepreneur** is a risk taker in the private enterprise system, a person who seeks a profitable opportunity and takes the necessary risks to set up and operate a business. Consider Sam Walton, Wal-Mart's founder, who started by franchising a few small Ben Franklin variety stores, and then opened his own Walton Five and Dime stores. Forty-five years later, this small venture has grown into a multibillion-dollar global business that is the largest company on earth.

Entrepreneurs differ from many small-business owners. Although many small-business owners possess the same drive, creative energy, and desire to succeed, what makes entrepreneurs different is their overwhelming desire to make their businesses grow. Sam Walton wasn't satisfied with just one successful Ben Franklin franchise, so he purchased others. And when that wasn't enough, he started and grew his own stores. Entrepreneurs combine their ideas and drive with money, employees, and other resources to create a business that fills a market need. That entrepreneurial role can make something significant out of a small beginning. Of the 500 CEOs in *Inc.* magazine's 500 fastest-growing U.S. companies, 38 percent have a net worth of more than $5 million.[2]

Entrepreneurs also differ from managers. Managers are employees who direct the efforts of others to achieve an organization's goals. Owners of some small start-up firms serve as owner–managers to implement their plans for their businesses and to offset human resource limitations at their fledgling companies. Entrepreneurs may also perform a managerial role, but their overriding responsibility is to use the resources of their organizations—employees, money, equipment, and facilities—to accomplish their goals. That is exactly how Jake Nickell and Jacob De Hart opened the Threadless T-shirt store on Chicago's north side. The two, who had met in college a few years earlier, entered an online T-shirt design competition; Nickell won. After working together on some online projects, they decided to start their own business, raised $1,000, and launched Threadless.com. At the Web site, people could submit T-shirt designs, visitors to the site could vote for their favorite, and the winning design would be printed. While Nickell and De Hart continued to work full-time in advertising, they spread the word about Threadless by using "street armies" to talk up the T-shirts. Eventually, both men quit their ad jobs and began hiring employees. Sales grew from $600,000 to $1.5 million in a year; recently, annual sales hit $15 million. With a successful business model on the Web, why add a retail store, a risky move that often fails? Says Nickell, "We really had no reason to open a store. It just seemed like a fun thing to do."[3] Some might call that crazy; some would call it the entrepreneurial spirit.

Studies have identified certain personality traits and behaviors common to entrepreneurs that differ from those required for managerial success. One of these traits is the willingness to assume the risks involved in starting a new venture. Some, like Jake Nickell and Jacob De Hart, leave their jobs to start their own companies and become successful entrepreneurs. Others find that they lack the skills required to start and grow a business. Entrepreneurial characteristics are examined in detail in a later section of this chapter.

Categories of Entrepreneurs

Entrepreneurs apply their talents in different situations. These differences can be classified into distinct categories: classic entrepreneurs, serial entrepreneurs, and social entrepreneurs.

Classic entrepreneurs identify business opportunities and allocate available resources to tap those markets. Jared Schiffman and Phillip Tiongson, graduates of the MIT Media Laboratory, exemplify classic entrepreneurs. They founded Potion Design, a small New York technology design firm that specializes in interactive retail installations. Through their business, they create innovative spaces that inform, educate, and entertain by integrating digital capabilities into physical structures. For example, the firm created an interactive exhibit for the Museum at Eldridge Street, on New York City's lower east side. By touching the top of a display table, visitors to the museum can navigate through photos, stories, and activities displayed on a screen above the table. For the Metropolitan Museum of Art, Potion created a system to find and read object labels for a Greek and Roman collection of 3,500 objects. Six kiosks along the wall show interactive maps of the gallery. Touching a case brings up photos of each object, and touching an object shows its label and alternative views of the object.[4]

While a classic entrepreneur starts a new company by identifying a business opportunity and allocating resources to tap a new market, serial entrepreneurs start one business, run it, and then start and run additional businesses in succession. Juha

classic entrepreneur person who identifies a business opportunity and allocates available resources to tap that market.

serial entrepreneur person who starts one business, runs it, and then starts and runs additional businesses in succession.

Entrepreneurs Jared Schiffman and Phillip Tiongson created this interactive exhibit for the Museum at Eldridge Street in New York City. By touching the top of the display table, visitors can navigate through the 3D diagrams and photos displayed on the screen above, read stories about the Jewish immigrants who settled the neighborhood, or participate in activities designed for young people. Schiffman and Tiongson are *classic entrepreneurs*, who identify a business opportunity and then marshall the resources to pursue it.

© Potion Design

Christensen is a serial entrepreneur. He never earned a college degree but gained experience working in his family's small aviation company outside Copenhagen. At age 17 he started a computer-reselling business. For over two decades he has been a big player in the wireless sector: he helped pioneer personal digital assistants before there was a Palm Pilot; he persuaded some of the world's top cell phone manufacturers to adopt a common operating system called Symbian; he headed Microsoft's move into smart phones; a few years later he moved on to Web start-up Macromedia and made millions when the company was sold to Adobe Systems. His latest venture, a Menlo Park, California, start-up called Sonopia, leases part of the radio communications spectrum owned by Verizon Wireless and resells it to other companies who sign up their own customers. Using customized handsets and customer support provided by Sonopia, small, diverse organizations can become phone companies with their own networks. Christensen has signed up more than 5,000 small organizations, including the National Wildlife Federation and the Atlantic League's Long Island Ducks in Central Islip, New York. The team uses Sonopia's services to offer fans green Motorola Razr phones with duck emblems and ringtones that quack.[5]

Some entrepreneurs focus on solving society's challenges through their businesses. **Social entrepreneurs** recognize a societal problem and use business principles to develop innovative solutions. Social entrepreneurs are pioneers of innovations that benefit humanity. Jane Addams founded Hull House in 1889 to improve living conditions in a poor immigrant neighborhood in Chicago, then expanded her efforts nationally. Maria Montessori, the first female physician in Italy, began working with children in 1906 and pioneered a revolutionary education method that supports individual development. Today, the Montessori method is used all over the world. Muhammad Yunus changed economics by founding the Grameen Bank, or "village bank," in Bangladesh in 1976 to offer very small business loans called *microloans* to help impoverished people become self-sufficient. That business model has been replicated in 58 countries.[6] Today, the world is filled with talented bankers, actors, and innovators turned social entrepreneurs. One example is eBay founder Pierre Omidyar, whose latest venture, Omidyar Network, pairs a traditional foundation with a for-profit venture fund. The Omidyar Network has already raised $120 million for worthy causes. Omidyar supports not-for-profit organizations like Donorschoose.org, which provides school supplies for children.[7]

Assessment Check ✓

1. Is a social entrepreneur simply a philanthropist?
2. What do classic entrepreneurs and social entrepreneurs have in common?

Reasons to Choose Entrepreneurship as a Career Path

If you want to run your own business someday, you'll have plenty of company. Studies indicate that more than 12 percent of Americans, about one of every eight people, run their own businesses.[8] Surveys, however, generally indicate that many more people, as many as half of Americans, want to start their own businesses. This interest is even stronger among 14- to 19-year-olds; nearly two-thirds want to start and run their own business.[9] While general interest in entrepreneurship is very high, how many Americans are actually taking steps to start their own businesses at any particular time? About 465,000 new businesses are started each month in America.[10]

The past two decades have witnessed a heightened interest in entrepreneurial careers, spurred in part by publicity celebrating the successes of entrepreneurs such as Michael Dell, who launched what would become personal computer giant Dell following his freshman year at the University of Texas; Martha Stewart, who parlayed her design skills into magazine publishing, TV production, and extensive product lines of home goods; and Bill Gates, who left Harvard to start Microsoft with friend Paul Allen.

People choose to become entrepreneurs for many different reasons. Some are motivated by dissatisfaction with the traditional work world, citing desires to escape unreasonable bosses or insufficient rewards and recognition. Other people start businesses because they believe their ideas represent opportunities to fulfill customer needs. George Naddaff has launched more than half a dozen companies, his most famous, Boston Chicken. When he was a kid in Boston, his father lost his job, so George and his brothers shined shoes. He would charge 10 cents back then, and when a customer gave him a quarter, he would rummage around in his pockets looking for change. Eventually, his customers, mostly sailors in the tough part of Boston, would get frustrated and tell him to keep the change. That was his first introduction to business, and that drive he had as a young boy with a father out of work never left him. He confesses, "I love to sell what I believe in." Now 77, his latest venture is UFood Grill, a restaurant chain for health-conscious consumers.[11]

As pointed out in Figure 6.1, people become entrepreneurs for one or more of four major reasons: a desire to be their own boss, succeed financially, attain job security, and improve their quality of life. Each of these reasons is described in more detail in the following sections.

Being Your Own Boss

Self-management is the motivation that drives many entrepreneurs. One entrepreneur who matches this portrait of the American independent professional as an individual who has control over when, where, and how she works is Liz Lange, the 40-something founder and CEO of Liz Lange Maternity. Lange recognized a real need while working as a designer's assistant. Expectant mothers seeking sophisticated maternity wear quickly discovered that they would have to make do with baby-doll dresses or pants with a hole cut in the front—and a Lycra panel to accommodate their unborn child. Lange found herself offended by what was available. So, she left her job to begin work designing a few basic items to show to retail buyers. They stated that pregnant women would not spend money on high-end maternity clothing. Undaunted, she borrowed $50,000 from family and friends and opened a small New York City office, where she sold her made-to-order clothes by appointment. Word of the high-fashion maternity

social entrepreneur person who recognizes societal problems and uses business principles to develop innovative solutions.

"They Said It"

"Social entrepreneurs are not content to just give a fish or teach how to fish. They will not rest until they have revolutionized the fishing industry."

—**Bill Drayton** (b. 1943) CEO and founder of Ashoka, a global nonprofit organization devoted to fostering social entrepreneurship

Figure 6.1

Why People Become Entrepreneurs

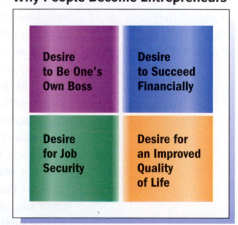

Desire to Be One's Own Boss

Desire to Succeed Financially

Desire for Job Security

Desire for an Improved Quality of Life

Liz Lange, founder of the trendsetting company Liz Lange Maternity, wanted to be her own boss. For many entrepreneurs, controlling when, where, and how they work is a major motivator.

© AP/Wide World Photos

clothing spread like wildfire and led to an article in *The New York Times* Style section. Sales exploded after that, and Lange decided to bypass department stores in favor of selected high-fashion boutiques. Soon her fashions were attracting stylish expectant moms, including some celebrities. According to Lange, "The trend is to look like anybody else who is fashionable."

Today, Lange runs stores in Beverly Hills, on New York's Madison Avenue, and on Long Island, New York, as well as producing an online catalog (http://www.lizlange.com) and a separate, less expensive line of clothes marketed at more than 1,300 Target stores nationwide. Her most recent introduction is the fourth-trimester line, postpartum pieces for the time before a woman is back to her pre-baby shape. Annual sales are about $10 million, not including her mass-market line. Both Lange and her satisfied customers agree that her decision to be her own boss was wise.[12] Marc Ecko is another entrepreneur who has followed his interest, this time in graffiti art and skateboard culture. Ecko has built an empire based on urban-style clothing, as the "Hit & Miss" feature describes.

Financial Success

Entrepreneurs are wealth creators. Many start their ventures with the specific goal of creating a profitable business and reaping its financial rewards. Why? Because they believe they won't get rich by working for someone else, and they're generally right. Research indicates that entrepreneurs are, on average, wealthier than wage earners. While entrepreneurs comprise less than 9 percent of U.S. households, they hold 39 percent of the wealth.[13]

The business press, of course, is quick to publish stories about the wealth and "self-made" successes of today's entrepreneurs. For example, it's common knowledge that Google founders Sergey Brin and Larry Page made more than $14 billion each when Google sold its shares in an initial public offering, and they are worth much more than that today. Less well known, though, are successful entrepreneurs such as Brett Hatton, who got his idea for a business while hitchhiking through Pakistan. On one of his stops, Hatton encountered a warehouse full of beautiful antiques and purchased several pieces. Later he started an antique store in Essex, England, before moving to Texas to open Four Hands, which manufactures antique reproductions in China and India. His company now employs 125 people with annual sales of $42 million. Crate & Barrel and Neiman Marcus sell his antique reproductions.[14]

Although entrepreneurs often mention financial rewards as a motive for starting their businesses, the path to riches can be long and uncertain. As you learned in Chapter 5, one-third of newly started small firms are out of business within two years, more than half within four years, 61 percent within six years, and 82 percent within ten years.[15] So there's clearly no guarantee of success. When Mel Zuckerman opened Canyon Ranch in Tucson, he was overweight and in poor health. He sold every asset he had to build a place where people with similar problems

Hit & Miss

Marc Ecko's Edgy Designs

You know Marc Ecko is unconventional when you watch his video of graffiti artists writing the words "Still Free" on Air Force One, then listen to him explain why he posted it on the Web—to support art, creativity, and free speech. You might guess that he's a former graffiti artist, but you may not surmise that he's the creator of a billion-dollar business.

Ecko (born Marc Milecofsky) is chairman and chief creative officer of Marc Ecko Enterprises, co-founded and owned with his twin sister, Marci Tapper, and friend Seth Gerszberg. Started in 1993, the company produces urban-edgy clothing, accessories, videogames, and a magazine and has annual sales of more than $1.5 billion.

Marc Ecko started in business at 14, painting T-shirts in the family garage. While a Rutgers University pharmacology student, he used his knowledge of graffiti art and skateboard and hip-hop culture to start a men's clothing line. The Eckō Unlimited brand (eckō unltd) with its urban style and rhinoceros mascot, was the first of the company's many brands. The company now has a lineup including Zoo York action sports, Avirex sportswear, the Red women's line, Cut 'N' Sew, and G-Unit Clothing, a joint venture with rapper Curtis "50 Cent" Jackson. Ecko clothing, watches, and other accessories are sold in specialty stores and large retailers like Macy's and Lord & Taylor and in 38 Eckō Unlimited outlets.

Quick expansion threatened the cash-strapped company in its early years. The partners looked for someone to buy them out, but no one wanted a company with sales of $16 million and debt of $7 million. An investor linked to a clothing company—with a warehouse, production shops, and computer systems—came to the rescue. Focused on marketing and production, the three founders took sales to $96 million in 18 months and repaid their creditor. The missteps weren't over, however. Ecko designed a new clothing line that bombed in retail stores. He then turned his focus from hands-on design to leading his team of artists.

The company has begun an ambitious expansion in the fiercely competitive retail industry. It plans to open 150 stores, including one in New York City's Times Square. "Retail expansion is a great cultural shift for our company, controlling our own destiny," Ecko says. He wants his destiny to include large-scale social projects in public school reform and public art. He and his partners founded and fully support a Ukrainian orphanage, to keep a pledge that they would donate a big portion of their profits to a children's charity if the company was able to pay back its large debts.

Meanwhile, Ecko publishes *Complex,* a bimonthly men's magazine and develops more videogames "just to have fun—that's the most important thing," he says. His first, *Getting Up: Contents Under Pressure,* features graffiti artists in a future universe. By the way, Ecko's Air Force One graffiti video (http://www.stillfree.com) looked realistic enough to prompt government officials to make sure the plane shown wasn't the real Air Force One.

Questions for Critical Thinking

1. What entrepreneurial characteristics describe Marc Ecko? Explain.
2. When the company needed cash in its early years, why do you think Ecko and his partners used debt financing rather than other funding methods?

Sources: Jake Chessum, "It's Going to Be Big," *Inc.*, March 2009, pp. 52–57; Andrea Cooper, "Who Wants to Be a Billionaire?" *Entrepreneur,* February 2008, http://www.entrepreneur.com; Lee Hawkins, "Marc Ecko's Urbanwear Line to Expand," *The Wall Street Journal,* March 9, 2007, p. B3.

could come to get back in shape and regain their health. In the first few years, Canyon Ranch almost went under. But Zuckerman believed in his concept and persevered; a few years later, as people became more fitness-conscious, Canyon Ranch became a vacation spot of choice. Today Canyon Ranch is an empire with $150 million in revenue, two resort spas, three SpaClubs, and Canyon Ranch Living condo complexes, but Mel Zuckerman, now 80 years old, knows it wasn't always that way.[16]

Job Security

Although the demand for skilled employees remains high in many industries, working for a company, even a *Fortune* 500 firm, is no guarantee of job security. In fact, over the past ten years, large companies sought efficiency by downsizing and actually eliminated more jobs than they created. As a result, a growing number of American workers—both first-time job seekers and laid-off long-term employees—are deciding to create their own job security by starting their own businesses. While running your own business doesn't guarantee job security, the U.S. Small Business Administration has found that most newly created jobs come from small businesses, with a significant share of those jobs coming from new companies.[17]

In his new book *The Breakthrough Company*, Keith McFarland examines how industry powerhouses are created. McFarland, a consultant and former CEO of Collectech Systems—a collection agency for telecom companies—studied nine of the *Inc.* 500 companies that had reached more than $250 million in annual sales. Why do some companies grow while others struggle? McFarland found that the "breakthrough" companies are not only great at hiring people but also great at developing people. At one of the companies examined, nuts and bolts distributor Fastenol, the average tenure among the top 25 employees was 23 years; the people running the company a couple decades ago when it was small are running it today, when it has $2 billion in sales. While such management stability isn't always the case, McFarland notes that successful entrepreneurs recognize that to grow and prosper, they must build a culture where ordinary workers can thrive and survive.[18]

Quality of Life

lifestyle entrepreneur person who starts a business to reduce work hours and create a more relaxed lifestyle.

Entrepreneurship is an attractive career option for people seeking to improve their quality of life. Starting a business gives the founder some choice over when, where, and how to work. A **lifestyle entrepreneur** is a person who starts a business to reduce work hours and create a more relaxed life. An individual seeking independence, freedom, and control over time may pursue this avenue. But this does not mean that success can be achieved by working less diligently or with less devotion. It is a common misconception that entrepreneurship is an easy route for someone tired of working and with a little extra cash to invest; many people lost their money with this attitude. In fact, individuals often find they become more involved and work more hours because the business is theirs, as are the risks and rewards. But by selecting an industry wisely, an entrepreneur can see an improvement in lifestyle, whether it be less travel, more control over hours worked, freedom from having a "boss," and so on. For instance, it is not complicated or expensive to go into Web development if your interests and talents lie there. Online ventures can be attractive to lifestyle entrepreneurs because they have more control over their time. Conversely, if you want to start a store that provides packaging and shipping services, you need a physical location, equipment, and employees, and you will probably need to put in long hours.

Entrepreneurs looking for a more relaxed lifestyle often find that pursuing a new venture is in their blood. Serial entrepreneur Dennis Pushkin sold his furniture manufacturing company at age 31 to spend more time boating and fishing. He started an automobile detailing franchise but sold it three years later because he wanted more time to coach kids' sports. Then he ran a dry-cleaning company, which he also left a few years later to play more golf. His most recent venture is MoreVisibility, an online search optimization company.[19]

> ## "They Said It"
>
> "You can turn the radar down a bit. But keep it on."
>
> —Dennis Pushkin (b. 1948) Founder, MoreVisibility

Assessment Check ✔

1. Are entrepreneurs more likely than employees to achieve financial success?
2. What factors affect the entrepreneur's job security?

The Environment for Entrepreneurs

If you are motivated to start your own company, several factors suggest that now may be the right time to begin. First, as discussed earlier in the chapter, the status of entrepreneurship as a career choice has been rising. Entrepreneurship began moving toward the business mainstream in the early 1980s after Steve Jobs of Apple Computers and other high-tech entrepreneurs gained national attention by going public—that is, selling stock in their companies. And, as discussed later in the chapter, today's entrepreneurs are also reaping the benefits of financial interest among investors. In addition to favorable public attitudes toward entrepreneurs and the growing number of financing options, several other factors—identified in Figure 6.2—also support and expand opportunities for entrepreneurs: globalization, education, information technology, and demographic and economic trends. Each of these factors is discussed in the following sections.

Figure 6.2

Factors Supporting and Expanding Opportunities for Entrepreneurs

Globalization

The rapid globalization of business, described in preceding chapters, has created many opportunities for entrepreneurs. Entrepreneurs market their products abroad and hire international talent. Among the fastest-growing small U.S. companies, almost two of every five have international sales. Lisa Knoppe Reed started Art for a Cause in her kitchen. The company creates and sells hand-painted tools and furniture. Knoppe Reed left the corporate world and was looking for a way to make a difference in the lives of others. After giving a speech to a special education class at a local school, Knoppe Reed was impressed with the students and thought of a way to help them and her company. She showed them how to sand and prime her tools and offered to donate a percentage of the revenue to the class. Today Knoppe Reed is assisted by special needs children and adults in classes throughout Michigan, and the company has moved well beyond its original boundaries. Art for a Cause markets its products to gift retailers and can be found in 4,000 stores around the world. She projects annual sales will reach $2.5 million.[20]

Growth in entrepreneurship is a worldwide phenomenon. The role of entrepreneurs is growing in most industrialized and newly industrialized nations, as well as in the emerging free-market countries in central and eastern Europe. However, as shown in Figure 6.3, the level of entrepreneurship varies considerably. Worldwide, more than 9 percent of adults are starting or managing a new business. Thailand leads in the number of adults engaged in entrepreneurial activity (27 percent), followed by Peru (26 percent), Colombia (23 percent), Venezuela (20 percent), Dominican Republic (17 percent), and China (16 percent). The United States, with more than 9 percent of adults qualifying as entrepreneurs, is currently in 13th place.[21]

Figure 6.3 also shows that entrepreneurs in many other countries, such as Japan (4 percent), Belgium and Puerto Rico (3 percent each), and Russia and Austria (2 percent each), find it much more difficult to start businesses. Obstacles include government regulations, high taxes, and political attitudes that favor big business. In the United Kingdom, which has a below-average rate of entrepreneurship (slightly less than 6 percent), five in ten small-business owners say they would not start a new company because of the heavy burden of government regulation.[22]

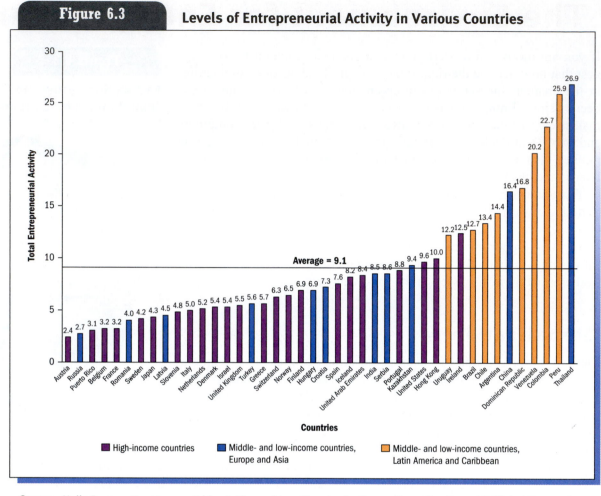

Figure 6.3   Levels of Entrepreneurial Activity in Various Countries

Source: Neils Bosma, Kent Jones, Erkko Autio, and Jonathan Levie, "2007 Executive Report," *Global Enterprise Monitor,* 2008, p. 16.

Education

The past two decades have brought tremendous growth in the number of educational opportunities for would-be entrepreneurs. Today, more than 100 U.S. universities offer full-fledged majors in entrepreneurship, dozens of others offer an emphasis in entrepreneurship, and hundreds more offer one or two courses in how to start a business.[23] Some schools, including Alfred University, University of St. Thomas, and Miami University of Ohio, offer entrepreneurship courses to nonbusiness students, on the assumption that people in other disciplines will eventually start businesses, too.

Another way business education is responding to the interest in entrepreneurship is by helping their students start firms. Babson College has a program in which a few students are permitted to replace several of the usual classes with launching an actual business under the direction of an entrepreneur-turned-professor. At the University of Maryland, entrepreneurship students live together in an exclusive, apartment-style residence hall that, with dedicated meeting rooms, offices, and computer labs, is designed to encourage interaction and ideas. Students are taught by entrepreneurship professors, experienced entrepreneurs, CEOs, and technology specialists from the engineering school and industry. Students in this program are not only expected to start a business but also given responsibility to run the university's business plan competition and technology start-up boot camp.[24]

Besides schools, many organizations have sprouted up in recent years to teach entrepreneurship to young people. The Kauffman Center for Entrepreneurial Leadership offers training programs for learners from kindergarten through community college. The center's Entreprep summer program, which is taught in conjunction with local colleges and universities, teaches high school juniors how to start and manage a company. Students in Free Enterprise (SIFE) is a worldwide not-for-profit organization in which college students, working with faculty advisors, teach grade school and high school students and other community members the value of private enterprise and entrepreneurship.[25] The Association of Collegiate Entrepreneurs has chapters on many college campuses in the United States and Canada.

The question, of course, is whether students who major in entrepreneurship or take entrepreneurship classes are any more likely to start a successful business. In fact, students who graduate from entrepreneurship programs are three times as likely to be self-employed and three times more likely to help start new companies.[26] Research studies have also shown that entrepreneurship education raises both attitudes and overall entrepreneurial intentions.[27] Take Brian Burns, a graduate of Clark University in Worcester, Massachusetts. Burns, as a consumer of extreme sports information, always had an idea of putting together maps and travel guides of the best running trails, bike routes, and swimming pools. While doing a case study on a high-end bike shop for a class in the university's Innovation and Entrepreneurship Program, Burns saw his idea crystallize: "I can still recall the night when things came together for me. What would the maps look like? How would I distribute them? What would I call this thing?" "This thing" became a new business called Multisport Maps.[28] Burns has since moved on to Startup Writing, a business specializing in writing copy for young companies.

Information Technology

The explosion in information technology (IT) has provided one of the biggest boosts for entrepreneurs. As computer and communications technologies have merged and dropped dramatically in cost, entrepreneurs have gained tools that help them compete with large companies. Information technology helps entrepreneurs work quickly and efficiently, provide attentive customer service, increase sales, and project professional images. In fact, technology has leveled the playing field to the point that, through the use of inexpensive and intelligent computer programming tools and instant Web distribution, a dorm-room innovator like Michael Dell can compete with a big company like IBM.[29] Charles Simonyi's programming start-up, Intentional Software, produces software so smart users can simply tell it what they want it to do. Once they enter a few basic instructions, the software will write its own code; users do not need any programming skills.[30]

Growing numbers of franchises are plunging into the information technology industry, with applications ranging from computer troubleshooting to network support. These IT franchises serve both business and residential consumers and can be found in shopping malls, electronic stores, and via toll-free phone numbers. Franchises to watch in this arena include Concerto Networks (www.concertonetworks.com), and Geeks in a Flash (www.geeksinaflash.com).[31]

The Internet and the Web have also created opportunities for entrepreneurs. In the finance industry, many entrepreneurs have used information technology to revolutionize stock-trading systems. John J. Lothian created a Web site called Markets Wiki to provide investors information about stocks.[32] Otis Chandler is a software engineer and entrepreneur who launched Goodreads (www.goodreads.com), an online site where visitors can exchange news about book titles, read reviews, and join an online book group.[33] Entrepreneurs are also using other networking sites to target customers. Restaurateur Sabena Puri created a profile page on Facebook for her upscale Indian restaurant, Junnoon, in Palo Alto, California. Diners can use Facebook to talk to one another, learn about the restaurant, and read reviews.[34]

Demographic and Economic Trends

Demographic trends, such as the aging of the U.S. population, the emergence of Hispanics as the nation's largest ethnic group, and the growth of two-income families, create opportunities for entrepreneurs to market new goods and services. Entrepreneurs take advantage of such trends to offer everything from retirement homes to grocery delivery services. For example, the active Baby Boomer market has provided an abundance of opportunity for one entrepreneur, Thom Hill. His company, Old Guys Rule, located in Ventura, California, produces apparel featuring vintage-inspired graphics targeted at aging Baby Boomers. According to Hill, "With the aging boomer population being as active as they are, we jumped on it and created a lifestyle brand for people who were active and have discretionary time and income." The brand is popular with golfers, surfers, bikers, and boaters.[35]

The changing population also influences who becomes an entrepreneur. For the last decade, adults aged 55 to 64 have been the age group most likely to start a business.[36] As Baby Boomers continue to age and control a large share of wealth in this country, the trend can only be expected to continue. Older entrepreneurs will also have access to their retirement funds and home equity for financing. Many Boomers also plan to work after retirement. Terry Alderete didn't have to work after 30 years at Pacific Bell, but the contacts she made as ethnic marketing director created an opportunity. Now she organizes events like Cinco de Mayo and Dia de los Muertos celebrations in Oakland, California.[37]

Characteristics of Entrepreneurs

The examples of entrepreneurship you've read about so far suggest that people who strike out on their own are a different breed. Successful entrepreneurs are more likely to have had parents who were entrepreneurs. They also tend to possess unique personality traits. Researchers who study successful entrepreneurs report that they are more likely to be inquisitive, passionate, self-motivated, honest, courageous, flexible, intelligent, and reliable people. The eight traits summarized in Figure 6.4 are especially important for people who want to succeed as entrepreneurs.

Figure 6.4

Characteristics of Entrepreneurs

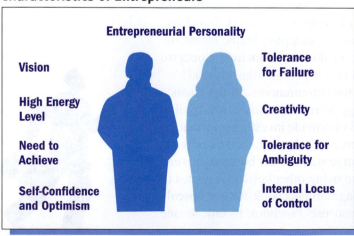

Entrepreneurial Personality

Vision

High Energy Level

Need to Achieve

Self-Confidence and Optimism

Tolerance for Failure

Creativity

Tolerance for Ambiguity

Internal Locus of Control

Vision

Entrepreneurs begin with a *vision*, an overall idea for how to make their business idea a success, and then they passionately pursue it. Bill Gates and Paul Allen launched Microsoft with the vision of a computer on every desk and in every home, all running Microsoft software. Their vision helped Microsoft become the world's largest marketer of computer software. It guided the company and provided clear direction for employees as Microsoft grew, adapted, and prospered in an industry characterized by tremendous technological change.

Arguably, every invention from the light bulb to the cell phone originated from a person with vision. In fact, some of the greatest innovators were so far ahead of their time they were labeled "crazy" or worse. Michael Lehrer was an accountant when his first child was born. While changing

Hit & Miss

Elon Musk: Rocket Man and More

Elon Musk is a man with lofty goals, like building rockets to take astronauts to and from the International Space Station by 2011 and making space transportation affordable enough to make it possible to populate another planet.

Musk is so serious about his dream that he founded SpaceX with $100 million of his own money. The El Segundo, California, start-up of 370 employees has launched two Falcon rockets. The first blew up. The second flew 200 miles into space before spinning out of control—the first time a privately financed rocket reached orbital altitude. After that record-breaking flight, SpaceX booked orders for 14 launches over the next few years, at the per-launch cost of $35 million to $55 million for a 178-foot high, 12-foot wide Falcon 9 rocket. SpaceX was profitable in the first year, with more than $100 million in revenue.

Musk has been called revolutionary, visionary, or crazy. "He is very much the person who, when someone says it's impossible, shrugs and says, 'I think I can do it,'" says Max Levchin, who cofounded PayPal with Musk.

From his first venture—creating and selling a video-game as a 12-year-old in South Africa—Musk has shown a hard-driving entrepreneurial spirit. After graduating from the University of Pennsylvania with degrees in finance and physics, he entered Stanford University's PhD program in physics. He quit after two days but stayed in Silicon Valley, where young techno-entrepreneurs were finding overnight success with big new ideas. "I wanted to be involved in something that would matter to the world and be important to the future of humanity," he says.

Interested in space, renewable energy, and the Internet, Musk first started Zip2, an Internet directory service that later sold for $307 million. With his 7 percent share of $22 million, Musk went right to work on a new idea—online banking, specifically payment processing. His second company, X.com, merged with another run by Levchin and Peter Thiel, and together they developed PayPal, which eBay bought for $1.5 billion.

Internet success enabled Musk to pursue his other big ideas. He founded Tesla Motors to develop electric cars that could compete with gasoline-powered cars. The $98,000 Tesla Roadster is by all accounts faster, cooler, and more fun to drive than similarly priced gas guzzlers. Musk intends to develop a Tesla sedan and open dealerships and service centers. His third current company also has an environmental focus. SolarCity, started by Musk and two cousins, designs and installs solar paneling systems in areas of California. Musk plans to go nationwide, with the goal of reducing the cost of solar so that everyone can adopt clean power.

Questions for Critical Thinking

1. How do you think the four environmental factors have influenced Elon Musk's success in previous ventures and his choice of current ones?
2. How important is it for an entrepreneur like Elon Musk to have a clear vision of what he wants to accomplish? Explain.

Sources: Michael Kanellos, "Elon Musk on Rockets, Sports Cars, and Solar Power," *CNET News*, February 15, 2008, http://www.news.com, accessed March 3, 2009; Richard Waters, "Elon Musk," *Financial Times*, December 26, 2007, http://www.FT.com, accessed October 14, 2008; Max Chafkin, "Entrepreneur of the Year '07: Elon Musk," *Inc.*, December 2007, pp. 115–125.

his son's bib, he realized he would have to change it, wash it, and get a clean one every time the baby spit up or drooled. He later launched Better Baby Products and sold Double Dribble bibs featuring interchangeable pieces to several large retailers. Although the business didn't bring much profit, it did give him confidence for his next venture, a golfing green in the backyard. At first, his neighbors thought he was crazy, especially when he replaced his lawn with a synthetic green that would need little maintenance. But within a year he was tearing up his neighbors' yards and building greens for them. Through referrals and quality work, he began taking on customers beyond his neighborhood. Now Lehrer's company, Home Green Advantage, builds 40 greens a year in places from suburban New York to Manhattan rooftops. It all started one day in a conference room when "Fairway to Heaven" struck Lehrer out of the blue.[38] Similarly, the vision of providing economically feasible space transportation, practical electronic cars, and affordable solar energy propelled Elon Musk to start three companies with his own money, as the "Hit & Miss" feature describes.

> ## "They Said It"
>
> "Vision is the art of seeing things invisible."
>
> —Jonathan Swift (1667–1745) English cleric and satirist

High Energy Level

Entrepreneurs willingly work hard to realize their visions. Starting and building a company require an enormous amount of hard work and long hours. Some entrepreneurs work full-time at their regular day jobs and spend weeknights and weekends launching their start-ups. Many devote seven days a week to their new ventures. The average time to start up a business is about two years, and working 50 hours a week is the norm.[39]

Many entrepreneurs work alone or with a very small staff. Therefore, a high energy level is a must. Truman and Minhee Cho grew up together, started dating in their twenties, then married. The couple started Paper+Cup+Design, a stationery and graphics company in Brooklyn. Minhee left her job as a magazine designer, while Truman still works full-time as a computer engineer. Minhee oversees a small staff of five, and Truman works several hours each evening at the office dealing with investors and new retail customers. The couple has expended enormous energy to place their note cards, journals, and gift tags in 250 stores nationwide.[40]

Because entrepreneurs like the Chos often work long hours, even two jobs, one of the major challenges they face is balancing the hard work with rest, recreation, and family time that are essential to good health, quality of life, and continued creativity.

At first, Michael Lehrer's neighbors scoffed at his vision of a backyard golfing green. Lehrer's company, Home Green Advantage, now builds 40 greens a year in suburban backyards.

© Michael Lehrer/Home Green Advantage

Need to Achieve

Entrepreneurs work hard because they want to excel. Their strong competitive drive helps them enjoy the challenge of reaching difficult goals and promotes dedication to personal success. A poll conducted by About.com showed Oprah Winfrey as the most admired entrepreneur. The first African American woman billionaire, Winfrey has built an empire stretching from television to magazines. Her own words best illustrate her strong drive: "I don't think of myself as a poor, deprived ghetto girl who made good. I think of myself as somebody who from an early age knew I was responsible for myself, and had to make good."[41]

During the past several years, most of PayPal's key players have left after selling out to eBay for $1.5 billion. Besides Elon Musk, with his SpaceX, Tesla Motors, and SolarCity, these PayPal alums have been building a variety of new ventures, including investment firms and several Internet companies. Co-founder Peter Thiel, who also had an early stake in Facebook, which is now worth about $1 billion, has founded a new venture capital firm that has Silicon Valley talking and runs a $3 billion hedge fund. Another PayPal cofounder, Max Levchin, runs a photo-sharing site called Slide and pulls in 134 million users a day. Thiel, Levchin, and other founders of the original PayPal run businesses worth an estimated $30 billion. A strong need to achieve pushes these successful serial entrepreneurs to further success.[42]

Self-Confidence and Optimism

Entrepreneurs believe in their ability to succeed, and they instill their optimism in others. Often their optimism resembles fearlessness in the face of difficult odds. They often see opportunities where others see danger lurking. Kevin Grauman founded and sold the Outsource Group—ranked number one on the *Inc.* 500—and now owns Emportal, a Web-based business that sells human resource tools such as online workforce management applications that track employees and vendors. In hard economic times, some firms are not looking for such products. Says Grauman, "I'm not a woe-is-me kind of guy." He knows that downturns in the economy are out of his

"They Said It"

"I'm not really interested in making money. That always comes as the result of success."

—*Steven Spielberg*
(b. 1946) American filmmaker

control, so he has to work with what he can control. While many business owners fear an economic downturn, Kevin Grauman sees more opportunities and thinks he will do well regardless of the economy.[43]

Some entrepreneurs have such confidence that they see what they want to see, and while this can be an asset, it can also be a limitation. *Rolling Stone* founder Jan Wenner has run the magazine according to his desires for 40 years. He has been a successful entrepreneur, but one shortcoming may be his limited use of the Web. The *Rolling Stone* site earns Wenner Media a few million dollars per year in licensing fees and some advertising revenue. Wenner, who says he's never lost a lot of money through what he calls "ridiculous online ideas," has been content with his company's Web site management, although he may look into some more lucrative ideas.[44]

Tolerance for Failure

Entrepreneurs often succeed by sheer will and the ability to try and try again when others would give up. They also view setbacks and failures as learning experiences and are not easily discouraged or disappointed when things don't go as planned. Bobbi Brown has built a big name in the cosmetics industry. Estée Lauder bought her company, and Brown stayed on in an active role. The brand faced some setbacks after its acquisition and sales went flat, but Brown never gave up. She met with the CEO, who said the problem was that the cosmetics were not setting themselves apart from the competition. Brown took the criticism in stride, learned from the setback, and decided to change the culture of the company. She moved out of the GM building to a loft in the SoHo section of Manhattan, made advertising photographs more editorial, and approached the cosmetics business as if it were a magazine. The company's numbers vastly improved and eventually hit half a billion dollars.[45]

Entrepreneurs often succeed simply because they won't give up. When sales of Bobbi Brown's cosmetics line stalled, she moved the company to a new location and revamped its advertising. In the process, she successfully differentiated her company from the competition.

© AP/Wide World Photos

Creativity

Entrepreneurs typically conceive new ideas for goods and services, and they devise innovative ways to overcome difficult problems and situations. If we look at the top entrepreneurs in the world, we can see that creativity is the common denominator. *Inc.* magazine presents an annual list of the 500 top small businesses, most of which were started by entrepreneurs. The word *solution* is in the name of 33 of these companies, and it captures the secret of their success: customers have a problem, and *Inc.* 500 companies find a creative solution. Many of these businesses outsource some of their functions; Attic Technologies offshores almost everything, including marketing, finance, and human resources. These companies have found creative ways to take in more without building costly facilities. Several of the companies, such as Szanca Solutions, provide cost-effective computer network support to the military.[46]

BusinessWeek publishes its 25 Under 25 list of the most promising young entrepreneurs in Europe, Asia, and the United States. Most of them wanted the independence and challenge of running their own business, and all have exhibited creativity in their ventures. Gabriel Erbst, 24, co-founded TableXChange, an online marketplace for reservations to top New York restaurants. For a fee of $15 to $40, TableXChange users can buy reservations from sellers, who also pay a transaction fee. Sarah Schupp is the 25-year-old founder of University Parent, a Boulder, Colorado, company that produces free, downloadable guides for parents visiting college campuses. Schupp attributes her success to a creative publishing model in which university partners are responsible for content and distribution while she takes care of advertising. It isn't surprising that most of the

25 Under 25 are building business around the Web, but it may surprise you that most of the businesses are already making a profit.[47]

Entrepreneurs like these young men and women often achieve success by making creative improvements, rather than single-handedly revolutionizing an industry. Research has shown that there is a substantial amount of creativity among entrepreneurs "at the tactical level"—in other words, in the ways entrepreneurs built their businesses, more so than in the product itself.[48]

Tolerance for Ambiguity

Entrepreneurs take in stride the uncertainties associated with launching a venture. Dealing with unexpected events is the norm for most entrepreneurs. Tolerance for ambiguity is different from the love of risk taking that many people associate with entrepreneurship. Successful entrepreneurship is a far cry from gambling because entrepreneurs look for strategies that they believe have a good chance of success, and they quickly make adjustments when a strategy isn't working. An important way entrepreneurs manage ambiguity is by staying close to customers so that they can adjust their offerings in keeping with customer desires.

When fuel costs rose dramatically, Robb Corwin, founder of Gorilla Fuel & Lube in Tempe, Arizona, found himself locked into hundreds of profit-draining contracts. Gorilla Fuel sells diesel and gasoline to businesses through flat-rate contracts. Corwin found himself in the unexpected position of selling fuel for less than he was paying for it. Corwin laments, "We were losing money on every drop." Faced with going out of business, Corwin began visiting his clients in person, telling them the contracts were killing his business. He risked his reputation by trying to renegotiate a contract before it is legally terminated, but only about a dozen refused. His company returned to profitability within six months.[49]

Internal Locus of Control

Entrepreneurs have an internal locus of control, which means they believe that they control their own fates. You won't find entrepreneurs gazing into a crystal ball, calling psychic help lines, or looking for a four-leaf clover; they take personal responsibility for the success or failure of their actions rather than believing in luck or fate. They neither make excuses for their shortcomings nor blame others for their setbacks and failures. Mario Barth is the owner and chief tattoo artist at Starlight Tattoo, with four profitable New Jersey studios and the Tattoo Super Store, an online tattoo supply business. One of Barth's tattoos costs $1,500, but most clients pay much more. Known in the industry as an innovator, he has celebrity clientele that includes Jason Kidd, Lenny Kravitz, Pamela Anderson, Def Leppard, and dozens more. With two more U.S. studios, four in Europe, and one in Asia under construction, Barth hopes to become the Starbucks of tattoo parlors. A business that has yet to shed its negative image, tattoo parlors can be found everywhere—1,500 in the U.S. alone by some estimates. If each shop generated $100 an hour for a 30-hour work week—a conservative estimate—the American tattoo industry is a $2.3 billion business. Research has shown that 36 percent of 18- to 25-year-olds have tattoos. Entrepreneurs have been reluctant to become involved in an industry that remains fragmented and dominated by small shops. But Barth doesn't worry about the stigma attached to the industry; in fact, he wants to improve it.[50]

After reading this summary of typical personality traits, maybe you're wondering if you have what it takes to become an entrepreneur. Take the test in Figure 6.5 to find out. Your results may help you determine whether you would succeed in starting your own company.

"They Said It"

"Being an entrepreneur doesn't mean jump off a ledge and make a parachute on the way down."

—Fred Smith (b. 1944)
Founder, FedEx

Assessment Check ✓

1. What is meant by an entrepreneur's vision?
2. Why is it important for an entrepreneur to have a high energy level and a strong need for achievement?
3. How do entrepreneurs generally feel about the possibility of failure?

Figure 6.5 **Quiz for Small Business Success**

Choose the answer you think is best for each question. There are no "wrong" answers. See page 211 for the scoring key.

1. What is the key to business success:
   a. business knowledge
   b. market awareness
   c. hands on management
   d. sufficient capital
   e. hard work

2. If a relative ever asks me for advice about starting a business I will tell them to:
   a. work for someone else in the field first
   b. write a business plan
   c. study marketing
   d. give up the idea
   e. learn about budgeting

3. Which is the largest potential trouble spot:
   a. too much growth
   b. too little growth
   c. too fast growth
   d. too slow growth
   e. sporadic growth

4. I trust: (select as many as apply)
   a. nobody
   b. myself
   c. my partner
   d. a few key employees
   e. my customers

5. I am unhappy when my employees are:
   a. late
   b. unhappy
   c. abrupt with customers
   d. resigning
   e. less dedicated than me

6. My customers are: (select as many as apply)
   a. always right
   b. too fussy
   c. demanding
   d. worth listening to
   e. dumb

7. Rank these in order of importance for small-business marketing success:
   a. word-of-mouth
   b. advertising
   c. signs
   d. location
   e. community events

8. When it comes to money I am:
   a. careful
   b. too carefree
   c. emotional
   d. shrewd
   e. hardnosed

9. Financially my firm:
   a. has trouble with cash-flow
   b. has a good line of credit
   c. is financed totally by receipt—no credit
   d. is making better profits this year than last
   e. knows exactly where it is all the time

10. In hiring people:
    a. I take far too long
    b. I look for the cheapest person
    c. personality is more Important than experience
    d. I look for the best person, and am willing to pay
    e. I only hire at the trainee level

11. With my employees:
    a. I treat everybody the same
    b. I try to talk privately to everybody once a week
    c. To whatever extent possible I tailor assignments to personalities
    d. I encourage them to talk to me about the business
    e. I try to work alongside them whenever possible

12. The real key to business success is:
    a. hard work and perseverance
    b. fine products and service
    c. advertising
    d. knowing the fundamentals of business
    e. employees

13. Competition is:
    a. dumb
    b. smart
    c. cunning
    d. everywhere
    e. a constant threat

14. The best competitive advantage is:
    a. experience
    b. understanding what the market wants
    c. confidence
    d. conducting a business ethically
    e. a detailed plan

15. I keep:
    a. careful financial records
    b. in touch with my customers
    c. in touch with my employees
    d. trying new techniques
    e. wanting to retire

16. My dream is:
    a. to grow the business until someone else can run it
    b. to work until I drop
    c. to give up these headaches and have more fun at work
    d. to try another business
    e. to take a vacation

17. I think business plans are:
    a. for the birds
    b. nice but not necessary
    c. something I can do with my accountant
    d. useful and informative
    e. essential—wouldn't do business without them

18. What makes a terrific entrepreneur?
    a. creativity
    b. discipline
    c. consumer orientation
    d. technical proficiency
    e. flexibility

19. What does a business need most?
    a. money
    b. market research
    c. help
    d. time
    e. a solid business plan

20. What is essential to marketing?
    a. "a sixth sense"
    b. market research
    c. customer awareness
    d. experience
    e. testing

Source: U.S. Small Business Administration, http://www.sba.gov/small/businessplanner/manage/makedecisions/serv_manage_q4.html, accessed October 20, 2008.

Starting a New Venture

The examples of entrepreneurs presented so far have introduced many ways to start a business. This section discusses the process of choosing an idea for a new venture and transforming the idea into a working business.

Selecting a Business Idea

In choosing an idea for your business, the two most important considerations are (1) finding something you love to do and are good at doing and (2) determining whether your idea can satisfy a need in the marketplace. People willingly work hard doing something they love, and the experience will bring personal fulfillment. The old adages "Do what makes you happy" and "To thine own self be true" are the best guidelines for deciding on a business idea.

Success also depends on customers, so would-be entrepreneurs must also be sure that the idea they choose has interest in the marketplace. The most successful entrepreneurs tend to operate in industries in which a great deal of change is taking place and in which customers have difficulty pinpointing their precise needs. These industries, including advanced technology and consulting, allow entrepreneurs to capitalize on their strengths, such as creativity, hard work, and tolerance of ambiguity, to build customer relationships. Nevertheless, examples of outstanding entrepreneurial success occur in every industry, such as Firefly Mobile, which sells mobile phones and accessories specifically targeted at children and tweens. The original Firefly Phone allows children to be connected to mom and dad and other important people and enables parents to restrict incoming and outgoing calls and monitor talking times.[51] The following guidelines may help you select an idea that represents a good entrepreneurial opportunity:

- List your interests and abilities. Include your values and beliefs, your goals and dreams, things you like and dislike doing, and your job experiences.

- Make another list of the types of businesses that match your interests and abilities.

- Read newspapers and business and consumer magazines to learn about demographic and economic trends that identify future needs for products that no one yet offers.

- Carefully evaluate existing goods and services, looking for ways you can improve them.

- Decide on a business that matches what you want and offers profit potential.

- Conduct marketing research to determine whether your business idea will attract enough customers to earn a profit.

- Learn as much as you can about the industry in which your new venture will operate, your merchandise or service, and your competitors. Read surveys that project growth in various industries.

Between the time Kara and Theo Goldin left corporate jobs and started a successful line of naturally flavored waters, they spent years raising questions, sorting out possibilities, and recognizing an opportunity, followed by months of research, experimentation, listening, and cold-calling potential distributors. After leaving her job at AOL at age 34, Kara joined her husband and two children at home in San Francisco. Theo, also 34, had already left his job at Netscape. Kara began studying the concerns of health-conscious mothers and found her idea in the heavily sugared juice boxes. She always thought water was a good alternative but realized kids preferred a flavor. She began collecting information from the beverage industry and testing fruit combinations on family and friends. Theo also began to devote more time to the project, and the couple soon launched Hint. They expect revenues to triple and exceed $10 million in three years.[52]

While Kara and Theo Goldin didn't invent a new product or process, many entrepreneurs who start new businesses do. When that happens, the inventor–entrepreneur needs to protect the rights to his or her invention by securing a patent. The U.S. Patent and Trademark Office's Web site (http://www.uspto.gov) provides information about this process, along with forms to apply for a patent. Inventors can also apply for a patent online.

Many entrepreneurs look for a successful, experienced business owner or executive to give them advice and help in refining their business idea and launching their venture. An ongoing relationship with a mentor can help an entrepreneur avoid pitfalls and achieve success. How to find and work with a mentor is outlined in the "Business Etiquette" feature.

BUYING AN EXISTING BUSINESS Some entrepreneurs prefer to buy established businesses rather than assume the risks of starting new ones. Buying an existing business

Developing a business idea that satisfies consumers' needs is an important step in conceiving a new business. After years of raising questions, sorting out possibilities, researching, experimenting, and listening, entrepreneurs Kara and Theo Goldwin left their corporate jobs to start Hint, a profitable line of naturally flavored waters.

© R. Alcorn, photographed for John Wiley & Sons

brings many advantages: employees are already in place to serve established customers and deal with familiar suppliers, the good or service is known in the marketplace, and the necessary permits and licenses have already been secured. Getting financing for an existing business also is easier than it is for most start-ups. Some sellers may even help the buyers by providing financing and offering to serve as consultants.

To find businesses for sale, contact your local chamber of commerce; brokers who sell businesses; and professionals such as lawyers, accountants, and insurance agents. It is important to analyze the performance of businesses under consideration. Most people want to buy a healthy business so that they can build on its success. When Bobby Kotick took over Activision, it was anything but healthy. Kotick, a serial entrepreneur and college dropout, threw himself into the near-bankrupt videogame company. He sold furniture to pay down debt and found new ways to sell old titles. Today Activision's annual revenues exceed $1.5 billion, making the Santa Monica firm the number two independent maker of videogames, behind Electronic Arts.[53]

BUYING A FRANCHISE Like buying an established business, buying a franchise offers a less risky way to begin a business than starting an entirely new firm. But franchising still involves risks. You must do your homework, carefully analyzing the franchisor's fees and capabilities for delivering the support it promises. Energetic preparation helps ensure that your business will earn a profit and grow. The franchising alternative was discussed in detail in Chapter 5.

Business Etiquette

MAKING THE MOST OF A MENTOR

Mentoring relationships are crucial for entrepreneurs launching their businesses. Experienced, impartial advisors can honestly assess an idea and what you are doing with your company as well as guide you around pitfalls and offer encouragement. Here are some pointers for working with a mentor.

1. List your goals for the mentoring relationship to have a clear focus and avoid wasting someone's time. Ask a person who has no financial interest in your business, so there won't be any conflict of interest or difficulty in being honest.
2. Learn about a potential mentor's company and background, then write or e-mail the person saying you are interested in getting input on what you're doing. Ask if you can meet for a quick coffee, breakfast, or lunch. Don't say you are looking for a mentor; that sounds like a big commitment and may scare people off.
3. Come to a meeting ready to discuss specific issues. Take notes. If a mentor says she has 20 minutes, let her know when the time is up and follow her lead before you continue talking. Pick up the tab for food or beverages.
4. Let the mentor set the pace of the relationship. At your first meeting, he may offer to meet again, look at your business plan, or help with a pitch to investors. If not, and you like what he's had to say, you can ask if he has time to meet again or have a phone conversation. Be sure to send a thank-you note after the meeting.
5. Show a willingness to learn. Act on advice and let your mentor know what actions you have taken.
6. Keep the relationship professional, with the focus on your business. Do not discuss personal issues.
7. While most mentoring lasts more than a few meetings, realize that neither of you is locked in long term. Continue the relationship only as long as it serves both of you well.

Sources: Scott Allen, "Choosing a Business Mentor (and Getting Them to Choose You)," accessed March 2009, http://www.entrepreneur.com; Gary Stern, "Use Mentoring to Jump Start Your Career," December 13, 2007, http://www.hispanicbusiness.com; Amy Barrett, "Why You Need a Mentor and How to Find One," *BusinessWeek SmallBiz,* February/March 2007, pp. 72–78.

Creating a Business Plan

Traditionally, most entrepreneurs launched their ventures without creating formal business plans. Although planning is an integral part of managing in contemporary business, entrepreneurs typically seize opportunities as they arise and change course as necessary. Flexibility seems to be the key to business start-ups, especially in rapidly changing markets. Fifty-eight percent of the most recent *Inc.* 500 CEOs did not create a formal written plan before launching their companies.[54] Entrepreneurial researcher Amar Bhidé attributes that surprising fact to the types of businesses that today's entrepreneurs start. When businesspeople do not need a large amount of cash to start their businesses, they often do not need financing from outside sources—which usually require plans.[55] Also, the rapid pace of change in some industries reduces the benefit of writing a plan.

Still, when an entrepreneur needs additional funds to start or grow a business, a business plan is indispensable.

Although the planning process for entrepreneurs differs from a major company's planning function, today's entrepreneurs are advised to construct business plans following the guidelines presented in Chapter 5 and Appendix D. Careful planning helps the entrepreneur prepare enough resources and stay focused on key objectives, and it provides an important tool for convincing potential investors and employees that the enterprise has the ingredients for success. Entrepreneurial business plans vary depending on the type of start-up, but the basic elements of such a plan—stating company goals, outlining sales and marketing strategies, and determining financial needs and sources of funds—apply to all types of ventures. The Internet also offers a variety of resources for creating business plans. Table 6.1 lists some of these online resources.

Finding Financing

seed capital initial funding needed to launch a new venture.

A key issue in any business plan is financing. How much money will you need to start your business and where will you get it? Requirements for ==seed capital,== funds used to launch a company, depend on the nature of your business and the type of facilities and equipment you need. On average, CEOs of the fastest-growing small businesses raised $1.5 million in seed capital to start their businesses. This average is highly skewed, though, by a few entrepreneurs who raised tens of millions of dollars for their business. Interestingly, companies started with less than $1,000 were about as likely to be profitable as those started with more than $100,000.[56]

Most entrepreneurs rely on personal savings and loans from business associates, family members, and friends to fund their start-ups. Table 6.2 lists the common sources of start-up capital. When two professors and two graduates of the College of Charleston formed Automated Trading Desk (ATD) with the objective of automating the financial markets, they raised $100,000 in seed capital from family and friends. ATD has experienced tremendous growth in South Carolina, trading more than 400 million shares on peak days.[57]

debt financing borrowed funds that entrepreneurs must repay.

DEBT FINANCING When entrepreneurs use ==debt financing,== they borrow money that they must repay. Loans from banks, finance companies, credit card companies, and family and friends are all sources of debt financing. Although many entrepreneurs charge business expenses to personal credit cards because they are relatively easy to obtain, high interest rates make this source of funding expensive. Annual interest charges on a credit card can run as high as 20 percent, while rates for a home equity loan (borrowing against the value of a home)

Table 6.1	Online Resources for Preparing a Business Plan
AllBusiness.com http://www.allbusiness.com	The "Business Advice" page provides links to examples, templates, and tips for writing a plan.
Inc. http://www.inc.com	Under "Departments," click "How-To-Guides" and then "Writing a Business Plan," which links to 150+ articles about how to write a business plan.
Kauffman eVenturing http://www.kauffman.org/eventuring	The "Explore Topics" section has links to information and resources for researching and writing a plan, as well as presenting it to lenders or investors.
MoreBusiness.com http://www.morebusiness.com	To see a sample plan, select "Business & Marketing Plans" from the list of templates.

Table 6.2	Funding Used by Entrepreneurs for Start-ups

Source	Percentage of Entrepreneurs*
Self-financing	82%
Loans from family, friends, or business associates	22%
Bank loans	18%
Lines of credit	18%
Venture capital	8%
SBA or other government funds	4%

*Percentages do not total 100 because entrepreneurs often use multiple sources to finance start-ups.
Source: "Entrepreneurial America: A Comprehensive Look at Today's Fastest-Growing Private Companies," *Inc. The Handbook of the American Entrepreneur,* accessed March 3, 2009, http://www.inc.com.

currently run between 6 and 8 percent. In exchange for a lower interest rate, borrowers with a home equity loan pledge the value of their home, so a borrower who does not repay the loan risks losing the home.

More and more people are using credit cards and lines of credit to finance new ventures. The most recent data available show an annual 25 percent increase in outstanding business loans under $100,000; the growth is composed primarily of credit cards or credit lines. The rise is attributed to the aggressive promotion of credit cards by banks and the ease customers have in obtaining them.[58] Nonetheless, the Small Business Administration (SBA) recommends avoiding the use of credit cards, if possible, and when necessary, using them for small amounts that can be easily paid out of cash flow.[59]

Karl Franz Williams opened Society Coffee, a chic espresso and wine bar, in New York's Harlem area just four blocks from Central Park. The entrepreneur, in his early 30s, wanted to offer his neighbors a peaceful spot to chat with friends. He financed the venture with $50,000 in personal savings, $150,000 from a SBA loan, and another $150,000 from a home equity loan. In addition to great shrimp and grits, Society Coffee has, as one customer put it, "the most delicious caramel cappuccino I've ever had." Williams has already planned his next venture, a bar and restaurant right down the street.[60] Home equity loans have been a popular method of financing new business start-ups. The rapid rise in housing prices in the early to mid-2000s enabled many entrepreneurs to borrow against their homes. But when housing prices began to slide, some homeowners found they owed more on their homes than they were worth. The slumping housing market discouraged the use of home equity loans by some entrepreneurs.[61]

Many banks turn down requests for loans to fund start-ups, fearful of the high risk such ventures entail. Only a small percentage of start-ups raise seed capital through bank loans, although some new firms can get SBA-backed loans, as discussed in Chapter 5. Applying for a bank loan requires careful preparation. Bank loan officers want to see a business plan and will evaluate the entrepreneur's credit history. Because a start-up has not yet established a business credit history, banks often base lending decisions on evaluations of entrepreneurs' personal credit histories. Banks are more willing to make loans to entrepreneurs who have been in business for a while, show a profit on rising revenues, and need funds to finance expansion. Some entrepreneurs have found that local community banks are more interested in their loan applications than are the major national banks.

equity financing funds invested in new ventures in exchange for part ownership.

EQUITY FINANCING To secure **equity financing,** entrepreneurs exchange a share of ownership in their company for money supplied by one or more investors. Entrepreneurs invest their own money along with funds supplied by other people and firms that become co-owners of the start-ups. An entrepreneur does not have to repay equity funds. Rather, the investors share in the success of the business. Sources of equity financing include family and friends, business partners, venture capital firms, and private investors.

Teaming up with a partner who has funds to invest may benefit an entrepreneur with a good idea and skills but little or no money. Investors may also have business experience, which they will be eager to share because the company's prosperity will benefit them. Like borrowing, however, equity financing has its drawbacks. One is that investment partners may not agree on the future direction of the business, and in the case of partnerships, if they cannot resolve disputes, one partner may have to buy out the other to keep operating. The "Solving an Ethical Controversy" feature discusses the pros and cons entrepreneurs face with equity financing. Women entrepreneurs are reluctant to use equity financing—perhaps for some of these reasons—leaving personal savings as the primary source of start-up and expansion capital.[62]

venture capitalists business firms or groups of individuals that invest in new and growing firms in exchange for an ownership share.

Venture capitalists are business organizations or groups of private individuals that invest in new and growing firms. These investors expect high rates of return, typically more than 30 percent, within short time periods of five years or less. Prior to the widespread failures of many dot-coms in the early years of the 21st century, a sizable portion of venture capital flowed into start-up Internet firms. Of all start-ups today, less than 8 percent receive any funds from venture capitalists.[63]

Venture capital (VC) remains a viable means for some entrepreneurs to raise capital. Shai Agassi raised $200 million in venture capital to fund his Silicon Valley company, Better Place. Agassi's company teamed with Renault and Nissan to sell electric cars and build a network of outlets where drivers can charge and replace batteries. The company chose to introduce the electric car in Israel, where the sales tax on gasoline-powered cars is as high as 60 percent. With sights on China, France, and Britain next, Agassi hopes to put a huge dent in the $1.5 trillion auto industry and the $1.5 trillion gasoline market.[64] Entrepreneurs seeking funding from venture capitalists can now share information about specific venture capital firms by posting anonymous blogs on an Internet site, TheFunded.com; some VC firms question whether the comments should be allowed to be anonymous.

angel investors wealthy individuals who invest directly in a new venture in exchange for an equity stake.

Angel investors, wealthy individuals who invest money directly in new ventures in exchange for equity, are a larger source of investment capital for start-up firms. In contrast to venture capitalists, angels focus primarily on new ventures. Many angel investors are successful entrepreneurs who want to help aspiring business owners through the familiar difficulties of launching their businesses. Angel investors back a wide variety of new ventures. Some invest exclusively in certain industries, others invest only in start-ups with socially responsible missions, and still others prefer to back only women entrepreneurs. Palo Alto–based Robotex, cofounded by Adam Gettings, recently introduced a robot designed to replace human soldiers on the battlefield. To design new weapons systems, military contractors generally obtain funding from federal agencies, which can take many months. Robotex is funded by angel investors and went from idea to product in six months.[65]

Because most entrepreneurs have trouble finding wealthy private investors, angel networks form to match business angels with start-ups in need of capital. As you learned in Chapter 5, the Small Business Administration's Active Capital provides online listings to connect would-be angels with small businesses seeking financing. Similar networks try to expand the old-boy network of venture capitalists to new investors and entrepreneurs as well. Venture capitalists that focus on women include Isabella Capital (http://www.fundisabella.com) and Springboard Enterprises (http://springboardenterprises.org). Those interested in minority-owned business include the U.S. Hispanic Chamber of Commerce (http://www.ushcc.com).

EQUITY FINANCING: GOLD MINE OR BOTTOMLESS PIT?

Entrepreneurs quickly learn that growing their business comes down to cold, hard cash. They often look for investors who are willing to buy a stake in the company in exchange for an infusion of capital. During an economic boom, investors are easier to find. But during a downturn, investment money is tight. Investors may require a high rate of return or a larger stake in the company. In addition, the terms may be tougher, giving the entrepreneur less control over the future of the business he or she created.

Is equity financing worth the trade-off for entrepreneurs to start or grow their businesses?

PRO

1. Capital raised through investors such as venture capitalists and angel investors can breathe new life into a firm, either by offering opportunities for growth or by saving a struggling small business from failure. The financial burden is then shared by more than one party, creating more security for the firm and its employees.
2. Active business partners can provide new ideas and more perspective on the marketplace. This can free entrepreneurs from some financial tasks, allowing them to concentrate on what they know and do best.

CON

1. The entrepreneur gives up some control of the company, including how capital may be used and perhaps even which products should be developed or dropped. This

could cause a rift between entrepreneur and investor and could also affect the future performance of the company. Entrepreneurs and investors may have widely differing objectives for the firm.
2. Investors don't have the same emotional stake in the company that the entrepreneur does. An investor might pump cash into several competitors in the same market or might simply have such diverse interests that little attention is paid to a single business. Finally, an investor who acquires a major stake in a firm may decide to sell the company.

Summary

All businesses need money to survive and grow. Experts suggest that small business owners attempt to raise capital when they are doing well, or at least when their projections are positive, instead of waiting until they are in a downturn or struggling to meet payroll. They are likely to get better terms this way, and their companies are more likely to remain

intact. Regardless of what condition a business is in, an entrepreneur would be well advised to become educated about the different types of investors and understand the terms thoroughly before entering into an agreement. Money is never "free"—an investor is not going to give a small business owner money without any strings. But if the entrepreneur is well informed and finds the right partner, the alliance can be beneficial to both.

Sources: "Raising Private Equity—Pros and Cons," *BizExchange*, http://www.bizexchange.com.au, accessed February 20, 2009; Kasey Wehrum, "Angel Investing 2009," *Inc.*, January 2009, http://www.inc.com; David Wanetick, "The Pros and Cons of Receiving Funding from Strategic Investors," *Vertical Pulse*, December 31, 2008, http://www.verticalpulse.com; Jim Casparie, "Raising Capital While Retaining Control," *Forbes*, August 16, 2008, http://www.forbes.com; Dileep Rao, "Raise Money When You Don't Need It," *Forbes*, August 11, 2008, http://www.forbes.com.

Solving an ETHICAL controversy

Government Support for New Ventures

Federal, state, and local governments support new ventures in a number of ways. *Business incubators,* discussed in Chapter 5, help entrepreneurs create new businesses from innovative ideas and in the process create new jobs and strengthen local, state, and national economies. Government subsidies for incubators represent a good investment. Research has shown that for every dollar of public investment, incubator clients and graduates generate about $30 in local tax revenue. More than 80 percent of incubator graduates remain in their communities and provide a return to their investors for years to come.[66] The Clean Energy Incubator (CEI) promotes the development of businesses focusing on clean energy. This joint venture between the Austin Technology Incubator and the National Renewable Energy Laboratory has served 18 companies within the renewable and energy-efficient sectors so far. CEI provides a support network of business and financial consultants with expertise in the clean energy field. CEI is supported by the Texas State Energy Conservation Office and has received funding from the U.S. Department of Energy.[67]

Another way to encourage entrepreneurship is through **enterprise zones,** specific geographic areas designated for economic revitalization. Enterprise zones encourage investment, often in distressed areas, by offering tax advantages and incentives to businesses locating within the boundaries of the zone. The state of Florida has 56 enterprise zones and allows a business located within urban zones to take tax credits for 20 or 30 percent of wages paid to new employees who reside within the urban enterprise zone. A business must create at least one new job to be eligible. For example, during a one-year period in an enterprise zone in Jacksonville, $900,000 in local incentives helped 433 businesses; 45 new businesses and 748 jobs were created.[68]

Government legislation can also encourage investment in the U.S. economy. The Immigration Act of 1990 (IMMACT 90) recognizes the growing globalization of business. It contains a provision that sets aside visas for immigrants wishing to invest money in a new venture in a *targeted employment area*—a rural area or an area that has experienced an unemployment rate of at least 150 percent of the national average. In addition, IMMACT 90 enables more experts in the fields such as science, engineering, and computer programming to be hired by U.S. firms.[69]

Assessment Check ✓

1. What are the two most important considerations in choosing an idea for a new business?
2. What is the purpose of a patent?
3. What is seed capital?

Intrapreneurship

intrapreneurship
process of promoting innovation within the structure of an existing organization.

Established companies try to retain the entrepreneurial spirit by encouraging **intrapreneurship,** the process of promoting innovation within their organizational structures. Today's fast-changing business climate compels established firms to innovate continually to maintain their competitive advantages.

Many companies encourage intrapreneurship. Perhaps none has benefited more from the practice than 3M. To foster creativity, 3M encourages engineers to "bootleg," or borrow up to 15 percent of their time from other assignments to explore new product ideas of their choosing. Bootlegging has led to some of 3M's most successful products including Scotch tape and those popular little squares of paper with the ability to stick to surfaces and be removed.[70] Post-it notes inventor Art Fry took advantage of 3M's bootlegging policy to explore a sticky substance that seemed to have no practical use. But the substance, when put on small sheets of paper, did work well for marking the pages of his hymnal while he sang in the church choir. After years of development, 3M introduced Post-it notes, and the rest is history.[71]

Established companies such as 3M support intrapreneurial activity in varied ways. In addition to allowing bootlegging time for traditional product development, 3M implements two intrapreneurial approaches: skunkworks and pacing programs. A **skunkworks** project is initiated by an employee who conceives an idea and then recruits resources from within 3M to turn it into a commercial product. **Pacing programs** are company-initiated projects that focus on a few products and technologies in which 3M sees potential for rapid marketplace winners. The company provides financing, equipment, and people to support such pacing projects.

Entrepreneurial environments created within companies can help firms retain valuable employees who might otherwise leave for another company or to start a business. As Google grew into a company with more than 12,000 employees, it only stood to reason that talented individuals would leave. Justin Rosenstein, a 24-year-old Google employee who invented its Website-building service, left to join Facebook. As a new generation of Internet start-ups continues

"They Said It"

"If it's a good idea ... go ahead and do it. It is much easier to apologize than it is to get permission."

—Grace Murray **Hopper** (1906–1992) Rear Admiral, U.S. Navy, and computer pioneer

to attract top technical staff from Google, the firm has begun experimenting with off-site skunkworks operations to develop cutting-edge products and separating parts of the business to be run as autonomous units and encourage intrapreneurship.[72] Google may be on the right track, as research has shown that allowing corporate entrepreneurs to launch a venture off-site and work in a culture free from that of its parent company will result in greater employee commitment for the new venture.[73] Whether or not it will stop the exodus of high-caliber people from Google, time will tell.

Assessment Check ✔

1. Why would large companies support intrapreneurship?
2. What is a skunkworks?

What's Ahead

The next chapter turns to a realm of business in which many entrepreneurs have been active during the past decade: e-business, or business use of the Internet. The chapter describes the technology behind electronic business. It introduces the challenges and opportunities available to entrepreneurs and other businesspeople who want to communicate with and sell to customers on the Internet. Not many years ago, Internet technology was a novelty except among high-tech firms and tech-savvy individuals. Today it is an integral factor in starting and growing a business.

Summary of Learning Goals

1 Define the term *entrepreneur,* and distinguish among entrepreneurs, small-business owners, and managers.

Unlike many small-business owners, entrepreneurs typically own and run their businesses with the goal of building significant firms that create wealth and add jobs. Entrepreneurs are visionaries. They identify opportunities and take the initiative to gather the resources they need to start their businesses quickly. Both managers and entrepreneurs use the resources of their companies to achieve the goals of those organizations.

Assessment Check Answers

1.1 What tools do entrepreneurs use to create a new business? Entrepreneurs combine their ideas and drive with money, employees, and other resources to create a business that fills a market need.

1.2 How do entrepreneurs differ from managers? Managers direct the efforts of others to achieve an organization's goals. The drive and impatience that entrepreneurs have to make their companies successful may hurt their ability to manage.

2 Identify the different types of entrepreneurs.

A classic entrepreneur identifies a business opportunity and allocates available resources to tap that market. A serial entrepreneur starts one business, runs it, and then starts and runs additional businesses in succession. A social entrepreneur uses business principles to solve social problems.

Assessment Check Answers

2.1 Is a social entrepreneur simply a philanthropist? A philanthropist generally promotes human welfare through charitable donations, while a social entrepreneur pioneers new ways to advance social causes and thus enhance social welfare.

2.2 What do classic entrepreneurs and social entrepreneurs have in common? They both identify opportunities and allocate resources to pioneer new innovations.

3 Explain why people choose to become entrepreneurs.

People choose this kind of career for many different reasons. Reasons most frequently cited include desires to be one's own boss, to achieve financial success, to gain job security, and to improve one's quality of life.

Assessment Check Answers

3.1 Are entrepreneurs more likely than employees to achieve financial success? While only one in five American workers is self-employed, more than two-thirds of all millionaires are self-employed. Consequently, if you run your own business, you're more likely to achieve financial success.

3.2 What factors affect the entrepreneur's job security? An entrepreneur's job security depends on the decisions of customers and investors and on the cooperation and commitment of the entrepreneur's own employees.

4 **Discuss factors that support and expand opportunities for entrepreneurs.**

A favorable public perception, availability of financing, the falling cost and widespread availability of information technology, globalization, entrepreneurship education, and changing demographic and economic trends all contribute to a fertile environment for people to start new ventures.

Assessment Check Answers

4.1 To what extent is entrepreneurship possible in different countries, and what opportunities does globalization create for today's entrepreneurs? More than 9 percent of adults worldwide are starting or managing a new business. As for globalization opportunities, entrepreneurs market their products abroad and hire international talent. Among the fastest-growing small U.S. companies, almost two of every five have international sales.

4.2 Identify the educational factors that help expand current opportunities for entrepreneurs. More than 100 U.S. universities offer majors in entrepreneurship, dozens of others offer an entrepreneurship emphasis, and hundreds more offer courses in how to start a business. Also, organizations such as the Kauffman Center for Entrepreneurial Leadership, Entreprep, and Students in Free Enterprise encourage and teach entrepreneurship.

4.3 Describe current demographic trends that suggest new goods and services for entrepreneurial businesses. The aging of the U.S. population, the emergence of Hispanics as the nation's largest ethnic group, and the growth of two-income families are creating opportunities for entrepreneurs to market new goods and services.

5 **Identify personality traits that typically characterize successful entrepreneurs.**

Successful entrepreneurs share several typical traits, including vision, high energy levels, the need to achieve, self-confidence and optimism, tolerance for failure, creativity, tolerance for ambiguity, and an internal locus of control.

Assessment Check Answers

5.1 What is meant by an entrepreneur's vision? Entrepreneurs begin with a vision, an overall idea for how to make their business idea a success, and then passionately pursue it.

5.2 Why is it important for an entrepreneur to have a high energy level and a strong need for achievement? Because start-up companies typically have a small staff and struggle to raise enough capital, the entrepreneur has to make up the difference by working long hours. A strong need for achievement helps entrepreneurs enjoy the challenge of reaching difficult goals and promotes dedication to personal success.

5.3 How do entrepreneurs generally feel about the possibility of failure? They view failure as a learning experience and are not easily discouraged or disappointed when things don't go as planned.

6 **Summarize the process of starting a new venture.**

Entrepreneurs must select an idea for their business, develop a business plan, obtain financing, and organize the resources they need to operate their start-ups.

Assessment Check Answers

6.1 What are the two most important considerations in choosing an idea for a new business? Two important considerations are finding something you love to do and are good at doing and determining whether your idea can satisfy a need in the marketplace.

6.2 What is the purpose of a patent? A patent protects the rights to a new invention, process, or product.

6.3 What is seed capital? Seed capital is the money that is used to start a company.

7 **Explain how organizations promote intrapreneurship.**

Organizations encourage intrapreneurial activity within the company in a variety of ways, including hiring practices, dedicated programs such as skunkworks, access to resources, and wide latitude to innovate within established firms.

Assessment Check Answers

7.1 Why would large companies support intrapreneurship? Large firms support intrapreneurship to retain an entrepreneurial spirit and to promote innovation and change.

7.2 What is a skunkworks? A skunkworks project is initiated by an employee who conceives an idea and then recruits resources from within the company to turn that idea into a commercial product.

Business Terms You Need to Know

entrepreneur 182

classic entrepreneur 183

serial entrepreneur 183

social entrepreneur 184

lifestyle entrepreneur 188

seed capital 200

debt financing 200

equity financing 202

venture capitalist 202

angel investor 202

intrapreneurship 204

Other Important Business Terms

enterprise zones 204

skunkworks 204

pacing programs 204

Review Questions

1. What are the similarities and differences among entrepreneurs, small-business owners, and managers? What tools do entrepreneurs use to create a new business?

2. How are classic entrepreneurs and social entrepreneurs similar, and how are they different?

3. Identify the three categories of entrepreneurs. How are they different from each other?

4. What are the four major reasons for becoming an entrepreneur? Why do you think entrepreneurs are more likely than employees to achieve financial success? What factors affect the entrepreneur's job security?

5. How have globalization and information technology created new opportunities for entrepreneurs? Describe current demographic trends that suggest new goods and services for entrepreneurial businesses.

6. Identify the eight characteristics that are attributed to successful entrepreneurs. Which trait or traits do you believe are the most important for success? Why? Why is it important for an entrepreneur to have a high energy level and a strong need for achievement? How do entrepreneurs generally feel about the possibility of failure?

7. What are the benefits and risks involved in buying an existing business or a franchise?

8. Why is creating a business plan an important step for an entrepreneur?

9. Describe the different types of financing that entrepreneurs may seek for their businesses. What are the risks and benefits involved with each?

10. Why do most entrepreneurs rely on personal savings, credit cards, and money from family and friends? Why is it difficult to obtain bank financing?

11. What is intrapreneurship? How does it differ from entrepreneurship?

Projects and Teamwork Applications

1. Think of an entrepreneur whom you admire or choose one of the following: Sergey Brin and Larry Page of Google, Jeff Bezos of Amazon.com, or Oprah Winfrey of Harpo Productions. Explain why you admire this entrepreneur, including ways in which the person has contributed to his or her industry as well as to the economy.

2. Current demographic and economic trends support entrepreneurs who create new businesses. One of these trends is the willingness of Americans to spend more money on certain goods and services, such as pet care. On your own or with a classmate, brainstorm a trend that may be a good idea for a new business. Write one or two paragraphs describing the trend and how it could be applied to a business.

3. Review the eight characteristics of successful entrepreneurs. Which characteristics do you possess? Do you think you would be a good entrepreneur? Why? Write a paragraph or two listing your strengths.

4. Many entrepreneurs are motivated by working in an area they love. Think about something you enjoy that you believe could be turned into a business. What aspect of the activity would actually be turned into a business? For example, if you love to play golf or shop at vintage clothing stores, how would you shape this interest into a business?

Web Assignments

1. **Young entrepreneurs.** Many entrepreneurs launch businesses at a young age. Visit the site listed here (http://www.businessweek.com/smallbiz/content/nov2007/sb20071112_320351.htm) to find out about *BusinessWeek SmallBiz* magazine's search for promising business talent. Read "The Winning Young Entrepreneurs, 2007." How were these young people selected? What were the judging criteria?

   Then click on the Slide Show of the best 25 entrepreneurs under 25 (http://images.businessweek.com/ss/07/10/1022_25and_under/index_01.htm?chan=smallbiz_smallbiz+index+page_best+u.s.+entrepreneurs+25+and+under+2007). Choose several to read about. What are their businesses? Could any of these business ideas be adapted for spin-offs?

2. **Business ideas.** Visit the Web site listed here (http://www.entrepreneur.com/businessideas/index.html) to explore ideas for business ventures. Look through some of the categories and ideas to find one that appeals to

you. Write a brief report to explain the idea, list what it would take to launch this business, and explain why it appeals to you.

3. **Selling a business idea to investors.** Visit the site listed (http://www.businessweek.com/smallbiz/content/oct2007/sb20071019_563293.htm) and read "Strategies to Make Your Pitch Perfect," by Tory Johnson, chief executive officer of the recruitment service, Women for Hire, and workplace contributor on *Good Morning, America*. What skills does she say are essential for selling yourself and your business? List some specific things you could do to practice those skills. List the four strategies Johnson recommends. How can you use those strategies in your career, whether or not you start your own business?

Note: Internet Web addresses change frequently. If you do not find the exact sites listed, you may need to access the organization's or company's home page and search from there.

Case 6.1	Entrepreneurs Help Revitalize New Orleans

An online trading company, a digital design firm, an online marketing business, a modular home company, restaurants and cafés, and a hip nightclub are vital part of the "new" New Orleans. The young entrepreneurs who have launched these and other ventures are helping the city's future while building their own.

Despite continuing problems—high crime rate, less-than-adequate infrastructure, still-abandoned areas, and high insurance costs—New Orleans is a "new entrepreneurial frontier," as a local development agency official describes it. Lifelong residents committed to the city's economic and civic development have been joined by an estimated 3,000 young professionals who have arrived since Hurricane Katrina to work in government and not-for-profit organizations or start their own firms.

Ambitious entrepreneurs are attracted by the city's rebuilding buzz and its low rents, relatively low salaries, and supply of qualified graduates from the local universities—Tulane, Loyola, the University of New Orleans, and Louisiana State in Baton Rouge. Business start-ups often are eligible for tax breaks and research and development grants, such as those offered by The Idea Village, a not-for-profit group that supports entrepreneurship. Of more than 1,000 applications Idea Village has received for grants, loans, or other assistance, nearly 40 percent have been for new ventures. "If you're into innovation and entrepreneurship, New Orleans is a laboratory for that," says Idea Village founder Tim Williamson. He calls the city an environment for social change and a magnet for fresh talent.

Many new businesses are in media and Internet technology, rather than the city's traditional industries of tourism, oil, and shipping. Internet-based businesses bring educated young workers, innovation, and the advantage of mobility and continued operations in the event of future storms. "New Orleans has extremely great long-term potential in the sense that we're crafting a new city," says Chris Brown, who has turned his digital design firm, Plaine Studios, into a full-time business. Other entrepreneurs and their start-ups, both techno and other types, include the following:

- Blake Killian started Killian Interactive, an online marketing firm.
- Neel Sus quit his job at Northrup Grumman to focus on his two companies, a business process improvement firm and a venture that provides a way to send patient information to doctors' smart phones, an innovation he hopes will help the city's hospitals improve care.
- Justin Brownhill, a former Citibank managing director, and Nicholas Perkin, a former videogame advertising executive, chose New Orleans over New York and San Francisco as a base for their online trading company, the New Orleans Exchange, which buys and sells accounts receivable, invoices, and other assets used as collateral for business loans. With plans to expand into global markets, they think New Orleans's widely recognized name is a good choice.
- Shawn Burst started a modular building materials company in his native city even though his target market is northern California. He licensed the innovative system from a German firm, invested $2 million, and built a prototype on New Orleans's Canal Boulevard.
- Robert LeBlanc opened Republic New Orleans, a nightclub and center frequented by natives and newcomers alike.
- Tony Osorio operates four *loncheras,* "taco trucks," and a Mexican restaurant, purchased for $120,000 cash.

For some, staying in New Orleans boosted their entrepreneurial spirit. Josh Besh, who fed red beans and rice and fried chicken to emergency workers free of charge after Katrina, kept his restaurant business afloat by reducing prices at his upscale Restaurant August and catering meals for workers brought in to clean up oil spills. Besh has since developed the catering side business and opened two new restaurants, La Provence and Luke, financed with cash flow from his original venues, Restaurant August and August Steak House. PJ's Coffee, a local tradition for 30 years, suffered damage at its roasting facility and in all 25 shops in the city. PJ's faced the challenge of getting supplies in and shipping coffee out

to franchisees throughout the Gulf Region and to out-of-state markets. While two locations never recovered, PJ's rebuilt and expanded from 42 regional stores to 60 and plans to franchise more. Renaming the brand PJ's Coffee of New Orleans emphasizes its proud heritage and commitment.[74]

Questions for Critical Thinking

1. Do you think the entrepreneurs featured in the case are lifestyle entrepreneurs? Explain.
2. How will entrepreneurship help revitalize New Orleans? What will be the effects of new information technology companies?

Social Entrepreneurs Run Business for the Common Good

Case 6.2

Social entrepreneurs start ventures to do well in business and do good in the world, and they often end up changing "business as usual." When actor Paul Newman and his friend A. E. Hotchner launched Newman's Own, the two had Newman's favorite salad dressing recipe, $40,000, and no business plan. The actor balked at having his picture on the bottle but then decided he could engage in "shameless exploitation" if the proceeds went to charity. Now Newman's Own is known for its all-natural products and its practice of donating 100 percent of its after-tax profits to worthy causes. The company has given more than $200 million to charities worldwide and founded Hole in the Wall Camps for children with cancer and other life-threatening illnesses to attend summer camp free.

Michael J. Fox is another of the rich and famous driven by a social mission. Diagnosed with Parkinson's disease, Fox started an organization to find new treatments for the disorder and got big-name investors to join the cause. While spending more than $100 million on research, the Michael J. Fox Foundation has tried to change how scientific funding works by reducing bureaucracy and staying

involved with researchers to get more accountability and faster results.

Not only the well known and well connected are social entrepreneurs. Record producer Louis Posen has given more than $1 million to charity through his small punk rock label. After a degenerative eye disease left him virtually blind and ended his plan of a film career, Posen started Hopeless Records, which employs nine workers and grosses about $5 million a year, a feat in the small punk rock segment. Artists can choose to release their records on either Hopeless or Posen's second label, Sub City—a name derived from subsidy and subculture—that donates 5 percent of the gross profits to charity. Half the money from the Sub City label comes from artists' royalties and half from Posen's profits. According to an executive at Warner Music Group, which helps distribute Posen's albums, "Louis has the spirit of an entrepreneur and a heart of gold."[75]

Questions for Critical Thinking

1. What characteristics do you think are common among social entrepreneurs?
2. What should be a social entrepreneur's primary goal? Why?

Who would have predicted that one day being a geek would be considered cool, much less heroic? Of course, heroic geekdom does have a few icons—Clark Kent, for one. But most people conjure up images of the Man of Steel—not the mild-mannered reporter—when they think about Clark Kent's fantastic deeds as Superman.

Entrepreneur Robert Stephens doesn't mind this perception. He also doesn't mind being called a geek, although he readily admits that he strives harder to emulate his own hero, James Bond, than he does Bill Gates, who transformed the world of computers with his company, Microsoft. But since Stephens does own a computer company—of sorts—he admits to his admiration to the geekish Gates as "having made everything easier for us."

Stephenzs is the epitome of an entrepreneur—so much so that associates joke that their dictionary definition of *entrepreneur* would read: see Robert Stephens. A decade ago, he recognized an opportunity—a gap in the technical service provided by computer companies for individuals and small businesses—and made a business out of filling it. "No one wanted to make house calls [to repair people's computers]," he recalls. But Stephens was willing to be on call 24/7 and to drive to the homes or offices of people who ran small businesses, to diagnose any problems with their computers, fix the problem on the spot, and even upgrade their computers on request. It was a simple business idea, designed to take advantage of an opportunity. Stephens also had the vision to realize that the Internet, even though at the time in its infancy in commercial applications, would have a huge impact on the way companies conducted their business by allowing people to work from home. And computers had begun popping up in homes for personal use and entertainment. So Stephens quit his computer programming job at the University of Minnesota and launched his computer-repair business with an initial investment of $200.

Stephens didn't have much money. He also didn't have any employees. But he was blessed with liberal amounts of creativity, intelligence, humor, and energy. He thought hard about what to call his company, wanting the name to make a lasting impression on potential customers. Finally,

he came up with The Geek Squad because he wanted to imply that he had a whole army of employees who could solve any computer-based trouble at a moment's notice. "The name is very important because it's what people think, say, and remember," Stephens explains.

When his customer base began to grow beyond his own service capabilities, he added his first employee, and then a few more. To support his company image, he designed badges identifying each employee as a member of The Geek Squad "intelligence network." He also designed uniforms for each serviceperson and provided a company car: a specially painted Volkswagen Beetle Geekmobile. Customers loved it—and so did The Geek Squad members.

For the most part, The Geek Squad serves customers operating home-based and other small businesses—ordinary people, such as lawyers who need fast repairs to their office computers. But sometimes glamour comes calling in the form of customers like U2 and the Rolling Stones. A few years ago, Geek Squad headquarters received an emergency call from U2's sound crew, who had encountered a host of computer problems in setting up the sound system for an Anaheim concert. They did such a bang-up job that the band called them in again during an appearance in Minneapolis.

Why did Stephens choose the entrepreneurial route for his career path? "I didn't want a boring job. I wanted to work for an international spy organization, and this is the closest I can get." He identified an important trend in the marketplace and built a business around it. His business model is based on his philosophy that he'd "rather be great at one thing than be mediocre at 15 things." The Geek Squad has progressed from a sole proprietorship begun in Minneapolis to a corporation with sizable offices in Chicago, Los Angeles, and San Francisco, as well as the Twin Cities. His intelligence network of service reps now numbers more than 50, and annual revenues have grown to several million dollars. His employees have job titles like "Dr. No" (the company's finance director) and "Counter Intelligence" (inside service representatives). He loves every minute of being a professional geek, even if he never did get his shot at being an international spy.[76]

Questions for Critical Thinking

1. Stephens identified two important trends in the environment—the need for on-site computer service and the growth of the Internet—that helped him predict his business would be a success. Identify at least one other factor in the environment that could be considered positive for The Geek Squad.

2. In what ways has Stephens and other entrepreneurs like him influenced the economy?

3. Describe some of the personal characteristics that probably contribute to Stephens's success.

4. Why was The Geek Squad a good business idea?

Figure 6.5

Scoring Key—Quiz for Small Business Success (page 197)

Scoring

1. a=5, b=4, c=3, d=2, e=1
2. a=5, e=4, b=3, c=2, d=1
3. c=5, a=4, b=3, d=2, e=1
4. b=5, e=4, d=3, c=2, a=1
5. b=5, d=4, c=3, a=2, e=1
6. d=5, c=4, a=3, b=2, e=1
7. a=5, d=4, c=3, b=2, e=1
8. a=5, d=4, e=3, b=2, c=1
9. e=5, d=4, b=3, a=2, c=1
10. d=5, a=4, c=3, b=2, e=1
11. c=5, d=4, e=3, b=2, a=1
12. e=5, d=4, a=3, b=2, c=1
13. e=5, d=4, c=3, b=2, a=1
14. a=5, b=4, c=3, e=2, d=1
15. b=5, a=4, c=3, d=2, e=1
16. e=5, a=4, b=3, c=2, d=1
17. e=5, d=4, c=3, b=2, a=1
18. c=5, a=4, b=3, e=2, d=1
19. b=5, e=4, a=3, d=2, c=1
20. c=5, b=4, e=3, d=2, a=1

Score	Your Business Success Quotient
75–100	You are a successful entrepreneur whose operations reflect tried and true business practices.
50–74	Your business is probably headed for long-term success. But success will come sooner if you sharpen your awareness of solid management skills and marketing techniques.
25–49	While you may be enjoying customer loyalty and repeat business, never forget that savvy competition is always looking for ways to take the lead. Don't let comfort lull you into false security. Be creatively assertive!
0–24	You may well have the right product. But to sell it successfully, you need to increase your market awareness and improve your operating philosophy. Reach out for practical classes, seminars, and advice from people who have good business track records. And—keep persevering. It's the key ingredient to winning!

chapter

7

E-Business: Doing Business Online

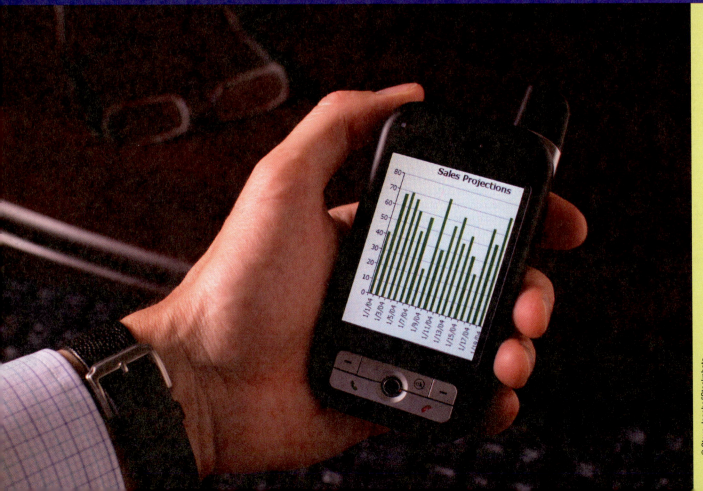

Twitter's E-Business Future: Cash or Trash?

Do you tweet? If so, you are one of the 6 million subscribers that San Francisco–based Twitter has picked up in its short existence. The free messaging service has attracted a lot of attention and about $55 million in venture capital funding. Twitter users focus on what is happening now—some have called it the 21st century version of the telegraph. In fact, Twitter broadcast the first news of the plane that crash-landed in New York's Hudson River without the loss of a single life. Survivors of the 2008 terrorist attacks in Mumbai, India, used it to tell the world what was happening during two desperate days. Workers laid off from Yahoo! provided moment-by-moment accounts of their departure from the firm. The Los Angeles Fire Department used it to send residents alerts of local wildfires, and surgeons at a Detroit hospital used Twitter to discuss the removal of a kidney patient's tumor.

Twitter has even become a favorite tool of President Barack Obama. It has connected people all over the world with like-minded people who have something to say—as well as some who have little more to impart than, "Going to the store now." It has spawned the development of countless applications that allow users to access photos and videos on the Internet.

Twitter's limitation is that messages, known as tweets, cannot exceed 140 keystrokes, what one observer calls the equivalent of a postcard. Once registered for their free account, users can sign up to track or "follow" the tweets of anyone they like—friends, family, colleagues, role models, superstars like Shaquille O'Neal and MC Hammer, political figures, even complete strangers. More than a quarter of a million users track President Obama, giving him the largest following of any subscriber. Users can also select the recipients of their own tweets, or they can choose to send messages to every Twitter subscriber. About one in five people between 18 and 34 with Internet service has used Twitter or a rival service at least once, and its popularity continues to grow.

What Twitter has not done so far is make any money. Founders Jack Dorsey, Biz Stone, and Evan Williams have refused to allow any advertising on the site, and they've turned down a $500 million takeover offer from Facebook. Yet the service's untapped potential for revenue is enormous, and its founders have promised to transform it into a sustainable business in the very near future.

But can it generate revenue, and if so, how? Because the founders have promised to keep the service free to individual subscribers, any money will have to come from somewhere else. Many industry observers see enormous commercial potential, even if paid advertising is not an option. For instance, JetBlue Airways already uses its Twitter account to find out what people are saying about its service. Online shoe store Zappos.com broadcasts promotions and collects customer feedback. Dell sends exclusive discounts to Twitter users and says its holiday promotions brought in sales worth more than $1 million. UPS and the Hyatt hotel chain have asked a programmer in Britain, where Twitter is wildly popular, to help them find better ways to monitor tweets about their businesses. "They are telling me about the sorts of services they would pay for," says programmer Iain Dodsworth.

If these firms and others like them are willing to pay for the continued ability to compile and search through millions of tweets, they might find a goldmine of data to analyze and a steady stream of marketing communications to enhance customer relationships. Twitter has said that search capabilities will be critical to its revenue-producing model. So it is taking a first step to integrate its search function on the site, which until now had to be accessed separately at www.search.twitter.com or through a separate search application.

Zappos, for one, says its willingness to pay for this type of service will depend on the asking price. But the CEO of a Texas consulting firm recently turned to Twitter's micro-blogging community for tech help relating to a crashed Web site. "It's the first place I go when I have a question," he said. "It's a continuous conversation going on right now around the world. It's immediate." That community and immediacy may prove to be Twitter's greatest assets, if only it can find a way to make them pay.[1]

Over the past decade, few developments in contemporary business have been as monumental as the Internet and related technologies. The Internet offers businesses and other organizations a source of information, a means of communication, and a channel for buying and selling, all rolled into one. With just a few clicks of a mouse, or a few keystrokes on a BlackBerry, the Internet has revolutionized virtually every aspect of business. Consumers across the globe use the Internet to pay bills, obtain product information, communicate with individuals and organizations, make purchases, and check their investments. Businesses use the Internet to exchange information with customers, advertise products, research market trends, and, of course, buy and sell a whole range of goods and services. New words have emerged such as *blog, podcast, RSS,* and *wiki,* and old words have new meanings: *Web, search marketing, banner, pop-up,* and *online.*

electronic business (e-business)
conducting business via the Internet.

"They Said It"

"The Internet will help achieve 'friction free capitalism' by putting buyer and seller in direct contact and providing more information to both about each other."

—Bill Gates (b. 1955) Co-founder, Microsoft Corporation

Electronic business (or **e-business**) refers to conducting business via the Internet. The size and scope of e-business is difficult to understate. In one recent year, U.S. online retail sales totaled nearly $134 billion, an increase of almost 5 percent from the prior year. By contrast, overall retail sales decreased by almost 1 percent during the same period.[2] According to a recent survey, more than seven in ten of adult Internet users have engaged in at least one online shopping activity.[3] Currently, e-business accounts for more than one-quarter of the value of all manufacturing shipments, sales, and revenues, totaling more than $1.3 trillion.[4] And it's not just the United States; e-business activity in Canada, for instance, has more than quadrupled in the last five years.[5]

E-business involves much more than just buying and selling. Some surveys suggest that the Web is the number-one medium for new-product information, eclipsing catalogs, print ads, and trade shows. The Internet allows retailers and vendors to exchange vital information, improving the overall functioning of inventory and supply, which lowers costs and increases profits. Moreover, an increasing number of Americans now get their news and information from blogs (short for *Web logs*, which are online journals) rather than from traditional media such as television, radio, and newspapers. Not surprisingly, a growing number of businesses are using blogs to put human faces on their organizations and communicate directly with customers.

Government agencies and not-for-profit organizations have also embraced the Internet. Organizations such as the American Diabetes Association and National Multiple Sclerosis Society use the Web to raise funds, highlight current activities, and discuss research and treatment options. Most states allow residents to register their cars online, saving trips to the motor vehicle office. The country of New Zealand is even considering offering an online voting option in national elections as early as 2011.[6]

In the past decade, the number of Internet users in the United States and worldwide has grown dramatically. Today more than 220 million Americans—close to 75 percent—access the Internet at home, at work, at school, or at public access sites. Worldwide, the number of Internet users exceeds 1.4 billion and in many places is growing faster than it is in the United States. For instance, China's Internet population—now the world's largest—has grown by more than 1,024 percent since the turn of the century.[7] As a testament to its importance, the Internet has become a significant presence in the daily lives of a majority of Americans. According to a recent study, six of every ten spend two or more hours online every day.[8]

In spite of the past success and future potential of the Internet and e-business, issues and concerns remain. Some highly touted e-business applications have proved less than successful, cost savings and profits have occasionally been elusive, and many privacy and security issues remain. Nevertheless, the benefits and potential of e-business clearly outweigh the concerns and problems.

This chapter examines the current state and potential of e-business. We begin by discussing the capabilities of e-business, the benefits of e-business, and the ways organizations use the Web. Next, we focus on business-to-business (B2B) transactions that make up the vast majority of e-business activity today. Then we explore business-to-consumer (B2C) e-business, which includes online shopping sites such as Amazon.com, Crutchfield.com, and Expedia.com. We also consider some of the challenges facing e-business. Next, we explain how organizations use the Web's communication functions to advance their objectives. The chapter concludes with discussions of the global reach of e-business and how to create, maintain, and manage an effective Web site.

What Is E-Business?

Today, the term *e-business* describes a wide range of business activities that take place on the Internet using any of the applications that rely on Web-based technology, such as e-mail and electronic shopping carts. E-business can be divided into the following five broad categories:

1. e-tailing or virtual storefronts on Web sites
2. online business-to-business transactions
3. electronic data interchange (EDI), the business-to-business exchange of data using compatible software
4. e-mail, instant messaging, blogs, and other Web-enabled communication tools for reaching prospective and existing customers
5. the gathering and use of demographic, product, and other information through Web contacts.

E-business provides a foundation for launching new businesses, extending the reach of existing companies, and building and retaining customer relationships. A Web presence builds awareness of a company's products and brands; provides the means for personalized, one-on-one communication with customers; and permits customers to place orders any time from almost anywhere in the world. E-business encompasses all of the following types of activities:

- researching digital cameras on CNet.com and then placing an order for a top-rated model on Crutchfield.com
- reviewing your class schedule for next term and paying your tuition bill at your school's Web site
- ordering a new pair of jeans at American Eagle's Web site
- booking a hotel in Chicago at Priceline.com.

The growth of e-business has attracted an army of specialized software firms and other service suppliers that provide expertise for firms taking their first steps into this competitive arena or trying to enhance their existing Web presence. Well-known examples include Accenture, Adobe, Hewlett-Packard, IBM, Microsoft, Oracle, and SAP. IBM, for instance, offers a wide range of software and services to business customers. While IBM was originally known as a manufacturer of computer hardware, the firm now generates more than half its revenue from

Maine.gov allows citizens of the state to complete many routine government transactions—and obtain important information—online. This is a valuable service for residents of the larger, mostly rural state, where winter weather often compromises traveling conditions.

Courtesy Maine.gov

global technology services, much of which is Web related. Moreover, IBM sells billions of dollars every year in software that provides the foundation for Web-enabled applications for thousands of businesses all over the world. Web-based services and software are such a significant part of IBM's future, that the company sold its PC manufacturing business several years ago.[9]

E-business has also had an impact on governments and others in the not-for-profit sector. The State of Maine's Web portal, http://www.maine.gov, has received an annual "Best of the Web" award each year since the site was first created and now attracts more than 4 million page visits per year. Maine.gov serves as the gateway to Maine's state and municipal government information and services. Among other features, residents can register motor vehicles, renew professional licenses, purchase hunting and fishing licenses, and pay traffic tickets. Dick Johnson, the state's former chief information officer, notes, "In this day and age when state budgets are tight, Maine.gov provides a cost-effective way to meet the public demand for convenient government transactions."[10]

Capabilities and Benefits of E-Business

Over the past two decades, the United States witnessed the shift from a manufacturing-based industrial economy to its service sector. An important component of the service-oriented economy is the use of electronic information, the Internet, and related technologies. Many people see e-business as a major driver of economic growth for the rest of the 21st century. Today, online retail sales make up more than 3 percent of total U.S. retail sales.[11] Some recent e-business successes are shown in Table 7.1.

Table 7.1	Some E-Business Successes

- Apple's iTunes has surpassed Wal-Mart as the number-one music retailer. Online sales of digital music rose 50 percent in a recent year while sales of CDs fell by 20 percent.

- Customer satisfaction with online retailers has surpassed that of traditional bricks-and-mortar retailers by almost 12 percent, according to the American Consumer Satisfaction Index released by the University of Michigan and ForeSee Results.

- Amazon.com, one of the oldest Web retailers, has annual sales of around $15 billion. Sales have been rising at an annual rate of more than 23 percent.

- Google and the Cleveland Clinic—a major medical center—have entered into a trial partnership that will better allow the clinic's current and past patients access to their medical records via the Web anywhere in the world.

Sources: Enid Burns, "E-Tailers Beat Offline Stores in Customer Satisfaction," *ClickZ Network,* http://www.clickz.com, accessed March 5, 2009; "When Will iTunes Replace Wal-Mart as No. 1 Music Retailer?" *CNET News,* February 26, 2008, http://www.news.com, accessed March 5, 2009; Company Report (Amazon.com), *MSN Money,* http://www.moneycentral.msn.com, accessed October 13, 2008; "Google Health Makes Its Pitch," *ZDNet Healthcare,* February 25, 2008, http://healthcare.zdnet.com, accessed October 13, 2008.

E-business offers a wide variety of capabilities and benefits to contemporary businesspeople.

- *Global reach.* The Web allows goods and services to be sold to customers regardless of geographic location. eBay, for example, is now the nation's largest used-car "dealer." Buyers and sellers meet in this virtual marketplace, where more than $17 billion worth of used vehicles are bought and sold annually.[12]

- *Personalization.* Only a handful of Dell computers are waiting for customers at any one time. The production process begins when an order is received and ends a day or two later when the new PC is shipped to the customer. Not only does this approach better satisfy customer needs, allowing for more personalization, but it also reduces the amount of inventory Dell has to carry.

- *Interactivity.* Customers and suppliers negotiate prices online in much the same manner as at a local flea market. The result is the creation of products that better satisfy both parties.

- *Right-time and integrated marketing.* Online retailers, such as Eddiebauer.com and Zappos.com, can provide products when and where customers want them. Moreover, the Internet enables the coordination of all promotional activities and communication to create a unified, customer-oriented promotional message.

- *Cost savings.* E-business can reduce the costs associated with operating and starting a business. For instance, Level 10 Design, a Web marketing consulting company, helped AT&T design a digital "coupon," allowing users to try AT&T's Wi-Fi service for free. The acquisition cost per digital coupon user worked out to less than $15. By comparison, the acquisition cost for traditional media was estimated to be above $60 per user.[13]

In addition to the benefits listed here, increasing evidence shows that an effective online presence improves the performance of traditional brick-and-mortar operations. As noted earlier, many consumers now use the Web as their primary source of product information. Research shows that 77 percent of consumer electronics purchases are influenced by online research. A majority of those using the Internet to research electronics actually made their purchase at a brick-and-mortar retailer.[14] According to ShopLocal, a multichannel marketing services company, purchases by so-called *Web-to-store shoppers*—those who research products online but purchase items in traditional retail stores—have risen faster than online purchases.[15]

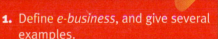

Assessment Check ✓

1. Define *e-business*, and give several examples.
2. List some benefits of e-business.
3. What is the impact of the Web on traditional brick-and-mortar companies?

Business Web Sites

Virtually all businesses today have Web sites. They may offer general product information; electronic shopping; and promotions such as games, contests, and online coupons. Type in the firm's Internet address, or use a search engine, and the company's home page appears.

Two types of company Web sites exist. Many firms have established **corporate Web sites** to increase their visibility, promote their offerings, and provide information for interested parties. Rather than selling products directly, these sites attempt to build customer goodwill and assist retailers and other resellers in their marketing efforts. For example, the Web site for bicycle manufacturer Cannondale contains detailed product information and reviews. Consumers who are actually interested in purchasing the company's products are directed to one of its retail dealers. There are also links to the Web sites of bicycle retailers who carry Cannondale products.

In addition to using the Web to communicate product information and build relationships with customers, many companies use their Web sites for other purposes as well. These include

corporate Web site
Web site designed to increase a firm's visibility, promote its offerings, and provide information to interested parties.

Business Etiquette

E-MAIL COURTESY

You probably know the general guidelines for using e-mail responsibly, such as following rules of grammar and spelling, avoiding all capital letters, and not e-mailing information you wouldn't mind seeing in the newspaper. Here's how to make your online business correspondence even more effective and appropriate.

1. Imagine every e-mail as a sheet of official company communication, and assume the highest level of courtesy and formality while you build business relationships. Always include a salutation ("Dear Ms. Robeson") and a closing ("Sincerely, Sanjeev Rao").
2. Choose a simple type font and avoid color, formatting, and emoticons.
3. Include a specific subject line, such as "Revised schedule for Diaz project." Don't leave it blank or vague ("Schedule"), and don't use an irrelevant subject line by digging out an old e-mail, hitting Reply, and starting to type.
4. Answer or acknowledge all incoming e-mails within 24 hours.
5. Keep your messages brief and to the point. Use professional business language and a pleasant, cordial tone. Say "please" and "thank you."
6. Include all necessary information, but make sure you are not providing information that should not leave the company.
7. When writing to a group of people who don't know each other, use the bcc (blind carbon copy) function to ensure that each recipient's e-mail address remains private.
8. Always proofread your entire e-mail, including the "to," "cc," and "subject" lines, and double-check attachments to be sure you're sending the right ones.
9. Never forward jokes, virus hoaxes, or chain letters to coworkers or customers.
10. E-mails are public documents. Avoid writing anything you wouldn't say in person, and take time to calm down before sending a hasty or overheated reply you might regret later.

Sources: Judith Kallos, "Business E-Mail Etiquette Basics," *NetManners*, http://www.netmanners.com, accessed March 5, 2009; Lydia Ramsey, "Business E-mail Etiquette: Maintaining a Professional Image," *The Sideroad*, http://www.sideroad.com, accessed March 5, 2009; "E-Mail Etiquette," *Emailreplies.com*, http://www.emailreplies.com, accessed March 5, 2009; "E-mail Etiquette," Online Writing Lab at Purdue University, http://owl.english.purdue.edu, accessed March 5, 2009; "E-mail Etiquette," *About.com*, http://careerplanning.about.com, accessed March 5, 2009; "E-mail Etiquette," *AllBusiness*, accessed March 5, 2009.

disseminating financial information to investors, enabling prospective employees to learn about career opportunities and even apply online for jobs, and providing e-mail and other communication tools for customers and other interested parties. Some tips for writing and using e-mail in a business setting are listed in the "Business Etiquette" feature.

marketing Web site
Web site whose main purpose is to increase purchases by visitors.

Although **marketing Web sites** often include information about company history, products, employment opportunities, and financial information, their goal is to increase purchases by site visitors. For instance, the Williams-Sonoma Web site contains all the information typically found on a corporate Web site, but it also includes an online store selling everything from $1,000 espresso machines to $15 cookbooks. Many marketing Web sites try to engage consumers in interactions that will move them closer to a demonstration, trial visit, purchase, or other marketing outcome. Some marketing Web sites, such as Apple.com, are quite complex. Visitors can investigate Apple products, such as iMac computers, iPhones, and iPods; view movie trailers on the QuickTime page; and purchase products from the online store. The site also offers games and contests, among other features.

Assessment Check ✔

1. Explain the differences between a corporate Web site and a marketing Web site.
2. Visit the Procter & Gamble Web site (http://www.pg.com). Is this site a corporate or marketing Web site?

Business–to–Business (B2B) E–Business

UPS.com is not designed to be flashy. The site has no fancy graphics or streaming video clips, no online games or contests, but it does have lots of practical information to assist the firm's customers. The site enables customers to check shipping rates, compare services, prepare and print package labels, schedule pickups and deliveries, track shipments, and order supplies. These services are vital to UPS customers, most of whom are businesses. Customers access the site thousands of time a day.

Business-to-business e-business, known as **B2B,** is the use of the Internet for business transactions between organizations. Although most people are more familiar with consumer-oriented (B2C) online firms, such as Buy.com and Expedia.com, B2C transactions are dwarfed by their B2B counterparts. According to data compiled by the U.S. Census Bureau, B2B e-business accounts for more than 94 percent of all e-business activity.[16] Manufacturers lead all industry sectors, with e-business accounting for more than 26 percent of total trade. Merchant wholesalers rank second, with e-business making up around 18 percent of total sales.[17]

In addition to generating sales revenue, B2B e-business also provides detailed product descriptions

The business page of the United States Postal Service's Web site offers a simple three-step shipping and mailing process. It also allows businesses to track their mail and helps managers reduce shipping costs.

whenever they are needed, and payments and other information are transferred on the Web. Moreover, B2B e-business can slash order-processing expenses. Business-to-business transactions, which typically involve more steps than consumer purchases, can be much more efficient on the Internet. Orders placed over the Internet typically contain fewer errors than handwritten ones, and when mistakes occur, the technology can quickly locate them. So the Internet is an attractive option for business buying and selling. In some industries, relying on the Internet to make purchases can reduce costs by almost 25 percent.

B2B e-business activity has become more varied in recent years. In addition to using the Web to conduct one-on-one sales transactions and provide product information, companies use such tools as EDI, extranets, private exchanges, electronic exchanges, and e-procurement.

business-to-business (B2B) e-business electronic business transactions between organizations using the Internet.

Electronic Data Interchanges, Extranets, and Private Exchanges

ELECTRONIC DATA INTERCHANGE One of the oldest applications of technology to business transactions is **electronic data interchange (EDI),** computer-to-computer exchanges of invoices, purchase orders, price quotations, and other sales information between buyers and sellers. EDI requires compatible hardware and software systems to exchange data over a network. Use of EDI cuts paper flow, speeds the order cycle, and reduces errors. In addition, by receiving daily inventory status reports from vendors, companies can set production schedules to match demand.

Wal-Mart was one of the first major corporations to adopt EDI in the early 1990s. In fact, the retailer refuses to do business with distributors and manufacturers that do not use compatible EDI standards. EDI is one of the major reasons Wal-Mart is able to operate with the efficiency that has made it the market leader in retailing. It can buy just the merchandise its customers want and just when it needs to restock its shelves, using a system known as *quick response*. Quick response is the retailing equivalent of just-in-time inventory, an inventory management system commonly used in manufacturing. (Just-in-time inventory is discussed in detail in Chapter 11.) Today, most large retailers have systems such as the one employed by Wal-Mart.

Early EDI systems were limited due to the requirement that all parties had to use the same computer operating system. That changed with the introduction of something called *Web services*—Internet-based systems that allow parties to communicate electronically with one another regardless of the computer operating system each uses. Web services rely on open-source XML (Extensible Markup Language) standards.

EXTRANETS Internet commerce also offers an efficient way for businesses to collaborate with vendors, partners, and customers through ==extranets,== secure networks used for e-business and accessible through the firm's Web site by external customers, suppliers, or other authorized users. Extranets go beyond ordering and fulfillment processes by giving selected outsiders access to internal information. As with other forms of e-business, extranets provide additional benefits such as enhanced relationships with business partners. For instance, recently, Microsoft helped Habitat for Humanity develop an extranet that links its various local offices, corporate partners, and volunteers. The result has been improved fund-raising efforts, increased volunteer productivity, and improved collaboration.[18]

Security and access authorization remain critical issues, and most companies create virtual private networks (VPN) that protect information traveling over public communications media. These networks control who uses a company's resources and what users can access. Also, they cost considerably less than leasing dedicated lines. Cisco Systems uses an extranet connection with VPN to connect its global partners with the firm's internal resources without compromising security. The importance of extranets to Cisco has increased in recent years as the firm has outsourced more of its noncore activities to partners. According to Julie Nordquist, Project Manager for Cisco's Internet Services Group, "With access to Cisco network resources, partners can manufacture with the same quality we do here."[19]

PRIVATE EXCHANGES The next generation of extranets is the **private exchange,** a secure Web site at which a company and its suppliers share all types of data related to e-business, from product design through order delivery. A private exchange is more collaborative than a typical extranet, so this type of arrangement has sometimes been called *c-business*. The participants can use it to collaborate on product ideas, production scheduling, distribution, order tracking, and any other functions a business wants to include. Partners in a private exchange often form strategic alliances, similar to those described in Chapter 4. Wal-Mart Stores has a private exchange it calls *Retail Link*. The system permits Wal-Mart employees to access detailed sales and inventory information. Suppliers such as Procter & Gamble and Nestlé, in turn, can look up Wal-Mart sales data and forecasts to manage their own inventory and logistics, helping them better meet the needs of the world's largest retailer and its millions of customers worldwide.

Another variant of extranets is an intranet, which provides similar capabilities but limits users to an organization's employees. Intranets are discussed in Chapter 15.

Electronic Exchanges and E-Procurement

The earliest types of B2B e-business usually consisted of a company setting up a Web site and offering information, as well as products, to any buyer willing to make online purchases.

extranet secure network used for e-business and accessible through an organization's Web site; available to external customers, suppliers, and other authorized users.

Then entrepreneurs created **electronic exchanges,** online marketplaces that bring buyers and sellers together and cater to a specific industry's needs. One of the earliest electronic exchanges, FreeMarkets, was set up by a former General Electric executive named Glen Meakem. FreeMarkets allowed suppliers to compete for the business of organizational buyers of everything from gears to printed circuit boards. The idea was to improve the efficiency of the purchase process for hundreds of business products.

Initially, many believed that electronic exchanges would become one of the most popular uses of the Internet. It didn't quite work out that way. Approximately 15,000 electronic exchanges were launched within a span of a few years. Today, however, fewer than 20 percent remain. The others either merged or simply disappeared. (FreeMarkets was acquired by the e-business software firm Ariba.) Only electronic exchanges specializing in electronic components and transportation services have proven consistently successful.[20]

Evolving from electronic exchanges has been something called **e-procurement,** Web-based systems that enable all types of organizations to improve the efficiency of their procurement processes. E-procurement has gained greater acceptance than electronic exchanges, and most experts believe that its use will continue to grow. Ariba, the company that acquired FreeMarkets, offers a variety of e-procurement software products. Many large corporations, such as British Airways (BA), use Ariba products to lower their procurement costs. More than 80 percent of the airline's purchases are now handled electronically. Average transaction cost has been cut by 40 percent, and employee productivity has increased by 48 percent. BA claims annual savings in excess of $150 million since implementing its e-procurement system. Moreover, the company has been able to reduce its engineering inventory by over $400 million since adopting e-procurement.[21]

E-procurement also benefits the public and not-for-profit sectors. For instance, states such as Kentucky and North Carolina have e-procurement systems that combine Internet technology with traditional procurement practices to streamline the purchasing process and reduce costs. State and local governmental agencies, public schools, and state-supported colleges can use the system to purchase products from state-approved vendors. According to the State of North Carolina, NC e-procurement @ Your Service has saved state taxpayers more than $350 million since the program was first implemented.[22] The University of Toronto uses SAP Supplier Relationship Management, the first standardized e-procurement transaction solution for higher education. Currently, 350-plus suppliers use the system, generating more than 120,000 transactions annually. Transactions that used to take 3.5 hours on average now take 20 minutes. The university estimates that annual savings from the system may exceed $20 million.[23]

Assessment Check ✔

1. What is B2B e-business? How large is it relative to B2C e-business?
2. Explain extranets and VPNs.
3. What is e-procurement?

Online Shopping and B2C E-Business

One area of e-business that has consistently grabbed news headlines is Internet, or online, shopping. Known as **business-to-consumer** (or **B2C**) **e-business,** the technology involves selling directly to consumers over the Web. Driven by convenience and improved security for transmitting credit-card numbers and other financial information, online retail sales, sometimes called *e-tailing*, account for more than 3 percent of total retail sales in the United States but are growing at an annual rate of 18 percent. By contrast, overall retail sales are increasing at an annual rate of around 4.5 percent. If these trends continue, online retail sales will soon exceed 10 percent of total retail sales.[24] Figure 7.1 shows the projected growth in online retail sales.

Most people generally think of the Web as a giant cybermall of retail stores selling millions of goods online. However, service providers are also important participants in e-business. These firms

business-to-consumer (B2C) e-business selling directly to consumers over the Internet.

Figure 7.1

Projected Online Retail Sales to 2011

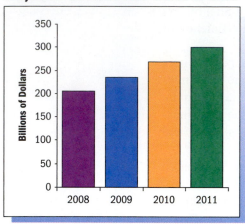

Source: U.S. Census Bureau, *Statistical Abstract of the United States: 2009,* http://www.census.gov, accessed March 5, 2009.

include providers of financial services. Brick-and-mortar banks, such as Bank of America and Wells Fargo, and brokerage firms, such as Fidelity Investments, have greatly expanded their online services in response to consumer demand. For instance, six in ten Americans now use the Internet for banking.[25]

Online financial services will be described in more detail in Chapter 17. In addition, many new online service providers are rapidly attracting customers who want to do more of their own banking and stock trading online. Airlines, too, use the power of the Web. Southwest Airlines, for instance, sells more than half of its tickets online, amounting to more than $5 billion annually. The airline also has several innovative Web-related services. One is called "Ding." Customers download a small program to their computers and specify their travel preferences (such as dates and destinations). If a special fare is offered that meets these preferences, a special icon pops up on their computer desktop.[26]

Another point to remember is that there are basically two types of B2C Web sites: shopping sites and informational sites. L.L. Bean (http://www.llbean.com) is a shopping site. Customers can view product information and place orders online. By contrast, Honda's Web site (http://automobiles.honda.com) is informational only. Consumers can view detailed product information, "build" their ideal Honda, compare financing alternatives, and even request a price quote from a local dealer. They *cannot*, however, buy a new car online.

E-Tailing and Electronic Storefronts

electronic storefront
company Web site that sells products to customers.

Retailers large and small have staked their claims in cyberspace by setting up **electronic storefronts,** Web sites that sell items to consumers. Wal-Mart received such a positive response to the launch of its electronic storefront that it expanded online product offerings from less than 2,500 to around 1 million items today.[27] Clothing retailer Lands' End used to generate virtually all of its orders by telephone. In 1995 the company opened one of the first electronic storefronts, offering only around 100 items. Today, every product, from every catalog, is available on Landsend.com, and the company offers separate Web sites for shoppers in the United Kingdom, Germany, and Japan. Along the way, it has pioneered several ways of enhancing the online shopping experience. Online customers can communicate with customer service representatives in real time, and two customers can even shop simultaneously—just as if they were shopping together in a brick-and-mortar store. Using a tool called "Virtual Model," shoppers can even "try on" clothes.[28] One of the most successful e-tailers, Amazon.com, is profiled in the "Hit & Miss" feature.

Generally, online retailers—such as Macys.com and Bestbuy.com—provide an online catalog where visitors click on items they want to buy. These items are placed in a file called an **electronic shopping cart.** When the shopper indicates that he or she wants to complete the transaction, the items in the electronic shopping cart are listed on the screen, along with the total amount due, so that the customer can review the whole order and make changes before making a payment.

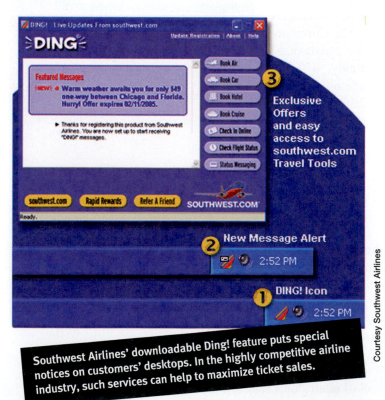

Courtesy Southwest Airlines

Southwest Airlines' downloadable Ding! feature puts special notices on customers' desktops. In the highly competitive airline industry, such services can help to maximize ticket sales.

Hit & Miss

Amazon.com's Profits Flow

Retailing can be a tough business. Many stores recently posted slumps in holiday sales, some announced layoffs, and others like Linens 'n Things filed for bankruptcy. But online store Amazon.com was enjoying a profit increase of 9 percent on sales that rose 18 percent. The company announced record annual revenues of $6.7 billion and was optimistic about the next year, sending its stock price soaring. It even saw its share of the online retail market jump from 6 to 10 percent. "Amazon is growing at a good two to three times the pace of everyone else," said one industry expert.

Now the Internet's biggest retailer, Amazon has grown by expanding into new product areas, offering free shipping, and delivering substantial product discounts. "We did do price comparisons among the big box stores that were local to us," said one holiday shopper in Virginia who spent $600 at Amazon, "and found time and time again that Amazon had the best price. I don't feel like I need to venture to any other site."

Amazon's new products are as varied as digital music downloads, motorcycle accessories, and hard-to-find CDs. It began with—and still sells—millions of books, and its newest innovation, the Kindle electronic-book reader, quickly became a best-seller. The firm uses sophisticated inventory tools that help keep its costs down and allow it to wait for favorable supplier prices before placing its orders. "Amazon was able to restock when nobody else was restocking," said one observer. "As demand was falling off a cliff [because other retailers had placed holiday orders much earlier], they could get better rates."

But behind its huge product array and complex operations have always been some fairly simple strategies. First is a customer focus. "Being customer-focused allows you to be more pioneering," founder and CEO Jeff Bezos claims. "We have found that, on the Internet, 'me too' strategies seem not to work very well. ... [and] you can't put into a spreadsheet how people are going to behave around a new product." Equally important, from its beginnings the company has worked to fill three enduring needs: vast selection, low prices, and fast, accurate delivery. Says Bezos, "It's impossible to imagine a world ten years from now where customers will say, 'I love Amazon, but I just wish your prices would be higher.'"

Questions for Critical Thinking

1. Why do you think Amazon has never opened any brick-and-mortar stores?
2. Jeff Bezos believes companies should have a long-term focus. What does that mean for an Internet firm whose competitive landscape changes daily?

Sources: Geoffrey A. Fowler, "Amazon's Sales Surge, Bucking Retail Slump," *The Wall Street Journal,* January 30, 2009, pp. B1 and B5; "Jeff Bezos, Corporate Executive: A Willingness to Be Misunderstood," *U.S. News & World Report,* December 1–8, 2008, p. 51; Kevin Maney, "Q&A with Jeff Bezos," *Portfolio,* June 2008, http://www.portfolio.com; Josh Quittner, "The Charmed Life of Amazon's Jeff Bezos," *Fortune,* April 15, 2008, http://money.cnn.com.

One factor that experts think will have a significant influence on the growth of online shopping is the increased availability and use of broadband technology. A study by research firm Leichtman Research Group estimates that more than half of U.S. households now have broadband Internet connections (mainly through DSL or cable modems). This percentage is expected to rise to more than 70 percent of households over the next few years.[29] Why is this trend significant for e-tailers? On average, broadband users are online more frequently and for longer periods of time, and they are more likely to make online purchases. Most important, broadband shoppers spend on average around one-third more online than narrowband shoppers.[30]

Who Are the Online Buyers and Sellers?

The Pew Internet and American Life Project periodically collects and analyzes data about Internet usage in the United States, including online buying behavior. Some of the key findings from the most recent survey are shown in Figure 7.2. While the typical online shopper is still relatively young, more highly educated, an urban or suburban resident, and affluent, there is also evidence that the demographics of online shoppers are changing. For instance, women are just as likely as men today

Figure 7.2   Demographics of Online Shoppers

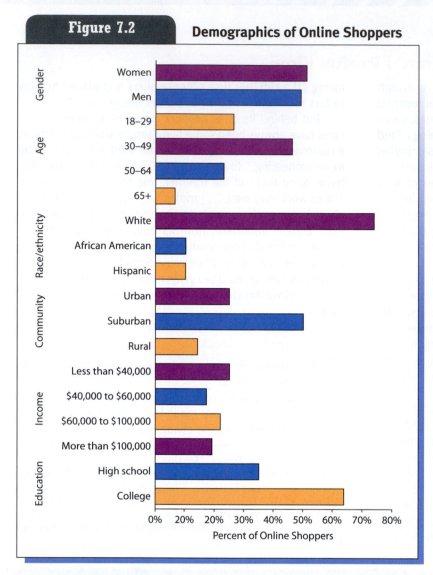

Gender
- Women
- Men

Age
- 18–29
- 30–49
- 50–64
- 65+

Race/ethnicity
- White
- African American
- Hispanic

Community
- Urban
- Suburban
- Rural

Income
- Less than $40,000
- $40,000 to $60,000
- $60,000 to $100,000
- More than $100,000

Education
- High school
- College

0% 20% 20% 30% 40% 50% 60% 70% 80%

Percent of Online Shoppers

Note: Within each demographic category (such as gender and age) is the breakdown of online shoppers. For instance, around 51 percent of online shoppers are female and 49 percent are male.
Source: Pew Internet and American Life Project, "Online Shopping," http://www.pewinternet.org, accessed March 5, 2009.

to purchase products online—a few years ago online shoppers were typically male. While consumers over age 50 still make up less than 30 percent of total online shoppers, the percentage of older consumers shopping on the Web is increasing faster than it is for younger consumers.[31] The bottom line: online buyers are beginning to look more and more like typical American consumers.

Early online sellers focused on offering products that consumers were familiar with and tended to buy frequently, such as books and music. Other popular online offerings included computer hardware and software, airline tickets, and hotel rooms. Figure 7.3 shows the projected growth in online sales of various products, excluding travel. As the figure illustrates, online sales of consumer electronics and home furnishings are expected to grow the fastest of the products listed. Many experts believe that if the demographics of Internet users continue to change, sales of products such as prescription drugs, kitchen products, and small and large appliances will benefit. These products are typically purchased more frequently by women and older consumers.

At the same time, however, online sales of other products appear to have reached a plateau. One example is travel. According to a recent study by Forrester Research, a technology consulting firm, the number of people booking travel online has fallen close to 10 percent in recent years. Moreover, even though revenues increased, the percentage of Internet users who usually book travel online fell from 68 to 62 percent. Forrester's online travel analyst Henry Harteveldt notes, "This is a wake-up call for the industry. Customers are tired of spending two or three hours [online] trying to find the airline or hotel or vacation package that meets their needs."[32] One explanation for this lengthy process is that most travel sites are, in effect, using extensions of technology built in the 1960s.

Benefits of B2C E-Business

Why do consumers shop online? Three main reasons are most often cited in consumer surveys: convenience, lower prices, and personalization.

CONVENIENCE The main advantage of online shopping, according to surveys is convenience. More than three-quarters of Internet users agreed that online shopping is convenient for them. Moreover, close to 70 percent agreed with the notion that cybershopping saves time.[33] Cybershoppers can order goods and services from around the world at any hour of the day or night. Most e-tailers allow customers to register their credit card and shipping information to streamline future purchases. Customers register with a user name and password, which they enter when they place another order. E-tailers typically send an e-mail message confirming an order and the amount charged to the buyer's credit card. Another e-mail is sent once the product is shipped, along with a tracking number that the customer can use to track the order through the delivery process.

LOWER PRICES Many products actually cost less online. Many of the best deals on airfares and hotels, for instance, are found at travel sites on the Internet. If you call Delta Airlines' toll-free number, before you speak to an agent a recorded voice invites you to visit Delta.com, "where lower fares may be available." Visitors to BN.com—the online store of bookseller Barnes & Noble—find that many best-sellers are discounted by up to 40 percent. At the brick-and-mortar stores, best-sellers are marked down

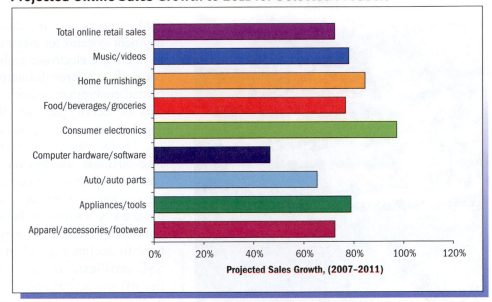

Figure 7.3

Projected Online Sales Growth to 2011 for Selected Products

Projected Sales Growth, (2007–2011)

Source: U.S. Census Bureau, *Statistical Abstract of the United States: 2009,* http://www.census.gov, accessed March 5, 2009.

only 30 percent. According to a recent survey, more than half of all Internet users agreed with the statement "The Internet is the best place to find bargains."[34]

The Web is an ideal method for savvy shoppers to compare prices from dozens—even hundreds—of sellers. Online shoppers can compare features and prices at their leisure. **Bots**— short for robots—make it easy to compare prices at dozens of e-tailers. For instance, say you're in the market for a new notebook computer. At Shopping.com, you can specify such things as screen size, processor speed, and weight. The bot finds the highest-rated notebook computers, the e-tailer offering the best price on each, and the estimated taxes and shipping expenses. The Web site even ranks the e-tailers by customer experience and tells you whether a particular model is in stock.

PERSONALIZATION While online shopping often operates with little or no human interaction, successful B2C e-business companies know how important personalization is to the quality of the shopping experience. Customer satisfaction is greatly affected by the firm's ability to offer service tailored to many customers. But each person expects a certain level of customer service. Consequently, most leading online retailers offer customized features on their Web sites. As a result, as was noted in Table 7.1, e-tailers often have higher customer satisfaction scores than traditional retailers.[35]

In the early years of e-business, Web marketers cast their nets broadly to land as many buyers as possible. Today, the emphasis has turned toward one-to-one marketing, creating loyal customers who are likely to make repeat purchases. How does personalized marketing work online? Say you buy a book at Amazon.com and register with the site. The site welcomes you back for your next purchase by name. Using software that analyzes your previous purchases, it also suggests other books you might like. You can even choose to receive periodic e-mails from Amazon.com informing you of new offerings. Many other leading e-tailers have adopted similar types of personalized marketing. As noted earlier, the number of customers using online travel sites has declined slightly. Experts suggest that more personalization is one key to renewing growth, and in fact, the travel sites that have done this are continuing to prosper.[36]

Developing Safe Online Payment Systems

In response to consumer concerns about the safety of sending credit card numbers over the Internet, companies have developed secure payment systems for e-business. The most common forms of online payment are electronic cash and electronic wallets. Internet browsers, such as Microsoft Internet Explorer and Firefox, contain sophisticated encryption systems. **Encryption** is the process of encoding data for security purposes. When such a system is active, users see a special icon indicating that they are at a protected Web site.

To increase consumer security, most companies involved in e-business use **Secure Sockets Layer (SSL)** technology to encrypt information and verify the identity of senders and receivers (called *authentication*). SSL consists of a public key and a private key—software that encrypts and decrypts information. The public key is used to encrypt information, and the private key is used to decipher it. When a browser points to a domain with an SSL certificate, the technology authenticates (verifies the identity of) the server and the visitor and establishes an encryption method and a unique session key. Both parties can then begin a secure session that guarantees a message's privacy and integrity. VeriSign is one of the leading providers of SSL technology, which is used by around 93 percent of *Fortune* 500 companies. The VeriSign Secured Seal is viewed more than 100 million times each day.[37]

An **electronic wallet** is another online payment method. An electronic wallet is a computer data file at an e-business site's checkout counter that contains not only electronic cash but credit card information, owner identification, and address. With electronic wallets, customers do not have to retype personal information each time they make a purchase at that site. Consumers simply click on the electronic wallet after selecting items, and their credit card payment information, name and address, and preferred mailing method are transmitted instantly.

Founded by American Express, Discover, JCB, MasterCard, and Visa, the PCI (payment card industry) Security Standards Council's mission is to enhance payment account data security. Its primary mission is to foster the broad adoption of PCI Security Standards among all companies engaged in e-business activity.[38]

VeriSign uses SSL encryption technology to protect businesses and their customers against online cyber attacks. The company also manages the registry of .com and .net domain names.

Assessment Check ✔

1. Visit the Web site of Starbucks (http://www.starbucks.com). Is this site an informational site or a shopping site? Explain your answer.

2. What are the major advantages cited by consumers of B2C e-business?

3. Outline how e-tailers are improving online payment systems.

E–Business Challenges

Not surprisingly, e-business has had its problems and challenges. Consumers are still concerned about protecting their privacy and security and being victimized by Internet fraud. In addition, consumers remain frustrated with unreliable and hard-to-use Web sites and annoyed over the inconveniences of scheduling deliveries and returning merchandise. Businesses are concerned about potential conflicts with business partners and difficulty in reaching customers electronically.

Privacy and Security Issues

Consumers worry that information about them will become available to others without their permission. In fact, research indicates that privacy remains one of the top concerns of Internet users and impedes the growth of e-business. As the earlier discussion of Internet payments explained, concern about the privacy of credit card numbers has led to the use of more secure payment systems and standards.

But businesses need to continue their efforts. The most recent survey on online shopping conducted by the Pew Internet and American Life Project showed that about three-quarters of Internet users agreed that they do not like giving out credit card or other personal information online. The survey's results also strongly suggest that more people would shop online, and shop more often, if they felt confident about e-business security and the privacy of their personal information.[39] Online retailers are developing new methods of paying for online purchases to allay consumer anxiety over privacy and security.

Because most consumers want assurances that any information they provide won't be sold to others without their permission, online merchants have adopted policies to protect consumer information. For example, many Internet companies have signed on with Internet privacy organizations such as TRUSTe. By displaying the TRUSTe logo on their Web sites, they indicate that they have promised to disclose how they collect personal data, what they do with the information, and how they follow the industry's best practices. Prominently displaying a privacy policy is an effective way to build customers' trust.

A policy is only as good as the company publishing it, though. Consumers have no assurances about what happens if a company is sold or goes out of business. For instance, Amazon.com has told customers openly that if it or part of its business is purchased at some point, its database would be one of the transferred assets.

Such privacy features may become a necessary feature of Web sites if consumer concerns continue to grow. They also may become legally necessary. Already in the United States, the Children's Online Privacy Protection Act (COPPA) requires that Web sites targeting children younger than age 13 obtain "verifiable parental consent" before collecting any data that could be used to identify or contact individual users, including names and e-mail addresses.

Security concerns are not limited to consumers. Employees are realizing that their employers can monitor their online behavior and e-mail messages at work. Some companies even specialize in helping employers use such information. Tacit Knowledge Systems builds a database from key terms in employees' e-mail. The primary objective is to help a company identify which employees have knowledge that they can contribute to the company—for example, knowledge about a particular competitor or type of product. Of course, many employees might be uncomfortable with their employer tracking what they write about. So Tacit's software allows employees to decide which aspects, if any, of their personal profile they want to make public.

Companies, too, are concerned about the privacy of their data, and with good reason. Bell Canada recently recovered stolen data on 3.4 million of its customers. Also, in one of the biggest cases of stolen consumer financial information ever, a data breach at retailer TJX (parent company of Marshalls and T.J. Maxx) affected more than 45 million credit and debit card accounts. TJX recently agreed to a settlement with Visa and a major bank, under which it would pay more than $40 million related to the data theft.[40]

To prevent such intrusions, companies install combinations of hardware and software called *firewalls* to keep unauthorized Net users from tapping into private corporate data. A **firewall** is an electronic barrier between a company's internal network and the Internet that limits access into and out of the network. However, an impenetrable firewall is difficult to find. Recently, researchers developed a simple method to steal encrypted information stored on computer hard disks and networks.[41] A determined and skilled hacker can often gain access, so it is important for firms to test their Web sites and networks for vulnerabilities regularly and back up critical data in case an intruder breaches security measures. Some of the newer technologies to prevent security breaches of computer networks are discussed in Chapter 15.

Internet Fraud

Fraud is another barrier to e-business. The Internet Crime Complaint Center (http://www.ic3.gov), run by the FBI and the White Collar Crime Taskforce, compiles complaints concerning Internet fraud. IC3 logged approximately 200,000 complaints during a recent year, although that represented a decline of around 10 percent from the prior year. About half of the total Internet-related fraud complaints dealt with online auctions. Auction fraud ranged from merchandise that did not match the description the bidder was given, such as fraudulent paintings, to products that were purchased but never delivered. Nondelivery of merchandise, credit and debit card fraud, investment fraud, and identify theft also made up major categories of Internet-related complaints referred to law enforcement agencies, according to the center.[42]

phishing high-tech scam that uses authentic looking e-mail or pop-up ads to get unsuspecting victims to reveal personal information.

One common type of Internet fraud, called **phishing,** is a high-tech scam that uses e-mail or pop-up messages claiming to be from familiar businesses or organizations, such as banks, Internet service providers, or even government agencies. The message usually asks the reader to "update" or "validate" account information, often stating that some dire consequence will occur if the reader doesn't respond. The purpose of phishing is to get unsuspecting victims to disclose personal information such as credit card numbers, bank account numbers, Social Security numbers, or computer passwords. Phishing is also a common method of distributing viruses and malicious spyware programs to computer users. As the Federal Trade Commission advises, if you receive an e-mail or pop-up message that asks for personal information, don't reply or click on the link in the message no matter how authentic the message or pop-up appears.[43] Legitimate companies don't ask for personal or financial information via e-mail or pop-ups. If in doubt, rather than following the link in the suspect e-mail, users should contact the organization directly, either by separately typing the Web address in a browser or by telephone.

© Internet Crime Complaint Center (a Federal Bureau of Investigation—NW3C partnership)

Fraud is a serious problem both for online customers and for trustworthy online businesses. Victims of Internet fraud can file criminal complaints on the Internet Crime Complaint Center's Web site.

Internet companies are increasing their antiphishing efforts. Recently, PayPal and eBay entered into a partnership with Yahoo! to use its antiphishing technology. This technology enables Internet service providers to determine whether messages are real and should be delivered to a customer's in box. It is hoped that the technology will significantly reduce the volume of fraudulent e-mail received by consumers and lower their risk of being victimized by phishing.[44]

A recent variation of phishing—dubbed **vishing** (for **v**oice ph**ishing**)—is a scam that involves an e-mail, text message, or telephone call to a consumer supposedly from a credit card company. The recipients are informed that their card needs to be "reactivated" and given a phone number to call or text that seems authentic. When the intended victims reach the sender, they receive a voice response directing them to enter their card number in order to "resolve a pending security issue." As with suspected phishing scams, if you receive such a message do not reply. Instead, contact the credit card issuer using an independently obtained telephone number or Web address.[45]

Payment fraud is another problem for many e-tailers. Orders are placed online, paid for with a credit card, and the merchandise is shipped. Then, the cardholder asks the credit card issuer for a chargeback to the e-tailer. The cardholder claims that he or she never made the purchase or never received the merchandise. Some claims are legitimate, but many involve fraud. Because an online purchase doesn't require a customer's signature or credit card imprint, the merchant, not the credit card issuer, bears the liability in most fraud cases. E-tailers are trying to reduce payment fraud by employing software that spots fraud before it happens, using payment verification services offered by credit card companies such as Visa, and even hiring companies who specialize in fighting credit card chargebacks.

Poor Web Site Design and Service

For e-business firms to attract customers—and keep them—companies must meet buyers' expectations. For instance, customers want to find items without frustration and get questions answered. However, Web sites are not always as well designed or easy to use as they should be. In fact, many Web shopping carts, perhaps 50 percent or more, are abandoned before a customer completes the purchase. Surveys indicate that almost 58 percent of Internet users have experienced one or more of the following when shopping online:

- lack of information
- inability to find the information they need
- feeling overwhelmed by too much information.[46]

Experts suggest that poor Web site design is the major cause of consumer frustration. This, in turn, impedes the growth of e-business.

Another challenge to successful e-business is merchandise delivery and returns. Retailers sometimes have trouble making deliveries to busy consumers. And consumers don't want to wait for packages to be delivered. Also, if customers aren't satisfied with products, they have to arrange for pickup or send packages back themselves.

Retailers are addressing these issues. Virtually all Web sites allow customers to track orders from placement to delivery. E-tailers have worked hard on returns—a process known as *reverse logistics*. Detailed directions on how to return merchandise, including preprinted shipping labels, are included in orders. A few, such as Nordstrom and Chef's Catalog, even pay the shipping cost for returns and arrange for package pickup.

Many of the so-called *pure-play dot-com retailers*—those without traditional stores or catalogs—didn't survive for very long. They had no history of selling and satisfying customers. Because of expertise in all parts of retailing, companies that combine their brick-and-mortar operations with e-business—such as Old Navy and REI—have generally been more successful than those with little or no retail experience.

The same lesson also applies to other service industries. To be successful at e-business, a firm must establish and maintain competitive standards for customer service. When it began enabling customers to check flight schedules and purchase tickets online, Southwest Airlines worked hard to make sure its Web site had the same high service standards the airline is known for. As noted earlier, Southwest.com has proved both very popular and profitable.

Channel Conflicts

Companies spend time and money to nurture relationships with their partners. But when a manufacturer uses the Internet to sell directly to customers, it can compete with its usual partners. Retailers often have their own Web sites. So they don't want their suppliers competing with them for sales. As e-business broadens its reach, producers must decide whether these relationships are more important than the potential of selling directly on the Web. Disputes between producers, wholesalers, and retailers are called **channel conflicts**.

> ## "They Said It"
>
> "The Internet is the most important single development in the history of human communication since the invention of call waiting."
>
> —**Dave Barry** (b. 1947) American writer and humorist

Mattel, well known for producing toys such as Barbie, Cabbage Patch dolls, and Matchbox cars, sells most of its products in toy stores and toy departments of other retailers, such as Target and Wal-Mart. The company wants an Internet presence, but it would cut the retailers out of this important source of revenue if it sold toys online to consumers. Mattel cannot afford to lose the goodwill and purchasing power of its giant retail partners. So the company sells only specialty products online, including pricey American Girl dolls, many of which are not available in retail stores.

Pricing is another potential area of conflict. In their eagerness to establish themselves as Internet leaders, some companies sell merchandise online at discount prices. However, while Vermont-based athletic footwear manufacturer Merrell does sell its products online, as well is at retail stores, the online store's prices are never lower than a customer would find at a local retail outlet. This policy helps minimize potential channel conflict. Bicycle and parts manufacturer Specialized Bicycle Components takes a slightly different approach. Prices on its online store are often slightly higher than they are at retail dealers. Specialized does this to provide a small incentive for shoppers to purchase items from one of its retailer dealers rather than the online store.

Using the Web's Communication Function

The Internet has four main functions: e-business, entertainment, information, and communication. Even though e-business is a significant activity and is growing rapidly, communication still remains the most popular Web function. The volume of e-mail today exceeds regular mail by an estimated ten to one. It's not surprising, then, that contemporary businesspeople use the communication function of the Internet to advance their organizational objectives.

Companies have long used e-mail to communicate with customers, suppliers, and other partners. Most companies have links on their Web sites that allow outside parties to send e-mails directly to the most appropriate person or division within the company. For instance, if you have a question concerning an online order from Eddie Bauer, you can click on a link on the retailer's Web site and send an e-mail to a customer service representative. Many online retailers have gone even further, offering their customers live help. Using a form of instant messaging, live help provides real-time communication between customers and customer service representatives.

Firms also use e-mail to inform customers about such company events as the introduction of new products and special promotions. While using e-mail in this manner can be quite cost effective, companies have to be careful. A growing number of customers consider such e-mails **spam**—the popular name for junk e-mail. In fact, in a recent survey, one of the leading reasons given by consumers for reducing online shopping was "receiving spam after online purchase." Many Internet users use spam filters to automatically eliminate junk e-mail from their in boxes.

Online Communities

In addition to e-mail, many firms use Internet forums, newsgroups, **electronic bulletin boards,** and Web communities that appeal to people who share common interests. All of these sites take advantage of the communication power of the Internet which, as noted earlier in the chapter, is still a main reason people go online. Members congregate online and exchange views and information on topics of interest. These communities may be organized for commercial or noncommercial purposes.

Online communities can take several forms, but all offer specific advantages to users and organizations alike. Online forums, for instance, are Internet discussion groups. Users log in and participate by sending comments and questions or receiving information from other forum members. Forums may operate as electronic bulletin boards, as libraries for storing information, or even as a type of classified ad directory. Firms often use forums to ask questions and exchange information with customers. Adobe, which designs such software as Acrobat and Photoshop, operates a "user-to-user" forum on its Web site as a support community for its customers. Customers who share common personal and professional interests can congregate, exchange industry news and practical product tips, share ideas, and—equally important—create publicity for Adobe products.

Newsgroups are noncommercial Internet versions of forums. Here people post and read messages on specific topics. Tens of thousands of newsgroups exist on the Internet, and the number continues to rise. Electronic bulletin boards center on a specific topic or area of interest. For instance, backpackers might check online bulletin boards such as Backpacker.net to find out about the latest equipment, new trails, or current weather conditions in popular backpacking locations. While newsgroups resemble two-way conversations, electronic bulletin boards are more like announcements.

Online communities are not limited to consumers. They also facilitate business-to-business marketing. Using the Internet to build communities helps companies find other organizations to benchmark against, including suppliers, distributors, and competitors that may be interested in forming an alliance. Business owners who want to expand internationally frequently seek advice from other members of their online community.

Blogs

Another type of online communication method that continues to gain popularity is the **blog.** Short for *Web log,* a blog is a Web page that serves as a publicly accessible personal journal for an individual or organization. Typically updated daily or even more frequently, these hybrid diary-guide sites are read regularly by many American Internet users. Using RSS (Really Simple Syndication) software, readers are continually alerted to new material posted on their favorite blogs whenever they are online. Unlike e-mail and instant messaging, blogs let readers post comments and ask questions aimed at the author (called a *blogger*). Some blogs today also incorporate wikis. A **wiki** is a Web page that anyone can edit, so a reader can, in addition to asking questions or posting comments, actually make changes to the Web page. The popular site Wikipedia.com is an online encyclopedia that users can edit and update. Video and audio blogs—called **podcasts**—are another relatively new technology. Bloggers can prepare a video or audio recording on a PC and then post it to a Web site, from which it can be downloaded to an MP3 player or smart phone. Podcasting is growing rapidly; the podcasting audience could soon reach 60 million. FeedBurner (a unit of Google), a leading provider of media distribution for blogs and RSS feeds, was recently serving almost 200,000 podcasts.[47]

With the growing interest in blogs, companies often incorporate them into their e-business strategies. Many believe that corporate blogs, if done properly, can also help build brand trust. An example of a successful blog is iLounge.com, a blog hosted by Apple, which lets users discuss their ideas for improving Apple products, such as the iPhone and iPod. The blog benefits Apple in two ways: (1) it helps build the iPod and iPhone brands; (2) it gives Apple ideas to improve the design and features of Apple's most successful products. Another successful corporate blog is Wal-Mart's Checkoutblog.com, the subject of the "Hit & Miss" feature. As the box notes, Wal-Mart's decision to stop selling HD DVDs, in favor of competing format Blu-ray, was first announced on the blog. Wal-Mart's decision effectively doomed the HD DVD format.

blog online journal written by a blogger.

Hit & Miss

Wal-Mart's Blog

Where can Wal-Mart employees speak their mind about the products their company sells? If you said, "Only in private," think again.

After two failed attempts to launch blogs aimed at shoppers in recent years, the retail giant (with annual sales approaching $400 billion) has finally gotten it right. Its newest blog, www.checkoutblog.com, is an unvarnished, uncensored Web site written by Wal-Mart buyers calling it as they see it. While sometimes personal—one blogger writes about her cat; others mention favorite novels—the Web site mainly focuses on electronics and has proven enormously influential. Checkoutblog.com was the first place the public learned that Wal-Mart had picked Sony's Blu-ray as the winner in the battle between high-definition DVD formats and would no longer stock Toshiba's HD DVD players. Toshiba accepted defeat in a decision likely to cost millions of dollars.

Meanwhile, back on the blog, "This decision will make my job so much easier," Susan Chronister wrote. "So ... if you bought the HD player like me, I'd retire it to the bedroom, kids' playroom, or give it to your parents ... and make space for a [Blu-ray disc] player for your awesome hi-def experience."

That kind of candor is what observers say make Wal-Mart's third try at blogging a success. Unlike the first two efforts, which were heavily corporate and quickly shut down, Checkoutblog, with about 1,000 hits a day, acknowledges that "readers can tell if people are being genuine or monitored," according to Wal-Mart's merchandise manager for entertainment.

In fact, if even cuddly Elmo Live can take the heat from a buyer ("It's a little creepy, but he actually seems alive"), then perhaps Wal-Mart has finally found its voice.

Questions for Critical Thinking

1. One Wal-Mart employee says, "If you are a vendor and you talk to your Wal-Mart buyer all the time, you are going to know their likes and dislikes anyway." Should the company give its vendors bad news about products before blogging about them? Why or why not?
2. How influential do you think a corporate blog like Checkoutblog.com can really be? Explain your answer.

Sources: Company Web site, http://checkoutblog.com, accessed March 5, 2009; Michael Barbaro, "Wal-Mart Tastemakers Write Unfiltered Blog," *The New York Times,* March 3, 2008, http://www.nytimes.com; Richard Wray and Justin McCurry, "Home Entertainment: Clearer Picture Emerges in Battle over High-Definition Viewing," *The Guardian* (London), February 19, 2008, http://www.guardian.co.uk.

Done poorly, however, a blog can do more harm than good. In fact, many Internet users still remain skeptical of company-sponsored blogs, viewing them as no more than extensions of the public relations department. One of the more notable PR failures was the *raging cow* blog sponsored by beverage maker Cadbury Schweppes. The company was criticized for attempting to fool readers into thinking that it was written by satisfied consumers, when in fact it was written by the company.[48] Table 7.2 lists five questions companies should ask before beginning a corporate-sponsored blog.

Of course, organizations are often the subject of blogs written by others. One type of blog that can make a company nervous is a personal blog written by an employee in which he or she muses about coworkers, bosses, and customers. Consequently, some firms have put into place policies on employee blogging. A few have even gone as far as prohibiting them.[49]

On a search engine, enter a well-known brand followed by a less-than-complimentary adjective, and see how many results turn up—probably thousands. Companies may dread to see these sites, many of which are blogs, but those written by angry customers are often doing the company a favor: they care enough about the company's products to say what went wrong and how to fix it. Experts suggest reading the writings of unhappy customers and trying to implement their suggestions.[50]

Table 7.2	Before Blogging: Some Questions to Ask
1	**What will the blog be about?** While the blog should be consistent with the company's overall message, it shouldn't just be about things the company sells.
2	**Who will write the blog?** Bloggers can be company insiders or outsiders. If the blog is written by nonemployees, make sure to note that the blog is company sponsored. Companies have gotten into trouble in the past by trying to fool readers by concealing their identities.
3	**How often will the blog be updated?** While daily updates are best, updating the blog a couple of times a week is generally okay. Many experts argue that the higher the quality of the posts, the less frequently the blog needs updating.
4	**How much should be spent on the blog?** While there are no-fee blogging services, they aren't designed to maximize keyword visibility or link popularity. Hiring a fee-based blogging service may be a sound investment.
5	**Will blogging really make a difference?** This is perhaps the most difficult question to answer. While a well-executed blog can produce a solid return on investment, a poorly executed one will do more harm than good. Just because blogging is considered trendy, doesn't mean it makes sense for every organization.

Sources: Adapted from, P. J. Fusco, "Five Getting-Started Blog Questions," *ClickZ Network*, January 30, 2008, http://www.clickz.com, accessed March 5, 2009.

Web-Based Promotions

Rather than relying completely on their Web sites to attract buyers, companies frequently expand their reach in the marketplace by placing ads on sites their prospective customers are likely to visit. **Banner ads,** the most common form of Internet advertising, are typically small messages placed in high-visibility areas of frequently visited Web sites. **Pop-up ads** are separate windows that contain an advertising message. The effectiveness of pop-up ads, however, is questionable. For one thing, scam artists use pop-ups. For another, many Internet users simply hate pop-up ads—even those from legitimate companies. Consequently, most Internet service providers now offer software that blocks pop-up ads. Google and Microsoft also offer free pop-up ad-blocking software.

One of the fastest growing types of online advertising is **pre-roll video ads.** An advertiser's short video clip runs as soon as a Web page loads. These video ads are typically anywhere from 15 to 30 seconds in length. Even though a survey by Burst Media found that more than half of all Internet users leave a Web site immediately when they see an ad starting to roll, most ad-buyers think they're as effective, if not more effective, than traditional 30-second TV spots.[51] As a result, spending on pre-roll ads could reach $3 billion, or more, within a couple of years.[52]

Another type of online advertising is so-called search marketing. Firms make sure that they are listed with the major search engines, such as Google and Microsoft Live Search. But that is not enough. A single search for an item—say, plastic fasteners—will yield thousands of sites, many of which might not even be relevant. To overcome this problem, companies pay online search engines to have their Web sites or ads pop up after a computer user enters certain words into the search engine or to make sure that their firm's listing appears toward the top of the search results. Google and other search engines now include "sponsored links" on the right side of the search results page. When a user clicks on one of the sponsored links, he or she is taken to that site, and the company pays the search engine a small fee. Many experts consider search marketing the most cost-effective form of Web-based advertising.

search marketing
paying search engines, such as Google, a fee to make sure that the company's listing appears toward the top of the search results.

Companies also use online coupons to promote their products via the Web. For instance, customers can visit Procter & Gamble's Web site (http://www.pg.com) to learn about a new product and then print a discount coupon redeemable at participating retailers. Consumers can also search for virtual coupons using such criteria as business name, location, and keyword, and then download and print them. ValPak Marketing Systems, a longtime leader in the paper coupon industry, now offers the online equivalent at its Web site (http://www.valpak.com).

The Global Environment of E-Business

For many companies, future growth is directly linked to a global strategy that incorporates e-business. While the United States still leads the world in technology, communications infrastructure, and ownership of PCs and other consumer technology products, other countries are rapidly catching up. This is also the case when it comes to Internet use. Figure 7.4 shows the top ten nations in terms of number of Internet users and the Internet penetration rates—the percentage of a country's population who are online. As the figures show, China leads the world in the number of Internet users, recently bypassing the United States. But China and the United States do not even rank in the top ten in terms of Internet penetration. The United States comes in at thirteenth, at 72.5 percent, and China is at only 19 percent. Greenland leads the way in Internet penetration, with more than 92 percent of citizens using the Internet. These statistics show that U.S. Internet usage is growing more slowly—at a little more than 130 percent in eight years—than in other countries. China and India, with their huge populations, both saw Internet usage grow more than 1,000 percent in the same time period.[53]

When it comes to e-business, the United States still leads, but the rest of the world is making major strides forward. U.S. firms cannot expect that their earlier experience with the Internet and e-business gives them a natural and permanent edge in foreign markets. For example, auction giant eBay may dominate most markets, but not in China. Chinese company Alibaba.com has an 83 percent share of the auction market in that country, compared with eBay's 7 percent.[54]

With so many users and so much buying power, the Internet creates an enormous pool of potential customers. Firms can market their goods and services internationally and locate distribution sources and trading partners abroad. Customers can search for products at their convenience, browsing through online catalogs that always show current information. Many companies divide their Web sites internationally.

Alibaba's online auction site serves fifteen global markets in three languages—Japanese, Mandarin Chinese, and English. The site, which serves businesses as well as individuals, offers everything from iron ore to MP3 players.

© R. Alcorn, photographed and edited for John Wiley & Sons; background image © Konstantin Inozemtsev/iStock International, Inc.

For instance, when you visit software company Symantec's Web site, you are first asked your country of origin; after entering the information, you are automatically taken to that country-specific portion of the Web site. A list of the products available for your country is shown, along with local distributors and service centers. And the information on the site is presented in the local language.

One practical implication of this global marketplace is the different languages that buyers and sellers speak. Reflecting the Internet's origins, about one-third of Internet users communicate in English. However, the remainder use other languages, led by Chinese, Spanish, Japanese, French, German, and Portuguese.[55] So far, roughly three of every four Web pages are still in English, slowing the adoption of the Internet in non-English-speaking countries. Other international differences are important, too. Auction site eBay initially goofed in the United Kingdom by launching an auction site with prices stated in U.S. dollars. After realizing that its British audience was offended and confused, the company quickly switched to British pounds.

E-business can heighten competition. In the virtual global marketplace, many manufacturers use the Internet to search online catalogs for the lowest-priced parts. No longer can local suppliers assume that they have locked up the business of neighboring firms. Furthermore, the Internet is a valuable way to expand a company's reach, especially for small businesses that would otherwise have difficulty finding customers overseas.

One issue that has proven problematic at times is adhering to local laws and customs. Obviously, U.S. companies should be sensitive to cultural differences, and they must respect local laws. The question, however, is how far they should go. Should they, for instance, allow their Web sites to be censored? How much should they cooperate with local law enforcement? The "Solving an Ethical Controversy" feature highlights the ethical dilemmas confronting American business internationally, specifically, Yahoo! in China, which provided information on two Chinese dissidents to the government.

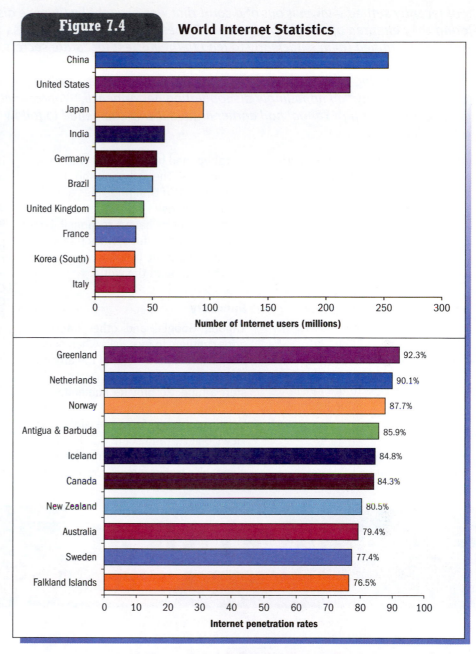

Figure 7.4 World Internet Statistics

Source: Internet World Stats, "Usage and Population Statistics," http://www.internetworldstats.com, accessed February 6, 2009.

Assessment Check ✓

1. Does the U.S. lead the world in Internet penetration? Is U.S. Web usage growing faster or slower when compared with other countries?

2. What kinds of advantages does e-business offer in a global context?

YAHOO! UNVEILS DISSIDENTS IN CHINA

Yahoo! recently settled a lawsuit out of a court that was brought by Chinese dissidents seeking damages for the suffering they endured after Yahoo! provided Chinese authorities with access to e-mails and other records. The information identified them sufficiently to lead to their arrest for "state secrets violations." Two dissidents are in prison; two others have lost jobs, investments, and personal property. Yahoo! CEO Jerry Yang apologized to the men's families during a U.S. Congressional hearing into the case, at which Representative Tom Lantos called the company's testimony "an appallingly disappointing performance." Yang admitted, "this is wrong and would not happen again," although Yahoo! had earlier argued it was compelled to follow the laws of the countries in which it does business.

Should U.S. online firms comply with other countries' regulations if they are unfair or repressive?

PRO

1. Yahoo! felt that if its employees violated Chinese law by disobeying the government's order, they could face prosecution and the company could lose its government license to operate there.
2. Without Yahoo! in China, thousands more people would be denied what little opportunity they have to gain access to the free exchange of ideas on the Internet.

CON

1. No one knows what the Chinese government would have done if Yahoo! had not complied with its demands. The company should have upheld U.S. principles and taken the risk.
2. Internet firms have a responsibility to stand up for privacy rights that ensure the free flow of information around the world.

Summary

Yahoo!, Google, and other Internet firms continue to face risks when operating abroad. As a result of the arrests and resulting backlash, Yahoo! will start a fund "to provide humanitarian and legal aid to dissidents who have been imprisoned for expressing their views online," and some U.S. lawmakers hope to make it a crime for U.S. companies to give foreign governments information about their customers without Justice Department permission.

Sources: K. Shu-Ling, "TSU Slams Yahoo over E-mail Tag," *Taipei Times,* January 7, 2009, http://www.taipeitimes.com; Dan Nystedt, "Yahoo Sued Again by Chinese Dissidents," *InfoWorld,* February 29, 2008, http://www.infoworld.com; Catherine Rampell, "Yahoo Settles with Chinese Families," *The Washington Post,* November 14, 2007, http://www.washingtonpost.com; Corey Boles, "Yahoo's Lashing Highlights Risks of China Market," *The Wall Street Journal,* November 7, 2007, http://online.wsj.com.

Solving an **ETHICAL** controversy

Managing a Web Site

Business Web sites serve many purposes. They broaden customer bases, provide immediate accessibility to current catalogs, accept and process orders, and offer personalized customer service. As technology becomes increasingly easy to use, anyone with a computer and Internet access can easily design and then publish a site on the Web. How people or organizations use their sites to achieve their goals determines whether their sites will succeed. Figure 7.5 lists some key questions to consider in developing a Web site.

Developing Successful Web Sites

Most Web experts agree that it is easier to build a bad Web site than a good one. When judging Web sites, success means different things to different organizations. One firm might feel

Figure 7.5   Questions to Consider in Developing a Web Site

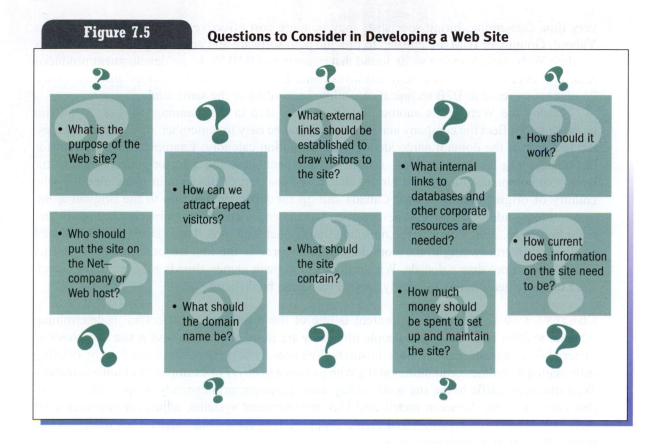

- What is the purpose of the Web site?

- Who should put the site on the Net—company or Web host?

- How can we attract repeat visitors?

- What should the domain name be?

- What external links should be established to draw visitors to the site?

- What should the site contain?

- What internal links to databases and other corporate resources are needed?

- How much money should be spent to set up and maintain the site?

- How should it work?

- How current does information on the site need to be?

satisfied by maintaining a popular site that conveys company information or reinforces name recognition—just as a billboard or magazine ad does—without requiring any immediate sales activity. Web sites like those of the *Los Angeles Times* and *USA Today* draw many visitors who want the latest news, and Yahoo!, Google, and ESPN are successful because they attract heavy traffic. To generate revenue, popular Web sites sell advertising space to other businesses.

Internet merchants need to attract customers who transact business on the spot. Some companies host Web sites that offer some value-added service to create goodwill for potential customers. Organizations such as the Mayo Clinic and accounting giant Ernst & Young provide useful information or links to related sites that people frequently visit. But to get people to stay at the site and complete a transaction, the site must also be secure, reliable, and easy to use.

PLANNING AND PREPARATION What is the company's goal for its Web site? Answering this question is the first and most important step in the Web site development process. For discount brokerage firm Charles Schwab, the primary objective is to sign up new customers. So the Web site designers put a link called "Open an Account" prominently on the site's home page. In addition, to reinforce Schwab's image as a respectable investment firm, the site uses a streamlined format that presents facts and other helpful information.

Objectives for the Web site also determine the scope of the project. If the company's goal is to sell merchandise online, the site must incorporate a way for customers to place orders and ask questions about products, as well as links to the firm's databases to track inventory and deliveries. As in this example, the plan includes not only the appearance of the Web site but also the company's behind-the-scenes resources for making the Web site deliver on its promises.

Other key decisions include whether to create and maintain a site in-house or to contract with outside experts. Some companies prefer to retain control over content and design by producing their own sites. However, because acquiring the expertise to develop Web sites can be very time consuming, hiring specialists may be more cost effective. Often companies such as Yahoo!, Google, or IBM are enlisted to provide both software and consulting services to clients for their Web sites. A recent study found that outsourcing B2B Web site development produced returns in excess of 2.5 times the initial investment. Moreover, outsourced solutions generated a 75 percent increase in B2B technical capabilities according to the same study.[56]

Naming the Web site is another important early step in the planning process. A domain name should reflect the company and its products and be easy to remember. For U.S. companies, the last part of the domain name identifies an affiliation category. Examples include .com for businesses, .org for organizations, .gov for government sites, and .edu for educational institutions. For companies outside the United States, the last part of the domain name identifies the country of origin, such as .ca for Canada and .jp for Japan. In addition to the original .com, .gov, and .org addresses, several new suffixes have been added to the Internet's naming system, including .aero, .biz, .coop, .info, .museum, .name, .net, and .pro. These suffixes were created to alleviate overcrowding in the .com domain and represent the first major addition of Internet addresses in more than a decade. With millions of domain names already registered, the search for a unique, memorable, and easily spelled name can be difficult.

CONTENT AND CONNECTIONS Content is one of the most important factors in determining whether visitors return to a site. People obviously are more inclined to visit a site that provides material that interests them. Many e-business Web sites try to distinguish themselves by offering information or online communities along with a chance to buy. For example, Williams-Sonoma's Web site lures traffic to the site with weekly menu planners; printer-ready recipes; and features that convert menus between metric and U.S. measurement systems, adjust measurements for different numbers of servings, and create shopping lists for menus. Many sites offer links to other sites that may interest visitors.

Standards for good content vary for every site, but available resources should be relevant to viewers, easy to access and understand, updated regularly, and written or displayed in a compelling, entertaining way. When the World Wide Web was a novelty, a page with a picture and a couple of paragraphs of text seemed entertaining. But such "brochureware" falls far short of meeting today's standards for interactivity, including the ability to accept customer data and orders, keep up-to-the-minute inventory records, and respond quickly to customer questions and complaints. Also, today's Internet users are less patient about figuring out how to make a site do what it promises. They won't wait ten minutes for a video clip to download or click through five different pages to complete a purchase.

After making content decisions and designing the site, the next step is connecting to the Internet by placing the required computer files on a server. Companies can have their own dedicated Web servers or contract to place their Web sites on servers at Internet Service Providers (ISPs) or other host companies. Most small businesses lack the necessary expertise to set up and run their own servers; they are better off outsourcing to meet their hosting and maintenance needs. They also need to draw business to their site. This usually requires a listing with the major search engines, such as Google and Ask.com.

Costs and Maintenance

As with any technological investment, Web site costs are an important consideration. The highly variable cost of a Web site includes not only development expenses but also the cost of placing the site on a Web server, maintaining and updating it, and promoting it. A reasonably tech-savvy employee with off-the-shelf software can create a simple piece of brochureware for a few hundred dollars. A Web site that can handle e-business will cost at least $10,000. Creating it requires understanding of how to link the Web site to the company's other information systems.

Although developing a commercial Web site with interactive features can cost tens of thousands of dollars, putting it online can cost as little as $20 or less a month for a spot on the server of a Web hosting company such as Godaddy.com or Yahoo!

It's also important for a Web site to stay current. Visitors don't return to a site if they know the information never changes or that claims about inventory or product selection are not current. Consequently, updating design and content is another major expense. In addition, site maintenance should include running occasional searches to test that links to the company's Web site are still active.

Measuring Web Site Effectiveness

How does a company gauge the return from investing in a Web site? Measuring the effectiveness of a Web site is tricky, and the appropriate process often depends on the purpose of the Web site. Figure 7.6 lists some measures of effectiveness. Profitability is relatively easy to measure in companies that generate revenues directly from online product orders, advertising, or subscription sales. As noted earlier, Southwest Airlines generates more than $5 billion annually in revenue from Southwest.com. However, what's not clear is how many of those tickets Southwest would have sold through other channels if Southwest.com did not exist. Moreover, and as noted earlier, evidence shows that so-called **Web-to-store** shoppers—a group that favors the Internet primarily as a research tool and time-saving device for retail purchases made in stores—are a significant consumer niche.

For many companies, revenue is not a major Web site objective. These Web sites are classified as corporate Web sites, not shopping sites. For such firms, online success is measured by increased brand awareness and brand loyalty, which presumably translates into greater profitability through offline transactions.

Some standards guide efforts to collect and analyze traditional consumer purchase data, such as how many Illinois residents bought new Honda Accords the previous year, watched *American Idol*, or tried the new coffee products at McDonald's. Still, the Internet presents several challenges for businesses. Although information sources are getting better, it is difficult to be sure exactly how many people use the Internet, how often, and what they actually do online. Some Web pages display counters that measure the number of visits. However, the counters can't tell whether someone has spent time on the page or skipped over it on the way to another site, or whether that person is a first-time or repeat viewer.

Advertisers typically measure the success of their ads in terms of **click-through rates,** meaning the percentage of people presented with a banner ad who click on it, thereby linking to a Web site or a pop-up page of information related to the ad. Recently, the average click-through rate has been declining to about 0.5 percent of those viewing an ad. This rate is much lower than the 1.0 to 1.5 percent response rate for direct-mail advertisements. Low click-through rates have

click-through rate
number of visitors who click on a Web banner ad.

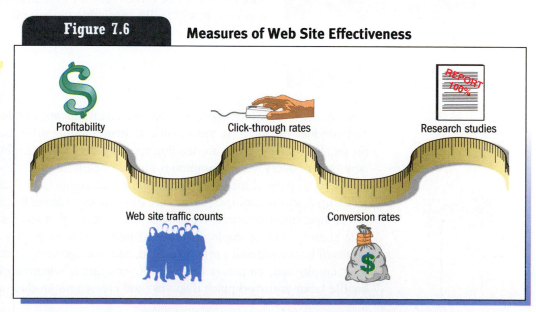

Figure 7.6 **Measures of Web Site Effectiveness**

Profitability — Click-through rates — Research studies — Web site traffic counts — Conversion rates

made traditional Web advertising, such as banner ads, less attractive than it was when they were novel and people were clicking on just about anything online.

As e-business gains popularity, new models for measuring its effectiveness are being developed. A basic measurement is the **conversion rate,** the percentage of Web site visitors who make purchases. A conversion rate of 3 to 5 percent is average by today's standards. A company can use its advertising cost, site traffic, and conversion rate data to find out the cost to win each customer. E-business companies try to boost their conversion rates by ensuring that their sites download quickly, are easy to use, and deliver on their promises. Many are turning to one of several firms that help companies improve the performance of their Web sites. Coremetrics is one such firm. The California-based company sells specialized software and provides consulting services to assist clients in various aspects of e-business. For instance, Coremetrics helped Petco improve the performance of its Web site (Petco.com) by, among other things, adding easily accessible customer product reviews. Shoppers who clicked on the reviews had a 50 percent higher conversion rate and spent 60 percent more than customers who didn't.[57]

Besides measuring click-through and conversion rates, companies can study samples of consumers. Research firms such as comScore, Jupiter Media Metrix, Nielsen/Net Ratings, and RelevantKnowledge recruit panels of computer users to track Internet site performance and evaluate Web activity; this service monitors Web audiences in much the same way that television audience viewing habits are rated. WebTrends provides information on Web site visitors, including where they come from; what they see; and the number of "hits," or visits to the site, during different times of the day. Other surveys of Web users investigate their brand awareness and their attitudes toward Web sites and brands. Nielsen Online—part of ACNielsen—plans to introduce an all-in-one ratings system that will measure viewership across television and the Internet.[58]

As Internet companies and advertisers continue to develop better measures of Web site effectiveness, new types of Internet advertising have emerged. One uses **display ads.** These ads are designed to reach targeted audiences and are the equivalent of glossy magazine ads or television commercials. Many consider display ads to be the future of Internet advertising. New computing tools and powerful analysis techniques have been developed to link online display ads to target markets. Rich LeFurgy, a principal at Archer Advisors, an Internet advertising consulting firm, notes, "The process is to be able to measure the reach and effectiveness of brand advertising as never before … if that happens, it will really accelerate the migration of brand advertisers online."[59]

conversion rate
percentage of visitors to a Web site who actually make a purchase.

Assessment Check ✔

1. When developing a Web site, what are some of the key questions to consider?

2. How does the type of Web site affect measures of effectiveness?

3. Explain *click-through rate* and *conversion rate*.

What's Ahead

The Internet is revolutionizing the way we communicate, obtain information, seek entertainment, and conduct business. It has created tremendous opportunities for B2B and B2C e-business. So far, B2B transactions are leading the way online. B2C e-business is growing and attracting new buyers every year. Companies are just beginning to harness the communication power of the Web to help achieve higher levels of customer satisfaction and loyalty. In spite of the challenges and roadblocks, the future of e-business looks bright.

In upcoming chapters, we look at other trends that are reshaping the business world of the 21st century. For example, in the next part of *Contemporary Business* we explore the critical issues of how companies organize, lead, and manage their work processes; manage and motivate their employees; empower their employees through teamwork and enhanced communication; handle labor and workplace disputes; and create and produce world-class goods and services.

Summary of Learning Goals

1 Define *e-business*, and discuss how it can help achieve business success.

E-business involves targeting customers by collecting and analyzing business information, conducting customer transactions, and maintaining online relationships with customers, suppliers, and other interested parties by means of the Internet. It consists of e-tailing, business-to-business transactions, electronic data interchanges, business-to-business exchange of data, and the use of Web-enabled communication tools such as e-mail. E-business increases a company's global reach, increases personalization, is interactive, offers right-time and integrated marketing, and can reduce costs.

Assessment Check Answers

1.1 Define *e-business*, and give several examples. E-business refers to conducting business via the Internet. Examples of e-business including e-tailing, business-to-business transactions, electronic exchange of data, and the use of Web-enabled communication tools.

1.2 List some of the benefits of e-business. The benefits of e-business include expanding global reach, increasing personalization and interaction with customers, offering right-time and integrated marketing, and reducing costs.

1.3 What is the impact of the Web on traditional brick-and-mortar companies? A Web site can improve the functioning of traditional brick-and-mortar companies. Even though consumers may purchase a product at a store, they often research it online beforehand. Evidence suggests that an effective Web presence can increase sales at traditional retail outlets.

2 Distinguish between a corporate Web site and a marketing Web site.

Virtually all businesses have Web sites. Generally, these sites can be classified as either corporate Web sites or marketing Web sites. Corporate Web sites are designed to increase the firm's visibility, promote its offerings, and provide information to interested parties. Marketing Web sites are also designed to communicate information and build customer relationships, but the main purpose of marketing Web sites is to increase purchases by site visitors.

Assessment Check Answers

2.1 Explain the differences between a corporate Web site and a marketing Web site. A corporate Web site is designed to increase a firm's visibility, promote its offerings, and provide information for interested parties. A marketing Web site generally includes the same information found on a corporate Web site but is also designed to increase sales to site visitors.

2.2 Visit the Procter & Gamble Web site (http://www. pg.com). Is this site a corporate Web site or a marketing Web site? The Procter & Gamble Web site is mainly a corporate Web site. However, consumers can download and print coupons for P&G products. So, in that sense, it is also a marketing Web site.

3 List the major forms of business-to-business (B2B) e-business.

Electronic data interchange was an early use of technology to conduct business transactions. E-business is the process of selling goods and services through Internet-based exchanges of data. It includes product information; ordering, invoicing, and payment processes; and customer service. In a B2B context, e-business uses Internet technology to conduct transactions between two organizations via extranets, private exchanges, electronic exchanges, and e-procurement.

Assessment Check Answers

3.1 What is B2B e-business? How large is it relative to B2C e-business? B2B e-business is the use of the Internet for business transactions between organizations. By some estimates, around 94 percent of all e-business activity consists of B2B e-business.

3.2 Explain extranets and VPNs. An extranet is a secure network accessible through a firm's Web site by authorized users. A virtual private network (VPN) is a secure Web site at which a company and its suppliers share all types of data from product design to the delivery of orders.

3.3 What is e-procurement? E-procurement consists of Web-based systems that enable all types of organizations to improve the efficiency of their procurement processes.

4 Explain business-to-consumer (B2C) e-business, and identify the products most often sold online.

B2C uses the Internet to connect companies directly with consumers. E-tailing and electronic storefronts are the major forms of online sales to consumers. Currently, online shoppers tend to be young, highly educated, affluent, and urban. However, in the coming years, online consumers will begin to look more like offline shoppers, and the kinds of products sold online will change as well. Benefits of B2C e-business include increased convenience, lower prices, and personalization. Payment methods include electronic cash, electronic wallets, and online transfers of cash. Major credit card issuers have formed the PCI Security Standards Council to establish standards to enhance the security of electronic payments.

Assessment Check Answers

4.1 Visit the Web site of Starbucks (http://www. starbucks.com). Is this site an informational site or a shopping site? Explain your answer. An informational site provides product information, technical support, and links to local retailers. A shopping Web site allows visitors to buy a firm's products. The Starbucks Web site is a shopping site because consumers can purchase everything from coffee to espresso machines.

4.2 What are the major advantages cited by consumers of B2C e-business? Consumers cite increased convenience, lower prices, and personalization as the major advantages of online shopping.

4.3 Outline how e-tailers are improving online payment systems. Online shopping sites use encryption—the process of encoding data for security purposes. Major firms involved in all aspects of e-business use Secure Sockets Layer (SSL) technology, an industrywide standard for secure Internet payment transactions. Electronic wallets are secure data files at Web sites that contain customer information so customers don't have to retype personal information each time they make a purchase. The PCI Security Standards Council has established standards to enhance payment account security.

5 Describe the major challenges confronting e-business.

The growth of e-business has been hampered by consumer security and privacy concerns, fraud, and system overload. In addition, poor Web design and service, unreliability of delivery and returns, and lack of retail expertise has limited e-business success. The Internet can also generate conflict among buyers and sellers.

Assessment Check Answers

5.1 List the major impediments to e-business. Impediments to e-business include protecting consumer privacy, fraud, unreliable and hard-to-use Web sites, problems with deliveries and returns, and potential channel conflicts.

5.2 What is phishing? Phishing is a high-tech scam that uses e-mail or pop-up messages that claim to come from banks or other organizations and attempt to get unsuspecting consumers to divulge personal information such as bank account, credit card, or Social Security numbers.

5.3 Explain how e-tailing can lead to channel conflicts. A channel conflict is a dispute between a producer, wholesaler, and/or retailer. E-tailing could lead to a channel conflict between a manufacturer and a retailer if the manufacturer sold the same products on its Web site retailers sold in their stores, but at lower prices.

6 Discuss how organizations use the communication functions of the Internet to advance their objectives.

Communication remains the most popular function of the Internet. Companies have long used e-mail to communicate with customers, suppliers, and other partners. Online communities are groups of people who share common interests. Companies use online communities such as forums and electronic bulletin boards to communicate with and obtain feedback from customers and other partners. Blogs are online journals that have gained popularity in recent years. Companies are exploring the potential of blogs with mixed success. Web-based promotions include advertising on other Web sites, search marketing, and online coupons.

Assessment Check Answers

6.1 Explain the differences between online forums and electronic bulletin boards. Online forums are Internet discussion groups and often resemble two-way conversations. Electronic bulletin boards are more like announcements.

6.2 How can blogs contribute to a successful e-business strategy? A blog, short for a *Web log*, is a Web page that serves as a publicly accessible journal for an individual or organization. If done properly, a blog can enhance brand trust and give a company customer input into improving existing products as well as developing new ones.

6.3 Define *banner ads, pop-up ads*, and *search marketing*. Banner ads are small messages placed in high-visibility areas of frequently visited Web sites. A pop-up ad is a separate window that contains an advertising message. Search marketing is an arrangement by which a firm pays a search engine—such as Google—a fee to make sure that the firm's listing appears toward the top of the search results.

7 Outline the global scope of e-business.

While China and the U.S. lead the world in Internet usage, other countries are rapidly catching up. Technology allows companies to compete in the global market and workplace. Even the smallest firms can sell products and find new vendors in international markets. Through its own Web site, a firm can immediately reach customers all over the world. Improved communications among employees in different locations create new ways to collaborate on projects. One problematic issue has been adhering to more restrictive local laws and customs by U.S. Internet companies.

Assessment Check Answers

7.1 Does the U.S. lead the world in Internet penetration? Is U.S. Web usage growing faster or slower when compared with other countries? The U.S. ranks only thirteenth in the world in Internet penetration (the percentage of a country's population going online). Web usage is growing faster in many other countries, such as India and China, than it is in the United States.

7.2 What kinds of advantages does e-business offer in a global context? The Internet creates an enormous pool of potential customers. Companies can market their products internationally and local distribution sources and trading partners abroad. Customers, regardless of location, can search for products at their convenience. The Web, at the same time, has heightened competition.

8 List the steps involved in developing successful Web sites, and identify methods for measuring Web site effectiveness.

Businesses establish Web sites to expand their customer bases, increase buyer awareness of their products, improve consumer communications, and provide better service. Before designing a Web site, a company's decision makers must first determine what they want to achieve with the site. Other important decisions include who should create, host, and manage the site; how to promote it; and how much funding to allocate. Successful Web sites contain informative, up-to-date, and visually appealing content. Sites should also download quickly and be easy to use. Finally, management must develop ways to measure how well a site accomplishes its objectives.

Assessment Check Answers

8.1 When developing a Web site, what are some of the key questions to consider? The first question deals with the purpose of the Web site. The second deals with whether the firm should develop the site itself or outsource it to a specialized firm. The third question is determining the name of the site.

8.2 How does the type of Web site affect measures of effectiveness? For a shopping site, profitability is an important measure of effectiveness, although profitability can be difficult to measure given the presence of so-called Web-to-store shoppers. For company Web sites, online success is measured by increased brand awareness and loyalty, which presumably translates into greater profitability through offline transactions.

8.3 Explain *click-through rate* and *conversion rate*. The click-through rate is the percentage of viewers who, when presented with a banner ad, click on it. The conversion rate is the percentage of Web site visitors who actually make purchases.

Business Terms You Need to Know

electronic business (e-business) 214

corporate Web site 217

marketing Web site 218

business-to-business (B2B) e-business 219

extranet 220

business-to-consumer (B2C) e-business 221

electronic storefront 222

phishing 228

blog 231

search marketing 233

click-through rate 239

conversion rate 240

Other Important Business Terms

electronic data interchange (EDI) 219

private exchange 220

electronic exchange 221

e-procurement 221

electronic shopping cart 222

bot 225

encryption 226

Secure Sockets Layer (SSL) 226

electronic wallet 226

firewall 227

vishing 228

channel conflict 229

spam 230

electronic bulletin board 230

newsgroup 231

wiki 231

podcast 231

banner ad 233

pop-up ad 233

pre-roll video ad 233

Web-to-store 239

display ad 240

Review Questions

1. List the five e-business categories.

2. Describe the type and purpose of information found on a corporate Web site.

3. Explain how an electronic data interchange operates. What is rapid response?

4. What is an electronic exchange? Why have they proven to be less successful than many originally projected?

5. What is a bot, and how do consumers use it to find the lowest price for a product online?

6. Define encryption and Secure Sockets Layer technology.

7. Describe some of the privacy concerns of online shoppers.

8. What is *phishing*? Explain *vishing*.

9. Discuss how companies can use blogs.

10. What are the challenges and benefits of e-business in the global business environment?

11. List the major questions that should be asked before venturing into e-business. What is the relationship between measures of effectiveness and the overall purpose of a Web site?

12. Assume a company spends $250,000 to attract 50,000 visitors to its Web site. If the conversion rate is 5 percent, how much did the company spend to acquire each customer? What are some of the ways a company can increase its conversion rate?

Projects and Teamwork Applications

1. Discuss how the profile of online buyers and sellers is changing. What are some of the implications of these trends for B2C e-business?

2. Communication is still the most popular Web function; team up with a partner and describe how a travel company could take advantage of online communication, including a blog, to market its travel services.

3. Identify a local company that has a significant online presence. Arrange to interview the person in charge of the company's Web site. Ask the following questions:

   a. How was the Web site developed?
   b. Did the company develop the site in-house, or did it outsource the task?
   c. How often does the company make changes to the site?
   d. In the opinion of your respondent, what are the advantages and disadvantages of going online?

4. Some consumers are reluctant to purchase online products that are perishable or that consumers typically like to touch, feel, or smell before buying. Working in a small group, suggest ways an e-business company might be able to reduce this reluctance. Visit the Web site of a food retailer that sells products online for some ideas.

5. Identify a local company that operates with little or no online presence. Outline a proposal that explains the benefits to the firm of either going online or significantly expanding its online presence. Sketch out what the firm's Web site should look like and the functions it should perform.

6. Choose one of the following types of companies, and describe how it could take advantage of the communication power of the Internet to market its products:

   a. travel agency that specializes in backpacking, mountain biking, and other types of outdoor activities
   b. local Thai restaurant
   c. firm that ships exotic spices and herbs throughout the country
   d. local hospital

7. Assume your company's management wants to start a company-sponsored blog. You've been given the task of developing the blog. Answer each of the questions in Table 7.2. Using a search engine, such as Google or Ask.com, find examples of two or three company-sponsored blogs. Review each blog. In your opinion, how effective are the blogs? Are they well organized? Are they updated frequently? Make sure to incorporate your reactions into the development plan for your company's blog.

Web Assignments

1. **Rating e-business Web sites**. Gomez.com is one of leading authorities on e-business. As such, it rates various e-business firms. Go its Web site (http://www.gomez.com) and read about its rankings of Internet electronics retailers. Which was ranked the highest? Why? What criteria does Gomez.com use when ranking e-business sites?

2. **Internet shopping**. Assume you're in the market for a new notebook computer. Visit the CNet Web site (http://www.cnet.com) and read about buying a notebook computer and current ratings. Then, after identifying at least two different notebook computers, go shopping on the Web, making sure to visit at least two different online retailers. Learn enough so you can describe each to a friend, including which you'd be more likely to purchase from and why.

3. **B2B**. IBM offers extensive consulting services, software, and hardware for firms engaged in e-business. Assume you're an entrepreneur and you'd like to expand your presence on the Web. Go to the IBM e-business Web site (http://www.ibm.com). Read about the products offered and review some of the case studies. Prepare a report on what you learned.

Note: Internet Web addresses change frequently. If you don't find the exact sites listed, you may need to access the organization's home page and search from there.

Ask.com Won't Tell

Ask a friend a question, and odds are he's forgotten it by the next day. Not your friendly online search engine. Most such programs, such as Google and Yahoo!, record your online searches, along with the identity of your particular computer, for up to 18 months regardless of the topic searched. Search engine companies claim that keeping this information helps them provide better search results, prevent spam and fraud, and offer users more relevant advertising. But the policy does raise privacy concerns. "A lot of information is recorded about people online that people don't have control over," says the editor-in-chief of online publication *Search Engine Land*. "It's time for us to get a better idea of what private information companies are keeping on us and what kind of control we have over it."

Enter Ask.com, the fourth-largest search engine. The company is introducing AskEraser, a one-click feature appearing on the home page and all search results. AskEraser allows users to delete their own queries from Ask.com servers, including their user ID, Internet address, session ID, and text of their search terms. Like a light switch, once on, the erase feature stays on until the user turns it off again. For users who choose not to erase, Ask.com keeps the search data anonymous and does not link it to individual users.

Although services are available to mask online activities, the ability to erase them with a simple user-controlled button is innovative for its speed and accessibility. AskEraser

is expected to lead the way to a new level of privacy protection in the industry, despite Google and Yahoo's dominance of the market. Ask.com has just under a 5 percent share of the search engine market, while Yahoo! has 23 percent and Google almost 60 percent. "It's really about building trust and the possibilities of personalization in the future," said a senior policy analyst at the Center for Democracy and Technology. "If people trust Ask services because they have the ability to turn them off, that's a significant move forward."

The 18-month holding period limit at other search engines was instituted after the public pressured the companies to make search logs anonymous. Even if competitors follow the lead of Ask.com, the executive director of the Electronic Privacy Information Center says, "Over the long term, we still need appropriate legislative safeguards." And in fact it is difficult to completely erase an electronic trail. Ask.com will continue to share some query information with Google, which uses it, with certain limits, to help shape the relevance of Ask.com's advertising.[60]

Questions for Critical Thinking

1. "Privacy only becomes important to the average consumer when something blows up," says the founder of an independent research company. Do you agree or disagree? Why?

2. Do you think AskEraser will bring about industry change in the area of online privacy? Why or why not? Does it have any potential drawbacks?

Real Money for Virtual Assets

The millions of players of subscription-based Internet games such as "Second Life," "Everquest II," and the hugely popular sword-and-sorcery quest "World of Warcraft" are often passionate about their pursuits. Many of these devotees spend countless hours working to make or acquire the powerful virtual weapons, armor, equipment, and currency they need to play. With these items, the virtual game characters they create earn enviably high status and advance through multiple levels of their respective contests. And unlike some earlier games, these

so-called *massively multiplayer online role-playing games* (MMORPGs for short) are also social experiences, in which each player can interact with dozens of others. According to the CEO of the firm that makes "World of Warcraft," for instance, the game is really "a social network with many entertainment components."

Some players, however, like to shortcut some of "the grind" of acquiring needed game items, so a new class of entrepreneurs called "gold farmers" has been willing to do the work for them—for a real-world price. Gold farmers, hundreds of thousands of players from China and the low-wage countries of eastern Europe, will play online games endlessly for no other purpose than to collect virtual goods and sell them to other players around the globe for real money. But some game publishers consider these transactions a form of cheating, and some players have been fleeced by fraudulent offers in what is essentially an unregulated marketplace. In addition, gold farmers, who may make no more than $100 a month, tend to hoard items without enriching the game experience for more dedicated players, a consequence many game fans resent.

"Publishers aren't participating," observes entrepreneur Mitch Davis, "and the gamers themselves don't have a particularly good experience."

Now Davis's start-up company, Live Gamer, proposes to solve these problems by creating a legitimate marketplace in which players can safely trade in virtual goods with the permission of the game publishers. It's difficult to gauge the real size of the market because most transactions to date have been unauthorized, but industry experts estimate its value between $1.8 and $2 billion annually. Live Gamer promises publishers it will keep unscrupulous gold farmers out of the market and let players who sell through its Web site keep 90 percent of the proceeds. The other 10 percent will be split between Live Gamer and the game publisher. According to its Web site, "Live Gamer provides a fully legitimate, publisher-supported virtual trading marketplace with security, convenience, and quality of service" that players can conveniently access in real time from within the game itself. So does anyone have a magic sword for sale?[61]

Questions for Critical Thinking

1. Do you think game publishers will support the concept of Live Gamer? Why or why not?

2. What advantages besides security does Live Gamer offer game players? Do you see any potential disadvantages to legitimizing the marketplace for virtual goods?

VIDEO   Case 7.3 — Manifest Digital: Putting the User First

What would you be willing to do to win a 61-inch plasma display projector? Would you be willing to test your ability to hurl office equipment farther than your opponents can? Would you make a mad dash through a busy office, leaping over coworkers, filing cabinets, and copy machines? Would you roll down a hallway in a runaway office chair, dodging stacks of boxes, office furniture, and pesky janitors? This is what scores of information technology professionals did during the IT Guy Games, an online game developed to promote technology company NEC Visual Systems.

The IT Guy Web site was created by Manifest Digital Inc., a user-centered marketing and design firm located in Chicago. The firm was founded by Jim Jacoby and Mike Davidson in 2001. According to Jacoby, Manifest Digital was "born of the dotcom fallout." After the dot-com bubble burst in 2000, the two joined forces to launch a company that would design and build Web sites based on "usability"—the ease with which a user can access, understand, and use a Web site. Although there are many Internet design firms, and a growing number of usability companies, Manifest Digital puts the target audience at the center of every decision they make.

Clients such as Sony, Texas Instruments, and Wynn Las Vegas have taken advantage of Manifest Digital's capabilities.

To serve the audience, Manifest Digital must learn about them. The company does this through research and testing. Research may start with purchasing data and sales analysis. Who is buying the product now? Who is the company trying to reach? This was the starting point when the company redesigned the Baseball section of the Wilson Sporting Goods Web site. Wilson knew that its audience was primarily teen and preteen boys. But the existing Web site was similar to a catalog. There was little on the site to involve the user. Manifest Digital redesigned the site around players at five different positions: pitcher, catcher, first base, infield, and outfield. Each position featured several Major League Baseball players. This gave users a chance to learn about Wilson's products through their favorite players. In addition, Manifest Digital made the site more active and interactive. They added animation, downloads, and video to engage the audience. Sales grew, and Wilson asked Manifest Digital to redesign other elements of their Web site.

Unlike many Internet design firms, which don't test their Web sites until late in the design process, Manifest Digital tests during every stage. Testing involves bringing in users and gives them tasks to accomplish, such as finding, comparing, and purchasing products online. Designers observe the users in action to see where they succeed and where they have trouble. This helps Manifest Digital make the structure of the site clearer. "You have to be careful not to ask them what they need or what they want," warns Carolyn Chandler, a User Experience professional at Manifest Digital. "You end up with many different solutions to the same problem, but none of them address what the real need is."

To discover the real need, Manifest Digital uses "contextual inquiry." This involves observing users in their "real-world" environment. While developing an intranet for YMCA, Jacoby noticed that the employees were "scrapbooking"—collecting information from a variety of sources and putting it into binders. Although no one had asked for this capability, once Manifest Digital built it into the Web site, the client realized it was exactly what they needed.

Creating a relationship with users helps attract and retain an audience. Manifest Digital experienced the growth of a vibrant community when they built the NEC IT Guy site. The site was publicized by banner ads featuring the IT Guy. The character was so popular, the games were so much fun, and the prize was so good that IT managers—the target audience—flocked to the site. Manifest Digital built a message board into the site, and users posted voraciously, offering tips to their fellow competitors about how to win the games. The campaign was so effective that NEC, which expected to spend $67 per click in advertising, ended up spending less than $3 per click. Even after the competition ended, the site remained online, because the community surrounding the game was so strong.

Web design has gone through several stages as the Internet has grown. During the past ten years, standards of design and functionality have developed. Now designers are innovating around those standards. Jim Jacoby sees usability as the latest way for companies to differentiate themselves. "Technology is a commodity," he says, "but usability is an art."[62]

Questions for Critical Thinking

1. Describe ways in which Manifest Digital helps its business customers achieve success.

2. Manifest Digital must understand the consumers who will buy its clients' goods and services. Describe ways in which you think Manifest Digital demonstrates this understanding.

3. Why is usability an important component of Web design? What sites have you encountered that are not "user friendly"?

4. Why do you think the NEC IT Guy site and the Wilson Baseball site are successful?

KANSAS

Saline River

Kansas City

Smoky Hill River

Salina

Greensburg

Garden City

Wichita

Greensburg KS.

© Getty Images

Greensburg: A Great Place to Start

Ashley Petty started taking massage therapy classes while studying for her business degree. After graduating, she worked for several years as a massage therapist, until the spa where she worked closed. Ashley was job hunting when the tornado hit her hometown of Greensburg, Kansas. Watching volunteers, residents, and relief workers exhaust themselves cleaning up the devastated town, she saw an opportunity. She would return home to start her own spa in Greensburg.

It was definitely a risky venture—the last thing she would have expected to find in Greensburg before the storm. Armed with a business plan she had written in college, Ashley drove to Town Hall and applied for one of the temporary trailers that were brought in to house displaced businesses. She got her trailer — a 1970s singlewide, complete with imitation wood paneling, stinky carpet, and a leaky roof. Not exactly the luxe spa she had envisioned in her business plan, but a good enough start. With a fresh coat of paint, some scented candles, and new drapes, she opened Elements Therapeutic Massage and Day Spa.

Ashley had expected that her spa would be a hard sell. The storm had destroyed the town's communications, so traditional advertising was out. To build a client base, Ashley turned to word of mouth. She went to town meetings, talked to old friends, met with volunteers from all over the country. Still, months went by and she still had barely enough clients to pay her expenses.

Winter hit. It was cold, the ancient furnace ran constantly, drafts blew in the new curtains, and rain soaked the freshly steamed carpet. Elements was the last place anyone would want to go to escape the stress of rebuilding—even Ashley couldn't stand to be there. Under normal circumstances, she would have considered more extensive capital improvements, but the trailer was only temporary and she was out of money.

At one town meeting, green architecture firm BNIM presented a plan for the new Downtown Greensburg, including a business incubator to sustain old businesses and promote new ones. Traditionally, a business incubator is reserved for start-ups, but in Greensburg, once-successful businesses needed help getting back on their feet. The incubator would be housed in a totally energy-efficient retail/office building with space for approximately ten new businesses. The rent would be reasonable, and the utility costs next to nothing. Ashley jumped at the chance to apply for a place in the building.

Questions

After viewing the video, answer the following questions:

1. What major challenges does Ashley Petty face in starting her business?
2. How will Greensburg's business incubator stimulate economic development?
3. What are some of the challenges Greensburg faces in recruiting new businesses? What incentives would you offer to encourage new business development there?
4. Would you start a new business in Greensburg? Why or why not?

Launching Your
Entrepreneurial
Career

Part 2

In Part 2, "Starting and Growing Your Business," you learned about the many ways that business owners have achieved their dreams of owning their own company and being their own boss. The part's three chapters introduced you to the wide variety of entrepreneurial or small businesses; the forms they can take—sole proprietorship, partnership, or corporation—and the reasons that some new ventures succeed and others fail. You learned that entrepreneurs are visionaries who build firms that create wealth and that they share traits such as vision and creativity, high energy, optimism, a strong need to achieve, and a tolerance for failure. Finally, you learned about the impact of computer technology in making e-business possible and about the importance of the Internet for business operations. By now you might be wondering how you can make all this information work for you. Here are some career ideas and opportunities in the small-business and e-business areas.

First, whatever field attracts you as a future business owner, try to acquire experience by working for someone else in the industry initially. The information and skills you pick up will be invaluable when you start out on your own. Lack of experience is often cited as a leading reason for small-business failure.[1]

Next, look for a good fit between your own skills, abilities, and characteristics and a market need or niche. For instance, the U.S. Department of Labor reports that opportunities in many healthcare fields are rising with the nation's increased demand for health services.[2] As the population of older people rises, and as young families find themselves increasingly pressed for time, the need for child care and elder services will also increase—and so will the opportunities for new businesses in those areas. So keep your eyes on trends to find ideas that you can use or adapt.

Another way to look for market needs is to talk to current customers or business associates. When the owner of Michigan-based Moon Valley Rustic Furniture wanted to retire, he went to see Rick Detkowski, who was in the real estate business. The owner intended to offer the buildings to Detkowski and close the business down. But the real estate agent, who owned several pieces of Moon Valley furniture himself, instead decided to buy, not just the buildings, but the furniture business, too. Before the sale was completed—and to determine whether he could run Moon Valley profitably—Detkowski talked with existing customers and furniture dealers, who had been hoping for years that the company would expand its line of sturdy cedar and pine items from the traditional summer lawn furniture into more innovative designs. Further

research showed that the general environmental trend among consumers was boosting demand for rustic furniture, in contrast with the overall housing slump. So Detkowski took the plunge and is now in the furniture manufacturing business. He has expanded the company's product lines and reorganized the factory floor for more efficiency—and cost savings.[3]

Are you intrigued by the idea of being your own boss but worried about risking your savings to get a completely new and untried business off the ground? Then owning a franchise, such as Quiznos or Dunkin' Donuts, might be for you. The Small Business Administration advises aspiring entrepreneurs that while franchising can be less risky than starting a new business from scratch, it still requires work and sacrifice. In addition, you need to completely understand both the resources to which you'll be entitled and the responsibilities you'll assume under the franchise agreement. Again, filling a market need is important for success. To find more information about franchising, access the Federal Trade Commission's consumer guide to buying a franchise at http://www.ftc.gov/bcp/edu/pubs/consumer/invest/inv05.shtm.

Are you skilled in a particular area of business, technology, or science? The consulting industry will be a rapidly growing area for several years, according to the Bureau of Labor Statistics.[4] Consulting firms offer their expertise to clients in private, government, not-for-profit, and even foreign business operations. Business consultants influence clients' decisions in marketing, finance, manufacturing, information systems, e-business, human resources, and many other areas including corporate strategy and organization. Technology consultants support businesses in all fields, with services ranging from setting up a secure Web site or training employees in the use of new software to managing an off-site help desk or planning for disaster recovery. Science consulting firms find plenty of work in the field of environmental consulting, helping businesses deal with pollution cleanup and control, habitat protection, and compliance with government's environmental regulations and standards.

But perhaps none of these areas appeal to you quite so much as tinkering with gears and machinery or with computer graphics and code. If you think you have the insight and creativity to invent something completely new, you need to make sure you're informed about patents, trademarks, and copyright laws to protect your ideas.[5] Each area offers different protections for your work, and none will guarantee success. Here again, hard work, persistence, and a little bit of luck will help you succeed.

Career Assessment Exercises in Entrepreneurship and Business Ownership

1. Find out whether you have what it takes to be an entrepreneur. Review the material on the SBA's Web site http://www.sba.gov/smallbusiness-planner/index.html. or take the Brigham Young University's Entrepreneurial Test at http://marriottschool.byu.edu/cfe/startingout/test.cfm. Answer the questions there. After you've finished, use the scoring guides to determine how ready you are to strike out on your own. What weak areas did your results disclose? What can you do to strengthen them?

2. Find an independent business or franchise in your area, and make an appointment to talk to the owner about his or her start-up experience. Prepare a list of questions for a 10- to 15-minute interview, and remember to ask about details such as the number of hours worked per week, approximate start-up costs, goals of the business, available resources, lessons learned since opening, and rewards of owning the business. How different are the owner's answers from what you expected?

3. Search online for information about how to file for a patent, trademark, or copyright. A good starting point is http://www.uspto.gov. Assume you have an invention you wish to protect. Find out what forms are required; what fees are necessary, if any; how much time is typically needed to complete the legal steps; and what rights and protections you will gain.

Part 3

Management: Empowering People to Achieve Business Objectives

>>>>>>>>>>>>>>

© Masterfile

chapter 8

Management, Leadership, and the Internal Organization

Digital Vision/Getty Images

Douglas Conant Heats Up Campbell's Soup

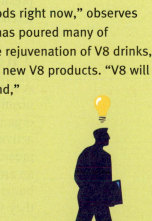

Trusted standbys are popular in trying times. Consumers look to comfort foods that remind them of their childhood, such as a simple bowl of Campbell's chicken noodle soup. Or they might pick one of Campbell's Chunky Soups. Your kid brother might want Chicken 'n Stars. And those counting calories might select one of the Healthy Request flavors such as New England chowder.

Campbell Soup Co. has been in existence for 140 years. Generations of U.S. consumers have grown up on its products, which include not only soups but other brands such as SpagettiOs pasta, V8 juice, Pepperidge Farm baked goods, Swanson broth, Prego spaghetti sauce, and Pace salsa. But during the last decade, the company fell on hard times. Its market value declined and employee morale was low. When Douglas R. Conant took over as CEO, he had a lot of work to do to reheat a company that many considered to be stale. Conant was adamant that Campbell's would not be the victim of a hostile takeover, no matter how grim the financial picture. "I don't think bigger is better," he explains. "I think focused food companies are the way to win." So he set about changing Campbell's organizational recipe.

Conant confronted the hard facts about his firm. Innovation was lacking—Campbell's was making the same products and operating the same way it had been since its founding. Nothing was wrong with its steaming bowl of chicken noodle soup, but competitors like Progresso had found different, tasty ways to serve their soups. As a result, consumers were choosing what appeared to be new and better products. So Conant began to cut the waste in his company's operations by dropping flagging products. He declared that the firm would continue producing only the products that ranked Number 1 or Number 2 in the food categories of simple meals including soup, snacks such as Pepperidge Farm cookies, or vegetable-based drinks such as V8. The company cut a number of items and sold off the delicious but unprofitable Godiva chocolate division.

Conant then reallocated resources to allow Campbell's to focus on products that would offer value and nutrition. The firm developed new packaging that emphasized consumer convenience, such as microwaveable soups and cans that would open with a single pull tab. Because Campbell's had been criticized for the amount of sodium and MSG flavor enhancer in its products, research and development teams came up with more healthful recipes for its soups, V8 drinks, and Pepperidge Farm snacks.

Trimming also included the managerial fat. During Conant's first three years as CEO, 300 of the firm's top 350 executives were replaced. Half of the new executives were promoted from within the company, and half were hired from the outside. The goal was to create a team with a mix of institutional knowledge and fresh ideas. They were tough decisions, but Conant insists they were necessary. "You can't talk your way out of something you behaved your way into," he says.

With ingredient prices for Campbell's soups and other products soaring, Conant has had to find a way to prune costs while developing new items and new markets. He stresses value to the consumer as a fundamental principle. "We're a value food company," he emphasizes, and he intends to keep it that way. New ads refer to Campbell's as "the original dollar menu," and grocery stores routinely run promotions offering ten cans of Campbell's soup for $10.

Nutrition has a new focus at Campbell's as well. A new line of soups called Select Harvest, which contain fewer calories and no MSG, recently hit supermarket shelves. Conant pledges to remove MSG from all its soups over the next few years. "Wellness is the Number 1 trend by far in consumer foods right now," observes Conant. To that end, Conant has poured many of Campbell's resources into the rejuvenation of V8 drinks, including the development of new V8 products. "V8 will be our next billion-dollar brand," he asserts.

Campbell's two major new markets are Russia and China, where 50 percent of the soup in the world is consumed. The challenge is that most soup eaten in those two countries is homemade. So Campbell's must convince Russian and Chinese consumers that it has something better to offer. Convenience might be easy to convey, but could Campbell's offer flavors that appeal to these populations? To find out, Campbell's sent teams of researchers to live with families and study how they make and eat their soup. They learned that consumers in these countries did not welcome ready-to-serve items—packaged convenience was not necessarily a value. So Campbell's has developed soup-starter products, which help cut some of the preparation time.

Conant knows that transforming a company takes time. But he has the patience to see Campbell's through to a new era of foods that are "'Mm 'Mm Good," as the firm's ads have claimed for years. "Give the organization time to do things right," he advises. "Do what you say you will; this is about performance, not intentions."[1]

Chapter 8 OVERVIEW

A management career brings challenges that appeal to many students in introductory business courses. When asked about their professional objectives, many students say, "I want to be a manager." You may think that the role of a manager is basically being the boss. But in today's business world, companies are looking for much more than bosses. They want managers who understand technology, can adapt quickly to change, can skillfully motivate subordinates, and realize the importance of satisfying customers. Managers who can master those skills will continue to be in great demand because their performance strongly affects their firms' performance.

This chapter begins by examining how successful organizations use management to turn visions into reality. It describes the levels of management, the skills that managers need, and the functions that managers perform. The chapter explains how the first of these functions, planning, helps managers such as Campbell's Douglas Conant meet the challenges of a rapidly changing business environment and develop strategies that guide a company's future. Other sections of the chapter explore the types of decisions that managers make, the role of managers as leaders, and the importance of corporate culture. The chapter concludes by examining the second function of management—organizing.

What Is Management?

management process of achieving organizational objectives through people and other resources.

Management is the process of achieving organizational objectives through people and other resources. The manager's job is to combine human and technical resources in the best way possible to achieve the company's goals.

Management principles and concepts apply to not-for-profit organizations as well as profit-seeking firms. A city administrator, a Salvation Army major, and the CEO of your local United Way organization all perform the managerial functions described later in this chapter. Managers preside over organizations as diverse as Miami-Dade Community College, the New York Stock Exchange, and the Dunkin Donuts shop down the street.

The Management Hierarchy

A local fast-food restaurant such as McDonald's typically works through a very simple organization that consists of an owner–manager and a few assistant managers. By contrast, large organizations develop more complex management structures. Southwest Airlines manages its activities through a chairperson of the board, a vice chairperson and chief executive officer, a president, three executive vice presidents, six senior vice presidents, and 25 vice presidents, plus an array of managers and supervisors.[2] All of these people are managers because they combine human and other resources to achieve company objectives. Their jobs differ, however, because they work at different levels of the organization.

A firm's management usually has three levels: top, middle, and supervisory. These levels of management form a management hierarchy, as shown in Figure 8.1. The hierarchy is the traditional structure found in most organizations. Managers at each level perform different activities.

The highest level of management is **top management.** Top managers include such positions as chief executive officer (CEO), chief financial officer (CFO), and executive vice president. Top managers devote most of their time to developing long-range plans for their organizations. They make decisions such as whether to introduce new products, purchase other companies, or enter new geographical markets. Top managers set a direction for their organization and inspire the company's executives and employees to achieve their vision for the company's future.

Many were skeptical when Robert Polet was named CEO of the Gucci Group. Polet had served as president of Unilever's ice cream and frozen foods division for several years. Once thought of as merely an "ice cream salesman," Polet has silenced his critics by leading Gucci through three years of sales and profit growth that have exceeded expectations. Gucci's CEO practices a hands-off management approach he calls "the art of letting go." Polet is cheerful and pleasant and can often be heard whistling in the office. His favorite expression for employees is "Break the rules." According to a former colleague at Unilever, Polet hates rules; this philosophy seems to be working at Gucci so far.[3]

Middle management, the second tier in the management hierarchy, includes positions such as general managers, plant managers, division managers, and branch managers. Middle managers' attention focuses on specific operations, products, or customer groups within an organization. They are responsible for developing detailed plans and procedures to implement the firm's strategic plans. If top management decided to broaden the distribution of a product, a sales manager would be responsible for determining the number of sales personnel required. Middle managers are responsible for targeting the products and customers who are the source of the sales and profit growth expected by their CEOs. To achieve these goals, middle managers might budget money for product development, identify new uses for existing products, and improve the ways they train and motivate salespeople. Middle managers are also responsible for solving unique company problems. Liz Holtz founded Liz Lovely Cookies with the intent of hand packing all cookies in clear bags tied with a ribbon. A *Philadelphia Inquirer* article attributed the cookies' addictive power at least in part to the packaging. But that packaging came with high costs, both in labor and time. To cut packaging time, Liz turned to Ilapak sales manager Scot Chin to come up with a package that was more efficient but stayed true to Liz Lovely's artisan spirit. Chin developed equipment to enclose the cookies in an inner wrap to lock in freshness and eliminate the need for employees to bag cookies by hand, which increased capacity 50 percent.[4]

Supervisory management, or first-line management, includes positions such as supervisor, section chief, and team leader. These managers are directly responsible for assigning nonmanagerial employees to specific jobs and evaluating their performance. Managers at this first level of the hierarchy work directly with the employees who produce and sell the firm's goods and services. They are responsible for implementing middle managers' plans by motivating workers to accomplish daily, weekly, and monthly goals. In *BusinessWeek*'s most recent annual ranking of customer service champs, all of the top-ranked firms have first-line managers who implement the firms' strategies to provide superior customer service. Whether it is L.L. Bean's acclaimed service department or Ace Hardware's "helpful hardware folks," these customer service champs have first-line managers who see that customer satisfaction is a top priority of service employees.[5]

Figure 8.1

The Management Hierarchy

- **Top Management**
  - Chief Executive Officer,
  - Chief Financial Officer,
  - Governor, Mayor
- **Middle Management**
  - Regional Manager,
  - Division Head,
  - Director, Dean
- **Supervisory (First-Line) Management**
  - Supervisor,
  - Department Chairperson,
  - Program Manager

Business Etiquette

SAYING THE RIGHT THING

Managers often face difficult workplace situations that call for quick thinking and tact. To help you avoid annoying a boss, alienating a colleague, or jeopardizing your job, here are some positive ways to handle potential traps.

1. If a boss or coworker belittles you in front of others, either ignore the behavior or disagree without arguing or bickering. Say something like, "That's not the way I see it." If the belittling continues, say, "You seem to have a problem with me. Let's talk about it in private."

2. If a coworker complains a lot about your boss or the company, it's best to neither agree nor disagree. Be respectful of the coworker's complaints without criticizing your employer by saying, "That doesn't sound good. What are your options?" If you are caught in a group gripe session, change the subject or politely excuse yourself and walk away.

3. If a colleague starts to tell you about a coworker's private life, stop the gossip. Diplomatically tell him you aren't interested in hearing about it—"too much information."

4. Give subordinates constructive criticism in a positive and supportive manner. Cushion the criticism between two upbeat statements, such as: "You always bring me good ideas. I'm going to have to say no this time. I just don't have room in the budget. Keep up the good work, and we'll talk again in a few months."

5. If a colleague continually asks for your help, resist the urge. Say, "I'm happy to help you out sometimes, but right now I've got too much of my own work that I need to get done."

6. If the long hours your boss demands are taking a toll on you and your family, ask if you can rearrange hours or get time off for a specific purpose. If you're being asked to work more hours than you agreed to, tell your boss, "I'm willing to put in some overtime, but I cannot physically continue to work this many hours each week." Suggest that another team member help.

7. If your boss or colleagues invite you to more social events than you'd care to attend, thank them for the invitation but say you have a previous commitment. Suggest an alternative get-together, like lunch, that doesn't cut into your personal time.

8. If you're quitting to join another firm, leave on good terms. Tell your boss, "I've taken another job. What can I do to make the transition as smooth as possible for you?" Offer to stay as long as you can to train your replacement, and then contribute maximum effort up through your final day.

Sources: "Business Etiquette Quiz," http://www.emilypost.com/business/business_ei_quiz.htm, accessed March 10, 2009; Don Gabor, "The Right Thing to Say in Difficult Situations on the Job," *Bottom Line Personal,* March 15, 2008, p. 5; Daniel Goleman, "'People Skills Are More Important Than IQ,'" *Bottom Line Personal,* March 1, 2008.

Skills Needed for Managerial Success

Managers at every level in the management hierarchy must exercise three basic types of skills: technical, human, and conceptual. All managers must acquire these skills in varying proportions, although the importance of each skill changes at different management levels.

Technical skills are the manager's ability to understand and use the techniques, knowledge, and tools and equipment of a specific discipline or department. Technical skills are especially important for first-line managers and become less important at higher levels of the management hierarchy. But most top executives started out as technical experts. The résumé of a vice president for information systems probably lists experience as a computer analyst and that of a vice president for marketing usually shows a background in sales. Many firms are increasing training programs for first-line managers to boost technical skills and worker productivity. Home Depot, with about 30,000 department supervisors, launched a new training program that includes more in-store training and workbook exercises such as analyzing sales reports. Dell also recently revamped its training program for first-line managers to include role-playing exercises, lectures, and question-and-answer sessions.[6]

Movéo is a brand consulting and marketing communications firm in Oakbrook Terrace, Illinois. The firm must stay on the cutting edge in the rapidly changing world of brand management and communications to serve clients like Motorola and Career Builder. Movéo accomplishes this by creating an environment in which employees freely share ideas and technical skills with one another. Fostering collaboration among staff and cross-training between first-line managers has also helped Movéo retain its most valued employees.[7]

Human skills are interpersonal skills that enable managers to work effectively with and through people. Human skills include the ability to communicate with, motivate, and lead employees to complete assigned activities. Managers need human skills to interact with people both inside and outside the organization. It would be tough for a manager to succeed without such

skills, even though they must be adapted to different forms—for instance, mastering and communicating effectively with staff through e-mail, cell phones, pagers, faxes, and text messaging, all of which are widely used in today's offices. Human skills remain equally critical at all levels of management. The "Business Etiquette" feature presents pointers on responding to tough workplace situations.

Conceptual skills determine a manager's ability to see the organization as a unified whole and to understand how each part of the overall organization interacts with other parts. These skills involve an ability to see the big picture by acquiring, analyzing, and interpreting information. Conceptual skills are especially important for top-level managers, who must develop long-range plans for the future direction of their organization. Howard Schultz returned as CEO of Starbucks, the company he founded, after the global coffee giant experienced a downturn in business. His plan to fix the company calls for shifting its focus from internal operations back to customers. This change will include doing more to reward Starbucks' best customers, opening fewer stores and even closing some in the United States, and redesigning some stores.[8]

Managerial Functions

In the course of a typical day, managers spend time meeting and talking with people, reading, thinking, and sending e-mail messages. As they perform these activities, managers are carrying out four basic functions: planning, organizing, directing, and controlling. Planning activities lay the groundwork, and the other functions are aimed at carrying out the plans.

PLANNING Planning is the process of anticipating future events and conditions and determining courses of action for achieving organizational objectives. Effective planning helps businesses crystallize their visions, which are described in the next section, avoid costly mistakes, and seize opportunities. Effective planning requires an evaluation of the business environment and a well-designed road map of the actions needed to lead a firm forward. To be effective, planning should be flexible and responsive and should involve managers from all levels of the organization. As global competition intensifies, technology expands, and the speed at which firms bring new innovations to market increases, planning for the future becomes even more critical. In a later section of this chapter, we elaborate on the planning process.

ORGANIZING Once plans have been developed, the next step in the management process typically is **organizing**—the means by which managers blend human and material resources through a formal structure of tasks and authority. This activity involves classifying and dividing work into manageable units by determining specific tasks necessary to accomplish organizational objectives, grouping tasks into a logical pattern or structure, and assigning them to specific personnel. Managers also must staff the organization with competent employees capable of performing the necessary tasks and assigning authority and responsibility to these individuals. Often organizing involves studying a company's existing structure and determining whether to reorganize it so that the company can better meet its objectives. The organizing process is discussed in detail later in this chapter.

DIRECTING Once plans have been formulated and an organization has been created and staffed, the management task focuses on **directing,** or guiding and motivating employees to accomplish organizational objectives. Directing includes explaining procedures, issuing orders, and seeing that mistakes are corrected. Managers may also direct in other ways, such as getting employees to agree on how they will meet objectives and inspiring them to care about customer satisfaction or their contribution to the company.

The directing function is a vital responsibility of supervisory managers. To fulfill their responsibilities to get things done through people, supervisors must be effective leaders. In addition, middle and top managers must be good leaders and motivators, and they must create an environment that fosters such leadership. A later section of this chapter discusses leadership, and Chapter 9 discusses motivating employees and improving performance.

planning process of anticipating future events and conditions and determining courses of action for achieving organizational objectives.

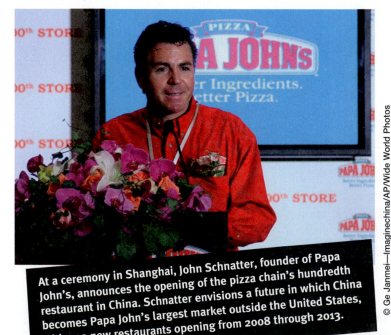

CONTROLLING Controlling is the function of evaluating an organization's performance to determine whether it is accomplishing its objectives. The basic purpose of controlling is to assess the success of the planning function. Controlling also provides feedback for future rounds of planning.

The four basic steps in controlling are to establish performance standards, monitor actual performance, compare actual performance with established standards, and take corrective action if required. Under the provisions of the Sarbanes-Oxley Act, for example, CEOs and CFOs must monitor the performance of the firm's accounting staff more closely. They must personally attest to the truth of financial reports filed with the Securities and Exchange Commission.

Setting a Vision and Ethical Standards for the Firm

As Chapter 1 discusses, business success usually begins with a **vision,** a perception of marketplace needs and the methods an organization can use to satisfy them. Vision serves as the target for a firm's actions, helping direct the company toward opportunities and differentiating it from its competitors. Michael Dell's vision of selling custom-built computers directly to consumers helped distinguish Dell from many other computer industry start-ups. John Schnatter, founder of Papa John's Pizza, keeps his vision—and his menu—focused to satisfy his pizza-loving customers.

A company's vision must be focused and yet flexible enough to adapt to changes in the business environment. The vision for pharmaceutical giant Merck is "to provide society with superior products and services by developing innovations and solutions that improve the quality of life and satisfy customer needs." In the long run, Merck's vision remains constant, to develop drugs ("innovations and solutions") that improve people's health. However, the way it is accomplished is adapted to industry changes as Merck's managers and researchers use natural or synthetic chemical compounds, high-tech gene-splicing equipment, or low-tech Petri dishes to grow biological substances.

Also critical to a firm's long-term success are the ethical standards that top executives set. As we saw in Chapter 2, a company's top managers can take an organization down a slippery slope if they operate unethically. Avoiding that path requires executives to focus on the organization's long-term success, not merely short-term gain. In recent years there have been numerous well-publicized instances of oversights or questionable behavior. In each case, the publicity hurt the organizations that executives were paid well to manage. Conversely, maintaining high ethical standards can build lasting success for a firm, as the "Hit & Miss" feature describes.

The ethical tone that a top management team establishes can also reap nonmonetary rewards. Setting a high ethical standard does not merely restrain employees from doing wrong, but it encourages, motivates, and inspires them to achieve goals they never thought possible. Such satisfaction creates a more productive, stable workforce—one that can create a long-term competitive advantage for the organization.

At a ceremony in Shanghai, John Schnatter, founder of Papa John's, announces the opening of the pizza chain's hundredth John's restaurant in China. Schnatter envisions a future in which China becomes Papa John's largest market outside the United States, with 500 new restaurants opening from 2008 through 2013.

© Ge Janmei—Imaginechina/AP/Wide World Photos

Hit & Miss

Kellogg's Brings Ethics to the Table

Today's news seems filled with stories about tainted products or substandard working conditions. But Kellogg's high ethical standards make it a refreshing bright spot. Founded in 1906, Kellogg Company is known worldwide for brands such as Special K and Corn Flakes cereals, Eggo waffles, Cheez-It crackers, Nutri-Grain breakfast bars, and hundreds of other products. The firm is dedicated to providing top-quality foods to consumers around the world. Its motto is "Bringing Our Best to You." But it is also working beyond the kitchen to protect the environment, provide employees with a safe workplace, and serve society.

Kellogg's does more than ship breakfast cereal to supermarket shelves; it educates the public about its foods. The firm developed the Kellogg Global Nutrient Criteria, a set of guidelines that establishes which products should be marketed to children, who are especially vulnerable to advertising. "We recognize that our success in the marketplace depends on continually earning consumers' trust by meeting their evolving needs for nutritious and enjoyable foods that are sourced, manufactured, and marketed responsibly," explains a senior vice-president. The firm is constantly researching nutritious options, reformulating recipes, and evaluating its foods' contributions to consumers' health.

Kellogg's is also concerned about the environment. The company has set a goal to reduce its energy and water use, greenhouse gas emissions, and waste by 15 to 20 percent by the year 2015. In addition, Kellogg's is exploring ways to encourage and support good agricultural practices around the world. One of the responsibilities of senior management is oversight of environmental sustainability, which means that accountability starts at the top of the company. Improved internal communications allow employees to share best practices throughout the company.

Kellogg's has a Global Code of Ethics that applies to both its employees and suppliers. Employees receive *K Values* training as part of their career development, and they can participate in the *Feeling Gr-r-reat* wellness program. The company continues to nurture diversity and ensure that all its approximately 32,000 employees are safe and have a chance to develop in their careers. Kellogg's also monitors working conditions at suppliers' facilities worldwide.

Kellogg's recognizes its role in the communities in which it operates and sells its food products. It is a founding member of the Global Food Banking Network and supports such organizations as United Way. It contributes large amounts of food to hunger-prevention and disaster-relief organizations, donating more than $40 million in cash and $120 million in food products to various organizations in the last five years.

Kellogg's has been recognized for its broad-based approach to ethics. The firm was recently named to Ethisphere's list of top ethical companies. Ethisphere is a think-tank devoted to researching and promoting the best practices in ethics and corporate responsibility—while maintaining a profit.

Questions for Critical Thinking

1. How would you describe the vision of Kellogg Company executives?
2. Why is it important for senior management at Kellogg's to adopt the ethical standards set forth by the company?

Sources: Company Web site, http://www.kelloggcompany.com, accessed February 23, 2009; *Corporate Responsibility Report,* http://www.kelloggcompany.com, accessed February 23, 2009; "A.D. David Mackay," *Forbes,* http://people.forbes.com, accessed February 23, 2009; "Kellogg Named to Most Ethical Companies List," *CloseUpMedia,* newsdesk@closeupmedia.com, accessed January 31, 2009; "Kellogg Company Releases Its First Global Responsibility Report," *Reuters,* January 13, 2009, http://www.reuters.com; "Kellogg Company Named to 2008's 'World's Most Ethical Companies' List by the Ethisphere," *Reuters,* June 4, 2008, http://www.reuters.com.

In practice, ethical decisions are not always clear-cut, and managers must make difficult decisions. Such situations are common, especially when a firm operates in a foreign country where the culture and norms are different from the firm's home country. A CEO of a large computer company faced such a dilemma when he decided to stop paying bribes to customs officials in India. The CEO was told that his decision, although ethically commendable, would mean disaster for the firm; the computers would be left in airport warehouses and the firm would lose money. But the CEO refused to change his

vision perception of marketplace needs and the methods an organization can use to satisfy them.

Assessment Check ✓

1. What is meant by a vision for the firm?
2. Why is it important for a top executive to set high ethical standards?

decision. He quietly informed officials in India that bribes would no longer be paid to speed up shipments. Realizing there was no advantage to holding up shipments, customs officials moved them faster than ever. While making the ethical choice may not always have this positive result, there is no strong evidence that consistent ethical behavior leads to financial losses.[9]

Still, a leader's vision and ethical conduct are only the first steps along an organization's path to success. Turning a business idea into reality takes careful planning and actions. The next sections examine the planning and implementation process.

Importance of Planning

At Home Depot's recent annual meeting of shareholders, CEO Frank Blake said, "We are at a turning point. We know that we have things to fix, but we also know that this is a great market and we need to invest now for the future." Reassuring shareholders about Home Depot's flat sales and languishing stock prices—attributed at least in part to the downturn in the housing market—Blake said the company would invest in stores and the workforce as part of its long-term plan to increase sales.[10] Let's take a closer look at the various types of planning companies like Home Depot engage in to achieve their goals.

Types of Planning

Planning can be categorized by scope and breadth. Some plans are very broad and long range, while others are short range and very narrow, affecting selected parts of the organization rather than all. Planning can be divided into the following categories: strategic, tactical, operational, and contingency, with each step including more specific information than the last. From the mission statement (described in the next section) to objectives to specific plans, each phase must fit into a comprehensive planning framework. The framework also must include narrow, functional plans aimed at individual employees and work areas relevant to individual tasks. These plans must fit within the firm's overall planning framework and help it reach objectives and achieve its mission.

STRATEGIC PLANNING The most far-reaching level of planning is **strategic planning**—the process of determining the primary objectives of an organization and then acting and allocating resources to achieve those objectives. After months of planning, Dell decided to sell computers through a limited number of retailers, including Best Buy, Wal-Mart, Staples, and musical instrument retailer Guitar Center. The PC maker has also linked up with several companies overseas like Gome Group in China and Bic Camera in Japan. The push into retailing is part of Dell's strategic planning effort to move beyond its original model of selling PCs directly via telephone or its Web site at a time when consumers have begun gravitating to stores for their computer purchases.[11]

TACTICAL PLANNING Tactical planning involves implementing the activities specified by strategic plans. Tactical plans guide the current and near-term activities required to implement overall strategies. When Wal-Mart first unveiled its plan to transform itself, the full scope of the changes wasn't clear at the time. That isn't the case any longer. After massive changes to make Wal-Mart more relevant to customers and to increase profitability, president and CEO of Wal-Mart Stores U.S.A. Eduardo Castro-Wright is ready to execute even more changes. Castro-Wright says the next part of the implementation plan includes refining merchandise assortments, improving the store experience, and adjusting store layouts.[12]

OPERATIONAL PLANNING Operational planning creates the detailed standards that guide implementation of tactical plans. This activity involves choosing specific work targets and assigning employees and teams to carry out plans. Unlike strategic planning, which focuses on the organization as a whole, operational planning deals with developing and implementing tactics in specific functional areas. For example, as part of its strategy to make stores more relevant and accessible to customers and revive its apparel business, Wal-Mart closed its product-development and sourcing teams and divided the unit into two hubs—brand merchandising based in New York and buying based at its headquarters in Bentonville, Arkansas. Said Wal-Mart spokeswoman Linda Blakely, "We needed to make changes to make sure our apparel was relevant and for speed to market." As part of the changes, dozens of jobs were cut at headquarters; these employees were offered other jobs in Bentonville or New York City.[13]

CONTINGENCY PLANNING Planning cannot foresee every possibility. Major accidents, natural disasters, and rapid economic downturns can throw even the best-laid plans into chaos. To handle the possibility of business disruption from events of this nature, many firms use **contingency planning,** which allows them to resume operations as quickly and as smoothly as possible after a crisis while openly communicating with the public about what happened. This planning activity involves two components: business continuation and public communication. Many firms have developed management strategies to speed recovery from accidents such as airline crashes, fires and explosions, chemical leaks, package tampering, and product failures.

A contingency plan usually designates a chain of command for crisis management, assigning specific functions to particular managers and employees in an emergency. Many issues have to be addressed once a crisis occurs, including identifying what people, facilities, systems, customers, data, and equipment are affected; communicating initially to employees, managers, and owners, then externally to customers and the public; activating operations critical to the organization's survival by bringing together the necessary people, equipment, information systems, and supplies; and resuming normal operations as soon as possible to minimize damage.[14] However, only 38 percent of *Fortune* 1000 companies responding to a survey indicated that their company had a formal crisis management plan.[15]

Planning at Different Organizational Levels

Although managers spend some time on planning virtually every day, the total time spent and the type of planning done differ according to the level of management. As Table 8.1 points out, top managers, including a firm's board of directors and CEO, spend a great deal of time on long-range planning, while middle-level managers and supervisors focus on short-term, tactical planning. Employees at all levels can benefit themselves and their company by making plans to meet their own specific goals.

Assessment Check

1. Outline the planning process.
2. Describe the purpose of tactical planning.
3. Compare the kinds of plans made by top managers and middle managers. How does their focus differ?

Table 8.1	Planning at Different Management Levels	
Primary Type of Planning	**Managerial Level**	**Examples**
Strategic	Top management	Organizational objectives, fundamental strategies, long-term plans
Tactical	Middle management	Quarterly and semiannual plans, departmental policies and procedures
Operational	Supervisory management	Daily and weekly plans, rules, and procedures for each department
Contingency	Primarily top management, but all levels contribute	Ongoing plans for actions and communications in an emergency

The Strategic Planning Process

Strategic planning often makes the difference between an organization's success and failure. Strategic planning has formed the basis of many fundamental management decisions:

- When John Donahoe took over as CEO of eBay in 2008, his first priority was revising the online auction site's core business, even at the short-term expense of investors. Donahoe plans to cut fees charged to sellers to draw more users and is planning large investments in technology to make shopping easier for buyers.[16]

- Financier Edward Lampert acquired control of Sears several years ago and relied on strategies that didn't depend on sales growth—cutbacks in spending, real estate sales, and aggressive investment of Sears Holdings Corporation's cash. Initially, stock prices soared, but more recently the strategy has been called into question as business at the firm's 3,800 stores has been falling.[17]

Successful strategic planners typically follow the six steps shown in Figure 8.2: defining a mission, assessing the organization's competitive position, setting organizational objectives, creating strategies for competitive differentiation, implementing the strategy, and evaluating the results and refining the plan.

Defining the Organization's Mission

mission statement
written explanation of an organization's business intentions and aims.

The first step in strategic planning is to translate the firm's vision into a **mission statement.** A mission statement is a written explanation of an organization's business intentions and aims. It is an enduring statement of a firm's purpose, possibly highlighting the scope of operations, the market it seeks to serve, and the ways it will attempt to set itself apart from competitors. A mission statement guides the actions of people inside the firm and informs customers and other stakeholders of the company's underlying reasons for existence. The mission statement should be widely publicized among employees, suppliers, partners, shareholders, customers, and the general public.

Merck's mission statement was outlined earlier in the section on establishing an organization's vision. Mission statements can vary in complexity and length.

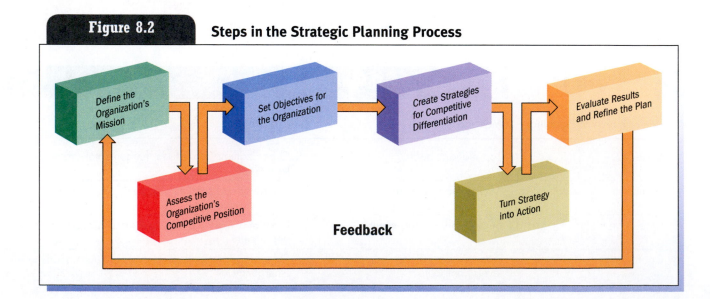

Figure 8.2   **Steps in the Strategic Planning Process**

Define the Organization's Mission → Set Objectives for the Organization → Create Strategies for Competitive Differentiation → Evaluate Results and Refine the Plan

Assess the Organization's Competitive Position

Turn Strategy into Action

Feedback

- Google's mission is "to organize the world's information and make it universally accessible and useful."[18]

- German chemical company Bayer's mission statement is, "Bayer: Science for a better life."[19]

- Toyota's mission is "to attract and attain customers with high-valued products and services and the most satisfying ownership experience in America."[20]

Developing a mission statement can be one of the most complex and difficult aspects of strategic planning. Completing these statements requires detailed considerations of a company's values and vision. Effective mission statements indicate specific, achievable, inspiring principles. They avoid unrealistic promises and statements.

Assessing Your Competitive Position

Once a mission statement has been created, the next step in the planning process is to assess the firm's current position in the marketplace. This phase also involves examining the factors that may help or hinder the organization in the future. A frequently used tool in this phase of strategic planning is SWOT analysis.

A **SWOT analysis** is an organized approach to assessing a company's internal strengths and weaknesses and its external opportunities and threats. SWOT is an acronym for *strengths, weaknesses, opportunities,* and *threats*. The basic premise of SWOT is that a critical internal and external reality check should lead managers to select the appropriate strategy to accomplish their organization's objectives. SWOT analysis encourages a practical approach to planning based on a realistic view of a firm's situation and scenarios of likely future events and conditions. The framework for a SWOT analysis appears in Figure 8.3.

Figure 8.3 Elements of SWOT Analysis

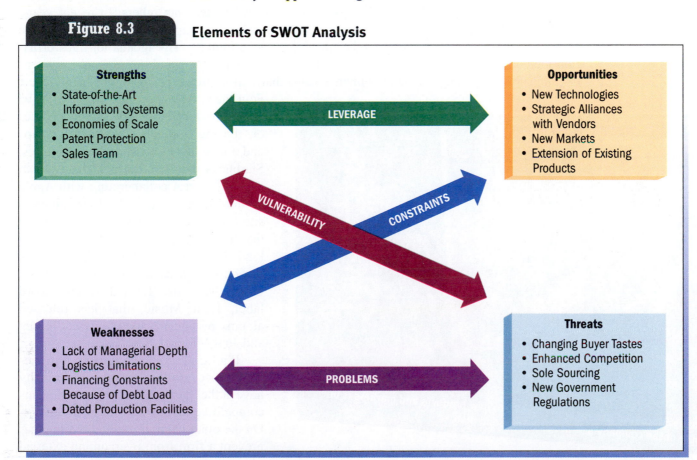

Strengths
- State-of-the-Art Information Systems
- Economies of Scale
- Patent Protection
- Sales Team

Opportunities
- New Technologies
- Strategic Alliances with Vendors
- New Markets
- Extension of Existing Products

LEVERAGE

VULNERABILITY

CONSTRAINTS

Weaknesses
- Lack of Managerial Depth
- Logistics Limitations
- Financing Constraints Because of Debt Load
- Dated Production Facilities

Threats
- Changing Buyer Tastes
- Enhanced Competition
- Sole Sourcing
- New Government Regulations

PROBLEMS

To evaluate a firm's strengths and weaknesses, the planners may examine each functional area such as finance, marketing, information technology, and human resources. Entrepreneurs may focus on the individual skills and experience they bring to a new business. Large firms may also examine strengths and weaknesses of individual decisions and geographical operations. Usually, planners attempt to look at their strengths and weaknesses in relation to those of other firms in the industry.

For Starbucks, a key strength is consumers' positive image of the company's brand, which gets them to stand in line to pay premium prices for coffee. That positive image comes from Starbucks's being one of the best 100 companies to work for in the United States, according to *Fortune,* and from its socially responsible corporate policies. The company's strategic plans have included various ways to build on Starbucks's strong brand loyalty by attaching it to new products and expanding into new markets. The expansion efforts have included creating a Web site, selling bottled Frappuccino iced coffee in supermarkets, and opening thousands of Starbucks outlets in Europe, Asia, and the Middle East. Weaknesses include saturating some markets with too many stores and not paying attention to store design.

SWOT analysis continues with an attempt to define the major opportunities and threats the firm is likely to face within the time frame of the plan. Possibilities include environmental factors such as market growth, regulatory changes, and increased competition. Starbucks saw an opportunity in the growth of the Internet and the interest in online shopping. Its Web site sells coffee and related accessories. In addition, Starbucks's experience in Japan, where its outlets' average sales top those in the United States, suggested that international expansion presented a solid opportunity. A threat is that consumers could tire of paying $3.50 or so for cappuccinos and lattés and switch to something else. The company has begun addressing that threat with the introduction of gourmet tea products.

Some aspects of Starbucks's strategy have succeeded better than others. In recent years, customer traffic slowed in U.S. stores. As noted earlier in the chapter, Howard Schultz came back as CEO to engineer a turnaround of the company he founded. His agenda for transformation includes improving U.S. business by introducing new products and programs for customers and suppliers, along with store enhancements that will improve the customers' experience. Four new rare and exotic coffees have been introduced, along with new choices on the menu such as sugar-free syrups and a new lunch program for U.S. stores. Starbucks also continues to innovate in the music area, collaborating with Apple to introduce a Starbucks Entertainment site on iTunes and a Wi-Fi Music Store that allows customers to buy and download digital music at participating coffeehouses. Starbucks and Concord Music Group have also formed a new record label, Hear Music, that has released albums by legends like Paul McCartney and Joni Mitchell.[21]

If a firm's strengths and opportunities mesh successfully, as they historically have at the Starbucks retail stores, it gains competitive leverage in the marketplace. On the other hand, if internal weaknesses prevent a firm from overcoming external

© Kevork/ Djansezian/AP/Wide World Photos

Extending Starbucks' strong brand loyalty to new products and markets is one example of the company's strategic turnaround plan.

threats, as in the case of Starbucks recently, it may face major difficulties. SWOT analysis is useful in the strategic planning process because it forces management to look at factors both inside and outside the organization and determine which steps it must take in the future to minimize external threats and take advantage of strategic opportunities.

Setting Objectives for the Organization

After defining the company's mission and examining factors that may affect its ability to fulfill that mission, the next step in planning is to develop objectives for the organization. **Objectives** set guideposts by which managers define the organization's desired performance in such areas as profitability, customer service, growth, and employee satisfaction. While the mission statement delineates a company's goals in general terms, objectives are more concrete statements. For instance, Toyota had the objective of selling 8.89 million vehicles in a recent year and inching by General Motors as the world's largest car company by sales volume for the year.[22] Toyota is also developing a hybrid version of every car model so that it can achieve its objective of selling 1 million hybrid cars a year.[23]

Also, more and more businesses are setting explicit objectives for performance standards other than profitability. As public concern about environmental issues mounts, many firms find that operating in an environmentally responsible manner pays off in good relations with customers. Others channel some of their profits into socially responsible causes, such as funding educational programs and scholarships.

objectives guideposts by which managers define the organization's desired performance in such areas as profitability, customer service, growth, and employee satisfaction.

Creating Strategies for Competitive Differentiation

Developing a mission statement and setting objectives point a business toward a specific destination. To get there, however, the firm needs to map the strategies it will follow to compete with other companies pursuing similar missions and objectives. The underlying goal of strategy development is **competitive differentiation,** the unique combination of a company's abilities and approaches that sets it apart from competitors. Common sources of competitive differentiation include product innovation, technology, and employee motivation. Smaller companies often have one source of competitive differentiation over much larger companies that are slower to adopt new technologies.[24]

Film-production studio Motion Theory is redefining its industry and changing the way advertisers connect with the public through a combination of creative development, filmmaking, and innovative visual effects. Co-founded by Mathew Cullen and Javier Jimenez, the company differentiates itself from competitors by uniting the efforts of directors, animators, designers, visual effects artists, and writers. The result is a creative approach to making commercials and music videos.[25] The Gatorade spot called "Inside Crosby," one of the most visually complex ads ever made, is an exploration of the engineering behind NHL star Sidney Crosby's wicked slap shot.[26]

Implementing the Strategy

Once the first four phases of the strategic planning process are complete, managers face even bigger challenges. They must put strategic plans into action by identifying specific points at which to pause and deploying the resources needed to implement the intended plans.

The Googling of the Web is an amazing story that began just a decade ago. That's when Larry Page and Sergey Brin officially incorporated their Silicon Valley garage operation, naming it after the mathematical term "googol"—10 followed by 100 zeroes. The pair had invented a unique approach to searching every word on every page of the entire Web, not simply the Web page title. Their secret was using as many computer processors at one time as necessary to conduct the searches; some estimate that Google uses from 175,000 to more than 450,000 processors today. A few years ago, Google patented its system for judging how closely each Web site matches the query. The strategy has paid off for Google, which has $12 billion cash and nearly 14,000 employees. A large part of this money comes from advertising fees; two programs called AdWords and AdSurvey work together to attract leads and turn them into sales at the lowest cost. For example, an advertiser can use AdWords to create an online ad and place it on the Web where it will reach the most qualified prospects. Google also joined with Salesforce.com, the leading hosted software service provider, to integrate AdWords into Salesforce.com's customer relationship management system.[27]

Monitoring and Adapting Strategic Plans

The final step in the strategic planning process, which naturally follows implementation, is to monitor and adapt plans when actual performance fails to match expectations. Monitoring involves establishing methods of securing feedback about actual performance. Common methods include comparing actual sales and market share data with forecasts, compiling information from supplier and customer surveys, monitoring complaints from the firm's customer hot line, and reviewing reports prepared by production, finance, marketing, and other company units.

Ongoing use of such tools as SWOT analysis and forecasting can help managers adapt objectives and functional plans as changes occur. An increase in the price of a key product component, for instance, could dramatically affect the firm's ability to maintain planned prices and still earn acceptable profits. An unexpected UPS strike may disrupt shipments of products to retail and business customers. In each instance, the original plan may require modification to continue to guide the firm toward achievement of its objectives.

Managers as Decision Makers

decision making process of recognizing a problem or opportunity, evaluating alternative solutions, selecting and implementing an alternative, and assessing the results.

In carrying out planning and the other management functions, executives must make decisions every day. **Decision making** is the process of recognizing a problem or opportunity and then dealing with it. Managers make two basic kinds of decisions: programmed decisions and nonprogrammed decisions.

Programmed and Nonprogrammed Decisions

A **programmed decision** involves simple, common, and frequently occurring problems for which solutions have already been determined. Examples of programmed decisions include assigning a starting salary for the new marketing assistant, reordering raw materials needed in the manufacturing process, and setting a discount schedule for large-volume customers. For these types of decisions, organizations develop rules, policies, and detailed procedures that managers apply to achieve consistent, quick, and inexpensive solutions to common problems. Because such solutions eliminate the time-consuming process of identifying and evaluating alternatives and making new decisions each time a situation occurs, managers can devote their time to the more complex problems associated with nonprogrammed decisions. For example, routine review of the inventory of fresh produce might allow a buyer at Whole Foods Market more time to seek other merchandising opportunities.

A **nonprogrammed decision** involves a complex and unique problem or opportunity with important consequences for the organization. Examples of nonprogrammed decisions include entering a new geographical market, acquiring another company, or introducing a new product. For example, CEO Steve Jobs made a bold decision when he introduced Apple's new MacBook Air computer. Using technologies taken from iPhone and iPod, Apple was able to reduce the size of the machine. The result was the world's thinnest laptop—at just 0.76 inch—and weighing three pounds. Intel also contributed by developing a smaller housing for MacBook's microprocessor chip. The laptop went on sale in the United States for $1,799 and is not without its critics. The battery is sealed inside the computer to reduce the size, but it only lasts four hours and doesn't allow the use of a second battery. The MacBook also requires a wireless Internet connection called *Wi-Fi,* but Wi-Fi is not available everywhere at this time. Jobs likes to quote hockey star Wayne Gretzsky, saying that Apple "skates to where the puck will be, not where it has been." The MacBook Air may not be for everyone, but it puts Apple on the cutting edge of technology once again.[28]

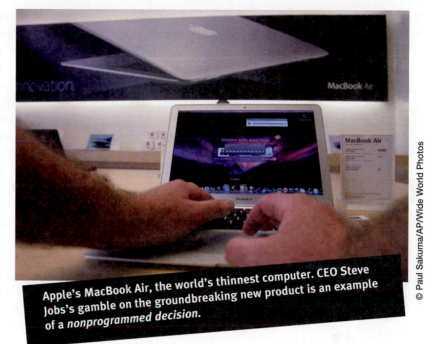
Apple's MacBook Air, the world's thinnest computer. CEO Steve Jobs's gamble on the groundbreaking new product is an example of a *nonprogrammed decision.*

© Paul Sakuma/AP/Wide World Photos

How Managers Make Decisions

In a narrow sense, decision making involves choosing among two or more alternatives, with the chosen alternative becoming the decision. In a broader sense, decision making involves a systematic, step-by-step process that helps managers make effective choices. This process begins when someone recognizes a problem or opportunity; it proceeds by developing potential courses of action, evaluating the alternatives, selecting and implementing one of them, and assessing the outcome of the decision. The steps in the decision-making process are illustrated in Figure 8.4. This systematic approach can be applied to all decisions, with either programmed or nonprogrammed features, in both for-profit and not-for-profit organizations.

The decision-making process does not yield the same results for every organization. For example, Best Buy and Circuit City, the leading U.S. electronics retailers, both faced the same challenging environment. Flat-screen television prices fell dramatically, and the lagging economy led to fewer purchases of electronic products. Yet Best Buy continued to expand its

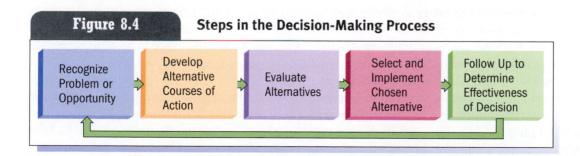

Figure 8.4	Steps in the Decision-Making Process

Recognize Problem or Opportunity → Develop Alternative Courses of Action → Evaluate Alternatives → Select and Implement Chosen Alternative → Follow Up to Determine Effectiveness of Decision

operations by opening more stores and pursuing acquisitions. Circuit City had planned to open half as many stores as Best Buy while closing some stores that were experiencing downturns; Circuit City filed for Chapter 11 bankruptcy and a year later closed for good. Industry analysts attribute Best Buy's success to selecting optimum store locations and moving quickly on new products, services, and partnerships with suppliers like Apple.[29] Managers are *human* decision makers, and while they can follow the decision-making process as shown in Figure 8.4 step-by-step, the outcome of their decisions depends on many factors, including the accuracy of their information and the experience, creativity, and wisdom of the person.

Making good decisions is never easy because it involves taking risks that can influence a firm's success or failure. Managers' decisions often have complex legal and ethical dimensions. *CRO Magazine* publishes an annual list of "The 100 Best Corporate Citizens." These companies make decisions that are ethical, environmentally responsible, fair toward employees, accountable to local communities, and provide responsible goods and services to customers and a healthy return to investors. These organizations prove that good corporate citizenship is good behavior. The ten best corporate citizens for a recent year include Green Mountain Coffee Roasters, Advanced Micro Devices, Nike, Motorola, Intel, IBM, Agilent Technologies, Timberland, Starbucks, and General Mills.[30] You can view the full list and most recent rankings at http://www.thecro.com.

Assessment Check ✓

1. Compare and contrast programmed and nonprogrammed decisions.
2. What are the steps in the decision-making process?

Managers as Leaders

leadership ability to direct or inspire people to attain organizational goals.

The most visible component of a manager's responsibilities is **leadership,** directing or inspiring people to attain organizational goals. Because effective leadership is so important to organizational success, a large amount of research has focused on the characteristics of a good leader. Great leaders do not all share the same qualities, but three traits are often mentioned: empathy, which is the ability to imagine yourself in another's position; self-awareness; and objectivity in dealing with others. Many great leaders share other traits, including courage, ability to inspire others, passion, commitment, flexibility, innovation, and willingness to experiment. Some leaders are so dedicated and passionate that they work around the clock to achieve their organization's goals, the subject of the "Solving an Ethical Controversy" feature.

Leadership involves the use of influence or power. This influence may come from one or more sources. One source of power is the leader's position in the organization. A national sales manager has the authority to direct the activities of the sales force. Another source of power is a leader's expertise and experience. A first-line supervisor with expert machinist skills will most likely be respected by employees in the machining department. Some leaders derive power from their personalities. Employees may admire a leader because they recognize an exceptionally kind and fair, humorous, energetic, or enthusiastic person.

A well-known example is Herb Kelleher, the retired CEO and now chairman of Southwest Airlines. Kelleher's legendary ability to motivate employees to outperform those at rival airlines came from his dynamic personality, boundless energy, love of fun, and sincere concern for his employees. Kelleher led by example, modeling the behavior he wanted to see in his employees. He pitched in to help serve snacks to passengers and load luggage. Employees, inspired by his example, now unload and reload a plane in 20 minutes—one-half of the average time for other airlines. Southwest Airlines was able to post its 35th straight year of profitability during the second-worst year in aviation history. In a year when more than a quarter of all U.S. flights arrived late and often packed with irate passengers, Southwest was on time the most, lost the fewest bags, and had the fewest customer complaints compared with other airlines.[31]

"They Said It"

"A great leader is not one who does the greatest things. He's the one who gets the people to do the greatest things."

—Ronald Reagan
(1911–2004) 40th president of the United States

DO CEOs OWE THEIR COMPANIES TOTAL COMMITMENT?

In recent years CEOs have been viewed as gurus, geniuses, or saviors, admired for their work ethic, toughness, and commitment to their jobs and companies. With globalization, the explosion of information technology, intense competition, corporate downsizing, mergers and acquisitions, and short-term performance expectations, executives are working harder than ever. For many CEOs, staying on top means nonstop work and little or no time or energy for family and personal lives.

Dominic Orr's experience as a CEO is not uncommon. As a marketing specialist for Hewlett-Packard (HP), he often put in 18 or 20 hours a day, traveled constantly, and for a few years even commuted from Japan to see his family in California. Changing jobs took him back home, but as CEO of Alteon WebSystems, a Silicon Valley data-networking company, he spent his few hours at home catching up on work. Orr now says he was "ruthlessly aggressive" at work and says his obsession with his job alienated him from his family. He began seeing a counselor to help restore balance in his life. Divorced, Orr left his position and took more than a year off to reconnect with his son and daughter and pursue some hobbies. Now CEO for wireless equipment firm Aruba Networks, Orr still works long hours but varies them to see his children.

Should boards, organizations, investors, clients—and CEOs themselves—expect total dedication no matter what the personal cost?

PRO

1. CEOs have ultimate responsibility for their company and all its employees, and their judgment is always on the line. Corporate boards are entitled to ask for an extreme level of commitment from their CEOs, who are well paid.
2. CEOs are a different breed from most people; they have tremendous energy and drive to sustain them through a career of nonstop work.

CON

1. Working continuously can wreck family and personal life. It does not create peak performance. Instead, it burns people out, erodes productivity, and can build anger and resentment toward colleagues and the employer.
2. An executive obsessed with work can become an unappealing boss and a poor leader who gives the message that the team can't run things on their own and makes others feel bad about having a life.

Summary

"Balance" has been a buzzword in the American workplace, but top executives are hard-pressed to balance their work and personal lives. Today's job market seems to have only two tracks—the fast track and the slow track—says Robert Reich, former U.S. Secretary of Labor. He says that only the fast track leads to better jobs. That means working all hours, giving up family time, and making very large sacrifices. CEOs who willingly make those sacrifices may find later that they've given up too much—any personal life. While it may seem impossible, work-obsessed CEOs must find ways to put time and energy into a personal life and to encourage employees to do the same.

Sources: Company Web site, http://www.arubanetworks.com, accessed March 10, 2009; Ray Williams, "Beware the Toxic Trap of Success," *Financial Post,* accessed March 2008, http://www.nationalpost.com; "Confessions of a CEO," *Fortune,* November 12, 2007, pp. 64–74; George Anders, "Business: For CEOs, Off-Duty Isn't an Option," *The Wall Street Journal,* November 7, 2007, p. A2; Michelle Conlin, "Do Us a Favor, Take a Vacation," *BusinessWeek,* May 21, 2007, p. 88.

Solving an ETHICAL controversy

Leadership Styles

The way a person uses power to lead others determines his or her leadership style. Researchers have identified a continuum of leadership styles based on the amount of employee participation allowed or invited. At one end of the continuum, **autocratic leadership** is centered on the boss. Autocratic leaders make decisions on their own without consulting employees. They reach decisions, communicate them to subordinates, and expect prompt implementation of instructions. An autocratic sales manager might assign quotas to individual salespeople without consulting them.

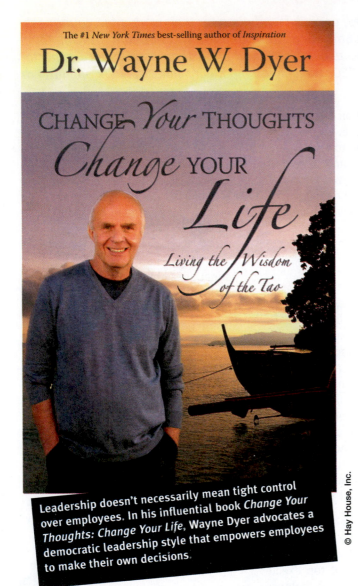

The #1 *New York Times* best-selling author of *Inspiration*

Dr. Wayne W. Dyer

CHANGE *Your* THOUGHTS *Change* YOUR *Life*

Living the Wisdom of the Tao

© Hay House, Inc.

Leadership doesn't necessarily mean tight control over employees. In his influential book *Change Your Thoughts: Change Your Life*, Wayne Dyer advocates a democratic leadership style that empowers employees to make their own decisions.

"They Said It"

"I praise loudly, I blame softly."

—Catherine II ("the Great") (1729–1796) Empress of Russia

Assessment Check ✔

1. How is *leadership* defined?
2. Identify the styles of leadership as they appear along a continuum of greater or lesser employee participation.

Democratic leadership involves subordinates in making decisions. Located in the middle of the continuum, this leadership style centers on employees' contributions. Democratic leaders delegate assignments, ask employees for suggestions, and encourage participation. An important trend that has developed in business during the past decade is the concept of **empowerment,** a practice in which managers lead employees by sharing power, responsibility, and decision making with them.

Wayne Dyer, an internationally known author and motivational speaker, thinks that we will eventually face resistance when we tell people what to do. In his most recent book, *Change Your Thoughts—Change Your Life: Living the Wisdom of the Tao,* Dyer cites the 17th verse of the *Tao Te Ching*, or "Great Way," written by Chinese philosopher Lao-tzu more than 2,500 years ago: "With the greatest leader above them, people barely know one exists ... The great leader speaks little ... When all is finished, the people say, 'We did it ourselves.'"[32] Many of the successful leaders we have mentioned in this chapter, whether it be Steve Jobs, Herb Kelleher, or Howard Schultz, let others make the right choices. Some of the best leaders, as Lao-tzu pointed out centuries ago, are not afraid to empower their employees.

At the other end of the continuum from autocratic leadership is **free-rein leadership.** Free-rein leaders believe in minimal supervision. They leave most decisions to their subordinates. Free-rein leaders communicate with employees frequently, as the situation warrants.

Which Leadership Style Is Best?

The most appropriate leadership style depends on the function of the leader, the subordinates, and the situation. Some leaders cannot work comfortably with a high degree of subordinate participation in decision making. Some employees lack the ability or the desire to assume responsibility. In addition, the specific situation helps determine the most effective style of interactions. Sometimes managers must handle problems that require immediate solutions without consulting employees. When time pressure is less acute, participative decision making may work better for the same people.

Democratic leaders often ask for suggestions and advice from their employees but make the final decisions themselves. A manager who prefers the free-rein leadership style may be forced by circumstances to make a particular decision in an autocratic manner. A manager may involve employees in interviewing and hiring decisions but take complete responsibility for firing an employee.

After years of research intended to determine the best types of leaders, experts agree that they cannot identify any single best style of leadership. Instead, they contend that the most effective style depends on the leader's base of power, the difficulty of the tasks involved, and the characteristics of the employees. Both extremely easy and extremely difficult situations are best suited to leaders who emphasize the accomplishment of assigned tasks. Moderately difficult situations are best suited to leaders who emphasize participation and good working relationships with subordinates.

Corporate Culture

The best leadership style to adopt often depends on the organization's **corporate culture,** its system of principles, beliefs, and values. Managerial philosophies, communications networks, and workplace environments and practices all influence corporate culture. When David Neeleman founded JetBlue Airways, his goal was to establish a culture in which all employees were on an equal footing. By creating a culture in which everyone could perform up to their potential, Neeleman hoped to create an airline known for customer service. Employees witness numerous acts of integrity by Neeleman and the other managers that are instilled in thousands of JetBlue employees who provide outstanding service to customers. JetBlue employees are not concerned about their individual status. New hires all receive a two-day orientation, and the flight crews attend their first week of training together to develop a strong culture. Neeleman himself presents "JetBlue 101" to each incoming class to leave a lasting impression. By most accounts, the soft-spoken Neeleman has achieved his goals. Within 13 months of its first flight, JetBlue was voted the number-two domestic airline, and it has received more than 100 additional awards during its existence. Even the well-publicized debacle during a February ice storm in New York City, when more than 1,000 JetBlue flights were canceled and six full planes sat on the tarmac for hours, was handled according to JetBlue's culture. Within days Neeleman introduced a "Customer Bill of Rights" to admit the airline's mistakes and compensate passengers affected by the delays and cancellations.[33]

A corporate culture is typically shaped by the leaders who founded and developed the company and by those who have succeeded them. One generation of employees passes on a corporate culture to newer employees. Sometimes this transfer is part of formal training. New managers who attend sessions at McDonald's Hamburger University may learn skills in management, but they also acquire the basic values of the organization's corporate culture established by McDonald's founder Ray Kroc: quality, service, cleanliness, and value.[34] Employees can absorb corporate culture through informal contacts, as well as by talking with other workers and through their experiences on the job.

Managers use symbols, rituals, ceremonies, and stories to reinforce corporate culture. The corporate culture at the Walt Disney Company is almost as famous as the Disney characters. According to Marty Sklar, vice chairman and principal creative executive, Walt Disney Imagineering, "From the beginning, starting with Walt Disney, we have had five things that make me proud to be part of the company: high-quality products, optimism for the future, great storytelling, an emphasis on family entertainment and great talent, passion and dedication from our Cast Members." That's correct, every employee is known as a cast member. All new employees attend Traditions I and are told stories about the company and its founder Walt Disney and are exposed to the language and elements of the organization's culture: a strong tradition of innovation; high-quality standards across all goods and services; a sense of community; timeless and engaging stories that delight and inspire; a sense of optimism; and honor and respect for the trust people place in Disney. The company has come a long way since Walt Disney introduced *Steamboat Willie,* but it is still true to the core value of Disney himself—providing quality entertainment.[35]

Corporate cultures can be very strong and enduring, as is the case with Disney. But corporate cultures can also be changed when circumstances require. Over several decades, General Electric's culture helped the company create generations of talented leaders and sustain its success. To achieve growth in its many business divisions around the globe, GE has shifted to a companywide culture of innovation. One result is its "ecoimagination" initiative for developing green products. Consistently ranked as one of the world's most innovative companies, GE considers its culture to be one of its innovations.[36] At times, growth can result in an organization's having more than one culture. With all their success, Google cofounders Larry Page and Sergey Brin and CEO Eric Schmidt recognized that as the company grew larger and larger, some aspects

corporate culture
organization's system of principles, beliefs, and values.

Assessment Check ✓

1. What is the relationship between leadership style and corporate culture?
2. What is a strong corporate culture?

of the culture would need to change. For example, YouTube has remained a separate division with its own culture that is different and works.[37]

In an organization with a strong culture, everyone knows and supports the same principles, beliefs, and values. A company with a weak or constantly shifting culture lacks a clear sense of purpose. To achieve goals, a business must also provide a framework that defines how employees should accomplish their tasks. This framework is the organization structure, which results from the management function of organizing.

Organizational Structures

organization
structured grouping of people working together to achieve common goals.

The management function of organizing is the process of blending human and material resources through a formal structure of tasks and authority. It involves arranging work, dividing tasks among employees, and coordinating them to ensure implementation of plans and accomplishment of objectives. The result of this process is an **organization,** a structured grouping of people working together to achieve common goals. An organization features three key elements: human interaction, goal-directed activities, and structure. The organizing process should result in an overall structure that permits interactions among individuals and departments needed to achieve company goals.

The steps involved in the organizing process are shown in Figure 8.5. Managers first determine the specific activities needed to implement plans and achieve goals. Next, they group these work activities into a logical structure. Then they assign work to specific employees and give the people the resources they need to complete it. Managers coordinate the work of different groups and employees within the firm. Finally, they evaluate the results of the organizing process to ensure effective and efficient progress toward planned goals. Evaluation often results in changes to the way work is organized.

Many factors influence the results of organizing. The list includes a firm's goals and competitive strategy, the type of product it offers, the way it uses technology to accomplish work, and its size. Small firms typically create very simple structures. The owner of a dry-cleaning business generally is the top manager, who hires several employees to process orders, clean the clothing, and make deliveries. The owner handles the functions of purchasing supplies such as detergents and hangers, hiring and training employees and coordinating their work, preparing advertisements for the local newspaper, and keeping accounting records.

As a company grows, its structure increases in complexity. With increased size comes specialization and growing numbers of employees. A larger firm may employ many salespeople, along with a sales manager to direct and coordinate their work, or organize an accounting department.

The organizing process should result in a well-defined structure so that employees know what expectations their jobs involve, to whom they report, and how their work contributes to

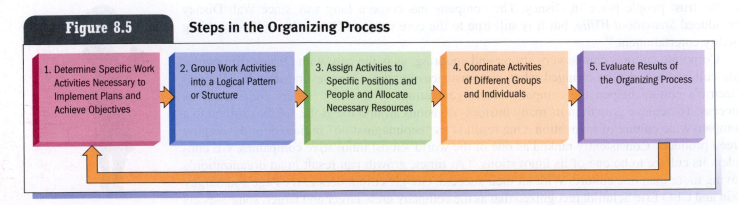

Figure 8.5 **Steps in the Organizing Process**

1. Determine Specific Work Activities Necessary to Implement Plans and Achieve Objectives
2. Group Work Activities into a Logical Pattern or Structure
3. Assign Activities to Specific Positions and People and Allocate Necessary Resources
4. Coordinate Activities of Different Groups and Individuals
5. Evaluate Results of the Organizing Process

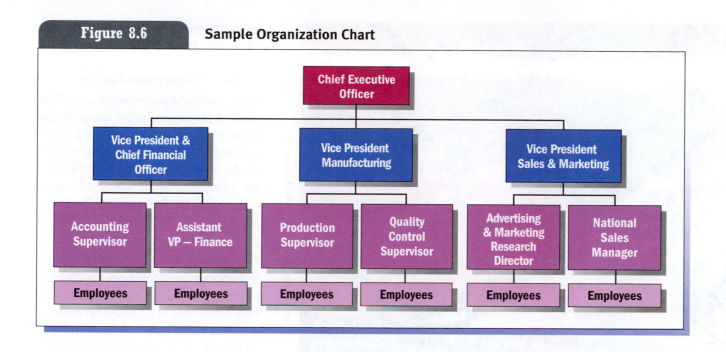

Figure 8.6   **Sample Organization Chart**

Chief Executive Officer

Vice President & Chief Financial Officer

Vice President Manufacturing

Vice President Sales & Marketing

Accounting Supervisor

Assistant VP — Finance

Production Supervisor

Quality Control Supervisor

Advertising & Marketing Research Director

National Sales Manager

Employees   Employees   Employees   Employees   Employees   Employees

the company's effort to meet its goals. To help employees understand how their work fits within the overall operation of the firm, managers prepare an **organization chart,** which is a visual representation of a firm's structure that illustrates job positions and functions. Figure 8.6 illustrates a sample organization chart. Each box in the chart would show a specific position. An organization chart depicts the division of a firm into departments that meet organizational needs.

Not-for-profit organizations also organize through formal structures that enable them to implement their plans. The Catholic Church, for example, is a hierarchy with clearly defined levels and strict lines of authority. The head of the church is the pope, based in the Vatican in Rome. The pope holds this position for life and is held to be preeminent in matters of church doctrine. Responsibility for administering the church's many other functions is dispersed downward throughout the organization. Next in the hierarchy are cardinals, appointed by the pope, who advise the pope and are responsible for electing a new pope upon the current pope's death. Reporting to the cardinals are archbishops who rule over a large area called an *archdiocese* and make sure bishops follow church rules. Next in rank are bishops, who are responsible for governing a diocese, the main administrative unit of the church, and for teaching church doctrine. Diocese are divided into parishes that are presided over by one or more priests, the final level in the church hierarchy.[38]

Departmentalization

Departmentalization is the process of dividing work activities into units within the organization. This arrangement lets employees specialize in certain jobs to promote efficient performance. The marketing effort may be headed by a sales and marketing vice president, who directs the work of salespeople, marketing researchers, and advertising and promotion personnel. A human resources manager may head a department made up of people with special skills in such areas as recruiting and hiring, employee benefits, and labor relations. The five major forms of departmentalization subdivide work by product, geographical area, customer, function, and process:

departmentalization
process of dividing work activities into units within the organization.

- *Product departmentalization.* This approach organizes work units based on the goods and services a company offers. IBM, which once struggled to turn its research and development ideas into competitive products, is now using independent divisions, called "emerging

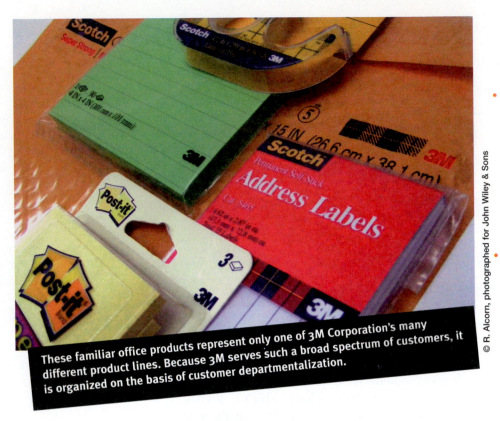

These familiar office products represent only one of 3M Corporation's many different product lines. Because 3M serves such a broad spectrum of customers, it is organized on the basis of customer departmentalization.

© R. Alcorn, photographed for John Wiley & Sons

business opportunities," or EBOs, to take ideas from the research lab to the marketplace. EBOs are a special kind of product departmentalization.

- *Geographical departmentalization.* This form organizes units by geographical regions within a country or, for a multi-national firm, by region throughout the world. Some retailers, such as Dillard's, are organized by divisions that serve different parts of the country. Railroads and gas and oil distributors also favor geographical departmentalization.

- *Customer departmentalization.* A firm that offers a variety of goods and services targeted at different types of customers might structure itself based on customer departmentalization. Management of 3M's wide array of products is divided among six business units: consumer and office; display and graphics; electro and communications; healthcare; industrial and transportation; and safety, security, and protection services.[39]

- *Functional departmentalization.* Some firms organize work units according to business functions such as finance, marketing, human resources, and production. An advertising agency may create departments for creative personnel (say, copywriters), media buyers, and account executives.

- *Process departmentalization.* Some goods and services require multiple work processes to complete their production. A manufacturer may set up separate departments for cutting material, heat-treating it, forming it into its final shape, and painting it.

Figure 8.7

Different Forms of Departmentalization within One Company

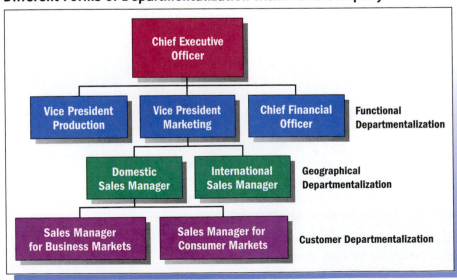

As Figure 8.7 illustrates, a single company may implement several different departmentalization schemes. The departments initially are organized by functions and then subdivided by geographical areas, which are further organized according to customer types. In deciding on a form of departmentalization, managers take into account the type of product they produce, the size of their company, their customer base, and the locations of their customers.

Delegating Work Assignments

After grouping activities into departments, managers assign this work to employees. The act of assigning activities to employees is called **delegation.** Managers delegate work to free their own time for planning and decision making. Subordinates to whom managers assign tasks thus receive responsibility, or obligations to perform those tasks. Along with responsibilities, employees also receive authority, or the power to make decisions and to act on them so they can carry out their responsibilities. Delegation of responsibility and authority makes employees accountable to their supervisor or manager. *Accountability* means that employees are responsible for the results of the ways they perform their assignments; they must accept the consequences of their actions.

Authority and responsibility tend to move downward in organizations, as managers and supervisors delegate work to subordinates. However, accountability moves upward, as managers assume final accountability for performance by the people they manage.

SPAN OF MANAGEMENT The **span of management,** or *span of control,* is the number of subordinates a manager supervises. The subordinates are often referred to as *direct reports.* First-line managers have wider spans of management, monitoring the work of many employees. The span of management varies considerably depending on many factors, including the type of work performed and employees' training. In recent years, a growing trend has brought ever wider spans of control, as companies have reduced their layers of management to flatten their organizational structures, in the process increasing the decision-making responsibility they give employees.

CENTRALIZATION AND DECENTRALIZATION How widely should managers disperse decision-making authority throughout an organization? A company that emphasizes **centralization** retains decision making at the top of the management hierarchy. A company that emphasizes **decentralization** locates decision making at lower levels. A trend toward decentralization has pushed decision making down to operating employees in many cases. Firms that have decentralized believe that the change can enhance their flexibility and responsiveness in serving customers.

Types of Organization Structures

The four primary types of organization structures are line, line-and-staff, committee, and matrix structures. These terms do not specify mutually exclusive categories, though. In fact, most modern organizations combine elements of one or more of these structures. The "Hit & Miss" feature describes how chairwoman and former CEO Anne Mulcahy changed the structure of Xerox when its profits were falling.

LINE ORGANIZATIONS A **line organization,** the oldest and simplest organization structure, establishes a direct flow of authority from the chief executive to subordinates. The line organization defines a simple, clear **chain of command**—a set of relationships that indicates who gives direction to whom and who reports to whom. This arrangement helps prevent buck passing. Decisions can be made quickly because the manager has authority to control subordinates' actions.

A line organization has an obvious defect, though. Each manager must accept complete responsibility for a number of activities and cannot possibly be an expert in all of them. This defect is apparent in midsize and large firms, where the pure line structure fails to take advantage of the specialized skills that are so vital to business today. Managers become overburdened with details and paperwork, leaving them little time for planning.

As a result, the line organization is an ineffective model in any but the smallest organizations. Hair-styling salons, so-called mom-and-pop grocery stores, and small law firms can operate effectively with simple line structures. The Coca-Cola Company, General Electric, and ExxonMobil cannot.

delegation act of assigning work activities to subordinates.

span of management number of subordinates a manager can supervise effectively.

chain of command set of relationships that indicates who directs which activities and who reports to whom.

Hit & Miss

Xerox Creates a New Image of Itself

Anne Mulcahy took the CEO position at Xerox when the company was facing possible bankruptcy. Shareholders wanted quick solutions to the company's complicated problems. Some dumped their stock, causing the price to drop 26 percent in one day. Mulcahy is a tough executive who is loyal to her company—she has been with Xerox for more than 25 years. She resisted the urge to declare bankruptcy, which would have cleared the firm's $18 billion in debt. "Bankruptcy is never a win," she says. But Xerox's organizational culture was so entrenched that few people thought she could succeed.

Despite advice that she should cut research and development or field sales, Mulcahy instead hacked away at Xerox's bloated organization. She met with top executives to determine whether they would accept her plans. Ninety-eight of the top 100 executives elected to stay. Mulcahy then visited customers, field staff, and workers at Xerox facilities. She authorized the sale of pieces of Fuji Xerox and outsourced portions of manufacturing. Entire divisions were shut down, and more than 30 percent of the company's workforce—roughly 30,000 jobs—were eliminated. Billions of dollars in expenses were cut. In the process, Xerox was transformed from a black-and-white copier manufacturer to an up-to-date supplier of office network services and color printing systems. Mulcahy's aim was to create a company that would be flexible enough to anticipate and meet the needs of its customers. "Focus on client service," she advises other companies that are facing similar fates. "I will fly anywhere to save any customer to Xerox."

The firm is on the comeback. Shareholders are now happy with Mulcahy's restructuring; the stock price has tripled from where it was just a few years ago. The firm's focus has shifted dramatically. "In a few years, we won't be selling black-and-white devices [at all]," predicts Mulcahy. "They will be output devices that are color-enabled, and the price will be at a point where customers will be indifferent." As the printing market continues to shift with the expansion of wireless communications systems, Xerox has launched 100 new printing technologies in three years. It is a leader in the specialized color printing market; its digital systems make it easy for customers to produce their own brochures, posters, and books. "This technology business is a never-ending process. You never get to sit back and say you're done. You're always looking for something new."

Unlike other executives who turn around companies and then depart for new challenges, Mulcahy has no intention of leaving Xerox. She calls herself a "lifer." Although she stepped down as CEO in May 2009, she is staying on as the company's chairwoman. Her ultimate goal is "restoring Xerox to a great company once again." It's likely she'll get the job done.

Questions for Critical Thinking

1. What type of organization do you think best represents the new direction of Xerox? Why?
2. Anne Mulcahy made some very bold moves. Do you agree with her approach? Why or why not?

Sources: Franklin Paul, "Xerox Profit Falls on Restructuring Costs," *Reuters,* January 23, 2009, http://www.reuters.com; Bill George, "The Courage to Say No to Wall Street," *U.S. News & World Report,* December 8, 2008, pp. 50–51; "Xerox Cutting 5 Percent of Workforce," *The Business Review,* October 24, 2008, http://albany.bizjournals.com; Jacquie McNish, "Xerox's Success Is a Reflection of Her Dedication," *The Globe and Mail,* September 11, 2008, http://www.theglobeandmail.com; "Anne Mulcahy—The 100 Most Powerful Women," *Forbes,* August 27, 2008, http://www.forbes.com.

LINE-AND-STAFF ORGANIZATIONS A **line-and-staff organization** combines the direct flow of authority of a line organization with staff departments that support the line departments. Line departments participate directly in decisions that affect the core operations of the organization. Staff departments lend specialized technical support. Examples of staff departments include labor relations, legal counsel, and information technology. Figure 8.8 illustrates a line-and-staff organization. Accounting, engineering, and human resources are staff departments that support the line authority extending from the plant manager to the production manager and supervisors.

A line manager and a staff manager differ significantly in their authority relationships. A **line manager** forms part of the primary line of authority that flows throughout the organization. Line managers interact directly with the functions of production, financing, or marketing—the functions needed to produce and sell goods and services. A **staff manager** provides information, advice, or technical assistance to aid line managers. Staff managers do not have authority to give orders outside their own departments or to compel line managers to take action.

The line-and-staff organization is common in midsize and large organizations. It is an effective structure because it combines the line organization's capabilities for rapid decision making and direct communication with the expert knowledge of staff specialists.

COMMITTEE ORGANIZATIONS A **committee organization** is a structure that places authority and responsibility jointly in the hands of a group of individuals rather than a single manager. This model typically appears as part of a regular line-and-staff structure. Examples of the committee structure emerge throughout organizations at one point in time. Nordstrom, the department store chain, once had an "office of the co-presidency" in which six members of the Nordstrom family shared the top job.

Committees also work in areas such as new-product development. A new-product committee may include managers from such areas as accounting, engineering, finance, manufacturing, marketing, and technical research. By including representatives from all areas involved in creating and marketing products, such a committee generally improves planning and employee morale because decisions reflect diverse perspectives.

Committees tend to act slowly and conservatively, however, and they often make decisions by compromising conflicting interests rather than by choosing the best alternative. The definition of a camel as "a racehorse designed by committee" provides an apt description of some limitations of committee decisions. At Nordstrom, the six-person office of the co-presidency was eventually abandoned for a more traditional structure.

MATRIX ORGANIZATIONS Some organizations use a matrix or product management design to capture the strengths and reduce the weaknesses of other organizational structures. The **matrix structure** links employees from different parts of the organization to work together on specific projects. Figure 8.9 diagrams a matrix structure.

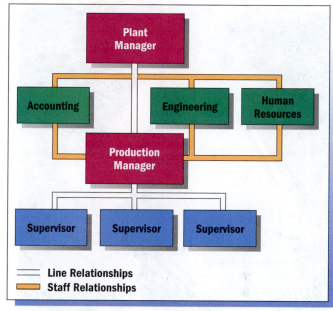

Figure 8.8

Line-and-Staff Organization

— Line Relationships
— Staff Relationships

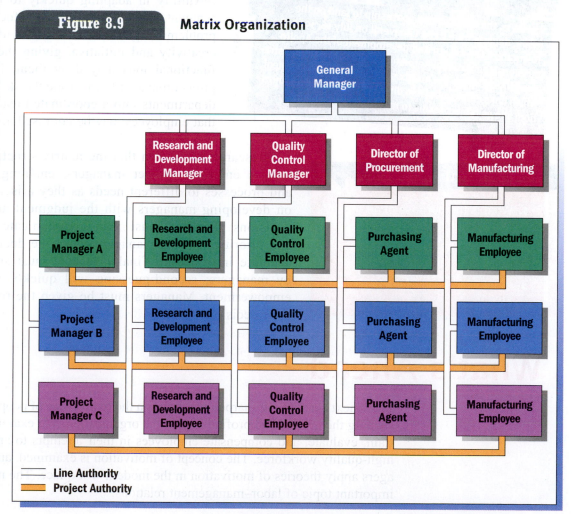

Figure 8.9 **Matrix Organization**

— Line Authority
— Project Authority

Apollo 11, the first manned spaceship to land on the moon, departs from Cape Canaveral on July 16, 1969. To organize the design and development of the Apollo missions, the National Aeronautics and Space Administration (NASA) chose the matrix structure. This arrangement, which links employees from different parts of the organization, allows project teams to react quickly to change.

Courtesy NASA

For a specific project, a project manager assembles a group of employees from different functional areas. The employees retain their ties to the line-and-staff structure, as shown in the vertical white lines. As the horizontal gold lines indicate, however, employees are also members of project teams. Upon completion of a project, employees return to their "regular" jobs.

In the matrix structure, each employee reports to two managers: one line manager and one project manager. Employees who are selected to work on a special project, such as development of a new product, receive instructions from the project manager (horizontal authority), but they continue as employees in their permanent functional departments (vertical authority). The term *matrix* comes from the intersecting grid of horizontal and vertical lines of authority.

The matrix structure has become popular at high-technology and multinational corporations, as well as hospitals, consulting firms, and aerospace firms. Dow Chemical and Procter & Gamble have both used matrix structures. The National Aeronautics and Space Administration used the matrix structure for its Mercury and Apollo space missions.

The major benefits of the matrix structure come from its flexibility in adapting quickly to rapid changes in the environment and its capability of focusing resources on major problems or products. It also provides an outlet for employees' creativity and initiative, giving them opportunities that their functional jobs may deny them. However, it challenges the project manager to integrate the skills of specialists from many departments into a coordinated team. Another disadvantage is that employees may be confused and frustrated in reporting to two bosses.

Research has shown that the matrix structure is most effective when leaders empower project managers, enabling them to adapt resources and processes to different needs as they arise. Emphasis must be placed on developing managers with the judgment and maturity to make good decisions. Leaders must also communicate organizational strategies and priorities so that managers can make decisions based on timely and accurate information. Finally, leaders must support the decisions made by managers; second-guessing will quickly undermine any attempt at empowerment. Managers must be given the resources needed to support their decisions.[40]

Assessment Check

1. What is the purpose of an organization chart?
2. What are the five major forms of departmentalization?
3. What does *span of management* mean?

What's Ahead

In the next chapter, we sharpen our focus on the importance of people—the human resource—in shaping the growth and profitability of the organization. We examine how firms recruit, select, train, evaluate, and compensate employees in their attempts to attract, retain, and motivate a high-quality workforce. The concept of motivation is examined, and we will discuss how managers apply theories of motivation in the modern workplace. The next chapter also looks at the important topic of labor–management relations.

Summary of Learning Goals

1 **Define *management* and the three types of skills necessary for managerial success.**

Management is the process of achieving organizational objectives through people and other resources. The management hierarchy depicts the levels of management in organizations: top managers provide overall direction for company activities, middle managers implement the strategies of top managers and direct the activities of supervisors, and supervisors interact directly with workers. The three basic managerial skills are technical skills, or the ability to apply the techniques, tools, and knowledge of a specific discipline or department; human skills, which involve working effectively with and through people; and conceptual skills, or the capability to see an overall view of the organization and how each part contributes to its functioning.

Assessment Check Answers

1.1 What is management? Management is the process of achieving organizational objectives through people and other resources. The manager's job is to combine human and technical resources in the best way possible to achieve the company's goals.

1.2 How do the jobs of top managers, middle managers, and supervisory managers differ? Top managers develop long-range plans, set a direction for their organization, and inspire managers and employees to achieve the company's vision. Middle managers focus on specific operations, products, or customer groups and develop detailed plans and procedures to implement the firm's strategic plans. Supervisory managers are directly responsible for evaluating the performance of nonmanagerial employees who produce and sell the firm's goods and services. They are responsible for implementing the plans developed by middle managers and motivating workers to accomplish daily, weekly, and monthly goals.

1.3 What is the relationship between the manager's planning and controlling functions? Controlling is evaluating an organization's performance to determine whether it is accomplishing its objectives. The basic purpose of controlling is to assess the success of the planning function. Controlling also provides feedback for future rounds of planning.

2 **Explain the role of vision and ethical standards in business success.**

Vision is the ability to perceive the needs of the marketplace and develop methods for satisfying those needs. Vision helps new businesses pinpoint the actions needed to take advantage of opportunities. In an existing firm, a clear vision of company purpose helps unify the actions of far-flung divisions, keep customers satisfied, and sustain growth. Setting high ethical standards helps a firm survive and be successful over the long term. Behaving ethically places an organization's constituents—those to whom it is responsible—at the top

of its priorities. It also goes beyond avoiding wrongdoing to encouraging, motivating, and inspiring employees.

Assessment Check Answers

2.1 What is meant by a vision for the firm? A vision serves as the target for a firm's actions, helping direct the company toward opportunities and differentiating it from its competitors. Vision must be focused and yet flexible enough to adapt to changes in the business environment.

2.2 Why is it important for a top executive to set high ethical standards? When top managers engage in unethical behavior, their actions encourage others to do the same. Legal charges, fines, prison time, financial losses, and bankruptcy can result. Because they set the standards for others, executives need to focus on achieving personal and organizational success in ethical ways.

3 **Summarize the major benefits of planning, and distinguish among strategic planning, tactical planning, and operational planning.**

The planning process identifies organizational goals and develops the actions necessary to reach them. Planning helps a company turn vision into action, take advantage of opportunities, and avoid costly mistakes. Strategic planning is a far-reaching process. It views the world through a wide-angle lens to determine the long-range focus and activities of the organization. Tactical planning focuses on the current and short-range activities required to implement the organization's strategies. Operational planning sets standards and work targets for functional areas such as production, human resources, and marketing.

Assessment Check Answers

3.1 Outline the planning process. Some plans are very broad and long range, focusing on key organizational objectives; others are more detailed and specify how particular objectives will be achieved. From the mission statement to objectives to specific plans, each phase must fit into a comprehensive planning framework.

3.2 Describe the purpose of tactical planning. The purpose of tactical planning is to determine which short-term activities should be implemented to accomplish the firm's overall strategy.

3.3 Compare the kinds of plans made by top managers and middle managers. How does their focus differ? Top managers focus on long-range, strategic plans. In contrast, middle-level managers and supervisors focus on short-term, tactical planning.

4 **Describe the strategic planning process.**

The first step of strategic planning is to translate the firm's vision into a mission statement that explains its overall intentions and aims. Next, planners must assess the firm's current competitive position using tools such as SWOT analysis, which weighs the firm's strengths, weaknesses, opportunities, and threats. Based on this information, managers set specific objectives that elaborate what the organization hopes to accomplish. The next step is to develop strategies for reaching objectives that will differentiate the firm from its competitors. Managers then develop an action plan that outlines the specific methods for implementing the strategy. Finally, the results achieved by the plan are evaluated, and the plan is adjusted as needed.

Assessment Check Answers

4.1 What is the purpose of a mission statement? A mission statement is a public declaration of a firm's purpose, the reason it exists, the customers it will serve, and the way it is different from competitors. A mission statement guides the actions of company managers and employees.

4.2 Which of the firm's characteristics does a SWOT analysis compare? A SWOT analysis determines a firm's strengths, weaknesses, opportunities, and threats relative to its competitors. In other words, SWOT analysis helps determine a firm's competitive position in the marketplace.

4.3 How do managers use objectives? Objectives, which are derived from the firm's mission statement, are used to define desired performance levels in areas such as profitability, customer service, and employee satisfaction.

5 **Contrast the two major types of business decisions, and list the steps in the decision-making process.**

A programmed decision applies a company rule or policy to solve a frequently occurring problem. A nonprogrammed decision forms a response to a complex and unique problem with important consequences for the organization. The five-step approach to decision making includes recognizing a problem or opportunity, developing alternative courses of action, evaluating the alternatives, selecting and implementing an alternative, and following up the decision to determine its effectiveness.

Assessment Check Answers

5.1 Compare and contrast programmed and nonprogrammed decisions. Because programmed decisions are simple and common and recur frequently, rules and policies can be established to eliminate the time-consuming process of identifying and evaluating alternatives and making new decisions each time a programmed situation occurs. By using rules and procedures to save time with programmed decisions, managers can devote more of their time to more complex nonprogrammed decisions.

5.2 What are the steps in the decision-making process? The decision-making process begins when someone recognizes a problem or opportunity, develops potential courses of action to solve the problem, evaluates the alternatives, selects and implements one of them, and assesses the outcome of the decision.

6 **Define *leadership,* and compare different leadership styles.**

Leadership is the act of motivating others or causing them to perform activities designed to achieve specific objectives. The basic styles are autocratic, democratic, and free-rein leadership. The best leadership style depends on three elements: the leader, the followers, and the situation. Today's leaders tend increasingly to involve employees in making decisions about their work.

Assessment Check Answers

6.1 How is leadership defined? Leadership means directing or inspiring people to attain organizational goals. Effective leaders share several traits, such as empathy, self-awareness, and objectivity in dealing with others. Leaders also use the power of their jobs, expertise, and experience to influence others.

6.2 Identify the styles of leadership as they appear along a continuum of greater or lesser employee participation. At one end of the continuum, autocratic leaders make decisions without consulting employees. In the middle of the continuum, democratic leaders ask employees for suggestions and encourage participation. At the other end of the continuum, free-rein leaders leave most decisions to their subordinates.

7 **Discuss the meaning and importance of corporate culture.**

Corporate culture refers to an organization's principles, beliefs, and values. It is typically shaped by a firm's founder and perpetuated through formal programs such as training, rituals, and ceremonies, as well as through informal discussions among employees. Corporate culture can influence a firm's success by giving it a competitive advantage.

Assessment Check Answers

7.1 What is the relationship between leadership style and corporate culture? The best leadership style to adopt often depends on the organization's corporate culture and its system of principles, beliefs, and values. Managerial philosophies, communications networks, and workplace environments and practices all influence corporate culture.

7.2 What is a strong corporate culture? A corporate culture is an organization's system of principles, beliefs, and values. In an organization with a strong culture, everyone knows and supports the same principles, beliefs, and values. A company with weak or constantly shifting culture lacks a clear sense of purpose.

8 **Identify the five major forms of departmentalization and the four main types of organization structures.**

The subdivision of work activities into units within the organization is called *departmentalization*. It may be based on products, geographical locations, customers, functions, or processes. Most firms implement one or more of four structures: line, line-and-staff, committee, and matrix structures. Each structure has advantages and disadvantages.

Assessment Check Answers

8.1 What is the purpose of an organization chart? An organization chart is a visual representation of a firm's structure that illustrates job positions and functions.

8.2 What are the five major forms of departmentalization? Product departmentalization organizes units by the different goods and services a company offers. Geographical departmentalization organizes units by geographical regions within a country or, for a multinational firm, by regions throughout the world. Customer departmentalization organizes units by different types of customers. Functional departmentalization organizes units by business functions such as finance, marketing, human resources, and production. Process departmentalization organizes units by the steps or work processes it takes to complete production or provide a service.

8.3 What does *span of management* mean? The span of management, or span of control, is the number of subordinates a manager supervises.

Business Terms You Need to Know

management 254	objectives 265	corporate culture 271	delegation 275
planning 257	decision making 266	organization 272	span of management 275
vision 258	leadership 268	departmentalization 273	chain of command 275
mission statement 262			

Other Important Business Terms

top management 255	controlling 258	nonprogrammed decision 267	line organization 275
middle management 255	strategic planning 260	autocratic leadership 269	line-and-staff organization 276
supervisory management 255	tactical planning 260	democratic leadership 270	line manager 276
technical skills 256	operational planning 260	empowerment 270	staff manager 276
human skills 256	contingency planning 261	free-rein leadership 270	committee organization 277
conceptual skills 257	SWOT analysis 263	organization chart 273	matrix structure 277
organizing 257	competitive differentiation 265	centralization 275	
directing 257	programmed decision 266	decentralization 275	

Review Questions

1. What is a management hierarchy? In what ways does it help organizations develop structure? In what ways could it be considered obsolete?

2. What are the three basic types of skills that managers must possess? Which type of skill is most important at each management level?

3. Identify and describe the four basic functions of managers.

4. Why is a clear vision particularly important for companies that have numerous operations around the country or around the world? Cite an example.

5. Which type of planning is most far-reaching? How does this type of planning affect other types of planning?

6. Suppose you planned a large cookout for your friends, but when you woke up on the morning of the party, it was pouring rain. What type of plan would allow you to cope with this situation? Specifically, what could you do?

7. As a student, you have a mission in school. Write your own mission statement for your education and program, including your goals and the ways you plan to accomplish them.

8. Identify each of the following as a programmed or non-programmed decision:

    a. reordering printer cartridges
    b. selecting a cell phone provider
    c. buying your favorite toothpaste and shampoo at the supermarket
    d. selecting a college to attend
    e. filling your car with gasoline

9. Identify the traits that are most often associated with great leaders. Which trait would be most important in the leader of a large corporation? A small company? Why?

10. Why is a strong corporate culture important to a company's success? Relate your answer to a specific firm.

Projects and Teamwork Applications

1. Create a résumé for yourself, identifying your technical skills, human skills, and conceptual skills. Which set of skills do you think is your strongest? Why?

2. Think of a company with which you are familiar—either one you work for or one with whom you conduct business as a customer. Consider ways in which the organization can meet the needs of its marketplace. Then write a sentence or two describing what you think the organization's vision is—or should be.

3. Conduct your own SWOT analysis for a company with which you are familiar. Visit the organization's Web site to learn as much about the company as you can before stating your conclusions. Be as specific as possible in identifying your perceptions of the company's strengths, weaknesses, opportunities, and threats.

4. Identify a classmate or college friend who you think is a good leader. Describe the traits that you think are most important in making this person an effective leader.

5. Your school has its own organizational culture. Describe what you perceive to be its characteristics. Is the culture strong or weak? How does the culture affect you as a student?

Web Assignments

1. **Contingency planning.** When Travelocity posted $51 fare to Fiji on its site, hundreds of people booked flights. CEO Michelle Peluso had to decide whether to lose $2 million by honoring the fare, a mistake made not by Travelocity but by an airline reservation center. Visit the Web site to find out how Travelocity executives resolved the problem (http://www.businessweek.com/managing/content/sep2007/ca20070923_089830.htm?chan=search). Watch the video, read the text, and take the reader poll. Write a brief report of the issue, Peluso's decision, the reasons behind it, and whether or not you agree with the decision and why.

2. **Mission statements.** Visit the Monsanto Web site (http://www.monsanto.com). At the bottom of the page, click on Monsanto Pledge to read the introductory page. What does the company state as its primary mission or purpose? What does Monsanto say is the "core of this agenda?" At left on the page, click on the Monsanto Pledge. What are the eight values included in the company's pledge?

3. **Leadership.** Visit the Web site listed here (http://podcast.amanet.org/edgewise/category/management/). Listen to the podcast of Dr. Susan Smith Kuczmarski and Thomas Kuczmarksi on "Changing the Way We Lead and Succeed," podcast #0807, dated February 15, 2008. They describe a new type of leader. What six qualities does such a leader possess? Which quality is the hardest for traditional leaders to develop? What do they say is the key ingredient for leadership?

Note: Internet Web addresses change frequently. If you don't find the exact sites listed, you may need to access the organization's home page and search from there.

At an annual meeting of shareholders several years ago, Merck CEO Ray Gilmartin presented his vision for the future. The company was coming off three quarters of poor earnings and had recently canceled two research programs for promising drugs. When shareholders heard that Gilmartin's turnaround plan focused on the development of three vaccines, the audience was skeptical; vaccines historically have not been thought of as game changers. Within five months, Gilmartin was out as CEO.

Today, after a period of poor stock performance and lawsuits against one of its most promising drugs, Merck is back on track. Ironically, it all began under Gilmartin's watch. All of the drugs he unveiled were eventually approved by the Food and Drug Administration. Taken together, they would generate $7 billion in annual revenue for Merck. Clearly, the vaccines have been much more successful than skeptics thought they would be.

Recently, Merck has performed well in all areas. It has gained FDA approval for more new drugs than any of its competitors. It has won most of the lawsuits over Vioxx, the arthritis drug that was linked to heart attacks and strokes and pulled from the market. A comprehensive settlement was reached in November 2007 for $4.85 billion, much less than originally expected. The company's stock has gone up 75 percent during this period.

Much of Merck's success has been attributed to the leadership of current CEO Richard Clark. Clark navigated the company through the Vioxx crisis, meeting regularly with small groups of employees. He broke down the cliques that had formed and established "one Merck," a phrase he uses often. Says Clark, "From the moment we begin talking about a particular drug franchise, I want researchers, marketers, and manufacturing people sitting in the same room."

Several other employees contributed significantly to Merck's turnaround. Chief scientist Peter Kim revamped Merck's once-productive labs, which had become stagnant and unprofitable. Kim changed Merck's insular culture, which rarely entered into the mergers and alliances that were gaining momentum in the industry. He developed a new system for Merck scientists to identify promising chemical compounds in the scientific literature. Kim also persuaded scientists to use their connections to identify licensing and acquisition opportunities; the number of such transactions rose quickly.

Another challenge facing Merck was restoring the fine reputation it had once enjoyed. Legal counsel Ken Frazier wanted to contest, rather than settle, the Vioxx crisis. The objective was to fairly compensate those who had suffered injury due to Vioxx but to defend the company against medical outcomes that were not caused by Vioxx. Frazier won enough cases to lead the way to a more favorable settlement.

While Merck has experienced a tremendous rebound, more rough waters may lie ahead. Vytorin, a blockbuster anticholesterol drug produced through a joint venture with Schering-Plough, is now under the microscope. A study conducted by both companies—but initially not released—found that the drug may not work as well as advertised. The fallout has caused the stock of both companies to drop, reduced the sales of Vytorin, and triggered several potential class-action lawsuits. Merck is confident that this pales in comparison to the problems they have been through.[41]

Questions for Critical Thinking

1. What role did leadership play in the turnaround at Merck?
2. Why was it important to change the existing culture at Merck's labs?

Live Nation Rocks On

While the music business remains in turmoil, Live Nation keeps rocking on. The two-year-old company, a spin-off of Clear Channel, generated more than $4 billion in revenue in a recent year. Michael Rapino produces more concert tours than any other company in the world, and he owns both large and small venues such as the House of Blues chain and a string of smaller clubs named after the famous Fillmore halls. As CEO of Live Nation, the 42-year-old Rapino is one of the few people in the music industry who has managed to grow revenue in recent years. Genesis, Roger Waters of Pink Floyd fame, and the newly reunited Police are some of the bands he has taken on the road.

The music business has changed dramatically, in large part due to file sharing and the iPod. Artists once made the bulk of their money selling CDs and toured to promote their albums. Today artists make most of their money touring, and Live Nation, the world's largest live-music company, is leading the way. But Rapino isn't stopping with concerts. Because he operates the tours of many musicians, he wants to turn Live Nation into a company that can handle all their musical needs. Rapino thinks he can offer one-stop service to musical artists creating their albums, selling their merchandise, and handling their Web sites. Live Nation also recently broke from Ticketmaster to form its own ticketing business.

In short, Rapino is mounting an all-out assault on record labels and believes he is in a great position to pull it off. Madonna has already left Warner Bros. to sign a ten-year contract with Live Music, who will handle every aspect of her business except publishing. According to her manager, Guy Oseary, companies have to be involved in all aspects of the music business today to do well. Rapino's strategy is fairly simple—to connect with the millions of people who attend a Live Nation show each year. According to Rapino, "I should be e-mailing you the morning after the Jay-Z concert, saying 'Want a CD? A download? Want a video of the show? Want a set list? Want a signed shirt with Jay-Z? We printed a limited edition.' The possibilities are endless."

Rapino's strategy is not without its critics. Some argue that he will need the resources of a major label to produce and market CDs; this job will eventually have to be licensed to a label. In addition, some record companies are following Rapino's lead and signing bands to similar comprehensive deals. Rapino's response to the critics is that he knows how to market and ultimately will sign many superstars in the years ahead. Investors appear skeptical, as Live Nation's stock fell 30 percent after the Madonna deal. But Rapino has complete confidence in his approach—while the CD business languished, live music is where the action is.[42]

Questions for Critical Thinking

1. What are some of Live Nation's strengths, weaknesses, opportunities, and threats?

2. What is Live Nation's strategy for competitive differentiation?

Made in the USA: American Apparel

American Apparel is on the cutting edge of fashion. Its hip T-shirts are designed specifically for a young, urban crowd. All are made in the United States by workers who earn far better wages than most others in the garment industry. A sign at the doorway to one of the firm's stores promises to "pioneer an industry standard in social responsibility." Founder Dov Charney likes to project an image of free expression. Yet all of these qualities have a familiar ring—they sound very much like concerns of the late 1960s and early 1970s. Dov Charney even sports the look—a mustache and muttonchop sideburns.

Charney has a vision—to provide young, urban consumers with logo-free cotton clothing made in the United States and *not* sold in shopping malls. He wants to accomplish this objective by running a factory with a safe and innovative working environment. He prices his clothing between $15 and $45, so his core customers can afford it. And he locates his stores in areas where young consumers are likely to shop, such as New York City's Lower East Side. Charney knows who his customers are, and he is interested in serving only his target group. "We don't design clothes for a 50-year-old," he says without apology. "We don't even care about them."

To achieve his goals, years ago Charney tapped Marty Bailey, who had already worked in the T-shirt industry for 20 years, including a stint at Fruit of the Loom. Bailey knew how to make the vision become a reality. Having watched most of the country's T-shirt production move offshore, he agreed with Charney that American Apparel should stay on American soil. But the manufacturing process itself needed to be streamlined and improved. "There were a lot of operators on the floor," recalls Bailey. "There was a lot of work in process. Material was sitting around for months. That means a lot of cash was tied up on the sewing floor. At Fruit of the Loom, I had instituted work teams. I did the same thing here." Over a period of about nine months, Bailey converted the entire operation to teams of 4 to 12 workers. Each worker would have responsibility for one portion of a garment—say, a sleeve or a neck—but the team would produce the final product. Each team would have access to a supervisor and a mechanic to help minimize delays. "We went from producing 30,000 pieces a day to 90,000, with no unfinished work in process," Bailey says of the conversion.

A successful company needs a leader and effective management. Dov Charney is clearly the leader of American Apparel. Sometimes he is called charismatic, sometimes controversial. But American Apparel is very much his company—he developed the style and continues to oversee all aspects of design, development, and marketing. Charney likes to visit American Apparel's 131 retail stores as often as he can; another 60 stores are planned for next year. "Dov is a huge part of the company," says Marty Bailey. "He is the face of the company, the passion, the drive. He's also the best marketer I've ever been associated with."

Bailey is also a top-notch manager. "I spend time in the stores, too. But I manage operations, which includes running the plant and handling distribution." Bailey acknowledges the difference in their two styles of leadership and management. "Dov is very animated, which is a huge part of our company. I'm pretty low key. But when I change pace, people know it's time to get serious." Yet Bailey points out that his goals and philosophies of leadership are really similar to Charney's. "I believe in managing people, not personnel," he says. "You ask people, you don't tell them."

Both men emphasize the importance of treating workers with respect. "My job is to support people, to train people, to listen to people, and to give them every opportunity to be successful," says Charney. Workers at American Apparel not only are paid better than the industry average but also have unique opportunities. Because the factory is located in Los Angeles, it attracts a substantial number of Hispanic employees. So the firm offers free English and citizenship classes, low-cost lunches, and free use of bicycles for commuting to and from work. A new health clinic has opened right at the factory to encourage employees to use their healthcare benefits.

Communication is also an important part of the American Apparel culture. "One of the main reasons people get upset is lack of information," Bailey observes. "You need to inform [employees], you let them know what's going on, and you let them know that they're needed. As a manager, the three most important things I can ever do is say please, thank you, and ask, 'What do you think?' "[43]

Questions for Critical Thinking

1. Describe the skills that you think Marty Bailey has that enable him to manage American Apparel's operations.

2. Based on what you have learned about the company, its leader, and its top manager, write your own mission statement for American Apparel.

3. Using the five-step approach to decision making, describe how American Apparel might make the nonprogrammed decision to add a new product to its line.

4. How would you describe Dov Charney's leadership style? How does it help shape the corporate culture?

chapter

9

1 Explain the importance of human resource management, the responsibilities of human resource managers, and the role of human resource planning in an organization's competitive strategy.

2 Describe how recruitment and selection contribute to placing the right person in a job.

3 Explain how training programs and performance appraisal help companies grow and develop their employees.

4 Outline the methods employers use to compensate employees through pay systems and benefit programs.

5 Discuss employee separation and the impact of downsizing and outsourcing.

6 Explain how Maslow's hierarchy of needs theory, expectancy theory, equity theory, goal setting, job design, and managers' attitudes relate to employee motivation.

7 Summarize the role of labor unions and the tactics of labor–management conflicts.

Human Resource Management, Motivation, and Labor–Management Relations

Tom Merton/Getty Images

NetApp Builds on Trust and Simplicity

NetApp may not be the flashiest young company in the high-tech industry. The Sunnyvale, California–based firm makes data storage equipment. With about 5,400 U.S. employees and another 3,000 abroad, it's not the biggest either. And despite experiencing tremendous growth since its founding, the company struggled recently with revenue shortfalls as recession forced its customers to cut their spending. But it is still getting attention.

NetApp rose to the top of two prestigious lists of the best companies to work for in the United States. Both *Fortune* and Great Places to Work Institute recognized the value of its down-to-earth, team-oriented corporate culture in attracting and retaining employees who simply love working there. When James Lau and David Hitz founded the company in 1992, they hired Dan Warmenhoven as CEO. Warmenhoven's top priorities were to build revenue and create an effective management team. Among the results: worldwide revenues topping $3 billion and more than 45,000 applicants for fewer than 600 job openings in a recent year.

NetApp's commitment to its employees shows up in large ways and small. Simplicity is a key value, and it is based largely on trust between employees and managers. A 12-page employee travel policy, for instance, was simplified to three straightforward sentences: "We are a frugal company. But don't show up dog-tired to save a few bucks. Use your common sense." Employees also are free to ask questions, share ideas, and make decisions. Says one, "I have been given lots of freedom to implement my ideas to make things better and also am able to make decisions in order to get the job done.... I can look back and see what I have been able to accomplish with a great feeling of satisfaction." Says another, "It is expected that you get your work done, and if you do that late at night or early in the morning, that is your choice ... the atmosphere is positive, creative, and the bar is higher, [but] no one is watching your movements; it is about performance."

Performance is rewarded through three separate programs that recognize and encourage knowledge sharing, sales success, and patent filings for new ideas. In a recent year, the company awarded over $1 million to 543 employees for creating patent-worthy innovations. But recognition goes beyond these one-time awards; it happens every day at NetApp. An employee explains, "I have never been at a company where the top executives actually *call* me to thank me for a job well done and great attitude. Even the 'little' people get noticed by ... our vice chairman.... Makes me much more committed to my career and job here."

Ongoing training gives employees the opportunities they need to learn new skills, develop their careers, and remain challenged to take risks. NetApp's U.S. employees recently completed more than 26,000 hours of annual training, and the company encourages self-assessment and the use of coaches. NetApp University promotes professional development. One assistant attended a week-long out-of-state training program to learn new Web site software. "To me, that is exciting and a great chance to learn a new skill! I will be spreading my wings a little and learning to lead a team."

At some firms, rapid growth builds layers between employees and managers, but NetApp strives to keep communication open. "I've personally experienced Dan, our CEO, choose to share difficult information in the spirit of candor rather than pushing it under the rug," says an employee. The company holds a Vice President's Forum every two weeks so that its leaders can share information about the industry and the economy and also asks employees about what is on their minds. After the meetings, the vice presidents share what they've learned with everyone on their teams. Recognizing that bad news is harder to share, the company even developed a communication kit for managers, called "Communicating with Employees during Tough Times."

Unlike some other firms, NetApp doesn't clean employees' clothes or change the oil in their cars. It does, however, serve fruit, bagels, and yogurt; offer five paid days off for volunteer work; provide same-sex couples with domestic partner benefits; offer child adoption benefits; sponsor community activities; donate equipment to needy organizations; and offer telecommuting, flexible schedules, and job sharing on the principle of "whatever works to get the job done." A unique NetApp medical benefit has paid 43 employees to cover treatment of autism for family members. All in all, it's little wonder that, in the words of a NetApp employee, "Everyone loves working here."[1]

The importance of people to the success of any organization is the very definition of **management:** the use of people and other resources to accomplish organizational objectives. In this chapter, we address the critical issues of human resource management and motivation. We begin with a discussion of the ways organizations attract, develop, and retain employees. Then we describe the concepts behind motivation and the way human resource managers apply them to increase employee satisfaction and organizational effectiveness.

We also explore the reasons for labor unions and focus on legislation that affects labor–management relations. The process of collective bargaining is then discussed, along with tools used by unions and management in seeking their objectives.

Human Resource Management Is Vital to All Organizations

human resource management function of attracting, developing, and retaining enough qualified employees to perform the activities necessary to accomplish organizational objectives.

As you saw with NetApp at the opening of the chapter, most organizations devote considerable attention to **human resource management,** the function of attracting, developing, and retaining enough qualified employees to perform the activities necessary to accomplish organizational objectives. Human resource managers are responsible for developing specific programs and activities as well as creating a work environment that generates employee satisfaction and efficiency.

The core responsibilities of human resource management include planning for staffing needs, recruitment and selection, training, evaluating performance, compensation and benefits, and employee separation. In accomplishing these five tasks, shown in Figure 9.1, human resource managers achieve their objectives of (1) providing qualified, well-trained employees for the organization; (2) maximizing employee effectiveness in the organization; and (3) satisfying individual employee needs through monetary compensation, benefits, opportunities to advance, and job satisfaction.

One of the key ways in which human resource managers accomplish those tasks is to develop *human resource plans* based on their organization's competitive strategies. They forecast the number of employees their firm will need and determine the types of skills necessary to implement its plans. Human resource managers are responsible for adjusting their company's workforce to meet the requirements of expanding in new markets; reducing costs, which may require laying off employees; or adapting to new technology. They formulate both long- and short-term plans to provide the right number of qualified employees.

Human resource managers also must plan how to attract and keep good employees with the right combination of pay,

Figure 9.1

Human Resource Management Responsibilities

benefits, and working conditions. At Trilogy Software, this aspect of human resource planning is at the core of the company's strategy. Trilogy develops software that handles information processing related to sales and marketing, an industry in which only fast-moving, highly sophisticated companies can succeed. So the company has a strategy to expand its staff of software developers. Knowing that it is competing for talent with software giants such as Microsoft and Cisco Systems, Trilogy targets college campuses, recruiting the brightest, most energetic students it can find. As a substitute for work experience, the company sends these young recruits to an intense three-month orientation program called Trilogy University, where they work on the firm's products as they learn about the software industry and the company culture. Trilogy appeals to recruits by emphasizing that their contribution to the company matters. "We are looking for people with big ideas and a dedication to transforming business," states the company's Web site.[2]

Assessment Check ✔

1. Why do human resource managers need to develop staffing plans?
2. How do human resource managers attract and keep good employees?

Recruitment and Selection

In recruiting and selecting employees, human resource managers strive to hire applicants who have skills the organization needs. To ensure that potential employees bring the necessary skills or have the capacity to learn them, most firms implement the recruitment and selection process shown in Figure 9.2.

Finding Qualified Candidates

Some organizations have great reputations, and people compete to be hired. Google, for instance, attracts 3,000 applicants daily without advertising.[3] Most firms, however, do not have the luxury of sorting through thousands of candidates to find the right person for a job. A survey conducted by Manpower found that 41 percent of employers across the globe are having a tougher time filling jobs.[4] More than 25 percent of human resource professionals report a shortage of job candidates with degrees in science, engineering, technology, and mathematics, according to the Society for Human Resource Management.[5] In addition, with 78 million baby boomers born between 1946 and 1964 beginning to retire and with only 46 million Generation X workers born between 1964 and 1984 to take their place, finding talented workers will be even more difficult.[6] So human resource managers must be creative in their search for qualified employees. Businesses look to both internal and external sources to find the best candidates for specific jobs. Policies of hiring from within emphasize internal sources, so many employers consider their own employees first for job openings. Internal recruiting is less expensive than external methods, and it helps boost employee morale. But if recruiters cannot find qualified internal candidates, they must look for people outside the organization. Recruitment from external sources involves advertising on the Internet and in newspapers and trade magazines; placing radio and television ads; and working through state and private employment agencies, college recruiting and internship offices, retiree job banks, and job fairs. One of the most effective external sources is employee referrals, in which employers ask current employees to recommend applicants, rewarding them with bonuses or prizes for new hires.

To recruit new workers, firms' Web sites often contain career sections that provide general employment information and list open positions. Applicants are often able to

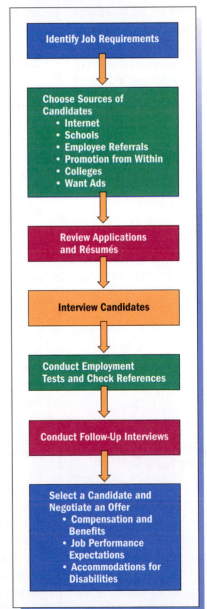

Figure 9.2

Steps in the Recruitment and Selection Process

Identify Job Requirements
↓
Choose Sources of Candidates
- Internet
- Schools
- Employee Referrals
- Promotion from Within
- Colleges
- Want Ads
↓
Review Applications and Résumés
↓
Interview Candidates
↓
Conduct Employment Tests and Check References
↓
Conduct Follow-Up Interviews
↓
Select a Candidate and Negotiate an Offer
- Compensation and Benefits
- Job Performance Expectations
- Accommodations for Disabilities

"They Said It"

"This may sound soft and mushy, but happy people are better for business. They are more creative and productive, they build environments where success is more likely, and you have a much better chance of keeping your best players."

—Shelly Lazarus (b. 1947)
Chairwoman and CEO, Ogilvy & Mather Worldwide

submit a résumé and apply for an open position online. Appendix E, Careers in Contemporary Business, points out that some firms also post job openings at employment Web sites, such as Monster.com. Internet recruiting is such a quick, efficient, and inexpensive way to reach a large pool of job seekers that the vast majority of companies currently use the Internet to fill job openings. Features that job hunters most want to see on recruiting Web sites include detailed company and job profiles, descriptions of ideal candidates, long-term career opportunities at the firm, and a clearly defined application process. Employers lacking in these areas are at a distinct disadvantage in recruiting young workers. Interactive features are often used to differentiate a firm's career Web site. Lockheed Martin added a real-time chat service that enables job hunters to write to the defense company's recruiters and get immediate responses.[7]

Recruiting techniques continue to evolve as technology advances. JobsinPods.com is an online library of podcast interviews with hiring managers and employees at a variety of U.S. companies, including AT&T, Intel, and IBM. New podcasts, also called *jobcasts,* are posted in a blog format, and older podcasts are archived. Some describe employers' hiring needs, while others discuss what employers look for in a new hire. Job seekers can also download the podcasts to an iPod and listen to them at their leisure.[8]

Selecting and Hiring Employees

In selecting and hiring employees, human resource managers must follow the requirements set out by federal and state laws. Title VII of the Civil Rights Act of 1964 prohibits employers from discriminating against applicants based on their race, religion, color, sex, or national origin. The Americans with Disabilities Act of 1990 prohibits employers from discriminating against disabled applicants. The Civil Rights Act created the Equal Employment Opportunity Commission (EEOC) to investigate discrimination complaints. The EEOC also helps employers set up **affirmative action programs** to increase job opportunities for women, minorities, disabled people, and other protected groups. The Civil Rights Act of 1991 expanded the alternatives available to victims of employment discrimination by including the right to a jury trial, punitive damages, and damages for emotional distress. At the same time, opponents to such laws have launched initiatives to restrict affirmative action standards and protect employers against unnecessary litigation. In one instance, California voters passed a proposition that prohibits the state from granting hiring preferences to minorities.

Failure to comply with equal employment opportunity legislation can expose an employer to fines and other penalties, negative publicity, and poor employee morale. The EEOC files hundreds of cases each year, with damages paid by businesses in the tens of millions annually. For example, AK Steel Holding Corp. agreed to pay $600,000 to settle EEOC charges that it condoned a racially hostile work environment at its Butler, Pennsylvania, plant. Employees at the plant are also receiving annual training in equal employment opportunity policies.[9]

Increases in discrimination lawsuits have elevated the importance of human resource managers in the hiring process. To prevent violations, human resource personnel must train managers involved in interviewing to follow employment law. For example, the law prohibits an interviewer from asking an applicant any questions relating to marital status, number of children, race, nationality, religion, or age. Interviewers also may not ask questions about applicants' criminal records, mental illness histories, or alcohol-related problems. For more information about employment litigation issues, visit the Web sites of the Society for Human Resource Management (http://www.shrm.org) and the EEOC (http://www.eeoc.gov).

Employers must also observe various other legal restrictions governing hiring practices. Some firms try to screen out high-risk employees by requiring drug testing for job applicants, particularly in industries in which employees are responsible for public safety, such as airlines and other public transportation. But drug testing is controversial because of concerns about

"They Said It"

"Treat others as ends, never as means."

—Dag Hammerskjöld
(1905–1961) Former Secretary General of the United Nations

privacy. Also, positive test results may not accurately indicate drug use, and traces of legal drugs, such as prescribed medications, may chemically resemble traces of illegal substances. Another legal issue is the practice of requiring employees to use only English in the workplace, viewed by the EEOC as discrimination on the basis of national origin and a violation of the law unless the employer can demonstrate a legitimate reason for the policy.[10]

Recruitment and selection are expensive processes because firms incur costs for advertising job openings, interviewing applicants, and conducting background checks, employment tests, and medical exams. A bad hiring decision is even more expensive, though. A hiring mistake causes a firm to spend money to train and motivate a less-than-optimal employee, as well as risk the potential costs of poor decisions by that employee. Other costs resulting from a bad hiring decision may include lawsuits, unemployment compensation claims, recruiting and training a replacement, and reductions in productivity and employee morale. It is estimated that problem employees cost the U.S. economy $382 billion annually in lost productivity.[11]

To avoid the costly results of a bad hiring decision, many employers require applicants to complete employment tests. These tests help verify the skills that candidates list on their application forms or résumés to ensure that they meet the performance expectations of the job. A variety of tests is available to gauge applicants' knowledge of mechanical, technical, language, and computer skills. One example is the Wonderlic Basic Skills Test, which measures basic math and verbal skills. The Wonderlic, and others like it, are **cognitive ability tests,** which measure job candidates' abilities in perceptual speed, verbal comprehension, numerical aptitude, general reasoning, and spatial aptitude. In other words, these tests indicate how quickly and how well people understand words, numbers, and logic. Cognitive ability tests accurately predict job performance in almost all kinds of jobs. Why is this so? Because people with strong cognitive or mental abilities are usually good at learning new things, processing complex information, solving problems, and making decisions, and these abilities are important in almost all jobs. As a result, if you were allowed to use just one selection test, a cognitive ability test would be the one to use. The Wonderlic test is such an effective way to determine whom to hire that it has been administered to more than 120 million people and is even taken by National Football League draftees. Because football requires mental as well as physical ability, one of the many factors NFL teams use to determine which players to draft are scores on the Wonderlic administered at the scouting combine.[12] Although the scores don't predict success or failure in the NFL, many general managers think that, all other things being equal, they would prefer to draft a player with greater cognitive abilities.

Assessment Check ✓

1. What are some of the costs associated with recruitment and selection?

2. What key federal and state laws apply to recruitment and selection?

Orientation, Training, and Evaluation

Once hired, employees need information about what is expected of them and how well they are performing. Companies provide this information through orientation, training, and evaluation. A newly hired employee often completes an orientation program administered jointly by the human resource department and the department in which the employee will work. During orientation, employer representatives inform employees about company policies regarding their rights and benefits. Many organizations give new hires copies of employee manuals that describe benefits programs and working conditions and expectations. They also provide different types of training to ensure that employees get a good start at the company.

Training Programs

Employees are increasing their requests for training so that they can build skills and knowledge that will prepare them for new job opportunities. Training is also a good investment from the employer's perspective. A firm should view employee training as an ongoing process throughout each employee's tenure with the company. Companies such as Trilogy, which was mentioned earlier, make training a vital part of selecting and hiring employees, as well as developing their careers. And everyone who is hired at online shoe retailer Zappos.com, regardless of position, attends a four-week training program that exposes new employees to the company's history, culture, and philosophies. They work the phones to get to know customers and spend time in the company's Kentucky warehouse to learn the

© 1999–2009 Zappos.com, Inc.

All new hires, regardless of position, attend a four-week training program at online shoe retailer Zappos.com. On-the-job training can help unify a company, increase productivity, and retain valuable employees.

different shipping operations. According to CEO Tony Hsieh, the training program "gets everyone on the same page."[13]

ON-THE-JOB TRAINING One popular instructional method is **on-the-job training,** which prepares employees for job duties by allowing them to perform tasks under the guidance of experienced employees. At Nike, assistant brand manager Julian Duncan participated in a training program that rotated him through six marketing assignments in 24 months. The training program exposed Duncan to people throughout the company and to situations that helped him learn the terrain.[14] A variation of on-the-job training is apprenticeship training, in which an employee learns a job by serving for a time as an assistant to a trained worker. Patio Enclosures, a construction firm based in Ohio, made its employees more productive and more committed to the company by setting up an apprenticeship program. Apprenticeship programs are much more common in Europe than in the United States. While American apprenticeships usually focus on blue-collar trades—such as plumbing and heating services—in Europe, many new entrants to white-collar professions complete apprenticeships.

CLASSROOM AND COMPUTER-BASED TRAINING Off-the-job training involves some form of classroom instruction such as lectures, conferences, audiovisual aids, computer instruction, and special machines to teach employees everything from basic math and language skills to complex, highly skilled tasks. At Johnson Controls-Unitary Products, which designs and manufactures heating and air conditioning systems, territory managers complete five days of classroom training that includes instruction about providing information and selling to customers and understanding the business's different areas: finance, operations, marketing, and human resources.[15]

Many firms are replacing classroom training with computer-based training programs. These programs can save employers money by reducing travel costs and employee time away from work. Global management consulting and technology services company Accenture offers employees about 80 percent more training hours than competitors. Training is tailored to individual needs, and with 18,000 courses on its Internet-based training Web site, employees can create their own training and development plans and monitor their progress at their own pace.[16] In addition, computer-based training offers consistent presentations, because the training content won't vary with the quality of the instructor. Audio and visual capabilities help these systems simulate the work environment better than some classroom training could, and employees benefit from greater control over the learning process. They can learn at their own pace and convenience, and they generally do not have to wait for the company to schedule a class. Despite these advantages, firms also offer traditional classroom training because it usually provides more opportunities for employees to interact with the instructor and with one another. Some people learn better through human interaction, and some have difficulty completing a computer-based learning program on their own.

Off-the-job training frequently involves use of the Internet. The Web provides a convenient means of delivering text, audio, and video training materials to employees wherever they are located. Online training programs also can offer interactive learning, such as simulations in which employees see the results of their decisions. Buffalo, New York–based Delaware North Companies (DNC) is a hospitality and food services provider with 40,000 employees worldwide. DNC relied on executives and human resource managers to train new supervisors, with mixed results. To improve its process, the company rolled out a new program for its 3,000 managers and executives that delivers self-paced interactive training on the Web, followed by virtual classes. DNC is one of a growing number of firms turning to the Web to train employees in a variety of areas ranging from teamwork to ethics and other management skills.[17]

MANAGEMENT DEVELOPMENT A **management development program** provides training designed to improve the skills and broaden the knowledge of current and potential executives. As noted earlier, the share of the workforce in their mid-20s to mid-40s, who traditionally have been developing their management skills, is shrinking, and many members of the workforce in their 60s are approaching retirement age. Without the luxury of developing executive talent slowly over the years, organizations instead must provide programs that help managers quickly learn how to lead a fast-moving company through turbulent times.

The content of management development programs may involve reviews of issues facing the company, as well as *benchmarking,* or learning the best practices of the best companies so they can serve as performance standards. The teachers may be the company's own executives. At other times, managers may be encouraged to receive counseling from an outside management coach, who helps them improve their skills.

Despite the importance of training talented employees for managerial jobs, many companies are searching for new hires to fill gaps in their executive ranks because they dropped the ball on developing future managers. A survey conducted by the Society for Human Resource Management found that 60 percent of the responding companies have no management succession plan of any kind. Employees who lack guidance and the development programs necessary to advance as managers are more likely to quit and look for a job elsewhere, even during an economic downturn.[18] So, organizations must identify individuals with the talent and desire to advance and develop their skills to keep them.

Performance Appraisals

Organizations also help employees improve their performance by providing feedback about their past performance. A **performance appraisal** is an evaluation of an employee's job performance that compares actual results with desired outcomes. Based on this evaluation, managers make objective decisions about compensation, promotions, additional training needs, transfers, or terminations. Rating employees' performance and communicating perceptions of their strengths and weaknesses are important elements in improving a firm's effectiveness, productivity, or profits. Government agencies, not-for-profit organizations, and academic institutions also conduct performance appraisals. Experts suggest that performance appraisals should be

performance appraisal evaluation of an employee's job performance that compares actual results with desired outcomes.

Employees value face-to-face feedback on their performance. Evaluations that are fair and consistent can improve an organization's productivity and profitability.

© iStockphoto

administered at least once a year, but a large human resource study found that workers are more satisfied with a frequency of three to four evaluations per year and that they value written, as well as face-to-face, feedback.[19]

Some firms conduct peer reviews, in which employees assess the performance of coworkers, while other firms ask employees to review their supervisors and managers. One type of performance appraisal is the **360-degree performance review,** a process that gathers feedback from a review panel of 8 to 12 people, including coworkers, supervisors, team members, subordinates, and sometimes customers. The idea is to get as much frank feedback from as many perspectives as possible. However, this approach to performance appraisal tends to generate considerable work for both employees and managers—each of whom may have to review 20 or more people—and volumes of paperwork. Fortunately, though, companies such as Halogen Software offer computer programs that automate the procedures and paperwork associated with 360-degree feedback.[20] A potential weakness of 360-degree performance reviews is that because the evaluations are anonymous, staff members might try to use the system to their advantage in personal disputes.

Regardless of the method used to evaluate job performance, to be effective it must be fair and consistent. Some managers are "hard" raters of performance, some "easy," and others fall in the middle. You probably have had the same experience with the grading standards of instructors. A study of nearly 6,000 employees reporting to two managers conducted by Personnel Decisions International (PDI) found that the majority of these employees received inconsistent performance ratings; employees rated outstanding by one manager received a lower rating from the other manager 62 percent of the time.[21] This lack of consistency is perceived by workers as unfair and has an adverse impact on the organization. Some companies are turning to the practice of *calibration* to ensure performance appraisals remain consistent across managers. This process involves face-to-face meetings that include the individuals responsible for conducting performance appraisals and the manager to whom they report, as well as a human resource person to facilitate the meeting. Involving these individuals not only ensures fairness in the appraisal process but also helps managers identify future managerial talent.

Assessment Check

1. Describe some aids in on-the-job training.
2. What is a management development program?
3. What is the main way an organization provides employees with feedback about their performance?

Compensation

Human resource managers work to develop an equitable compensation system spanning wages and salaries plus benefits. Because human resource costs represent a sizable percentage of any firm's total product costs, excessive wage rates may make its goods and services too expensive to compete effectively in the marketplace. Inadequate wages, however, lead to difficulty in attracting qualified people, high turnover rates, poor morale, and inefficient production. One of the common denominators of *Fortune* magazine's list of "The 100 Best Companies to Work For" is a very good compensation package. For instance, an ambitious management trainee at Four Seasons Hotels and Resorts can become a general manager in a dozen years, earning $200,000 to $300,000 annually.[22] In recent years, shareholders and business experts have sometimes viewed the compensation of executives as excessive and called for CEO pay to be linked more closely to the company's performance, an issue described in the "Hit & Miss" feature.

The terms *wages* and *salary* are often used interchangeably but are different. **Wages** represent compensation based on an hourly pay rate or the amount of output produced. Firms

wage compensation based on an hourly pay rate or the amount of output produced.

Hit & Miss

The Good, Bad, and Ugly of Executive Pay

One of Barack Obama's first actions as president was to sign into law an economic stimulus package. The legislation directed $787 billion of taxpayer money to a wide array of programs to boost the faltering U.S. economy. Some of that money will help prop up struggling banks and financial firms on Wall Street. Executives at those institutions are used to—and demand—huge compensation packages and multimillion-dollar bonuses. That may be fine when their firms are raking in profits. The problem is that they have received the fat paychecks despite steep financial losses. Such compensation practices had already drawn public outrage a few months before. After former President Bush's Troubled Assets Relief Program (TARP) doled out billions of dollars to ailing U.S. banks, some of those firms continued to pay out a near-record total of $18 billion in executive bonuses. Four top executives at Merrill Lynch & Co., for instance, took home $121 million among them.

Congress reacted to taxpayer criticism by enacting new rules. Top executives and the most highly paid employees at firms receiving government assistance must accept limits on their cash bonuses. Lavish severance packages—called "golden parachutes"—are banned, and shareholders must vote on executive pay. Congress is also reviewing bonuses already paid to executives at TARP recipients and negotiating reimbursement, known as "clawbacks," of those it thinks are "inconsistent with the purposes" of the plan.

How ugly did the picture get? Profit at SunTrust Banks had dropped by half, along with its stock price, but the board of directors approved a 75 percent increase in total compensation, including stock options, for CEO James Wells, bringing his package to $8.1 million. Merrill Lynch CEO John Thain was fired after Bank of America bought his firm and discovered underreported losses in the billions of dollars there. But just before the merger was completed, Merrill distributed $4 billion in executive bonuses, and Thain completed a $1.22 million renovation of his private office.

On the flip side, General Electric CEO Jeffrey Immelt declined a 2008 bonus and millions in performance awards because of the company's falling profits. Morgan Stanley CEO John Mack took no bonuses for 2007 or 2008 because the company's stock price had declined even though it made a profit. Aflac announced its CEO, Daniel Amos, would forgo a bonus of nearly $3 million, and its chief financial officer trimmed his award by over a third. Top executives at ailing Ford Motor Company opted to cut their pay 30 percent, and members of the automaker's board of directors refused cash compensation for 2009.

Of his colleagues' big rewards amid massive losses, Morgan Stanley's John Mack said, "Executive compensation is something that without question has gotten out of hand, and we need to fix it."

Questions for Critical Thinking

1. Some critics of the proposed changes in executive compensation argue that reducing performance rewards will encourage talented managers to go elsewhere. Do you think this is a valid objection to pay limits? Why or why not?

2. Do you think shareholders should have input on the size of compensation packages for CEOs? Why or why not?

Sources: Nick Bunkley, "Ford Executives Cut Own Pay 30% for 2 Years," *The New York Times,* February 25, 2009, http://www.nytimes.com; "Thain Arrives at Cuomo's Office for Merrill Bonus Question," *CNN Money*, February 24, 2009, http://money.cnn.com; Del Jones, "SunTrust Board OK'd a 75% Raise in CEO's Compensation," *USA Today*, February 24, 2009, http://www.usatoday.com; "Aflac CEO to Forgo $2.8 Million Bonus," *USA Today*, February 24, 2009, http://www.usatoday.com; Christine Harper, "Morgan Stanley's Mack Sees Some Businesses Curtailed," *Bloomberg News*, February 23, 2009, http://www.bloomberg.com; Matthew Benjamin, "Geithner May Have Little Leeway on Executive Compensation Rules," *Bloomberg News*, February 20, 2009, http://www.bloomberg.com; Stephen Manning, "General Electric CEO Declines Bonus for 2008," *Associated Press*, February 19, 2009, http://www.google.com; Maria Bartiromo, "Nell Minow on Outrageous CEO Pay—and Who's to Blame," *BusinessWeek*, February 19, 2009, http://www.businessweek.com; Jonathan Stempel and Elinor Comlay, "Thain Ousted from Bank of America Amid Losses," Reuters, January 22, 2009, http://news.yahoo.com.

pay wages to production employees, maintenance workers, and sometimes retail salespeople. **Salaries** represent compensation calculated periodically, such as weekly or monthly. Office personnel, executives, and professional employees usually receive salaries.

salary compensation calculated on a periodic basis, such as weekly or monthly.

An effective compensation system should attract well-qualified workers, keep them satisfied in their jobs, and inspire them to succeed. Most firms base their compensation policies on the following five factors:

1. salaries and wages paid by other companies that compete for the same people

2. government legislation, including the federal, state, or local minimum wage

3. the cost of living
4. the firm's ability to pay
5. worker productivity.

Figure 9.3

Four Forms of Incentive Compensation

Profit Sharing Bonus based on company profits	**Gain Sharing** Bonus based on productivity gains, cost savings, or quality improvements
Lump-Sum Bonus One-time cash payment or option to buy shares of company stock based on performance	**Pay for Knowledge** Salary increase based on learning new job tasks

Many employers balance rewarding workers with maintaining profits by linking more of their pay to superior performance. They try to motivate employees to excel by offering some type of incentive compensation in addition to salaries or wages. Today, almost one-tenth of the compensation of salaried workers is some form of variable pay. These programs include the following:

- profit sharing, which awards bonuses based on company profits
- gain sharing, when companies share the financial value of productivity gains, cost savings, or quality improvements with their workers
- lump-sum bonuses and stock options, which reward one-time cash payments and the right to purchase stock in the company based on performance
- pay for knowledge, which distributes wage or salary increases as employees learn new job tasks.

Figure 9.3 summarizes the four types of incentive compensation programs.

Employee Benefits

employee benefits
rewards such as retirement plans, health insurance, vacation, and tuition reimbursement provided for employees either entirely or in part at the company's expense.

In addition to wages and salaries, firms provide benefits to employees and their families as part of their compensation. **Employee benefits,** such as retirement plans, health and disability insurance, sick leave, child care and elder care, and tuition reimbursement, are paid entirely or in part at the company's expense. Benefits represent a large component of an employee's total compensation. Although wages and salaries account for around 70 percent of the typical employee's earnings, the other 30 percent takes the form of employee benefits.[23]

Historically, many companies have picked up most of the tab for healthcare benefits, with employees paying little of the cost. However, with costs increasing nearly 15 percent per year, employers are requiring employees to pay a larger share of their healthcare benefits. Companies, such as GE, Halliburton, and IBM, have placed caps on what they will pay for employee and retiree health benefits. After the caps are reached, individuals are responsible for the remaining costs.

Some companies have begun providing incentives to encourage employees to remain healthy. Workers at many companies have the benefit of on-site fitness facilities. Some of the best include SAS Institute, which has everything from a pool to a putting green; employees can have their dry cleaning done while working out. The gym at Goldman Sachs offers rock climbing and massage therapy. Workers at eBay have access to full-time certified trainers and nutritionists.[24] Other employers provide incentives for employees to stay in shape. Currently, Chicago police officers earn $250 annually if they pass a yearly physical fitness test.[25]

Some benefits are required by law. U.S. firms are required to make Social Security and Medicare contributions, as well as payments to state unemployment insurance and workers' compensation programs, which

Ann Heisenfelt/© AP/Wide World Photos

Benefits like on-site fitness facilities improve both the company's health and that of employees. This public relations manager is working out at General Mills, named one of the 100 best companies for working mothers.

SHOULD PAID SICK LEAVE BE REQUIRED BY LAW?

The United States is the only one of the world's major economic powers that does not require employers to provide paid sick days. Advocates say the country should follow the lead of other developed nations and make paid sick days a basic labor standard.

U.S. businesses voluntarily provide paid sick days for about 52 percent of employees. That means about 59 million American workers, mostly in entry-level or low-paid jobs, do not get even one paid day off to stay home when they are sick. For them, missing work means lost wages and sometimes a reprimand or dismissal. Many employees who are sick show up at work anyway. In one study, 77 percent of the respondents said they go to the office when they are sick, hampering their performance and exposing coworkers to illnesses like the flu. Employees without paid sick leave also take their children to school or day care, which spreads illnesses to other children. They also jeopardize the public health, because employees who don't have paid sick days often work in service industries: hotels, restaurants, healthcare facilities, and child care centers.

Proponents are pushing for mandatory sick-day laws on the state and federal levels. One measure would require companies with 15 or more employees to provide seven paid sick days a year for people who work at least 20 hours each week.

Should employers be forced to provide paid sick leave?

PRO

1. Paid sick days are a human right; employees without that benefit must choose between their incomes and their health.
2. Paid sick days could reduce costs for employers by increasing productivity, stopping the spread of illnesses like the flu in the workplace, and reducing turnover.

CON

1. Employers can provide only so much in benefits. When government mandates a specific benefit like paid sick leave, businesses must respond by cutting other types of benefits.
2. An increase in per-employee costs, especially in companies that employ a large number of entry-level workers, can reduce company profits. Employers are forced to cut hours, lay people off, or even go out of business.

Summary

Those who want paid sick leave say it's a matter of economic justice; the policy would benefit mostly low-income and minority workers, many of whom are in the hospitality and food-service industries (85 percent of food-service workers have no paid sick days). They say employers also will benefit by boosting productivity and reducing costly turnover. One proponent says companies will save about $8 billion annually. Opponents say that less-skilled, lower-paid workers are the ones who would most likely lose jobs through employer cost-cutting. According to one estimate, seven paid sick days would increase per-employee costs by up to 5 percent a year. Businesses that already provide paid time off (PTO) also oppose the legislation, which would add seven days to companies' existing PTO benefits, unless their policies specifically designate paid sick days. That requirement would force some employers to redesign their flexible PTO plans because many provide paid leave without distinguishing between sick days and days taken for other reasons.

Sources: "Mandated Paid Sick Leave a Bad Move," *Marquette Tribune*, February 10, 2009, http://media.marquettetribune.org; Christine Vestal, "Sick Day Blues," *Lexington Herald-Leader,* February 27, 2008, p. B8; Jeffrey Pfeffer, "It's Time to Live Up to Family Values," *Business 2.0,* October 2007, p. 54; Mark Schoeff Jr., "Paid Sick Leave Mandate Raises Employer Ire," *Workforce Management,* September 10, 2007, p. 6; Richard Berman, "A Sickening Amount of Ignorance," *Retailing Today,* August 13, 2007, p. 9.

Solving an ETHICAL controversy

protect workers in case of job-related injuries or illnesses. The Family and Medical Leave Act of 1993 requires covered employers to offer up to 12 weeks of unpaid, job-protected leave to eligible employees. Firms voluntarily provide other employee benefits, such as child care and health insurance, to help them attract and retain employees. California is the first state to make paid family leave into law.[26] As the "Solving an Ethical Controversy" feature discusses, some advocates are pressing state and federal lawmakers to require businesses to provide paid sick leave, a move many employers oppose.

Pensions and other retirement plans have been another area of concern for U.S. companies. Some companies have reduced the amount of matching contributions they will make to workers' **401(k) plans,** retirement savings plans to which employees can make pretax contributions to retirement accounts. Some companies have been cutting back on cash contributions to their employees' plans and are contributing company stock instead. Four Seasons Hotels and Resorts contributes 3 percent of each employee's salary to a 401(k) and another 3 to 5 percent in profit sharing.[27]

Flexible Benefits

In response to the increased diversity of the workplace, human resource managers are developing creative ways to tailor their benefit plans to the varying needs of employees. One approach sets up **flexible benefit plans,** also called *cafeteria plans.* Such a benefit system offers employees a range of options from which they can choose, including different types of medical insurance, dental and vision plans, and life and disability insurance. This flexibility allows one working spouse to choose his or her firm's generous medical coverage for the entire family, and the other spouse can allocate benefit dollars to purchasing other types of coverage. Typically, each employee receives a set allowance (called *flex dollars* or *credits*) to pay for purchases from the benefits menu. A healthy, single employee might choose to allocate fewer flex dollars to health insurance, say, by choosing a higher deductible, and put more flex dollars toward an optional dental or vision plan. By contrast, an older employee might earmark some flex dollars to pay for elder care for aging parents.

Contributions to cafeteria accounts are commonly made by both the employee and employer. Cafeteria plans also offer tax benefits to both employees and employers. Employee contributions are made using so-called *pretax dollars,* meaning that employees don't pay taxes on their contributions. Also, employers don't have to pay unemployment taxes or Social Security and Medicare taxes on the amount deducted from employee paychecks. Molson Coors Brewing allows employees to trade holidays—to buy or sell up to five days per year—and offers flexible working policies such as sabbatical leaves.[28]

Another way of increasing the flexibility of employee benefits involves time off from work. Instead of establishing set numbers of holidays, vacation days, and sick days, some employers give each employee a bank of **paid time off (PTO).** Employees use days from their PTO accounts without having to explain why they need the time. According to a study by the Alexander Hamilton Institute (AHI), about 56 percent of the companies surveyed use PTO programs; more than half of them claim they have reduced unscheduled absences. Other benefits cited include easier record keeping, less confusion among employees, and better recruiting and retention.[29] Banner Health, a healthcare provider in seven Western states including Alaska, provides PTO hours for eligible employees. Hours can be used for sick days, vacation time, holidays, bereavement, doctor's appointments, and personal time. Hours can also be donated to other employees in need. Banner Health allows employees to cash out earned PTO days and pays remaining PTO balances upon termination of employment, a policy adopted by most companies using PTO accounts.[30]

Flexible Work

Another part of the trend toward responsiveness to employee needs is the option of **flexible work plans.** Flexible work plans are benefits that allow employees to adjust their working hours and places of work to accommodate their personal needs. Flexible work plan options include flextime, compressed workweeks, job sharing, and home-based work. By implementing these benefit programs, employers have reduced employee turnover and absenteeism and boosted productivity and job satisfaction.

Flextime is a scheduling system that allows employees to set their own work hours within constraints specified by the firm. Rather than requiring everyone to work the regular work hours of 8 a.m. to 5 p.m., an employer may require employees to be at work between the core hours of 10 a.m. and 3 p.m. Outside the core hours, employees can choose when to start and end their workdays, opting either to arrive at work early, say at 6 a.m., and leave early, or to arrive later and work later. Flextime works well in jobs in which employees can work relatively independently, but not so well when they must work together in teams, such as in manufacturing, or when they must provide direct customer service. The practice is common in European countries; an estimated 40 percent of the Swiss workforce and 25 percent of German workers have flextime schedules. Growing numbers of U.S. firms are offering flextime, and increasing numbers of employees are taking advantage of this benefit. Ivy Exec, a New York job board, matches screened professionals and graduates from top universities with flexible jobs. Cofounder Elena Bajic notes that "the new generations coming into the work force are going to demand" flexibility.[31]

Even hospitals, where work takes place around the clock and for longer shifts than normal, are embracing flexible scheduling for nurses. With the help of programs from BidShift, a San Diego company that specializes in Internet-based scheduling software, the logistic problems of flexible scheduling are solved. BidShift's programs allow managers to post schedules online, where employees log in and request certain shifts or schedule changes. BidShift and similar products offered by other organizations have been introduced into hundreds of hospitals in recent years. The University of Southern California in Los Angeles uses BidShift's ShiftRewards program to award nurses for offering to take an extra shift or signing up early for a shift; a shift on Mother's Day earns more points than on a typical weekday. Points can be redeemed for a range of awards.[32]

The **compressed workweek** is a scheduling option that allows employees to work the regular number of weekly hours in fewer than the typical five days. Employees might work four 10-hour days and then have three days off each week. Such arrangements not only reduce the number of hours employees spend commuting each week but can stretch out the company's overall workday, providing more availability to customers in other time zones. Hospitals, police and fire departments, and airlines often offer work schedules that allow several long days matched by several days off. According to Ed Cooney, Macy's senior vice president of human resources, employees value benefits like flextime and compressed workweeks second only to pay and health insurance. Cooney rates these types of benefits as inexpensive to offer and help retain talented employees when their children are young, their parents require care, or they face other personal demands. These work options also increase loyalty and reduce absenteeism, according to Cooney. Forty percent of Macy's employees are on a compressed workweek schedule.[33]

A **job sharing program** allows two or more employees to divide the tasks of one job. This plan appeals to a growing number of people who prefer to work part-time rather than full-time—such as older workers, students, working parents, and people of all ages who want to devote time to personal interests or leisure—so companies are offering this option and even suggest these arrangements to help attract and retain valuable employees. Job

A two-career couple heads for the day care center and work. Many employees use flextime to mesh their work schedules with opening and closing times at schools and day care programs.

Ryan McVay/Photodisc/Alamy

sharing requires a high degree of cooperation and communication between the partners, but it can let a company benefit from the talents of people who do not want to work full-time. A successful job sharing arrangement requires partners who work well together, ongoing communication, and dedication to making the partnership work. Physicians Jessica Whitley and Amanda Lenhard have done just that. Together they work seven days on, followed by seven days off, as physicians who specialize in the care of hospitalized patients at Lake West Hospital in Willoughby, Ohio. Job sharing is relatively uncommon for physicians because of the personal contact involved. Both wives and mothers, Whitley and Lenhard make it work with an open communication style, a cooperative attitude, respect for each other, and flexibility.[34]

A *home-based work program* allows employees to perform their jobs from home instead of at the workplace. Home-based workers are sometimes called *teleworkers* or **telecommuters** because many "commute" to work via telephones, e-mail, computers, and fax machines. Working from home has great appeal to employees with disabilities, older workers, and parents with small children. Because telecommuters work with minimal supervision, they need to be self-disciplined and reliable employees. They also need managers who are comfortable with setting goals and managing from afar.

With the advent of high-speed Internet connections, millions of Americans are telecommuting from their homes, and the number continues to rise. According to studies conducted by IDC, a Framingham, Massachusetts–based marketing research firm, nearly 75 percent of the U.S. workforce will soon have the ability to telecommute from home—or almost anywhere else. Telecommuting is especially appealing to the younger generation of workers who value flexibility and have a higher comfort level with technology.[35] Between 6 and 10 percent of Hewlett-Packard's 68,000 U.S. employees telecommute from home or some other remote location. CEO Lew Platt believes that telework helps HP recruit and retain high-tech employees.[36]

Flexible work is critical in attracting and keeping talented human resources. More than 70 percent of Generation Y professionals—those just entering the workforce—are concerned with balancing career with personal life. This is placing increasing pressure on companies to offer options like job sharing, compressed workweeks, and telecommuting.[37] Employees who work for companies without a flexible plan may be successful in requesting one. The "Business Etiquette" feature outlines how.

Assessment Check

1. Explain the difference between *wage* and *salary*.
2. What is another name for a *cafeteria plan*?
3. What types of organizations typically use a compressed workweek?

Employee Separation

Employee separation is a broad term covering the loss of an employee for any reason, voluntary or involuntary. It also includes businesses' efforts to control the cost of their workforces, such as downsizing or outsourcing.

Voluntary and Involuntary Turnover

Either employer or employee can decide to terminate employment. *Voluntary turnover* occurs when employees leave firms to start their own businesses, take jobs with other firms, move to another city, or retire. Some firms ask employees who leave voluntarily to participate in *exit interviews* to find out why they decided to leave. These interviews give employers a chance to learn about problems in the workplace, such as unreasonable supervisors or unfair work practices. Because of recruitment and replacement costs, as well as lost productivity, the best companies actively work to minimize turnover by creating a positive work environment, training

Business Etiquette

How to Ask for a Flexible Work Schedule

Flexible work plans are the benefit jackpot for many employees. With them, dependable, disciplined workers can perform their jobs well *and* take care of children or elderly parents, see soccer games, volunteer, run errands, or avoid commuting in rush hour. For younger employees, having a schedule that permits them to spend more time with their families is one of the most important factors in choosing a job. Employers gain, too, as flexible setups contribute to employee wellness, job satisfaction, loyalty, and retention of valued employees. If your employer hasn't offered this benefit, you could ask for one. Here are some tips:

1. Rate your performance. If it isn't outstanding, focus on improving before asking for special consideration. "Flextime is an accommodation, not an entitlement," says one recruiting firm CEO. "Slackers and clock-watchers won't get the benefit of the doubt."

2. Research other departments in your company. Other successes with flexible work schedules could help convince your boss to try it. Also look at employers in your area and your industry for success stories.

3. Join forces with coworkers who might also benefit from flexible scheduling. You'll gain strength in numbers if you work together on a proposal.

4. Make a plan. List the tasks you can perform off-site. Write down when you will be out of the office and how you will maintain communication. Be ready to compromise. You may need to share your office space with others or choose a day other than Friday for your time away from the workplace.

5. If you're concerned that working away from the office will reduce your chance for promotion, plan to go in for most of the workweek. Working from home on one or two days or going to the office other than the usual 9 to 5 may make all the difference in your life.

6. Think of the benefits your plan will provide for you and your company. Figure out why your boss might say no and think of ways to counter these arguments.

7. Write a formal proposal describing your plan and the benefits for you and your boss. Address the possible opposing reasons. Present the proposal in writing, so your boss can take your proposal to the next management level, if needed.

8. In your proposal and any discussion, be upbeat about your work. Instead of saying, "I just can't take the long commute anymore," explain how working from home will give you more time to devote to work and less stress, because you won't be sitting in a car for hours each day.

9. Suggest a trial period and outline ways to measure the success of your plan. Managers may be more comfortable if there is an option for stopping the arrangement.

10. If your request is turned down, ask for feedback and a time frame for looking at the issue again. Go back with a positive attitude.

Sources: "How to Build Your Confidence to Ask," *WorkOptions*, http://workoptions.com, accessed March 10, 2009; Jeff Stimpson, "The New Equilibrium: Work/Life Balance," *The Practical Accountant,* February 2008, pp. 16–25; Tory Johnson, "Flex Your Choices," *Incentive,* January 2008, p. 52; Jeffrey Pfeffer, "It's Time to Live Up to Family Values," *Business 2.0,* October 2007, p. 54; Robery Carey, "Striking a Balance," *Successful Meetings,* October 2007, pp. 24–28.

bosses to be good managers, and offering competitive compensation and benefits. When scheduled bus operator National Express noticed it was experiencing high turnover, it discovered that a lack of employee benefits was the main cause. The company added a wide array of benefits, including a cash-based loyalty award, discounted travel, and on-site health checks. So far, turnover has fallen from 50 percent to 27 percent.[38]

Some turnover is the result of environmental factors and is difficult to minimize. Microsoft, for instance, had to lay off employees for the first time in its history, as the "Hit & Miss" feature describes. During the recent weakening economy, some Silicon Valley start-ups found employees gravitating to larger companies they thought could better withstand an economic downturn. Workers switching

Hit & Miss

Microsoft's Misses Force First Layoffs

Microsoft recently announced the first significant employee layoffs in its history. It had plenty of company; other big tech companies like Intel, Dell, and Advanced Micro Devices are also feeling the pinch of recession. "Our financial position is solid," CEO Steve Ballmer told employees. But "consumers and businesses have reined in spending, which is affecting PC shipments and IT expenditures." Microsoft's quarterly profit was more than half a billion dollars less than the same quarter a year before, and the company expected revenues to be lower than normal for the rest of the year.

Some part of the decline, and the company's lowered share price, did reflect an economy-wide slowdown. But the layoffs—cuts of up to 5,000 jobs, or 5 percent of the company's workforce—were widely attributed to problems and missteps by the Redmond, Washington, firm. The growing popularity of small and inexpensive netbook computers hurt sales of Microsoft's operating system. Less powerful than PCs, netbooks cannot accommodate the firm's Vista software, so it must substitute the older, more compact Windows XP operating system. It loses money by selling XP at a discount to compete with free open-source software from Linux.

Vista, said to be plagued with problems, hasn't gained traction with PC customers either. "Windows Vista didn't do well," said one industry observer. "Based on our data, a lot of clients are skipping Windows Vista." Some are even skipping new PC purchases altogether or postponing them. Corporate clients are following suit. Over a third of Microsoft's PC software revenue comes from renewable corporate subscriptions to its operating systems like Vista and XP, but budget cuts among its clients mean fewer profitable renewals for the firm.

Other drags on Microsoft's profitability include its less-than-successful attempts to enter new markets like Web search, where it lags behind Google, and so-called cloud computing, which delivers software via the Internet and competes with Microsoft Office. The firm also lost market share to Apple, which successfully expanded into the cell phone market and continues to deliver innovative laptops. Summing up these problems, Ballmer said, "We are certainly in the midst of a once-in-a-lifetime set of economic conditions."

In addition to the layoffs, Microsoft is cutting its travel and marketing budgets, shutting down production at some plants, and postponing new acquisitions. Expensive but morale-boosting employee perks like free snacks and shuttle buses will remain, however. Ballmer admits the company may not bounce back quickly and that profits and revenues may continue below expectations for some time. "Our model is not for a quick rebound," he said. "Our model is things go down, and then they reset. The economy shrinks."

The firm is taking up to 18 months to eliminate the 5,000 jobs in stages and does plan to make hundreds of new hires, particularly in the area of Internet search, for future competitiveness.

Questions for Critical Thinking

1. What might be the impact on current and future employees of Microsoft's large and staggered layoff? How can the firm minimize any negative effects?
2. Do you think any of the layoffs could have been avoided? If yes, how, and if not, why not?

Sources: Franklin Paul and Bill Rigby, "Microsoft Stuns with Profit Miss, Job Cuts," Reuters, January 22, 2009, http://news.yahoo.com; Ashlee Vance, "Microsoft Slashes Jobs as Sales Fall," *The New York Times*, January 22, 2009, http://www.nytimes.com; Tom Sullivan, "Vista Main Culprit in Microsoft Layoffs," *InfoWorld*, January 22, 2009, http://www.infoworld.com; Ina Fried, "Where Will Microsoft Cut?" *CNET News*, January 20, 2009, http://news.cnet.com.

---

to large companies appear more likely to hold onto their jobs, at least for the time being.[39] As the working population in the United States and abroad is aging, many organizations are concerned about the skills and knowledge that is being lost. According to the HRfocus Aging Workforce Survey, the best way to retain these older workers is, by far, the use of part-time or flextime programs.[40]

Involuntary turnover occurs when employers terminate employees because of poor job performance, negative attitudes toward work and coworkers, or misconduct such as dishonesty or sexual harassment. Terminating poor performers is necessary because they lower productivity and employee morale. Coworkers resent employees who receive the same pay and benefits as they do without contributing fairly to the company's work. But employers need to carefully document reasons when terminating employees. Protests against wrongful dismissal are often involved in complaints filed by the EEOC or by lawsuits brought by fired employees.

Interestingly, one study reported that involuntary turnover of senior managers is about 7.5 percent when the CEO is stable. With a new CEO from inside the company, involuntary turnover jumps to 12.5 percent; turnover reaches 26 percent with a new CEO from outside the company.[41]

Downsizing

During the early years of the 21st century, employers terminated thousands of employees, including many middle managers, through downsizing. **Downsizing** is the process of reducing the number of employees within a firm by eliminating jobs. Many downsizing firms have reduced their workforces by offering early retirement plans, voluntary severance programs, and opportunities for internal reassignment to different jobs. Employers who value their employees have helped them find jobs with other companies and set up job counseling centers.

Companies downsize for many reasons. The two most common objectives of downsizing are to cut overhead costs and streamline the organizational structure. A lean economy caused music firm EMI to announce sweeping job cuts, a move that angered employees and artists.[42] A slowing economy generally means fewer jobs are created and more downsizing occurs, according to John Challenger, CEO of Challenger, Gray, and Christmas, an outplacement consulting firm. Challenger notes that in those times, human resource executives must adjust their focus to programs that develop and retain people rather than attracting new people.[43]

While some firms report improvements in profits, market share, employee productivity, quality, and customer service after downsizing, studies show that downsizing doesn't guarantee those improvements. Why? A big reason is that eliminating jobs through downsizing can have devastating effects on employee morale. Workers who remain after a downsizing worry about job security and become angry when they have to work harder for the same pay. As commitment to their jobs and their firms weakens, many employees will leave to seek employment offering greater job security. In general, corporate downsizing has encouraged employees to put individual career success before employer loyalty, which has declined in the last two decades.

Employee surveys reveal that many workers are more interested in career security than job security. Specifically, the typical employee may seek training to improve the skills needed for the next job. People are willing to work hard at their current jobs, but they also want to share in the success of their companies in the form of pay-for-performance and stock options. For human resource managers, the new employee–employer relationship requires developing continuous training and learning programs for employees.

Outsourcing

In their continuing efforts to remain competitive against domestic and international rivals, a growing number of firms hold down costs by evolving into leaner organizations. Functions that were performed previously by company employees may be contracted to other firms, a practice called **outsourcing.** Outsourcing began on a small scale, with firms contracting out services such as maintenance, cleaning, and delivery. Services commonly outsourced today include housekeeping; architectural design; grounds, building, utility, and furniture maintenance; food service; security; and relocation services. Today, outsourcing has expanded to include outside contracting of many tasks once considered fundamental internal functions.

Outsourcing complements today's focus on business competitiveness and flexibility. It allows a firm to continue performing the functions it does best, while hiring other companies to do tasks that they can handle more competently and cost effectively. Another benefit of outsourcing is the firm's ability to negotiate the best price among competing bidders and the chance to avoid the long-term

downsizing process of reducing the number of employees within a firm by eliminating jobs.

"They Said It"

"No passion so effectively robs the mind of all its power of acting and reasoning as fear."

—Edmund Burke (1729–1797) English statesman, orator, and writer

outsourcing contracting with another business to perform tasks or functions previously handled by internal staff members.

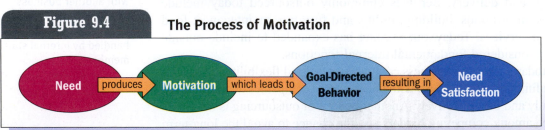

resource costs associated with in-house operations. Firms that outsource also gain flexibility to change vendors at the end of contract periods if they desire. The key to successful outsourcing is a strong commitment by both parties to form a partnership from which each derives benefits. Southwest Airlines is reconsidering some of its operating plans, including outsourcing maintenance overseas, following highly publicized maintenance lapses. Southwest outsources 60 percent of its maintenance domestically, but none overseas. Other airlines outsource maintenance to places like El Salvador, although mechanics unions generally oppose this practice.[44]

Motivating Employees

Employee motivation is the key to effective management. And motivation starts with good employee morale. **Morale** is the mental attitude of employees toward their employer and jobs. It involves a sense of common purpose among the members of work groups and throughout the organization as a whole. High morale is a sign of a well-managed organization because workers' attitudes toward their jobs affect the quality of their work. One of the most obvious signs of poor manager–worker relations is poor morale. It lurks behind absenteeism, employee turnover, and strikes. It shows up in falling productivity and rising employee grievances.

In contrast, high employee morale occurs in organizations in which employees feel valued and heard and can contribute what they do best. This climate reinforces a human tendency—that people perform best when they believe they are capable of succeeding. High morale also results from an organization's understanding of human needs and its success at satisfying those needs in ways that reinforce organizational goals.

Each person is motivated to take action designed to satisfy needs. A need is simply a lack of some useful benefit. It reflects a gap between an individual's actual state and his or her desired state. A motive is an inner state that directs a person toward the goal of satisfying a felt need. Once the need—the gap between where a person is now and where he or she wants to be—becomes important enough, it produces tension. The individual is then moved—the root word for *motive*—to reduce the tension and return to a condition of equilibrium. Figure 9.4 depicts the principle behind this process. A need produces a motivation, which leads to goal-directed behavior, resulting in need satisfaction.

Generally speaking, managers use rewards and punishments to motivate employees. *Extrinsic rewards* are external to the work itself, such as pay, fringe benefits, and praise. *Intrinsic rewards* are related directly to performing the job and include feeling good about achieving a goal or about being able to make job-related decisions without consulting a supervisor. *Punishment* involves giving an undesirable consequence for a particular behavior. For instance, a supervisor may punish a frequently tardy worker by docking that person's pay for the time missed. Both types of rewards produce higher levels of performance than punishment does. To motivate workers intrinsically, managers could create more interesting jobs or allow workers greater control over their work. To motivate workers extrinsically, managers might explore new alternative compensation programs such as accumulation of paid time off rather than overtime or encourage promotion from within. Now we turn our attention to some of the traditional theories of motivation.

Figure 9.4 The Process of Motivation

Need → *produces* → Motivation → *which leads to* → Goal-Directed Behavior → *resulting in* → Need Satisfaction

Maslow's Hierarchy of Needs Theory

The studies of psychologist Abraham H. Maslow suggest how employers can motivate employees. **Maslow's hierarchy of needs** has become a widely accepted list of human needs based on these important assumptions:

- People's needs depend on what they already possess.

- A satisfied need is not a motivator; only needs that remain unsatisfied can influence behavior.

- People's needs are arranged in a hierarchy of importance; once they satisfy one need, at least partially, another emerges and demands satisfaction.

In his theory, Maslow proposed that all people have basic needs such as hunger and protection that they must satisfy before they can consider higher-order needs such as social relationships or self-worth. He identified five types of needs:

1. *Physiological needs.* These basic human needs include food, shelter, and clothing. In the workplace, employers satisfy these needs by paying salaries and wages and establishing comfortable working environments.

2. *Safety needs.* These needs refer to desires for physical and economic protection. Employers satisfy these needs by providing benefits such as retirement plans, job security, and safe workplaces.

3. *Social (belongingness) needs.* People want to be accepted by family and other individuals and groups. At work, employees want to maintain good relationships with their coworkers and managers and to participate in group activities.

4. *Esteem needs.* People like to receive attention, recognition, and appreciation from others. Employees feel good when they are recognized for good job performance and respected for their contributions.

5. *Self-actualization needs.* These needs drive people to seek fulfillment, realizing their own potential and fully using their talents and capabilities. Employers can satisfy these needs by offering challenging and creative work assignments and opportunities for advancement based on individual merit. According to several workplace satisfaction studies, the attainment of meaning—not money—is the best predictor of satisfaction and productivity in the workplace.[45]

Maslow's hierarchy of needs theory of motivation proposed by Abraham Maslow. According to the theory, people have five levels of needs that they seek to satisfy: physiological, safety, social, esteem, and self-actualization.

Everyone, including employees, has a need to belong. Occasional office parties allow workers to relax and socialize, lifting their morale and motivating them to do a good job.

John Guistina/Iconica/Getty Images

According to Maslow, people must satisfy the lower-order needs in the hierarchy (physiological and safety needs) before they are motivated to satisfy higher-order needs (social, esteem, and self-actualization needs).

Herzberg's Two-Factor Model of Motivation

In the 1950s, Frederick Herzberg, a social psychologist and consultant, proposed a work motivation model that is still popular today. Herzberg surveyed accountants and engineers, asking them to describe when they felt good or bad about their jobs. He found that one set of job and personal factors produced good feelings and that another created bad feelings. Of particular interest was that while the presence of one condition like having meaningful work made participants feel good, the absence of that condition did not make them feel bad. Herzberg concluded that while certain motivators lead to satisfaction, their absence does not necessarily lead to dissatisfaction; he labeled these two sets of factors hygiene and motivators.

Hygiene factors (or maintenance factors), if present, are essential to job satisfaction, although they cannot motivate an employee. They refer to aspects of work that are not directly related to the task itself but related to the job environment, including salary, job security, personal life, working conditions, status, interpersonal relations, technical supervision, and company policies. **Motivator factors** can produce high levels of motivation when they are present. They relate directly to the specific aspects of a job and include achievement, recognition, advancement, the job itself, growth opportunities, and responsibility. As you can see, hygiene factors are extrinsic, while motivators are intrinsic. Managers need to remember that hygiene factors, though not motivational, can result in satisfaction. But if managers wish motivate employees, they should emphasize recognition, achievement, and growth. Nuggett Markets, ranked 12th on *Fortune* magazine's list of "The 100 Best Companies to Work For," throws a year-end bash to recognize workers.[46]

Expectancy Theory and Equity Theory

expectancy theory theory that describes the process people use to evaluate the likelihood their effort will yield the desired outcome and how much they want the outcome.

Victor Vroom's **expectancy theory** of motivation describes the process people use to evaluate the likelihood that their effort will yield the desired outcome and the degree to which they want the outcome. Expectancy theory suggests that people use three factors to determine the degree of effort to put forth. First is the individual's subjective assessment that an effort will lead to job performance. This is the "can do" component of an employee's approach to work. Second is the value of the outcome (reward) to the individual. Desirable rewards encourage effort while undesirable rewards discourage effort. Third is the employee's assessment of how likely a successful task performance will lead to a desirable reward. Vroom's expectancy theory is summarized in Figure 9.5. In short, an employee is motivated if he or she thinks he or she can complete a task. Next, the employee assesses the reward for accomplishing the task and is motivated if the reward is worth the effort.

Expectancy theory provides practical guidelines that managers can use to motivate employees. First, by asking what outcomes workers want the most, managers will not run the risk of providing rewards that workers do not value. For instance, workers may prefer to get time off to care for a child or elderly parent rather than receive promotions or bonuses. Second, by providing workers with the tools, information, and other support systems they need to carry out their work, managers help them translate effort into performance. Third, managers should communicate clearly the relationship between performance and rewards. Once workers understand that performance leads to desirable outcomes,

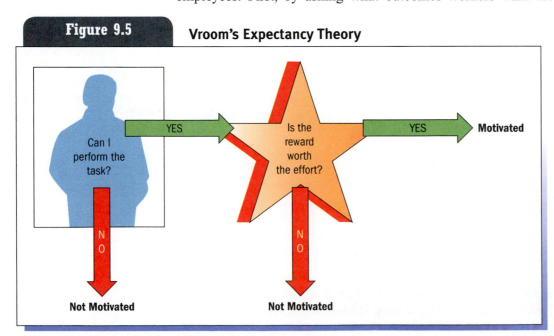

Figure 9.5

Vroom's Expectancy Theory

Can I perform the task?
YES → Is the reward worth the effort? → YES → **Motivated**
NO → **Not Motivated**
NO → **Not Motivated**

they are likely to work harder. For example, managers should let workers know the level of performance required for promotions and bonuses. Finally, because some rewards are intrinsic, such as pride in workmanship, managers should establish a work environment conducive to such rewards

Equity theory is concerned with the individual's perception of fair and equitable treatment. In their work, employees first consider their input or effort and then their outcomes or rewards. Next, employees compare their perceived ratio of effort to reward to the ratios of other workers performing the same job. As shown in Figure 9.6, if employees feel they are

Figure 9.6   **Equity Theory**

underrewarded for their work, in comparison with others doing similar work, equity theory suggests they will decrease their effort to restore the balance. Conversely, if employees feel they are overrewarded, they will feel guilty and put more effort into their job to restore equity and reduce guilt.

Note that a worker's effort and rewards need not be in exact balance with everyone else's. That is, a worker may feel that he or she is working very hard but may not feel unfairly treated as long as his or her comparison workers are also working very hard. Many workers are willing to work hard as long as the burden is shared. Equity theory helps explain workers' feelings of mistreatment by highly paid managers. For instance, the average pay of the 20 highest-paid CEOs in the United States is more than $85,000 a day, more than most Americans earn in a year.[47] If employees feel this is unfair—especially if they think the CEO is underachieving—equity theory suggests they may reduce their effort.

equity theory theory concerned with the individual's perception of fair and equitable treatment.

Goal-Setting Theory and Management by Objectives

As shown earlier in Figure 9.4, a need produces motivation, which leads to goal-directed behavior, which results in need satisfaction. In other words, needs motivate people to direct their behavior toward something that will satisfy their needs. That something is a goal. A **goal** is a target, objective, or result that someone tries to accomplish. **Goal-setting theory** says that people will be motivated to the extent to which they accept specific, challenging goals and receive feedback that indicates their progress toward goal achievement. As shown in Figure 9.7, the basic components of goal-setting theory are goal specificity, goal difficulty, goal acceptance, and performance feedback.

Goal specificity is the extent to which goals are detailed, exact, and unambiguous. Goals such as "we want to lower our costs" are not as motivating as goals that are more specific, such as "we want to lower our costs by 2 percent." *Goal difficulty* is the extent to which a goal is hard or challenging to accomplish. More difficult goals, such as "we want to lower costs by 5 percent," are more motivating than less difficult goals, such as "we want to lower costs by 2 percent." *Goal acceptance* is the extent to which people consciously understand and agree to goals. If the stated goal was to "lower costs by 20 percent," people might not accept or be committed to that goal because they view it as unreasonable and unattainable. Finally, *performance feedback* is information about the quality or quantity of past performance and indicates whether progress is being

goal target, objective, or result that someone tries to accomplish.

goal-setting theory theory that people will be motivated to the extent to which they accept specific, challenging goals and receive feedback that indicates their progress toward goal achievement.

Figure 9.7

Components of Goal-Setting Theory

Goal Specificity

Goal Difficulty

Performance Feedback

Goal Acceptance

made toward accomplishing a goal. When people know how near they are to their goals, they adjust their strategies to reach them. Goal setting typically won't work unless performance feedback is provided.

How does goal setting work? To start, challenging goals focus employees' attention on the critical aspects of their jobs and away from unimportant areas. Goals also energize behavior, motivating employees to develop plans and strategies to reach them. Goals also create tension between the goal, which is the desired future state of affairs, and the employee's or company's current state. This tension can be satisfied in only two ways: by achieving or abandoning the goal. Finally, goals influence the persistence of employee efforts. Because goals "go away" only when they are accomplished, employees are more likely to persist in their attempts when they have goals. Simply put, goal-setting theory suggests that people who set goals outperform those who don't.

Goal-setting principles are evident in a motivation technique introduced by Peter Drucker in 1954 in his book *The Practice of Management.* **Management by objectives (MBO)** is a systematic and organized approach that enables managers to focus on attainable goals and to achieve the best results based on the organization's resources. MBO helps motivate individuals by aligning their objectives with the goals of the organization, increasing overall organizational performance. MBO clearly delineates what everyone should be doing and how these actions benefit the organization. MBO is a collaborative process between managers and subordinates; when the parts work together, the whole also works smoothly. Also, by concentrating on objectives, employees can quickly distinguish between tasks that *must* be completed and those that are a waste of time. MBO principles include the following:

- a series of related organizational goals and objectives
- specific objectives for each individual
- participative decision making
- set time period to accomplish goals
- performance evaluation and feedback.

Job Design and Motivation

In their search for ways to improve employee productivity and morale, a growing number of firms are focusing on the motivation inherent in the job itself. Rather than simplifying the tasks involved in a job, employers are broadening tasks to add meaning and satisfaction to employees' work. Two ways employers are applying motivational theories to restructure jobs are job enlargement and job enrichment.

job enlargement job design that expands an employee's responsibilities by increasing the number and variety of tasks assigned to the worker.

Job enlargement is a job design that expands an employee's responsibilities by increasing the number and variety of tasks they entail. Some firms have successfully applied job enlargement by redesigning the production process. A typical approach is to replace assembly lines on which each worker repeats the same step on each product with modular work areas in which employees perform several tasks on a single item. Similarly, many companies have enlarged administrative assistants' jobs in areas such as communications.

Job enrichment is a change in job duties to increase employees' authority in planning their work, deciding how it should be done, and learning new skills that help them grow. Many companies have developed job enrichment programs that empower employees to take responsibility for their work. The Pampered Chef, a direct seller of kitchen products that is owned by Warren Buffett's Berkshire Hathaway, gives its managers and consultants the power to make decisions about many aspects of their work. Kitchen consultants, who organize selling and demonstration parties at customers' homes, can choose how much or how little they want to work and receive various incentive rewards for performance. "Over the years, thousands of people from all walks of life have joined our Pampered Chef family. They've found a truly unlimited opportunity and life-changing possibilities," notes founder and chairman Doris Christopher.[48]

Job rotation involves systematically moving employees from one job to another. Job rotation increases the range of activities by introducing workers to more jobs and therefore more tasks. The goal is not only to reduce worker dissatisfaction caused by specialization but also to increase work interest and motivation. For instance, employees in a tool factory might work on a machine one week, conduct stress tests the next week, and pack orders the next. Collegeville, Pennsylvania–based Wyeth Pharmaceuticals uses its rotational training manager (RTM) program to develop employees and identify future leaders. Participants in the two-year program develop training materials, work with brand teams, and learn by striving to be better sales representatives, better managers, and future leaders of the company.[49] The major drawback of job rotation is that it does little to change the nature of the work itself. Rather than performing one task over and over again, a worker performs a variety of tasks. But the jobs remain highly specialized, and workers can grow bored or dissatisfied. Inefficiencies might also result because workers must be trained for several jobs.

job enrichment change in job duties to increase employees' authority in planning their work, deciding how it should be done, and learning new skills.

job rotation systematically moving employees from one job to another.

© R. Alcorn, photographed for John Wiley & Sons

This kitchen consultant for the Pampered Chef gives in-home demonstrations on her own schedule. Empowering consultants to make their own decisions increases their motivation.

Managers' Attitudes and Motivation

The attitudes that managers display toward employees also influence worker motivation. Managers' traditional view of workers as cogs in the production process—much like lathes, drill presses, and other equipment—led them to believe that money was the best way to motivate employees. Maslow's theory has helped managers understand that employees feel needs beyond those satisfied by monetary rewards.

Psychologist Douglas McGregor, a student of Maslow, studied motivation from the perspective of how managers view employees. After observing managers' interactions with employees, McGregor coined the terms *Theory X* and *Theory Y* as labels for the assumptions that different managers make about worker behavior and how these assumptions affect management styles.

Theory X assumes that employees dislike work and try to avoid it whenever possible. So managers must coerce or control them or threaten punishment to achieve the organization's goals. Managers who accept this view feel that the average person prefers to receive direction, wishes to avoid responsibility, has relatively little ambition, and can be motivated only by money and job security. Managers who hold these assumptions are likely to keep their subordinates under close and constant observation, hold out the threat of disciplinary action, and demand that they adhere closely to company policies and procedures.

Theory Y assumes that the typical person likes work and learns, under proper conditions, to accept and seek responsibilities to fulfill social, esteem, and self-actualization needs. Theory Y managers consider the expenditure of physical and mental effort in work as an ordinary activity, as natural as play or rest. They assume that most people can think of creative ways to solve work-related problems but that most organizations do not fully utilize the intelligence that most employees bring to their jobs. Unlike the traditional management philosophy that relies on external control and constant supervision, Theory Y emphasizes self-control and self-direction.

Theory Y requires a different management approach that includes worker participation in decisions that Theory X would reserve for management. If people actually behave in the manner described by Theory X, they may do so because the organization satisfies only their lower-order needs. If the organization instead designs ways to satisfy their social, esteem, and self-actualization needs as well, employees may be motivated to behave in different ways.

Another perspective on management proposed by management professor William Ouchi has been labeled Theory Z. Organizations structured on **Theory Z** concepts attempt to blend the best of American and Japanese management practices. This approach views worker involvement as the key to increased productivity for the company and improved quality of work life for employees. Many U.S. firms have adopted the participative management style used in Japanese firms by asking workers for suggestions to improve their jobs and then giving them the authority to implement proposed changes.

Labor–Management Relations

In nations throughout the world, employees have joined together to increase their power to achieve the goals of improved wages and benefits, fewer working hours, and better working conditions. These efforts have succeeded, especially in the United States; today's workplace is far different from that of a century ago, when child labor, unsafe working conditions, and a 72-hour workweek (six 12-hour days a week) were common. In this section, we review the development of labor unions, labor legislation, the collective bargaining process, settling labor–management disputes, and competitive tactics of unions and management.

Development of Labor Unions

labor union group of workers who have banded together to achieve common goals in the areas of wages, hours, and working conditions.

A **labor union** is a group of workers who have banded together to achieve common goals in the areas of wages, hours, and working conditions. Workers gradually learned that bargaining as a unified group could bring them improvements in job security, wages, working conditions, and other areas. The organized efforts of Philadelphia printers in 1786 resulted in the first U.S. minimum wage—$1 a day. After 100 more years, New York City streetcar conductors were able to negotiate a reduction in their workday from 17 to 12 hours.

Labor unions can be found at the local, national, and international levels. A *local union* represents union members in a specific area, such as a single community, while a *national union* is a labor organization consisting of numerous local chapters. An *international union* is a national union with membership outside the United States, usually in Canada. Large national and international unions in the United States include the United Auto Workers, the National Education Association, the Teamsters, the International Brotherhood of Electrical Workers, the International Association of Machinists and Aerospace Workers, the United Steelworkers of America, and the American Federation of Teachers. More than half of U.S. union members belong to one of these giant organizations.

Almost 16 million U.S. workers—close to 12 percent of the nation's full-time workforce—belong to labor unions.[50] Although only about 8 percent of workers in the private sector are

"They Said It"

"Union gives strength."

—**Aesop** (620–560 B.C.) Greek fable writer

unionized, more than one in three government workers belong to unions. The largest union in the United States is the 3.2 million-member National Education Association (NEA), representing public school teachers and other support personnel. Other large unions include the 1.9 million members of the Service Employees International Union (SEIU), the 1.4 million members of the International Brotherhood of Teamsters, the 1.3 million members of the United Food and Commercial Workers, and the 640,000 members of the United Auto Workers.

Labor Legislation

Government attitudes toward unions have varied considerably over the past century. These shifting attitudes influenced major pieces of legislation enacted during this period. Let's look at the major pieces of labor legislation:

- *National Labor Relations Act of 1935 (Wagner Act).* Legalized collective bargaining and required employers to negotiate with elected representatives of their employees. Established the National Labor Relations Board (NLRB) to supervise union elections and prohibit unfair labor practices such as firing workers for joining unions, refusing to hire union sympathizers, threatening to close if workers unionize, interfering with or dominating the administration of a union, and refusing to bargain with a union.

- Fair Labor Standards Act of 1938. Set the initial federal minimum wage (25 cents an hour, with exceptions for farm workers and retail employees) and maximum basic workweek for workers employed in industries engaged in interstate commerce. Outlawed child labor.

- *Taft-Hartley Act of 1947 (Labor–Management Relations Act).* Limited unions' power by prohibiting such practices as coercing employees to join unions; coercing employers to discriminate against employees who are not union members, except for failure to pay union dues under union shop agreements; discrimination against nonunion employees; picketing or conducting secondary boycotts or strikes for illegal purposes; featherbedding; and excessive initiation fees under union shop agreements.

- *Landrum-Griffin Act of 1959 (Labor–Management Reporting and Disclosure Act).* Amended the Taft-Hartley Act to promote honesty and democracy in running unions' internal affairs. Required unions to set up a constitution and bylaws and to hold regularly scheduled elections of union officers by secret ballot. Set forth a bill of rights for members. Required unions to submit certain financial reports to the U.S. Secretary of Labor.

The Collective Bargaining Process

Labor unions work to increase job security for their members and to improve wages, hours, and working conditions. These goals are achieved primarily through collective bargaining, the process of negotiation between management and union representatives for the purpose of arriving at mutually acceptable wages and working conditions for employees.

collective bargaining process of negotiation between management and union representatives for the purpose of arriving at mutually acceptable wages and working conditions for employees.

Issues covered in collective bargaining include wages, work hours, benefits, union activities and responsibilities, grievance handling and arbitration, layoffs, and employee rights and seniority. As in all types of negotiations, the collective bargaining process involves demands, proposals, and counterproposals that ultimately result in compromise and agreement. The initial demands represent a starting point in negotiations. They are rarely, if ever, accepted by the other party without some compromise. The final agreement depends on the negotiating skills and relative power of management and union representatives.

Union contracts, which typically cover a two- or three-year period, are often the result of weeks or more of discussion, disagreement, compromise, and eventual agreement. Once agreement is reached, union members must vote to accept or reject the contract. If the contract is rejected, union representatives may resume the bargaining process with management representatives, or union members may strike to obtain their demands. U.S. Airways CEO Doug Parker was hampered by union issues in negotiating labor agreements after the merger with America West. The stickiest point was pilot seniority. Pilots work for years for the right to fly the biggest jets and earn the highest salaries. The Airline Pilots Association (ALPA) took exception with the way Parker wanted to negotiate seniority. According to ALPA spokesman Peter Janhunen, "You can have colonels reporting to lieutenants."[51]

Settling Labor–Management Disputes

Although strikes make newspaper and television headlines, most labor–management negotiations result in a signed agreement without a work stoppage. Of the thousands of union contracts in force in the United States, roughly 20 work stoppages involving 1,000 or more workers take place each year, averaging about 10.5 days.[52] The courts are the most visible and familiar vehicle for dispute settlement, but most disagreements are settled by negotiations. Dispute resolution mechanisms, such as grievance procedures, mediation, and arbitration, are quicker, cheaper, and less complicated procedurally and receive less publicity.

The union contract serves as a guide to relations between the firm's management and its employees. The rights of each party are stated in the agreement. But no contract, regardless of how detailed, will eliminate the possibility of disagreement. Such differences can be the beginning of a **grievance,** a complaint—by a single employee or by the entire union—that management is violating some provision of the union contract. Almost all union contracts require these complaints to be submitted to a formal grievance procedure similar to the one shown in Figure 9.8.

The procedure typically begins with the employee's supervisor and then moves up the company's chain of command. If the highest company officer cannot settle the grievance, it is submitted to an outside party for mediation or arbitration.

Mediation is the process of settling labor–management disputes through recommendations of an impartial third party. Although the mediator does not serve as a decision maker, union and management representatives can be assisted by the mediator's suggestions, advice, and compromise solutions.

When disputes cannot be solved voluntarily through mediation, the parties can turn to **arbitration**—bringing in an impartial third party, called an *arbitrator,* who renders a legally binding decision. The arbitrator must be acceptable both to the union and to management, and his or her decision is legally enforceable. In essence, the arbitrator acts as a judge, making a decision after listening to both sides of the argument. Most union contracts call for the use of arbitration if union and management representatives fail to reach an agreement.

Competitive Tactics of Unions and Management

Although most differences between labor and management are settled through the collective bargaining process or through a formal grievance

Figure 9.8

Steps in the Grievance Procedure

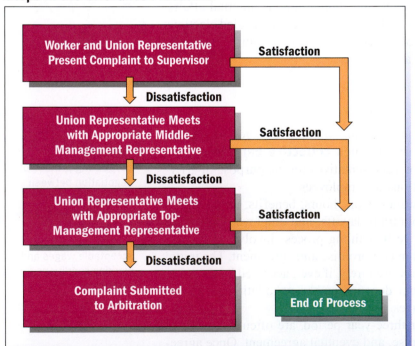

procedure, both unions and management occasionally resort to various tactics to make their demands known.

UNION TACTICS The chief tactics of unions are strikes, picketing, and boycotts. The **strike,** or *walkout,* is one of the most effective tools of the labor union. It involves a temporary work stoppage by employees until a dispute has been settled or a contract signed. Although strikes are relatively rare, they do make headlines. The strike by members of the Writers Guild of America drew national attention when it shut down late-night talk shows including *Late Show with David Letterman* and *The Tonight Show with Jay Leno.*[53] The strike lasted 100 days, accounting for 409,500 lost workdays.[54]

Although the power to strike represents unions' ultimate tactic, they do not wield it lightly because strikes can do damage in a number of ways, affecting an entire industry, as well as related businesses. The strike by Local 1 of Broadway Stagehands darkened 27 Broadway productions, costing theatres as much as $17 million a day. Broadway contributes an estimated $5 billion annually to New York City through ticket sales and visitor spending.[55] Restaurants were hit especially hard. Even Sardi's, the 650-seat Broadway landmark, saw business fall 30 to 40 percent.[56]

Picketing—workers marching at the entrances of the employer's business as a public protest against some management practice—is another effective form of union pressure. As long as picketing does not involve violence or intimidation, it is protected under the U.S. Constitution as freedom of speech. Picketing may accompany a strike, or it may be a protest against alleged unfair labor practices. Broadway stagehands picketed in the theatre district during their strike, protesting theatre owners' and producers' demand for a 38 percent cut in jobs and wages. The strike caused losses of about $2 million a day for businesses around the theatre district.[57] Because members of other unions often refuse to cross picket lines, the picketed firm may be unable to obtain deliveries and other services. Unions occasionally stage "informational" picketing during contract negotiations to pressure management while still working.

A **boycott** is an organized attempt to keep the public from purchasing the products of a firm. Some unions have been quite successful in organizing boycotts, and some unions even fine members who defy a primary boycott. Pennsylvania brewery D.G. Yuengling & Son unexpectedly withdrew its union recognition, declaring it would no longer negotiate with Teamsters Local 830, even though the existing contract had not expired. Local 830 filed charges with the National Labor Relations Board. In support of the Local 830 workers, the Pennsylvania Conference of Teamsters urged Philadelphia area union workers and their families and friends, as well as local tavern owners and licensed liquor establishments, not to purchase Yuengling brands.[58]

MANAGEMENT TACTICS Management also has tactics for dealing with organized labor. In the past, it has used the **lockout**—in effect, a management strike to put pressure on union members by closing the firm. However, other than a few high-profile cases, the lockout is not commonly used unless a union strike has partially shut down a plant or engaged in a work slowdown. Firms can easily recruit strikebreakers in high-status fields such as professional sports and in

Picket lines went up on Broadway as members of the Stagehands' union went on strike. Strikes are a last-ditch tactic that can empty union coffers, injure an entire industry, and even damage the economy.

high-paying industries located in areas of high unemployment. Yet even in favorable conditions, management frequently has difficulties securing enough replacement workers with required skills. Some employers get around these difficulties by using supervisors and nonunion replacement employees to continue operations during strikes. When the International Longshore and Warehouse Union (ILWU) and the Pacific Maritime Association began negotiations on a new West Coast waterfront contract, issues such as work hours, wages, and benefits were put on the table. The ILWU, whose members work on the docks loading and unloading ships, has the most lucrative contract in blue-collar America. The previous negotiation was marked by ILWU work slowdowns and a ten-day lockout by employers, delaying the shipment of goods from ports and tarnishing the reputation of both West Coast labor and management.[59]

The Future of Labor Unions

Union membership and influence grew through most of the 20th century by giving industrial workers a voice in decisions about their wages, benefits, and working conditions. Unions have improved life for working Americans by helping pass laws ending child labor, establishing the eight-hour workday, and protecting workers' safety and health. Today, however, union members and influence are declining. As the United States, western Europe, and Japan have shifted from manufacturing economies to information and service economies, the makeup of the workforce has become less favorable for unions. While almost 8 percent of private-sector workers are union members today, that's down from nearly 17 percent in 1983. That is a historically low percentage. In fact, unions have been unable to organize any of the Japanese-owned automobile plants in the United States—Toyota, Honda, Nissan. Their biggest lack of success has been their inability to organize Wal-Mart's 1.9 million U.S. workers.

How do you explain the decline in union membership over the past several decades? A thoughtful review of the decline in union membership points to a number of demographic factors. One is a shift in the labor force away from unionized industries. Most of the new jobs created during this period were white collar, in the service sector, with small to medium-sized businesses, and part-time or flexible work. In addition, employers became more concerned about creating the working conditions that support a productive workforce, including collaboration with employees. More laws today constrain the manner in which employers deal with employees; as a result, working conditions are vastly improved from those that fueled the growth of unions in the 1930s. Finally, many employees today simply think that union membership offers little advantage to them.

Have unions lost their ability to deliver greater pay and benefits to their members? The most recent data from the U.S. Department of Labor suggest that union workers still have several advantages over nonunion workers, as Table 9.1 shows. Union workers are paid more than nonunion workers. A higher percentage of union workers are covered by employer-provided health insurance, and union workers have more vacation days. Of course, the counterargument is that the cost of these benefits increases the cost of running a business, leaving firms vulnerable to nonunion competitors. GM has faced about a $25 per hour labor cost disparity with its Japanese competition, making it very difficult for GM to compete on price.[60]

How will labor unions have to change to maintain their relevance? More than anything else, they will need to appeal to a broader range of workers. With the number of U.S. manufacturing jobs shrinking because of increasing productivity and overseas outsourcing, labor unions are reaching out to nonmanufacturing workers, such as healthcare, high-tech, and service workers. Another possibility is offering affiliate or partial union memberships, which offer the same benefits as full memberships except for collective bargaining

Assessment Check

1. How many U.S. workers are represented by labor unions?
2. Identify the major issues covered in the collective bargaining process.
3. Explain picketing, boycotts, and lockouts.

Table 9.1	Comparison of Union and Nonunion Wages and Benefits	
	Union Workers	Nonunion Workers
Median weekly earnings	$886	$691
Women's median weekly earnings	$809	$615
African American workers' median weekly earnings	$720	$564
Percent of workers covered by employer-provided health plans	78%	49%
Percent of workers *without* health insurance	2.5%	15%
Percent of workers covered by guaranteed pensions	67%	15%
Percent of workers covered by short-term disability plans	60%	35%
Average days of paid vacation	15 days	11.75 days

Sources: U.S. Department of Labor, Bureau of Labor Statistics, "Union Members in 2008," January 28, 2009; U.S. Department of Labor, Bureau of Labor Statistics, "National Compensation Survey: Employee Benefits in Private Industry in the United States, March 2007," August 2007; Economic Policy Institute; Employee Benefits Research Institute, May 2005.

or grievance issues. Finally, labor unions will have to overcome the widespread belief that they can't succeed unless a company's management loses. Today, most workers realize that they prosper when their companies prosper and that management and workers must work together in positive, rather than adversarial, relationships. Some bright signs already appear on the horizon. In the last decade, 2.5 million workers have formed new unions. Union leaders believe that the tide will turn in their favor as wages stagnate and more companies cut back on health care and pensions while increasing work hours.[61]

What's Ahead

Treating employees well by enriching the work environment will continue to gain importance as a way to recruit and retain a highly motivated workforce. In addition, managers can tap the full potential of their employees by empowering them to make decisions, leading them to work effectively as teams, and fostering clear, positive communication. The next chapter covers these three means of improving performance. By involving employees more fully through empowerment, teamwork, and communication, companies can benefit from their knowledge while employees enjoy a more meaningful role in the company.

Summary of Learning Goals

1 **Explain the importance of human resource management, the responsibilities of human resource managers, and the role of human resource planning in an organization's competitive strategy.**

Organizations devote considerable attention to attracting, training, and retaining employees to help maintain their competitiveness. Human resource managers are responsible for recruiting, selecting, training, compensating, terminating, and motivating employees. They accomplish these tasks by developing specific programs and creating a work environment that generates employee satisfaction and efficiency. A human resource plan is designed to implement a firm's competitive strategies by providing the right number of employees, training them to meet job requirements, and motivating them to be productive and satisfied workers.

Assessment Check Answers

1.1 Why do human resource managers need to develop staffing plans? Staffing plans help managers determine how many employees their firms will need and the kinds of skills those employees will need.

1.2 How do human resource managers attract and keep good employees? Using the right combination of pay, benefits, and working conditions helps managers attract and keep good employees.

2 **Describe how recruitment and selection contribute to placing the right person in a job.**

Firms use internal and external methods to recruit qualified employees. For needs that the company cannot meet with existing employees, it may find candidates by encouraging employee referrals, advertising, accepting résumés at its Web site, and using job search Web sites. In selecting qualified candidates, human resource managers must follow legal requirements designed to promote equal employment opportunity. Employment tests, such as cognitive ability tests, are often used to assess job candidates' capabilities and help companies hire more qualified workers.

Assessment Check Answers

2.1 What are some of the costs associated with recruitment and selection? Firms incur costs for advertising job openings, interviewing applicants, and conducting background checks, employment tests, and medical exams. Hiring mistakes increase training costs, can result in lawsuits and unemployment compensation claims, and reduce productivity and employee morale.

2.2 What key federal and state laws apply to recruitment and selection? Recruitment and selection practices must adhere to Title VII of the Civil Rights Act of 1964, the Americans with Disabilities Act of 1990, the Civil Rights Act of 1991, and other regulations of the Equal Employment Opportunity Commission.

3 **Explain how training programs and performance appraisals help companies grow and develop their employees.**

Human resource managers use a variety of training techniques, including on-the-job training, computerized training programs, and classroom methods. In addition, management development programs help managers make decisions and improve interpersonal skills. Companies conduct performance appraisals to assess employees' work, as well as their strengths and weaknesses.

Assessment Check Answers

3.1 Describe some aids in on-the-job training. In on-the-job training, you learn how to perform tasks under the guidance of experienced employees. A variation of on-the-job training is apprenticeship training, in which an employee learns a job by serving for a longer time as an assistant to a trained worker.

3.2 What is a management development program? A management development program provides training designed to improve the skills and broaden the knowledge of current and potential executives.

3.3 What is the main way an organization provides employees with feedback about their performance? The main method is a performance appraisal, in which an employee's job performance is compared with desired outcomes. Peer reviews and 360-degree performance reviews are also used to provide feedback.

4 **Outline the methods employers use to compensate employees through pay systems and benefit programs.**

Firms compensate employees with wages, salaries, and incentive pay systems, such as profit sharing, gain sharing, lump-sum bonuses, stock options, and pay-for-knowledge programs. Benefit programs vary among firms, but most companies offer healthcare programs, insurance, retirement plans, paid time off, and sick leave. A growing number of companies are offering flexible benefit plans and flexible work plans, such as flextime, compressed workweeks, job sharing, and home-based work.

Assessment Check Answers

4.1 Explain the difference between *wage* and *salary*. Wages represent compensation based on an hourly pay rate or the amount of output produced. Salaries represent compensation calculated periodically, such as weekly or monthly.

4.2 What is another name for a *cafeteria plan*? Cafeteria plans are also called *flexible benefit plans.*

4.3 What types of organizations typically use a compressed workweek? Hospitals, police and fire departments, airlines, and manufacturing organizations often use compressed work-weeks. However, many other kinds of companies are now finding success with compressed workweeks.

5 **Discuss employee separation and the impact of downsizing and outsourcing.**

Either employers or employees can decide to terminate employment (called *involuntary turnover* and *voluntary turnover,* respectively). Downsizing reduces a company's workforce to reduce labor costs in an effort to improve the firm's competitive position. The company may transfer some responsibilities to contractors, a practice called *outsourcing.* The goals of outsourcing are to reduce costs by giving work to more efficient specialists and to allow the company to focus on the activities it does best.

Assessment Check Answers

5.1 What is the difference between voluntary and involuntary turnover? Voluntary turnover occurs when employees leave firms to start their own businesses, take jobs with other firms, move to another community, or retire. Involuntary turnover occurs when employers terminate employees because of poor job performance, negative attitudes toward work and coworkers, or misconduct.

5.2 What is downsizing? How is it different from outsourcing? Downsizing is the process of reducing the number of employees within a firm by eliminating jobs. Downsizing is done to cut overhead costs and streamline the organizational structure. With outsourcing, companies contract with other firms to perform noncore jobs or business functions, such as housekeeping, maintenance, or relocation services. This allows companies to focus on what they do best, and can result in a downsized workforce.

6 **Explain how Maslow's hierarchy of needs theory, expectancy theory, equity theory, goal setting, job design, and managers' attitudes relate to employee motivation.**

Employee motivation starts with good employee morale. Maslow's hierarchy of needs theory states that all people have basic needs (physiological and safety) that they must satisfy before they can consider higher-order needs (social, esteem, and self-actualization). Expectancy theory and equity theory stress the importance of employee expectations and perceptions of fairness in determining how much effort they will put forth. Goal-setting theory, job enlargement, and job enrichment are three ways in which managers can motivate employees and satisfy various levels of needs. Managers' attitudes can also affect employee motivation. Theory X managers keep their subordinates under close and constant observation. Theory Y managers emphasize workers' self-control

and self-direction. Theory Z managers believe that worker involvement is the key to increased productivity for the company and improved quality of work life for employees.

Assessment Check Answers

6.1 In an organization, what conditions are likely to produce high morale? High employee morale occurs when employees feel valued and heard and can contribute what they do best. High morale also results from an organization's understanding of human needs and its success at satisfying those needs in ways that reinforce organizational goals.

6.2 Explain how goal setting works. People will be motivated to the extent to which they accept specific, challenging goals and receive feedback that indicates their progress toward goal achievement.

6.3 Identify three ways that employers structure jobs for motivation. Three ways that employers apply motivational theories to restructure jobs are job enlargement, job enrichment, and job rotation. Job enlargement is a job design that expands an employee's responsibilities by increasing the number and variety of tasks they entail. Job enrichment is a change in job duties to increase employees' authority in planning their work, deciding how it should be done, and learning new skills that help them grow. Job rotation involves systematically moving employees from one job to another.

6.4 Compare and contrast Theory X, Theory Y, and Theory Z. Theory X assumes that employees dislike work and try to avoid it whenever possible. Theory Y assumes that the typical person likes work and learns, under proper conditions, to accept and seek responsibilities to fulfill social, esteem, and self-actualization needs. Theory Z views worker involvement as the key to increased productivity for the company and improved quality of work life for employees.

7 **Summarize the role of labor unions and the tactics of labor–management conflicts.**

A labor union is a group of workers who have banded together to achieve common goals in the key areas of wages, working hours, and working conditions. Labor unions exist at local, national, and international levels. Government attitudes toward unions have varied considerably during the past century and are reflected in the major pieces of labor legislation enacted during this period. Labor unions work to achieve their goals of increased job security and improvements in wages, hours, and working conditions through a process known as *collective bargaining.* Most labor–management negotiations result in a signed agreement without a work stoppage. Even after an agreement is signed, disputes can arise. A grievance is a complaint that management is violating some provision of the union contract. Mediation is the process of settling labor–management disputes through recommendations of an impartial third party. Arbitration is a process in which an impartial third party renders a legally binding decision. Some tactics available to labor unions during disputes include strikes (walkouts), picketing, and boycotts. Tactics available to management include lockouts and hiring replacement workers.

Assessment Check Answers

7.1 How many U.S. workers are represented by labor unions? Almost 16 million U.S. workers—close to 13 percent of the nation's full-time workforce—belong to labor unions. Although only about 8 percent of workers in the private sector are unionized, more than one in three government workers belong to unions.

7.2 Identify the major issues covered in the collective bargaining process. The major issues covered in collective bargaining include wages, work hours, benefits, union activities and responsibilities, grievance handling and arbitration, layoffs, and employee rights and seniority.

7.3 Explain picketing, boycotts, and lockouts. Picketing is when workers march at the entrances of the employer's business to protest against some management practice. A boycott is an organized attempt to keep the public from purchasing the products of a firm. A lockout is a management strike, in which company management pressures labor union members by closing the operation.

Business Terms You Need to Know

human resource
    management 288
performance appraisal 293
wage 294
salary 295

employee benefits 296
downsizing 303
outsourcing 303
Maslow's hierarchy of
    needs 305

expectancy theory 306
equity theory 307
goal 307
goal-setting theory 307
job enlargement 308

job enrichment 309
job rotation 309
labor union 310
collective bargaining 311

Other Important Business Terms

management 288
affirmative action
    programs 290
cognitive ability tests 291
on-the-job training 292
management development
    program 293
360-degree performance
    review 294

401(k) plan 298
flexible benefit plan 298
paid time off (PTO) 298
flexible work plan 298
flextime 299
compressed workweek 299
job sharing program 299
telecommuter 300
morale 304

hygiene factors 306
motivator factors 306
management by objectives
    (MBO) 308
Theory X 309
Theory Y 309
Theory Z 310
grievance 312
mediation 312

arbitration 312
strike 313
picketing 313
boycott 313
lockout 313

Review Questions

1. What are the core responsibilities of human resource management? What are the three main objectives of human resource managers?

2. What methods do companies use to recruit and select employees?

3. What types of training programs are popular today? How does 360-degree feedback work?

4. On what five factors are compensation policies usually based? Name at least three employee benefits that are required by law and three more that are provided voluntarily by many firms.

5. Describe four types of flexible work plans. Identify an industry that would be well suited to each type of plan and explain why.

6. Outline the major reasons for terminating employees. Why do companies downsize? What are some of the difficulties they may encounter in doing so?

7. Select three different theories of motivation, and explain how each can be used by managers to motivate employees.

8. How is goal setting related to need satisfaction? What mistakes need to be avoided when setting goals?

9. How do companies use job design to motivate employees?

10. What are the chief tactics of unions and management in their contract negotiations? Are they usually effective? Why or why not?

Projects and Teamwork Applications

1. Choose one of the following organizations (or select one of your own) and write a memo outlining a plan for outsourcing some of the tasks currently performed by employees. Cite reasons for your choices.
   a. summer resort in Wisconsin
   b. regional high school in Arizona
   c. software development firm in California
   d. major hospital in Massachusetts
   e. manufacturing plant in Kentucky

2. Would you accept a job you didn't particularly like because the firm offered an attractive benefits package? Why or why not? Do you think your answer would change as you get older?

3. Not every unionized worker has the right to strike. All federal employees and many state and municipal employees—such as police officers and firefighters—cannot strike. Suppose you were a teacher or an airline pilot. Do you think members of your union should be allowed to strike? Why or why not?

4. Do you think the downward trend in union membership will continue? In what ways might this trend change the relationship between companies and employees over the next decade?

5. Suppose you are a human resource manager and you have determined that your company would benefit from hiring some older workers. Write a memo explaining your reasons for this conclusion.

Web Assignments

1. **Hiring.** Visit the Web site listed (http://www.businessweek.com/managing/content/mar2008/ca20080313_241443.htm). Read the article "Netting the Net Generation" and watch the slide show. Jot down the slide show's ten recommendations to employers who want to recruit bright young employees. Which of these steps would most help an employer trying to recruit you (whether or not you are a Gen Y or Millennial)?

2. **Performance reviews.** Visit the Web site listed here (http://harvardbusinessonline.hbsp.harvard.edu/flatmm/hbrextras/200803/garvin/index.html) and watch the video, "US Army's After-Action Reviews." What are the seven characteristics of AARs? Could AARs be beneficial in business settings? Why or why not? Think of an example where AARs could be used in the business world.

3. **Employee needs and peak performance.** Visit the Web site listed (http://www.bnet.com/2422-13724_23-182940.html) and watch the video, "Peak," by Chip Conley, whose company, Joie de Vivre Hospitality, operates hotels, spas, and restaurants in California. How does Conley apply Abraham Maslow's hierarchy of needs theory to his business? Which specific practices does he use to create a culture of recognition and help employees find meaning in their jobs?

Note: Internet Web addresses change frequently. If you do not find the exact sites listed, you may need to access the organization's or company's home page and search from there.

Looking for a great company to work for? Your search might take you to Google. It was named the best company to work for in *Fortune* magazine's annual rankings for two years in a row. Now recognized as the fastest-growing media company in history, Google is run by managers who believe happy people are more productive.

Co-founder Larry Page notes that labor has come a long way since his grandfather worked on the auto assembly line in Flint, Michigan. During sit-down strikes, he carried a lead pipe to protect himself from company strongmen. That was two generations ago. Google employees don't need to carry weapons to work, says Page with extreme understatement.

Google's strategy is to "hire great people and encourage them to make their dreams a reality." The company has transformed human resource management like no other. Google grew from a handful of employees to more than 12,000 worldwide through a creative approach to recruiting, motivating, and retaining top talent. The results have been spectacular. The average employee generates more than $1 million in annual revenue, compared with $564,000 for Yahoo! and $647,000 for Microsoft.

With no advertising, Google receives more than 760,000 job applications a year. The process begins when individuals search the Web site and apply for a job. If their skills fit a job, the applicants are interviewed by phone for 30 to 40 minutes to assess their technical skills and determine whether an in-person interview is warranted. During on-site interviews, candidates meet engineers from different teams to get a firsthand view of work life at Google. Interviewers question applicants about their areas of interest, present them with a typical problem, and expect immediate solutions. Right or wrong answers are not as important as showing a thoughtful process and creativity, and applicants may even go to the whiteboard to demonstrate some computer-coding skills. Every prospective Google employee completes at least four interviews, and all the interviewers' opinions count. The company's philosophy is that great people hire more great people.

Once you're hired at Google, the fun literally begins. Co-founders Larry Page and Sergey Brin never believed work and fun were mutually exclusive. From its innovative training program to generous benefits, Google does everything possible to make sure employees enjoy their jobs and have fun. Instead of traditional training programs, Google's employee development is decentralized, with courses playing only a small part. The work changes quickly, so most employees don't end up in positions they were hired for anyway. Because Google hires self-starters with a thirst

for learning, most training is shifted to employees, with 30 percent of their time allocated to their own development and innovation. Development also takes place through on-the-job learning by continual rotation to new projects, use of new-hire mentors, department "tech-talks," and on-site speakers like former TV news anchor Tom Brokaw.

Google's approach to motivation and performance management is also innovative. Motivation is spurred by constant change, rapid decision making, and a culture that expects ambitious ideas. Limited bureaucracy lets employees be free to make decisions and take risks without fearing the consequences of failure. Ideas are approved in days, not months. Google managers believe all employees are high performers and accept the blame should someone fall short. The company supports its culture with a generous benefit package that is as highly publicized as Google's search tools.

The company knows employees have diverse needs and celebrates this diversity through flexible and individually directed benefits. The basics include the choice among three medical insurance carriers, comprehensive dental insurance, vision insurance, and a flexible spending account. An employee assistance program provides employees and dependents free short-term counseling, legal consultations, child care referrals, and financial counseling. Life and accidental death insurance is offered at two times annual salary, employees may select additional voluntary life insurance, they receive short-term and long-term disability, and the company provides business travel accident insurance. Employees also receive stock options along with a generous 401(k) retirement plan. Vacation policies are generous, with 15 vacation days for new employees, 20 days after four years, and 26 after six. Other paid time off includes 12 paid holidays, a variety of leaves and sabbaticals, and unlimited sick leave.

Beyond the basics, Google gives tuition reimbursement of up to $8,000 per year, a $2,000 bonus for referring a new hire, back-up child care, a child care center, and up to $5,000 reimbursement for the costs of adopting a child. Going way beyond the basics, Google also provides free lunch and dinner at 17 cafés at the Mountain Valley, California, campus and between-meal snacks. There's also an on-site doctor, shuttle service to several East Bay and South Bay locations, financial planning classes, oil changes and car washes for employees' cars, dry cleaning, gym facilities, and massage therapy. Google employees, the thinking goes, are too valuable to spend time running to a dry cleaner. Other fabulous benefits include ski trips, picnics, movies, and an outdoor volleyball court.

Google's founders like to say they are only serious about search. Google puts users first when it comes to its online search engine, and it puts employees first when it comes to daily life at work. Says CEO Eric Schmidt: "The goal is to strip away everything that gets in our employees way … Let's face it: programmers want to program, they don't want to do their laundry. So we make it easy for them to do both."[62]

Questions for Critical Thinking

1. How does Google's training program differ from more traditional programs?

2. Which motivation theories can be used to explain how human resource managers motivate employees at Google?

During its glory days from the mid-1950s into the 1970s, General Motors ruled the auto world and beyond. While GM is still one of the world's largest auto manufacturers, its sales and status have dropped for years while foreign competitors gained significant ground. Vehicle quality and style contributed to GM's decline, but so have production costs: GM couldn't build vehicles as inexpensively as Japanese firms do.

Labor accounts for much of the difference between U.S. and Japanese production costs. GM faced a $25 per hour labor cost difference with Japanese competitors, much of it coming from healthcare costs, which added about $1,400 to the cost of every GM car and truck built in North America. Toyota's healthcare costs ranged from $200 to $300 per vehicle. The inequality created a dilemma for CEO Rick Wagoner and his predecessors, who were torn between the responsibility to employees and retirees and the future of the company.

The cost of labor, particularly healthcare costs for 340,000 GM retirees, has long been a point of contention between GM and the United Auto Workers (UAW), one the UAW was not willing to concede. In September 2007 the two sides reached an impasse in contract negotiations. The 74,000 UAW members went out on the first nationwide strike against GM in 37 years. After only two days, the strike ended with an agreement that placed retirees' healthcare benefits in the hands of the union by establishing a union-administered trust, to which GM will contribute $29.5 billion. UAW president Ron Gettlefinger said he was pleased that the trust would secure retirees'

benefits. The UAW's national negotiating committee and GM's executive board both unanimously recommended ratification. "There's no question this was one of the most complex and difficult bargaining sessions in the history of the GM-UAW relationship," CEO Wagoner said, thanking the UAW bargaining team for its work in reaching the agreement.

The new contract also created a two-tier wage structure, with some newly hired workers receiving lower pay—in line with Toyota's. The union also agreed to early-retirement plans for thousands of current workers. Some analysts estimated that the new healthcare trust alone will save GM as much as $3.4 billion annually once it fully kicks in.

Six months after GM's agreement with the UAW, chairman and CEO Wagoner received a 33 percent raise, bringing his salary to $2.2 million, and stock shares worth at least $1.68 million for his performance in a year for which the automaker reported a loss of $38.7 billion. He also received stock options for a half-million shares. UAW president Gettlefinger questioned the fairness of big payouts for executives after workers agreed to concessions and while GM is still losing money. [63]

Questions for Critical Thinking

1. Why do you think, after many years, the UAW conceded on the retiree healthcare issue?

2. How do you think GM shareholders and employees, both current and retired, would react to CEO Wagoner's compensation? Explain.

How would you like to take your dog to work? That's everyday life at Replacements, Ltd., the world's largest supplier of old and new china and silverware, located in Greensboro, North Carolina. With a 415,000-square-foot facility, Replacements has an inventory of 13 million pieces in more than 297,000 patterns, some more than 100 years old. Owner and founder Bob Page built Replacements into a $70 million-a-year business and has been bringing his two dachshunds to work for years, and he encourages Replacement's more than 500 employees to do the same. But please be careful around the fragile china!

Although pets have traditionally been banned from most offices, Replacements is one of a growing number of firms that allow dogs at work. About 20 percent of U.S. firms, including giants like Google, allow dogs in the office. According to psychologist Dr. Rose Perrine, author of the study "Critters in the Cube Farm," "Employees perceive that [pets at work] reduce stress. Employees also thought pets improved mental and physical health, and organization effects, such as attendance and productivity." Page echoes these sentiments, welcoming dogs not only in the office, but also in the warehouse and even the showroom.

According to Page, it's a perk that pays off. According to one survey, 46 million workers would work longer hours if they were allowed to bring companions to the office. The theory is simple: dogs reduce stress—and that is good for business.

The dogs seem to get along well at Replacements, and only occasionally express themselves with a loud bark. Although there have been a few "accidents," dogs have become part of the firm's culture. The company has been named as a "Best Place" to work in a number of publications. If you are ever in Greensboro, feel free to stop in; well-behaved pets are welcome.[64]

Questions for Critical Thinking

1. Why does Bob Page, founder of Replacement, Ltd., allow employees to bring their dogs to work?

2. In what ways does having dogs at work help Replacements, Ltd. recruit and retain quality employees?

3. Which of the motivation theories that we discussed explain why 46 million Americans would work longer if they could bring a companion to work?

4. How do you feel about working in an office that would allow dogs? Can you see any drawbacks to such a policy?

chapter

10

Improving Performance through Empowerment, Teamwork, and Communication

© iStockphoto

IDEO's Innovative Design Teams

How do businesses generate new ideas? Are they the result of inspiration or perspiration? IDEO's customers would probably answer, "Both," because they have experienced the wizardry of founder David Kelley's collaborative approach to product design. Palo Alto, California–based IDEO uses teams to create breakthroughs in products that people really use—everything from Apple's first computer mouse to new train interiors for Amtrak to baby strollers for Evenflo. IDEO's clients include a variety of organizations, such as Procter & Gamble, Intel, the Mayo Clinic, and the American Red Cross.

IDEO uses cross-functional design teams—groups of professionals with different areas of expertise, such as industrial design, mechanical engineering, architecture, psychology, and anthropology. Considering the human factor is central to IDEO's philosophy—that empathy is vital to the successful design of every product. So IDEO teams are dispatched all over the world to observe consumers using goods and services in their daily lives. Team members watch how consumers use items and note ways in which they could be improved. Whenever possible, they put themselves in the place of the consumer. One IDEO team member had himself strapped to a hospital gurney and wheeled through the emergency room admission process so that he could learn how a hospital could improve its services.

IDEO also believes that teamwork is the foundation of creativity and innovation. IDEO executives and staff use teams to share and improve ideas, build problem-solving skills, and spark a multitude of new ideas. A single team meeting can generate ideas for a variety of tasks or projects, not just the one at hand. At IDEO, team brainstorming and discussion sessions aren't secret. Members are encouraged to test ideas with family, friends, and colleagues. This way, simultaneous innovation occurs—an idea that may not work for one product may work beautifully for another.

With all of this information sharing and "thinking outside the box," it may seem that IDEO's designs result from creative chaos. But the design process itself is careful and thorough. IDEO teams take a five-step approach for every project:

- They start by researching existing goods and services.
- They observe consumers using these products.
- They visualize improvements or solutions.
- They evaluate their initial ideas.

- Finally, they refine and implement their solutions to their clients' problems—perhaps in the form of an improvement or a new product altogether.

The human factor lies at the core of everything IDEO does. Tim Brown, IDEO's president and CEO, notes that design and innovation "encourage us to take a human-centered, empathic approach to business problems as well as social problems," and by viewing problems or ideas that way, IDEO is able to make connections between seemingly unrelated areas. From the human-centered focus came the idea of strapping a team member to a hospital gurney. What did the team learn from this experiment? They discovered that patients often become confused and disoriented when lying on a gurney simply because they can't see signs on the hospital walls. They don't necessarily know which room they've been in or where they are going—particularly if they are handed off from one staff member to another. So the IDEO team came up with a Patient Journey Punch Card that would show each person where he or she had been, what had taken place, and what would be happening next.

But the IDEO team didn't stop there. They figured they might also be able to learn something from smooth-functioning, precise NASCAR pit crews that could be applied to hospital emergency room (ER) procedures. So the team took their clients to watch the pit crews during a race. They discovered that those teams work under similarly stressful, time-constrained conditions. They realized that ER staff and pit crews ultimately want to make everyone comfortable and happy—as quickly as possible. "Seeing something that is analogous can be inspirational," notes Chris Flink, a partner at IDEO. "The pit crew's behavior was something the ER team could consider. The sense of wanting to help people, for example in the health care professions, can get lost over time." But viewing the race teams helped the ER employees reconnect and rethink how they approached their business from the patient's point of view. Flink continued, "It's deeply inspirational to them because they do care."

When given the task of developing a better baby stroller for Evenflo, the four members of the IDEO stroller team immediately dismantled just about every stroller on the market to see how they worked. Evenflo wanted a stroller that would be compatible with any infant car seat. It also wanted a stroller that would grab people's attention, maneuver easily, and be comfortable. Armed with this objective and knowledge about existing strollers, the team hit the street. They watched how parents and nannies

pivoted, pushed, and pulled their strollers. They observed how strollers handled bumps and curbs. "We watch and talk to people and try to figure out why they do what they do and how they use things," explains team member Bryan Walker. The IDEO team generated literally hundreds of possible solutions to the problems raised by Evenflo, and in the end delivered several models for Evenflo's approval.

IDEO's team approach to every project works because its members collaborate to find solutions. "IDEO likes to hire people whose mindset allows them to see opportunities rather than problems," says Chris Flink.[1]

Chapter 10   OVERVIEW

Top managers at most firms recognize that teamwork and communication are essential for encouraging employees and helping them improve organizational performance. This chapter focuses on how organizations involve employees by sharing information and empowering them to make critical decisions, allowing them to work in teams, and fostering communication. We begin by discussing the

ways managers are expanding their employees' decision-making authority and responsibility. Then we explain why and how a growing number of firms rely on teams of workers rather than individuals to make decisions and carry out assignments. Finally, we discuss how effective communication allows workers to share information that improves decision making.

Empowering Employees

empowerment giving employees authority and responsibility to make decisions about their work without traditional managerial approval and control.

An important component of effective management is **empowerment** of employees. Managers promote this goal by giving employees authority and responsibility to make decisions about their work without traditional managerial approval and control. Empowerment seeks to tap the brainpower of all workers to find improved ways of doing their jobs and executing their ideas. Empowerment frees managers from hands-on control of subordinates. It also motivates workers by adding challenges to their jobs and giving them a feeling of ownership. Managers empower employees by sharing company information and decision-making authority and by rewarding them based on company performance.

Sharing Information and Decision-Making Authority

One of the most effective methods of empowering employees is to keep them informed about the company's financial performance. Companies such as Virginia-based engineering firm Anderson & Associates provide regular reports to their employees on key financial information, such as profit-and-loss statements. Anderson, which designs roads, water and sewer lines, and water-treatment facilities, posts financial statements, training schedules, policy documents, and other information on the company's internal Web site.[2] Any employee can visit the site and look up the company's cash flow, design standards, and photos of coworkers in other cities, as well as basic measures of financial performance.

Like other companies that practice this strategy of open-book management, Anderson also trains its employees to interpret financial statements so that they can understand how their work contributes to company profits. Using information technology to empower employees does carry some risks. One is that information may reach competitors. Although Anderson & Associates considered this problem, management decided that sharing information was essential to the company's strategy.

The second way in which companies empower employees is to give them broad authority to make workplace decisions that implement a firm's vision and its competitive strategy. Even among nonmanagement staff, empowerment extends to decisions and activities traditionally handled by managers. Employees might be responsible for such tasks as purchasing supplies, making hiring decisions, scheduling production or work hours, overseeing the safety program, and granting pay increases. The original Westinghouse Air Brake Company was founded in 1869 when George Westinghouse invented the first air brake system for locomotive engines. The company maintained worldwide leadership throughout the 20th century by developing rail equipment technologies that improved the safety and productivity of customers. Wabtec Corporation was formed when Westinghouse Air Brake merged with MotivePower Industries.[3] Through employee empowerment, assembly-line workers that once attached a single bolt now assemble an entire brake directly from a customer's order. Management and line workers hold brainstorming sessions several times each year. According to CEO Albert Neupaver: "If you listen to the operators, they'll give you the solutions."[4] The "Hit & Miss" feature describes how Nugget Market empowers employees to deliver excellent service.

Linking Rewards to Company Performance

Some companies give employees special privileges, called *perks*, to motivate them, as the "Solving an Ethical Controversy" feature on page 330 describes. But perhaps the ultimate step in convincing employees of their stake in the prosperity of their firm is worker ownership. Two widely used ways that companies provide worker ownership are employee stock ownership plans and stock options. Table 10.1 compares these two methods of employee ownership.

EMPLOYEE STOCK OWNERSHIP PLANS More than 11 million workers participate in nearly 10,000 **employee stock ownership plans (ESOPs)** worth more than $900 billion.[5] These plans benefit employees by giving them ownership stakes in their companies, leading to potential profits as the value of their firm increases. Under ESOPs, the employer buys shares of the company stock on behalf of the employee as a retirement benefit. The accounts continue to grow in value tax-free, and when employees leave the company, they can cash in their stock shares. Employees are motivated to work harder and smarter than they would without ESOPs because, as part owners, they share in their firm's financial success.

As retirement plans, ESOPs must comply with government regulations designed to protect pension benefits. Because ESOPs can be expensive to set up, they are more common in larger firms than in smaller ones. Public companies with ESOPs average around 14,000 employees, while private companies average about 1,500 employees.[6] One danger with ESOPs is that if the majority of an employee's retirement funds are in company stock and the value falls dramatically, the employee may be severely harmed.[7]

STOCK OPTIONS Another popular way for companies to share ownership with their employees is through the use of **stock options,** or rights to buy a specified amount of company stock at a given price within a given time period. In contrast to an ESOP, in which the company holds stock for the benefit of employees, stock options give employees a chance to own the stock themselves if they exercise their options by completing the stock purchase. According to the National Center for Employee Ownership, stock options work like this: "A stock option plan grants employees the right to buy company stock at a specified price

Hit & Miss

Nugget Market Employees: The Power of Gold

Nugget Market is more than a supermarket; it's a shopping destination. The upscale stores in the California chain feature hand-painted murals and statues at the entrance, elegant merchandise displays, a vast selection—600 varieties of produce and 400 types of cheese—fresh meat and fish, restaurant-quality ready-to-cook entrees and ready-to-eat meals, baked-from-scratch treats, a deli, tea and espresso bar, sushi bar, olive bar, soup and hot pizza counters, a café with wine by the glass, and more.

Nugget offers a unique blend of gourmet fare, products for the health-conscious, and the usual supermarket goods. But the chain is known for more than that. Nugget prices its goods competitively and delivers first-rate service. Employees are called "associates," and customers are "guests." When choosing associates, managers look for "can-do people that want to enjoy what they do for a living." CEO Eric Stille says Nugget's success comes from the family feeling in the stores. His goal is to make Nugget "a great place to be every day" for both associates and guests. The company, which has made the *Fortune* 100 Best Companies to Work For list several times, gives employees generous benefits, training and opportunities for personal development and promotion, and the responsibility to serve customers well.

As Nugget is committed to associates, so are the associates committed to guests. They provide prompt, friendly service and take initiative when needed. For example, when a guest asked about the availability of a specific type of green chili pepper, a produce director whipped out his cell phone, found out that the pepper is available only from August to October, and told the customer, "Come back in August. We'll take care of you."

Nugget associates are also trusted to develop their own departments. Wine steward Larry Otterness stocks the wine, beer, and spirits in Nugget's Roseville, California, store with a huge selection of domestic and imported beers and wines, including those from California vintners. At Friday night wine tastings, he interacts with guests and teaches them about wine. He says he loves his job. "We're all running our own shows … We've all got each other to support and help us … In the same way that I'm able to take chances in ordering, I can also takes chances in other areas, because I know everyone will rise to the occasion. We are empowered to think big."

For Wayne Rudi, assistant director of meat operations, thinking big has meant creating a new product. "It is my vision to bring back sausage as a healthy, wholesome lifestyle choice that's good for you," he says. From his first batch of five pounds of mild Italian links, he has developed a line of handmade, low-fat, low-sodium sausage made from natural, organic beef, pork, veal, and boneless/skinless chicken thighs and seasoned with natural herbs and spices. The vision of this empowered employee has produced results that Nugget guests are eating up.

Questions for Critical Thinking

1. What do you think is the first step in empowering employees at Nugget Market?
2. How does calling employees "associates" contribute to empowerment at Nugget stores?

Sources: Mike Roberts, "Employees Treated Like Gold at Nugget Market," *Village Life*, February 4, 2009, http://www.villagelife.com; Tim Menicutch, "A Shiny, New Nugget Opens Today," El Dorado Hills, California, *Telegraph*, January 30, 2008, http://www.edhtelegraph.com, accessed October 21, 2008; Meg Major, "Striking Gold," *Progressive Grocer*, September 1, 2007, pp. 40–48.

Table 10.1	Employee Stock Ownership Plans and Stock Options
ESOP	**Stock Options**
• Company-sponsored trust fund holds shares of stock for employees	• Company gives employees the option to buy shares of its stock
• Usually covers all full-time employees	• Can be granted to one, a few, or all employees
• Employer pays for the shares of stock	• Employees pay a set price to exercise the option
• Employees receive stock shares (or value of stock) upon retiring or leaving the company	• Employees receive shares of stock when (and if) they exercise the option, usually during a set period

Sources: Based on "Employee Stock Options Fact Sheet," "How an Employee Stock Ownership Plan (ESOP) Works" "A Comprehensive Overview of Employee Ownership," National Center for Employee Ownership, accessed March 2009, http://www.nceo.org.

during a specified period once the option has vested. So if an employee gets an option on 100 shares at $10 and the stock price goes up to $20, the employee can 'exercise' the option and buy those 100 shares at $10 each, sell them on the market for $20 each, and pocket the difference. But if the stock price never rises above the option price, the employee will simply not exercise the option."[8]

Although options were once limited to senior executives and members of the board of directors, some companies now grant stock options to employees at all levels. Federal labor laws allow stock options to be granted to both hourly and salaried employees. It is estimated that 7 to 10 million employees in thousands of companies hold stock options.[9] About one-third of all stock options issued by U.S. corporations go to the top five executives at each firm. Much of the remainder goes to other executives and managers, who make up only about 2 percent of the U.S. workforce. Yet there is solid evidence that stock options motivate regular employees to perform better. Some argue that to be most effective as motivators, stock options need to be granted to a much broader base of employees.

Stock options have turned hundreds of employees at firms such as Home Depot, Microsoft, and Google into millionaires. But such success stories are no guarantee, especially when stock prices drop during economic downturns. As with ESOPs, employees face risks when they rely on a single company's stock to provide for them. The National Center for Employee Ownership estimates the total lost value of stock options in the hundreds of billions of dollars.[10]

Teams

A **team** is a group of people with complementary skills who are committed to a common purpose, approach, and set of performance goals. All team members hold themselves mutually responsible and accountable for accomplishing their objectives. Teams are widely used in business and in many not-for-profit organizations such as hospitals and government agencies. Teams are one of the most frequently discussed topics in employee training programs, in which individuals often learn how to work with others. Many firms emphasize the importance of teams during their hiring processes, asking job applicants about their previous experiences as team members. Why? Because companies want to hire people who can work well with other people and pool their talents and ideas to achieve more together than they could achieve working alone. Today, as shown in Figure 10.1, there are five basic types of teams: work teams, problem-solving teams, self-managed teams, cross-functional teams, and virtual teams.

About two-thirds of U.S. firms currently use **work teams,** which are relatively permanent groups of employees. In this approach, people with

Assessment Check ✓

1. What is empowerment?
2. What kinds of information can companies provide employees to help them share decision-making responsibility?
3. What are some of the risks of sharing this information?
4. How do employee stock ownership plans and stock options reward employees and encourage empowerment?

team group of employees who are committed to a common purpose, approach, and set of performance goals.

work team relatively permanent group of employees with complementary skills who perform the day-to-day work of organizations.

Figure 10.1   **Five Species of Teams**

Five Species of Teams

Self-Managed Teams: Teams that are empowered to decide how they complete their daily tasks.

Cross-Functional Teams: Teams that are made up of members from different functions, or parts, of a firm.

Virtual Teams: Groups of geographically and/or organizationally dispersed co-workers who use a combination of telecommunications and information technologies to accomplish an organizational task.

Work Teams: An increasingly popular species, work teams do just that—the daily work. When empowered, they are self-managed teams.

Problem-Solving Teams: This most popular of types comprises knowledge workers who gather to solve specific problems and then disband.

EXECUTIVE PERKS—NOT BUSINESS AS USUAL?

Executives often receive not just cash rewards such as stock options and bonuses, but also special perks, or privileges, that other employees do not. Perks range from country club memberships to corporate jets to use of company cars and free dry-cleaning services. But these gifts are getting extra scrutiny now, when companies are cutting costs to stay afloat.

After accepting about $1.5 billion from the federal Troubled Asset Relief Program, Northern Trust Corp. flew hundreds of clients and employees to Los Angeles for a star-studded weekend of entertainment at a golf tournament. The company had just laid off 450 workers, causing speculation about the source of the funds for the outing. The bank later said it would repay the bailout funds it received. The heads of the three Detroit auto manufacturers—Ford, General Motors, and Chrysler—were ridiculed for flying to Washington, DC, in corporate jets for a meeting with Congress to ask for bailout funds.

Should companies receiving government assistance or cutting costs be allowed to give their executive perks?

PRO

1. Companies should be allowed to compensate executives in whatever ways will make them more competitive in the marketplace. Business experts defend the practice of generous executive perks because they allow a firm to retain its best talent.

2. The top executives in any firm are also the risk takers. The same traits—including healthy doses of confidence—that make them good at what they do are also those that value high salaries and perks.

CON

1. If a company receives government assistance or is in trouble financially, it should be held accountable for the way it spends its funds. "There is no doubt there has been an increase in companies disclosing cutbacks in executive perks," observes one compensation researcher.

2. Executive perks should be tied to company performance, particularly in the case of those receiving federal assistance. Employee morale, already at a low point, suffers even more when average workers see executives not sharing their pain.

Summary

Whether they receive federal aid or not, more companies are cutting back on executive perks such as luxury travel, country club memberships, entertainment, and bonuses. Severance packages have been reduced as well. "Our advice is to eliminate [perks] except for those that are critically necessary for business needs," says one executive pay expert. In these times, companies that don't take that advice risk bad publicity.

Sources: Alfonso Serrano, "Reining in CEO Perks," *Portfolio,* February 29, 2009, http://www.portfolio.com; Becky Yerak, "Northern Trust May Card Bogey on Los Angeles Golf Tournament Sponsorship," *Chicago Tribune,* February 25, 2009, http://www.chicagotribune.com; Nanette Byrnes and Theo Francis, "Will the Big Bucks Stop Here?" *Spiegel Online International,* February 5, 2009, http://www.spiegel.de/international/business; Daniel Trotta, "For CEOs, Thirst for Perks May Be in their DNA," *Financial Post,* January 30, 2009, http://www.financialpost.com; Barbara De Lollis, "Business Events Turn Practical," *USA Today,* p. 4B; Martha Graybow, "For CEOs, Giving Up Perks May Be Hard to Do," *Reuters,* November 19, 2008, http://www.reuters.com.

Solving an ETHICAL controversy

complementary skills perform the day-to-day work of the organization. Most of Wal-Mart's major vendors maintain offices near its headquarters in Bentonville, Arkansas. Typically, the vendor offices operate as work teams, and the head of these vendor offices often has the title of "team leader."

In contrast to work teams, a **problem-solving team** is a temporary combination of workers who gather to solve a specific problem and then disband. They differ from work teams in important ways, though. Work teams are permanent units designed to handle any business problem that arises, but problem-solving teams pursue specific missions. These missions can be broadly stated, such as finding out why customers are satisfied or how to transition from one major computer

problem-solving team temporary combination of workers who gather to solve a specific problem and then disband.

system to another, or narrowly defined, such as solving the overheating problem in Generator 4 or determining the best way and time to move from an old office location to a new one. Once the team completes its task by solving the assigned problem, it usually disbands.

A work team empowered with the authority to decide how its members complete their daily tasks is called a **self-managed team.** A self-managed team works most effectively when it combines employees with a range of skills and functions. Members are cross-trained to perform each other's jobs as needed. Distributing decision-making authority in this way can free members to concentrate on satisfying customers. Whole Foods Market, a national chain of upscale food stores, has a structure based on self-managed work teams. Company managers decided that Whole Foods could be most innovative if employees made decisions themselves. Every employee is part of a team, and each store has about ten teams handling separate functions, such as groceries, bakery, and customer service. Each team handles responsibilities related to setting goals, hiring and training employees, scheduling team

Although members of a *virtual team* rarely meet in person, they stay in touch through new technologies like videoconferencing. In today's global marketplace, the flexibility of virtual teams is a distinct advantage.

Image Source/Getty Images

members, and purchasing goods to stock. Teams meet at least monthly to review goals and performance, solve problems, and explore new ideas. Whole Foods awards bonuses based on the teams' performance relative to their goals.[11] The "Hit & Miss" feature describes another company that has used teamwork effectively to change customers' opinions for the better.

A team made up of members from different functions, such as production, marketing, and finance, is called a **cross-functional team.** Most often, cross-functional teams work on specific problems or projects, but they can also serve as permanent work team arrangements. The value of cross-functional teams comes from their ability to bring many different perspectives to a work effort. When J. B. Hunt Transport Services identified an increase in overdue and delinquent bills, the Lowell, Arkansas–based transportation company began the "perfect invoice initiative." Cross-functional teams found several problems, including a lack of integration between the sales system and the billing system and difficulty tracking driver delay charges. Teams set priorities enabling Hunt to improve its invoicing system and gain $5.9 million in increased revenue, labor savings, and faster payments.[12]

Virtual teams are groups of geographically or organizationally dispersed coworkers who use a combination of telecommunications and information technologies to accomplish an organizational task. Because of the availability of e-mail, videoconferencing, and group communication software, members of virtual teams rarely meet face-to-face. The principal advantage of virtual teams is that they are very flexible. Employees can work with each other regardless of physical location, time zone, or organizational affiliation. Virtual teams can be difficult to manage. But some companies have found strategies that help coordinate virtual teamwork. ON Semiconductor has information technology staff around the globe who support sales staff in Slovakia, where it has a factory; in Hong Kong, where there is a sales office; in Shenzhen, China, where there is a customer service center; and in Kuala Lumpur, Malaysia, where its regional development center is located. One team member at ON's Phoenix,

self-managed team work team that has the authority to decide how its members complete their daily tasks.

cross-functional team team made up of members from different functions, such as production, marketing, and finance.

virtual team group of geographically or organizationally dispersed coworkers who use a combination of telecommunications and information technologies to accomplish an organizational task.

Assessment Check ✓

1. What is a team?
2. What are the five types of teams, and how are they different?

United's Clean Teams Send Customer Satisfaction Soaring

Any traveler who has logged even a few hundred miles in the air knows that it's not pleasant to sit for several hours shoulder-to-shoulder with fellow passengers in a dirty plane. In the wake of soaring fuel costs and fewer passengers willing to pay full fare, airlines pruned their cleaning staff and materials to cut expenses. United Airlines admits that its aircraft would go from 6 to 18 months between thorough cleanings, which entails heavy scrubbing of the cabin from top to bottom. But leaving crumbs on the cabin floor and wadded up paper towels in the bathroom isn't the same as reducing food service to pretzels and nuts. To many consumers, an unclean plane represents a new low. In fact, airlines discovered that dirty planes affect travelers' perceptions of all services. "You ask people to rate the planes; they notice dirty," says one travel writer, who notes that people who are forced to fly in dirty cabins also assume that planes will arrive late and luggage will be lost.

So airlines—United in particular—have begun reversing this trend. Recognizing the need to attract more passengers to stay in business, they now dispatch teams to scour their aircraft from top to bottom more frequently. Paul Sanders, United's general manager for cabin appearance—dubbed Mr. Clean by his team—operates with military precision and thoroughness. He runs his finger over each surface and sniffs in each corner. He makes sure that intensive cleanings are accomplished on United jets every 15 to 30 days—carpets are shampooed, seat cushions removed and checked for stains, every nook and cranny of the planes searched for dirt. He is responsible for helping to set United's cleaning standards worldwide, making sure that cleaning teams in Europe and Asia are trained to the same standards as those in the United States. He points out that a clean plane looks and feels like new.

Moments after a United flight taxis to the gate, a cleaning team swarms onto the empty plane, plucking coffee cups, tissues, and other trash from the seats and floor. Reading materials are placed in their seat-back pockets, trays are wiped, bathrooms and galleys are scrubbed to gleaming. Overhead bins are checked for belongings, and blankets are folded. If a team leader notices a suspicious odor or smudge of grime, he or she points it out to the cleaning crew.

Clean has struck a chord with United's passengers. The airline's passenger ratings for cabin cleanliness increased dramatically just a few months after the new cleaning program was put in place. Satisfied travelers are likely to pass the good word to friends, family, and colleagues. Something as simple as a clean passenger cabin may actually give United a competitive advantage.

Questions for Critical Thinking

1. How would you classify the type of cleaning teams that work for United? Do you think any other type of team would be as effective? Why or why not?
2. How does United's focus on teamwork positively differentiate it from its competitors?

Sources: Carl Unger, "American, United Aim for Cleaner Planes," *Smarter Travel,* January 30, 2009, http://www.smatertravel.com; "Airlines Clean Up Planes to Bring Back Flyers," *AHN,* January 30, 2009, http://www.allheadlinenews.com; Julie Johnson, "United, Others Get Serious about Clean Planes," *Chicago Tribune,* January 29, 2009, http://www.chicagotribune.com; Matt Bartosik, "Airlines Clean Up Their Act," *NBC Chicago,* January 29, 2009, http://www.nbcchicago.com.

Arizona, headquarters sets objectives and distributes work to team members wherever they reside. Recognizing the importance of in-person meetings, the firm also brings team members to its corporate headquarters to work on key projects.[13]

Team Characteristics

Effective teams share a number of characteristics. They must be an appropriate size to accomplish their work. In addition to size, teams also can be categorized according to the similarities and differences among team members, called *level* and *diversity.* We discuss these three characteristics next.

Team Size

Teams can range in size from as small as 2 people to as large as 150 people. In practice, however, most teams have fewer than 12 members. Although no ideal size limit applies to every team, research on team effectiveness indicates that they achieve maximum results with about six or seven members. A group of this size is big enough to benefit from a variety of diverse skills, yet small enough to allow members to communicate easily and feel part of a close-knit group.

Certainly, groups smaller or larger than this ideal size can do effective work, but they can create added challenges for a team leader. Participants in small teams of two to four members often show a desire to get along with each other. They tend to favor informal interactions marked by discussions of personal topics, and they make only limited demands on team leaders. A large team with more than 12 members poses a different challenge for team leaders because decision making may work slowly and participants may feel less committed to team goals. Larger teams also tend to foster disagreements, absenteeism, and membership turnover. Subgroups may form, leading to possible conflicts among various functions. As a general rule, a team of more than 20 people should be divided into subteams, each with its own members and goals.

Team Level and Team Diversity

Team level is the average level of ability, experience, personality, or any other factor on a team. For example, a high level of team experience means that a team has members who, on average, are very experienced. This does not mean that *every* member of the team has considerable experience but that enough team members do to significantly raise the average level of experience on the team. Businesses consider team level when they need teams with a particular set of skills or capabilities to do their jobs well.

While team level represents the average level or capability on a team, **team diversity** represents the variances or differences in ability, experience, personality, or any other factor on a team. In other words, strong teams not only have talented members—as demonstrated by their team level—but also members who are different in terms of ability, experience, or personality. Team diversity is an important consideration for teams that must complete a wide range of different tasks or particularly complex tasks. For instance, the British Broadcasting Corporation (BBC) routinely creates teams for a variety of events such as the FIFA World Cup or the Olympic Games. These teams involve production and broadcast groups larger than 100 people, many of whom are part-time employees. Team members typically come from more than 15 different countries, with skills ranging from electrician to statistician, or from scheduling to producing. And because an event at any of the sports venues only takes place once, the BBC teams have one chance to get it right.[14]

team level average level of ability, experience, personality, or any other factor on a team.

team diversity variances or differences in ability, experience, personality, or any other factor on a team

Assessment Check ✓

1. Teams reach maximum effectiveness, diversity, and communication flow with how many members?

2. Explain team level and team diversity.

Stages of Team Development

Teams typically progress through five stages of development: forming, storming, norming, performing, and adjourning. Although not every team passes through each of these stages, teams that do tend to be better performers. These stages are summarized in Figure 10.2.

STAGE 1: FORMING The first stage, forming, is an orientation period during which team members get to know each other and find out what behaviors are acceptable to the group. Team members begin with curiosity about expectations of them and whether they will fit in with the group. An effective team leader provides time for members to become acquainted.

Figure 10.2   Stages of Team Development

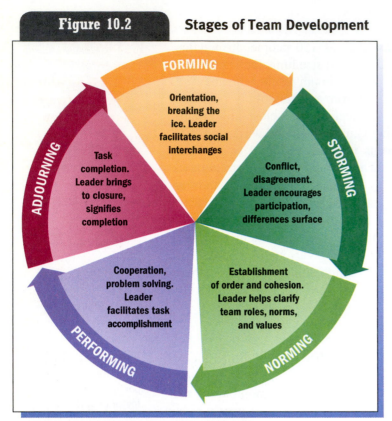

FORMING — Orientation, breaking the ice. Leader facilitates social interchanges

STORMING — Conflict, disagreement. Leader encourages participation, differences surface

NORMING — Establishment of order and cohesion. Leader helps clarify team roles, norms, and values

PERFORMING — Cooperation, problem solving. Leader facilitates task accomplishment

ADJOURNING — Task completion. Leader brings to closure, signifies completion

STAGE 2: STORMING The personalities of team members begin to emerge at the storming stage as members clarify their roles and expectations. Conflicts may arise, as people disagree over the team's mission and jockey for position and control of the group. Subgroups may form based on common interests or concerns. At this stage, the team leader must encourage everyone to participate, allowing members to work through their uncertainties and conflicts. Teams must move beyond this stage to achieve real productivity.

STAGE 3: NORMING During the norming stage, members resolve differences among them, accept each other, and reach broad agreement about the roles of the team leader and other participants. This stage is usually brief, and the team leader should use it to emphasize the team's unity and the importance of its objectives.

STAGE 4: PERFORMING Team members focus on solving problems and accomplishing tasks at the performing stage. They interact frequently and handle conflicts in constructive ways. The team leader encourages contributions from all members. He or she should attempt to get any nonparticipating team members involved.

STAGE 5: ADJOURNING The team disbands at the adjourning stage after members have completed their assigned task or solved the problem. During this phase, the focus is on wrapping up and summarizing the team's experiences and accomplishments. The team leader may recognize the team's accomplishments with a celebration, perhaps handing out plaques or awards.

Assessment Check ✔

1. Explain how teams progress through the stages of team development.
2. Explain the difference between the storming and performing stages.

Team Cohesiveness and Norms

team cohesiveness
extent to which team members feel attracted to the team and motivated to remain part of it.

Teams tend to maximize productivity when they form into highly cohesive units. **Team cohesiveness** is the extent to which team members feel attracted to the team and motivated to remain part of it. This cohesiveness typically increases when members interact frequently, share common attitudes and goals, and enjoy being together. When cohesiveness is low, morale suffers. By contrast, cohesive groups have a better chance of retaining their members. As a result, cohesive groups typically experience lower turnover. In addition, team cohesiveness promotes cooperative behavior, generosity, and a willingness on the part of team members to help each other. When team cohesiveness is high, team members are more motivated to contribute to the team, because they want the approval of other team members. Not surprisingly, studies have clearly established that cohesive teams quickly achieve high levels of performance and consistently perform better. Team-building retreats are an effective way to encourage cohesiveness and improve satisfaction and retention.[15] Many team training approaches also emphasize building cohesion through techniques like cross-training team members in each others' roles or training team members to develop the skills needed to support the team task.[16]

"They Said It"

"The team that trusts—their leader and each other—is more likely to be successful."

—**Mike Krzyzewski** (b. 1947)
Head basketball coach, Duke University

A **team norm** is a standard of conduct shared by team members that guides their behavior. Norms are not formal written guidelines; they are informal standards that identify key values and clarify team members' expectations. In highly productive teams, norms contribute to constructive work and the accomplishment of team goals. For instance, the Rutherford County public school system, the sixth largest in Tennessee, launched a systemwide effort to create work teams in every school to improve teaching. Team norms represent commitments to behave in certain ways that guide members in working together. Each team has a leader who encourages the team to focus on a few essential norms such as when and how teams will meet and how they will interact with students.[17]

team norm informal standard of conduct shared by team members that guides their behavior.

Assessment Check ✔

1. How does cohesiveness affect teams?

2. Explain how team norms positively and negatively affect teams.

Team Conflict

Conflict is an antagonistic interaction in which one party attempts to thwart the intentions or goals of another. Conflict and disagreement are inevitable in most teams. But this shouldn't surprise anyone. People who work together are naturally going to disagree about what and how things are done. What causes conflict in teams? Although almost anything can lead to conflict—casual remarks that unintentionally offend a team member or fighting over scarce resources—the primary cause of team conflict is disagreement over team goals and priorities. Other common causes of team conflict include disagreements over task-related issues, interpersonal incompatibilities, simple fatigue, and team diversity.

conflict antagonistic interaction in which one party attempts to thwart the intentions or goals of another.

Earlier in this chapter we noted how teams can experience diversity among members. Chapter 1 discussed how diversity in gender, ethnic background, culture, religion, age, and physical and mental abilities can enhance a firm's success. While diversity brings stimulation, challenge, and energy, it can also lead to conflict. The job of the manager is to create an environment in which differences are appreciated and in which a team of diverse individuals works productively together. Diversity awareness training programs can reduce conflict by bringing these differences out in the open and identifying the unique talents of diverse individuals.

Lothar Schulz/Getty Images

Successful teams are *cohesive*—that is, they hold together well. In sports and in business, their low turnover and high productivity give them a competitive edge.

Although most people think conflict should be avoided, it is essential for teams to mature and perform at the highest level; mature teams encourage members to address their differences.[18] The key to dealing with conflict is making sure that the team experiences the right kind of conflict. **Cognitive conflict** focuses on problem-related differences of opinion, and reconciling these differences strongly improves team performance. With cognitive conflict, team members disagree because their different experiences and expertise lead them to different views of the problem and its solutions. Cognitive conflict is also characterized by a willingness to examine, compare, and reconcile differences to produce the best possible solution. By contrast, **affective conflict** refers to the emotional reactions that can occur when disagreements become personal rather than professional, and these differences strongly decrease team performance. Because affective conflict often results

"They Said It"

"I don't like to work in a group. I don't get along well with other people."

—Jimmy Breslin (b. 1930) Columnist

in hostility, anger, resentment, distrust, cynicism, and apathy, it can make people uncomfortable, cause them to withdraw, decrease their commitment to a team, lower the satisfaction of team members, and decrease team cohesiveness. So, unlike cognitive conflict, affective conflict undermines team performance by preventing teams from engaging in activities that are critical to team effectiveness.

What can managers do to manage team conflict? Emphasizing cognitive conflict alone isn't enough, because cognitive and affective conflict can occur together in the same teams. Attempts to agree on a difficult issue can quickly deteriorate from cognitive to affective conflict if the discussion turns personal and tempers and emotions flare. So while cognitive conflict is clearly the better approach to take, encouraging conflict of any type should be approached with caution.

Perhaps the team leader's most important contribution to conflict resolution can be facilitating good communication so that teammates respect each other and are free to disagree with each other. Ongoing, effective communication ensures that team members perceive each other accurately, understand what is expected of them, and obtain the information they need. Improved communication increases the chances of working cooperatively as a team. The remainder of this chapter discusses the importance of effective communication and the development of good communication skills.

Assessment Check ✔

1. What is cognitive conflict, and how does it affect teams?
2. Explain affective conflict and its impact on teams.

The Importance of Effective Communication

Countries like China, Thailand, and Mexico are home to a number of manufacturing businesses that sell products to companies in the United States. But the more parties that are involved in the production process, the harder it is to maintain good communication among them. This was never more obvious than when poor communication led to toy giant Mattel's recall of 21 million products made in China. Breakdowns occurred all along the communication chain—from inadequate product specifications, to faulty assumptions on how and where the toys were being produced, to pressure to stay on schedule at all cost. After concerns were raised about lead paint and small magnets that children could swallow, the massive recalls were issued and finger pointing began.[19]

communication
meaningful exchange of information through messages.

Communication can be defined as a meaningful exchange of information through messages. Few businesses, including those as large and successful as Mattel, can succeed without effective communication. Managers spend about 80 percent of their time—six hours and 24 minutes of every eight-hour day—in direct communication with others, whether on the telephone, in meetings, via e-mail, or in individual conversations. Company recruiters consistently rate effective communication, such as listening, conversing, and giving feedback, as the most important skill they look for when hiring new employees. In this last half of the chapter, you'll learn about the communication process, the basic forms of communication, and ways to improve communication within organizations.

The Process of Communication

Every communication follows a step-by-step process that involves interactions among six elements: sender, message, channel, audience, feedback, and context. This process is illustrated in Figure 10.3.

In the first step, the *sender* composes the message and sends it through a communication carrier, or channel. Encoding a message means that the sender translates its meaning into understandable terms and a form that allows transmission through a chosen channel. The sender can communicate a particular message through many different channels, including written messages, face-to-face conversations, and electronic mail. A promotional message to the firm's customers may be communicated through such forms as radio and television ads, billboards, magazines, and sales presentations. The *audience* consists of the people who receive the message. In decoding, the receiver of the message interprets its meaning. *Feedback* from the audience—in response to the sender's communication—helps the sender determine whether the audience has correctly interpreted the intended meaning of the message.

Every communication takes place in some sort of situational or cultural context. The *context* can exert a powerful influence on how well the process works. A conversation between two people in a quiet office, for example, may be a very different experience from the same conversation held in a crowded and noisy restaurant. A request by an American to borrow a flashlight from an Australian friend might produce only confusion; what Americans call *flashlights,* Australians call *torches.* Anthropologists classify cultures as low context and high context. Communication in **low-context cultures** tends to rely on explicit written and verbal messages. Examples include Switzerland, Austria, Germany, and the United States. In contrast, communication in **high-context cultures**—such as those of Japan, Latin America, and India—depends not only on the message itself but also on the conditions that surround it, including nonverbal cues, past and present experiences, and personal relationships between the parties. Westerners must carefully temper their low-context style to the expectations of colleagues and clients from high-context countries. Although Americans tend to favor direct interactions and want to "get down to business" soon after shaking hands or sitting down to a business dinner, businesspeople in Mexico and Asian countries prefer to become acquainted before discussing details. When conducting business in these cultures, wise visitors allow time for relaxed meals during which business-related topics are avoided.

Senders must pay attention to audience feedback, even requesting it if none is forthcoming, because this response clarifies whether the communication has conveyed the intended message. Feedback can indicate whether the receiver paid attention to a message and was able to decode it accurately. Even when the receiver tries to understand, the communication may fail if the message was poorly encoded with difficult or ambiguous words. Managers sometimes become fond of using fuzzy language such as *transparency, forward*

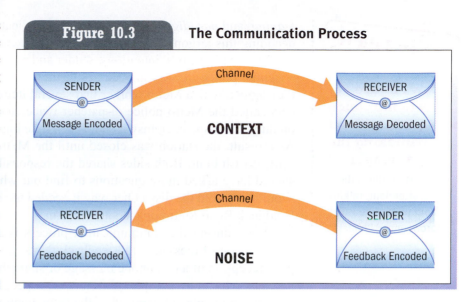

Figure 10.3 **The Communication Process**

SENDER
@
Message Encoded

Channel

RECEIVER
@
Message Decoded

CONTEXT

RECEIVER
@
Feedback Decoded

Channel

SENDER
@
Feedback Encoded

NOISE

At a toy store in California, a stock clerk pulls potentially dangerous products from the shelves after a manufacturer's recall. Because of poor communication between U.S. toy companies and Chinese suppliers, many toys manufactured in China contain poisonous lead paint or small magnets that pose a choking hazard to children.

© Paul Sakuma/AP/Wide World Photos

"They Said It"

"I can't figure out how to introduce the captain without panicking the passengers."

—Delta Airlines flight attendant, talking about pilot Mike Hyjek (pronounced "hijack")

leaning, and *paradigm shift.* Feedback can indicate whether the sender's audience succeeded in decoding this jargon—or even bothered to try.

Even with the best intentions, sender and receiver may not communicate. When Alexandria, Virginia, police officers arrived at rail transit Metro's Braddock Road station after 3:00 a.m., they agreed with a Metro worker that several items found in the area were suspicious. The officers called the Metro police dispatcher twice, asking whether Metro had a bomb-sniffing dog on duty; the dispatcher answered no each time but did not notify the bomb squad to request one. As a result, the station was closed until the Metro bomb squad arrived two hours later, at the start of rush hour. Both sides shared the responsibility for the delay. Metro says its dispatcher should have asked more questions to find out what was happening, and the Alexandria police should have told the dispatcher why it needed the dog. Fortunately, no bomb was found, and the Braddock Road Metro opened at 7:25 a.m.[20]

Noise during the communication process is some type of interference that influences the transmission of messages and feedback. Noise can result from simple physical factors such as poor reception of a cell phone message or static that drowns out a radio commercial. It can also be caused by more complex differences in people's attitudes and perceptions. Consequently, even when people are exposed to the same communications, they can end up with very different perceptions and understandings because of communication noise. Noise can be present at any point in the communication process. This is why communication can be so difficult and frustrating for managers. As part of its strategic effort to improve its internal communications program, the Volvo Group compared its own practices with those of other industry leaders.

Internal communication is focused on relaying the company's mission and strategic objectives to more than 90,000 employees worldwide. Volvo found that the most effective channel for communicating information about mission and strategy was a face-to-face dialogue between a supervisor and his or her employees. So Volvo began using face-to-face communication to create a clear connection between the individual's job and the strategic direction of the company. Today, nearly 85 percent of all employees claim to understand the company's mission and strategic objectives, a significant increase from 67 percent before the change.[21]

Assessment Check

1. What is the difference between communication in low-context and high-context cultures?
2. In the context of the communication process, what is noise?

"They Said It"

"Talk low, talk slow, and don't say too much."

—John Wayne (1907–1979) American actor

Basic Forms of Communication

People communicate in many different ways. Some obvious methods include calling a meeting of team members or writing a formal mission statement. Other much less obvious methods include gestures and facial expressions during a conversation or leaning forward when speaking to someone. These subtle variations can significantly influence the reception of the message. As Table 10.2 points out, different communications can assume various forms: oral and written, formal and informal, and nonverbal.

ORAL COMMUNICATION Managers spend a great deal of their time engaged in oral communication, both in person and on the phone. Some people prefer to communicate this way, believing that oral channels more accurately convey messages. Face-to-face oral communication allows people to combine words with such cues as facial expressions and tone of voice. Oral communication over the telephone lacks visual cues, but it offers some of the advantages of face-to-face communication, such as opportunities to hear the tone of voice and provide immediate feedback by asking questions about anything the receiver doesn't understand or raising new issues related to the message.

Oral communication, because of its immediacy, can result in poor communication. If a person gets agitated or nervous during a conversation, noise enters the communication process. Messages that are not clearly encoded may also fail to communicate the intended idea.

Table 10.2	Forms of Communication	
Form	**Description**	**Examples**
Oral communication	Communication transmitted through speech	Personal conversations, speeches, meetings, voice mail, telephone conversations, videoconferences
Written communication	Communication transmitted through writing	Letters, memos, formal reports, news releases, e-mail, faxes, online discussion groups, Internet messaging
Formal communication	Communication transmitted through the chain of command within an organization to other members or to people outside the organization	Internal—memos, reports, meetings, written proposals, oral presentations, meeting minutes External—letters, written proposals, oral presentations, speeches, news releases, press conferences
Informal communication	Communication transmitted outside formal channels without regard for the organization's hierarchy of authority	Rumors spread informally among employees via the grapevine
Nonverbal communication	Communication transmitted through actions and behaviors rather than through words	Gestures, facial expressions, posture, body language, dress, makeup

A hurried manager may give an oral instruction such as, "I don't care what you have to do; just get the sale," without thinking through the consequences. Does the manager really mean to do *anything*—no matter what? In addition, even though feedback is immediate with oral communication, it might be given without thought, also reducing the quality of the exchange. Unfortunately, some feel compelled to respond immediately in a face-to-face situation, when thinking before responding might be more productive.

In any medium, a vital component of oral communication is **listening**—receiving a message and interpreting its genuine meaning by accurately grasping the facts and feeling conveyed. Although listening is the first communication skill that people learn and the one they use most often, it is also the one in which they receive the least formal training.

Listening may seem easy, because the listener makes no obvious effort. This apparent passivity creates a deceptive picture, however. The average person talks at a rate of roughly 150 words per minute, but the brain can handle up to 400 words per minute. This discrepancy can lead to boredom, inattention, and misinterpretation. In fact, immediately after listening to a message, the average person can recall only half of it. After several days, the proportion of a message that a listener can recall falls to 25 percent or less.

Certain types of listening behaviors are common in both business and personal interactions:

- *Cynical listening.* This defensive type of listening occurs when the receiver of a message feels that the sender is trying to gain some advantage from the communication.

- *Offensive listening.* In this type of listening, the receiver tries to catch the speaker in a mistake or contradiction.

- *Polite listening.* In this mechanical type of listening, the receiver listens to be polite rather than to communicate. Polite listeners are usually inattentive and spend their time rehearsing what they want to say when the speaker finishes.

- *Active listening.* This form of listening requires involvement with the information and empathy with the speaker's situation. In both business and personal life, active listening is the basis for effective communication.

listening receiving a message and interpreting its intended meaning by grasping the facts and feelings it conveys.

"They Said It"

"Words are, of course, the most powerful drug used by mankind."

—Rudyard Kipling (1865–1936) Nobel Prize winner in literature

Learning how to be an active listener is an especially important goal for business leaders because effective communication is essential to their role. To become better listeners, managers should avoid sending signals to subordinates, even if unintentional, that discourage frank input. For instance, if managers change the subject, employees may assume the subject is closed.[22]

WRITTEN COMMUNICATION Channels for written communication include reports, letters, memos, online discussion boards, and e-mail messages. Most of these channels permit only delayed feedback and create a record of the message. So it is important for the sender of a written communication to prepare the message carefully and review it to avoid misunderstandings.

Effective written communication reflects its audience, the channel carrying the message, and the appropriate degree of formality. When writing a formal business document, such as a complex report, a manager must plan in advance and carefully construct the document. The process of writing a formal document involves planning, research, organization, composition and design, and revision. Written communication via e-mail may call for a less-formal writing style, including short sentences, phrases, and lists.

E-mail can be a very effective communication channel, especially for delivering straightforward messages and information. But e-mail's effectiveness also leads to its biggest problem: too much e-mail! Many workers find their valuable time being consumed with e-mail. To relieve this burden and leave more time for performing the most important aspects of the job, some companies are looking into ways to reduce the time employees spend sending and reading e-mail. For instance, two outsourcing companies in India answer e-mails for busy managers at a number of U.S. companies.[23]

Other e-mail issues are security and retention. Because e-mail messages are often informal, senders occasionally forget that they are creating a written record. Even if the recipient deletes an e-mail message, other copies exist on company e-mail servers. E-mails on company servers can be used as evidence in a lawsuit. After Advanced Micro Devices filed a lawsuit accusing Intel of violating antitrust laws by discounting its microprocessor chips, Intel spent millions of dollars to recover e-mails needed in the case. Intel said its e-mail retention lapses were caused partly because its system automatically deletes unsaved e-mails in 35 to 45 days. Intel filed papers with the court listing hundreds of employees and their actions regarding the retention of e-mail.[24]

Presiding over a departmental meeting is an example of *formal communication*. Although formal communication often occurs within a top-down command structure, employees should feel free to communicate their thoughts and suggestions openly.

FORMAL COMMUNICATION A **formal communication channel** carries messages that flow within the chain of command structure defined by an organization. The most familiar channel, *downward communication,* carries messages from someone who holds a senior position in the organization to subordinates. Managers may communicate downward by sending employees e-mail messages, presiding at department meetings, giving employees policy manuals, posting notices on bulletin boards, and reporting news in company newsletters. The most important factor in formal communication is to be open and honest. "Spinning" bad news to make it look better almost always backfires. In a work environment characterized by open communication, employees feel free to express opinions, offer suggestions, and even voice complaints. Research has shown that open communication has the following seven characteristics:

1. *Employees are valued.* Employees are happier and more motivated when they feel they are valued and their opinions are heard.

2. *A high level of trust exists.* Telling the truth maintains a high level of trust; this forms the foundation for open communication and employee motivation and retention.

3. *Conflict is invited and resolved positively.* Without conflict, innovation and creativity are stifled.

4. *Creative dissent is welcomed.* By expressing unique ideas, employees feel they have contributed to the company and improved performance.

5. *Employee input is solicited.* The key to any company's success is input from employees, which establishes a sense of involvement and improves working relations.

6. *Employees are well informed.* Employees are kept informed about what is happening within the organization.

7. *Feedback is ongoing.* Both positive and negative feedback must be ongoing and provided in a manner that builds relationships rather than assigns blame.[25]

Many firms also define formal channels for *upward communications.* These channels encourage communication from employees to supervisors and upward to top management levels. Some examples of upward communication channels are employee surveys, suggestion boxes, and systems that allow employees to propose new projects or voice complaints. Upward communication is also necessary for managers to evaluate the effectiveness of downward communication. Figure 10.4 illustrates the forms of organizational communication, both formal and informal.

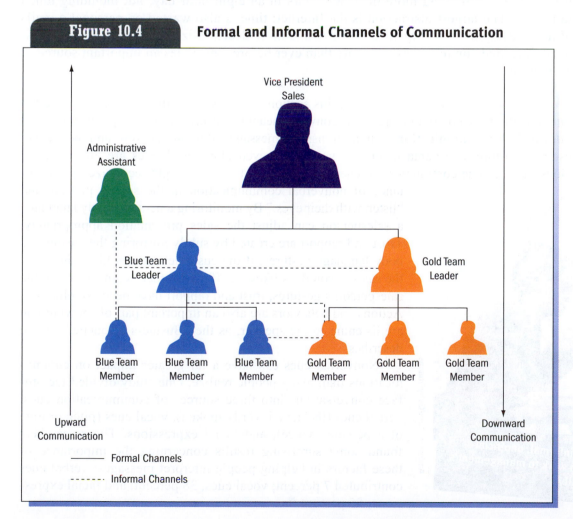

Figure 10.4 — **Formal and Informal Channels of Communication**

Vice President Sales

Administrative Assistant

Blue Team Leader

Gold Team Leader

Blue Team Member

Blue Team Member

Blue Team Member

Gold Team Member

Gold Team Member

Gold Team Member

Upward Communication

Downward Communication

——— Formal Channels

- - - - - Informal Channels

INFORMAL COMMUNICATION **Informal communication channels** carry messages outside formally authorized channels within an organization's hierarchy. A familiar example of an informal channel is the **grapevine,** an internal channel that passes information from unofficial sources. All organizations, large or small, have grapevines; it is futile for managers to try to eliminate this informal channel. Grapevines disseminate information with speed and economy and are surprisingly reliable. Conversely, communications must be managed effectively so that the grapevine is not the main source of information. When properly nurtured, the grapevine can help managers get a feel for the morale of companies, understand the anxieties of the workforce, and evaluate the effectiveness of formal communications. Managers can improve the quality of information circulating through the company grapevine by sharing what they know, even if it is preliminary or partial information. By feeding information to selected people, smart lenders can harness the power of the grapevine.[26]

The spontaneity of informal communication may diminish when a company's employees are spread among many locations. Employees who telecommute or travel frequently may miss opportunities to build smooth working relationships or exchange ideas. In those situations, communication technology can help firms promote informal communication. Some companies establish online chat areas for employees so that they can visit each other during breaks. Some also encourage their workers to create home pages that describe their interests and hobbies. But communication technology must be managed carefully to avoid lost productivity. According to a survey by America Online and Salary.com, the average worker admits to wasting more than two hours in an eight-hour day, not including lunch and breaks. The largest distraction is the Internet; time is also wasted on personal e-mails and text messaging.[27] As organizations become more decentralized and more globally dispersed, informal communication—more than ever before—provides an important source of information.

NONVERBAL COMMUNICATION So far, this section has considered different forms of verbal communication, or communication that conveys meaning through words. Equally important is **nonverbal communication,** which transmits messages through actions and behaviors. Gestures, posture, eye contact, tone of voice, and even clothing choices are all nonverbal actions that become communication cues. For instance, top salespeople recognize the importance of nonverbal communication in the selling process and "listen with their eyes." By monitoring a person's body language, a salesperson can adjust the sales presentation appropriately. Trust and rapport are created by subtly mirroring the customer's body language gestures; if the customer crosses his or her legs, the salesperson does likewise. If a customer begins to match the salesperson's gestures, trust and rapport have been established.[28] Actions and behaviors are also an important part of showing you are listening to the speaker, as the "Business Etiquette" feature describes.

Nonverbal cues can have a far greater impact on communications than many people realize. One study divided face-to-face conversations into three sources of communication cues: verbal cues (the actual words spoken), vocal cues (pitch or tone of a person's voice), and facial expressions. The researchers found some surprising results concerning the importance of these factors in helping people interpret messages: verbal cues contributed 7 percent; vocal cues, 38 percent; and facial expressions, 55 percent.[29]

"They Said It"

"The difference between the right word and the almost right word is the difference between lightning and lightning bugs."

—Mark Twain (1835–1910)
American novelist

Anderson Ross/Getty Images

The company grapevine—an informal, unofficial communication channel—can work to management's advantage if it is used carefully.

Business Etiquette

LISTEN UP: HOW TO BE AN EFFECTIVE LISTENER IN BUSINESS

When someone is speaking to you, you can learn a great deal—and be a more effective businessperson—if you listen carefully. In general, you listen for one or more of four reasons: to obtain information, to understand something, to enjoy the message, to learn. In the workplace, if your boss is giving you an assignment, you'll know what is expected of you. Listening to your co-workers helps you build empathy, support, and a good working relationship. Skilled listening can help you perform better as part of a team. If you listen well, you'll resolve problems more efficiently with co-workers and customers. You can answer a question more accurately if you have heard it correctly. And if you know the speaker well or at least understand the context of the conversation, you'll be able to root out any underlying meanings.

Here are some tips for becoming a more effective listener:

- *Pay attention to your speaker and what he or she is saying*. Maintain eye contact, if appropriate for the culture. Turn off your cell phone or pager. Refrain from interrupting or changing the subject before the speaker is through.
- *Demonstrate that you are listening actively*. Nod your head occasionally. Smile, frown, or use other expressions appropriate to the context of the conversation. Show empathy.
- *Withhold judgment until the speaker is finished*. Don't finish the speaker's sentences or jump in to argue halfway through his or her point. Let the speaker finish—you might be surprised by the ending and change your response.
- *Give the speaker feedback*. Repeat any instructions and ask questions pertaining to the conversation when the speaker has finished. Paraphrase or summarize the important points, such as "It sounds as though you are saying this."
- *Respond appropriately at the conclusion*. Be honest in your responses, but respectful, even if you disagree. Everyone is entitled to a point of view. If you treat the person with respect, likely you will have good communication in the future.

Despite your best intentions, sometimes listening goes awry. Here are some barriers to good listening that you can monitor:

- *Your own biases or prejudices*. Make an effort to understand your own biases so that you can listen as objectively as possible.
- *Language, accent or dialect, or cultural differences*. Try to be aware of cultural differences such as gestures or body language. Listen intently. If you don't understand something, it's better to ask a person politely to repeat it than to walk away with a misunderstanding.
- *Background noise*. If you are in a crowded room or on a busy street corner, try to move to a quieter place. If that's impossible, do your best to tune out the distractions.
- *Strong emotions*. If you are angry, afraid, or even excited about what's being said, it can be difficult to receive a message accurately. Try to save your emotions for later.

Listening is one of the most important skills you will develop as a businessperson. It takes time and practice to become an effective listener, just as it does to learn how to drive or use a new software program. Take the time to become a skilled listener—both you and your career will benefit.

Sources: "Active Listening: Hear What People Are Really Saying," *Mind Tools,* http://www.mindtools.com, accessed February 27, 2009; Dawn Rosenberg McKay, "Now Pay Attention," *About.com,* http://careerplanning.about.com, accessed February 27, 2009; Larry Alan Nadig, "Tips on Effective Listening," http://www.drnadig.com, accessed February 27, 2009.

Even personal space—the physical distance between people who are engaging in communication—can convey powerful messages. Figure 10.5 shows a continuum of personal space and social interaction with four zones: intimate, personal, social, and public. In the United States, most business conversations occur within the social zone, roughly between 4 and 12 feet apart. If one person tries to approach closer than that, the other will likely feel uncomfortable or even threatened.

Interpreting nonverbal cues can be especially challenging for people with different cultural backgrounds. Concepts of appropriate personal space differ dramatically throughout most of the world. Latin Americans conduct business discussions in positions that most Americans and

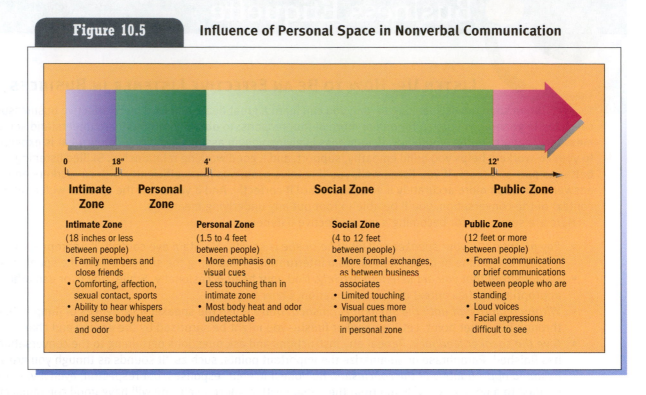

Figure 10.5 Influence of Personal Space in Nonverbal Communication

0   18"   4'   12'

Intimate **Personal**   **Social Zone**   **Public Zone**
Zone   **Zone**

Intimate Zone   **Personal Zone**   **Social Zone**   **Public Zone**
(18 inches or less   (1.5 to 4 feet   (4 to 12 feet   (12 feet or more
between people)   between people)   between people)   between people)
• Family members and   • More emphasis on   • More formal exchanges, • Formal communications
  close friends   visual cues   as between business   or brief communications
• Comforting, affection, • Less touching than in   associates   between people who are
  sexual contact, sports   intimate zone   • Limited touching   standing
• Ability to hear whispers• Most body heat and odor • Visual cues more   • Loud voices
  and sense body heat   undetectable   important than   • Facial expressions
  and odor   in personal zone   difficult to see

Assessment Check ✔

1. What are four common listening behaviors? Characterize each.

2. What are some advantages of e-mail as a communication medium? What are some disadvantages?

3. What are the differences between formal and informal communication?

4. Why do we pay more attention to nonverbal communication cues than to verbal communication cues?

Northern Europeans would find uncomfortably close. Americans often back away to preserve their personal space, a gesture that Latin Americans perceive as a sign of cold and unfriendly relations. To protect their personal space, some Americans separate themselves across desks or tables from their Latin American counterparts—at the risk of challenging their colleagues to maneuver around those obstacles to reduce the uncomfortable distance.

People send nonverbal messages even when they consciously try to avoid doing so. Sometimes nonverbal cues convey a person's true attitudes and thoughts, which may differ from spoken meanings. Generally, when verbal and nonverbal cues conflict, receivers of the communication tend to believe the nonverbal content. This is why firms seeking to hire people with good attitudes and a team orientation closely watch nonverbal behavior during job interviews in which job applicants participate in group sessions with other job candidates applying for the same job. If in those group interviews an applicant frowns or looks discouraged when a competing candidate gives a good answer, that nonverbal behavior suggests that this person may not be strongly team oriented.

External Communication: Crisis Management

external communication
meaningful exchange of information through messages transmitted between an organization and its major audiences.

External communication is a meaningful exchange of information through messages transmitted between an organization and its major audiences, such as customers, suppliers, other firms, the general public, and government officials. Businesses use external communication to keep their operations functioning, to maintain their positions in the marketplace, and to build customer relationships by supplying information about topics such as product modifications and price changes.

Every communication with customers—including sales presentations and advertisements—should create goodwill and contribute to customer satisfaction. However, all of this is threatened when companies experience a public crisis that threatens their reputation or goodwill. Yum Brands, one of the largest fast-food companies in the world, faced such a crisis after a video showed a dozen large rats crawling around the floor nibbling crumbs and climbing on children's high chairs at a Manhattan restaurant shared by Taco Bell and KFC. This crisis, on the heels of an *E. coli* bacterial outbreak at Taco Bell restaurants in New York and the Northeast, temporarily damaged the reputation of Yum Brands' businesses.[30]

How a company like Yum handles a public crisis after a damaging event can determine whether the company survives and whether its reputation can be restored. Putting together a plan of action and dealing with facts and rumors immediately could be the difference between regaining trust and disaster.[31] The following steps should be taken when dealing with a public crisis.

First, when a crisis occurs, companies must respond quickly. Before the initial news contact, which might be a press conference or an interview with a print or TV reporter, prepare by writing a statement—no matter how short—and stick to it. The statement should mention the time, place, initial description of what occurred (not the cause), and the number and status of the people involved.

Second, as soon as possible, put top company management in front of the press. Because the public will hold top management accountable, it's best to have top managers responding to reporters' questions.

Third, when answering reporters' questions, stick to the facts. Don't wing it. If you don't know the details about what happened, then don't speculate. If you speculate and are proven wrong, it will look like you were lying. So tell people only what you know.

Fourth, if you don't know, offer to find out. You don't have to know the answer to each question off the top of your head. When you don't know, say so: "I don't know the answer to that question." When you can find out an answer, say that, too. But then be sure to deliver the answer in a timely manner.

Fifth, never say "no comment." "No comment" is perceived as a statement of guilt. It's better to say, "I don't know."

Sixth, identify and speak to your audience. When speaking to an audience, it's important to recognize that what you say is likely to be only a small part of a TV, print, or radio story. Accordingly, you can speak more effectively to your audience by using visual or word images instead of facts. Most people don't have the time or are reluctant to immerse themselves in the details of a story. Facts are easily forgotten. Images are easily remembered.

Finally, acknowledge problems and explain solutions. If a question or factual statement puts your organization in a negative light, acknowledge the problem, and then explain how you're correcting it.

The crisis faced by Yum Brands illustrates the danger of damaging images captured in video. Shot through the window by a local television crew on a Friday morning before the restaurant opened, the film was the most viewed item at Web sites and was shown on television stations across the country. KFC and Taco Bell immediately issued a joint statement: "This is an isolated incident at a single restaurant at 3316th Avenue in Greenwich Village, New York, and is totally unacceptable. The restaurant is closed and we will not allow it to be reopened until it has been sanitized and given a complete clean bill of health." But Peter Blackshaw, chief marketing officer of Nielsen BuzzMetrics, said Yum failed to use the Web to defend itself or make sure positive messages were heard and easily accessible. Instead, consumers looking for reassurance had to work hard to find it.[32] No image is more vile than rats in restaurant food, and that image is not easily forgotten.

Assessment Check ✔

1. What is external communication?
2. During a company crisis, why is it dangerous for a spokesperson to say "no comment" when answering reporters' questions?

What's Ahead

Today's consumers expect the products they buy to be of the highest value for the price. Firms ensure this value by developing efficient systems for producing goods and services, as well as maintaining high quality. The next chapter examines the ways in which businesses produce world-class goods and services, efficiently organize their production facilities, purchase what they need to produce their goods and services, and manage large inventories to maximize efficiency and reduce costs.

Summary of Learning Goals

1 Describe why and how organizations empower employees.

By empowering employees, a firm finds better ways to perform jobs, motivates people by enhancing the challenges and satisfaction in their work, and frees managers from hands-on control so that they can focus on other tasks. Employers empower workers by sharing information, distributing decision-making authority and responsibility, and linking rewards to company performance through employee stock ownership plans and stock options.

Assessment Check Answers

1.1 What is empowerment? Empowerment is giving employees authority and responsibility to make decisions about their work without traditional managerial approval and control.

1.2 What kinds of information can companies provide employees to help them share decision-making responsibility? Sharing information about company performance, particularly financial performance, is one of the best ways to share decision-making responsibility.

1.3 What are some of the risks of sharing this information? One risk is that proprietary competitive or financial information may reach your competitors.

1.4 How do employee stock ownership plans and stock options reward employees and encourage empowerment? Employee stock ownership plans (ESOPs) benefit employees by giving them ownership stakes in their companies. Employees are motivated to work harder and smarter than they would without ESOPs because they share in their firm's financial success. In contrast to an ESOP, in which the company holds stock for the benefit of employees (when employees leave the company, they cash in their stock), stock options give employees a chance to own the stock themselves if they exercise their options by completing the stock purchase.

2 Distinguish among the five types of teams in the workplace.

The five basic types of teams are work teams, problem-solving teams, self-managed teams, cross-functional teams,
and virtual teams. Work teams are permanent groups of coworkers who perform the day-to-day tasks necessary to operate the organization. Problem-solving teams are temporary groups of employees who gather to solve specific problems and then disband. Self-managed teams have the authority to make decisions about how their members complete their daily tasks. Cross-functional teams are made up of members from different functions, such as production, marketing, and finance. Virtual teams are groups of geographically or organizationally dispersed coworkers who use a combination of telecommunications and information technologies to accomplish an organizational task.

Assessment Check Answers

2.1 What is a team? A team is a group of employees who are committed to a common purpose, approach, and set of performance goals.

2.2 What are the five types of teams, and how are they different? Work teams are permanent, while problem-solving teams are temporary. Unlike work teams, self-managed teams have the authority to change how they get their work done. Cross-functional teams are composed of people from different backgrounds, while virtual teams are composed of people from different locations.

3 Identify the characteristics of an effective team.

Three important characteristics of a team are its size, team level, and team diversity. Effective teams typically contain between 5 and 12 members, with about 6 or 7 members being the ideal size. Team level is the average level of ability, experience, personality, or any other factor on a team. For example, a high level of team experience means that members have, on average, particular expertise in some area. Instead of considering similarities, team diversity represents the variances or differences in ability, experience, personality, or any other factor on a team. In other words, strong teams not only have talented members but also benefit from the differences in terms of ability, experience, or personality of individual members. Diverse teams tend to display broader ranges of viewpoints and produce more innovative solutions to problems than do homogeneous teams.

Assessment Check Answers

3.1 Teams reach maximum effectiveness, diversity, and communication flow with how many members? Six or seven members is typically the best size for a team.

3.2 Explain team level and team diversity. While team level represents the average level or capability on a team, team diversity represents the variances or differences in ability, experience, personality, or any other factor on a team.

4 Summarize the stages of team development.

Teams pass through five stages of development: (1) Forming is an orientation period during which members get to know each other and find out what behaviors are acceptable to the group. (2) Storming is the stage during which individual personalities emerge as members clarify their roles and expectations. (3) Norming is the stage at which differences are resolved, members accept each other, and consensus emerges about the roles of the team leader and other participants. (4) Performing is characterized by problem solving and a focus on task accomplishment. (5) Adjourning is the final stage, with a focus on wrapping up and summarizing the team's experiences and accomplishments.

Assessment Check Answers

4.1 Explain how teams progress through the stages of team development. Teams pass through five stages of development: forming, storming, norming, performing, and adjourning.

4.2 Explain the difference between the storming and performing stages. The primary difference is how teams handle conflict in these stages. In the storming stage, people disagree over the team's mission and jockey for position and control of the group. But in the performing stage, those issues have been settled, so team members handle conflicts in constructive ways; in other words, they encourage cognitive conflict to solve problems.

5 Relate team cohesiveness and norms to effective team performance.

Team cohesiveness is the extent to which team members feel attracted to the team and motivated to remain on it. Team norms are standards of conduct shared by team members that guide their behavior. Highly cohesive teams whose members share certain standards of conduct tend to be more productive and effective.

Assessment Check Answers

5.1 How does cohesiveness affect teams? Members of cohesive teams interact more often, share common attitudes and goals, have higher morale, and are more likely to help each other. Cohesive teams also perform better.

5.2 Explain how team norms positively and negatively affect teams. Norms are informal standards that identify key values and clarify team members' expectations. But those norms can be positive or negative. Positive norms contribute to constructive work and the accomplishment of team goals. Negative norms can, for example, contribute to reduced work effort, reduced quality, and poor job attendance.

6 Describe the factors that can cause conflict in teams and ways to manage conflict.

Conflict and disagreement are inevitable in most teams. Conflict can stem from many sources: disagreements about goals and priorities, task-related issues, interpersonal incompatibilities, scarce resources, and simple fatigue. Although most people view conflict negatively, the key to dealing with team conflict is not avoiding it, but making sure that the team experiences the right kind of conflict. Cognitive conflict focuses on problem-related differences of opinion and, when reconciled, strongly improves team performance. By contrast, affective conflict refers to the emotional reactions that can occur when disagreements become personal rather than professional, and these differences strongly decrease team performance. A team leader can limit conflict by focusing team members on broad goals, clarifying participants' respective tasks and areas of authority, acting as mediator, and facilitating effective communication.

Assessment Check Answers

6.1 What is cognitive conflict, and how does it affect teams? With cognitive conflict, team members disagree because their different experiences and expertise lead them to different views of the problem and its solutions. Cognitive conflict is characterized by a willingness to examine, compare, and reconcile differences to produce the best possible solution.

6.2 Explain affective conflict and its impact on teams. Because affective conflict often results in hostility, anger, resentment, distrust, cynicism, and apathy, it can make people uncomfortable, cause them to withdraw, decrease their commitment to a team, lower the satisfaction of team members, and decrease team cohesiveness.

7 Explain the importance and process of effective communication.

Managers and employees spend much of their time exchanging information through messages. Communication helps all employees understand the company's goals and values and the parts they play in achieving those goals. Every communication follows a step-by-step process that involves interactions among six elements: sender, message, channel, audience, feedback, and context.

Assessment Check Answers

7.1 What is the difference between communication in low-context and high-context cultures? Communication in low-context cultures tends to rely on explicit written and verbal messages. By contrast, communication in high-context cultures depends not only on the message itself but also on the conditions that surround it, including nonverbal cues, past and present experiences, and personal relationships between the parties.

7.2 In the context of the communication process, what is noise? Noise interferes with the transmission of messages and feedback. Noise can result from physical factors such as poor reception of a cell phone message or differences in people's attitudes and perceptions.

8 **Compare the different types of communication.**

People exchange messages in many ways: oral and written, formal and informal, verbal and nonverbal communication. Effective written communication reflects its audience, its channel, and the appropriate degree of formality. Formal communication channels carry messages within the chain of command. Informal communication channels, such as the grapevine, carry messages outside the formal chain of command. Nonverbal communication plays a larger role than most people realize. Generally, when verbal and nonverbal cues conflict, the receiver of a message tends to believe the meaning conveyed by nonverbal elements.

Assessment Check Answers

8.1 What are four common listening behaviors? Characterize each. Cynical listening occurs when the receiver of a message feels that the sender is trying to gain some advantage from the communication. Offensive listening occurs when the receiver tries to catch the speaker in a mistake or contradiction. Polite listening occurs when the receiver acts politely but, rather than listening, is rehearsing what he or she wants to say when the speaker finishes. Active listening requires involvement with the information and empathy with the speaker's situation.

8.2 What are some advantages of e-mail as a communication medium? What are some disadvantages? E-mail can be a very effective communication channel, especially for delivering straightforward messages and information. But too much e-mail and poor security, meaning that it's easy for people who weren't intended to read a particular e-mail to do so, are some of its disadvantages.

8.3 What are the differences between formal and informal communication? Formal communication occurs within the formal chain of command defined by an organization. Informal communication occurs outside the organization's hierarchy.

8.4 Why do we pay more attention to nonverbal communication cues than to verbal communication cues? Nonverbal cues can reveal what senders are really thinking or feeling, particularly when nonverbal cues don't match verbal communication.

9 **Explain external communication and methods of managing a public crisis.**

External communication is a meaningful exchange of information through messages transmitted between an organization and its major audiences, such as customers, suppliers, other firms, the general public, and government officials. Every communication with customers should create goodwill and contribute to customer satisfaction. However, all of this is threatened when companies experience a public crisis that threatens their reputations or goodwill. To manage a public crisis, businesses should respond quickly when a crisis occurs with a prepared statement; quickly put top company management in front of the press; answer reporters' questions with facts; offer to find out answers; never say, "No comment"; identify and speak to their audience by using visual or word images; and acknowledge problems and explain solutions.

Assessment Check Answers

9.1 What is external communication? External communication occurs when organizations communicate with and receive messages from key external groups, such as customers, suppliers, other firms, the general public, and government officials.

9.2 During a company crisis, why is it dangerous for a spokesperson to say "no comment" when answering reporters' questions? "No comment" is perceived as a statement of guilt. It's better to say, "I don't know."

Business Terms You Need to Know

empowerment 326	self-managed team 331	team diversity 333	communication 336
team 329	cross-functional team 331	team cohesiveness 334	listening 339
work team 329	virtual team 331	team norm 335	grapevine 342
problem-solving team 330	team level 333	conflict 335	external communication 344

Other Important Business Terms

employee stock ownership plan (ESOP) 327	cognitive conflict 335	high-context culture 337	informal communication channel 342
stock options 327	affective conflict 335	formal communication channel 340	nonverbal communication 342
	low-context culture 337		

Review Questions

1. Describe the ways employers can empower their employees. Give a specific example of each.

2. Identify and briefly explain the approaches companies use to provide for worker ownership. What are the main differences between them?

3. How does each of the five team types function? In what instances might a company use each type?

4. How do team level and team diversity affect team performance?

5. What are the characteristics of an effective team? Why are these features so significant?

6. Identify and briefly describe the five stages of team development. At what stages might a team not be able to move forward?

7. How does affective conflict hinder group effectiveness?

8. What are the major elements in the communication process? Briefly define each element.

9. Outline the two channels for formal communication. Give an example of each.

10. What is the central focus of a company's external communication?

Projects and Teamwork Applications

1. Consider your current job or one you have held in the past. Did your employer practice any kind of employee empowerment? If so, what? If not, why not? Or think of your family as a company. Did your parents empower their children? If so, in what ways? In either scenario, what do you think were the consequences of empowerment or nonempowerment?

2. Identify a firm that makes extensive use of teams. Then interview someone from the firm to assess how their teams operate.

3. Do you consider yourself a good listener? First, identify which listening style you think you practice. Then describe the listening styles outlined in this chapter to a friend, family member, or classmate and ask that person what type of listening style he or she thinks you practice. Finally, compare the two responses. Do they agree

or disagree? *Note:* You can take this exercise a step further by asking more than one person what type of listening style you practice and then comparing all of the responses.

4. The grapevine is one of the strongest communication links in any organization, from large corporation to college classroom to family. Do you rely on information that travels along the grapevine? Why or why not?

5. Take a seat in the library or dorm lounge, in a mall, in a restaurant, or wherever there is a flow of people whom you can watch without being noticed. For at least 15 minutes, observe and jot down the nonverbal cues that you see pass between people. Then try to interpret these cues. How would your interpretation affect any actual communication you might have with one of these people?

Web Assignments

1. **Stock options.** Visit the Web site listed (http://investing. businessweek.com). Click on the "Learning Center" link. Under "Subject," click on "Options." Then click on "What Are Stock Option Plans?" Read the article. How does a company benefit by offering stock options to employees? How do employees benefit?

2. **Team conflict.** As a student, you've probably been part of a team for a class project. If not, you no doubt will. Visit the site listed for Penn State's Web page, "Teaching and Learning with Technology," on conflict (http://tlt.psu. edu/suggestions/teams/student/index.html). Click on "Conflict Resolution Tips." Read through the information, especially the sections on Depersonalizing Team Internal Conflict, Structuring Discussion, and Key Questions.

   At question 10, click on the word *unproductive* to access the table comparing productive and unproductive behaviors. Use the table to evaluate a project team experience

you have had. Did team members display more productive or unproductive behaviors? How about you? If you haven't yet been on a project team, ask yourself which behaviors would you most likely display when working on a team.

3. **Listening skills.** Visit the Web site listed (http://www. infoplease.com/homework/listeningskills1.html). Click on "Homework Center." Then select the "Skills" link. Click on "Speaking and Listening," then on "Listening Skills." Read the article. What are the three steps in the listening process? What are seven tips for building listening skills? Which tip do you think would help you most in becoming a better listener? Why?

Note: Internet Web addresses change frequently. If you do not find the exact sites listed, you may need to access the organization's or company's home page and search from there.

After carefully crafting a positive public image for years, Southwest Airlines faced a crisis. The low-fare carrier was hit with a $10.2 million fine by the Federal Aviation Administration (FAA) for lapses in maintenance record keeping. The media seized the story, and Southwest received immediate scrutiny and criticism. This was unfamiliar territory for the airline with a stellar safety record—having flown more than a billion people without a single fatal accident—and which was considered the most successful in the industry. One crisis-management and litigation specialist said that Southwest's success and solid reputation triggered the harsh criticism.

The crisis was sparked by a congressional investigation finding that FAA supervisors ignored their inspectors' concerns and left in service Southwest jets that did not comply with safety standards. Media reports alleged that FAA officials presented misleading testimony about airline maintenance. In a letter, investigative committee members told the FAA, "Your testimony conveyed inaccurate and misleading information about whether aviation safety inspectors and managers ... were ordered to conduct special meetings with all airlines, repair stations and other regulated entities to deliver and discuss" the FAA's Customer Service Initiative.

While Southwest's reputation took the first hit, most other major airlines also grounded planes to check for compliance with FAA safety procedures. Airlines eventually cancelled thousands of flights—more than 1,000 by American Airlines in a single day—to inspect planes and perform scheduled maintenance. The stranding of hundreds of thousands of passengers cost the airlines millions of dollars in refunds, rebooking costs, employee overtime, and vouchers for passengers trapped overnight. The groundings also created uncertainty with investors, according to a Morgan Stanley analyst, who noted, "At worst [maintenance] noncompliance could lead companies to incur significant costs in the future." Not good news for an industry experiencing financial woes for years.

Southwest CEO Gary Kelly immediately apologized to customers and safety regulators for the maintenance lapses. "I am not satisfied we are as compliant or as safe as we could be," he said. Kelly promised to revamp maintenance procedures to ensure safety and indicated the airline would fully cooperate with the FAA. He also acknowledged the fallout from such a crisis: "There are

some that have lost trust in Southwest Airlines. We will have to regain that trust."

Besides acknowledging the problem publicly, Kelly began working on a solution. Southwest placed on leave three employees being investigated by the FAA. The airline grounded 38 planes until it could determine whether safety inspections had been done properly. Aviation safety experts said none of the planes posed a serious safety hazard. Four planes were repaired for some fuselage cracks; all were back in service shortly.

Kelly also moved quickly to restore Southwest's damaged relationship with the FAA. He approached officials to work together on a solution and showed a willingness to accept responsibility for the maintenance lapses. He apologized to the agency and gave his word Southwest would improve maintenance record keeping. In addition, Kelly ordered a comprehensive review of all maintenance procedures and record keeping.

One strategic communications strategist recommended that Southwest pay careful attention to blogs, because "that's where consumers are talking and where reporters are getting their ideas." Marketing experts also suggested that the airline with the lighthearted image may need to show it takes flying seriously. Southwest is known for humorous advertisements and employees who like to have fun, so some suggested a more serious demeanor would be appropriate.

Kelly is concerned about restoring customer confidence and proving the airline deserves the trust of the public. He realizes it will take time to win back some passengers. According to BrandIndex, a daily survey of thousands of brands, Southwest's image and reputation slipped after the crisis surfaced. In the meantime, Kelly has vowed to make Southwest "the safest airline in the world." That goal is a tall order, because stories of airline safety for years to come will likely mention Southwest.[33]

Questions for Critical Thinking

1. Why was it important for Gary Kelly to address the safety concerns immediately? Did he do an effective job in managing the crisis?

2. What are the likely lingering effects of the public crisis for Southwest Airline and for the entire airline industry? How can they be overcome?

Interaction Associates Team Puts Its Expertise to Work

Interaction Associates is a consulting firm with offices in San Francisco and Cambridge, Massachusetts. The company specializes in developing collaborative approaches to coaching, leadership, managing change, and team building. Co-founders David Straus and Michael Doyle wrote the book *How to Make Meetings Work,* and Straus wrote *How to Make Collaboration Work.* Their firm has helped hundreds of firms around the world improve performance by building collaborative workplaces. How do you suppose the firm would put its expertise to work on itself? By using teams to find a new office.

When the lease on its San Francisco office was about to expire, Interaction Associates set up employee teams to decide where to move. "You need to give people a voice in what they're doing and how they're going to experience their work every day," says president and CEO Linda Dunkel, named one of America's best bosses by workplace assessment organization Winning Workplaces. She chose a five-member team to find a location closer to the city's center and to save at least $100,000 a year on the lease. While staying in the present building was an option, Dunkel wanted to be closer to downtown where employees were involved in volunteer work and where mass transit was available.

The diverse team members came from marketing, consulting, operations, information technology, and fulfillment and logistics. Team leader Beth O'Neill was chosen for her frankness and wide range of experience with the company. The team met for about an hour a week in the beginning and involvement increased as time went on. The task took eight months before the final move. During that period, team members met with brokers, selected a location, developed a floor plan, and even picked office colors. Occasionally, team members checked in with the president for guidance, but they generally managed themselves.

The road to the new office contained a few bumps along the way. For instance, while the relocation team debated the pros and cons of one desirable office space, another tenant snapped it up. But the team eventually selected an office with lots of windows near Union Station. It wasn't Dunkel's first choice of the final three buildings the team considered, but she realized the importance of letting team members complete the task and did not want to override their decision. In the end, she came around to the team's way of thinking. Says Dunkel, "Now that I see the final result, it's a better decision than if I'd made it on my own, and that's a powerful message. It speaks to the power of a group to pull out a variety of interests and thrash things through and ultimately come up with a better decision." [34]

Questions for Critical Thinking

1. What were the benefits of selecting a diverse team to find the new office location? Why did Beth O'Neill make a good team leader?
2. Why was it important for the president to let the team select the final location even though it wasn't her first choice? What could have been some negative consequences of overriding the team?

VIDEO Case 10.3 — Meet the People of BP

London-based BP (British Petroleum) is a major player in the oil and energy industry, with more than 100,000 workers in 100 countries. Imagine what 100,000 workers can accomplish if they all perform at the highest level. From human resources managers, to sales and marketing managers, to finance executives, to retail store managers, to geologists, BP employees are part of an organizational culture that fosters empowerment, communication, and effective teamwork. "Experience isn't essential to join us … it's your attitude that's important to us," says one part of the careers section of the BP Web site. This outlook prevails throughout the many BP divisions.

Some years ago, BP instituted a training program designed to build better communication and teamwork among its top-level managers. Called the Projects Academy, the program—based at the Massachusetts Institute of Technology (MIT)—provided top managers with new ways to examine complex problems, work with colleagues and staff, and find solutions for developing new products. Program director Jim Breson observed that getting these individuals to work together as a group was initially a challenge—they simply weren't accustomed to it. "When we were creating the program, we noted the high-level managers were rather like the Tom Cruise character in the movie *Top Gun*." These managers, he says, were already highly competent, but they needed to find ways to perform even better, through teamwork and communication. The managers who emerged from the course say they are better for having taken it. "I think what Projects Academy provides is a framework that gives us the best of what we can learn from others while preserving the best of BP's unique approach," remarks David Dalton, a geologist who recently became BP's general manager in Abu Dhabi. "What's happening here is a real effort to keep people engaged and linked together on an ongoing basis. My classmates and I are focused ... on how we, as a broad community of project people, can learn from each other and create new insights into how we perform our jobs." Dalton and his colleagues now communicate regularly from anywhere around the world. He likes the fact that he can call on the expertise of others who have similar concerns and responsibilities to his own. "It's positively wonderful to be part of a growing connectivity that allows us to share and communicate these responsibilities," he says.

Far from the oil fields of the Middle East—and from MIT—management trainees for BP's retail stores, which include convenience stores and cafés adjacent to BP stations, are learning the same concepts. During their training, they become familiar with the BP culture of empowerment. As part of the Customer Assistant team, they develop skills in working with others. They learn the norms of the team, including how to communicate with each other and with customers.

As a large firm, BP operates teams that serve different purposes; however, they all share the goal of communicating effectively and taking personal responsibility to improve performance, provide customer service, and gain a competitive advantage. Teams are so important to the firm that it gives awards to those that perform especially well. One award-winning problem-solving team found a better way to predict pressure in deep-water drilling operations, thus avoiding dangerous accidents and oil spills. A cross-functional team with members from refining and marketing worked together to launch Masana Petroleum Solutions in South Africa, a firm owned and run by local residents. Still another team found a new way to reduce CO_2 emissions at the Salah Gas Project in Algeria.

One of the more unusual BP teams is known as Operation People. During a time when the firm was cutting costs and morale was beginning to sag, BP convened an Operation People group to turn things around. They developed some corporate initiatives—and they also started a band, which took popular songs and rewrote the lyrics to apply to BP. The band played at one meeting and were a hit. So they began to perform at other venues, including the Rock and Roll Hall of Fame. With this creative form of communication, they spread the word about their company.

Some years ago, BP introduced a new global management framework that gives the financial controllers more independence to run their units. This change meant the firm needed to retrain the controllers in their new roles. So BP created a training course that put participants in teams in which they had to solve real-work problems together, even if it meant resolving personal conflicts. BP spokesperson Sarah Harvey explains, "The program is designed to help our people develop a deeper knowledge of their role and accountabilities and also the interpersonal awareness to build the right relationships with their business partners so that they can remain connected yet independent." One team leader in the program notes the importance of understanding his teammates' behavior so that he could manage their relationships. But all of the relationship building took place within the context of real situations that BP financial controllers would face.

BP uses nearly every available medium of communication, including publishing its own very substantial magazine, called *The BP Magazine*. The publication is filled with all types of articles that focus on economics, culture, the environment, and even the foods of the nations in which BP does business. Not only does the magazine help BP employees around the world stay connected, but it also provides a forum for good publicity, such as announcements of awards the firm has won or achievements particular divisions or employees have accomplished. New events are happening somewhere every day at BP—and the company wants all 100,000 employees, and its many customers, to know.[35]

Questions for Critical Thinking

1. Describe ways that BP empowers its employees. Do you think this approach is effective in such a large company? Why or why not?

2. BP uses a variety of teams to accomplish many of its goals. What makes them effective? What are the benefits of this approach?

3. A company as large as BP must rely on many forms of communication. How might managers use teams as a basis for managing informal communication?

4. External communication is vital to a firm such as BP. Suppose an environmental accident such as an oil spill occurred involving BP. What steps would you recommend the firm take to communicate the circumstances of the incident and maintain goodwill with its customers and the general public?

Goals

1 Outline the importance of production and operations management.
2 Explain the roles of computers and related technologies in production.
3 Identify the factors involved in a plant location decision.
4 Explain the major tasks of production and operations managers.
5 Compare alternative layouts for production facilities.
6 List the steps in the purchasing process.
7 Outline the advantages and disadvantages of maintaining large inventories.
8 Identify the steps in the production control process.
9 Explain the benefits of quality control.

Production and Operations Management

© AP/Wide World Photos

Honda's Manufacturing Turns on a Dime

Business success depends on giving customers what they want. But when your manufacturing and production facilities are set up to make what customers *don't* want, turning the process around quickly can be challenging, especially in the auto industry. Assembly lines are long and complex and, for many years, were set up to build just one model at a time. Change is expensive and time-consuming, sometimes requiring a whole new manufacturing process to be designed, as Ford and General Motors both know. Ford's retooling of an SUV plant in Michigan is costing the company $75 million, and it will be 13 months before it can turn out any of the new smaller cars U.S. drivers now prefer. General Motors is investing $350 million to transform an Ohio plant to enable it to produce a new model.

But at Honda's East Liberty facility in Ohio, change is easy. After 120 new Civic compacts rolled off the line one recent morning, workers ran over and switched the hand-like parts on some welding robots. A few minutes later, the machines were assembling the company's CR-V sport utility vehicles.

Most automakers' assembly operations can produce minor variations on a theme, but Honda's legendary ability to switch with such ease from one model to another— and even from trucks to cars and back again—has long been a unique advantage. Now, as auto sales are declining around the country and gasoline prices remain unpredictable, Honda can quickly and inexpensively switch a given factory from building pickup trucks to making smaller and more fuel-efficient cars. If demand for larger vehicles picks up in the future, the firm can switch some of its facilities back just as easily. Honda can also quickly lower production of slower-selling models like the Acura RDX to favor those that sell fast like the Accord, responding to changes in consumer preferences almost as soon as they happen. "We have the flexibility to do what is necessary," says a senior manufacturing executive in Ohio.

One key to Honda's manufacturing flexibility is those hand-like devices on its assembly robots, which the company engineered itself. Different vehicles call for different "hands" to manipulate components, but the robots themselves remain. Another advantage is that almost all Honda products are deliberately designed so they can be assembled the same way. At the East Liberty plant that switched from Civics to CR-Vs, for instance, robots install doors and attach side panels for both vehicles at the same point in the manufacturing process, greatly minimizing the number of assembly-line changes needed between models.

Honda can also rearrange production among its facilities, as well as within each one. For instance, to allow its Canadian plant to make more best-selling Civics, the firm is moving production of its Ridgeline pickup truck out of Canada to Lincoln, Alabama. The Alabama plant, which already makes the Odyssey minivan and the Pilot SUV, will also start building the Accord soon. The Accord was the first Japanese passenger car made in the United States—in 1982—and is now the first car to be made in Lincoln since the truck plant opened in 2001. Given Honda's forward thinking, however, the change was easy to accommodate. And thanks to the built-in flexibility of its three Ohio plants, Honda was able to stop importing CR-Vs from the United Kingdom a few years ago, when the weak dollar cut profits, and switch to making them in the United States instead.

"They have total model flexibility," one car industry official said. "They can go from building 100 percent Accords on Friday, to 100 percent Civics on Monday. Their only limitation is the response time for ordering vehicles."

Honda builds a higher percentage of vehicles in the United States than any other international automaker and has been improving the efficiency and flexibility of its U.S. plants for many years. "We are leveraging our flexible manufacturing network to meet the needs of our customers for more fuel-efficient products," says the executive vice president of American Honda Motor Co. That might help keep Honda's ability to turn on a dime unsurpassed for some time.[1]

By producing and marketing desired goods and services, businesses satisfy their commitment to society as a whole. They create what economists call *utility*—the want-satisfying power of a good or service. Businesses can create or enhance four basic kinds of utility: time, place, ownership, and form. A firm's marketing operation generates time, place, and ownership utility by offering goods and services to customers when they want to buy at convenient locations where ownership of the products can be transferred.

Production, by contrast, creates form utility by converting raw materials and other inputs into finished products, such as Honda's automobiles and trucks. **Production** applies resources such as people and machinery to convert materials into finished goods and services. The task of **production and operations management** is to oversee the application of people and machinery in converting materials into finished goods and services. Figure 11.1 illustrates the production process.

People sometimes use the terms *production* and *manufacturing* interchangeably, but doing so ignores an important difference. Production is a broader term that spans both manufacturing and nonmanufacturing industries. For instance, companies in extractive industries such as fishing, lumber, and mining engage in production, and so do service providers. Services are intangible outputs of production systems. They include outputs as diverse as trash hauling, education, haircuts, tax accounting, dental care, mail delivery, transportation, and lodging. Figure 11.2 lists five examples of production systems for a variety of goods and services.

Figure 11.1   **The Production Process: Converting Inputs to Outputs**

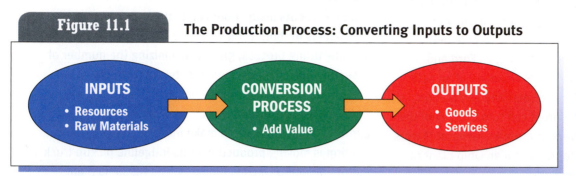

Figure 11.2   **Typical Production Systems**

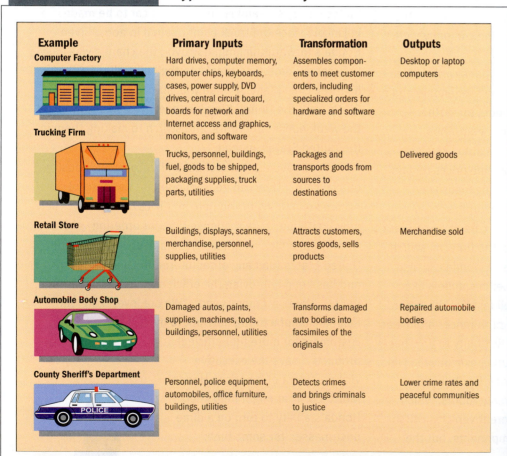

Example	Primary Inputs	Transformation	Outputs
Computer Factory	Hard drives, computer memory, computer chips, keyboards, cases, power supply, DVD drives, central circuit board, boards for network and Internet access and graphics, monitors, and software	Assembles components to meet customer orders, including specialized orders for hardware and software	Desktop or laptop computers
Trucking Firm	Trucks, personnel, buildings, fuel, goods to be shipped, packaging supplies, truck parts, utilities	Packages and transports goods from sources to destinations	Delivered goods
Retail Store	Buildings, displays, scanners, merchandise, personnel, supplies, utilities	Attracts customers, stores goods, sells products	Merchandise sold
Automobile Body Shop	Damaged autos, paints, supplies, machines, tools, buildings, personnel, utilities	Transforms damaged auto bodies into facsimiles of the originals	Repaired automobile bodies
County Sheriff's Department	Personnel, police equipment, automobiles, office furniture, buildings, utilities	Detects crimes and brings criminals to justice	Lower crime rates and peaceful communities

But whether the production process results in a tangible good or an intangible service, it always converts inputs into outputs. This conversion process may make major changes in raw materials or simply combine already finished parts into new products. A cabinet-maker combines wood, tools, and skill to create finished kitchen cabinets for a new home. A transit system combines buses, trains, and employees to create its output: passenger transportation. Both of these production processes create utility.

This chapter describes the process of producing goods and services. It looks at the importance of production and operations management and discusses the new technologies that are transforming the production function. It then discusses the tasks of the production and operations manager, the importance of quality, and the methods businesses use to ensure high quality.

Strategic Importance of the Production Function

Along with marketing and finance, production is a vital business activity. Without a good or service to sell, companies cannot generate money to pay their employees, lenders, and stockholders. And without the profits from products, firms quickly fail. The production process is just as crucial in nonprofit organizations, such as the Mayo Clinic and Goodwill Industries, because the goods or services they offer justify their existence. Effective production and operations management can lower a firm's costs of production, boost the quality of its goods and services, allow it to respond dependably to customer demands, and enable it to renew itself by providing new products. Let's look at the differences among mass, flexible, and customer-driven production.

Mass Production

From its beginnings as a colonial supplier of raw materials to Europe, the United States evolved into an industrial giant. Much of this remarkable change resulted from **mass production,** a system for manufacturing products in large amounts through effective combinations of employees with specialized skills, mechanization, and standardization. Mass production makes outputs available in large quantities at lower prices than individually crafted items would cost. It is mass production that brought cars, refrigerators, televisions, and even homes to the majority of the population. That's right, even homes. William Levitt, featured on the cover of *Time* magazine in 1950, made homes affordable to the average American by removing the most expensive items—the basements—and mass-producing them at the rate of one every 16 minutes.[2]

Mass production begins with *specialization of labor,* dividing work into its simplest components so that each worker can concentrate on performing one task. By separating jobs into small tasks, managers create conditions for high productivity through *mechanization,* in which machines perform much of the work previously done by people. *Standardization,* the third element of mass production, involves producing uniform, interchangeable goods and parts. Standardized parts simplify the replacement of defective or worn-out components. For instance, if your car's windshield wiper blades wear out, you can easily buy replacements at a local auto parts store such as AutoZone.

A logical extension of these principles of specialization, mechanization, and standardization led to development of the <mark>assembly line.</mark> This manufacturing technique moves the product along a conveyor belt past a number of workstations, where workers perform specialized tasks such as welding, painting, installing individual parts, and tightening bolts. Henry Ford's application of this concept revolutionized auto assembly. Before the assembly line, it took Ford's workers 12 hours to assemble a Model T car. But with an assembly line, it took just 1.5 hours to make the same car. Not surprisingly, dozens of other industries soon adopted the assembly line technique.

Although mass production has important advantages, it has limitations, too. While mass production is highly efficient for producing large numbers of similar products, it is highly inefficient when producing small batches of different items. This trade-off tempts some companies to focus on efficient production methods rather than on making what customers really want. In addition, the labor specialization associated with mass production can lead to boring jobs, because workers keep repeating the same task. To improve their competitive capabilities, many firms adopt flexible production and customer-driven production systems. These techniques may not replace mass production altogether but may simply improve a company's use of mass production.

Flexible Production

While mass production efficiently creates large batches of similar items, flexible production can cost effectively produce smaller batches. Flexible production can take many forms, but it generally involves using information technology to share the details of customer orders, programmable equipment to fulfill the orders, and skilled people to carry out whatever tasks are needed to fill a particular order. This arrangement is useful when combined with lean production methods that use automation and information technology to reduce requirements for workers and inventory. Flexible production also requires a high degree of communication and cooperation among customers and employees throughout the organization.

Flexible production has been widely adopted in the auto industry. Changing from mass production to flexible production enabled companies to produce different kinds of cars at the same plant. For instance, Toyota Motor Manufacturing Kentucky produces Camrys, Camry Hybrids, Avalons, and Solaras at its Georgetown plant.[3] Even though the Camry is the best-selling car in America, the Georgetown plant would not operate at peak efficiency if it only produced this car.

At this auto plant in Georgetown, Kentucky, Toyota uses flexible production techniques to turn out several different models. The auto industry, which developed mass production methods, now finds flexible production to be more efficient.

© Al Behrman/AP/Wide World Photos

Customer-Driven Production

A customer-driven production system evaluates customer demands to link what a manufacturer makes with what customers want to buy. Many firms have implemented this approach with great success. One method is to establish computer links between factories and retailers' scanners, using data about sales as the basis for creating short-term forecasts and designing production schedules to meet those forecasts. Another approach to customer-driven production systems is simply not to make the product until a customer orders it. For example,

Dell builds computers to customers' specifications when they order over the telephone or through Dell's Web site.

Volvo is one of the world's leading manufacturers of luxury cars. The company has a relatively small share of the global auto market; it relies heavily on Europe, in particular Sweden, for a significant share of its sales. The company's flexible production operations are driven by customer demand. This focus on producing what will sell has helped Volvo reduce its inventory and remain competitive as low-cost Asian automobile manufacturers have expanded their operations in Europe.[4]

Assessment Check ✓

1. What are the advantages and disadvantages of mass production?
2. What are the characteristics of flexible production?
3. Describe a customer-driven production system.

Production Processes

Not surprisingly, the production processes and time required to make an Apple iPod and a gallon of gasoline are different. Production processes use either an analytic or synthetic system, and time requirements call for either a continuous or an intermittent process.

An *analytic production system* reduces a raw material to its component parts in order to extract one or more marketable products. For example, petroleum refining breaks down crude oil into several marketable products, including gasoline, heating oil, and aviation fuel. When corn is processed further, the resulting marketable food products include animal feed and corn sweetener.

By contrast, a *synthetic production system* is the reverse of an analytic system. It combines a number of raw materials or parts or transforms raw materials to produce finished products. Dell's assembly line produces personal computers by assembling the various components ordered by each customer. Ford's assembly line uses a variety of metal, plastic, and rubber components to produce cars and trucks. Other synthetic production systems make drugs, chemicals, computer chips, and canned soup.

A *continuous production process* generates finished products over a lengthy period of time. The steel industry provides a classic example. Its blast furnaces never completely shut down except for malfunctions. Petroleum refineries, chemical plants, and nuclear power facilities also practice continuous production. A shutdown can damage sensitive equipment, with extremely costly results.

An *intermittent production process* generates products in short production runs, shutting down machines frequently or changing their configurations to produce different products. Most services result from intermittent production systems. For instance, accountants, plumbers, and dentists traditionally have not attempted to standardize their services because each service provider confronts different problems that require individual approaches. However, some companies, including Jiffy Lube (auto service) and Terminix (pest control services), offer standardized services as part of a strategy to operate more efficiently and compete with lower prices. In contrast, McDonald's has moved toward a more intermittent production model. The fast-food chain invested millions in new cooking equipment to set up kitchens for preparing sandwiches quickly to order, rather than producing large batches ahead of time and then keeping them warm under heat lamps.

Technology and the Production Process

Like other business functions, production has changed dramatically as computers and related technologies have developed. For example, in manufacturing, a "lights out" factory is completely automated. In other words, because of computers, software, robots, and other kinds of integrated technology systems, no workers are needed to make what a "lights out" factory produces. You could literally turn all the lights off, and the factory would keep producing

Hit & Miss

Boeing's 787 Dreamliner Set to Take Off

After weathering many design changes, production delays, and even a labor strike, the manufacture of Boeing Company's long-awaited 787 Dreamliner passenger plane is back on track. The Everett, Washington–based production facility will fulfill its outstanding orders for almost 900 of the planes to customers around the world, at the rate of about 10 per month.

The Dreamliner, which is sold to commercial airlines like Japan's All Nippon Airways, lists for between $150 million and $200 million each. The plane pioneers a new carbon-fiber composite material for the frame, which makes it lighter and more fuel-efficient than existing airliners. It also consists of thousands of parts. But what makes Boeing's production process truly unusual is the number of places around the world where those parts are made and partially assembled before being sent to the massive Washington plant for the final production stages. Boeing has even set aside a special cargo plane for picking up and delivering the parts, a modified 747 craft nicknamed the Dreamlifter.

The Dreamliner's tail fins are made in Fredrickson, Washington, while the back half of the fuselage, or body, comes from Charleston, South Carolina. The front section is made in Kansas. Engine parts come from Chula Vista, California, fuel lines from New Jersey, and metal parts for the oxygen masks from New York State. The fairing, which reduces wind drag, is made in Canada. Going even farther afield, the passenger doors are made in France, the wings and front section in Japan, and the cargo doors in Sweden. Other parts of the fuselage are from Italy, and the engine and landing gear are from the United Kingdom. In all, Boeing outsourced design work to about 50 different partner firms and found more than 100 parts suppliers on four continents. Many of these suppliers in turn subcontracted the manufacture of specialized components to smaller firms.

Boeing believes that its vast outsourcing program, while complex, allows it to partner with the best specialist manufacturers, reduce risk, and keep production costs down. The company, which has increased its reliance on outsourcing with each new plane it produces, now acts as more of a project manager than a manufacturer. "Subassemblies are produced across the globe, which then come together in Boeing's U.S. facilities. Today's rule: To sell around the world, produce around the world," says one observer of Boeing's Dreamliner process.

Holding everything together is a French company's sophisticated database management and computer-aided design system. This software lets Boeing and all its design and manufacturing engineers not only simulate the appearance of the plane and its flight in virtual 3D but also view virtual production lines and manufacturing processes before the real ones are constructed. These simulations are critical in preventing costly errors, such as doors that don't open properly or parts that don't fit.

When everything all comes together in Everett, the seven major airplane assemblies are snapped together to form the wings, fuselage, cockpit, and tail. From there, the Dreamliner is ready to take to the air. But Boeing isn't done with the revolutionary 787; a cargo version of the plane is already in the works.

Questions for Critical Thinking

1. What are the advantages and disadvantages of Boeing's reliance on parts suppliers all over the world?
2. Some observers believe the manufacture of the Dreamliner will revolutionize the production of aircraft throughout the aviation industry. Do you agree? Why or why not?

Sources: Lee Hochberg, "Airplane Production Evolves with New Technology," *Online News Hour,* http://www.pbs.org, accessed February 27, 2009; "Boeing Working on 787 Again," *Wichita Business Journal,* February 3, 2009, http://www.bizjournals.com; Phaedra Hise, "The Remarkable Story of Boeing's 787," *Fortune,* July 9, 2007, http://money.cnn.com, accessed February 27, 2009; "Boeing 787 Virtual Rollout Causes Dassault Great Sigh of Relief," *3D CAD News,* January 12, 2007, http://3dcadnews.blog.com, accessed February 27, 2009; Michael Mecham, "Boeing: 2009 Soft but Stable," *Aviation Week,* February 2, 2009, http://www.aviationweek.com; Kari J. Bodnarchuk, "Warbirds and Wonderbirds," *The Boston Globe,* December 8, 2008, http://www.boston.com; John Teresko, "Planning the Factory of the Future," *IndustryWeek,* December 1, 2008, http://www.industryweek.com; Sholnn Freeman, "Darling of Jet Industry, Bane of the Picket Line," *The Washington Post,* September 10, 2008, http://.www.washingtonpost.com.

finished products. In addition to boosting efficiency in production, automation and information technology allow firms to redesign their current methods to enhance flexibility. These changes allow a company to design and create new products faster, modify them more rapidly, and meet customers' changing needs more effectively than it could achieve with traditional methods. Technology also helps Boeing design and produce its new 787 Dreamliner airplane at different facilities and then assemble the pieces in Everett, Washington, as the "Hit & Miss" feature describes. Important production technologies today include robots, computer-aided design and manufacturing, flexible manufacturing systems, and computer-integrated manufacturing.

Robots

A growing number of manufacturers have freed people from boring, sometimes dangerous assignments by replacing them with robots. A **robot** is a reprogrammable machine capable of performing a variety of jobs that require manipulation of materials and tools. Robots can repeat the same tasks many times without varying their movements. Many factories use robots today to "palletize" their products for shipping. This means stacking finished products on a wood, plastic, or steel pallet and then shrink-wrapping the items onto the pallet with plastic. Not only do robots lift pallets into place, they also use their gripping "hands" and lifting "arms" to put products into neat rows and layers for shipping. IBM's vast computer-chip production facility in New York's Hudson Valley has hundreds of chipmaking machines the size of train locomotives. Within the machines, robotic hands pass disks from one workstation to the next, where surfaces are either etched, coated with chemicals, or baked. Each disk can hold from 500 to 1,000 chips.[5]

Initially, robots were most common in automotive and electronics manufacturing, but growing numbers of industries are adding robots to production lines as improvements in technology make them less expensive and more useful. Firms operate many different types of robots. The simplest kind, a *pick-and-place robot,* moves in only two or three directions as it picks up something from one spot and places it in another. So-called *field robots* assist people in nonmanufacturing, often hazardous, environments such as nuclear power plants, the international space station, and even battlefields. Police use robots to remotely dispose of suspected bombs. However, the same technology can be used in factories. Using vision systems, infrared sensors, and bumpers on mobile platforms, robots can automatically move parts or finished goods from one place to another, while either following or avoiding people, whichever is necessary to do the job. For instance, machine vision systems are being used more frequently for complex applications such as computer-chip manufacturing inspection. The advancements in machine vision components like cameras, illumination systems, and processors have greatly improved their capabilities.[6]

Computer-Aided Design and Manufacturing

A process called **computer-aided design (CAD)** enables engineers to design parts and buildings on computer screens faster and with fewer mistakes than they could achieve working with traditional drafting systems. Using an electronic pen, an engineer can sketch three-dimensional (3-D) designs on an electronic drafting board or directly on the screen. The computer then provides tools to make major and minor design changes and to analyze the results for particular characteristics or problems. Engineers can put a new car design through a simulated road test to project its real-world performance. If they find a problem with weight distribution, for example, they can make the necessary changes virtually—without actually test-driving the car. In other words, with advanced CAD software, prototyping is as much "virtual" as it is "hands-on." Actual prototypes or parts aren't built

robot reprogrammable machine capable of performing numerous tasks that require manipulation of materials and tools.

computer-aided design (CAD) system for interactions between a designer and a computer to create a product, facility, or part that meets predetermined specifications.

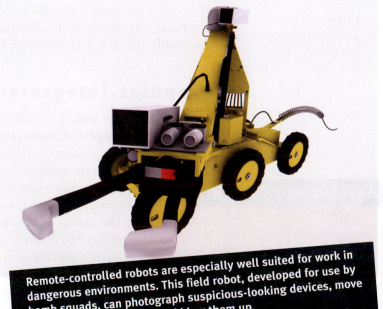

Remote-controlled robots are especially well suited for work in dangerous environments. This field robot, developed for use by bomb squads, can photograph suspicious-looking devices, move them to a safer location, and blow them up.

Daniel Bringmann/iStockphoto

until the engineers are satisfied that the required structural characteristics in their virtual designs have been met. Computer-aided design has contributed to the rapid advancement in golf club technology. CAD has enabled club manufacturers to develop larger club heads, springier club faces, and innovative designs that shift the center of gravity to create straighter shots.[7]

The process of **computer-aided manufacturing (CAM)** picks up where the CAD system leaves off. Computer tools enable a manufacturer to analyze the steps that a machine must take to produce a needed product or part. Electronic signals transmitted to processing equipment provide instructions for performing the appropriate production steps in the correct order. Both CAD and CAM technologies are now used together at most modern production facilities. These so-called *CAD/CAM systems* are linked electronically to automatically transfer computerized designs into the production facilities, saving both time and effort. They also allow more precise manufacturing of parts.

computer-aided manufacturing (CAM) electronic tools to analyze CAD output and determine necessary steps to implement the design, followed by electronic transmission of instructions to guide the activities of production equipment.

Flexible Manufacturing Systems

A **flexible manufacturing system (FMS)** is a production facility that workers can quickly modify to manufacture different products. The typical system consists of computer-controlled machining centers to produce metal parts, robots to handle the parts, and remote-controlled carts to deliver materials. All components are linked by electronic controls that dictate activities at each stage of the manufacturing sequence, even automatically replacing broken or worn-out drill bits and other implements.

Flexible manufacturing systems have been enhanced by powerful new software that allows machine tools to be reprogrammed while they are running. This capability allows the same machine to make hundreds of different parts without the operator having to shut the machine down each time to load new programs. The software also connects to the Internet to receive updates or to control machine tools at other sites. And because the software resides on a company's computer network, engineers can use it to diagnose production problems any time, from anywhere they can access the network. BMW's flexible manufacturing system enables customers to make as many changes as they like—cloth or leather seats, spoiler or sunroof—until six days before a car goes into production. Although BMW won't say how much the flexibility increases costs, the system has generated more revenue from last-minute add-ons. The company has mastered flexible manufacturing to the point where no two cars coming down the assembly line at a given time are identical.[8]

Computer-Integrated Manufacturing

Companies integrate robots, CAD/CAM, FMS, computers, and other technologies to implement **computer-integrated manufacturing (CIM),** a production system in which computers help workers design products, control machines, handle materials, and control the production function in an integrated fashion. This type of manufacturing does not necessarily imply more automation and fewer people than other alternatives. It does, however, involve a new type of automation organized around the computer. The key to CIM is a centralized computer system running software that integrates and controls separate processes and functions. The advantages of CIM include increased productivity, decreased design costs, increased equipment utilization, and improved quality.

CIM is widely used in the printing industry to coordinate thousands of printing jobs, some very small. CIM saves money by combining many small jobs into one larger one and by automating the printing process from design to delivery. According to Yves Rogivue, former CEO of printing company

Assessment Check

1. List some of the reasons businesses invest in robots.
2. Distinguish among computer-aided design, computer-aided manufacturing, flexible manufacturing, and computer-integrated manufacturing.

MAN Roland, "CIM is the cornerstone upon which the future of this industry will be built. Implementing CIM cuts costs and improves productivity."[9] One of the world's largest printers with headquarters near Chicago, MAN Roland has been a proponent of CIM for over a decade. The firm has used it to reduce costs and increase profit margins while attracting new customers with specialized printing needs.[10]

The Location Decision

The decision of where to locate a production facility hinges on transportation, human, and physical factors, as shown in Table 11.1. Transportation factors include proximity to markets and raw materials, along with availability of alternative modes for transporting both inputs and outputs. For instance, automobile assembly plants are located near major rail lines. Inputs—such as engines, plastics, and metal parts—arrive by rail, and the finished vehicles are shipped out by rail. Shopping malls are often located adjacent to major streets and freeways in suburban areas, because most customers arrive by car.

Physical variables involve such issues as weather, water supplies, available energy, and options for disposing of hazardous waste. Theme parks, such as Walt Disney World, are often located in warm climates so they can be open, and attract visitors, year-round. A firm that wants to locate near a community often must prepare an **environmental impact study** that analyzes how a proposed plant would affect the quality of life in the surrounding area. Regulatory agencies typically require these studies to cover topics such as the impact on transportation facilities; energy requirements; water and sewage treatment needs; natural plant life and wildlife; and water, air, and noise pollution. The "Hit & Miss" feature explains how a small company uses renewable energy resources to power its production facility.

Human factors include an area's labor supply, local regulations, and living conditions. Management considers local labor costs, as well as the availability of workers with needed qualifications. For instance, software makers and other computer-related firms concentrate in areas with the technical talent they need, including California's Silicon Valley, Boston, and Austin,

Table 11.1	Factors in the Location Decision
Location Factor	**Examples of Affected Businesses**
Transportation	
Proximity to markets	Baking companies and manufacturers of other perishable products, dry cleaners, hotels, other services
Proximity to raw materials	Paper mills
Availability of transportation alternatives	Brick manufacturers, retail stores
Physical Factors	
Water supply	Computer chip fabrication plants
Energy	Aluminum, chemical, and fertilizer manufacturers
Hazardous wastes	All businesses
Human Factors	
Labor supply	Auto manufacturers, software developers
Local zoning regulations	Manufacturing and distribution companies
Community living conditions	All businesses

Hit & Miss

NRG Models Energy Efficiency

When Vermont-based NRG Systems needed more space, the decision for the wind-energy company was not whether to go green but how. The answer: a new 46,000-square-foot building featuring energy-efficient technology and powered mostly by renewable energy. The facility provides much more than just space for the company's growth. "We also wanted to create a workplace that was healthy, functional, and beautiful for our employees, while supporting our company's mission of furthering the use of renewable energy," says president and CEO Jan Blittersdorf. She owns the company with her husband, David, NRG's founder.

NRG makes wind assessment systems, towers, instruments, and sensors that measure and analyze wind speed, direction, and other data to locate and operate wind-energy projects. NRG's products can be found in 110 countries, with about half of its sales in the United States. Customers include electric utilities, wind-farm developers, research facilities, universities, government agencies, and homeowners.

NRG chose the latest in green design and technology for its new facility, which includes a café, kitchen, swimming pool, and fitness center in addition to space for offices, manufacturing, tower production and assembly, and shipping. The facility consumes about a third of the energy that conventional buildings of the same size do. Solar panels and a wind turbine behind the facility supply two-thirds of the company's electricity, which also avoids the emission of 105,000 pounds of carbon dioxide a year. Wood pellets from lumber milling waste are used for its heating needs. Water-saving devices such as dual-flushing toilets and faucet aerators save more than 100,000 gallons of water per year. Motion sensors that detect when spaces are occupied turn lights off when they aren't needed. Rows of skylights and windows take advantage of natural light, provide natural ventilation, and give workers views of the outdoors. Employees use laptop computers and Energy Star–rated office equipment, which were selected to reduce electricity use and heat gain. NRG also uses "smart" production technology that automates processes. For example, machinery runs only during the manufacturing process and is in a no-power mode at other times.

Making the building energy efficient increased costs about 8 percent. "We spent more money to build our facility green," says David Blittersdorf, "but we see it as a long-term investment that will more than pay for itself in terms of productivity gains and energy and operating savings costs." The green, energy-lean building has brought NRG some gold. It is one of a small number of industrial buildings to be LEED Gold certified. The designation—LEED stands for Leadership in Energy and Environmental Design—recognizes a high level of performance in building design, construction, and operation based on national standards developed by the U.S. Green Building Council.

Question for Critical Thinking

1. What environmental impact do you suppose NRG's green facility will have on the community in which it is located?
2. In the future, do you think many businesses will pay more to make their facilities energy efficient? Why or why not?

Sources: "NRG Holds Grand Opening for New Building," http://www.nrgsystems.com, accessed March 12, 2009; "Walking the Talk in a Global Market," http://www.winningworkplaces.org; accessed March 12, 2009; Lisa Sutor, "Green Manufacturing Comes of Age," *Control Engineering,* November 2007, p. 69.

Texas. By contrast, some labor-intensive industries have located plants in rural areas with readily available labor pools and limited high-wage alternatives. And some firms with headquarters in the United States and other industrialized countries have moved production offshore in search of low wages. Apparel is a classic example. But no matter what business you're in, a production and operations manager's facility location decision must consider the following factors:

- proximity to suppliers, warehouses, and service operations
- insurance and taxes
- availability of such employee needs as housing, schools, mass transportation, day care, shopping, and recreational facilities

- size, skills, and costs of the labor force
- ample space for current and future needs of the firm
- distance to market for goods
- receptiveness of the community
- economical transportation for materials and supplies, as well as for finished goods
- climate and environment that matches the industry's needs and employees' lifestyle
- amount and cost of energy services.

A recent trend in location strategy is bringing production facilities closer to final markets. This has led some business developers to label Central America "the new Asia." Companies including Dell, IBM, and Procter & Gamble have moved facilities from Asia to Central America due to its proximity to the United States. Central America is in the same time zone as some U.S. cities and only a three- or four-hour flight from many companies' U.S. headquarters. For fast-moving consumer goods and electronics, U.S. distribution centers are moving to regional locations closer to retailers.[11] Although he declined to give a timetable, Volkswagen's U.S. CEO, Stefan Jacoby, indicated that he plans to build a production facility in Chattanooga, Tennessee, to make the company "a local player" in the U.S. market.[12]

The Job of Production Managers

Production and operations managers oversee the work of people and machinery to convert inputs (materials and resources) into finished goods and services. As Figure 11.3 shows, these managers perform four major tasks. First, they plan the overall production process. Next, they determine the best layout for the firm's facilities. Then they implement the production plan. Finally, they control the manufacturing process to maintain the highest possible quality. Part of the control process involves continuous evaluation of results. If problems occur, managers return to the first step and make adjustments.

Planning the Production Process

Production planning begins by choosing what goods or services to offer to customers. This decision is the essence of every company's reason for operating. Other decisions such as machinery

Figure 11.3 Tasks of Production Managers

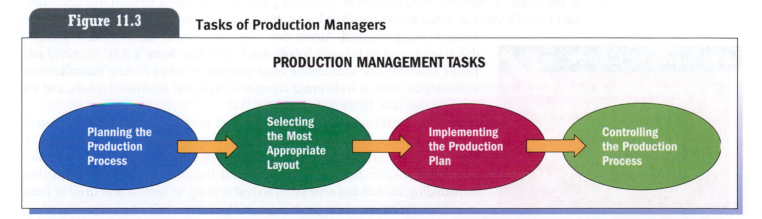

PRODUCTION MANAGEMENT TASKS

Planning the Production Process → Selecting the Most Appropriate Layout → Implementing the Production Plan → Controlling the Production Process

purchases, pricing decisions, and selection of retail outlets all grow out of product planning. But with product planning, it's not enough to plan products that satisfy customers. Products must satisfy customers *and* be produced as efficiently and inexpensively as possible. So while marketing research studies determine consumer reactions to proposed products and estimate potential sales and profitability levels, production departments focus on planning the production process when they (1) convert original product ideas into final specifications and (2) design the most efficient facilities to produce those products.

Chapter 8 presented different organizational structures, depending on the needs and goals of the company. It is important for production managers to understand how a project fits into the company's structure because this will affect the success of the project. In a traditional manufacturing organization, each production manager is given a specific area of authority and responsibility such as purchasing or inventory control. One drawback to this structure is that it may actually pit the purchasing manager against the inventory control manager. As more organizations have moved toward team-oriented structures, some organizations assign team members to specific projects reporting to the production manager. Each team is responsible for the quality of its products and has the authority to make changes to improve performance and quality. The major difference between the two approaches is that all workers on teams are responsible for their output, and teamwork avoids the competitiveness between managers often found in traditional structures.

Determining the Facility Layout

The next production management task is determining the best layout for the facility. An efficient facility layout can reduce material handling, decrease costs, and improve product flow through the facility.[13] This decision requires managers to consider all phases of production and the necessary inputs at each step. Figure 11.4 shows three common layout designs: process, product, and fixed-position layouts. It also shows a customer-oriented layout typical of service providers' production systems.

A process layout groups machinery and equipment according to their functions. The work in process moves around the plant to reach different workstations. A process layout often facilitates production of a variety of nonstandard items in relatively small batches. Its purpose is to process goods and services that have a variety of functions. For instance, a typical machine shop generally has separate departments where machines are grouped by functions such as grinding, drilling, pressing, and lathing. Process layouts accommodate a variety of production functions and use general-purpose equipment that can be less costly to purchase and maintain than specialized equipment.

A product layout, sometimes referred to as an *assembly line,* sets up production equipment along a product-flow line, and the work in process moves along this line past workstations. This type of layout efficiently produces large numbers of similar items, but it may prove inflexible and able to accommodate only a few product variations. Although product layouts date back at least to the Model T assembly line, companies are refining this approach with modern touches. Many auto manufacturers continue to use a product layout, but robots perform many of the activities that humans once performed. Automation overcomes one of the major drawbacks of this system—unlike humans, robots don't get bored doing a dull, repetitive job. Future assembly-line architecture must continue to adapt to new manufacturing technologies, such as widespread computerization and automated robots, and the need for low-cost, lightweight buildings.[14]

A fixed-position layout places the product in one spot, and workers, materials, and equipment come to it. This approach suits production of very large, bulky, heavy, or fragile products. For example, a bridge cannot be built on an assembly line. Fixed-position layouts dominate several industries including construction, shipbuilding, aircraft and aerospace, and oil drilling, to name a few. In all of these industries, the nature of the product generally dictates a fixed-position layout.

Assessment Check ✔

1. Differentiate among the three most common layout designs: process, product, and fixed position.

2. Describe a customer-oriented layout that is typically used by service providers.

Service organizations also must decide on appropriate layouts for their production processes. A service firm should arrange its facilities to enhance the interactions between customers and its services—also called *customer-oriented layout*. If you think of patients as inputs, a hospital implements a form of the process layout. Banks, libraries, and universities also use process layouts. Sometimes the circumstances surrounding a service require a fixed-position layout. For instance, doctors, nurses, and medical devices are brought to patients in a hospital emergency room.

Implementing the Production Plan

After planning the production process and determining the best layout, a firm's production managers begin to implement the production plan. This activity involves (1) deciding whether to make, buy, or lease components; (2) selecting the best suppliers for materials; and (3) controlling inventory to keep enough, but not too much, on hand.

MAKE, BUY, OR LEASE DECISION One of the fundamental issues facing every producer is the **make, buy, or lease decision**—choosing whether to manufacture a needed product or component in house, purchase it from an outside supplier, or lease it. This decision is critical in many contemporary business situations.

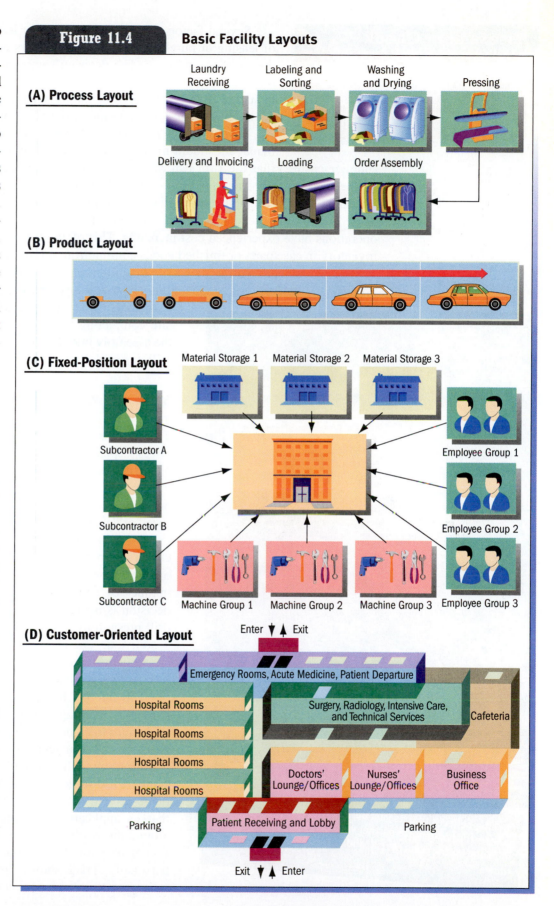

Figure 11.4 **Basic Facility Layouts**

(A) Process Layout

Laundry Receiving — Labeling and Sorting — Washing and Drying — Pressing

Delivery and Invoicing — Loading — Order Assembly

(B) Product Layout

(C) Fixed-Position Layout

Material Storage 1   Material Storage 2   Material Storage 3

Subcontractor A   Subcontractor B   Subcontractor C

Machine Group 1   Machine Group 2   Machine Group 3

Employee Group 1   Employee Group 2   Employee Group 3

(D) Customer-Oriented Layout

Enter ▼ ▲ Exit

Emergency Rooms, Acute Medicine, Patient Departure

Hospital Rooms | Surgery, Radiology, Intensive Care, and Technical Services | Cafeteria

Hospital Rooms

Hospital Rooms | Doctors' Lounge/Offices | Nurses' Lounge/Offices | Business Office

Hospital Rooms

Parking | Patient Receiving and Lobby | Parking

Exit ▼ ▲ Enter

Assessment Check ✓

1. What factors affect the make, buy, or lease decision?
2. What factors should firms consider when selecting vendors?

Several factors affect the make, buy, or lease decision, including the costs of leasing or purchasing parts from vendors compared with the costs of producing them in house. The decision sometimes hinges on the availability of outside suppliers that can dependably meet a firm's standards for quality and quantity. The need for confidentiality sometimes affects the decision, as does the short- or long-term duration of the firm's need for supplies.

Even when the firm decides to purchase from outside vendors, production managers should maintain access to multiple supply sources. An alternative supplier ensures that the firm can obtain needed materials despite strikes, quality-assurance problems, or other situations that may affect inputs. Outsourcing has its disadvantages. The main reason companies say they use outsourcing is a desire to lower costs, but a study conducted by AMR Research found that 56 percent of companies that are outsourcing production operations have experienced cost increases. This often occurs because of the need to stockpile inventory in case parts or finished goods coming from distant locations are late.[15] The problems Boeing encountered with its new 787 Dreamliner airplane—the most complex machine in mass production—underscore the potential hazards of outsourcing. Boeing had to delay delivery of its plane several times because its overseas suppliers were late completing their components, delaying their arrival at the assembly line. The airline company had to pay customers millions of dollars in penalty payments and incentives.[16]

Boeing believes that its vast outsourcing program allows the company to partner with the best specialist manufacturers, reduces risk, and keeps production costs down.

Jim Bryant/UPI/Landov LLC

SELECTION OF SUPPLIERS Once a company decides what inputs to purchase, it must choose the best vendors for its needs. To make this choice, production managers compare the quality, prices, dependability of delivery, and services offered by competing companies. Different suppliers may offer virtually identical quality levels and prices, so the final decision often rests on factors such as the firm's experience with each supplier, speed of delivery, warranties on purchases, and other services.

For a major purchase, negotiations between the purchaser and potential vendors may stretch over several weeks or even months, and the buying decision may rest with a number of colleagues who must say yes before the final decision is made. The choice of a supplier for an industrial drill press, for example, may require a joint decision by the production, engineering, purchasing, and quality-control departments. These departments often must reconcile their different views to settle on a purchasing decision.

The Internet has given buyers powerful tools for finding and comparing suppliers. Buyers can log on to business exchanges to compare specifications, prices, and availability. Ariba Spend Management, at http://www.ariba.com, offers organizations software and other tools that allow them to source $120 billion worth of goods and services from suppliers around the world. Ariba Spend Management claims that its applications operate on nearly 4 million desktops around the world.[17] Networking provides a way for production managers to learn about suppliers and get to know them personally. Trade shows, conferences, and seminars enable managers to meet suppliers and others in their industry.

The "Business Etiquette" feature advises managers on how to make the most of industry events.

Firms often purchase raw materials and component parts on long-term contracts. If a manufacturer requires a continuous supply of materials, a one-year or two-year contract with a vendor helps ensure availability. Today, many firms are building long-term relationships with suppliers and slashing the number of companies with which they do business. At the same time, they are asking their vendors to expand their roles in the production process.

INVENTORY CONTROL Production and operations managers' responsibility for **inventory control** requires them to balance the need to keep stocks on hand to meet demand against the costs of carrying inventory. Among the expenses involved in storing inventory are warehousing costs, taxes, insurance, and maintenance. Firms waste money if they hold more inventory than they need. On the other hand, having too little inventory on hand means a shortage of raw materials, parts, or goods for sale that often leads to delays and unhappy customers. Firms lose business when they consistently miss promised delivery dates or turn away orders. That was the case during the holiday season for three big-selling books: *Artisan Bread in Five Minutes a Day, Roast Chicken and Other Stories,* and *Gallop!* The main reason for the shortage of these books was that publishers didn't anticipate their popularity, printing too few copies and leaving retail stores caught out-of-stock.[18] Therefore, managers must balance this threat against the cost of holding inventory to set acceptable stocking levels.

Efficient inventory control can save a great deal of money. In one common technique, many firms maintain **perpetual inventory** systems to continuously monitor the amounts and locations of their stocks. Such inventory control systems

Business Etiquette

MAKING THE MOST OF INDUSTRY CONFERENCES

Conferences, trade shows, and seminars can be valuable experiences. You can find out about new technology and products, make contacts with suppliers, get ideas on managing production and operations, and meet other facility managers. Here are tips for making an industry event productive and enjoyable.

1. Before you go, make sure you take plenty of business cards. Your purpose is to meet people and bring back business to your company or find suppliers or other contacts.
2. Find out the dress code so that you will have the right clothes for special events like dinners or awards ceremonies.
3. When you get your "welcome packet," scan it to figure out which attendees you would especially like to meet. Make it your mission to network with those people.
4. Wear your name badge, preferably on on the right side of your clothing so that others can read it easily when you shake hands.
5. Attend all the social functions or networking sessions, meet and greet first and eat later. Carrying a plate and a drink makes it impossible to shake hands with someone and more difficult to converse comfortably.
6. If you are alone at the opening session, start by going up to another individual or a small group of two or three people. It can be awkward to approach a larger group of people you don't know and begin a one-to-one conversation.
7. After you've introduced yourself to someone and talk a bit, exchange business cards. If this is someone with whom you would like to speak again, set up another time to meet during the conference or a time to call when you get back to work. Shake hands, thank the person, and move on to someone else.
8. Get to educational sessions on time. Sit close to the front, next to someone instead of leaving empty seats between you, and introduce yourself. End the conversation when the speaker begins. If the person next to you continues to talk, politely tell them right away you'd like to talk afterward.
9. Respect the speaker and those around you. Resist the urge to use laptops, hand-held computers, and cell phones during sessions. Constantly being turned on is a turnoff for other people and divides your attention. Taking notes is fine, but remember to look at the speaker, listen well, and contribute by asking a question or providing feedback when requested.
10. At a luncheon or dinner, introduce yourself to everyone at the table. If possible, meet everyone before you sit down, or move around the table. Don't reach over the table to shake hands.
11. At meals or other times when there's a group, don't monopolize the conversation. Avoid inappropriate topics such as personal health (yours and others'), personal finances, controversial subjects, or gossip.
12. Back at work, follow up with new contacts and write thank-you notes when appropriate, for example, if someone picked up your tab at a meal not included in the conference.

Sources: Rob Hard, "Etiquette Mistakes at Business Events," http://eventplanning.about.com, accessed March 12, 2009; Jessica Guynn, "Meetings Etiquette: Turning These Off," *Los Angeles Times,* April 6, 2008, http://www.newsday.com; Colleen A. Rickenbacher, "Conference Etiquette: Tools to Survive Your Next Industry Event, *SuperVision*, March 2008, pp. 11–12.

An employee stocks shelves with Colgate toothpaste at a Target store in Tallahassee, Florida. Target uses an electronic scanning system in all of its stores to keep an updated record of its inventory.

© Phil Coale/AP/Wide World Photos

typically rely on computers, and many automatically generate orders at the appropriate times. Many supermarkets link their scanning devices to perpetual inventory systems that reorder needed merchandise without human interaction. As the system records a shopper's purchase, it reduces the inventory count stored in the computer. Once inventory on hand drops to a predetermined level, the system automatically reorders the merchandise. Target keeps perpetual inventories in its stores, created by what is scanned. This practice allows Target to know what its inventory is at all times and keeps out-of-stocks to a minimum.[19]

Some companies go further and hand over their inventory control functions to suppliers. This concept is known as *vendor-managed inventory*. For instance, Digi-Key Corp., an electronics company in Thief River Falls, Minnesota, has implemented vender-managed inventory with its suppliers that have good logistics control and centralized stores. According to Steve Vecchiarelli, vice president of Digi-Key: "These centralized stores allow suppliers more control without underperforming pockets of inventory impacting supplier costs. With good logistics, suppliers can provide superior on-time delivery with upside potential and protection against the downside."[20]

JUST-IN-TIME SYSTEMS A **just-in-time (JIT) system** implements a broad management philosophy that reaches beyond the narrow activity of inventory control to influence the entire system of production and operations management. A JIT system seeks to eliminate anything that does not add value in operations activities by providing the right part at the right place at just the right time—right before it is needed in production.

JIT systems are being used in a wide range of industries, including medical supplies. DePuy, a subsidiary of Johnson & Johnson and one of the oldest manufacturers of orthopedic implants in the United States, ships medical supplies to support more than 500,000 surgeries annually. At its distribution center in Bridgewater, Massachusetts, DePuy uses a JIT system to ship necessary supplies on time with the assurance of quality to 10,000 hospitals nationwide. According to Dave Johnson, director of distribution for DePuy, "Hospitals don't want to keep a lot of inventory. They're always looking to cut costs, and they don't like to have a lot of costs from a space standpoint." DePuy's JIT approach enables a doctor preparing for surgery to order the necessary tools and parts, which are delivered on time.[21]

Production using JIT shifts much of the responsibility for carrying inventory to vendors, which operate on forecasts and keep stocks on hand to respond to manufacturers' needs. Suppliers that cannot keep enough high-quality parts on hand are often assessed steep penalties by purchasers. Another risk of using JIT systems is what happens if manufacturers underestimate demand for a product. Strong demand will begin to overtax JIT systems, as suppliers and their customers struggle to keep up with orders with no inventory cushion to tide them over.

MATERIALS REQUIREMENT PLANNING Besides efficiency, effective inventory control requires careful planning to ensure the firm has all the inputs it needs to make its products. How do production and operations managers coordinate all of this information? They rely on **materials requirement planning (MRP),** a computer-based production planning system that

just-in-time (JIT) system management philosophy aimed at improving profits and return on investment by minimizing costs and eliminating waste through cutting inventory on hand.

materials requirement planning (MRP) computer-based production planning system by which a firm can ensure that it has needed parts and materials available at the right time and place in the correct amounts.

lets a firm ensure that it has all the parts and materials it needs to produce its output at the right time and place and in the right amounts.

Production managers use MRP programs to create schedules that identify the specific parts and materials required to produce an item. These schedules specify the exact quantities needed and the dates on which to order those quantities from suppliers so that they are delivered at the correct time in the production cycle. A small company might get by without an MRP system. If a firm makes a simple product with few components, a telephone call may ensure overnight delivery of crucial parts. For a complex product, however, such as a technologically advanced loader or harvester manufactured by Madill Equipment at its plant in Kalama, Washington, longer lead times are necessary. Madill purchased its MRP program "to forecast long lead-time components and manage the rescheduling of materials, as well as determine critical shortages for the assembly and fabrication departments," according to CEO Rich Enners.[22]

Controlling the Production Process

The final task of production and operations managers is controlling the production process to maintain the highest possible quality. **Production control** creates a well-defined set of procedures for coordinating people, materials, and machinery to provide maximum production efficiency. Suppose that a watch factory must produce 80,000 watches during October. Production control managers break down this total into a daily production assignment of 4,000 watches for each of the month's 20 working days. Next, they determine the number of workers, raw materials, parts, and machines the plant needs to meet the production schedule. Similarly, a manager in a service business such as a restaurant must estimate how many dinners the outlet will serve each day and then determine how many people are needed to prepare and serve the food, as well as what food to purchase.

Figure 11.5 illustrates production control as a five-step process composed of planning, routing, scheduling, dispatching, and follow-up. These steps are part of the firm's overall emphasis on total quality management.

PRODUCTION PLANNING The phase of production control called **production planning** determines the amount of resources (including raw materials and other components) an organization needs to produce a certain output. The production planning process develops a bill of materials that lists all needed parts and materials. By comparing information about needed parts and materials with the firm's perpetual inventory data, purchasing personnel can identify necessary purchases. Employees or automated systems establish delivery schedules to provide needed parts and materials when required during the production process. Production planning also ensures the availability of needed machines and personnel. The second the clock hits zero on the final

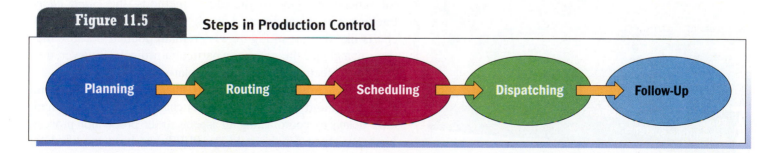

Figure 11.5 **Steps in Production Control**

Planning → Routing → Scheduling → Dispatching → Follow-Up

football playoff game determining who will play in the Super Bowl, 150 employees at the Wilson Sporting Goods factory in Ada, Ohio, begin working double shifts. The Ada plant makes 120 footballs for the Super Bowl—one cowhide makes about ten footballs—not to mention thousands of $130 replica game balls.[23] Although material inputs contribute to service-production systems, production planning for services tends to emphasize human resources more than materials.

ROUTING Another phase of production control, called **routing**, determines the sequence of work throughout the facility and specifies who will perform each aspect of the work at what location. Routing choices depend on two factors: the nature of the good or service and the facility layouts discussed earlier in the chapter—product, process, fixed position, or customer oriented.

Observing production activities can improve routing decisions. At the Fenton, Michigan, factory of TRW Chassis Systems, a team of employees charged with improving work processes on an assembly line discovered that one worker's job consisted of simply moving parts from the end of a conveyor line to a test stand. The team moved the test stand, placing it next to the end of the assembly line so that the tester could unload the items. The unnecessary worker moved to another—probably more gratifying—job in a different part of the plant.[24]

scheduling development of timetables that specify how long each operation in the production process takes and when workers should perform it.

SCHEDULING In the **scheduling** phase of production control, managers develop timetables that specify how long each operation in the production process takes and when workers should perform it. Efficient scheduling ensures that production will meet delivery schedules and make efficient use of resources. Wine and spirits maker Pernod Ricard increased productivity in its plants significantly and reduced inventory 15 percent with a more efficient scheduling system that resulted in greater certainty for the production team.[25]

Scheduling is an extremely important activity for a manufacturer of a complex product with many parts or production stages. Think of all the parts needed to make a computerized tomography (CT) or magnetic resonance imaging (MRI) scanner or other complex hospital equipment. Scheduling must make each one available in the right place at the right time and in the right amounts to ensure a smooth production process.

Scheduling practices vary considerably in service-related organizations. Printing shops or hair stylists may use relatively unsophisticated scheduling systems, resorting to such devices as "first come, first served" rules, appointment schedules, or take-a-number systems. They may call in part-time workers and use standby equipment to handle demand fluctuations. On the other hand, hospitals typically implement sophisticated scheduling systems similar to those of manufacturers.

Production managers use a number of analytical methods for scheduling. One of the oldest methods, the *Gantt chart,* tracks projected and actual work progress over time. Gantt charts like the one in Figure 11.6 remain popular because they show at a glance the status of a particular project. However, they are most effective for scheduling relatively simple projects.

A complex project might require a **PERT (Program Evaluation and Review Technique)** chart, which seeks to minimize delays by coordinating all aspects of the production process. First developed for the military, PERT has been modified for

Even small service businesses, like barber shops, use scheduling systems.

Jeffrey Hochstrasser/iStockphoto. Edited by R. Alcorn

Figure 11.6

Sample Gantt Chart

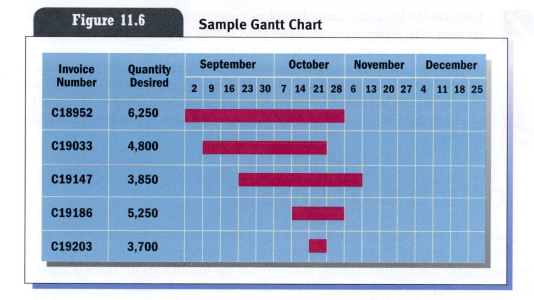

Invoice Number	Quantity Desired	September					October				November				December			
		2	9	16	23	30	7	14	21	28	6	13	20	27	4	11	18	25
C18952	6,250																	
C19033	4,800																	
C19147	3,850																	
C19186	5,250																	
C19203	3,700																	

industry. The simplified PERT diagram in Figure 11.7 summarizes the schedule for purchasing and installing a new robot in a factory. The heavy gold line indicates the **critical path**—the sequence of operations that requires the longest time for completion. In this case, the project cannot be completed in fewer than 17 weeks.

In practice, a PERT network may consist of thousands of events and cover months of time. Complex computer programs help production managers develop such a network and find the critical path among the maze of events and activities. The construction of a huge office building requires complex production planning of this nature.

DISPATCHING The phase of production control in which the manager instructs each department on what work to do and the time allowed for its completion is called **dispatching**. The dispatcher authorizes performance, provides instructions, and lists job priorities. Dispatching may be the responsibility of a manager or a self-managed work team.

Figure 11.7

PERT Diagram for the Purchase and Installation of a New Robot

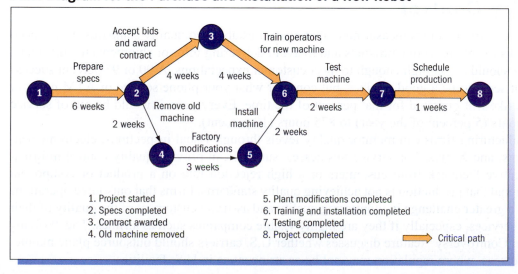

1. Project started
2. Specs completed
3. Contract awarded
4. Old machine removed
5. Plant modifications completed
6. Training and installation completed
7. Testing completed
8. Project completed

→ Critical path

Assessment Check ✓

1. What five steps are involved in controlling the production process?
2. What is the difference between a PERT chart and a Gantt chart?
3. What is the critical path?

FOLLOW-UP Because even the best plans sometimes go awry, production managers need to be aware of problems that arise. **Follow-up** is the phase of production control in which employees and their supervisors spot problems in the production process and determine needed changes. Problems take many forms: machinery malfunctions, delayed shipments, and employee absenteeism can all affect production. The production control system must detect and report these delays to managers or work teams so they can adjust schedules and correct the underlying problems.

Importance of Quality

benchmarking process of determining other companies' standards and best practices.

Although "quality" can be defined several ways, perhaps the most common definition of quality is a good or service free of deficiencies. Quality matters because fixing deficient products is costly. If Seagate makes a defective computer hard drive, it has to either fix the drive or replace it to keep a customer happy. If an airline books too many passengers for a flight, it has to offer vouchers worth several hundred dollars to encourage passengers to give up their seats and take a later flight.

For most companies, the costs of poor quality can amount to 20 percent of sales revenue, if not more. Some typical costs of poor quality include downtime, repair costs, rework, and employee turnover. Production and operations managers must set up systems to track and reduce such costs.

One process that companies use to ensure that they produce high-quality products from the start is **benchmarking**—determining how well other companies perform business functions or tasks. In other words, benchmarking is the process of determining other firms' standards and best practices. Automobile companies routinely purchase each other's cars and then take them completely apart to examine and compare the design, components, and materials used to make even the smallest part. They then make improvements to match or exceed the quality found in their competitors' cars. Companies may use many different benchmarks, depending on their objectives. For instance, some organizations that want to make more money may compare their operating profits or expenses to those of other firms. Retailers concerned with productivity may want to benchmark sales per square foot.[26]

Quality Control

quality control measuring goods and services against established quality standards.

Quality control involves measuring output against established quality standards. Firms need such checks to spot defective products and to avoid delivering inferior shipments to customers. Standards should be set high enough to meet customer expectations. A 90 or 95 percent success rate might seem to be a good number, but consider what your phone service or ATM network would be like if it operated for that percent of the time. Every year, it would be out of service for 438 hours (5 percent of the year) to 875 hours (10 percent).

Manufacturing firms can monitor quality levels through visual inspections, electronic sensors, robots, and X-rays. For service businesses, surveys can provide quality-control information. Negative feedback from customers or a high rejection rate on a product or component sends a signal that production is not achieving quality standards. Firms that outsource operations may face a greater challenge in monitoring quality and assuring customers of the quality of their goods or services, especially if they are highly visible companies such as airlines. The "Solving an Ethical Controversy" feature discusses whether U.S. carriers should outsource plane maintenance overseas, where regulation may not be as stringent as in U.S. facilities.

SHOULD AIRLINES OUTSOURCE MAINTENANCE ABROAD?

At an airport in San Salvador, jet maintenance technicians work on planes owned by companies based in the United States and some European countries. The same scene takes place in facilities in many parts of the world. Critics question the safety of outsourcing aircraft maintenance abroad, where operations may be beyond the reach of the Federal Aviation Administration.

Airline maintenance, repair, and overhaul is a $41 billion industry, expected to reach nearly $63 billion by 2017. Many countries, among them El Salvador, Mexico, China, Korea, Singapore, and Dubai, have invested heavily in operations to attract work from the world's airlines. The Federal Aviation Administration (FAA) oversees the nearly 4,200 facilities in the United States and more than 700 abroad, although many overseas shops are not certified by the FAA. The U.S. Transportation Department says American carriers outsource two-thirds of their maintenance to facilities both inside and outside the United States. Officials for major U.S. airlines express confidence in the maintenance and repair operations.

Unions, consumer groups, and business-travel associations, however, are waging campaigns against outsourcing maintenance to other countries. Critics say that quality and regulatory oversight diminish when maintenance is sent abroad. "You can't keep track as these airline companies outsource to the Third World—there aren't enough FAA inspectors to cover El Salvador, South Korea, and China," says one mechanics union spokesman. The Department of Transportation's inspector general has questioned the FAA's oversight of overseas maintenance.

Should U.S. air carriers use overseas maintenance and repair facilities?

PRO

1. Airlines choose maintenance operators based on the quality of work, as well as cost and completion time. Overseas facilities regularly undergo audits by quality inspectors and regulators from several countries.
2. Federal officials have never cited overseas maintenance mistakes as the cause of a major U.S. airplane crash.

CON

1. The FAA does not have the resources to effectively monitor the overseas maintenance facilities under its jurisdiction. It is very difficult to perform surprise inspections. Unlike U.S.-based facilities, overseas shops do not have as many requirements, such as criminal-background checks and random drug and alcohol tests on mechanics.
2. Even more worrisome to critics is the fact that many facilities offering various airline maintenance services are not certified by the FAA.

Summary

Despite union concerns, some carriers have continued to outsource aircraft maintenance domestically but have delayed plans to send planes for work abroad. At least one airline is looking at retiring older planes faster to ease the burden of refurbishing them. Facing criticism over aircraft maintenance, the FAA has taken a stricter approach on how maintenance work is completed. Congress has taken up the issues of increased FAA inspections of overseas repair shops and required drug and alcohol testing for maintenance workers. Stepped-up regulations would help advance public and industry confidence in overseas operations, which will be needed to help maintain the 27,000 planes expected to be in the air by the next decade.

Sources: Geri Smith and Justin Bachman, "Flying In For a Tune-Up Overseas," *BusinessWeek,* April 21, 2008, http://www.businessweek.com, accessed March 12, 2009; Geri Smith and Justin Bachman, "The Offshoring of Airplane Care," *BusinessWeek,* April 10, 2008, http://www.businessweek.com, accessed October 21, 2008; Andy Pasztor and Melanie Trottman, "Southwest Rethinks Plane Retirement, Shelves Outsource Plan," *The Wall Street Journal,* March 17, 2008, p. A2; Edward H. Phillips, "Happy Days Here Again," *Aviation Week & Space Technology,* April 16, 2007, p. 123.

Solving an ETHICAL controversy

Because the typical factory can spend up to half its operating budget identifying and fixing mistakes, a company cannot rely solely on inspections to achieve its quality goals. Instead, quality-driven production managers identify all processes involved in producing goods and services and work to maximize their efficiency. The causes of problems in the processes must be found and eliminated. If a company concentrates its efforts on better designs of products and processes with clear quality targets, it can ensure virtually defect-free production.[27]

General Electric, Ford, DuPont, Nokia, and Sony are just a few of the growing number of major manufacturers using the Six Sigma concept to achieve quality goals. *Six Sigma* means a company tries to make error-free products 99.9997 percent of the time—a tiny 3.4 errors per million opportunities. The goal of Six Sigma programs is for companies to eliminate virtually all defects in output, processes, and transactions. Computer networking firm Sun Microsystems has developed its own rigorous, data-driven version of Six Sigma that keeps the company focused on customer requirements. Sun Sigma is a companywide effort to measure how well existing processes are meeting customer requirements and to improve processes. A Sun Sigma team developed a new way to install highly complex servers so that they are ready to go once connected to power and the customer's network. Through preconfigured systems, installations that used to take weeks now take just hours. Customers receive orders in five days and realize a 15 percent cost savings.[28]

ISO Standards

For many goods, an important measure of quality is to meet the standards of the **International Organization for Standardization,** known as **ISO** for short—not an acronym but a shorter name derived from the Greek word *isos,* meaning "equal." Established in Europe in 1947, ISO includes representatives from more than 146 nations. Its mission is to promote the development of standardized products to facilitate trade and cooperation across national borders. ISO standards govern everything from the format of banking and telephone cards to freight containers to paper sizes to metric screw threads. The U.S. member body of ISO is the American National Standards Institute.

The ISO 9000 family series of standards sets requirements for quality processes; these standards define how a company should ensure that its products meet customers' requirements. The ISO 14000 series sets standards for operations that minimize harm to the environment. ISO accredits organizations in member countries to evaluate performance against these standards. To receive an ISO 9000 family certification, a company must undergo an on-site audit. The audit ensures that documented quality procedures are in place and that all employees understand and follow the procedures. Production managers meet these requirements through an ongoing process involving periodic recertification.

Many organizations have received significant benefits from ISO 9000. Many consumers prefer to buy from companies that are ISO 9000–certified. In addition, research has shown that ISO 9000 certification enhances a company's competitiveness, which in turn helps to improve business performance.[29]

International Organization for Standardization, (ISO) organization whose mission is to promote the development of standardized products to facilitate trade and cooperation across national borders.

Assessment Check

1. What are some ways in which a company can monitor the quality level of its output?

2. What does Six Sigma mean?

3. List some of the benefits of acquiring ISO 9000 certification.

What's Ahead

Maintaining high quality is an important element of satisfying customers. Product quality and customer satisfaction are also objectives of the business function of marketing. The next part consists of three chapters that explore the many activities involved in customer-driven marketing. These activities include product development, distribution, promotion, and pricing.

Summary of Learning Goals

1 | Outline the importance of production and operations management.

Production and operations management is a vital business function. Without a quality good or service, a company cannot create profits, and it soon fails. The production process is also crucial in a not-for-profit organization, because the good or service it produces justifies the organization's existence. Production and operations management plays an important strategic role by lowering the costs of production, boosting output quality, and allowing the firm to respond flexibly and dependably to customers' demands.

Assessment Check Answers

1.1 What are the advantages and disadvantages of mass production? Mass production leads to high productivity, mechanization, and standardization, all of which make outputs available in large quantities at lower prices than individually crafted items would cost. The disadvantages are inefficiency when making small batches of items and specialized tasks leading to boring, repetitive jobs.

1.2 What are the characteristics of flexible production? Flexible production is characterized by cost-effective production of small batches, use of information technology to share the details of customer orders, programmable equipment to fulfill the orders, and skilled people to carry out whatever tasks are needed to fill a particular order.

1.3 Describe a customer-driven production system. Customer-driven production systems directly link what manufacturers make with what customers want to buy. One way to do this is to establish computer links between factories and retailers' scanners. Another is to not make a product until a customer orders it.

2 | Explain the roles of computers and related technologies in production.

Computer-driven automation allows companies to design, create, and modify products rapidly and produce them in ways that effectively meet customers' changing needs. Important design and production technologies include robots, computer-aided design (CAD), computer-aided manufacturing (CAM), and computer-integrated manufacturing (CIM).

Assessment Check Answers

2.1 List some of the reasons businesses invest in robots. Businesses use robots to free people from boring, sometimes dangerous assignments and to move heavy items from one place to another in a factory.

2.2 Distinguish among computer-aided design, computer-aided manufacturing, flexible manufacturing, and computer-integrated manufacturing. Computer-aided design (CAD) enables engineers to design parts and buildings on computer screens faster and with fewer mistakes than they could achieve working with traditional drafting systems.

Computer-aided manufacturing (CAM) uses the CAD specifications to determine the steps that machines must take to produce products or parts. CAD and CAM are typically used together. Computer-integrated manufacturing (CIM) is a system in which companies integrate robots, CAD/CAM, FMS, computers, and other technologies to design products, control machines, handle materials, and control the production function in an integrated fashion.

3 | Identify the factors involved in a plant location decision.

Criteria for choosing the best site for a production facility fall into three categories: transportation, human, and physical factors. Transportation factors include proximity to markets and raw materials, along with availability of transportation alternatives. Physical variables involve such issues as water supply, available energy, and options for disposing of hazardous wastes. Human factors include the area's labor supply, local regulations, and living conditions.

Assessment Check Answers

3.1 What is the purpose of an environmental impact study, and how does it influence the location decision? The purpose is to analyze how a proposed plant would affect the quality of life in the surrounding area. The effects on transportation facilities; energy requirements; water and sewage treatment needs; natural plant life and wildlife; and water, air, and noise pollution are studied.

3.2 What human factors are relevant to the location decision? Human factors include an area's labor supply, labor costs, local regulations, and living conditions.

4 | Explain the major tasks of production and operations managers.

Production and operations managers use people and machinery to convert inputs (materials and resources) into finished goods and services. Four major tasks are involved. First, the managers must plan the overall production process. Next, they must pick the best layout for their facilities. Then they implement their production plans. Finally, they control the production process and evaluate results to maintain the highest possible quality.

Assessment Check Answers

4.1 What is the key responsibility of production managers? Production managers must oversee the work of people and machinery to convert inputs (materials and resources) into finished goods and services.

4.2 List the four major tasks of production and operations managers. The four tasks are planning overall production, laying out the firm's facilities, implementing the production plan, and controlling manufacturing to achieve high quality.

5 Compare alternative layouts for production facilities.

Process layouts effectively produce nonstandard products in relatively small batches. Product layouts are appropriate for the production of a large quantity of relatively similar products. Fixed-position layouts are common when production involves very large, heavy, or fragile products. Customer-oriented layouts are typical for service facilities where success depends on interaction between customers and service providers.

Assessment Check Answers

5.1 Differentiate among the three most common layout designs: process, product, and fixed position. A process layout groups machinery and equipment according to their functions. The work in process moves around the plant to reach different workstations. A product layout sets up production equipment along a product-flow line, and the work in process moves along this line past workstations. A fixed-position layout places the product in one spot, and workers, materials, and equipment come to it.

5.2 Describe a customer-oriented layout that is typically used by service providers. A customer-oriented layout enhances the interactions between a company and its customers. For example, a hospital will make sure that the nurses' station is close to all of the patients' beds in a hospital wing.

6 List the steps in the purchasing process.

In the make, buy, or lease decision, production and operations managers determine whether to manufacture needed inputs in house, purchase them, or lease them from an outside supplier. Managers determine the correct materials to purchase, select appropriate suppliers, and develop an efficient ordering system. The objective is to buy the right materials in the right amounts at the right time and in the right place.

Assessment Check Answers

6.1 What factors affect the make, buy, or lease decision? The costs of leasing or purchasing parts from vendors, versus producing them in house, the availability of dependable outside suppliers, and the need for confidentiality affect this decision.

6.2 What factors should firms consider when selecting vendors? Firms should compare quality, prices, speed, warranties, and the dependability of delivery and services offered by vendors.

7 Outline the advantages and disadvantages of maintaining large inventories.

The task of inventory control is to balance the need to maintain adequate supplies against the need to minimize funds invested in inventory. Excessive inventory results in unnec-

essary expenditures for warehousing, taxes, insurance, and maintenance. Inadequate inventory may mean production delays, lost sales, and inefficient operations.

Assessment Check Answers

7.1 What balance must managers seek when controlling inventory? Managers must balance the need to keep stocks on hand to meet demand against the costs of carrying inventory.

7.2 Explain perpetual inventory and vendor-managed inventory. Perpetual inventory systems continuously monitor the amount and location of inventory and automatically generate orders at the appropriate times. Vendor-managed inventory is a system in which companies have their suppliers control and manage their inventory.

7.3 What is a just-in-time inventory system, and what are some of its advantages? With a just-in-time inventory system, component parts arrive from suppliers just as they are needed at each stage of production. By having parts arrive "just in time," the manufacturer keeps little inventory on hand and thus avoids the costs associated with holding inventory.

7.4 What is MRP used for? Production managers use MRP programs to create schedules that identify the specific parts and materials required to produce an item. These schedules specify the exact quantities required and when to order those quantities from suppliers so that needed inventory is delivered at the best time within the production cycle.

8 Identify the steps in the production control process.

The production control process consists of five steps: planning, routing, scheduling, dispatching, and follow-up. Quality control is an important consideration throughout this process. Coordination of each of these phases should result in high production efficiency and low production costs.

Assessment Check Answers

8.1 What five steps are involved in controlling the production process? The five steps are planning, routing, scheduling, dispatching, and follow-up.

8.2 What is the difference between a PERT chart and a Gantt chart? PERT charts, which seek to minimize delays by coordinating all aspects of the production process, are used for more complex projects; Gantt charts, which track projected and actual work progress over time, are used for scheduling relatively simple projects.

8.3 What is the critical path? In a PERT chart, a red line indicates the critical path, which is the sequence of steps or operations that will take the longest time to complete.

9 Explain the benefits of quality control.

Quality control involves evaluating goods and services against established quality standards. Such checks are necessary to spot defective products and to see that they are not shipped to customers. Devices for monitoring quality levels of the firm's output include visual inspection, electronic sensors, robots, and X-rays. Companies are increasing the quality of their goods and services by using Six Sigma techniques and by becoming ISO 9000 and 14000 certified.

Assessment Check Answers

9.1 What are some ways in which a company can monitor the quality level of its output? Benchmarking, quality control, Six Sigma, and ISO standards are ways of monitoring quality.

9.2 What does Six Sigma mean? Six Sigma means a company tries to make error-free products 99.9997 percent of time—just 3.4 errors per million opportunities.

9.3 List some of the benefits of acquiring ISO 9000 certification. These standards define how a company should ensure that its products meet customers' requirements. Studies show that customers prefer to buy from companies that are ISO 9000 certified.

Business Terms You Need to Know

production 356	computer-aided design (CAD) 361	materials requirement planning (MRP) 370	International Organization for Standardization (ISO) 376
production and operations management 356	computer-aided manufacturing (CAM) 362	scheduling 372	
assembly line 358	just-in-time (JIT) system 370	benchmarking 374	
robot 361		quality control 374	

Other Important Business Terms

mass production 357	environmental impact study 363	perpetual inventory 369	Evaluation and Review Technique) 372
flexible manufacturing system (FMS) 362	make, buy, or lease decision 367	production control 371	critical path 373
computer-integrated manufacturing (CIM) 362	inventory control 369	production planning 371	dispatching 373
		routing 372	follow-up 374
		PERT (Program	

Review Questions

1. What is utility? Define and briefly describe the four different types of utility.

2. Distinguish between production and manufacturing. In what ways does each of the following perform a production function?
   a. delicatessen
   b. dentist
   c. local transit system
   d. music store

3. Why is production such an important business activity? In what ways does it create value for the company and its customers?

4. How does mass production work? Describe a good or service that would lend itself well to mass production and one that would not lend itself well to mass production.

5. How does flexible production compare with mass production?

6. Briefly describe the four different production systems. Give an example of a good or service that is produced by each.

7. Describe the four major tasks of production and operations managers: planning the production process, selecting the most appropriate layout, implementing the production plan, and controlling the production process.

8. What would be the best facility layout for each of the following?
   a. card shop
   b. chain of economy motels
   c. car wash
   d. accountant's office
   e. large auto dealer's service facility

9. Describe a flexible manufacturing system.

10. What are the benefits of producing a quality product? Briefly describe the International Organization for Standardization (ISO).

Projects and Teamwork Applications

1. Imagine that you have been hired as a management consultant for one of the following types of service organizations to decide on an appropriate layout for its facility. Select one and sketch or describe the layout that you think would be best.

   a. dry-cleaners
   b. doctor's office
   c. small, elegant lakeside restaurant
   d. coffee house

2. Imagine that you have been hired as production manager for a snowboard manufacturer (or choose another type of manufacturer that interests you). What type of inventory control would you recommend for your company? Write a brief memo explaining why.

3. Nissan and Hyundai have built auto assembly plants in Mississippi and Alabama, respectively. What factors do you think Nissan and Hyundai considered when choosing their plant location?

4. Suggest two or three ways in which each of the following firms could practice effective quality control:

   a. pharmaceutical firm
   b. miniature golf course
   c. Internet florist
   d. agricultural packing house

Web Assignments

1. **Production.** Visit the National Association of Manufacturers' Web site, (www.shopfloor.org). Click on the link "Cool Stuff Being Made." Browse through the selection of videos showing the manufacture of various products. Watch a video that interests you. Write a brief report containing these elements: company name, location, years in business, and products. Describe the production process in a few sentences.

2. **PERT charts.** Visit the Web site listed (http://learn.midsouthcc.edu/LearningObjects/softchalk/project_management/pert/index.html) to practice completing a PERT chart for a project. Use information from the table to complete the chart, then take the two-question quiz and see how you score. Did you complete the chart correctly? Congratulations! If not, try again.

3. **Environmental impact.** Visit the U.S. Green Building Council's Web site (http://www.usgbc.org). Click on "LEED," then click on "Project Certification." Read the information about the benefits of earning LEED certification. What benefits can businesses obtain by becoming LEED certified? What kinds of building are eligible to be certified?

Note: Internet Web addresses change frequently. If you do not find the exact sites listed, you may need to access the organization's or company's home page and search from there.

Case 11.1 Zara: Zippy Production Means Fast Fashion

At Zara, fashion paradise awaits shoppers constantly on the lookout for chic new clothing. New designs appear twice a week, and the items showcased in the windows are in stock. Regular Zara shoppers know they should scan the clothes on the black plastic hangers for the latest looks.

Zara leads the industry in making and shipping "fast fashion"—inexpensive trendy clothing. Its parent company is Spain-based Inditex, whose seven brands include Massimo Dutti and Bershka. With 3,700 stores in 68 countries and annual sales of $12 billion, Inditex is the world's second-largest clothing retailer by sales after Gap. Inditex is famous for opening a new store every day of the year in some part of the world and for getting products to the stores at lightning speed. Zara makes up 60 percent of Inditex's business.

When it opened the first store in a Spanish port town, Zara capitalized on two strengths: a keen sense for customer tastes and a production process that began with the final price and worked back to the most efficient operations. Later Zara brought a local business-school professor on board to refine shipping and distribution and consulted with professors from the MIT Sloan School of Management to develop the best system of replenishing stores rapidly. Zara collections are small and often sell out, and the company prefers to move a clothing group out of a store if some pieces or sizes are out of stock. The MIT group designed a mathematical model to handle the enormous number of decisions involved in determining every garment and every size needed at every store.

At Inditex company headquarters outside La Coruña, Spain, sales managers at computers monitor sales at every store around the world. When apparel sells well—or doesn't—they tell nearby designers to come up with new designs. Downstairs other designers decide on window displays and store layouts. They set up displays in mock store windows lining a simulated street full of shops. The designers take pictures to show how different storefronts should look, from London's Regent Street to New York's Fifth Avenue. Every two weeks, new displays are photographed and e-mailed to stores to replicate.

Zara store managers use hand-held computers that show how garments rank by sales, so clerks can reorder fast-moving merchandise in less than an hour. These orders arrive, with new items, two days later. Alarm tags are attached at the factory, to save sales staff's time and allow them to spend more time serving customers. Clothes are shipped directly from the factory to stores. Unlike competitors that manufacture most of their clothing in Asia, Inditex produces only a third of its goods there. Factories in Spain, Portugal, Morocco, and Turkey make two-thirds of the merchandise. While labor costs are higher in these countries than in Asia, Inditex wants the flexibility of having most of its production near its warehouses, which are all in Spain. The company combines merchandise for its various store brands and ships the large volume of goods twice a week via Air France Cargo or Emirates Airline. Planes from Spain fly to Bahrain with merchandise for Inditex stores in the Middle East, proceed to Asia, and return to Spain with raw materials and partially finished clothing.

Some retail specialists question whether Zara's local production can continue to be successful. Producing the majority of its merchandise so close to home may lose some benefit as more stores open farther away. Zara has been able to make up some of its production and distribution costs by charging more for its clothing sold overseas. In the United States, for example, Zara pieces cost as much as 40 percent more than in Spain. That inconsistency, critics say, could be risky in a global business. Meanwhile, Zara's quick production and distribution has prompted other retailers to increase the number of new styles they offer each year and to get the new looks into stores faster.[30]

Questions for Critical Thinking

1. Do you think the advantages of locating most of Zara's production in Spain and other nearby countries outweigh the disadvantages?

2. Describe Zara's inventory control system. How does it affect production?

Sprint's Emergency Call for Service

Case 11.2

Service businesses face many of the same production and operations problems that plague companies producing cars and electronics. Banks, car washes, hospitals, and telecommunication firms must produce high-quality services or lose business as customers turn elsewhere. Providing superior service may appear to be fairly straightforward, and many providers, like retailer Amazon.com, Ritz-Carlton Hotels, and online shoestore Zappos.com, do get it right. It is anything but easy, however. Sprint is a case in point.

Sprint was once the third-largest U.S. long-distance company. It was known for high-quality phone service and ads saying that its fiber-optic network was so sensitive you could "hear a pin drop." When Sprint merged with Nextel, industry observers thought the move made a lot of sense; combined, the two would be better positioned to compete with the two wireless leaders, AT&T and Verizon. Nextel, famous for its "push-to-talk" technology enabling a cell phone user to connect to other cell phones in less than a second by pushing only one button, had the best customer retention in the industry. "The combination of Sprint and Nextel builds strength on strength," said Sprint's CEO at the time. Unfortunately, the result was a drop in Sprint's service, reputation, and stock value. Since the merger, the company has fallen to last in customer service among the nation's leading wireless carriers, according to J.D. Power's annual survey. Customers jumped in droves to other long-distance providers.

What went wrong at Sprint? The numbers-driven management approach implemented after the merger has been blamed for much of the company's downfall. For instance, call centers were viewed and measured as profit centers, rather than service centers. Employees previously focused on solving customers' problems, no matter how long it took, were pressured to keep conversations with customers short. Managers began tracking employee computer use and tightly monitoring all activities. Call center workers were asked to be more involved in sales; some say they had quotas on how many contracts they should renew each month. The changes resulted in low morale and poor customer service.

To reverse course, Sprint Nextel CEO Daniel Hesse and his managers are revising the postmerger approach and making service the priority. Gone is the limit on how long service representatives can spend on the phone with customers. Management now tracks how quickly calls are answered and how often employees resolve problems on the customer's first call. The executives know it will take time to restore consumer confidence in Sprint. As one employee put it, "I don't think customer service is extinct here, just endangered." [31]

Questions for Critical Thinking

1. Why is quality control extremely important for a service business like Sprint Nextel?
2. How effective do you think the new quality-control measures will be in Sprint Nextel's effort to regain its reputation for service?

VIDEO Case 11.3 — Washburn Guitars: Sound Since 1883

Well-run businesses tend to stay sound for a long time. They grow, they change, they add and delete products, they open and close manufacturing plants, they streamline and expand their operations. But their basic business foundation remains strong, no matter what happens.

Washburn Guitars has been making beautiful sounds since it was founded in Chicago in 1883. Location has always been a key component of the company's overall strategy; when the firm became Washburn International nearly 100 years later, it wasn't long before its manufacturing, office headquarters, and warehouse divisions were consolidated into a single 130,000-square-foot facility outside Mundelein, Illinois. This allowed the firm to incorporate its SoundTech speaker division, which had been operating elsewhere, into the same facility. Perhaps the most important reason for the move, however, was the availability of a skilled workforce nearby. Company president Rudy Schlacher explained that moving to the new location allowed the firm to "tap into an exceptional local workforce." About three years after the move, Washburn International morphed again—into U.S. Music Corporation—which now includes even more divisions, such as Randall Amplifiers, Vinci Strings and Accessories, SoundTech Professional Audio, and Oscar Schmidt folk instruments. The organizational change "gives us the opportunity to clearly separate the parent corporation [U.S. Music] from the name of its producing division, Washburn Guitars," explained Schlacher.

Building fine musical instruments is an art in itself, and the production crew at Washburn takes its job seriously. "Every guitar that is shipped from the Chicago area factory is constructed with passion only a musician can feel," says the Washburn Web site. Each acoustic guitar is built by one craftsperson—called a luthier—from start to finish. "These guitars are crafted with the hard-working spirit and quality standards of the luthiers that have crafted Washburn guitars since the late 1800s for musicians and songwriters around the world."

"I like working with wood, taking it from raw lumber to an actual musical instrument with its own voice," says luthier John Stover. Stover has built acoustic guitars for such musical stars as Dolly Parton and Dan Donegan of Chicago-based metal band Disturbed.

Even though the guitars are built by hand, Washburn uses computer-aided design and manufacturing (CAD/CAM) technologies in its manufacturing process. A CAD/CAM engineer helps design and draw new guitar models. The electric models that are built on an assembly line are still guided by expert craftspeople whose jobs may be assembly lead or neck lead (the worker in charge of building and assembling guitar necks).

Building only 2,500 guitars a year for the general public while maintaining Washburn's high quality standards is expensive. But Washburn finds ways to save in production costs so that it can charge customers reasonable prices for its products; many of its models retail for between $500 and $1,000. Some models are manufactured in Indonesia, where labor is less expensive. Also, although Washburn accepts customized requests through dealers on its current line of guitars and basses made in the United States, the firm does not offer individual custom designs. So a customer could ask for a different paint finish or a left-handed conversion—but not an entirely different design. This system means that customers generally get what they want—without paying exorbitant prices. And it allows Washburn to carefully control its inventory of raw materials and components.

Occasionally Washburn creates an alliance with a musician such as Dan Donegan for a particular series of instruments. Together with Washburn's luthiers and production team, Donegan designed a new series of guitars called Maya (after Donegan's daughter). "Washburn really went above and beyond to make sure my guitars are to my exact specification. I really wanted to create a guitar that is somewhat unique but appeals to artists of all musical genres," said Donegan of his experience with Washburn. The Maya standard and Maya Pro guitars are both built in the United States and come with a range of components. The Maya standard is made of poplar and retails at about $1,500, while the Pro is made of mahogany and retails for just under $2,700. Washburn is also producing a limited customized edition of the Maya line that will be available through select dealers.

Building a guitar is clearly a labor of love for those who work at Washburn. These craftspeople understand the needs of their customers because most of them are musicians themselves. So working with someone like Dan Donegan is as smooth a process as strumming an old tune. Production manager Gil Vasquez explains his job at Washburn this way: "My knowledge of guitars is vast, and I am constantly searching for the ultimate tone, whether it is in the way the guitar is constructed or in the electronics that are being used." Vasquez knows what he is talking about; his customers include Lenny Kravitz, Eric Clapton, Jimmy Page—and Dan Donegan. [32]

Questions for Critical Thinking

1. How do production and operations management contribute to the long-term success of Washburn Guitars?

2. Describe the manufacturing technique(s) you think are applicable to Washburn. Also, explain how CAD and CAM contribute to the design and production processes at Washburn.

3. Describe the physical variables and human factors involved in Washburn's choice of location for its headquarters and production facility in Mundelein, Illinois.

4. What are the benefits of quality control at Washburn? What methods might the firm use for controlling quality?

KANSAS

Saline River · Kansas City
Smoky Hill River · Salina
Greensburg
Garden City
Wichita

© Getty Images

Greensburg KS.

No Time to Micromanage

"This is a stepping stone for me," thought Greensburg's town administrator, Steve Hewitt. Hewitt, who had grown up in Greensburg, had moved back home and taken a position in the tiny rural town of 1500. Standing in what was left of his kitchen on the night of Friday, May 4, 2007, he realized he had gotten more than he bargained for.

Across town, Mayor Lonnie McCollum and his wife had survived by clinging to a mattress as the storm ravaged their home. A write-in candidate in the past election, McCollum had accepted the job and set out to revive the dying town. Among his many ideas, the most innovative had been green building. McCollum was no tree-hugger; he was simply looking for a way to save money on fuel and utilities, to conserve the town's resources.

Like many people in town, Hewitt and McCollum had no idea of the extent of the damage. They would later learn that the two-mile-wide F5 tornado drove right through the two-mile-wide town. By the end of the weekend, though, they knew that Greensburg was gone. At a press conference, McCollum announced that the town would rebuild, and would do it using green technology.

By May 2008, the town was on its third mayor since the disaster, but Steve Hewitt was still the town administrator. He had expanded his staff from 20 to 35 people, establishing a full-time fire department, a planning department, and a community development department. Each week Hewitt spent hours giving interviews to reporters from all over the world. "He's very open as far as information," said Recovery Coordinator and Assistant Town Administrator Kim Alderfer. "He's very good about delegating authority. He gives you the authority to do your job. He doesn't have time to micromanage."

Meanwhile, residents Janice and John Haney had rebuilt their family farm on the outskirts of town. Although their new home, an earth berm structure, was full of energy-efficient features, Janice wasn't convinced that the plan to rebuild Greensburg using green technology was the right one. "I do worry that it will be a T-shirt slogan," said Haney. "I personally don't think the persons that are living in Greensburg right now are really committed to it. We didn't have a choice. You MUST go green. That's really not everybody's option." She added that many people feared higher taxes would force some families out of town.

Questions

After viewing the video, answer the following questions:

1. What kind of leader is Steve Hewitt?
2. How would you describe Greensburg's culture?
3. Do you believe that as town administrator, Hewitt had the right to impose green building codes on residents and businesses?
4. Perform a SWOT analysis of Greensburg's green initiative.

Launching Your Management Career

Part 3, "Management: Empowering People to Achieve Business Objectives," covers Chapters 8 through 11, which discuss management, leadership, and the internal organization; human resource management, motivation, and labor–management relations; improving performance through empowerment, teamwork, and communication; and production and operations management. In those chapters, you read about top executives and company founders who not only direct their companies' strategy but lead others in their day-to-day tasks to keep them on track, middle managers who devise plans to turn the strategies into realities, and supervisors who work directly with employees to create strong teams that satisfy customers. An incredible variety of jobs is available to those choosing management careers. And the demand for managers will continue to grow. The U.S. Department of Labor estimates that managerial jobs will grow by nearly 15 percent over the next decade.[1]

So what kinds of jobs might you be able to choose from if you launch a management career? As you learned in Chapter 8, three types of management jobs exist: supervisory managers, middle managers, and top managers. Supervisory management, or first-line management, includes positions such as supervisor, office manager, department manager, section chief, and team leader.

Managers at this level work directly with the employees who produce and sell a firm's goods and services.

Middle management includes positions such as general managers, plant managers, division managers, and regional or branch managers. They are responsible for setting objectives consistent with top management's goals and planning and implementing strategies for achieving those objectives.

Top managers include such positions as chief executive officer (CEO), chief operating officer (COO), chief financial officer (CFO), chief information officer (CIO), and executive vice president. Top managers devote most of their time to developing long-range plans, setting a direction for their organization, and inspiring a company's executives and employees to achieve their vision for the company's future. Top managers travel frequently between local, national, and global offices as they meet and work with customers, suppliers, and company managers and employees.

Most managers start their careers in areas such as sales, production, or finance, so you likely will start in a similar entry-level job. If you do that job and other jobs well, you may be considered for a supervisory position. Then, if you are interested and have the technical, human, and conceptual skills to succeed, you'll begin your

management career path. But what kinds of supervisory management jobs are typically available? Let's review the exciting possibilities.

Administrative service managers manage basic services—such as clerical work, payroll, travel, printing and copying, data records, telecommunications, security, parking, and supplies—without which no organization could operate. On average, administrative service managers earn $68,000 a year.[2]

Construction managers plan, schedule, and coordinate the building of homes, commercial buildings such as offices and stores, and industrial facilities such as manufacturing plants and distribution centers. Unlike administrative service managers, who work in offices, construction managers typically work on building sites with architects, engineers, construction workers, and suppliers. On average, construction managers earn almost $74,000 a year.[3]

Food service managers run restaurants and services that prepare and offer meals to customers. They coordinate workers and suppliers in kitchens, dining areas, and banquet operations; are responsible for those who order and purchase food inventories; maintain kitchen equipment; and recruit, hire, and train new workers. Food service managers can work for chains such as Ruby Tuesday or Olive Garden, for local restaurants, and for corporate food service departments in organizations. On average, food service managers earn more than $43,000 a year.[4]

Human resource managers help organizations follow federal and local labor laws; effectively recruit, hire, train, and retain talented workers; administer corporate pay and benefits plans; develop and administer organizational human resource policies; and, when necessary, participate in contract negotiations or handle disputes. Human resource management jobs vary widely, depending on how specialized the requirements are. On average, human resource managers earn from $43,000 to $89,000 a year, depending on the area in which they specialize.[5]

Lodging managers work in hotels and motels but also help run camps, ranches, and recreational resorts. They may oversee guest service, front desk, kitchen, restaurant, banquet, house cleaning, and maintenance workers. Because they are expected to help satisfy customers around the clock, they often work long hours and may be on call when not at work. On average, lodging managers earn about $42,000 a year.[6]

Medical and health service managers work in hospitals, nursing homes, doctors' offices, and corporate and university settings. They run departments that offer clinical services; ensure that state and federal laws are followed; and handle decisions related to the management of patient care, nursing, surgery, therapy, medical records, and financial payments. On average,

medical and health service managers earn $73,000 a year.[7]

Purchasing managers lead and control organizational supply chains that ensure that companies have needed materials to produce the goods and services they sell, purchase materials at reasonable prices, and oversee deliveries when and where they are needed. Purchasing managers work with wholesale and retail buyers, buying goods that are then resold to others; purchasing agents, who buy supplies and raw materials for their organizations; and contract specialists, who negotiate and supervise purchasing contracts with key suppliers and vendors. On average, purchasing managers earn nearly $82,000 a year.[8]

Production managers direct and coordinate operations that manufacture goods. They work with employees who produce parts and assemble products, help determine which new machines should be purchased and when existing machines need maintenance, and are responsible for achieving production goals that specify the quality, cost, schedule, and quantity of units to be produced. On average, production managers earn almost $78,000 a year.[9]

Career Assessment Exercises in Management

1. The American Management Association is a global, not-for-profit professional organization that provides a range

of management development and educational services to individuals, companies, and government agencies. Access the AMA's Web site at http://www.amanet.org. Explore the "Free Resources" link there (you will have to register). Pick an article or research area that interests you. Provide a one-page summary of the management issues discussed in the feature.

2. Go online to a business news service, such as Yahoo! News or Google News, or look at the business section of your local newspaper. Find a story relating to a first-line supervisor, middle manager, or top executive. Summarize that person's duties. What decisions does that person make and how do those decisions affect his or her organization?

3. Pick a supervisory management position from the descriptions provided here that interests you. Research the career field. What skills do you possess that would make you a good candidate for a management position in that field? What work and other experience do you need to help you get started? Create a list of both your strengths and weaknesses and formulate a plan to add to your strengths.

Part 4

Marketing Management

© Masterfile

chapter 12

Customer-Driven Marketing

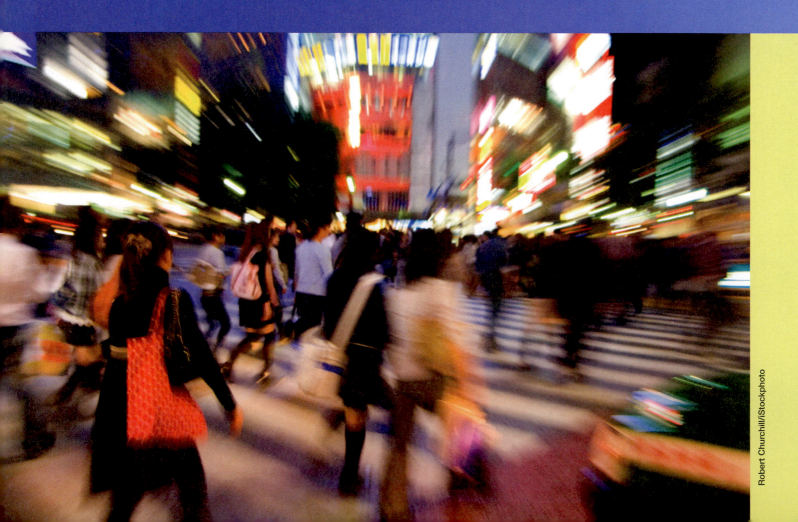

PetSmart Pampers Pooches

Purebred poodle or Pomeranian, hybrid of hound and husky, everyone loves the family dog. But some people's attachment goes deeper, and PetSmart, the largest U.S. pet-store chain, aims to meet the needs of the finickiest owner. The company has pinpointed a group of consumers whose passion for their pets is so great that the animals are considered full-fledged family members. PetSmart calls these customers "pet parents" and offers services geared directly to them.

Pet owners can pick up a dog leash, toy, or food in one of nearly 1,000 PetSmart retail stores. But several hundred stores now also offer upscale lodging in their PetSmart PetsHotels. The PetsHotel provides personalized day and overnight care for dogs and cats. At a PetsHotel, family pooches enjoy extended play time, salon services, and healthful snacks including lactose-free soft-serve ice cream. The facilities are sparkling clean, resembling a luxury hotel, and the staff is knowledgeable and well trained. A PetsHotel suite, which goes for about $31 per night, includes a room with a window, dog beds with lamb-skin blankets, and a TV that plays videos such as Disney's *101 Dalmations*. Pet owners often say they wouldn't mind staying at the hotel themselves. Doggie Day Camp, the day-care option located inside the PetsHotel, is a program that provides hours of supervised play with other dogs in climate-controlled playrooms. Doggie Day Camp is open seven days a week—except for Thanksgiving and Christmas—and has flexible drop-off and pick-up times.

Pet owners use both of these programs for a number of reasons. Some are traveling. Others use the day care as an alternative to leaving a dog home alone. Some drop their dogs off for a few hours of exercise and interaction with other dogs to prevent mischievous behavior from occurring at home.

PetSmart markets its services to pet parents who want specialized care for their dogs, pointing out on its Web site the benefits of its own programs over those of competitors. Each dog is carefully screened to identify those that are best suited to the programs and to make certain that the programs can meet customers' needs. The pet parent is interviewed, then the health and temperament of the dog is assessed, including confirmation of specific vaccinations. Finally, the dog is introduced to the group with which it will play for the duration of its stay. If all three stages go well, the dog becomes a member of the PetSmart family. PetSmart Pet Care Specialists are safety certified and trained in behavior assessment—not just part-time pet sitters. The indoor facilities provide a safe, clean environment for all the dogs that stay either for the day program or overnight.

PetSmart offers a frequent-user program to pet parents who plan to use Doggie Day Camp regularly. For every 10 sessions purchased during select months with a PetPerks Savings Card, customers receive 1 session free. Coupons for the free sessions are mailed to customers, but program users can also check their rewards status online.

How successful is PetSmart at recognizing the needs of passionate pet owners? Its revenues from its PetsHotel and Doggie Day Camp services have increased more than 25 percent each year since their start. The services are twice as profitable as the sale of pet toys, accessories, and food.

But success should come as no surprise when more than 80 percent of dog owners refer to their pooches as family members. "We are benefiting from the trend toward the humanization of pets," says PetSmart spokesperson David Lenhardt. "It's that passion for pets that makes the pet hotel work."[1]

Business success in the 21st century is directly tied to a company's ability to identify and serve its target markets. In fact, all organizations—profit-oriented and not-for-profit, manufacturing and retailing—*must* serve customer needs to succeed, just as PetSmart does by offering pet parents day care and overnight stays for their canine family members. Marketing is the link between the organization and the people who buy and use its goods and services. It is the way organizations determine buyer needs and inform potential customers that their firms can meet those needs by supplying a quality product at a reasonable price. And it is the path to developing loyal, long-term customers.

Although consumers who purchase goods for their own use and enjoyment or business purchasers seeking products to use in their firm's operation may seem to be huge, undifferentiated masses, marketers see distinct wants and needs for each group. To understand buyers, from huge manufacturers to Web surfers to shoppers in the grocery aisles, companies gather mountains of data on every aspect of consumer lifestyles and buying behaviors. Marketers use the data to understand the needs and wants

of both final customers and business buyers so that they can better satisfy them. Satisfying customers goes a long way toward building relationships with them. It's not always easy. To establish links with the buying public, Whole Foods CEO John Mackey invites e-mails from consumers who may—or may not—be customers. After several weeks of electronic debate with an animal welfare activist over Whole Foods's practice of selling duck meat from a particular source, Mackey asked the activist to help rewrite his firm's policies on farm animal treatment. This relationship, which developed through direct communication between the CEO and a consumer, has helped Whole Foods cement its relationship with customers who have certain food-source concerns.

This chapter begins with an examination of the marketing concept and the way businesspeople develop a marketing strategy. We then turn to marketing research techniques, leading to an explanation of how businesses apply data to market segmentation and understanding customer behavior. The chapter closes with a detailed look at the important role customer relationships play in today's highly competitive business world.

What Is Marketing?

Every organization—from profit-seeking firms such as Dunkin' Donuts and Whole Foods to such not-for-profits as the United Way and the M. D. Anderson Cancer Center—must serve customer needs to succeed. Perhaps retail pioneer J. C. Penney best expressed this priority when he told his store managers, "Either you or your replacement will greet the customer within the first 60 seconds."

marketing organizational function and set of processes for creating, communicating, and delivering value to customers and for managing customer relationships in ways that benefit the organization and its stakeholders.

According to the American Marketing Association, **marketing** is "an organizational function and a set of processes for creating, communicating, and delivering value to customers and for managing customer relationships in ways that benefit the organization and its stakeholders."[2] In addition to selling goods and services, marketing techniques help people advocate ideas or viewpoints and educate others. The American Diabetes Association mails out questionnaires that ask, "Are you at risk for diabetes?" The documents help educate the general public about this widespread disease by listing its risk factors and common symptoms and describing the work of the association.

Department store founder Marshall Field explained marketing quite clearly when he advised one employee to "give the lady what she wants." The phrase became the company motto, and it remains a business truism today. The best marketers not only give consumers what they want but even anticipate consumers' needs before those needs surface. Ideally, they can get a jump on the competition by creating a link in consumers' minds between the new need and the fulfillment of that need by the marketers' products. Principal Financial Group markets employee retirement plans to other firms as a strategy for retaining the best employees. NetJets offers fractional jet ownership to executives who want the luxury and flexibility of private ownership at a reduced cost. Samsung offers its next generation of high-definition TV with its trademarked Cinema Smooth Light Engine. "Stop watching TV," says its promotion. "Start living it."

As these examples illustrate, marketing is more than just selling. It is a process that begins with discovering unmet customer needs and continues with researching the potential market; producing a good or service capable of satisfying the targeted customers; and promoting, pricing, and distributing that good or service. Throughout the entire marketing process, a successful organization focuses on building customer relationships.

When two or more parties benefit from trading things of value, they have entered into an **exchange process.** When you purchase a cup of coffee, the other party may be a convenience store clerk, a vending machine, or a Dunkin' Donuts server. The exchange seems simple—some money changes hands, and you receive your cup of coffee. But the exchange process is more complex than that. It could not occur if you didn't feel the need for a cup of coffee or if the convenience store or vending machine were not available. You wouldn't choose Dunkin' Donuts unless you were aware of the brand. Because of marketing, your desire for a flavored blend, decaf, or plain black coffee is identified, and the coffee manufacturer's business is successful.

exchange process activity in which two or more parties give something of value to each other to satisfy perceived needs.

How Marketing Creates Utility

Marketing affects many aspects of an organization and its dealings with customers. The ability of a good or service to satisfy the wants and needs of customers is called **utility.** A company's production function creates *form utility* by converting raw materials, component parts, and other inputs into finished goods and services. But the marketing function creates time, place, and ownership utility. **Time utility** is created by making a good or service available when customers want to purchase it. **Place utility** is created by making a product available in a location convenient for customers. **Ownership utility** refers to an orderly transfer of goods and services from the seller to the buyer. Firms may be able to create all three forms of utility. Papa John's manages to do this by taking orders at its restaurants, by telephone, online, and via cell phone text messages. Not to be outdone, competitor Domino's Pizza now accepts orders from Web-enabled mobile devices, in addition to texted and conventional phone orders. The firm's mobile ordering site is similar to its regular Web site but adapted for even quicker transactions. Mobiledominos.com is designed for a small screen, has a streamlined interface, and saves previous orders in the system so that loyal customers can reorder their favorites with a few clicks. "With so many people living life on the go, Domino's mobile ordering delivers even more convenience for our customers' busy lifestyles," says Rob Weisberg of Domino's. "With the addition of yet another order-taking channel, Domino's is thrilled to lead the market with this breakthrough technology that continues to change the way people think about ordering pizza."[3] Both pizza chains create all three types of utility by allowing customers to purchase the foods they want, where and when it is most convenient. Retailer Moosejaw Mountaineering has also created several forms of utility for its customers through wireless technology, as described in the "Hit & Miss" feature.

utility want-satisfying power of a good or service.

Assessment Check

1. What is utility?
2. Identify ways in which marketing creates utility.

Hit & Miss

Moosejaw Mountaineering Markets a Little Mobile Madness

Moosejaw Mountaineering may sound like a tongue twister. Yet, the outdoor gear and apparel retailer's marketing efforts are anything but twisted. Founder Robert Wolfe and his crew, including his brother and sister, believe that the key to a successful exchange with consumers is interactivity and creating utility—time, place, and ownership. "Moosejaw's goal is to sell the finest outdoor, surf, skate, and snowboard products in the world and have as much fun as possible while doing it," says Wolfe. "The customer experience, which we call Moosejaw Madness, is the core of our entire strategy." Some of the fun activities offered at Moosejaw's retail stores include in-store whiffle-ball games or a concert of dueling xylophones. Go online to the firm's Web site and you can enter a contest to win an invisible coffee mug.

Fun involves interactions with customers, which is the foundation of Moosejaw's marketing strategy. Recently the company launched a text-messaging campaign in which customers could sign up to receive biweekly messages from Moosejaw. It was a huge success. Instead of sending out coupons or sales alerts, Moosejaw texted games and trivia questions designed to spark consumers' interest. One text read: "Text me back with rock, paper, or scissors. I already know what I'm throwing and if you beat me, I'll add 100 Moosejaw Points to your [frequent buyer] account now." The text generated a 66-percent response and helped build a closer bond with customers.

Another wireless initiative is a bit more practical—providing customers the option to receive their order numbers and UPS tracking information via text message. This offer creates both time and place utility—quick information conveniently sent to a cell phone and a confirmation of a product order and shipment. People love it. "Twenty percent of our customers have signed up," notes Wolfe with a little surprise. "I would've expected less than 1 percent." But after launching the initiative, he realized why it was popular. Is it important to have your tracking information sent to your phone rather than waiting a couple of hours to check your e-mail? Certainly not. "But it is cool, and will you tell three friends about the service? Absolutely."

Questions for Critical Thinking

1. Describe another way that Moosejaw could use text messaging to create marketing utility.
2. Why is interactivity such a vital component to Moosejaw's marketing efforts?

Sources: Tiffany Meyers, "Innovate in a Recession," *Entrepreneur,* February 2009, p. 110; "Moosejaw Mountaineering Embarks on New Online Effort to Engage the Socially Connected Customer," *Yahoo! Finance,* September 30, 2008, http://biz.yahoo.com; "Moosejaw Spreading the Madness across Channels," *PRWeb,* September 4, 2008, http://www.prweb.com; Tom Dellner, "A Method to Their Madness," *Electronic Retailer Magazine,* January 2008, http://www.eletronicretailermag.com.

Evolution of the Marketing Concept

Marketing has always been a part of business, from the earliest village traders to large 21st-century organizations producing and selling complex goods and services. Over time, however, marketing activities evolved through the four eras shown in Figure 12.1: the production, sales, and marketing eras, and now the relationship era. Note that these eras parallel some of the time periods discussed in Chapter 1.

For centuries, organizations of the *production era* stressed efficiency in producing quality products. Their philosophy could be summed up by the remark, "A good product will sell itself." Although this production orientation continued into the 20th century, it gradually gave way to the *sales era,* in which businesses assumed that consumers would buy as a result of energetic sales efforts. Organizations didn't fully recognize the importance of their customers until the *marketing era* of the 1950s, when they began to adopt a consumer orientation. This focus has intensified in recent years, leading to the emergence of the *relationship era* in the 1990s, which continues to this day. In the relationship era, companies emphasize customer satisfaction and building long-term business relationships.

Emergence of the Marketing Concept

The term **marketing concept** refers to a company-wide customer orientation with the objective of achieving long-run success. The basic idea of the marketing concept is that marketplace success begins with the customer. A firm should analyze each customer's needs and then work backward to offer products that fulfill them. The emergence of the marketing concept can be explained best by the shift from a *seller's market,* one with a shortage of goods and services, to a *buyer's market,* one with an abundance of goods and services. During the 1950s, the United States became a strong buyer's market, forcing companies to satisfy customers rather than just producing and selling goods and services. Today, much competition among firms centers on the effort to satisfy customers. Apple's iPhone followed on the heels of its wildly successful iPod, with the combined features of a cell phone, wide-screen iPod with touch controls, and Internet link. The iPhone operates completely by touch screen, has a 3.5-inch display, contains a full Safari Web browser, and even takes pictures with a 2-megapixel camera. The more recent iPod Touch borrowed some of the iPhone's revolutionary features, and Apple recently introduced an ultrathin notebook computer called the Air, which will fit inside an 8½-inch by 11-inch envelope. Apple is well known for anticipating and responding quickly to consumers' needs. "Apple is executing on all cylinders right now," says one industry watcher. "They … appear to be an unstoppable force."[4]

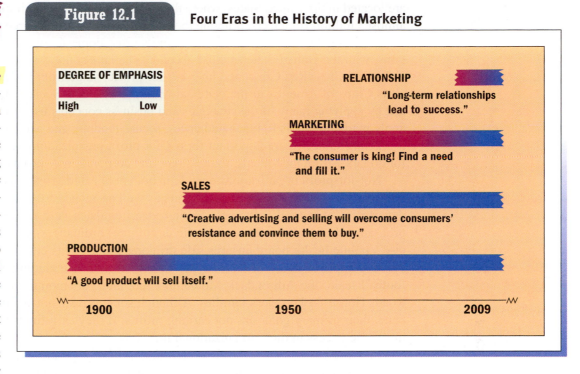

Figure 12.1 Four Eras in the History of Marketing

DEGREE OF EMPHASIS
High — Low

RELATIONSHIP
"Long-term relationships lead to success."

MARKETING
"The consumer is king! Find a need and fill it."

SALES
"Creative advertising and selling will overcome consumers' resistance and convince them to buy."

PRODUCTION
"A good product will sell itself."

1900   1950   2009

marketing concept
companywide consumer orientation to promote long-run success.

Assessment Check ✔

1. What is the marketing concept?
2. How is the marketing concept tied to the relationship era of marketing?

Not-for-Profit and Nontraditional Marketing

The marketing concept has traditionally been associated with products of profit-seeking organizations. Today, however, it is also being applied to not-for-profit sectors and other nontraditional areas ranging from religious organizations to political campaigns.

Not-for-Profit Marketing

Residents of every continent benefit in various ways from the approximately 20 million not-for-profit organizations currently operating around the globe. Some 1.9 million of them are located in the United States, where they employ more than 9 million workers and benefit from almost 5 million volunteers, bringing the total not-for-profit workforce to about 14 million people.[5] Canada leads the world in contributions to its gross domestic product by not-for-profit organizations, with the United States a close second.[6] The largest not-for-profit organization in the world is the Red Cross/Red Crescent. Other not-for-profits range from Habitat for Humanity to Boys & Girls Clubs of America to the National Multiple Sclerosis Society. These organizations all benefit by applying many of the strategies and business concepts used by profit-seeking firms. They apply marketing tools to reach audiences, secure funding, and accomplish their overall missions. Marketing strategies are important for not-for-profit organizations because they are all competing for dollars—from individuals, foundations, and corporations—just as commercial businesses are.

Not-for-profit organizations operate in both public and private sectors. Public groups include federal, state, and local government units as well as agencies that receive tax funding. A state's department of natural resources, for instance, regulates land conservation and environmental programs; the local animal control officer enforces ordinances protecting people and animals; a city's public health board ensures safe drinking water for its citizens. The private not-for-profit sector comprises many different types of organizations, including West Virginia University's football team, the Adirondack Mountain Club, and Portsmouth, New Hampshire–based Cross Roads House for homeless families. Although some private not-for-profits generate surplus revenue, their primary goals are not earning profits. If they earn funds beyond their expenses, they invest the excess in their organizational missions.

In some cases, not-for-profit organizations form a partnership with a profit-seeking company to promote the firm's message or distribute its goods and services. This partnership usually benefits both organizations. Wal-Mart and Sam's Club associates raise funds to contribute to the Children's Miracle Network, an alliance of premier children's hospitals across the United States.

Athletes are particularly visible campaigning for not-for-profit organizations—their own as well as others. NFL quarterback Peyton Manning's Peyback Foundation grants money to other organizations that help at-risk children and teens put their lives back on track. In addition, Peyton Manning's Children's Hospital, which is part of the St. Vincent's healthcare network, provides a wide range of physical and emotional services for children and their families.[7]

Nontraditional Marketing

Not-for-profit organizations often engage in one or more of five major categories of nontraditional marketing: person marketing, place marketing, event marketing, cause marketing, and organization marketing. Figure 12.2 provides examples of these types of marketing. Through each of these types of marketing, an organization seeks to connect with the audience that is most likely to offer time, money, or other resources. In some cases, the effort may reach the market the organization intends to serve.

PERSON MARKETING Efforts designed to attract the attention, interest, and preference of a target market

Figure 12.2

Categories of Nontraditional Marketing

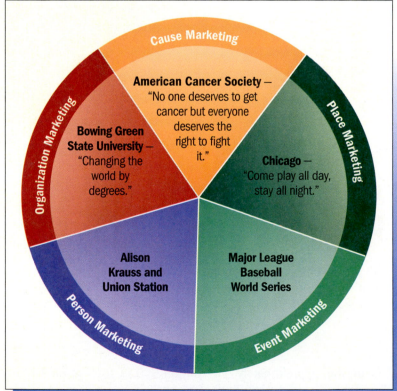

Cause Marketing

Place Marketing

Organization Marketing

Person Marketing

Event Marketing

American Cancer Society — "No one deserves to get cancer but everyone deserves the right to fight it."

Bowling Green State University — "Changing the world by degrees."

Chicago — "Come play all day, stay all night."

Alison Krauss and Union Station

Major League Baseball World Series

toward a person are called **person marketing.** Campaign managers for a political candidate conduct marketing research; identify groups of voters and financial supporters; and then design advertising campaigns, fund-raising events, and political rallies to reach them. AT&T ensured a full crowd of spectators by signing on Tiger Woods to host its AT&T National golf tournament, which also honored U.S. military members.[8]

Many successful job seekers apply the tools of person marketing. They research the wants and needs of prospective employers, and they identify ways they can meet them. They seek employers through a variety of channels, sending messages that emphasize how they can benefit the employer.

PLACE MARKETING As the term suggests, **place marketing** attempts to attract people to a particular area, such as a city, state, or nation. It may involve appealing to consumers as a tourist destination or to businesses as a desirable business location. A strategy for place marketing often includes advertising.

Place marketing may be combined with event marketing, such as the Olympics. The city of Vancouver, Canada, used three mythical cartoon critters, named Quatchi, Miga, and Sumi, to promote the Olympic and Paralympic Winter Games. Merchandise featuring the mascots was available for sale to the public more than two years before the actual games took place.[9]

EVENT MARKETING Marketing or sponsoring short-term events such as athletic competitions and cultural and charitable performances is known as **event marketing.** Target recently sponsored the first women's junior professional surfing competition. The American Diabetes Association sponsored the "Tour de Cure," a series of fund-raising events held across the United States to raise funds to support its mission to prevent and cure diabetes.[10]

Event marketing often forges partnerships between not-for-profit and profit-seeking organizations. Many businesses sponsor events such as 10K runs to raise funds for health-related charities. These occasions require a marketing effort to plan the event and attract participants and sponsors. Events may be intended to raise money or awareness, or both.

CAUSE MARKETING Marketing that promotes awareness of, or raises money for, a cause or social issue, such as drug abuse prevention, childhood hunger, or homelessness, is **cause marketing.** Cause marketing seeks to educate the public and may or may not attempt to directly raise funds. An advertisement often contains a phone number or Web site address through which people can obtain more information about the organization or issue. Then they can either donate money or take other actions of support. Jumpstart is a program that pairs college students with at-risk preschoolers who need better connections with adults to have successful school experiences and family lives. Through its Web site, the organization markets its successes, recruits college volunteers, and seeks donations. It is now one of the fastest-growing not-for-profit organizations in the United States.[11]

Profit-seeking companies look for ways to contribute to their communities by joining forces with charities and causes, providing

This sightseeing guide, an example of *place marketing*, is published by the state of California to encourage tourism.

DON'T SERVE ALCOHOL TO TEENS.

It's unsafe. It's illegal. It's irresponsible.

This advertisement, part of the U.S. government's We Don't Serve Teens campaign, is an example of *cause marketing*. Created as a public service by brewer Anheuser-Busch, it is an expression of corporate social responsibility.

financial, marketing, and human resources. Timberland is well known for its City Year program, through which young adults contract to perform a year of volunteer service in their communities. For-profit firms can also combine their goods and services with a cause. Mary Beth Sieminski and her sisters created a line of stylish, reusable shopping bags for sale to consumers in an effort to combat the environmental damage caused by the estimated 100 billion plastic shopping bags that are manufactured—and thrown away—each year. Their company, called Skeeda, currently sells eight different designs, and its Web site offers other "easy green" tips to interested consumers. In addition, the partners offer opportunities for consumers to sell Skeeda bags at fund-raising events.[12]

ORGANIZATION MARKETING The final category of nontraditional marketing, **organization marketing,** influences consumers to accept the goals of, receive the services of, or contribute in some way to an organization. The U.S. Postal Service, the American Cancer Society, and Oprah Winfrey's Angel Network are all examples of organizations that engage in marketing. They use their own Web sites, advertise in magazines, and send mail directly to consumers in their efforts to market their organizations. The Angel Network was established by Oprah Winfrey more than a decade ago in an order to "encourage people around the world to make a difference in the lives of others." The organization initiates its own charitable projects as well as supports the projects of other not-for-profits such as Habitat for Humanity and The Boys & Girls Clubs of America.[13]

Figure 12.3

Target Market and Marketing Mix within the Marketing Environment

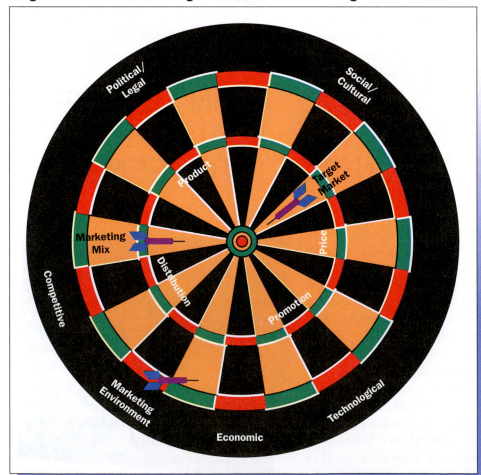

Developing a Marketing Strategy

Decision makers in any successful organization, for-profit or not-for-profit, follow a two-step process to develop a *marketing strategy*. First, they study and analyze potential target markets and choose among them. Second, they create a marketing mix to satisfy the chosen market. Figure 12.3 shows the relationship among the target market, the marketing mix variables, and the marketing environment. Later discussions refer back to this figure as they cover each topic. This section describes the development of a marketing strategy designed to build attract and build relationships with customers. Sometimes, in an effort to do this, marketers use questionable methods, as described in the "Solving an Ethical Controversy" feature.

WHEN FREE CREDIT REPORTS AREN'T FREE

When times are tough and credit is tight, consumers are naturally concerned about their credit scores. They are more apt to search for and monitor their scores. The Fair Credit Reporting Act (FCRA) mandates each of the three major consumer reporting companies—Equifax, Experian, and TransUnion—to provide consumers with a free copy of their credit report once a year. Consumers must make this request through the official Annual Credit Report Request Service by phone, mail, or online at AnnualCreditReport.com.

Consumers are regularly bombarded with marketing messages claiming to offer free credit reports. Some may be free, but many contain hidden charges. Some of these firms' advertising practices leave consumer advocates frustrated and concerned. FreeCreditReport.com and Freetriplescore.com have come under government scrutiny for their advertising practices.

Should firms be allowed to use the word "free" in advertising for credit reports if the service contains hidden charges?

PRO

1. If the credit score itself is free, but related services are not, then the advertising is truthful. "It absolutely is the free credit report," argues Mike Dean, chief marketing officer for a division of Experian that operates FreeCreditReport.com. "It's not

the one by the government, which is why we put the link on our front page of the landing site."
2. Some promotional offers contain free credit scores, with a tie-in to additional services for which there is a charge. Other industries make similar offers for such services as a free month of phone, cable, or Internet service.

CON

1. The word "free" is a powerful enticement in advertising. "It's of great concern," says Linda Sherry of Consumer Action, "when strings are attached."
2. Consumer advocates say firms are preying unnecessarily on people's fears. "It's what I call a protection racket," says Edmund Mierzwinski of the U.S. Public Interest Research Group. "The sites are designed to trick people into taking on over-priced, useless credit monitoring, and they do so by attempting to

make it appear as if you're going to get something for free."

Summary

The Federal Trade Commission warns consumers about sites other than AnnualCreditReport.com, but consumer groups want more. "I don't think they've cracked down hard enough on the television and other kinds of radio ads that are deceptive to consumers because there's no room to put adequate disclosure," remarks Linda Sherry.

Sources: "Your Access to Free Credit Reports," *Federal Trade Commission,* http://www.ftc.gov, accessed March 2, 2009; "Free Credit Report," *CreditCards. com,* http://www.creditcards.com, accessed March 2, 2009; Justin Pritchard, "Are Free Credit Reports Really Free?" *About.com,* September 3, 2008; Stephanie Clifford, "The High Cost of a Free Credit Report," *The New York Times,* August 5, 2008, http://www. nytimes.com.

Solving an ETHICAL controversy

Earlier chapters of this book introduced many of the environmental factors that affect the success or failure of a firm's business strategy, including today's rapidly changing and highly competitive world of business, a vast array of sociocultural factors, economic challenges, political and legal factors, and technological innovations. Although these external forces frequently operate outside managers' control, marketers must still consider the impact of environmental factors on their decisions.

A marketing plan is a key component of a firm's overall business plan. The marketing plan outlines its marketing strategy and includes information about the target market, sales and revenue goals, the marketing budget, and the timing for implementing the elements of the marketing mix.

Selecting a Target Market

The expression "find a need and fill it" is perhaps the simplest explanation of the two elements of a marketing strategy. A firm's marketers find a need through careful and continuing study of the individuals and business decision makers in its potential market. A market consists of people with purchasing power, willingness to buy, and authority to make purchase decisions.

Markets can be classified by type of product. **Consumer products**—often known as business-to-consumer (B2C) products—are goods and services, such as GPS systems, tomato sauce, and a haircut, that are purchased by end users. **Business products**—or business-to-business (B2B) products—are goods and services purchased to be used, either directly or indirectly, in the production of other goods for resale. Some products can fit either classification depending on who buys them and why. A computer or credit card can be used by a business or a consumer.

An organization's **target market** is the group of potential customers toward whom it directs its marketing efforts. Customer needs and wants vary considerably, and no single organization has the resources to satisfy everyone. *Forbes* is geared toward businesspeople and consumers who are interested in business, while *Teen Vogue* is aimed at teenagers who are interested in fashion.

Decisions about marketing involve strategies for four areas of marketing activity: product, distribution, promotion, and pricing. A firm's **marketing mix** blends the four strategies to fit the needs and preferences of a specific target market. Marketing success depends not on the four individual strategies but on their unique combination.

Product strategy involves more than just designing a good or service with needed attributes. It also includes decisions about package design, brand names, trademarks, warranties, product image, new-product development, and customer service. Think about your favorite pair of jeans. Do you like them because they fit the best, or do other attributes—such as styling and overall image—also contribute to your brand preference? *Distribution strategy,* the second marketing mix variable, ensures that customers receive their purchases in the proper quantities at the right times and locations. *Promotional strategy,* another marketing mix element, effectively blends advertising, personal selling, sales promotion, and public relations to achieve its goals of informing, persuading, and influencing purchase decisions.

Pricing strategy, the final mix element, is also one of the most difficult areas of marketing decision making in setting profitable and justifiable prices for the firm's product offerings. Such actions are sometimes subject to government regulation and considerable public scrutiny. They also represent a powerful competitive weapon and frequently produce responses by the other firms in the industry, who match price changes to avoid losing customers. Think about your jeans again. Would you continue to purchase them if they were priced either much higher or much lower?

CVS Caremark knows that women are its best customers, so the pharmacy chain looks for ways to attract and serve them. "Women are really stressed out across the country," says Gordon Howard, head of the firm's mid-Atlantic region. So CVS marketers decided to find out how to make women's lives easier. After talking with women customers about their needs in focus groups, CVS redesigned its stores to make them easier—and faster—to navigate, shortened wait times for prescriptions, and stocked up on more beauty products. The stores are now larger and more contemporary looking, and the shelves are filled with the products that women want. Longer-range plans include the installment of MinuteClinics and other health services such as obesity-prevention and smoking-cessation programs.[14]

Developing a Marketing Mix for International Markets

Marketing a good or service in foreign markets means deciding whether to offer the same marketing mix in every market *(standardization)* or to develop a unique mix to fit each market

target market group of people toward whom an organization markets its goods, services, or ideas with a strategy designed to satisfy their specific needs and preferences.

marketing mix blending the four elements of marketing strategy—product, distribution, promotion, and pricing—to satisfy chosen customer segments.

"They Said It"

"We're always looking to see what we can do to make our customers' lives easier or save them money. It pervades every part of the company."

—Michael Dell (b. 1965) Founder, Dell Inc.

(adaptation). The advantages of standardizing the marketing mix include reliable marketing performance and low costs. This approach works best with B2B goods, such as steel, chemicals, and aircraft, which require little sensitivity to a nation's culture.

Adaptation, on the other hand, lets marketers vary their marketing mix to suit local competitive conditions, consumer preferences, and government regulations. Consumer tastes are often shaped by local cultures. Because consumer products generally tend to be more culture dependent than business products, they more often require adaptation. In China, McDonald's serves its Big Mac but also offers a plastic cup of corn and traditional bean curd dessert pies. Wal-Mart sells eels and turtles in its supermarket department instead of its pet center. And Starbucks offers mooncakes while providing wait service. Why do these firms go out of their way to adapt to Chinese preferences? China represents a potential market of 1.3 billion consumers.[15]

Marketers also try to build adaptability into the designs of standardized goods and services for international and domestic markets. *Mass customization* allows a firm to mass produce goods and services while adding unique features to individual or small groups of orders. Toyota and its partner Isuzu have partnered to develop and produce small diesel engines for the European market, where most vehicles run on diesel fuel instead of gasoline. The cars look the same in the U.S. and Europe, but their engines reflect the preferences of each market.[16]

Marketing Research

Marketing research involves more than just collecting data. Researchers must decide how to collect data, interpret the results, convert the data into decision-oriented information, and communicate those results to managers for use in decision making. **Marketing research** is the process of collecting and evaluating information to help marketers make effective decisions. It links business decision makers to the marketplace by providing data about potential target markets that help them design effective marketing mixes.

marketing research collecting and evaluating information to support marketing decision making.

Obtaining Marketing Research Data

Marketing researchers need both internal and external data. Firms generate *internal data* within their organizations. Financial records provide a tremendous amount of useful information, such as changes in unpaid bills, inventory levels, sales generated by different categories of customers or product lines, profitability of particular divisions, or comparisons of sales by territories, salespeople, customers, or product lines.

Researchers gather *external data* from outside sources, including previously published data. Trade associations publish reports on activities in particular industries. Advertising agencies collect information on the audiences reached by various media. National marketing research firms offer information through subscription services. Some of these professional research firms specialize in specific markets, such as teens or ethnic groups. This information helps companies make decisions about developing or modifying products. The Forum to Advance the Mobile Experience conducted a survey of cell phone users to find out how satisfied they were with the features on cell phones. What researchers discovered may come as a surprise. While manufacturers keep packing phones with more new features such as cameras and recording devices, they may have overlooked the fact that many consumers just want a phone with good reception and voice quality. "There are too many product features that consumers don't use, or don't know how to use, and it frustrates them," the survey reported.[17]

"They Said It"

"It's tough to make predictions, especially about the future."

—Yogi Berra (b. 1925) Major League Baseball player and coach

What will we put our stamp on next?

Pitney Bowes mailstream solutions use satellite imagery to [let you see] For the first time, business can see the big picture for what it really is: a composite of precise demographic [...] reflect differen [...]

Pitney Bowes, best known for its postage meters, also makes a business of organizing demographic and lifestyle data by Zip code and street address. This approach to organizing information, called *geocoding*, uses satellite imagery to allow marketers to zoom in on their customers.

Consumer goods manufacturer Procter & Gamble has excelled in marketing research for a long time; it created its own marketing research department in 1923. The department conducts observations and works with more than 4 million consumers in 60 countries to learn about their needs and preferences.[18]

Secondary data, or previously published data, are low cost and easy to obtain. Federal, state, and local government publications are excellent data sources, and most are available online. The most frequently used government statistics include census data, which contain the population's age, gender, education level, household size and composition, occupation, employment status, and income. Even private research firms such as Teenage Research Unlimited, which studies the purchasing habits of teens, provide some free information on their Web sites. This information helps firms evaluate consumers' buying behavior, anticipate possible changes in the marketplace, and identify new markets.

Even though secondary data represent a quick and inexpensive resource, marketing researchers sometimes discover that this information isn't specific or current enough for their needs. If so, researchers may conclude that they must collect *primary data*—data collected firsthand through such methods as observation and surveys.

Marketing researchers sometimes collect primary data through observational studies, in which they view the actions of consumers either directly or through mechanical devices. Procter & Gamble spends about $200 million on consumer observation each year, citing it as the firm's most important type of marketing research. "We're spending far more time living with consumers in their homes, shopping with them in stores and being part of their lives," explains CEO A. G. Lafley. "This leads to much richer insights. It helps us identify innovation opportunities that are often missed by traditional research."[19]

Simply observing customers cannot provide some types of information. A researcher might observe a customer buying a red sweater, but have no idea why the purchase was made—or for whom. When researchers need information about consumers' attitudes, opinions, and motives, they need to ask the consumers themselves. They may conduct surveys by telephone, in person, online, or in focus groups.

A *focus group* gathers 8 to 12 people in a room or over the Internet to discuss a particular topic. A focus group can generate new ideas, address consumers' needs, and even point out flaws in existing products. Pottery Barn Kids, a division of Pottery Barn, developed its Learning Toys Collection through observation, reading, and focus groups. Focus groups that included both parents and children were gathered and observed as they played with and talked about the new toys.[20]

Applying Marketing Research Data

As the accuracy of information collected by researchers increases, so does the effectiveness of resulting marketing strategies. One field of research is known as **business intelligence,** which uses various activities and technologies to gather, store, and analyze data to make better competitive decisions. Dell established its IdeaStorm Web site to gather information, criticism, compliments, and ideas for developing new computer products and improving existing ones. New users must register at the site and follow guidelines in order to post their ideas and reactions. Submitted ideas receive scores for their popularity, which helps Dell sort through material and decide which items to pursue. "Our commitment is to listen to your input and ideas to improve our products and services, and the way we do business," reads a welcoming note to the site. "We will do our best to keep you posted on how Dell brings customer ideas to life."[21]

Data Mining

Once a company has built a database, marketers must be able to analyze the data and use the information it provides. **Data mining,** part of the broader field of business intelligence, is the task of using computer-based technology to evaluate data in a database and identify useful trends. These trends or patterns may suggest predictive models of real-world business activities. Accurate data mining can help researchers forecast recessions, weed out credit card fraud, and pinpoint sales prospects.

data mining computer searches of customer data to detect patterns and relationships.

Data mining uses **data warehouses,** which are sophisticated customer databases that allow managers to combine data from several different organizational functions. Wal-Mart's data warehouse, considered the largest in the private sector, contains more than 500 terabytes (trillions of characters) of data. The retail giant uses data mining to assess local preferences for merchandise so that it can tailor the inventory of each store to the tastes of its neighborhood. Google created its enterprise Search Appliance, which allows corporate users to search through data and prioritize information in specific categories.[22] Sulake, a Finnish company that created an online virtual world called Habbo that is popular with teens, has conducted several research projects aimed at finding out more about teen preferences and buying habits. But one recent survey was particularly unusual. Instead of gathering information from actual teens, the firm tapped into the life habits of the avatars—imaginative digital characters—that teens had created on the Habbo site. The results produced more data than Sulake marketers had anticipated. "We wanted to focus on how users are behaving and what they are buying," explained marketer Emmi Kuusikko. "At first, we thought we would simply use the [information] for internal purposes, for product development. Then we saw that we could do global research about teens' lives."[23]

Assessment Check ✔

1. What is the difference between primary data and secondary data?
2. What is data mining?

Market Segmentation

Market segmentation is the process of dividing a market into several relatively homogeneous groups. Both profit-seeking and not-for-profit organizations use segmentation to help them reach desirable target markets. Market segmentation is often based on the results of research, which attempts to identify trends among certain groups of people. For instance, one survey of online teens revealed that 89 percent of these consumers believed that devices such as cell phones, iPods, and digital cameras made their lives easier. But their parents did not feel quite the same—only 71 percent of their parents agreed.[24] Information such as this can help marketers decide what types of products to develop and to whom they should be marketed.

market segmentation process of dividing a total market into several relatively homogeneous groups.

Market segmentation attempts to isolate the traits that distinguish a certain group of customers from the overall market. However, segmentation doesn't automatically produce marketing success. Table 12.1 lists several criteria that marketers should consider. The effectiveness of

Table 12.1	Criteria for Market Segmentation
Criterion	**Example**
A segment must be a measurable group.	Data can be collected on the dollar amount and number of purchases by college students.
A segment must be accessible for communication.	A growing number of seniors are going online, so they can be reached through Internet channels.
A segment must be large enough to offer profit potential.	In a small community, a store carrying only large-size shoes might not be profitable. Similarly, a specialty retail chain may not locate in a small market.

a segmentation strategy depends on how well the market meets these criteria. Once marketers identify a market segment to target, they can create an appropriate marketing strategy.

Toy retailing giant Toys 'R' Us identified several hot toy trends among children during one recent holiday season, so the firm kicked into gear to stock the toys it thought would sell to kids and their parents. "Internet connectivity is a really strong trend," noted a spokesman for the retailer. "As the Internet becomes incorporated into more and more everyday tasks, we've seen a lot of different toys that are able to connect to the Internet." Armed with this information, Toys 'R' Us made sure it could offer plenty of toys with online links.[25]

How Market Segmentation Works

An immediate segmentation distinction involves whether the firm is offering goods and services to customers for their own use or to purchasers who will use them directly or indirectly in providing other products for resale (the so-called B2B market). Depending on whether their firms offer consumer or business products, marketers segment their target markets differently. Four common bases for segmenting consumer markets are geographical segmentation, demographic segmentation, psychographic segmentation, and product-related segmentation. Business markets can segment on only three criteria: customer-based segmentation, end-use segmentation, and geographical segmentation. Figure 12.4 illustrates the segmentation methods for these two types of markets.

Segmenting Consumer Markets

Market segmentation has been practiced since people first began selling products. Tailors made some clothing items for men and others for women. Tea was imported from India for tea drinkers in England and other European countries. In addition to demographic and geographical segmentation, today's marketers also define customer groups based on psychographic—lifestyle and values—criteria as well as product-related distinctions.

GEOGRAPHICAL SEGMENTATION The oldest segmentation method is **geographical segmentation**—dividing a market into homogeneous groups on the basis of their locations. Geographical location does not guarantee that consumers in a certain region will all buy the same kinds of products, but it does provide some indication of needs. For instance, suburbanites buy more lawn care products than central-city dwellers. However, many suburbanites choose instead to purchase the services of a lawn maintenance firm. Consumers who live in northern states, where winter is more severe, are more likely to buy ice scrapers, snow shovels, and snowblowers than those who live in warmer climates. They are also more likely to contract with firms who plow driveways. Marketers also look at the size of the population of an area, as well as who lives there—are residents old or young? Do they reflect an ethnic background? What is the level of their income?

Figure 12.4   Methods of Segmenting Consumer and Business Markets

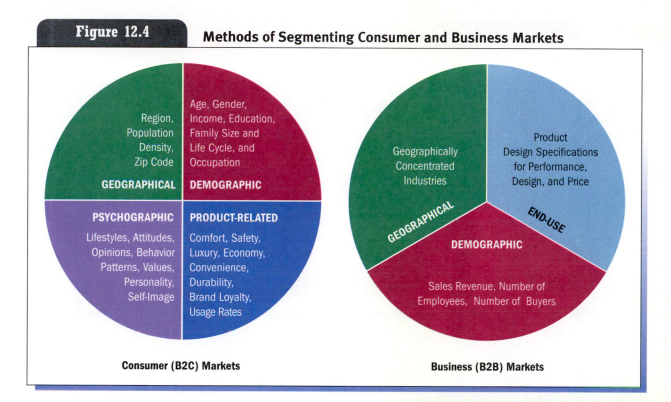

Consumer (B2C) Markets

GEOGRAPHICAL — Region, Population Density, Zip Code

DEMOGRAPHIC — Age, Gender, Income, Education, Family Size and Life Cycle, and Occupation

PSYCHOGRAPHIC — Lifestyles, Attitudes, Opinions, Behavior Patterns, Values, Personality, Self-Image

PRODUCT-RELATED — Comfort, Safety, Luxury, Economy, Convenience, Durability, Brand Loyalty, Usage Rates

Business (B2B) Markets

GEOGRAPHICAL — Geographically Concentrated Industries

END-USE — Product Design Specifications for Performance, Design, and Price

DEMOGRAPHIC — Sales Revenue, Number of Employees, Number of Buyers

Some of the U.S.'s top restaurateurs have discovered that preferences regarding service vary from coast to coast. Tom Colicchio learned this the hard way when he opened a new restaurant outside Los Angeles. Already a successful restaurant owner in New York and head judge on the reality series *Top Chef,* Colicchio thought he knew his market well. But it turned out that California diners had some different expectations from their counterparts in New York when it came to service. Colicchio quickly made changes to reflect these preferences. Some were as detailed as training the lounge staff to automatically transfer bar tabs to dinner tabs to avoid bothering customers with two bills. Others were more subjective, such as educating the team to determine when to designate a dining party as "VIP" and give them seating preference.[26]

Job growth and migration patterns are important considerations as well. Some businesses combine areas or even entire countries that share similar population and product-use patterns instead of treating each as an independent segment.

DEMOGRAPHIC SEGMENTATION By far the most common method of market segmentation, **demographic segmentation** distinguishes markets on the basis of various demographic or socioeconomic characteristics. Common demographic measures include gender, income, age, occupation, household size, stage in the family life cycle, education, and racial or ethnic group. The U.S. Census Bureau is one of the best sources of demographic information for the domestic market. Figure 12.5 lists some of the measures used in demographic segmentation.

This Lands' End kids catalog illustrates *demographic segmentation* by stage of the family life cycle (parents with small children). To appeal to the targeted market segment, Lands' End ran a children's holiday drawing contest; winning entries were showcased in the catalog.

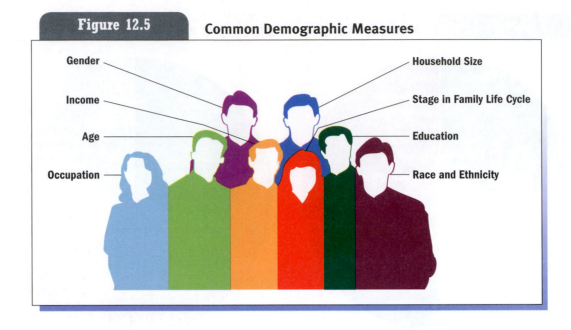

Figure 12.5 **Common Demographic Measures**

Gender

Income

Age

Occupation

Household Size

Stage in Family Life Cycle

Education

Race and Ethnicity

Gender used to be a simple way to define markets for certain products—clothes, jewelry, and skin care products for women; tools and motorcycles for men. Much of that has changed—dramatically. Men now buy clothes, jewelry, and skin care products, and women buy tools and motorcycles. But marketers have also found that even though these shifts have occurred, blurring the lines between products, there are still differences in the *way* that women and men shop. One study revealed that men are "purpose driven" when shopping for clothes, searching out specific items and ending the trip when those items are found and purchased. Women are more "possibility driven" when clothes shopping, browsing through selections to see what's available before making their purchases.[27]

Another shift involves purchasing power. Women now control an estimated 85 percent of the $7 trillion spent each year on personal consumption items, and one expert predicts that women will soon control 60 percent of all wealth in the United States, in part because of their tendency to live longer than men.

Age is perhaps the most volatile factor in demographic segmentation in the United States, with our rapidly aging population. Of the 300-plus million people who live in the United States, more than 97 million will be age 65 or older by the year 2020.[28] Based on these statistics, marketers for travel and leisure products, as well as retirement and business investments, are working hard to attract the attention of this age group, who represent the aging Baby Boomer group—those born between 1946 and 1964. Active-adult housing communities are one result of these efforts. Older adults who continue to remain active but who might not want the responsibility of home maintenance, are attracted to communities in which they can live comfortably and spend their time pursuing sports, travel, and classes that might include cooking or wine tasting. Some developers have built communities with a resort-style atmosphere in places such as Colorado ski country or the outskirts of a desirable city such as Chicago or San Francisco. One architect who conducted marketing research for such developers concludes, "Affluent baby boomers want a certain level of lifestyle for themselves as they get older and downsize."[29]

Teens are another rapidly growing market. The entire scope of Generation Y—those born between 1976 and 1997—encompasses about 113 million young Americans, or a little more than one-third of the total population. These consumers are tech-savvy shoppers who influence not only their own purchases but also those of their families and friends. They are educated consumers who comparison shop and usually avoid impulse purchases, often because they are spending their own money.[30] "This is such an important age group for us to focus on," emphasizes Mike Nevins, a marketer for a 77-million-square-foot shopping center in southern California. "Their influence cannot be overestimated, not only when we merchandise the property but when we give feedback to our retailers on their shopping habits."[31]

The 100 million consumers who represent minority groups hold a combined purchasing power of more than $1 trillion a year—about 10 percent of the total consumer market—in the United States alone.[32] This means that about one in three U.S. residents represents a minority group, the largest of which are Hispanics, African Americans, and Asian Americans. Four states and the District of Columbia are now what the U.S. Census Bureau refers to as "majority-minority," meaning that more than half the people who live in those areas represent minority groups. Hawaii has the greatest minority population, at 75 percent; followed by the District of Columbia, 69 percent; New Mexico and California, 57 percent each; and Texas, 52 percent.[33]

This television ad combined an English caption with a Spanish voiceover to appeal to both English- and Spanish-speaking viewers. Such advertisements recognize the purchasing power of Hispanics, the fastest growing demographic group in the United States.

Statistics can be helpful, but they don't tell the whole story. Marketers must also learn where people live, how old they are, what language they speak, and how much income they have in order to serve them well. Finally, they must learn cultural tastes and preferences, as described in the "Hit & Miss" feature.

Above all, companies must avoid stereotyping if they are going to market successfully to a diverse group of consumers. One way to do this is to break a large group into smaller segments. For instance, the Hispanic market is made up of many smaller segments, based on country of origin, language, lifestyle, and cultural values. In an attempt to target a younger Hispanic audience, three television networks have begun to offer bilingual, Spanish, and English-language programming with Hispanic themes. Because many Hispanic American teens and young adults are bilingual, the networks are trying to capture their attention while their parents and grandparents continue to watch Spanish-only programming. "This is a demographic that is going to get bigger and bigger and bigger," notes Alex Pels, general manager at the mun2 network. "But, what we've seen is that most of these young Latino Americans don't identify with a specific brand or company. There is not a lot of media out there that is designed with them in mind."[34] These TV marketers want to change that.

Entrepreneurs who are members of minority groups may start their own businesses out of frustration at not being able to find food, clothing, entertainment, or other goods and services that fit their tastes and needs. Rajbhog Foods was started by an Indian family living in Queens, New York, because they and their community wanted to be able to purchase the vegetarian products of their traditional diet. Within the first few years the company had 70 employees, three plants, and a catering business that handled Indian weddings and conventions. Then the business began opening franchises in locations that had concentrated Indian populations. "We try to reach out to every corner where there is an Indian community," explains Sachin Mody, son of the firm's founders and also its chief executive, "so they don't have to drive all the way to one location to get what they need."[35]

Hit & Miss

Pollo Campero and Wal-Mart Cater to Hispanic Tastes

Hungry Wal-Mart shoppers can visit such restaurant chains as McDonald's, Blimpie's, and Subway for a quick bite. Now another company has joined the roster, this one with a definite Hispanic flavor: Pollo Campero.

Guatemala-based Pollo Campero, which means *country chicken* in Spanish, was founded by the Gutierrez family 30 years ago. Its food began to cross the border when passengers traveling to the United States brought the takeout chicken aboard their flights. The firm opened its first U.S. restaurant in 2002, which was an immediate hit. Known mostly for its fried chicken and authentic side dishes such as yucca fries and sweet plantains, Pollo Campero is a family friendly restaurant where diners can eat in or take out.

Wal-Mart serves a large segment of Hispanic customers, so the pairing between the retail giant and Pollo Campero seems natural. "They've always said that they had a very big Hispanic component in their customer base," explains Pollo Campero's Rodolfo Jiminez, referring to Wal-Mart. Wal-Mart is installing about 20 Pollo Campero restaurants in its stores and intends to increase the number over time. Pollo Campero remains a small portion of Wal-Mart's overall restaurant offerings—currently about 1,000 McDonald's and 1,400 Subway sandwich outlets operate in Wal-Mart stores. But marketers at both Pollo Campero and Wal-Mart are confident the partnership will grow.

Because Wal-Mart's total customer base is diverse, Pollo Campero isn't limiting its offerings to traditional Latin cuisine. The restaurant is expanding its menu to other products. The new offerings include such items as bone-in grilled chicken seasoned with a blend of lime and orange juice, red bell peppers, and herbs. Other choices include grilled chicken Caesar salads and grilled chicken wraps. However, Pollo's famous fried chicken remains the most popular.

The exposure that Pollo Campero gets through its Wal-Mart locations is perhaps more valuable than any of its marketing efforts to date. "Most people didn't know the brand," notes Jiminez. "But just the fact of being there, it's an open space and looks nice. We just said we were about chicken, so [people] came over and tried the product and they were very pleased. Our strategy is to offer the best chicken in the U.S."

Questions for Critical Thinking

1. What type(s) of segmentation strategy is being used by Pollo Campero and Wal-Mart? Do you think it will be effective? Why or why not?
2. What steps could both firms take to increase traffic in the Pollo Campero restaurants that are located in Wal-Mart stores?

Sources: Company Web site, http://www.pollocampero.com, accessed March 11, 2009; Amanda Jones Hoyle, "Guatemalan Eatery Pollo Campero Makes Raleigh a Regional HQ," May 30, 2008, http://triangle.bizjournals.com; "Pollo Campero Franchise Expanding to Wal-Mart," *New York Daily News,* May 12, 2008, http://www.nydailynews.com; "Pollo Campero Beats Competition to Market with Choice of Grilled and Fried Bone-In Chicken," company press release, March 14, 2008.

PSYCHOGRAPHIC SEGMENTATION Lifestyle is the sum of a person's needs, preferences, motives, attitudes, social habits, and cultural background. In recent years, marketing researchers have tried to formulate lifestyle portraits of consumers. This effort has led to another strategy for segmenting target markets, **psychographic segmentation,** which divides consumer markets into groups with similar psychological characteristics, values, and lifestyles.

Psychographic studies have evaluated motivations for purchases of hundreds of goods and services, ranging from soft drinks to healthcare services. Using the resulting data, firms tailor their marketing strategies to carefully chosen market segments. A frequently used method of developing psychographic profiles involves the use of *AIO statements*—verbal descriptions of various activities, interests, and opinions. Researchers survey a sample of consumers, asking them whether they agree or disagree with each statement. The answers are then tabulated and analyzed for use in identifying various lifestyle categories.

Another way to get current information from consumers about their lifestyles is to create *blogs* to which consumers may respond. Companies including Stonyfield Farm, Verizon, and Microsoft have hired bloggers to run online Web journals as a way to connect with and receive information from consumers. Other firms encourage employees at all levels to use blogs to communicate with consumers. General Motors has several blogs at its Gmblogs.com site, each tailored to a specific brand or consumer interest. The FastLane blog discusses GM cars and trucks, inviting consumers to offer their thoughts and ideas. The Cadillac Drivers' Log chronicles the adventures of two engineers who are test-driving the new Cadillac CTS around the United States and the world. GM Tuner Source provides news updates and photos from racing and driving events across America.[36]

Although demographic classifications such as age, gender, and income are relatively easy to identify and measure, researchers also need to define psychographic categories. Often marketing research firms conduct extensive studies of consumers and then share their psychographic data with clients. In addition, businesses look to studies done by sociologists and psychologists to help them understand their customers. For instance, while children may fall into one age group and their parents in another, they also live certain lifestyles together. Recent marketing research reveals that today's parents are willing and able to spend more on goods and services for their children than parents were a generation or two ago. Spending on food, clothing, personal care, and entertainment, including reading materials, for children has already topped $100 billion annually in the United States, and researchers expect it to top $140 billion in the next few years. "[Parents] are the most well-informed consumer group that you can look at," says one entrepreneur who founded a company that manufactures high-end baby chairs.[37] These are just a few trends identified by the researchers, but they provide valuable information to firms that may be considering developing convenience foods, designing the interiors of family vehicles, or implementing new wireless plans.

PRODUCT-RELATED SEGMENTATION Using **product-related segmentation,** sellers can divide a consumer market into groups based on buyers' relationships to the good or service. The three most popular approaches to product-related segmentation are based on benefits sought, usage rates, and brand loyalty levels.

Segmenting by *benefits sought* focuses on the attributes that people seek in a good or service and the benefits they expect to receive from it. As more firms shift toward consumer demand for products that are eco-friendly, marketers find ways to emphasize the benefits of these products. Home goods retailer Crate & Barrel has begun to offer tables and chairs made of mango wood, which is harvested only after the trees' fruit-bearing capabilities have passed. Consumers can also select a sofa whose cushions are made of recycled fibers that are filled with a natural, soy-based foam. "We are responding to consumer interest," says a company spokesperson. "And it's the right thing to do."[38]

Consumer markets can also be segmented according to the amounts of a product that people buy and use. Segmentation by *product usage rate* usually defines such categories as heavy users, medium users, and light users. The 80/20 principle states that roughly 80 percent of a product's revenues come from only 20 percent of its buyers. Companies can now pinpoint which of their customers are the heaviest users—and even the most profitable customers—and direct their heaviest marketing efforts to those customers.

The third technique for product-related segmentation divides customers by *brand loyalty*— the degree to which consumers recognize, prefer, and insist on a particular brand. Marketers define groups of consumers with similar degrees of brand loyalty. They then attempt to tie loyal customers to a good or service by giving away premiums, which can be anything from a logo-emblazoned T-shirt to a pair of free tickets to a concert or sports event.

Segmenting Business Markets

In many ways, the segmentation process for business markets resembles that for consumer markets. However, some specific methods differ. Business markets can be divided through geographical segmentation; demographic, or customer-based, segmentation; and end-use segmentation.

Age, gender, ethnicity, and language are examples of consumer traits used in demographic segmentation. This particular Ford Focus ad, published in *Latina* magazine, sells to a young Hispanic audience. The Spanish language caption "Salta ala vista" translates to "It jumps at sight."

Geographical segmentation methods for business markets resemble those for consumer markets. Many B2B marketers target geographically concentrated industries, such as aircraft manufacturing, automobiles, and oil field equipment. Especially on an international scale, customer needs, languages, and other variables may require differences in the marketing mix from one location to another.

Demographic, or *customer-based, segmentation* begins with a good or service design intended to suit a specific organizational market. Sodexho Marriott Services is the largest provider of food services in North America. Its customers include healthcare institutions, business and government offices, schools, and colleges and universities. Within these broad business segments, Sodexho identifies more specific segments, which might include colleges in the South, or universities with culturally diverse populations—and differing food preferences or dining styles. Sodexho uses data obtained from surveys that cover students' lifestyles, attitudes, preferences for consumer products in general, services, and media categories. In addition, it uses targeted surveys that identify preferences for restaurant brands or certain foods, meal habits, amount of spending, and the like. Marketers evaluate the data, which sometime reveal surprising trends. At one university in the rural Northeast, students indicated that they liked foods with an international flavor. So Sodexho adapted its offerings accordingly.[39]

To simplify the process of focusing on a particular type of business customer, the federal government has developed a system for subdividing the business marketplace into detailed segments. The six-digit *North American Industry Classification System (NAICS)* provides a common classification system used by the member nations of NAFTA (the United States, Canada, and Mexico). It divides industries into broad categories such as agriculture, forestry, and fishing; manufacturing; transportation; and retail and wholesale trade. Each major category is further subdivided into smaller segments—such as gas stations with convenience food and warehouse clubs—for more detailed information and to facilitate comparison among the member nations.

Another way to group firms by their demographics is to segment them by size based on their sales revenues or numbers of employees. Consolidated Freightways collects data from visitors to its Web site and uses the data to segment customers by size. Modern information processing also enables companies to segment business markets based on how much they buy, not just how big they are.

End-use segmentation focuses on the precise way a B2B purchaser will use a product. Resembling benefits-sought segmentation for consumer markets, this method helps small and midsize companies target specific end-user markets rather than competing directly with large firms for wider customer groups. A company might also design a marketing mix based on certain criteria for making a purchase.

Consumer Behavior

A fundamental marketing task is to find out why people buy one product and not another. The answer requires an understanding of consumer behavior, the actions of ultimate consumers directly involved in obtaining, consuming, and disposing of products and the decision processes that precede and follow these actions.

Determinants of Consumer Behavior

By studying people's purchasing behavior, businesses can identify consumers' attitudes toward and uses of their products. This information also helps marketers reach their targeted customers. Both personal and interpersonal factors influence the way buyers behave. Personal influences on **consumer behavior** include individual needs and motives, perceptions, attitudes, learned experiences, and self-concept. For instance, today people are constantly looking for ways to save time, so firms do everything they can to provide goods and services designed for convenience. However, when it comes to products such as dinner foods, consumers want convenience, but they also want to enjoy the flavor of a home-cooked meal and spend quality time with their families. So companies such as Stouffer's offer frozen lasagna or manicotti in family sizes, and supermarkets have entire sections devoted to freshly prepared take-out meals that range from roast turkey to filet mignon.

McDonald's is betting that consumers who drink premium coffee beverages also like to buy them at bargain prices. In a selected number of U.S. locations, McDonald's has begun to place McCafe coffee bars—serving cappuccino, lattes, and mochas—near the cash register. "This is the biggest endeavor for McDonald's since our introduction of breakfast 35 years ago," says John Betts, vice president of the firm's national beverage strategy. Its success will depend on how well McDonald's knows its customers.[40]

The interpersonal determinants of consumer behavior include cultural, social, and family influences. In the area of convenience foods, cultural, social, and family influences come into play as much as an individual's need to save time. Understanding that many consumers value the time they spend with their families and want to care for them by providing good nutrition, marketers often emphasize these values in advertisements for convenience food products.

Sometimes external events influence consumer behavior. When crude oil prices spiked to $100 a barrel, forcing hikes at the gas pump, consumers responded by cutting back on clothing purchases, eating out in restaurants, vacations and trips, and the number of channels they receive on their cable service. Especially hard hit were low-income consumers, who used more and more of their budgets for gasoline and heating oil in certain climates.[41]

Determinants of Business Buying Behavior

Because a number of people can influence purchases of B2B products, business buyers face a variety of organizational influences in addition to their own preferences. A design engineer may help set the specifications that potential vendors must satisfy. A procurement manager may invite selected companies to bid on a purchase. A production supervisor may evaluate the operational aspects of the proposals that the firm receives, and the vice president of manufacturing may head a committee making the final decision.

Steps in the Consumer Behavior Process

Consumer decision making follows the sequential process outlined in Figure 12.6, with interpersonal and personal influences affecting every step. The process begins when the consumer

consumer behavior
actions of ultimate consumers directly involved in obtaining, consuming, and disposing of products and the decision processes that precede and follow these actions.

Figure 12.6

Steps in the Consumer Behavior Process

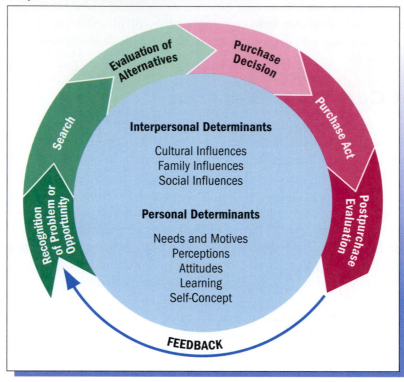

recognizes a problem or opportunity. If someone needs a new pair of shoes, that need becomes a problem to solve. If you receive a promotion at work and a 20 percent salary increase, that change may also become a purchase opportunity.

To solve the problem or take advantage of the opportunity, the consumer seeks information about his or her intended purchase and evaluates alternatives, such as available brands. The goal is to find the best response to the problem or opportunity.

Eventually, the consumer reaches a decision and completes the transaction. Later, he or she evaluates the experience by making a postpurchase evaluation. Feelings about the experience serve as feedback that will influence future purchase decisions. The various steps in the sequence are affected by both interpersonal and personal factors.

Relationship Marketing

The past decade has brought rapid change to most industries, as customers have become better-informed and more-demanding purchasers through closely comparing competing goods and services. They expect, even demand, new benefits from the companies that supply them, making it harder for firms to gain a competitive advantage based on product features alone.

In today's hypercompetitive era, businesses need to find new ways of relating to customers if they hope to maintain long-term success. Businesses are developing strategies and tactics that draw them into tighter connections with their customers, suppliers, and even employees. As a result, many firms are turning their attention to the issues of relationship marketing. **Relationship marketing** goes beyond an effort toward making the sale. Instead, it develops and maintains long-term, cost-effective exchange relationships with partners. These partners include individual customers, suppliers, and employees. As its ultimate goal, relationship marketing seeks to achieve customer satisfaction.

Managing relationships instead of simply completing transactions often leads to creative partnerships. However, customers enter into relationships with firms only if they are assured that the relationship will somehow benefit them. As the intensity of commitment increases, so does the likelihood of a business continuing a long-term relationship with its customers. Businesses are building relationships by partnering with customers, suppliers, and other businesses. Timberland, maker of footwear and clothing, creates many partnerships that foster long-term relationships. The firm partners with not-for-profit organizations such as CARE, City Year, and Clean Air–Cool Planet to complete service projects for communities and the environment. Through its Serve-a-Palooza, hundreds of Timberland employees engage in volunteer tasks in their communities. Those opportunities even extend to customers who have expressed interest in participating in programs in their own regions. If you want to volunteer for a food drive or to help restore a marsh, just log on to the Timberland Web site to see what's available. All of these activities help build relationships with customers, communities, and other organizations.[42]

An "emergency vehicle" equipped with consumer electronics brings tongue-in-cheek relief to teens bored by a slow summer. This Save Your Summer! marketing campaign was conceived by Panasonic to develop long-term relationships with youthful customers.

PRNewsFoto/Panasonic Consumer Electronics Company/ © AP/Wide World Photos

relationship marketing developing and maintaining long-term, cost-effective exchange relationships with partners.

Benefits of Relationship Marketing

Relationship marketing helps all parties involved. In addition to providing mutual protection against competitors, businesses that forge solid links with vendors and customers are often rewarded with lower costs and higher profits than they would generate on their own. Long-term agreements with a few high-quality suppliers frequently reduce a firm's production costs. Unlike onetime sales, these ongoing relationships encourage suppliers to offer customers preferential treatment, quickly adjusting shipments to accommodate changes in orders and correcting any quality problems that might arise.

Good relationships with customers can be vital strategic weapons for a firm. By identifying current purchasers and maintaining positive relationships with them, organizations can efficiently target their best customers. Studying current customers' buying habits and preferences can help marketers identify potential new customers and establish ongoing contact with them. Attracting a new customer can cost five times as much as keeping an existing one. Not only do marketing costs go down, but long-term customers usually buy more, require less service, refer other customers, and provide valuable feedback. Together, these elements contribute to a higher **lifetime value of a customer**—the revenues and intangible benefits (referrals and customer feedback) from the customer over the life of the relationship, minus the amount the company must spend to acquire and serve that customer. Keeping that customer may occasionally require some extra effort, especially if the customer has become upset or dissatisfied with a good or service. But good marketers can overcome this particular challenge, as described in the "Business Etiquette" feature.

Business Etiquette

CALMING THE ANGRY CUSTOMER

An angry customer is a challenge to any business. This customer represents not only an immediate problem but also a potential loss of future business. The person might be emotional about poor service or a broken product, frustrated by lack of attention from the company, or just plain demanding. Your job as a businessperson is to view this customer as a challenge rather than a disruption—and if at all possible, turn his or her dissatisfaction into satisfaction. With a little bit of common sense, good personal skills, and knowledge about your company and its products, you can very likely succeed at the task.

1. *Stay calm.* Nothing adds more fuel to a fire than hot air. So listen calmly to the person's problem. Take notes, if necessary. Most people begin to calm down if they believe someone is actually listening. Don't argue. Acknowledge the customer's anger, but don't take it personally. You can respond by saying, "No wonder you're frustrated and angry!"

2. *Repeat the customer's stated problem.* Make sure you understand the problem before offering a solution. For instance, you might say, "You lost Internet service between the hours of 10:00 a.m. and 2:00 p.m.," or "The book you ordered arrived too late to give as a gift."

3. *Focus on a solution.* Act as quickly and as authoritatively as your position allows. If you cannot solve the problem, contact someone who can do so as soon as possible. Remember that your firm has somehow caused a customer distress, and you want to keep that customer from doing business with another company.

4. *Thank the customer for his or her patience.* Empathy at this stage not only may surprise a customer but can be the final interaction that he or she will remember. It closes the conversation on a positive note.

5. *Follow up.* If appropriate, send an e-mail or call the person to make sure that service was restored or a replacement product was received. By handling the situation professionally, you are likely to reinforce your firm's relationship with the customer—instead of breaking it.

Sources: Lynne McClure, "Handling Angry Customers," *Impact Publications,* http://www.impactpublications.com, accessed March 24, 2009; Ken Lansford, "Tips on Handling Angry Customers," *PowerHomeBiz.com,* http://www.powerhomebiz.com, accessed March 24, 2009; "Handling Angry Customers," *Gaebler Ventures,* http://www.gaebler.com, accessed March 24, 2009; "Top 5 Tips for Handling Angry Customers," *Knowledge Associates,* http://www.knowledgence.com, accessed March 24, 2009.

Businesses also benefit from strong relationships with other companies. Purchasers who repeatedly buy from one business may find that they save time and gain service quality as the business learns their specific needs. Some relationship-oriented companies also customize items based on customer preferences. Because many businesses reward loyal customers with discounts or bonuses, some buyers may even find that they save money by developing long-term relationships. Alliances with other firms to serve the same customers also can be rewarding. The partners combine their capabilities and resources to accomplish goals that they could not reach on their own. In addition, alliances with other firms may help businesses develop the skills and experience they need to successfully enter new markets or improve service to current customers.

Tools for Nurturing Customer Relationships

Although relationship marketing has important benefits for both customers and businesses, most relationship-oriented businesses quickly discover that some customers generate more profitable business than others. If 20 percent of a firm's customers account for 80 percent of its sales and profits—the 80/20 principle mentioned earlier in the chapter—a customer in that category undoubtedly has a higher lifetime value than a customer who buys only once or twice or who makes small purchases.

While businesses shouldn't ignore any customer, they need to allocate their marketing resources wisely. A firm may choose to customize goods or services for high-value customers while working to increase repeat sales of stock products to less-valuable customers. Differentiating between these two groups also helps marketers focus on each in an effort to increase their commitment.

FREQUENCY MARKETING AND AFFINITY MARKETING PROGRAMS Popular techniques through which firms try to build and protect customer relationships include frequent buyer or user programs. These so-called **frequency marketing** programs reward purchasers with cash, rebates, merchandise, or other premiums. Frequency programs have grown more sophisticated over the years. They offer more personalization and customization than in the past. Airlines, hotel groups, restaurants, and many retailers including supermarkets offer frequency programs.

Customers who join the Marriott Rewards program have the option to spend their earned points at nearly 3,000 hotels, resorts, spas, and golf locations in 67 countries and territories worldwide.[43]

Affinity programs are another tool for building emotional links with customers. An affinity program is a marketing effort sponsored by an organization that solicits involvement by individuals who share common interests and activities. Affinity programs are common in the credit card industry. For instance, a person can sign up for a credit card emblazoned with the logo of a favorite charity, a sports or entertainment celebrity, or a photograph of his or her college. Bank of America offers credit cards featuring the logos of all the Major League Baseball teams.

Many businesses also use comarketing and cobranding. In a **comarketing** deal, two businesses jointly market each other's products. When two or more businesses link their names to a single product, **cobranding** occurs. When two seemingly unlikely businesses team up, the marketing sparks fly—and two very different groups of consumers may come together to buy the same product. Nike and iPod have marketed the Nike+iPod Sport kit, which allows a runner to insert a special sensor into a built-in pocket in a Nike+ shoe, which synchronizes the runner's activity with workout data and music that plays through the iPod. Enthusiasts can also purchase specially designed Nike workout apparel that has pockets designed to hold an iPod nano itself.[44]

ONE-ON-ONE MARKETING The ability to customize products and rapidly deliver goods and services has become increasingly dependent on technology such as computer-aided design and manufacturing (CAD/CAM). The Internet offers a way for businesses to connect with customers in a direct and intimate manner. Companies can take orders for customized products, gather data about buyers, and predict what items a customer might want in the future. Computer databases provide strong support for effective relationship marketing. Marketers can maintain databases on customer tastes, price-range preferences, and lifestyles, and they can quickly obtain names and other information about promising prospects. Amazon.com greets each online customer with a list of suggested books he or she might like to purchase. Many online retailers send their customers e-mails about upcoming sales, new products, and special events.

Small and large companies often rely on *customer relationship management (CRM)* software technology that helps them gather, sort, and interpret data about customers. Software firms develop this software in order to help businesses build and manage their relationships with customers. Queue Buster is one such product. The software offers callers the choice of receiving an automated return call instead of waiting on hold for the next available operator or service representative. After implementing the software, travel agency STA reported that its customer satisfaction ratings had improved to 98 percent. This simple solution to customers' frustration probably not only helped build customer loyalty but also helped save STA from lost business as well.[45]

What's Ahead

The next two chapters examine each of the four elements of the marketing mix that marketers use to satisfy their selected target markets. Chapter 13 focuses on products and their distribution through various channels to different outlets. Chapter 14 covers promotion and the various methods marketers use to communicate with their target customers, along with strategies for setting prices for different products.

Assessment Check ✓

1. What is the lifetime value of a customer?
2. Discuss the increasing importance of one-on-one marketing efforts.

Summary of Learning Goals

1 **Summarize the ways in which marketing creates utility.**

Utility is the ability of a good or service to satisfy the wants and needs of customers. The production function creates form utility by converting inputs to finished goods and services. Marketing creates time, place, and ownership utility by making the product available when and where consumers want to buy and by arranging for orderly transfers of ownership.

Assessment Check Answers

1.1 What is utility? Utility is the ability of a good or service to satisfy the wants and needs of customers.

1.2 Identify ways in which marketing creates utility. Marketing creates time utility by making a good or service available when customers want to purchase it; place utility by making the product available in a convenient location; and ownership utility by transferring the product from the buyer to the seller.

2 **Discuss the marketing concept.**

The marketing concept refers to a companywide customer orientation with the objective of achieving long-run success. This concept is essential in today's marketplace, which is primarily a buyer's market, meaning buyers can choose from an abundance of goods and services. Marketing now centers on the satisfaction of customers and building long-term relationships with those customers.

Assessment Check Answers

2.1 What is the marketing concept? The marketing concept is a companywide customer orientation with the objective of achieving long-run success. According to the marketing concept, success begins with the customer.

2.2 How is the marketing concept tied to the relationship era of marketing? Most marketing now centers on the satisfaction of customers and building long-term relationships with them, rather than simply producing and selling goods and services.

3 **Describe not-for-profit marketing, and identify the five major categories of nontraditional marketing.**

Not-for-profit organizations must engage in marketing just as for-profit firms do. Not-for-profit organizations operate in both the public and private sectors, and use marketing to obtain volunteers and donations, make people aware of their existence, achieve certain goals for society, and so on. Not-for-profit organizations may engage in several types of nontraditional marketing—person, place, event, cause, or organization marketing. They may rely on one type or a combination.

Assessment Check Answers

3.1 Why do not-for-profit organizations engage in marketing? Not-for-profit organizations use marketing to attract volunteers and donors, communicate their message, and achieve their societal goals.

3.2 What are the five types of nontraditional marketing used by not-for-profit organizations? The five types of nontraditional marketing are person, place, event, cause, and organization marketing.

4 **Outline the basic steps in developing a marketing strategy.**

All organizations develop marketing strategies to reach customers. This process involves analyzing the overall market, selecting a target market, and developing a marketing mix that blends elements related to product, distribution, promotion, and pricing decisions. Often company marketers develop a marketing plan that expresses their marketing strategy.

Assessment Check Answers

4.1 Distinguish between business consumer products and business products. Business products are goods and services purchased to be used, either directly or indirectly, in the production of other goods for resale. Consumer products are purchased by end users.

4.2 What are the steps in developing a marketing strategy? The steps in developing a marketing strategy are to analyze the overall market, select a target market, and develop a marketing mix.

5 **Describe the marketing research function.**

Marketing research is the information-gathering function that links marketers to the marketplace. It provides valuable information about potential target markets. Firms may generate internal data or gather external data. They may use secondary data or conduct research to obtain primary data. Data mining, which involves computer searches through customer data to detect patterns or relationships, is one helpful tool in forecasting various trends such as sales revenues and consumer behavior.

Assessment Check Answers

5.1 What is the difference between primary data and secondary data? Secondary data are previously published facts that are low cost to retrieve and easy to obtain. Primary data are collected firsthand through observation or surveys.

5.2 What is data mining? Data mining involves computer searches through customer data in order to evaluate the data and identify useful trends.

6 **Identify and explain each of the methods available for segmenting consumer and business markets.**

Consumer markets can be divided according to four criteria: demographic characteristics, such as age and family size; geographical factors; psychographic variables, which involve behavioral and lifestyle profiles; and product-related variables, such as the benefits consumers seek when buying a product or the degree of brand loyalty they feel toward it.

Business markets are segmented according to three criteria: geographical characteristics, customer-based specifications for products, and end-user applications.

Assessment Check Answers

6.1 What is the most common form of segmentation for consumer markets? Demographics is the most commonly used consumer market segmentation method.

6.2 What are the three approaches to product-use segmentation? The three approaches to product-use segmentation are by benefits sought, product usage rate, and brand loyalty.

6.3 What is end-use segmentation in the B2B market? End-use segmentation focuses on the precise way a B2B purchaser will use a product.

7 Outline the determinants of consumer behavior.

Consumer behavior refers to the actions of ultimate consumers with direct effects on obtaining, consuming, and disposing of products, as well as the decision processes that precede and follow these actions. Personal influences on consumer behavior include an individual's needs and motives, perceptions, attitudes, learned experiences, and self-concept. The interpersonal determinants include cultural influences, social influences, and family influences. A number of people within a firm may participate in business purchase decisions, so business buyers must consider a variety of organizational influences in addition to their own preferences.

Assessment Check Answers

7.1 Define *consumer behavior.* Consumer behavior refers to the actions of ultimate consumers directly involved in obtaining, consuming, and disposing of products, along with the decision processes surrounding these actions.

7.2 What are some determinants of consumer behavior? Determinants of consumer behavior include both personal influences and interpersonal influences. Personal influences include an individual's needs and motives; perceptions, attitudes, experiences; and self-concept. Interpersonal influences include cultural, social and family influences.

8 Discuss the benefits of and tools for relationship marketing.

Relationship marketing is an organization's attempt to develop long-term, cost-effective links with individual customers for mutual benefit. Good relationships with customers can be a vital strategic weapon for a firm. By identifying current purchasers and maintaining a positive relationship with them, an organization can efficiently target its best customers, fulfill their needs, and create loyalty. Information technologies, frequency and affinity programs, and one-on-one efforts all help build relationships with customers.

Assessment Check Answers

8.1 What is the lifetime value of a customer? The lifetime value of a customer incorporates the revenues and intangible benefits from the customer over the life of the relationship with a firm, minus the amount the company must spend to acquire and serve the customer.

8.2 Discuss the increasing importance of one-on-one marketing efforts. One-on-one marketing is increasing in importance as consumers demand more customization in goods and services. It is also increasingly dependent on technology such as computer-aided design and manufacturing (CAD/CAM). The Internet also offers a way for businesses to connect with customers in a direct and personal manner.

Business Terms You Need to Know

marketing 390	marketing concept 393	marketing research 399	consumer behavior 409
exchange process 391	target market 398	data mining 401	relationship marketing 411
utility 391	marketing mix 398	market segmentation 401	

Other Important Business Terms

time utility 391	organization marketing 396	demographic segmentation 403	lifetime value of a customer 411
place utility 391	consumer (B2C) product 398	psychographic segmentation 406	frequency marketing 412
ownership utility 391	business (B2B) product 398	product-related segmentation 407	affinity program 413
person marketing 395	business intelligence 400	end-use segmentation 408	comarketing 413
place marketing 395	data warehouse 401		cobranding 413
event marketing 395	geographical segmentation 402		
cause marketing 395			

Review Questions

1. Define the four different types of utility and explain how marketing contributes to the creation of utility. Then choose one of the following companies and describe how it creates each type of utility with its goods or services:
   a. Subway sandwiches
   b. Carnival Cruises
   c. Barnes & Noble books
   d. BoRics hair salons
   e. Wal-Mart health clinics

2. Describe the shift from a seller's market to a buyer's market. Why was this move important to marketers?

3. Describe how an organization might combine person marketing and event marketing. Give an example.

4. Describe how an organization might combine cause marketing and organization marketing. Give an example.

5. Identify each of the following as a consumer product or a business product, or classify it as both:
   a. cup of coffee
   b. iPod
   c. gasoline
   d. forklift truck
   e. toothbrush
   f. travel agency

6. Identify and describe the four strategies that blend to create a marketing mix.

7. What is a target market? Why is target market selection usually the first step in the development of a marketing strategy?

8. Identify the two strategies that a firm could use to develop a marketing mix for international markets. What are the advantages and disadvantages of each?

9. Describe the types of data that someone who is thinking of starting a limousine service might choose to gather. How might this businessperson use the data in making the startup decision?

10. Explain each of the methods used to segment consumer and business markets. Which methods do you think would be most effective for each of the following and why? (Note that a combination of methods might be applicable.)
    a. supermarket featuring Mexican foods
    b. air conditioning units
    c. motorcycles
    d. line of pet food
    e. dental insurance
    f. spa treatments

11. What are the three major determinants of consumer behavior? Give an example of how each one might influence a person's purchasing decision.

12. What are the benefits of relationship marketing? Describe how frequency and affinity programs work toward building relationships.

Projects and Teamwork Applications

1. On your own or with a classmate, choose one of the following products and create an advertisement that illustrates how your firm creates time, place, and form utility in its delivery of the product to the customer.
   a. computer repair service
   b. kayaks
   c. special-order cakes
   d. pet-sitting service

2. Choose one of the following nonprofit organizations or find one of your own. Research the organization online to learn more about it. Outline your proposed contents for a fund-raising event based on the chapter discussion of nontraditional marketing, such as cause marketing or organization marketing.
   a. Juvenile Diabetes Research Foundation
   b. Oprah's Angel Network

   c. Toys for Tots
   d. Salvation Army

3. As a marketer, if you can find ways to classify your firm's goods and services as both business and consumer products, most likely your company's sales will increase as you build relationships with a new category of customers. On your own or with a classmate, choose one of the following products, and outline a marketing strategy for attracting the classification of customer that is *opposite* from the one listed in parenthesis.
   a. hybrid car (consumer)
   b. exercise class (consumer)
   c. package delivery service (business)
   d. restaurant supplies (business)

4. Think of two situations in which you have been a customer: one in which you have been satisfied with the

merchandise you received and one in which you have not. Make a list of the reasons you were satisfied in the first case and another list of the reasons you were not satisfied in the second case. Would you say that the failure was the result of the seller not understanding your needs?

5. Comarketing and cobranding are techniques that organizations often use to market their own and each other's

products, such as Nike and iPod. On your own or with a classmate, choose two firms with goods and/or services you think would work well together for comarketing separate products or cobranding a single product. Then create an advertisement for your comarketing or cobranding effort.

Web Assignments

1. **Census data.** The U.S. Census Bureau collects and publishes a massive amount of demographic data on U.S. households. Visit the Census Bureau's Web site (http://www.census.gov) and review the available reports. Using some of these reports, answer at least two of the following questions:

   a. What are the five fastest-growing counties in the United States?
   b. Which county has the highest per-capita income?
   c. Which county has the highest percentage of college graduates?
   d. Which county has the highest percentage of its population under the age of 18?

2. **Market segmentation.** You probably know that Scion and Lexus are both Toyota brands, yet they are targeted to very different markets. Visit the Scion, Lexus, and

Toyota U.S. Web sites (http://www.lexus.com; http://www.scion.com; http://www.toyota.com). Based on your review of all three sites, prepare a brief report discussing Toyota's market segmentation strategy.

3. **Marketing for not-for-profit organizations.** Virtually all not-for-profit organizations have their own Web sites. Most use their sites to market their organizations to prospective donors and clients. Visit at least two not-for-profit organization Web sites. Identify and evaluate the impact on you personally (positive, negative, or neutral) of the Web marketing strategies employed. Would you be more willing or less willing to support the organization now?

Note: Internet Web addresses change frequently. If you do not find the exact sites listed, you may need to access the organization's or company's home page and search from there.

Green Marketing: Good for Customers, Businesses, and the Earth — Case 12.1

Green marketing has finally grown up. Once considered a quirky trend that appealed to a certain niche of environmentally concerned consumers, it has now become part of the overall business and marketing strategy of both small companies and major global corporations. As awareness of the importance of protecting and maintaining the resources of the planet has seeped into the mainstream, the idea of sustainability—meeting the needs of humans without damaging the environment—has become the basis of a new direction for many firms. Global consumer products manufacturer Unilever, which produces everything from Dove soap and Sunsilk shampoo to Lipton tea and Wishbone dressing, keeps the environment in mind in all of its processes. As part of its overall mission, the firm strives to improve people's health through nutrition and hygiene, minimize its environmental footprint, obtain renewable supplies of raw materials, and add wealth and other benefits to developing communities.

As it researches, develops, produces, and markets its products, Unilever undertakes projects designed to improve the lives of people and their environment. In Brazil, the firm funds a farming program that is helping tomato growers convert to environmentally friendly drip irrigation and recycles 17 tons of waste each year at its toothpaste factory. In Ghana, the firm is teaching palm oil producers to reuse plant waste. Unilever also reports publicly the amount of carbon dioxide and hazardous waste its factories discharge each year—all while taking steps to reduce those emissions.

These efforts are not only good for consumers, producers, and the environment but also necessary for the survival of companies like Unilever. Environmental regulations are tightening in the United States, Europe, and many other places around the world. If companies do not invest in technologies that preserve the environment in which they operate, eventually they will go out of business. "You can't ignore the impact your company has on the community and environment," warns Unilever CEO Patrick Cescau. "It's also about growth and innovation. In the future, it will be the only way to do business."

Unilever is just one of many companies moving in this direction. Toyota, the leading manufacturer of hybrid vehicles, is also now one of the largest auto manufacturers in the world. Toyota's reputation as a green corporation has propelled its sales past the competition. Marketing firm Interbrand reports that since the launch of the Prius and subsequent roll-outs of hybrid models of the Highlander, Camry, and others, Toyota's brand value has accelerated by nearly 50 percent. Meanwhile, automakers that were late to the game missed out not only on sales but on the opportunity to create a positive image in the minds of consumers. "We didn't appreciate the image value of hybrids," admits Larry Burns, chief of research and development at GM. "We missed that."

Meanwhile, not-for-profit organizations are working on new forms of green marketing as well. Instead of emphasizing individual endangered species such as the aardvark or the dugong, they are beginning to see the value of focusing on "flagship" or "heartland" areas around the world, chunks of land that contain intense concentrations of wildlife. Land conservation is not new, but this approach includes hotspots with a huge variety of plant and animal species. Marketed properly—for instance, allowing consumers to "adopt" a square of landscape—organizations like the African Wildlife Foundation and Conservation International are discovering that they can raise the money needed to implement important conservation projects.

Organizations have come to realize that consumers want to participate in environmental sustainability and that marketing messages informing shoppers of a company's green practices are helpful both to its image and its bottom line. As Dow Chemical increases its research on products such as roof tiles that deliver solar power, CEO Andrew N. Liveris explains why. "There is 100 percent overlap between our business drivers and social environmental interests." Going forward, a company can't have one without the other.[46]

Questions for Critical Thinking

1. Go online and research any of the companies mentioned—or another one that interests you—to find out more about the firm's green marketing. Then create a new slogan reflecting the company's green marketing practices.

2. How might green marketing affect consumer behavior and help build customer relationships?

Case 12.2 — *High School Musical* Draws New Audience for Disney

Rarely do sequels post the same success as the original story, but *High School Musical 2* debuted on the Disney Channel to an estimated 17.2 million preteens and teens. Those viewers had eagerly awaited the continuation of the story line about Troy (Zac Efron), Gabriella (Vanessa Hudgens), Sharpay (Ashley Tisdale), and their friends at East High. The number of viewers made the sequel the most-watched basic cable program in history, compared with the debut of the original *High School Musical,* which attracted an audience of about 7.7 million. But it's the staying power among this group of consumers that has Disney marketers excited about *High School Musical* and its sequel. Hit singles, including "We're All in This Together," along with DVD sales and productions by what seems to be every high school drama club in the nation, have kept the two movies in the minds of kids and their parents. Just in case that's not enough, Disney has created a live concert tour, a live stage show, and even a live version of *High School Musical* on ice.

Why are these movies such a hit with the preteen and teen set? "I think kids like having role models to look up to and enjoy singing along," explains one mom. The story is simple—a high school jock and a "brainiac" both surprise their friends by breaking out of their social roles and auditioning for the high school play. They land the parts, taking them away from two previous high school stars—and shock everyone further by giving a stellar performance. Not surprisingly, the two fall in love. But it's more than just the story or the catchy tunes. Preteens and teens can watch the movies with their friends, their siblings, even their parents. In fact, marketers determined that the premier of *HSM2* became a social event. According to one study, more than 35 percent of teens watched the debut outside their homes—at the homes of friends or other locations. "Because the first movie became a sort of 'lifestyle' for kids, it was only natural that teens would want to watch the sequel with friends, which accounts for the high out-of-home viewership," explains Amanda Welsh, head of research for Integrated Media Measurement. Teens also sent text messages to friends while they watched the movie. "The first night it aired, the texting numbers at all the major cell phone carriers went up during the movie," reports *HSM* author Peter Barsocchini.

For years, Disney has sought to draw teens back into the fold at a time in their lives when Mickey and Minnie have lost their appeal. It's possible that Troy and Gabriella could be the couple to lure these consumers back to the Disney family.[47]

Questions for Critical Thinking

1. Describe what you think would be a successful marketing mix for the first two *High School Musical* movies as well as any upcoming sequels.
2. The market for the movies is segmented primarily by age, but how might marketers further segment this market?

VIDEO   Case 12.3   WBRU Listens to Its Customers

Everyone has a favorite radio station, whether it's rock, folk, urban, or news. Just like other businesses, radio stations use strategies for segmenting markets and target those who are most likely to listen to their format. But unlike some other businesses, radio stations must engage in marketing both to consumers (listeners) and businesses (potential advertisers). WBRU is no exception. Based in Providence, Rhode Island, WBRU serves a mainly college-educated audience spread throughout Rhode Island and southeastern Massachusetts.

WBRU presents what it calls a "modern rock format" with nine commercial breaks each hour. Calling itself "music interactive," WBRU concentrates on hot new music groups, boasting that its programming contains "no endless morning talk, no off-color or offensive humor...We only feature targeted lifestyle programs and promotions...with the most dynamic, exciting playlists in the business."

Local advertisers and listeners meet on the common ground of WBRU's radio waves. According to a past demographic survey for the station, 29 percent of WBRU's listeners are employed full-time; 28 percent have a home mortgage; 13 percent own a computer; 11 percent drive a Lexus, BMW, or Saab; and 10 percent work in executive or managerial positions. During a past 12-month period, WBRU listeners spend $21 million on furniture, $17 million on appliances, $26 million on clothing, $9 million on TV sets, and $9 million on jewelry. WBRU attracts its advertisers by providing them with this listener profile information. Through the years, such corporate heavyweights as Blockbuster Video, Dunkin' Donuts, and New England Sports Network have signed on for commercials at the station—to gain its listeners' ears.

Segmenting the market is important for attracting advertisers, but it is even more important for attracting listeners. If WBRU knows who its listeners are, it can fine-tune its programming to offer selections they want to hear. To get such information, the station conducts an online survey at its Web site—listeners can answer questions about other stations they like, what they do in their free time, what consumer items they purchase, and who their favorite recording artists are. In one marketing segment, the station targets African Americans by offering gospel music on Sundays by its DJ Brother Don, followed by DJs Cas Casion and Commish, who specialize in hip-hop and rhythm and blues. Other programming slots include "Retro Lunch" and jazz at 2 a.m. Each of those time slots is targeted to a specific listening market.

Listeners can get music news and win free CDs and other prizes at the WBRU Web site, as well as look up future programming schedules. They can browse through the BRU Store, view the message board and photo gallery, and download interviews with the likes of Dave Matthews. All of these opportunities to interact with the station help WBRU sharpen its understanding of its listeners. If you want to go see Big Dumb Face at Lupo's on Friday, you can find out about it at WBRU. If you prefer Papa Roach or Alien Ant Farm, keep listening to the station for you chance to win free tickets. And if you're not sure whether you want to plunk down your cash for the new Buckcherry CD, check out the review first on WBRU. Falling asleep while pulling an all-nighter? Tune into SBRU LOUD at 10 p.m. on Thursday nights, and you're guaranteed to stay awake. If all of this sounds good to you, you're probably the perfect SBRU listener, even if you don't own a Lexus or your own company—yet.[48]

Questions for Critical Thinking

1. In what ways does WBRU attempt to add value to its basic service?
2. In addition to providing businesses with demographic information about listeners, what types of marketing efforts might WBRU make to attract businesses to advertise on its airwaves and Web site?
3. Describe a typical WBRU listener from what you have read in the case.
4. Go to the WBRU Web site at www.wbru.com and look for ways that the station conducts research about its listeners, either directly or indirectly.

Goals

1 Explain marketing's definition of a product and list the components of a product strategy.

2 Describe the classification system for consumer and business goods and services.

3 Distinguish between a product mix and a product line.

4 Briefly describe each of the four stages of the product life cycle.

5 List the stages of the new-product development process.

6 Explain how firms identify their products.

7 Outline and briefly describe each of the major components of an effective distribution strategy.

8 Identify the various categories of distribution channels, and discuss the factors that influence channel selection.

chapter
13

Product and Distribution Strategies

Eightfish/Stone/Getty Images

The Buckle Shines Amid Retail Gloom

Retailers are smarting from the pinch of consumers' tightened wallets. Many reported slow sales even during the usually busy holiday season. But one clothing retailer has actually seen its sales grow by double digits. At youth-oriented retail chain The Buckle, sales climbed more than 13 percent recently—and more than 20 percent during a holiday season when other stores saw declines. The Buckle's 388 mall stores are keeping up the momentum, too. Annual sales are expected to soon reach $780 million, a stellar performance in a generally dismal shopping year.

What accounts for the chain's continued growth and popularity? One key is the racks of fresh merchandise arriving at stores every day. Another factor is the stores' 15- to 25-year-old customers, who are keen shoppers with money to spend. "This is their first recession," notes one retail expert. "They're not as scared as everyone else. Their home equity is not at stake, and their 401(k) [retirement plan] is just getting started." But like any other retailer, The Buckle ultimately rises and falls on the quality of its merchandise. And that's where The Buckle is shining with its inventory of high-fashion shirts, jeans, shoes, and accessories for men and women.

The chain stocks the hottest high-quality brands, like Fossil and Guess, which make up about 70 percent of its sales. The rest comes from the store's own BKE brand of mostly denim pieces. But whatever the manufacturer, The Buckle usually carries each style in only a few sizes. It restocks in different colors or different designs than the ones that have already sold. This strategy ensures that the chain's most loyal customers won't see their friends wearing the same outfits they've just chosen, a benefit Buckle fans prize. One teen in a customer focus group said, "I shop The Buckle because it seems to offer more opportunity to look different from everyone else. I buy classic pieces and edgy accessories and create my own look."

Another young shopper agreed. "I feel I can create a distinctive style with their clothes," he said. The wide product assortment and constantly changing choices that keep fashion-conscious customers coming back might present a logistical challenge to a chain with stores in 38 states. But the Nebraska-based firm runs a highly efficient distribution system that keeps items flowing. That's important considering that despite its narrow range for each item, the store carries some unusual sizes, such as extra extra extra long jeans. One happy shopper reported, "I was always stretching my jeans to make them as long as possible, but then a friend recommended I try out The Buckle."

The store also trains its young and energetic salespeople carefully to help promote its merchandise. One important strategy is to get the customer into a dressing room. Once there, the shopper is fed a stream of suggestions for coordinating a look. A salesperson whose customer is trying on jeans, for instance, will deliver, unasked, a couple of T-shirts and a belt to go with them. "I end up trying on clothes faster and faster, finding more stuff I like, then never even taking the time to look at the prices," said one young shopper. "I know I buy more because of it."

The Buckle is careful about where its clothing comes from, too. It has a corporate goal of providing the most enjoyable shopping experience possible—with high-quality products at the best value in the most equitable manner. That requires "sound business and human rights ethics from our suppliers" as set out in the company's Code of Conduct and Standards of Engagement. The code includes health, safety, employment, and environmental practices. The Buckle gives a copy to all its suppliers to sign.

Top-quality products in the right assortment with attentive service—it all adds up to a store full of products that customers love.[1]

In this chapter we examine ways in which organizations design and implement marketing strategies that address customers' needs and wants. Two of the most powerful such tools are strategies that relate to products, which include both goods and services, and those that relate to the distribution of those products.

As the story of The Buckle illustrates, successful companies cater to the tastes of their customers. The retail chain continues to perfect its recipe for success with customers by offering the clothes and styles they want to wear in limited quantities to avoid duplication with other teen wardrobes. In addition, the creation of new products is the lifeblood of an organization. Because products do not remain economically viable forever, companies must constantly develop new ones to ensure their survival and long-term growth. Providing new styles continually to meet fashion's changing tastes keeps The Buckle on the upswing in a depressed retail market.

This chapter focuses on the first two elements of the marketing mix: product and distribution. Our discussion of product strategy begins by describing the classifications of goods and services, customer service, product lines and the product mix, and the product life cycle. Companies often shape their marketing strategies differently when they are introducing a new product, when the product has established itself in the marketplace, and when it is declining in popularity. We also discuss product identification through brand name and distinctive packaging, and the ways in which companies foster loyalty to their brands to keep customers coming back for more.

Distribution, the second mix variable discussed, focuses on moving goods and services from producer to wholesaler to retailer to buyers. Managing the distribution process includes making decisions such as what kind of wholesaler to use and where to offer products for sale. Retailers can range from specialty stores to factory outlets and everything in between, and they must choose appropriate customer service, pricing, and location strategies in order to succeed. The chapter concludes with a look at logistics, the process of coordinating the flow of information, goods, and services among suppliers and on to final consumers.

Product Strategy

product bundle of physical, service, and symbolic attributes designed to satisfy buyers' wants.

Most people respond to the question "What is a product?" by listing its physical features. By contrast, marketers take a broader view. To them, a **product** is a bundle of physical, service, and symbolic attributes designed to satisfy consumer wants. The chief executive officer of a major tool manufacturer once startled his stockholders with this statement: "Last year our customers bought over 1 million quarter-inch drill bits, and none of them wanted to buy the product. They all wanted quarter-inch holes." Product strategy involves considerably more than just producing a good or service; instead, it focuses on benefits.

The marketing conception of a product includes decisions about package design, brand name, trademarks, warranties, product image, new-product development, and customer service. Think, for instance, about your favorite soft drink. Do you like it for its taste alone, or do other attributes, such as clever ads, attractive packaging, ease of purchase from vending machines and other convenient locations, and overall image, also attract you? These other attributes may influence your choice more than you realize.

Assessment Check

1. What is a product?
2. What is the marketing view of a product?

Classifying Goods and Services

Marketers have found it useful to classify goods and services as either B2C or B2B, depending on whether the purchasers of the particular item are consumers or businesses. These classifications can be subdivided further, and each type requires a different competitive strategy.

Classifying Consumer Goods and Services

The classification typically used for ultimate consumers who purchase products for their own use and enjoyment and not for resale is based on consumer buying habits. **Convenience products** are items the consumer seeks to purchase frequently, immediately, and with little effort. Items stocked in gas-station markets, vending machines, and local newsstands are usually convenience products—for example, newspapers, snacks, candy, coffee, and bread.

Shopping products are those typically purchased only after the buyer has compared competing products in competing stores. A person intent on buying a new sofa or dining room table may visit many stores, examine perhaps dozens of pieces of furniture, and spend days making the final decision. **Specialty products,** the third category of consumer products, are those that a purchaser is willing to make a special effort to obtain. The purchaser is already familiar with the item and considers it to have no reasonable substitute. The nearest Mini Cooper dealer may be 75 miles away, but if you have decided you want one, you will make the trip.

Note that a shopping product for one person may be a convenience item for someone else. Each item's product classification is based on buying patterns of the majority of people who purchase it.

The interrelationship of the marketing mix factors is shown in Figure 13.1. By knowing the appropriate classification for a specific product, the marketing decision maker knows quite a bit about how the other mix variables will adapt to create a profitable, customer-driven marketing strategy.

CLASSIFYING BUSINESS GOODS *Business products* are goods and services such as paycheck services and huge multifunction copying machines used in operating an organization; they also include machinery, tools, raw materials, components, and buildings used to produce other items for resale. While consumer products are classified by buying habits, business products are classified based on how they are used and by their basic characteristics. Products that are long-lived and relatively expensive are called *capital items.* Less costly products that are consumed within a year are referred to as *expense items.*

Five basic categories of B2B products exist: installations, accessory equipment, component parts and materials, raw materials, and supplies. *Installations* are major capital items, such as new factories, heavy equipment and machinery, and custom-made equipment. Installations are expensive and often involve buyer and seller negotiations that may last for more than a year before a purchase actually is made. Purchase approval

IT'S TIME TO DRIVE LIKE THERE IS A TOMORROW.

To hug trees and corners at the same time. And for adrenaline to be regarded as a renewable resource. It's time for a little more turn and a little less burn. For the letters RPM to play nice with the letters MPG. And for the road and earth to finally find some middle ground. It's time to maximize our fun. To minimize our impact. And to start getting the most out of every single mile we drive. It's time to think about our Carfun Footprint.

MINIUSA.COM/MINIMALISM

MINI COOPER

Buying a *specialty product* takes extra effort. The Mini Cooper—known to environmentally conscious consumers as a green auto—isn't sold in many places.

Figure 13.1   **Marketing Impacts of Consumer Product Classifications**

Marketing Strategy Factor	Convenience Product	Shopping Product	Specialty Product
· **Purchase Frequency**	· Frequent	· Relatively infrequent	· Infrequent
· **Store Image**	· Unimportant	· Very important	· Important
· **Price**	· Low	· Relatively high	· High
· **Promotion**	· By manufacturer	· By manufacturer and retailers	· By manufacturer and retailers
· **Distribution Channel**	· Many wholesalers and retailers	· Relatively few wholesalers and retailers	· Very few wholesalers and retailers
· **Number of Retail Outlets**	· Many	· Few	· Very small number; often one per market area

frequently involves a number of different people—production specialists, representatives from the purchasing department, and members of top management—who must agree on the final choice.

Although *accessory equipment* also includes capital items, they are usually less expensive and shorter lived than installations and involve fewer decision makers. Examples include hand tools and fax machines. *Component parts and materials* are finished business goods that become part of a final product, such as disk drives that are sold to computer manufacturers or batteries purchased by automakers. *Raw materials* are farm and natural products used in producing other final products. Examples include milk, iron ore, leather, and soybeans. *Supplies* are expense items used in a firm's daily operation that do not become part of the final product. Often referred to as MRO (maintenance, repair, and operating supplies), they include paper clips, light bulbs, and copy paper.

CLASSIFYING SERVICES Services can be classified as either B2C or B2B. Child and elder care centers and auto detail shops provide services for consumers, while the Pinkerton security patrol at a local factory and Kelly Services' temporary office workers are examples of business services. In some cases, a service can accommodate both consumer and business markets. For example, when ServiceMaster cleans the upholstery in a home, it is a B2C service, but when it spruces up the painting system and robots in a manufacturing plant, it is a B2B service.

Like tangible goods, services can also be convenience, shopping, or specialty products depending on the buying patterns of customers. However, they are distinguished from goods in several ways. First, services, unlike goods, are intangible. In addition, they are perishable because firms cannot stockpile them in inventory. They are also difficult to standardize, because they must meet individual customers' needs. Finally, from a buyer's perspective, the service provider is the service; the two are inseparable in the buyer's mind.

Marketing Strategy Implications

The consumer product classification system is a useful tool in marketing strategy. As described in Figure 13.1, once a new refrigerator has been classified as a shopping good, its marketers have a better idea of its promotion, pricing, and distribution needs.

Each group of business products, however, requires a different marketing strategy. Because most installations and many component parts frequently are marketed directly from manufacturer to business buyer, the promotional emphasis is on personal selling rather than on advertising. By contrast, marketers of supplies and accessory equipment rely more on advertising, because their products often are sold through an intermediary, such as a wholesaler. Producers of installations and component parts may involve their customers in new-product development, especially when the business product is custom made. Finally, firms selling supplies and accessory equipment place greater emphasis on competitive pricing strategies than do other B2B marketers, who tend to concentrate more on product quality and customer service.

Assessment Check

1. Differentiate among convenience, shopping, and specialty products.
2. How do business products differ from consumer items?

Product Lines and Product Mix

Few firms operate with a single product. If their initial entry is successful, they tend to increase their profit and growth chances by adding new items to offer their customers. The next generation of videogames will allow players to skip standalone game consoles and go right to their PCs. The new games offer enhanced visuals that are the result of collaboration among videogame developers, graphics cards manufacturers, and Microsoft. Fine-tuning of Microsoft's Vista operating system provides new features for game players, including the ability to zoom in on details such as a game character's freckles.[2]

A company's **product line** is a group of related products marked by physical similarities or intended for a similar market. A **product mix** is the assortment of product lines and individual goods and services that a firm offers to consumers and business users. The Coca-Cola Company and PepsiCo both have product lines that include old standards—Coke Classic and Diet Coke, Pepsi and Diet Pepsi. But recently, both firms have decided to expand their mix to include new carbonated drinks that are fortified with vitamins and minerals. Diet Coke Plus and Pepsi's Tava are both called "sparkling beverages" and intended to appeal to consumers who prefer not to drink traditional soft drinks because of concerns about the calorie count or caffeine content.[3]

Marketers must assess their product mix continually to ensure company growth, to satisfy changing consumer

product line group of related products that are physically similar or are intended for the same market.

product mix company's assortment of product lines and individual offerings.

A *product line* includes several related products designed to have the same appearance, like these NASCAR auto care products.

PRNewsFoto/Ecolab/© AP/Wide World Photos

needs and wants, and to adjust to competitors' offerings. To remain competitive, marketers look for gaps in their product lines and fill them with new offerings or modified versions of existing ones. A helpful tool that is frequently used in making product decisions is the product life cycle.

Product Life Cycle

product life cycle four basic stages—introduction, growth, maturity, and decline—through which a successful product progresses.

Once a product is on the market, it usually goes through a series of four stages known as the **product life cycle:** introduction, growth, maturity, and decline. As Figure 13.2 shows, industry sales and profits vary depending on the life-cycle stage of an item.

Product life cycles are not set in stone; not all products follow this pattern precisely, and different products may spend different periods of time in each stage, as the "Hit & Miss" feature describes. The concept, however, helps the marketing planner anticipate developments throughout the various stages of a product's life. Profits assume a predictable pattern through the stages, and promotional emphasis shifts from dispensing product information in the early stages to heavy brand promotion in the later ones.

"They Said It"

"I like to tell people that all of our products and business will go through three phases. There's vision, patience, and execution."

—Steve Ballmer (b. 1956)
CEO, Microsoft

Stages of the Product Life Cycle

In the *introduction stage,* the firm tries to promote demand for its new offering; inform the market about it; give free samples to entice consumers to make a trial purchase; and explain its features, uses, and benefits. Sometimes companies partner at this stage to promote new products, as did General Mills and Curves International when the two launched four new weight-management cereal and breakfast bars under the Curves name. The two firms conducted a contest, called "Real Change, Real Women," in which women were invited to write essays about what motivated them to switch to a healthy lifestyle. The grand prize included the chance to appear on Curves Cereal boxes, along with a year-long supply of the new products.[4] The developers of Crocs sandals spent the introduction stage selling their product from booths at boat shows. That product moved to the next stage very quickly.

New-product development costs and extensive introductory promotional campaigns to acquaint prospective buyers with the merits of the innovation, though essential to later success, are expensive and commonly lead to losses in the introductory stage. Losses also occur due to the relatively low sales and high costs of promotions, establishing distribution channels, and training the sales force about the new product's advantages. In addition, only about 45 percent of firms actually meet their launch dates, incurring expenses related to delays.[5] But such expenditures are necessary if the firm is to profit later.

During the *growth stage,* sales climb quickly as new customers join early

Figure 13.2   Stages in the Product Life Cycle

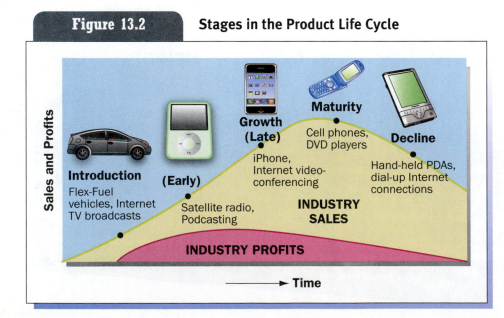

Hit & Miss

Chattem Breathes Life into Old Brands

Where do brands go to die? If they're lucky, they don't die at all. They are bought by Chattem instead. The 130-year-old company succeeds these days, not by creating new products, but by pouring new life into old brand-name health products, toiletries, and pain relievers.

Chattem has put Gold Bond brand back on the map by updating its packaging and expanding the product line from a decades-old remedy for itches and rashes to an array of about two dozen different items. They're now sold in nearly 70,000 U.S. drug and grocery stores, including Wal-Mart, which accounts for about one-third of Chattem's revenue.

Chattem carries about 26 brands and is always looking for more, from such parent firms as Procter & Gamble and Johnson & Johnson. The company recently purchased Selsun Blue dandruff shampoo, Kaopectate stomach soother, and Balmex diaper rash cream. It spent $410 million for five brands it purchased from Johnson & Johnson in a recent year. "Things that are very important to us are an afterthought for other companies," said Chattem's CEO.

A Chattem product makeover can take up to 18 months and usually begins with a customer focus group to identify the product's potential. Next comes packaging redesign. That involves more than a facelift, though a new look is often important for reviving a product's fortunes. But streamlining the packaging lets the company fit more units on store shelves, where space is allotted competitively on a per-product basis.

The company also adds new touches to products that need them. When it purchased over-the-counter sleep aid Unisom, it reformulated it as a meltable tablet that can be swallowed without water. Occasionally, Chattem's efforts to save a product are in vain. After it spent almost $100 million to purchase diet drug Dexatrim, the FDA recalled it and other remedies that contained an ingredient believed to increase the risk of stroke. Chattem withdrew all its Dexatrim brand products but was still on the hook for nearly 400 consumer claims that cost it over $56 million to settle.

Chattem usually spends about $120 million a year on advertising and promotion, including 15-second TV spots, catchy jingles and slogans, and sometimes even a celebrity spokesperson. Model Christie Brinkley is endorsing ACT mouthwash, now available in seven versions. Chattem has already promoted the product's ability to restore tooth enamel and doubled ACT's sales to $60 million.

Some companies try to revive their own brands, but for those who want to unload a product line, Chattem is ready to step in. And with sales of $450 million and a growth rate around 12 percent a year, it seems to have found a winning strategy. After all, said one observer, "In a financial meltdown, people still have arthritis and dandruff."

Questions for Critical Thinking

1. How does Chattem determine whether an aging product is still viable in the marketplace? What other measures do you think it might use to tell good products from bad, and why?
2. Why would a company sell a viable brand-name product to a firm like Chattem?

Sources: Company Web site, http://www.chattem.com, accessed March 4, 2009; "Chattem Unbottles Potent Profits, Defying Economy," *iStockAnalyst,* January 30, 2009, http://www.istockanalyst.com; Jonathan Heller, "Chattem Creates Value in Consumer Products," *Real Money,* January 27, 2009, http://biz.yahoo.com; Helen Coster, "Old Brands in New Bottles," *Forbes,* October 27, 2008, pp. 134–137.

---

users who now are repurchasing the item. Word-of-mouth referrals and continued advertising and other special promotions by the firm induce others to make trial purchases. At this point, the company begins to earn profits on the new product. This success encourages competitors to enter the field with similar offerings, and price competition develops. After its initial success in the digital music market, Apple is faced with competitors for its iPod. Yahoo!, SanDisk, and the start-up Zing have collaborated to jump into the arena with a product called Sansa Connect. The device has WiFi capabilities that allow users to buy the music they want directly from the device without being linked to a computer, which was Yahoo!'s contribution to the project.[6]

In the *maturity stage,* industry sales at first increase, but they eventually reach a saturation level at which further expansion is difficult. Competition also intensifies, increasing the availability of the product. Firms concentrate on capturing competitors' customers, often dropping prices to further the appeal. Cell phones are in the maturity stage: competitors compete not only on price but also on features such as calendars, e-mail and attachments, messaging capability, full-color screens, keyboards, and fax and word-processing functions. Flat-screen TVs are also in the maturity stage, so companies are trying to entice consumers to buy new ones by offering even bigger TVs than they have before, topping the 50-inch mark. Sony has committed itself to the larger models, reporting that soon these TVs will account for 68 percent of its line. The firm is sending 500 spokespeople out to retail stores nationwide to promote the benefits of the giant screens.[7]

Sales volume fades late in the maturity stage, and some of the weaker competitors leave the market. During this stage, firms promote mature products aggressively to protect their market share and to distinguish their products from those of competitors. As Starbucks has hit the maturity stage, the firm is making an effort to boost sales by adding more coffee shops. Some marketers applaud this move, but others warn that it could actually contribute to a decline by saturating the marketplace with too many outlets.

Sales continue to fall in the *decline stage,* the fourth phase of the product life cycle. Profits decline and may become losses as further price-cutting occurs in the reduced overall market for the item. Competitors gradually exit, making some profits possible for the remaining firms in the shrinking market. The decline stage usually is caused by a product innovation or a shift in consumer preferences. Sometimes technology change can hasten the decline stage for a product. Eighty percent of U.S. residences contains at least one DVD player, and high-definition DVDs have already replaced old DVD technology. Online sites where consumers can simply download movies or television shows are becoming another major competitor for entertainment as the link between computer and television is becoming faster and more reliable.[8]

Marketing Strategy Implications of the Product Life Cycle

Like the product classification system, the product life cycle is a useful concept for designing a marketing strategy that will be flexible enough to accommodate changing marketplace characteristics. These competitive moves may involve developing new products, lowering prices, increasing distribution coverage, creating new promotional campaigns, or any combination of these approaches. Wal-Mart has adopted a unique marketing strategy, as the "Hit & Miss" feature explains. In general, the marketer's objective is to extend the product life cycle as long as the item is profitable. Some products can be highly profitable during the later stages of their life cycle, because all the initial development costs already have been recovered.

A commonly used strategy for extending the life cycle is to increase customers' frequency of use. Wal-Mart and Target offer grocery sections in their stores in order to increase the frequency of shopper visits. Another strategy is to add new users. Marketers for Old Spice grooming products decided that Old Spice didn't have to be old hat. So they came up with a campaign to freshen up the product line's image and attract younger men. Called "Experience Is Everything," the television, print, and online campaign poked fun at the idea of modern masculinity while reminding consumers of the benefits of Old Spice products.[9]

Arm & Hammer used a third approach: finding new uses for its products. The original use of the firm's baking soda in baking has been augmented by its newer uses as a toothpaste, refrigerator freshener, and flame extinguisher. A fourth product life cycle extension strategy is changing package sizes, labels, and product designs. Many times, changing the product design means finding a way to give it an online application. Toymaker Mattel did this with Barbie by creating plastic hand-held MP3 players called Barbie Girls that could be accessorized like dolls and connected to the Internet to retrieve special animations and to shop in a virtual world on the Web. Mattel marketers view this move as vital to maintaining the doll's relevance with the next generation of consumers. "There is a large group of girls who still love Barbie; they're just playing with it in a different way," explains Rosie O'Neil,

Assessment Check ✔

1. What are the stages of the product life cycle?
2. What are the marketing implications of each stage?

Wal-Mart's Winning Strategy

With many retailers seeing drops in sales as consumers reduce spending, you might expect competitor Wal-Mart to feel the pinch, too. But the world's largest retailer reports sales increases of about 5 percent per store, double-digit growth in profits, and a stock price that rose 20 percent. How does Wal-Mart do it? Low price is a key factor. "Save money, live better" still applies as consumers hunt for budget-stretching bargains. "Look," said one shopper piling 10 shopping bags into his car. "All that for $54!"

Not long ago Wal-Mart was struggling from overexpansion and battling Target for high-end customers. Now the firm has a new marketing strategy it calls "win, play, show." These categories are based on an item's growth potential, price competitiveness, and credibility with customers. "Win" products have all three qualities; they're hot items the retailer can offer at low prices—like flat-screen TVs, for which Wal-Mart recently doubled its market share.

"Play" items exist in markets where the company competes without dominating, such as clothing. It limits its offerings here to quick-selling items like L.E.I. jeans that are priced at $20 and is easing out of the high end of the market.

"Show" merchandise are essentials like hardware that the chain has to carry to maintain its one-stop shopping reputation, but it doesn't need to offer huge variety. "It's important we have hammers and tape measures" to compete with Lowe's and Home Depot, "but not 28 tape measures, which ... we actually carried at one time," says the chain's merchandising chief.

To compete during a recent holiday season, the company switched its strategy from slashing most prices as much as 30 percent to offering a handful of popular brands like Hot Wheels and Barbie for a rock-bottom $10. Wal-Mart is also promoting its redesigned private-label groceries. "Great Value is the largest brand at Wal-Mart," says its senior vice president. "It plays across more than 100 categories. ... We have plans to make this brand even stronger with improved value and quality."

Questions for Critical Thinking

1. Wal-Mart's plans for its Great Value food line include new packaging, an 800 number for consumers, reformulated recipes, and more prominent merchandise guarantees. How will these product changes influence customers' buying decisions?
2. Customers will likely remain unaware of the store's "win, play, show" categories. How will the new strategy affect sales?

Sources: Warren Thayer, "Changes in the Wind at Wal-Mart," *Refrigerated and Frozen Foods,* February 17, 2009, http://www.rffretailer.com; "Wal-Mart's Same-Store Sales Rise in January," *Forbes,* February 5, 2009, http://www.forbes.com; "Merchants Ensure that Categories 'Win, Play, or Show," *MMR,* December 15, 2008, http://findarticles.com; Christopher Palmeri, "Wal-Mart Is Up for this Downturn," *BusinessWeek,* October 30, 2008, p. 34; Kimberly Morrison, "Wal-Mart Pursues a Brand Identity," *The Morning News,* September 4, 2008, http://www.nwaonline.net.

brand manager for Mattel. "We found that with girls 7 to 12, they love the online experience. This is a fusion of those worlds."[10]

Stages in New-Product Development

New-product development is expensive, time consuming, and risky, because only about one-third of new products become success stories. Products can fail for many reasons. Some are not properly developed and tested, some are poorly packaged, and others lack adequate promotional support or distribution or do not satisfy a consumer need or want. Even successful products eventually reach the end of the decline stage and must be replaced with new-product offerings.

Most of today's newly developed items are aimed at satisfying specific consumer demands. New-product development is becoming increasingly efficient and cost-effective because marketers use a systematic approach in developing new products. As Figure 13.3 shows, the new-product development process has six stages. Each stage requires a "go/no-go" decision by management before moving on to subsequent stages. Because items that go through each development stage only to be rejected at one of the final stages involve significant investments

Figure 13.3

Process for Developing New Goods and Services

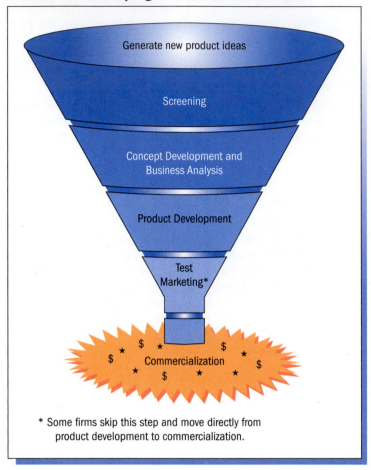

Generate new product ideas

Screening

Concept Development and Business Analysis

Product Development

Test Marketing*

Commercialization

* Some firms skip this step and move directly from product development to commercialization.

in both time and money, the sooner decision makers can identify a marginal product and drop it from further consideration, the less time and money will be wasted.

The starting point in the new-product development process is generating ideas for new offerings. Ideas come from many sources, including customer suggestions, suppliers, employees, research scientists, marketing research, inventors outside the firm, and competitive products. The most successful ideas are directly related to satisfying customer needs. Dannon introduced a yogurt product called Activia after its researchers realized that they had identified a bacteria that could be added to yogurt to aid customers' digestion. Consumers ate it up—literally. Industry experts report that Activia is one of the most successful food product launches in recent years.[11]

In the second stage, screening eliminates ideas that do not mesh with overall company objectives or cannot be developed given the company's resources. Some firms hold open discussions of new-product ideas with specialists who work in different functional areas in the organization.

During the concept development and business analysis phase, further screening occurs. The analysis involves assessing the new product's potential sales, profits, growth rate, and competitive strengths and determining whether it fits with the company's product, distribution, and promotional resources. *Concept testing*—marketing research designed to solicit initial consumer reaction to new-product ideas—may be used at this stage. For example, potential consumers might be asked about proposed brand names and other methods of product identification. *Focus groups* are formal sessions in which consumers meet with marketers to discuss what they like or dislike about current products and perhaps test or sample a new offering to provide some immediate feedback.

Next, an actual product is developed, subjected to a series of tests, and revised. Functioning prototypes or detailed descriptions of the product may be created. These designs are the joint responsibility of the firm's development staff and its marketers, who provide feedback on consumer reactions to the proposed product design, color, and other physical features. The U.S. Army recently developed a new uniform at the Army's Soldier Systems Center in Natick, Massachusetts. But to learn if the uniform was really up to standards, the center outfitted the Third Brigade, Second Infantry, in a prototype during a deployment overseas. The soldiers reported that they liked the new digital-pixel camouflage, a collar that does not chafe the neck, and expansion pleats along the shoulders for freedom of movement.[12]

test marketing
introduction of a new product supported by a complete marketing campaign to a selected city or TV coverage area to examine both consumer responses to the new offering and the marketing effort used to support it.

Test marketing introduces a new product supported by a complete marketing campaign to a selected city or TV coverage area. Marketers look for a location or television coverage area with a manageable size, where residents match their target market's demographic profile, to test their product. During the test marketing stage, the item is sold in a limited area while the company examines both consumer responses to the new offering and the marketing effort used to support it. Test market results can help managers determine the product's likely performance in a full-scale introduction. Some firms skip test marketing, however, because of concerns that the test could reveal their product strategies to the competition. Also, the expense of doing limited production

Table 13.1		The Five Worst Cars in the Last 100 Years
Rank	**Auto**	**Typical Owner Comment**
1	Yugo	"At least it had heated rear windows—so your hands would stay warm while you pushed."
2	Chevy Vega	"Burned so much oil, it was singlehandedly responsible for the formation of OPEC."
3	Ford Pinto	"The car would do 75 mph in 2nd gear, shaking apart and sounding like a bat out of hell. In 4th gear, the top speed was 70 mph. What's wrong with this picture? You do the math."
4	AMC Gremlin	"Calling it a pregnant roller skate would be kind."
5	Chevy Chevette	"If I got on the Interstate without being run over, the car would creep toward 55. About an hour later, I'd reach it. Then the shaking would begin."

Source: Reported in "Car Talk," http://www.cartalk.com, accessed March 24, 2009.

runs of complex products such as a new auto or refrigerator is sometimes so high that the test marketing stage is skipped and the development process moves directly to the next stage.

In the final stage, commercialization, the product is made available in the marketplace. Sometimes this stage is referred to as a product launch. Considerable planning goes into this stage, because the firm's distribution, promotion, and pricing strategies must all be geared to support the new product offering. After several years of distributing packets of its Pur water purifying powder to developing countries where clean water is scarce, Procter & Gamble marketers realized that the single-use packets would be ideal for camping, fishing, picnics, and other outdoor activities where drinkable water might not be available. So in a venture with Reliance Products, which makes reusable water containers and other outdoor products, P&G began selling the packets commercially.[13]

The need for a steady stream of new products to offer the firm's customers, the chances of product failure, and the tens of millions of dollars needed to complete a successful new-product launch make new-product development a vital process for 21st-century firms. However, as Table 13.1 illustrates, success is not guaranteed until the new-product offering achieves customer acceptance. Microsoft introduced a virtual character called Bob that was designed to improve the Program Manager interface for Windows, but it just never caught on. Another computer device was supposed to bring the sense of smell to online shopping or browsing. But the company, DigiScent, didn't think through its plan carefully. Aside from rejecting the idea of being assaulted with unwanted aromas in addition to pop-up ads, consumers turned a thumbs-down on the product's name—iSmell.[14]

Assessment Check ✓

1. What are the stages of the new-product development process?

2. Where do ideas for new products come from?

Product Identification

A major aspect of developing a successful new product involves methods used for identifying a product and distinguishing it from competing offerings. Both tangible goods and intangible services are identified by brands, brand names, and trademarks. A **brand** is a name, term, sign, symbol, design, or some combination thereof used to identify the products of one firm and to differentiate them from competitive offerings. Tropicana, Pepsi, and Gatorade are all made by PepsiCo, but a unique combination of name, symbol, and package design distinguishes each brand from the others.

brand name, term, sign, symbol, design, or some combination that identifies the products of one firm and differentiates them from competitors' offerings.

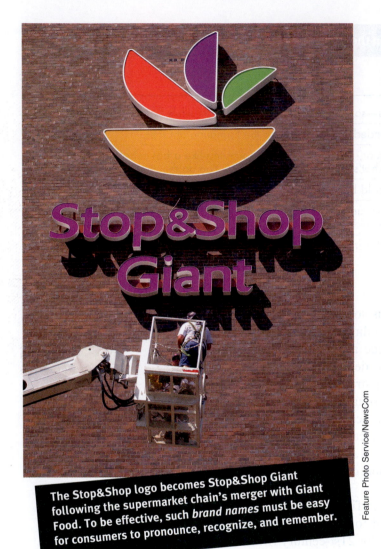

The Stop&Shop logo becomes Stop&Shop Giant following the supermarket chain's merger with Giant Food. To be effective, such *brand names* must be easy for consumers to pronounce, recognize, and remember.

Feature Photo Service/NewsCom

A **brand name** is that part of the brand consisting of words or letters included in a name used to identify and distinguish the firm's offerings from those of competitors. The brand name is the part of the brand that can be vocalized. Many brand names, such as Coca-Cola, McDonald's, American Express, Google, and Nike, are famous around the world. Likewise, the "golden arches" brand mark of McDonald's also is widely recognized.

A **trademark** is a brand that has been given legal protection. The protection is granted solely to the brand's owner. Trademark protection includes not only the brand name but also design logos, slogans, packaging elements, and product features such as color and shape. A well-designed trademark, such as the Nike "swoosh," can make a definite difference in how positively consumers perceive a brand.

Selecting an Effective Brand Name

Good brands are easy to pronounce, recognize, and remember: Crest, Visa, and Avis are examples. Global firms face a real problem in selecting brand names, because an excellent brand name in one country may prove disastrous in another. Most languages have a short *a,* so Coca-Cola is pronounceable almost anywhere. But an advertising campaign for E-Z washing machines failed in the United Kingdom because the British pronounce *z* as "zed."

Brand names should also convey the right image to the buyer. One effective technique is to create a name that links the product with its positioning strategy. The name Dial reinforces the concept of 24-hour protection; Dove soap and beauty products give an impression of mildness, and Taster's Choice instant coffee supports the promotional claim "Tastes and smells like ground roast coffee."

Brand names also must be legally protectable. Trademark law specifies that brand names cannot contain words in general use, such as *television* or *automobile.* Generic words—words that describe a type of product—cannot be used exclusively by any organization. On the other hand, if a brand name becomes so popular that it passes into common language and turns into a generic word, the company can no longer use it as a brand name. Once upon a time, aspirin, linoleum, and zipper were exclusive brand names, but today they have become generic terms and are no longer legally protectable.

Brand Categories

A brand offered and promoted by a manufacturer is known as a **manufacturer's** (or **national**) **brand.** Examples are Tide, Cheerios, Gatorade, Fossil, and Nike. But not all brand names belong to manufacturers; some are the property of retailers or distributors. A **private** (or **store**) **brand** identifies a product that is not linked to the manufacturer but instead carries a wholesaler's or retailer's label. Sears's Craftsman tools and Wal-Mart's Ol' Roy dog food are examples.

Another branding decision marketers must make is whether to use a family branding strategy or an individual branding strategy. A **family brand** is a single brand name used for several related products. KitchenAid, Johnson & Johnson, Hewlett-Packard, and Dole use a family name for their entire line of products. When a firm using family branding introduces a new product, both customers and retailers recognize the familiar brand name. The promotion of individual products within a line benefits all the products because the family brand is well known.

Other firms use an **individual branding** strategy by giving each product within a line a different name. For example, Procter & Gamble has individual brand names for its different laundry detergents, including Tide, Cheer, and Dash. Each brand targets a unique market segment. Consumers who want a cold-water detergent can choose Cheer over Tide or Dash, instead of purchasing a competitor's brand. Individual branding also builds competition within a firm and enables the company to increase overall sales.

Brand Loyalty and Brand Equity

Brands achieve varying consumer familiarity and acceptance. While a homeowner may insist on Anderson windows when renovating, the consumer buying a loaf of bread may not prefer any brand. Consumer loyalty increases a brand's value, so marketers try to strengthen brand loyalty. When a brand image suffers, marketers try to re-create a positive image.

BRAND LOYALTY Marketers measure brand loyalty in three stages: brand recognition, brand preference, and brand insistence. *Brand recognition* is brand acceptance strong enough that the consumer is aware of the brand, but not strong enough to cause a preference over other brands. A consumer might have heard of L'Oréal hair care products, for instance, without necessarily preferring them to Redken. Advertising, free samples, and discount coupons are among the most common ways to increase brand recognition.

Brand preference occurs when a consumer chooses one firm's brand over a competitor's. At this stage, the consumer usually relies on previous experience in selecting the product. Furniture and other home furnishings fall into this category. A shopper who purchased an IKEA dining room table and chairs and was satisfied with them is likely to return to purchase a bedroom set. While there, this shopper might pick up a set of mixing bowls for the kitchen or a lamp for the family room—because he or she knows and likes the IKEA brand. *Brand insistence* is the ultimate degree of brand loyalty, in which the consumer will look for it at another outlet, special-order it from a dealer, order by mail, or search the Internet. Shoppers who insist on IKEA products for their homes may drive an hour or two—making a day excursion of the venture—to visit an IKEA store.[15]

Good design can make the everyday a little better.

IKEA
Everyday Fabulous Exhibit

IKEA installed this clever showpiece, meant to look like a bus stop, in New York City during Design Week. The retailer of affordable, well-designed contemporary furniture enjoys *brand insistence*—the ultimate expression of brand loyalty. For devoted IKEA fans, no other brand will do.

Feature Photo Service/NewsCom

Brand-building strategies were once limited to the consumer realm, but now they are becoming more important for B2B brands as well. Intel, Xerox, IBM, and service providers such as Manpower and ServiceMaster are among the suppliers who have built brand names among business customers.

BRAND EQUITY Brand loyalty is at the heart of <mark>brand equity,</mark> the added value that a respected and successful name gives to a product. This value results from a combination of factors, including awareness, loyalty, and perceived quality, as well as any feelings or images the customer associates with the brand. High brand equity offers financial advantages to a firm, because the product commands a relatively large market share and sometimes reduces price sensitivity, generating higher profits. Figure 13.4 shows the world's ten most valuable brands and their estimated worth.

Brand awareness means the product is the first one that comes to mind when a product category is mentioned. If someone says "coffee," do you think of Starbucks, Dunkin' Donuts, or Folgers? Brand association is the link between a brand and other favorable images. In one survey of 1,000 undergraduate students, respondents were asked where they thought certain brands originated and then make statements about the quality of those brands. Researchers discovered that participants tended to mistakenly identify well-known brands as Japanese, American, or German. For instance, they thought Nokia was Japanese, when in fact the company is based in Finland. They thought Adidas was from the United States, when it is actually German. In addition, students who identified Nokia as Japanese gave the company a high quality rating because they associated Japan with quality products.[16]

Large companies have typically assigned the task of managing a brand's marketing strategies to a *brand manager,* who may also be called a *product manager* at some firms. This marketing professional plans and implements the balance of promotional, pricing, distribution, and product arrangements that leads to strong brand equity. A **category manager,** a newer concept, oversees an entire group of products. Unlike traditional brand or product managers, category managers have profit responsibility for their product group. These managers are assisted by associates, usually called *analysts.* Part of the shift to category management was initiated by large retailers, which realized they could benefit from the marketing muscle of large grocery and household goods producers such as Kraft and Procter & Gamble. As a result, producers began to focus their attention on in-store merchandising instead of mass-market advertising. A few years ago, Kraft reorganized its sales force so that each representative was responsible for a retailer's needs instead of pushing a single brand.

A <mark>category advisor</mark> functions in the B2B context. This vendor is the major supplier designated by a business customer to assume responsibility for dealing with all the other vendors for a project and presenting the entire package to the business buyer.

brand equity added value that a respected and successful name gives to a product.

category advisor vendor that is designated by the business customer as the major supplier to deal with all other suppliers for a special purchase and to present the entire package to the business buyer.

Figure 13.4

The World's Ten Most Valuable Brands (billions)

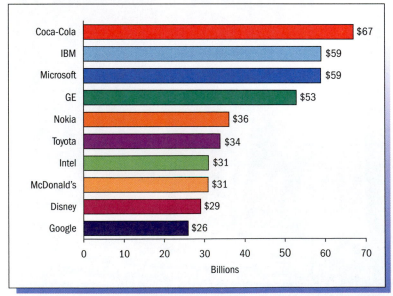

Coca-Cola	$67
IBM	$59
Microsoft	$59
GE	$53
Nokia	$36
Toyota	$34
Intel	$31
McDonald's	$31
Disney	$29
Google	$26

Source: Data from "The 100 Top Brands," *BusinessWeek,* September 29, 2008, http://www.businessweek.com, accessed March 24, 2009.

Packages and Labels

Packaging and labels are important in product identification. They also play an important role in a firm's overall product strategy. Packaging affects the durability, image, and convenience of an item and is responsible for one of the biggest costs in many consumer products. Due to a growing demand to produce smaller, more environmentally friendly packages, box manufacturers and chemical companies are now working harder to create more compact packaging that is made from renewable sources and is recyclable. Wal-Mart has been a leader in the push for "greener" packaging. Recently, the company announced an initiative to reduce its packaging by 5 percent in the next five years. That move could not only be helpful to the environment but could also save the company about $3.4 billion. "If you go to a smaller package, it means you can put more of them in a shipping container, which means you can get more product on a truck; it lowers the amount of energy and fuel used to transport the product," explains Robert Anstine, vice president of marketing at International Paper Company, which is working with Wal-Mart on the program.[17]

Choosing the right package is especially crucial in international marketing because marketers must be aware of such factors as language variations and cultural preferences. Consumers in African nations often prefer bold colors, but use of the country's flag colors may be problematic. Some countries frown on other uses of their flag. Also, in Africa red is often associated with death or witchcraft. Package size can vary according to the purchasing patterns and market conditions of a country. In countries with small refrigerators, people may want to buy their beverages one at a time rather than in six-packs. Package weight is another important issue, because shipping costs are often based on weight.

Labeling is an integral part of the packaging process as well. In the United States, labeling must meet federal laws requiring companies to provide enough information to allow consumers to make value comparisons among competitive products and, in the case of food packaging, provide nutrition information on the label. Marketers who ship products to other countries have to comply with labeling requirements in those nations. This means knowing the answers to such questions as the following:

- Should the labels be in more than one language?

- Should ingredients be specified?

- Do the labels give enough information about the product to meet government standards?

While the Food and Drug Administration (FDA) is considering whether symbols containing nutrition information

PepsiCo's Smart Spot label identifies Lay's baked chips as a low-fat product. Busy consumers appreciate easy-to-read labels that shorten their shopping trips.

© R. Alcorn, photographed for John Wiley & Sons

should be added to food labels, some companies have already gone ahead with the move. PepsiCo applies its "Smart Spot" symbol to Diet Pepsi, Baked Lay's chips, and other low-calorie or low-fat products. Portland, Maine–based supermarket chain Hannaford Brothers uses a 0-to-3 star system to rate the nutritional value of the food items it sells. Consumers report that they like the labeling system because it gives them more information quickly on the ingredients. An added bonus could be that the symbols also become recognizable as part of a firm's brand.[18]

Another important aspect of packaging and labeling is the *Universal Product Code (UPC)*, the bar code read by optical scanners that print the name of the item and the price on a receipt. For many stores, these identifiers are useful not just for packaging and labeling but also for simplifying and speeding retail transactions and for evaluating customer purchases and controlling inventory. Radio-frequency identification (RFID) technology—embedded chips that can broadcast their product information to receivers—may replace UPC bar codes, however, as we'll discuss later in this chapter.

Assessment Check

1. Differentiate among a brand, a brand name, and a trademark.
2. Define *brand equity*.

Distribution Strategy

The next element of the marketing mix, **distribution strategy,** deals with the marketing activities and institutions involved in getting the right good or service to the firm's customers. Distribution decisions involve modes of transportation, warehousing, inventory control, order processing, and selection of marketing channels. Marketing channels typically are made up of intermediaries such as retailers and wholesalers that move a product from producer to final purchaser.

The two major components of an organization's distribution strategy are distribution channels and physical distribution. **Distribution channels** are the paths that products—and title to them—follow from producer to consumer or business user. They are the means by which all organizations distribute their goods and services. **Physical distribution** is the actual movement of these products from the producer to the user. Physical distribution covers a broad range of activities, including customer service, transportation, inventory control, materials handling, order processing, and warehousing.

distribution channel
path through which products—and legal ownership of them—flow from producer to consumers or business users.

physical distribution
actual movement of products from producer to consumers or business users.

Distribution Channels

In their first decision for distribution channel selection, marketers choose which type of channel will best meet both their firm's marketing objectives and the needs of their customers. As shown in Figure 13.5, marketers can choose either a **direct distribution channel,** which carries goods directly from producer to consumer or business user, or distribution channels that involve several different marketing intermediaries. A *marketing intermediary* (also called a *middleman*) is a business firm that moves goods between producers and consumers or business users. Marketing intermediaries perform various functions that help the distribution channel operate smoothly, such as buying, selling, storing, and transporting products; sorting and grading bulky items; and providing information to other channel members. The two main categories of marketing intermediaries are wholesalers and retailers.

Figure 13.5   Alternative Distribution Channels

Consumer Goods

Producer				Consumer
Producer			Retailer	Consumer
Producer		Wholesaler	Retailer	Consumer
Producer	Agent/Broker	Wholesaler	Retailer	Consumer

Business Goods

Producer			Business User
Producer	Agent/Broker		Business User
Producer		Wholesaler	Business User
Producer	Agent/Broker	Wholesaler	Business User

Services

| Service Provider | | Consumer or Business User |
| Service Provider | Agent/Broker | Consumer or Business User |

No one channel suits every product. The best choice depends on the circumstances of the market and on customer needs. The most appropriate channel choice may also change over time as new opportunities arise and marketers strive to maintain their competitiveness. When you're on your way to school or work, sometimes you just want to grab one piece of fruit to eat along the way. The trouble is, usually you have to buy an entire bunch of bananas or bag of apples, and you may have to go to the supermarket. Chiquita Brands is trying to change that by working with convenience stores, coffee shops, drugstores, and other convenience outlets to place single ripe bananas where consumers can grab one instead of a bag of chips. Marketing research revealed that consumers would eat more bananas if they were available in more locations, so Chiquita is listening to the request. "This allows us to meet consumer demand for eating more bananas," says Chiquita spokesman Mike Mitchell. "And it's great for Chiquita because we can charge a premium price."[19]

DIRECT DISTRIBUTION The shortest and simplest means of connecting producers and customers is direct contact between the two parties. This approach is most common in the B2B market. Consumers who buy fresh fruits and vegetables at rural roadside stands use direct distribution, as do services ranging from banking and ten-minute oil changes to ear piercing and Mary Kay Cosmetics.

"They Said It"

"The universe is really big. It's even bigger than Wal-Mart."

—Richard Belzer (b. 1944)
American comedian

Direct distribution is commonly found in the marketing of relatively expensive, complex products that may require demonstrations. Most major B2B products such as installations, accessory equipment, component parts, business services, and even raw materials are typically marketed through direct contacts between producers and business buyers. The Internet has also made direct distribution an attractive option for many retail companies and service providers. Netflix allows movie enthusiasts to rent DVDs through a U.S. call center, and recently it has begun to offer instant viewing of movies online. The firm actually eliminated its e-mail ordering system because it was not as efficient as Netflix hoped it would be. However, CEO Reed Hastings predicts that direct downloading of movies from the Internet will increase a great deal in the next few years, particularly among consumers ages 25 and younger.[20]

DISTRIBUTION CHANNELS USING MARKETING INTERMEDIARIES Although direct channels allow simple and straightforward connections between producers and their customers, the list of channel alternatives in Figure 13.5 suggests that direct distribution is not the best choice in every instance. Some products sell in small quantities for relatively low prices to thousands of widely scattered consumers. Makers of such products cannot cost effectively contact each of their customers, so they distribute products through specialized intermediaries called *wholesalers* and *retailers*.

Although you might think that adding intermediaries to the distribution process would increase the final cost of products, more often than not this choice actually lowers consumer prices. Intermediaries such as wholesalers and retailers often add significant value to a product as it moves through the distribution channel. They do so by creating utility, providing additional services, and reducing costs.

Marketing utility is created when intermediaries help ensure that products are available for sale when and where customers want to purchase them. If you want something warm to eat on a cold winter night, you don't call up Campbell Soup and ask them to ship a can of chicken noodle soup. Instead, you go to the nearest grocery store, where you find utility in the form of product availability. In addition, intermediaries perform such important services as transporting merchandise to convenient locations. Finally, by representing numerous producers, a marketing intermediary can cut the costs of buying and selling. As Figure 13.6 shows, if four manufacturers each sold directly to four consumers, this would require 16 separate transactions. Adding a marketing intermediary, such as a retailer, to the exchange cuts the number of necessary transactions to 8.

Figure 13.6

Reducing Transactions through Marketing Intermediaries

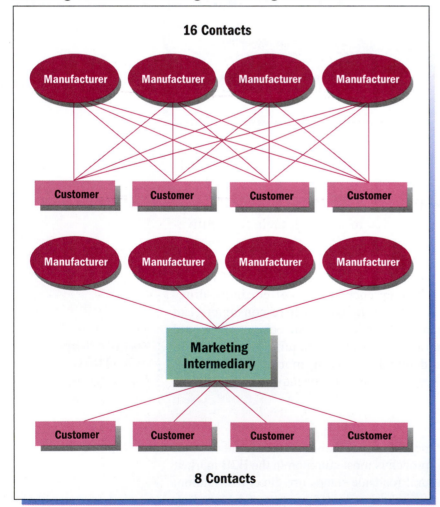

Wholesaling

A **wholesaler** is a distribution channel member that sells primarily to retailers, other wholesalers, or business users. For instance, Sysco is a wholesaler that buys food products from producers and then resells them to restaurants, hotels, and other institutions in the United States and Canada.

Wholesaling is a crucial part of the distribution channel for many products, particularly consumer goods and business supplies. Wholesaling intermediaries can be classified on the basis of ownership; some are owned by manufacturers, some are owned by retailers, and others are independently owned. The United States has about 435,000 wholesalers, 90 percent of which have fewer than 20 employees. Approximately 20 percent of wholesalers are self-employed.[21]

Manufacturer-Owned Wholesaling Intermediaries

A manufacturer's marketing manager may decide to distribute goods directly through company-owned facilities to control distribution or customer service. Firms operate two main types of manufacturer-owned wholesaling intermediaries: sales branches and sales offices.

Sales branches stock the products they distribute and fill orders from their inventories. They also provide offices for sales representatives. Sales branches are common in the chemical, petroleum products, motor vehicle, and machine and equipment industries.

A *sales office* is exactly what its name implies: an office for a producer's salespeople. Manufacturers set up sales offices in various regions to support local selling efforts and improve customer service. Some kitchen and bath fixture manufacturers maintain showrooms to display their products. Builders and decorators can visit these showrooms to see how the items would look in place. Unlike sales branches, however, sales offices do not store any inventory. When a customer orders from a showroom or other sales office, the merchandise is delivered from a separate warehouse.

Independent Wholesaling Intermediaries

An independent wholesaling intermediary is a business that represents a number of different manufacturers and makes sales calls on retailers, manufacturers, and other business accounts. Independent wholesalers are classified as either merchant wholesalers or agents and brokers, depending on whether they take title to the products they handle.

Merchant wholesalers, like apparel wholesaler WholesaleSarong.com, are independently owned wholesaling intermediaries that take title to the goods they handle. Within this category, a *full-function merchant wholesaler* provides a complete assortment of services for retailers or industrial buyers, such as warehousing, shipping, and even financing. A subtype of full-function merchant is a *rack jobber,* such as Ohio-based Arrow Distributing, which handles distribution of CDs and DVDs to retail stores. This type of firm stocks, displays, and services particular retail products, such as paperback books or greeting cards in a drugstore or supermarket. Usually, the retailer receives a commission based on actual sales as payment for providing merchandise space to a rack jobber.

A *limited-function merchant wholesaler* also takes legal title to the products it handles, but it provides fewer services to the retailers to which it sells. Some limited-function merchant wholesalers only warehouse products but do not offer delivery service. Others warehouse and deliver products but provide no financing. One type of limited-function merchant wholesaler is a *drop shipper* such as Kate Aspen, an Atlanta-based wholesaler of wedding favors. Drop shippers also operate in such industries as coal and lumber, characterized by bulky products for which no single producer can provide a complete assortment. They give access to many related goods by contacting numerous producers and negotiating the best possible prices. Cost considerations call for producers to ship such products directly to the drop shipper's customers.

Another category of independent wholesaling intermediaries consists of *agents* and *brokers.* They may or may not take possession of the goods they handle, but they never take title, working mainly to bring buyers and sellers together. Stockbrokers such as Charles Schwab and real estate agents such as RE/MAX perform functions similar to those of agents and brokers, but at the retail level. They do not take possession of or title to the sellers' property; instead, they create time and ownership utility for both buyer and seller by helping carry out transactions.

Manufacturers' reps act as independent sales forces by representing the manufacturers of related but noncompeting products. These agent intermediaries, sometimes referred to as *manufacturers' agents,* receive commissions based on a percentage of the sales they make.

Retailer-Owned Cooperatives and Buying Offices

Retailers sometimes band together to form their own wholesaling organizations. Such organizations can take the form of either a buying group or a cooperative. The participating retailers set up the new operation to reduce costs or to provide some special service that is not readily available in the marketplace. To achieve cost savings through quantity purchases, independent retailers may form a buying group that negotiates bulk sales with manufacturers. One such buying group is Florida-based Retail Advantage Group, which buys products for its member hospital gift shops and gift shop chains. Members join for a year at a time and can receive up to 10 percent discounts on orders they place, while remaining free to buy from any other vendors.[22] In a cooperative, an independent group of retailers may decide to band together to share functions such as shipping or warehousing.

Retailing

retailer channel member that sells goods and services to individuals for their own use rather than for resale.

Retailers, in contrast to wholesalers, are distribution channel members that sell goods and services to individuals for their own use rather than for resale. Consumers usually buy their food, clothing, shampoo, furniture, and appliances from some type of retailer. The supermarket where you buy your groceries may have bought some of its items from a wholesaler such as Unified Grocers and then resold them to you.

Retailers are the final link—the so-called last three feet—of the distribution channel. Because they are often the only channel members that deal directly with consumers, it is essential that retailers remain alert to changing shopper needs. For instance, soaring gas prices affect consumers' budgets, so they may make fewer trips to the mall or cut back on nonessential purchases. As a result, retailers may need to offer special sales or events to lure customers to their shops. It is also important for retailers to keep pace with developments in the fast-changing business environment, such as the disruption in delivery of supplies from widespread wildfires or storms.

Nonstore Retailers

Two categories of retailers exist: store and nonstore. As Figure 13.7 shows, nonstore retailing includes four forms: direct-response retailing, Internet retailing, automatic merchandising, and direct selling. *Direct-response retailing* reaches prospective customers through catalogs; telemarketing; and even magazine, newspaper, and television ads. Shoppers order merchandise by mail, telephone, computer, and fax machine and then receive home delivery or pick the merchandise up at a local store. Lands' End has long stood out as a highly successful direct-response retailer; its well-known clothing catalog and stellar customer service have set the standard for this type of distribution channel. With the retailer's purchase by Sears, however, customers can now see, feel, and try on its clothing at Lands' End Shops in Sears locations around the country.

Internet retailing, the second form of nonstore retailing, has grown rapidly. Tens of thousands of retailers have set up shop online, with sales growing at a rate of about 5 percent a year (as compared with declines in total retail sales). Today, online sales account for more than 3 percent of total retail sales.[23] A severe shakeout saw hundreds of Internet enterprises shut down during the first few years of the 21st century, but firms that survived have stronger business models than those that failed. Two examples of success by pure dot-coms are Amazon and eBay. A major shift in retailing has seen traditional brick-and-mortar retailers competing with pure dot-com start-ups by setting up their own Web sites as an option for shoppers. Nordstrom, JCPenney, and Wal-Mart report strong online sales. Shopping sites are among the most popular Internet destinations, and sales of clothing and DVDs in particular have risen.

The last two forms of nonstore retailing are automatic merchandising and direct selling. *Automatic merchandising* provides convenience through the use of vending machines. ATMs may soon join the ranks of vending machines as banks find new ways to compete for customers. Some ATMs offer extra services such as check cashing and stamps, as well as concert tickets and road maps. Future ATMs will be able to connect wirelessly to cell phones to allow customers to download and pay for games and music. *Direct selling* includes direct-to-consumer sales by Pampered Chef kitchen representatives and salespeople for Silpada sterling silver jewelry through party-plan selling methods. Both are forms of direct selling.

Companies that previously relied heavily on telemarketing in generating new customers have encountered consumer resistance to intrusive phone calls. Among the growing barriers are caller ID, call-blocking devices such as the TeleZapper, and the National Do Not Call list, which made it illegal for most companies to call people who are registered. As a result, dozens of companies, including telecommunications and regional utilities, have sent direct-mail pieces to promote such services as phones, cable television, and natural gas distributors.

Figure 13.7 — Types of Nonstore Retailing

Nonstore Retailers

Direct-Response Retailing
Examples: sales through catalogs, telemarketing, and magazine, newspaper, and television ads

Internet Retailing
Examples: sales through virtual storefronts, Web-based sellers, and the Web sites of brick-and-mortar retailers

Direct Selling
Examples: direct manufacturer-to-consumer sales through party plans and direct contact by Amway, Home & Garden Party decorations, and Electrolux vacuum cleaner salespeople

Automatic Merchandising
Examples: sales of such consumer products as candy, soft drinks, ice, chewing gum, sandwiches, and soup through vending machines

This Proactiv Solution kiosk dispenses skin care products automatically, just as an ATM dispenses cash. *Automatic merchandising* is a form of nonstore retailing.

PRNewsFoto/Zoom Systems/NewsCom

Store Retailers

In-store sales still outpace nonstore retailing methods like direct-response retailing and Internet selling. Store retailers range in size from tiny newsstands to multistory department stores and multiacre warehouselike retailers such as Sam's Club. Table 13.2 lists the different types of store retailers, with examples of each type. Clearly, there are many approaches to retailing and a variety of services, prices, and product lines offered by each retail outlet.

THE WHEEL OF RETAILING Retailers are subject to constant change as new stores replace older establishments. In a process called the **wheel of retailing,** new retailers enter the market by offering lower prices made possible through reductions in service. Supermarkets and discount houses, for example, gained their initial market footholds through low-price, limited-service appeals. These new entries gradually add services as they grow and ultimately become targets for new retailers.

As Figure 13.8 shows, most major developments in retailing appear to fit the wheel pattern. The low-price, limited-service strategy characterized supermarkets, catalog retailers, discount stores, and, most recently, Internet retailers and giant "big-box" stores, such as PetSmart, Borders, and Office Depot. Most of these retailers have raised price levels gradually as they added new services. Corner grocery stores gave way to supermarkets and then to warehouse clubs such as Costco or BJ's. Department stores lost market share to discount clothing retailers such as Target and Marshalls. Independent bookstores have lost business to giant chains like Barnes & Noble, Books-A-Million, Borders, and such online-only sellers as Amazon.com and Buy.com.

Even though the wheel of retailing does not fit every pattern of retail evolution—for example, automatic merchandising has always been a relatively high-priced method of retailing—it does

Table 13.2	Types of Retail Stores	
Store Type	**Description**	**Example**
Specialty store	Offers complete selection in a narrow line of merchandise	Bass Pro Shops, Dick's Sporting Goods, Williams-Sonoma
Convenience store	Offers staple convenience goods, easily accessible locations, long store hours, and rapid checkouts	7-Eleven, Mobil Mart, QuikTrip
Discount store	Offers wide selection of merchandise at low prices; off-price discounters offer designer or brand-name merchandise	Target, Wal-Mart, Nordstrom Rack, Marshalls
Warehouse club	Large, warehouse-style store selling food and general merchandise at discount prices to membership cardholders	Costco, Sam's Club, BJ's
Factory outlet	Manufacturer-owned store selling seconds, production overruns, or discontinued lines	Adidas, Coach, Pottery Barn, Ralph Lauren
Supermarket	Large, self-service retailer offering a wide selection of food and nonfood merchandise	Safeway, Whole Foods Market, Kroger
Supercenter	Giant store offering food and general merchandise at discount prices	Wal-Mart Supercenter, Super Target
Department store	Offers a wide variety of merchandise selections (furniture, cosmetics, housewares, clothing) and many customer services	Nordstrom, Macy's, Neiman Marcus

give retail managers a general idea of what is likely to occur during the evolution of retailing. It also shows that business success involves the "survival of the fittest." Retailers that fail to change fail to survive.

How Retailers Compete

Retailers compete with each other in many ways. Nonstore retailers focus on making the shopping experience as convenient as possible. Shoppers at stores such as Saks Fifth Avenue enjoy a luxurious atmosphere and personal service. In fact, those who visit the new shoe department at the flagship store in New York have the run of the entire eighth floor—with its own Zip code. "It's a marketing strategy," explains the public relations director for Saks. "We wanted the department to be a destination, and that required a Zip code."[24]

Like manufacturers, retailers must develop marketing strategies based on goals and strategic plans. Successful retailers convey images that alert consumers to the stores' identities and the shopping experiences they provide. To create that image, all components of a retailer's strategy must complement each other. After identifying their target markets, retailers must choose merchandising, customer service, pricing, and location strategies that will attract customers in those market segments.

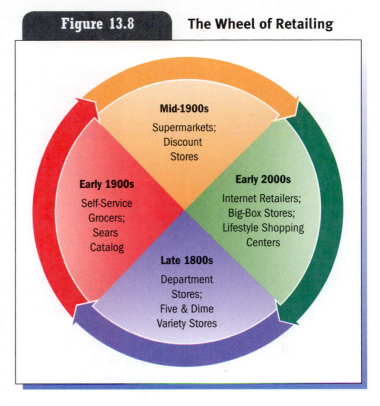

Figure 13.8 **The Wheel of Retailing**

Mid-1900s
Supermarkets; Discount Stores

Early 2000s
Internet Retailers; Big-Box Stores; Lifestyle Shopping Centers

Late 1800s
Department Stores; Five & Dime Variety Stores

Early 1900s
Self-Service Grocers; Sears Catalog

IDENTIFYING A TARGET MARKET The first step in developing a competitive retailing strategy is to select a target market. This choice requires careful evaluation of the size and profit potential of the chosen market segment and the current level of competition for the segment's business. Bargain stores such as Family Dollar target consumers who are extremely price conscious, for example, while convenience stores like 7-Eleven target consumers who want an easy way to purchase items they buy frequently. To attract a younger generation of car buyers, Toyota created the Scion brand of sporty small cars. Scion vehicles sell for under $20,000 and are marketed separately from the company's other brands: Toyota and Lexus. After experimenting with a few hybrid models and finding success with them, Toyota may place all of its hybrid vehicles under the Prius brand, to appeal to environmentally conscious consumers.

SELECTING A PRODUCT STRATEGY Next, the retailer must develop a product strategy to determine the best mix of merchandise to carry to satisfy that market. Retail strategists must decide on the general product categories, product lines, and variety to offer. Sometimes that involves expanding the product mix and sometime it involves contracting it. Nike is considering selling its Nike Bauer Hockey subsidiary, which produces hockey skates, clothing and equipment, along with equipment for in-line skating and street and roller hockey, to concentrate on its general fitness sports lines.[25]

SHAPING A CUSTOMER SERVICE STRATEGY A retailer's customer service strategy focuses on attracting and retaining target customers to maximize sales and profits. Some stores offer a wide variety of services, such as gift wrapping, alterations, returns, interior design services, and delivery. Other stores offer bare-bones customer service, stressing low price instead. Some grocery shoppers, for instance, can find convenience online through a service like Peapod, which handles product selection, packing, and delivery. They can visit a supermarket and make their own selections. Or they can go to a discount supermarket like Minnesota-based Cub Foods, a division of SuperValu, where they not only assemble their orders but also bag their purchases.

SELECTING A PRICING STRATEGY Retailers base their pricing decisions on the costs of purchasing products from other channel members and offering services to customers. Pricing can play a major role in consumers' perceptions of a retailer, and not just because they appreciate low prices. Grocery retailer Trader Joe's offers organic and gourmet foods under its own private labels at rock-bottom prices. Customers enjoy shopping for "Trader Jose's" Mexican specialties and Trader Darwin's nutritional supplements at prices lower than other gourmet or organic markets.[26] Pricing strategy is covered in more detail in Chapter 14.

CHOOSING A LOCATION A good location often marks the difference between success and failure in retailing. The location decision depends on the retailer's size, financial resources, product offerings, competition, and, of course, its target market. Traffic patterns, the visibility of the store's signage, parking, and the location of complementary stores also influence the choice of a retail location. The rivalry between PetSmart and Petco could be described as a dogfight. Petco tends to have smaller stores in greater numbers, located in strip malls, than PetSmart, whose strategy is to build bigger "power centers" right beside other large discount chains. PetSmart recently added pet services—adoption, grooming, day care, and boarding—in some of its stores. Petco uses its stores to promote a broader selection of goods for offbeat pets, such as tarantulas and unusual reptiles.[27]

A *planned shopping center* is a group of retail stores planned, coordinated, and marketed as a unit to shoppers in a geographical trade area. By providing single convenient locations with free parking, shopping centers have largely replaced downtown shopping in many urban areas. But time-pressed consumers are increasingly looking for more efficient ways to shop, including catalogs, Internet retailers, and one-stop shopping at large free-standing stores such as Wal-Mart Supercenters. To lure more customers, shopping centers are recasting themselves as entertainment destinations, with art displays, carousel rides, and musical entertainment. The giant Mall of America in Bloomington, Minnesota, features a seven-acre amusement park and an aquarium.

Shopping malls are well-known magnets for teens, who often meet there to socialize with friends. Businesses want to welcome their teen customers, but sometimes the cluster of teens hanging around the mall causes difficulties for other customers and some retailers, as described in the "Solving an Ethical Controversy" feature.

In recent years, large regional malls have also witnessed a growing shift in shopping center traffic to smaller strip centers, name-brand outlet centers, and *lifestyle centers,* open-air complexes containing retailers that often focus on specific shopper segments and product interests. Lifestyle centers such as Rushmore Crossing in South Dakota represent a microcosm of a small town. Instead of being anchored by one giant department store, lifestyle centers generally take shoppers back outdoors, where they can walk along sidewalks, dine in courtyards, and enjoy a neighborhood atmosphere. "They've become more of a place to spend leisure time, while indoor malls are a place solely to shop," says Erin Hershkowitz of the International Council of Shopping Centers.[28]

BUILDING A PROMOTIONAL STRATEGY A retailer designs advertisements and develops other promotions to stimulate demand and to provide information such as the store's location,

TEENS AT THE MALL: A GOOD MATCH?

For decades, the words teens *and* mall *have been closely linked. But now, some mall managers and executives are rethinking the shopping center's role as a hangout for teens.*

The problem, they say, is that malls packed with unsupervised minors actually deter other shoppers from visiting and making purchases. Walkways and handicapped ramps may be blocked by chatting teens, and some officials say baby strollers have been overturned and seniors jostled by teens engaged in horseplay. So some mall officials are taking action: sending teens home by early evening, unless they are accompanied by an adult. "I hate to call it a curfew," says one chief of police. But that's what many people believe it is.

Should shopping centers and malls be allowed to impose curfews on teens?

PRO

1. If teens are routinely disrupting the activities of other customers, then mall officials should take appropriate action, which may include limiting the hours during which unsupervised teens can occupy the shopping center. "As a business we have an obligation to listen to our customers and retailers, and look out for their best interests," explains one mall manager.
2. The mall should not be responsible for supervising teens while they are shopping. "Some parents just drop their kids off like we're some kind of babysitter," says a mall official. "I tell them they have to go; this isn't a game or a playground. It's a place of business."

CON

1. Teens represent a huge amount of buying power, and it would be unwise to reject them or upset them. Even those who do not spend a lot now will be the big spenders of the future.
2. The majority of teens are well behaved. They shouldn't have to pay for the bad behavior of others.

Summary

For many teens, the mall is a place they can spend time with their friends—without their parents. It also represents a place where they can make their own decisions about purchases. But the behavior of some teens, along with their sheer numbers, is causing mall officials enough concern to try to solve the problem. "Most of our teenage shoppers behave appropriately, but there are groups from time to time that we know like to loiter in the mall on weekends," reports a shopping center manager. Whether we like it or not, more and more malls are looking into restricting teen access at night.

Sources: International Council of Shopping Centers, http://www.icsc.org, accessed March 24, 2009; "Crossroads to Impose Weekend Teen Curfew," National Youth Rights Association, October 18, 2007, http://www.youthrights.org, Julie Rawe, "Bye-Bye, Mall Rats," *Time,* July 9, 2007, pp. 41–42; Betsy Taylor, "Malls Try Teen Curfews to Draw Shoppers," *Associated Press,* April 5, 2007, http://abcnews.go.com, accessed October 13, 2008; Judy Keen, "Malls' Night Restrictions on Teens Paying Off," *USA Today,* March 15, 2007, p. 3A.

Solving an ETHICAL controversy

merchandise offerings, prices, and hours. Starbucks plans and executes several promotions to generate interest in its products. It hosts a national book group where readers can read and discuss books. It also promotes current films and CDs on racks in stores. Starbucks also launched a series of television ads—its first ever—to reach consumers who might not be aware of the Starbucks brand or who might not know that a Starbucks coffeehouse is nearby.[29] Nonstore retailers provide their phone numbers and Web site addresses. More recently, online retailers have scaled back their big advertising campaigns and worked to build traffic through word of mouth and clever promotions. Promotional strategy is also discussed in depth in Chapter 14.

Assessment Check

1. Define *distribution channels*.
2. What is a marketing intermediary?
3. Differentiate between a merchant wholesaler and an agent or broker in terms of title to the goods.
4. What are the elements of a retailer's marketing strategy?

CREATING A STORE ATMOSPHERE A successful retailer closely aligns its merchandising, pricing, and promotion strategies with *store atmospherics,* the physical characteristics of a store and its amenities, to influence consumers' perceptions of the shopping experience. Atmospherics begin with the store's exterior, which may use eye-catching architectural elements and signage to attract customer attention and interest. Interior atmospheric elements include store layout, merchandise presentation, lighting, color, sound, and cleanliness. A high-end store such as Nordstrom, for instance, features high-ceilinged selling areas that spotlight tasteful and meticulously cared-for displays of carefully chosen items of obvious quality. Dick's Sporting Goods, on the other hand, crams an ever-changing array of moderately priced clothing and gear into its warehouselike settings furnished with industrial-style display hardware.

Distribution Channel Decisions and Logistics

Every firm faces two major decisions when choosing how to distribute its goods or services: selecting a specific distribution channel and deciding on the level of distribution intensity. In deciding which distribution channel is most efficient, business managers need to consider four factors: the market, the product, the producer, and the competition. These factors are often interrelated and may change over time. In today's global business environment, strong relationships with customers and suppliers are important for survival. One way of helping cement those relationships is to take the time to thank your customers and partners, as the "Business Etiquette" feature explains.

Selecting Distribution Channels

Market factors may be the most important consideration in choosing a distribution channel. To reach a target market with a small number of buyers or buyers concentrated in a geographical area, the most feasible alternative may be a direct channel. In contrast, if the firm must reach customers who are dispersed or who make frequent small purchases, then the channel may need to incorporate marketing intermediaries to make goods available when and where customers want them.

In general, products that are complex, expensive, custom made, or perishable move through shorter distribution channels involving few—or no—intermediaries. On the other hand, standardized products or items with low unit values usually pass through relatively long distribution channels. Levi's tried selling its basic jeans products through its Web site but quickly realized it was impractical to fill orders for a single order of pants available at local stores. Greek entrepreneur Stelios Haji-Ioannou, however, finds the Internet the perfect channel for easyGroup, the private investment group for his "easy" brand. The company represents a variety of businesses with the "easy" tag—including easyJet.com, easyCar.com, easyJobs.com, and easyPizza.com. Each business offers a no-frills, low-cost approach to service that consumers can order online. EasyJet is one of Europe's biggest Internet retailers, selling 95 percent of its seats online.[30]

Producers that offer a broad product line, with the financial and marketing resources to distribute and promote it, are more likely to choose a shorter channel. Instead of depending on marketing intermediaries, financially strong manufacturers with broad product lines typically use their own sales representatives, warehouses, and credit departments to serve both retailers and consumers.

In many cases, start-up manufacturers turn to direct channels because they can't persuade intermediaries to carry their products, or they want to extend their sales reach. Dale and Thomas is known for its gourmet popcorn flavors, which include peanut butter, caramel, and chocolate. But the firm wanted to spread the word a little farther. So it hired chef Ed Doyle to stir up even more delectable flavors and talk about them on video. Posted on YouTube, the videos have developed a following with consumers. Dale and Thomas marketer Paul Goodman notes that the campaign will probably be extended to blogs and podcasts to reach even more customers directly.[31]

Competitive performance is the fourth key consideration when choosing a distribution channel. A producer loses customers when an intermediary fails to achieve promotion or product delivery. Channels used by established competitors as well as new market entries also can influence decisions. Sometimes, a joint venture between competitors can work well. Best Buy and Apple have teamed up to sell their products under the same roof. Under the agreement, Apple controls its own retail space within Best Buy stores. Although Apple has a well-established retail business, it can't match the size of electronics giant Best Buy. Best Buy benefits by generating more traffic from customers who want to see and buy Apple's innovative products in convenient locations. The strategy has worked well, as the sales of Macs in particular have increased.[32]

Selecting Distribution Intensity

A second key distribution decision involves *distribution intensity*—the number of intermediaries or outlets through which a manufacturer distributes its goods. Only one BMW dealership may be operating in your immediate area, but you can find Coca-Cola everywhere—in supermarkets, convenience stores, gas stations, vending machines, and restaurants. BMW has chosen a different level of distribution intensity than that used for Coca-Cola. In general, market coverage varies along a continuum with three different intensity levels:

1. **Intensive distribution** involves placing a firm's products in nearly every available outlet. Generally, intensive distribution suits low-priced convenience goods such as milk, newspapers, and soft drinks. This kind of market saturation requires cooperation by many intermediaries, including wholesalers and retailers, to achieve maximum coverage.

2. **Selective distribution** is a market-coverage strategy in which a manufacturer selects only a limited number of retailers to distribute its product lines. Selective distribution can reduce total marketing costs and establish strong working relationships within the channel.

3. **Exclusive distribution,** at the other end of the continuum from intensive distribution, limits market coverage in a specific geographical region. The approach suits relatively expensive specialty products such as Rolex watches. Retailers are carefully selected to enhance the product's image to the market and to ensure that well-trained personnel will contribute to customer satisfaction. Although producers may sacrifice some market coverage by granting an exclusive territory to a single intermediary, the decision usually pays off in developing and maintaining an image of quality and prestige.

When companies are offloading excess inventory, even high-priced retailers may look to discounters to help them clear the merchandise from their warehouses. To satisfy consumers' taste for luxury goods, designer outlet malls offer shoppers a chance to buy status items at lower prices. Philadelphia Premium Outlets shopping center contains more than 100 stores carrying such brands as Calphalon kitchenware, Coach handbags, and Neiman Marcus Last Call.[33]

Logistics and Physical Distribution

supply chain sequence of suppliers that contribute to creating a good or service and delivering it to business users and final consumers.

A firm's choice of distribution channels creates the final link in the **supply chain,** the complete sequence of suppliers that contribute to creating a good or service and delivering it to business users and final consumers. The supply chain begins when the raw materials used in production are delivered to the producer and continues with the actual production activities that create finished goods. Finally, the finished goods move through the producer's distribution channels to end customers.

logistics activities involved in controlling the flow of goods, services, and information among members of the supply chain.

The process of coordinating the flow of goods, services, and information among members of the supply chain is called **logistics.** The term originally referred to strategic movements of military troops and supplies. Today, however, it describes all of the business activities involved in the supply chain with the ultimate goal of getting finished goods to customers.

PHYSICAL DISTRIBUTION A major focus of logistics management—identified earlier in the chapter as one of the two basic dimensions of distribution strategy—is *physical distribution,* the activities aimed at efficiently moving finished goods from the production line to the consumer or business buyer. As Figure 13.9 shows, physical distribution is a broad concept that includes transportation and numerous other elements that help link buyers and sellers. An effectively managed physical distribution system can increase customer satisfaction by ensuring reliable movements of products through the supply chain. For instance, Wal-Mart studies the speed with which goods can be shelved once they arrive at the store because strategies that look efficient at the warehouse, such as completely filling pallets with goods, can actually be time-consuming or costly in the aisles.

A technology called *radio-frequency identification (RFID)* relies on a computer chip implanted somewhere on a product or its packaging that emits a low-frequency radio signal identifying the item. The radio signal doesn't require a line of sight to register on the store's computers the way a bar code does, so a hand-held RFID reader can scan crates and cartons without unloading them. Because the chip can store information about the product's progress through the distribution channel, retailers can efficiently manage inventories, maintain stock levels, reduce loss, track stolen goods, and cut costs. The technology is similar to that already used to identify lost pets and speed vehicles through toll booths. Wal-Mart, Target, the U.S. Department of Defense, and the German retailer Metro Group already require their suppliers to use RFID technology. The U.S. Army is now using solar power to activate battery-powered RFIDs, which are particularly useful in remote areas. Automakers are also using RFID technology to improve their production processes by tracking parts and other supplies.[34]

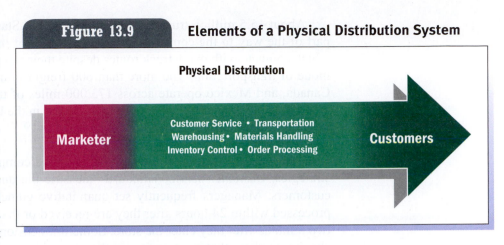

Figure 13.9 Elements of a Physical Distribution System

Warehousing is the physical distribution activity that involves the storage of products. *Materials handling* is moving items within factories, warehouses, transportation terminals, and stores. Inventory control involves managing inventory costs, such as storage facilities, insurance, taxes, and handling. The physical distribution activity of *order processing* includes preparing orders for shipment and receiving orders when shipments arrive.

The wide use of electronic data interchange (EDI) and the constant pressure on suppliers to improve their response time have led to **vendor-managed inventory,** in which the producer and the retailer agree that the producer (or the wholesaler) will determine how much of a product a buyer needs and automatically ship new supplies when needed.

The form of transportation used to ship products depends primarily on the kind of product, the distance involved, and the cost. The logistics manager can choose from a number of companies and modes of transportation. As Table 13.3 shows, the five major transport modes are—in order of total expenditures—trucks (with about 75 percent of total expenditures), railroads (approximately 12 percent), water carriers (6 percent), air freight (4 percent), and pipelines (3 percent). The faster methods typically cost more than the slower ones. Speed, reliable delivery, shipment frequency, location availability, handling flexibility, and cost are all important considerations when choosing the most appropriate mode of transportation.

Table 13.3	Comparison of Transportation Modes					
Mode	Speed	Dependability in Meeting Schedules	Frequency of Shipments	Availability in Different Locations	Flexibility in Handling	Cost
Truck	Fast	High	High	Very extensive	Average	High
Rail	Average	Average	Low	Low	High	Average
Water	Very slow	Average	Very low	Limited	Very high	Very low
Air	Very fast	High	Average	Average	low	Very high
Pipeline	Slow	High	High	Very limited	Very Low	Low

About 15.5 million trucks operate in the United States, carrying most finished goods all or part of the way to the consumer. Nearly 2 million of these are tractor trailers.[35] But railroads, which compete with many truck routes despite their recent loss of market share, are still a viable mode of transportation. The more than 600 freight railroads that operate in the United States, Canada, and Mexico operate across 173,000 miles of track and earn about $42 billion in revenues. Seventy percent of all autos manufactured in the United States travel to their destinations by train, as does 30 percent of the country's grain.[36]

CUSTOMER SERVICE Customer service is a vital component of both product and distribution strategies. *Customer service standards* measure the quality of service a firm provides for its customers. Managers frequently set quantitative guidelines—for example, that all orders be processed within 24 hours after they are received or that salespeople approach shoppers within two minutes after they enter the store. Sometimes customers set their own service standards and choose suppliers that meet or exceed them.

The customer service components of product strategy include warranty and repair service programs. *Warranties* are firms' promises to repair a defective product, refund money paid, or replace a product if it proves unsatisfactory. Repair services are also important. Consumers want to know that help is available if something goes wrong. Those who shop for home computers, for example, often choose retailers that not only feature low prices but also offer repair services and tech support centers. Products with inadequate service backing quickly disappear from the market as a result of word-of-mouth criticism.

Consumers' complaints of the impersonal service they received at Web sites led dot-coms to take a number of steps to "humanize" their customer interactions and deal with complaints. Many Web sites contain button help icons that link the visitor to a representative.

Assessment Check

1. What is distribution intensity?
2. Define *supply chain*.
3. What do customer service standards measure?

What's Ahead

This chapter covered two of the elements of the marketing mix: product and distribution. It introduced the key marketing tasks of developing, marketing, and packaging want-satisfying goods and services. It also focused on the three major components of an organization's distribution strategy: the design of efficient distribution channels; wholesalers and retailers who make up many distribution channels; and logistics and physical distribution. We turn to the remaining two—promotion and pricing—in Chapter 14.

Summary of Learning Goals

1 **Explain marketing's definition of a product and list the components of a product strategy.**

A product is a bundle of physical, service, and symbolic attributes designed to satisfy consumer wants. The marketing conception of a product includes the brand, product image, warranty, service attributes, packaging, and labeling, in addition to the physical or functional characteristics of the good or service.

Assessment Check Answers

1.1 What is a product? A product is a bundle of physical, service, and symbolic attributes designed to satisfy consumer wants.

1.2 What is the marketing view of a product? The marketing view of a product includes the brand, product image, warranty, service attributes, packaging, and labeling, in addition to the physical or functional characteristics of the good or service.

2 **Describe the classification system for consumer and business goods and services.**

Goods and services can be classified as consumer (B2C) or business (B2B) products. Consumer products are those purchased by ultimate consumers for their own use. They can be convenience products, shopping products, or specialty products depending on consumer habits in buying them. Business products are those purchased for use either directly or indirectly in the production of other goods and services for resale. They can be classified as installations, accessory equipment, component parts and materials, raw materials, and supplies. This classification is based on how the items are used and product characteristics. Services can be classified as either consumer or business services.

Assessment Check Answers

2.1 Differentiate among convenience, shopping, and specialty products. Convenience products are items the consumer seeks to purchase frequently, immediately, and with little effort. Shopping products are typically purchased after the buyer has compared competing products in competing stores. Specialty products are those a purchaser is willing to make a special effort to obtain.

2.2 How do business products differ from consumer items? Business products, such as drill presses, are sold to firms or organizations. Consumer products, such as personal care items, are sold to final users.

3 **Distinguish between a product mix and a product line.**

A product mix is the assortment of goods and services a firm offers to individual consumers and B2B users. A product line is a series of related products.

Assessment Check Answers

3.1 What is a product line? A product line is a series of related products.

3.2 What is a product mix? A product mix is the assortment of goods and services a firm offers to individual consumers and B2B users.

4 **Briefly describe each of the four stages of the product life cycle.**

Every successful new product passes through four stages in its product life cycle: introduction, growth, maturity, and decline. In the introduction stage, the firm attempts to elicit demand for the new product. In the product's growth stage, sales climb, and the company earns its initial profits. In the maturity stage, sales reach a saturation level. In the decline stage, both sales and profits decline. Marketers sometimes employ strategies to extend the product life cycle, including increasing the frequency of use, adding new users, finding new uses for the product, and changing package size, labeling, or product quality.

Assessment Check Answers

4.1 What are the stages of the product life cycle? In the introduction stage, the firm attempts to elicit demand for the new product. In the product's growth stage, sales climb, and the company earns its initial profits. In the maturity stage, sales reach a saturation level. In the decline stage, both sales and profits decline.

4.2 What are the marketing implications of each stage? Marketers sometimes employ strategies to extend the product life cycle, including increasing frequency of use, adding new users, finding new uses for the product, and changing package size, labeling, or product quality.

5 **List the stages of the new-product development process.**

Six stages exist in the new-product development process for most products: idea generation, screening, business analysis, product development, test marketing, and commercialization. At each stage, marketers must decide whether to continue to the next stage, modify the new product, or discontinue the development process. Some new products skip the test marketing stage due to the desire to quickly introduce a new product with excellent potential, a desire not to reveal new-product strategies to competitors, and the high costs involved in limited production runs characteristic of expensive items.

Assessment Check Answers

5.1 What are the stages of the new-product development process? Six stages exist in the new-product development process for most products: idea generation, screening, business analysis, product development, test marketing, and commercialization.

5.2 Where do ideas for new products come from? New-product ideas come from many sources including customer suggestions, suppliers, employees, research scientists, marketing research, investors outside the firm, and competitive products.

6 **Explain how firms identify their products.**
Products are identified by brands, brand names, and trademarks, which are important elements of product images. Effective brand names are easy to pronounce, recognize, and remember, and they project the right images to buyers. Brand names cannot contain generic words. Under certain circumstances, companies lose exclusive rights to their brand names if common use makes them generic terms for product categories. Some brand names belong to retailers or distributors rather than to manufacturers. Brand loyalty is measured in three degrees: brand recognition, brand preference, and brand insistence. Some marketers use family brands to identify several related items in a product line. Others employ individual branding strategies by giving each product within a line a different brand name.

Assessment Check Answers

6.1 Differentiate among a brand, a brand name, and a trademark. A brand is a name, term, sign, symbol, design, or some combination thereof used to identify the products of one firm and differentiate them from competitive offerings. A brand name is that part of the brand consisting of words or letters included in a name used to identify and distinguish the firm's offerings from those of competitors. A trademark is a brand that has been given legal protection.

6.2 Define _brand equity_. Brand equity is the added value that a respected and successful brand name gives to a product.

7 **Outline and briefly describe each of the major components of an effective distribution strategy.**
A firm must consider whether to move products through direct or indirect distribution. Once the decision is made, the company needs to identify the types of marketing intermediaries, if any, through which it will distribute its goods and services. The Internet has made direct distribution an attractive option for many retail companies. Another component is distribution intensity. The business must decide on the amount of market coverage—intensive, selective, or exclusive—needed to achieve its marketing strategies. Finally, attention must be paid to managing the distribution channel. It is vital to minimize conflict between channel members.

Assessment Check Answers

7.1 Define _distribution channels_. Distribution channels are the paths that products, and title to them, follow from producer to consumer or business user.

7.2 What is a marketing intermediary? A marketing intermediary (also called a middleman) is a business firm that moves goods between producers and consumers or business users.

7.3 Differentiate between a merchant wholesaler and an agent or broker in terms of title to the goods. Merchant wholesalers are independently owned wholesaling intermediaries that take title to the goods they handle. Agents and brokers may or may not take possession of the goods they handle, but they never take title, working mainly to bring buyers and sellers together.

7.4 What are the elements of a retailer's marketing strategy? After identifying their target markets, retailers must choose merchandising, customer service, pricing, and location strategies that will attract customers in those market segments.

8 **Identify the various categories of distribution channels, and discuss the factors that influence channel selection.**
Marketers can choose either a direct distribution channel, which moves goods directly from the producer to the consumer, or indirect distribution channels, which involve marketing intermediaries in the paths through which products—and legal ownership of them—flow from producer to the final customer. Ideally, the choice of a distribution channel should support a firm's overall marketing strategy. Before selecting distribution channels, firms must consider their target markets, the types of goods being distributed, their own internal systems and concerns, and competitive factors.

Assessment Check Answers

8.1 What is distribution intensity? Distribution intensity is the number of intermediaries or outlets through which a manufacturer distributes its goods.

8.2 Define _supply chain_. A supply chain is the sequence of suppliers that contribute to creating a good or service and delivering it to business users and final consumers.

8.3 What do customer service standards measure? Customer service standards measure the quality of service a firm provides for its customers.

Business Terms You Need to Know

product 422	test marketing 430	distribution channel 436	supply chain 448
product line 425	brand 431	physical distribution 436	logistics 448
product mix 425	brand equity 434	wholesaler 439	
product life cycle 426	category advisor 434	retailer 440	

Other Important Business Terms

convenience product 423
shopping product 423
specialty product 423
brand name 432
trademark 432

manufacturer's (national)
  brand 432
private (store) brand 432
family brand 432
individual branding 433

category manager 434
distribution strategy 436
direct distribution
  channel 436
wheel of retailing 442

intensive distribution 448
selective distribution 448
exclusive distribution 448
vendor-managed
  inventory 449

Review Questions

1. Classify each of the following business-to-consumer (B2C) and business-to-business (B2B) goods and services. Then choose one and describe how it could be classified as both.
   a. *Vogue* or *Men's Health* magazine
   b. six-pack of bottled water
   c. delivery truck
   d. tech support for a communications system
   e. day spa
   f. Thai restaurant

2. What is the relationship between a product line and a product mix? Give an example of each.

3. Identify and briefly describe the six stages of new-product development.

4. What is the difference between a manufacturer's brand and a private brand? What is the difference between a family brand and an individual brand?

5. What are the three stages of brand loyalty? Why is the progression to the last stage so important to marketers?

6. What are the advantages of direct distribution? When is a producer most likely to use direct distribution?

7. What is a wholesaler? Why is the wholesaler important to the distribution of many products?

8. What is the wheel of retailing? How has the Internet affected the wheel of retailing?

9. Identify and briefly describe the four different types of nonstore retailers. Give an example of at least one type of good or service that would be suited to each type of nonstore retailer.

10. What are the three intensity levels of distribution? Give an example of two products for each level.

11. What types of products would most likely be shipped through each transport mode (see Table 13.3). Give an example for each mode.

12. Define *logistics*. How does it relate to physical distribution?

Projects and Teamwork Applications

1. On your own or with a classmate, choose one of the following goods or services. Decide whether you want to market it as a consumer product or a business product. Now create a brand name and marketing strategy for your product.
   a. photocopier
   b. meal service
   c. cell phone
   d. fitness class
   e. tax preparation

2. Choose one of the following products that is either in the maturity or decline stage of its life cycle (or select one of your own), and develop a marketing strategy for extending its life cycle.
   a. oatmeal
   b. burger restaurant
   c. land-line telephones
   d. music CDs
   e. paper stationery or notecards

3. On your own or with a classmate, choose a product whose brand name (including its name, symbol, colors, and so forth) you think could be improved. You can search the Internet, look at magazines, or watch television commercials to make your selection. Outline why you think the brand name is weak—then create a new one for the product, illustrating it with a poster, advertisement, or other visual presentation. Include packaging or labeling if applicable. Explain why you think your new brand name will be more effective than the old one.

4. Choose one of the following products and describe how you would market it through direct distribution:
   a. handmade jewelry
   b. gourmet cheeses
   c. digital photography
   d. lawn-mowing service
   e. closet organizers

5. Where do you do most of your shopping—in stores or online? Choose your favorite retailer and analyze why you like it. Outline your reasons for shopping there, then add two or three suggestions for improvement.

6. Choose one of the following products and select a distribution intensity for the product. Describe specifically where and how your product would be sold. Then describe the reasons for your strategy.

   a. line of clothing made of fabric manufactured from recycled materials

   b. home furnishings made by skilled craftspeople
   c. custom candles
   d. pet items
   e. radio show

7. Suppose you were in charge of coordinating transportation for a touring entertainment show such as a circus, a rock concert, or an ice show. Outline your strategy for getting your show from one location to another, taking into account modes of transportation, flow of information, customer service, and the like.

Web Assignments

1. **Product packaging standards.** Wal-Mart established a new set of standards for product packaging. Visit the Web site listed here (http://www.walmartfacts.com/articles/4564.aspx) and review these standards. Prepare a report discussing the new standards and the way they differ from previous standards. Why do you think Wal-Mart implemented these new packaging standards? What are the overall goals?

2. **Patents.** Visit the Web site of the U.S. Patent and Trademark Office (http://www.uspto.gov/web/offices/pac/doc/general/index.html). Review the information on patents. Make a list of five interesting facts on patents and bring the list with you to participate in a class discussion on the topic.

3. **Transportation statistics.** The Bureau of Transportation Statistics publishes a wide variety of

data on transportation. Visit the Bureau's Web site (http://www.bts.gov) and access the most recent report you can find on container shipping. Review the report and answer the following questions:

   a. What are some regional port trends in the United States?
   b. Which goods are most frequently inbound (shipping to the U.S.) and outbound (shipped to other countries) via containers?
   c. What are the top 20 container ports in the world?

Note: Internet Web addresses change frequently. If you do not find the exact sites listed, you may need to access the organization's or company's home page and search from there.

Case 13.1   Neiman Marcus Attempts to Attract Teens

Neiman Marcus and YouTube? The high-end retailer, known for catering to customers of a certain age and income, might be considered an unlikely candidate for an appearance on the Internet site that is dominated by youth. But that's exactly what Neiman Marcus did to promote its 100th anniversary. Its marketers created a video showing off the store's latest styles, and they admit the move was a little unusual given its traditional clients. But that's the point: the retail chain wants to open its doors to teens. The store still represents a luxury brand, but Neiman Marcus is determined to attract teen consumers because they eventually will become adult consumers with more money to spend. If Neiman can nab teens now, get them interested in its luxury goods, and turn them into loyal customers, they are less likely to drift off to a

rival later in life. Thus the leap to YouTube. "Like with anything, you hear people in meetings say, 'Did you see the thing on YouTube?'" explains Ginger Reeder, vice president of corporate communications for Neiman Marcus. "And if it starts to permeate our consciousness, we can only assume it's in our customers' as well."

Each generation has its own idea of what luxury is, so Neiman Marcus is making an effort to identify the preferences of the next generation even as it serves affluent customers who are middle-aged. The firm has already launched a chain of stores called Cusp, targeted at younger consumers, and is tracking their progress closely. Located in well-to-do areas such as Los Angeles, Washington, D.C., and suburban Chicago, these stores are stocked with trendy, casual clothing at slightly lower prices than consumers might typically find at Neiman Marcus stores. The atmosphere is less formal than the chandelier-laden traditional stores; in fact, the Cusp store in Los Angeles features displays made of artificial tree branches and twig fences. And while Neiman Marcus promotes heavily through its famous catalog called *The Book*, the Cusp boutiques are marketed online. Still, although the Cusp stores don't bear the Neiman Marcus name, shoppers can use their Neiman credit cards there.

According to Ginger Reeder and other Neiman marketers, YouTube and other such outlets are a logical step. "[Neiman Marcus] is making a concerted pitch, strategic pitch to young people to say, 'We're not your grandmother's store—we're your store too,'" notes one consultant in the luxury retail market. The YouTube pitch wasn't cheap. Purchasing the homepage space for a single day cost about $250,000. But considering how many young people might view the video, the price could be a bargain.

Although estimates of teenage spending vary widely, Teenage Research Unlimited says that consumers between the ages of 12 and 19 spend about $180 billion a year. "[Teens] don't have mortgages to pay, and they don't have rent," explains an industry watcher. "They have disposable income." Luxury items such as designer jeans, handbags, shoes, and sunglasses that celebrities wear are particularly popular. Neiman Marcus is happy to supply these items to young consumers. Using video to reach them and tell them about these products makes sense. "What people really wanted to see is merchandise," says Ginger Reeder of the YouTube video. "But they're also looking to us [to see] what's hot, what's trendy. One way to get that across is through ... those videos on YouTube. You can see them on our site, but you may have a whole other audience that sees them on YouTube."[37]

Questions for Critical Thinking

1. How might the introduction of Cusp stores and the YouTube video affect Neiman Marcus's brand equity?
2. Describe Neiman Marcus's distribution strategy.

Teens Turn to Net for TV

Will the television become extinct? Networks and movie studios will make sure that we always have programs to watch, but is the television set itself on the way out? Perhaps, among some groups of viewers. According to a survey by E-Poll, more than 25 percent of young men between the ages of 13 and 34 now watch video on devices other than televisions. In addition, three out of every four consumers ages 13 and older have watched videos on their desktop computers at some time. Portable laptops, cell phones, and iPods are other video outlets. Young teens between the ages of 12 and 14 own and use a variety of electronics regularly, including computers, TVs, DVD players, and cell phones, according to another survey. About 2 percent of U.S. households do not contain TVs, despite the push for larger screens and the move to high-definition programming, because people can watch their favorite broadcasts online.

What do all these statistics mean? Basically, that consumers' viewing habits—from news to movies to music videos and TV shows—is shifting. "Things are changing quickly, and it's likely that the teens surveyed by E-Poll ... are much more familiar with the various ways they can watch video," observes industry expert Debra Aho Williamson.

"In fact, I believe that young people will expect to be able to watch TV [shows] anywhere, anytime. It will be a part of their everyday life, just as mobile phones are today." Networks and movie studios are beginning to take serious notice of this trend. Although paid video downloads are still the most profitable for producers of the content, ad-supported video streaming is becoming increasingly common. One research firm estimates that this business will bring in $117 million in revenues for the producers of primetime and daytime TV programming in a recent year. That's not a huge sum, but it is nearly triple the figure for the previous year.

These changes affect the product life cycle of televisions and the way marketers may be able to generate consumer interest in turning on the TV. One way is to promote an easy and inexpensive way to transfer online video to TV. Online download services like Amazon Unbox and AppleTV are slowly catching on. But another, obvious direction the television industry could take is Internet TV networks. Already, the founders of Internet phone service Skype are offering Joost.com, an Internet TV network. Users can visit the network's Web site, download the most recent version of the Joost software, and sit back to watch TV shows and movies from such content providers as Warner Brothers, Sony, CNN, PBS, Major League Baseball, and the NHL. Joost doesn't offer a broad selection yet—you can catch a current episode of 'CSI' or the classic 'Lassie' series—but the mere fact that it exists signals a change in the way consumers will be viewing TV programming. "We have good content and an increasingly larger library," CEO Mike Volpi points out. "If you showed up as a user six months ago, you saw a couple music videos and some old movies. Now we have a lot of good stuff, and we are adding new content everyday."

Whether Joost succeeds in the long run, establishing its brand in the minds of consumers, or morphs into something else is a key challenge for marketers. As rivals begin to compete for online viewers, Joost has an opportunity to capture the attention—and perhaps loyalty—of viewers. One expert suggests that the site create an overall look or theme and ensure that all Joost ads, both online and offline, follow the same format in order to send unified messages to consumers. They say that viewers should be able to glance at an ad, logo, or slogan and know instantly that it belongs to Joost, just as they do when they see the NBC peacock and the CBS eye.[38]

Questions for Critical Thinking

1. At what stage would you say television is in the product life cycle? What strategies might TV networks and manufacturers employ to extend the life cycle of their products?

2. The Internet is changing the way entertainment is delivered to consumers. Do you think in the near future more Internet TV networks will be created? Why or why not?

VIDEO   Case 13.3   Monopoly: America's Love of Rags-to-Riches Game Is Timeless

Maybe you've never been to Atlantic City, but if you've played Monopoly, the names Park Place, Boardwalk, and Atlantic Avenue are as familiar to you as the streets around your own hometown. Monopoly, invented in 1934 by entrepreneur Charles B. Darrow, is based on real streets in Atlantic City. When Darrow first showed his game to executives at Parker Brothers, they weren't interested. But the gamemaker's disinterest failed to discourage him. Darrow and a printer friend made 5,000 sets anyway and convinced a department store in Philadelphia to carry them. When all 5,000 quickly sold out, Darrow went back to Parker Brothers, who soon changed their minds after learning of the consumer response to the unknown—and untested— new game. Their decision to add it to their product line was perhaps the most important move in Parker Brothers' history. Within 12 months following its launch, Monopoly had become the best-selling game in the U.S. By 2005, Parker Brothers, now a division of Hasbro Inc., had sold more than 200 million sets of Monopoly worldwide.

But the huge popularity of Monopoly poses a problem for its manufacturer: the game lasts, and repeat sales are difficult to secure. Once a family or an individual consumer buys a Monopoly set, there's no need to buy another. And if the idea of commerce—or rampant greed—doesn't appeal to someone, he or she is likely to pass on the game. Until recently, young children were left out of the game unless they had guidance from parents or older brothers and sisters, simply because the rules, concepts, and numbers were too complicated for them to follow. So Monopoly marketers began to evaluate ways to extend the product line. They examined new age groups, new socioeconomic groups likely to have market potential, and different interest groups and considered commemorative editions to mark or celebrate certain events in history. They also researched new platforms using interactive technology.

"Line extensions are all additives to Monopoly No. 9 [the official name of the original game]," explains Holly Riehl, director of marketing for Monopoly. The original game captures a universal truth that we all aspire to wealth, according to Riehl. In fact, Monopoly is such a universal game that, as Riehl says, "it has been adapted so thoroughly by every country that every country thinks it's their own." These ideas have combined to set the stage for a burst of new Monopoly editions targeted to different consumers.

Several years ago, Hasbro introduced a premium-priced Deluxe Monopoly with eye-catching new features for the collector—special tokens, title and deed carousels (making it easier to see and organize them during the game), and wooden houses and hotels. At around the same time, the company brought out Monopoly Junior for younger players. Based on an amusement park theme, in which game participants buy and sell amusement park rides and attractions, Monopoly Junior has attracted a younger generation of players ages 5 to 8. There's also the Dig'n Dinos edition for even younger children, and a Disney edition for players ages 8 to adult. Also in the product line are Monopoly 60th Anniversary and Monopoly Millennium, both developed to mark those anniversaries—and sold at a higher price of $39.95. If you are feeling particularly patriotic, pick up the America edition; if you speak Spanish, you can purchase the Spanish edition. And if you are a Star Wars or Pokemon fan, fear not—a Monopoly edition has been created for you, too.

Hasbro has also ventured into the interactive realm with a new subsidiary, Hasbro Interactive. The division sold 1 million copies of the first Monopoly CD-ROM, which became the fifth best-selling PC game of all time. "On the computer, Boardwalk and Park Place came to life," says Holly Riehl. Four years after the first release, an updated version hit the market, in which players could customize the 3-D board properties with their own street names and landmarks. Then came Monopoly PlayStation, Monopoly Hand-held, and Monopoly Nintendo, along with an e-mail version of the game.

Hasbro isn't trying to flood the market with Monopoly games, although certainly its marketers would like to see at least one edition in every household. But to reach as many consumers as possible, marketers conduct extensive product planning to make sure that each new version "makes sense," as Riehl puts it. "For instance, Monopoly Star Wars and Pokemon were a good fit," she says. The company tries to balance the basic concepts of the original Monopoly game with every one of its extensions, including such additions as a new token to the game. Several years ago, Hasbro conducted a search for a new

Monopoly playing token, finally narrowing it down to three candidates: a biplane, a piggybank, and a sack of money. Then consumers were invited to vote for their favorite among the three. Over 2 million consumers cast their vote for the sack of money, which is now part of the game.

Riehl reports that Hasbro is planning even more extensions to attract new—and loyal—customers to the Monopoly experience. Monopoly slot machines are already very popular in Las Vegas, and game fanciers can watch for a Monopoly café as well as Monopoly books and other media. In short, Hasbro hopes Monopoly will eventually have a monopoly (of sorts) on all kinds of entertainment.[39]

Questions for Critical Thinking

1. How would you classify Monopoly as a consumer product? Why?

2. At what stage would you place Monopoly in the product life cycle? How does this relate to Hasbro's decision to extend the product line?

3. Monopoly marketing director Holly Riehl says that the idea for each new Monopoly edition goes through extensive planning before it is manufactured and brought to market. Even so, do you think that Hasbro is taking on more risk by introducing so many different types of Monopoly to the marketplace? Why or why not?

4. Visit the Monopoly Web site at http://www.monopoly.com or open up your own Monopoly game. Identify as many elements of the product image as you can. Do you think that Monopoly is a strong brand? Why or why not?

chapter 14

Promotion and Pricing Strategies

George Doyle/Stockbyte/Getty Images

The E*Trade Baby Talks Value

Babies and young children often utter funny, surprising, and insightful comments on the world around them. Online stock trading, investing, and banking firm E*Trade has bet its advertising budget on cuteness, creating a series of television commercials featuring a talking baby who knows more about investing than the average adult. He's adorable, funny, and smart. He text messages friends and even hires a clown with his profits, commenting that he underestimated the clown's creepiness. But at the conclusion of the most talked-about of the ads, he spits up on his computer keyboard—reminding viewers that, after all, he is just a baby. E*Trade debuted new installments of the Talking Baby series during Super Bowl broadcasts over a period of three years. The third commercial was so popular that it was rated higher than ads for Pepsi starring Justin Timberlake, Doritos, Coca-Cola, and even Bud Light.

Making stock trading funny or even memorable is not easy, especially during difficult economic times. But E*Trade succeeded—viewers remembered the cute wisecracking baby. Despite the daunting task of trying to understand online stock trading, they came away with the impression that E*Trade makes it so easy that even a smart child can do it. By advertising during such a visible program as the Super Bowl, and in such a challenging economy, E*Trade was taking a risk. But it was a calculated one that has been part of E*Trade's promotional strategy all along. "History repeatedly has shown that those who continue to make smart marketing investments when economic times are uncertain are best positioned for success when the economy rebounds," explains Nicholas Utton, chief marketing officer for E*Trade. "That's why, in this uncertain economic climate, reinforcing the strength of our brand and value proposition is critical."

The talking toddler fits squarely with E*Trade's image as a firm that thumbs its nose at large, traditional brokerages. E*Trade encourages investors to take control of their own portfolios instead of leaving all the decisions in the hands of professionals. By doing so, investors can take advantage of the better deals that E*Trade can offer because it doesn't have the overhead costs associated with traditional brokerage firms. The company's Web site promises that its "pricing is clear, competitive, and fair." Trades can be made for $9.99 or less, and the firm provides special deals that go even lower for qualified customers. "E*Trade has always flown in the face of traditional brokerages," notes Tor Myhren of Grey New York, the advertising agency that created the talking baby ads. "And this little, financially savvy, street-wise baby has seemed to really tap a nerve with more independent investors. He shows that anyone can do it. Seeing how easy it is for him helps people overcome their fears of what they perceive as complicated technology."

The talking baby spots didn't just appear on TV. To generate interest in the commercial, particularly among young adults, E*Trade launched the talking baby on the Web prior to the Super Bowl. Several days before the game, E*Trade posted selected outtakes of the commercial—footage that didn't make it to the final version—on its branded YouTube channel. The company even created a Facebook page for the famous baby. By the time the actual commercial aired on game night, people were already talking about it. "We succeeded in creating something memorable that engages retail investors in a meaningful way through multiple channels, and more importantly, has produced significant return on investment," notes Myhren. The baby actually got nervous adult investors to give online investing with E*Trade a try. And that's not child's play.[1]

This chapter focuses on the different types of promotional activities and the way prices are established for goods and services. **Promotion** is the function of informing, persuading, and influencing a purchase decision. This activity is as important to not-for-profit organizations such as the Boys & Girls Clubs of America and the Huntington's Disease Society of America as it is to profit-seeking companies such as Nationwide Insurance and the Boston Red Sox.

Some promotional strategies try to develop *primary demand,* or consumer desire for a general product category. The objective of such a campaign is to stimulate sales for an entire industry so that individual firms benefit from this market growth. A popular example is the dairy industry's "Got Milk?" campaign. Print and television messages about the nutritional benefits of milk show various celebrities, including NFL quarterback Brett Favre and TV host Meredith Vieira. The American Heart Association has also become a part of these ads. Other promotional campaigns aimed at hiking per-capita consumption have been commissioned by the California Strawberry Commission and the National Cattlemen's Beef Association.

Most promotional strategies, in contrast, seek to stimulate *selective demand*—desire for a specific brand. Every driver needs some type of car insurance, and the Geico gecko wants consumers to pick its firm for low rates. Country-western star Toby Keith promotes Ford F-150 trucks, which encourages his fans to choose that brand over competitors. Sales promotions that offered teens a free iTunes song download for trying on a pair of Gap jeans also encouraged shoppers to purchase a specific brand.

Marketers choose among many promotional options to communicate with potential customers. Each marketing message a buyer receives—through a television or radio commercial, newspaper or magazine ad, Web site, direct-mail flyer, or sales call—reflects on the product, place, person, cause, or organization promoted in the content. Through **integrated marketing communications (IMC),** marketers coordinate all promotional activities—advertising, sales promotion, personal sales presentations, and public relations—to execute a unified, customer-focused promotional strategy. This coordination is designed to avoid confusing the consumer and to focus positive attention on the promotional message.

This chapter begins by explaining the role of IMC and then discusses the objectives of promotion and the importance of promotional planning. Next, it examines the components of the promotional mix: advertising, sales promotion, personal selling, and public relations. Finally, the chapter addresses pricing strategies for goods and services.

Cookies aren't the only things that can be dipped with milk.

Nothing keeps me going during a night out, like the refreshing sensation of milk. It tastes great and keeps my body limber and my bones strong – necessities for the twists and twirls of the tango!

got milk?

Got milk? This ad, part of the dairy industry's long-running series featuring the milk mustache, is meant to increase *primary demand* for milk.

PRNewsFoto/Milk Processor Education Program/© AP/Wide World Photos

---

promotion function of informing, persuading, and influencing a purchase decision.

integrated marketing communications (IMC) coordination of all promotional activities—media advertising, direct mail, personal selling, sales promotion, and public relations—to produce a unified customer-focused message.

Integrated Marketing Communications

An integrated marketing communications strategy focuses on customer needs to create a unified promotional message in the firm's ads, in-store displays, product samples, and presentations by company sales representatives. To gain a competitive advantage, marketers that implement IMC need a broad view of promotion. Media options continue to multiply, and marketers cannot simply rely on traditional broadcast and print media and direct mail. Plans must include all forms of customer contact. Packaging, store displays, sales promotions, sales presentations, and online and interactive media also communicate information about a brand or organization. With IMC, marketers create a unified personality and message for the good, brand, or service they promote. Coordinated activities also enhance the effectiveness of reaching and serving target markets.

Marketing managers set the goals and objectives for the firm's promotional strategy with overall organizational objectives and marketing goals in mind. Based on these objectives, marketers weave the various elements of the strategy—personal selling, advertising, sales promotion, publicity, and public relations—into an integrated communications plan. This document becomes a central part of the firm's total marketing strategy to reach its selected target market. Feedback, including marketing research and sales reports, completes the system by identifying any deviations from the plan and suggesting improvements.

In its stepped-up IMC campaign for Axe men's body spray and deodorant, Unilever combined a number of marketing promotions. It invited college students to help make "The World's Dirtiest Film" by being videotaped while jumping into mounds of mashed potatoes or giant chocolate ice-cream sundaes—and, of course, providing Axe products to clean up at a shower station afterward. The film included other customer videos and some professional skits, and it aired on *Jimmy Kimmel Live.* Facebook was a partner in the Axe campaign, and creators of the best user-generated content were eligible to win a trip to Los Angeles. Unilever also redesigned the product packaging and projected ads for Axe on the sides of buildings in Tampa and Milwaukee, among other places, and as billboards in the videogame "Rainbow Six Vegas."[2]

The Promotional Mix

Just as every organization creates a marketing mix combining product, distribution, promotion, and pricing strategies, each also requires a similar mix to blend the many facets of promotion into a cohesive plan. The promotional mix consists of two components—personal and nonpersonal selling—that marketers combine to meet the needs of their firm's target customers and effectively and efficiently communicate its message to them. Personal selling is the most basic form of promotion: a direct person-to-person promotional presentation to a potential buyer. The buyer–seller communication can occur during a face-to-face meeting or via telephone, videoconference, or interactive computer link.

Nonpersonal selling consists of advertising, sales promotion, direct marketing, and public relations. Advertising is the best-known form of nonpersonal selling, but sales promotion accounts for about half of these marketing expenditures. Spending for sponsorships, which involves marketing messages delivered in association with another activity such as a golf tournament or a benefit concert, is on the rise as well. Marketers need to be

Assessment Check

1. What is the objective of an integrated marketing communications program?
2. What types of media are used in integrated marketing communications?

promotional mix combination of personal and nonpersonal selling techniques designed to achieve promotional objectives.

personal selling interpersonal promotional process involving a seller's face-to-face presentation to a prospective buyer.

Table 14.1 — Comparing the Components of the Promotional Mix

Component	Advantages	Disadvantages
Advertising	Reaches large consumer audience at low cost per contact Allows strong control of the message Message can be modified to match different audiences	Difficult to measure effectiveness Limited value for closing sales
Personal selling	Message can be tailored for each customer Produces immediate buyer response Effectiveness is easily measured	High cost per contact High expense and difficulty of attracting and retaining effective salespeople
Sales promotion	Attracts attention and creates awareness Effectiveness is easily measured Produces short-term sales increases	Difficult to differentiate from similar programs of competitors Nonpersonal appeal
Public relations	Enhances product or firm credibility Creates a positive attitude about the product or company	Difficult to measure effectiveness Often devoted to nonmarketing activities
Sponsorships	Viewed positively by consumers Enhances brand awareness	Difficult to control message

careful about the types of promotion they choose or risk alienating the very people they are trying to reach.

Figure 14.1

Five Major Promotional Objectives

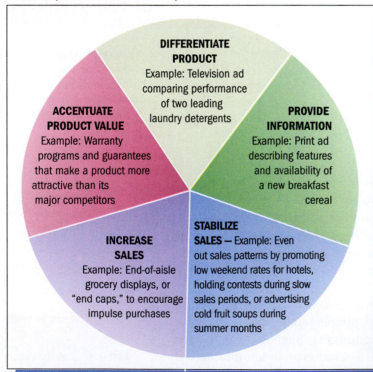

DIFFERENTIATE PRODUCT — Example: Television ad comparing performance of two leading laundry detergents

ACCENTUATE PRODUCT VALUE — Example: Warranty programs and guarantees that make a product more attractive than its major competitors

PROVIDE INFORMATION — Example: Print ad describing features and availability of a new breakfast cereal

INCREASE SALES — Example: End-of-aisle grocery displays, or "end caps," to encourage impulse purchases

STABILIZE SALES — Example: Even out sales patterns by promoting low weekend rates for hotels, holding contests during slow sales periods, or advertising cold fruit soups during summer months

Each component in the promotional mix offers its own advantages and disadvantages, as Table 14.1 demonstrates. By selecting the most effective combination of promotional mix elements, a firm may reach its promotional objectives. Spending within the promotional mix varies by industry. Manufacturers of many business-to-business (B2B) products typically spend more on personal selling than on advertising because those products—such as a new telecommunications system—may require a significant investment. Consumer-goods marketers may focus more on advertising and sponsorships. Later sections of this chapter discuss how the parts of the mix contribute to effective promotion.

Objectives of Promotional Strategy

Promotional strategy objectives vary among organizations. Some use promotion to expand their markets, and others use it to defend their current positions. As Figure 14.1 illustrates, common objectives include providing information, differentiating a product, increasing sales, stabilizing sales, and accentuating a product's value.

Marketers often pursue multiple promotional objectives at the same time. To promote its Microsoft Office software, Microsoft has to convince business owners, who buy the software, and their employees, who use the software, that the product is a worthwhile investment.

Marketers need to keep their firm's promotional objectives in mind at all times. Sometimes the objectives are obscured by a fast-paced, creative ad campaign. In this case, the message—or worse, the brand name or image—is lost. The series of comic Geico ads that featured grumpy Neanderthals and the tag line "So easy a caveman could do it" were an instant hit. They were widely viewed on YouTube and even inspired a short-lived TV sitcom. But despite their quirky originality, the ads allowed humor to overtake the message; few viewers remembered the product—car insurance.

PROVIDING INFORMATION A major portion of U.S. advertising is information oriented. Credit card ads provide information about benefits and rates. Ads for hair-care products include information about benefits such as shine and volume. Ads for breakfast cereals often contain nutritional information. Television ads for prescription drugs, a nearly $2 billion industry, are sometimes criticized for relying on emotional appeals rather than providing information about the causes, risk factors, and especially the prevention of disease.[3] But print advertisements for drugs often contain an entire page of warnings, side-effects, and usage guidelines.

DIFFERENTIATING A PRODUCT Promotion can also be used to differentiate a firm's offerings from the competition. Applying a concept called **positioning**, marketers attempt to establish their products in the minds of customers. The idea is to communicate to buyers meaningful distinctions about the attributes, price, quality, or use of a good or service.

Baby's First Gift.

Is it the toy you give her? Or the amazing new type of stem cell she gives your family?

Introducing the Plureon® Placental Stem Cell Service exclusively from Cryo-Cell.

For the first time ever, you have the opportunity to have next-generation stem cells collected at the birth of your baby and preserved for your family's future health. Highly adaptable Plureon stem cells, *derived from the placenta,* have already produced bone, heart muscle, nerve, liver, and pancreatic cells in the laboratory. Combining them with the proven therapeutic value of cord blood stem cells delivers the potential to treat a far wider range of diseases than ever before. Invest in your family's future well-being with our new Plureon Service.

Another innovation from Cryo-Cell, your stem cell solution source.

To learn more, call 1-800-786-7235 or visit www.cryo-cell.com today.

CryoCell INTERNATIONAL

This award-winning ad for cryogenic storage of stem cells was recognized for its simplicity and ability to evoke an emotional response. Often, the emotional appeals in medical ads overshadow the information they provide.

PRNewsFoto/Corbett Worldwide Healthcare Communications/© AP/Wide World Photos

When you set out to purchase a car, you have hundreds of brands from which to choose. How do you decide which one to buy? Carmakers do their best to differentiate their vehicles by style, performance, safety features, and price. They must make their vehicles stand out to individual consumers. Buick positions its Enclave SUV as a luxury brand worthy of comparison with Lexus and Mercedes-Benz. General Motors sold 30,000 of the crossover vehicle in its first six months, and with rave reviews for its price, features, quality, and interior and exterior styling, it might have sold more. But the company deliberately limited the initial output, which only helped boost the Enclave's image as an upscale vehicle. In fact, 90 percent of sales have been of the high-end CXL model.[4]

INCREASING SALES Increasing sales volume is the most common objective of a promotional strategy. Naturalizer became the third-largest seller of women's dress shoes by appealing to Baby Boomers. But as these women have grown older, they have bought fewer pairs of shoes each year. Naturalizer wants to keep these customers but also attract the younger generation. So the firm developed a new line of trendy shoes. The promotional strategy included ads in magazines read by younger women—such as *Elle* and *Marie Claire*—featuring young women in beach attire and Naturalizer shoes. The response to this strategy was a substantial increase in Naturalizer's sales through department stores.

STABILIZING SALES Sales stabilization is another goal of promotional strategy. Firms often use sales contests during slack periods, motivating salespeople by offering prizes such as vacations, TVs, camera phones, and cash to those who meet certain goals. Companies distribute sales promotion materials—such as calendars, pens, and notepads—to customers to stimulate sales during the off-season. Jiffy Lube puts that little sticker on your windshield to remind you when to have your car's next oil change—the regular visits help stabilize sales. A stable sales pattern brings several advantages. It evens out the production cycle, reduces some management and production costs, and simplifies financial, purchasing, and marketing planning. An effective promotional strategy can contribute to these goals.

McDonald's came up with new iced-coffee flavors in its campaign to boost coffee sales in the summer. Vanilla and hazelnut flavors joined plain iced-coffee drinks offered at 700 stores in major cities like Boston, Chicago, New York, and Seattle. Coffee mugs frozen in ice appeared in the Seattle locations, and Boston stores gave out free coffee. Public-transit ads and TV commercials were part of the Chicago campaign, along with ads on cocktail napkins and more free samples at the Accenture Chicago Triathlon.[5]

ACCENTUATING THE PRODUCT'S VALUE Some promotional strategies enhance product values by explaining hidden benefits of ownership. Carmakers offer long-term warranty programs; life insurance companies promote certain policies as investments. The creation of brand awareness and brand loyalty also enhances a product's image and increases its desirability. Advertising with luxurious images supports the reputation of premium brands like Jaguar, Tiffany, and Rolex.

Promotional Planning

Today's marketers can promote their products in many ways, and the lines between the different elements of the promotional mix are blurring. Consider the practice of **product placement**. A growing number of marketers pay placement fees to have their products showcased in various media, ranging from newspapers and magazines to television and movies. Coca-Cola gets prominent placement on *American Idol,* for instance, and *America's Next Top Model* and *Extreme Makeover: Home Edition* are other popular shows with high product-placement appeal.[6] Television shows and movies account for 98 percent of all product placements, with videogame and online placements projected to grow.[7]

Another type of promotional planning must be considered by firms with small budgets. **Guerrilla marketing** is innovative, low-cost marketing efforts designed to get consumers' attention in unusual ways. Guerrilla marketing is an increasingly popular tactic for marketers, especially those with limited promotional budgets. Even unintentional exposure can have remarkable effects. A famous YouTube video shows how dropping Mentos candy into a 2-liter bottle of Diet Coke triggers a chemical reaction along the lines of a gushing, wet volcano. While the video undoubtedly motivated at least some of its millions of viewers to buy Mentos and Diet Coke, Steve Spangler, science editor for a Colorado TV station and an amateur toy maker, was inspired to produce his Geyser Tube toy. The toy re-created the explosion in a plastic tube with a pin and string to control the timing. "We don't have any relationship with YouTube," said Spangler. "But I couldn't be happier for [the attention the video makers generated]. Science is for everybody."[8]

Marketers for larger companies have caught on and are using guerrilla approaches as well, with mixed success. In a famous misfire, Sam Ewen's start-up guerrilla marketing agency, Interference, attracted widespread negative attention with its light-up boards featuring characters from a new Cartoon Network show called *Aqua Teen Hunger Force.* Agency employees hung the boards up in ten U.S. cities including Boston, where jittery citizens called police to "defuse" what they thought were potential bombs. Then CNN picked up the story. "Whoever thought this up needs to find another job," said Massachusetts Congressman Edward Markey. But "once you take the emotion out of it, it was a really innovative campaign," said Donna Sokolsky, cofounder of Spark PR. "That's what people will remember."[9]

From this overview of the promotional mix, we now turn to discussions of each of its elements. The following sections detail the major components of advertising, sales promotion, personal selling, and public relations.

Advertising

Consumers receive about 5,000 marketing messages each day, many of them in the form of advertising.[10] Advertising is the most visible form of nonpersonal promotion—and the most effective for many firms. **Advertising** refers to paid nonpersonal communication usually targeted at large numbers of potential buyers. Although U.S. citizens often think of advertising as a typically American function, it is a global activity. Six of the top 20 firms that advertise in the United States are headquartered in other countries: GlaxoSmithKline, Unilever, Toyota, Sony, Daimler AG, and Honda. The top five advertisers in the United States are, in order, Procter & Gamble, AT&T, General Motors, Time Warner, and Verizon.[11]

Advertising expenditures vary among industries, companies, and media. Automotive, retail, and telecommunications take top honors for spending in the United States—carmakers spend a whopping $20 billion per year. Top car advertiser General Motors spends more than $3 billion a year alone. Magazine and newspaper are the two highest-ranked media in advertising revenues, at $20 billion each.[12] Because advertising expenditures are so great, and because consumers are bombarded with so many messages, firms need to be more and more creative and efficient at getting consumers' attention.

Types of Advertising

The two basic types of ads are product and institutional advertisements. **Product advertising** consists of messages designed to sell a particular good or service. Advertisements for Nantucket Nectars juices, iPods, and Capital One credit cards are examples of product advertising. **Institutional advertising** involves messages that promote concepts, ideas, philosophies, or goodwill for industries, companies, organizations, or government entities. Each year, the Juvenile Diabetes Research Foundation promotes its "Walk for the Cure" fund-raising event, and your college may place advertisements in local papers or news shows to promote its activities.

A form of institutional advertising that is growing in importance, **cause advertising,** promotes a specific viewpoint on a public issue as a way to influence public opinion and the legislative process about issues such as literacy, hunger and poverty, and alternative energy sources. Both not-for-profit organizations and businesses use cause advertising, sometimes called *advocacy advertising*. The Bill and Melinda Gates Foundation is a not-for-profit organization dedicated to raising public awareness and generating legislation and other efforts in the fight against poverty, lack of education, and disease. Funded through grants from the Gateses and investment guru Warren Buffett, the foundation operates in all 50 states, the District of Columbia, and 100 countries. Through well-publicized grants of nearly $1.6 billion to the United Negro College fund for its Millennium Scholars Program and tours abroad to personally oversee vaccination programs, the Gateses generate interest in their causes. For their efforts they received a recent *Time* Person of the Year award.[13]

advertising
paid nonpersonal communication delivered through various media and designed to inform, persuade, or remind members of a particular audience.

"They Said It"

"Advertising isn't a *science*. It's persuasion. And persuasion is an *art*."

—William Bernbach
(1911–1982)
U.S. advertising executive

Advertising and the Product Life Cycle

Both product and institutional advertising fall into one of three categories based on whether the ads are intended to inform, persuade, or remind. A firm uses *informative advertising* to build initial demand for a product in the introductory phase of the product life cycle. Highly publicized new-product entries attract the interest of potential buyers who seek information about the advantages of the new products over existing ones, warranties provided, prices, and places that offer the new products. Ads for new cell phones boast of new features, colors, designs, and pricing options to attract new customers.

Persuasive advertising attempts to improve the competitive status of a product, institution, or concept, usually in the growth and maturity stages of the product life cycle. One of the most popular types of persuasive product advertising, *comparative advertising,* compares products directly with their competitors—either by name or by inference. Tylenol advertisements mention the possible stomach problems that aspirin could cause, stating that its pain reliever does not irritate the stomach. But advertisers need to be careful when they name competing brands in comparison ads because they might leave themselves open to controversy or even legal action by competitors. Notice that Tylenol does not mention a specific aspirin brand in its promotions.

Reminder-oriented advertising often appears in the late maturity or decline stages of the product life cycle to maintain awareness of the importance and usefulness of a product, concept, or institution. Triscuits have been around for a long time, but Nabisco attempts to mobilize sales with up-to-date advertising that appeals to health and fitness–conscious consumers. The advertising mentions its new no-trans-fat formulations.

Advertising Media

Marketers must choose how to allocate their advertising budgets among various media. All media offer advantages and disadvantages. Cost is an important consideration in media selection, but marketers must also choose the media best suited for communicating their message. As Figure 14.2 indicates, advertising on television, in newspapers, and in magazines represent the three leading media outlets. However, Internet advertising is growing fast. Consumers now receive ads when they download news and other information to their hand-held wireless devices.

Advertising executives agree that firms need to rethink traditional ad campaigns to incorporate new media as well as updated uses of traditional media. Google is looking for ways to combine the targeting capabilities of Internet advertising and the richness of the television medium, and it is not alone. "If we can combine the addressability of direct advertising with the accountability of the Internet, with the emotion of television—that's when we see television ad spend[ing] growing again," says Google's head of TV technology.[14] Google is already partnering with EchoStar Communications, a satellite broadcaster, to test ways to let advertisers like E*Trade and 1–800-Flowers select regional or national area coverage, as well as time of day and channel, for broadcasting their ads.[15]

TELEVISION Television is still one of America's leading national advertising media. Television advertising can be classified as network, national, local, and cable ads. The four major national networks—ABC, CBS, NBC, and Fox—along with the CW, broadcast almost

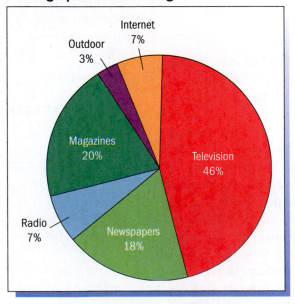

Figure 14.2

Carving up the Advertising Media Pie

Internet 7%
Outdoor 3%
Magazines 20%
Radio 7%
Newspapers 18%
Television 46%

Note: Percentages do not total to 100% due to rounding. Direct mail was not measured in these data.
Source: Data from "100 Leading National Advertisers," *Advertising Age,* June 22, 2009; http://adage.com/datacenter.

one-fifth of all television ads. Despite a decline in audience share and growing competition from cable, network television remains the easiest way for advertisers to reach large numbers of viewers—10 million to 20 million with a single commercial. Automakers, fast-food restaurants, and food manufacturers are heavy users of network TV advertising.

Nearly two-thirds of U.S. households with TVs now subscribe to cable, drawn to the dozens or even hundreds of channels available through cable or satellite services. As these services broaden their offerings to Internet and interactive programming, their audience is expected to continue growing. The variety of channels on cable and satellite networks lets advertisers target specialized markets and reach selected demographic groups, such as consumers who watch Animal

Here are recent contestants from *Project Runway*, one of cable TV's most successful reality shows. Cable channels like Bravo and Lifetime allow advertisers to target specific markets and demographic groups.

Planet. Recent research suggests that even people who can use their digital video recorders (DVRs) to skip TV ads don't always do so. According to the Nielsen Company, many DVR users still watch shows at their scheduled times, when they must watch the ads, and even those who record shows for later viewing watch almost half the ads they could skip.[16]

Although television reaches the greatest number of consumers at once, it is the most expensive advertising medium. The price to air a 30-second ad during weeknight prime time on network television generally ranges from $100,000 to more than $500,000 for the most popular shows. Super Bowl ads have been known to command prices of nearly $3 million for 30 seconds. So marketers want to be certain that their commercials reach the greatest number of viewers. Because of the high cost, advertisers may demand guarantees of audience size and receive compensation if a show fails to deliver the promised number of viewers.

NEWSPAPERS Daily and weekly newspapers continue to dominate local advertising. Marketers can easily tailor newspaper advertising for local tastes and preferences. Advertisers can also coordinate advertisements with other promotional efforts such as discount coupons from supermarkets and one-day sales at department stores. A disadvantage comes from the relatively short life span; people usually discard their newspapers soon after reading. Retailers and automobile dealers rank first among newspaper advertisers. Most newspapers now maintain Web sites, some of which offer separate material and features, to complement their print editions.

RADIO Despite the proliferation of other media, the average U.S. household owns five radios—including those in cars—a market penetration that makes radio an important advertising medium. Advertisers like the captive audience of listeners as they commute to and from work. As a result, morning and evening drive-time shows command top ad rates. In major markets, many stations serve different demographic groups with targeted programming. Internet radio programming also offers opportunities for yet more focused targeting.

Satellite stations offer great potential for advertisers. Although Sirius still offers commercial-free music stations—it has always carried ads on its talk shows—competitor XM recently frustrated some subscribers by airing commercials on the four music channels controlled by Clear Channel, which sued to run the ads. Each satellite network has more than 6 million subscribers, and more advertising may be in listeners' future. As one industry analyst said of satellite radio broadcasters, "As they grow and gain subscribers, I can't imagine them giving up the millions in revenue they could take in from advertisers."[17]

MAGAZINES Magazines include consumer publications and business trade journals. *Time, Reader's Digest,* and *Sports Illustrated* are consumer magazines, whereas *Advertising Age* and *Oil & Gas Journal* fall into the trade category.

Magazines may customize their publications and target advertising messages to different regions of the country. One method places local advertising in regional editions of the magazine. Other magazines attach wraparounds—half-size covers on top of full-size covers—to highlight articles inside that relate to particular areas; different wraparounds appear in different parts of the country.

Magazines are a natural choice for targeted advertising. Media buyers study demographics of subscribers and select magazines that attract the desired readers. American Express advertises in *Fortune* and *Forbes* to reach businesspeople, while PacSun clothes and Clearasil skin medications are advertised in *teenVogue.*

DIRECT MAIL The average U.S. household receives about 550 pieces of direct mail each year, including 100 catalogs. The huge growth in the variety of direct-mail offerings combined with the convenience they offer today's busy, time-pressed shoppers has made direct-mail advertising a multibillion-dollar business. Even consumers who like to shop online often page through a catalog before placing an online order. Although direct mail is expensive per person, a small business may be able to spend less on a limited direct-mail campaign than on a television or radio ad. For businesses with a small advertising budget, a carefully targeted direct-mail effort can be highly effective. E-mail is a low-cost form of direct marketing. Marketers can target the most interested Internet users by offering Web site visitors an option to register to receive e-mail. Companies like Amazon.com, Spring Hill Nurseries, and Abercrombie & Fitch routinely send e-mail to regular customers.

Address lists are at the heart of direct-mail advertising. Using data-mining techniques to segment markets, direct-mail marketers create profiles that show the traits of consumers who are likely to buy their products or donate to their organizations. Catalog retailers sometimes experiment by sending direct-mail pieces randomly to people who subscribe to particular magazines. Next, they analyze the orders received from the mailings and develop profiles of purchasers. Finally, they rent lists of additional subscriber names that match the profiles they have developed.

Studies have shown that most U.S. consumers are annoyed by the amount of "junk mail" they receive every day, including catalogs, advertising postcards, and flyers. Among Internet users, a major pet peeve is *spam,* or junk e-mail. Many states have outlawed such practices as sending e-mail promotions without legitimate return addresses, although it is difficult to track down and catch offenders.

The Direct Marketing Association (DMA; www.the-dma.org) helps marketers combat negative attitudes by offering its members guidelines on ethical business practices. The DMA also provides consumer information at its Web site, as well as services that enable consumers to opt out of receiving unsolicited offers. In addition, Federal Trade Commission regulations have taken effect for direct mail in certain industries. Now when you receive that unsolicited, preapproved credit card application in the mail, it must be accompanied by a prominent notice telling you how to get off the bank's mailing list. This law will affect millions of consumers, because each household receives almost six applications every month; that amounts to 1.4 billion applications sent per quarter. Consumers can also opt out of receiving such offers for two years.[18]

OUTDOOR ADVERTISING Outdoor advertising accounts for nearly $7 billion in advertising expenditures.[19] The majority of spending on outdoor advertising is for billboards, but spending for other types of outdoor advertising, such as signs in transit stations, stores, airports, and sports stadiums, is growing fast. Advertisers are exploring new forms of outdoor media, many of which involve technology: computerized paintings, video billboards, "trivision" that displays three revolving images on a single billboard, and moving billboards mounted on trucks. Other innovations include ads displayed on the Goodyear blimp, using an electronic system that offers animation and video. Tens of thousands of New York City drivers signed up to earn $800 a month by allowing ads to be wrapped around their cars and trucks by advertisers like Verizon and Jamba Juice.[20] PepsiCo used vinyl material to wrap its logo on Seattle city buses, and the History Channel did the same to transform an entire Amtrak train into a gallery of famous faces from the 1960s to promote one of its shows.[21] Outdoor advertising suffers from several disadvantages, however. The medium requires brief messages, and billboards are often attacked by preservation and conservation groups.

This humorous ad was the first in Chick-fil-A's long-running series of cow-themed billboards. The popular series, which featured renegade cows bent on convincing people to eat chicken instead of beef, was recognized by the outdoor advertising industry's hall of fame.

PRNewsFoto/Chick-fil-A, Inc./NewsCom

INTERNET ADVERTISING Marketing experts reported that sales from online advertising have surpassed $20 billion per year and could soon surpass $50 billion.[22] Search engine marketing, display ads, and even classified ads are surging.

Online and interactive media have already changed the nature of advertising. Starting with simple banner ads, Internet advertising has become much more complex and sophisticated. Miniature television screen images, called *widgets* or *gadgets,* can carry marketing messages only a few inches high on a Web site, blog, or desktop display. And they contain embedded links to their home sites. CarDomain.com, a car lover's Web site, saw an increase of 60,000 page views per day after hundreds of other sites downloaded its widget, spreading the word about CarDomain.com in the process. Google experimented with overlay advertisements on YouTube, which it now owns. But it has already found that viewers object to *pre-rolls*—ads they are forced to watch before a video clip can play. Google now inserts ads only in videos created by select marketing partners and offers viewers a simple way to click them off without viewing. YouTube's head of advertising sales predicts further innovations that will create better and more user-friendly ways of offering ads with videos.[23]

Another example is *viral advertising,* which creates a message that is novel or entertaining enough for consumers to forward it to others, spreading it like a virus. The great advantage is that spreading the word online, which often relies on social networking on sites like MySpace and Facebook, costs the advertiser nothing. While viral marketing can be risky, the best campaigns are edgy and often funny. "It's really not easily defined," said one actor in a viral campaign for a software company, "which I think is kind of cool. It seems to engage people faster if they can't identify who it is."[24] However, not all online advertising is well received.

Some viral campaigns rely on personal word-of-mouth promotions, and when ordinary consumers are recruited as "brand ambassadors" for pay, questions can arise about ethics. One company, BzzAgent, gives its members products instead of money. But these ambassadors are not required to tell others that they're being paid or receiving free gifts to discuss products, which some view as problematic.[25]

SPONSORSHIP One of the hottest trends in promotion offers marketers the ability to integrate several elements of the promotional mix. **Sponsorship** involves providing funds for a sporting or cultural event in exchange for a direct association with the event. Sports sponsorships attract two-thirds of total sponsorship dollars in the United States alone. Entertainment, festivals, causes, and the arts divide up the remaining third of sponsorship dollars.

NASCAR, the biggest spectator sport in the United States, thrives on sponsorships. Because it can cost as much as $15 to $20 million a year to run a top NASCAR team, drivers depend on sponsorships from companies to keep the wheels turning.[26] Firms may also sponsor charitable or other not-for-profit awards or events. In conjunction with sports network ESPN, Gatorade sponsors its High School Athlete of the Year award, presented to the top male and female high school athletes who "strive for their best on and off the field."

Sponsors benefit in two major ways: exposure to the event's audience and association with the image of the activity. If a celebrity is involved, sponsors usually earn the right to use his or her name along with the name of the event in advertisements. They can set up signs at the event, offer sales promotions, and the like. Sponsorships play an important role in relationship marketing, bringing together the event, its participants, and the sponsoring firms.

OTHER MEDIA OPTIONS As consumers filter out familiar advertising messages, marketers look for novel ways to catch their attention. In addition to the major media, firms promote through many other vehicles such as infomercials and specialized media. **Infomercials** are a form of broadcast direct marketing, also called *direct response television (DRTV)*. These 30-minute programs resemble regular television programs but are devoted to selling goods or services such as exercise equipment, skin-care products, or kitchenware. The long format allows an advertiser to thoroughly present product benefits, increase awareness, and make an impact on consumers. Advertisers also receive immediate responses in the form of sales or inquiries because most infomercials feature toll-free phone numbers. Infomercial stars may become celebrities in their own right, attracting more customers wherever they go. The most effective infomercials tend to be for auto care products, beauty and personal care items, investing and business opportunities, collectibles, fitness and self-improvement products, and housewares and electronics.[27]

Advertisers use just about any medium they can find. They place messages on subway tickets in New York City and toll receipts on the Massachusetts Turnpike. A more recent development is the use of ATMs for advertising. Some ATMs can play 15-second commercials on their screens, and many can print advertising messages on receipts. An ATM screen has a captive audience because the user must watch the screen to complete a transaction. Directory advertising includes the familiar Yellow Pages listings in telephone books and thousands of other types of directories, most presenting business-related promotions. Besides local and regional directories, publishers also have produced special versions of the Yellow Pages that target ethnic groups.

Assessment Check

1. What are the two basic types of advertising? Into what three categories do they fall?
2. What is the leading advertising medium in the United States?
3. In what two major ways do firms benefit from sponsorship?

Sales Promotion

sales promotion nonpersonal marketing activities other than advertising, personal selling, and public relations that stimulate consumer purchasing and dealer effectiveness.

Traditionally viewed as a supplement to a firm's sales or advertising efforts, sales promotion has emerged as an integral part of the promotional mix. Promotion now accounts for more than half as many marketing dollars as are spent on advertising, and promotion spending is rising faster than ad spending. **Sales promotion** consists of forms of promotion such as coupons, product samples, and rebates that support advertising and personal selling.

Both retailers and manufacturers use sales promotions to offer consumers extra incentives to buy. Beyond the short-term advantage of increased sales, sales promotions can also help marketers build brand equity and enhance customer relationships. Examples include samples, coupons, contests, displays, trade shows, and dealer incentives.

Consumer-Oriented Promotions

The goal of a consumer-oriented sales promotion is to get new and existing customers to try or buy products. In addition, marketers want to encourage repeat purchases by rewarding current users, increase sales of complementary products, and boost impulse purchases. Figure 14.3 shows how marketers allocate their consumer-oriented spending among the categories of promotions.

Promotions can also popularize an idea, such as the growing awareness of how much pollution plastic shopping bags contribute to the environment. The "Hit & Miss" feature discusses the growing trend of eco-friendly shopping bags.

PREMIUMS, COUPONS, REBATES, AND SAMPLES Nearly 6 of every 10 sales promotion dollars are spent on *premiums*—items given free or at a reduced price with the purchase of another product. Cosmetics companies such as Clinique offer sample kits with purchases of their products. Fast-food restaurants are also big users of premiums. McDonald's and Burger King include a toy with every children's meal—the toys often tie in with new movies or popular cartoon shows. In general, marketers choose premiums that are likely to get consumers thinking about and caring about the brand and the product. People who purchase health foods at a grocery store may find an offer for a free personal training session at a local health club printed on the back of their sales receipt.

Customers redeem *coupons* for small price discounts when they purchase the promoted products. Such offers may persuade a customer to try a new or different product. Some large supermarket chains double the face value of manufacturers' coupons. Coupons have the disadvantage of focusing customers on price rather than brand loyalty. Other discounters such as Wal-Mart prefer to lure customers with their own low-priced brands. While some consumers complain that clipping coupons is too time consuming, others relish the savings, particularly when prices seem to be high. Still, coupon redemption has dropped steadily in the United States since 1992, partly because more consumers are choosing discount retailers and frequent-shopper programs instead.[28]

Rebates offer cash back to consumers who mail in required proofs of purchase. Rebates help packaged-goods manufacturers increase purchase rates, promote multiple purchases, and reward product users. Other types of companies also offer rebates, especially for electronics, computers and their accessories, and automobiles. Processing rebates gives marketers a way to collect data about their customers, but many shoppers find it inconvenient to collect the required receipts, forms, and UPC codes and then wait several weeks for their refund. Some stores are phasing out mail-in rebates; Best Buy has already replaced them with "instant savings" that the consumer can pocket at the cash register.[29]

A *sample* is a gift of a product distributed by mail, door to door, in a demonstration, or inside packages of another product. On any given day you might receive a sample moisturizer,

Figure 14.3

Spending on Consumer-Oriented Promotions

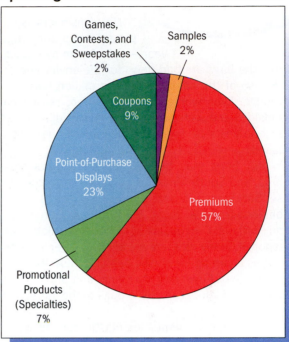

Source: Data from Kathleen M. Joyce, "Higher Gear," *Promo Magazine,* http://promomagazine.com, accessed March 26, 2009.

Hit & Miss

Promoting Green Totes: It's in the Bag

U.S. consumers use 85 billion plastic shopping bags every year—1,500 for an average family of four. The bags are bad news for the environment. Annual U.S. use of the bags requires 12 million barrels of oil to produce. Even worse, once discarded, plastic bags clog roadsides and waterways, endanger wildlife, and take up to 1,000 years to degrade. Only about 1 percent are ever reused.

But hope may be on the horizon. France, Ireland, China, and South Africa have banned or discouraged their use. San Francisco and 30 Alaskan villages have banned nonbiodegradable bags. Boston, Santa Cruz, Annapolis, and Portland, Oregon, are considering similar measures. In response, many retailers are offering "green" alternatives, such as charging for plastic bags, as IKEA does, encouraging bring-your-own-bag shopping, and providing recycling bins so customers can return bags to the store, sometimes for a rebate.

Some replacements for plastic can do double duty as promotional tools, and consumers seem to like them. Some shopping bags, in fact, are highly desirable fashion items. The most sought-after accessory in England recently wasn't a sleek Coach pouch or Fendi clutch. It was a humble $15 cotton canvas tote bag with the words "I'm not a plastic bag" embroidered on the front. The eco-friendly bag, created by high-end British designer Anya Hindmarch and produced in a limited edition in partnership with nonprofit group We Are What We Do, also sold in Dublin, Taiwan, and Hong Kong. In fact, in Hong Kong a near-riot broke out, and buyers feared being robbed of their bags on the way home. Planned sales of the tote were then canceled in Beijing, Shanghai, and Singapore. The Hindmarch bag was a hit with trendsetters like actresses Keira Knightley and Reese Witherspoon, and it was one of the premiums given to guests at *Vanity Fair*'s Oscar party. It sold out in less than half an hour at New York's Whole Foods stores. Whole Foods also sells its own reusable bag, made of organic cotton, for 99 cents.

Other designers are getting into the act. Marc Jacobs, tongue in cheek, produced a $12 canvas hold-all that reads "Jacobs by Marc Jacobs for Marc by Marc Jacobs in collaboration with Marc Jacobs for Marc by Marc Jacobs." Fellow designers Jack Spade, Stella McCartney, Hermes, and Louis Vuitton are selling similar tote bags, but at designer prices.

Meanwhile, the Hindmarch bag has also turned up on eBay, giving new meaning to "reduce, reuse, recycle" by selling for hundreds of dollars. What does Anya Hindmarch think about all the fuss? "I hate the idea of making the environment trendy," she says, "but you need to make it cool and then it becomes a habit."

Questions for Critical Thinking

1. Can stores that provide eco-friendly shopping bags or other ways to reduce the polluting effects of plastic reap promotional benefits from their efforts?
2. What other ways can you think of to promote the idea of recycling plastic bags or reducing their use?

Sources: Christopher Bodeen, "Shoppers: It's BYO Bag in China," *Associated Press,* January 10, 2008, http://news.yahoo.com, accessed March 26, 2009; Lisa McLaughlin, "Paper, Plastic or Prada?" *Time,* August 13, 2007, pp. 49–51; Erin Byers Murray, "Saving the Planet (One Trendy Bag at a Time)," *The Boston Globe,* July 26, 2007, http://www.boston.com, accessed October 14, 2008; Denise Winterman, "It's in the Bag, Darling," *BBC News Magazine,* April 25, 2007, http://news.bbc.co.uk, accessed October 14, 2008.

---

a bar of soap, or a packet of laundry detergent. Three of every four consumers who receive samples will try them.

GAMES, CONTESTS, AND SWEEPSTAKES Contests, sweepstakes, and games offer cash, merchandise, or travel as prizes to participating winners. Firms often sponsor these activities to introduce new goods and services and to attract additional customers. Games and contests require entrants to solve problems or write essays and sometimes provide proof of purchase. Sweepstakes choose winners by chance and require no product purchase. Consumers typically prefer them because games and contests require more effort. Companies like sweepstakes, too, because they are inexpensive to run and determine the number of winners from the beginning. With games and contests, the company cannot predict the number of people who will correctly complete a puzzle or gather the right number of symbols from scratch-off cards. Sweepstakes, games, and contests can reinforce a company's image and advertising message, but consumer attention may focus on the promotion rather than the product.

In recent years, court rulings and legal restrictions have limited the use of games and contests. Companies must proceed carefully in advertising their contests and games and the prizes they award. Marketers must indicate the chances of winning and avoid false promises such as implying that a person has already won.

SPECIALTY ADVERTISING Do you have any pens, T-shirts, or refrigerator magnets imprinted with a business name that you received for free? These offers are examples of **specialty advertising** or *advertising specialties.* This type of sales promotion involves the gift of useful merchandise carrying the name, logo, or slogan of a profit-seeking business or a not-for-profit organization. Because those products are useful and sometimes personalized with recipients' names, people tend to keep and use them, giving advertisers repeated exposure. Originally designed to identify and create goodwill for advertisers, advertising specialties now generate sales leads and develop traffic for stores and trade show exhibitors. Like premiums, these promotions should reinforce the brand's image and its relationship with the recipient.

Trade-Oriented Promotions

Sales promotion techniques can also contribute to campaigns directed to retailers and wholesalers. **Trade promotion** is sales promotion geared to marketing intermediaries rather than to consumers. Marketers use trade promotion to

Here is the winner of retailer Old Navy's search for a new mascot. A form of sales promotion, contests can either call attention to a product or become the center of attention themselves.

encourage retailers to stock new products, continue carrying existing ones, and promote both new and existing products effectively to consumers. Successful trade promotions offer financial incentives. They require careful timing, attention to costs, and easy implementation for intermediaries. These promotions should bring quick results and improve retail sales. Major trade promotions include point-of-purchase advertising and trade shows.

Point-of-purchase (POP) advertising consists of displays or demonstrations that promote products when and where consumers buy them, such as in retail stores. When the Swiffer floor cleaner was being introduced, Procter & Gamble used in-store demonstrations to show consumers how it worked. Marketing research has shown that consumers are more apt to purchase certain products when such displays are present. Sunscreen, painting supplies, and snacks are typically displayed this way. A high-tech version of POP advertising is digital advertising consoles mounted on grocery carts. After four years of research and development, Microsoft Corp. is offering retailers consoles that not only show video ads but also help shoppers locate, scan, and pay for their purchases.[30]

Manufacturers and other sellers often exhibit at *trade shows* to promote goods or services to members of their distribution channels. These shows are often organized by industry trade associations, typically during annual meetings or conventions. Each year, thousands of trade shows attract millions of exhibitors and hundreds of millions of attendees. Such shows are particularly important in fast-changing industries like those for computers, toys, furniture, and fashions. The annual Consumer Electronics Show, which is held in Las Vegas and attracts more than 100,000 visitors, is the nation's largest. But shows in the medical and healthcare, RV and camping, and even woodworking machinery fields remain strong. These shows are especially effective for introducing new products and generating sales leads.

Personal Selling

Many companies consider personal selling—a person-to-person promotional presentation to a potential buyer—the key to marketing effectiveness. Unless a seller matches a firm's goods or services to the needs of a particular client or customer, none of the firm's other activities produces any benefits. Today, sales and sales-related jobs employ about 16 million U.S. workers.[31] Businesses often spend five to ten times as much on personal selling as on advertising. Given the significant cost of hiring, training, benefits, and salaries, businesses are very concerned with the effectiveness of their sales personnel. One of their continuing concerns is with the way representatives communicate with others. The "Business Etiquette" feature discusses how salespeople can build relationships with customers by expressing empathy.

How do marketers decide whether to make personal selling the primary component of their firm's marketing mix? In general, firms are likely to emphasize personal selling rather than advertising or sales promotion under four conditions:

1. Customers are relatively few in number and geographically concentrated.
2. The product is technically complex, involves trade-ins, or requires special handling.
3. The product carries a relatively high price.
4. It moves through direct-distribution channels.

Selling Piper Cub airplanes is a good example. Customers tend to be wealthy people who value their freedom and privacy, not to mention the luxury of having their own plane. They can also be reclusive or unpredictable, yet salespeople must turn the controls over to them during demonstration rides despite knowing nothing about their piloting skill. "It is a way of life I am selling," says veteran sales rep Bruce Keller, "not just aluminum. I want the customer to share that with me. If you look at my airplane and you sit in it, you are going flying."[32]

The sales functions of most companies are experiencing rapid change. Today's salespeople are more concerned with establishing long-term buyer–seller relationships and acting as consultants to their customers than in the past.

Personal selling can occur in several environments, each of which can involve business-to-business or business-to-consumer selling. Sales representatives who make sales calls on prospective customers at their homes or businesses are involved in *field selling*. Companies that sell major industrial equipment typically rely heavily on field selling. *Over-the-counter selling* describes sales activities in retailing and some wholesale locations, where customers visit the seller's facility to purchase items. *Telemarketing* sales representatives make their presentations over the phone. A later section reviews telemarketing in more detail.

Sales Tasks

All sales activities involve assisting customers in some manner. Although a salesperson's work can vary significantly from one company or situation to another, it usually includes a mix of three basic tasks: order processing, creative selling, and missionary selling.

ORDER PROCESSING Although both field selling and telemarketing involve this activity, **order processing** is most often related to retail and wholesale firms. The salesperson identifies customer needs, points out merchandise to meet them, and processes the order. Route sales personnel process orders for such consumer goods as bread, milk, soft drinks, and snack foods. They check each store's stock, report inventory needs to the store manager, and complete the sale. Most of these jobs include at least minor order-processing functions.

CREATIVE SELLING Sales representatives for most business products and some consumer items perform **creative selling,** a persuasive type of promotional presentation. Creative selling promotes a good or service whose benefits are not readily apparent or whose purchase decision requires a close analysis of alternatives. Sales of intangible products such as insurance rely heavily on creative selling, but sales of tangible goods benefit as well.

Many retail salespeople just process orders, but many consumers are looking for more in the form of customer service, which is where creative selling comes in. Trained sales staff at Talbots women's clothing stores hold seasonal wardrobe-building workshops at the stores, helping customers select and purchase coordinating clothing, accessories, and shoes from the Talbots line—which they might not have purchased without such advice.

MISSIONARY SELLING Sales work also includes an indirect form of selling in which the representative promotes goodwill for a company or provides technical or operational assistance to the customer; this practice is called **missionary selling.** Many businesses that sell technical equipment, such as Oracle and Fujitsu, provide systems specialists who act as consultants to customers. These salespeople work to solve problems and sometimes help their clients with questions not directly related to their employers' products. Other industries also use missionary selling techniques. Pharmaceutical company representatives—called *detailers*—visit physicians to describe the firm's latest products, although some firms are finding success with more subtle methods including Web-based sales calls outside office hours.[33] The actual sales, in any case, are handled through pharmacies, which fill the prescriptions.

Business Etiquette

IN HARD TIMES, TAKE CARE OF YOUR CUSTOMERS

Despite a slow economy, consumers and businesses still need to make purchases. They need to buy goods and services to keep their organizations functioning—and in many cases their workers employed. The difference is, they may think longer about each purchase and look for the greatest value in every transaction. Here is where you, as a salesperson, can help—and create a competitive advantage for yourself.

- *Be respectful of your customer's time.* In a tight economy, your customer may be doing the jobs of several people. Be organized and efficient with your presentation. Of course, always arrive on time for an appointment. If you are talking on the phone, make the call brief and to the point.
- *Feel your customer's pain.* Perhaps a customer has had to cut back on an order or is looking for a better deal. Show empathy for the situation—you may be in the same boat. If your product can actually help alleviate some of the customer's economic stress, then be sure to point that out.
- *Try to find the best deal for your customer.* Work hard to create the best deal for your customer, whether it's a percentage off, added free features, an extended warranty at no charge, or something else. Your efforts very likely will pay off with a solid relationship that lasts long after the economy turns around.
- *Give the relationship attention.* Even if your customer has to postpone or cancel an order for a period of time, give the relationship the same courtesy and attentiveness you would during better times. If you do, your customer will be more likely to return to you for a purchase in the future.
- *Be positive.* Everyone needs a bit of encouragement now and then. You don't have to be excessively happy, but try to present at least one positive outcome of the current situation. And if your business is slow, don't complain about it to your customers. Let them know that you are working hard, too, but that you have an optimistic outlook about your own business and theirs.

Sources: Jeremy Gislason, "Maximizing Sales in an Economic Downturn," *Selfgrowth.com,* http://www.selfgrowth.com, accessed March 4, 2009; "3 Sales Etiquette Skills to Keep Sharp," *SalesBlogShots,* January 8, 2009, http://salesblogshots.7dayshootout.com; Paul Keegan, "Sales Slip-ups," *Fortune,* September 29, 2008, p. 108; Debbie Mrazek, "Counterintuitive Selling Rules during a Recession," *True You Marketing,* February 20, 2008, http://www.trueyoumarketing.com.

TELEMARKETING **Telemarketing,** personal selling conducted by telephone, provides a firm's marketers with a high return on their expenditures, an immediate response, and an opportunity for personalized two-way conversation. Many firms use telemarketing because expense or other obstacles prevent salespeople from meeting many potential customers in person. Telemarketers can use databases to target prospects based on demographic data. Telemarketing takes two forms. A sales representative who calls you is practicing *outbound telemarketing*. On the other hand, *inbound telemarketing* occurs when you call a toll-free phone number to get product information or place an order.

Outbound telemarketers must abide by the Federal Trade Commission's 1996 Telemarketing Sales Rule. Telemarketers must disclose that they are selling something and on whose behalf they are calling before they make their presentations. The rule also limits calls to between 8 a.m. and 9 p.m., requires sellers to disclose details on exchange policies, and requires them to keep lists of people who do not want to receive calls. In some states, it is also against the law for telemarketers to leave messages on consumers' answering machines. Despite opposition from the Direct Marketing Association, Congress enacted another law in 2003 creating a national "do not call" registry intended to help consumers block unwanted telemarketing calls. Consumers who want to be on the list must call a special number or visit a Web site to register. Telemarketers stop calling registered numbers within 31 days or face stiff fines of up to $11,000 for each violation.[34] Charities, surveys, and political campaign calls are exempt from these restrictions. Businesses with which consumers already have a relationship, such as the bank where they have accounts or the dealership where they buy their cars, may conduct telemarketing calls under the guidelines of the Telemarketing Sales Rule.

Figure 14.4

Seven Steps in the Sales Process

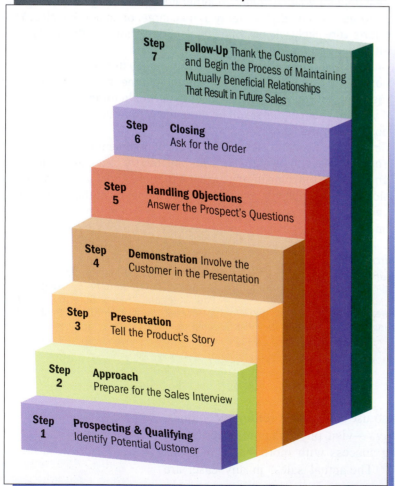

Step 7 — **Follow-Up** Thank the Customer and Begin the Process of Maintaining Mutually Beneficial Relationships That Result in Future Sales

Step 6 — **Closing** Ask for the Order

Step 5 — **Handling Objections** Answer the Prospect's Questions

Step 4 — **Demonstration** Involve the Customer in the Presentation

Step 3 — **Presentation** Tell the Product's Story

Step 2 — **Approach** Prepare for the Sales Interview

Step 1 — **Prospecting & Qualifying** Identify Potential Customer

The Sales Process

The sales process typically follows the seven-step sequence shown in Figure 14.4: prospecting and qualifying, the approach, the presentation, the demonstration, handling objections, the closing, and the follow-up. Remember the importance of flexibility, though; a good salesperson is not afraid to vary the sales process based on a customer's responses and needs. The process of selling to a potential customer who is unfamiliar with a company's products differs from the process of serving a long-time customer.

PROSPECTING, QUALIFYING, AND APPROACHING

At the prospecting stage, salespeople identify potential customers. They may seek leads for prospective sales from such sources as existing customers, friends and family, and business associates. The qualifying process identifies potential customers who have the financial ability and authority to buy.

Companies use different tactics to identify and qualify prospects. Some companies rely on business development teams to do this legwork. They use the responses from direct mail to provide leads to sales reps. Other companies believe in personal visits from sales representatives; others use e-mail, which is inexpensive and boasts a good response rate.[35]

Successful salespeople make careful preparations, analyzing available data about a prospective customer's product lines and other pertinent information before making the initial contact. They realize the importance of a first impression in influencing a customer's future attitudes toward the selling company and its products.

PRESENTATION AND DEMONSTRATION At the presentation stage, salespeople communicate promotional messages. They may describe the major features of their products, highlight the advantages, and cite examples of satisfied consumers. A demonstration helps reinforce the message that the salesperson has been communicating—a critical step in the sales process. Department-store shoppers can get a free makeover at the cosmetics counter. Anyone looking to buy a car will take it for a test drive before deciding whether to purchase it.

Some products are too large to transport to prospective buyers or require special installation to demonstrate. Using laptop computers, multimedia presentations, graphic programs like SmartDraw, Web conferences, and even podcasts, sales representatives can demonstrate these products for customers.[36] Others, such as services, are intangible. So a presentation including testimonials from satisfied customers or graphs illustrating results may be helpful.

HANDLING OBJECTIONS Some salespeople fear potential customers' objections because they view the questions as criticism. But a good salesperson can use objections as an opportunity to answer questions and explain how the product will benefit the customer. As a general rule, the key is to sell benefits, not features: How will this product help the customer?

CLOSING The critical point in the sales process—the time at which the salesperson actually asks the prospect to buy—is the closing. If the presentation effectively matches product benefits to customer needs, the closing should be a natural conclusion. If there are more bumps in the process, the salesperson can try some different techniques, such as offering alternative products, offering a special incentive for purchase, or restating the product benefits. Closing the sale—and beginning a relationship in which the customer builds loyalty to the brand or product—is the ideal outcome of this interaction. But even if the sale is not made at this time, the salesperson should regard the interaction as the beginning of a potential relationship anyway. The prospect might very well become a customer in the future.

FOLLOW-UP A salesperson's actions after the sale may determine whether the customer will make another purchase. Follow-up is an important part of building a long-lasting relationship. After closing, the salesperson should process the order efficiently. By calling soon after a purchase, the salesperson provides reassurance about the customer's decision to buy and creates an opportunity to correct any problems.

Public Relations

A final element of the promotional mix, public relations (PR)—including publicity—supports advertising, personal selling, and sales promotion, usually by pursuing broader objectives. Through PR, companies attempt to improve their prestige and image with the public by distributing specific messages or ideas to target audiences. Cause-related promotional activities are often supported by PR and publicity campaigns. In addition, PR helps a firm establish awareness of goods and services, then builds a positive image of them.

Public relations refers to an organization's communications with its various public audiences, such as customers, vendors, news media, employees, stockholders, the government, and the general public. Many of these communication efforts serve marketing purposes. Public relations is an efficient, indirect communications channel for promoting products. It can publicize products and help create and maintain a positive image of the company.

public relations organization's communications and relationships with its various audiences.

The PR department links a firm with the media. It provides the media with news releases and video and audio clips, as well as holding news conferences to announce new products, the formation of strategic alliances, management changes, financial results, and similar developments. Publications issued by the PR department include newsletters, brochures, and reports.

publicity stimulation of demand for a good, service, place, idea, person, or organization by disseminating news or obtaining favorable unpaid media presentations.

Publicity

The type of public relations that is tied most closely to promoting a company's products is publicity—nonpersonal stimulation of demand for a good, service, place, idea, event, person, or organization by unpaid placement of information in print or broadcast media. Press releases generate publicity, as does news coverage. Ironically, sometimes even criticism can generate publicity. Protests against violent videogames such as "Manhunt 2" create media attention that has been known to cause sales of these products to rise rather than decline.[37]

Not-for-profit organizations benefit from publicity when they receive coverage of events such as the Susan G. Komen "Race for the Cure" that raises money for breast cancer research.[38] When a for-profit firm teams up with a not-for-profit firm in a fund-raising effort, the move usually generates good publicity for both organizations.

While good publicity can promote a firm's positive image, negative publicity can cause problems. When JetBlue stranded passengers for hours on runways at New York's JFK Airport in an ice storm, the aftermath was so bad that an Airline Passenger's Bill of Rights was introduced in Congress and JetBlue's founder was forced to resign from his position as CEO.[39]

wrinkled?
wonderful?

When did beauty become limited by age? It's time to think, talk and learn how to make beauty real again. Join Dove and the debate at campaignforrealbeauty.com

© Unilever, Inc.

Instead of young professional models, Dove's Campaign for Real Beauty featured striking women of all ages, shapes, and sizes. The highly successful campaign was based on a pulling strategy, meant to increase the demand for Dove products.

Pushing and Pulling Strategies

Marketers can choose between two general promotional strategies: a pushing strategy or a pulling strategy. A **pushing strategy** relies on personal selling to market an item to wholesalers and retailers in a company's distribution channels. So companies promote the product to members of the marketing channel, not to end users. Sales personnel explain to marketing intermediaries why they should carry particular merchandise, usually supported by offers of special discounts and promotional materials. Marketers also provide **cooperative advertising** allowances, in which they share the cost of local advertising of their firm's product or line with channel partners. All of these strategies are designed to motivate wholesalers and retailers to push the good or service to their own customers.

A **pulling strategy** attempts to promote a product by generating consumer demand for it, primarily through advertising and sales promotion appeals. Potential buyers will then request that their suppliers—retailers or local distributors—carry the product, thereby pulling it through the distribution channel. Dove used this strategy when it launched a highly popular advertising campaign—called "Campaign for Real Beauty"—for its products featuring everyday women instead of professional models. The ads for soap, shampoo, and lotions were placed in magazines, on billboards and buildings, and even along the sides of buses. The strategy was so successful that it also generated good publicity—including a segment on NBC's *Today Show*.[40]

Most marketing situations require combinations of pushing and pulling strategies, although the primary emphasis can vary. Consumer products usually depend more heavily on pulling strategies than do B2B products, which favor pushing strategies.

Pricing Objectives in the Marketing Mix

Products offer utility, or want-satisfying power. However, we as consumers determine how much value we associate with each one. In the aftermath of a disaster, we may value electricity and food and water above everything else. If we commute a long distance or are planning a vacation, fuel may be of greater concern. But all consumers have limited amounts of money and a variety of possible uses for it. So the **price**—the exchange value of a good or service—becomes a major factor in consumer buying decisions.

Businesspeople attempt to accomplish certain objectives through their pricing decisions. Pricing objectives vary from firm to firm, and many companies pursue multiple pricing objectives. Some try to improve profits by setting high prices; others set low prices to attract new business. As Figure 14.5 shows, the four basic categories of pricing objectives are (1) profitability, (2) volume, (3) meeting competition, and (4) prestige.

price exchange value of a good or service.

Profitability Objectives

Profitability objectives are perhaps the most common objectives included in the strategic plans of most firms. Marketers know that profits are the revenue the company brings in, minus its expenses. Usually a big difference exists between revenue and profit. Large automakers try to produce at least one luxury vehicle for which they can charge $50,000 or more instead of relying entirely on the sale of $15,000 to $25,000 models, thus making a greater profit typical of luxury models.

Some firms maximize profits by reducing costs rather than through price changes. Companies can maintain prices and increase profitability by operating more efficiently or by modifying the product to make it less costly to produce. One strategy is to maintain a steady price while reducing the size or amount of the product in the package—something that manufacturers of candy, coffee, and cereal have done over the years. But the recent increase in firms that are following this practice has brought criticism, as the "Solving an Ethical Controversy" feature explains.

Volume Objectives

A second approach to pricing strategy—**volume objectives**—bases pricing decisions on market share, the percentage of a

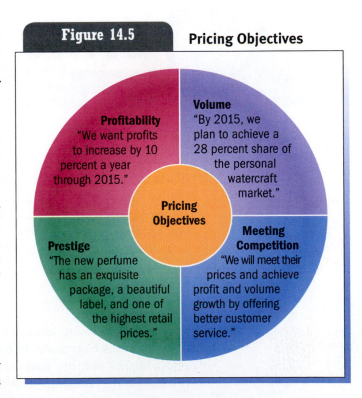

Figure 14.5 Pricing Objectives

Profitability "We want profits to increase by 10 percent a year through 2015."

Volume "By 2015, we plan to achieve a 28 percent share of the personal watercraft market."

Pricing Objectives

Prestige "The new perfume has an exquisite package, a beautiful label, and one of the highest retail prices."

Meeting Competition "We will meet their prices and achieve profit and volume growth by offering better customer service."

SOARING PRICES, SHRINKING PACKAGES

If the container of ice cream you just bought seems smaller than it used to be or the box of cereal feels lighter, it's not your imagination. As the prices of ingredients soar, manufacturers find ways to cut costs instead of charging more for their goods. One way is to reduce the size of each package. Consumer goods firms such as General Mills, Kellogg, Unilever, and Procter & Gamble have been quietly cutting the amount of cereal, ice cream, coffee, paper towels, and other products in a single box or bag. Meanwhile, they are not cutting prices. In fact, some are even raising prices. Is this legal? Yes, as long as firms don't lie about how much product is actually in the container.

Should firms be required to announce when they reduce the amount of product that comes in a package?

PRO

1. "If companies are going to do this, they need to be transparent about it and let consumers know," says Chris Waldrop, director of the Food Policy Institute at the Consumer Federation of America.
2. Even though companies are required to put the weight or volume of a product on its package, most busy consumers won't notice that the jar of Skippy peanut butter now contains 16.3 ounces instead of 18 ounces. This practice makes it more difficult for consumers to comparison shop.

CON

1. Grocery producers need to trim costs, attract consumers, and stay in business. In many cases, reducing package sizes and contents is preferable to increasing prices. "The reality is, people pay more attention to prices than sizes," notes one marketing professor.
2. Keeping the price stable and reducing the product amount is a win-win for both grocery producers and consumers. Producers are able to control costs, and consumers do not see an increase in out-of-pocket expenses.

Summary

In a tight economy, sellers and buyers are faced with difficult choices. Probably the best advice is for consumers to be aware of unit pricing and package size. Differences can be subtle. It might take a few moments to read a package label, but at least you'll know what you are buying. When you see the word "giant" on a box of cereal or can of coffee, look at the weight or volume before putting the item in your shopping cart.

Sources: Jerry Hirsch, "Grocers, Name-Brand Food Producers at Odds Over Prices," *Los Angeles Times,* March 2, 2009, http://wwwlatimes.com; "Haagen-Dazs Shrinks Package, Says It's to Preserve Quality," *Slashfood,* January 20, 2009, http://www.slashfood.com; Chris Serres, "Freshly Squeezed: The Ever-Shrinking Box and Carton," *Star Tribune,* December 2, 2008, http://www.startribune.com; Susan Koeppen, "Downsized Products Giving Consumers Less," *CBS News,* October 23, 2008, http://www.cbsnews.com; Michael Brush, "The Incredible Shrinking Doritos Bag," *MSN Money,* August 1, 2008, http://articles.moneycentral.msn.com.

Solving an **ETHICAL** *controversy*

> ## "They Said It"
>
> **"Free is good—but read the fine print."**
>
> —Anonymous

market controlled by a certain company or product. One firm may seek to achieve a 25 percent market share in a certain industry, and another may want to maintain or expand its market share for particular products. As a market becomes saturated—like the PC market—firms need to find ways to get consumers to upgrade or try new products. Setting a lower price can accomplish that objective, as long as the firm still makes a profit. Many PC makers—and retailers—have begun to offer their products at lower prices, particularly at the start of the school year.[41]

Pricing to Meet Competition

A third set of pricing objectives seeks simply to meet competitors' prices so that price essentially becomes a nonissue. In many lines of business, firms set their own prices to match those of established industry leaders. However, companies may not legally work together to agree on prices or force retailers to sell at a set price.

Because price is such a highly visible component of a firm's marketing mix, businesses may be tempted to use it to obtain an advantage over competitors. But sometimes the race to match competitors' prices results in a *price war*, which has happened periodically in the airline and fast-food industries. The ability of competitors to match a price cut leads many marketers to try to avoid price wars by favoring other strategies, such as adding value, improving quality, educating consumers, and establishing relationships.

Wal-Mart's decision to sell 42-inch flat-panel TVs for under $1,000 during the Christmas selling season was daring, and it paid off in more than holidays sales. Competitors like CompUSA fell victim to the price-slashing, laying off workers and closing stores in the months that followed. "The tube business and big-screen business just dropped off a cliff," said the CEO of Rex Stores, a regional chain that was also hurting. "We expected a dropoff, but nowhere near the decline that we had."[42]

Prestige Objectives

The final category of objectives encompasses the effect of prices on prestige. **Prestige pricing** establishes a relatively high price to develop and maintain an image of quality and exclusiveness. Marketers set such objectives because they recognize the role of price in communicating an overall image for the firm and its products. People expect to pay more for a Lexus vehicle, a Louis Vuitton purse, or a vacation on St. Kitts or Nevis in the Caribbean. "It's phenomenal to me to watch the young girls—I'm talking 15-year-old girls—pining after a Marc Jacobs bag, and these bags are $2,000," said the vice president for fashion direction at Bloomingdale's. "It's beyond belief."[43]

Scarcity can create prestige. Products that are limited in distribution or so popular that they become scarce generate their own prestige—allowing businesses to charge more for them. The scarcity of "hot" ticket concerts, for instance, although created artificially in part by online buyers "whose only job is to buy and sell seats," has created a secondary market where prices rise into the hundreds of dollars. Online ticket brokers snatched up enough Hannah Montana tickets to shut out many of the teenage singer's real fans during her recent 54-city tour.[44]

REACH HIGHER.
SHOW US WHAT "LINCOLN LUXURY" MEANS TO YOU.

In this ad, Lincoln challenges aspiring filmmakers to "Reach Higher. Show us what 'Lincoln Luxury' means to you." High-end advertising is a hallmark of luxury brands, as is *prestige pricing*. Both make a product seem more desirable, contributing to its mystique.

Assessment Check

1. Define *price*.
2. Which pricing objective actually results in diverting consumer attention from price?

Pricing Strategies

People from different areas of a company contribute their expertise to set the most strategic price for a product. Accountants, financial managers, and marketers provide relevant sales and cost data, along with customer feedback. Designers, engineers, and systems analysts all contribute important data as well.

Prices are determined in two basic ways: by applying the concepts of supply and demand discussed in Chapter 3, and by completing cost-oriented analyses. Economic theory assumes that a market price will be set at the point at which the amount of a product desired at a given price equals the amount that suppliers will offer for sale at that price. In other words, this price occurs at the point at which the amount demanded and the amount supplied are equal. Online auctions, such as those conducted on eBay, are a popular application of the demand-and-supply approach.

Price Determination in Practice

cost-based pricing
adding a percentage (markup) to the base cost of a product to cover overhead costs and generate profits.

Economic theory might lead to the best pricing decisions, but most businesses do not have all the information they need to make those decisions, so they adopt <mark>cost-based pricing</mark> formulas. These formulas calculate total costs per unit and then add markups to cover overhead costs and generate profits.

Cost-based pricing totals all costs associated with offering a product in the market, including research and development, production, transportation, and marketing expenses. An added amount, the markup, then covers any unexpected or overlooked expenses and provides a profit. The total becomes the price. Although the actual markup used varies by such factors as brand image and type of store, the typical markup for clothing is determined by doubling the wholesale price (the cost to the merchant) to arrive at the retail price for the item.

Breakeven Analysis

breakeven analysis
pricing technique used to determine the minimum sales volume a product must generate at a certain price level to cover all costs.

Businesses often conduct a <mark>breakeven analysis</mark> to determine the minimum sales volume a product must generate at a certain price level to cover all costs. This method involves a consideration of various costs and total revenues. *Total cost* is the sum of total variable costs and total fixed costs. *Variable costs* change with the level of production, as labor and raw materials do, while *fixed costs* such as insurance premiums and utility rates charged by water, natural gas, and electric power suppliers remain stable regardless of the production level. *Total revenue* is determined by multiplying price by the number of units sold.

FINDING THE BREAKEVEN POINT The level of sales that will generate enough revenue to cover all of the company's fixed and variable costs is called the *breakeven point*. It is the point at which total revenue just equals total costs. Sales beyond the breakeven point will generate profits; sales volume below the breakeven point will result in losses. The following formulas give the breakeven point in units and dollars:

$$\text{Breakeven point (in units)} = \frac{\text{Total fixed costs}}{\text{Contribution to fixed costs per unit}}$$

$$\text{Breakeven point (in dollars)} = \frac{\text{Total fixed costs}}{1 - \text{Variable cost per unit/Price}}$$

A product selling for $20 with a variable cost of $14 per unit produces a $6 per-unit contribution to fixed costs. If the firm has total fixed costs of $42,000, then it must sell 7,000 units to break even on the product. The calculation of the breakeven point in units and dollars is as follows:

$$\text{Breakeven point (in units)} = \frac{\$42,000}{\$20 - \$14} = \frac{\$42,000}{\$6} = 7,000 \text{ units}$$

$$\text{Breakeven point (in dollars)} = \frac{\$42,000}{1 - \$14/\$20} = \frac{\$42,000}{1 - 0.7} = \frac{\$42,000}{0.3} = \$140,000$$

Figure 14.6 illustrates this breakeven point in a graph.

Marketers use breakeven analysis to determine the profits or losses that would result from several different proposed prices. Because different prices produce different breakeven points, marketers could compare their calculations of required sales to break even with sales estimates from marketing research studies. This comparison can identify the best price—one that would attract enough customers to exceed the breakeven point and earn profits for the firm.

Most firms add consumer demand—determining whether enough customers will buy the number of units the firm must sell

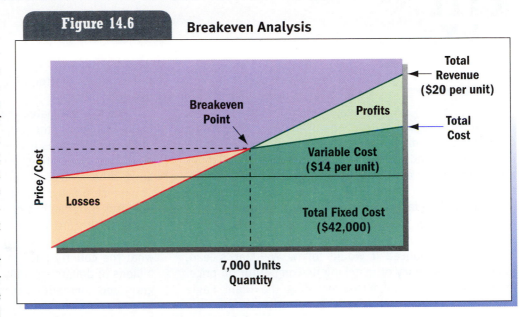

Figure 14.6 **Breakeven Analysis**

at a particular price to break even—by developing estimates through surveys of likely customers, interviews with retailers that would be handling the product, and assessments of prices charged by competitors. Then the breakeven points for several possible prices are calculated and compared with sales estimates for each price. This practice is referred to as *modified breakeven analysis*.

Alternative Pricing Strategies

The strategy a company uses to set its prices should grow out of the firm's overall marketing strategy. In general, firms can choose from four alternative pricing strategies: skimming, penetration, discount or everyday low pricing, and competitive pricing.

SKIMMING PRICING A **skimming pricing** strategy sets an intentionally high price relative to the prices of competing products. The term comes from the expression "skimming the cream." This pricing strategy often works for the introduction of a distinctive good or service with little or no competition, although it can be used at other stages of the product life cycle as well. A skimming strategy can help marketers set a price that distinguishes a firm's high-end product from those of competitors. It can also help a firm recover its product development costs before competitors enter the field. This is often the case with prescription drugs.

PENETRATION PRICING By contrast, a **penetration pricing** strategy sets a low price as a major marketing weapon. Businesses may price new products noticeably lower than competing offerings when they enter new industries characterized by dozens of competing brands. Once the new product achieves some market recognition through consumer trial purchases stimulated by its low price, marketers may increase the price to the level of competing products. However, stiff competition might prevent the price increase.

EVERYDAY LOW PRICING AND DISCOUNT PRICING Everyday low pricing (EDLP) is a strategy devoted to maintaining continuous low prices rather than relying on short-term price-cutting tactics such as cents-off coupons, rebates, and special sales. This strategy has been used successfully by retailers such as Wal-Mart and GNC to consistently offer low prices to consumers; manufacturers also use EDLP to set stable prices for retailers. Many stores, led by Wal-Mart, have slashed the price of generic drugs to $4 per prescription as a way of encouraging more shoppers to come to their stores; this strategy is discussed in the "Hit & Miss" feature.

Hit & Miss

Wal-Mart Leads the Wave of $4 Generic Drugs

A few years ago Wal-Mart, which also owns Sam's Club and Neighborhood Market stores, announced it would sell dozens of generic prescription drugs for $4 no matter what kind of insurance coverage the customer had, or even if the customer didn't have any insurance at all. The third-largest seller of prescription drugs in the United States, Wal-Mart debuted the program in Florida as a test market and quickly rolled it out to more than 4,000 locations throughout the United States.

Target announced it would follow Wal-Mart's lead, in line with its policy of matching its competitor on price. Other chains soon followed, including the Giant Eagle supermarket chain, which said about two-thirds of the prescriptions it filled were for generic drugs, and the Publix and Meijer grocery chains, which both promised to give out several generic antibiotics free to customers with or without insurance.

For the grocery chains, free prescriptions are loss leaders. "The main thing is to get people into the stores," said an editor at *Supermarket News*. And at Publix, which is Florida's top grocery chain and has stores in four other states, the strategy works. Most of its prescription customers go on to purchase other items in the store. "We are constantly looking at ways to build our loyal pharmacy customer base," said a company spokesperson.

Wal-Mart recently added more medicines to the program, including those prescribed for glaucoma, attention deficit disorder, fungal infections, and acne. Drugs for fertility and birth control were priced at $9, compared with nationwide averages between $24 and $30 a month. The additions mean that about 95 percent of prescriptions written in most categories can be filled at discount prices.

Wal-Mart estimated it saved customers over $600 million in the first year of the program, covering nearly 40 percent of the prescriptions it filled. "This program has exceeded all of our expectations," said the company's chief operating officer. Even a former Deputy Undersecretary of Commerce praised the program. "Wal-Mart's $4 prescription drug program has had a major impact at a time when rising healthcare costs are on everyone's mind," said Paul A. London. "This program has the potential to lower what the country pays for prescription drugs by tens of billions of dollars annually as customers learn of the program and competitors match it. Wal-Mart is applying its basic business model to lower prices and make affordable health care available to more Americans."

Questions for Critical Thinking

1. The drug chains Walgreens, CVS, and Rite Aid have promised to respond to Wal-Mart's price cuts for prescription drugs. Does it make sense for them to do so by matching the $4 price? Why or why not?
2. Do prescription drugs make good loss leaders for a retailer? Why or why not?

Sources: Company Web site, http://www.walmartstores.com, accessed March 26, 2009; "Giant Eagle Expands Discount Drug Program, Lowers HBC Prices," *Progressive Grocer,* November 8, 2007, http://www.progressivegrocer.com, accessed October 14, 2008; "Wal-Mart Launches Phase Two of Prescription Program with New $4 Medications and Increased Savings," company press release, September 27, 2007, http://www.walmartfacts.com, accessed October 14, 2008; Madhusmita Bora, "7 Antibiotics Free at Publix," *St. Petersburg Times,* August 7, 2007, http://www.sptimes.com, accessed October 14, 2008.

With *discount pricing,* businesses hope to attract customers by dropping prices for a set period of time. Automakers usually offer consumers special discounts on most or all of their vehicles during the holiday shopping season. After the holidays, prices usual rebound. But experts warn that discounting must be done carefully, or profits can disappear. Businesses should offer discounts only for a specified period of time and with a clear understanding of what they are trying to accomplish with the strategy. They should advertise the discount, so customers know it is a special deal. When the time period has elapsed, so should the discount.

COMPETITIVE PRICING Although many organizations rely heavily on price as a competitive weapon, even more implement **competitive pricing** strategies. They try to reduce the emphasis on price competition by matching other firms'

Assessment Check ✓

1. What is a cost-based pricing formula?
2. What might be considered the most stable of the alternative pricing strategies?

prices and concentrating their own marketing efforts on the product, distribution, and promotional elements of the marketing mix. In fact, in industries with relatively homogeneous products, competitors must match one another's price reductions to maintain market share and remain competitive. By pricing their products at the levels of competing offerings, marketers largely negate the price variable in their marketing strategies.

Consumer Perceptions of Prices

How do you perceive prices for certain products? Marketers must consider this. If large numbers of potential buyers consider a price too high or too low, businesses must correct the situation. Price–quality relationships and the use of odd pricing are important considerations in setting prices.

Price–Quality Relationships

Research shows that a consumer's perception of product quality is closely related to an item's price. Most marketers believe that this perceived price–quality relationship remains steady over a relatively wide range of prices, although extremely high or low prices have less credibility. The price–quality relationship can critically affect a firm's pricing strategy.

Many consumers associate prestige, quality, and high price together—believing that paying a high price for an item such as an Infiniti car or a Kate Spade bag not only conveys prestige but also ensures quality. Others believe that eating at an expensive restaurant automatically means the food will be better than food served at a fast-food chain. Conversely, consumers may view an extremely low price as an indication that corners have been cut and quality will suffer. Interestingly, a recent taste test at the California Institute of Technology found that 20 people perceived the *same* wine as better tasting when it was marked at $90 a bottle than when it was marked $10. Only the prices were varied, but the taste testers didn't know that. This study supports the price–quality link in consumers' minds.[45]

Odd Pricing

Have you ever wondered why retailers set prices like $1.99 instead of $2 or $9.99 instead of $10? Before the age of cash registers and sales taxes, retailers reportedly followed this practice of odd pricing to force clerks to make correct change as part of cash control efforts. But now **odd pricing** is commonly used because many retailers believe that consumers favor uneven amounts or amounts that sound less than they really are: it's easier to justify a purchase of $299 than one of $300. However, some retailers also use this method to identify items that have been marked down. The odd price lets sales personnel—and customers—know the item is on sale.

Assessment Check

1. How does the price–quality relationship affect a firm's pricing strategy?
2. Why is odd pricing used?

What's Ahead

The chapters in Part 4 have explained the main principles underlying marketing management and described how each fits a firm's overall business strategy. The next few chapters will help you understand how companies manage the technology and information that are available to businesses to create value for their customers and enhance their competitiveness in the marketplace. You'll also learn how firms manage their financial resources.

Summary of Learning Goals

1 Discuss how integrated marketing communications relates to a firm's overall promotional strategy.

In practicing integrated marketing communications, a firm coordinates all promotional activities to produce a unified, customer-focused message. IMC identifies consumer needs and then shows how a company's products meet those needs. Marketers select the promotional media that best target and reach customers. Teamwork and careful promotional planning to coordinate IMC strategy components are important elements of these programs.

Assessment Check Answers

1.1 What is the objective of an integrated marketing communications program? An integrated marketing communications strategy focuses on customer needs to create a unified promotional message about a firm's goods or services.

1.2 What types of media are used in integrated marketing communications? Media used in integrated marketing communications include broadcast, print, direct mail, packaging and store displays, sales promotions, presentations, and online and interactive media.

2 Explain the concept of a promotional mix and outline the objectives of promotion.

A company's promotional mix integrates two components: personal selling and nonpersonal selling, which includes advertising, sales promotion, and public relations. By selecting the appropriate combination of promotional mix elements, marketers attempt to achieve the firm's five major promotional objectives: provide information, differentiate a product, increase demand, stabilize sales, and accentuate the product's value.

Assessment Check Answers

2.1 Which component of the promotional mix reaches the largest audience? Nonpersonal selling reaches the largest audience.

2.2 Why do firms pursue multiple promotional objectives at the same time? Firms pursue multiple promotional objectives because they may need to convey different messages to different audiences.

2.3 What are product placement and guerrilla marketing? Product placement involves paying a fee to have a product showcased in certain media, such as movies and television. Guerrilla marketing is innovative, low-cost marketing efforts designed to get consumers' attention in unusual ways.

3 Summarize the different types of advertising and advertising media.

Advertising, the most visible form of nonpersonal promotion, is designed to inform, persuade, or remind. Product advertising promotes a good or service, while institutional advertising promotes a concept, idea, organization, or philosophy. Television, newspapers, and magazines represent the largest advertising media categories. Others include direct mail, radio, and outdoor advertising. Interactive media such as the Internet represent the fastest-growing type of advertising. Interactive advertising directly involves the consumer, who controls the flow of information.

Assessment Check Answers

3.1 What are the two basic types of advertising? Into what three categories do they fall? The two basic types of advertising are product and institutional. They fall into the categories of informative, persuasive, and reminder-oriented advertising.

3.2 What is the leading advertising medium in the United States? According to the most recent numbers listed in Figure 14.2, television is the leading advertising medium in the United States.

3.3 In what two major ways do firms benefit from sponsorship? Firms benefit from sponsorship in two ways: they gain exposure to the event's audience and are associated with the image of the activity.

4 Outline the roles of sales promotion, personal selling, and public relations in promotional strategy.

Sales promotion accounts for greater expenditures than does advertising. Consumer-oriented sales promotions such as coupons, games, rebates, samples, premiums, contests, sweepstakes, and promotional products offer an extra incentive to buy a product. Point-of-purchase advertising displays and trade shows are sales promotions directed to the trade markets. Personal selling involves face-to-face interactions between seller and buyer. The primary sales tasks are order processing, creative selling, and missionary selling. The seven-step sales process entails prospecting and qualifying, approach, presentation, demonstration, handling objections, closing, and follow-up. Public relations is nonpaid promotion that seeks to enhance a company's public image through press releases, news conferences, articles, and news broadcasts.

Assessment Check Answers

4.1 Why do retailers and manufacturers use sales promotions? Retailers and manufacturers use sales promotions to offer consumers extra incentives to buy their products.

4.2 When does a firm use personal selling instead of nonpersonal selling? Personal selling is generally used when customers are few and geographically concentrated, the product is technically complex or requires special handling, the price is high, or the product moves through direct-distribution channels.

4.3 How does public relations serve a marketing purpose?
Public relations can be an efficient, indirect communications channel for promoting products. It can publicize products and help create and maintain a positive image of the company.

5 **Describe pushing and pulling promotional strategies.**
A pushing strategy relies on personal selling to market a product to wholesalers and retailers in a company's distribution channels. Marketers promote the product to members of the marketing channel, not to end users. A pulling strategy promotes the product by generating consumer demand for it, through advertising and sales promotion.

Assessment Check Answers

5.1 Give an example of a pushing strategy. A classic example of a pushing strategy is drug manufacturers, who used to market solely to physicians and hospitals. (Today, they also use a pulling strategy by marketing directly to patients through advertising, which encourages patients to ask their doctors about medications.)

5.2 Give an example of a pulling strategy. Pulling strategies are used by retailers and by manufacturers of consumer goods like cosmetics, automobiles, and clothing.

6 **Outline the different types of pricing objectives.**
Pricing objectives can be classified as profitability, volume, meeting competition, and prestige. Profitability objectives are probably the most common. Volume objectives base pricing decisions on market share. Meeting competitors' prices makes price a nonissue in competition. Prestige pricing establishes a high price to develop and maintain an image of quality or exclusiveness.

Assessment Check Answers

6.1 Define *price.* Price is the exchange value of a good or service.

6.2 Which pricing objective actually results in diverting consumer attention from price? Pricing to meet the competition diverts consumer attention from price.

7 **Discuss how firms set prices in the marketplace, and describe the four alternative pricing strategies.**
Although economic theory determines prices by the law of demand and supply, most firms use cost-based pricing, which adds a markup after costs. They usually conduct a breakeven analysis to determine the minimum sales volume a product must generate at a certain price in order to cover costs. The four alternative pricing strategies are skimming, penetration, everyday low pricing and discounting, and competitive pricing. A skimming strategy sets a high price initially to recover costs and then lowers it; a penetration strategy sets a lower price to attract customers and then raises it later. Discounting offers a lower price for a certain period of time. Competitive pricing matches other firms' prices and emphasizes nonprice benefits of a product.

Assessment Check Answers

7.1 What is a cost-based pricing formula? A cost-based pricing formula calculates the total costs per unit and then adds markups to cover overhead costs and generate profits.

7.2 What might be considered the most stable of the alternative pricing strategies? Everyday low pricing or discount pricing would be the most stable pricing strategy by offering consistently low prices.

8 **Discuss consumer perceptions of price.**
Marketers must consider how consumers perceive the price–quality relationship of their products. Consumers may be willing to pay a higher price if they perceive a product to be of superior quality. However, extreme prices—either high or low—may turn consumers away. Marketers often use odd pricing to convey a message to consumers.

Assessment Check Answers

8.1 How does the price-quality relationship affect a firm's pricing strategy? Consumers must believe that the price of an item reflects its quality, except in extreme cases. So a firm must try to set its prices accordingly.

8.2 Why is odd pricing used? Odd pricing is commonly used because retailers believe that consumers favor uneven amounts or amounts that sound less than they really are. Odd pricing may also be used to indicate a sale item.

Business Terms You Need to Know

promotion 460	promotional mix 461	sales promotion 470	price 479
integrated marketing communications (IMC) 460	personal selling 461 advertising 465	public relations 477 publicity 478	cost-based pricing 482 breakeven analysis 482

Other Important Business Terms

nonpersonal selling 461

positioning 463

product placement 464

guerrilla marketing 464

product advertising 465

institutional
advertising 465

cause advertising 465

sponsorship 470

infomercial 470

specialty advertising 473

trade promotion 473

point-of-purchase (POP)
advertising 473

order processing 475

creative selling 475

missionary selling 475

telemarketing 476

pushing strategy 478

cooperative advertising 478

pulling strategy 478

profitability objectives 479

volume objectives 479

prestige pricing 481

skimming pricing 483

penetration pricing 483

everyday low pricing
(EDLP) 483

competitive pricing 484

odd pricing 485

Review Questions

1. What is the purpose of integrated marketing communications?

2. What are the five major objectives of a promotional strategy?

3. Identify and define each of the three categories of advertising based on their purpose. Which type of advertising might marketers use for the following products?
   a. shampoo
   b. videogame console
   c. juice boxes for kids
   d. healthcare insurance

4. What are the benefits of online and interactive advertising? What might be some drawbacks?

5. For each of the following, describe potential benefits and drawbacks of a sponsorship relationship:
   a. Jeep and snowboard racing
   b. World Cup Soccer and Corona

   c. Wrangler and the Wrangler Football Golf Classic (a golf tournament that raises money for high school football programs)

6. If you were a marketer for Stouffer's Lean Cuisine, what kind of sales promotion might you use for your line of packaged dinners?

7. Under what circumstances are firms likely to emphasize personal selling?

8. Describe the seven-step sales process.

9. Identify and define the four basic categories of pricing objectives.

10. What are the four alternative pricing strategies used by marketers? Give an example of the circumstances under which each might be selected.

Projects and Teamwork Applications

1. On your own or with a classmate, choose a product that one or both of you purchased recently. Identify the various media that were used to promote the product and analyze the promotional mix. Do you agree with the company's marketing strategy, or would you recommend changes to the mix? Why? Create your own print ad for the product you chose, using any business strategies or knowledge you have learned in this course so far.

2. Evaluate the price of the product you selected in the preceding exercise. What appears to be the pricing strategy used by its manufacturer? Do you think the price is fair? Why or why not? Choose a different strategy and develop a new price for the product based on the strategy. Poll your classmates to learn

whether they would purchase the product at the new price—and why.

3. Some schools have received financial benefits by allowing companies to promote their goods and services to students within the school. Others have decided against the practice, and some states are even considering laws banning this type of promotion. With your class, discuss the pros and cons of promotion in public schools and on college campuses. In your view, is there a distinction between a public school and a college campus? Why or why not?

4. On your own or with a classmate, research a recent situation that has caused a business, a not-for-profit organization, or a government agency to suffer from bad publicity. Evaluate the situation and create a program

outlining steps the firm or organization might take to obtain better publicity and build good public relations.

5. Imagine that the town where your college or university is located has decided to build and develop a new baseball stadium for a minor-league team. As a marketer, what kind of approach would you take for establishing ticket prices?

Web Assignments

1. **Online advertising.** Visit the Web site of ClickZ Network, a leading Internet marketing research firm (http://www.clickz.com). In the search box, type "online advertising trends." You'll likely find hundreds of articles and reports. Review two or three of the most current ones, and prepare a brief report highlighting recent trends in online advertising and promotion. Some questions you might address include the following:

   a. What are some of the key trends in online advertising?
   b. Which types of marketers spend the highest percentages of their promotional budgets online?
   c. What are some of the target markets of online promotional campaigns?

2. **Product placements.** Nielsen Media compiles information and statistics on product placements in such media as film and television. Visit Nielsen Media's Web site (http://www.nielsenmedia.com) and review the most recent report you can find on product placement. Make a list of three or four interesting facts on product placement that you can use in a class discussion of the topic.

3. **Pricing strategies.** Assume you're in the market for a high-definition television (HDTV). Make a list of the major brands including LG, Panasonic, Samsung, and Sony. Select some general specifications for your new HDTV (for instance, 32-inch, LCD display, 1080p resolution). Next visit several online retailers including those with bricks-and-mortar stores (e.g., Wal-Mart, Sears, and Best Buy) and Web-only electronics retailers (e.g., Crutchfield). Check prices on your specified HDTV among the retailers and the brands. Based on your research, how much variation in prices did you find—both among brands as well as among retailers? What does your research tell you about the pricing strategies employed by various retailers and manufacturers?

   http://www.walmart.com
   http://www.sears.com
   http://www.bestbuy.com
   http://www.crutchfield.com

   Note: Internet Web addresses change frequently. If you do not find the exact sites listed, you may need to access the organization's or company's home page and search from there.

Dollar Stores Muscle In on the Big Discounters | Case 14.1

Dollar stores, low-priced convenience retailers with limited assortments of basic goods, are spreading. Chains like Dollar General, Family Dollar, and 99¢ Only are among the fastest growing channels for food, drugs, and mass retailing in the United States. "Dollar stores combine pricing power, efficient operations, and small stores to make the model work," says one industry observer. But the chains will need to maintain their supplier relationships, manage their inventory, and keep operating expenses down by, for example, extending employees' hours instead of going to the expense of recruiting, hiring, and training extra workers during busy times.

Despite these challenges, dollar store chains are adding to their product offerings, increasing the number of food and household items they stock. Some might add national brands, if they can purchase them cheaply enough. That means suppliers that price and package their products for the dollar stores' needs will be able to take advantage of this new opportunity. At most dollar stores, prices are very low, but seldom just a dollar.

With consumer spending trending downward, dollar stores are likely to find plenty of room for expansion. "These low-priced, limited-assortment retailers are very entrenched among low-income households," said a senior vice president at ACNielsen. In fact, although they can't compete on volume with chains like Kohl's, Target, and Wal-Mart—sales of the top three dollar chains combined are only about 6 percent of Wal-Mart's—they do seem able to attract customers away from the big chains, particularly shoppers who can't afford Wal-Mart. Dollar stores are also quick and easy to open. Unlike some of Wal-Mart's huge superstores, "You'll never hear them going up against the planning commission," said one retail consultant. They can close down just as quickly to cut their losses if a location isn't profitable.

Another advantage is their small size, which allows customers to get in and out quickly. To capitalize on this advantage, Dollar General and Family Dollar plan to carry less clothing and more food, health and beauty products, and household goods like laundry detergent that require more trips to the store.[46]

Questions for Critical Thinking

1. If dollar stores carry low-end merchandise, are they really competing with stores like Wal-Mart and Target on price? Why or why not?

2. What are some of the ways dollar stores are able to keep their prices so low?

Case 14.2 Marketing to the Over-40 Crowd

Baby Boomers—members of the superlarge generation born in the 20 or so years following World War II—are among the most technologically savvy and most affluent consumers in the marketplace.

Surprised? More than 70 percent of the country's 78 million Boomers have cell phones that can access the Internet, about half own camera phones, and more than a quarter of them send text messages every day (but fewer of them text while driving than younger consumers do). Women between 35 and 54—most of whom fall into the category of younger Boomers—made up the single largest category of Internet surfers, and not surprisingly they also account for a high proportion of online shoppers. "This generation of women is on the run, and they're much more high-tech oriented than you would guess," says one researcher.

Adult women in general are among the most powerful consumers, controlling about 80 percent of the more than $2 trillion the Boomers as a whole spend on consumer goods and services. After all, most of the boom generation is still in its peak earning years. Boomer women also make most of the buying decisions in their households, choosing brands carefully after considering quality, service, and company reputation. While they tend to spend heavily in product categories like personal care, beauty, and health, they are not looking for eternal youth. With health and wellness issues converging for many, Boomer women see themselves neither as seniors nor as rail-thin models of youthful perfection. They think of themselves as vital, adventurous, and open to continuous personal development and are willing to form relationships with companies that see them the same way.

Boomer men share women's concerns for their future as they enter retirement. "Boomers may spend twenty, thirty or more years in retirement, however we define it," says the director of Metlife's Mature Market Institute. "It may turn out to be their longest lifestage.... Boomers will explore new kinds of living arrangements ... so they can age in place with 'families of choice' to share expenses and to care for one another should they need assistance some day."

Because of their numbers, Baby Boomers have had a big impact on cultural trends, product innovation, and economics for many years. There's no question they still represent a vital market. In fact, after climbing steadily for some years, the median age of the prime-time audience for the four major networks is now over 40, up from the mid-30s a few years ago. But some marketers are focusing their efforts on youth-oriented advertising and promotion channels like cable/satellite radio and television, the Internet, and word-of-mouth and buzz campaigns. Are some marketers leaving the lucrative Boomers out?[47]

Questions for Critical Thinking

1. Do you think marketers should be paying more attention to the Baby Boom generation with specially tailored promotional campaigns for such goods and services as vacation travel, second homes, autos, health care, beauty and fashion, retirement and financial planning, technology products, home appliances, and so on? Why or why not?

2. How can marketers best target Boomers so as to appeal to their interests, concerns, and goals but without making them feel old, irrelevant, or even middle-aged? Suggest a marketing or promotional theme for one product that you think would appeal to a member of the Boom generation.

It's the American Dream: four inner-city kids, steeped in hip-hop, start their own clothing business and make it big. Really big. It began when childhood friends Daymond John, Alexander Martin, Carl Brown, and Keith Perrin were looking for the tight-fitting tie-top hats that were popular among hip-hop fans. They left their Queens, New York, neighborhood and drove into downtown Manhattan in search of the hats. When they finally found them, the four realized quickly that they could easily make similar ones and sell them to their friends. So they bought fabric and made 40 hats, which sold right away. By then, they were thinking about starting a business. John was a homeowner, so he took out a mortgage to fund the business and turned half his house into a clothing factory for tie-top hats, T-shirts, and baseball caps—all with the logo FUBU embroidered on them. The name, which has a hip-hop ring to it, stands for the company philosophy: "For us, by us." The founders now laugh about those early beginnings. "Our entire business model was to get enough money to buy food to eat," they recall.

Selling some clothes to friends got their business off the ground, but the FUBU (pronounced foo-boo) founders needed more than that. Money was an obstacle. Even if they could place some socks in one retail store and some shirts and hats in another, they didn't have a way to promote them. And to be successful, they needed a way to promote their goods to get the message out to prospective customers. The messenger came in the form of rap artist and actor L. L. Cool J, who happened to be from Queens as well. Cool J liked FUBU's stuff, but he wasn't ready to wear it in a show or music video until the owners made some design and color changes. FUBU listened and came up with the right T-shirt for him, which resulted in Cool J becoming an early spokesperson for the brand. Since then, supporters have included Mariah Carey, Boys II Men, Will Smith, and Sean "P Diddy" Combs. Placements of FUBU clothing in music videos, feature films, and on stage have gone a long way toward building the brand's identity.

With the financing that came with a promotion and distribution agreement with Samsung, FUBU was able to open the doors to many of the 500 retailers who now stock FUBU clothing, including Macy's, Foot Locker, Champs, and Nordstrom. Eventually, the FUBU founders were able to afford a booth at the glamorous "Magic: The Business of Fashion" trade show in Los Angeles, where celebrities and department store buyers now flock to put in their orders as soon as possible—which generates sales as well as publicity for FUBU. And when the NBA approached FUBU about a licensing agreement, both sides realized immediately that it was the perfect match. The NBA's customers are often FUBU customers as well. NBA clothing by FUBU is expected to generate $25 million to $50 million for FUBU, and potentially more. Each organization promotes the other, to the benefit of both.

Price has been an issue from the beginning for FUBU. The four founders wanted to produce high-quality clothing at prices somewhat lower than other manufacturers. Still, the clothes aren't cheap. Jeans run from $44.99 to $69.99, and a T-shirt with the official Harlem Globetrotters logo can be priced from $55 to $89. The company also has a women's line, where women can pick up a velour dress for $64.99, a stretch denim shirt dress for $55, and some graphic tees for $22.99. Clearly, consumers don't seem to be griping about price—today, FUBU is a $350 million global business, selling its products in countries as near as Canada and Mexico and as far away as Japan and Malaysia.

FUBU's relationship with customers is an important part of its promotional effort—all four founders say they are comfortable talking with anyone they meet on the street. They like to stop and listen to the experiences and ideas of the people who buy and wear their clothing, and they never forget their roots. Their personal presence gives them a connection with consumers that other designers and manufacturers simply can't achieve. When shoppers can't be near a FUBU store or the headquarters in New York, they can log on to the company's Web site at http://www.y2g.com to find out about company-sponsored parties, trips, and tours, and read celebrity interviews, all of which enhance their relationship with FUBU. "We're a lifestyle brand," say the founders. And shoppers seem to be happy to live their lives in FUBU clothes. [48]

Questions for Critical Thinking

1. FUBU has coordinated its promotional activities to produce a unified, customer-focused message. How would you state that message?

2. How would you characterize FUBU's promotional objectives?

3. Which advertising medium would be the most effective for FUBU at its present stage? Why?

4. How do you think consumers perceive FUBU's pricing?

© Getty Images

Think Green, Go Green, Save Green

Not long ago, the phrase "hybrid SUV" would have seemed an oxymoron. But in just a few short years, fuel-efficient hybrids of all shapes and sizes have appeared in showrooms. This new generation of vehicles combines fuel-efficient gas engines, natural gas engines, and hydrogen fuel cells. As gas prices soar and concern over the environment grows, consumers will become more and more interested in them.

Enter Lee Lindquist, Alternative Fuels Specialist at Scholfield Honda in Wichita, Kansas. A passionate environmentalist, Lee was researching alternative-fuel vehicles when he learned that Honda had been selling a natural gas Civic GX in New York and California since 1998. Originally marketed to municipalities and corporations as a way of addressing air quality issues, the Civic GX seemed the perfect way for cost-conscious Kansans to combat rising fuel prices. It was also a way to promote local resources, since Kansas is a major producer of natural gas.

Lee took the idea of the Civic GX to his boss, Owner Roger Scholfield, who was skeptical of it at first. Scholfield had long promoted the Honda as a fuel-efficient vehicle and didn't want to muddy the waters with this new vehicle. But eventually he warmed to the idea and began offering the car to his corporate customers.

When the tornado hit Greensburg in May 2007, the idea of going green took on a whole new life at Scholfield Honda. One of the problems with offering the Civic GX had been the lack of natural gas fueling stations, as well as the high cost of constructing one. Well aware of the media attention surrounding Greensburg, Scholfield decided to donate a natural gas Civic to the town, along with a fueling station.

Scholfield was up-front about the decision to donate the car. The investment was a costly one, and there were many less expensive ways of reaching his customers in Wichita. Scholfield admits he questioned his decision even as he drove into Greensburg for the presentation. But the bottom line was that it was the right thing to do. Today, when customers come into Scholfield's dealership, they are more interested in alternative-fuel and high-efficiency vehicles.

If you want to buy a Civic GX from Scholfield Honda today, get in line, because the staff can't keep them in stock. While you wait, enjoy a nice cup of coffee served in a compostable, corn-based disposable cup. Toss those old soda cans rattling around in your back seat into Scholfield's recycling bins. And on your way out, don't forget to take your complimentary Scholfield Honda reusable green shopping bag and water bottle.

Questions

After viewing the video, answer the following questions:

1. Do you think Scholfield's green marketing campaign will change consumers' opinions of hybrid and alternative-fuel cars?

2. Do you think Scholfield's donation of a natural gas Civic to the town of Greensburg will drive business to his dealership in Wichita? Why or why not?

Launching Your Marketing Career

In Part 4, "Marketing Management," you learned about the goals and functions of marketing. The three chapters in this part emphasized the central role of customer satisfaction in defining value and developing a marketing strategy in traditional and nontraditional marketing settings. You learned about the part played by marketing research and the need for relationship marketing in today's competitive environment. You discovered how new products are developed and how they evolve through the four stages of the product life cycle, from introduction through growth and maturity to decline. You also learned about the role of different channels in creating effective distribution strategies. Finally, you saw the impact of integrated marketing communications on the firm's promotional strategy, the role of advertising, and the way pricing influences consumer behavior. Perhaps you came across some marketing tasks and functions that sounded especially appealing to you. Here are a few ideas about careers in marketing that you may want to pursue.

The first thing to remember is that, as the chapters in this part made clear, marketing is about a great deal more than personal selling and advertising. For instance, are you curious about why people behave the way they do? Are you good at spotting trends? *Marketing research analysts* seek answers to a wide range of questions about business competition, customer preferences, market trends, and past and future sales. They often design and conduct their own consumer surveys, using the telephone, mail, the Internet, or personal interviews and focus groups. After they analyze the data they've collected, their recommendations form input for managerial decisions about whether to introduce new products, revamp current ones, enter new markets, or abandon products or markets where profitability is low. As members of a new-product development team, marketing researchers often work directly with members of other business departments such as scientists, production and manufacturing personnel, and finance employees. Also, marketing researchers are increasingly asked to help clients implement their recommendations. With today's highly competitive economy, jobs in this area are expected to grow. Annual earnings for marketing research analysts average about $59,000.[1]

Another career path in marketing is sales. Do you work well with others and read their feelings accurately? Are you a self-starter? Being a *sales representative* might be for you. Selling jobs exist in every industry, and because many use a combination of salary and performance-based commissions, they can pay handsomely. Sales jobs are often a first step on the ladder to upper-management positions as well. Sales representatives work for wholesalers and manufacturing companies (and even for publishers such as the one that produces this book). They sell automobiles, computer systems and technology, pharmaceuticals, advertising, insurance, real estate, commodities and financial services, and all kinds of consumer goods and services.

If you're interested in mass communications, note that print and online magazines, newspapers, and broadcast companies such as ESPN and MTV generate most of their revenue from advertising, so sales representatives who sell space and time slots in the media contribute a great deal to the success of these firms.[2] And if you like to travel, consider that many sales jobs involve travel.

Advertising, marketing management, and *public relations* are other categories of marketing. In large companies, marketing managers, product managers, promotion managers, and public relations managers often work long hours under pressure; they may travel frequently or transfer between jobs at headquarters and positions in regional offices. Their responsibilities include directing promotional programs, overseeing advertising campaigns and budgets, and conducting communications such as press releases with the firm's publics. Thousands of new positions are expected to open up in the next several years; the field is expected to grow 14 percent over the next decade. Growth of the Internet and new media has especially increased demand for advertising and public relations specialists.[3]

Advertising and public relations firms employed about 458,000 people in a recent year.[4] About one in five U.S. advertising firms are located in New York or California, and more than a quarter of advertising industry workers live in those two states. Most advertising firms develop specialties; many of the largest are international in scope and earn a major proportion of their revenue abroad. Online advertising is just one area in which new jobs will be opening in the future, as more and more client firms expand their online sales operations.

Career Assessment Exercises in Marketing

1. Select a field that interests you. Use the Internet to research types of sales positions available in that field. Locate a few entry-level job openings and see what career steps that position can lead to. (You might wish to start with a popular job-posting site such as Monster.com.) Note the job requirements, the starting salary, and the form of compensation—straight salary? salary plus commission?—and write a one-page summary of your findings.

2. Use the Internet to identify and investigate two or three of the leading advertising agencies in the United States, such as Young & Rubicam or J. Walter Thompson. What are some of their recent ad campaigns, or who are their best-known clients? Where do the agencies have offices? What job openings do they currently list, and what qualifications should applicants for these positions have? Write a brief report comparing the agencies you selected, decide which one you would prefer to work for, and give your reasons.

3. Test your research skills. Choose an ordinary product, such as toothpaste or soft drinks, and conduct a survey to find out why people chose the brand they most recently purchased. For instance, suppose you wanted to find out how people choose their shampoo. List as many decision criteria as you can think of, such as availability, scent, price, packaging, benefits from use (conditioning, dandruff-reducing, and so on), brand name, and ad campaign. Ask eight to ten friends to rank these decision factors, and note some simple demographics about your research subjects such as their age, gender, and occupation. Tabulate your results. What did you find out about how your subjects made their purchase decision? Did any of your findings surprise you? Can you think of any ways in which you might have improved your survey?

Part 5

Managing Technology and Information

© Mark Hall/Photoedit/Getty Images, Inc.

chapter 15

Using Technology to Manage Information

Glowimages/Getty Images

BlackBerry Storm Takes on the iPhone

Many technology experts predict that cell phones will soon rival PCs in computing capabilities. They already surpass them in compactness and convenience. Canada-based Research In Motion (RIM), the firm that brought us the BlackBerry, has been working feverishly to bring one more option to mobile computing—an innovative new smart phone to rival Apple's iPhone.

After two years of development and a $100 million marketing campaign, RIM finally released the Storm, which immediately lived up to its name by generating a whirlwind of marketing buzz. The phone, which sold 500,000 units in its first month and soon reached 1 million units, was developed in conjunction with Verizon Wireless, one of the largest U.S. telecommunications providers and the sole U.S. carrier for the Storm. The first touch-screen BlackBerry, the Storm lacks a physical keyboard and comes packed with multiple communications features designed to help executives stay in touch with the office, suppliers, and customers. It also contains 128 megabytes of memory, so no matter how the user wants to communicate—via voice, text, or images—he or she has plenty of room to store applications, pictures, sound files, documents, and data. The SurePress "clickable" touch screen, which has earned a technology award, offers the physical sensation of a real keyboard, the first innovation in touch-screen technology in some time.

Despite some early complaints from technophiles about software glitches, which RIM calls the "new reality" of releasing complex cell phones and which it rushed to correct, the Storm is winning praise for its user-friendly features. They include a high-resolution touch screen with navigation control keys, a programmable shortcut key, adjustable font type and size, powerful search capabilities, and the screen's ability to automatically rotate from portrait to landscape when the handset is turned sideways. The phone provides e-mail and Internet browsing, along with a satellite mapping system and a 3.2-megapixel digital camera with flash and video. The device also has a media player that can handle both music and video.

The Storm weighs less than 6 ounces and boasts simple finger controls to zoom, cut and paste, or scroll through e-mails and text. Users can instantly edit Word documents, Excel spreadsheets, and PowerPoint slides. A software upgrade is available to allow the creation of new documents. Preloaded instant message programs include those of Yahoo!, Windows Live, AOL, and ICQ. Networking applications include Facebook, MySpace, and Flickr; other options are available for downloading.

In fact, RIM is benchmarking not just Apple's iPhones but also its ground-breaking service for downloadable applications. Users of the BlackBerry Storm—and of other RIM devices including the Pearl, Curve, and Bold—now can enjoy the new applications center called BlackBerry App World, the equivalent of Apple's hugely popular App Store. RIM is offering games, networking and messaging applications, and a wide assortment of other software to improve personal productivity, check news headlines, schedule events, track stock tickers, and manage other communications tasks. Some applications are free; others are priced competitively but at rates starting a little higher than for the iPhone. That price differential signals RIM's intention to target the BlackBerry line to business users, who, at least in theory, are less interested in the simpler applications that many consumer cell phone users crave.

The Storm does offer a specific benefit in addition to all its communications options. Purchased applications from App World can be uploaded up to three separate times for one fee, a boon for users who upgrade their handsets regularly, as executives on the go tend to do. And for those whose business travels take them abroad, the Storm offers another breakthrough. The phone works with high-speed data services on both Verizon's and Vodafone's networks, giving it true built-in global capacity. Says one technology analyst, "For a lot of users, Verizon is the network of choice and a BlackBerry is the device of choice."

Building on its initial success with the Storm, RIM is manufacturing a million units a month in response to market demand. Selling for the same price as the iPhone after a mail-in rebate, the Storm is aiming to match or surpass the iPhone's 25 percent share of the still-expanding smart phone market in North America. RIM considers the Storm "an overwhelming suc-

cess," and for those who still quibble over potential flaws, one financial consultant who is pleased with his new Storm has an answer: "No single device is going to be the end-all be-all for everyone."[1]

Chapter 15 OVERVIEW

This chapter explores how businesses manage information as a resource, particularly how they use technology to do so. Today, virtually all business functions—from human resources to production to supply chain management—rely on information systems. The chapter begins by differentiating between information and data and then defines an information system. The components of information systems are presented, and two major types of information systems are described. Because of their importance to organizations, the chapter discusses databases, the heart of all information systems.

Then the chapter looks at the computer hardware and software that drive information systems. Today, specialized networks make information access and transmission function smoothly, so the chapter examines different types of telecommunications and computer networks to see how businesses are applying them for competitive advantage. The chapter then turns to a discussion of the ethical and security issues affecting information systems, followed by a description of how organizations plan for, and recover from, information system disasters. A review of the current trends in information systems concludes the chapter.

Data, Information, and Information Systems

data raw facts and figures that may or may not be relevant to a business decision.

information knowledge gained from processing data.

information system organized method for collecting, storing, and communicating past, present, and projected information on internal operations and external intelligence.

"They Said It"

"Information is not knowledge."

—Albert Einstein (1879–1955) Physicist

Every day, businesspeople ask themselves questions such as the following:

- How well is our product selling in Atlanta compared with Tampa? Have sales among consumers aged 25 to 45 increased or decreased within the past year?

- How will rising energy prices affect production and distribution costs?

- If employees can access the benefits system through our network, will this increase or decrease benefit costs?

- Can we communicate more efficiently and effectively with our increasingly dispersed workforce?

An effective information system can help answer these and many other questions. **Data** consist of raw facts and figures that may or may not be relevant to a business decision. **Information** is knowledge gained from processing those facts and figures. So although businesspeople need to gather data about the demographics of a target market or the specifications of a certain product, the data are useless unless they are transformed into relevant information that can be used to make a competitive decision. For instance, data might be the sizes of various demographic groups in a country. Information drawn from that data could be how many of those individuals are potential customers for a firm's products. Technology has advanced so quickly that all businesses, regardless of size or location, now have access to data and information that can make them competitive in a global arena.

An **information system** is an organized method for collecting, storing, and communicating past, present, and projected information on internal operations and external intelligence. Most information systems today use computer and telecommunications technology. A large organization typically assigns responsibility for directing its information systems and related operations to an executive called the **chief information officer (CIO).** Often, the CIO reports directly to the firm's chief executive officer (CEO). An effective CIO can understand and harness technology so that the company can communicate internally and externally in one seamless operation. But small companies rely just as much on information systems as do large ones, even if they do not employ a manager assigned to this area on a full-time basis.

The role of the CIO is both expanding and changing as the technology to manage information continues to develop. Over the past ten years, the role of a CIO has transitioned from being a technical one to that of a business partner who often exerts strong influence over his or her company's strategy. Moreover, CIOs and former CIOs are beginning to appear on company boards more often.[2]

Information systems can be tailored to assist many business functions and departments—from marketing and manufacturing to finance and accounting. They can manage the overwhelming flood of information by organizing data in a logical and accessible manner. Through the system, a company can monitor all components of its operations and business strategy, identifying problems and opportunities. Information systems gather data from inside and outside the organization; they then process the data to produce information that is relevant to all aspects of the organization. Processing steps could involve storing data for later use, classifying and analyzing it, and retrieving it easily when needed.

Many companies—and nations—combine high-tech and low-tech solutions to manage the flow of information. E-mail, wireless communications, and videoconferencing haven't totally replaced paper memos, phone conversations, and face-to-face meetings, but they are increasingly common. Information can make the difference between staying in business and going bankrupt. Keeping on top of changing consumer demands, competitors' actions, and the latest government regulations will help a firm fine-tune existing products, develop new winners, and maintain effective marketing.

Components and Types of Information Systems

The definition of *information system* in the previous section does not specifically mention the use of computers or technology. In fact, information systems have been around since the beginning of civilization and were, by today's standards, very low tech. Think about your college or university's library. At one time the library probably had card catalog files to help you find information. Those files were information systems because they stored data about books and periodicals in an organized manner on 3-by-5-inch index cards. Users could flip through the cards and locate library materials by author, title, or subject, although the process could be tedious and time consuming.

Today, however, when businesspeople think about information systems, they are most likely thinking about **computer-based information systems.** These systems rely on computer and related technologies to store information electronically in an organized, accessible manner. So, instead of card catalogs, your college library probably uses a computerized information system that allow users to search through library holdings much faster and easier.

Computer-based information systems consist of four components and technologies:

- computer hardware
- computer software
- telecommunications and computer networks
- data resource management.

Computer hardware consists of machines that range from supercomputers to smart phones. It also includes the input, output, and storage devices needed to support computing machines. Software includes operating systems, such as Microsoft Vista and Linux, and applications programs, such as Adobe Acrobat and Oracle's PeopleSoft Enterprise applications. Telecommunications and computer networks encompass the hardware and software needed to provide wired or wireless voice and data communications. This includes support for external networks such as the Internet and private internal networks. Data resource management involves developing and maintaining an organization's databases so that decision makers are able to access the information they need in a timely manner.

In the case of your college or university library, the computer-based information system is generally made up of computer hardware, such as monitors and keyboards, which are linked to the library's network and a database containing information on the library's holdings. Specialized software allows users to access the database. In addition, the library's network is likely also connected to a larger private network and the Internet. This connection gives users remote access to the library's database, as well as access to other computerized databases such as LexisNexis.

Databases

The heart of any information system is its **database,** a centralized integrated collection of data resources. A company designs its databases to meet particular information processing and retrieval needs of its workforce. Businesses obtain databases in many ways. They can hire a staff person to build them on site, hire an outside source to do so, or buy packaged database programs from specialized vendors, such as Oracle. A database serves as an electronic filing cabinet, capable of storing massive amounts of data and retrieving it within seconds. A database should be continually updated; otherwise, a firm may find itself with data that are outdated and possibly useless. One problem with databases is that they can contribute to information overload—too much data for people to absorb or data that are not relevant to decision making. Because computer processing speed and storage capacity are both increasing rapidly, and because data have become more abundant, businesspeople need to be careful that their databases contain only the facts they need. If they don't, they can waste time wading through unnecessary data. Another challenge with databases is keeping them safe, as the "Hit & Miss" feature describes.

Decision makers can also look up online data. Online systems give access to enormous amounts of government data, such as economic data from the Bureau of Labor Statistics and the Department of Commerce. One of the largest online databases is that of the U.S. Census Bureau. The census of population, conducted every ten years, attempts to collect data on more than 120 million households across the United States. After attempting to count everyone in the country, the Census Bureau has selected participants fill out forms containing questions about marital status, place of birth, ethnic background, citizenship, workplaces, commuting time, income, occupation, type of housing, number of telephones and vehicles, even grandparents as caregivers. Households receiving the most recent questionnaire could respond in English as well as a variety of other languages including Spanish, Chinese, Vietnamese, and Korean. Not surprisingly, sifting through all the collected data takes time. Although certain restrictions limit how businesspeople can access and use specific census data, the general public may access the data via the American FactFinder on the Census Bureau's Web site (http://factfinder.census.gov), as well as at state data centers and public libraries.

Another source of free information is company Web sites. Interested parties can visit firms' home pages to look for information about customers, suppliers, and competitors. Trade associations and academic institutions also maintain Web sites with information on topics of interest.

Hit & Miss

Heartland Payments Systems Breached

Electronic payments are simple and convenient. But what happens when databases are compromised? One payment-processing company announced that card data for millions of debit and credit card users may have been exposed to fraud. This security breach could prove to be the largest and most costly to date—but probably not the last. "If you add it all up, including legal costs, it could be as much as half a billion dollars in losses," said a data security analyst.

Princeton, New Jersey–based Heartland Payments Systems processes more than 100 million credit and debit card transactions a month for its more than 250,000 business customers—from retailers to gas stations to payroll system companies. Heartland's security broke down when intruders placed programs into its system, perhaps as early as May 2008. Card information, including account numbers, expiration dates, and internal bank codes, was extracted by the hackers as it traveled through Heartland's internal network. Data for up to 600 million Visa, MasterCard, American Express, and Discover cardholders issued by over 200 institutions in 40 states was left vulnerable.

Heartland, which now faces at least 15 civil lawsuits from individual and bank customers, admits it doesn't know exactly how long the bad software, an "extremely sophisticated code," had been in its system. Because Heartland didn't detect any suspicious activity until Visa and MasterCard International alerted it in fall 2008, some observers say the company wasn't using all the security controls required by the Payment Card Industry (PCI) Data Security Standard. If it had been, it would have been monitoring all its files and directories for unauthorized activity.

In addition, it seems that Heartland was not sufficiently monitoring the traffic leaving its network or analyzing logs created by its security systems. "If you do some kind of data leak prevention type of analysis," says one software security vendor, "you would be able to say, 'Why is a server on my internal payment network sending data outside the network?' Even if the data is encrypted, you should see the traffic flows."

Two investigative companies Heartland hired after hearing from Visa and MasterCard also missed the intrusion. Finally, on Presidential Inauguration Day in January 2009,

when media attention was diverted, Heartland quietly announced the data theft.

In the aftermath of the announcement, banks had to decide whether to reissue all their credit and debit cards—an enormously expensive option due to the tens of thousands of cards involved—or simply ask consumers to monitor their individual accounts for suspicious activity. As lawsuits began piling up and investigations by the Securities and Exchange Commission and Federal Trade Commission got under way, Heartland promised to surpass PCI standards in the future. It is creating a new department dedicated to encrypting data on its internal networks. Meanwhile Florida police arrested three suspects said to have used card numbers from stolen Visa gift cards to spend over $100,000 at local Wal-Mart stores, buying items they later sold for cash.

But many questions remained unanswered, not least of which is, Could it happen again? Said the president of another card processing company, "Everybody who processes card information is dying to know exactly how this happened."

Questions for Critical Thinking

1. What could Heartland have done differently to prevent a security breach? What do you think it will do in the future?
2. The PCI standards do not require firms to encrypt data on their internal networks, although Heartland says it will now do so. Should all firms be required to take this step? Why or why not?

Sources: Jaikumar Vijayan, "Banks, Credit Unions Begin to Sue Heartland over Data Breach," *ComputerWorld,* March 2, 2009, http://www.computerworld.com; Robert McMillan, "SEC, FTC Investigating Heartland after Data Theft," *PCWorld,* February 25, 2009, http://www.pcworld.com; Warwick Ashford, "First Arrests in Connection with Heartland Data Breach," *ComputerWeekly,* February 17, 2009, http://www.computerweekly.com; Thomas Claburn, "Three Arrested for Using Stolen Heartland Credit Card Numbers," *Information Week,* February 17, 2009, http://www.informationweek.com; Jaikumar Vijayan, "Heartland Data Breach Sparks Security Concerns in Payment Industry," *ComputerWorld,* January 22, 2009, http://www.computerworld.com; Brennon Slattery, "Heartland Has No Heart for Violated Customers," *PCWorld,* January 21, 2009, http://www.pcworld.com; Eric Dash and Brad Stone, "Credit Card Processor Says Some Data Was Stolen," *The New York Times,* January 21, 2009, http://www.nytimes.com.

Types of Information Systems

Many different types of information systems exist. In general, however, information systems fall into two broad categories: operational support systems or management support systems.

OPERATIONAL SUPPORT SYSTEMS

Operational support systems are designed to produce a variety of information on an organization's activities for both internal and external users. Examples of operational support systems include transaction processing systems and process control systems. **Transaction processing systems** record and process data from business transactions. For example, major retailers use point-of-sale systems, which link electronic cash registers to the retailer's computer centers. Sales data are transmitted from cash registers to the computer center either immediately or at regular intervals. **Process control systems** monitor and control physical processes. A steel mill, for instance, may have electronic sensors linked to a computer system monitoring the entire production process. The system makes necessary changes and alerts operators to potential problems.

Commercial airplane manufacturer Airbus relies on a sophisticated information system based on RFID (radio-frequency identification) technology to track parts and tools used in the production and maintenance of its products. The information system follows parts from warehouses to production facilities to the specific lines where they are attached to aircraft. The system also tracks how and where tools are used. Airbus expects the information system to improve overall supply chain management, reduce required inventory levels, and increase productivity.[3]

MANAGEMENT SUPPORT SYSTEMS

Information systems that are designed to provide support for effective decision making are classified as **management support systems.** Several different types of management support systems are available. A **management information system (MIS)** is designed to produce reports to managers and other professionals. A **decision support system (DSS)** gives direct support to businesspeople during the decision-making process. For instance, a marketing manager might use a decision support system to analyze the impact on sales and profits of a product price change. An **executive support system (ESS)** lets senior executives access the firm's primary databases, often by touching the computer screen, pointing with a mouse, or even using voice recognition. The typical ESS allows users to choose from many kinds of data, such as the firm's financial statements and sales figures, as well as stock market trends for the company and for the industry as a whole. If they wish, managers can start by looking at summaries and then access more detailed information when needed. Finally, an **expert system** is a computer program that imitates human thinking through complicated sets of "if-then" rules. The system applies human knowledge in a specific subject area to solve a problem. Expert systems are used for a variety of business purposes: determining credit limits for credit card applicants, monitoring machinery in a plant to predict potential problems or breakdowns, making mortgage loans, and determining optimal plant layouts. They are typically developed by capturing the knowledge of recognized experts in a field whether within a business itself or outside it.

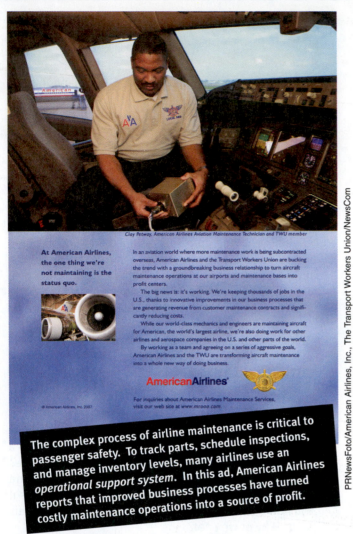

Clay Petway, American Airlines Aviation Maintenance Technician and TWU member

At American Airlines, the one thing we're not maintaining is the status quo.

In an aviation world where more maintenance work is being subcontracted overseas, American Airlines and the Transport Workers Union are bucking the trend with a groundbreaking business relationship to turn aircraft maintenance operations at our airports and maintenance bases into profit centers.

The big news is: it's working. We're keeping thousands of jobs in the U.S., thanks to innovative improvements in our business processes that are generating revenue from customer maintenance contracts and significantly reducing costs.

While our world-class mechanics and engineers are maintaining aircraft for American, the world's largest airline, we're also doing work for other airlines and aerospace companies in the U.S. and other parts of the world.

By working as a team and agreeing on a series of aggressive goals, American Airlines and the TWU are transforming aircraft maintenance into a whole new way of doing business.

AmericanAirlines®

© American Airlines, Inc. 2007

For inquiries about American Airlines Maintenance Services, visit our web site at www.mraaa.com.

PRNewsFoto/American Airlines, Inc., The Transport Workers Union/NewsCom

The complex process of airline maintenance is critical to passenger safety. To track parts, schedule inspections, and manage inventory levels, many airlines use an *operational support system.* In this ad, American Airlines reports that improved business processes have turned costly maintenance operations into a source of profit.

operational support systems information systems designed to produce a variety of information on an organization's activities for both internal and external users. **management support systems** information systems that are designed to provide support for effective decision making.

Assessment Check ✔

1. List the four components of a computer-based information system.

2. What is a database?

3. What are the two general types of information systems? Give examples of each.

Computer Hardware and Software

It may be hard to believe, but only a few decades ago computers were considered exotic curiosities, used only for very specialized applications and understood by only a few people. The first commercial computer, UNIVAC I, was sold to the U.S. Census Bureau in the early 1950s. It cost $1 million, took up most of a room, and could perform about 2,000 calculations per second.[4] The invention of transistors and then integrated circuits (microchips) quickly led to smaller and more powerful devices. By the 1980s, computers could routinely perform several million calculations per second. Now, computers perform billions of calculations per second, and some fit into the palm of your hand.

These Sperry UNIVAC mainframe computers, built in 1964, are still in use today at the Philadelphia office of the IRS. The huge machines are housed in a special climate-controlled room.

When the first personal computers were introduced in the late 1970s and early 1980s, the idea of a computer on every desk, or in every home, seemed far-fetched. Today they have become indispensable to both businesses and households. Not only have computers become much more powerful and faster over the past 25 years, but they are less expensive as well. IBM's first personal computer (PC), introduced in 1981, cost well over $5,000 fully configured. Today, the typical PC sells for under $800.

Types of Computer Hardware

Hardware consists of all tangible elements of a computer system—the input devices, the components that store and process data and perform required calculations, and the output devices that present the results to information users. Input devices allow users to enter data and commands for processing, storage, and output. The most common input devices are the keyboard and mouse. Storage and processing components consist of the hard drive as well as various other storage components, including DVD drives and flash memory devices. Flash memory devices are becoming increasingly popular because they are small, hold large amounts of data, are portable, and fit in a pocket. To gain access to the data they hold, users just plug them into an unused USB (universal serial bus) port found on today's computers. Output devices, such as monitors and printers, are the hardware elements that transmit or display documents and other results of a computer system's work.

Different types of computers incorporate widely varying memory capacities and processing speeds. These differences define four broad classifications: mainframe computers, midrange systems, personal computers, and hand-held devices. A mainframe computer is the largest type of computer system with the most extensive storage capacity and the fastest processing speeds. Especially powerful mainframes called *supercomputers* can handle extremely rapid, complex calculations involving thousands of variables, such as weather modeling and forecasting. Today's supercomputers can perform a trillion or more calculations per second.

Midrange systems consist of high-end network servers and other types of computers that can handle large-scale processing needs. They are less powerful than mainframe computers but more powerful than most personal computers. A **server** is the heart of a computer network, supporting applications and allowing the sharing of output devices, software, and databases

hardware all tangible elements of a computer system.

server computer that supports network applications and allows for the sharing of software, output devices, and databases by all networked computers.

Business Etiquette

COURTEOUS COMMUNICATIONS VIA WIRELESS DEVICES

It's easy to get hooked on your BlackBerry or other smart phone. You take a quick peek during dinner or while someone is speaking during a meeting. You think you are being productive—you don't want to miss that important message—but in fact, you are practicing poor etiquette. And if someone catches in you the act, you could even lose the deal or the promotion you wanted so badly. Instead, follow a few tips for proper use of communication technology, and you'll earn the respect and goodwill of customers and coworkers alike.

1. Know when to silence your phone or PDA and put it away. Don't be tempted to answer calls or return messages when your attention should be focused on the task and people at hand.

2. If you must take a call or answer an emergency message, excuse yourself. Don't engage in separate conversations or e-mail in front of the people with whom you are meeting.

3. When you send a business message to or from a mobile device, be concise but not cute. Avoid shorthand like "cu@5" instead of "see you at 5." Don't pack the message with unnecessary information.

4. Check your message before sending it to avoid misspellings and other typos. The recipient shouldn't have to try to figure out what you wanted to say.

5. Follow up promptly with more information when it's needed. Call or e-mail the person from your PC as soon as you can to make sure the message came through and to fill in the blanks.

Sources: Christopher Elliott, "E-Mail Etiquette for Your Wireless Device," *Office Live Small Business*, http://office.microsoft.com, accessed March 26, 2009; Stephanie Whittaker, "Can You Wait? I'm Getting a Message," *The Gazette (Montreal)*, http://www.canada.com/montrealgazette, accessed April 11, 2008; Kevin Hill, "A Little BlackBerry Etiquette," *CrackBerry.com*, June 11, 2007, http://www.crackberry.com, accessed October 20, 2008.

"They Said It"

"Knowing a great deal is not the same as being smart; intelligence is not information alone but also judgment, the manner in which information is collected and used."

—Carl Sagan (1934–1996) American astronomer and writer

among networked users. Many Internet-related functions at organizations are handled by mid-range systems. Midrange systems are also commonly employed in process control systems, computer-aided manufacturing (CAM), and computer-aided design (CAD).

Personal computers are everywhere today—in homes, businesses, schools, nonprofit organizations, and government agencies. Recent estimates of PC ownership say that more than two-thirds of American households have at least one personal computer. They have earned increasing popularity because of their ever-expanding capability to handle many of the functions that large mainframes performed only a few decades ago. Most desktop computers are linked to networks, such as the Internet.

Desktop computers used to be the standard PC seen in offices and homes. While millions of desktop computers remain on the job, notebook computers now account for more than half of all new PCs sold. The increasing popularity of notebooks can be explained by their lower prices, better displays, faster processing speeds, larger storage capacities, and more durable designs. At the same time they are becoming more powerful, notebooks have never been lighter or thinner. A new model from Sony, the Vaio SZ, weighs under four pounds and is less than one inch thick when closed. For many users, the size, weight, and portability of notebooks offsets the fact that notebooks still cost more than comparable desktop computers.

One of the newest types of notebook computer is the so-called *netbook*. These devices are very small and inexpensive; some cost less than $300. While they don't have the computing capability of larger, more expensive notebooks, netbooks can still perform basic tasks (such as e-mail, word processing, and spreadsheet calculations) and can access the Internet through a wireless connection.

Hand-held devices—made by companies such as Apple, RIM, Nokia, Palm, and Samsung—are even smaller. Two kinds of hand-held devices are available to most business and consumer users. The original type is the personal digital assistant (PDA). PDAs keep schedules and contact information and have limited software applications such as word processing and spreadsheets. Most PDAs today allow users to access the Internet through wireless networks.

The other type of hand-held device is the so-called *smart phone*. A smart phone is essentially a device that combines a cell phone with a PDA. Examples include Apple's iPhone, Palm's Treo, RIM's BlackBerry Storm, and Samsung's Blackjack. In addition to making and receiving calls and text messages, smart phones allow users to surf the Internet, receive and send e-mail, check their schedules, and even open and edit documents. The typical smart phone is only slightly larger and heavier than a regular cell phone. On short trips, many businesspeople find that they just rely on their smart phone. Given their added capability, it's not surprising that smart phone sales are growing much faster than sales of traditional PDAs. Moreover, most of the recent overall growth in the sale of cell phones can be attributed to smart phones.[5]

While smart phones can be terrific tools that boost productivity, some people overuse or even misuse them. The "Business Etiquette" feature describes some do's and don'ts when it comes to smartphone use in a business environment.

In addition to PDAs and smart phones, specialized hand-held devices are used in a variety of businesses for different applications. Some restaurants, for example, have small wireless devices that allow servers to swipe a credit card and print out a receipt right at the customer's table. Drivers for UPS and FedEx use special hand-held devices to track package deliveries. The driver scans each package as it is delivered, and the information is transmitted to the delivery firm's network. Within a few seconds, the sender, using an Internet connection, can obtain the delivery information and even see a facsimile of the recipient's signature.

Computer Software

Software includes all of the programs, routines, and computer languages that control a computer and tell it how to operate. The software that controls the basic workings of a computer system is its *operating system*. More than 80 percent of personal computers use a version of Microsoft's popular Windows operating system. Personal computers made by Apple use the Mac operating system. Most hand-held devices use either the Palm operating system or a special version of Windows called Windows Mobile. But the iPhone and BlackBerry models use their own operating systems. Other operating systems include Unix, which runs on many midrange computer systems, and Linux, which runs on both PCs and midrange systems.

A program that performs the specific tasks that the user wants to carry out—such as writing a letter or looking up data—is called *application software*. Examples of application software include Adobe Acrobat, Microsoft PowerPoint, and Quicken. Table 15.1 lists the major categories of application software. Most application programs are currently stored on individual computers. As the chapter's opening vignette discussed, the future of applications

software all the programs, routines, and computer languages that control a computer and tell it how to operate.

Assessment Check ✓

1. List two input and output devices.
2. What accounts for the increasing popularity of notebook computers?
3. What is software? List the two categories of software.

Table 15.1	Common Types of Applications Software	
Type	**Description**	**Examples**
Word processing	Programs that input, store, retrieve, edit, and print various types of documents.	Microsoft Word
Spreadsheets	Programs that prepare and analyze financial statements, sales forecasts, budgets, and similar numerical and statistical data.	Microsoft Excel
Presentation software	Programs that create presentations. Users can create bulleted lists, charts, graphs, pictures, audio, and even short video clips.	Microsoft PowerPoint
Desktop publishing	Software that combines high-quality type, graphics, and layout tools to create output that can look as attractive as documents produced by professional publishers and printers.	Adobe Acrobat, Microsoft Publisher
Financial software	Programs that compile accounting and financial data to create financial statements, reports, and budgets; they perform basic financial management tasks such as balancing a checkbook.	Quicken, QuickBooks
Database programs	Software that searches and retrieves data from a database; it can sort data based on various criteria.	Microsoft Access, Approach
Personal information managers	Specialized database programs that allow people to track communications with personal and business contacts; some combine e-mail capability.	Microsoft Outlook, Lotus Organizer
Enterprise resource planning	Integrated cross-functional software that controls many business activities, including distribution, finance, and human resources.	SAP Enterprise Resource Planning

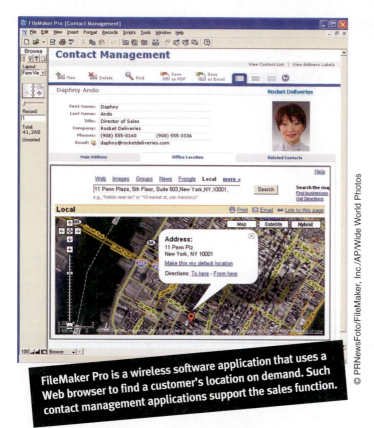

FileMaker Pro is a wireless software application that uses a Web browser to find a customer's location on demand. Such contact management applications support the sales function.

software is uncertain. Some believe much of it will eventually become Web based, with the programs themselves stored on Internet-connected servers. Others disagree, arguing that most computer users will not want to rely on an Internet connection to perform tasks such as preparing a spreadsheet using Microsoft Excel.

Computer Networks

As mentioned earlier, virtually all computers today are linked to networks. In fact, if your PC has Internet access, you're linked to a network. Local area networks and wide area networks allow businesses to communicate, transmit and print documents, and share data. These networks, however, require businesses to install special equipment and connections between office sites. But Internet technology has also been applied to internal company communications and business tasks, tapping a ready-made network. Among these new Internet-based applications are intranets, virtual private networks (VPNs), and voice over Internet protocol (VoIP). Each has contributed to the effectiveness and speed of business processes, so we discuss them next.

Local Area Networks and Wide Area Networks

Most organizations connect their offices and buildings by creating **local area networks (LANs)**, computer networks that connect machines within limited areas, such as a building or several nearby buildings. LANs are useful because they link computers and allow them to share printers, documents, and information, as well as provide access to the Internet. Figure 15.1 shows what a small business computer network might look like.

Wide area networks (WANs) tie larger geographical regions together by using telephone lines and microwave and satellite transmission. One familiar WAN is long-distance telephone service. Companies such as AT&T and Verizon provide WAN services to businesses and consumers. Firms also use WANs to conduct their own operations. Typically, companies link their own network systems to outside communications equipment and services for transmission across long distances.

In Troy, Michigan, Sysco employees use the WiFi network at Panera Bread to hold an informal sales meeting. WiFi hotspots depend on *wireless local networks.*

Wireless Local Networks

A wireless network allows computers, printers, and other devices to be connected without the hassle of stringing cables in traditional office settings. The current standard for wireless networks is called WiFi. **WiFi**—short for *wireless fidelity*—is a wireless network that connects various devices and allows them to communicate with one another through radio waves. Any PC with a WiFi receptor can connect with the Internet at so-called *hot spots*—locations with a wireless router and a high-speed Internet modem. There are probably 100,000 or more hot spots worldwide today. They are found in a variety of places, including airports, libraries, and coffee shops. Examples include Panera Bread's 1,100 stores in the United States and Kansai International Airport in Osaka, Japan. Some locations provide free access, while others charge a fee. Many believe that the successor to WiFi will be something dubbed *Wi-Max.* Unlike WiFi's relatively limited geographic coverage area—generally around 300 feet—a single Wi-Max access point can provide coverage over many miles. In addition, cell phone service providers, such as Sprint Nextel and AT & T, offer broadband network cards for notebook PCs. These devices allow users to access the provider's mobile broadband network from virtually any location where cell phone reception is available.

Intranets

A broad approach to sharing information in an organization is to establish a company network patterned after the Internet. Such a network is called an **intranet.** Intranets are similar to the Internet, but they limit access to employees or other authorized users. An intranet blocks outsiders without valid passwords from entering its network by incorporating both software and hardware known as a **firewall.** Firewalls limit data transfers to certain locations and log system use so that managers can identify attempts to log on with invalid passwords and other threats to a system's security. Highly sophisticated packages immediately alert system administrators about suspicious activities and permit authorized personnel to use smart cards to connect from remote terminals.

Intranets solve the problem of linking different types of computers. Like the Internet, intranets can integrate computers running all kinds of operating systems. In addition, intranets are relatively easy and inexpensive to set up because most businesses already have some of the required hardware and software. For instance, a small business can simply purchase a DSL router and a few cables and create an intranet using phone jacks and internal phone lines. All the business's computers will be linked with each other and with the Internet.

Intranets also support teamwork among employees who travel or work from home. Any intranet member with the right identification, a PC, and some sort of Internet connection—either dial-up or broadband—can link to the intranet and gain access to group calendars, e-mail, documents, and other files. Intranets can also be used for videoconferencing and other forms of virtual meetings. Marathon Oil—a petroleum company with offices throughout the United States and seven other countries including Aberdeen, Scotland; Findlay, Ohio; and Houston, Texas—uses an intranet to allow employees access to its document management system via a Web browser from anywhere in the world.[6]

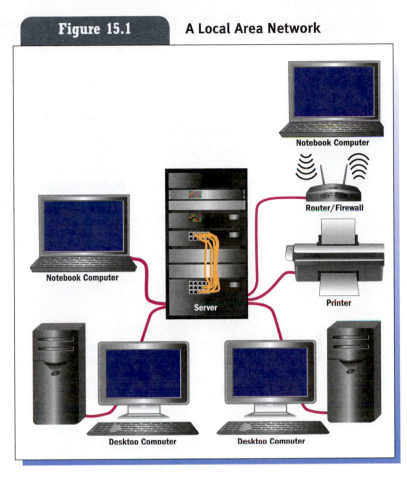

Figure 15.1   **A Local Area Network**

Notebook Computer

Router/Firewall

Notebook Computer

Printer

Server

Desktop Computer   Desktop Computer

intranet computer network that is similar to the Internet but limits access to authorized users.

Virtual Private Networks

To gain increased security for Internet communications, companies often turn to virtual private networks (VPNs), secure connections between two points on the Internet. These VPNs use firewalls and programs that encapsulate data to make them more secure during transit. Loosely defined, a VPN can include a range of networking technologies, from secure Internet connections to private networks from service providers like IBM. A VPN is cheaper for a company to use than leasing several of its own lines. It can also take months to install a leased line in some parts of the world, but a new user can be added to a VPN in a day. Because a VPN uses the Internet, it can be wired, wireless, or a combination of the two.

With a limited budget and small computer staff, Milwaukee-based Equitable Bank decided that a secure VPN was the most cost-effective way to connect its many branches. The system gives loan officers instant access to centralized information and helps speed loan applications through the system. The VPN also ensures a high level of customer privacy and data security required by company policy and state and federal regulations.[7]

VoIP

VoIP—which stands for *voice over Internet protocol*—is an alternative to traditional telecommunication services provided by companies such as Verizon and Qwest. The VoIP telephone is not connected to a traditional phone jack but rather is connected to a personal computer with any type of broadband connection. Special software transmits phone conversations over the Internet, rather than through telephone lines. A VoIP user dials the phone as usual. The person can make and receive calls to and from those with traditional telephone connections (landline or wireless).

A growing number of consumers and businesses have embraced VoIP, mainly due to its cost savings and extra features. One of the largest BMW dealers in North America, Circle BMW in Eatontown, New Jersey, recently switched to VoIP. Not only did the system save the dealership around $2,500 per month, but it also improved customer service. When a call comes in, a new window automatically pops up on a computer screen with the customer's information and history. The system also routes office line calls to a salesperson's hand-held device when the employee isn't at his or her desk.[8]

In spite of VoIP's apparent advantages, there are several potential drawbacks to replacing traditional telephony with Internet telephony. For one thing, your Internet phone service will be only as reliable as your broadband connection. If your broadband connection goes out, so will your phone service. Also, without extensive safeguards, VoIP can expose a phone system to the havoc affecting the rest of the Internet, such as worms and viruses.

Security and Ethical Issues Affecting Information Systems

Numerous security and ethical issues affect information systems. As information systems become increasingly important business assets, they also become progressively harder and more expensive to replace. Damage to information systems or theft of data can have disastrous consequences. When computers are connected to a network, a problem at any individual computer can affect the entire network. Two of the major security threats are e-crime and so-called *malware*.

E-Crime

Computers provide efficient ways for employees to share information. But they may also allow people with more malicious intentions to access information. Or they may allow pranksters—who have no motive other than to see whether they can hack into a system—to gain access to private information. Common e-crimes involve stealing or altering data in several ways:

- Employees or outsiders may change or invent data to produce inaccurate or misleading information.
- Employees or outsiders may modify computer programs to create false information or illegal transactions or to insert viruses.
- Unauthorized people can access computer systems for their own benefit or knowledge or just to see if they can get in.

Individuals, businesses, and government agencies are all vulnerable to computer crime. Computer hackers—unauthorized users—sometimes work alone and sometimes in groups. Sometimes hackers break into computer systems just to show that they can do it; other times they have more sinister motives. Recently, Okemo Mountain Resort in Vermont and Maine-based Hannaford Brothers Supermarket chain were the victims of computer hacking. In both instances, hackers penetrated the firms' information systems and stole customer credit and debit card information. Republican vice presidential candidate Sarah Palin was the victim of e-mail hacking as well.[9]

Information system administrators implement two basic protections against computer crime: they try to prevent access to their systems by unauthorized users and the viewing of data by unauthorized system users. To prevent access, the simplest method requires authorized users to enter passwords. The company may also install firewalls, described earlier. To prevent system users from reading sensitive information, the company may use encryption software, which encodes, or scrambles, messages. To read encrypted messages, users must use an electronic key to convert them to regular text. But as fast as software developers invent new and more elaborate protective measures, hackers seem to break through their defenses. Thus, security is an ongoing battle.

Another form of computer theft is as old as crime itself: theft of equipment. As the size of computer hardware diminishes, it becomes increasingly vulnerable to theft. Hand-held devices, for instance, can easily vanish with a pickpocket or purse snatcher. And because these machines may contain all kinds of important information for a business, employees need to be especially careful not to leave them unattended or within easy reach of others. A vendor for Agilent Technologies recently had a notebook computer stolen. The computer contained unencrypted personal data on 51,000 current and former employees of Agilent Technologies, including Social Security numbers. In another recent case, a hard drive containing the Social Security numbers of 38,000 past and present students, faculty, and staff of Georgetown University was reported stolen.[10] Many notebook computers and hand-held devices contain special security software or passwords that makes it difficult for a thief or any unauthorized person to access the data stored in the computer's memory. If you have a notebook computer, and it contains sensitive personal information, you should consider having such safeguards.

Computer Viruses, Worms, Trojan Horses, and Spyware

Viruses, worms, Trojan horses, and spyware, collectively referred to as **malware,** are malicious software programs designed to infect computer systems. These programs can destroy data, steal sensitive information, and even render information systems inoperable. By one estimate, more than 5.5 million malware programs were unleashed on computer users during one recent year.[11] Malware attacks cost consumers and businesses billions of dollars annually.

malware any malicious software program designed to infect computer systems.

Computer **viruses** are programs that secretly attach themselves to other programs (called *hosts*) and change them or destroy data. According to computer security company Symantec, there are currently in excess of 1 million active computer viruses worldwide.[12] Viruses can be programmed to become active immediately or to remain dormant for a period of time, after which the infections suddenly activate themselves and cause problems. A virus can reproduce by copying itself onto other programs stored in the same drive. It spreads as users install infected software on their systems or exchange files with others, usually by exchanging e-mail, accessing electronic bulletin boards, trading disks, or downloading programs or data from unknown sources on the Internet.

A **worm** is a small piece of software that exploits a security hole in a network to replicate itself. A copy of the worm scans the network for another machine that has a specific security hole. It copies itself to the new machine using the security hole and then starts replicating from there as well. Unlike viruses, worms don't need host programs to damage computer systems.

A **Trojan horse** is a program that claims to do one thing but in reality does something else, usually something malicious. For example, a Trojan horse might claim, and even appear, to be a game. When an unsuspecting user clicks the Trojan horse, the program might erase the hard drive or steal any personal data stored on the computer.

Spyware is software that secretly gathers user information through the user's Internet connection without his or her knowledge, usually for advertising purposes. Spyware applications are typically bundled with other programs downloaded from the Internet. Once installed, the spyware monitors user activity on the Internet and transmits that information in the background to someone else.

Attacks by malware are not limited to computers and computer networks; hand-held devices, including cell phones, have been affected as well. Smart phone users have reported a sharp increase in viruses, worms, and other forms of malware. According to Luis Corrons, technical director of computer security firm PandaLabs, "Trojans designed to steal confidential data like email passwords, instant messaging contacts, etc., are the most prevalent. This shows attacks against cell phones are becoming increasingly sophisticated."[13] In spite of this threat, however, most mobile device users still take few, if any, security precautions.[14]

As viruses, worms, and Trojan horses become more complex, the technology to fight them must increase in sophistication as well. The simplest way to protect against computer viruses is to install one of the many available antivirus software programs, such as Norton AntiVirus and McAfee VirusScan. These programs, which also protect against worms and some Trojan horses, continuously monitor systems for viruses and automatically eliminate any they spot. Users should regularly update them by downloading the latest virus definitions. In addition, computer users should also install and regularly update antispyware programs because many Trojan horses are forms of spyware.

But management must begin to emphasize security at a deeper level: during software design, in corporate servers, at Web gateways, and through Internet service providers. Because more than 80 percent of the world's PCs run on Microsoft operating systems, a single virus, worm, or Trojan horse can spread quickly among them. Individual computer users should carefully choose the files they load onto their systems, scan their systems regularly, make sure their antivirus software is up-to-date, and install software only from known sources. They should also be very careful when opening attachments to e-mails because many viruses, worms, and Trojan horses are spread that way.

Information Systems and Ethics

The scope and power of today's information systems not surprisingly raise a number of ethical issues and concerns. These affect both employees and organizations. For instance, it is not uncommon for organizations to have specific ethical standards and policies regarding the use of information systems by employees and vendors. These standards include obligations

SHOULD EMPLOYERS BE WATCHING EMPLOYEES' EVERY MOVE?

When the subject of online shopping, personal e-mailing, and surfing the Web at work comes up, most people shrug and acknowledge that it happens at every workplace where employees have access to the Internet.

If some of this behavior is acceptable, who draws the line—and where—separating what is permitted personal use and what is not? Employers often say that they do, because employee activity in the workplace, during work hours, is their business. But some people disagree, arguing that employers often go too far in their oversight.

Should employers monitor the online activities of their employees?

PRO

1. Estimates say that employees spend between one and three hours each day online conducting personal business at work. Because employers are paying their employees to work, this lost productivity is significant. Websense Inc. estimates that U.S. businesses lose $85 billion each year due to Internet misuse during work hours. Monitoring employees' activities is the only way to make sure they are working.
2. Certain online activities could cause a security breach to a firm. In addition, employees admit to visiting adult sites, social networking sites, and entertainment sites, all of which could compromise the security and reputation of a company. Some firms choose to block access to these types of sites.

CON

1. Using technology to monitor employee activities raises concerns about privacy, particularly if employees are not informed beforehand about the technology being implemented—and the consequences of being caught.
2. Some companies decide that the expense, along with problems that arise when employees are terminated for Internet misuse, is not worth the trouble.

Summary

Companies typically monitor employee Internet use by tracking message content, keystrokes, and time spent at the computer. While most experts agree that this is often necessary, they note that employers could do a better job of informing employees about the behavior that is both expected of them and prohibited. "Where employers often fall short is that they tell employees that they will be monitored but they don't describe exactly what behavior is expected or not expected," explains Manny Avramadis, senior vice president of global human resources for the American Management Association (AMA). "To explain exactly what their expectations are about the policy is important. Educated employees and explaining the definition of what is fair and acceptable Internet and e-mail use annually is recommended."

Sources: Susan M. Heathfield, "Surfing the Web at Work," *About.com,* http://humanresources.about.com, accessed March 26, 2009; Christian Humphries, "Look Who's Talking (and Chatting and Surfing)," *WindowsITPro,* February 29, 2008, http://windowsitpro.com, accessed March 26, 2009; Kaylyn Kendall Dines, "Office Watch," *Black Enterprise,* September 2007, http://www.blackenterprise.com, accessed October 20, 2008; Aaron Letto, "Managing Risk from Within: Monitoring Employees the Right Way," *Risk Management,* April 2007, http://www.rmmag.com, accessed October 20, 2008.

Solving an ETHICAL controversy

to protect system security and the privacy and confidentiality of data. Policies also may cover the personal use of computers and related technologies, both hardware and software, by employees.

Ethical issues also involve organizational use of information systems. Organizations have an obligation to protect the privacy and confidentiality of data about employees and customers. Employment records contain sensitive personal information, such as bank account numbers, which, if not protected, could lead to identity theft. Another ethical issue is the use of computer technology to monitor employees while they are working. The "Solving an Ethical Controversy" feature debates the issue of employee monitoring further.

Assessment Check ✓

1. Explain computer hacking.
2. What is malware?
3. How does a computer virus work?

"The moment when confidence becomes conviction." This Japanese advertisement, timed to coincide with the Red Sox–Oakland A's game at the Tokyo Dome, touts EMC²'s disaster recovery service.

Disaster Recovery and Backup

Natural disasters, power failures, equipment malfunctions, software glitches, human error, and terrorist attacks can disrupt even the most sophisticated computer information systems. These disruptions can cost businesses and other organizations billions of dollars. Even more serious consequences can occur. For example, one recent study found that more than 90 percent of firms that sustained a loss of critical data went out of business within two years.[15]

When the Delaware River flooded a while back, the water damaged a bakery and café owned by Jane and Joel Vitart in New Hope, Pennsylvania. The flood caused about $120,000 in damage and cleanup costs, but the biggest blow was the loss of the business's computer system. As Jane Vitart noted, "I ran my whole business on that computer—all my financial data, inventory, vendor bills, my marketing materials, customer lists, menus." She had backed up some of her financial data, but the backup disk was defective. The business was closed for six weeks and then reopened only after the couple stretched their credit to the limit and used all their personal savings. Jane Vitart said, "I feel like I'm starting from scratch." Now, at the first hint of flooding, she makes sure the computer system is among the first items evacuated.[16]

Software glitches are no less serious. Recently, software malfunctions created problems for thousands of customers of the Dallas, Texas, Water Utilities, from double-billing and other erroneous charges to trouble paying bills online. In another instance, a software problem prevented apparel-maker Levi Strauss & Company from getting some shipments to the United States on time. Sales and profits were adversely affected by the delay. And computer problems were at least partly responsible for the cancellation of more than 400 British Airways flights on a recent day, costing the airline millions of dollars.[17]

Disaster recovery planning—deciding how to prevent system failures and continue operations if computer systems fail—is a critical function of all organizations. Disaster prevention programs can avoid some of these costly problems. The most basic precaution is routinely backing up software and data—at the organizational and individual levels. However, the organization's data center cannot be the sole repository of critical data because a single location is vulnerable to threats from both natural and man-made disasters. Consequently, off-site data backup is a necessity.

According to security experts, there are five important tasks regarding off-site data storage. First is planning. The organization needs to decide what data need to be protected. Priority should be given to data having severe legal or business consequences should they be lost. Second, a backup schedule must be established and closely adhered to. Third, when data are transmitted off-site, they must be protected by the highest level of security possible. Fourth, care should be taken in selecting the right security vendor. There are dozens of vendors offering different services and having different areas of expertise. Finally, the backup system should be continually tested and evaluated.

Assessment Check ✓

1. What are the types of disasters to which information systems are vulnerable?

2. List the tasks regarding off-site data storage.

Hit & Miss

Google Takes Cloud Computing to Business Users

If you've ever experienced a hard-drive crash, you can appreciate the benefit of computer applications that store all your programs and data on external servers instead of your own computer. That's the concept behind cloud computing.

Google is hoping to capitalize on cloud computing by taking its suite of online software, called Google Apps, into business computing to square off against Microsoft Office. Google Apps includes e-mail, instant messaging, calendars, word processing, chat, voice mail, spreadsheets, and document creation and collaboration. The applications are free and simple to use and allow users to conduct business via "the cloud"—Google's remote computers and data centers accessible online. Gmail, Google's e-mail program, earns revenue from advertising.

Some users prefer Google's simpler applications to the feature-rich applications of Microsoft Office, which dominate desktop computers. While Google is nimble, however, Microsoft has deep pockets for product development and marketing. One industry observer says that despite the fact that half a million companies have signed up for Google Apps, "it's a raindrop" compared with Office's 500 million users.

Still, Google has dedicated 600 employees to ramping up the business side of its cloud computing efforts. Their leader, Google's engineering director, likes to pitch the idea of freeing yourself from your computer and offers to delete and reformat the hard drives of skeptics' computers along with his own, to prove his point that a computer is "just an appliance to access the cloud." No one has taken him up on the offer so far, but he remains confident people will come to see the cloud as a valuable communication service.

"Work when you want to work," he insists. "Don't worry about where things are. Just go to a browser and do your work." Even collaboration on documents can be easier in the cloud, where everyone can work on a text at once and the computer sorts out any conflicts.

With customers such as biotech pioneer Genentech, General Electric, the government of Washington, DC, and many consultants, marketing firms, and health care providers, Google's servers must provide nearly failproof service. The firm currently offers a service level agreement (SLA) promising Gmail will be available 99.9 percent of the time; it's putting together SLAs for Google Calendar and Google Docs and introducing an online dashboard showing the status of each service. To those who point out that 99.9 percent availability means the server can be down nearly 9 hours a year—high-end services promise downtime of as little as 5 minutes a year—Google's product manager says, "We talk to customers, and 99.9 percent is … much higher than most organizations [get] with their internal service today."

Questions for Critical Thinking

1. Google believes the success of cloud computing depends on keeping applications simple. Do you think business customers see such simplicity as a strength or a weakness? Why?

2. Is reliability of 99.9 percent sufficient for business customers? Why or why not? What should users of cloud computing do to protect their data and programs in the cloud in case of outages?

Sources: Tom Kaneshige, "Can Google Apps Move Up-Market?" *Computerworld,* March 7, 2009, http://www.computerworld.com; company Web site, http://www.google.com, accessed March 6, 2009; Michael Agger, "Kill Your Computer: The Cloud Wants to Set You Free," *Slate,* March 2, 2009, http://www.slate.com; John Naughton, "There's a Silver Lining to Google's Cloud Computing Glitch," *The Observer,* March 1, 2009, http://www.guardian.co.uk; Stephen Shankland, "Can You Trust Your Business to Google's Cloud?" *CNET News,* July 11, 2008, http://news.cnet.com.

Information System Trends

Computer information systems are constantly—and rapidly—evolving. To keep their information systems up-to-date, firms must continually keep abreast of changes in technology. Some of the most significant trends in information systems today include the growing demands of the so-called *distributed workforce*, the increased use of application service providers, on-demand computing, and cloud and grid computing (see the accompanying "Hit & Miss" feature).

The Distributed Workforce

As discussed in earlier chapters, many companies are relying more and more on a distributed workforce—employees who no longer work in traditional offices but rather in what are called *virtual offices*, including at home. Information technology makes a distributed workforce possible. Computers, networks, and other components of information systems allow many workers the ability to do their jobs effectively almost anywhere. For instance, none of JetBlue's reservations agents work in offices; they all work at home, connected to the airline's information system. JetBlue is hardly alone in its use of home-based workers. Boeing, Starbucks, Agilent Technologies, Sun Microsystems, and many other companies maintain "virtual" offices with thousands of workers. According to the Bureau of Labor Statistics (BLS), more than 20 million full-time employees do the majority of their work at home.[18] The BLS statistics show that the vast majority of at-home workers use computers and related technologies. Most experts believe that the number of people working in virtual offices will increase and could constitute around 40 percent of the workforce within a few years. The increasing demands of the distributed workforce will likely lead to more innovative and increasingly powerful information systems.

application service provider (ASP) outside supplier that provides both the computers and the application support for managing an information system.

Application Service Providers

As with other business functions, many firms find that outsourcing at least some of their information technology function makes sense. Because of the increasing cost and complexity of obtaining and maintaining information systems, many firms hire an **application service provider (ASP),** an outside supplier that provides both the computers and the application support for managing an information system. An ASP can simplify complex software for its customers so that it is easier for them to manage and use. When an ASP relationship is successful, the buyer can then devote more time and resources to its core businesses instead of struggling to manage its information systems. Other benefits include stretching the firm's technology dollar farther and giving smaller companies the kind of information power that in the past has been available only to much larger organizations. Even large companies turn to ASPs to manage some or all of their information systems. Recently, the Walt Disney Company outsourced much of its information technology (IT) functions to IBM and Affiliated Computer Services to save money. Approximately 1,000 Disney employees transferred to new jobs with the two vendors.[19] Companies that decide to use ASPs should check the backgrounds and references of these firms before hiring them to manage critical systems. In addition, customers should try to ensure that the service provider has strong security measures to block computer hackers or other unauthorized access to the data, that its data centers are running reliably, and that adequate data and applications backups are maintained.

SOME OF THE GREATEST VICTORIES ARE CELEBRATED IN SILENCE

You've earned a great trust. And inherited a great responsibility—to those whose success depends on you. Accomplishing your mission demands vision. Resolve. And proven technologies packaged in broad, integrated mission solutions. In defining, developing and delivering these solutions, Raytheon is sharing your mission. Every day. In ways both great and small. www.raytheon.com/ads/aw3

Raytheon
Customer Success Is Our Mission

Raytheon Company/PRNewsFoto/NewsCom

"Some of the greatest victories are celebrated in silence." Raytheon, an *applications service provider (ASP)*, offers services such as Joint Battlespace Integration, which coordinates the information available to the U.S. armed forces, Missile Defense Agency, and Department of Homeland Security. ASPs free their customers from the complex task of information management, allowing them to concentrate on their core missions.

On-Demand, Cloud, and Grid Computing

Another recent trend is **on-demand computing,** also called *utility computing*. Instead of purchasing and maintaining expensive software, firms essentially rent the software time from application providers and pay only for their usage of the software, similar to purchasing electricity from a utility. On-demand computing is particularly useful for firms that experience annual peaks in demand or seasonal spikes in customer usage of their applications. By renting the service they need only when they need it, they can avoid buying the software that is not routinely required. On-demand computing can also help companies remain current with the most efficient software on the market without purchasing huge upgrades.

Cloud computing uses powerful servers to store applications software and databases. Users access the software and databases via the Web using anything from a PC to a smart phone. The software as service movement championed by Google among others and described in the "Hit & Miss" feature on page 513 is an example of cloud computing.

Small and medium-size companies occasionally find themselves with jobs that require more computing power than their current systems offer. A cost-effective solution for these firms may be something called *grid computing*. **Grid computing** consists of a network of smaller computers running special software. The software breaks down a large, complex job into smaller tasks and then distributes them to the networked computers. The software then reassembles the individual task results into the finished job. By combining multiple small computers, grid computing creates a virtual mainframe or even supercomputer.

The new laws of physics.

Cloud computing supports this mobile desktop solution, which makes data available to users by smart phone at any time or place, regardless of the file size or location.

PRNewsFoto/Transmedia/AP/Wide World Photos

Assessment Check ✔

1 What is an application service provider?
2 Explain on-demand computing.

What's Ahead

This is the first of two chapters devoted to managing technology and information. The next chapter, "Understanding Accounting and Financial Statements," focuses on accounting, financial information, and financing reporting. Accounting is the process of measuring, interpreting, and communicating financial information to enable people inside and outside the firm to make informed decisions. The chapter describes the functions of accounting and role of accountants; the steps in the accounting cycle; the types, functions, and components of financial statements; and the role of budgets in an organization.

Summary of Learning Goals

1 Distinguish between data and information, and explain the role of information systems in business.

It is important for businesspeople to know the difference between data and information. Data are raw facts and figures that may or may not be relevant to a business decision. Information is knowledge gained from processing those facts and figures. An information system is an organized method for collecting, storing, and communicating past, present, and projected information on internal operations and external intelligence. Most information systems today use computer and telecommunications technology.

Assessment Check Answers

1.1 Distinguish between data and information. Data consist of raw facts and figures that may or may not be relevant to a decision. Information is the knowledge gained from processing data.

1.2 What is an information system? An information system is an organized method for collecting, storing, and communicating past, present, and projected information on internal operations and external intelligence.

2 List the components and different types of information systems.

When people think about information systems today they're generally thinking about computer-based systems, those that rely on computers and related technologies. Computer-based information systems rely on four components: computer hardware, software, telecommunications and computer networks, and data resource management. The heart of an information system is its database, a centralized integrated collection of data resources. Information systems fall into two broad categories: operational support systems and management support systems. Operational support systems are designed to produce a variety of information for users. Examples include transaction processing systems and process control systems. Management support systems are those designed to support effective decision making. They include management information systems, decision support systems, executive support systems, and expert systems.

Assessment Check Answers

2.1 List the four components of a computer-based information system. The four components of a computer-based information system are computer hardware, software, telecommunications and computer networks, and data resource management.

2.2 What is a database? A database is a centralized integrated collection of data resources.

2.3 What are the two general types of information systems? Give examples of each. The two categories of information systems are operational support systems (such as transactions processing and process control systems) and management support systems (such as management information, decision support, executive support, and expert systems).

3 Outline how computer hardware and software are used to manage information.

Hardware consists of all tangible elements of a computer system, including input and output devices. Major categories of computers include mainframes, supercomputers, midrange systems, personal computers (PCs), and hand-held devices. Computer software provides the instructions that tell the hardware what to do. The software that controls the basic workings of the computer is its *operating system*. Other programs, called *application software*, perform specific tasks that users want to complete.

Assessment Check Answers

3.1 List two input and output devices. Input devices include the keyboard and mouse. Output devices include the monitor and printer.

3.2 What accounts for the increasing popularity of notebook computers? Notebook computers account for over half of all new personal computers sold. Their increased popularity is due to better displays, lower prices, more rugged designs, increasing computing power, and slimmer designs.

3.3 What is software? List the two categories of software. Computer software provides the instructions that tell the hardware what to do. The software that controls the basic workings of the computer is its *operating system*. Other programs, called *application software*, perform specific tasks that users want to complete.

4 Describe networking and telecommunications technology and the types of computer networks.

Local area networks connect computers within a limited area. Wide area networks tie together larger geographical regions by using telephone lines, microwave, or satellite transmission. A wireless network allows computers to communicate through radio waves. Intranets allow employees to share information on a ready-made company network. Access to an intranet is restricted to authorized users and is protected by a firewall. Virtual private networks (VPNs) provide a secure Internet connection between two or more points. VoIP—voice over Internet protocol—uses a personal computer running special software and a broadband Internet connection to make and receive telephone calls over the Internet rather than over traditional telephone networks.

Assessment Check Answers

4.1 What is a LAN? A local area network (LAN) is a computer network that connects machines within a limited area, such as a building or several nearby buildings.

4.2 What are the differences between an intranet and a VPN? An intranet is a computer network patterned after the Internet. Unlike the Internet, access to an intranet is limited to employees and other authorized users. A virtual private network (VPN) is a way of gaining increased security for Internet connections.

4.3 Briefly explain how VoIP works. The VoIP phone is connected to a personal computer with any type of broadband connection. Special software transmits phone conversations over the Internet. A VoIP user can make and receive calls to and from those with traditional telephone connections (either landline or wireless).

5 **Discuss the security and ethical issues involving computer information systems.**

Numerous security and ethical issues affect information systems. Two of the main security threats are e-crime and malware. E-crimes range from hacking—unauthorized penetration of an information system—to the theft of hardware. Malware are malicious software programs designed to infect computer systems. Examples include viruses, worms, Trojan horses, and spyware. Ethical issues affecting information systems include the proper use of the systems by authorized users. Organizations also have an obligation to employees, vendors, and customers to protect the security and confidentiality of the data stored in information systems.

Assessment Check Answers

5.1 Explain computer hacking. Computer hacking is a breach of a computer systems by unauthorized people. Sometimes the hackers' motive is just to see if they can get in. Other times, hackers have more sinister motives, including stealing or altering data.

5.2 What is malware? Malware are malicious software programs designed to infect computer systems.

5.3 How does a computer virus work? A virus is a program that secretly attaches itself to another program (called a *host*). The virus then changes the host, destroys data, or even makes the computer system inoperable.

6 **Explain the steps that companies go through in anticipating, planning for, and recovering from information systems disasters.**

Information system disasters, whether man-made or due to natural causes, can cost businesses billions of dollars. The consequences of a disaster can be minimized by routinely backing up software and data, both at an organizational level and at an individual level. Organizations should back up critical data at an off-site location. Some may also want to invest in extra hardware and software sites, which can be accessed during emergencies.

Assessment Check Answers

6.1 What are the types of disasters to which information systems are vulnerable? Natural disasters, power failures, equipment malfunctions, software glitches, human error, and even terrorist attacks can disrupt even the most powerful, sophisticated computer information systems.

6.2 List the tasks regarding off-site data storage. The five tasks are planning and deciding which data to back up, establishing and following a backup schedule, protecting data when they are transmitted off-site, choosing the right vendor, and continually testing and refining the backup system.

7 **Review the current trends in information systems.**

Information systems are continually and rapidly evolving. Some of the most significant trends are the increasing demands of the distributed workforce, the increased use of application service providers, on-demand computing, and grid computing. Many people now work in virtual offices, including at home. Information technology makes this possible. Application service providers allow organizations to outsource most of their IT functions. Rather than buying and maintaining expensive software, on-demand computing offers users the option of renting software time from outside vendors and paying only for their usage. Grid computing consists of a network of smaller computers running special software creating a virtual mainframe or even supercomputer.

Assessment Check Answers

7.1 What is an application service provider? An application service provider (ASP) is an outside vendor that provides both the computers and application support for managing an information system. By using an ASP, the organization effectively outsources some, or all, of its IT function.

7.2 Explain on-demand computing. Instead of purchasing and maintaining expensive software, some organizations use on-demand computing. In this arrangement, software is rented from a vendor and the organization only pays for its actual usage.

Business Terms You Need to Know

data 498

information 498

information system 498

operational support
  systems 502

management support
  systems 502

hardware 503

server 503

software 505

intranet 507

malware 509

application service
  provider (ASP) 514

Other Important Business Terms

chief information officer
(CIO) 499
computer-based
information systems 499
database 500
transaction processing
system 502

process control system 502
management information
system (MIS) 502
decision support system
(DSS) 502
executive support system
(ESS) 502

expert system 502
local area network
(LAN) 506
WiFi 507
firewall 507
VoIP 508
virus 510

worm 510
Trojan horse 510
spyware 510
on-demand computing 514
grid computing 515

Review Questions

1. Distinguish between data and information. Why is the distinction important to businesspeople in their management of information?

2. What are the four components of an information system?

3. Describe the two different types of information system, and give an example of how each might help a particular business.

4. Explain decision support systems, executive support systems, and expert systems.

5. What are the major categories of computers? What is a smart phone?

6. What is an intranet? Give specific examples of benefits for firms that set up their own intranets.

7. Briefly explain how VoIP works. Why might a business switch from regular telephony to Internet telephony?

8. What steps can organizations and individuals take to prevent computer crime?

9. How does a computer virus work? What can individuals and organizational computer users do to reduce the likelihood of acquiring a computer virus?

10. Why is disaster recovery important for businesses? Relate your answer to a natural disaster such as a hurricane or fire.

11. Describe four information system trends.

Projects and Teamwork Applications

1. Do you believe that information overload is a serious problem in your life? What steps do you (or can you) take to reduce this overload so that you can function more effectively in all areas of your life?

2. Suppose you've been hired to design an information system for a midsize retailer. Describe what that information system might look like, including the necessary components. Would the system be an operational support system, a management support system, or both?

3. Select a local company and contact the person in charge of its information system for a brief interview. Ask that individual to outline his or her company's information system. Also, ask the person what he or she likes most about the job. Did this interview make you more or less interested in a career in information systems?

4. Working with a partner, research the current status of Wi-Max. Prepare a short report on its growth, its current uses, and its future for business computing.

5. Do you think computer hacking is a serious crime? Defend your answer.

6. Your supervisor has asked your advice. She isn't sure the company's information system needs any elaborate safeguards because the company has little Web presence beyond a simple home page. However, employees use e-mail extensively to contact suppliers and customers. Make a list of the threats to which the company's information system is vulnerable. What types of safeguards would you suggest?

7. Your college or university probably has a set of ethical guidelines and policies regarding the use of its information system by students, faculty, and staff. Review the guidelines and write a brief report summarizing your findings.

8. After recent man-made and natural disasters, interest in data backup and recovery software for critical computer data increased dramatically. Visit the following Web sites and, working with a partner, prepare a report outlining some of the key features of these programs with the goal of convincing the owner of a small business that he or she should invest in critical data backup and recovery software.
http://www.baymountain.com
http://www.unitrends.com

Web Assignments

1. **Finding the right PC.** Assume you're in the market for a new personal computer. First, make a list of your needs. Needs represent the basic configuration that will meet your individual computing requirements. Next, make a list of your wants. Wants represent features you'd like to have in your new PC but don't necessarily need. Finally, decide between a notebook computer and a desktop computer. List the reasons you chose a desktop or a notebook.

   a. Visit the CNET (http://www.cnet.com) Web site. Research different computer makes and models that meet your specifications. Make a list of the five top-rated systems. What criteria did CNET consider when developing the rankings?

   b. Decide where you will buy your new computer. Will you order it from a direct seller, such as Dell, purchase it from an online retailer, such as Newegg.com, or buy it at a retail store, such as Office Depot? What are the advantages and disadvantages of each option?

   c. Repeat the exercise, assuming you're buying a computer for your job. Explain any differences between a computer purchased for personal and school use and one purchased for business use.

2. **Software as service.** Visit the Web sites of Google Apps and Microsoft Office (http://www.google.com/a/help/intl/en/var_3.html; http://www.microsoft.com/office). What are Google Apps? What types of programs are offered? How do the features of Google Apps compare with those of the Microsoft Office Suite?

3. **Malware.** Symantec is a leading computer security company. One of its products is Norton AntiVirus. It keeps a record of currently active malware. Go to the firm's Web site (http://www.symantec.com/security_response/index.jsp) and answer the following questions:

   a. Approximately how many different malware programs have been discovered?

   b. How many new ones are discovered each month?

   c. Which are more common: viruses, worms, or Trojan horses?

   d. What are the names of the most recently discovered malware programs?

Note: Internet Web addresses change frequently. If you do not find the exact site listed, you may need access the organization's or company's home page and search from there.

HP Rebounds Overseas

Case 15.1

Just as the U.S. economy was tilting and some tech companies were sliding toward potential disaster, Hewlett-Packard (HP) surprised the experts by reporting substantial growth—in Brazil, China, India, Russia, and South Africa. In fact, the PC unit of the company reported sales growth of 24 percent during one quarter when other firms were posting flat growth or losses. Most of this revenue came from countries in which consumer markets are new and businesses are building their customer base. HP reported that 69 percent of its total revenue came from outside the United States, a significantly higher percentage than that of other high-tech firms. The four fastest-growing markets—Brazil, China, India, and Russia—accounted for a 35 percent jump in revenue.

But the African market has heads turning. HP Africa recently predicted growth of 25 percent per year for the next several years. Managing Director of HP Africa Rainer Koch explains the importance of that market, especially in light of a softer U.S. market and the amount of outsourcing occurring in India. "Because of outsourcing, salaries in India are skyrocketing, so I think you will see people recruiting in Africa," notes Koch. "Africa has a large English-speaking population and a large French-speaking population. I think it will really compete with India in 10 years." As global firms begin to hire qualified workers in Africa, they will need computers to conduct business. "In some places the market is exploding," he continues.

Despite some skepticism, Koch is optimistic about HP's future in Africa. "I was in Eastern Europe 15 years ago, and in some ways it is a similar picture. People thought things would never take off in Romania or Bulgaria, but they did." One important factor in the growth of technology and business throughout Africa is the introduction of cell phones, whose use has mushroomed over the last few years. Small businesses and average consumers now have an easier time with phone and Internet connections.

Africa's largest economy is South Africa, where the tech market is already well developed. But exciting opportunities are opening up in emerging, oil-rich countries such as Nigeria, Libya, Angola, and Ghana. All of these signs suggest a strong future for HP, which is making the most of its opportunities—and its own strengths—in overseas markets, where PCs and their accessories are newly in demand.

"We like our position in many of the markets we are in," says CEO Mark Hurd. It's likely to get even stronger.[20]

Questions for Critical Thinking

1. Visit the Hewlett-Packard Web site to learn more about its goods and services for a global market. In what ways do you think HP can serve small businesses in emerging countries in Africa, Asia, and South America? How might the company have to adapt to conditions in these countries?

2. How might HP have to adapt its products and business practices to succeed in countries like India, China, and South Africa? What about other nations?

Case 15.2   Trend Micro Busts Computer Bugs

It's happened to everyone. You send an important e-mail to your instructor or your boss, and it bounces back "undeliverable." Or you're trying to finish a last-minute report, but your computer doesn't cooperate, acting sluggish. Or your manager calls you into the office to ask you why you were visiting weird Web sites at odd hours on your computer. When you add all these incidents up, you conclude that your computer has a bug.

A variety of software programs are designed to catch viruses and worms, but Trend Micro is rapidly becoming one of the most popular. This preference is partly because company CEO Eva Chen decided several years ago that consumers would become loyal customers if they found out about Trend Micro's software and had the opportunity to try it. So Chen directed some of the firm's marketing resources away from corporate customers and began to focus on individual consumers. She approached Best Buy, which agreed to give Trend Micro's software a big chunk of shelf space.

The strategy worked. Trend Micro offers its products at a lower price than either industry giants McAfee or Symantec, and reviewers report that its security software is very easy to install and use. It also takes less time than others to complete an entire scan of a laptop or PC—about 90 minutes to scan a desktop PC and about 45 minutes to scan a laptop. Even better, it does not gobble up a computer's entire memory while scanning. In fact, Trend Micro's newest software consumes only half the amount of memory during scans than its previous products. This means that during a scan, you can surf the Web, write a memo, and do other activities at nearly normal speed.

If Trend Micro's software detects a potentially damaging spyware program, it is automatically deleted. But if the program is friendly—one that enables a favorite Web site to recognize your computer without a log on—it leaves it intact. In addition, if a threatening program tries to attack your computer, the software automatically ropes it off and removes it. Trend Micro also identifies vulnerabilities in your computer that could lead to an outside user taking over your data, programs, and applications.

Despite its success, however, even Trend Micro has fallen victim to Web attacks. During one, malicious software infected tens of thousands of Web pages, attempting to install passwords that would steal software from people who visited the company sites. Although it might seem embarrassing that a security vendor would sustain such an attack, other vendors have had the same experience. It simply underscores how rapidly hackers are able to adapt to and overcome security systems and programs. Trend Micro was able to defuse the situation quickly. Eva Chen notes that her company has a "continuous commitment to stay one step ahead of new threats and provide our customers with the freedom to use their computers as they desire without worrying about protecting their systems and data against a growing range of Web threats." Like a digital ghost buster, Trend Micro is ready to root out and blast away even the tiniest and most silent of bugs.[21]

Questions for Critical Thinking

1. Why is it so important for Trend Micro—as a business—to stay ahead of new computer threats?

2. Do you agree with Eva Chen's move into the consumer market for security software? Why or why not?

A freshly brewed cup of coffee is one of life's simple pleasures; there's nothing high-tech about it. Or is there? California-based Peet's Coffee & Tea has specialized in offering consumers the richest, freshest coffee beans and select teas for more than 40 years. Although Peet's roasts its coffee beans in small batches by hand—every day—technology is still involved in the way the firm handles customer orders, processes information, and sends out shipments.

Peet's sells 32 different kinds of coffee—single bean, blends, and decaffeinated. It also sells a variety of teas. The coffee beans are roasted daily, and some are then ground to order in a variety of styles. Each order, large or small, is packaged and shipped the same day for freshness. Managing information in order to accomplish these tasks quickly and sell through five different channels—the company's 100-plus retail stores, mail order, the Internet, grocery stores, and corporate food services—requires the right technology. An individual customer may place an order through Peets.com, while grocery stores use an extranet at Peets.net. Or a customer may phone the call center, which transfers the order to the company's intranet. The firm also offers the Peetniks program, which automatically generates reorders for customers. Online customers have until midnight Pacific Standard Time to place an order for the next day.

Peet's relies on an order-fulfillment system designed by software producer Great Plains and modified over the years to meet the changing needs of the firm as it has grown. The system creates a roasting spreadsheet, which shows the roasters how many pounds of each kind of coffee to roast on a given day. The system also generates reports that show how big the order size of each type of coffee is and where it is going, which determines which roasting machine will be used. Once the coffee has finished the roasting process, the system indicates how much of each type of coffee will go to each channel. Because each channel uses different packaging, the system diverts the right amount of each coffee to the correct order-fulfillment department for packaging. A spreadsheet tells workers how much coffee goes into grocery packaging, how much goes into five-pound "pillow packs" for Peet's retail stores, and how much goes into one-pound bags for mail-order and Internet customers.

Finally, the system produces labels for the packages and shipping labels. The labels designate the type of coffee and the roasting date, so groceries and Peet's stores can monitor their inventory for freshness. This ordering process takes place continually throughout the day, with the system sorting information and directing the right coffee to the right place. "Before we had this system, the roasting staff just estimated what they needed to roast each day," recalls Mike Cloutier of Peet's. "This system is far more efficient."

Computer software can't physically transport a package of coffee from one location to another. So Peet's uses the FloShipper system, an automated conveyor system that boxes and tapes each packaged order of coffee, weighs it, and slots it into the appropriate shipping lane. The system is designed specially to handle individual orders from consumers. The hand-roasted coffee then gets to customers more quickly. Before Peet's adopted this system, Peet's workers took two shifts to complete an order manually; now the time is down to one shift. "We could not meet our same day roast-and-ship standards without the FloShipper system," says Peet's director of plant operations.

Throughout the Peet's organization, technology meets craftsmanship every day. Without the order-fulfillment software and automated shipping systems, customers would not receive the freshest coffee—which is still roasted by hand every day, the way it was 40 years ago.[22]

Questions for Critical Thinking

1. What are some of the data that Peet's order-fulfillment system gathers? What kind of information does it provide to workers?
2. How does technology help Peet's devote more time and resources to its core business?
3. How might Peet's use an enterprise resource planning (ERP) system?
4. How might Peet's use desktop publishing systems to communicate with consumers and business customers?

chapter **16**

Understanding Accounting and Financial Statements

Image Source/© Corbis

Mark-to-Market Accounting: Who Takes the Hit?

© David Zalubowski/AP/Wide World Photos

Small business owners, everyday investors, and those with pension or retirement funds are rightfully worried about the value of their holdings these days. Certain accounting rules and practices receive extra scrutiny when markets nosedive. One of those rules, known as *mark-to-market accounting*, values the assets on a company's balance sheet based on their current, fair market value—if they were to be sold that day—not to the price that was paid for them. This accounting rule, formally known as Financial Accounting Standard No. 157, is overseen by the Financial Accounting Standards Board (FASB) and enforced by the Securities and Exchange Commission (SEC). The rule was adopted in the wake of the collapse of the savings-and-loan industry in the 1980s. Its goal was to create more accurate, reliable reporting by banks and financial institutions in particular, although it affects other organizations as well.

But critics see problems with the mark-to-market rules, and banks are probably the hardest hit by what many experts believe are weak points in the regulations. When the value of an asset such as a home drops or a loan holder defaults, according to mark-to-market rules a bank must mark down the value of those assets, even though the value might increase later. Some industry experts believe that tying an asset to the market is not necessarily the best way to establish its value. Further complicating the situation is that not every type of investment instrument, such as those involving home mortgages, is traded every day. But they must be lumped in with those that *are* traded daily. So banks are forced to hold essentially worthless assets that they can't sell in the collapsed market. As a result, some argued that today's financial climate demanded that FAS 157 should be suspended or at least modified. "The current framework for accounting oversight, though well intentioned, has proved inadequate and must be fundamentally revised," noted Ed Yingling, president of the American Bankers Association.

Even banks that were hardest hit by the credit crisis and the consequences of having to apply the mark-to-market rules to their balance sheets said that they could live with a revision instead of an outright abandonment of the accounting law. "Most of the banks that are hurting—if they were allowed to let these loans work themselves out over time as opposed to being forced to write them down and liquidate them—they

would survive just fine," remarks Michael Chaffin, CEO and president of the First Choice Community Bank in Georgia. "It's just common sense," he argues. "We're throwing billions and even trillions of dollars into a hole that we could plug if we just adjusted accounting standards temporarily. I'm not saying give it to us forever." Chaffin pointed out that community banks like his were not the ones involved in making risky mortgage loans—yet his bank suffered because of the housing industry's downturn and the accounting rules apply to all.

Yet those on the other side of the debate believe that mark-to-market accounting practices are fair and valid. They argued that any temporary gains made by relaxing the rules would just delay the problem of valuing mortgage investments and create more doubt. Some maintained that the mark-to-market rules actually benefit investors. "I think that mark-to-market [accounting] does help the investor," said Conrad Hewitt, former chief accountant for the SEC. "Mark-to-market brought to focus the problems we have had in our financial institutions much faster." Despite requests to repeal the rule before he left office, Hewitt declined to do so.

To resolve the issue, legislation was proposed to create a new federal oversight agency that would make the ultimate decision about accounting practices. The proposed Federal Accounting Oversight Board (FAOB) would not replace the FASB but would approve the standards being set and decide how they would be applied. The new five-member board would include top officials from the Federal Reserve, the U.S. Treasury, the SEC, the Federal Deposit Insurance Corporation, and the Public Company Oversight Board. If you think this sounds like another layer of government bureaucracy, you are not alone. In addition, critics charged that creating a new board would dilute the authority of the SEC and FASB, undermining the government's efforts to stabilize the financial sector of the U.S. economy.

Meanwhile, as bankers and lawmakers continued to press hard for changes in the mark-to market regulations, the FASB finally agreed to relax the rules—at least temporarily. Starting in the second quarter of 2009, bank managers were allowed to value their assets according to what they would go for in an "orderly" sale, not one forced in a distressed market. Still, some critics said the changes did not go far enough, while others said they only clouded the true picture of the banking industry. This issue will no doubt raise itself again.[1]

Chapter 16 OVERVIEW

Accounting professionals prepare the financial information that organizations present in their annual reports. Whether you begin your career by working for a company or by starting your own firm, you need to understand what accountants do and why their work is so important in contemporary business.

Accounting is the process of measuring, interpreting, and communicating financial information to enable people inside and outside the firm to make informed decisions. In many ways, accounting is the language of business. Accountants gather, record, report, and interpret financial information in a way that describes the status and operation of an organization and aids in decision making.

Millions of men and women throughout the world describe their occupation as accountant. In the United States alone, more than 1.2 million people, around half of whom are women, work as accountants. According to the Bureau of Labor Statistics, the number of accounting-related jobs is expected to increase by around 18 percent between now and 2016.[2] The availability of jobs and relatively high starting salaries for talented graduates—starting salaries for accounting graduates average around $50,000 per year—have made accounting one of the most in-demand majors on college campuses. In the last five years, the number of accounting majors has risen by more than 11 percent. Even that increase, however, may not be sufficient to keep up with the rising demand for accountants.[3]

This chapter begins by describing who uses accounting information. It discusses business activities involving accounting statements: financing, investing, and operations. It explains the accounting process, defines double-entry bookkeeping, and presents the accounting equation. We then discuss the development of financial statements from information about financial transactions. The methods of interpreting these statements and the roles of budgeting in planning and controlling a business are described next. The chapter concludes with a discussion of the development and implementation schedule of a uniform set of accounting rules for global business.

Users of Accounting Information

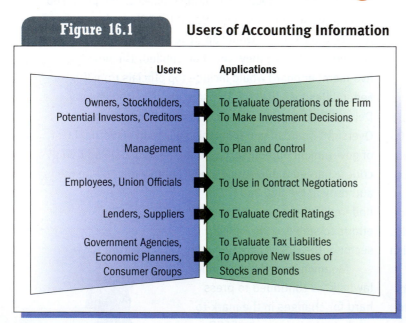

Figure 16.1 **Users of Accounting Information**

Users	Applications
Owners, Stockholders, Potential Investors, Creditors	To Evaluate Operations of the Firm / To Make Investment Decisions
Management	To Plan and Control
Employees, Union Officials	To Use in Contract Negotiations
Lenders, Suppliers	To Evaluate Credit Ratings
Government Agencies, Economic Planners, Consumer Groups	To Evaluate Tax Liabilities / To Approve New Issues of Stocks and Bonds

People both inside and outside an organization rely on accounting information to help them make business decisions. Figure 16.1 lists the users of accounting information and the applications they find for that information.

Managers with a business, government agency, or not-for-profit organization are the major users of accounting information, because it helps them plan and control daily and long-range operations. Business owners and boards of directors of not-for-profit groups also rely on accounting data to determine how well managers are operating the organizations. Union officials use accounting data in contract negotiations, and employees refer to it as they monitor their firms' productivity and profitability performance.

To help employees understand how their work affects the bottom line, many companies share sensitive financial information with their employees and teach them how to understand and use financial statements. Proponents of what is often referred to as **open book management** believe that allowing employees to view financial information helps them better understand how their work contributes to the company's success, which, in turn, benefits them.

Outside a firm, potential investors evaluate accounting information to help them decide whether to buy a firm's stock. As we'll discuss in more detail later in the chapter, any company whose stock is traded publicly is required to report its financial results on a regular basis. So anyone, for example, can find out what Cisco System's sales were last year or how much money Boeing made during the past three months. Bankers and other lenders use accounting information to evaluate a potential borrower's financial soundness. The Internal Revenue Service (IRS) and state tax officials use it to determine a company's tax liability. Citizens' groups and government agencies use such information in assessing the efficiency of operations such as Massachusetts General Hospital; the Salem, Oregon school system; Henry Ford Community College; and the Art Institute of Chicago.

Accountants play fundamental roles not only in business but also in other aspects of society. Their work influences each of the business environments discussed earlier in this book. They clearly contribute important information to help managers deal with the competitive and economic environments.

Less obvious contributions help others understand, predict, and react to the technological, regulatory, and social and cultural environments. For instance, thousands of people volunteer each year to help people with their taxes. One of the largest organized programs is Tax-Aide, sponsored by AARP (formally known as the American Association of Retired Persons). Its program has in excess of 32,000 IRS-trained volunteers helping more than 1.8 million low- and middle-income persons over 60 file their state and federal tax returns. Thousands of clients use the free service each year.[4]

Business Activities Involving Accounting

The natural progression of a business begins with financing. Subsequent steps, including investing, lead to operating the business. All organizations, profit oriented and not-for-profit, perform these three basic activities, and accounting plays a key role in each one:

- Financing activities provide necessary funds to start a business and expand it after it begins operating.

- Investing activities provide valuable assets required to run a business.

- Operating activities focus on selling goods and services, but they also consider expenses as important elements of sound financial management.

Michael and Steven Roberts, of St. Louis–based Roberts Hotel Group, performed all three activities during the start-up and growth of their various business ventures. The Roberts brothers, recently named by accounting firm Ernst & Young as Entrepreneurs of the Year, purchase and totally refurbish historic hotel properties in cities throughout the United States. They finance each purchase using a combination of personal funds, bank loans, and money from outside investors. The Roberts brothers invest these funds in hotel properties and other assets. Operating activities include hiring contractors and professional staff, and finding hotel chains, such as Wyndham Hotels & Resorts, to lease the finished properties.[5]

Accounting Professionals

Accounting professionals work in a variety of areas in and for business firms, government agencies, and not-for-profit organizations. They can be classified as public, management, government, and not-for-profit accountants.

accounting process of measuring, interpreting, and communicating financial information to support internal and external business decision making.

"They Said It"

"You have to know accounting. It's the language of practical business life. It was a very useful thing to deliver to civilization. I've heard it came to civilization through Venice, which of course was once the great commercial power in the Mediterranean."

—Charlie Munger (b. 1924) American businessperson and vice chairman of Berkshire Hathaway (and Warren Buffett's right-hand man)

Assessment Check ✔

1. Define *accounting*.
2. Who uses accounting information?
3. What are the three business activities that involve accounting?

KPMG.
Where the fun factor and the growth factor work side by side.

From global opportunities to career building to cool experiences and community involvement, work at KPMG has a definite fun component built in. Whether as an intern or a new associate, you get to grow as an individual as you team with others who share your enthusiasm and energy. There are networks, clubs and volunteer activities to join as well as the chance to enjoy parks and events. For an inside look at how fun and work exist side by side at KPMG, go to youtube.com/KPMGGo.

kpmgcareers.com

KPMG.
A great place to build your career.

AUDIT • TAX • ADVISORY

KPMG, one of the Big Four accounting firms, recruits on hundreds of college campuses and hires thousands of new accountants every year. This advertisement stresses the career-building opportunities available at KPMG.

Public Accountants

A **public accountant** provides accounting services to individuals or business firms for a fee. Most public accounting firms provide three basic services to clients: (1) auditing, or examining, financial records; (2) tax preparation, planning, and related services; and (3) management consulting. Because public accountants are not employees of a client firm, they can provide unbiased advice about the firm's financial condition.

While there are hundreds of public accounting firms in the United States, a handful of firms dominate the industry. The four largest public accounting firms—Deloitte & Touche, Ernst & Young, KPMG, and PricewaterhouseCoopers (PWC)—collect more than $100 billion annually from global clients.[6] By contrast, Minneapolis-based RSM McGladrey, which ranks as the nation's fifth-largest accounting firm, has annual revenues of approximately $1.3 billion.[7]

Several years ago, public accounting firms came under sharp criticism for providing management consulting services to many of the same firms they audited. Critics argued that when a public accounting firm does both—auditing and management consulting—an inherent conflict of interest is created. In addition, this conflict of interest may undermine confidence in the quality of the financial statements accounting firms audit. The bankruptcies of such high-profile firms as Enron and WorldCom increased pressure on public accounting firms to end the practice. Legislation also established strict limits on the types of consulting services auditors can provide. For example, an accounting firm that audits a company's books cannot provide any other services to that company, including tax services. As a result, three of the four largest public accounting firms either sold large portions of their consulting practices or spun them off into separate companies, and they now concentrate on providing auditing and tax services. PWC, for instance, sold much of its consulting business to IBM.

In spite of tougher rules regarding audits, public accounting firms are still criticized occasionally over the quality of audits and their relationships with clients. For instance, recently one of the so-called big four firms, KPMG, drew sharp fire over its audits of New Century Financial Corporation, once one of the largest subprime mortgage lenders in the country.

As the "Hit & Miss" feature outlines, a growing number of public accountants describe themselves as *forensic accountants,* and several smaller public accounting firms actually specialize in forensic accounting. These professionals, and the firms that employ them, focus on uncovering potential fraud in a variety of organizations.

Certified public accountants (CPAs) demonstrate their accounting knowledge by meeting state requirements for education and experience and successfully completing a number of rigorous tests in accounting theory and practice, auditing, law, and taxes. Other accountants who meet specified educational and experience requirements and pass certification exams carry the title *certified management accountant, certified fraud examiner,* or *certified internal auditor.*

public accountant
accountant who provides accounting services to other organizations.

"They Said It"

"I was never a Certified Public Accountant. I just had a degree in accounting. It would require passing a test, which I would not have been able to do."

—Bob Newhart (b. 1929)
American comedian

Forensic Accountants: Calculating "Who Done It"

Accountants as crime fighters? Until recently, no one would have thought so or considered accounting to be a daring job. But with the rash of white-collar crimes ranging from business fraud to illegal investment schemes, the idea of accountant-as-sleuth has come of age.

Forensic accounting is accounting in preparation for legal review. Forensic accountants may investigate charges of fraud, embezzlement, improper financial reporting, shareholder lawsuits, or insurance claims. A private company or the government may hire a forensic accounting firm to sift through financial information, e-mails, inventories, and other documents to find evidence of trouble. A Forensic Certified Public Accountant uses all the accounting and auditing skills learned as a CPA, along with specialized investigative training to dig out exactly what happened in a company and why.

Take Harry Markopolos, who spent almost a decade gathering information about the fraudulent investment practices of Bernard Madoff, including attempts to notify the authorities. Suspicious that Madoff's claims of steady profits were untrue, Markopolos used computer analyses of Madoff's supposed trading deals to deconstruct his claims and methods and found they could not be duplicated. "You can't dominate all markets," Markopolos says. "You have to have some losses." When the Madoff case broke, Markopolos became an instant celebrity.

Other accountants have worked long hours on less-publicized cases, but they remain optimistic about their investigations. With an increase in bankruptcies, credit crises, and other financial troubles, the need for forensic accounting is on the rise. "Generally, when business is in for a rough ride, that's good for what we do," explains forensic accountant Richard Boulton. "The credit crisis, in broad terms, should create a wave of litigation and disputes where investigative accounting skills come to the fore." Cases involving oil and gas companies also provide a lucrative market. E-discovery—extracting sensitive financial data from computer hard drives—is a new branch of forensic accounting receiving attention. This type of detective work can provide important electronic data to support a legal case.

Crime fighting accountants may not be the stuff of superhero comic books, but they represent a new breed of financial investigator. "There will be plenty of opportunity out there for 'Who killed the company and why did it fail?' types of investigations," predicts another forensic accountant.

Questions for Critical Thinking

1. Describe how a shift in the economy has created a new career path for accounting students.
2. How might forensic accounting change the world of business?

Sources: "What Is Forensic Accounting?" *Journal of Forensic Accounting,* http://www.rtedwards.com, accessed March 6, 2009; "Recession Bolstering Demand for Forensic Accounting Services," *A.E. Feldman,* February 9, 2009, http://blog.aefeldman.com; "Potential for Bailout Money Fraud Prompts Expansion of Forensic Accounting Firm," *PRWeb,* January 15, 2009, http://www.topix.com; Ross Kerber, "Dogged Pursuer of Madoff Wary of Fame," *The Boston Globe,* January 8, 2009, http://www.boston.com; Greg Barr, "Forensic Accountants Arrive in Tough Times," *Houston Business Journal,* August 29, 2008, http://www.bizjournals.com; Jennifer Nycz-Conner, "Forensic Accountant Digs into Suspicious Numbers," *Washington Business Journal,* July 25, 2008, http://washington.bizjournals.com.

Management Accountants

An accountant employed by a business other than a public accounting firm is called a **management accountant.** Such a person collects and records financial transactions and prepares financial statements used by the firm's managers in decision making. Management accountants provide timely, relevant, accurate, and concise information that executives can use to operate their firms more effectively and more profitably than they could without this input. In addition to preparing financial statements, a management accountant plays a major role in interpreting them. A management accountant should provide answers to many important questions:

- Where is the company going?
- What opportunities await it?
- Do certain situations expose the company to excessive risk?
- Does the firm's information system provide detailed and timely information to all levels of management?

Linkin Park members Joe Hahn and Chester Bennington help rebuild New Orleans after Katrina. Not-for-profit institutions are the fastest-growing segment of accounting because these firms are being asked to verify how they spend the money they raise.

Sean Gardner/Getty Images

Management accountants frequently specialize in different aspects of accounting. A cost accountant, for example, determines the cost of goods and services and helps set their prices. An internal auditor examines the firm's financial practices to ensure that its records include accurate data and that its operations comply with federal, state, and local laws and regulations. A tax accountant works to minimize a firm's tax bill and assumes responsibility for its federal, state, county, and city tax returns. Some management accountants achieve a **certified management accountant (CMA)** designation through experience and passing a comprehensive examination.

Management accountants are usually involved in the development and enforcement of organizational policies on such items as employee travel. As part of their job, many employees travel and accumulate airline frequent flyer miles and hotel reward points. While some organizations have strict policies over the personal use of travel perks, many do not.

Changing federal regulations affecting accounting and public reporting have increased the demand for management accountants in recent years. As a result, salaries for these professionals are rising.

Government and Not-for-Profit Accountants

Federal, state, and local governments also require accounting services. Government accountants and those who work for not-for-profit organizations perform professional services similar to those of management accountants. Accountants in these sectors concern themselves primarily with determining how efficiently the organizations accomplish their objectives. Among the many government agencies that employ accountants are the National Aeronautics and Space Administration, the Federal Bureau of Investigation, the Internal Revenue Service, the Commonwealth of Pennsylvania, and the City of Fresno, California. The federal government alone employs thousands of accountants.

Not-for-profit organizations, such as churches, labor unions, charities, schools, hospitals, and universities, also hire accountants. In fact, the not-for-profit sector is one of the fastest growing segments of accounting practice. An increasing number of not-for-profits publish financial information because contributors want more accountability from these organizations and are interested in knowing how the groups spend the money that they raise.

The Foundation of the Accounting System

generally accepted accounting principles (GAAP) principles that encompass the conventions, rules, and procedures for determining acceptable accounting practices at a particular time.

To provide reliable, consistent, and unbiased information to decision makers, accountants follow guidelines, or standards, known as **generally accepted accounting principles (GAAP).** These principles encompass the conventions, rules, and procedures for determining acceptable accounting and financial reporting practices at a particular time.

All GAAP standards are based on four basic principles: consistency, relevance, reliability, and comparability. Consistency means that all data should be collected and presented in the same manner across all periods. Any change in the way in which specific data are collected or presented must be noted and explained. Relevance states that all information being reported should be appropriate and assist users in evaluating that information. Reliability implies that the accounting data presented in financial statements is reliable and can be verified by an independent party such as an outside auditor. Finally, comparability ensures that one firm's financial statements can be compared with those of similar businesses. The "Business Etiquette" feature provides some tips for preparing for an audit.

In the United States, the **Financial Accounting Standards Board (FASB)** is primarily responsible for evaluating, setting, or modifying GAAP. The U.S. Securities and Exchange Commission (SEC), the chief federal regulator of the financial markets and accounting industry, actually has the statutory authority to establish financial accounting and reporting standards for publicly held companies. (A publicly held company is one whose stock is publicly traded in a market such as the New York Stock Exchange.) However, the SEC's policy has been to rely on the accounting industry for this function, as long as the SEC believes the private sector is operating in the public interest. Consequently, the Financial Accounting Foundation—an organization made up of members of many different professional groups—actually appoints the seven members of FASB, although the SEC does have some input. Board members are all experienced accounting professionals and serve five-year terms. They may be reappointed for a second five-year term. Board members must sever all connections with the firms they served prior to joining the board. The board is supported by a professional staff of approximately 70 individuals.[8]

The FASB carefully monitors changing business conditions, enacting new rules and modifying existing rules when necessary. It also considers input and requests from all segments of its diverse constituency, including corporations and the SEC. One major change in accounting rules recently dealt with executive and employee stock options. Stock options give the holder the right to buy stock at a fixed price. The FASB now requires firms that give employees stock options to calculate the cost of the options and treat the cost as an expense, similar to salaries.

In response to well-known cases of accounting fraud, and questions about the independence of auditors, the Sarbanes-Oxley Act—commonly known as SOX—created the Public Accounting Oversight Board. The five-member board has the power to set audit standards and to investigate

AUDITING ETIQUETTE

The words *tax audit* strike fear into many business owners' hearts. But the auditor and the auditee can both ease the pain and inconvenience of the process by preparing for their meeting ahead of time. Remember, not all audits result in the payment of extra taxes.

If you're being audited:

1. Review your return—with your preparer if you have one—beforehand, and be prepared to explain where your figures came from.
2. Find and organize all your records, receipts, sales slips, canceled checks, bank statements, checkbooks, cash register tapes, and other documents, whether paper or electronic. If they're electronic, print them out.
3. Locate automobile records and travel and entertainment receipts if they are relevant to your business or your return.
4. Avoid dragging a messy stack of papers to the audit. Neatness counts, and it may help auditors give you the benefit of the doubt where they can.
5. Don't attempt to cater to the auditor's needs or try to influence him or her in any way. Be professional.
6. Answer all questions but don't volunteer any information. If you use a tax preparer, follow his or her advice to the letter.

If you're performing the audit:

1. Be on time for your meeting. Begin by thanking everyone for attending, and then stay on schedule.
2. Use titles like Mr. and Ms. for the auditees, and make frequent use of courteous words like "please," "thank you," "may I," and "you're welcome."
3. Avoid making special requests such as for food, coffee, or a cigarette break. Bring your own paper, pens, and calculator.
4. Respect the auditee's privacy by asking permission before taking any photographs and by knocking on doors—whether open or closed—before entering.
5. Be tactful and polite. Don't tell the auditee how to do his or her accounting or run the business, and never correct a colleague in front of others. Avoid criticizing your own or other organizations.
6. Don't be boastful if you find an error. Be sensitive to the auditee's situation.

Sources: Russell's Rules of Etiquette for Auditors, J. P. Russell and Associates, http://www.jp-russell.com, accessed March 31, 2009; "Preparing for a Business Audit," Nolo, http://www.nolo.com, accessed March 31, 2009; Rosemary Carolson and Kay Bell, "How to Prepare for an Audit," *Bankrate,* http://www.bankrate.com, accessed October 20, 2008.

Financial Accounting Standards Board (FASB) organization that interprets and modifies GAAP in the United States.

THE BURDEN OF SARBANES-OXLEY ON SMALL BUSINESS

While passage of the Sarbanes-Oxley Act (SOX) has helped improve the quality of financial reporting, the benefit has not been free. Internal costs of compliance have inched down as companies have finished setting up necessary procedures, but external costs for mandated audits, compensation to board members, and legal fees all have risen nearly every year.

External audits, for instance, nearly tripled over five years for companies with less than $1 billion in annual revenue. This rise brought the total cost of compliance to nearly $3 million. SOX's most expensive provision, Section 404, requires companies to assess their own financial reporting controls, then pay a third-party auditor for an independent assessment.

So far, smaller companies have been exempt from Section 404, and the SEC will postpone the external audit requirement until 2009. Firms will have to make their own assessment but not pay for the independent audit. "For a company our size, [the audit savings] is in the $75,000 range," says the CFO for Epic Bancorp of San Rafael. California. That's big. While small firms have complained from the beginning that full compliance will be staggeringly expensive, not everyone agrees that postponing it is a good idea.

Is it fair to expect the same degree of Sarbanes-Oxley compliance from small and large firms?

PRO

1. Section 404 has greatly improved the quality of financial reporting, and investors want to see its full implementation across the board.
2. Small companies are often plagued by weak controls, restatements of financial position, and fraud and therefore are most in need of improvements to internal controls.

CON

1. The cost of external audits has continued to rise rapidly and will impose a severe financial hardship on small firms, which have smaller budgets.
2. Other costs include labor. "The untold man hours are what kills you to try to keep up with this," said the president of Hennessy Advisors, which recently spent more than $500,000 to comply with SOX.

Summary

Some observers believe small companies might eventually be exempted entirely from Section 404, and business lobbyists continue to fight it as invasive and ineffective—as well as costly. But others believe that in the wake of the mortgage crisis, the government may respond with more regulation, not less.

Sources: "Costs: Financial Impact of Sarbanes-Oxley Compliance," http://www.sox-online.com, accessed March 31, 2009; Nikki Swartz, "SOX Costs Sock Small Firms," *Information Management Journal,* March/April 2008, http://www.arma.org; "Lifting the Lid—SarbOx Rules Get Reprieve in Subprime Mess," *Forbes,* March 28, 2008, http://www.forbes.com; William Jason, "Small Public Companies Given Some Sarbanes-Oxley Reprieve," *North Bay Business Journal,* February 11, 2008, http://www.northbaybusinessjournal.com; "Grant Thornton LLP Disagrees with SEC Delays on 404," *Business Wire,* December 14, 2007, http://www.businesswire.com.

Solving an ETHICAL controversy

Assessment Check ✓

1. Define *GAAP*.
2. What are the four basic requirements to which all accounting rules must adhere?
3. What is the role played by the FASB?

and sanction accounting firms that certify the books of publicly traded firms. Members of the Public Accounting Oversight Board are appointed by the SEC. No more than two of the five members of the board can be certified public accountants.

In addition to creating the Public Accounting Oversight Board, SOX also added to the reporting requirements for publicly traded companies. Senior executives including the CEO and chief financial officer (CFO), for example, must personally certify that the financial information reported by the company is correct. As we noted earlier, these requirements have increased the demand for accounting professionals, especially managerial accountants. One result of this increased demand has been higher salaries.

It is expensive for firms to adhere to GAAP standards and SOX requirements. Audits, for instance, can cost millions of dollars each year. These expenses can be especially burdensome for small businesses. Consequently, some have proposed modifications to GAAP and SOX for smaller firms, arguing that some accounting rules were really designed for larger companies. Others disagree. The issue of whether GAAP and SOX requirements should be eased for small businesses is debated in the "Solving an Ethical Controversy" feature.

The Accounting Cycle

Accounting deals with financial transactions between a firm and its employees, customers, suppliers, and owners; bankers; and various government agencies. For example, payroll checks result in a cash outflow to compensate employees. A payment to a vendor results in receipt of needed materials for the production process. Cash, check, and credit purchases by customers generate funds to cover the costs of operations and to earn a profit. Prompt payment of bills preserves the firm's credit rating and its future ability to earn a profit. The procedure by which accountants convert data about individual transactions to financial statements is called the **accounting cycle.**

Figure 16.2 illustrates the activities involved in the accounting cycle: recording, classifying, and summarizing transactions. Initially, any transaction that has a financial impact on the business, such as payments to suppliers or wages, should be documented. All of these transactions are recorded in journals, which list transactions in chronological order. Journal listings are then posted to ledgers. A ledger shows increases or decreases in specific accounts such as cash or wages. Ledgers are used to prepare the financial statements, which summarize financial transactions. Management and other interested parties use the resulting financial statements for a variety of purposes.

The Accounting Equation

Three fundamental terms appear in the accounting equation: assets, liabilities, and owners' equity. An **asset** is anything of value owned or leased by a business. Assets include land, buildings, supplies, cash, accounts receivable (amounts owed to the business as payment for credit sales), and marketable securities.

accounting cycle set of activities involved in converting information and individual transactions into financial statements.

asset anything of value owned by a firm.

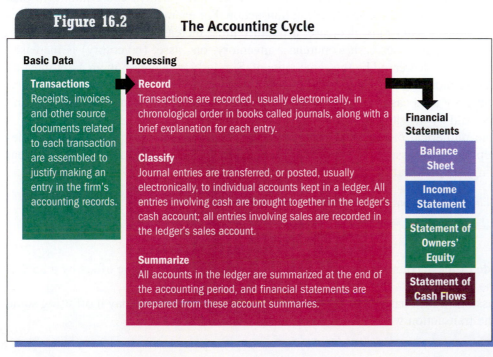

Figure 16.2 The Accounting Cycle

Basic Data

Transactions
Receipts, invoices, and other source documents related to each transaction are assembled to justify making an entry in the firm's accounting records.

Processing

Record
Transactions are recorded, usually electronically, in chronological order in books called journals, along with a brief explanation for each entry.

Classify
Journal entries are transferred, or posted, usually electronically, to individual accounts kept in a ledger. All entries involving cash are brought together in the ledger's cash account; all entries involving sales are recorded in the ledger's sales account.

Summarize
All accounts in the ledger are summarized at the end of the accounting period, and financial statements are prepared from these account summaries.

Financial Statements

Balance Sheet

Income Statement

Statement of Owners' Equity

Statement of Cash Flows

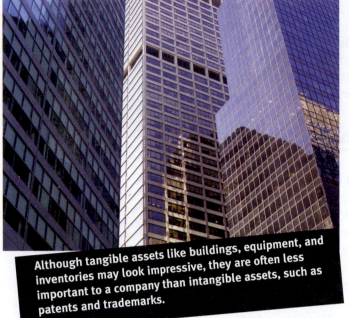

Although tangible assets like buildings, equipment, and inventories may look impressive, they are often less important to a company than intangible assets, such as patents and trademarks.

Frank Schwere/Getty Images

Although most assets are tangible assets, such as equipment, buildings, and inventories, intangible possessions such as patents and trademarks are often some of a firm's most important assets. This kind of asset is especially essential for many companies, including computer software firms, biotechnology companies, and pharmaceutical companies. For instance, Johnson & Johnson—which has both biotechnology and pharmaceutical operations—reported around $28 billion in intangible assets in one recent year, out of a total of almost $81 billion in assets.[9]

Two groups have claims against the assets of a firm: creditors and owners. A **liability** of a business is anything owed to creditors—that is, the claims of a firm's creditors. When a firm borrows money to purchase inventory, land, or machinery, the claims of creditors are shown as accounts payable, notes payable, or long-term debt. Wages and salaries owed to employees also represent liabilities (known as *wages payable* or *accrued wages*).

Owners' equity represents the owner's initial investment in the business plus profits that were not paid out to owners over time in the form of cash dividends. A strong owners' equity position often is used as evidence of a firm's financial strength and stability.

The **accounting equation** (also referred to as the *accounting identity*) states that assets must equal liabilities plus owners' equity. This equation reflects the financial position of a firm at any point in time:

$$\text{Assets} = \text{Liabilities} + \text{Owners' equity}$$

Because financing comes from either creditors or owners, the right side of the accounting equation also represents the business's financial structure.

The accounting equation also illustrates **double-entry bookkeeping**—the process by which accounting transactions are recorded. Because assets must always equal liabilities plus equity, each transaction must have an offsetting transaction. For example, if a company increases an asset, either another asset must decrease, a liability must increase, or owners' equity must increase. So if a company uses cash to purchase inventory, one asset (inventory) is increased while another (cash) is decreased by the same amount. Similarly, a decrease in an asset must be offset by either an increase in another asset, a decrease in a liability, or a decrease in owners' equity. If a company uses cash to repay a bank loan, both an asset (cash) and a liability (bank loans) decrease, and by the same amount.

Two simple numerical examples will help illustrate the accounting equation and double-entry bookkeeping. First, assume the owner of a photo studio purchases a new camera system for $5,000 using her personal funds. The accounting transaction would look as follows:

Increase plant, property, and equipment (an asset) by $5,000

Increase owners' equity by $5,000

So, the left side of the accounting equation would increase by $5,000 and be offset by a $5,000 increase on the right side.

Second, assume a firm has a $100,000 loan from a bank and decides to pay it off using some of its cash. The transaction would be recorded as:

liability claims against assets by creditors.

owners' equity funds contributed by owners plus profits not distributed to owners in the form of cash dividends.

accounting equation relationship that states that assets must always equal the sum of liabilities and owners' equity.

double-entry bookkeeping process by which accounting transactions are entered; each individual transaction always has an offsetting transaction.

Decrease bank loan (liability) by $100,000
Decrease cash (asset) by $100,000

In this second example, the left side and right side of the accounting equation would both decrease by $100,000.

The relationship expressed by the accounting equation underlies development of the firm's financial statements. Three financial statements form the foundation: the balance sheet, the income statement, and the statement of owners' equity. The information found in these statements is calculated using the double-entry bookkeeping system and reflect the basic accounting equation. A fourth statement, the statement of cash flows, is also prepared to focus specifically on the sources and uses of cash for a firm from its operating, investing, and financing activities.

The Impact of Computers and the Internet on the Accounting Process

For hundreds of years, bookkeepers recorded, or posted, accounting transactions as manual entries in journals. They then transferred the information, or posted it, to individual accounts listed in ledgers. Computers have streamlined the process, making it both faster and easier. For instance, point-of-sale terminals in retail stores perform a number of functions each time they record sales. These terminals not only recall prices from computer system memory and maintain constant inventory counts of individual items in stock but also automatically perform accounting data entry functions.

Accounting software programs are used widely in both large and small businesses today. They allow a do-it-once approach, in which a single input leads to automatic conversion of a sale into a journal entry, which then is stored until needed. Decision makers can then request up-to-date financial statements and financial ratios instantly. Improvements in accounting software continue to make the process even faster and easier. The town of Groton, Massachusetts, uses a Sage Software product called MIP Fund Accounting—a product specifically designed to meet the accounting needs of government agencies and not-for-profit organizations. Town accountant Valarie Jenkins immediately saw the advantage of using a computer-based accounting system. "The old books were really beautiful, with manual entries in tidy handwriting," she notes, "but it was almost impossible to generate useful information from them."[10]

Because the accounting needs of entrepreneurs and small businesses differ from those of larger firms, accounting software makers have designed programs that meet specific user needs. Some examples of accounting software programs designed for entrepreneurs and small businesses, and designed to run on personal computers, include QuickBooks, Peachtree, and BusinessWorks. Software programs designed for larger firms, often requiring more sophisticated computer systems, include products from Oracle and SAP.

For firms that conduct business worldwide, software producers have introduced new accounting programs that handle all of a company's accounting information for every country in which it operates. The software handles different languages and currencies, as well as the financial, legal, and tax requirements of each nation in which the firm conducts business.

The Internet also influences the accounting process. Several software producers offer Web-based accounting products designed for small and medium-sized businesses. Among other benefits, these products allow users to access their complete accounting systems from anywhere using a standard Web browser.

Assessment Check

1. List the steps in the accounting cycle.
2. What is the accounting equation?
3. Briefly explain double-entry bookkeeping.

Financial Statements

Financial statements provide managers with essential information they need to evaluate the liquidity position of an organization—its ability to meet current obligations and needs by converting assets into cash; the firm's profitability; and its overall financial health. The balance sheet, income statement, statement of owners' equity, and statement of cash flows provide a foundation on which managers can base their decisions. By interpreting the data provided in these statements, the appropriate information can be communicated to internal decision makers and to interested parties outside the organization.

Of the four financial statements, only the balance sheet is considered to be a permanent statement; its amounts are carried over from year to year. The income statement, statement of owners' equity, and statement of cash flows are considered temporary because they are closed out at the end of each year.

Public companies are required to report their financial statements at the end of each three-month period, as well as at the end of each fiscal year. Annual statements must be examined and verified by the firm's outside auditors. These financial statements are public information available to anyone. A fiscal year does not have to coincide with the calendar year, and companies set different fiscal years. For instance, Starbucks's fiscal year runs from October 1 to September 30 of the following year. Nike's fiscal year consists of the twelve months between June 1 and May 31. By contrast, GE's fiscal year is the same as the calendar year, running from January 1 to December 31.

The Balance Sheet

balance sheet statement of a firm's financial position—what it owns and claims against its assets—at a particular point in time.

A firm's **balance sheet** shows its financial position on a particular date. It is similar to a photograph of the firm's assets together with its liabilities and owners' equity at a specific moment in time. Balance sheets must be prepared at regular intervals, because a firm's managers and other internal parties often request this information every day, every week, or at least every month. On the other hand, external users, such as stockholders or industry analysts, may use this information less frequently, perhaps every quarter or once a year.

The balance sheet follows the accounting equation. On the left side of the balance sheet are the firm's assets—what it owns. These assets, shown in descending order of liquidity (in other words, convertibility to cash), represent the uses that management has made of available funds. Cash is always listed first on the asset side of the balance sheet.

On the right side of the equation are the claims against the firm's assets. Liabilities and owners' equity indicate the sources of the firm's assets and are listed in the order in which they are due. Liabilities reflect the claims of creditors—financial institutions or bondholders that have loaned the firm money, suppliers that have provided goods and services on credit, and others to be paid, such as federal, state, and local tax authorities. Owners' equity represents the owners' claims (those of stockholders, in the case of a corporation) against the firm's assets. It also amounts to the excess of all assets over liabilities.

Figure 16.3 shows the balance sheet for Diane's Java, a small California-based coffee wholesaler. The accounting equation is illustrated by the three classifications of assets, liabilities, and owners' equity on the company's balance sheet. Remember, total assets must always equal the sum of liabilities and owners' equity. In other words, the balance sheet must always balance.

The Income Statement

income statement financial record of a company's revenues and expenses, and profits over a period of time.

Whereas the balance sheet reflects a firm's financial situation at a specific point in time, the **income statement** represents the flow of resources that reveals the performance of the organization over a specific time period. Resembling a video rather than a photograph, the income

Figure 16.3

Diane's Java Balance Sheet (Fiscal Year, Ending December 31)

① Current Assets:
Cash and other liquid assets that can or will be converted to cash within one year.

② Plant, Property, and Equipment (net):
Physical assets expected to last for more than one year; shown net of accumulated depreciation —the cumulative value that plant, property, and equipment have been expensed (depreciated).

③ Value of assets such as patents and trademarks.

④ Current Liabilities:
Claims of creditors that are to be repaid within one year; accruals are expenses, such as wages, that have been incurred but not yet paid.

⑤ Long-Term Debt:
Debts that come due one year or longer after the date on the balance sheet.

⑥ Owners' (or shareholders') Equity: Claims of the owners against the assets of the firm; the difference between total assets and total liabilities.

Diane's Java

Balance Sheet

($ thousands)	2011	2010
Assets		
① Current Assets		
Cash	$ 800	$ 600
Short-term investments	1,250	940
Accounts receivable	990	775
Inventory	2,200	1,850
Total current assets	5,240	4,165
② Plant, property, and equipment (net)	3,300	2,890
③ Goodwill and other intangible assets	250	250
Total Assets	8,790	7,305
Liabilities and Shareholders' Equity		
④ Current Liabilities		
Accruals	$ 350	$ 450
Accounts payable	980	900
Notes payable	700	500
Total current liabilities	2,030	1,850
⑤ Long-term debt	1,100	1,000
Total liabilities	3,130	2,850
⑥ Shareholders' equity	5,660	4,455
Total Liabilities and Equity	8,790	7,305

Figure 16.4

Diane's Java Income Statement (Fiscal Year Ending December 31)

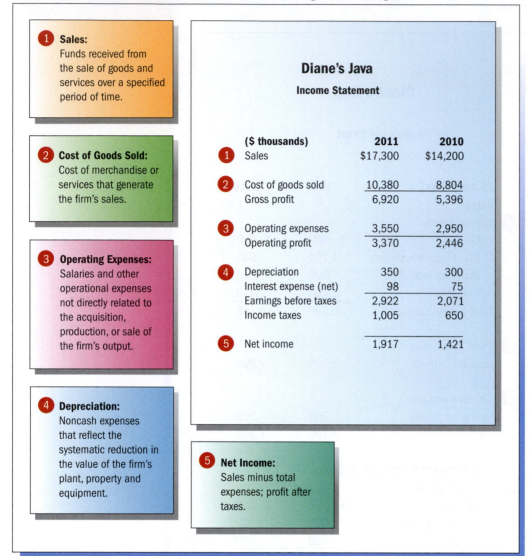

1 Sales:
Funds received from the sale of goods and services over a specified period of time.

2 Cost of Goods Sold:
Cost of merchandise or services that generate the firm's sales.

3 Operating Expenses:
Salaries and other operational expenses not directly related to the acquisition, production, or sale of the firm's output.

4 Depreciation:
Noncash expenses that reflect the systematic reduction in the value of the firm's plant, property and equipment.

5 Net Income:
Sales minus total expenses; profit after taxes.

Diane's Java
Income Statement

($ thousands)	2011	2010
1 Sales	$17,300	$14,200
2 Cost of goods sold	10,380	8,804
Gross profit	6,920	5,396
3 Operating expenses	3,550	2,950
Operating profit	3,370	2,446
4 Depreciation	350	300
Interest expense (net)	98	75
Earnings before taxes	2,922	2,071
Income taxes	1,005	650
5 Net income	1,917	1,421

statement is a financial record summarizing a firm's financial performance in terms of revenues, expenses, and profits over a given time period, say, a quarter or a year.

In addition to reporting the firm's profit or loss results, the income statement helps decision makers focus on overall revenues and the costs involved in generating these revenues. Managers of a not-for-profit organization use this statement to determine whether its revenues from contributions and other sources will cover its operating costs. Finally, the income statement provides much of the basic data needed to calculate the financial ratios managers use in planning and controlling activities. Figure 16.4 shows the income statement for Diane's Java.

An income statement (sometimes called *a profit-and-loss, or P&L, statement*) begins with total sales or revenues generated during a year, quarter, or month. Subsequent lines then deduct all of the costs related to producing the revenues. Typical categories of costs include those involved in producing the firm's goods or services, operating expenses, interest, and taxes. After all of them have been subtracted, the remaining net income may be distributed to the firm's owners (stockholders, proprietors, or partners) or reinvested in the company as retained earnings. The final figure on the income statement—net income after taxes—is the so-called *bottom line*.

Keeping costs under control is an important part of running a business. Too often, however, companies concentrate more on increasing revenue than on controlling costs. Regardless of how much money a company collects in revenues, it wouldn't stay in business for long unless it eventually earns a profit.

statement of owners' equity record of the change in owners' equity from the end of one fiscal period to the end of the next.

Statement of Owners' Equity

The **statement of owners',** or shareholders', **equity** is designed to show the components of the change in equity from the end of one fiscal year to the end of the next. It uses information from both the balance sheet and income statement. A somewhat simplified example is shown in Figure 16.5 for Diane's Java.

Note that the statement begins with the amount of equity shown on the balance sheet at the end of the prior year. Net income is added, and cash dividends paid to owners are subtracted (both are found on the income statement for the current year). If owners contributed any additional capital, say, through the sale of new shares, this amount is added to equity. On the other hand, if owners withdrew capital, for example, through the repurchase of existing shares, equity declines. All of the additions and subtractions, taken together, equal the change in owners' equity from the end of last fiscal year to the end of the current one. The new amount of owners' equity is then reported on the balance sheet for the current year.

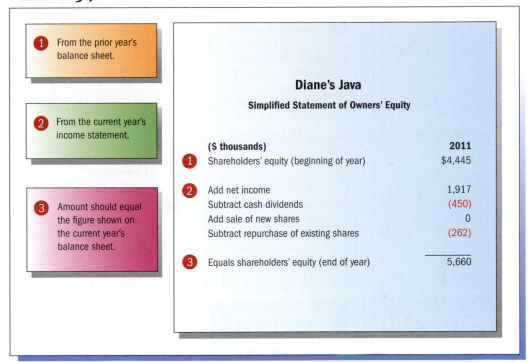

Figure 16.5

Diane's Java Simplified Statement of Owners' Equity (Fiscal Year Ending December 31)

1. From the prior year's balance sheet.

2. From the current year's income statement.

3. Amount should equal the figure shown on the current year's balance sheet.

Diane's Java

Simplified Statement of Owners' Equity

($ thousands)	2011
1 Shareholders' equity (beginning of year)	$4,445
2 Add net income	1,917
Subtract cash dividends	(450)
Add sale of new shares	0
Subtract repurchase of existing shares	(262)
3 Equals shareholders' equity (end of year)	5,660

The Statement of Cash Flows

In addition to the statement of owners' equity, the income statement, and the balance sheet, most firms prepare a fourth accounting statement—the **statement of cash flows.** Public companies are required to prepare and publish a statement of cash flows. In addition, commercial lenders often require a borrower to submit a statement of cash flows. The statement of cash flows provides investors and creditors with relevant information about a firm's cash receipts and cash payments for its operations, investments, and financing during an accounting period. Figure 16.6 shows the statement of cash flows for Diane's Java.

Companies prepare a statement of cash flows due to the widespread use of accrual accounting. **Accrual accounting** recognizes revenues and costs when they occur, not when actual cash changes hands. As a result, there can be differences between what is reported as sales, expenses, and profits, and the amount of cash that actually flows into and out of the business during a period of time. An example is depreciation. Companies depreciate fixed assets—such as machinery and buildings—over a specified period of time, meaning that they systematically reduce the value of the asset. Depreciation is reported as an expense on the firm's income statement—see Figure 16.4—but does not involve any actual cash. The fact that depreciation is a noncash expense means that what a firm reports as net income (profits after tax) for a particular period actually understates the amount of cash the firm took in, less expenses, during that period of time. Consequently, depreciation is added back to net income when calculating cash flow.

The fact that **cash flow** is the lifeblood of every organization is evidenced by the business failure rate. Many former owners of failed firms blame inadequate cash flow for their company's demise. Those who value the statement of cash flows maintain that its preparation and scrutiny by various parties can prevent financial distress for otherwise profitable firms, too many of which are forced into bankruptcy due to a lack of cash needed to continue day-to-day operations.

statement of cash flows statement showing the sources and uses of cash during a period of time.

accrual accounting accounting method that records revenues and expenses when they occur, not necessarily when cash actually changes hands.

Figure 16.6

Diane's Java Statement of Cash Flows (Fiscal Year Ending December 31)

1 Operating Activities:
The nuts and bolts of day-to-day activities of a company carrying out its regular business; Increases in accounts receivable and inventory are uses of cash, while increases in accruals and accounts payables are sources of cash; in financially healthy firms, net cash flow from operating activities should be positive.

2 Investing Activities:
Transactions to accumulate or use cash in ways that affect operating activities in the future; often a use of cash.

3 Financing Activities:
Ways to transfer cash to or from creditors and to or from owners; can be either positive or negative.

4 Net Cash Flow:
The sum of cash flow from operating, investing, and financing activities, a reconcilement of cash from the beginning to the end of the accounting period (one year in this example).

Diane's Java
Statement of Cash Flows

($ thousands)	2011
Cash Flow from Operating Activities	
1 Net income	$1,917
Depreciation	350
Change in accounts receivable	(215)
Change in inventory	(350)
Change in accruals	(100)
Change in accounts payable	80
Total cash flow from operating activities	1,682
2 Cash Flow from Investing Activities	
Capital expenditures	(760)
Change in short-term investments	(310)
Total cash flow from investing activities	(1,070)
3 Cash Flow from Financing Activities	
Cash dividends	(450)
Sale/repurchase of shares	(262)
Change in notes payable	200
Change in long-term debt	100
Total cash flow from financing activities	(412)
4 Net Cash Flow	200
Cash (beginning of year)	600
Cash (end of year)	800

Even for firms for which bankruptcy is not an issue, the statement of cash flows can provide investors and other interested parties with vital information. For instance, assume that a firm's income statement reports rising earnings. At the same time, however, the statement of cash flows shows that the firm's inventory is rising faster than sales—often a signal that demand for the firm's products is softening, which may in turn be a sign of impending financial trouble.

Financial Ratio Analysis

Accounting professionals fulfill important responsibilities beyond preparing financial statements. In a more critical role, they help managers interpret the statements by comparing data about the firm's current activities to that for previous periods and to results posted by other companies in the industry. **Ratio analysis** is one of the most commonly used tools for measuring the firm's liquidity, profitability, and reliance on debt financing, as well as the effectiveness of management's resource utilization. This analysis also allows comparisons with other firms and with the firm's own past performance.

Ratios assist managers by interpreting actual performance and making comparisons to what should have happened. Comparisons with ratios of similar companies help managers understand their firm's performance relative to competitors' results. These industry standards serve as important yardsticks and help pinpoint problem areas, as well as areas of excellence. Ratios for the current accounting period also may be compared with similar calculations for previous periods to spot developing trends. Ratios can be classified according to their specific purposes. The four major categories of financial ratios are summarized in Table 16.1. The ratios for Diane's Java for the 2010 and 2011 fiscal years are shown in Table 16.2.

Liquidity Ratios

A firm's ability to meet its short-term obligations when they must be paid is measured by **liquidity ratios.** Increasing liquidity reduces the likelihood that a firm will face emergencies caused by the need to raise funds to repay loans. On the other hand, firms with low liquidity may be

Table 16.1	Major Categories of Financial Ratios	
Category	**Ratio**	**Description**
Liquidity ratios	Current ratio	Current assets divided by current liabilities
	Quick (acid-test) ratio	Current assets (minus inventory) divided by current liabilities
Efficiency ratios	Inventory turnover	Cost of goods sold divided by average inventory
	Receivables turnover	Credit sales divided by average accounts receivable
	Total asset turnover	Revenue or sales divided by average total assets
Leverage ratios	Debt ratio	Total liabilities divided by total assets
	Long term debt to equity	Long-term debt divided by owners' equity
Profitability ratios	Gross profit margin	Gross profit divided by revenue or sales
	Net profit margin	Net profit divided by revenue or sales
	Return on equity	Net profit divided by average owners' equity

Table 16.2	Financial Ratios for Diane's Java	
Financial Ratio	**2011 Fiscal Year**	**2010 Fiscal Year**
Current ratio	2.58	2.25
Quick ratio	1.50	1.25
Inventory turnover	5.13	5.03
Receivables turnover	19.60	19.32
Total asset turnover	2.15	2.15
Debt ratio	35.6%	39.0%
Long-term debt to equity	19.4%	22.4%
Gross profit margin	40.0%	38.0%
Net profit margin	11.1%	10.0%
Return on equity	37.9%	36.6%

forced to choose between default or borrowing from high-cost lending sources to meet their maturing obligations.

Two commonly used liquidity ratios are the current ratio and the acid-test, or quick, ratio. The current ratio compares current assets to current liabilities, giving executives information about the firm's ability to pay its current debts as they mature. The current ratio of Diane's Java can be computed as follows (unless indicated, all amounts from the balance sheet or income statement are in thousands of dollars):

$$\text{Liquidity ratio} = \frac{\text{Current assets}}{\text{Current liabilities}} = \frac{5,240}{2,030} = 2.58$$

In other words, Diane's Java has $2.58 of current assets for every $1.00 of current liabilities. In general, a current ratio of 2 to 1 is considered satisfactory liquidity. This rule of thumb must be considered along with other factors, such as the nature of the business, the season, and the quality of the company's management team. Diane's Java's management and other interested parties are likely to evaluate this ratio of 2.58 to 1 by comparing it with ratios for previous operating periods and with industry averages.

The acid-test (or quick) ratio measures the ability of a firm to meet its debt payments on short notice. This ratio compares quick assets—the most liquid current assets—against current liabilities. Quick assets generally consist of cash and equivalents, short-term investments, and accounts receivable. So, generally quick assets equal total current assets minus inventory.

Diane's Java's current balance sheet lists total current assets of $5.24 million and inventory of $2.2 million. Therefore, its quick ratio is as follows:

$$\text{Acid-test ratio} = \frac{\text{Current assets} - \text{Inventory}}{\text{Current liabilities}} = \frac{(5,240 - 2,200)}{2,030} = 1.50$$

Because the traditional rule of thumb for an adequate acid-test ratio is around 1 to 1, Diane's Java appears to have a strong level of liquidity. However, the same cautions apply here as for the current ratio. The ratio should be compared with industry averages and data from previous operating periods to determine whether it is adequate for the firm.

Activity Ratios

Activity ratios measure the effectiveness of management's use of the firm's resources. One of the most frequently used activity ratios, the inventory turnover ratio, indicates the number of times merchandise moves through a business:

$$\text{Inventory turnover} = \frac{\text{Cost of goods sold}}{\text{Average inventory}} = \frac{10,380}{[(2,200 + 1,850)/2]} = 5.13$$

Average inventory for Diane's Java is determined by adding the inventory as of December 31, 2011 ($2.2 million) with the inventory as of December 31, 2010 ($1.85 million) and dividing it by 2. Comparing the 5.13 inventory turnover ratio with industry standards gives a measure of efficiency. It is important to note, however, that inventory turnover can vary substantially depending on the products a company sells and the industry in which it operates. For example,

Kroger, primarily a grocery retailer, has an inventory turnover ratio of about 11.4, while Nike's turns its inventory slightly less than 4.5 times per year.

If a company makes a substantial portion of its sales on credit, measuring receivables turnover can provide useful information. Receivables turnover can be calculated as follows:

$$\text{Receivables turnover} = \frac{\text{Credit sales}}{\text{Average accounts receivable}}$$

Because Diane's Java is a wholesaler, let's assume that all of its sales are credit sales. Average receivables equals the simple average of 2011's receivables and 2010's receivables. The ratio for the company is:

$$\text{Receivables turnover} = \frac{17,300}{[(990 + 775)/2]} = 19.60$$

Taking the figure for receivables turnover, 19.6, and dividing it into 365 equals the average age of receivables, 18.62 days. Assume Diane's Java expects its retail customers to pay outstanding bills within 30 days of the date of purchase. Given that the average age of its receivables are less than 30 days, Diane's Java appears to be doing a good job collecting its credit sales.

Another measure of efficiency is total asset turnover. It measures how much in sales each dollar invested in assets generates:

$$\text{Total asset turnover} = \frac{\text{Sales}}{\text{Average total assets}}$$

$$= \frac{17,300}{[(8,790 + 7,305)/2]} = 2.15$$

Average total assets for Diane's Java equals total assets as of December 31, 2011 ($8.79 million) plus total assets as of December 31, 2010 ($7.305 million) divided by 2.

Diane's Java generates about $2.15 in sales for each dollar invested in assets. Although a higher ratio generally indicates that a firm is operating more efficiently, care must be taken when comparing firms that operate in different industries.

Some industries simply require higher investment in assets than do other industries. For example, retailer Costco has an asset turnover ratio of 3.5, while electric and gas utility Southern Companies has an asset turnover of only 0.3. Although the utility's ratio appears quite small, it is actually only slightly lower than the average for all electric and gas utility companies.

Profitability Ratios

Some ratios measure the organization's overall financial performance by evaluating its ability to generate revenues in excess of operating costs and other expenses. These measures are called **profitability ratios.** To compute these ratios, accountants compare the firm's earnings with total sales or investments.

This AFLAC advertisement, aimed at investors rather than insurance buyers, boasts a ten-year total return to shareholders of 18.3 percent. *Return on equity* is one measure of a company's profitability.

© Aflac

Over a period of time, profitability ratios may reveal the effectiveness of management in operating the business. Three important profitability ratios are gross profit margin, net profit margin, and return on equity:

$$\text{Gross profit margin} = \frac{\text{Gross profit}}{\text{Sales}} = \frac{6{,}920}{17{,}300} = 40.0\%$$

$$\text{Net profit margin} = \frac{\text{Net income}}{\text{Sales}} = \frac{1{,}917}{17{,}300} = 11.1\%$$

$$\text{Return on equity} = \frac{\text{Net income}}{\text{Average equity}} = \frac{1{,}917}{[(5{,}660 + 4{,}455)/2]} = 37.9\%$$

All of these ratios indicate positive evaluations of the current operations of Diane's Java. For example, the net profit margin indicates that the firm realizes a profit of slightly more than 11 cents on each dollar of merchandise it sells. Although this ratio varies widely among business firms, Diane's Java compares favorably with wholesalers in general, which have an average net profit margin of around 5 percent. However, this ratio, like the other profitability ratios, should be evaluated in relation to profit forecasts, past performance, or more specific industry averages to enhance the interpretation of results. Similarly, while the firm's return on equity of almost 38 percent appears outstanding, the degree of risk in the industry also must be considered.

Leverage Ratios

Leverage ratios measure the extent to which a firm relies on debt financing. They provide particularly interesting information to potential investors and lenders. If management has assumed too much debt in financing the firm's operations, problems may arise in meeting future interest payments and repaying outstanding loans. As we discuss in Chapter 18, borrowing money does have advantages. However, relying too heavily on debt financing may lead to bankruptcy. More generally, both investors and lenders may prefer to deal with firms whose owners have invested enough of their own money to avoid overreliance on borrowing. The debt ratio and long-term debt to equity ratio help analysts evaluate a firm's leverage:

$$\text{Debt ratio} = \frac{\text{Total liabilities}}{\text{Total assets}} = \frac{3{,}130}{8{,}790} = 35.6\%$$

$$\text{Long-term debt to equity} = \frac{\text{Long-term debt}}{\text{Owners' equity}} = \frac{1{,}100}{5{,}660} = 19.64\%$$

A total liabilities to total assets ratio greater than 50 percent indicates that a firm is relying more on borrowed money than owners' equity. Because Diane's Java's total liabilities to total assets ratio is 35.6 percent, the firm's owners have invested considerably more than the total amount of liabilities shown on the firm's balance sheet. Moreover, the firm's long-term debt to equity ratio is only 19.64 percent, indicating that Diane's Java has only about 19.6 cents in long-term debt to every dollar in equity. The long-term debt to equity ratio also indicates that Diane's Java hasn't relied very heavily on borrowed money.

The four categories of financial ratios relate balance sheet and income statement data to one another, help management pinpoint a firm's strengths and weaknesses, and indicate areas in need of further investigation. Large, multiproduct firms that operate in diverse markets use their information systems to update their financial ratios every day or even every hour. Each company's management must decide on an appropriate review schedule to avoid the costly and time-consuming mistake of overmonitoring.

In addition to calculating financial ratios, managers, investors, and lenders should pay close attention to how accountants applied a number of accounting rules when preparing financial statements. GAAP gives accountants leeway in reporting certain revenues and expenses. Public companies are required to disclose, in footnotes to the financial statements, how the various accounting rules were applied.

Budgeting

Although the financial statements discussed in this chapter focus on past business activities, they also provide the basis for planning in the future. A **budget** is a planning and controlling tool that reflects the firm's expected sales revenues, operating expenses, and cash receipts and outlays. It quantifies the firm's plans for a specified future period. Because it reflects management estimates of expected sales, cash inflows and outflows, and costs, the budget serves as a financial blueprint and can be thought of as a short-term financial plan. It becomes the standard for comparison against actual performance.

budget organization's plans for how it will raise and spend money during a given period.

Budget preparation is frequently a time-consuming task that involves many people from various departments within the organization. The complexity of the budgeting process varies with the size and complexity of the organization. Large corporations such as United Technologies, Clorox, and Motorola maintain complex and sophisticated budgeting systems. Their budgets help managers integrate their numerous divisions in addition to serving as planning and controlling tools. But budgeting in both large and small firms is similar to household budgeting in its purpose: to match income and expenses in a way that accomplishes objectives and correctly times cash inflows and outflows.

Because the accounting department is an organization's financial nerve center, it provides much of the data for budget development. The overall master, or operating, budget is actually a composite of many individual budgets for separate units of the firm. These individual budgets typically include the production budget, cash budget, capital expenditures budget, advertising budget, and sales budget.

Technology has improved the efficiency of the budgeting process. The accounting software products discussed earlier—such

Figure 16.7

Four-Month Cash Budget for Birchwood Paper Company

Birchwood Paper Company
Four-Month Cash Budget

($ thousands)	May	June	July	August
Gross sales	$1,200.0	$3,200.0	$5,500.0	$4,500.0
Cash sales	300.0	800.0	1,375.0	1,125.0
One month prior	600.0	600.0	1,600.0	2,750.0
Two months prior	300.0	300.0	300.0	800.0
Total cash inflows	1,200.0	1,700.0	3,275.0	4,675.0
Purchases				
Cash purchases	1,040.0	1,787.5	1,462.5	390.0
One month prior	390.0	1,040.0	1,787.5	1,462.5
Wages and salaries	250.0	250.0	250.0	250.0
Office rent	75.0	75.0	75.0	75.0
Marketing and other expenses	150.0	150.0	150.0	150.0
Taxes		300.0		
Total cash outflows	1,905.0	3,602.5	3,725.0	2,327.5
Net cash flow				
(Inflows − Outflows)	(705.0)	(1,902.5)	(450.0)	2,347.5
Beginnning cash balance	250.0	150.0	150.0	150.0
Net cash flow	(705.0)	(1,902.5)	(450.0)	2,347.5
Ending cash balance	(455.0)	(1,752.5)	(300.0)	2,497.5
Target cash balance	150.0	150.0	150.0	150.0
Surplus (deficit)	(605.0)	(1,902.5)	(450.0)	2,347.5
Cumulative surplus (deficit)	(605.0)	(2,507.5)	(2,957.5)	610.0

as QuickBooks—all include budgeting features. Moreover, modules designed for specific businesses are often available from third parties. The University of Missouri, for example, has developed a series of QuickBooks modules designed to meet the budgeting needs of the state's dairy farmers.[11]

One of the most important budgets prepared by firms is the **cash budget.** The cash budget, usually prepared monthly, tracks the firm's cash inflows and outflows. Figure 16.7 illustrates a sample cash budget for Birchwood Paper—a small Maine-based paper products company. The company has set a $150,000 target cash balance. The cash budget indicates months in which the firm will need temporary loans—May, June, and July—and how much it will need (close to $3 million). The document also indicates that Birchwood will generate a cash surplus in August and can begin repaying the short-term loan. Finally, the cash budget produces a tangible standard against which to compare actual cash inflows and outflows.

International Accounting

Today, accounting procedures and practices must be adapted to accommodate an international business environment. The Coca-Cola Company and McDonald's both generate more than half their annual revenues from sales outside the United States. Nestlé, the giant chocolate and food products firm, operates throughout the world. It derives 98 percent of its revenues from outside Switzerland, its home country. International accounting practices for global firms must reliably translate the financial statements of the firm's international affiliates, branches, and subsidiaries and convert data about foreign currency transactions to dollars. Also, foreign currencies and exchange rates influence the accounting and financial reporting processes of firms operating internationally.

As market economies in countries such as Poland and China have developed, the demand for accountants has increased. The "Hit & Miss" feature describes the recent development of the accounting profession in Vietnam.

In Pakistan, a truck driver delivers Nestlé food products. Because the Swiss corporation operates around the world, its profits and its financial statements are affected by foreign exchange rates.

Ilyas Dean/NewsCom

Exchange Rates

As defined in Chapter 4, an exchange rate is the ratio at which a country's currency can be exchanged for other currencies. Currencies can be treated as goods to be bought and sold. Like the price of any product, currency prices change daily according to supply and demand. So exchange rate fluctuations complicate accounting entries and accounting practices.

Accountants who deal with international transactions must appropriately record their firms' foreign sales and purchases. Today's sophisticated accounting software helps firms handle all of their international transactions within a single program. An international firm's consolidated financial statements must reflect any gains or losses due to changes in exchange rates during specific periods of time. Financial statements that cover operations in two or more countries also need to treat fluctuations consistently to allow for comparison.

In the United States, GAAP requires firms to make adjustments to their earnings that reflect changes in exchange rates. In general, a weakening dollar increases the earnings of a U.S. firm that has international operations because the same units of a foreign currency will translate into more U.S. dollars. By the same token, a strengthening dollar will have the opposite effect on earnings—the same number of units of a foreign currency will translate into fewer dollars. In one recent year, for instance, the declining value of the U.S. dollar added more than $514 million to McDonald's earnings.[12]

Accounting Is Booming in Vietnam

Vietnam's economy is booming, thanks to the government's encouragement of connections with the global economy, and to foreign direct investment by overseas companies attracted by low labor costs and low overhead. Vietnam's state-of-the-art facilities include E-Town, a high-rise building reserved for high-tech firms and located a mile from the international airport in Ho Chi Minh City, the capital. Local entrepreneurs are thriving too, adding to the growing number of wealthy business owners.

What does all this activity and revenue add up to? Taxes. And that means Vietnam's fledging accounting industry is coming into its own. Begun in the 1990s, accounting in Vietnam has grown as rapidly as the manufacturing sector. The Big Four firms already book about $15 to $20 million worth of tax consulting business, a figure expected to grow as the government encourages increasing prosperity to widen the country's tax base among its 85 million citizens.

The industry is divided in several ways. At the top are PricewaterhouseCoopers, Ernst & Young, KPMG, and Deloitte & Touche, offering accounting, taxation, and corporate financial services, along with consulting, project management, and software engineering. Next are a handful of state-owned auditing firms that serve the country's remaining government-run businesses. One of these, Vietnam Auditing Company (VACO), was among the first to comply with new regulations that require accounting firms to be independent of the state, by becoming a full member of the Deloitte Global network. Midsize firms are next—some local and at least one foreign owned, Grant Thornton.

Another division is between north and south. The southern region, where the capital is located, is growing faster and will probably require more accounting services, at least in the near future.

Growth may create staffing and retention problems for Vietnamese accounting firms. At Grant Thornton, for instance, although salaries are rising, the biggest problem is how to motivate staff to stay. With the high demand for qualified auditors, the company pays its staff on par with international firms. But the firm is also looking at other factors that employees may value, such as "a sense of belonging, training, and salary, also the ability to balance home and work life. Several of our audit staff resigned in the past because of the hours," says the company's managing partner. "Managers are the key. . . . If you lose one [employee], a whole lot can go."

International accounting requires specialized knowledge of foreign accounting regulations and tax codes. This advertisement reminds customers that Grant Thornton International has offices in 112 countries, including Vietnam.

Questions for Critical Thinking

1. How might the mandate to privatize accounting firms in Vietnam affect those firms' operations and ethical standards?
2. What can Vietnamese accounting firms do to improve staffing and retention?

Sources: Company Web site, Grant Thornton Vietnam, http://www.gt.com.vn, accessed March 31, 2009; "Interview: Grant Thornton Vietnam: Opening the Doors," *International Accounting Bulletin,* June 22, 2007, http://o-www.lexisnexis.com; "Deloitte Global Admits Full Member Firm in Vietnam," *International Accounting Bulletin,* May 12, 2007, http://o-www.lexisnexis.com; David Hannon, "Business in Vietnam Defies Misconceptions," *Purchasing,* February 15, 2007, http://www.purchasing.com, accessed October 20, 2008.

International Accounting Standards

The International Accounting Standards Committee (IASC) was established in 1973 to promote worldwide consistency in financial reporting practices. The IASC soon developed its first set of accounting standards and interpretations and, in 2001, became the **International Accounting Standards Board (IASB). International Financial Reporting Standards (IFRS)** are the standards and interpretations adopted by the IASB. The IASB operates in much the same manner as the FASB does in the United States, interpreting and modifying IFRS.

Because of the boom in worldwide trade, there is a real need for comparability of and uniformity in international accounting rules. Trade agreements such as NAFTA and the expansion of the European Union have only heightened interest in creating a uniform set of global accounting rules. In addition, an increasing number of investors are buying shares in foreign multinational corporations, and they need a practical way to evaluate firms in other countries. To assist global investors, more and more firms are beginning to report their financial information according to international accounting standards. This practice helps investors make informed decisions.

Nearly 100 other countries currently require, permit the use of, or have a policy of convergence with IFRS. These nations include members of the European Union, India, Australia, Canada, and Hong Kong. At first, the United States was skeptical of IFRS, even though major American accounting organizations have been involved with the IASB since its inception. In fact, the SEC used to require all firms whose shares were publicly traded in the United States to report financial results using GAAP. This rule applied regardless of where firms were located.

This requirement started to change a few years ago, when the FASB and the IASB met and committed to the eventual convergence of IFRS with GAAP. This agreement was further clarified in 2005. Around the same time, the SEC began to loosen its rules on the use of IFRS by foreign firms whose shares trade in the United States. Today, many foreign companies can report results using IFRS as long as they reconcile these results to GAAP in a footnote. Recently, the SEC went further. Some large U.S. companies were allowed to use international accounting standards beginning in 2009. By 2016, all U.S. firms will be required to do so.[13]

Assessment Check

1. How are financial statements adjusted for exchange rates?
2. What is the purpose of the IASB?

How does IFRS differ from GAAP? Although many similarities between IFRS and GAAP exist, there are some important differences. For example, under GAAP, plant, property, and equipment is reported on the balance sheet at the historical cost minus depreciation. Under IFRS, on the other hand, plant, property, and equipment is shown on the balance sheet at current market value. This gives a better picture of the real value of a firm's assets. Many accounting experts believe that IFRS is overall less complicated than GAAP and more transparent.[14]

What's Ahead

This chapter describes the role of accounting in an organization. Accounting is the process of measuring, interpreting, and communicating financial information to interested parties both inside and outside the firm. The next two chapters discuss the finance function of an organization. Finance deals with planning, obtaining, and managing the organization's funds to accomplish its objectives in the most efficient and effective manner possible. Chapter 17 outlines the financial system, the system by which funds are transferred from savers to borrowers. Organizations rely on the financial system to raise funds for expansion or operations. The chapter includes a description of financial institutions, such as banks; financial markets, such as the New York Stock Exchange; financial instruments, like stocks and bonds; and the role of the Federal Reserve System. Chapter 18 discusses the role of finance and the financial manager in an organization.

Summary of Learning Goals

1 Explain the functions of accounting, and identify the three basic activities involving accounting.

Accountants measure, interpret, and communicate financial information to parties inside and outside the firm to support improved decision making. Accountants gather, record, and interpret financial information to management. They also provide financial information on the status and operations of the firm for evaluation by outside parties, such as government agencies, stockholders, potential investors, and lenders. Accounting plays key roles in financing activities, which help start and expand an organization; investing activities, which provide the assets it needs to continue operating; and operating activities, which focus on selling goods and services and paying expenses incurred in regular operations.

Assessment Check Answers

1.1 Define *accounting*. Accounting is the process of measuring, interpreting, and communicating financial information in a way that describes the status and operation of an organization and aids in decision making.

1.2 Who uses accounting information? Managers of all types of organizations use accounting information to help them plan, assess performance, and control daily and long-term operations. Outside users of accounting information include government officials, investors, creditors, and donors.

1.3 What are the three business activities that involve accounting? The three activities involving accounting are financing, investing, and operating activities.

2 Describe the roles played by public, management, government, and not-for-profit accountants.

Public accountants provide accounting services to other firms or individuals for a fee. They are involved in such activities as auditing, tax statement preparation, management consulting, and accounting system design. Management accountants collect and record financial transactions, prepare financial statements, and interpret them for managers in their own firms. Government and not-for-profit accountants perform many of the same functions as management accountants, but they analyze how effectively the organization or agency is operating, rather than its profits and losses.

Assessment Check Answers

2.1 List the three services offered by public accounting firms. The three services offered by public accounting firms are auditing, management consulting, and tax services.

2.2 What tasks do management accountants perform? Management accountants work for the organization and are responsible for collecting and recording financial transactions, and preparing and interpreting financial statements.

3 Identify the foundations of the accounting system, including GAAP and the role of the Financial Accounting Standards Board (FASB).

The foundation of the accounting system in the United States is GAAP (generally accepted accounting principles), a set of guidelines or standards that accountants follow. There are four basic requirements to which all accounting rules should adhere: consistency, relevance, reliability, and comparability. The Financial Accounting Standards Board (FASB), an independent body made up of accounting professionals, is primarily responsible for evaluating, setting, and modifying GAAP. The U.S. Securities and Exchange Commission (SEC) also plays a role in establishing and modifying accounting standards for public companies, firms whose shares are traded in the financial markets.

Assessment Check Answers

3.1 Define *GAAP*. GAAP stands for generally accepted accounting principles and is a set of standards or guidelines that accountants follow in recording and reporting financial transactions.

3.2 What are the four basic requirements to which all accounting rules must adhere? The four basic requirements to which all accounting rules must adhere are consistency, relevance, reliability, and comparability.

3.3 What is the role played by the FASB? The Financial Accounting Standards Board (FASB) is an independent body made up of accounting professionals and is primarily responsible for evaluating, setting, and modifying GAAP.

4 Outline the steps in the accounting cycle, and define *double-entry bookkeeping* and the *accounting equation*.

The accounting process involves recording, classifying, and summarizing data about transactions and then using this information to produce financial statements for the firm's managers and other interested parties. Transactions are recorded chronologically in journals, posted in ledgers, and then summarized in accounting statements. Today, much of this takes place electronically. The basic accounting equation states that assets (what a firm owns) must always equal liabilities (what a firm owes creditors) plus owners' equity. This equation also illustrates double-entry bookkeeping—the process by which accounting transactions are recorded. Under double-entry bookkeeping, each individual transaction must have an offsetting transaction.

Assessment Check Answers

4.1 List the steps in the accounting cycle. The accounting cycle involves the following steps: recording transactions, classifying these transactions, summarizing transactions, and using the summaries to produce financial statements.

4.2 What is the accounting equation? The accounting equation states that assets (what a firm owns) must always equal liabilities (what a firm owes) plus owners' equity. Therefore, if assets increase or decrease, there must be an offsetting increase or decrease in liabilities, owners' equity, or both.

4.3 Briefly explain double-entry bookkeeping. Double-entry bookkeeping means that all transactions must have an offsetting transaction.

Explain the functions and major components of the four principal financial statements: the balance sheet, the income statement, the statement of owners' equity, and the statement of cash flows.

The balance sheet shows the financial position of a company on a particular date. The three major classifications of balance sheet data represent the components of the accounting equation: assets, liabilities, and owners' equity. The income statement shows the results of a firm's operations over a specific period. It focuses on the firm's activities—its revenues and expenditures—and the resulting profit or loss during the period. The major components of the income statement are revenues, cost of goods sold, expenses, and profit or loss. The statement of owners' equity shows the components of the change in owners' equity from the end of the prior year to the end of the current year. Finally, the statement of cash flows indicates a firm's cash receipts and cash payments during an accounting period. It outlines the sources and uses of cash in the basic business activities of operating, investing, and financing.

Assessment Check Answers

5.1 List the four financial statements. The four financial statements are the balance sheet, the income statement, the statement of owners' equity, and the cash flow statement.

5.2 How is the balance sheet organized? Assets (what a firm owns) are shown on one side of the balance sheet and are listed in order of convertibility into cash. On the other side of the balance sheet are claims to assets, liabilities (what a firm owes), and owners' equity. Claims are listed in the order in which they are due, so liabilities are listed before owners' equity. Assets always equal liabilities plus owners' equity.

5.3 Define *accrual accounting*. Accrual accounting recognizes revenues and expenses when they occur, not when cash actually changes hands. Most companies use accrual accounting to prepare their financial statements.

Discuss how financial ratios are used to analyze a company's financial strengths and weaknesses.

Liquidity ratios measure a firm's ability to meet short-term obligations. Examples are the current ratio and the quick, or acid-test, ratio. Activity ratios, such as the inventory turnover ratio, accounts receivable turnover, and the total asset turnover ratio, measure how effectively a firm uses its resources. Profitability ratios assess the overall financial performance of the business. The gross profit margin, net profit margin, and return on owners' equity are examples. Leverage ratios, such as the total liabilities to total assets ratio and the long-term debt to equity ratio, measure the extent to which the firm relies on debt to finance its opera-

tions. Financial ratios help managers and outside evaluators compare a firm's current financial information with that of previous years and with results for other firms in the same industry.

Assessment Check Answers

6.1 List the four categories of financial ratios. The four categories of ratios are liquidity, activity, profitability, and leverage.

6.2 Define the following ratios: *current ratio, inventory turnover, net profit margin,* and *debt ratio*. The current ratio equals current assets divided by current liabilities; inventory turnover equals cost of goods sold divided by average inventory; net profit margin equals net income divided by sales; and the debt ratio equals total liabilities divided by total assets.

7 Describe the role of budgets in a business.

Budgets are financial guidelines for future periods reflecting expected sales revenues, operating expenses, and cash receipts and outlays. They represent management expectations for future occurrences based on plans that have been made. Budgets serve as important planning and controlling tools by providing standards against which actual performance can be measured. One important type of budget is the cash budget, which estimates cash inflows and outflows over a period of time.

Assessment Check Answers

7.1 What is a budget? A budget is a planning and control tool that reflects the firm's expected sales revenues, operating expenses, cash receipts, and cash outlays.

7.2 How is a cash budget organized? Cash budgets are generally prepared monthly. Cash receipts are listed first. They include cash sales as well as the collection of past credit sales. Cash outlays are listed next. These include cash purchases, payment of past credit purchases, and operating expenses. The difference between cash receipts and cash outlays is net cash flow.

8 Outline accounting issues facing global business and the move toward one set of worldwide accounting rules.

One accounting issue that affects global business is exchange rates. An exchange rate is the ratio at which a country's currency can be exchanged for other currencies. Daily changes in exchange rates affect the accounting entries for sales and purchases of firms involved in international markets. These fluctuations create either losses or gains for particular companies. The International Accounting Standards Board (IASB) was established to provide worldwide consistency in financial reporting practices and comparability of and uniformity in international accounting standards. It has developed International Financial Reporting Standards (IFRS). Many countries have already adopted IFRS, and the United States is in the process of transitioning to it.

8.1 How are financial statements adjusted for exchange rates? An exchange rate is the ratio at which a country's currency can be exchanged for other currencies. Fluctuations of exchange rates create either gains or losses for particular companies since data about international financial transac-

tions must be translated into the currency of the country in which the parent company resides.

8.2 What is the purpose of the IASB? The International Accounting Standards Board (IASB) was established to provide worldwide consistency in financial reporting practices and comparability and uniformity of international accounting rules. The IASB has developed the International Financial Reporting Standards (IFRS).

Business Terms You Need to Know

accounting 524

public accountant 526

generally accepted accounting principles (GAAP) 528

Financial Accounting Standards Board (FASB) 529

accounting cycle 531

asset 531

liability 532

owners' equity 532

accounting equation 532

double-entry bookkeeping 532

balance sheet 534

income statement 534

statement of owners' equity 536

statement of cash flows 537

accrual accounting 537

budget 543

Other Important Business Terms

open book management 525

certified public accountant (CPA) 526

management accountant 527

certified management accountant (CMA) 528

cash flow 537

ratio analysis 539

liquidity ratios 539

activity ratios 540

profitability ratios 541

leverage ratios 542

cash budget 544

International Accounting Standards Board (IASB) 546

International Financial Reporting Standards (IFRS) 546

Review Questions

1. Define *accounting*. Who are the major users of accounting information?

2. What are the three major business activities in which accountants play a major role? Give an example of each.

3. What does the term *GAAP* mean? Briefly explain the role of the Financial Accounting Standards Board and the Securities and Exchange Commission.

4. Explain the accounting equation.

5. What is double-entry bookkeeping? Give a brief example.

6. List the four major financial statements. Which financial statements are permanent and which are temporary?

7. What is the difference between a current asset and a long-term asset? Why is cash typically listed first on a balance sheet?

8. List and explain the major items found on an income statement.

9. What is accrual accounting? Give an example of how accrual accounting affects a firm's financial statement.

10. List the four categories of financial ratios and give an example of each. What is the purpose of ratio analysis?

11. What is a cash budget? Briefly outline what a simple cash budget might look like.

12. What is the International Accounting Standards Board (IASB)? Which countries have adopted IFRS?

Projects and Teamwork Applications

1. Your grandmother sends you a large check for your birthday, asking that you use the money to buy shares of stock in a company. She recommends that you review the company's financial statements before investing. What can a company's financial statements tell you about the investment potential of its stock?

2. Contact a local public accounting firm and set up an interview with one of the firm's partners. Ask the individual what his or her educational background is, what attracted the individual to the accounting profession, and what he or she does during a typical day. Prepare a brief report on your interview. Do you now want to learn

more about the accounting profession? Are you more interested in possibly pursuing a career in accounting?

3. Suppose you work for a U.S. firm that has extensive European operations. You need to restate data from the various European currencies in U.S. dollars in order to prepare your firm's financial statements. Which financial statements and which components of these statements will be affected?

4. One of the current issues in accounting is whether the SEC is beginning to infringe on FASB's independence. Working in a small group, research this issue and write a report outlining the arguments.

5. With a partner, identify two public companies operating in different industries. Collect at least three years' worth of financial statements for the firms. Calculate the financial ratios listed in Table 16.1. Prepare an oral report summarizing your findings.

6. You've been appointed treasurer of a local not-for-profit organization. You would like to improve the quality of the organization's financial reporting to existing and potential donors. Describe the kinds of financial statements you would like to see the organization's accountant prepare. Why do you think better quality financial statements might help reassure donors?

7. Adapting the format of Figure 16.7, prepare on a sheet of paper your personal cash budget for next month. Keep in mind the following suggestions as you prepare your budget:

   a. *Cash inflows.* Your sources of cash would include your earnings, if any, gifts, scholarship monies, tax refunds, dividends and interest, and income from self-employment.

   b. *Cash outflows.* When estimating next month's cash outflows, include any of the following that may apply to your situation:

      i. Household expenses (rent or mortgage, utilities, maintenance, home furnishings, telephone/cell phone, cable TV, household supplies, groceries)
      ii. Education (tuition, fees, textbooks, supplies)
      iii. Work (transportation, clothing)
      iv. Clothing (purchases, cleaning, laundry)
      v. Automobile (auto payments, fuel, repairs)
      vi. Insurance premiums
         • Renters (or homeowners)
         • Auto
         • Health
         • Life
      vii. Taxes (income, property, Social Security, Medicare)
      viii. Savings and investments
      ix. Entertainment/recreation (health club, vacation/travel, dining, movies)
      x. Debt (credit cards, installment loans)
      xi. Miscellaneous (charitable contributions, child care, gifts, medical expenses)

   c. *Beginning cash balance.* This amount could be based on a minimum cash balance you keep in your checking account and should include only the cash available for your use; therefore, money such as that invested in retirement plans should not be included.

Web Assignments

1. **Careers in accounting.** The so-called big four accounting firms are some of the largest employers of recent college graduates. Go the career section of the Ernst & Young Web site (http://www.ey.com/global/content.nsf/US/_Careers_Home). Click on "For students" and review the information. What types of careers are offered by Ernst & Young? What is the firm looking for in new hires? What does a typical career path look like for a new hire? After reviewing this information, are you more or less interested in pursuing a career in public accounting?

2. **Financial Accounting Standards Board.** Visit the Web site of the FASB (http://www.fasb.org). Review some of the recent and proposed rule changes. Pick one and prepare a brief report, including a description of the issue, who originally proposed the change, and when the change will become effective.

3. **Understanding financial reporting requirements.** As discussed in the chapter, public companies are required to report financial results on a regular basis and file these reports with the Securities and Exchange Commission. These reports are public documents, available to anyone. Choose a public company and visit the SEC's Web site (http://www.sec.gov). Click on "Edgar" and search for recent filings for your firm. Prepare a report summarizing what you found.

Note: Internet addresses change frequently. If you do not find the exact sites listed, you may need to access the organization's or company's home page and search from there.

Everybody wants to save time and money. So with more and more companies looking for new ways to streamline their operations and management processes, improve productivity, and reduce costs, opportunities are growing for software providers that can help automate time-consuming operations and reporting tasks.

One such firm, Lawson Software, has more than 500 customers in the healthcare industry who rely on its integrated software products to help run more than 4,500 facilities around the country. Holland Hospital, a not-for-profit health facility in Holland, Michigan, has only 205 beds and 1,600 employees. But as Lawson's marketing director says, "Community hospitals, like their larger peers, want business software that's easy to deploy and use." Holland's old systems for managing its physical resources, purchasing supplies, and recording financial data for reporting were time consuming, wasteful, and slow. They held back employee productivity and made it difficult to share information across departments. Paper-based reports also made it necessary to input the same data multiple times. Management wanted to improve these operations, and do it quickly and cheaply.

Lawson's packaged software application that was developed especially for community hospitals helped Holland achieve its goals. First, Lawson worked to make it easy for Holland to adopt the new program, to reduce the cost and effort of changing systems. Then it brought the new software in and showed Holland's employees how it standardized materials management, made data entry easier and more accurate, and increased the efficiency of the hospital's office operations.

Now Holland employees can share information such as purchase orders across departments, use automated processes for tasks that used to be manual such as paying for supplies, and speed the preparation of reports that managers use to make decisions. Employees were soon spending one full hour a day *less* on tracking and replenishing supplies, for instance. "We're already starting to achieve time and cost savings," acknowledges Holland's director of information systems.

Another firm that's benefited from adopting Lawson software is Bassett Healthcare, a large regional healthcare system with four hospitals and 24 community health centers in upstate New York. Bassett has more than twice as many employees as Holland and relied on similar paper-based methods. Proving that "our industry-leading software and healthcare expertise help customers like Bassett simplify the business of healthcare so they can focus on enhancing patient care," Lawson introduced a standardized computer-based budgeting system.

The new software automated what used to be a cumbersome process for getting budget approvals. It not only frees up valuable management time but also includes security measures that ensure employees see only the information they need to do their jobs. This was important to Bassett because confidentiality of information is critical in the healthcare industry. New cost controls included in the software package are also helping Bassett meet its profitability goals.

Even government offices are able to benefit from automated accounting and administrative software like Lawson's. In Wyandotte County, Kansas, a Lawson package helps centralize administrative functions so that government administrators can eliminate the manual processes for budgeting, purchasing, and human resource operations. The county's Unified Government, which is responsible for nearly 160,000 citizens, can increase employee productivity, end redundant data-entry procedures, simplify reporting, and reduce costs in the process.[15]

Questions for Critical Thinking

1. Do you see any potential disadvantages in using software to automate administrative processes like accounting and financial reporting? If so, what are they?

2. Why is it important for users of financial accounting and other software packages to restrict access to certain kinds of information in the system?

Who Is RSM McGladrey?

In the middle of the Roaring Twenties in Cedar Rapids, Iowa, an ambitious young accountant named Ira B. McGladrey started his own firm by buying out his employers' seven-person operation and adding a couple of one-person branch offices around the state. Ten years later, after pulling through the Great Depression, the company added two new partners—George Hansen and Keith Dunn—and began a decades-long period of growth and expansion. Company founder McGladrey remained an active partner in the firm and a leader in the accounting profession until his death in the 1950s.

By the 1970s McGladrey, Hansen, Dunn & Company, as it was by then called, had 29 offices in eight states and had added consulting services to its client offerings. Two big mergers in ten years helped the company more than double in size, adding 12 more states to its range of operations and extending its offices from the East Coast to the West Coast and from Minnesota to Florida. In 1987 the company changed its name to McGladrey & Pullen, and since 1999 it has operated as two separate and independent business partners, RSM McGladrey and McGladrey & Pullen LLP.

RSM McGladrey offers financial accounting, tax, and business consulting. Some of its services are assisting with bankruptcy and reorganization, assisting with payroll fulfillment, setting up retirement plans, performing business valuation, assisting with mergers and acquisitions, e-accounting, making financial projections and modeling, and reviewing operations for efficiency and productivity. McGladrey & Pullen LLP is a partner-owned CPA firm that offers tailored and industry-specific auditing services.

Together, the two firms make up the country's fifth-largest provider of accounting, tax, and business consulting services and employ more than 8,000 professionals and associates in 120 offices around the United States.

They also hire several hundred interns and entry-level employees every year. The partner firms specialize in working with medium-sized companies in industries ranging from construction to real estate, financial services, health care, auto dealerships, and manufacturing. Other clients include not-for-profits and government agencies.

Both firms are members of RSM International, a worldwide affiliation of accounting and consulting firms operating in 70 countries. Thus, they are able to help clients with all sorts of international accounting questions, whether customers are simply looking for best practices from around the world to use or getting ready to take the big step and expand their operations overseas.

RSM McGladrey also operates the RSM McGladrey Institute, which supports accounting research, holds public forums on accounting and auditing concerns, and provides professional research and educational materials to students and the media about accounting, auditing, and the stock market. The firm recently began distributing to its clients the results of its annual survey of almost 1,000 U.S. CEOs and CFOs representing different-sized companies in various industries. The survey explores current business conditions and global opportunities and includes a jobs forecast.[16]

Questions

1. What historical and economic factors do you think might have contributed to the growth and expansion of the accounting industry, and Ira McGladrey's firm, from the Great Depression to the present day?

2. Do you think it's a good idea for RSM McGladrey and McGladrey & Pullen LLP to operate as separate firms? Why or why not? How might the arrangement benefit the two firms' clients?

Taking Account: The Little Guys

Accounting is a vital part of every business, large and small. The Little Guys—an independent retailer based in the Chicago suburbs that specializes in selling and installing home theater equipment—is no exception. How does The Little Guys stay ahead of big guys such as Best Buy and Wal-Mart? By focusing carefully on what its customers want and purchasing and stocking merchandise wisely. The firm has made a name for itself through customer service, including hiring a friendly, knowledgeable staff that is eager to educate customers on the latest high-tech equipment. And it has adapted to changes in the market. "The biggest change in the industry is that five years ago brands drove people to our store," observes co-founder David Wexler. "Today, the manufacturers' brands are everywhere, so the brand is now us. It's 'The Little Guys' name that's most important." In fact, industry surveys confirm that consumers now care more about customer service and financial incentives than they do about big brand names in consumer electronics.

Making decisions about such issues as merchandise and staff payroll is all part of accounting—both short term and long term. Co-founder Evie Wexler handles most of the day-to-day accounting for The Little Guys with the help of the software program QuickBooks. Many small-business owners use such commercially available programs to help run their firms. Wexler reports that QuickBooks simplifies many accounting tasks, automatically placing data in the correct category. "[QuickBooks] writes all the checks, so that when you balance the checkbook, it's all there," she says. "When we started, we were small enough that someone could have kept the books by hand. What we've grown into—the amount of things we receive each day, the amount that goes out, the number of employees we have—it's too complex. The program gives us a better picture of what goes on in the business every day."

For more complex accounting issues, the Wexlers turn to an outside accountant, whom they view as a business consultant—not just someone who fills out forms and reports. They have relied on their accountant's expertise from the beginning. "When we first opened the store, we worked with the accountant as a consultant," recalls David. "He helped us understand some of the technicalities of opening a business. We wrote out a business plan." The business plan specified how much they would spend on advertising, rent, utilities, payroll, and other expenses.

Operating expenses such as payroll and overhead must be tracked carefully. Payroll in particular is a complicated accounting task for The Little Guys. The sales staff is paid based on a percentage of sales, providing an incentive for each salesperson to perform. "Because we pay on a percentage, payroll is difficult," explains Evie Wexler. "There are percentages and base pay. There are lots of idiosyncracies—401k, federal tax, [state] tax, Social Security, and Medicare. You have to track all of this." Overhead expenses such as warehousing and truck maintenance are another part of the accounting puzzle. And the retail store also needs to be insured. "When you look at your profit/loss statement, you can see how much it costs you to do business every day," says Evie.

The Wexlers and their business partner meet to review financial statements for each quarter. They evaluate each expense category to determine whether they are spending too much or not enough to get the results they want. David focuses on the sales figures for each month and compares them with the same month of the previous year. He notes that when they started their business, he tried to look at the sales figures for every day. But he learned that "you can't do that—you'll drive yourself crazy. Now I'll look every week or ten days. You need a bigger slice of time." He points out that variables such as snowstorms, five Saturdays in a month, or a major sale can all skew the numbers. But he explains that they examine overall trends to make decisions. Perhaps surprisingly, Evie says, "We don't set financial goals. We look at how we did for the year. Then we'll decide how much better we're doing this year."

The Little Guys prides itself on offering customers the latest, highest-quality home theater products. With those high-end products come high prices. But the firm's customers don't pay the ticket price. Instead, they negotiate a deal for a full home theater system, including installation. This customization affects the firm's cash flow. "Sometimes we find ourselves in hot water, and then we react," says Evie. During one season, customers were placing special orders for items that The Little Guys had to pay the manufacturers for up-front. Meanwhile, in-stock items were sitting on the shelves. So the Wexlers instructed the sales staff to concentrate on selling those in-stock items in order to improve the store's cash flow.

Because The Little Guys is—yes—little, it can be more flexible in the way it handles buying decisions than larger firms can. "Most businesses are more structured," says Evie. "Because we own the business, we don't buy new things without talking to each other. We have to be a little bit risky in order to be flexible and offer our customers the best products." As a result, the business doesn't have a rigid budget for the products it purchases. But the Wexlers wouldn't operate any other way. Evie admits that worrying about bills sometimes keeps her up at night. But years of experience have taught these business owners that they can compete successfully against the big guys.[17]

Questions for Critical Thinking

1. What role does an outside accountant play for a small firm like The Little Guys?

2. How might accounting help The Little Guys grow as a business?

3. For The Little Guys, create a table with three columns and list the major classifications of data in the accounting equation—assets, liabilities, and owners' equity—that could be used later in the firm's balance sheet.

4. Evie Wexler says that her firm does not have a rigid budget for purchasing items to sell in the store. But what role does a budget play in planning and providing standards by which The Little Guys can measure its performance?

KANSAS

Saline River
Kansas City

Smoky Hill River
Salina

Greensburg

Garden City

Wichita

© Getty Images

Greensburg KS.

The Dog Ate My Laptop

The night of the tornado, Superintendent of Schools Darin Headrick heard the storm sirens go off on his way home from work. He stopped at the home of High School Principal Randy Fulton and the two men headed for the basement, just in case. The next thing they knew, the entire school system was gone. Textbooks were scattered everywhere, computers destroyed.

For the first three months after the storm, no one could live in town. People stayed in shelters or with friends and family outside of town. No one had a home phone anymore, but people were eager to connect with each other and find out what was happening. Although the Federal Emergency Management Agency (FEMA) was distributing information at checkpoints on the edges of town, people had to go to town to get it.

Like 95 percent of the town's 1,500 residents, Headrick himself was homeless. With just four months to rebuild an entire school system, all he had were his laptop and cell phone, so he got into his truck and began searching for a wireless signal. Taking a lesson from his students, he used text messaging to distribute information. Although very few people still had computers, almost everyone had a cell phone. Residents who subscribed to the text service could receive updates and instant messages over the phone, wherever they were.

Rebuilding the schools was a bigger task. Headrick secured temporary trailers for grades K–12 and received generous donations of desks and school supplies. By August 15, he had the basics needed to start the school year, but he still lacked textbooks. Technology would have to fill in the gaps, so the students didn't fall behind.

One of the school system's existing programs was ITV, for Interactive Distance Learning Network. ITV allowed Greensburg's rural schools to log in to classrooms around the state via Web cam. This type of real-time distance learning is referred to as *synchronous learning,* as opposed to the asynchronous online courses given on college campuses. After the tornado, all that was needed to get the program up and running again were a computer, an Internet connection, and a Web cam.

Early in the winter of 2007 each of Greensburg High's students got an unexpected gift: a laptop computer containing e-books, handwriting recognition software, and a tablet screen for note taking. The new laptops replaced their tattered textbooks. Students would hand in their assignments via e-mail and receive feedback from their teachers via instant messaging.

Questions

After viewing the video, answer the following questions:

1. Was Greensburg Public Schools' investment in technology a smart move?
2. Would you consider enrolling in an asynchronous online course? What might be the benefits and drawbacks?
3. Do you think hand-held devices and text messaging improve productivity and communication or distract their users?

Launching Your
Information Technology and Accounting Career

Part 5, "Managing Technology and Information," includes Chapters 15 and 16, which discuss using computers and related technology to manage information and accounting and financial statements. In Chapter 15, we discussed well-known technology companies such as Google and Oracle, as well as a host of smaller organizations that use computer technology to manage information. In Chapter 16, you read about giant accounting firms such as Ernst & Young and a variety of public and private organizations, large and small, that generate and use accounting data. These examples illustrate that all organizations need to manage technology and information. And with the complexity and scope of technology and information likely to increase in the years ahead, the demand for accounting and information systems professionals is expected to grow.

According to the U.S. Department of Labor, employment in occupations such as accounting, auditing, computer software engineering and support specialists, and network systems administrators is expected to grow faster than the average for all occupations in the next decade. In fact, two of the top five occupations in which employment is expected to grow the fastest over the next few years are related to information systems.[1] In addition, recent graduates with bachelor's degrees in accounting and information systems have among the highest average starting salaries of all business graduates. The median annual salary for accountants and auditors is almost $55,000, with the top 10 percent earning about $94,000.[2] Salaries in information systems vary widely based on education and experience. But starting salaries for computer engineering graduates average more than $56,000, and graduates in computer science average nearly $54,000.[3] Those who are information systems managers earn about $102,000 per year.[4]

What types of jobs are available in information systems and accounting? What are the working conditions like? What are the career paths? Information systems and accounting are both fairly broad occupations and encompass a wide variety of jobs. In some cases you'll work in the accounting or information systems department of a business such as Procter & Gamble or Shell. In other cases, you'll work for a specialized accounting or information systems firm, such as PricewaterhouseCoopers or IBM, that provides these services to governments, not-for-profit organizations, and businesses.

Accounting and information systems are popular business majors, and many entry-level positions are available each year. For instance, many accounting graduates start their careers working for a public accounting firm. Initially, their job duties involve auditing or tax services, usually working with more senior accountants. As their careers progress, accounting graduates take on more and more supervisory responsibilities. Some may move from public accounting firms to take accounting positions at other organizations. Many accounting and information systems graduates spend their entire careers in these fields, while others move into other areas. People who began their careers in accounting or information systems are well represented in the ranks of senior management today. Let's look briefly at some of the specific jobs you might find after earning a degree in accounting or information systems.

Public accountants perform a broad range of accounting, auditing, tax, and consulting services for their clients, which include businesses, governments, not-for-profit organizations, and individuals. Auditing is one of the most important services offered by public accountants, and many accounting graduates begin their careers in auditing. Auditors examine a client's financial statements and accounting procedures to make sure they conform with all applicable laws and regulations. Public accountants either own their own businesses or work for public accounting firms. Many public accountants are certified public accountants (CPAs). To become a CPA, you have to meet educational and experience requirements and pass a comprehensive examination.

Management accountants work for an organization other than a public accounting firm. They record and analyze financial information and financial statements for their organizations. Management accountants are also involved in budgeting, tax preparation, cost management, and asset management. Internal auditors verify the accuracy of their organization's internal controls and check for irregularities, waste, and fraud.

Technical support specialists are troubleshooters who monitor the performance of computer systems; provide technical support and solve problems for computer users; install, modify, clean, and repair computer hardware and software; and write training manuals and train computer users.

Network administrators design, install, and support an organization's computer networks, including its local area network, wide area network, Internet, and intranet systems. They provide administrative support for software and hardware users and ensure that the design of an organization's computer networks and all of the components fit together efficiently and effectively.

Computer security specialists plan, coordinate, and implement an organization's information security. They educate users about how to protect computer systems, install antivirus and similar software, and monitor the networks for security breaches. In recent years, the role and importance of computer security specialists have increased in response to the growing number of attacks on networks and data.

Career Assessment Exercises in Information Systems and Accounting

1. The American Institute of Certified Public Accountants is a professional organization dedicated to the enhancement of the public accounting profession. Visit the organization's Web site (http://www.aicpa.org). Review the information on CPA standards and examinations. Write a brief summary on what you learned about how to become a CPA.

2. Assume you're interested in a career as a systems administrator. Go to the following Web site: http://www.sage.org. Prepare a brief report outlining the responsibilities of a systems administrator, who hires for these positions, and what kind of educational background you need to become one.

3. Identify a person working in your local area in the accounting field and arrange an interview with that person (your college career center may be able to help you). Ask that person about his or her job responsibilities, educational background, and the best and worst aspects of his or her job as an accountant.

Part 6

Managing Financial Resources

© Masterfile

chapter 17

The Financial System

Chris Maluszynski/Moment/Redux Pictures

Citigroup Closes Out the Financial Supermarket

The merger seemed like a good idea at the time. The stock market was up, money was flowing freely, and huge acquisitions were commonplace. A little over a decade ago Travelers Group, a big insurance company, merged with Citibank's growing stable of banking and other financial businesses in a $76 billion deal.

Under the management of Sanford Weill, Travelers had already bought up brokerage firm Smith Barney, insurance firm Aetna, and Wall Street investment banking firm Salomon Brothers. The merger with Citibank, the nation's largest bank, made history by consolidating so many lines of financial business—banking, insurance, investments—into one huge conglomerate. Weill emerged as CEO of the new company, which some observers said offered one-stop shopping, calling it a financial supermarket. At its height Citigroup, as the new giant was called, had 374,000 employees in more than 100 countries. It seemed the only place it could go was up.

But the huge profits expected from the deal proved elusive, and executives at the top of the merged firm did not see eye-to-eye. Problems and infighting among the board members and the managers spread, costs ballooned, and the company's technology fell behind the times. Meanwhile, Citigroup's stock price plummeted—at one point sinking more than 75 percent to a 16-year low. Then the bottom dropped out in 2008 and 2009. Losses mounted into tens of billions of dollars as Citigroup was caught in the economic crisis that hit so many other financial players. The company had badly overextended itself by buying up highly risky mortgage-backed securities that even its own executives failed to understand.

"I cannot think of one positive that developed as a result of [merging] these two companies," said one industry observer. "The miracle of Citigroup is that it still is in the position it is in, given the massive mismanagement."

As economic conditions and losses worsened, Citigroup was at last forced to take some painful medicine to try to find its way back to financial health. It had to sell most of its business units—dismantling the financial supermarket. Sanford Weill had retired in 2006, leaving the company in the hands of Charles Prince III. Prince, a lawyer by training, had steered the company through some of the biggest corporate accounting and conflict-of-interest scandals of the late 1990s—the collapse of Enron and WorldCom—in both of which the titanic firm was said to be involved. However, not even Prince could save the company this time. As losses from mortgage investments climbed, Citigroup had to accept $45 billion under the U.S. government's Troubled Assets Relief Program. Prince was forced out, to be replaced by Vikram Pandit.

Prince had already sold the Travelers insurance business, so Pandit's first step was to streamline the remainder of the firm. Pandit sold the very businesses Weill had acquired. The first unit to go was brokerage firm Smith Barney. Morgan Stanley paid $2.7 billion for a 51 percent ownership stake and an option to complete the purchase in three years. Citigroup also announced plans to eliminate noncore businesses like consumer finance and a private-label credit card unit, to cut back its stock trading activities, and to sell its overseas brokerage and asset management firms. These changes came quickly, under pressure from federal regulators. Most observers applauded the breakup as the right solution, saying it had just come a few years too late.

Many factors likely contributed to the failure of the financial supermarket, including management mistakes, a scattered market focus, and bloated costs. Unchecked risk taking was another element, according to some experts. In addition, the growing ease of Internet banking with its favorable rates and terms helped undercut what Citigroup hoped would be major money makers among its operating units. Customers no longer needed to be physically present in a financial institution to purchase products. Some critics now question whether a financial supermarket was what banking customers really wanted after all.[1]

Businesses, governments, and individuals often need to raise capital. Assume a businessperson forecasts a sharp increase in sales for the coming year, and this expected increase requires additional inventory. If the business lacks sufficient cash to purchase the needed merchandise, it may turn to a bank for a short-term loan. On the other hand, some individuals and businesses have incomes that are greater than their current expenditures and wish to earn a rate of return on the excess funds. For instance, say your income this month is $3,000 but your expenditures are only $2,500. You can take the extra $500 and deposit it in your bank savings account, which pays you a rate of interest.

The two transactions just described are small parts of what is known as the **financial system,** the process by which money flows from savers to users. Virtually all businesses, governments, and individuals participate in the financial system, and a well-functioning one is vital to a nation's economic well-being. The financial system is the topic of this chapter.

We begin by describing the financial system and its components in more detail. Then, the major types of financial instruments, such as stocks and bonds, are outlined. Next we discuss financial markets, where financial instruments are bought and sold. We then describe the world's major stock markets, such as the New York Stock Exchange. Next, banks and other financial institutions are described in depth. The structure and responsibilities of the U.S. Federal Reserve System, along with the tools the Fed uses to control the supply of money and credit, are detailed. The chapter concludes with an overview of the major laws and regulations affecting the financial system and a discussion of today's global financial system.

Understanding the Financial System

Figure 17.1

Overview of the Financial Systems and Its Components

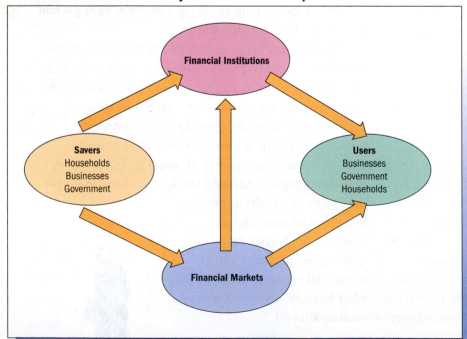

Households, businesses, government, financial institutions, and financial markets together form what is known as the financial system. A simple diagram of the financial system is shown in Figure 17.1.

On the left are savers—those with excess funds. For a variety of reasons, savers choose not to spend all of their current income, so they have a surplus of funds. Users are the opposite of savers; their spending needs exceed their current income, so they have a deficit. They need to obtain additional funds to make up the difference. Savings are provided by some households, businesses, and the government, but borrowers also consist of other households, businesses, and the government. Households may need money to buy automobiles or homes. Businesses may need money to purchase inventory or build new production facilities. Governments may need money to build highways and courthouses.

Generally, in the United States, households are net savers—meaning that as a whole they save more funds than they use—while businesses and governments are net users—meaning that they use more funds than they save. The fact that most of the net savings in the U.S. financial system are provided by households may be a bit of a surprise initially, because Americans do not have a reputation of being thrifty. Yet even though the savings rate of American households is low compared with those of other countries, American households still save hundreds of billions of dollars each year.

How much an individual saves is a function of many variables. One of the most important is the person's age. People often transition from net borrowers to net savers as they get older. When you graduate from college and begin a career, you likely have little in the way of savings. In fact, you may be deeply in debt. In the early years of your career, you may spend more than you make as you acquire major assets, such as a home. So in these early years your *net worth*—the difference between what you own and what you owe—is very low and may even be negative. However, as your career progresses and your income rises, you will begin to build a financial nest egg to fund retirement and other needs. Your net worth will also increase. It will continue to increase until you retire and begin drawing on your retirement savings.

Funds can be transferred between savers and users in two ways: directly and indirectly. A direct transfer means that the user raises the needed funds directly from savers. While direct transfers occur, the vast majority of funds flow through either financial markets or financial institutions. For example, assume a local school district needs to build several new schools. The district doesn't have enough cash on hand to pay for the school construction costs, so it sells bonds to investors (savers) in the financial market. The district uses the proceeds from the sale to pay for the new schools and in return pays bond investors interest each year for the use of their money.

The other way in which funds can be transferred indirectly is through financial institutions—for example, a commercial bank such as Cincinnati-based Fifth Third Bank or Alabama-based Regions Bank. The bank pools customer deposits and uses the funds to make loans to businesses and households. These borrowers pay the bank interest, and it, in turn, pays depositors interest for the use of their money.

HSBC, "the world's local bank," maintains this branch office in Altrincham, Pennsylvania. Commercial banks like HSBC pool customers' deposits and lend them to businesses and consumers.

Dave Thompson/PA Photos/Landov LLC

financial system process by which funds are transferred from those having excess funds (savers) to those needing additional funds (users).

Assessment Check

1. What is the financial system?
2. In the financial system, who are the borrowers and who are the savers?
3. List the two most common ways in which funds are transferred between borrowers and savers.

Types of Securities

For the funds they borrow from savers, businesses and governments provide different types of guarantees for repayment. **Securities,** also called financial instruments, represent obligations on the part of issuers—businesses and governments—to provide purchasers with expected or stated returns on the funds invested or loaned. Securities can be classified into three categories: money market instruments, bonds, and stock. Money market instruments and bonds are both debt securities, and stocks are units of ownership in corporations like General Electric, Best Buy, 3M, and PepsiCo.

securities financial instruments such as stocks and bonds.

Money Market Instruments

Money market instruments are short-term debt securities issued by governments, financial institutions, and corporations. All money market instruments mature within one year from the date of issue. Investors are paid interest by the issuer for the use of their funds. Money market instruments are generally low-risk securities and are purchased by investors when they have surplus cash. Examples of money market instruments include U.S. Treasury bills, commercial paper, and bank certificates of deposit.

Treasury bills are short-term securities issued by the U.S. Treasury and backed by the full faith and credit of the U.S. government. Treasury bills are sold with a maturity of 30, 90, 180, or 360 days and have a minimum denomination of $1,000. They are considered virtually risk free and easy to resell. Commercial paper is securities sold by corporations, such as General Electric, that mature from 1 to 270 days from the date of issue. Although slightly riskier than Treasury bills, commercial paper is still generally considered a very low-risk security.

A certificate of deposit (CD) is a time deposit at a financial institution, such as a commercial bank, savings bank, or credit union. The sizes and maturity dates of CDs vary considerably and can often be tailored to meet the needs of purchasers. CDs with denominations of $100,000 or less per depositor are federally insured. CDs with larger denominations are not federally insured but can be sold more easily prior to maturity.

Bonds

Bondholders are creditors of a corporation or government body. By selling bonds, a firm obtains long-term debt capital. Federal, state, and local governments also acquire funds through bonds. Bonds are issued in various denominations—face values—usually between $1,000 and $25,000. Each issue indicates a rate of interest to be paid to the bondholder—stated as a percentage of the bond's face value—as well as a maturity date on which the bondholder is paid the bond's face value. Because bondholders are creditors, they have a claim on the firm's assets that must be satisfied before any claims of stockholders in the event of the firm's bankruptcy, reorganization, or liquidation.

TYPES OF BONDS A prospective bond investor can choose among a variety of bonds. The major types of bonds are summarized in Table 17.1. **Government bonds** are bonds sold by the U.S. Department of the Treasury. Because government bonds are backed by the full faith and credit of the U.S. government, they are considered the least risky of all bonds. The Treasury sells bonds that mature in 2, 5, 10, and 30 years from the date of issue.

Municipal bonds are bonds issued by state or local governments. Two types of municipal bonds exist. A *revenue bond* is a bond issue whose proceeds are to be used to pay for a project that will produce revenue—such as a toll road or bridge. The Oklahoma Turnpike Authority has issued such bonds. A *general obligation bond* is a bond whose proceeds are to be used to pay for a project that will not produce any revenue—such as a new Indiana State Police post. General obligation bonds can only be sold by states or local governmental units—such as Toledo, Ohio, or Bergen County, New Jersey—that have the power to levy taxes. An important feature of municipal bonds is the exemption of interest payments from federal income tax. Because of this attractive feature, municipal bonds generally carry lower interest rates than either corporate or government bonds.

Corporate bonds are a diverse group and often vary based on the collateral—the property pledged by the borrower—that backs the bond. For example, a *secured bond* is backed by a specific pledge of company assets. These assets serve as collateral, just like a home serves as collateral for a mortgage. However, many firms also issue *unsecured bonds,* called **debentures.** These bonds are backed only by the financial reputation of the issuing corporation.

Table 17.1	Types of Bonds		

Issuer	Types of Securities	Risk	Special Features
U.S. Treasury (government bonds)	Notes: Mature in 10 years or fewer from date of issue. Bonds: Mature in 30 years from date of issue	Treasury bonds and notes have virtually no risk.	Interest is exempt from state income taxes.
State and local governments (municipal bonds)	General obligation: Issued by state or local governmental units with taxing authority; backed by the full faith and credit of the state where issued. Revenue: Issued to pay for projects that generate revenue—such as water systems or toll roads; revenue from project used to pay principal and interest.	Risk varies depending on the financial health of the issuer. Most large municipal bond issues are rated in terms of credit risk (AAA or Aaa is the highest rating).	Interest is exempt from federal income taxes and may be exempt from state income taxes.
Corporations	Secured bonds: Bonds are backed by specific assets. Unsecured bonds (debentures): Backed by the financial health and reputation of the issuer.	Risk varies depending on the financial health of the issuer. Most corporate bond issues are rated in terms of credit risk (AAA or Aaa is the highest rating).	A few corporate bonds are convertible into shares of common stock of the issuing company.
Financial institutions	Mortgage pass-through securities.	Generally very low risk.	They pay monthly income consisting of both interest and principal.

Another popular type of bond is the *mortgage pass-through security.* These securities are backed by a pool of mortgage loans purchased from lenders, such as savings banks. As borrowers make their monthly mortgage payments, these payments are "passed through" to the holders of the securities. Most mortgage pass-through securities are relatively safe because all mortgages in the pool are insured. However, in recent years, mortgage pass-through securities consisting of pools of so-called **subprime mortgages,** loans made to borrowers with poor credit ratings, were issued. Many of these securities turned out to be quite risky and, in part, triggered what became known as the *credit crisis.* The extent of the crisis forced the federal government to undertake a massive bailout of the financial system. The Office of Financial Stability—part of the U.S. Treasury department—was created to purchase poor-quality mortgage-backed and other securities from financial institutions.

QUALITY RATINGS FOR BONDS Two factors determine the price of a bond: its risk and its interest rate. Bonds vary considerably in terms of risk. One tool used by bond investors to assess the risk of a bond is its so-called *bond rating.* Several investment firms rate corporate and municipal bonds, the best known of which are Standard & Poor's (S&P), Moody's, and Fitch. Table 17.2 lists the S&P bond ratings. Moody's and Fitch use similar rating systems. Bonds with the lowest level of risk are rated AAA. As ratings descend, risk increases. Bonds with ratings of BBB and above are classified as **investment-grade bonds.** By contrast, bonds with ratings of BB and below are classified as **speculative,** or so-called **junk, bonds.** Junk bonds attract investors by offering high interest rates in exchange for greater risk. Today, junk bonds pay about 50 percent more in interest than do investment-grade corporate bonds.

Table 17.2	Standard & Poor's Bond Ratings	
Highest	AAA	
	AA	Investment grade
	A	
	BBB	
	BB	
	B	
	CCC	Speculative grade
	CC	
Lowest	C	

Note: Standard & Poor's occasionally assigns a plus or minus following the letter rating. For instance, AA+ means that the bond is higher quality than most AA bonds but hasn't quite met AAA standards. Ratings below C indicate that the bond is currently not paying interest.

The credit crisis of recent years generated a great deal of criticism of the ratings companies. Problems with the system are discussed in more depth in the "Hit & Miss" feature.

The second factor affecting the price of a bond is its interest rate. Other things being equal, the higher the interest rate, the higher the price of a bond. However, everything else usually is not equal; the bonds may not be equally risky, or one may have a longer maturity. Investors must evaluate the trade-offs involved.

Another important influence on bond prices is the market interest rate. Because bonds pay fixed rates of interest, as market interest rates rise, bond prices fall, and vice versa. For instance, the price of a ten-year bond, paying 5 percent per year, would fall by about 8 percent if market interest rates rose from 5 percent to 6 percent.

Most corporate and municipal bonds, and some government bonds, are callable. A **call provision** allows the issuer to redeem the bond before its maturity at a specified price. Not surprisingly, issuers tend to call bonds when market interest rates are declining. For example, if York County, Pennsylvania, had $50 million in bonds outstanding with a 5 percent annual interest rate, it would pay $2.5 million annually in interest. If interest rates decline to 3 percent, the county may decide to call the 5 percent bonds, repaying the principal from the proceeds of newly issued 3 percent bonds. Calling the 5 percent bonds and issuing 3 percent bonds will save the county $1 million a year in interest payments. The savings in annual interest expense should more than offset the cost of retiring the old bonds and issuing new ones.

Stock

common stock
ownership claims in corporations.

The basic form of corporate ownership is embodied in **common stock.** Purchasers of common stock are the true owners of a corporation. Holders of common stock vote on major company decisions, such as purchasing another company or electing a board of directors. In return for the money they invest, they expect to receive some sort of return. This return can come in the form of cash dividend payments, expected price appreciation, or both. Dividends vary widely from stock to stock. DuPont, for instance, pays an annual dividend of more than $1.60 per share. In contrast, Starbucks pays no annual dividend to its shareholders. As a general rule, faster growing companies pay less in dividends because they need more funds to finance their growth. Consequently, investors expect stocks paying little or no cash dividends to show greater price appreciation compared with stocks paying more generous cash dividends.

Hit & Miss

Ratings Companies Get an F

Credit-rating agencies such as Standard & Poor's, Moody's, and Fitch are charged with providing consumers with unbiased appraisals, or ratings, on which to base their investment decisions. The key word is *unbiased*. As the House Oversight and Government Reform Committee held hearings recently into problems with credit ratings, it became clear the raters may have been giving distorted information.

"The story of the credit-rating agencies is the story of a colossal failure," said California's Representative Henry Waxman, the committee chairperson. "Millions of investors rely on them for independent, objective assessments. The ratings agencies broke this bond of trust, and federal regulators ignored the warning signs."

The problem? Ratings agencies are paid by the very companies they are evaluating—the issuers of the securities. This situation presents what many now consider to be a built-in conflict of interest. Moody's CEO admitted in a confidential memo that raters and their bosses are "continually 'pitched' by bankers, issuers, investors ... whose views can color credit judgment. We 'drink the Kool-aid.' Unchecked, competition on this basis can place the entire financial system at risk."

That conflict of interest is what many now believe helped contribute to the economic crisis, in which major firms collapsed and worldwide recession loomed. In fact, some of the riskiest mortgage-backed securities being traded were given the highest ratings. As subprime mortgage holders all over the country began defaulting on their loans, it exposed how overvalued the securities were that included them. Only then did the agencies adjust their ratings. But by that time, the damage had been done—the stock market was already tanking.

All three major ratings firms admitted their mistakes and the consequences of those mistakes. They further promised to institute future safeguards and make their rating procedures more transparent. Their errors were not intentional, they claimed. "We have to earn our credibility back," said the president of Standard & Poor's.

Consumers may take some time to put their faith in credit ratings again. Internal memos made clear that some raters knew they were overvaluing many securities. One Standard & Poor's instant-message exchange between two of its analysts ran like this:

"That deal is ridiculous."

"I know right ... model def [definition] does not capture half of the ... risk."

"We should not be rating it."

"We rate every deal. It could be structured by cows and we would rate it."

One rater's managing director admitted, "We had blinders on and never questioned the information we were given. These errors make us look either incompetent at credit analysis or like we sold our soul to the devil for revenue, or a little bit of both."

While Moody's CEO told a World Economic Forum panel that the problem was bad information whose "completeness and veracity was deteriorating," Congressional critics were skeptical of that explanation. "When the referee is being paid by the players, no one should be surprised when the game spins out of control," said former Connecticut Representative Christopher Shays.

Questions for Critical Thinking

1. Ratings agencies' business model appears flawed, because they profit by promoting the securities of the firms that "pitch" them. How could they avoid this conflict of interest? Where else should they look for revenue?

2. How can agencies solve the problem of incomplete or misleading information about the securities they rate?

Sources: Michael Pomerleano, "The Failure of Financial Regulation," *Financial Times,* January 15, 2009, http://blogs.ft.com; Amit R. Paley, "Credit-Rating Firms Grilled over Conflicts," *The Washington Post,* October 23, 2008, http://www.washingtonpost.com; "Hot Docs: Credit Rating Agencies 'a Colossal Failure,' U.S. Economic Recovery in Late 2009," *U.S. News & World Report,* October 23, 2008, http://www.usnews.com; Andrew Ross Sorkin, "Rating Agencies Draw Fire on Capitol Hill," *The New York Times,* October 22, 2008, http://dealbook.blogs.nytimes.com; Roger Lowenstein, "Triple-A Failure," *The New York Times,* April 27, 2008, http://www.nytimes.com; Floyd Norris, "Moody's Official Concedes Failures in Some Ratings," *The New York Times,* January 26, 2008, http://www.nytimes.com.

Common stockholders benefit from company success, and they risk the loss of their investments if the company fails. If a firm dissolves, claims of creditors must be satisfied before stockholders receive anything. Because creditors have a senior claim to assets, holders of common stock are said to have a residual claim on company assets.

The market value of a stock is the price at which the stock is currently selling. For example, Johnson & Johnson's stock price fluctuated between $59 and $69 per share during a recent year. What determines this market value is complicated; many variables cause stock prices to fluctuate up and down. Throughout the summer and fall of 2008, stock prices were very volatile, partly due to the credit crisis. However, in the long run stock prices tend to follow a company's profits. For instance, over the past ten years, both Johnson & Johnson's earnings and stock price have risen by more than 300 percent.

PREFERRED STOCK In addition to common stock, a few companies also issue preferred stock—stock whose holders receive preference in the payment of dividends. General Motors and Bank of America are examples of firms with preferred stock outstanding. Also, if a company is dissolved, holders of preferred stock have claims on the firm's assets that are ahead of the claims of common stockholders. On the other hand, preferred stockholders rarely have any voting rights, and the dividend they are paid is fixed, regardless of how profitable the firm becomes. Therefore, although preferred stock is legally classified as equity, many investors consider it to be more like a bond than common stock.

CONVERTIBLE SECURITIES Companies may issue bonds or preferred stock that contains a conversion feature, so they are called **convertible securities.** This feature gives the bondholder or preferred stockholder the right to exchange the bond or preferred stock for a fixed number of shares of common stock. Peabody Energy has an outstanding convertible bond that can be exchanged for 17.1 shares of the firm's common stock. Convertible bonds pay lower interest rates than those lacking conversion features, helping to reduce the interest expense of the issuing firms. Investors are willing to accept these lower interest rates because they value the potential for additional gains if the price of the firm's stock increases. For instance, at a price of $61 per share, Peabody Energy's convertible bond would have a common stock value of at least $1,043 ($61 × 17.1). Should the price of Peabody's common stock increase by $10 per share, the value of the convertible will increase by at least $171.

Assessment Check ✓

1. What are the major types of securities?
2. What is a government bond? A municipal bond?
3. Why do investors purchase common stock?

Financial Markets

financial market market in which securities are bought and sold.

primary market financial market in which new security issues are first sold.

Securities are issued and traded in **financial markets.** While there are many different types of financial markets, one of the most important distinctions is between primary and secondary markets. In the **primary market,** firms and governments issue securities and sell them initially to the public. When a company needs capital to purchase inventory, expand a plant, make major investments, acquire another firm, or pursue other business goals, it may sell a bond or stock issue to the investing public. For example, Oracle once sold about $5 billion in bonds, using the proceeds to purchase software maker BEA Systems.[2] Similarly, when Washington State needs capital to build a new highway, to buy a new ferry, or to fulfill other public needs, its leaders may also decide to sell bonds.

A stock offering gives investors the opportunity to purchase ownership shares in a firm such as well-known drug maker Amgen and to participate in its future growth, in exchange for providing current capital. When a company offers stock for sale to the general public for the first time, it is called an **initial public offering (IPO).** During a recent 12-month period, around 160 initial public offerings raised a total of more than $35 billion. These companies, on average, had been in existence for seven years prior to going public.[3]

Both profit-seeking corporations and government agencies also rely on primary markets to raise funds by issuing bonds. For example, the federal government sells treasury bonds to finance part of federal outlays such as interest on outstanding federal debt. State and local governments sell bonds to finance capital projects such as the construction of sewer systems, streets, and fire stations.

Announcements of new stock and bond offerings appear daily in business publications such as *The Wall Street Journal*. These announcements are often in the form of a simple black-and-white ad called a *tombstone*.

Securities are sold to the investing public in two ways: in open auctions and through investment bankers. Virtually all securities sold through open auctions consist of U.S. Treasury securities. A week before an upcoming auction, the Department of the Treasury announces the type and number of securities it will be auctioning. Treasury bills are auctioned weekly, but longer-term Treasury securities are auctioned once a month or once a quarter. Sales of most corporate and municipal securities are made via financial institutions such as Morgan Stanley. These institutions purchase the issue from the firm or government and then resell the issue to investors. This process is known as *underwriting*.

Financial institutions underwrite stock and bond issues at a discount, meaning that they pay the issuing firm or government less than the price the financial institution charges investors. This discount is compensation for services rendered, including the risk financial institutions incur whenever they underwrite a new security issue. Although the size of the discount is often negotiable, it usually averages around 5 percent for all types of securities. The size of the underwriting discount, however, is generally higher for stock issues than it is for bond issues. For instance, underwriting discounts for IPOs are generally between 7 and 10 percent.

On its building in Times Square, New York City, Morgan Stanley displays current stock prices and foreign stock indexes.

Kay Nietfeld/NewsCom

Corporations and governments are willing to pay for the services provided by financial institutions because they are financial market experts. In addition to locating buyers for the issue, the underwriter typically advises the issuer on such details as the general characteristics of the issue, its pricing, and the timing of the offering. Several financial institutions commonly participate in the underwriting process. The issuer selects a lead, or primary, financial institution, which in turn forms a syndicate consisting of other financial institutions. Each member of the syndicate purchases a portion of the security issue, which it resells to investors.

Media reports of stock and bond trading are most likely to refer to trading in the <mark>secondary market,</mark> a collection of financial markets in which previously issued securities are traded among investors. The corporations or governments that originally issued the securities being traded are not directly involved in the secondary market. They neither make any payments when securities are sold nor receive any of the proceeds when securities are purchased. The New York Stock Exchange (NYSE), for example, is a secondary market. In terms of the dollar value of securities bought and sold, the secondary market is four to five times as large as the primary market. In a recent year, more than $30 trillion worth of stock was traded on the NYSE alone.[4] The characteristics of the world's major stock exchanges are discussed in the next section.

Assessment Check ✔

1. What is a financial market?
2. Distinguish between a primary and secondary financial market.
3. Briefly explain the role of financial institutions in the sale of securities.

secondary market
financial market in which already issued securities are traded between investors.

Understanding Stock Markets

Stock markets, or **exchanges,** are probably the best-known of the world's financial markets. In these markets, shares of stock are bought and sold by investors. The two largest stock markets in the world, the New York Stock Exchange and the Nasdaq stock market, are located in the United States.

The New York Stock Exchange

The New York Stock Exchange—sometimes referred to as the Big Board—is the most famous and one of the oldest stock markets in the world, having been founded in 1792. Today, more than 3,000 common- and preferred-stock issues are listed on the NYSE. These stocks represent most of the largest, best-known companies in the United States and have a total market value exceeding $13 trillion. In terms of the total value of stock traded, the NYSE is the world's largest stock market.

For a company's stock to be traded on the NYSE, the firm must apply to the exchange for listing and meet certain listing requirements. In addition, the firm must continue to meet requirements each year to remain listed on the NYSE. Corporate bonds are also traded on the NYSE, but bond trading makes up less than 1 percent of the total value of securities traded there during a typical year.

Trading on the NYSE takes place face-to-face on a trading floor. Buy and sell orders are transmitted to a specific post on the floor of the exchange. Buyers and sellers then bid against one another in an open auction. Only investment firms that are designated members of the NYSE and that own at least one trading license are allowed to trade on the floor of the exchange. The NYSE issues up to 1,500 trading licenses at a cost of about $40,000 each.[5]

Each NYSE stock is assigned to a specialist firm. Specialists are unique investment firms that maintain an orderly and liquid market in the stocks assigned to them. Specialists must be willing to buy when there are no other buyers and sell when there are no other sellers. Specialists also act as auctioneers and catalysts, bringing buyers and sellers together.

Some observers portray the NYSE and its trading practices as somewhat old-fashioned, especially in this technological age. Most markets, they note, have abandoned their trading floors in favor of electronic trading. However, even though the NYSE still retains a trading floor, the exchange has become highly automated in recent years. Its computer systems automatically match and route most orders, which are typically filled within a few seconds.

The Nasdaq Stock Market

The world's second-largest stock market is the Nasdaq stock market. It is very different from the NYSE. Nasdaq—which stands for National Association of Securities Dealers Automated Quotation System—is actually a computerized communications network that links member investment firms. It is the world's largest intranet. All trading on Nasdaq takes place through its intranet, rather than on a trading floor. Buy and sell orders are entered into the network and executed electronically. All Nasdaq-listed stocks have two or more market makers—investment firms that perform essentially the same functions as NYSE specialists.

Around 5,000 companies have their stocks listed on Nasdaq. Compared with firms listed on the NYSE, Nasdaq-listed corporations tend to be smaller, less well-known firms. Some are relatively new businesses and cannot meet NYSE listing requirements. It is not uncommon for firms eventually to transfer the trading of their stocks from Nasdaq to the NYSE—16 did so in a recent year. However, dozens of major companies currently trade on Nasdaq—such as Amgen, Cisco Systems, Dell, Intel, and Microsoft—that would easily meet NYSE listing requirements. For a variety of reasons, these firms have decided to remain listed on Nasdaq.

Other U.S. Stock Markets

In addition to the NYSE and Nasdaq Stock Market, several other stock markets operate in the United States. The American Stock Exchange, or AMEX, focuses on the stocks of smaller firms, as well as other financial instruments such as options. In comparison with the NYSE and Nasdaq, the AMEX is tiny. Daily trading volume is generally less than 100 million shares compared with the 2+ billion shares on each of the larger two exchanges.

Several regional stock exchanges also operate throughout the United States. They include the Chicago, Pacific (San Francisco), Boston, Cincinnati, and Philadelphia Stock Exchanges. Originally established to trade the shares of small, regional companies, the regional exchanges now list securities of many large corporations as well. In fact, more than half of the companies listed on the NYSE are also listed on one or more regional exchanges.

Unlike the New York Stock Exchange, the NASDAQ does not have a trading floor; all transactions are done electronically. Firms listed on the NASDAQ tend to be smaller and younger than the large, established firms listed on the New York Stock Exchange.

© UPI Photo/Landov

Foreign Stock Markets

Stock markets exist throughout the world. Virtually all developed countries and many developing countries have stock exchanges. Examples include Bombay, Helsinki, Hong Kong, Mexico City, Paris, and Toronto. One of the largest stock exchanges outside the United States is the London Stock Exchange. Founded in the early 17th century, the London Stock Exchange lists approximately 2,900 stock and bond issues, more than 500 of which are shares of companies located outside the United Kingdom and Ireland. Trading on the London Stock Exchange takes place using a Nasdaq-type computerized communications network.

The London Stock Exchange is perhaps the most international of all stock markets. Approximately two-thirds of all cross-border trading in the world—for example, the trading of stocks of American companies outside the United States—takes place in London. It is not uncommon for institutional investors in the United States to trade NYSE- or Nasdaq-listed stocks in London. These investors claim they often get better prices and faster order execution in London than they do in the United States.

ECNs and the Future of Stock Markets

For years a so-called *fourth market* has existed. The fourth market is the direct trading of exchange-listed stocks off the floor of the exchange, in the case of NYSE-listed stocks, or outside the network, in the case of Nasdaq-listed stocks. Until recently, trading in the fourth market was limited to institutional investors buying or selling large blocks of stock.

Now the fourth market has begun to open up to smaller, individual investors through markets called *electronic communications networks* (ECNs). In ECNs, buyers and sellers meet in a virtual stock market and trade directly with one another. No specialist or market maker is involved. ECNs have become a significant force in the stock market in recent years. Around half of all trades involving Nasdaq-listed stocks take place on INET or Archipelago—the two largest ECNs—rather than directly through the Nasdaq system. Some have suggested that ECNs represent the future for stock markets, given that INET and Archipelago were acquired within the last few years by Nasdaq and the NYSE, respectively.

"They Said It"

"There's always a bull market somewhere."

—Jim Cramer (b.1955)
Host of *Mad Money* on CNBC

Investor Participation in the Stock Markets

Assessment Check ✔

1. What are the world's two largest stock markets?

2. Why is the London Stock Exchange unique?

3. Explain the difference between a market order and a limit order.

financial institution
intermediary between savers and borrowers, collecting funds from savers and then lending the funds to individuals, businesses, and governments.

Because most investors aren't members of the NYSE, or any other stock market, they need to use the services of a brokerage firm to buy or sell stocks. Examples of brokerage firms include Edward Jones and TD Ameritrade. Investors establish an account with the brokerage firm and then enter orders to trade stocks. The brokerage firm executes the trade on behalf of the investor, charging the investor a fee for the service. While some investors phone in orders or visit the brokerage firm in person, many today use their PCs and trade stocks online. The requirements for setting up an account vary from broker to broker. Selecting the right brokerage firm is one of the most important decisions investors make.

The most common type of order is called a **market order.** It instructs the broker to obtain the best possible price—the highest price when selling and the lowest price when buying. If the stock market is open, market orders are filled within seconds. Another popular type of order is called a **limit order.** It sets a price ceiling when buying or a price floor when selling. If the order cannot be executed when it is placed, the order is left with the exchange's market maker. It may be filed later if the price limits are met.

Financial Institutions

One of the most important components of the financial system is **financial institutions.** They serve as an intermediary between savers and borrowers, collecting funds from savers and then lending the funds to individuals, businesses, and governments. Financial institutions greatly increase the efficiency and effectiveness of the transfer of funds between savers and users. Because of financial institutions, savers earn more, and users pay less, than they would without them. In fact, it is difficult to imagine how any modern economy could function without well-developed financial institutions. Think about how difficult it would be for a businessperson to obtain inventory financing or an individual to purchase a new home without financial institutions. Prospective borrowers would have to identify and negotiate terms with each saver individually.

Traditionally, financial institutions have been classified into depository institutions—institutions that accept deposits that customers can withdraw on demand—and nondepository institutions. Examples of depository institutions include commercial banks, such as US Bancorp and Sun Trust; savings banks, such as Golden West and Ohio Savings; and credit unions, such as the State Employees Credit Union of North Carolina. Nondepository institutions include life insurance companies, such as Northwestern Mutual; pension funds, such as the Florida state employee pension fund; and mutual funds. In total, financial institutions have trillions of dollars in assets. Figure 17.2 illustrates the size of the most prominent financial institutions.

Figure 17.2 — **Assets of Major Financial Institutions**

Source: Insurance Information Institute, *2009 Financial Services Fact Book*, http://www.iii.org, accessed February 19, 2009.

Commercial Banks

Commercial banks are the largest and probably most important financial institution in the United States, and in most other countries as well. In the United States today, the approximately 7,300 commercial banks have total assets of roughly $11.1 trillion. Commercial banks offer the most services of any financial institution. These services include a wide range of checking and savings deposit accounts, consumer loans, credit cards, home mortgage loans, business loans, and trust services. Commercial banks also sell other financial products, including securities and insurance.

Although 7,300 may sound like a lot of banks, the number of banks has actually declined dramatically in recent years; 25 years ago there were 14,000 commercial banks. At the same time, banks have grown larger: today, the typical commercial bank is about five times as large as it was ten years ago. Both changes can be explained by the fact that bank mergers are commonplace.

Although the overall trend in the banking industry has been toward fewer, larger banks, a countertrend has also emerged: the growth of small community banks. It is not uncommon for several dozen of these banks to begin operation in any one year. Community banks typically serve a single city or county and have millions, rather than billions, of dollars in assets and deposits. Many consumers and small-business owners prefer smaller banks because they believe they offer a higher level of personal service and often pay lower fees.

HOW BANKS OPERATE Banks raise funds by offering a variety of checking and savings deposits to customers. The banks then pool these deposits and lend most of them out in the form of consumer and business loans. At the end of a recent year, banks held roughly $7.3 trillion in deposits and had about $6.5 trillion in outstanding loans.[6] The distribution of outstanding loans is shown in Figure 17.3. As the figure shows, banks lend a great deal of money to both households and businesses for a variety of purposes. Commercial banks are an especially important source of funds for small businesses. When evaluating loan applications, banks consider the borrower's ability and willingness to repay the loan. Occasionally, banks reject applications. The "Business Etiquette" features details the right and wrong way to handle a loan rejection.

Banks make money primarily because the interest rate they charge borrowers is higher than the rate of interest they pay depositors. Banks also make money from other sources, such as fees charged customers for checking accounts and using automated teller machines. Fees and other noninterest income now make up around one-third of total bank revenue.

ELECTRONIC BANKING More and more funds each year move through electronic funds transfer systems (EFTSs), computerized systems for

Despite the recent trend toward consolidation of the banking industry, small community banks have been growing in importance. Many customers prefer the personal service offered by local institutions like Park National Bank.

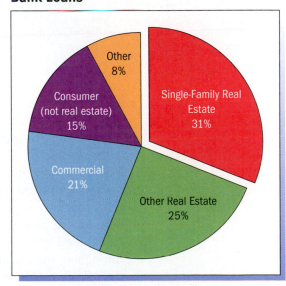

Figure 17.3

Distribution of Outstanding Commercial Bank Loans

- Single-Family Real Estate 31%
- Other Real Estate 25%
- Commercial 21%
- Consumer (not real estate) 15%
- Other 8%

Source: Federal Deposit Insurance Corporation (FDIC), "Statistics on Banking," http://www.fdic.gov, accessed February 19, 2009.

Business Etiquette

When the Answer Is "No"

As a consumer or small business owner, at some point in your career you will apply for credit. Whether it's a car loan, a mortgage, a credit card, or a small business loan, you are borrowing someone else's money for a certain length of time at a specified interest rate. Naturally, you assume that the bank or other financial institution would be delighted to lend you the amount you request; you know you are a responsible person, and you have every intention of repaying the loan. But a lot of factors are considered when making loans, and you might be declined for any number of reasons. If this happens to you, don't take it personally. Instead, follow these tips for handling the word "no"—and ultimately turning the answer into a "yes."

1. *Know your rights.* When you apply for a credit card or loan, you have certain rights. This does *not* mean that the institution must lend you money. But the Fair Credit Reporting Act requires the lender to follow certain procedures when evaluating your application. For example, you have the right to ask for your credit score, and you have the right to know what information is in your file. For more information visit the Federal Trade Commission's Web site at http://www.ftc.gov/credit.

2. *Find out why you were denied.* By law, the lender must explain in writing within 30 days of your application why your loan was turned down. It may be something as simple as the fact that you have not been employed long enough, or you may have too many outstanding debts.

3. *Review your credit history.* Make sure you have made previous payments on time and that you haven't forgotten to pay a bill. This includes doctor's bills and rent, in addition to credit card bills. If you do not think your credit score is accurate, you may dispute it. Visit http://ftc.gov/credit for further information. If you owe payments on several credit cards, take the time to pay them off before applying for another loan. Make sure your other bills are paid as well.

4. *Apply to another lender.* Not every lender has the same standards, and you might have been turned down for reasons beyond your control—for example, if the institution has already issued its quota of loans for a certain period of time.

5. *Find out what would make your finances more attractive to a lender.* It's all right to ask the lender what steps you can take to improve your chances of being granted a loan or credit. Criteria might include obtaining a full-time job, having a certain amount of cash flow, carrying no other debts, and securing a secondary source of repayment. If you are looking for money to help start a small business venture, you want to be able to present a strong business plan and management team and find a lender with whom you can develop a long-term business relationship.

Sources: "A Summary of Your Rights Under the Fair Credit Reporting Act," FTC Web site, http://www.ftc.gov/credit, accessed March 31, 2009; "Managing Your Banker Relationship: It Does Matter!" *The Daniel Group*, http://www.danielgroup.com, accessed October 21, 2008; "Mortgage Center," *Yahoo! Finance*, http://loan.yahoo.com, accessed October 21, 2008; Robert A. Woods, "When Your Banker Says 'No'," Busop1.com, http://www.busop1.com, accessed October 21, 2008; "Managing Credit Tutorial," *SmartEdge*, http://www.gmacfs.com, accessed October 21, 2008; Robert Rosen, "Know How: Bank on It," Worcester Business Journal, November 26, 2007, http://wbjournal.com, accessed October 21, 2008.

conducting financial transactions over electronic links. Millions of businesses and consumers now pay bills and receive payments electronically. Most employers, for example, directly deposit employee paychecks in their bank accounts, rather than issuing employees paper checks. Today nearly all Social Security checks and other federal payments made each year arrive as electronic data rather than paper documents.

One of the original forms of electronic banking, the automated teller machine (ATM), continues to grow in popularity. ATMs allow customers to make banking transactions at any time by inserting an electronic card into the machine and entering a personal identification number. Networked systems enable ATM users to access their bank accounts in distant states and even throughout the world. Most banks now offer customers debit cards—also called *check cards*—that allow customers to make purchases directly from their checking or savings account. A debit card looks like a credit card but acts like a check and replaces the customer's ATM card. Many large retailers—including Home Depot, Supervalu, Target, Wal-Mart, and Walgreen's—have installed special terminals that allow customers to use their ATM or debit cards to make purchases. Customers are required to enter their personal identification numbers and can often get cash back. Consumers enjoy the convenience of this feature; at the same time, it eliminates the problem of bad checks for retailers. The number of annual ATM and debit card transactions is expected to exceed 42.5 billion within the next couple of years.[7]

ONLINE BANKING Today, many consumers do some or all of their banking on the Internet. According to one survey, more than one-third of American households use some online banking services regularly.[8] Two types of online banks exist: Internet-only banks, such as ING Direct, and traditional brick-and-mortar banks with Web sites, such as JPMorgan Chase and Citibank. A major reason people are attracted to online banking is convenience. Customers can transfer money, check account balances, and pay bills at any time.

FEDERAL DEPOSIT INSURANCE Most commercial bank deposits are insured by the **Federal Deposit Insurance Corporation (FDIC),** a federal agency. Deposit insurance means that, in the event the bank fails, insured depositors are paid in full by the FDIC, up to $250,000. The amount was increased (up from $100,000) as a result of the 2008 financial panic. Federal deposit insurance was enacted by the Banking Act of 1933 as one of the measures designed to restore public confidence in the banking system. Before deposit insurance, so-called *runs* were common as people rushed to withdraw their money from a bank, often just on a rumor that the bank was in precarious financial condition. With more and more withdrawals in a short period, the bank was eventually unable to meet customer demands and closed its doors. Remaining depositors often lost most of the money they had in the bank. Deposit insurance shifts the risk of bank failures from individual depositors to the FDIC. Although banks still fail today, no insured depositor has ever lost any money.

Federal Deposit Insurance Corporation (FDIC) government agency that insures deposits at commercial and savings banks.

Savings Banks and Credit Unions

Commercial banks are by far the largest depository financial institution in the United States, but savings banks and credit unions also serve a significant segment of the financial community. Today savings banks and credit unions offer many of the same services as commercial banks.

Savings banks used to be called *savings and loan associations* or *thrift institutions*. They were originally established in the early 1800s to make home mortgage loans. Savings and loans originally raised funds by accepting only savings deposits and then lent these funds to consumers to buy homes. Today, there are around 1,250 savings banks with total assets of about $1.9 trillion.[9] Although savings banks offer many of the same services as commercial banks, including checking accounts, they are not major lenders to businesses. More than 85 percent of their outstanding loans are real estate loans.[10] Deposits in savings banks are now FDIC insured.

Credit unions are cooperative financial institutions that are owned by their depositors, all of whom are members. Around 85 million Americans belong to one of the nation's approximately 8,100 credit unions. Combined, credit unions have more than $750 billion in assets.[11] By law, credit union members must share similar occupations, employers, or membership in certain organizations. This law effectively caps the size of credit unions. In fact, the nation's largest bank—Bank of America—holds more deposits than all the country's credit unions combined. The "Hit & Miss" feature profiles the nation's largest credit union, Navy Federal Credit Union.

Credit unions are designed to serve consumers, not businesses. Credit unions raise funds by offering members a number of demand and saving deposits—checking accounts at credit unions are referred to as share draft accounts—and then, in turn, lend these funds to members. Because credit unions are not-for-profit institutions, they often pay savers higher rates of interest, charge lower rates of interest on loans, and have fewer fees than other financial institutions. Credit unions can have either state or federal charters, and deposits are insured by a federal agency, the National Credit Union Administration (NCUA), which functions essentially the same way that the FDIC does.

Hit & Miss

Navy Federal Gets It Right on Time

In business, timing can be everything. During the recent subprime mortgage lending fiasco, Navy Federal Credit Union didn't change its course. The firm didn't participate in the practice of subprime lending, considering those loans too risky. Instead, it continued to lend money to its members for homes, autos, and education. Navy Federal is regularly audited by an independent firm, and it provides guidance to members about the right loan products for them. So when other lending institutions began to falter, Navy Federal remained in a sound financial position. And as other lenders reduced the number of products they offered, Navy Federal was able to add new products, such as its Active Duty Choice mortgage.

Navy Federal was founded in 1933 by seven civilian Navy personnel and has since grown to more than 3 million members, making it one of the largest credit unions in the world. NFCU provides U.S. Navy and Marine Corps personnel and their families with a variety of financial services, ranging from personal checking accounts and credit cards to insurance and mortgages. "Once a member, always a member," promises the NFCU, which means that even if a member of the military becomes a civilian, the privileges afforded by the NFCU remain. Its business practices have helped it weather a number of economic storms, including the subprime mortgage crisis.

In addition to a focus on its borrowers, NCFU thinks about its employees. To create a better work environment, NCFU built a corporate campus that has received praise and an award for its "green" operations. When senior vice president of construction and improvements Ebb Ebbeson started the project, he wasn't trying to make an environmental statement. "There was no sustainability road map at the time," he concedes. But turnover among certain groups of employees, in particular the phone operators, was so high that the firm decided changes were necessary. Ebbeson and his team discovered that sustainable architecture met the needs of their assignment, so they pursued it with military vigor. The plan not only created a more healthful environment for employees but also saved NFCU money and earned the firm the coveted LEED rating for sustainability. All around, the new campus represents good business. "We're not fooling around here," says Ebbeson. "This is serious business. We can't afford to be down for an hour or half a day." The new campus features state-of-the-art green building technologies and provides spacious, sunny, and beautiful workplaces. Employees are happier at work, NFCU has posted significant savings on energy, and it still makes sensible loans to qualified members. It's a firm that plans on being around for a long, long time.

Questions for Critical Thinking

1. What is the difference between a credit union like NFCU and a bank?
2. NFCU did not yield to the trend toward riskier loans. While it's easy to say that this was the right choice to make, are there any conditions under which you think it might be a good business decision to take the risk? Explain your answer.

Sources: "About Navy Federal," company Web site, http://www.navyfcu.org, accessed March 31, 2009; "Navy Federal Credit Union Is Making Its Mark within the Financial Services Industry," *PR Newswire*, January 17, 2008, http://www.prnewswire.com; Andrew Blum, "The Accidental Environmentalists," *MetropolisMag*, January 16, 2008, http://www.metropolismag.com, accessed October 21, 2008; Helen Walters, "Navy Federal Credit Union," *BusinessWeek*, November 28, 2007, http://www.businessweek.com, accessed October 21, 2008.

Nondepository Financial Institutions

Nondepository financial institutions accept funds from businesses and households, much of which they then invest. Generally, these institutions do not offer checking accounts (demand deposits). Three examples of nondepository financial institutions are insurance companies, pension funds, and finance companies.

INSURANCE COMPANIES Households and businesses buy insurance to transfer risk from themselves to the insurance company. The insurance company accepts the risk in return for a series of payments, called *premiums*. Underwriting is the process insurance companies use to determine whom to insure and what to charge. During a typical year, insurance companies collect more in premiums than they pay in claims. After they pay operating expenses, they invest this difference.

Insurance companies are a major source of short- and long-term financing for businesses. Life insurance companies alone have total assets of more than $4.7 trillion invested in everything from bonds and stocks to real estate.[12] Examples of life insurers include Prudential and New York Life.

PENSION FUNDS Pension funds provide retirement benefits to workers and their families. They are set up by employers and are funded by regular contributions made by employers and employees. Because pension funds have predictable long-term cash inflows and very predictable cash outflows, they invest heavily in assets, such as common stocks and real estate. By some estimates, more than 25 percent of all common stocks are owned by pension funds. In total, pension funds have more than $8.5 trillion in assets.[13]

FINANCE COMPANIES Consumer and commercial finance companies, such as Ford Credit, John Deere Capital Corporation, and Pennsylvania-based Dollar Financial, offer short-term loans to borrowers. A commercial finance company supplies short-term funds to businesses that pledge tangible assets such as inventory, accounts receivable, machinery, or property as collateral for the loan. A consumer finance company plays a similar role for consumers. Finance companies raise funds by selling securities or borrowing funds from commercial banks. Many finance companies, such as GMAC, are actually subsidiaries of a manufacturer. GMAC finances dealer inventories of new cars and trucks, as well as provides loans to consumers and other buyers of General Motors products.

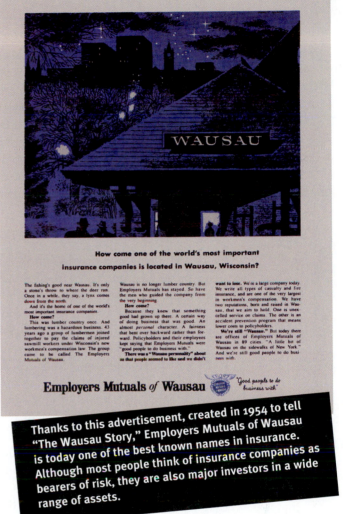

Thanks to this advertisement, created in 1954 to tell "The Wausau Story," Employers Mutuals of Wausau is today one of the best known names in insurance. Although most people think of insurance companies as bearers of risk, they are also major investors in a wide range of assets.

PRNewsFoto/NewsCom

Mutual Funds

One of the most significant types of financial institutions today is the mutual fund. **Mutual funds** are financial intermediaries that raise money from investors by selling shares. They then use the money by investing in securities that are consistent with the mutual fund's objectives. For example, a stock mutual fund invests mainly in shares of common stocks. Mutual funds have become extremely popular over the last few decades. The United States's more than 8,000 mutual funds have more than $12 trillion in assets and almost 300 million shareholder accounts; 20 years ago, there were fewer than 3,000 funds with a total of $800 billion in assets. One reason for this growth is the increased popularity of 401(k) and similar types of retirement plans. It is estimated that well over half of all 401(k) assets are invested in mutual fund shares.[14]

Mutual fund investors are indirect owners of a portfolio of securities. As the value of the securities owned by the mutual fund changes, so too will the value of the mutual fund's shares. Moreover, investment income such as bond interest and stock dividends are passed through to fund shareholders.

About half of mutual fund assets, around $6.5 trillion, are invested in stock funds. Money market mutual funds—those that invest in money market instruments such as commercial paper—are also popular. These funds have total assets of around $3 trillion.[15]

Assessment Check ✔

1. What are the two main types of financial institutions?
2. What are the primary differences between commercial banks and savings banks?
3. What is a mutual fund?

The Role of the Federal Reserve

Federal Reserve System (Fed) the U.S. central bank.

Created in 1913, the **Federal Reserve System,** or **Fed,** is the central bank of the United States and is an important part of the nation's financial system. The Fed has four basic responsibilities: regulating commercial banks, performing banking-related activities for the U.S. Department of the Treasury, providing services for banks, and setting monetary policy. Not all banks belong to the Fed. Banks with federal charters are required to belong to the Fed, but membership is optional for state-chartered banks. Because the largest banks in the country are all federally chartered, the bulk of banking assets is controlled by Fed members. The Fed acts as the banker's bank for members. It provides wire transfer facilities, clears checks, replaces worn-out currency, and lends banks money.

Organization of the Federal Reserve System

The nation is divided into 12 federal reserve districts, each with its own federal reserve bank. Each district bank supplies banks within its district with currency and facilitates the clearing of checks. District banks are run by a nine-member board of directors, headed by a president.

The governing body of the Fed is the board of governors. The board consists of seven members, including a chair and vice chair, appointed by the president and confirmed by the Senate. A full term for a Fed governor is 14 years. If a governor serves a full term, he or she cannot be reappointed. A governor can be reappointed if he or she was initially appointed to an unexpired term. The chair and vice chair serve in that capacity for four years and can be reappointed. The chair of the board of governors is a very important position. Some have commented, only half jokingly, that the Fed chair is the second most powerful person in the nation.

The Fed is designed to be politically independent. Terms for Fed governors are staggered in such a way that a president could not appoint a majority of members, assuming that all members serve their entire terms. The Fed also has its own sources of revenue and does not depend on congressional appropriations.

An important part of the Fed is the **Federal Open Markets Committee (FOMC).** The FOMC sets most policies concerning monetary policy and interest rates. It consists of 12 members—the 7 Fed board governors plus 5 representatives of the district banks, who serve on a rotating basis. The Fed chair is also chair of the FOMC.

Check Clearing and the Fed

As mentioned earlier, one of the Fed's responsibilities is to help facilitate the clearing of checks. Even in this age of electronic and online banking, Americans still write billions of paper checks each year. The clearing of a check is the process by which funds are transferred from the check writer to the recipient.

Assume the owner of Gulf View Townhouses of Tampa buys a $600 carpet cleaner from the local Home Depot and writes a check. If Home Depot has an account at the same bank as Gulf View, the bank will clear the check in-house. It will decrease the balance in the owner's account by $600 and increase the balance in Home Depot's account by $600. If Home Depot has an account at another bank in Tampa, the two banks may still clear the check directly with one another. This process is cumbersome, however, so it is more likely that the banks will use the services of a local check clearinghouse.

But if Home Depot has its account with a bank in another state—perhaps in Atlanta, where Home Depot is based—the check will likely be cleared through the Federal Reserve System. Home Depot will deposit the check in its Atlanta bank account. Its bank, in turn, will deposit the check in the Federal Reserve Bank of Atlanta. The Atlanta Federal Reserve bank will present the check to Gulf View's bank for payment, which pays the check by deducting $600 from Gulf View's account. Regardless of the method used, the Check Clearing for the 21st Century Act allows banks and the Fed to use electronic images of checks—rather than the paper documents themselves—during the clearing process. Because these images are transferred electronically, the time it takes to clear a check has been reduced substantially, often to less than 48 hours.

Monetary Policy

The Fed's most important function is controlling the supply of money and credit, or monetary policy. The Fed's job is to make sure that the money supply grows at an appropriate rate, allowing the economy to expand and inflation to remain in check. If the money supply grows too slowly, economic growth will slow, unemployment will increase, and the risk of a recession will increase. If the money supply grows too rapidly, inflationary pressures will build. The Fed uses its policy tools to push interest rates up or down. If the Fed pushes interest rates up, the growth rate in the money supply will slow, economic growth will slow, and inflationary pressures will ease. If the Fed pushes interest rates down, the growth rate in the money supply will increase, economic growth will pick up, and unemployment will fall.

Two common measures of the money supply exist, called M1 and M2. M1 consists of currency in circulation and balances in bank checking accounts. M2 equals M1 plus balances in some savings accounts and money market mutual funds. Figure 17.4 shows the approximate breakdowns of M1 and M2. The Fed has four major policy tools for controlling the growth in the supply of money and credit: reserve requirements, the discount rate, open market operations, and Term Auction Facility loans.

The Fed requires banks to maintain reserves—defined as cash in their vaults plus deposits at district Federal Reserve banks or other banks—equal to a certain percentage of what the banks hold in deposits. For example, if the Fed sets the reserve requirement at 5 percent, a bank that receives a $500 deposit must reserve $25, so it has only $475 to invest or lend to individuals or businesses. By changing the reserve requirement, the Fed can affect the amount of money available for making loans. The higher the reserve requirement, the less banks can lend out to consumers and businesses. The lower the reserve requirement, the more banks can lend out. Because any change in the reserve requirement can have a sudden and dramatic impact on the money supply, the Fed rarely uses this tool. In fact, the Fed has not changed reserve requirements in more than ten years. Reserve requirements range from 0 to 10 percent, depending on the type of account.

Another policy tool is the so-called *discount rate,* the interest rate at which Federal Reserve banks make short-term loans to member banks. A bank might need a short-term loan if transactions leave it short of reserves. If the Fed wants to slow the growth

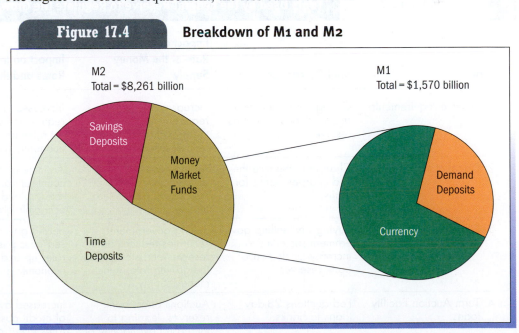

Figure 17.4   **Breakdown of M₁ and M₂**

M2
Total = $8,261 billion

Savings Deposits

Money Market Funds

Time Deposits

M1
Total = $1,570 billion

Demand Deposits

Currency

Source: Board of Govenors of the Federal Reserve System, *Federal Reserve Bulletin,* http://www.federalreserve.gov, accessed February 20, 2009.

rate in the money supply, it increases the discount rate. This increase makes it more expensive for banks to borrow funds. Banks, in turn, raise the interest rates they charge on loans to consumers and businesses. The end result is a slowdown in economic activity. Lowering the discount rate has the opposite effect.

The third policy tool, and the one used most often, is **open market operations,** the technique of controlling the money supply growth rate by buying or selling U.S. Treasury securities. If the Fed buys Treasury securities, the money it pays enters circulation, increasing the money supply and lowering interest rates. When the Fed sells Treasury securities, money is taken out of circulation and interest rates rise. When the Fed uses open market operations it employs the so-called *federal funds rate*—the rate at which banks lend money to one another overnight—as its benchmark.

A relatively new monetary policy tool is the *Term Auction Facility.* In these auctions, the Fed makes extra funds available to banks at low interest rates. A recent auction resulted in the Fed making $50 billion of 28-day loans to banks.[16] The more funds the Fed offers, and the lower the rate, the greater the impact on market interest rates, the supply of credit, and economic activity. Table 17.3 illustrates how the tools used by the Federal Reserve can stimulate or slow the economy.

The Federal Reserve has the authority to exercise selective credit controls when it thinks the economy is growing too rapidly or too slowly. These credit controls include the power to set margin requirements—the percentage of the purchase price of a security that an investor must pay in cash on credit purchases of stocks or bonds.

The Fed can also inject capital into the financial system in response to a financial crisis. During the recent 2008 credit crisis, the Fed pumped hundreds of billions of dollars into the financial system. The Fed even came to the rescue of AIG, a major insurance company, by purchasing some of the firm's stock.

Table 17.3	Tools Used by the Federal Reserve to Regulate the Growth in the Money Supply			
Tool	Brief Description	Impact on the Growth Rate of the Money Supply	Impact on Interest Rates and the Economy	Frequency of Use
1. Reserve requirements	Change in the percentage of deposits held as reserves.	Increases in reserve requirements slow the growth rate in the money supply.	Increases in reserve requirements push interest rates up and slow economic growth.	Rarely used.
2. Discount rate	Change in the rate the Fed charges banks for loans.	An increase in the discount rate slows the growth rate in the money supply.	An increase in the discount rate pushes interest rates up and slows economic growth.	Used only in conjunction with open market operations.
3. Open market operations	Buying and selling government securities to increase or decrease bank reserves.	Selling government securities reduces bank reserves and slows the growth rate in the money supply.	Selling government securities pushes interest rates up and slows economic growth.	Used frequently.
4. Term Auction Facility loans	Fed auctions 28-day loans to banks.	Auctions boost bank reserves, leading to increased availability of credit.	Increased availability of credit pushes interest rates lower and spurs economic activity.	Relatively new; used frequently when first introduced.

Transactions in the foreign exchange markets also affect the U.S. money supply and interest rates. The Fed can lower the exchange value of the dollar by selling dollars and buying foreign currencies, and it can raise the dollar's exchange value by doing the opposite—buying dollars and selling foreign currencies. When the Fed buys foreign currencies, the effect is the same as buying securities because it increases the U.S. banking system's reserves. Selling foreign currencies, on the other hand, is like selling securities, in that it reduces bank reserves.

Regulation of the Financial System

Given the importance of the financial system, it is probably not surprising that many components are subject to government regulation and oversight. In addition, industry self-regulation is commonplace.

Bank Regulation

Banks are among the nation's most heavily regulated businesses. The main purpose of bank regulation is to ensure public confidence in the safety and security of the banking system. Banks are critical to the overall functioning of the economy, and a collapse of the banking system can have disastrous results. Many believe that one of the major causes of the Great Depression was the collapse of the banking system that started in the late 1920s.

All banks, whether commercial or savings, and credit unions have either state or federal charters. Most commercial banks are state chartered; however, federally chartered banks control more than half of all banking assets. State-chartered banks are regulated by the appropriate state banking authorities; federally chartered commercial banks are regulated by the Federal Reserve, the Federal Deposit Insurance Corporation, and the Comptroller of the Currency. Furthermore, state-chartered commercial banks that are federally insured—and virtually all are—are also subject to FDIC regulation.

At the federal level, savings banks are regulated by the Office of Thrift Supervision and the FDIC. Federal credit unions are subject to NCUA regulation. State-chartered savings banks and credit unions are also regulated by state authorities.

Banks and credit unions are subject to periodic examination by state or federal regulators. Examinations ensure that the institution is following sound banking practices and is complying with all applicable regulations. These examinations include the review of detailed reports on the bank's operating and financial condition, as well as on-site inspections. Regulators can impose various penalties on institutions deemed not in compliance with sound banking practices, including forcing the delinquent financial institution into a merger with a healthier one.

Government Regulation of the Financial Markets

Regulation of U.S. financial markets is primarily a function of the federal government, although states also regulate them. Federal regulation grew out of various trading abuses during the 1920s. To restore confidence and stability in the financial markets after the 1929 stock market crash, Congress passed a series of landmark legislative acts that have formed the basis of federal securities regulation ever since.

As noted in Chapter 16, the U.S. Securities and Exchange Commission, created in 1934, is the principal federal regulatory overseer of the securities markets. The SEC's mission is to administer securities laws and protect investors in public securities transactions. The SEC has broad enforcement power. It can pursue civil actions against individuals and corporations, but actions requiring criminal proceedings are referred to the U.S. Justice Department.

The SEC requires virtually all new public issues of corporate securities to be registered. As part of the registration process for a new security issue, the issuer must prepare a prospectus. The typical prospectus gives a fairly detailed description of the company issuing the securities, including financial data, products, research and development projects, and pending litigation. It also describes the stock or bond issue and underwriting agreement in detail. The registration process seeks to guarantee full and fair disclosure. The SEC does not rule on the investment merits of a registered security. It is concerned only that an issuer gives investors enough information to make their own informed decisions.

Besides primary market registration requirements, SEC regulation extends to the secondary markets as well, keeping tabs on trading activity to make sure it is fair to all participants. Every securities exchange must by law follow a set of trading rules that have been approved by the SEC. In addition, the Market Reform Act of 1990 gave the SEC emergency authority to halt trading and restrict practices such as program trading—when computer systems are programmed to buy or sell securities if certain conditions arise—during periods of extreme volatility.

insider trading use of material nonpublic information to make investment profits.

One area to which the SEC pays particular attention is insider trading. **Insider trading** is defined as the use of material nonpublic information about a company to make investment profits. Examples of material nonpublic information include a pending merger or a major oil discovery, which could affect the business's stock price. The SEC's definition of insider trading goes beyond corporate insiders—people such as the company's officers and directors. It includes lawyers, accountants, investment bankers, and even reporters—anyone who uses nonpublic information to profit in the stock market at the expense of ordinary investors. While some actions or communications are clearly insider trading, others are more ambiguous. Consequently, all employees of public companies have to be mindful of what is and isn't permitted.

Securities laws also require every public corporation to file several reports each year with the SEC; the contents of these reports become public information. The best known, of course, is the annual report. Public corporations prepare annual reports for their shareholders, and they file another report containing essentially the same information, Form 10-K, with the SEC. The SEC requires additional reports each time certain company officers and directors buy or sell a company's stock for their own accounts (Form 4) or anytime an investor accumulates more than 5 percent of a company's outstanding stock (Form 13-d). All of these reports are available for viewing and download at the Free Edgar Web site (http://www.freeedgar.com).

The Securities and Exchange Commission is a governmental agency charged with regulating financial markets. Its Web site featured here is a good source of information for would-be investors.

Industry Self-Regulation

The securities markets are also heavily self-regulated by professional associations and the major financial markets. The securities industry recognizes that rules and regulations designed to ensure fair and orderly markets promote investor confidence and benefit all participants. Two examples of self-regulation are the rules of conduct established by the various professional organizations and the market surveillance techniques used by the major securities markets.

PROFESSIONAL RULES OF CONDUCT Prodded initially by federal legislation, the National Association of Securities Dealers (NASD) established and periodically updates rules of conduct for members—both individuals and firms. These rules try to ensure that brokers perform their basic functions honestly and fairly, under constant supervision. Failure to adhere to rules of conduct can result in disciplinary actions. The NASD also established a formal arbitration procedure through which investors can attempt to resolve disputes with brokers without litigation.

MARKET SURVEILLANCE All securities markets use a variety of methods to spot possible violations of trading rules or securities laws. For example, the NYSE continuously monitors trading activity throughout the trading day. A key technical tool used by the NYSE is called Stock Watch, an electronic monitoring system that flags unusual price and volume activity. The NYSE then seeks explanations for unusual activity from the member firms and companies involved. In addition, all market participants must keep detailed records of every aspect of every trade (called an *audit trail*). The NYSE's enforcement division may impose a variety of penalties on members for rule violations. In addition, the exchange turns over evidence to the SEC for further action if it believes that violations of federal securities laws may have occurred.

While industry self-regulation has been an important component of securities market regulation, some contend that the industry can never truly regulate itself effectively in today's market environment. The "Solving an Ethical Controversy" feature debates the pros and cons of industry self-regulation.

In Frankfurt, Germany, a sculpture of the euro—the symbol for the European Union's currency—stands outside the headquarters of Europe's central bank. The 12 gold stars represent all the peoples of Europe.

Alex Grimm/Reuters/Landov LLC

Assessment Check

1. Who regulates banks?
2. Define *insider trading*.
3. List two ways in which the securities markets are self-regulated.

The Financial System: A Global Perspective

Not surprisingly, the global financial system is becoming more and more integrated each year. As we've noted, financial markets exist throughout the world. Shares of U.S. firms trade in other countries while shares of international companies trade in the United States. In fact, investors in China and Japan own more U.S. Treasury securities than do domestic investors.

Financial institutions have also become a global industry. Major U.S. banks—such as JPMorgan Chase and Bank of America—have extensive international operations. They have offices, lend money, and accept deposits from customers throughout the world. According to recent statistics, U.S. banks have more than $200 billion in outstanding loans to international customers.

Although most Americans recognize large U.S. banks such as Citibank among the global financial giants, only 3 of the 30 largest banks in the world (measured by total assets) are U.S. institutions—Bank of America, Citibank, and JPMorgan Chase—and the largest of the three, Bank of America, ranks only tenth. The other 27 are based in Belgium, China, France, Germany, Holland, Italy, Japan, Switzerland, and the United Kingdom. The world's largest bank, Swiss-based UBS AG, has almost $2 trillion in assets. These international banks also operate worldwide, including in the United States.[17]

Virtually all nations have some sort of a central bank, similar to the U.S. Federal Reserve. Examples include the Banks of

CAN THE SECURITIES INDUSTRY REGULATE ITSELF?

Since enactment of the Securities Act of 1933 and the Securities Exchange Act of 1934, securities regulation in the United States has been the combined responsibility of the government (primarily the Securities and Exchange Commission, or SEC) and industry self-regulatory organizations (often called SROs). Professional organizations, such as the National Association of Securities Dealers, along with the major financial markets formed the backbone of industry self-regulation. These SROs established rules for professional and ethical conduct. Individuals or firms that violate rules were subjected to a variety of penalties. The SEC, along with enforcing securities laws and regulations, also oversaw the functioning of SROs. This unique government–industry regulatory partnership was emulated by many other countries.

Arguments in favor of self-regulation, as opposed to government regulation, include added flexibility, minimized resistance by the industry, and expertise. Recently, however, the SEC, investor advocacy groups, and even members of the industry itself have begun to question the fairness and efficiency of securities industry self-regulation in light of market developments, new technologies, and growing global competition. Moreover, a number of other countries, such as Canada and the United Kingdom, have started to move away from self-regulation toward an increased role for government.

Can the securities industry adequately regulate itself?

PRO

1. Self-regulation has worked well in the United States for more than 70 years. The U.S. financial markets are considered to be among the fairest and most open in the world.
2. The securities industry has a strong economic incentive to guarantee that all investors are treated in a fair and ethical manner. The industry is best equipped to enforce such guarantees.

CON

1. Many small investors believe that self-regulation is not designed to protect them from Wall Street, but rather to protect Wall Street from them. The system, some argue, favors large investors and insiders at the expense of small investors.
2. SROs are almost entirely financed by the industry, raising questions about their independence and effectiveness. This financing arrangement also creates a potential conflict of interest.

Summary

At this point, there seems little question that the SEC will revise the ways in which the securities industry regulates itself. While some industry self-regulation will likely remain, it is equally likely that the scale and scope of government oversight will increase.

Sources: "Self Regulation in Today's Securities Markets," Centre for Financial Market Integrity, CFA Institute, http://www.cfainstitute.org, accessed March 31, 2009; "SEC Publishes Regulatory Actions to Streamline SRO Rule Filing Process," Securities and Exchange Commission press release, July 3, 2008, http://www.sec.gov, accessed September 28, 2008; Doug Halonen, "SEC Plan Could Cost Managers," *Pensions and Investments*, March 31, 2008, http://www.pionline.com, accessed September 28, 2008; Ross Kerber, "Probe Is Not a Clear Loss for Fidelity," *The Boston Globe*, March 7, 2008, http://www.boston.com, accessed September 28, 2008; Jonathan Chevreau, "Protecting Bay Street from You," *The Financial Post*, November 3, 2007, http://www.lexisnexis.com, accessed September 28, 2008; Sara Hansard, "Report: Independent SRO Needed for Global Markets, Exchanges," *Investment News*, October 1, 2007, http://www.lexisnexis.com, accessed September 28, 2008.

Solving an **ETHICAL** controversy

Canada, England, and Japan and the European Central Bank. These central banks play roles much like the Fed, such as controlling the money supply and regulating banks. Policymakers at other nations' central banks often respond to changes in the U.S. financial system by making similar changes in their own systems. For example, if the Fed pushes U.S. interest rates lower, central banks in Japan and Europe may also push their interest rates lower.

These changes can influence events in countries around the world. Lower U.S. and European interest rates not only decrease the cost of borrowing for U.S. and European firms but also increase the amount of money available for loans to borrowers in other countries such as Chile and India.

What's Ahead

This chapter explored the financial system, a key component of the U.S. economy and something that affects many aspects of contemporary business. The financial system is the process by which funds are transferred between savers and borrowers and includes securities, financial markets, and financial institutions. The chapter also described the role of the Federal Reserve and discussed the global financial system. In the next chapter, we discuss the finance function of a business including the role of the financial managers, financial planning, asset management, and sources of short- and long-term funds.

Summary of Learning Goals

1 Outline the structure and importance of the financial system.

The financial system is the process by which funds are transferred between those having excess funds (savers) and those needing additional funds (users). Savers and users consist of individuals, businesses, and governments. Savers expect to earn a rate of return in exchange for the use of their funds. Financial markets, financial institutions, and financial instruments (securities) make up the financial system. While direct transfers are possible, most funds flow from savers to users through the financial markets or financial institutions, such as commercial banks. A well-functioning financial system is critical to the overall health of a nation's economy.

Assessment Check Answers

1.1 What is the financial system? The financial system is the process by which funds are transferred between those having excess funds (savers) and those needing additional funds (users).

1.2 In the financial system, who are the borrowers and who are the savers? Savers and borrowers consist of individuals, businesses, and governments. Generally, individuals are net savers, meaning they spend less than they make, while businesses and governments are net borrowers.

1.3 List the two most common ways in which funds are transferred between borrowers and savers. The two most common ways funds are transferred are through the financial markets and through financial institutions.

2 List the various types of securities.

Securities, also called *financial instruments,* represent obligations on the part of issuers—businesses and governments—to provide purchasers with expected or stated returns on the funds invested or loaned. Securities can be classified into three categories: money market instruments, bonds, and stock. Money market instruments and bonds are debt instruments. Money market instruments are short-term debt securities and tend to be low-risk securities. Bonds are longer-term debt securities and pay a fixed amount of interest each year. Bonds are sold by the U.S. Department of the Treasury (government bonds), state and local governments (municipal bonds), and corporations. Mortgage pass-through securities are bonds backed by a pool of mortgage loans. Most municipal and corporate bonds have risk ratings. Common stock represents ownership in corporations. Common stockholders have voting rights and a residual claim on the firm's assets.

Assessment Check Answers

2.1 What are the major types of securities? The major types of securities are money market instruments, bonds, and stock.

2.2 What is a government bond? A municipal bond? A government bond is one issued by the U.S. Treasury. Municipal bonds are issued by state and local governments.

2.3 Why do investors purchase common stock? There are two primary motives for purchasing common stock. One is to receive dividends, cash payments to shareholders by the firm. The other is potential price appreciation of the shares.

3 Define *financial market*, and distinguish between primary and secondary financial markets.

A financial market is market where securities are bought and sold. The primary market for securities serves businesses and governments that want to sell new security issues to raise funds. Securities are sold in the primary market either through an open auction or via a process called *underwriting*. The secondary market handles transactions of previously issued securities between investors. The New York Stock Exchange is a secondary market. The business or government that issued the security is not directly involved in secondary market transactions. In terms of the dollar value of trading volume, the secondary market is about four to five times larger than the primary market.

Assessment Check Answers

3.1 What is a financial market? A financial market is a market in which securities are bought and sold.

3.2 Distinguish between a primary and secondary financial market. The primary market for securities serves businesses and governments that want to sell new security issues to raise funds. The secondary market handles transactions of previously issued securities between investors.

3.3 Briefly explain the role of financial institutions in the sale of securities. Financial institutions purchase new securities issues from corporations or state and local governments and then resell the securities to investors. The institutions charge a fee for their services.

4 Describe the characteristics of the major stock exchanges.

The best known financial markets are the stock exchanges. They exist throughout the world. The two largest—the New York Stock Exchange and Nasdaq—are located in the United States. The NYSE is bigger, measured in terms of the total value of stock traded. Larger and better-known companies dominate the NYSE. Buy and sell orders are transmitted to the trading floor for execution. The Nasdaq stock market is an electronic market in which buy and sell orders are entered into a computerized communication system for execution. Most of the world's major stock markets today use similar electronic trading systems. They may represent the future stock markets.

Assessment Check Answers

4.1 What are the world's two largest stock markets? The world's two largest stock markets are the New York Stock Exchange and the Nasdaq stock market.

4.2 Why is the London Stock Exchange unique? The London Stock Exchange is probably the most international of the world's stock markets because a large percentage of the shares traded are not those of domestic firms.

4.3 Explain the difference between a market order and a limit order. A market order instructs the investor's broker to obtain the best possible price when buying or selling securities. A limit order sets a maximum price (if the investor wants to buy) or a minimum price (if the investor wants to sell).

5 Discuss the organization and functioning of financial institutions.

Financial institutions act as intermediaries between savers and users of funds. Depository institutions—commercial banks, savings banks, and credit unions—accept deposits from customers that can be redeemed on demand. Commercial banks are the largest and most important of the depository institutions offering the widest range of services. Savings banks are a major source of home mortgage loans. Credit unions are not-for-profit institutions offering financial services to consumers. Government agencies, most notably the FDIC, insure deposits at these institutions. Nondepository institutions include pension funds and insurance companies. Nondepository institutions invest a large portion of their funds in stocks, bonds, and real estate. Mutual funds are another important financial institution. These companies sell shares to investors and, in turn, invest the proceeds in securities. Many individuals today invest a large portion of their retirement savings in mutual fund shares.

Assessment Check Answers

5.1 What are the two main types of financial institutions? The two major types of financial institutions are depository institutions (those that accept checking and similar accounts) and nondepository institutions.

5.2 What are the primary differences between commercial banks and savings banks? Today commercial and savings banks offer many of the same services. However, commercial banks lend money to businesses, as well as individuals. Savings banks lend money primarily to individuals, principally in the form of home mortgage loans.

5.3 What is a mutual fund? A mutual fund is an intermediary that raises money by selling shares to investors. It then pools investor funds and purchases securities that are consistent with the fund's objectives.

6 Explain the functions of the Federal Reserve System and the tools it uses to control the supply of money and credit.

The Federal Reserve System is the central bank of the United States. The Federal Reserve regulates banks, performs banking functions for the U.S. Department of the Treasury, and acts as the banker's bank (clearing checks, lending money to banks, and replacing worn-out currency). It controls the supply of credit and money in the economy to promote growth and control inflation. The Federal Reserve's tools include reserve requirements, the discount rate, open market operations, and Term Auction Facility loans. Selective credit controls and purchases and sales of foreign currencies also help the Federal Reserve manage the economy.

Assessment Check Answers

6.1 What is the Federal Reserve? The Federal Reserve is the U.S. central bank. It is responsible for regulating banks, providing banking-related services for the federal government, acting as the banker's bank, and setting monetary policy.

6.2 How is the Fed organized? The country is divided into 12 districts, each of which has a Federal Reserve Bank. The Fed is run by a seven-member Board of Governors headed by a chair and vice chair. An important part of the Fed is the Federal Open Markets Committee, which sets monetary and interest rate policy. The Fed is designed to be politically independent.

6.3 List the four tools the Fed uses to control the supply of money and credit. The four tools are the following: reserve requirements, the discount rate, open market operations, and Term Auction Facility loans.

7 Evaluate the major features of regulations and laws affecting the financial system.

Commercial banks, savings banks, and credit unions in the United States are heavily regulated by federal or state banking authorities. Banking regulators require institutions to follow sound banking practices and have the power to close noncompliant ones. In the United States, financial markets are regulated at both the federal and state levels. Markets are also heavily self-regulated by the financial markets and professional organizations. The chief regulatory body is the Securities and Exchange Commission. It sets a number of requirements for both primary and secondary market activity, prohibiting a number of practices, including insider trading. The SEC also requires public companies to disclose financial information regularly. Professional organizations and the securities markets also have rules and procedures that all members must follow.

Assessment Check Answers

7.1 Who regulates banks? All banks have either state or federal charters. Federally chartered banks are regulated by the Federal Reserve, the FDIC, and the Comptroller of the Currency. State-chartered banks are regulated by state banking authorities and the FDIC.

7.2 Define *insider trading.* Insider trading is defined as the use of material nonpublic information to make an investment profit.

7.3 List two ways in which the securities markets are self-regulated. Professional organizations like the National Association of Securities Dealers have codes of conduct that members are expected to follow. Major financial markets have trading rules and procedures to identify suspicious trading activity.

8 Describe the global financial system.

Financial markets exist throughout the world and are increasingly interconnected. Investors in other countries purchase U.S. securities while U.S. investors purchase foreign securities. Large U.S. banks and other financial institutions have a global presence. They accept deposits, make loans, and have branches throughout the world. Foreign banks also operate worldwide. The average European or Japanese bank is much larger than the average American bank. Virtually all nations have central banks that perform the same roles as the U.S. Federal Reserve System. Central bankers often act together, raising and lowering interest rates as economic conditions warrant.

Assessment Check Answers

8.1 Where do U.S. banks rank compared with international banks? Banks in Asia and Europe are generally much larger than U.S. banks. In fact, only 3 out of the world's 30 largest banks are based in the United States.

8.2 Do other countries have organizations that play roles similar to those played by the Federal Reserve? Yes, all nations have central banks that perform many of the same functions that the U.S. Federal Reserve System does.

Business Terms You Need to Know

financial system 560	primary market 566	financial institution 570	Federal Reserve System
securities 561	secondary market 567	Federal Deposit Insurance	(Fed) 576
common stock 564	stock market (exchange)	Corporation (FDIC) 573	Insider trading 580
financial market 566	568		

Other Important Business Terms

money market instruments 562	subprime mortgage 563	convertible securities 566	mutual fund 575
government bonds 562	investment-grade bond 563	initial public offering (IPO) 566	Federal Open Markets Committee (FOMC) 576
municipal bonds 562	speculative (junk) bond 563	market order 570	open market operations 578
debenture 562	call provision 564	limit order 570	

Review Questions

1. What is the financial system? Why is the direct transfer of funds from savers to users rare?

2. What is a security? Give several examples.

3. List the major types of bonds. Explain a mortgage pass-through.

4. What are the differences between common stock and preferred stock?

5. Explain the difference between a primary financial market and a secondary financial market.

6. Compare and contrast the New York Stock Exchange and the Nasdaq stock market.

7. Why are commercial banks, savings banks, and credit unions classified as depository financial institutions? How do the three differ?

8. Why are life insurance companies, pension funds, and mutual funds considered financial institutions?

9. Briefly explain the role of the Federal Reserve and list the tools it uses to control the supply of money and credit.

10. What does bank regulation entail? Why are state-chartered banks also regulated by the FDIC?

11. Which federal agency is primarily responsible for regulating the financial markets?

12. Explain how the Federal Reserve, acting in conjunction with other central banks, could affect exchange rates.

Projects and Teamwork Applications

1. Collect current interest rates on the following types of bonds: U.S. Treasury bonds, AAA-rated municipal bonds, AAA-rated corporate bonds, and BBB-rated corporate bonds. Arrange the interest rates from lowest to highest. Explain the reasons for the ranking.

2. You've probably heard of U.S. savings bonds—you may even have received some bonds as a gift. What you may not know is that two different types of savings bonds exist. Do some research and compare and contrast the two types of savings bonds. What are their features? Their pros and cons? Assuming you were interested in buying savings bonds, which of the two do you find more attractive?

3. With a partner, assume you are considering buying shares of Lowe's or Home Depot. Describe how you would go about analyzing the stocks and deciding which, if either, you would buy.

4. Compared with most businesses, is a bank more vulnerable to failure? Why or why not? How does federal deposit insurance help protect the soundness of the banking system?

5. Working in a small team, identify a large bank. Visit that bank's Web site and obtain its most recent financial statements. Compare the bank's financial statements to those of a nonfinancial company, such as a manufacturer or retailer. Report on your findings.

6. Go to the MSN Money Web Site (http://moneycentral.msn.com). Click "Fund Research." Assume you're investing money for retirement. Specify several investment criteria you believe are most important. Identify at least three mutual funds that best meet your criteria. Choose one of the funds and research it. Answer the following questions:
   a. What was the fund's average annual return for the past five years?
   b. How well did the fund perform relative to its peer group and relative to an index such as the S&P 500?
   c. What are the fund's ten largest holdings?

7. An exchange rate is the rate at which one currency can be exchanged for another. Working with a partner, use the Internet to find the current exchange rate between the U.S. dollar and the following currencies: Australian dollar, euro, British pound, Japanese yen, and Brazilian real. Has the dollar been rising or falling in value relative to these currencies? Assume that there was general agreement that the dollar was "undervalued." Why would an increase in U.S. interest rates help increase the value of the dollar relative to other currencies? Explain how the Federal Reserve could push U.S. interest rates higher.

Web Assignments

1. **Stock market indexes.** One measure of the overall level of stock prices is the index. The best known indexes are the Dow Jones 30 and the Standard & Poor's 500. Visit the two Web sites listed here (www.djindexes.com; www2.standardandpoors.com/portal/site/sp/en/us/page) and research how both indexes are calculated. Prepare a brief report on your findings.

2. **Insider trading cases.** Visit the SEC's Web site (http://www.sec.gov) and review two current cases of alleged

insider trading. What firms are involved? Who is involved? What actions allegedly constituted insider trading?

3. **Online banking.** Visit your bank's Web site (or choose another bank). Make a list of the online services the bank offers and review the details. Do you currently do any banking online? Did a closer inspection of online banking services make you more or less inclined to do more banking transactions using your PC?

Note: Internet addresses change frequently. If you don't find the exact site listed, you may need to access the organization's or company's home page and search from there.

Vanguard: A Frontrunner with Investors

Case 17.1

The Vanguard Group is the top seller of mutual funds in the United States, with more than $1 trillion in assets. Although it isn't the world's largest mutual fund company—American Funds earned that title—it is still the best seller among U.S. consumers. Many credit Vanguard's recent offering of ETFs (exchange traded funds), which took in a net of nearly $17 billion in one year, as a significant contributor to the firm's success. But Michael Miller, managing director for planning and development at Vanguard, points to the value the company creates for its customers. "We believe back to the basics made a difference with shareholders," he says. "[It's] low cost and high value."

Vanguard is well known for providing affordable investment opportunities to the average consumer. "Vanguard is the low-cost leader in the mutual fund realm, and their ETFs are often the lowest-cost option," observes Dan Colluton, an analyst with mutual fund rating firm Morningstar. This strategy is particularly effective when the economy appears uncertain or when consumers lack the confidence to spend more. "People focus on cost more when returns are low in the market," explains Dan Wiener, editor of *The Independent Advisor* for Vanguard investors.

But Vanguard has suffered somewhat in recent years from the perception that it is something of a maverick in the investment industry. In particular, some financial advisors complain that Vanguard doesn't reach out to them with phone calls, e-mails, and other communications to provide information about its products. "I've probably gotten mail from Vanguard, but their efforts are noticeably less intensive than those of rivals such as Barclays or State Street Global Advisors," says Rick Miller, a financial planner. Mark Balasa, another advisor, agrees with Miller, remarking that Vanguard doesn't communicate much even when it launches new products. Unfortunately, this does not strengthen relationships with the advisors who could be offering Vanguard's products. "In some ways, we kind of dismissed them," concludes Balasa. While many agree that Vanguard falls short in this way, they are quick to agree on the value of Vanguard funds. "In the end, they have a great brand," admits Tom Lydon, president of Global Trends Investments.

"Are we perfect?" questions Vanguard chairman John J. Brennan. "No. Will we ask advisors if we can do better? Absolutely." In fact, Vanguard has launched a number of initiatives designed to help professionals, including the addition of new features to its advisor Web site to attract new clients, manage current clients, and even build their own careers. The firm holds financial symposiums for advisors and provides them with online services that allow them to earn education credits. If Vanguard handles this portion of its business well, it could create as much value for advisors as it does for their clients. [18]

Questions for Critical Thinking

1. Do you think it is just as important for Vanguard to reach out to financial advisors as it is to reach out to investors who want to buy its funds? Why or why not?

2. How does Vanguard create value for its clients?

Community Banks: Thriving in a Land of Giants

If you're like many U.S customers of the country's increasingly large banks, you transact business online, by phone, or by machine. You may not have seen a human bank teller in months. But small community banks are staging a quiet revolution aimed at bringing back the human touch. The movement has gained clout through trade organization America's Community Bankers (ACB), which was founded in 1892 under the name United States League of Local Building and Loan Associations.

Community banks play several important roles in the U.S. economy. They support small businesses, focus on lending to local businesses and individuals, emphasize the retail portion of their business (individuals and families), and offer personalized service. Sometimes small banks offer additional incentives such as a free tank of gas or a countertop grill for opening a new account. Other times, they provide affordable car loans for a college student. "When you provide customers with good service, a good rate of return on their deposits and also provide affordable loans for homeowners, then you have a simple recipe for success," explains Gary Nation, CEO of Central Federal Savings & Loan, a community bank in Illinois. While larger banks may be able to offer a greater variety of financial products, community banks offer more personal interaction. A local bank gets to know its community, its residents, and their needs—and is better able to serve them all. In many cases, the bank's employees live in the same town where the bank is located.

Community banks are also less likely to fail amid nationwide financial swings and crises. That's because they are generally well funded and conservative in their outlook. "We've always maintained a very strong capital position, which has allowed us to operate in shaky times," notes Rocky Seiler, CEO of Jackson Federal in Minnesota. His bank employs just five people and is one of only two banks in town. "We have to provide good service, because our competitors are a block away," he continues. Community banks are also less likely to offer risky or complex financial products such as subprime mortgage loans or derivative investments. "The business has changed somewhat, but we've remained ... focused on deposits and home loans," observes Gary Nation. "The principles of serving the customers have pretty much stayed the same."

Banks like Jackson Federal benefit from membership in America's Community Bankers through the organization's training programs and networking at conventions. ACB also gives small banks a voice in Congress at the national level that might otherwise go unheard. "We are effective because we are highly respected by people on the Hill and by the regulators," notes Mark Macomber of ACB. "They respect us for our currency, and after 115 years, that's something hard to maintain."[19]

Questions for Critical Thinking

1. In what ways do community banks do a better job of serving their customers than larger banks might be able to?
2. Why is an organization like ACB important to the banking industry?

Morgan Stanley Likes Educated Customers

Whether or not they have money invested in the securities market, people seem fascinated by the bulls and bears who make and lose fortunes. They enjoy a thrill when the market is riding high, and they hold their breath when the market takes a plunge. Investment firms like Morgan Stanley want their business customers to feel confident that their money is safely invested with them—and will gain them a handsome return over the long run. Regardless of an individual business's or consumer's investment objectives, from

growth in capital to growth in income, Morgan Stanley seeks to help its customers meet their financial goals.

Morgan Stanley is a global financial services company that holds significant market positions in three business segments: securities, asset management, and credit services, including credit cards and real-estate loans. Morgan Stanley offers a variety of investment instruments and services, from bond trading 24 hours a day, 5 days a week, to customized programs like NetWorth, in which a customer can gain access to all of his or her online account information on one secure Web page. With its wireless trading service called TradeRunner, customers can trade anytime, anywhere. The company even has a service called the Blue Chip Basket, in which a customer can buy ten stocks for a trading fee of $49.95. On the Web site alone, customers are offered free delayed quotes and graphs, a look at the 5,600 mutual funds located in the Mutual Fund Center, and access to historical analyses modeling that describes interesting market activity. All of these services have one aim in mind—convenience and value for customers, whatever their needs.

Because it is vital for investors to understand the information presented in stock, bond, and mutual fund quotations, the Morgan Stanley Web site offers an Investment Basics section to newcomers. The section offers a variety of information, including a glossary of terms such as *maturity, price-earnings ratio,* and *interest rates,* so customers can learn more about the financial markets. Such additional assistance helps new investors understand the information that is being provided to them when they look at their investment statements.

As the Internet continues to offer opportunities for financial services, Morgan Stanley has expanded its global online reach. The company has placed a total of 10,000 employees in 500 U.S. locations as well as Europe and Asia. "We'll be the benchmark for online buying in financial services," predicts Gerry Fitzmaurice, director of national purchasing from Morgan Stanley.

In spite of Morgan's strength and prominence, the firm found itself tested as never before by the 2008 credit crisis. Investors were so unnerved by the health of the financial industry that the value of Morgan Stanley's stock fell by more than 80 percent during the first nine months of 2008. Other giant investment firms—such as Bear Stearns and Merrill Lynch—were acquired by commercial banks while another, Lehman Brothers, ended up in bankruptcy. Morgan Stanley struggled to remain independent. It converted itself into a bank holding company, making it easier for the firm to borrow from the Federal Reserve. A large Japanese bank, Mitsubishi, bought a 20 percent stake in Morgan, providing a much needed injection of capital. Many investors viewed the deal as a sign of confidence in Morgan's future.

No one can truly predict what will happen to an economy in the future. It's like trying to pinpoint where a tornado will touch down or how many inches of rain will fall to feed bumper crops. The rises and falls of the stock market can seem as fickle as the weather. But economists at companies like Morgan Stanley need to act like meteorologists, using their knowledge, experience, financial tools, and the information they have at hand to help their customers make the best investment decisions possible. "We believe in educated customers," says one slogan on the firm's Web site. But the statement is more than a mere slogan; it is part of Morgan Stanley's goal to create enhanced value for its customers by teaching them what they need to know in order to become investment partners and make sound decisions and, ultimately, decisions about their future.[20]

Questions for Critical Thinking

1. How important is it for Morgan Stanley's customers to identify their investing objectives? In what ways might the firm help customers make this determination?

2. Would you feel comfortable making investments online? Why or why not?

3. Access the company's Web site at www.morganstanleyindividual.com, and check out the services and information that are offered. Do you find the site helpful and informative?

Goals

1 Define *finance,* and explain the role of financial managers.

2 Describe the components of a financial plan and the financial planning process.

3 Outline how organizations manage their assets.

4 Compare the two major sources of funds for a business, and explain the concept of leverage.

5 Identify sources of short-term financing for business operations.

6 Discuss long-term financing options.

7 Describe mergers, acquisitions, buyouts, and divestitures.

chapter

18

Financial Management

Digital Vision/Getty Images

Intel Places Its Chips on the Table—At Home

An old business saying advises, "It takes money to make money." Smart business owners know that they must invest a portion of their revenues for their firms to survive and grow. While this approach may be obvious in profitable times, you might question a company that sinks cash into new products and facilities when the economy is faltering and the future is far from certain. But that's exactly what Intel, the U.S. manufacturer of computer microprocessors, pledged to do. Just when thousands of companies were laying off workers, trimming operations, closing facilities, and removing products from their lines, Intel announced plans to expand existing manufacturing sites in Arizona, New Mexico, and Oregon, supporting about 7,000 jobs in those locations. In addition, the firm unveiled a strategy that included a new assembly test facility in Vietnam and a new factory in China. Why take such an aggressive stand as other firms retreated? "You never save your way out of recession," asserts Intel spokesman Chuck Mulloy. "You invest your way."

The total price tag for Intel's strategy is a whopping $7 billion. Even more eye popping is that Intel is not raising capital in the financial markets to fund the expansion. Instead, the company is using internal cash to pay for what it is calling its largest-ever investment in a new manufacturing process. Although some experts might question the size of the investment during an economic downturn, no one argues with the necessity of continually moving ahead in the technology industry.

Intel's new product—its next-generation chip made with 32-nanometer technology—is critical to the firm's future growth. In the new chips, tiny transistors are squeezed together so tightly that one billion of them will fit on a chip the size of a dime. This innovation creates two forms of efficiency—less electricity is consumed, and the cost of producing each chip is lower. The 32-nanometer circuitry occupies only 71 percent of the space of current microchips.

Intel outlined plans for producing the new chips long before the economy dropped, and executives believed that if the firm waited for a turnaround, it would lose the opportunity to be the first to bring the chips to market. At this time, Intel can launch the new microprocessors at a reasonable price. "One of the best ways to use this capacity [32-nanometer technology] is for what I call 'square-wave transition,' to bring massive amounts of new technology at a great price point," explains Intel CEO Paul Otellini. With lower costs, computer manufacturers can afford to use the new chips in such mainstream products as PCs, creating higher sales for Intel.

In this light, "it would be hard to argue that they shouldn't be making this investment," notes one observer. Even so, Intel must consider its commitment to retaining U.S. employees, whose wages are typically higher than those of workers in countries like China or India. "Our standard of living doesn't allow us to compete for low-wage jobs," states Otellini, who urges continued investment in education if the U.S. technology industry is to remain competitive.

Although paying higher wages for U.S. workers may appear to be a luxury, Intel views it as a necessity for keeping a close eye on the manufacturing process, including quality and schedule. "One of Intel's tremendous strengths is process control [in manufacturing chips]," comments an industry expert. If highly technical manufacturing stays in the United States, the company can promote its quality and avoid the cost in dollars and time of setting up its technical manufacturing in foreign facilities. Otellini advocates keeping as much of Intel's manufacturing in the United States as possible to reap the advantage of getting new products to market quickly and monitoring quality more easily. Intel has closed some plants in Southeast Asia for financial and quality reasons. But the company does send certain processes overseas in specified plants in Vietnam and China.

Aside from the value of keeping operations close to home, Otellini says Intel benefits from the "feel good" factor, particularly when bad economic news seems to be everywhere. "For a variety of reasons, the factories where we are in the best position to ramp this [32-nanometer] technology fast were the ones that happened to be in the United States," he says. "And there is a nice statement to be made by an American company to be investing in America right now."[1]

Previous chapters discuss two essential functions that a business must perform. First, the company must produce a good or service or contract with suppliers to produce it. Second, the firm must market its good or service to prospective customers. This chapter introduces a third, equally important, function: a company's managers must ensure that it has enough money to perform its other tasks successfully, in both the present and the future, and that these funds are invested properly. Adequate funds must be available to buy materials, equipment, and other assets; pay bills; and compensate employees. This third business function is **finance**—planning, obtaining, and managing the company's funds in order to accomplish its objectives as effectively and efficiently as possible.

An organization's financial objectives include not only meeting expenses and investing in assets but also maximizing its overall worth, often determined by the value of the firm's common stock. Financial managers are responsible for meeting expenses, investing in assets, and increasing profits to shareholders. Solid financial management is critical to the success of a business. A glance through the daily news provides examples of firms that, even though they offered good products to the marketplace, failed because funds were not managed properly.

This chapter focuses on the finance function of organizations. It begins by describing the role of financial managers, their place in the organizational hierarchy, and the increasing importance of finance. Next, the financial planning process and the components of a financial plan are outlined. Then the discussion focuses on how organizations manage assets as efficiently and effectively as possible. The two major sources of funds—debt and equity—are then compared, and the concept of leverage is introduced. The major sources of short-term and long-term funding are described in the following sections. A description of mergers, acquisitions, buyouts, and divestitures concludes the chapter.

The Role of the Financial Manager

finance planning, obtaining, and managing the company's funds to accomplish its objectives as effectively and efficiently as possible.

financial manager executive who develops and implements the firm's financial plan and determines the most appropriate sources and uses of funds.

Because of the intense pressures they face today, organizations are increasingly measuring and reducing the costs of business operations, as well as maximizing revenues and profits. As a result, **financial managers**—executives who develop and implement their firm's financial plan and determine the most appropriate sources and uses of funds—are among the most vital people on the corporate payroll.

Figure 18.1 shows what the finance function of a typical company might look like: at the top is the chief financial officer (CFO). The CFO usually reports directly to the company's chief executive officer (CEO) or chief operating officer (COO). In some companies, the CFO is also a member of the board of directors. In the case of software maker Oracle, both the current CFO and former CFO serve on that company's board, the latter as its chairman. Moreover, it's not uncommon for CFOs to serve as independent directors on other firms' boards, such as Hewlett-Packard, Microsoft, and Target. As noted in Chapter 16, the CFO, along with the firm's CEO, must certify the accuracy of the firm's financial statements.

Reporting directly to the CFO are often three senior managers. While titles can vary, these three executives are commonly called the *vice president for financial management* (or *planning*), the *treasurer,* and the *controller.* The vice president for financial management or planning is responsible for preparing financial forecasts and analyzing major investment decisions, such as new products, new production facilities, and acquisitions. The treasurer is responsible for all of the company's financing activities, including cash management, tax planning and preparation, and shareholder relations. The treasurer also works on the sale of new security issues to investors. The controller is the chief accounting manager. The controller's functions include keeping the company's books, preparing financial statements, and conducting internal audits.

The growing importance of financial professionals is reflected in an expanding number of CEOs promoted from financial positions. Indra Nooyi, CEO of PepsiCo, and Jim Marsh, CEO of British telecommunications company Cable and Wireless, both served as their firm's CFO prior to assuming the top job. The importance of finance professionals is also reflected in how much CFOs earn today. According to a survey by executive compensation consulting firm Equilar, the median annual salary for CFOs of *Fortune* 500 companies is around $2.8 million.[2] The CFO of investment firm Berkshire Hathaway is actually paid more than the company's famous chairman, Warren Buffett.[3]

In performing their jobs, financial professionals continually seek to balance risks with expected financial returns. Risk is the uncertainty of gain or loss; return is the gain or loss that results from an investment over a specified period of time. Financial managers strive to maximize the wealth of their firm's shareholders by striking the optimal balance between risk and return. This balance is called the ==risk-return trade-off.== For example, heavy reliance on borrowed funds may increase the return to shareholders, but the more money a firm borrows, the greater the risks to shareholders. An increase in a firm's cash on hand reduces the risk of meeting unexpected cash needs. However, because cash does not earn much, if any, return, failure to invest surplus funds in an income-earning asset—such as in securities—reduces a firm's potential return or profitability. Many illustrations of the risk-return trade-off are provided throughout the chapter.

Every financial manager must perform this risk-return balancing act. For example, in the late 1990s, Airbus wrestled with a major decision: whether to begin development and production of the giant A380 jetliner. The development costs for the aircraft—the world's largest jetliner—were initially estimated at more than $10 billion. Before committing to such a huge investment, financial managers had to weigh the potential profits of the A380 with the risk that the profits would not materialize. With its future on the line, Airbus decided to go ahead with the development of the A380. After spending more than $15 billion, the A380 entered commercial service a few years ago. Airbus currently has orders for approximately 200 jetliners at a list price of around $285 million each.[4] At this point, however, it's still unclear whether the A380 investment will turn out to be a smart, and profitable, decision.

Figure 18.1

What the Finance Organization at a Typical Firm Looks Like

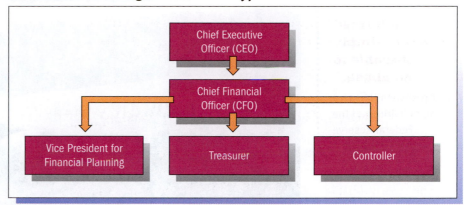

risk-return trade-off process of maximizing the wealth of the firm's shareholders by striking the optimal balance between risk and return.

More and more, today's CEOs are being drawn from the ranks of CFOs. Jim Marsh, CEO of a British telecommunications company, is one example of the trend.

"Any informed borrower is simply less vulnerable to fraud and abuse."

—Alan Greenspan (b. 1926)
Former Chairman of the
Federal Reserve

An Airbus A380 touches down at the Dubai Air Show in the United Arab Emirates. The double-deck luxury liner features a bar, a mini-spa, and first-class suites with showers and double beds.

© The Canadian Press, Nathan Denette/AP/Wide World Photos

Assessment Check ✔

1. What is the structure of the finance function at the typical firm?
2. Explain the risk-return trade-off.

Financial managers must also learn to adapt to changes in the financial system. The recent credit crisis has made it more difficult for some companies to borrow money from traditional lenders such as banks. This, in turn, has forced firms to scale back expansion plans or seek funding from other sources such as commercial financing companies. In addition, financial managers must adapt to internal changes as well. The "Hit & Miss" feature discusses how financial policies at UPS have evolved since the company went public.

Financial Planning

financial plan document that specifies the funds needed by a firm for a period of time, the timing of inflows and outflows, and the most appropriate sources and uses of funds.

Financial managers develop their organization's **financial plan,** a document that specifies the funds needed by a firm for a period of time, the timing of inflows and outflows, and the most appropriate sources and uses of funds. Some financial plans, often called *operating plans,* are short-term in nature, focusing on projections no more than a year or two in the future. Other financial plans, sometimes referred to as *strategic plans,* have a much longer time horizon, perhaps up to five or ten years.

Regardless of the time period, a financial plan is based on forecasts of production costs, purchasing needs, plant and equipment expenditures, and expected sales activities for the period covered. Financial managers use forecasts to determine the specific amounts and timing of expenditures and receipts. They build a financial plan based on the answers to three questions:

1. What funds will the firm require during the planning period?
2. When will it need additional funds?
3. Where will it obtain the necessary funds?

Hit & Miss

UPS: Balancing Risks and Returns

Managing the risks and returns for a company as large as UPS is no easy task. UPS is the largest package delivery firm in the world and a leader in supply chain services for other businesses. But CFO Kurt Kuehn is happy to do the job. Kuehn has worked for Brown—the firm's nickname, from its huge brown delivery trucks—for more than 30 years. Most recently he served as senior vice president of global sales and marketing and was a member of the UPS management committee. Prior to that, he was vice president of investor relations. So he knows the company's finances from the inside out.

When Kuehn took over the CFO job, one of the first tasks he faced was a restructuring of the company's financial policy regarding its capital structure. The new structure is designed to create greater value for UPS's major stakeholders—its shareholders. Essentially, UPS plans to restructure its balance sheet in such a way that it increases its debt by reinvesting in the company, using a target debt ratio of up to 60 percent funds-from-operations to total debt. "We have been studying our capital structure options for some time," explained Kuehn when the plan was announced. "This change in policy will permit us to make increased investments in the business, pursue selective acquisitions, and undertake larger share repurchases."

In this case, debt is positive for the company, allowing it to plough more resources back into the business.

CEO Scott Davis was quick to reassure shareholders and business customers of this fact. "UPS has had a long-standing commitment to a very strong balance sheet for decades, and that will not change," he insisted. "Indeed, we are putting the balance sheet strength to work more efficiently to deploy capital for the benefit of our shareholders. UPS's consistent, stable cash flows mean we can accept a higher degree of debt while continuing to strategically grow our business." A day after the new plan was announced, UPS stock rose more than 4 percent, indicating that investors approved of the strategy and felt secure in their investment.

Questions for Critical Thinking

1. Describe Kurt Kuehn's role as a financial manager at UPS.
2. Why is the idea of restructuring the firm's balance sheet to increase debt possibly a good business move for UPS?

Sources: "UPS Adopts New Financial Policy to Enhance Shareholder Value," company press release, January 9, 2008, http://reuters.com; accessed April 2, 2009; Ruthie Ackerman, "UPS Manages Expectations," *Forbes*, April 23, 2008, http://www.forbes.com; Melanie Lindner, "Investors Impressed by UPS," *Forbes*, January 10, 2008, http://www.forbes.com; Roy Harris, "What Did Brown Do for Scott Davis? Made Him CEO," *CFO*, October 15, 2007, http://www.cfo.com.

Some funds flow into the firm when it sells its goods or services, but funding needs vary. The financial plan must reflect both the amounts and timing of inflows and outflows of funds. Even a profitable firm may face a financial squeeze as a result of its need for funds when sales lag, when the volume of its credit sales increases, or when customers are slow in making payments.

In general, preparing a financial plan consists of three steps. The first is a forecast of sales or revenue over some future time period. This projection is, in fact, the key variable in any financial plan because without an accurate sales forecast, the firm will have difficulty accurately estimating other variables, such as production costs and purchasing needs. The best method of forecasting sales depends on the nature of the business. For instance, a retailer's CFO might begin with the current sales-per-store figure. Then he or she would look toward the near future, factoring in expected same-store sales growth, along with any planned store openings or closings, to come up with a forecast of sales for the next period. If the company sells merchandise through other channels, such as online, the forecast would be adjusted to reflect those additional channels.

Next, the CFO uses the sales forecast to determine the expected level of profits for future periods. This longer-term projection involves estimating expenses such as purchases, employee compensation, and taxes. Many expenses are themselves functions of sales. For instance, the more a firm sells, generally the greater its purchases. Along with estimating future profits, the CFO should

A Caribbean flamingo nurtures her chick at the San Diego Zoo. Good financial planning helped the zoo weather an outbreak of a rare bird disease.

UPI Photo/Ken Bohn/San Diego Zoo/Landov LLC

also determine what portion of these profits will likely be paid to shareholders in the form of cash dividends.

After coming up with the sales and profit forecast, the CFO then needs to estimate how many additional assets the firm will need to support projected sales. Increased sales, for example, might mean the company needs additional inventory, stepped-up collections for accounts receivable, or even new plant and equipment. Depending on the nature of the industry, some businesses need more assets than do other companies to support the same amount of sales. The technical term for this requirement is **asset intensity.** For instance, chemical manufacturer DuPont has approximately $0.94 in assets for every dollar in sales. So, for every $100 increase in sales, the firm would need about $94 of additional assets. Warehouse retailer Costco, by contrast, has only roughly $0.31 in assets for every dollar in sales. It would require an additional $31 of assets for every $100 of additional sales. This difference is not surprising; manufacturing is a more asset-intensive business than retailing.

A simplified financial plan illustrates these steps. Assume a growing company is forecasting that sales next year will increase by $40 million to $140 million. After estimating expenses, the CFO believes that after-tax profits next year will be $12 million and the firm will pay nothing in dividends. The projected increase in sales next year will require the firm to invest another $20 million in assets, and because increases in assets are uses of funds, the company will need an additional $20 million in funds. The company's after-tax earnings will contribute $12 million, meaning that the other $8 million must come from outside sources. So, the financial plan tells the CFO how much money will be needed and when it will be needed. Armed with this knowledge, and given that the firm has decided to borrow the needed funds, the CFO can then begin negotiations with banks and other lenders.

The cash inflows and outflows of a business are similar to those of a household. The members of a household depend on weekly or monthly paychecks for funds, but their expenditures vary greatly from one pay period to the next. The financial plan should indicate when the flows of funds entering and leaving the organization will occur and in what amounts. One of the most significant business expenses is employee compensation. The "Business Etiquette" feature discusses the right and wrong way to ask for a pay raise.

A good financial plan also includes financial control, a process of comparing actual revenues, costs, and expenses with forecasts. This comparison may reveal significant differences between projected and actual figures, so it is important to discover them early to take quick action.

Paula Brock, CFO of the Zoological Society of San Diego, which operates the famous San Diego Zoo, credits the zoo's financial plan and planning process with helping it weather an outbreak of an exotic bird disease in Southern California a few years ago. When the disease first appeared, the zoo took immediate action to protect its valuable bird collection, which drew a significant number of visitors—and generated revenue. Thanks to these actions, no birds got sick, and the damage to the zoo's finances were minimal, even though the zoo spent more than a half-million dollars. The financial plan raised the alarm, and resources were redirected to fight the disease, allowing managers to make the necessary adjustments.[5]

Assessment Check

1. What three questions does a financial plan address?
2. Explain the steps involved in preparing a financial plan.

Managing Assets

As we noted in Chapter 16, assets consist of what a firm owns. But assets also represent uses of funds. To grow and prosper, companies need to obtain additional assets. Sound financial management requires assets to be acquired and managed as effectively and efficiently as possible.

Short-Term Assets

Short-term, or current, assets consist of cash and assets that can be, or are expected to be, converted into cash within a year. The major current assets are cash, marketable securities, accounts receivable, and inventory.

CASH AND MARKETABLE SECURITIES The major purpose of cash is to pay day-to-day expenses, much like individuals maintain balances in checking accounts to pay bills or buy food and clothing. In addition, most organizations strive to maintain a minimum cash balance in order to have funds available in the event of unexpected expenses. As noted earlier, because cash earns little, if any, return, most firms invest excess cash in so-called **marketable securities**—low-risk securities that either have short maturities or can be easily sold in secondary markets. Money market instruments—described in Chapter 17—are popular choices for firms with excess cash. The cash budget, which we discussed in Chapter 16, is one tool for managing cash and marketable securities because it shows expected cash inflows and outflows for a period of time. The cash budget indicates which months the firm will have surplus cash and can invest in marketable securities and which months it will need additional cash.

Critics of some companies' budgeting practices contend that occasionally firms hoard cash. Recently, Cisco Systems had more than $22 billion in cash and marketable securities. Yet, firms may have good reasons for holding large amounts of cash and marketable securities. They may plan on using these funds shortly to make a large investment, pay dividends to shareholders, or repurchase outstanding bonds.

ACCOUNTS RECEIVABLE Accounts receivable represent uncollected credit sales and can be a significant asset. For example, almost one-quarter of Nike's total assets consist of accounts receivable. The financial manager's job is to collect the funds owed the firm as quickly as possible while still offering sufficient credit to customers to generate increased sales. In general, a more liberal credit policy means higher sales but also increased collection expenses, higher levels of bad debt, and a higher investment in accounts receivable.

Management of accounts receivable is composed of two functions: determining an overall credit policy and deciding which customers will be offered credit. Formulating a credit policy involves deciding whether the firm will offer credit and, if so, on what terms. Will a discount be offered to customers who pay in cash? Often, the overall credit policy is dictated by competitive pressures or general industry practices. If all your competitors offer customers credit, your firm will likely have to as well. The other aspect of a credit policy is deciding which customers will be offered credit. Managers must consider the importance of the customer as well as its financial health and repayment history.

One simple tool for assessing how well receivables are being managed is calculating accounts receivable turnover over successive time periods. We showed how this ratio is calculated in Chapter 16. If receivables turnover shows signs of slowing, it means that the average credit customer is paying later. This trend warrants further investigation.

At Bed Bath & Beyond, inventory is the most valuable asset. Managing inventory can be a costly and highly complicated undertaking, especially for retailers.

Mark Peterson/Redux Pictures

INVENTORY MANAGEMENT For many firms, such as retailers, inventory represents the largest single asset. At home furnishings retailer Bed Bath & Beyond, inventory makes up almost 40 percent of total assets. Even for nonretailers, inventory is an important asset. At heavy equipment manufacturer Caterpillar, inventory is around 13 percent of total assets. On the other hand, some types of firms, such as electric utilities and transportation companies, have no inventory. For the majority of firms, which do carry inventory, proper management of it is vital.

Managing inventory can be complicated. The cost of inventory includes more than just the acquisition cost. It also includes the cost of ordering, storing, insuring, and financing inventory, as well as the cost of stock outs, lost sales due to insufficient inventory. Financial managers try to minimize the cost of inventory. But production, marketing, and logistics also play important roles in determining proper inventory levels. The production considerations of inventory management were discussed in Chapter 11. In Chapter 13, we outlined the marketing and logistics issues surrounding inventory.

Trends in the inventory turnover ratio—described in Chapter 16—can be an early warning sign of impending trouble. For instance, if inventory turnover has been slowing for several consecutive quarters, it indicates that inventory is rising faster than sales. In turn, this may suggest that customer demand is softening and the firm needs to take action, such as reducing production or increasing promotional efforts.

Capital Investment Analysis

In addition to current assets, firms also invest in long-lived assets. Unlike current assets, long-lived assets are expected to produce economic benefits for more than one year. These investments often involve substantial amounts of money. For example, as noted earlier in the chapter, Airbus invested more than $15 billion in development of the A380. In another example, auto manufacturer BMW recently announced a $750 million expansion of its production facility in South Carolina, bringing its total investment in the state to more than $5.4 billion.[6]

The process by which decisions are made regarding investments in long-lived assets is called **capital investment analysis.** Firms make two basic types of capital investment decisions: expansion and replacement. The A380 and the BMW South Carolina plant investments are examples of expansion decisions. Replacement decisions involve upgrading assets by substituting new ones. A retailer, such as Wal-Mart, might decide to replace an old store with a new Supercenter, as it did recently in Oxford, Ohio.

Financial managers must estimate all of the costs and benefits of a proposed investment, which can be quite difficult, especially for very long-lived investments. Only those investments that offer an acceptable return—measured by the difference between benefits and costs—should be undertaken. BMW's financial managers must believe that the benefits of expanding the South Carolina production facility outweigh the high cost. The expansion will allow BMW to produce three new models designed mainly for the North American market, so the expected profit from the sale of these models would be considered in the decision. Some other benefits cited by BMW include lower production costs and improved logistics. During the announcement, Josef Kerscher, president of BMW [U.S.] Manufacturing noted, "The boost in the production capacity at BMW Manufacturing will positively impact the logistics, supplier and distribution networks that support the manufacturing processes."[7]

Managing International Assets

Today, firms often have assets worldwide. Both McDonald's and The Coca-Cola Company generate more than half of their annual sales outside the United States. The vast majority of sales for Unilever and Nestlé occur outside their home countries (the Netherlands and Switzerland, respectively). Managing international assets creates several challenges for the financial manager, one of the most important of which is the problem of exchange rates.

As we discussed in several other chapters, an exchange rate is the rate at which one currency can be exchanged for another. Exchange rates can vary substantially from year to year, creating a problem for any company with international assets. As an example, assume a U.S. firm has a major subsidiary in the United Kingdom. Assume that the U.K. subsidiary earns an annual profit of £750 million. Over the past five years, the exchange rate between the U.S. dollar and the British pound has varied between 1.74 (dollars per pound) and 2.09.[8] This means the dollar value of the U.K. profits ranged from less than $1.3 billion to almost $1.6 billion.

Consequently, many global firms engage in activities that reduce the risks associated with exchange rate fluctuations. Some are quite complicated. However, one of the simplest, and most widely used, is called a *balance sheet hedge.* Essentially, a balance sheet hedge creates an offsetting liability to the non-dollar-denominated asset, one that is denominated in the same currency as the asset. In our example, the U.K. subsidiary is a pound-denominated asset. To create an offsetting liability, the firm could take out a loan, denominated in British pounds, creating a pound-denominated liability. If done correctly, this hedge will reduce or even eliminate the risk associated with changes in the value of the dollar relative to the pound. This will improve the financial performance of the firm, which can have a positive impact on its stock price.

"They Said It"

"You never save your way out of recession. You invest your way."

—**Paul Otellini** (b. 1950)
Intel CEO on his firm's plans to invest $7 billion in U.S. chip manufacturing plants

Assessment Check ✓

1. Why do firms often choose to invest excess cash in marketable securities?

2. What are the two aspects of accounts receivable management?

3. Explain the difference between an expansion decision and a replacement decision.

Sources of Funds and Capital Structure

Recall the accounting equation introduced in Chapter 16:

$$Assets = Liabilities + Owners'\ equity.$$

If you view this equation from a financial management perspective, it reveals that there are only two sources of funds: debt and equity. **Debt capital** represents funds obtained through borrowing. **Equity capital** consists of funds provided by the firm's owners when they reinvest earnings, make additional contributions, liquidate assets, issue stock to the general public, or raise capital from outside investors. The mix of a firm's debt and equity capital is known as its **capital structure.**

capital structure mix of a firm's debt and equity capital.

Companies often take very different approaches to capital structure. For instance, pharmaceutical giant Bristol Myers Squibb has a debt ratio (the ratio of total liabilities to total assets) of around 60 percent, meaning that more than half of its total funds have been borrowed. By contrast, Pfizer—another large drug company—has a debt ratio of less than 40 percent. Also, a company's capital structure can change over time. In five years, Nike's debt ratio fell from 41 percent to 34 percent. On the other hand, during the same period, Home Depot's debt ratio rose from 35 percent to 59 percent.

leverage increasing the rate of return on funds invested by borrowing funds.

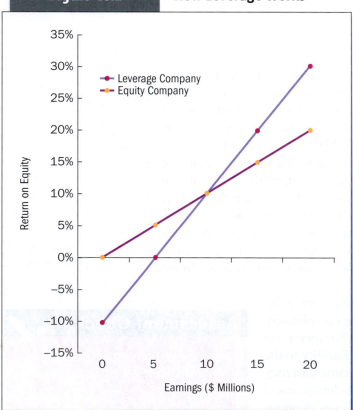

Figure 18.2   **How Leverage Works**

Return on Equity (y-axis): 35%, 30%, 25%, 20%, 15%, 10%, 5%, 0%, –5%, –10%, –15%

Earnings ($ Millions) (x-axis): 0, 5, 10, 15, 20

— Leverage Company
— Equity Company

Note: The example assumes that both companies have $100 million in capital. Leverage company consists of $50 million in equity and $50 million in bonds (with an interest rate of 10 percent). Equity company consists of $100 million in equity and no bonds. This example also assumes no corporate taxes.

Leverage and Capital Structure Decisions

Raising needed cash by borrowing allows a firm to benefit from the principle of **leverage,** increasing the rate of return on funds invested by borrowing funds. The key to managing leverage is to ensure that a company's earnings remain larger than its interest payments, which increases the leverage on the rate of return on shareholders' investment. Of course, if the company earns less than its interest payments, shareholders lose money on their original investments.

Figure 18.2 shows the relationship between earnings and shareholder returns for two identical hypothetical firms that choose to raise funds in different ways. Leverage Company obtains 50 percent of its funds from lenders who purchase company bonds. Leverage Company pays 10 percent interest on its bonds. Equity Company raises all of its funds through sales of company stock.

Notice that if earnings double, from say $10 million to $20 million, returns to shareholders of Equity Company also double—from 10 percent to 20 percent. But returns to shareholders of Leverage Company more than double—from 10 percent to 30 percent. However, leverage works in the opposite direction as well. If earnings fall from $10 million to $5 million, a decline of 50 percent, returns to shareholders of Equity Company also fall by 50 percent—from 10 percent to 5 percent. By contrast, returns to shareholders of Leverage Company fall from 10 percent to zero. Thus, leverage increases potential returns to shareholders but also increases risk.

Another problem with borrowing money is that an overreliance on borrowed funds may reduce management's flexibility in future financing decisions. If a company raises equity capital this year and needs to raise funds next year, it will probably be able to raise either debt or equity capital. But if it raises debt capital this year, it may be forced to raise equity capital next year.

Equity capital has drawbacks as well. Because shareholders are owners of the company, they usually have the right to vote on major company issues and elect the board of directors. Whenever new equity is sold, the control of existing shareholders is diluted, and the outcome of these votes could potentially change. One contentious subject today between companies and shareholders is whether shareholders should be able to vote on executive pay packages. The "Solving an Ethical Controversy" feature debates the issue.

Another disadvantage of equity capital is that it is more expensive than debt capital. First, creditors have a senior claim to the assets of a firm relative to shareholders. Because of this advantage, creditors are willing to accept a lower rate of return than shareholders are. Second, the firm can deduct interest payments on debt, reducing its taxable income and tax bill. Dividends paid to shareholders, on the other hand, are not tax deductible. A key component of the financial manager's job is to weigh the advantages and disadvantages of debt capital and equity capital, creating the most appropriate capital structure for his or her firm.

Mixing Short-Term and Long-Term Funds

Another decision financial managers face is determining the appropriate mix of short-and long-term funds. Short-term funds consist of current liabilities, and long-term funds consist of long-term debt and equity. Short-term funds are generally less expensive than long-term funds, but they also expose the firm to more risk. This is because short-term funds have to be renewed, or rolled over, frequently. Short-term interest rates can be volatile. During a recent 12-month period, for example, rates on commercial paper, a popular short-term financing option, ranged from a high of 5.3 percent to a low of less than 2 percent.[9]

Because short-term rates move up and down frequently, interest expense on short-term funds can change substantially from year to year. For instance, if a firm borrows $50 million for ten years at 5 percent interest, its annual interest expense is fixed at $2.5 million for the entire ten years. On the other hand, if it borrows $50 million for one year at a rate of 4 percent, its annual interest expense of $2 million is only fixed for that year. If interest rates increase the following year to 6 percent, $1 million will be added to its interest expense bill. Another potential risk of relying on short-term funds is availability. Even financially healthy firms can occasionally find it difficult to borrow money.

Because of the added risk of short-term funding, most firms choose to finance all of their long-term assets, and even a portion of their short-term assets, with long-term funds. Johnson & Johnson is typical of this choice. Figure 18.3 shows a recent balance sheet broken down between short- and long-term assets, and short- and long-term funds.

Dividend Policy

Along with decisions regarding capital structure and the mix of short- and long-term funds, financial managers also make decisions regarding a firm's dividend policy. Dividends are periodic cash payments to shareholders. The most common type of dividend is paid quarterly and is often labeled as a

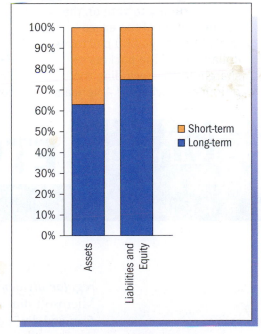

Figure 18.3

Johnson & Johnson's Mix of Short- and Long-Term Funds

- Short-term
- Long-term

Source: Johnson & Johnson financial statements, www.investor.jnj.com, accessed April 2, 2009.

EXECUTIVE PAY: WHO SHOULD DECIDE THE SALARIES OF CEOs?

The press is often filled with reports of astronomical salaries of CEOs and other top executives at large corporations.

For example, Lloyd Blankfein, CEO of investment firm Goldman Sachs, received nearly $70 million in compensation during one recent year. Some people say that this kind of pay package is well deserved—if it weren't for the talent and expertise of such business leaders, companies would not perform as well as they do. During the year that Blankfein received this premium salary, his firm earned almost $12 billion in profits. But sometimes executives receive enormous packages even as their companies falter, which causes many to question the wisdom and ethics of such compensation. As a result, some people are calling for a change in the way executive pay is decided.

Should company shareholders help determine how much top executives are paid?

PRO

1. Corporations that are publicly held are actually owned by shareholders, who should have the opportunity to vote on the compensation of top executives. "Excessive CEO pay takes dollars out of the pockets of shareholders—including the retirement savings of America's working families," argues the AFL-CIO labor union.

2. Companies such as insurance firm Aflac, which recently conducted a shareholder vote to determine its CEO's pay, benefit financially as well as from an improved image. "I think it will build trust in U.S. companies and in corporate America," predicts Hey-Won Choi, senior vice president for financial services firm TIAA-CREF.

CON

1. Companies that allow shareholders to vote on executive salaries may not be able to attract the top leaders in their field. Companies need to be free to compensate executives at the market rate. Shareholders may not necessarily know what the appropriate pay is because they are not experts in the field.

2. A shareholder vote may actually result in a higher rate of pay, as has happened with the CEOs of a number of firms. Those CEOs' compensation continued to rise between 5 percent and 11 percent after votes aligned their pay with the company's performance.

Summary

Shareholders of more than 100 large companies—including The Coca-Cola Company, IBM, General Motors, ExxonMobil, Citigroup, Anheuser-Busch, General Electric, and Wal-Mart—are insisting on having a say in their CEO's pay. As these firms hold their annual meetings, they are receiving increasing pressure to give in to a "say on pay" vote. In addition, investors and representatives from a wide range of companies including Pfizer, Morgan Stanley, Dell, Sara Lee, and others have met and discussed the issue—and it isn't going away. "This isn't an attack on companies in general," explains Timothy Smith, a senior executive at Goldman Sachs who actually favors the move. "This is good governance, just like ratification of auditors or majority vote for directors."

Sources: Simon Avery and Janet McFarland, "How Much Is Too Much?" *Globe Investor*, April 2, 2009, http://www.globeinvestor.com; Mary Thompson, "Aflac Shareholders Approve First Vote on CEO Pay," *CNBC*, May 8, 2008, http://www.cnbc.com; Josiah Ryan, "Union Targets Excessive Executive Pay," *CNSNews*, April 15, 2008, http://www.cnsnews.com; Barbara Kiviat, "Giving Investors a Say on CEO Pay," *Time*, April 9, 2008, http://www.time.com.

Solving an ETHICAL controversy

regular dividend. Occasionally, firms make one-time special or extra dividend payments, as Microsoft did several years ago. Earnings that are paid in dividends are not reinvested in the firm and don't contribute additional equity capital.

Firms are under no legal obligation to pay dividends to shareholders. While some companies pay generous dividends, others pay nothing. Starbucks has never paid a dividend to its shareholders. In contrast, 3M has paid dividends for 30-plus consecutive years, during which time the amount has more than quadrupled. Companies that pay dividends try to increase them or at the very least hold them steady from year to year. However, in rare cases firms must cut or eliminate dividends. This happened recently to General Motors, which eliminated its common stock dividend. Slowing auto sales made it necessary for GM to conserve cash, thus forcing the decision to stop paying dividends.[10]

Many factors determine a company's dividend policy, one of which is its investment opportunities. If a firm has numerous investment opportunities and wishes to finance some or all of them with equity funding, it will likely pay little, if any, of its earnings in dividends. Shareholders may actually want the company to retain earnings, because by reinvesting them, the firm's future profits, and the value of its shares, will increase faster. By contrast, a firm with more limited investment opportunities generally pays more of its earnings in dividends.

In addition to dividends, some firms buy back a portion of their outstanding stock. Home Depot, for instance, has repurchased more than $1 billion of stock over the past couple of years. Generally, shares are purchased on the secondary markets. The main purpose of share buy-backs is to raise the market value of the remaining shares, thus benefiting shareholders.

© Jim Mone/AP/Wide World Photos

3M, known for its innovation, is headquartered in Maplewood, Minnesota. The company has paid dividends to investors for more than 30 years.

Short-Term Funding Options

Many times throughout a year, an organization may discover that its cash needs exceed its available funds. Retailers generate surplus cash for most of the year, but they need to build up inventory during the late summer and fall to get ready for the holiday shopping season. Consequently, they often need funds to pay for merchandise until holiday sales generate revenue. Then they use the incoming funds to repay the amount they borrowed. In these instances, financial managers evaluate short-term sources of funds. By definition, short-term sources of funds are repaid within one year. Three major sources of short-term funds exist: trade credit, short-term loans, and commercial paper. Large firms often rely on a combination of all three sources of short-term financing.

Assessment Check ✔

1. Explain the concept of leverage.

2. Why do firms generally rely more on long-term funds than short-term funds?

3. What is an important determinant of a firm's dividend policy?

Trade Credit

Trade credit is extended by suppliers when a firm receives goods or services, agreeing to pay for them at a later date. Trade credit is common in many industries such as retailing and manufacturing. Suppliers routinely ship billions of dollars of merchandise to retailers each day and are paid at a later date. Without trade credit, the retailing sector would probably look much different—with fewer selections. Under this system, the supplier records the transactions as an account receivable, and the retailer records it as an account payable. Target alone currently has more than $6.5 billion of accounts payable on its books. The main advantage of trade credit is its easy availability because credit sales are common in many industries. The main drawback to trade credit is that the amount a company can borrow is limited to the amount it purchases.

"They Said It"

"Business is not financial science; it's about trading . . . buying and selling. It's about creating a product or service so good that people will pay for it."

—Anita Roddick (1942–2007)
Founder of The Body Shop

What is the cost of trade credit? If suppliers do not offer a cash discount, trade credit is effectively free. For example, assume a supplier offers trade credit under the terms net 30—meaning that the buyer has 30 days to pay. This is similar to borrowing $100 and repaying $100 in 30 days. The effective rate of interest is zero. However, some suppliers offer a discount if they are paid in cash. If one is offered, trade credit can get quite expensive. Now assume that a 2 percent discount is offered to cash buyers. If the discount is not taken, they have 30 days to pay. Essentially, then, if the buyer doesn't pay cash, it is borrowing $98 today and repaying $100 30 days later. The annual interest rate on such a loan exceeds 24 percent.

Short-Term Loans

Loans from commercial banks are a significant source of short-term financing for businesses. Often these loans are used to finance inventory and accounts receivable. For example, a small manufacturer of ski equipment's period of highest sales is late fall and early winter. To meet this demand, it has to begin building inventory during the summer. The manufacturer also has to finance accounts receivable (credit sales to customers) during the fall and winter. So, it takes out a bank loan during the summer. As the inventory is sold and accounts receivable collected, the firm repays the loan.

There are two types of short-term bank loans: lines of credit and revolving credit agreements. A line of credit specifies the maximum amount the firm can borrow over a period of time, usually a year. The bank is under no obligation to actually lend the money, however. It does so only if funds are available. Most lines of credit require the borrower to repay the original amount, plus interest, within one year. By contrast, a revolving credit agreement is essentially a guaranteed line of credit—the bank guarantees that the funds will be available when needed. Banks typically charge a fee, on top of interest, for revolving credit agreements.

The cash budget is an important tool for determining the size of a line of credit because it shows the months in which additional financing will be needed or borrowed funds can be repaid. For instance, assume the ski manufacturer's cash budget indicates that it will need $2.5 million for the June through November period. The financial manager might set up a line of credit with the bank for $2.8 million. The extra $300,000 is for any unexpected cash outflows.

In addition to commercial banks, commercial finance companies also make short-term loans to businesses. While most bank loans are unsecured, meaning that no specific assets are pledged as collateral, loans from commercial finance companies are often secured with accounts receivable or inventory.

Another form of short-term financing using accounts receivable is called **factoring.** The business sells its accounts receivable to either a bank or finance company—called a *factor*—at a discount. The size of the discount determines the cost of the transaction. Factoring allows the firm to convert its receivables into cash quickly without worrying about collections.

The cost of short-term loans depends not only on the interest rate but also on the fees charged by the lender. In addition to fees, some lenders require the borrower to keep so-called *compensating balances*—5 to 20 percent of the outstanding loan amount—in a checking account. Compensating balances increase the effective cost of a loan since the borrower doesn't have full use of the amount borrowed.

Say, for example, that a firm borrows $100,000 for one year at 5 percent interest. The borrower will pay $5,000 in interest (5 percent × $100,000). If the lender requires that 10 percent of the loan amount be kept as compensating balance, the firm only has use of $90,000. However, because it still will pay $5,000 in interest, the effective rate on the loan is actually 5.56 percent ($5,000 divided by $90,000).

Commercial Paper

Commercial paper is a short-term IOU sold by a company; this concept was briefly described in Chapter 17. Commercial paper is typically sold in multiples of $100,000 to $1 million and has a maturity that ranges from one to 270 days. Most commercial paper is unsecured. It is an attractive source of financing because large amounts of money can be raised at rates that are typically 1 to 2 percent less that those charged by banks. At the end of a recent year, almost $1.8 trillion in commercial paper was outstanding.[11] While commercial paper is an attractive short-term financing alternative, only a small percentage of businesses can issue it. That is because access to the commercial paper market has traditionally been restricted to large, financially strong corporations.

Sources of Long-Term Financing

Funds from short-term sources can help a firm meet current needs for cash or inventory. A larger project or plan, however, such as acquiring another company or making a major investment in real estate or equipment, usually requires funds for a much longer period of time. Unlike short-term sources, long-term sources are repaid over many years.

Organizations acquire long-term funds from three sources. One is long-term loans obtained from financial institutions such as commercial banks, life insurance companies, and pension funds. A second source is bonds—certificates of indebtedness—sold to investors. A third source is equity financing acquired by selling stock in the firm or reinvesting company profits.

Public Sale of Stocks and Bonds

Public sales of securities such as stocks and bonds represent a major source of funds for corporations. Such sales provide cash inflows for the issuing firm and either a share in its ownership (for a stock purchaser) or a specified rate of interest and repayment at a stated time (for a bond purchaser). Because stock and bond issues of many corporations are traded in the secondary markets, stockholders and bondholders can easily sell these securities. During a recent year, nonfinancial U.S. companies publicly sold more than $344 billion in bonds and about $60 billion in common stock.[12] Public sales of securities, however, can vary substantially from year to year depending on conditions in the financial markets. Bond sales, for instance, tend to be higher when interest rates are lower.

In Chapter 17, we discussed the process by which most companies sell securities publicly—through investment bankers via a process called *underwriting*. Investment bankers purchase the securities from the issuer and then resell them to investors. The issuer pays a fee to the investment banker, called an *underwriting discount*.

Private Placements

Some new stock or bond issues are not sold publicly but instead to a small group of major investors such as pension funds and insurance companies. These sales are referred to as

private placements. Most private placements involve corporate debt issues. More than $120 billion in corporate bonds were sold privately in a recent year in the United States.[13]

It is often cheaper for a company to sell a security privately than publicly, and there is less government regulation with which to contend because SEC registration is not required. Institutional investors such as insurance companies and pension funds buy private placements because they typically carry slightly higher interest rates than publicly issued bonds. In addition, the terms of the issue can be tailored to meet the specific needs of both the issuer and the institutional investors. Of course, the institutional investor gives up liquidity because privately placed securities do not trade in secondary markets.

Venture Capitalists

Venture capitalists are an important source of long-term financing, especially to new companies. **Venture capitalists** raise money from wealthy individuals and institutional investors and invest these funds in promising firms. Venture capitalists also provide management consulting advice as well as funds. In exchange for their investment, venture capitalists become part owners of the business. If the business succeeds, venture capitalists can earn substantial profits.

One of the largest venture capital firms is Draper Fisher Jurvetson, based in Menlo Park, California. During the past 20 years, DFJ has invested in more than 300 small, start-up companies including Hotmail (acquired by Microsoft) and Skype (acquired by eBay). Currently the firm has more than $5.5 billion in capital commitments in companies throughout the world.[14]

Private Equity Funds

Similar to venture capitalists, **private equity funds** are investment companies that raise funds from wealthy individuals and institutional investors and use those funds to make large investments in both public and privately held companies. Unlike venture capital funds, which tend to focus on small, start-up companies, private equity funds invest in all types of businesses, including mature ones. For example, a private equity fund, Cerberus Capital Management, bought automaker Chrysler a couple of years ago for more than $7 billion. Cerberus has also made equity investments recently in Air Canada and financing company GMAC.[15] Often, private equity funds invest in transactions that take public companies private, or leveraged buyouts (LBOs). In these transactions, discussed in more detail in the next section, a public company reverts to private status. The "Hit & Miss" feature profiles another large private equity fund, TPG Capital (formerly Texas Pacific Group).

A variation of the private equity fund is the so-called **sovereign wealth fund.** These companies are owned by governments and invest in a variety of financial and real assets, such as real estate. Although sovereign wealth funds generally make investments based on the best risk-return trade-off, political, social, and strategic considerations also play roles in their investment decisions.

Recently, several sovereign wealth funds made large investments in major U.S. financial firms, including Morgan Stanley and Citigroup. For instance, the Abu Dhabi Investment Authority invested $7.5 billion in Citigroup, becoming the giant bank's largest single shareholder in the process.[16] The assets of the ten largest sovereign wealth funds are shown in Figure 18.4. Together, these ten funds have over $2.3 trillion in assets.

Hit & Miss

TPG Hunts for the Hottest Deals

TPG is always hot on the trail of a good deal. The firm specializes in buyouts and investments in companies that are struggling, and it focuses on the United States, Europe, and Asia. TPG manages funds emphasizing private equity, venture capital, public equity, and debt investments. In general, TPG looks for companies that need an equity investment of anywhere between $100 million and $750 million in order to survive—companies that are established or even at the mature stage of their product offerings. Their goods and services may be suffering from obsolescence, or they may not be able to manage costs.

Some people might view TPG as a scavenger hunting for fallen prey, but founding partner David Bonderman views his firm in a more heroic light. Previously, he focused on investing in ailing corporations—those owned by shareholders—and taking them private in order to bring them back to life. If he succeeded, he and his company made a lot of money. "Private equity allows me to make long-term decisions and make investments in companies that are not valued by the market," Bonderman explained of this practice. But recently, Bonderman has taken the opposite approach: investing less in a company and keeping it public. One of these firms was Washington Mutual—the large mortgage lender. TPG invested $1.35 billion in Washington Mutual only to lose that investment several months later when the FDIC seized control of the bank.

Which approach is better business? The answer may depend on the state of the economy. When more credit is available, the public-to-private approach can result in enormous profits, although the risk is high. TPG made several billion dollars taking wireless carrier Alltel private and then selling it a year later to Verizon. When less credit is available, investing private money in public companies is a necessity. Some good deals can be made, but even they carry some risk, as the Washington Mutual loss illustrates. Still, David Bonderman and his partners show no signs of slowing down. TPG has holdings in upscale Texas retail chain Neiman Marcus Group, Pennsylvania-based disaster recovery firm SunGard Data Systems, Italian motorcycle manufacturer Ducati, and others. Despite a business environment that sometimes resembles a bucking bronco, Bonderman isn't jumping from the saddle anytime soon.

Questions for Critical Thinking

1. Describe some of the risks encountered by a firm like TPG.
2. Why is it important for TPG to adjust its strategy to changes in the economic environment such as availability of credit? What other changes in the environment might require alternative strategies?

Sources: "TPG," profile from *BusinessWeek*, http://investing.businessweek.com, accessed April 2, 2009; Amerendra Bhushan, "Texas Pacific Group Investor Letter—Humbled by WAMU Losses," *CEOWORLD Magazine*, September 27, 2008, http://ceoworld.biz; "TPG Capital," company profile, *Google Finance*, http://finance.google.com, accessed May 21, 2008; Andrew Ross Sorkin, "New Path for Kings of Buyouts," *The New York Times*, April 8, 2008, http://www.nytimes.com; Alistair Barr, "WaMu Gets $7 Billion from Group Led by Texas Pacific," *MarketWatch*, April 8, 2008, http://www.marketwatch.com.

Hedge Funds

Hedge funds are private investment companies open only to qualified, large investors. In recent years, hedge funds have become a significant presence in the U.S. financial markets. By some estimates, hedge funds account for about 60 percent of all secondary bond market trading and around one-third of all activity on stock exchanges.[17] They are also significant investors in noninvestment grade, or junk, bonds. Hedge funds are estimated to have total assets that exceed $1.4 trillion.[18] Unlike mutual funds, hedge funds are not regulated the SEC.

Traditionally, hedge funds, unlike venture capitalists and private equity funds, did not make direct investments in companies, preferring instead to purchase existing stock and bond issues. Recently, however, evidence suggests that hedge funds are beginning to make some direct investments in firms, both debt as well as equity, and therefore have become a source of long-term capital.

Assessment Check ✓

1. What is the most common type of security sold privately?
2. Explain venture capital.
3. What is a sovereign wealth fund?

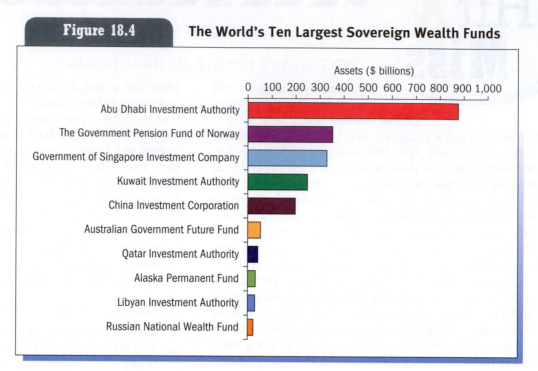

Figure 18.4   The World's Ten Largest Sovereign Wealth Funds

Assets ($ billions)

0 100 200 300 400 500 600 700 800 900 1,000

- Abu Dhabi Investment Authority
- The Government Pension Fund of Norway
- Government of Singapore Investment Company
- Kuwait Investment Authority
- China Investment Corporation
- Australian Government Future Fund
- Qatar Investment Authority
- Alaska Permanent Fund
- Libyan Investment Authority
- Russian National Wealth Fund

Source: "The Rise of Sovereign Wealth Funds Coverage from 2006 to Today," *Euromoney,* http:// www.euromoney.com, accessed April 2, 2009; "Sovereign Wealth Funds: The New Hedge Fund?" *The New York Times,* http://www.nytimes.com, accessed May 16, 2008; "The World's Most Expensive Club," *The Economist,* http://www.economist.com, accessed May 16, 2008; "Sovereign Wealth Fund," *Wikipedia,* http://en.wikipedia.org, accessed May 16, 2008.

Mergers, Acquisitions, Buyouts, and Divestitures

Chapter 5 briefly described mergers and acquisitions. A merger is a transaction in which two or more firms combine into one company. In an acquisition, one firm buys the assets and assumes the obligations of another firm. Chapter 5 also listed the classifications of mergers and acquisitions—vertical, horizontal, and conglomerate—and noted that many of these transactions involve large sums of money. A recent example is Mars acquiring Wm. Wrigley Company for $23 billion. In this section, we focus on the financial implications of not only mergers and acquisitions but also buyouts and divestitures.

Note that even in a merger, there is a buyer and seller. The seller is often referred to as the *target.* Financial managers evaluate a proposed merger or acquisition in much the same way they would evaluate any large investment—by comparing the costs and benefits. To acquire another company, the buying firm typically has to offer a premium for the target's shares—in other words, a higher price than the current market price. For instance, Mars offered $80 for each share of Wrigley, a premium of almost 30 percent over the existing price.[19]

When the buyer makes what is known as a **tender offer** for the target's shares, it specifies a price and the form of payment. The buyer can offer cash, securities, or a combination of the two. The Mars offer to Wrigley shareholders was all cash. The tender offer can be friendly, meaning it is endorsed by the target's board of directors, or unfriendly. Shareholders of both the buyer and target must vote to approve a merger.

Justifying such a premium requires the financial manager also to estimate the benefits of a proposed merger. These benefits could take the form of cost savings from economies of scale or reduced workforces or the buyer getting a bargain price for the target's assets. Sometimes, a buyer finds that the most cost-effective method of entering a new market is simply to buy an existing company that serves the market. Johnson & Johnson has a long history of making such acquisitions. When it decided to enter the contact lens market several years ago, Johnson & Johnson bought Vistakon, the firm that invented disposable contact lenses under the brand name Acuvue. Whatever the reasons, the term used to describe the benefits produced by a merger or acquisition is **synergy**—the notion that the combined firm is worth more than the buyer and target are individually.

Leveraged buyouts, or **LBOs,** were briefly introduced in the preceding section. In an LBO, public shareholders are bought out, and the firm reverts to private status. The term *leverage* comes from the fact that many of these transactions are financed with high degrees of debt—often in excess of 75 percent. Private equity companies and hedge funds provide equity and debt financing for many LBOs. The firm's existing senior management is often part of the buyout group. LBO activity has increased sharply in the last few years. In one recent year, for instance, there were more than 1,800 LBOs valued in excess of $575 billion; five years earlier, the value of LBO activity was less than $90 billion.[20] One of the largest was the buyout of wireless carrier Alltel for almost $25 billion.

Why do so many LBOs occur? One reason is that private companies enjoy benefits that public companies do not. Private companies are not required to publish financial results, are subject to less SEC oversight, and are not pressured to produce the short-term profits often demanded by Wall Street. Some argue that LBOs, because of the high degree of debt, enforce more discipline on management to control costs. While LBOs do have advantages, history has shown that many companies that go private reemerge as public companies several years later.

In a sense, a **divestiture** is the reverse of a merger, that is, a company sells assets such as subsidiaries, product lines, or production facilities. Two types of divestitures exist: sell-offs and spin-offs. In a **sell-off,** assets are sold by one firm to another. Recently Pfizer sold its consumer health products division to Johnson & Johnson, including such popular products as antismoking gum Nicorette and allergy medicine Zyrtec.

The other type of a divestiture is a **spin-off.** In this transaction, the assets sold form a new firm. Shareholders of the divesting firm become shareholders of the new firm as well. For example, Cadbury Schweppes decided to split its soft drink business from its confectionery unit. Cadbury shareholders received shares of the new beverage company, called Dr Pepper Snapple Group.

Firms divest assets for several reasons. Sometimes divestitures result from prior acquisitions that didn't work out as well as expected. German automaker Daimler Benz's recent divestiture of Chrysler is one such example. In other cases, a firm makes a strategic decision to concentrate on its core businesses and decides to divest anything that falls outside this core. That was the explanation Pfizer gave for selling its consumer health products division. Still another explanation relates to antitrust issues. Government authorities occasionally require divestitures of certain assets as a condition for approving a merger.

tender offer offer made by a firm to the target firm's shareholders.

leveraged buyout (LBO) transaction in which public shareholders are bought out and the firm reverts to private status.

divestiture sale of assets by a firm.

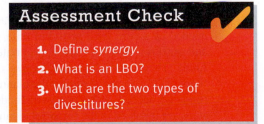

Assessment Check ✔

1. Define *synergy*.
2. What is an LBO?
3. What are the two types of divestitures?

What's Ahead

Contemporary Business concludes with five appendixes. Appendix A, "Business Law," outlines the main legal issues concerning business. It reviews the types of laws, the regulatory environment of business, and the core of business law, including discussions of contract law and property law. Appendix B examines risk management and insurance. It describes the concept of risk, alternative ways of dealing with risk, and the various kinds of insurance available to business and individuals. Appendix C discusses some of the important components of personal financial planning, such as budgeting, credit, and retirement planning. Appendix D describes how to write an effective business plan, and Appendix E discusses career searches and options to help you prepare for your future in business.

Summary of Learning Goals

1 Define *finance*, and explain the role of financial managers.

Finance deals with planning, obtaining, and managing a company's funds to accomplish its objectives efficiently and effectively. The major responsibilities of financial managers are to develop and implement financial plans and determine the most appropriate sources and uses of funds. The chief financial officer (CFO) heads a firm's finance organization. Three senior executives reporting to the CFO are the vice president for financial management, the treasurer, and the controller. When making decisions, financial professionals continually seek to balance risks with expected financial returns.

Assessment Check Answers

1.1 What is the structure of the finance function at the typical firm? The head of the finance function of a firm has the title of chief financial officer (CFO) and generally reports directly to the firm's chief executive officer. Reporting to the CFO are the treasurer, the controller, and the vice president for financial management.

1.2 Explain the risk-return trade-off. Financial managers strive to maximize the wealth of their firm's shareholders by striking the optimal balance between risk and return. Often, decisions involving the highest potential returns expose the firm to the greatest risks.

2 Describe the components of a financial plan and the financial planning process.

A financial plan is a document that specifies the funds needed by a firm for a period of time, the timing of inflows and outflows, and the most appropriate sources and uses of funds. The financial plan addresses three questions: what funds will be required during the planning period, when will funds be needed, and where will funds be obtained? Three steps are involved in the financial planning process: forecasting sales over a future period of time, estimating the expected level of profits over the planning period, and determining the additional assets needed to support additional sales.

Assessment Check Answers

2.1 What three questions does a financial plan address? The financial plan addresses three questions: what funds will be required during the planning period, when will funds be needed, and where will funds be obtained?

2.2 Explain the steps involved in preparing a financial plan. The first step is to forecast sales over a future period of time. Second, the financial manager must estimate the expected level of profits over the planning period. The final step is to determine the additional assets needed to support additional sales.

3 Outline how organizations manage their assets.

Assets consist of what a firm owns and also represent the uses of its funds. Sound financial management requires assets to be acquired and managed as effectively and efficiently as possible. The major current assets are cash, marketable securities, accounts receivable, and inventory. The goal of cash management is to have sufficient funds on hand to meet day-to-day transactions and pay any unexpected expenses. Excess cash should be invested in marketable securities, which are low-risk securities with short maturities. Managing accounts receivable, which are uncollected credit sales, involves collecting funds owed the firm as quickly as possible while also offering sufficient credit to customers to generate increased sales. The main goal of inventory management is to minimize the overall cost of inventory. Production, marketing, and logistics also play roles in determining proper inventory levels. Capital investment analysis is the process by which financial managers make decisions on long-lived assets. This involves comparing the benefits and costs of a proposed investment. Managing international assets poses additional challenges for the financial manager, including the problem of fluctuating exchange rates.

3.1 Why do firms often choose to invest excess cash in marketable securities? Cash earns no rate of return, which is why excess cash should be invested in marketable securities. These are low-risk securities that have short maturities and can be easily sold in the secondary markets. As a result, they are easily converted back into cash, when needed.

3.2 What are the two aspects of accounts receivable management? The two aspects of accounts receivable management are deciding on an overall credit policy (whether to offer credit and, if so, on what terms) and determining which customers will be offered credit.

3.3 Explain the difference between an expansion decision and a replacement decision. An expansion decision involves decisions about offering new products or building or acquiring new production facilities. A replacement decision is one that considers whether to replace an existing asset with a new one.

4 Compare the two major sources of funds for a business, and explain the concept of leverage.

Businesses have two sources of funds: debt capital and equity capital. Debt capital represents funds obtained through borrowing, and equity capital consists of funds provided by the firm's owners. The mix of debt and equity capital is known as the firm's capital structure, and the financial manager's job is to find the proper mix. Leverage is a technique of increasing the rate of return on funds invested by borrowing. Yet, leverage increases risk. Also, overreliance on borrowed funds may reduce management's flexibility in future financing decisions. Equity capital also has drawbacks. When additional equity capital is sold, the control of existing shareholders is diluted. In addition, equity capital is more expensive than debt capital. Financial managers are also faced with decisions concerning the appropriate mix of short- and long-term funds. Short-term funds are generally less expensive than long-term funds but expose firms to more risk. Another decision involving financial managers is determining the firm's dividend policy.

4.1 Explain the concept of leverage. Leverage is a technique of increasing the rate of return by borrowing funds. But leverage also increases risk.

4.2 Why do firms generally rely more on long-term funds rather than short-term funds? Although short-term funds are generally less expensive than long-term funds, short-term funds expose the firm to additional risks. The cost of short-term funds can vary substantially from year to year. In addition, at times short-term funds can be difficult to obtain.

4.3 What is an important determinant of a firm's dividend policy? The main determinant of a firm's dividend policy is its investment opportunities. Firms with more profitable investment opportunities often pay less in dividends than do firms with fewer such opportunities.

5 Identify sources of short-term financing for business operations.

The three major short-term funding options are trade credit, short-term loans from banks and other financial institutions, and commercial paper. Trade credit is extended by suppliers when a firm receives goods or services, agreeing to pay for them at a later date. Trade credit is relatively easy to obtain and costs nothing unless a supplier offers a cash discount. Loans from commercial banks are a significant source of short-term financing and are often used to finance accounts receivable and inventory. Loans can be either unsecured or secured, with accounts receivable or inventory pledged as collateral. Commercial paper is a short-term IOU sold by a company. While large amounts of money can be raised through the sale of commercial paper, usually at rates below those charged by banks, access to the commercial paper market is limited to large, financially strong corporations.

5.1 What are the three sources of short-term funding? The three sources of short-term funding are trade credit, short-term loans from banks and other financial institutions, and commercial paper.

5.2 Explain trade credit. Trade credit is extended by suppliers when a buyer agrees to pay for goods and services at a later date. Trade credit is relatively easy to obtain and costs nothing unless a cash discount is offered.

5.3 Why is commercial paper an attractive short-term financing option? Commercial paper is an attractive financing option because large amounts can be raised by selling commercial paper at rates that are generally less than those charged by banks.

6 Discuss long-term financing options.

Long-term funds are repaid over many years. There are three sources: long-term loans obtained from financial institutions, bonds sold to investors, and equity financing. Public sales of securities represent a major source of funds for corporations. These securities can generally be traded in secondary markets. Public sales can vary substantially from year to year depending on the conditions in the financial markets. Private placements are securities sold to a small number of institutional investors. Most private placements involve debt securities. Venture capitalists are an important source of financing for new companies. If the business succeeds, venture capitalists stand to earn large profits. Private equity funds are investment companies that raise funds from wealthy individuals and institutional investors and use the funds to make investments in both public and private companies. Unlike venture capitalists, private equity funds invest in all types of businesses. Sovereign wealth funds are investment companies owned by governments. While hedge funds generally invest in existing stock and bond issues, they have begun to make direct investments in companies and are another source of long-term funds.

Assessment Check Answers

6.1 What is the most common type of security sold privately? Corporate debt securities are the most common type of security sold privately.

6.2 Explain venture capital. Venture capitalists are important sources of funding, especially for small companies. Venture capitalists invest in these companies by taking an ownership position. If the business succeeds, venture capitalists can earn substantial profits.

6.3 What is a sovereign wealth fund? A sovereign wealth fund is a government-owned investment company. These companies make investments in a variety of financial and real assets, such as real estate. While most investments are based on which offers the best risk-return trade-off, political, social, and strategic considerations play roles as well.

7 | Describe mergers, acquisitions, buyouts, and divestitures.

A merger is a combination of two or more firms into one company. An acquisition is a transaction in which one company buys another. Even in a merger, there is a buyer and a seller (called the *target*). The buyer offers cash, securities, or a combination of the two in return for the target's shares. Mergers and acquisitions should be evaluated as any large

investment is, by comparing the costs with the benefits. *Synergy* is the term used to describe the benefits a merger or acquisition is expected to produce. A leveraged buyout (LBO) is a transaction in which shares are purchased from public shareholders and the company reverts to private status. Usually LBOs are financed with substantial amounts of borrowed funds. Private equity companies are often major financers of LBOs. Divestitures are the opposite of mergers, in which companies sell assets such as subsidiaries, product lines, or production facilities. A sell-off is a divestiture in which assets are sold to another firm. In a spin-off, a new firm is created from the assets divested. Shareholders of the divesting firm become shareholders of the new firm as well.

Assessment Check Answers

7.1 Define *synergy*. Synergy is the term used to describe the benefits produced by a merger or acquisition. It is the notion that the combined firm is worth more than the buyer and target are individually.

7.2 What is an LBO? An LBO—a leveraged buyout—is a transaction whereby public shareholders are bought out and the firm reverts to private status. LBOs are usually financed with large amounts of borrowed money.

7.3 What are the two types of divestitures? A sell-off is a divestiture in which assets are sold to another firm. In a spin-off, a new firm is created from the assets divested. Shareholders of the divesting firm become shareholders of the new firm as well.

Business Terms You Need to Know

finance 592	financial plan 594	venture capitalist 606	leveraged buyout (LBO) 609
financial manager 592	capital structure 600	tender offer 609	divestiture 609
risk-return trade-off 593	leverage 600		

Other Important Business Terms

asset intensity 596	debt capital 600	private placements 606	synergy 609
marketable securities 597	equity capital 600	private equity funds 606	sell-off 609
capital investment analysis 599	trade credit 603	sovereign wealth funds 606	spin-off 609
	factoring 604		

Review Questions

1. Define *finance*.
2. Explain the risk-return trade-off, and give two examples.
3. Describe the financial planning process. How does asset intensity affect a financial plan?
4. What are the principal considerations when determining an overall credit policy? How do the actions of competitors affect a firm's credit policy?
5. Briefly explain capital investment analysis.

6. Why do exchange rates pose a challenge for financial managers of companies with international operations?

7. Discuss the concept of leverage. Use a numerical example to illustrate the effect of leverage.

8. What are the advantages and disadvantages of both debt and equity financing?

9. Compare and contrast the three sources of short-term financing.

10. Define *venture capitalist, private equity fund, sovereign wealth fund,* and *hedge fund.* Which of the four invests the most money in start-up companies?

11. Briefly describe the mechanics of a merger or acquisition.

12. Why do firms divest assets?

Projects and Teamwork Applications

1. Assume you would like to start a business. Put together a rough financial plan that addresses the three financial planning questions listed in the text.

2. Your business has really grown, but now it needs a substantial infusion of capital. A venture capital firm has agreed to invest the money you need. In return, the venture capital firm will own 75 percent of the business, and you will be replaced as CEO by someone chosen by the venture capitalist. You will retain the titles of founder and chairman of the board. Would you be willing to take the money but lose control over your business?

3. Working with a partner, assume that a firm needs $10 million in additional long-term capital. It currently has no debt and $40 million in equity. The options are a ten-year bond (with an interest rate of 7 percent) or selling $10 million in new equity. You expect next year's earnings before interest and taxes to be $5 million (the firm's tax rate is 35 percent). Prepare a memo outlining the advantages and disadvantages of debt and equity financing. Using the numbers provided, prepare a numerical illustration of leverage similar to the one shown in Figure 18.2.

4. Collect at least five years' worth of balance sheet data on three publicly traded companies; choose companies operating in different industries. Has each company become more or less leveraged in recent years? Why do some firms appear to rely more on debt than others? (*Note:* A good source of recent financial statements is MSN Money Central, http://investor.msn.com).

5. Working in a small team, select three publicly traded companies. Visit each firm's Web site. Most have a section devoted to information for investors. Review each firm's dividend policy. Does the company pay dividends? If so, when did it begin paying dividends? Have dividends increased each year, or have they fluctuated from year to year? Is the company currently repurchasing shares? Has it done so in the past? Prepare a report summarizing your findings.

6. As noted in the chapter, one of the largest recent LBOs involved wireless carrier Alltel. Research this transaction. Who purchased Alltel? How was the transaction financed? By whom? What has happened to Alltel since then?

7. Select a large retailer, such as Target or Lowe's, and then identify two to three of the retailer's large suppliers. Use each firm's financial statements to illustrate the use of accounts receivable management and trade credit.

Web Assignments

1. **Careers in finance.** Visit the Web site of *CFO* magazine (http://www.cfo.com). Click on the "Careers" link and then select "Career Paths." Review and summarize three of the articles you find. What did you learn about finance careers? What are some of the current issues affecting the field? Did this exercise make you more or less likely to pursue a finance-related career?

2. **Merger activity.** Merger activity tends to occur in waves. The Deal.com (http://www.thedeal.com) is a Web site containing data on merger and LBO activity. Visit the Web site and access the most recent data you can find. Has merger and LBO activity increased or decreased during the past few years—both in terms of number of deals and the total value of deals? Reviewing current merger activity, do current interest rates and stock prices appear to be related to the increase or decrease in merger activity you observed?

3. **Asset-backed commercial paper.** As noted in the chapter, most commercial paper is unsecured. However, in recent years a new type of commercial paper—called *asset-backed commercial paper*—has emerged. Use a search engine to find one or two articles on asset-backed commercial paper. What is it? How is it different from unsecured commercial

paper? Who issues asset-backed commercial paper? Then visit the Web site of the Federal Reserve (http://www.federalreserve.gov) and click on the "Statistical Releases" link. One of the series tracks new commercial paper issues. How large are sales of asset-backed commercial paper relative to unsecured commercial paper? Note any other trends you can identify.

Note: Internet Web addresses change frequently. If you do not find the exact site listed, you may need to access the organization's or company's home page and search from there.

Case 18.1 — Does Microsoft Have Too Much Cash?

Imagine having too much cash. *Right,* you're thinking; *that's impossible.* But for companies, sometimes cash becomes a liability because it is not being used in more productive ways—to pay down debt, invest in new-product development, enter new markets, or reward employees and shareholders. Recently, Microsoft found itself in this position. With more than $7.4 billion in cash and $13.6 billion in short-term investments, some experts worry that the firm simply has too much money in its treasure chest.

So in an effort to divest itself of cash and use some of that money to secure its position in new markets, Microsoft recently made a bid for a major stake in Yahoo! Securing a stake in a major search engine would help Microsoft compete online against Google. But Yahoo! not only rejected the offer, the possibility of a deal between Yahoo! and Google began to loom. Microsoft continued to pursue the purchase of specific divisions of Yahoo!, including its search-advertising business. But so far that proposal has remained unanswered. Microsoft then approached Facebook founder Mark Zuckerberg, also unsuccessfully, although Microsoft did purchase a $240 million stake in Facebook. "You can tell, from our history and what we've done, that we really wanted to keep the company independent, by focusing on building and focusing on the long-term," explained Zuckerberg.

Regardless of Yahoo!'s or Facebook's response to Microsoft, the software giant needs to determine how to use its cash on hand to its best advantage. CEO Steve Ballmer declared recently that Microsoft's goal is to acquire 20 companies a year over the next five years, ranging from $50 million to $1 billion. Of course, achieving this goal will mean that Microsoft will have to raise additional funds.

In addition, Microsoft has been doing what a number of other companies are also currently doing: buying back shares of stock that are on the market. This practice is intended to increase the price of the shares and limit the number that are selling on the open market. But some experts warn that what looks good on paper doesn't necessarily translate to true business success. "The tendency is to assume that corporate share repurchases lead to a sustained uptick in stock performance, and the more activity the better," explain Stewart Glickman and Todd Rosenbuth of Standard & Poor's equity research group. But the two experts point to a surprising result of their study: "The companies that used buybacks most aggressively actually generated the weakest returns." Companies with the largest buybacks of their own stock over the past few years include Microsoft, ExxonMobil, IBM, Procter & Gamble, Cisco Systems, Bank of America, and General Electric. While experts warn that it's not a magic bullet, the practice can be beneficial if combined with other business-generating activities.

Meanwhile, Microsoft still has plenty of spare change, although if it does acquire 20 smaller companies each year and buy back a portion of its outstanding stock, that nest egg is likely to diminish. Will that be a good event? Time will tell.[21]

Questions for Critical Thinking

1. Do you agree with the idea that Microsoft needs to spend some of its cash? Why or why not? Explain the benefits and drawbacks of hoarding cash from a business perspective.

2. Imagine that you are an advisor to the CFO of Microsoft. In what ways would you suggest the company use its excess cash?

Recently the value of the U.S. dollar hit a historic low against such currencies at the euro and Canadian dollar. While U.S. executives are optimistic about its rebound, European and Asian businesspeople are less certain about the greenback's return to glory. Regardless of the ultimate outcome, a declining dollar does not necessarily spell disaster for everyone.

First, the downside of the decline. Companies that outsource manufacturing or services overseas are likely to reap fewer profits. A weaker dollar also drives the price of foreign goods upward, along with the price of commodities such as oil. While the oil producers are unlikely to suffer, both U.S. consumers and the producers of foreign consumer goods will take a hit—because American consumers cannot afford to buy as many products made by foreign companies. Finally, businesses associated with travel overseas will attract fewer U.S. vacationers. Families that might have planned a trip to Europe or a vacation in the Bahamas will be more apt to stay closer to home.

Now the upside. Families that alter their extravagant travel plans will probably still take a vacation, but they might rent a cottage at a nearby beach or lake. They might take a day trip to a local amusement park and stop for pizza or burgers on the way home instead of dining at a more lavish eatery. This is good news for local restaurants, ice cream stands, and recreational destinations. Some U.S. manufacturing and service industries may also cash in on the declining dollar. Because their goods and services are now relatively cheaper on the global market, they are more attractive to foreign businesses. Organizational buyers are also much more apt to snap up U.S. goods and services than they were a decade ago. In fact, some experts believe that the increase in U.S. exports is having a positive impact on the economy. "It's a powerful shock absorber for the economy," notes one expert. He predicts that the weak dollar will eventually become a "net positive" for growth in the overall U.S. economy. Finally, many companies are now finding that outsourcing work overseas is no longer less expensive than keeping it at home, which could mean an increase in job opportunities and spending in the United States.

No one can predict with certainty when or how much the U.S. dollar will rise or fall. But smart businesses will know how to make the most of the opportunities created either way.[22]

Questions for Critical Thinking

1. How might a U.S. company change the way it manages its assets during a period in which the dollar is weak?
2. How might financing options change when the dollar is strong?

VIDEO **Case 18.3** **Southwest Bucks Airline Industry Headwinds**

In 2008, the U.S. airline industry losses were projected to range from $7 to $10 billion—one of the industry's worst years ever. Over the past few years, four of the nation's largest airlines were reorganized under Chapter 11 of the Bankruptcy Code. Airlines have responded to tough economic times by laying off thousands of workers, cutting service to dozens of cities, and grounding hundreds of jets. On the other hand, Southwest Airlines is likely to turn a profit in 2008 and is the only U.S. airline to have made money in each of the last 10 years. In fact, Southwest has turned an annual profit every year since it started flying in the early 1970s. As other airlines have cut back, Southwest has expanded. In an industry prone to labor unrest, Southwest has never experienced a strike, even though 90 percent of its employees belong to unions, and has never had to resort to mass layoffs. No wonder Southwest ranks high in surveys of the best companies to work for. And unlike most of its competition, Southwest hasn't started charging fees for such things as drinks, checked bags, or even window seats. Its ads even like to poke fun at the competition with the tag line "low fares, no hidden fees."

How has Southwest achieved this enviable record? Sound financial management has played a major role. Southwest's operating expenses are among the lowest in the airline industry. Unlike most airlines, Southwest operates only one type of aircraft, the Boeing 737. Airlines such as American, Delta, and United operate as many as 11 different types. Having only one type of aircraft saves millions of dollars every year in maintenance and crew training. Southwest also doesn't have to keep as large an inventory of spare parts. It saves money in other ways as well. With one class of service and no assigned seats, Southwest's fleet spends less time on the ground and more time in the air making money. The typical turnaround time spent at the gates averages less than 20 minutes—far less than any other airline. Since Southwest doesn't serve meals on any of its flights, only drinks, it saves money on galleys and aircraft cleaning. Good employee–management relations mean less turnover, greater worker productivity, and therefore major cost savings.

While most airlines rely on expensive hub-and-spoke systems, where passengers are funneled through large airports such as Dallas–Ft. Worth, Southwest emphasizes point-to-point service. It avoids the nation's busiest airports, like Chicago's O'Hare and Atlanta's Hartsfield–Jackson, with their corresponding high fees and frequent delays. For instance, instead of serving Washington's Reagan National airport, Southwest operates out of nearby Baltimore–Washington International airport. Reagan National charges airlines landing fees of around $12 per passenger, per flight. Baltimore charges less than $4.50. In August 2008, less than 75 percent of flights arrived at Chicago's O'Hare airport on time. By contrast, Chicago Midway, where Southwest is the dominant carrier, had an on time arrival rate that same month that exceeded 86 percent.

During the first eight months of 2008, oil prices soared. Remember $4-a-gallon gas? Soaring oil prices added something like $61 billion to the fuel bill of U.S. airlines. Airlines were paying the equivalent of $112 per barrel for fuel, but Southwest was paying only $51. How did it manage to pay less than half as much for fuel as its competition? A few years earlier, Southwest's financial managers arrived at the conclusion that fuel prices were headed higher and decided to do something about it. So, Southwest hedged higher fuel prices by buying oil futures contracts. A futures contract fixes the future delivery price of a commodity. As the price of oil rose, the futures position held by Southwest made money, which effectively lowered the price it paid for fuel. Southwest estimates that its hedging program has saved the company more than $2 billion in fuel expenses. Most other airlines didn't hedge against rising oil prices and spent billions more on fuel.

While Southwest's record of profitability and sound financial management is the envy of the industry, it is facing challenges. For one, as oil prices fell throughout the fall of 2008, Southwest's cost advantage over its competition began to disappear. The credit crisis and poor economy has started to take its toll. Southwest has dramatically scaled back its expansion plans. It has also begun to move into markets where large airlines maintain hubs. For years, Southwest stayed out of Denver, where United has a giant hub. A couple of years ago, Southwest began serving Denver and has continually added flights. More recently, Southwest entered the Minneapolis market, long dominated by Northwest. United and Delta, which acquired Northwest in 2008, are aggressively defending their turf. Some analysts question the wisdom of this, and other recent moves.[23]

Questions for Critical Thinking

1. What accounts for Southwest Airlines' record of success?

2. Explain how Southwest's business model leads to cost savings.

3. What is hedging? How did hedging allow Southwest to effectively pay less for fuel than its competition?

4. What are some of the current challenges facing Southwest? Do you think its business model will continue to work in the coming years?

So Much to Do, So Little Cash

When Dan Wallach started Greensburg GreenTown, he knew it wouldn't be easy. A self-proclaimed idea guy, he admits that the details of high finance elude him. What he is good at is rallying people around a cause and getting them to write a few big checks. This time, though, Wallach decided to involve the largest number of people possible. Greensburg GreenTown's One Million $5.00 Donations campaign was the result.

The money that is raised will be used to cover GreenTown's operating expenses, as well as to fund gaps in municipal projects, build model green homes, and educate residents about green building practices. Another aspect of GreenTown's work is to provide information and access to media organizations. Shortly after the tornado, the Planet Green cable channel began production on a television series that would chronicle the town's rebuilding. Wallach thought the exposure created by that show and others like it would be valuable in his fund-raising efforts.

As a not-for-profit organization, Greensburg GreenTown is heavily regulated by the IRS, because the donations it receives are fully tax deductible. It falls into the same category as religious organizations and educational institutions, which are exempt from federal income taxes but must pay other federal taxes, such as employment taxes. Because working through the red tape required to obtain this IRS status can take time, many organizations, GreenTown included, work through an approved intermediary while their applications are processed.

Although Greensburg GreenTown supports and educates Greensburg's residents, the town itself must rely on other sources of funding. All towns have budgets for repairs and improvements, but no one expected to have to rebuild the entire town. After the tornado, Greensburg had no roads, no hospital, no school system, no utilities, or any of the other services one might expect to find in a town. Money was tight even before the tornado, so rebuilding seemed an impossible task.

Luckily, various government and corporate organizations chipped in. The Federal Emergency Management Agency (FEMA) and the U.S. Department of Agriculture (USDA) provided aid in the form of grants. Corporations like Frito-Lay donated significant amounts of money to support the town's innovative business incubator. With millions of dollars at stake and hundreds of projects under way at once, Assistant Town Administrator and Recovery Coordinator Kim Alderfer says the hardest part is keeping track of it all.

Questions

After viewing the video, answer the following questions:

1. What are the key legal and financial distinctions of Greensburg GreenTown?
2. If you were in Kim Alderfer's shoes, what kind of financial contingency plan would you put in place for Greensburg's future?
3. Should not-for-profit organizations be required to open their books to donors? Why or why not?

Part 6   Launching Your Finance Career

Part 6, "Managing Financial Resources," describes the finance function in organizations. Finance deals with planning, obtaining, and managing an organization's funds to accomplish its objectives in the most effective way possible. In Chapter 17, we discussed the financial system, including the various types of securities, financial markets and institutions, the Federal Reserve System, financial regulators, and global financial markets. In Chapter 18, we examined the role financial managers play in an organization; financial planning; short- and long-term financing options; and mergers, acquisitions, buyouts, and divestitures. Throughout both chapters, we described the finance functions of a variety of businesses, governments, and not-for-profit organizations. As Part 6 illustrates, finance is a very diverse profession and encompasses many different occupations. According to the U.S. Department of Labor, over the next decade most finance-related occupations are expected to experience employment growth that is a little better than average for all occupations. However, employment in several finance occupations is expected to grow faster than average. Employment in the financial investment industry should be strong because of the number of Baby Boomers in their peak earning years with funds to invest and the globalization of securities markets.[1]

In most business schools, finance is either the most popular or second most popular major among undergraduates. Combining finance with accounting is a common double major. Those with degrees in finance also enjoy relatively high starting salaries. A recent survey found that the average starting salary for a person with an undergraduate degree in finance was nearly $49,000 per year.[2]

All organizations need to obtain and manage funds, so they employ finance professionals. Financial institutions and other financial services firms employ a large percentage of finance graduates. These businesses provide important finance-related services to businesses, governments, and not-for-profit organizations. Some graduates with finance degrees take jobs with financial services firms such as Bank of America and J.P. Morgan Chase, while others begin their careers working in the finance departments of businesses in other industries such as 3M and Boeing, governments, or not-for-profit organizations. You may begin your career evaluating commercial loan applications for a bank, analyzing capital investments for a business, or helping a not-for-profit organization decide how to invest its endowment. Often finance professionals work as members of a team, advising top management. Some individuals spend their entire

careers working in finance-related occupations; others use their finance experience to move into other areas of the firm. Today, the chief financial officer—the senior finance executive—holds one of the most critical jobs in any organization. In addition, the number of CEOs who began their careers in finance is growing.

Finance is a diverse, exciting profession. Here are a few of the specific occupations you might find after earning a degree in finance.

Financial managers prepare financial reports, direct investment activities, raise funds, and implement cash management strategies. Computer technology has significantly reduced the time needed to produce financial reports. Many financial managers spend less time preparing reports and more time analyzing financial data. All organizations employ financial managers, although roughly 30 percent of all financial managers work for financial services firms such as commercial banks and insurance companies.[3] Specific responsibilities vary with titles. For instance, credit managers oversee the firm's issuance of credit, establish standards, and monitor the collection of accounts. Cash managers control the flow of cash receipts and disbursements to meet the needs of the organization.

Most *loan officers* work for commercial banks and other financial institutions. They find potential clients and help them apply for loans. Loan officers typically specialize in commercial, consumer, or mortgage loans. In many cases, loan officers act in a sales capacity, contacting individuals and organizations about their need for funds and trying to persuade them to borrow the funds from the loan officer's institution. Thus, loan officers often need marketing as well as finance skills.

Security analysts generally work for financial services firms such as Fidelity or Raymond James & Associates. Security analysts review economic data, financial statements, and other information to determine the outlook for securities such as common stocks and bonds. They make investment recommendations to individual and institutional investors. Many senior security analysts hold a chartered financial analyst (CFA) designation. Obtaining a CFA requires a specific educational background, several years of related experience, and a passing grade on a comprehensive, three-stage examination.

Portfolio managers manage money for an individual or institutional client. Many portfolio managers work for pension funds or mutual funds for which they make investment decisions to benefit the funds' beneficiaries. Portfolio managers generally have extensive experience as financial managers or security analysts, and many are CFAs.

Personal financial planners help individuals make decisions in areas such as insurance, investments, and retirement planning. Personal financial planners meet with their clients, assess their needs and goals, and make recommendations. Approximately 30 percent of personal financial planners are self-employed, and many hold certified financial planner (CFP) designations. Like the CFA, obtaining a CFP requires a specific educational background, related experience, and passing a comprehensive examination.

Career Assessment Exercises in Finance

1. Assume you're interested in pursuing a career as a security analyst. You've heard that the CFA is an important designation and can help enhance your career. Visit the CFA's Web site (http://www.cfainstitute.org) to learn more about the CFA. Specifically, what are the requirements to obtain a CFA, and what are the professional benefits of having a CFA?

2. Arrange for an interview with a commercial loan officer at a local bank. Ask the loan officer about his or her educational background, what a typical day is like, and what the loan officer likes and doesn't like about his or her job.

3. Ameriprise Financial offers financial planning services to individuals and organizations. Visit the firm's careers Web site (http:///www.ameriprise.com/careers). Review the material and write a brief summary of what you learned about being a personal financial planner. Does such a career interest you? Why or why not?

Business Law

Apple's iPhone: Don't Touch the Patents!

Smart phone users knew right away they really liked the iPhone, and it quickly grabbed a big chunk of the cell phone market. The innovative device also spawned a long line of imitators. What most users probably didn't know is that for many of the iPhone's ground-breaking features Apple has, or is seeking, patents to protect them. A patent gives an inventor exclusive rights to an invention for a period of time.

One key protection that Apple sought back in September 2007 was a patent for the iPhone's multifunction touch screen. Recently granted by the United States Patent and Trademark Office, Patent number 7,479,949 covers not only the screen itself but also the technology underlying the phone's hardware and some of its software. Included in that patent are its operating system and some of its phone and camera functions.

Apple is taking the right steps, says one lawyer whose own firm is changing its wireless carrier to AT&T to allow its attorneys to use the iPhone themselves. He continues, "It's the only way to protect market share. What they're patenting is what happens when the touch screen senses the finger movements. From a user application standpoint, it's a market differentiator … a big part of its success is due to this touch screen technology."

Apple, in fact, might have effectively closed out a lot of the iPhone's competition by gaining broad enough protection to allow it to block even products with merely similar designs. "Apple has a patent on a new feature that everyone's going to want to have," said the lawyer. "When you use another device that doesn't have the same functionality, it's like night and day."

Rival firms are concerned that the breadth of Apple's patent, which is allowed by law, may leave them out in the cold. As long as a company meets the many rigorous descriptive and other legal patent requirements in its application, said another lawyer, "patentees can obtain coverage on features found in competitors' products. … [Apple's] length specification—over 300 pages—and copious drawings" mean that it will be issued more patents, which builds the iPhone patent portfolio for possible lawsuits against competitors.

In fact, according to one iPhone market observer, "instead of calling it Patent number 7,479,949, the Patent and Trademark Office should have called it 'Death to the Pre." The Pre is Palm's newest entry in the cell phone market, which boasts a multitouch interface that allows finger-touch navigation of Web sites. It received rave reviews when it was previewed. But the observer predicted that Apple's patent "will definitely give Apple's legal team a lot of ammunition in going after and stopping the Pre before it ever reaches the market. The Pre, by all accounts, was the most worthy competitor to the iPhone, and the first one to really have a feel when using that was 'iPhonish' in response and capability."

Other industry watchers think it's too early to tell whether Palm will have a patent infringement problem with Apple. One Palm spokesperson points out that "Apple was not the first to do multi-touch." Others agree. "Palm, like Apple, has a rich heritage in touch technology," said one expert, and "a lot of companies have intellectual property [IP] relating to multi-touch."

Palm says it will go ahead with its launch of the Pre. Yet Apple seems to be making its own intentions clear. Its chief operating officer recently said, "We are watching the landscape. We like competition. … However, we will not stand for having our IP ripped off, and we'll use whatever weapons we have at our disposal." Is the Pre doomed before it's launched? Apple wouldn't name names.[1]

No one starts a business or invents a product expecting someone to sue the company. But unfortunately, lawsuits do occur. So it makes sense for every businessperson to understand the laws governing the industry, trade, employment, and consumers. You don't need a law degree, but it's wise to be educated and informed before you hang a sign above your store or make a promise that could be misunderstood.

Legal issues affect every aspect of business. Despite the best efforts of most businesspeople, legal cases do arise. A dispute may arise over a contract, an employee may protest being passed over for a promotion, or a town may challenge the environmental impact of a new gas station. Unfortunately, the United States has the dubious distinction of being the world's most litigious society. Lawsuits are as common as business deals. Consider Wal-Mart, which is involved in as many as 7,000 legal cases at any one time. Even if you are never involved in a lawsuit, the cost still affects you. The average U.S. family pays a hidden "litigation tax" of $10,000 each year because of the costs of lawsuits that force businesses to increase their prices. Small businesses, like dentists' offices, doctors' offices, and day care providers are often the hardest hit and may cut back on their services or close. The total cost of frivolous lawsuits—those brought for petty reasons—runs about $865 billion a year.[2]

On the lighter side, every day brings news reports of proposed laws intended to protect businesses, consumers, and the general public—but somehow miss the mark. In addition, old laws are still on the books that no longer serve a purpose and are all but forgotten. For instance, in Alaska, it's illegal to wake a bear to take its picture, but it is perfectly legal to shoot a bear while it is sleeping. In Hawaii, it is against the law to insert pennies in your ear. In Louisiana, it is illegal to gargle in public. In Montana, it is against the law to operate a vehicle with ice picks attached to the wheels. In North Carolina, it is illegal to use elephants to plow cotton fields. And in Arizona, it's illegal to hunt camels.[3] How these laws came to be raises about as many questions as the laws themselves.

Legislation that specifically affects the business functions is analyzed in each chapter of this book. Chapter 2 presents an overview of the legal environment, and legislation affecting international operations is covered in Chapter 4. Chapter 5 discusses laws related to small businesses. Laws regarding human resource management and labor unions are examined in Chapter 9. Laws affecting other business operations, such as environmental regulations and product safety, are one of the topics in Chapter 13, and marketing-related legislation is examined in Chapter 14. Finally, legislation pertaining to banking and the securities markets is discussed in Chapters 17 and 18.

In this appendix, we provide a general perspective of legislation at the federal, state, and local levels, and point out that, while business executives may not be legal experts, they do need to be knowledgeable in their specific area of responsibility. A good dose of common sense also helps avoid potential legal problems. This appendix looks at the general nature of business law, the court system, basic legal concepts, and the changing regulatory environment for U.S. business. Let's start with some initial definitions and related examples.

Legal System and Administrative Agencies

judiciary court system, or branch of government that is responsible for settling disputes by applying laws.

The **judiciary,** or court system, is the branch of government responsible for settling disputes among parties by applying laws. This branch consists of several types and levels of courts, each with a specific jurisdiction. Court systems are organized at the federal, state, and local levels. Administrative agencies also perform some limited judicial functions, but these agencies are more properly regarded as belonging to the executive or legislative branches of government.

At both the federal and state levels, **trial courts**—courts of general jurisdiction—hear a wide range of cases. Unless a case is assigned by law to another court or to an administrative agency, a court of general jurisdiction will hear it. The majority of cases, both criminal and civil, pass through these courts. Within the federal system, trial courts are known as *U.S. district courts,* and at least one such court operates in each state. In the state court systems, the general jurisdiction courts are often called *circuit courts,* and states typically provide one for each county. Other names for general jurisdiction courts are superior courts, common pleas courts, or district courts.

State judiciary systems also include many courts with lower, or more specific, jurisdictions. In most states, parties can appeal the decisions of these lower courts to the general jurisdiction courts. Examples of lower courts are probate courts—which settle the estates of people who have died—and small-claims courts—where people can represent themselves in suits involving limited amounts of money. For example, a landlord might go to small-claims court to settle a dispute with a tenant over a security deposit.

Decisions made at the general trial court level may be appealed in **appellate courts.** Both the federal and state systems have appellate courts. For instance, the U.S. Fourth Circuit Court of Appeals, which is based in Richmond, Virginia, covers the states of Maryland, Virginia, West Virginia, North Carolina, and South Carolina.[4] The appeals process allows a higher court to review the case and correct any lower court error indicated by the appellant, the party making the appeal.

Appeals from decisions of the U.S. circuit courts of appeals can go all the way to the nation's highest court, the U.S. Supreme Court. Appeals from state courts of appeal are heard by the highest court in each state, usually called the *state supreme court.* In a state without intermediate appellate courts, the state supreme court hears appeals directly from the trial courts. Parties who are not satisfied by the verdict of a state supreme court can appeal to the U.S. Supreme Court and may be granted a hearing if they can cite grounds for such an appeal, and if the Supreme Court considers the case significant enough to be heard. The Supreme Court typically has more than 7,000 cases on the docket per year. However, only about 100 are granted review with oral arguments by attorneys. Formal written decisions are delivered for 80 to 90 of those cases.[5]

While most cases are resolved by the system of courts described here, certain highly specialized cases require particular expertise. Examples of specialized federal courts are the U.S. Tax Court for tax cases and the U.S. Court of Claims, which hears claims against the U.S. government itself. Similar specialized courts operate at the state level.

Administrative agencies, also known as bureaus, commissions, or boards, decide a variety of cases at all levels of government. These agencies usually derive their powers and responsibilities from state or federal statutes. Technically, they conduct hearings or inquiries rather than trials. Examples of federal administrative agencies are the Federal Trade Commission (FTC), the National Labor Relations Board (NLRB), and the Federal Energy Regulatory Commission (FERC). The FTC has the broadest power of any of the federal regulatory agencies. It enforces laws regulating unfair business practices, and it can stop false and deceptive advertising practices. Examples at the state level include public utility commissions and boards that govern the licensing of various trades and professions. Zoning boards, planning commissions, and boards of appeal operate at the city or county level.

Types of Law

Law consists of the standards set by government and society in the form of either legislation or custom. This broad body of principles, regulations, rules, and customs that govern the actions of all members of society, including businesspeople, is derived from several sources. **Common law** refers to the body of law arising out of judicial decisions, some of which can be

"They Said It"

"It usually takes a hundred years to make a law; and then, after it has done its work, it usually takes a hundred years to get rid of it."

—Henry Ward Beecher (1813–1887) U.S. clergyman

"They Said It"

"When you go into court, you are putting your fate into the hands of 12 people who weren't smart enough to get out of jury duty."

—Norm Crosby (b. 1927) American comedian

law standards set by government and society in the form of either legislation or custom.

common law body of law arising out of judicial decisions, some of which can be traced back to early England.

traced back to early England. For example, in some states, an unmarried couple who has lived together for a certain period of time is said to be legally husband and wife by common law.

Statutory law, or written law, includes state and federal constitutions, legislative enactments, treaties of the federal government, and ordinances of local governments. Statutes must be drawn precisely and reasonably to be constitutional, and thus enforceable. Still, courts must frequently interpret their intentions and meanings.

With the growth of the global economy, knowledge of international law becomes crucial. **International law** refers to the numerous regulations that govern international commerce. Companies must be aware of the domestic laws of trading partners, trade agreements such as NAFTA, and the rulings of such organizations as the World Trade Organization. International law affects trade in all kinds of industries. When a range of defective or tainted products manufactured in China—but sold in the United States—was recalled, companies discovered that although the goods came from China, the liability for their defects lay squarely within the United States. Tainted or defective toothpaste, pet food, toys, tires, and shrimp all fell under the scrutiny of the Food and Drug Administration (FDA), the Consumer Product Safety Commission (CPSC), and other agencies, which hold U.S. manufacturers responsible for the quality of their foreign-made products. When pet owners, parents, and other consumers filed lawsuits against the U.S. firms, these companies quickly discovered that suing the Chinese companies that made the goods brought very little result.[6]

In a broad sense, all law is business law because all firms are subject to the entire body of law, just as individuals are. In a narrower sense, however, **business law** consists of those aspects of law that most directly influence and regulate the management of various types of business activity. Specific laws vary widely in their intent from business to business and from industry to industry. The legal interests of airlines, for example, differ from those of oil companies.

State and local statutes also have varying applications. Some state laws affect all businesses that operate in a particular state. Workers' compensation laws, which govern payments to workers for injuries incurred on the job, are an example. Other state laws apply only to certain firms or business activities. States have specific licensing requirements for businesses, such as law firms, funeral directors, and hair salons. Many local ordinances also deal with specific business activities. Local regulations on the sizes and types of business signs are commonplace. Some communities even restrict the sizes of stores, including height and square footage.

statutory law written law, including state and federal constitutions, legislative enactments, treaties of the federal government, and ordinances of local governments.

business law aspects of law that most directly influence and regulate the management of business activity.

At a PetSmart store in Toronto, Canada, recalled pet food collects in a bin. Although the tainted food was manufactured in China, the Western companies that outsourced its production were held liable for damages to consumers.

Norm Bets/Landov LLC

Regulatory Environment for Business

Government regulation of business has changed over time. Depending on public sentiment, the economy, and the political climate, we see the pendulum swing back and forth between increased regulation and deregulation. But the goal of both types of legislation is protection of healthy competition. One industry that has experienced some deregulation in the past is still subject to relatively tight regulations: banking. Despite the relaxation of banking regulations across state lines and the advent of online banking, laws governing everything from stock trading to retirement investing remain strict. In response to a crisis in which lending institutions granted mortgages to home buyers who were then unable to meet payments that later increased dramatically—precipitating record numbers of foreclosures—a new bill was introduced in Congress. The Mortgage Reform and Anti-Predatory Lending Act of 2007 modifies the Truth in Lending Act. This legislation is an effort to protect consumers by establishing fair lending practices, which ultimately helps the housing market. The first part of the bill requires licensing or registration of mortgage originators (the lenders). The second part states that no lender can make a residential mortgage loan without ensuring that the consumer can pay it back. The third part of the bill puts greater restrictions on fees and penalties.[7]

Let's look at the issues surrounding regulation and deregulation and the legislation that has characterized them.

Antitrust and Business Regulation

John D. Rockefeller's Standard Oil monopoly launched antitrust legislation. Breaking up monopolies and restraints of trade was a popular issue in the late 1800s and early 1900s. In fact, President Theodore Roosevelt always promoted himself as a "trust-buster." The highly publicized Microsoft case of the 1990s is another example of antitrust litigation.

During the 1930s, several laws designed to regulate business were passed. The basis for many of these laws was protecting employment. The world was in the midst of the Great Depression during the 1930s, so the government was focused on keeping its citizens employed. Recently, government officials became concerned with the security aspects of international business transactions, Internet usage, the sources of funds, and their effects on U.S. business practices. So, new regulatory legislation in the form of the USA Patriot Act was enacted in 2001. In 2005, Congress voted to reauthorize the Patriot Act indefinitely, adding several new provisions.[8]

The major federal antitrust and business regulation legislation includes the following:

Law	What It Did
Sherman Act (1890)	Set a competitive business system as a national policy goal. The act specifically banned monopolies and restraints of trade.
Clayton Act (1914)	Put restrictions on price discrimination, exclusive dealing, tying contracts, and interlocking boards of directors that lessened competition or might lead to a monopoly.
Federal Trade Commission Act (1914)	Established the FTC with the authority to investigate business practices. The act also prohibited unfair methods of competition.
Robinson-Patman Act (1936)	Outlawed price discrimination in sales to wholesalers, retailers, or other producers. The act also banned pricing designed to eliminate competition.
Wheeler-Lea Act (1938)	Banned deceptive advertising. The act gave the FTC jurisdiction in such cases.
USA Patriot Act (2001; extended in 2005)	Limited interactions between U.S. and foreign banks to those with "know your customer" policies; allowed the U.S. Treasury Department to freeze assets and bar a country, government, or institution from doing business in the United States; gave federal authorities broad powers to monitor Internet usage and expanded the way data is shared among different agencies. Reauthorization (2005) created a new Assistant Attorney General for Security, enhanced penalties for terrorism financing, and provided clear standards and penalties for attacks on mass transit systems.

The protection of fair competition remains an issue in industries today. Despite the fact that in some parts of the country only one cable company is willing or able to invest the millions of dollars it takes to set up cable service in a small town, an apartment building, or rural area, consumers want a choice. If they are locked into a multiyear contract with the original provider, they can't switch to a new provider without paying penalties. The Federal Communications Commission (FCC) now prohibits long-term contracts between cable TV providers and the owners of apartment buildings, condominium complexes, and planned subdivisions in an effort to promote competition by giving consumers the same choice they might have in other markets.[9]

Business Deregulation

Deregulation was a child of the 1970s whose influence continues today. Many formerly regulated industries were freed to pick the markets they wanted to serve. The deregulated industries, such as utilities and airlines, were also allowed to price their products without the guidance of federal regulations. For the most part, deregulation led to lower consumer prices. In some cases, it also led to a loss of service. Many smaller cities and airports lost airline service for a while because of deregulation. But small and discount airlines such as Southwest and JetBlue began to focus on and serve those locations, with great success.

Following are several major laws related to deregulation:

Law	What It Did
Airline Deregulation Act (1978)	Allowed airlines to set fares and pick their routes.
Motor Carrier Act and Staggers Rail Act (1980)	Permitted the trucking and railroad industries to negotiate rates and services.
Telecommunications Act (1996)	Cut barriers to competition in local and long-distance phone, cable, and television markets.
Gramm-Leach-Bliley Act (1999)	Permitted banks, securities firms, and insurance companies to affiliate within a new financial organizational structure; required them to disclose to customers their policies and practices for protecting the privacy of personal information.

Consumer Protection

Numerous laws designed to protect consumers have been passed in the last 100 years. In many ways, business itself has evolved to reflect this focus on consumer safety and satisfaction. Recently, Congress passed the broadest changes in the country's consumer protection system in decades, including stricter regulations governing toy manufacturing, public access to complaints about products, and a major overhaul of the Consumer Product Safety Commission (CPSC) designed to improve communication and efficiency. One provision includes stricter limits on the amount of lead in children's toys, and another requires mandatory safety standards for nursery items like cribs and playpens.[10] The new Food and Drug Administration Amendments Act (FDAA) of 2007 reauthorizes existing laws and includes new provisions designed to enhance drug safety, encourage the development of pediatric medical devices, and enhance food safety.[11]

The major federal laws related to consumer protection include the following:

Law	What It Did
Federal Food and Drug Act (1906)	Banned adulteration and misbranding of foods and drugs involved in interstate commerce.
Consumer Credit Protection Act (1968)	Required disclosure of annual interest rates on loans and credit purchases.
National Environmental Policy Act (1970)	Established the Environmental Protection Agency to deal with various types of pollution and organizations that create pollution.
Public Health Cigarette Smoking Act (1970)	Prohibited tobacco advertising on radio and television.
Consumer Product Safety Act (1972)	Established the Consumer Product Safety Commission with authority to specify safety standards for most products.
Nutrition Labeling and Education Act (1990)	Stipulated detailed information on the labeling of most foods.
Dietary Supplement Health and Education Act (1994)	Established standards with respect to dietary supplements including vitamins, minerals, herbs, amino acids, and the like.
Food and Drug Administration Amendments Act of 2007 (2007)	Reauthorized several laws dealing with prescription drugs and added new ones enhancing food safety, drug safety, development of pediatric medical devices, and clinical trial registries.

Employee Protection

Chapters 2 and 9 cover many of the issues employers face in protecting their employees from injury and harm while on the job. But employees must also be protected from unfair practices by employers. The Equal Employment Opportunity Commission (EEOC) recently ruled that employers could reduce or eliminate the benefits they offer to retirees when they turn 65, because those retirees would then be eligible for Medicare. The new regulation allows employers to designate two classifications—those who are under 65 and those who are over 65—and tailor their benefits accordingly. More than 10 million retirees depend on employee-sponsored healthcare plans for all or some of their coverage. Arguing that the ruling "gives employers free rein to use age as a basis for reducing or eliminating health care benefits for retirees 65 and older," the American Association of Retired Persons (AARP) is attempting to overturn the regulation.[12]

Some of the relevant laws related to employee protection include the following:

Law	What It Did
Fair Labor Standards Act (1938)	For hourly workers, provided payment of the minimum wage, overtime pay for time worked over 40 hours in a workweek, restricted the employment of children, and required employers to keep records of wages and hours.
OSHA Act (1970)	Required employers to provide workers with workplaces free of recognized hazards that could cause serious injury or death and requires employees to abide by all safety and health standards that apply to their jobs.
Americans with Disabilities Act (1991)	Banned discrimination against the disabled in public accommodations, transportation, and telecommunications.

(Continued)

Law	What It Did
Family and Medical Leave Act (1993)	Required covered employers to grant eligible employees up to 12 workweeks of unpaid leave during any 12-month period for the birth and care of a newborn child of the employee, placement with the employee of a son or daughter for adoption or foster care, care of an immediate family member with a serious health condition, or medical leave for the employee if unable to work because of a serious health condition.
Uniformed Services Employment and Reemployment Rights Act (1994)	Protects the job rights of individuals who voluntarily or involuntarily leave their jobs to perform military service. Also prohibits employment discrimination in such cases.
American Jobs Creation Act (2004)	Reduced taxes for manufacturing in the United States, provided temporary tax breaks for income repatriated to the United States, and encouraged domestic job growth.
Pension Protection Act (2006)	Required companies with underfunded pension plans to pay extra premiums; made it easier for companies to automatically enroll employees in defined contribution plans; provided greater access to professional advice about investing.

Investor Protection

Chapters 16, 17, and 18 describe the institutions subject to investor protection laws and some of the events that brought the Sarbanes-Oxley law into being. (See the entry in the following table for specific provisions of Sarbanes-Oxley.) Following is a summary of legislation to protect investors:

Law	What It Did
Securities Exchange Act (1934)	Created the Securities and Exchange Commission with the authority to register, regulate, and oversee brokerage firms, transfer agents, clearing agencies, and stock exchanges; the SEC also has the power to enforce securities laws and protect investors in public transactions.
Bank Secrecy Act (1970)	Deterred laundering and use of secret foreign bank accounts; created an investigative paper trail for large currency transactions; imposed civil and criminal penalties for noncompliance with reporting requirements; improved detection and investigation of criminal, tax, and regulatory violations.
Sarbanes-Oxley Act (2002)	Required top corporate executives to attest to the validity of the company's financial statements; increased the documentation and monitoring of internal controls; prohibited CPA firms from providing some types of consulting services for their clients; established a five-member accounting oversight board.

Cyberspace and Telecommunications Protection

Computers and widespread use of the Internet and telecommunications have dramatically expanded the reach of businesses. They have also raised some thorny issues such as computer fraud and abuse, online privacy, cyberbullying, and cyberterrorism. Under a Supreme Court ruling, Internet file-sharing services are now held accountable if their intention is for consumers to use software to exchange songs and videos illegally. This ruling helps protect copyrights, which are covered later in this appendix. Recently Viacom—the parent company of MTV and Comedy Central—sued YouTube and its parent company, Google, for $1 billion in federal court, claiming "massive intentional copyright infringement." Google and YouTube denied the claim, but later Google unveiled a copyright filter designed to catch unauthorized use of copyrighted videos and other materials. The filter is basically a database of copyrighted videos that can be used to match videos that are uploaded on YouTube. The filter system automatically notifies someone who is uploading video that the material is copyrighted, and the copyright holder that the video has been placed on the site. Both parties can then decide how they want to proceed.[13]

Following are some of the major laws enacted to regulate cyberspace and telecommunications:

Law	What It Did
Computer Fraud and Abuse Act (1986)	Clarified definitions of criminal fraud and abuse for federal computer crimes and removed legal ambiguities and obstacles to prosecuting these crimes; established felony offenses for unauthorized access of "federal interest" computers and made it a misdemeanor to engage in unauthorized trafficking in computer passwords.
Children's Online Privacy Protection Act (1998)	Authorized the FTC to set rules regarding how and when firms must obtain parental permission before asking children marketing research questions.
Identity Theft and Assumption Deterrence Act (1998)	Made it a federal crime to knowingly transfer or use, without lawful authority, a means of identification of another person with intent to commit, aid, or abet any violation of federal, state, or local law.
Anticybersquatting Consumer Protection Act (1999)	Prohibited people from registering Internet domain names similar to company or celebrity names and then offering them for sale to these same parties.
Homeland Security Act (2002)	Established the Department of Homeland Security; gave government wide new powers to collect and mine data on individuals and groups, including databases that combine personal, governmental, and corporate records including e-mails and Web sites viewed; limited information citizens can obtain under the Freedom of Information Act; gave government committees more latitude for meeting in secret.
Amendments to the Telemarketing Sales Rule (2003), extended by the Do-Not-Call Improvement Act of 2007 and the Do-Not-Call Fee Extension Act of 2007	Created a national "do not call" registry, which prohibits telemarketing calls to registered telephone numbers; restricted the number and duration of telemarketing calls generating dead air space with use of automatic dialers; cracked down on unauthorized billing; and required telemarketers to transmit their caller ID information. Telemarketers must check the do-not-call list quarterly, and violators could be fined as much as $11,000 per occurrence. Excluded from the registry's restrictions are charities, opinion pollsters, and political candidates. The 2007 DNC Improvement Act allowed registered numbers to remain on the list permanently, unless consumers call to remove them themselves; the FTC will remove disconnected and reassigned numbers from the list. The Fee Extension Act of 2007 set annual fees telemarketers must pay to access the registry.
Check Clearing for the 21st Century Act (2003)	Created a substitute check, allowing banks to process check information electronically and to deliver substitute checks to banks that want to continue receiving paper checks. A substitute check is the legal equivalent of the original check.

The Core of Business Law

Contract law and the law of agency; the Uniform Commercial Code, sales law, and negotiable instruments law; property law and the law of bailment; trademark, patent, and copyright law; tort law; bankruptcy law; and tax law are the cornerstones of U.S. business law. The sections that follow set out the key provisions of each of these legal concepts.

Contract Law and Law of Agency

Contract law is important because it is the legal foundation on which business dealings are conducted. A **contract** is a legally enforceable agreement between two or more parties regarding a specified act or thing.

CONTRACT REQUIREMENTS As Figure A.1 points out, the four elements of an enforceable contract are agreement, consideration, legal and serious purpose, and capacity. The parties must reach *agreement* about the act or thing specified. For such an agreement, or contract, to be valid and legally enforceable, each party must furnish *consideration*—the value or benefit that a party provides to the others with whom the contract is made. Assume that a builder hires an electrician to install wiring in a new house. The wiring job and the resulting payment are the considerations in this instance. In addition to consideration, an enforceable contract must involve a *legal and serious purpose*. Agreements made as a joke or involving the commission of crimes are not enforceable as legal contracts. An agreement between two competitors to fix the prices for their products is not enforceable as a contract because the subject matter is illegal.

The last element of a legally enforceable contract is *capacity,* the legal ability of a party to enter into agreements. The law does not permit certain people, such as those judged to be insane, to enter into legally enforceable contracts. Contracts govern almost all types of business activities. You might sign a contract to purchase a car or cell phone service, or to lease an apartment.

BREACH OF CONTRACT A violation of a valid contract is called a **breach of contract.** The injured party can go to court to enforce the contract provisions and, in some cases, collect **damages**—financial payments to compensate for a loss and related suffering.

LAW OF AGENCY All types of firms conduct business affairs through a variety of agents, such as partners, directors, corporate officers, and sales personnel. An **agency** relationship exists when one party, called the *principal,* appoints another party, called the *agent,* to enter into contracts with third parties on the principal's behalf.

The law of agency is based on common-law principles and case law decisions of state and federal courts. Relatively little agency law has been enacted into statute. The law of agency is important because the principal is generally bound by the actions of the agent.

The legal basis for holding the principal liable for acts of the agent is the Latin maxim *respondeat superior* ("let the master answer"). In a case involving agency law, the court must decide the rights and obligations of the various parties. Generally, the principal is held liable if an agency relationship exists and the agent has some type of authority to do the wrongful act. The agent in such cases is liable to the principal for any damages.

Figure A.1

Four Elements of an Enforceable Contract

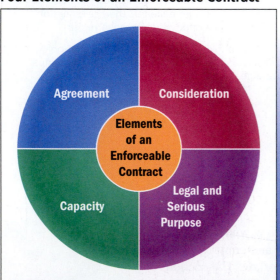

Uniform Commercial Code

Most U.S. business law is based on the **Uniform Commercial Code**—usually referred to simply as the UCC. The UCC covers topics such as sales law, warranties, and negotiable instruments. All 50 states have adopted the UCC, although Louisiana also relies on elements of civil law based on French, German, and Spanish codes, in addition to Roman law. While the other U.S. states rely on the tenets of English common law, which is also known as judge-based law, Louisiana's civil law system is found in most European nations. The UCC is actually a "model law" first written by the National Conference of Commissioners on Uniform State Laws, which states can then review and adopt, adopt with amendments, or replace with their own laws. The idea of the UCC is to create at least some degree of uniformity among the states.[14]

Sales law governs sales of goods or services for money or on credit. Article 2 of the UCC specifies the circumstances under which a buyer and a seller enter into a sales contract. Such agreements are based on the express conduct of the parties. The UCC generally requires written agreements for enforceable sales contracts for products worth more than $500. The formation of a sales contract is quite flexible because certain missing terms in a written contract or other ambiguities do not prevent the contract from being legally enforceable. A court will look to past dealings, commercial customs, and other standards of reasonableness to evaluate whether a legal contract exists.

Courts also consider these variables when either the buyer or the seller seeks to enforce his or her rights in cases in which the other party fails to perform as specified in the contract, performs only partially, or performs in a defective or unsatisfactory way. The UCC's remedies in such cases usually involve the award of monetary damages to injured parties. The UCC defines the rights of the parties to have the contract performed, to have it terminated, and to reclaim the goods or place a lien—a legal claim—against them.

WARRANTIES Article 2 of the UCC also sets forth the law of warranties for sales transactions. Products carry two basic types of warranties: an *express warranty* is a specific representation made by the seller regarding the product, and an *implied warranty* is only legally imposed on the seller. Generally, unless implied warranties are disclaimed by the seller in writing, they are automatically in effect. Other provisions govern the rights of acceptance, rejection, and inspection of products by the buyer; the rights of the parties during manufacture, shipment, delivery, and passing of title to products; the legal significance of sales documents; and the placement of the risk of loss in the event of destruction or damage to the products during manufacture, shipment, or delivery.

NEGOTIABLE INSTRUMENTS The term **negotiable instrument** refers to commercial paper that is transferable among individuals and businesses. The most common example of a negotiable instrument is a check. Drafts, certificates of deposit (CDs), and notes are also sometimes considered negotiable instruments.

Article 3 of the UCC specifies that a negotiable instrument must be written and must meet the following conditions:

1. It must be signed by the maker or drawer.
2. It must contain an unconditional promise or order to pay a certain sum of money.
3. It must be payable on demand or at a definite time.
4. It must be payable to order or to bearer.

Checks and other forms of commercial paper are transferred when the payee signs the back of the instrument, a procedure known as *endorsement*.

Property Law and Law of Bailment

Property law is a key feature of the private enterprise system. *Property* is something for which a person or firm has the unrestricted right of possession or use. Property rights are guaranteed and protected by the U.S. Constitution. However, under certain circumstances property may be legally seized under the *law of eminent domain*. In a U.S. Supreme Court ruling, the city of

sales law law governing the sale of goods or services for money or on credit.

negotiable instrument commercial paper that is transferable among individuals and businesses.

Three Basic Types of Property

New London, Connecticut, was granted permission to seize a distressed area of real estate—owned by individual citizens—for future economic development by private business. In response, several states are now proposing laws to ban such practices. California has enacted tighter, more specific standards for what is considered blight, or a distressed area. New Jersey requires that property owners be given at least 45 days' notice before their property can be taken under eminent domain.[15]

As Figure A.2 shows, property can be divided into three basic categories. *Tangible personal property* consists of physical items such as equipment, supplies, and delivery vehicles. *Intangible personal property* is nonphysical property such as mortgages, stocks, and checks that are most often represented by a document or other written instrument, although it may be as vague and remote as a computer entry. You are probably familiar with certain types of intangible personal property such as checks or money orders. But other examples include bonds, notes, letters of credit, and receipts.

A third category of property is *real property,* or real estate. All firms have some interaction with real estate law because of the need to buy or lease the space in which they operate. Some companies are created to serve these real estate needs. Real estate developers, builders, contractors, brokers, appraisers, mortgage companies, escrow companies, title companies, and architects all deal with various aspects of real property law.

The law of bailment deals with the surrender of personal property by one person to another when the property is to be returned at a later date. The person delivering the property is known as the *bailor,* and the person receiving the property is the *bailee.* Some bailments benefit bailees, others benefit bailors, and still others provide mutual benefits. Most courts now require that all parties practice reasonable care in all bailment situations. The degree of benefit received from the bailment is a factor in court decisions about whether parties have met the reasonable-care standards.

Bailment disputes are most likely to arise in business settings such as hotels, restaurants, banks, and parking lots. A series of rules have been established to govern settlement of these disagreements. The law focuses on actual delivery of an item. For instance, a restaurant owner is not liable if a customer's coat or purse is stolen from the back of his or her chair. This is because the customer has not given the item to the restaurant for safekeeping. However, if the customer delivers the coat or purse to the restaurant checkroom, receives a claim check, and the item is stolen, then the restaurant is liable.

Trademarks, Patents, and Copyrights

Trademarks, patents, and copyrights provide legal protection for key business assets by giving a firm the exclusive right to use those assets. A **trademark** consists of words, symbols, or other designations used by firms to identify their offerings. The Lanham Act (1946) provides for federal registration of trademarks. Trademarks are a valuable commercial property. Coca-Cola and McDonald's are two of the world's most widely recognized trademarks, so they are very valuable to the companies that own them.

If a product becomes too well known, its fame can create problems. Once a trademark becomes a part of everyday usage, it loses its protection as a legal trademark. Consider the names *aspirin, cola, nylon, kerosene,* and *linoleum.* All these product names were once the exclusive property of their manufacturers, but they have passed into common language, and now anyone can use them. Companies sometimes attempt to counter this threat by advertising that a term is actually a registered trademark. Although most people know the iPhone as an Apple trademark, Cisco Systems actually sued Apple over use of the name, claiming that it had owned the name prior to Apple's use. In an unusual turn of events, after negotiations both firms agreed to find ways to make their identically named products work together in certain applications.[16]

By law, a **patent** guarantees an inventor exclusive rights to an invention for 17 years. Copyrights and patents have a constitutional basis; the U.S. Constitution specifies that the federal government has the power "to promote the progress of science and useful arts, by securing for limited times to authors and inventors the exclusive rights to their respective writings or discoveries." Recently, the patent process and patent laws have been under scrutiny, and the Patent Reform Act was introduced in 2007. Under the act, which is supported by the information technology industry, it is now more difficult for firms to sue for patent infringement. Instead of filing for a patent on a first-to-invent basis, firms will receive patents on a first-to-file basis, which is more common around the world.[17]

A **copyright** protects written or printed material such as books, designs, cartoon illustrations, photos, computer software, music, and videos. This class of business property is referred to as *intellectual property.* Copyrights are filed with the Library of Congress. Congress recently extended copyright protection for creative material by an additional 20 years, covering artistic works for the lifetime of the creator plus 70 years; for companies the time is 95 years. Not surprisingly, the Internet has opened up a whole new realm of copyright infringement, ranging from downloading music files to illegally sharing video footage. Recently toy and game manufacturer Mattel served a copyright notice against the creators of the popular online game Scrabulous, claiming that the online version is too similar to its own game—Scrabble. Although Scrabulous had appeared online at other sites, when it hit Facebook, Mattel took action. "Mattel values its intellectual property and actively protects its brands and trademarks," said a Mattel spokesperson.[18]

As mentioned earlier, the U.S. Supreme Court has ruled that Internet file-sharing services will be held accountable if they intend for their customers to use the software illegally. Even greater restrictions exist in Europe, where Apple has been trying to establish a version of its legal iTunes movie rental service, allowing users to stream films or television shows to their computers and TVs. Laws are fragmented among the 27 member countries of the European Union, making such a service difficult to set up. As a result, consumers have fewer legal options for online content. "Europe's content sector is suffering under its regulatory fragmentation, under its lack of clear, consumer-friendly rules of accessing copyright-protected online content, and serious disagreements between stakeholders about fundamental issues," notes a commissioner who oversees media for the European Commission.[19]

Mattel, maker of the popular board game Scrabble, has charged the creators of an online version of the game with copyright violation. The U.S. Supreme Court has held some owners of online file-sharing programs liable for such violations.

Raine Vara/Alamy

Despite publicity about Internet copyright infringement, many people engage in the practice unintentionally. In an effort to educate children, the director of the U.S. Patent and Trademark Office recently gave a commencement speech to a group of elementary school students in Utah about the seriousness of downloading music, movies, and games illegally from the Internet.

Law of Torts

A **tort** (French for "wrong") refers to a civil wrong inflicted on another person or the person's property. The law of torts is closely related to the law of agency because a business entity, or principal, can be held liable for torts committed by its agents in the course of business dealings. Tort law differs from both criminal and contract law. While criminal law is concerned with crimes against the state or society, tort law deals with compensation for injured people who are the victims of noncriminal wrongs.

Tort cases are often extremely complex and may result in large monetary awards. It is typical to read or hear about cases in which patients are awarded millions of dollars in compensation for inadequate medical care. But what about pets? Lawsuits have surged around pets, their owners, and veterinarians. In the last few years, courts in several states have awarded damages to pet owners whose pets became ill or died from eating contaminated pet food. Although Menu Foods recalled 60 million containers of 90 brands of pet food that was contaminated by the toxin melamine, the firm was sued by pet owners for unfair and deceptive trade practices. Plaintiffs alleged that the firm had not provided adequate quality control for its foods and had failed to act quickly enough when it became apparent that something was wrong. Some even claimed emotional trauma caused by the deaths or illnesses of their pets, while others asked for compensation for vet bills, including euthanasia costs.[20]

TYPES OF TORTS A tort may be intentional, or it may be caused by negligence. Assault, slander, libel, and fraud are all examples of intentional torts. Businesses can become involved in such cases through the actions of both owners and employees. A security guard who uses excessive force to apprehend an alleged shoplifter may have committed a tort. Under agency law, the guard's employers, such as a shopping mall or retailer, can be also held liable for any damages or injury caused by the security guard.

The other major group of torts result from negligence. This type of tort is based on carelessness rather than intentional behavior that causes injury to another person. Under agency law, businesses can also be held liable for the negligence of their employees or agents. A delivery truck driver who kills a pedestrian while delivering goods creates a tort liability for his or her employer if the accident results from negligence.

PRODUCT LIABILITY An area of tort law known as **product liability** has been developed by both statutory and case law to hold businesses liable for negligence in the design, manufacture, sale, or use of products. Some states have extended the theory of tort law to cover injuries caused by products, regardless of whether the manufacturer is proven negligent. This legal concept is known as *strict product liability*.

The business response to product liability has been mixed. To avoid lawsuits and fines, some recall defective products voluntarily; others decide to fight recall mandates if they believe the recall is not justified. Auto manufacturers and toy makers typically issue voluntary recalls, as do drug manufacturers.

Class–Action Fairness

A *class-action suit* groups a number of individual plaintiffs, such as consumers with adverse reactions to medications, to allow for efficient processing under one lawsuit. Several years ago, Congress passed the **Class-Action Fairness Act of 2005.** The act imposes certain restrictions on class-action lawsuits. First, it automatically moves most large, multistate class actions—those with potential damages exceeding $5 million and in which more than two-thirds of the plaintiffs are geographically dispersed—from state courts into federal courts. This restriction prevents "shopping around" for sympathetic locations but lets cases that belong within a particular state remain there. Second, judges must consider the actual monetary value of any damage done so that plaintiffs receive true compensation for injury instead of large, arbitrary awards. Third, attorneys now receive payment differently. Under the old system, attorneys would receive a percentage of the gross settlement amount, regardless of whether all plaintiffs collected. Now judges can require uncollected awards to go to charity or government agencies, instead of into the pockets of lawyers. If the attorneys' fees are not based on a percentage, then they must charge based on the time they spent on the case.

Effects of the act are already being felt. In many states, the tide has already begun to turn away from huge, long, expensive lawsuits. Some states have passed their own laws restricting the types of suits that can be filed. Michigan has virtually eliminated class-action suits against drug manufacturers, and New York threw out a case accusing investment firms of manipulating the price of certain initial stock offerings. Twenty-three states have instituted statutes prohibiting suits against fast-food restaurants for causing obesity. And damage limits in many states have restricted medical malpractice suits. As the act helps achieve balance, both consumers and businesses will benefit.

Bankruptcy Law

Bankruptcy, legal nonpayment of financial obligations, is a common occurrence in contemporary society. The term *bankruptcy* is derived from *banca rotta,* or "broken bench," referring to the medieval Italian practice of creditors breaking up the benches of merchants who did not pay their bills.

Federal legislation passed in 1918 and revised several times since then provides a system for handling bankruptcies. Bankruptcy has two purposes. One is to protect creditors by providing a way to obtain compensation through debtors' assets. The second goal, which is almost unique to the United States, is to also protect debtors, allowing them to get a fresh financial start.

Federal law recognizes two types of bankruptcy. Under voluntary bankruptcy, a person or firm asks to be judged bankrupt because of inability to repay creditors. Under involuntary bankruptcy, creditors may request that a party be judged bankrupt.

Personal Bankruptcies

With a growing number of individuals amassing large personal debt—often through credit cards—Congress recently revised personal bankruptcy law to make it more difficult for people to erase their debt instead of being held accountable for it. Under the Bankruptcy Abuse Prevention and Consumer Protection Act of 2005, it is harder for individuals to file Chapter 7

bankruptcy legal nonpayment of financial obligations.

bankruptcy, which traditionally has wiped out most debt. If their earnings exceed their state's median income, they will instead be required to file Chapter 13 bankruptcy, which sets up a repayment plan as designed by the court. Despite criticism by consumer groups that say that banks and credit card companies have caused the problem by encouraging personal debt, many people agree that the revisions are fair.[21]

Business Bankruptcies

Businesses can also go bankrupt for a variety of reasons—mismanagement, plunging sales, an inability to keep up with changes in the marketplace. Under Chapter 11 a firm may reorganize and develop a plan to repay its debts. Chapter 11 also permits prepackaged bankruptcies, in which companies enter bankruptcy proceedings after obtaining approval of most—but not necessarily all—of their creditors. Often companies can emerge from prepackaged bankruptcies sooner than those that opt for conventional Chapter 11 filings. Airlines have managed to accomplish this, as well as some large retailers.

Tax Law

tax assessment by a governmental unit.

A branch of law that affects every business, employee, and consumer in the United States is tax law. A **tax** is an assessment by a governmental unit. Federal, state, and local governments and special taxing authorities all levy taxes. Appendix C, "Personal Financial Planning," also covers tax law.

Some taxes are paid by individuals and some by businesses. Both have a decided impact on contemporary business. Business taxes reduce profits, and personal taxes cut the disposable incomes that individuals can spend on the products of industry. Governments spend their revenue from taxes to buy goods and services produced by businesses. Governments also act as transfer agents, moving tax revenue to other consumers and transferring Social Security taxes from the working population to retired or disabled people.

Governments can levy taxes on several different bases: income, sales, business receipts, property, and assets. The type of tax varies from one taxing authority to the other. The individual income tax is the biggest source of revenue for the federal government. Many states also rely heavily on income taxes as well as sales taxes, which vary widely. Cities and towns may collect property taxes in order to operate schools and improve roads. So-called *luxury taxes* are levied on items like yachts, and *sin taxes* are levied on items such as cigarettes and alcohol. During the past decade, the issue of whether to tax different types of Internet services and use has been hotly debated.

> ### "They Said It"
>
> "Clearly everyone wants a tax cut, but you can't have a tax cut from a surplus that you don't have."
>
> —Charles B. Rangel (b. 1930) U.S. Congressman from New York and Chair of the House Ways and Means Committee

Business Terms You Need to Know

judiciary A-2	statutory law A-4	agency A-10	bankruptcy A-15
law A-3	business law A-4	sales law A-11	tax A-16
common law A-3	contract A-10	negotiable instrument A-11	

Other Important Business Terms

trial courts A-3
appellate courts A-3
international law A-4
deregulation A-6

breach of contract A-10
damages A-10
Uniform Commercial
  Code A-10

trademark A-12
patent A-13
copyright A-13
tort A-14

product liability A-14
Class-Action Fairness Act
  of 2005 A-15

Projects and Teamwork Applications

1. Many firms incorporate in Delaware because the state offers a business-friendly environment, including complete incorporation services, flexible corporate laws, a respected court, and a business-oriented staff at the Delaware Division of Corporations. Do you think that Delaware's approach to business creates a competitive edge for the state? For the businesses that locate there? Discuss your views in class.

2. To be effective, laws must be practical and enforceable; they must also be changed periodically to reflect changes in societal views and values. You've already seen some of the wacky laws enacted by states. Go online and research your home state or community to find more outdated, unenforceable, or wacky laws that affect business. Present them in class and discuss how they might be revised so that they could actually work.

3. Go online to research a federal business-related law enacted during the past five years. Why was this legislation passed? What were the arguments for and against it? How has the new law affected both businesses and consumers thus far? Can you foresee any revisions or amendments to the law?

4. Go online or flip through a magazine to find a recognizable trademark. Print or tear out a copy of the ad or Web site containing the trademark. Study the trademark and evaluate it. Why is it so recognizable? How has it benefited the company? Has it changed over time? If not, *should* it change to meet today's styles or attitudes? Is there any way it could be made more effective? What is your personal response to the trademark as a consumer? Present your evaluation to the class.

5. Because it can copy and distribute material anywhere in the world at lightning speed, the Internet has created a whole new challenge for those who create intellectual property—text, music, videos, and software. Some people argue that old copyright laws are obsolete; they may actually stifle technological creativity. Others claim that creators must be protected at all costs. Recently, the National Music Publishers' Association, Viacom, and other groups filed suit against YouTube and its parent Google, claiming that YouTube was breaking copyright law by hosting copyrighted video clips. In addition, two groups representing Chinese musicians have filed suit against Baidu, China's most popular search engine, for similar actions.[22] Imagine you are acting as the judge hearing these lawsuits. Write your own opinion of how they should be settled, including any changes you think should occur in copyright law as it pertains to the Internet.

Appendix B

Insurance and Risk Management

Crisis on the Coasts: Homeowner's Insurance Is Swept Away

When insurance companies issue policies to homeowners, they do so based on detailed calculations of risk. Among the considerations is whether a home is located in an area that is prone to natural disasters such as flooding, earthquakes, wildfires, hurricanes, or tornadoes. To stay in business, insurance firms need to take in more premium revenues than they pay out in claims. But sometimes, major disasters—like hurricanes in the South or massive wildfires that sweep across the West—play havoc with insurers' predictions. Huge claims may result in such a severe hike in rates that homeowners can't afford the coverage, or in some cases, the insurer leaves the state or the region altogether.

Nowhere has this situation been more critical than along the U.S. coast, in southern states like Florida, Louisiana, North Carolina, and Texas. Up north, Massachusetts homeowners face an insurance crisis as the beachfront along Cape Cod erodes, damaging the foundations of houses perched atop dunes. In fact, the ten states with the highest average homeowners' insurance premiums all contain some coastline: Texas, Florida, Louisiana, Oklahoma, Mississippi, California, Massachusetts, Rhode Island, Alabama, and Connecticut. Texans pay the highest premiums of all, an average of $1,409 per year. Florida, Louisiana, and Oklahoma all exceed $1,000, while the national average for homeowners' insurance premiums is $804 per year. Insurance industry officials insist that Texas is prone to the most

unpredictable weather—including hurricanes, hailstorms, and tornadoes—often all in one year. A decade ago, an epidemic of mold spreading throughout Texas homes ate up claims that would have covered other disasters. The mold crisis actually resulted in the passage of a major insurance law designed to restrict the amount of premium increases, but Texas rates continued to rise.

In Florida, the situation became critical when State Farm Insurance announced

Distraught residents look for personal belongings in the aftermath of a tornado. Natural disasters such as tornadoes, hurricanes, and earthquakes not only can cause catastrophic damage but huge increases in claims and subsequent rate hikes for homeowners' insurance.

The Colorado Springs Gazette, Bryan Oller/© AP/Wide World Photos

that it was pulling out of the state, after having done business there for more than 60 years. The company had requested permission of state insurance regulators to raise its rates by 47 percent in one year but was denied. State Farm responded by announcing that it would not renew homeowner policies for its 1.2 million customers and would not issue any new ones. "This is not an action we wanted to take, but one we must take given the realities of the Florida property insurance market," explained State Farm Florida's president.

Consumer advocates and state legislators were angry with the company's action. The move not only signaled lost insurance coverage but also meant more than 5,000 State Farm Florida employees would lose their jobs. Some homeowners said they would simply have to sell their homes. Referring to a state law designed to prohibit insurers from keeping their profitable businesses and dumping the others, one state legislator commented, "You can't just cherry-pick the lines you want to write." But State Farm said it was discontinuing all its homeowners' insurance business, ranging from multimillion dollar mansions to modest dwellings. State Farm had set up its Florida business as a separate entity from its parent company because of what the firm referred to as "the unique risks"—meaning hurricanes and flooding—of conducting business there. Several years ago, it borrowed $750 million from the parent firm and could never repay the money. Unable to raise additional money through rate hikes, State Farm Florida had no other choice but to leave.

Along the North Carolina coast, the insurance commissioner has been locked in a battle with insurance companies over rate hikes and plans for the cost of another major hurricane. The Beach Plan, a state-sanctioned insurance program, is supposed to cover roughly 170,000 properties worth $72 billion along the coast. But the plan doesn't have enough money to do so. The Beach Plan already charges up to 15 percent more than other insurers do—and may have to charge as much as 25 percent. Across the state to the west, residents pay lower premiums, which upsets those who live near the water. Inland homeowners are worried that the Beach Plan may approve surcharges to pass costs along to their properties in the event a catastrophic hurricane sweeps up the coast. If the increase passes, all agree that it will be a hardship to homeowners everywhere across North Carolina. "It's a huge increase—huge," observes one real-estate agent who is fighting the rate hike. "It could take people out of their homes. We can't give up. We have to try to fight this out."[1]

Appendix B OVERVIEW

Risk is a daily fact of life for both individuals and businesses. Sometimes it appears in the form of a serious illness or premature death. In other instances, it takes the form of property loss, such as the extensive damage to homes and businesses due to forest fires in Idaho or hurricanes in Louisiana. Risk can also occur as the result of the actions of others—such as a pizza delivery driver running a red light and striking another vehicle. In still other cases, risk may occur as a result of our own actions—we may not eat as many healthful foods as we should or occasionally drive too fast in the rain.

Businesspeople must understand the types of risk they face and develop methods for dealing with them. One approach to risk is to shift it to specialized firms called *insurance companies*. This appendix discusses the concept of insurance in a business setting. It begins with a definition of risk. We then describe the various ways in which risk can be managed. Next, we list some of the major insurance concepts, such as what constitutes an insurable risk. The appendix concludes with an overview of the major types of insurance.

The Concept of Risk

Risk is uncertainty about loss or injury. Consider the risks faced by a typical business. A factory or warehouse faces the risk of fire, burglary, water damage, and storm damage. Accidents, judgments due to lawsuits, and natural disasters are just some of the risks faced by businesses. Risks can be divided into two major categories: speculative risk and pure risk.

Speculative risk gives the firm or individual the chance of either a profit or a loss. Purchasing shares of stock on the basis of the latest hot tip from an acquaintance at the local health club can result in profits or losses. Expanding operations into a new market may result in higher profits or the loss of invested funds.

Pure risk, on the other hand, involves only the chance of loss. Motorists, for example, always face the risk of accidents. If they occur, both financial and physical losses may result. If they do not occur, however, drivers do not profit. Insurance often helps individuals and businesses protect against financial loss resulting from some types of pure risk.

Risk Management

Because risk is an unavoidable part of business, managers must find ways to deal with it. The first step in any risk management plan is to recognize what's at risk and why it's at risk. After that, the manager must decide how to handle the risk. In general, businesses have four alternatives in handling risk: avoid it, minimize it, assume it, or transfer it.

Executives must consider many factors when evaluating risks, both at home and abroad. These factors include a nation's economic stability; social and cultural factors, such as language; available technologies; distribution systems; and government regulations. International businesses are typically exposed to less risk in countries with stable economic, social and cultural, and political and legal environments.

Avoiding Risk

Some of the pure risks facing individuals can be avoided by taking a healthy approach to life. Abstaining from smoking, getting regular exercise and staying physically fit, and not driving during blizzards and other hazardous conditions are three ways of avoiding personal risk. By the same token, businesses can also avoid some of the pure risks they face. For example, a manufacturer can locate a new production facility away from a flood-prone area.

Reducing Risk

Managers can reduce or even eliminate many types of risk by removing hazards or taking preventive measures. Many companies develop safety programs to educate employees about potential hazards and the proper methods of performing certain dangerous tasks. For instance, any employee who works at a hazardous waste site is required to have training and medical monitoring that meet the federal Occupational Safety and Health Administration (OSHA) standards. The training and monitoring not only reduce risk but pay off on the bottom line. Aside from the human tragedy, accidents cost companies time and money.

Although many actions can reduce the risk involved in business operations, they cannot eliminate risk entirely. Most major insurers help their clients avoid or minimize risk by offering the services of loss-prevention experts to conduct thorough reviews of their operations. These health and safety professionals evaluate customers' work environments and recommend procedures and equipment to help firms minimize worker injuries and property losses.

By the same token, individuals can take actions to reduce risk. For instance, obeying all traffic laws and keeping a car in good working condition can reduce the risks associated with driving. Boarding up windows or using hurricane shutters often reduces the damage caused by hurricane winds. Taking these and other actions, however, can't entirely eliminate risk.

Self-Insuring against Risk

Instead of purchasing insurance against certain types of pure risk, some companies accumulate funds to cover potential losses. So-called *self-insurance funds* are special funds created by periodically setting aside cash reserves that the firm can draw on in the event of a financial loss resulting from a pure risk. A firm makes regular payments to the fund, and it charges losses to the fund. Such a fund typically accompanies a risk-reduction program aimed at minimizing losses.

One of the most common forms of self-insurance is employee health insurance. Most employers provide health insurance coverage to employees as a component of their fringe benefit programs. Many, especially larger ones, find it more economical to create a self-insurance fund covering projected employee healthcare expenses, as opposed to purchasing a health insurance policy from a health insurance company, like Indiana-based WellPoint. Self-insured employers, however, almost always contract with a health insurer to administer their employee health plans.

Shifting Risk to an Insurance Company

Although organizations and individuals can take steps to avoid or reduce risk, the most common method of dealing with it is to shift it to others in the form of **insurance**—a contract by which an insurer, for a fee, agrees to reimburse another firm or individual a sum of money if a loss occurs. The insured party's fee to the insurance company for coverage against losses is called a **premium.** Insurance substitutes a small, known loss—the insurance premium—for a larger, unknown loss that may or may not occur. In the case of life insurance, the loss—death—is a certainty; the main uncertainty is the date when it will occur.

It is important for the insurer to understand the customer's business, risk exposure, and insurance needs. Firms that operate in several countries usually do business with insurance companies that maintain global networks of offices.

> **insurance** contract by which the insurer for a fee agrees to reimburse the insured a sum of money if a loss occurs.

> **premium** amount paid by the insured to the insurer to exchange for insurance coverage.

Basic Insurance Concepts

Figure B.1 illustrates how an insurance company operates. The insurer collects premiums from policyholders in exchange for insurance coverage. The insurance company uses some of these funds to pay current claims and operating expenses. What's left over is held in the form of reserves, which are in turn invested. Reserves can be used to pay for unexpected losses. The returns from insurance company reserves may allow the insurer to reduce premiums, generate profits, or both. By investing reserves, the insurance industry represents a major source of long-term financing for other businesses.

An insurance company is a professional risk taker. For a fee, it accepts risks of loss or damage to businesses and individuals. Four basic principles underlie insurance: the concept of insurable interest, the concept of insurable risk, the rule of indemnity, and the law of large numbers.

Insurable Interest

To purchase insurance, an applicant must demonstrate an **insurable interest** in the property or life of the insured. In other words, the policyholder must stand to suffer a loss, financial or otherwise, due to fire, storm damage, accident, theft, illness, death, or lawsuit. A homeowner,

> **insurable interest** demonstration that a direct financial loss will result if some event occurs.

How an Insurance Company Operates

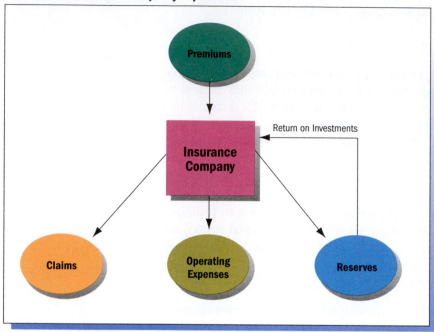

for example, has an insurable interest in his or her home and its contents. In the case of life insurance coverage purchased for someone providing the bulk of a household's income, the policyholder's spouse and minor children have a clear insurable interest.

A firm can purchase property and liability insurance on physical assets—such as offices and factories—to cover losses due to such hazards as fire and theft because the company can demonstrate an obvious insurable interest. Similarly, because top executives are important assets to a company, a business often purchases key person life insurance, which compensates the business should an important individual die.

Insurable Risk

Insurable risk refers to the requirements that a risk must meet in order for the insurer to provide protection. Only some pure risks, and no speculative ones, are insurable. There are four basic requirements for a pure risk to be considered an insurable risk:

insurable risk requirement that a pure risk must meet for an insurer to agree to provide coverage.

1. The likelihood of loss should be reasonably predictable. If an insurance company cannot reasonably predict losses, it has no basis for setting affordable premiums.
2. The loss should be financially measurable.
3. The loss should be accidental, or fortuitous.
4. The risk should be spread over a certain geographic area.

underwriting process used by an insurance company to determine who, or what, to insure and how much to charge.

The insurance company has the right to set standards for accepting risk. This process of setting these standards, and deciding what to charge, is known as **underwriting.**

Rule of Indemnity

rule of indemnity requirement that the insured cannot collect more than the amount of the loss and cannot collect for the same loss more than once.

The **rule of indemnity** states that the insured cannot collect more than the amount of the loss. Nor can the insured collect for that loss more than once. For instance, assume a drycleaner's delivery van is damaged in an accident. If the total damage amounts to $2,500, that is the maximum amount the business can collect from the insurance company.

Occasionally a loss may be covered by more than one policy. For instance, assume that a $5,000 loss is covered by two different policies. The rule of indemnity means that the insured individual or business can only collect a total of $5,000 from both insurance companies. It is up to the insurers to decide which pays how much based on policy specifics.

The Law of Large Numbers

Insurance is based on the law of averages, or statistical probability. Insurance companies simply cannot afford to sell insurance policies unless they can reasonably predict losses. As a result, insurance companies have studied the chances of occurrences of deaths, injuries, property damage, lawsuits, and other types of hazards. Table B.1 is an example of the kind

Table B.1	Relationship between the Age of the Driver and the Number of Motor Vehicle Accidents

Age Group	Accident Rate (per 100 drivers)
19 years old and under	23
16 years old	21
17 years old	21
18 years old	21
19 years old	19
20 to 24 years old	15
20 years old	17
21 years old	16
22 years old	14
23 years old	14
24 years old	13
25 to 34 years old	9
35 to 44 years old	7
45 to 54 years old	8
55 to 64 years old	7
65 to 74 years old	5
75 years old and over	5

Source: U.S. Census Bureau, 2009 Statistical Abstract of the United States, http://www.census.gov, accessed April 17, 2009.

of data insurance companies examine. It shows the automobile accident rate, by the age of the driver, for a recent year. From their investigations, insurance companies have developed **actuarial tables,** which predict the number of fires, automobile accidents, or deaths that will occur in a given year. Premiums charged for insurance coverage are based on these tables. Actuarial tables are based on the law of large numbers. In essence, the **law of large numbers** states that seemingly random events will follow a predictable pattern if enough events are observed.

An example can demonstrate how insurers use the law of large numbers to calculate premiums. Previously collected statistical data on a city with 50,000 homes indicates that the city will experience an average of 500 fires a year, with damages averaging $30,000 per occurrence. What is the minimum annual premium an insurance company would charge to insure one residence?

To simplify the calculations, assume that the premiums would not produce profits or cover any of the insurance company's operating expenses—they would just produce enough income to pay policyholders for their losses. In total, fires in the city would generate claims of $15 million (500 homes damaged × $30,000). If these losses were spread over all 50,000 homes, each homeowner would be charged an annual premium of $300 ($15 million ÷ 50,000 homes). In reality, though, the insurer would set the premium at a higher figure to cover operating expenses, build reserves, and earn a reasonable profit. For instance, during a recent year, life insurers collected almost $150 billion in premiums while paying out approximately $94 billion in claims.[2]

actuarial table probability of the number of events that are expected to occur within a given year.

law of large numbers concept that seemingly random events will follow predictable patterns if enough events are observed.

Some losses are easier for insurance companies to predict than others. Life insurance companies, for example, can predict with high accuracy the number of policyholders who will die within a specified period of time. Losses from such hazards as automobile accidents and weather events are much more difficult to predict. For example, in a recent year U.S. homeowners insurance claims were 32 percent less than they were in 2005, the year of several major hurricanes including Katrina.[3]

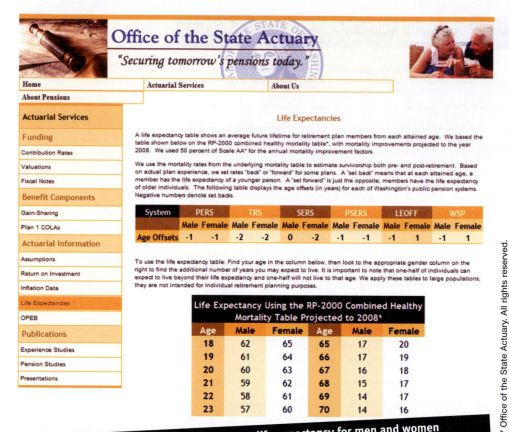

Life Expectancies

A life expectancy table shows an average future lifetime for retirement plan members from each attained age. We based the table shown below on the RP-2000 combined healthy mortality table*, with mortality improvements projected to the year 2008. We used 50 percent of Scale AA* for the annual mortality improvement factors.

We use the mortality rates from the underlying mortality table to estimate survivorship both pre- and post-retirement. Based on actual plan experience, we set rates "back" or "forward" for some plans. A "set back" means that at each attained age, a member has the life expectancy of a younger person. A "set forward" is just the opposite; members have the life expectancy of older individuals. The following table displays the age offsets (in years) for each of Washington's public pension systems. Negative numbers denote set backs.

System	PERS		TRS		SERS		PSERS		LEOFF		WSP	
	Male	Female	Male	Female	Male	Female	Male	Female	Male	Female	Male	Female
Age Offsets	-1	-1	-2	-2	0	-2	-1	-1	-1	1	-1	1

To use the life expectancy table: Find your age in the column below, then look to the appropriate gender column on the right to find the additional number of years you may expect to live. It is important to note that one-half of individuals can expect to live beyond their life expectancy and one-half will not live to that age. We apply these tables to large populations; they are not intended for individual retirement planning purposes.

Life Expectancy Using the RP-2000 Combined Healthy Mortality Table Projected to 2008*					
Age	Male	Female	Age	Male	Female
18	62	65	65	17	20
19	61	64	66	17	19
20	60	63	67	16	18
21	59	62	68	15	17
22	58	61	69	14	17
23	57	60	70	14	16

These actuarial tables show the current life expectancy for men and women between the ages of 18 and 110. They were prepared for residents of Washington State by the Office of the State Actuary.

Sources of Insurance Coverage

The insurance industry includes both for-profit companies, such as Prudential, State Farm, and Geico (part of famed investor Warren Buffett's firm Berkshire Hathaway), and a number of public agencies that provide insurance coverage for business firms, not-for-profit organizations, and individuals. Let's look at the primary features of this array of insurers.

Public Insurance Agencies

A **public insurance agency** is a state or federal government unit established to provide specialized insurance protection for individuals and organizations. It provides protection in such areas as job loss (unemployment insurance) and work-related injuries (workers' compensation). Public insurance agencies also sponsor specialized programs, such as deposit, flood, and crop insurance.

UNEMPLOYMENT INSURANCE Every state has an unemployment insurance program that assists unemployed workers by providing financial benefits, job counseling, and placement services. Compensation amounts vary depending on workers' previous incomes and the states in which they file claims. These insurance programs are funded by payroll taxes paid by employers.

WORKERS' COMPENSATION Under state laws, employers must provide workers' compensation insurance to guarantee payment of wages and salaries, medical care costs, and such rehabilitation services as retraining, job placement, and vocational rehabilitation to employees who are injured on the job. In addition, workers' compensation provides benefits in the form of weekly payments or single, lump-sum payments to survivors of workers who die as a result of work-related injuries. Premiums are based on the company's payroll, the on-the-job hazards to which it exposes workers, and its safety record.

SOCIAL SECURITY The federal government is the nation's largest insurer. The Social Security program, established in 1935, provides retirement, survivor, and disability benefits to millions of Americans. **Medicare** was added to the Social Security program in 1965 to provide health insurance for people age 65 and older and certain other Social Security recipients. More than nine out of ten workers in the United States and their dependents are eligible for Social Security program benefits. The program is funded through a payroll tax, half of which is paid by employers and half by workers. Self-employed people pay the full tax.

Private Insurance Companies

Much of the insurance in force is provided by private firms. These companies provide protection in exchange for the payment of premiums. Some private insurers are stockholder owned, and therefore are run like any other business, and others are so-called *mutual associations*. Most, though not all, mutual insurance companies specialize in life insurance. Technically, mutual insurance companies are owned by their policyholders, who may receive premium rebates in the form of dividends. In spite of this, however, there is no evidence that an insurance policy from a mutual company costs any less than a comparable policy from a stockholder-owned insurer. In recent years some mutual insurance companies have reorganized as stockholder-owned companies, including Prudential, one of the nation's largest insurers.

Types of Insurance

Individuals and businesses spend hundreds of billions of dollars each year on insurance coverage. Figure B.2 shows how much insurance companies collected in premiums for selected types of insurance in a recent year. All too often, however, both business firms and individual households make poor decisions when buying insurance. There are four commonsense tips to remember when buying insurance:

1. Insure against large losses, not small ones. It is generally much more cost effective to self-insure against small losses.

2. Buy insurance with broad coverage, not narrow coverage. For example, it is much less expensive generally to buy a homeowners policy that protects you from multiple events (perils such as fire and theft) than to buy several policies that cover individual events.

3. Shop around. Premiums for similar policies can vary widely from company to company.

4. Buy insurance only from financially strong companies. Insurance companies occasionally go bankrupt. If that happens, the insured is left with no coverage and little hope of getting premiums back.

Although insurers offer hundreds of different policies, they all fall into three broad categories: property and liability insurance, health and disability insurance, and life insurance.

Figure B.2

Premiums Collected by Insurance Companies for Selected Types of Insurance

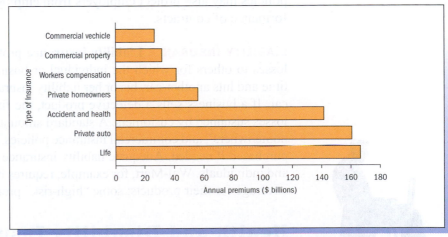

Note: Accident and health includes long-term care and disability insurance.
Source: Insurance Information Institute, *2009 Insurance Fact Book,* http://www.iii.org.

Property and Liability Insurance

Insurance that protects against fire, accident, theft, or other destructive events, or perils, is called **property and liability insurance.** Examples of this insurance category include homeowners' insurance, auto insurance, business or commercial insurance, and liability insurance. Most property and liability policies are subject to deductibles. A deducible is the amount of the loss the insured pays out of pocket.

HOMEOWNERS' INSURANCE Homeowners' insurance protects homeowners from damage to their residences due to various perils. If a home is destroyed by fire, for example, the homeowners' policy will pay to replace the home and its contents. Virtually all homeowners carry coverage of this nature.

Homeowners' insurance premiums have risen sharply in recent years. Moreover, homeowners in several states, including Texas and Florida, are finding it increasingly difficult to obtain homeowners' insurance because an increasing number of insurance companies are refusing to sell new policies or renew existing policies. Not only have premiums risen, but insurance companies are also revising coverage concerning damage caused by catastrophic perils such as hurricanes, other windstorms, and hail. For instance, in many states the deductible on a homeowners' policy is now based on the percentage of the home's value, not a specified dollar amount. And this percentage is often higher if the damage was caused by a hurricane.[4]

Although standard policies cover a wide range of perils, most do not cover damage from widespread catastrophes such as floods and earthquakes. Homeowners must purchase separate policies to protect against damage caused by these perils. Flood insurance is available through the National Flood Insurance Program. Earthquake coverage is offered in several earthquake-prone states such as California and Washington but is very expensive.

AUTO INSURANCE With more than $150 billion in annual premiums, automobile insurance is the country's largest category of property and liability insurance. Automobile insurance policies cover losses due to automobile accidents or theft, including personal and property claims. Virtually all states require drivers to have a minimum amount of auto insurance coverage.

COMMERCIAL AND BUSINESS INSURANCE Commercial and business insurance protects firms from financial losses resulting from the suspension of business operations (**business interruption insurance**) or physical damage to property as a result of destructive events. These policies may also protect employers from employee dishonesty or losses resulting from nonperformance of contracts.

LIABILITY INSURANCE Liability insurance protects an individual or business against financial losses to others for which the individual or business was responsible. If a driver fails to stop in time and hits another car, his or her liability insurance would pay to repair the damage to the other car. If a business sells a defective product, the firm's liability insurance would pay for financial losses sustained by customers. A standard amount of liability coverage is usually attached to auto, homeowners', and commercial insurance policies. Additional amounts of liability insurance can be purchased if needed. Adequate liability insurance is critically important today for both businesses and individuals. Wal-Mart, for example, requires its suppliers to have at least $2 million in liability coverage for their products; some "high-risk" products require a minimum of $10 million.[5]

Health and Disability Insurance

Each of us faces the risk of getting sick or being injured in some way. Even a relatively minor illness can result in substantial healthcare bills. To guard against this risk, most Americans have some form of **health insurance**—insurance that provides coverage for expenses due to sickness or accidents. With soaring costs in health care, this type of insurance has become an important consideration for both businesses and individuals.

Sources of health insurance include private individual policies, private group policies, and the federal government, through Medicare and Medicaid (health insurance for lower-income people). More than 60 percent of Americans are covered by private group health insurance provided by their employer as an employee benefit. Four of every five U.S. employees work for businesses and not-for-profits that offer some form of group health insurance. Group policies resemble individual health insurance policies but are offered at lower premiums. Individual health insurance policies are simply too expensive for most people. Of every $10 spent by employers on employee compensation (wages, salaries, and employee benefits), more than $1 goes to cover the cost of health insurance. Health insurance costs have soared in recent years, and employers have responded by cutting back on benefits, requiring employees to pay more of the premium, charging higher deductibles, or even dropping coverage altogether.

Private health insurance plans fall into one of two general categories: fee-for-service plans and managed care plans. In a **fee-for-service plan,** the insured picks his or her doctor and has almost unlimited access to specialists. Fee-for-service plans charge an annual deductible and copayments. By contrast, a **managed care plan** pays most of the insured's healthcare bills. In return, the program has a great deal of say over the conditions of healthcare provided for the insured. Most managed care plans, for example, restrict the use of specialists and may specify which hospitals and pharmacies can be used. Some employers offer employees a choice between a fee-for-service and a managed care plan. Multiple managed care plans are sometimes available.

Managed care plans have become extremely popular in recent years. More than 150 million Americans are enrolled in some form of managed care plan, and many fee-for-service plans have adopted some elements of managed care. A primary reason for the popularity of managed care is simply cost: managed care plans generally cost employers and employees less than fee-for-service plans. Managed care, however, is not without its critics. The effort to control costs has caused a backlash because of restrictions placed on doctors and patients. Legislation at both the federal and state level has forced managed care plans to give patients and physicians more control over medical decisions.

TYPES OF MANAGED CARE PLANS Two types of managed care plans can be found in the United States: health maintenance organizations and preferred provider organizations. Although both manage health care, important differences exist between the two.

Health maintenance organizations (HMOs) do not provide health insurance, they provide health care. An HMO supplies all of the individual's healthcare needs, including prescription drugs and hospitalization. The individual must use the HMO's own doctors and approved treatment facilities in order to receive benefits. Doctors and other healthcare professionals are actually employees of the HMO. Individuals pick a primary care physician and cannot see a specialist without a referral. An HMO charges no deductibles and only a low, fixed-dollar copayment.

The second type of managed care plan is the preferred provider organization (PPO). In the United States, more individuals are covered by PPOs than by HMOs. A PPO is an arrangement in which an

health insurance
category of insurance that pays for losses due to illness or injury.

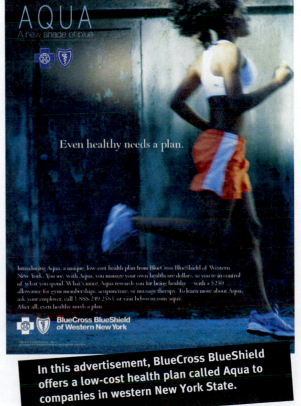

In this advertisement, BlueCross BlueShield offers a low-cost health plan called Aqua to companies in western New York State.

PRNews Foto/Jay Advertising, Inc/NewsCom

employer negotiates a contract between local healthcare providers (physicians, hospitals, and pharmacies) to provide medical care to its employees at a discount. These plans have low fixed-dollar copayments. They are generally much more flexible than HMOs. Members can choose their primary care physician from a list of doctors. If a referral is given or hospitalization is required, the member again chooses from a list of approved healthcare providers. A member who obtains treatment from a healthcare provider outside the PPO network may be reimbursed for only part of the cost.

DISABILITY INCOME INSURANCE Not only is **disability income insurance** one of the most overlooked forms of insurance, but many workers don't have enough coverage. The odds of a person developing a disability are considerably higher than most people realize. Take a group of five randomly selected 45-year-olds. There is approximately a 95 percent chance that one of the five will develop some form of a disability during the next 20 years. Disability income insurance is designed to replace lost income when a wage earner cannot work due to an accident or illness.

Two sources of disability income insurance exist: Social Security and private disability insurance policies. Social Security disability benefits are available to virtually all workers, but they have very strict requirements. Private disability insurance is available on either an individual or group basis. As with health insurance, a group policy is much cheaper than an individual policy. Many employers provide at least some disability coverage as an employee benefit. Employees often have the option of obtaining additional coverage by paying more.

life insurance protects people against the financial losses that occur with premature death.

Among other benefits, many businesses offer life insurance to their employees. Although groups usually get a better deal on insurance than individuals, young employees may do better with an individual insurance policy.

Photodisc/Getty Images

Life Insurance

Life insurance protects people against the financial losses that occur with premature death. Three of every four Americans have some form of life insurance. The main reason people buy life insurance is to provide financial security for their families in the event of their death. With assets totaling more than $4 trillion, the life insurance industry is one of the nation's largest businesses.

TYPES OF LIFE INSURANCE As with health and disability insurance, both individual and group life insurance policies are available. Many employers offer life insurance to employees as a component of the firm's benefit program. However, unlike health and disability insurance, an individual life insurance policy is usually cheaper than a group policy for younger people.

The different types of life insurance fall neatly into two categories: term policies and so-called *cash value policies*. **Term policies** provide a death benefit if the policyholder dies within a specified period of time. It has no value at the end of that period. **Cash value policies**—sometimes called whole life and universal life—combine life insurance protection with a savings or investment feature. The cash value represents the amount of the savings or investment portion of the policy. Although there are arguments in favor of cash value policies, many experts believe that term life insurance is a better choice for most consumers. For one thing, a term policy is much cheaper than a cash value policy, especially for younger people.

HOW MUCH LIFE INSURANCE SHOULD YOU HAVE? People can purchase life insurance policies for almost any amount. Life insurance purchases are limited only by the amount of premiums people can afford and their ability to meet medical qualifications. The amount of life insurance a person needs, however, is a very personal decision. The general rule of thumb is that a person needs life insurance if he or she has family members who financially depend on that individual. A young parent with three small children could easily need $500,000 or more of life insurance. A single person with no dependents would reasonably see little or no need for a life insurance policy.

Businesses, as well as individuals, buy life insurance. The death of a partner or a key executive is likely to result in a financial loss to an organization. Key person insurance reimburses the organization for the loss of the services of an essential senior executive and to cover the executive search expenses needed to find a replacement. In addition, life insurance policies may be purchased for each member of a partnership to be able to repay the deceased partner's survivors for his or her share of the firm and permit the business to continue.

Business Terms You Need to Know

risk A-20	insurable risk A-22	law of large numbers A-23	life insurance A-28
insurance A-21	underwriting A-22	property and liability	
premium A-21	rule of indemnity A-22	insurance A-26	
insurable interest A-21	actuarial table A-23	health insurance A-27	

Other Important Business Terms

speculative risk A-20	Medicare A-25	fee-for-service plan A-27	term policy A-28
pure risk A-20	business interruption	managed care plan A-27	cash value policy A-28
public insurance	insurance A-26	disability income	
agency A-24	liability insurance A-26	insurance A-28	

Projects and Teamwork Applications

1. Assume you're the owner of a small plumbing supply warehouse and delivery company. Working with a partner, list some of some of the major risks your business faces. How should each risk be handled (avoided, reduced, assumed, or transferred)? What types of insurance will your business likely have to have, including those types of insurance required by law?

2. Assess your own personal insurance needs. What types of coverage do you currently have? How do you see your insurance needs changing in the next five to ten years?

3. Insurance terminology is often very confusing. Visit the Web site listed (http://www.iii.org/media/glossary) and define the following insurance terms: adverse selection, declaration, floater, reinsurance, and waiver.

4. The U.S. Census Bureau and Kaiser Family Foundation prepare reports periodically on health insurance. Visit the Web sites listed (http://www.census.gov/hhes/www/hlthins/hlthins.html; http://www.kff.org/insurance/index.cfm) and access the latest reports you can find. Make a list of five or six highlights about the state of health insurance in the United States.

5. As health insurance costs have risen, some employers have responded by instituting wellness programs, encouraging employees to stop smoking, exercise, lose weight, and generally pursue healthier lifestyles. A few organizations go further, mandating such programs as a condition of continued employment. Go to the library and research several examples of employer wellness programs. What are the pros and cons, including the ethics, of such programs? How would you feel if your employer had such a program?

Personal Financial Planning

The Credit Card Hustle

In one recent student-loan survey of college graduates, nearly half said they wished they had learned more in college about managing their finances. You have the chance now to become one of the other 50 percent. Start by thinking hard about any credit cards you carry and the way you use them.

According to student loan company Nellie Mae, by the end of his or her first year in college, the average student is $1,500 in debt thanks to the easy availability of credit cards. Many companies offer credit cards to students who have no job, no credit history, and no income, and the firms provide incentives to sign up that range from free meals to T-shirt giveaways. Credit card companies also use sophisticated strategies to pitch their cards. Advertising online and via cell phone has proliferated. Chase has a Facebook page for online sign-ups, Visa partners with trendy makeup vendor Urban Decay, and Bank of America hosts on-campus promotions. Says a senior vice president at Chase, "If we can put content in places where people are already spending their time, we can create a different kind of relationship with them. We think it will translate to a more loyal and active customer base."

While some credit companies also offer credit education and free financial handbooks, critics say these efforts are not enough. "The whole point is to establish a relationship with a naïve consumer with a free gift that makes it look like they're your friend and that they're thinking in your best interest," says Robert Manning, author of *Credit Card Nation* and a professor at the Rochester Institute of Technology. Others agree that

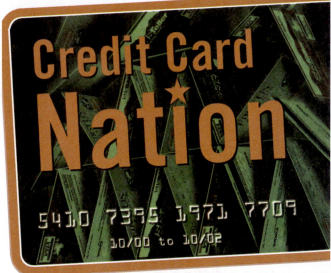

Reproduced with permission of Perseus Books, Cambridge, MA

Credit Card Nation

5410 7395 1971 7709

10/00 to 10/02

THE CONSEQUENCES

OF AMERICA'S ADDICTION

TO CREDIT

Robert D. Manning

"*Credit Card Nation* should be required reading for the tens of millions of Americans in debt to the Visas of the world and deeply immersed in our credit-card-driven consumer culture." *

Beware the lure of easy credit. Banks are only too willing to extend credit to naïve consumers, as Robert Manning, author of *Credit Card Nation*, warns.

credit card companies take advantage of students. Defenders such as the American Bankers Association respond that it insults students' intelligence to assume they will take on unnecessary debt for the sake of a free T-shirt or other incentive. Credit card providers claim students use credit cards for educational needs like textbooks and for emergencies.

Because they're not forking over cash, few students realize how much money they are spending with plastic, how difficult it is to pay it back, or how quickly interest can accumulate on unpaid balances. Credit problems also damage the borrower's credit history if payments lag. "There is an aura or a freedom that a credit card gives a student, and that can very quickly turn into something financially dangerous," says the chief executive of a Web site that offers credit card comparisons. Many credit providers cushion young debtors at first, by raising their credit limits—and their interest rates—or offering supplemental loans.

Widespread publicity related to student debt has led some companies to pull back on their promotions, and many colleges offer debt counseling in free seminars and workshops. Still, some states are considering legislation to restrict solicitations on college campuses. But almost half of all college students already carry credit cards, and many react like Mallory Parker did in her first year at Arizona State: "I charged everything on it," she says of her card, until she found herself with $2,200 of debt plus interest.

Read on for some specific strategies for managing your finances, including debt, and remember, as a spokesperson for Money Management International says, "Credit is a tool of convenience, not an extension of income."[1]

Appendix C OVERVIEW

You are studying business, but much of what you learn in this course will also apply to your personal life. For instance, you learn about each of the important functions of a business—from accounting to marketing, from finance to management. Learning about each business function will help you choose a career, and a career choice is one of the most important personal financial decisions you will make. You will learn why firms prepare budgets and financial statements. But budgets and financial statements are also important tools for individuals and households.

Everyone, regardless of age or income, can probably do a better job of managing his or her finances. As a group, Americans are much better at making money than they are at managing money. This appendix introduces you to personal financial management. **Personal financial management** deals with a variety of issues and decisions that affect a person's financial well-being. It includes basic money management, credit, tax planning, major consumer purchases, insurance, investing, and retirement planning.

The appendix will draw from many of the topics you will learn while studying business, but it introduces you to some new concepts as well. It is hoped that after completing the appendix, you will be a better-informed financial consumer and personal money manager and that you will be motivated to learn more about personal finance. The rewards, in both monetary and nonmonetary terms, can be tremendous.

The Meaning and Importance of Personal Finance

personal financial management study of the economic factors and personal decisions that affect a person's financial well-being.

Personal finance is the study of the economic factors and personal decisions that affect a person's financial well-being. Personal finance affects, and is affected by, many things we do and many decisions we make throughout our lives.

Your lifestyle affects your finances. Skiing at expensive resorts won't leave much money in your savings account.

On one level, personal finance involves money know-how. It is essential to know how to earn money, as well as how to save, spend, invest, and control it in order to achieve goals. The reward of sound money management is an improvement in one's standard of living. **Standard of living** consists of the necessities, comforts, or luxuries an individual seeks to attain or maintain.

On another level, personal finance is intertwined with each person's lifestyle—the way we live our daily lives. Our choice of careers, friends, hobbies, communities, and possessions is determined by personal finances, and yet our personal finances can also be determined by our lifestyles. If, for example, you're a college student living independently on a shoestring budget, you will probably have to make many financial sacrifices to achieve your educational goals. Where you live is determined by what school you attend and how much you can afford to pay for rent; your vacation is set by your academic schedule and your checkbook balance; your clothing depends on the climate and your budget. All these lifestyle decisions are largely determined by your personal finances.

Ryan McVay/The Image Bank/Getty Images

standard of living
necessities, comforts, and luxuries one seeks to obtain or to maintain.

The Importance of Personal Finance Today

Good money management has always been important, but major changes in the external environment over the past couple of decades have made personal finance even more important today. And this is true whether you're a 20-year-old college student, a 40-year-old parent with a mortgage, or a 60-year-old thinking about retirement. Let's look at three reasons why personal financial planning is so important in today's environment.

SLUGGISH GROWTH IN PERSONAL INCOME Personal income in the United States has grown very slowly in recent years. For example, median income, adjusted for inflation, rose at an annual rate of less than 1 percent over the past decade.[2] Will this trend continue? Perhaps. Many experts forecast that annual increases in wages and salaries will barely keep pace with the rate of inflation in the coming years.

The sluggish growth in personal income makes sound money management very important. You cannot count on rising personal income by itself to improve your standard of living. Rather, you need to save and invest more money, stick to a budget, and make major purchases wisely.

CHANGES IN THE LABOR MARKET Job security and the notion of work have changed in recent years. The traditional model of working for the same company for one's entire career is very rare today. Recent data show that job tenure—the length of time a person has worked for his or her current employer—has declined sharply over the past 20 years. Moreover, the probability of someone entering the workforce today and working for the same employer in ten years has also noticeably declined.[3]

The fact is you and your classmates will likely change jobs and even employers several times during your careers. Some will end up working part-time or on a contract basis, with little job security and fewer benefits. Others will take time off to care for small children or elderly parents. And a goal many people have today is to start their own business and work for themselves.

Furthermore, it is estimated that one in four workers today will be unemployed at some point during their working lives. Frankly, you never know when your employer will "downsize," taking your job with it, or "outsource" your job to someone else. Just review today's headlines, and you will see that announcements of prominent companies downsizing and outsourcing are common.

These changes make sound personal financial management even more important. You have to keep your career skills up-to-date and accumulate sufficient financial resources to weather an unexpected crisis.

MORE OPTIONS The number of choices today in such areas as banking, credit, investments, and retirement planning can be bewildering. Today you can do most of your banking with a brokerage firm and then buy mutual fund shares at a bank. Even the simple checking account has become more complicated. The typical bank offers several different types of checking accounts, each with its own features and fees. Choosing the wrong account could easily cost you a hundred dollars or more in unnecessary fees each year.

Fifteen years ago, few college students carried credit cards, and those who did typically had cards tied to their parents' accounts. Banks and other credit card issuers didn't consider college students to be reasonable risks. The situation is considerably different today. Most college students have their own credit card accounts; many have multiple accounts. Approximately half of all college students carry a balance from month to month, and credit problems are a major reason some students drop out of college.

One of the first things you'll do when you start a new job is make decisions concerning employee benefits. The typical employer may offer lots of choices in such areas as health insurance, disability insurance, group life insurance, and retirement plans. Select the wrong health insurance plan, for example, and you could end up paying thousands of dollars more in out-of-pocket costs. Making the wrong decisions concerning retirement, even if you're still in your 20s, could make it more difficult to achieve a financially secure retirement.

Most people believe that choice is a good thing, and having more choices in the personal finance arena means the consumer is likely to find what he or she seeks. At the same time, however, a longer menu of choices means it's easier to make mistakes. The more informed you are, the better choices and fewer costly mistakes you are likely to make.

Personal Financial Planning—A Lifelong Activity

Personal financial planning is as important an activity whether you're 20, 40, or 60; whether you're single or married with children; and whether your annual income is $20,000 or $200,000. Many experts say that if you can't stick to a budget and control your spending when you're making $25,000 a year, you'll find it difficult to live within your means even if your income doubles or triples.

The fact that sound planning is a lifelong activity, of course, doesn't mean your financial goals and plans remain constant throughout your life—they won't. The major goal when you're young may be to buy your first home or pay off your college loans. For older people, the major goal is probably making their retirement funds last for the rest of their lives.

Also, the importance of personal finance goals will change as you go through life. Although we should all begin planning for retirement as soon as we begin our careers, the relative importance of retirement and estate planning increases as retirement nears. Choosing the right life insurance policy is a major decision for a 30-year-old father of two, but not for a 65-year-old grandfather. On the other hand, estate planning may be far more important for the 65-year-old than it is for the 30-year-old.

"They Said It"

"Never spend your money before you have it."

—Thomas Jefferson (1743–1826) 3rd president of the United States

A Personal Financial Management Model

financial plan guide to help a person reach desired financial goals.

A **financial plan** is a guide to help you reach targeted goals in the future, closing the gap between where you are currently and where you'd like to be in the future. Goals could include buying a home, starting your own business, sending children to college, or retiring early. Developing a personal financial plan consists of several steps, as illustrated in Figure C.1.

The first step in the process is to establish a clear picture of where you currently stand financially. Next, develop a series of short- and long-term goals. These goals should be influenced by your values, as well as an assessment of your current financial situation. The next step is to establish a set of financial strategies—in each of the personal planning areas—designed to help close the gap between where you are now and where you want to be in the future. Next, put your plan into action and closely monitor its performance. Periodically evaluate the effectiveness of your financial plan and make adjustments when necessary.

Financial plans cannot be developed in a vacuum. They should reflect your available resources—especially salary and fringe benefits, such as health insurance and retirement plans. For example, your goals and financial strategies must be based on a realistic estimate of your future income. If you cannot reach your financial goals through your present career path, you will have to scale back your goals or consider switching careers.

In addition, external factors—such as economic conditions and employment prospects—will influence your financial plan and decisions. For instance, assume you currently rent an apartment but have a goal of buying a home. You can afford to buy a home right now but also believe there is a good chance you'll be offered a much better job in a new city within the next year. A wise financial move might be to postpone buying a home until your employment future becomes clearer.

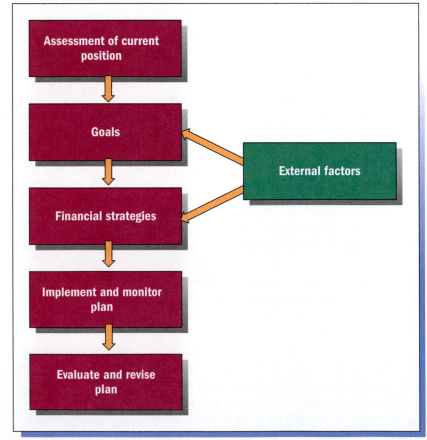

Figure C.1

A Model of Personal Financial Management

General Themes Common to All Financial Plans

Regardless of the specifics, all financial plans revolve around three general themes: (1) maximizing income and wealth, (2) using money more effectively, and (3) monitoring expenditures.

MAXIMIZING INCOME AND WEALTH Maximizing your income and wealth means getting more money. Work smarter; seek retraining for a better, higher-paying job; take career risks that may pay off in the long run; make sound investment decisions—all these are examples of the implementation of the first step. The amount of money you earn is a vital part of any financial plan, and it is up to you to make the most of your opportunities.

USING MONEY MORE EFFECTIVELY Money has two basic uses: consumption and savings. Even if you are a regular saver, you'll still spend most of your income, probably more than 90 percent. You must try to spend every dollar wisely and make every major buying decision part of your overall financial plan. Avoid impulsive spending or giving in to a hard sell.

And it's not just big expenditures you need to watch. Cutting back your spending on small items can make a difference. Little purchases do add up. For example, taking your lunch a couple of times a week rather than eating out could save about $15 a week. Invest that savings at 3 percent interest (per year) and you'll have almost $38,000 in 30 years.

MONITORING EXPENDITURES Budgeting is the key to controlling expenditures. A budget focuses on where the money is going and whether a person's goals are being met. It also suggests appropriate times for reevaluating priorities. If your budget doesn't reflect what you want from life both now and in the future, change it.

Information also helps you keep your expenditures under control. The more you know about real estate, consumer loans, insurance, taxes, and major purchases, the more likely you are to spend the least money to purchase the greatest value.

Small expenses add up. Over time, bringing your own lunch to the office instead of eating out can really beef up your bank account.

Sean Justice/Getty Images

The Pitfalls of Poor Financial Planning

Unfortunately, too many people fail to effectively plan their financial future. Not only do many of these people find it difficult to improve their standard of living, but quite a few also find themselves with mounting debts and a general inability to make ends meet. In a recent year, around 800,000 Americans filed for bankruptcy.[4] What happens to people when they cannot meet their debt obligations?

Creditors will not ignore missed or consistently late payments. First, they will send written inquiries concerning your failure to make required payments on time. Unless you make the payment or contact them about making other arrangements, your creditors are likely to take further actions. Examples of actions creditors can take include repossessing your property, garnishing your wages, or even sending you into personal bankruptcy. At the very least, your ability to obtain credit will be seriously damaged.

"They Said It"

"My problem lies in reconciling my gross habits with my net income."

—Errol Flynn (1909–1959)
Actor

Setting Personal Goals

Whatever your personal financial goals, they should reflect your values. Values are a set of fundamental beliefs of what is important, desirable, and worthwhile in your life. Your values will influence how you spend your money and, therefore, should be the foundation of your financial plan. Each person's financial goals will be determined by the individual's values because every individual considers some things more desirable or important than others. Start by asking yourself some questions about your values, the things that are most important to you, and what you would like to accomplish in your life.

Figure C.2

Relationship between Age and Household Net Worth

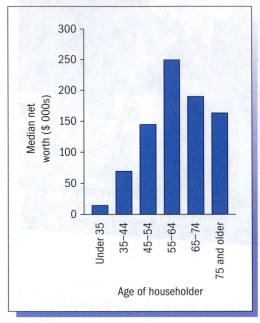

Source: Federal Reserve Board of Governors, Survey of Consumer Finances, http://www.federalreserve.gov, accessed April 7, 2009.

net worth the difference between an individual or household's assets and liabilities.

Your goals are also influenced by your current financial situation. Prepare a set of current financial statements for yourself and update them maybe once a year. Just like a business, a personal income statement reflects income and expenditures during a year. A balance sheet is a statement of what you own (assets) and what you owe (liabilities) at a specific point in time. For an individual or household, the difference between assets and liabilities is called **net worth.** As shown in Figure C.2, not surprisingly as people accumulate assets over their lives, net worth increases.

After reviewing your current financial statements, you should prepare a budget. It is an excellent tool for monitoring your expenditures and cash flow and permits you to track past and current expenditures and plan future ones. Budgets are generally prepared on a monthly basis. Most budgeters divide expenditures into fixed expenses (those that don't change much from month to month) and variable expenses (those that vary). Your monthly apartment rent is probably a fixed expense while the amount you spend each month on utilities (like cell phone, electricity, and cable TV) is most likely a variable expense. One key to effective budgeting is to make sure that the budgeted amounts are realistic.

Next, establish a series of financial goals based on your values and current financial situation. Separate your goals into short-term goals (those you would like to accomplish within the next year or so) and long-term goals (those you would like to accomplish within a longer time span). An example of a short-term goal is "pay off the outstanding balance on my Visa card by this time next year." A long-term goal might be to buy a house by age 30. It is important, of course, that your short-term goals support your long-term goals. For instance, if your long-term goal is to buy a house, short-term goals should include starting a regular savings program and paying off credit card debt.

In addition, some of your goals will be monetary in nature—meaning you can put a price tag on them—while other goals will be nonmonetary. If you want to pay off the outstanding balance on your Visa card by this time next year, and the current balance is $1,000, that is an example of a monetary goal. By contrast, constructing and following a monthly budget is an example of a nonmonetary goal.

Whether short-term or long-term, monetary or nonmonetary, your financial goals should be defined as specifically as possible and focus on results. Goals should also be realistic and attainable. Paying off the $1,000 balance on your Visa card within the next 12 months may be realistic; paying it off in the next 2 months may not be. If your monthly take-home pay is $3,000, and your fixed monthly expenses—such as rent, utilities, transportation, and loan payments—amount to $2,000, setting a goal of saving $750 per month is probably not very realistic. On the other hand, setting a monthly savings goal of $150 may be much more reasonable.

Financial goals change throughout a person's lifetime, and for this reason they should be written down and reviewed periodically. To be effective, goals should reflect changes in circumstances, such as education, family, career, the economic environment, and even your emotional and physical well-being.

Your Personal Financial Decisions

An individual's economic future is charted via financial strategies in such personal planning areas as career choice, credit management, and tax planning. These strategies should reflect your goals and be designed to close the gap between where you are and where you want to be.

Career Choice

No factor exerts as strong an influence on an individual's personal finances as does career choice. Virtually all of your income, especially when you're just starting out, will come from wages and salaries. It is through work that all of us acquire the income needed to build a lifestyle; to buy goods and services, including insurance protection; to save and invest; and to plan for retirement. Your job is also the source of many important fringe benefits, such as health insurance and retirement savings plans, that are important components of your financial future. Throughout *Contemporary Business*, we've discussed ways to select a career that fits your skills and interests, find a job, and perform in that job.

Basic Money Management

Basic money management involves managing checking and savings accounts. Properly managing these relatively simple financial assets is an important first step toward proper management of more complicated financial assets such as investment and retirement accounts. You must choose a bank or other financial institution and then select the right checking account. Banks today offer several different types of checking accounts, each with its own set of features and fees.

Table C.1 lists several commonsense tips for selecting and managing a checking account. Managing a savings account involves understanding the importance of savings, setting savings goals, and picking the best savings option.

Credit Management

Not surprisingly, credit is the area of personal finance that gets more people into financial difficulties than any other area. And Americans love credit. According to recent data from the Federal Reserve, Americans now owe in excess of $2.5 trillion, excluding home mortgage loans. This amount has almost doubled over the past ten years.[5]

Credit allows a person to purchase goods and services by borrowing the necessary funds from a lender, such as a bank. The borrower agrees to repay the loan over a specified period of time, paying a specified rate of interest. The **finance charge** is the difference between the amount borrowed and the amount repaid. Credit is available from many sources today, but rates vary, so it pays to shop around.

credit receiving money, goods, or services on the basis of an agreement between the lender and the borrower that the loan is for a specified period of time with a specified rate of interest.

finance charge the difference between the amount borrowed and the amount repaid on a loan.

Table C.1	Some Commonsense Tips for Choosing and Managing a Checking Account
•	Shop around. There are lots of financial institutions that offer checking accounts. Fees and services vary considerably.
•	Choose the right account for the way you bank. Consider such factors as the number of checks you write each month, how often you use ATMs, and your average monthly balance.
•	Keep good records and regularly balance your checking account.
•	Use your personal computer to pay bills electronically, balance your checkbook, and perform other banking tasks.
•	Watch how you use your ATM card. Know which ATMs are owned by your bank and how much you're charged to use another bank's ATM. Be careful when using an ATM to check your current balance.
•	Notify your bank immediately if your ATM card is lost or stolen.
•	Sign up for overdraft protection.
•	Understand how your bank computes minimum monthly balance.
•	Read the fine print in your monthly statement.

There are two broad types of consumer credit: revolving (or open-end) credit and installment credit. Revolving credit is a type of credit arrangement that enables consumers to make a number of different purchases up to a credit limit, specified by the lender. The consumer has the option of repaying some or all of the outstanding balance each month. If the consumer carries a balance from month to month, finance charges (interest) are levied. An example of revolving credit is a credit card, such as Visa or MasterCard.

An installment loan is a credit arrangement in which the borrower takes out a loan for a specified amount, agreeing to repay the loan in regular installments over a specified period of time. Part of each payment is interest and part goes to repay principal (the amount borrowed). Generally, installment loan payments are made monthly and are for the same amount. Most student loans, auto loans, and home mortgage loans are examples of installment loans.

People have good reasons for borrowing money. They include purchasing large, important goods and services (cars, homes, or a college education), dealing with financial emergencies, taking advantage of opportunities or of convenience, and establishing or improving your credit rating. All of these reasons are appropriate uses of credit if you can repay the loans in a timely manner.

However, a wrong reason for borrowing money is using credit to live beyond your means. For instance, you may want to go to Cancun for vacation but really cannot afford to, so you charge the trip. Using credit to live beyond your means often leads to credit problems. Watch for these warning signs of potential credit problems:

- You use credit to meet basic living expenses.
- You use credit to make impulse purchases.
- You take a cash advance on one credit card to repay another.
- The unpaid balance on your credit cards increases month after month.

Consumers who think of credit purchases as a series of small monthly payments are fooling themselves. As we noted earlier, most college students, more than 80 percent, have at least one credit card today, and more than half carry balances from month to month averaging around $2,100.[6] How long would it take someone with the average balance to become debt free, assuming he or she made only the minimum payment each month (the minimum payment is typically $25 or 2.5 percent of the outstanding balance, whichever is greater) and is charged the average rate of interest (around 17 percent)? The answer is almost 11 years (129 months to be exact), during which time the borrower would pay more than $2,000 in interest. What's more, the preceding example assumes that the person does not charge anything else while paying off the balance.

If you feel as though you have a problem with credit, or may be developing one, you should seek help as soon as possible. Your college or university may offer credit counseling services. If not, contact a local not-for-profit credit counseling service or the National Foundation for Credit Counseling (800–388–2227 or http://www.nfcc.org). According to the experts, one of the keys to the wise use of credit is education. Learning about the pros and cons of borrowing money, as well as learning about responsible spending, can help people avoid future problems with credit.

Tax Planning

Everyone pays a variety of taxes to federal, state, and local governments. The major taxes paid by individuals include federal and state income taxes, Social Security and Medicare taxes, real estate taxes, and sales taxes. The median-income family paid almost 38 percent of its income in taxes during a recent year. Think about your own situation and the taxes you pay. You have federal income taxes withheld from each paycheck. In addition, if you live in one of the 41 states with a state income tax, you have state income tax withheld also. Social Security and Medicare taxes amount to 15.3 percent of your wages split between you and your employer (you pay the entire amount if you're self-employed). If you rent an apartment, part of your monthly rent goes to pay the landlord's property tax bill. Every time you buy something, you likely pay sales tax to your state and local governments.

Unfortunately, there is very little you can do to legally reduce some of the taxes you pay. The only tax over which you have some control is the federal and state income tax. But even in these cases, people have only a handful of ways to lower their tax bill. Still, you need to understand the federal income tax system and know what kinds of tax records to keep. Even though millions of Americans pay someone else to do their taxes, many people have relatively simple returns and preparing a tax return is one of the best ways of learning more about your personal finances. The Internal Revenue Service (IRS) has several excellent publications to help you prepare a federal income tax return. One of the best is IRS Publication #17 *(You and Your Federal Income Tax)*. This and all other IRS publications are available free of charge from local IRS offices or the IRS Web site (http://www.irs.gov). Using one of the tax preparation software programs (TurboTax or TaxCut) and your personal computer to prepare your federal and state income tax returns simplifies the process. Electronic filing of tax returns is another good choice.

Major Purchases

Even if you follow a strict budget and manage to save money regularly, you will still spend most of your income each year. Effective buying is an important part of your financial plan.
Within personal budget limits, an individual exercises his or her rights as a consumer to select or reject the wide range of goods and services that are available. As you purchase an automobile, a home, or any other major item, you need to carefully evaluate alternatives, separate needs from wants, and determine how you are going to finance the purchase. Your goal is to make every dollar you spend count.

Americans spend more than $900 billion annually on transportation, most of which goes to purchasing and maintaining automobiles. Given that new vehicles average more than $20,000 today, and even good used cars can cost in excess of $14,000, buying an automobile is a substantial purchase. On top of that, most car purchases are financed. Buying a car involves weighing many factors, including whether you want a new or used car, what makes and models appeal to you, and how much you can afford to pay. Many consumers today choose not to buy a new car but rather to lease one. While leasing has advantages, it also has drawbacks and, overall, is often more expensive than buying.

For most people, housing consumes the largest share of their monthly budgets. Most Americans—almost 70 percent—own their own homes, and home ownership is a goal of most people. Owning a home has a number of advantages, both financial and nonfinancial. Some of the financial benefits include tax savings (home mortgage interest and property taxes are both tax deductible) and the potential increase in the home's value. Nonfinancial benefits include pride of ownership. For those who don't own homes, the major barrier to home ownership is the down payment required to get a mortgage loan, along with other so-called closing costs. Even buying an average priced home will require the

Although leasing a car has some advantages, over the long run it costs more than buying the same car.

REUTERS/Shannon Stapleton/Landov LLC

buyer to have around $25,000 in cash. The so-called subprime mortgage crisis—discussed in Chapter 17—has led many mortgage lenders to require at least 10 percent of the purchase price as a down payment.

The other major housing option is renting. Renting also offers a number of advantages, including cost savings (the landlord takes care of maintenance and repairs) and mobility. It is much easier to move if you rent than if you own a home. People who plan on staying in an area for a short period of time are usually better off renting even if they can afford to buy a home. The choice between buying and renting is obviously a major financial decision that needs to be approached rationally, not emotionally.

Insurance

Another important personal planning area is insurance. Insurance is an admittedly expensive but necessary purchase. Americans spend close to $150 billion each year on auto insurance alone. Some of the basic principles and the various types of insurance are described in Appendix B. Although the focus of that appendix is business insurance, much of what is discussed applies to your personal insurance needs as well.

Your goal is to have adequate and appropriate coverage in each of the major insurance types—life, health, disability, and property and liability. Insurance needs can vary substantially from individual to individual. As noted earlier in *Contemporary Business*, some types of insurance are provided to employees as fringe benefits. They typically include health insurance, disability insurance, and life insurance. In the standard arrangement, the premium is split between the employee and employer. A few employers contract with insurance companies to offer employees auto and homeowners' insurance at discounts.

Investment Planning

Investing is a process by which money acquired through work, inheritance, or other sources is preserved and increased. Sound investment management is an important component of the financial plan and can make it easier to attain other personal goals, such as buying a home, sending children to college, starting a business, or retiring comfortably. Furthermore, it is very difficult today to substantially increase wealth without investing. And, given the changes to the external environment—such as employer-sponsored retirement plans—it is likely that everyone will have to make investment decisions at some point during his or her life.

The investment process consists of four steps. The first step is to complete some preliminary tasks, including setting overall personal goals, having a regular savings program, and managing credit properly. The second step is to establish a set of investment goals—why you want to invest, what you want to accomplish, and what kind of time frame you have. Obviously, your investment goals should be closely related to your overall personal goals. Next, you need to assess risk and return. You invest because you expect to earn some future rate of return. At the same time, however, all investing exposes you to a variety of risks. You need to find the proper balance between risk and return because investments offering the highest potential returns also expose you to more risk. Your age, income, and short- or long-term investment time frames all have an impact on the risk/return trade-off.

The final step is to select the appropriate investments. As discussed in Chapter 17 of *Contemporary Business*, there are three general types of investments: money market instruments, bonds, and common stock. The proper mix of these three investments depends on such factors as your investment goals and investment time horizon. For instance, a 25-year-old investing for retirement should have close to 100 percent of his or her funds invested in common stocks because growth in capital is the overriding investment objective. Even with the recent turmoil in the stock market, stocks have generally outperformed all other investment alternatives over longer periods of time. On the other hand, if the 25-year-old is investing to have sufficient funds for a down payment on a house within the next couple of years, the investor should have most of his or her funds invested in money market instruments or bonds given the short time horizon. Even after selecting the appropriate investments, the investor must monitor their performance and be prepared to make changes when necessary.

Financial Planning for Tomorrow

The last major personal planning area deals with future financial issues, such as sending children to college and retirement and estate planning. As you know, college is expensive and college costs are rising at a rate that exceeds the overall rate of inflation. By beginning a college savings program early, parents can ensure that they will have sufficient financial resources to send their children to college when the time comes. Today a variety of college savings programs exist, some of which provide parents with tax benefits.

Most people want to eventually retire with sufficient funds to ensure a degree of financial security. Social Security will provide only a fraction of what you will need; you will be responsible for the rest. According to the experts, you will need to have a savings nest egg of at least $1.5 million by the time you retire. Four important principles apply when it comes to saving for retirement: start early, save as much as you can each month, take advantage of all tax-deferred retirement savings plans to which you are entitled, and invest your retirement savings appropriately.

Aside from Social Security, two other major sources of retirement income exist: employer-sponsored retirement plans and individual retirement plans. Most employers offer their workers a retirement plan; some offer more than one plan. For most people, employer-sponsored retirement plans will likely provide the bulk of their retirement income. Essentially, two types of employer-sponsored retirement plans exist. A defined benefit plan guarantees a worker a certain retirement benefit each year. The size depends on a number of factors, including the worker's income and the length of time he or she worked for the employer. Pension plans are classified as defined benefit plans.

The other type of employer-sponsored retirement plan is the defined contribution plan. In this type of retirement plan, you contribute to your retirement account and so does your employer. You are given some choice of where your retirement funds can be invested. Often you are given a list of mutual funds in which to invest your money. A 401(k) is an example of a defined contribution plan. Defined contribution plans are becoming more common and are in many cases replacing defined benefit plans.

Millions of Americans have some sort of individual retirement plan not tied to any employer. These workers may be self-employed or may merely want to supplement their employer-sponsored retirement savings. Examples of individual retirement plans include regular IRAs (individual retirement accounts), Roth IRAs, Keogh plans, and simplified employee pension (SEP) plans. To set up one of these retirement plans, you must meet certain eligibility requirements.

Another element of financial planning for tomorrow is estate planning. Of all the personal planning areas, estate planning is probably the least relevant for you, although your parents and grandparents probably face some estate-planning issues. However, all adults, regardless of age, need to have two documents: a valid will (naming a guardian if you have any minor children) and a durable power of attorney (the name varies from state to state, but it is a document that gives someone else the power to make financial and medical decisions if you are incapacitated).

This appendix has just scratched the surface of personal financial planning. We hope it has encouraged you to learn more. Dozens of helpful books, Web sites, and other resources are available. If you can fit it into your class schedule, consider taking a class in personal financial planning. Your college or university probably offers one. Taking such a class may be one of the smartest decisions you make while you're in college.

Business Terms You Need to Know

personal financial
management A-31

standard of living A-32
financial plan A-34

net worth A-36
credit A-37

finance charge A-37

Projects and Teamwork Applications

1. Prepare a current set of financial statements for yourself. What do you think your financial statements will look like a year from now? Five years from now?

2. One of the most important tools for managing your personal finances is a budget. The earlier you learn to prepare and follow a budget, the better off you will be. There are a number of interactive budgeting programs available online. Go to http://www.nelliemae.com/calculators and fill out the budget worksheet. Compare your entries with the guidelines listed. Remember, a budget has to be realistic and support your overall goals. How difficult will it be for you to follow the budget you prepared?

3. You have probably heard of credit files (or reports). In fact, if you have a credit card, a student loan, or some other form of credit, you already have a credit file. Working with a partner, visit the Federal Trade Commission's Web site (http://ftc.gov), searching under the "For Consumers" category, and the TransUnion Bank Web site (http://truecredit.com/), searching under the "Credit Learning Center." Review the materials that these Web sites provide on credit files and credit reporting.
   a. What is a credit file?
   b. What information is contained in a credit file?
   c. Who compiles the information contained in a credit file?
   d. Who has access to a credit file?
   e. Regarding your credit file, what rights do you have?

4. Even though you are still in college, you face a number of important financial issues, everything from paying college expenses to dealing with credit cards. Visit http://www.nhheaf.org/pdfs/10steps.pdf and click "10 Steps to Financial Fitness." What are the ten steps? Which of these will be easiest for you to complete? Which will be the most difficult?

5. Analyze your current credit situation. What are your existing debts? How much are you paying each month? Did you borrow for the right reasons? List some steps you think you should take to improve your management of credit. Compare your findings with those of a classmate.

Developing a Business Plan

Feed Granola: A Healthy Business

Jason Osborn and Jason Wright had all the ingredients: a tasty product, the desire to start their own company, and a dose of good luck. But they also had good business sense. Having studied business management, advertising, and hotel and tourism management in college, the two landed in New York where they roomed together while working for a modeling agency. Both were entrepreneurs at heart—with a passion for healthful foods—so Osborn and Wright began making their own blend of granola for themselves and their friends. They offered their original raisin nut crunch flavor to a local restaurant, which immediately added the granola to its menu. Then they asked a dietician to test the product for nutritional value. When she reported that they had "a really healthy product here" and that she believed a market existed for it, they decided to launch Feed Granola.

Just as many other entrepreneurs have done, Osborn and Wright started their business in their own apartment, making batches in their kitchen. They knocked on doors in the neighborhood, offering free samples of their granola to gyms and natural food stores. When they outgrew their own location, they found space in the kitchen of a meal delivery service, where they could make their granola at night and exchange a portion of each batch in payment. Eventually, they moved to larger and larger production spaces as word spread about their granola. Meanwhile, they needed money to finance their growth, which meant that they had to come up with a formal business plan for prospective investors.

While every business plan contains some essential information and planning, the way business plans actually evolve varies with the circumstances and imaginations of the start-up entrepreneurs. Jason Osborn recalls, "In the beginning, we were just flying by the seat of our pants. Early on we sought out SCORE [a not-for-profit group of retired business consultants] and spoke to them literally via e-mail. They helped us with questions about incorporating and starting a business plan. Then

© Feed Granola Co., Hoboken, New Jersey

Entrepreneurs Jason Osborn and Jason Wright translated their passion for healthful foods into this new product, Feed Granola.

we created the business plan ourselves. It was really just cursory. It laid out how we'd run the business and outlined some of our market and financial milestones. We used that plan to secure our loan from the SBA [Small Business Administration]." Once they received their loan, the business partners were ready to launch Feed at a national tradeshow. They expanded their business plan to include the packaging and branding—including the name Feed.

Osborn and Wright went from that tradeshow to others, continuing to peddle their granola at local establishments like coffee shops and health-food stores. Then the big break came: Whole Foods Market wanted to stock Feed. Now the granola is sold in eight states in stores that include Earth Fare, Fresh Market, Fairway Market, Westerly, and Zabars—as well as Whole Foods. Customers can munch on granola flavors such as Cranberry Coconut Crunch, Blueberry Almond Crunch, and Apple a Day. Osborn still maintains that the original raisin nut crunch is his favorite, but perhaps that's because he is sentimental about Feed's first recipe.

Both men acknowledge that while their modeling jobs didn't lead them directly to business ownership, "models are independent contractors virtually running their own business," explains Osborn. "I was in charge of my finances, budgeting, tracking down payments, scheduling conflicts, finding new business, managing my career choices and most importantly, building relationships." All of these skills apply to running Feed Granola. Osborn advises other budding entrepreneurs to "get a clear vision and stick to it." Even if that vision is packed with fruits and nuts.[1]

Appendix D OVERVIEW

Many entrepreneurs and small-business owners have written business plans to help them organize their businesses, get them up and running, and raise money for expansion. In this appendix, we cover the basics of business planning: what business plans are, why they're important, and who needs them. We also explain the steps involved in writing a good plan and the major elements it should contain. Finally, we cover additional resources to get you started with your own business plan—to help you bring your unique ideas to reality with a business of your own.

What Is a Business Plan?

You may wonder how the millions of different businesses operating in the United States and throughout the world today got their start. Often it is with a formal business plan. A **business plan** is a written document that articulates what a company's objectives are, how these objectives will be achieved, how the business will be financed, and how much money the company expects to bring in. In short, it describes where a company is, where it wants to go, and how it intends to get there.

Why a Business Plan Is So Important

A well-written business plan serves two key functions:

1. It organizes the business and validates its central idea.
2. It summarizes the business and its strategy to obtain funding from lenders and investors.

First, a business plan gives a business formal direction, whether it is just starting, going through a phase of growth, or struggling. The business plan forces the principals—the owners—through rigorous planning, to think through the realities of running and financing a business. In their planning, they consider many details. How will inventory be stored, shipped, and stocked? Where should the business be located? How will the business use the Internet? And most important, how will the business make enough money to make it all worthwhile?

A business plan also gives the owners a well-reasoned blueprint to refer to when daily challenges arise, and it acts as a benchmark by which successes and disappointments can be measured. Additionally, a solid business plan will sell the potential owner on the validity of the idea. In some cases, the by-product of developing the plan is demonstrating to a starry-eyed person that he or she is trying to start a bad business. In other words, the process of writing a plan benefits a would-be businessperson as much as the final plan benefits potential investors.

Finally, a business plan articulates the business's strategy to financiers who can fund the business, and it is usually required to obtain a bank loan. Lenders and venture capitalists need to see that the business owner has thought through the critical issues and presented a promising idea before they will consider investing in it. They are, after all, interested in whether it will bring them significant returns.

Who Needs a Business Plan?

Some people mistakenly believe that they need a business plan only if it will land on the desk of a venture capitalist or the loan committee of the company's bank. Others think that writing a plan is unnecessary if their bank or lending institution doesn't require it. Such assumptions miss the point of planning, because a business plan acts as a map to guide the way through the often tangled roads of running a business. The answer to the question of who needs a plan is anyone who is serious about being successful. Every small-business owner should develop a business plan because it empowers that person to take control.

How Do I Write a Business Plan?

Developing a business plan should mean something different to everyone. Think of a business plan as a clear statement of a business's identity. A travel agency has a different identity from a newly launched magazine, which has yet a different identity from a restaurant hoping to expand its share of the market. Each business has unique objectives and processes, and each faces different obstacles.

At the same time, good business plans contain some similar elements no matter who the business owner is, what he or she sells, or how far the owner is into the venture. A savvy business owner molds the elements of a business plan into a professional and personal representation of the firm's needs and goals. The plan should also realistically assess the risks and obstacles specific to the business and present solutions for overcoming them.

Because the document is important, it takes time to collect needed information and organize it. Don't be misled into believing that you will simply sit down and begin writing. Before any writing begins, the business owner must become an expert in his or her field. Readying important information about the company and the market will make the writing easier and faster. Some critical pieces of information to have on hand are the following items:

- The company's name, legal form of organization, location, financial highlights, and owners or shareholders (if any).

"They Said It"

"In preparing for battle, I have always found that plans are useless, but planning is indispensable."
—Dwight D. Eisenhower (1890–1969) General and 34th president of the United States

"They Said It"

"I never think of the future. It comes soon enough."
—Albert Einstein (1879–1955) American scientist

- Organization charts, list of top managers, consultants or directors, and employee agreements.
- Marketing research, customer surveys, and information about the company's major competitors.
- Product information, including goods and services offered; brochures; patents, licenses, and trademarks; and research and development plans.
- Marketing plans and materials.
- Financial statements (both current and forecasted).

The business owner also must do a lot of soul searching and brainstorming to answer important questions necessary to build the backbone of a healthy business. Figure D.1 lists some critical questions to ask yourself.

Once equipped with these answers, you can begin writing the document, which can be anywhere between 10 and 50 pages long. The length of the plan depends on the complexity of the company, whether the company is a start-up (established companies have longer histories to detail), and what the plan will be used for. Regardless of size, the document should be well organized and easy to use, especially if the business plan is intended for external uses, such as to secure financing. Number all pages, include a table of contents, and make sure the format is attractive and professional. Include two or three illustrative charts or graphs and highlight the sections and important points with headings and bulleted lists. Figure D.2 outlines the major sections of a business plan.

The following paragraphs discuss the most common elements of an effective business plan. When you need additional instruction or information as you write, refer to the "Resources" section at the end of the appendix.

Executive Summary

The primary purpose of an executive summary is to entice readers sufficiently to read more about the business. An **executive summary** is a one- to two-page snapshot of what the overall business plan explains in detail. Consider it a business plan within a business plan. Through its enthusiasm and quick momentum, the summary should capture the reader's imagination. Describe your strategy for succeeding in a positive, intriguing, and realistic way and briefly yet thoroughly answer the first questions anyone would have about your business:

Figure D.1   Self-Evaluation Questions

Take a few minutes to read and answer these questions.
Don't worry about answering in too much detail at this point.
The questions are preliminary and
intended to help you think through your venture.

1. In general terms, how would you explain your idea to a friend?

2. What is the purpose or objective of your venture?

3. What service are you going to provide, or what goods are you going to manufacture?

4. Is there any significant difference between what you are planning and what already exists?

5. How will the quality of your product compare with competitive offerings?

6. What is the overview of the industry or service sector you are going to enter? Write it out.

7. What is the history, current status, and future of the industry?

8. Who is your customer or client base?

9. Where and by whom will your good or service be marketed?

10. How much will you charge for the product you are planning?

11. Where is the financing going to come from to initiate your venture?

12. What training and experience do you have that qualifies you for this venture?

13. Does such training or experience give you a significant edge?

14. If you lack specific experience, how do you plan to gain it?

who, what, why, when, where, and how. Financiers always turn to the executive summary first. If it isn't well presented or lacks the proper information, they will quickly move on to the next business plan in the stack. The executive summary is just as important to people funding the business with personal resources, however, because it channels their motivations into an articulate mission statement. It is a good idea to write the summary last, because it will inevitably be revised once the business plan takes final shape.

To write an effective executive summary, focus on the issues that are most important to your business's success and save the supporting matters for the body. The executive summary should describe the business's strategy and goals, the good or service it is selling, and the advantages it has over the competition. It should also give a snapshot of how much money will be required to launch the business, how it will be used, and how the lenders or investors will recoup their funds.

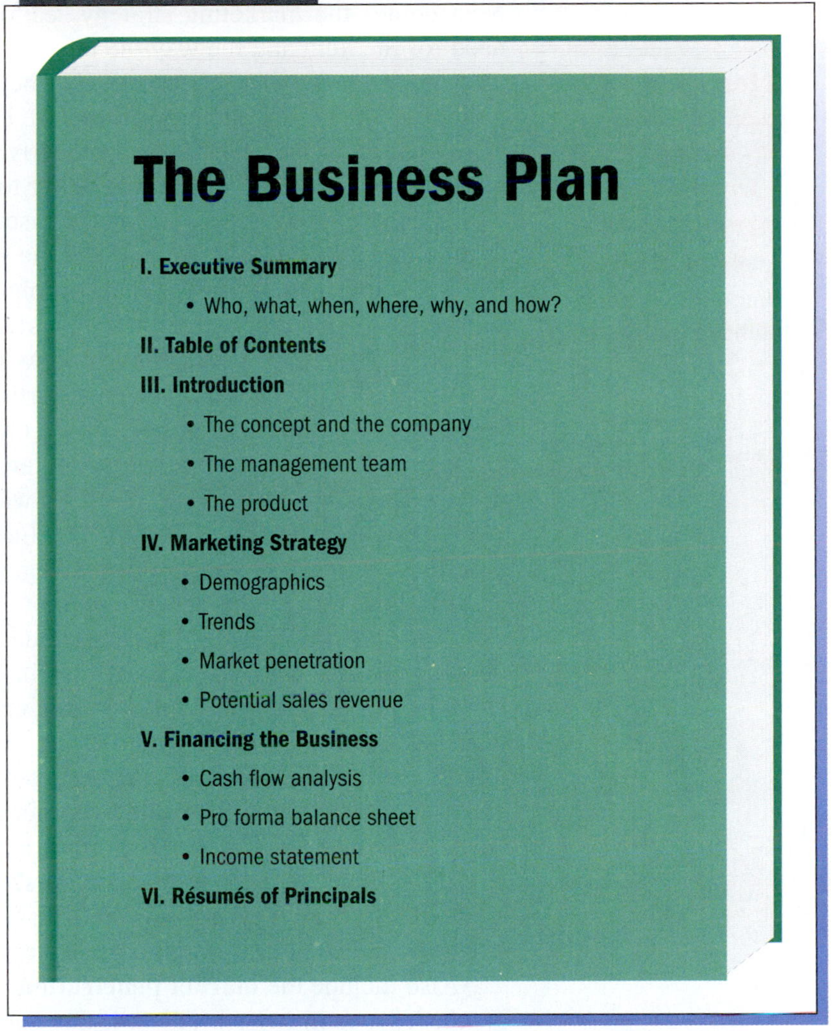

Introduction

The **introduction** follows the executive summary. After the executive summary has offered an attractive synopsis, the introduction should begin to discuss the fine details of the business. It should be crafted to include any material the upcoming marketing and financing sections do not cover. The introduction should describe the company, the management team, and the product in detail. If one of these topics is particularly noteworthy for your business, you may want to present that topic as its own section. Listen to what you write and respond as the plan takes shape.

Include basic information about the company—its past, present, and future. What are the company's roots, what is its current status, and what actions need to be taken to achieve its goals? If you are starting a company, include a description of the evolution of the concept. Be sure to tie all of the business's goals and plans to the industry in which it will operate, and describe the industry itself.

A business doesn't run itself, of course. People are the heart of a business, so write an appealing picture of the business's management team. Who are the key players and how does their experience resonate with the company's goals? Describe their—or your, if you are a sole proprietor—education, training, and experience, and highlight and refer to their résumés included later in the plan. Be honest, however—not all businesses are started by experts. If you lack demonstrated experience in a certain area, explain how you plan to get it.

Also describe the product, the driving force behind the venture. What are you offering, and why is it special? What are the costs of the service or price tag on the good? Analyze the features of the offering and the effect these features have on the overall cost.

Figure D.2   **Outline of a Business Plan**

The Business Plan

I. Executive Summary
- Who, what, when, where, why, and how?

II. Table of Contents

III. Introduction
- The concept and the company
- The management team
- The product

IV. Marketing Strategy
- Demographics
- Trends
- Market penetration
- Potential sales revenue

V. Financing the Business
- Cash flow analysis
- Pro forma balance sheet
- Income statement

VI. Résumés of Principals

Marketing Strategy

Next comes the marketing strategy section. The **marketing strategy** describes the market's need for the item and the way the business will fulfill it. Marketing strategies are not based on informal projections or observations. They are the result of a careful market analysis. So formulating a marketing strategy allows the business owner to become familiar with every aspect of the particular market. If done properly, it will allow you to define your target market and position your business within that sector to get its share of sales.

The marketing strategy includes a discussion of the size of the customer base that will want to purchase your good or service and the projected rate of growth for the product or category. Highlight information on the demographics of your customers. **Demographics** are statistical characteristics of the segment of the market, such as income, gender, and age. What types of people will purchase your product? How old are they, and where do they live? What is their lifestyle like? For example, someone starting an interior design business will want to report how many homeowners live within a certain radius of the business, as well as their median income. Of course, this section of the marketing analysis will be quite different for a company that conducts all of its business online. You will want to know the types of people who will shop at your Web site, but your discussion won't be limited to one geographic area. It is also a good idea to describe the trends in your product category. **Trends** are consumer and business tendencies or patterns that business owners can exploit to gain market share in an industry.

The marketing strategy should also detail your distribution, pricing, and promotional goals. Discuss the average price of your offering and the reasons behind the price you have chosen. How do you intend to let your potential customers know that you have a product to sell? How will you sell it—through a catalog, in a retail location, online, or perhaps a combination of all three? The effectiveness of your distribution, pricing, and promotional goals determines the extent to which you will be able to garner market share.

Competitors are another important part of your marketing strategy. What companies are already selling products similar to yours? Include a list of your competitors to show that you know exactly who they are and what you are up against. Describe what you think are their major strengths and weaknesses and how successful they have been within your market.

Also include the **market penetration,** which is the percentage of total customers who have purchased a company's product. If there are 10,000 people in your market, and 5,000 have purchased your product, your market penetration is 50 percent. The **potential sales revenue,** also an important figure to include, is the total revenue of a company if it captured 100 percent market penetration. In other words, this figure represents the total dollar value of sales you would bring in if everyone who is a potential customer purchased your product.

Financing the Business

The goal of a business is to make money. Everything in the business plan lays the foundation for the **financing section.** Business owners should not skip this section even if they are not seeking outside money. While it is crucial to have an accurate financial analysis to get financing, it also is a necessary exercise for business owners funding the venture themselves. The financing section demonstrates the cost of the product, operating expenses, expected sales revenue and profit, and the amount of the business owner's own funds that will be invested to get the business up and running. The financial projections should be compelling but accurate and based on realistic assumptions. The owner should be able to defend them.

Any assumptions made in the body of the business plan should be tied into the financial section. For instance, if you think you will need a staff of five, your cash flow analysis should explain how you are going to pay them. A cash flow analysis, a mandatory component of a financial analysis, shows how much money will flow through your business throughout the year. It helps you plan for staggered purchasing, high-volume months, and slow periods. Your business may be cyclical or seasonal, so the cash flow projection lets you know if you need to arrange a line of credit to cover periodic shortfalls. In addition, an income statement is a critical component. The income statement is a statement of income and expenses your company has accrued over a period of time.

Remember that leaving out important details can undercut your credibility, so be thorough. The plan must include your assumptions about the conditions under which your business will operate. It should cover details such as market strength; date of start-up; sales buildup; gross profit margin; equipment, furniture, and fixtures required; and payroll and other key expenses that will affect the financial plan. In addition, a banker will want a pro forma balance sheet, which provides an estimate of what the business owns (assets), what it owes (liabilities), and what it is worth (owner's equity). Refer to Chapters 16, 17, and 18 of *Contemporary Business* for additional details on accounting, financial statements, and financial management.

Résumés of Principals

The final element of the business plan is the inclusion of the résumés of the principals behind the business: the management team. Each résumé should include detailed employment information and accomplishments. If applicable to your business, consider expanding on the traditional résumé by including business affiliations, professional memberships, hobbies, and leisure activities.

However you choose to develop a business plan, make sure that *you* develop the plan. It should sound as though it was written by the entrepreneur, not by some outside "expert."

Resources

A tremendous amount of material is available to help business owners—whether existing or prospective—write effective business plans. The biggest task is narrowing it down to which resources are right for you. The Internet delivers an abundance of sound business-planning tools and advice, much of which are free. It allows you to seek diverse examples and opinions, which is important because no one source will match your situation exactly. Your school library and career center also have a wealth of resources. Following are some helpful resources for business planning.

Books

Dozens of books exist on how to write a business plan. Examples include the following:

- Gerald Watts, *The New Venture Coursebook: The Business Plan,* 5th ed. (Oxford, U.K.: Butterworth-Heinemann, 2008).
- Edward Blackwell, *How to Prepare a Business Plan,* 6th ed. (London: Kogan Page Ltd., 2008).
- Mike McKeever, *How to Write a Business Plan,* 8th ed. (Berkeley, CA: Nolo Press, 2007).
- K. Dennis Chambers, *Entrepreneur's Guide to Writing Business Plans and Proposals* (Westport, CT: Greenwood Publishing Group, 2007).
- Joseph Covello and Brian Hazelgren, *The Complete Book of Business Plans,* 2nd ed. (Naperville, IL: Sourcebooks, Inc., 2006).

Web Sites

- *Entrepreneur, Inc.,* and *BusinessWeek* magazines offer knowledgeable guides to writing a business plan. *Entrepreneur's* Web site also contains sample business plans.

http://www.entrepreneur.com
http://www.inc.com
http://www.businessweek.com

- If you are hoping to obtain funding with your business plan, you should familiarize yourself with what investors are looking for. Two professional associations for the venture capital industry are the following:
  http://www.nvca.org (National Venture Capital Association)
  http://www.nasbic.org (National Association of Small Business Investment Companies)

- New Enterprise Associates and PricewaterhouseCoopers have useful Web sites:
  http://www.nea.com
  http://www.pwc.com ("The Second Key: Writing the Business Plan" link)

Software

Business-planning software can give an initial shape to your business plan. However, a word of caution is in order if you write a business plan using the software's template. Bankers and potential investors, such as venture capitalists, read so many business plans that those based on templates may sink to the bottom of the pile. Also, if you aren't looking for funding, using software can undercut a chief purpose of writing a plan—learning about your unique idea. So think twice before you deprive yourself of that experience. Remember, software is a tool. It can help you get started, stay organized, and build a professional-looking business plan, but it can't actually write the plan for you.

The Small Business Administration's website, www.sba.gov, offers a wealth of information on starting, managing, and expanding a small business.

© U.S. Small Business Administration

Associations and Organizations

Many government and professional organizations provide assistance to would-be business owners. Here is a partial list:

- The U.S. Small Business Administration offers planning materials, along with other resources.
  http://www.sba.gov/smallbusinessplanner

- The SBA also has a center specifically designed for female entrepreneurs.
  http://www.sba.gov/aboutsba/sbaprograms/onlinewbc

- One of the missions of the Ewing Marion Kauffman Foundation is to encourage entrepreneurship across the United States. The foundation's Web sites offer online resources for new and growing businesses.
  http://www.kauffman.org

Other Important Business Terms

business plan A-44
executive summary A-46
introduction A-47

marketing strategy A-48
demographics A-48

trends A-48
market penetration A-48

potential sales revenue A-48
financing section A-48

Careers in Contemporary Business

You'll be hitting the job market soon—if you haven't already. Regardless of what industry you want to work in—financial services, marketing, travel, construction, hospitality, manufacturing, wireless communications—you need an education. Attending college and taking a business course like this one gives you an edge because business skills and knowledge are needed in many different fields. But education comes in many forms. In addition to taking classes, you should try to gain related experience, either through a job or participation in campus organizations. Cooperative education programs, internships, or work-study programs can also give you hands-on experience while you pursue your education. These work experiences will often set you apart from other job seekers in the eyes of recruiters or human resource professionals—people who hire employees.

Every one of you will be responsible for making a living once you leave school. Education influences that, as well. Based on the most recent data, if you have a high school degree, your median income is likely to be $30,134 per pear. If you have a two-year college (associate's) degree, it will be around $41,903. If you graduate from a four-year college or university, you can expect to earn a median of $51,700 annually. A master's degree can earn you $64,468, while a doctorate may command $76,937 per year. Finally, if you earn a professional degree, you may be earning $90,878 or more. A person with at least a four-year college or university degree earns, on average, around $500,000 more over a career lifetime than the person who has only a high school degree.[1] However, keep in mind that while a degree may help you get in the door for certain job interviews and may put you on a path for advancement, it doesn't guarantee success; you have to achieve that yourself.

Companies plan their hiring strategies carefully in order to attract and keep the most productive, creative employees and avoid the cost of rehiring. So, soon-to-be graduates still need to be on their toes. But creativity has never been in short supply among business students, and by the time you finish this class—and college—you will be well equipped to take on the challenge. You'll be able to think of your hunt for employment as a course in itself, at the end of which you will have a job. And you will be on your way toward a rewarding business career.

During this course, you are exposed to all the functional areas of business. You learn how firms are organized and operated. You find out who does what in a company. Gradually, you identify industries and disciplines—such as sales, finance, or product design—that interest you. And you learn about many organizations, large and small—who founded them, what products they offer, how they serve their customers, and what types of decisions they make. In short, you gain knowledge about business that you can apply to your career search and life.

Choosing a career is an important life decision. It sets you on a path that will influence where you live, how much money you earn, what type of people you meet, and what you do every day. And whether your goal is to operate an organic farm or to rise high in the ranks of a major corporation, you'll need to understand the principles of business. Even if you think you're headed down a different path, business skills may prove to be important. In addition, many fields are beginning to recognize the importance of a broader base of knowledge than specialized technical skills, and business knowledge is part of that base. For example, engineers used to rely almost solely on a foundation of technical skill and expertise. But experts in the industry now report a trend toward a more well-rounded education. While engineers still need a strong technical foundation, they need additional skills as well. "Engineers who want to be

competitive in the coming years need to have both a strong technical foundation and a broader nontraditional skill set," notes Jim Jones, a professor at Purdue University. These skills include the ability to communicate well and understand the global environment for business.[2] That's why this appendix discusses the best way to approach career decisions and to prepare for an *entry-level job*—your first permanent employment after leaving school. We then look at a range of business careers and discuss employment opportunities in a variety of fields.

It's important to remember that you'll be looking for a job regardless of the state of the overall economy, whether it's sluggish or booming. You may find it a bit tougher or easier than your classmates who graduate two years ahead of you or two years behind. You'll read about job cuts and unemployment rates, hiring freezes and wage increases. But if you stay flexible and are ready to work—just about any time and anywhere—you'll succeed.[3]

Internships—A Great Way to Acquire Real-World Experience

Many business students complete one or more *internships* prior to completing their academic careers. Some arrange internships during the summer, while others work at them during a semester away from college. An internship gives you hands-on experience in a real business environment, whether it's in banking, the hotel industry, or retailing. Not only does an internship teach you how a business runs, but it can also help you decide whether you want to pursue a career in a particular industry. You might spend a summer interning in the admissions department of a hospital and then graduate with your job search focused on hospital administration. Or you might decide you'd much rather work for a magazine publisher or a construction company.

When you apply for an internship, don't expect to be paid much, if at all. The true value of an internship lies in its hands-on experience. An internship bridges the theory–practice educational gap. It will help carry you from your academic experience to your professional future. Also keep in mind that, as an intern, you will not be running a department. People may not ask for your input or ideas. You may work in the warehouse or copy center. You might be answering phones or entering data. But it is important to make the most of your internship. Because many companies make permanent job offers—or offers to enter paid training programs—to the best interns, you'll want to stand out.

Internships can serve as critical networking and job-hunting tools. In many instances, they lead to future employment opportunities, allowing students to demonstrate technical proficiency while providing cost-effective employee training for the company. Even if you don't end up being hired by the company for which you interned, the experience is extremely valuable to your job hunt. One study estimates that almost one-third of all entry-level hires had internships prior to being hired. "It's the primary entry point to full-time employment," says the former managing director of one financial services firm.[4]

Internships provide invaluable experience to business students. They also help students decide whether to pursue a career in a specific industry.

Duluth News-Tribune, Clint Austin/© AP/Wide World Photos

With this information in mind, start thinking the way a professional does now. Here are some tips for a successful internship experience. These guidelines are also helpful for your first job.

- **Dress like a professional.** Dress appropriately for your future career. During an interview visit, look around to see what employees are wearing. If you have any questions, ask your supervisor.

- **Act like a professional.** Arrive on time to work. Be punctual for any meetings or assignments. Ask questions and listen to the answers carefully. Complete your work thoroughly and on time. Maintain good etiquette on the phone, in meetings, and in all interactions with other people.

- **Stand out.** Work hard and show initiative, but behave appropriately. Don't try to use authority that you do not have. Show that you are willing to learn.

- **Be evaluated.** Even if your internship does not include a formal evaluation, ask your employer how you are doing to learn about your strengths and weaknesses.

- **Keep in touch.** Once you complete your internship, stay in touch periodically with the firm so that people know what you are currently doing.

An excellent source of information about the nation's outstanding internships can be found at your local bookstore—*The Best 109 Internships,* Ninth Edition, published by The Princeton Review. The same organization also publishes *The Internship Bible,* which is also helpful.

In addition to an internship, you can build your résumé with work and life experience through volunteer opportunities, extracurricular activities, and summer or off-campus study programs. *Cooperative education* also provides valuable experience. Cooperative education programs are similar to internships, but the jobs themselves usually pay more. These programs may take place during the summer or during the school year—typically, students might take classes one semester and hold jobs the next semester. Most cooperative programs are specific to a major field of study, such as retailing or information technology. At your cooperative job, you'll be treated like a real full-time employee, meaning you'll work long hours and probably have more responsibility that you would as an intern. And depending on how these programs are scheduled, you might add a semester or two to your college education. But in the long run, you will gain knowledge and work experience that will serve you well as you build your career.[5]

Self–Assessment for Career Development

You are going to spend a lot of time during your life working, so why not find a job—or at least an industry—that interests you? To choose the line of work that suits you best, you must first understand yourself. Self-assessment involves looking in the mirror and seeing the real you—with all your strengths and weaknesses. It means answering some tough questions. But being honest with yourself pays off because it will help you find a career that is challenging, rewarding, and meaningful to you. As you get to know yourself better, you may discover that helping other people really makes you happy. You may realize that to feel secure, you need to earn enough to put away substantial savings. Or you might learn that you are drawn to risks and the unknown, characteristics that might point you toward owning your own business someday. Each of these discoveries provides you with valuable information in choosing a career.

Many resources are available to help you in selecting a career. They include school libraries, career guidance and placement offices, counseling centers, and online job-search services. They include alumni from your college, as well as friends, family, and neighbors. Don't forget the contacts you make during an internship—they can help you in many ways. Ask questions of

anyone you know—a local retailer, banker, or restaurant owner. Most people will be happy to speak with you or arrange a time to do so.

If you are interested in a particular industry or company, you might be able to arrange an informational interview—an appointment with someone who can provide you with more knowledge about an industry or career path. This type of interview is different from one that follows your application for a specific job, although it may ultimately lead to that. The informational interview can help you decide whether you want to pursue a particular avenue of employment. It also gives you some added experience in the interview process—without the pressure. To arrange an interview, tap anyone you know—friends of your parents, local businesspeople, or coordinators of not-for-profit organizations. Colleges often have databases of graduates who are working in various fields who are willing to talk with students on an informational basis, so be sure to start your search right at your own school.

To help you get started asking and answering the questions that will help you begin looking in the right direction, you can visit a number of Web sites that offer online career assessment tests. Career Explorer, at http://www.careerexplorer.net, is one such site. LiveCareer at http://www.livecareer.com and JobDiagnosis at http://www.JobDiagnosis.com are two more.[6] These sites and others, such as Monster's Career Fit Indicator at http://www.monster.com, help you identify your interests, strengths, and weaknesses—including some that may surprise you. In addition, follow the self-assessment process outlined in the next section to learn more about yourself.

The Self-Assessment Process

For a thorough assessment of your goals and interests, follow these steps:

1. **Outline your career interests.** What field or work activities interest you? What rewards do you want to gain from work?

2. **Outline your career goals.** What do you want to achieve through your career? What type of job can you see yourself doing? Where do you see yourself in a year? In five years? Do you have an ultimate dream job? How long are you willing to work to reach it? Write your goals down so that you can refer to them later.

3. **Make plans to reach your goal.** Do you need more education? Does the career require an apprenticeship or a certain number of years on the job? Write down the requirements you'll need to meet in order to reach your goal.

4. **List your skills and specific talents.** Write down your strengths—job skills you already have, as well as skills you have developed in life. For instance, you might know how to use financial software, and you might be good at negotiating with people. In addition, your school's career development office probably has standardized tests that can help determine your aptitude for specific careers. However, take these only as a guideline. If you really want to pursue a certain career, go for it.

5. **List your weaknesses.** This can be tough—it can also be fun. If you are shy about meeting new people, put shyness on your list. If you are quick to argue, admit it. If you aren't the best business-letter writer or think you're terrible at math, confess to yourself. This list gives you an opportunity to see where you need improvement—and take steps to turn weaknesses into strengths.

6. **Briefly sketch out your educational background.** Write down the schools, colleges, and special training programs you have attended, along with any courses you plan to complete before starting full-time employment. Make a candid assessment of how your background matches up with the current job market. Then make plans to complete any further education you may need.

7. **List the jobs you have held.** Include jobs that paid, internships, and volunteer opportunities. They all gave you valuable experience. As you make your list, think about what you liked and disliked about each. Maybe you liked working with the general public as a supermarket cashier. Perhaps you enjoyed caring for animals at a local shelter.

8. **Consider your hobbies and personal interests.** Many people have turned hobbies and personal pursuits into rewarding careers. Mick Jagger, lead singer of the Rolling Stones, has a master's degree from the London School of Economics. Without it, he probably wouldn't have been able to manage his rock group's vast business dealings. Jake Burton Carpenter earned a bachelor's degree in economics, but he loved winter sports. So he started a snowboard manufacturing company—and revolutionized the way people get from the top of a snowy mountain to the bottom. Cooking and catering star Paula Deen needed to support her young family. She loved the cooking from her own region—the South—so she opened a small business in which she and her boys delivered freshly made bag lunches to local businesses. Today she is a celebrity with her own television show, cookbooks, Web site, retail products, and more.[7] Turning a hobby into a career doesn't happen overnight, though, nor is it easy. It requires the same amount of research and hard work as any other business. But for many people, it is a labor of love—and ultimately succeeds because they refuse to give up.

Job Search Guidelines

Once you have narrowed your choice of career possibilities to two or three that seem right for you, get your job search under way. The characteristics that made these career choices attractive to you are also likely to catch the attention of other job seekers, so you must expect competition. Locate available positions that interest you; then be resourceful! Your success depends on gathering as much information as possible.

Register at Your Career Center

Register at your school's career center. Establish an applicant file, including letters of recommendation and supporting personal information. Most placement offices send out periodic lists of new job vacancies by e-mail, so be sure to get your name and e-mail address on the list. Visit the office regularly, and become a familiar face. Find out how the office arranges interviews with company representatives who visit campus. If your school has a career event, be sure to attend.

Preparing Your Job Credentials

Most placement or credential files include the following information:

1. letters of reference from people who know you well—instructors and employers
2. transcripts of course work to date
3. personal data form to report factual information
4. statement of career goals.

The career center will provide you with special forms to help you to develop your file. Often, these forms can be completed online. Prepare the forms carefully, since employers are always interested in your written communication skills. Keep a copy of the final file for later use in preparing similar information for other employment sources. Check back with the career center to make sure your file is in order, and update it whenever necessary to reflect additional academic accomplishments and added work experiences.

Letters of reference are very important, because they give prospective employers both personal and professional insights about you. They can influence a hiring decision. So, make a careful list of people who might be willing to write letters of reference. Your references should not be family members or close friends. Instead, choose a coach, an instructor, a former employer, or someone else whose knowledge could contribute to your job application. A soccer coach could vouch for your hard work and determination. A music teacher might be able to detail how well you accept instruction. A former employer might describe your punctuality and ability to get along with others. If possible, include someone from your school's business faculty on your list of references, or at least one of your current instructors.

Always ask people personally for letters of reference. Be prepared to give them brief outlines of your academic preparation, along with information about your job interests and career goals. This information will help them prepare their letters quickly and efficiently. It also shows that you are serious about the task and respect their time. Remember, however, that these people are very busy. Allow them at least a couple of weeks to prepare their reference letters; then follow up politely on missing ones. Always call or write to thank them for writing the letters.

Finding Employment through the Internet

The Internet plays an important role in connecting employers and job seekers. Companies of all sizes post their job opportunities on the Web, both on their own sites and on job sites such as Monster.com, Yahoo! HotJobs.com, and CareerBuilder.com. Specialized or niche sites such as Accounting.com and TechCareers.com are also gaining popularity. Some sites are free to applicants, while others charge a subscription fee. Figure E.1 provides a sampling of general and more-focused career sites.

Career Web sites typically offer job postings, tips on creating an effective résumé, a place to post your résumé, and advice on interviews and careers. If this sounds easy, keep in mind that these sites may receive hundreds of thousands of hits each day from job hunters, which means you have plenty of competition. This doesn't mean you shouldn't use one of these sites as part of your job search; just don't make it your sole source. Savvy job seekers often find that their time is better spent zeroing in on niche boards offering more focused listings. Naturally, if a particular company interests you, go to the firm's Web site, where available positions will be posted. If you are interested in applying for a job at the accounting firm Ernst & Young, go to http://www.ey.com. If you are looking for a job with Whole Foods Market, visit http://www.wholefoods.com. And if you fancy yourself working for an outdoor retailer, go to Recreational Equipment Inc. (REI) at http://www.rei.com.

Newspapers, the source for traditional classified want ads, also post their ads on the Web. Job seekers can even visit sites that merge ads from many different newspapers into one searchable database, such as CareerBuilder (http://www.careerbuilder.com). Some sites go a step farther and create separate sections for each career area. For example, entire sections may be devoted to accounting, marketing, and other business professions. Searches can then be narrowed

| Figure E.1 | Internet Job Sites |

General
CareerBuilder.com
Monster.com
Yahoo! HotJobs.com

Industry or Employer Focused
USAJOBS and Federaljobs.com—job listings by the federal government
eFinancialCareers.com—jobs in the financial industry
WomensJobSearch.net and WomenSportsJobs.com—listings open to both men and women
Recruiting.com and hrcareerpage.com—jobs in human resources
Salesjobs.com—jobs in sales
Msajobs.com and MedZilla.com—sales jobs in the medical and biotechnical industries
Technicalsalesjobsblog.com—jobs in computers and telecommunications
TechCareers.com—jobs in information technology and other tech fields
Accounting.com—jobs in accounting

Source: Sarah E. Needleman, "Pounding the Pavement on Wall Street, Virtually," *CollegeJournal,* www.collegejournal.com, accessed April 7, 2008; and Emily Steel, "Job-Search Sites Face a Nimble Threat," *CollegeJournal,* October 11, 2007, http://www.collegejournal.com/jobhunting.

according to geographic location, entry level, company name, job title, job description, and other categories.

As mentioned earlier, you can connect with potential employers by posting your résumé on job sites. Employers search the résumé database for prospects with the right qualifications. One commonly used approach is for an employer to list one or more *keywords* to select candidates for personal interviews—for example, "field sales experience," "network architecture," or "auditing"—and then browse the résumés that contain all the required keywords. Employers also scan résumés into their human resource database, and then when a manager requests, say, ten candidates, the database is searched by keywords that have been specified as part of the request. Job seekers are responding to this computer screening of applicants by making sure that relevant keywords appear on their résumés.

The *Contemporary Business* Web site hosts a comprehensive job and career assistance section. The site is updated frequently to include the best job and career sites for identifying and landing the career you want, as well as current strategies for getting the best results from your Web-based career-search activities.

Finding Employment through Other Sources

We've already mentioned the importance of registering at your college's career planning or placement office. If you have completed formal academic coursework at more than one institution, you may be able to set up a placement file at each. In addition, you may want to contact private and public employment services available in your location or in the area where you would like to live.

PRIVATE EMPLOYMENT AGENCIES These firms often specialize in certain types of jobs—such as marketing, finance, sales, or engineering—offering services for both employers and job candidates that are not available elsewhere. Many private agencies interview, test, and screen job applicants so that potential employers do not have to do so. Job candidates benefit from the service by being accepted by the agency and because the agency makes the first contact with the potential employer.

A private employment agency usually charges the prospective employer a fee for finding a suitable employee. Other firms charge job seekers a fee for helping find them a job. Be sure that you understand the terms of any agreement you sign with a private employment agency.

STATE EMPLOYMENT OFFICES Don't forget to check the employment office of your state government. Remember that in many states, these public agencies process unemployment compensation applications along with other related work. Because of the mix of duties, some people view state employment agencies as providing services for semiskilled or unskilled workers. However, these agencies *do* list jobs in many professional categories and are often intimately involved with identifying job finalists for major new facilities moving to your state. In addition, many of the jobs listed at state employment offices may be with state or federal government agencies and may include professionals such as accountants, attorneys, healthcare professionals, and scientists.

Learning More about Job Opportunities

Carefully study the various employment opportunities you have identified. Obviously, you will like some more than others, but you can examine a variety of factors when assessing each job possibility:

- actual job responsibilities
- industry characteristics

- nature of the company
- geographic location
- salary and opportunities for advancement
- contribution of the job to your long-range career objectives.

Too many job applicants consider only the most striking features of a job, perhaps its location or the salary offer. However, a comprehensive review of job openings should provide a balanced perspective of the overall employment opportunity, including both long-run and short-run factors.

Building a Résumé

Regardless of how you locate job openings, you must learn how to prepare and submit a *résumé,* a written summary of your personal, educational, and professional achievements. The résumé is a personal document covering your educational background, work experience, career preferences and goals, and major interests that may be relevant. It also includes such basic contact information as your home and e-mail addresses, as well as your telephone number. It should *not* include information on your age, marital status, race, or ethnic background.

Your résumé is usually your formal introduction to an employer, so it should present you in the best light, accentuating your strengths and potential to contribute to a firm as an employee. However, it should *never* contain embellishments or inaccuracies. You don't want to begin your career with unethical behavior, and an employer is bound to discover any discrepancies in fact— either immediately or during the months following your employment. Either event typically results in short-circuiting your career path.

Organizing Your Résumé

The primary purpose of a résumé is to highlight your qualifications for a job, usually on a single page. An attractive layout facilitates the employer's review of your qualifications. You can prepare your résumé in several ways. You may use narrative sentences to explain job duties and career goals, or you may present information in outline form. A résumé included as part of your credentials file at the career center on campus should be quite short. Remember to design it around your specific career objectives.

Figures E.2, E.3, and E.4 illustrate different ways to organize your résumé—by *reverse chronology,* or time; by *function;* and by *results.* Regardless of which format you select, you will want to include the following: a clearly stated objective, your work or professional experience, your education, your personal interests such as sports or music, and your volunteer work. While all three formats are acceptable, one study showed that 78 percent of employers preferred the reverse chronological format—with the most recent experience listed first—because it was easiest to follow.

Tips for Creating a Strong Résumé

Your résumé should help you stand out from the crowd, just as your college admissions application did. A company may receive hundreds or even thousands of résumés, so you want yours to be on the top of the stack. Here are some do's and don'ts from the pros:

Do:

- State your immediate objective clearly. If you are applying for a specific job, say so. State why you want the job and why you want to work at this particular company.
- Use terms related to your field, so that a busy human resource manager can locate them quickly.

If you are submitting your résumé online, use words that will create an automatic "match" with a job description or field. If you are applying for an entry-level job in marketing, the phrase "communication skills" is likely to generate a match. You can identify such words and phrases by reading job descriptions online or in the newspaper.

- Provide facts about previous jobs, internships, cooperative education programs, or volunteer work, including results or specific achievements. Include any projects or tasks you undertook through your own initiative. If these activities are unrelated to the job for which you are applying, highlight the related skills such as letter writing or organizing a team.

- Highlight your strengths and skills.

- Write clearly and concisely. Keep your résumé to a single page.

- Proofread your résumé carefully for grammar, usage, and typographical errors. Refer to a dictionary or style manual if you have any uncertainty about these issues.[8]

| Figure E.2 | Chronological Résumé |

FELICIA SMITH-WHITEHEAD
4265 Popular Lane
Cleveland, Ohio 44120
216-555-3296
FeliciaSW@gmail.com

OBJECTIVE
Challenging office management position in a results-oriented company where my organizational and people skills can be applied; leading to an operations management position.

WORK EXPERIENCE
ADM Distribution Enterprises, Cleveland, Ohio   2010–Present
Office Manager of leading regional soft-drink bottler. Coordinate all bookkeeping, correspondence, scheduling of 12-truck fleet to serve 300 customers, promotional mailings, and personnel records, including payroll. Install computerized systems.

Merriweather, Hicks & Bradshaw Attorneys, Columbus, Ohio   2008–2010
Office Supervisor and Executive Assistant for Douglas H. Bradshaw, Managing Partner. Supervised four clerical workers and two paraprofessionals, automated legal research and correspondence functions, and assisted in coordinating outside services and relations with other firms and agencies. Promoted three times from Secretary to Office Supervisor.

Conner & Sons Custom Coverings, Cleveland, Ohio   2004–2008
Secretary in father's upholstery and awning company. Performed all office functions over the years, running the office when the owner was on vacation.

EDUCATION

McBundy Community College, Associate's Degree in Business	2008
Mill Valley High School, Honors	2004

COMPUTER SKILLS
Familiar with Microsoft Office and Adobe Acrobat

LANGUAGE SKILLS
Fluent in Spanish (speaking and writing)
Adequate speaking and writing skills in Portuguese

PERSONAL
Member of various community associations; avid reader; enjoy sports such as camping and cycling; enjoy volunteering in community projects.

DON'T:

- Offer any misleading or inaccurate information.
- Make vague statements, such as "I work well with others," or "I want a position in business."
- State your objective as, "to run this company" or to "advance as quickly as possible."
- Include a salary request.
- Make demands about vacation time, work hours, or excessive benefits.

Enrique Garcia
Five Oceanside Drive, Apt. 6B
Los Angeles, CA 90026
215-555-7092
EGARCIA@hotmail.com

Objective
Joining a growth-oriented company that values highly productive employees. Seeking an opportunity that leads to senior merchandising position.

Professional Experience
Administration
Management responsibilities in a major retailing buying office, coordinated vendor-relation efforts. Supervised assistant buyers.

Category Management
Experience in buying home improvement and sport and recreation categories.

Planning
Chaired a team charged with reviewing the company's annual vendor evaluation program.

Problem Solving
Successfully developed a program to improve margins in the tennis, golf, and fishing lines.

Work Experience

Senior Buyer for Southern California Department Stores	2009–Present
Merchandiser for Pacific Discount Stores, a division of Southern California Department Stores	2007–2009

Education
Bachelor's Degree

California State University–San Bernardino	2005–2007

Associate's Degree

Los Angeles City College	2003–2005

- Highlight your weaknesses.
- Submit a résumé with typos or grammatical errors.
- Use slang or other inappropriate phrases or comments.
- Include pictures or graphics, or use fancy type fonts.[9]

Take your time with your résumé; it is one of the most important documents you'll create during your career. If you need help, go to your school's career center. If you are dealing with an employment agency, a counselor there should be able to help as well.

Keep in mind that you will probably have to modify your résumé at times to tailor it to a particular company or job. Again, take the time to do this; it may mean the difference between standing out and being lost in a sea of other applicants.

Preparing Your Cover Letter

In most cases, your résumé will be accompanied by a *cover letter*. This letter should introduce you, explain why you are submitting a résumé (cite the specific job opening if possible), and let the recipient know where you can be reached for an interview. An effective cover letter will make the recipient want to take the next step and read your résumé. Here are a few tips for preparing an outstanding letter:

- Write the letter to a specific person, if possible. A letter addressed to "to whom it may concern" may never reach the right person. Call the company or check its Web site for the name of the person to whom you should send your letter. It might be someone in human resources or a person in the department where you'd actually be working. Be sure to obtain the person's title if possible (such as editor or director), and spell the person's name correctly.

- Introduce yourself and explain the purpose of your letter—to apply for a job.

- Get right to the point, and keep it simple. Explain why you are the ideal candidate for the job.

- Describe in a few sentences either a special project you are currently working on or something unique about a job you have recently held that relates to the qualifications you will need on the job for which you are applying.

- Keep it short—a page is acceptable, half a page even better.

- Request an interview.

- Thank the person for his or her time and consideration.

- Make sure all your contact information is in the letter—name, address, home phone number, cell phone number, and e-mail address.

- Proofread your letter carefully.[10]

Submitting Your Online Résumé

You may write a sparkling cover letter and stellar résumé, but if your online submission is blocked or tossed aside by an automated processing system, it won't have a chance to impress the person for whom it was intended. Here are a few tips for making certain your letter and résumé reach their mark.

- As mentioned earlier, identifying words and phrases that create a match—and allow your materials through the filter—is often the key to a successful online submission. This applies to the subject line of your e-mail, as well. Don't write, "seeking employment." Instead, write "application for marketing assistant position." If you are responding to a published job advertisement, include the job code from the advertisement.

- Include your cover letter in the e-mail.

Figure E.4   **Results-Oriented Résumé**

ANTONIO PETTWAY
101 Beverly Road
Upper Montclair, NJ 07043
820-555-1234
apettway@yahoo.com

OBJECTIVE
To apply my expertise as a construction supervisor to a management role in an organization seeking improvements in overall production, long-term employee relationships, and the ability to attract the best talent in the construction field.

PROFESSIONAL EXPERIENCE
DAL Construction Company, Orange, NJ   2010–Present
    Established automated, on-site recordkeeping system improving communications and morale between field and office personnel, saving 400 work hours per year, and reducing the number of accounting errors by 20 percent. Developed a crew selected as "first choice crew" by most workers wanting transfers. Completed five housing projects ahead of deadline and under budget.

NJ State Housing Authority, Trenton, NJ   2008–2010
    Created friendly, productive atmosphere among workers enabling first on-time job completion in 4 years and one-half of usual materials waste. Initiated pilot materials delivery program with potential savings of 3.5 percent of yearly maintenance budget.

Essex County Housing Authority, Montclair, NJ   2008
    Produced information pamphlets increasing applications for county housing by 22 percent. Introduced labor-management discussion techniques saving jobs and over $29,000 in lost time.

Payton, Durnbell & Associates Architects, Glen Ridge, NJ   2007–2008
    Developed and monitored productivity improvements, saving 60 percent on information transfer costs for firm's 12 largest jobs.

EDUCATION
Montclair State University, Bachelor's Degree in Business   2003–2007

COMPUTER SKILLS
Familiar with Microsoft Office and Adobe Acrobat

PERSONAL
Highly self-motivated. Willing to relocate. Enjoy tennis and hiking.

- Send your résumé in the body of the e-mail—not as an attachment. This is more convenient for the recipient, and it also avoids the disaster of having your attachment automatically deleted by an antivirus system.

- Do not send graphics, because they may be blocked or deleted as well.

- If you are answering an ad, read the instructions for application and follow them exactly.[11]

The Job Interview

Congratulations! You've prepared an effective résumé, and you've been contacted for an interview. An interview is more than a casual conversation. During an interview, at least one company manager will learn about you, and you'll learn more about the company and the job.

Although you may feel nervous about the interview, you can control some of its outcome by doing your homework: planning and preparing for this important encounter with your potential employer. Before you meet with an interviewer, learn everything you can about the firm. The simplest way to do this is to visit the company's Web site. You can also check with your school's career center. If you know anyone who works for the company, you may ask the person about the firm. Try to learn the answers to the following questions about the organization:

- What does the firm do—manufacture clothing, market snack foods, produce films, sell cars? If you are applying for a job at a large corporation, zero in on the division for which you would be working.

- What is the company's mission? Many firms include a statement about their purpose in the business world—to supply affordable energy to communities, to serve fresh food, to make communication easier. Understanding why the company exists will help you grasp where it is headed and why.

- Where, when, and by whom was the company founded? Learn a little about the history of the firm.

- What is its position in the marketplace? Is it a leader or is it trying to gain a competitive advantage? Who are its main competitors?

- Where is the firm based? Does it have facilities located around the country and the world, or is it purely local?

- How is the company organized? Are there multiple divisions and products?

Learning about the firm indicates to the interviewer that you have initiative and motivation, as well as an interest in the firm's culture and history. You have taken the time and effort to find out more about the organization, and your enthusiasm shows.

Dress appropriately for a job interview. Be prompt, polite, and friendly.

Stockbyte/Getty Images

Tips for Successful Interviewing

An interview is your personal introduction to the company. You want to make a good impression, but you also want to find out whether you and the firm make a good fit. Although the interviewer will be asking most of the questions, you will want to ask some, as well. People who conduct interviews say that the most important qualities candidates can exhibit are self-confidence, preparedness, and an ability to communicate clearly.

When you are contacted for an interview, find out the name(s) of the person or people who will be interviewing you. It's also appropriate to ask whether the initial interview will be with a human resource manager or with the person to whom you would be reporting on the job, or both. Many people who conduct initial job interviews work in their firms' human resource divisions. These interviewers act as gatekeepers and can make recommendations to managers and supervisors about which individuals to interview further or hire. Managers who head the units in which an applicant will be employed may get involved later in the hiring process. Some hiring decisions come from human resource personnel together with the immediate supervisor of the prospective employee. In other cases, immediate supervisors make the decision alone. At your interview, keep in mind the following tips.

Do:

- **Dress appropriately.** Dress as if it is your first day of work at the firm. Conceal any tattoos or body piercings and wear simple jewelry.

- **Arrive a few minutes early.** This gives you time to relax and take in the surroundings. It also shows that you are punctual and care about other people's time.
- **Introduce yourself with a smile and a handshake.** Be friendly, but not overly familiar.
- **Be yourself—at your best.** Don't suddenly adopt a new personality. But try to be confident, polite, respectful, and interested in the people who are spending time with you. Be sure to thank each person who interviews you.
- **Listen.** Pay attention to what the interviewer is saying. If something is unclear to you, ask for clarification. Turn off your cell phone. Your full attention should be on the conversation you are having in the interview.
- **Use appropriate language.** As in your résumé and cover letter, be sure to use correct English. You don't need to be stiff or formal, but avoid slang or phrases that you know are inappropriate for the situation.

DON'T:

- **Talk too much.** Avoid telling the interviewer a lot about your personal life, or why you left a particular job. Answer questions honestly and thoroughly, but don't dip into irrelevant details.
- **Be arrogant or aggressive.** Self-confidence is a good trait, but don't miss the mark by behaving in an arrogant or condescending manner. Certainly don't become aggressive, demanding that the interviewer offer you the job or even another interview.
- **Act indifferent or bored.** This may not be the job you ultimately want, but treat the interview and the interviewer with respect and attention. If you make a good impression, the firm is likely to keep your name on file—and that dream job may appear after all.[12]

Answering and Asking Questions

In a typical format, the interviewer tries to talk as little as possible, giving you a chance to talk about yourself and your goals. You want to present your thoughts clearly and concisely, in an organized fashion, without rambling on to unrelated topics. The interviewer may wait until you are finished or prompt you to talk about certain subjects by asking questions. Be as specific as possible when answering questions. The questions that interviewers ask often include the following:

- "Why do you want this job?"
- "Why do you want to work in this field?"
- "What are your short-term goals? Long-term objectives?"
- "Where do you see yourself in five years? In ten years?"
- "What are your strengths? What are your weaknesses?"
- "What motivates you?"
- "Describe a situation in which you made a tough decision or solved a problem."
- "What did you like best about your last job? What did you like least?"
- "Why should my firm hire you?"
- "Are you considering other jobs or companies?"

One way to prepare for these questions is to role-play an interview with a friend or classmate. Take turns playing the interviewer and the job candidate. If possible, videotape the interview so that you can watch your own body language and hear the sound of your voice.[13]

At some point, the interviewer will probably ask you whether you have any questions of your own. It's a good idea to come prepared with some questions, but others may arise during the interview. Try to keep your list concise, say three or four of your most important questions. The questions you ask reflect just as much about you as the answers you give to the interviewer's questions. Here is a sample of appropriate questions for the initial interview:

- "Could you clarify a certain aspect of the job responsibilities for me?"
- "Do people who start in entry-level jobs at this company tend to develop their careers here?"
- "In what ways could I perform above and beyond the job requirements?"

At some point during your conversation, the interviewer may give you an idea of the salary range for the job. If not, he or she will do so during a subsequent interview. You may ask about the range, but do not ask exactly how much you will be paid if you get the job. Keep in mind that usually there is little or no negotiation of an entry-level salary. However, you may ask if there is a probationary period with a review at the end of the period. Here are a few other questions *not* to ask:

- "When will I be promoted?"
- "How much time off do I get?"
- "When will I get my first raise?"
- "How many people are applying for this job?"
- "What are my chances of getting this job?"

At the end of the interview, be sure to thank the interviewer with a smile and a handshake, even if you both know the job is not for you. Again, another opportunity may come along in the future and you want to leave the door open. When you get home, write a note or e-mail the interviewer, thanking him or her for time spent with you. Thank-you notes really do make a lasting impression on a person, and it gives you another chance to reinforce your interest.

A successful first interview often leads to a second. The purpose of this interview is to better determine your specific qualifications and fit with the company. You may be introduced to more people—potential coworkers, people in other divisions, or sales staff. You may have another meeting with human resource staff members in which you'll learn more about salary, employee benefits, the firm's code of ethics, and the like. Depending on the type of job, you might be asked to take some skills tests. If you are entering a training program for a bank, you might be required to take some math-oriented tests. If you are going to work for a publisher, you might be asked to take an editing test or do some proofreading. If you are applying for a job as a sales representative, you may be given a test that assesses your personality traits. Don't be intimidated by these tests—you are not expected to know everything or be perfect—just do your best.

Making the Employment Decision

After receiving your résumé, conducting one or two interviews, and administering a skills test, a potential employer knows a lot about you. You should also know a lot about the company. If the experience has been positive on both sides, you may be offered a job. If you have interviewed at several companies and are offered more than one job, congratulations! You may receive a phone call, followed by a letter outlining the offer in writing. Whether you receive one offer or several, thank the person making the offer. If you choose to accept immediately, feel free to do so. If you have doubts about the job or need to decide between two, it is appropriate to ask for 24 hours to respond. If you must decline an offer, do so promptly and politely. After all, you may end up working for that firm sometime in the future. If you get a few rejections before you receive an offer, don't give up. Every application and interview adds to your experience.

As you think about an offer, consider the aspects that are most important. You'll want to choose a job that comes closest to your career interests and objectives. But don't rule out the element of surprise—you might wind up with a job you like in an industry you'd never considered before. Don't worry too much about the salary. The point of an entry-level job is to set you on a forward path. And keep in mind that your first job won't be your last. Once you have accepted an offer, you'll be given a start date as well as the name of the person to whom you should report on arrival. Congratulations, you are now a member of the workforce!

Nontraditional Students

Take a quick glance around your class. You'll likely see classmates of all ages. Some will fall into the traditional college age group of 18 to 22, but many don't. Perhaps you are a veteran returning from military duty overseas. Maybe you have been engaged in a full-time career but want to broaden your education. Students who fall outside the 18- to 22-year-old age group are often referred to as *nontraditional students,* but these students have become the norm on many campuses. Homemakers returning to school to freshen up their résumés before returning to the workforce and workers who have been laid off due to an economic downturn are other examples of nontraditional students. As diverse as this group is, they share one thing in common: they are older than traditional students. This means that they face different challenges—but also enjoy some advantages over their younger classmates.

One major challenge faced by nontraditional students is scheduling. Often they are juggling the responsibilities of work, school, and family. They may have to study at odd times—during meals, while commuting, or after putting the kids to bed. If they are switching careers, they may be learning an entirely new set of skills, as well. But nontraditional students have an important advantage: experience. Even experience in an unrelated field is a plus. Older students know how organizations operate. Often, they have developed useful skills in human relations, management, budgeting, and communications. Even a former stay-home parent has skills in all of these areas. Through observing other people's successes and failures—as well as living through their own—they have developed an inventory of what to do and what not to do. So, in some ways, these students have a head start on their younger counterparts. But they also face the reality that they have fewer years in which to develop a career.

The Job Market: Where Do You Fit In?

The industry you choose, and the career you follow within it, are part of a bigger picture. They reflect the needs of society, changing populations, developing technology, and the overall economy. For instance, the U.S. population is expected to increase at a slower rate of growth than during the previous two decades. The U.S. workforce will continue to become more diverse, with Hispanics accounting for the largest share of jobs among minorities, while Asians represent the fastest-growing group of employees. White, non-Hispanic workers will make up a declining share of the workforce, falling from approximately 69 percent to about 65 percent.[14]

The number of women in the workforce is still growing at a faster rate than that of men. The male labor force is expected to grow by about 8 percent by the year 2016, compared with almost 9 percent for women. So the men's share of the labor force will likely continue to decrease, while the women's share will increase.[15]

All of these facts combine to shape a picture of the needs of U.S. society and the workforce available to serve it. As the Baby Boom generation ages, the age group between 55 and 64 will

increase by about one third. Thus, the United States will need more healthcare services, as well as other services for an aging population, such as assisted living facilities and leisure and hospitality. The group between the ages 35 and 44 will decrease by almost 6 percent, while the youth population between 16 and 24 will decline by about 1 percent. But today's younger workers are receiving more education and training to fill the need for professional and business service workers. These projections affect both the workforce and the types of goods and services needed to satisfy consumers. So jobs in education and healthcare services will increase by more than 5 million and in professional and business services by a little over 4 million.[16]

Careers in service-providing industries continue a long-term rise. Service jobs will likely represent almost 16 million new jobs by 2016, while goods-producing jobs will decline. But industries that produce certain types of goods, such as those related to the needs of an aging population and those related to green technologies or products, will probably increase. Employment in construction, especially commercial construction, will increase by around 10 percent because of the need to replace aging U.S. roads, bridges, and tunnels, while manufacturing jobs will continue to drop, declining about 11 percent. And as just mentioned, employment in professional and business services, as well as in information technology and finance, will increase.[17]

The good news is that even in a weaker job market, employers are looking to hire recent college graduates. In fact, some continue to offer signing bonuses and other incentives in order to secure the best workers. Why? Continuing to hire entry-level employees makes good business sense. "Employers are nervous that if they don't continue to hire, they'll turn back when we're seeing an uptick in the economy, and they will have lost out on some of the talent they need," explains Mitch Barnes, an expert in human resources. "I do know of employers that are keeping the spigot open because they're going to miss out if they don't. They feel there's a scramble in the market to bring in new people." Some of the hot jobs can be found in accounting, sales, management training, engineering, and business services.[18] So keep your résumé current and your outlook positive: a job is out there for you.

A Long-Range View of Your Career

As we said earlier, choosing a career is an important life decision. A career is a professional journey—regardless of whether you want to run a small restaurant or a branch bank, whether you are fascinated by language or math, whether you prefer to work with animals or people. In the end, you hope to contribute something good to society while enjoying what you do—and make a reasonable living at it.

Throughout your career, it is important to stay flexible and continue learning. Challenging new skills will be required of managers and other businesspeople during these first decades of the 21st century. Remain open to unexpected changes and opportunities that can help you learn and develop new skills. Keep in mind that your first job will not be your last. But tackle that first job with the same enthusiasm you'd have if someone asked you to run the company itself, because everything you learn on that job will be valuable at some point during your career—and someday you may actually run the company.

Finally, if you haven't already started your career search, begin now. Do this by talking with various resources, lining up an internship, looking for a part-time job on or off campus, or volunteering for an organization. Register with the campus career center long before you graduate. Then, when you reach your final semester, you'll be well on your way to beginning the career you want.

We are confident that this textbook presents a panorama of career options for you. Whatever you decide, be sure it is right for you—not your friends, your instructors, or your parents. As the old saying goes, "You pass this way just once." Enjoy the journey!

More Career Information on the *Contemporary Business* Web Site

More career information is available to students using *Contemporary Business* at the book's Web site.

The "Management Careers" section on the Web site enables you to learn more about business careers and to locate currently posted job opportunities. The site provides a vast number of career resources such as links to job sites, career guidance sites, and the like. Also, many links include extensive career information and guidance, such as interviewing techniques and tips for résumé writing.

Projects and Teamwork Applications

1. Prepare your résumé following the procedures outlined earlier in this section. Ask your business instructor and classmates to critique it. Then revise and proofread it.

2. Arrange to interview someone in your community who is working in a profession that interests you. Write, call, or e-mail to request an appointment. The interview can take place by phone or in person and should take no more than 15 to 20 minutes. Be prepared with questions to ask. Report to your class about what you learned about the realities of working in the profession.

3. Select a partner and take turns interviewing each other for a job in front of the class. Use the interview questions mentioned earlier, and develop two or three of your own. After completing the interviews, ask the class to give you feedback on how you looked and acted during your interview. Would they advise you to do or say anything differently?

4. Visit one of the job Web sites such as CareerBuilder or Monster and research an industry in which you think you might be interested. Prepare a report on what you learned about the field. Was the site helpful? What types of jobs were available in the field? Based on your report, do you plan to pursue this industry or select another field?

5. Go online to the Web site for a specific company for which you might be interested in working. Click on the "Careers" or "Job Opportunities" section of the site, and read carefully the job descriptions for any entry-level positions and the procedure for applying for them. Review also any general information about career development at the firm. Present your findings to the class.

Glossary

360-degree performance review employee performance review that gathers feedback from co-workers, supervisors, managers, and sometimes customers.

401(k) plan retirement savings plan to which employees can make pretax contributions; employers often make additional contributions to the plan.

accounting process of measuring, interpreting, and communicating financial information to support internal and external business decision making.

accounting cycle set of activities involved in converting information and individual transactions into financial statements.

accounting equation relationship that states that assets must always equal the sum of liabilities and owners' equity.

accrual accounting accounting method that records revenues and expenses when they occur, not necessarily when cash actually changes hands.

acquisition procedure in which one firm purchases the property and assumes the obligations of another.

activity ratios measures of how efficiently a firm utilizes its assets.

actuarial table probability of the number of events that are expected to occur within a given year.

advertising paid nonpersonal communication delivered through various media and designed to inform, persuade, or remind members of a particular audience.

affective conflict disagreement that focuses on individuals or personal issues.

affinity program marketing effort sponsored by an organization that solicits involvement by individuals who share common interests and activities.

affirmative action programs programs designed by employers to increase job opportunities for women, minorities, disabled people, and other protected groups

agency legal relationship whereby one party, called a *principal,* appoints another party, called an *agent,* to enter into contracts with third parties on the principal's behalf.

alien corporation firm incorporated in one nation and operating in another nation.

angel investors wealthy individuals who invest directly in a new venture in exchange for an equity stake.

appellate courts courts that hear appeals of decisions made at the general trial court level; both the federal and state systems have appellate courts.

application service provider (ASP) outside supplier that provides both the computers and the application support for managing an information system.

arbitration bringing in an impartial third party called an arbitrator to render a binding decision in a dispute.

assembly line manufacturing technique that carries the product on a conveyor system past several workstations where workers perform specialized tasks.

asset anything of value owned by a firm.

asset intensity amount of assets needed to generate a given level of sales.

autocratic leadership management approach whereby leaders make decisions on their own without consulting employees.

balance of payments overall money flows into and out of a country.

balance of trade difference between a nation's exports and imports.

balance sheet statement of a firm's financial position—what it owns and claims against its assets—at a particular point in time.

balanced budget situation in which total revenues raised by taxes and fees equal total proposed government spending for the year.

bankruptcy legal nonpayment of financial obligations.

banner ad ad placed by an organization on another organization's Web site; interested parties click on the ad for more information.

benchmarking process of determining other companies' standards and best practices.

blog online journal written by a blogger.

board of directors elected governing body of a corporation.

bot short for *robot*—a program that allows online shoppers to compare prices for a specific product at several e-tailers.

boycott effort to prevent people from purchasing a firm's goods or services.

brand name, term, sign, symbol, design, or some combination that identifies the products of one firm and differentiates them from competitors' offerings.

brand equity added value that a respected and successful name gives to a product.

brand name part of a brand consisting of words or letters that form a name that identifies and distinguishes an offering from those of competitors.

branding process of creating an identity in consumers' minds for a good, service, or company; a major marketing tool in contemporary business.

breach of contract violation of a valid contract.

breakeven analysis pricing technique used to determine the minimum sales volume a product must generate at a certain price level to cover all costs.

budget organization's plan for how it will raise and spend money during a given period of time.

budget deficit funding shortfall in which government spends more than the amount of funds raised through taxes and fees.

budget surplus excess funding that occurs when government spends less than the amount of funds raised through taxes and fees.

business all profit-seeking activities and enterprises that provide goods and services necessary to an economic system.

business (B2B) product good or service purchased to be used, either directly or indirectly, in the production of other goods for resale.

business ethics standards of conduct and moral values involving right and wrong actions arising in the work environment.

business incubator organization that provides temporary low-cost, shared facilities to small start-up ventures.

business intelligence activities and technologies for gathering, storing, and analyzing data to make better competitive decisions.

business interruption insurance type of insurance that protects firms from financial losses resulting from the suspension of business operations.

business law aspects of law that most directly influence and regulate the management of business activity.

business plan written document that provides an orderly statement of a company's goals, the methods by which it intends to achieve those goals, and the standards by which it will measure achievements.

business-to-business (B2B) e-business electronic business transactions between organizations using the Internet.

business-to-consumer (B2C) e-business selling directly to consumers over the Internet.

call provision right of the issuer to buy a bond back from the investor before maturity at a specified price.

capital production inputs consisting of technology, tools, information, and physical facilities.

capital investment analysis process of comparing the costs and benefits of a long-term asset investment.

capital structure mix of a firm's debt and equity capital.

capitalism economic system that rewards firms for their ability to perceive and serve the needs and demands of consumers; also called the private enterprise system.

cash budget budget that shows cash inflows and outflows during a period of time.

cash flow sources of cash minus uses of cash during a specified period of time.

cash value policy type of life insurance that combines insurance protection with a savings feature.

category advisor vendor that is designated by the business customer as the major supplier to deal with all other suppliers for a special purchase and to present the entire package to the business buyer.

category manager person who oversees an entire group of products and assumes profit responsibility for the product group.

cause advertising form of institutional advertising that promotes a specific viewpoint on a public issue as a way to influence public opinion and the legislative process.

cause marketing marketing that promotes a cause or social issue, such as preventing child abuse, anti-littering efforts, and stop-smoking campaigns.

Central America–Dominican Republic Free Trade Agreement (CAFTA-DR) agreement among the United States, Costa Rica, the Dominican Republic, El Salvador, Guatemala, Honduras, and Nicaragua to reduce tariffs and trade restrictions.

centralization decision making based at the top of the management hierarchy.

certified management accountant (CMA) management accountant who meets specified educational and experience requirements and has passed an examination covering management accounting topics.

certified public accountant (CPA) public accountant who meets specified educational and experiential requirements and has passed a comprehensive examination on accounting theory and practice.

chain of command set of relationships that indicates who directs which activities and who reports to whom.

channel conflict conflict between two or more members of a supply chain, such as a manufacturer, wholesaler, or retailer.

chief information officer (CIO) executive responsible for managing a firm's information system and related computer technologies.

Class-Action Fairness Act of 2005 law that moves most large, multistate class-action lawsuits to federal courts, ensures judicial oversight of plaintiffs' compensation, bases lawyers' compensation on awards actually distributed or actual time spent, and ensures plaintiffs' interests are protected equally with their lawyers'.

classic entrepreneur person who identifies a business opportunity and allocates available resources to tap that market.

click-through rate number of visitors who click on a Web banner ad.

cobranding cooperative arrangement in which two or more businesses team up to closely link their names on a single product.

code of conduct formal statement that defines how the organization expects employees to resolve ethical issues.

cognitive ability tests tests that measure job candidates' abilities in perceptual speed, verbal comprehension, numerical aptitude, general reasoning, and spatial aptitude.

cognitive conflict disagreement that focuses on problem- and issue-related differences of opinion.

collective bargaining process of negotiation between management and union representatives for the purpose of arriving at mutually acceptable wages and working conditions for employees.

comarketing cooperative arrangement in which two businesses jointly market each other's products.

committee organization organizational structure that places authority and responsibility jointly in the hands of a group of individuals rather than a single manager.

common law body of law arising out of judicial decisions, some of which can be traced back to early England.

common stock shares of ownership in a corporation.

communication meaningful exchange of information through messages.

communism planned economic system in which private property is eliminated, goods are owned in common, and factors of production and production decisions are controlled by the state.

competition battle among businesses for consumer acceptance.

competitive differentiation unique combination of organizational abilities, products, and approaches that sets a company apart from competitors in the minds of customers.

competitive pricing pricing strategy that tries to reduce the emphasis on price competition by matching other firms' prices and concentrating marketing efforts on the product, distribution, and promotional elements of the marketing mix.

compressed workweek scheduling option that allows employees to work the regular number of hours per week in fewer than the typical five days.

computer-aided design (CAD) system for interactions between a designer and a computer to create a product, facility, or part that meets predetermined specifications.

computer-aided manufacturing (CAM) electronic tools to analyze CAD output and determine necessary steps to implement the design, followed by electronic transmission of instructions to guide the activities of production equipment.

computer-based information systems information systems that rely on computer and related technologies to store information electronically in an organized, accessible manner.

computer-integrated manufacturing (CIM) production system that integrates computer tools and human workers to design products, control machines, handle materials, and control production.

conceptual skills ability to see the organization as a unified whole and to understand how each part interacts with others.

conflict antagonistic interaction in which one party attempts to thwart the intentions or goals of another.

conflict of interest situation in which an employee must make a decision about a business's welfare versus personal gain.

conglomerate merger combination of two or more unrelated firms, usually with the goal of diversification, spurring sales growth, or spending a cash surplus that might otherwise make the firm a tempting target for a takeover attempt.

consumer (B2C) product good or service that is purchased by end users.

consumer behavior actions of ultimate consumers directly involved in obtaining, consuming, and disposing of products and the decision processes that precede and follow these actions.

consumer orientation business philosophy that focuses first on determining unmet consumer needs and then designing products to satisfy those needs.

Consumer Price Index (CPI) monthly measure of changes in retail price levels by comparisons of changes in the prices of a "market basket" of goods and services most commonly purchased by urban consumers.

consumerism public demand that a business consider the wants and needs of its customers in making decisions.

contingency planning plans that allow a firm to resume operations as quickly and as smoothly as possible after a crisis while openly communicating with the public about what happened.

contract legally enforceable agreement between two or more parties regarding a specified act or thing.

controlling function of evaluating an organization's performance to determine whether it is accomplishing its objectives.

convenience product item the consumer seeks to purchase frequently, immediately, and with little effort.

conversion rate percentage of visitors to a Web site who actually make a purchase.

convertible securities bonds or preferred stock issues that are convertible into a set number of shares of the issuing company's common stock.

cooperative organization whose owners join forces to collectively operate all or part of the functions in their business.

cooperative advertising allowances provided by marketers in which they share the cost of local advertising of their firm's product or product line with channel partners.

copyright protection of written material such as textbooks, designs, cartoon illustrations, photos, and computer software.

core inflation rate the underlying inflation rate of the economy after energy and food prices are removed.

corporate charter legal document that formally establishes a corporation.

corporate culture organization's system of principles, beliefs, and values.

corporate philanthropy act of an organization making a contribution to the communities in which it earns profits.

corporate Web site Web site designed to increase a firm's visibility, promote its offerings, and provide information to interested parties.

corporation business that stands as a legal entity with assets and liabilities separate from those of its owner(s).

cost-based pricing adding a percentage (markup) to the base cost of a product to cover overhead costs and generate profits.

countertrade barter agreement whereby trade between two or more nations involves payment made in the form of local products instead of currency.

creative selling personal selling that involves skillful solutions for the customer's needs.

creativity capacity to develop novel solutions to perceived organizational problems.

credit receiving money, goods, or services on the basis of an agreement between the lender and the borrower that the loan is for a specified period of time with a specified rate of interest.

critical path sequence of operations that requires the longest time for completion.

critical thinking ability to analyze and assess information to pinpoint problems or opportunities.

cross-functional team team made up of members from different functions, such as production, marketing, and finance.

damages financial payments to compensate for a loss and related suffering.

data raw facts and figures that may or may not be relevant to a business decision.

data mining computer searches of customer data to detect patterns and relationships.

data warehouse customer database that allows managers to combine data from several different organizational functions.

database centralized integrated collection of data resources.

debenture unsecured corporate bond.

debt capital funds obtained from borrowing.

debt financing borrowed funds that entrepreneurs must repay.

decentralization decision makeup based at lower levels of the organization.

decision making process of recognizing a problem or opportunity, evaluating alternative solutions, selecting and implementing an alternative, and assessing the results.

decision support system system designed to give direct support to personnel during the decision-making process.

deflation falling prices caused by a combination of reduced consumer demand and decreases in the costs of raw materials, component parts, human resources, and other factors of production.

delegation act of assigning work activities to subordinates.

demand willingness and ability of buyers to purchase goods and services.

demand curve graph of the amount of a product that buyers will purchase at different prices; generally slopes downward to reflect larger quantities likely to be purchased as prices decline.

democratic leadership management approach whereby leaders delegate assignments, ask employees for suggestions, and encourage their participation.

demographic segmentation dividing markets on the basis of various demographic or socio-economic characteristics such as gender, age, income, occupation, household size, stage in family life cycle, education, or ethnic group.

demographics statistical characteristics of the segment of the market that might purchase a product.

departmentalization process of dividing work activities into units within the organization.

deregulation regulatory trend toward elimination of legal restraints on competition in industries previously served by a single firm in an attempt

to improve customer service and lower prices through increased competition.

devaluation reduction in a currency's value relative to other currencies or to a fixed standard.

direct distribution channel marketing channel that moves goods directly from producer to ultimate user.

directing guiding and motivating employees to accomplish organizational objectives.

disability income insurance type of insurance that pays benefits to those who cannot work due to some sort of disability.

discrimination biased treatment of a job candidate or employee.

dispatching phase of production control in which the manager instructs each department on what work to do and the time allowed for its completion.

display ad glossy-looking online ad often targeted at a specific user.

distribution channel path through which products— and legal ownership of them—flow from producer to consumers or business users.

distribution strategy planning that ensures that customers find their products in the proper quantities at the right times and places.

diversity blending individuals of different genders, ethnic backgrounds, cultures, religions, ages, and physical and mental abilities to enhance a firm's chances of success.

divestiture sale of assets by a firm.

domestic corporation firm that operates in the state where it is incorporated.

double-entry bookkeeping process by which accounting transactions are entered; each individual transaction always has an offsetting transaction.

downsizing process of reducing the number of employees within a firm by eliminating jobs.

dumping selling products abroad at prices below production costs or below typical prices in the home market to capture market share from domestic competitors.

economics social science that analyzes the choices people and governments make in allocating scarce resources.

electronic bulletin board Internet chat room that allows users to post and read messages on a specific topic.

electronic business (e-business) conducting business via the Internet.

electronic data interchange (EDI) computer-to-computer exchanges of invoices, purchase orders, price quotations, and other information between buyers and sellers.

electronic exchange online marketplace that caters to an industry's specific needs.

electronic shopping cart file that holds items that the online shopper has chosen to buy.

electronic storefront company Web site that sells products to customers.

electronic wallet secure computer data file set up by an online shopper at an e-business site that contains credit card and personal identification information.

embargo total ban on importing specific products or a total halt to trading with a particular country.

employee benefits rewards such as retirement plans, health insurance, vacation, and tuition reimbursement provided for employees either entirely or in part at the company's expense.

employee ownership business in which workers purchase shares of stock in the firm that employs them.

employee stock-ownership plan (ESOP) plan that benefits employees by giving them ownership stakes in the companies for which they work.

empowerment giving employees authority and responsibility to make decisions about their work without traditional managerial approval and control.

encryption process of encoding data for security purposes, using software that encodes and scrambles messages.

end-use segmentation marketing strategy that focuses on the precise way a B2B purchaser will use a product.

enterprise zones specific geographic areas designated for economic revitalization.

entrepreneur person who seeks a profitable opportunity and takes the necessary risks to set up and operate a business.

entrepreneurship willingness to take risks to create and operate a business.

environmental impact study analyzes how a proposed plant would affect the quality of life in the surrounding area.

e-procurement use of the Internet by business and government agencies to solicit bids and purchase goods and services from suppliers.

Equal Employment Opportunity Commission (EEOC) government agency created to increase job opportunities for women and minorities and to help end discrimination based on race, color, religion, disability, gender, or national origin in any personnel action.

equilibrium price prevailing market price; the point at which the quantity demanded of a product equals the quantity supplied.

equity capital funds obtained from owners.

equity financing funds invested in new ventures in exchange for part ownership.

equity theory theory concerned with the individual's perception of fair and equitable treatment.

European Union (EU) 27-nation European economic alliance.

event marketing marketing or sponsoring short-term events such as athletic competitions and cultural and charitable performances.

everyday low pricing (EDLP) pricing strategy devoted to maintaining continuous low prices rather than relying on short-term price cuts such as cents-off coupons, rebates, and special sales.

exchange control restriction on importation of certain products or against certain companies to reduce trade and expenditures of foreign currency.

exchange process activity in which two or more parties give something of value to each other to satisfy perceived needs.

exchange rate value of one nation's currency relative to the currencies of other countries.

exclusive distribution distribution strategy involving limited market coverage by a single retailer or wholesaler in a specific geographical territory.

executive summary one- to two-page snapshot of what the overall business plan explains in detail.

executive support system system that allows senior executives access to a firm's primary database.

expectancy theory theory that describes the process people use to evaluate the likelihood their effort will yield the desired outcome and how much they want the outcome.

expert system system that imitates human thinking through a complicated set of "if-then" rules.

exports domestically produced goods and services sold in other countries.

external communication meaningful exchange of information through messages transmitted between an organization and its major audiences.

extranet secure network used for e-business and accessible through an organization's Web site; available to external customers, suppliers, and other authorized users.

factoring selling receivables to another party, called a factor, for cash.

factors of production four basic inputs for effective operation: natural resources, capital, human resources, and entrepreneurship.

family brand brand name used to identify several different, but related, products.

family leave granting up to 12 weeks of unpaid leave annually for employees who have or adopt a child, are becoming foster parents, are caring for a seriously ill relative or spouse, or are themselves seriously ill.

Federal Deposit Insurance Corporation (FDIC) government agency that insures deposits at commercial and savings banks.

Federal Open Markets Committee Fed body that has primary responsibility for money policy.

Federal Reserve System (Fed) the U.S. central bank.

fee-for-service plan traditional form of health insurance in which the insured chooses his or her healthcare provider, pays for treatment, and is reimbursed by the insurance company; also called an indemnity plan.

finance planning, obtaining, and managing the company's funds to accomplish its objectives as effectively and efficiently as possible.

finance charge the difference between the amount borrowed and the amount repaid on a loan.

Financial Accounting Standards Board (FASB) organization that interprets and modifies GAAP in the United States.

financial institution intermediary between savers and borrowers, collecting funds from savers and then lending the funds to individuals, businesses, and governments.

financial manager executive who develops and implements the firm's financial plan and determines the most appropriate sources and uses of funds.

financial market market in which securities are bought and sold.

financial plan document that specifies the funds needed by a firm for a period of time, the timing of inflows and outflows, and the most appropriate sources and uses of funds; guide to help a person reach desired financial goals.

financial system process by which funds are transferred from those having excess funds (savers) to those needing additional funds (users).

financing section section of a business plan that demonstrates the cost of the product, operating expenses, expected sales revenue and profit, and the amount of the business owner's own funds that will be invested to get the business up and running.

firewall electronic barrier between a company's internal network and the Internet that limits access into and out of the network.

fiscal policy government spending and taxation decisions designed to control inflation, reduce unemployment, improve the general welfare of citizens, and encourage economic growth.

flexible benefit plan benefit system that offers employees a range of options from which they may choose the types of benefits they receive.

flexible manufacturing system (FMS) facility that workers can quickly modify to manufacture different products.

flexible work plan employment that allows personnel to adjust their working hours and places of work to accommodate their personal needs.

flextime scheduling system that allows employees to set their own work hours within constraints specified by the firm.

follow-up phase of production control in which employees and their supervisors spot problems in the production process and determine needed adjustments.

foreign corporation firm that operates in states where it is not incorporated.

foreign licensing agreement international agreement in which one firm allows another to produce or sell its product, or use its trademark, patent, or manufacturing processes, in a specific geographical area in return for royalties or other compensation.

formal communication channel messages that flow within the chain of command defined by an organization.

franchise contractual agreement in which a franchisee gains the right to produce and/or sell the franchisor's products under that company's brand name if they agree to certain operating requirements.

franchisee small-business owner who contracts to sell the good or service of a supplier (the franchisor) in exchange for a payment (usually a flat fee plus a percentage of sales).

franchising contractual agreement that specifies the methods by which a dealer can produce and market a supplier's good or service.

franchisor business owner who permits the franchisee to sell its products and use its name, as well as providing a variety of marketing, management, and other services in return for the payment of various fees and a percentage of sales.

free-rein leadership management style of leaders who believe in minimal supervision and leave most decisions to their subordinates.

frequency marketing marketing initiative that rewards frequent purchases with cash, rebates, merchandise, or other premiums.

General Agreement on Tariffs and Trade (GATT) international trade accord that substantially reduced worldwide tariffs and other trade barriers.

generally accepted accounting principles (GAAP) principles that encompass the conventions, rules, and procedures for determining acceptable accounting practices at a particular time.

geographical segmentation dividing an overall market into homogeneous groups on the basis of their locations.

global business strategy offering a standardized, worldwide product and selling it in essentially the same manner throughout a firm's domestic and foreign markets.

goal target, objective, or result that someone tries to accomplish.

goal-setting theory theory that people will be motivated to the extent to which they accept specific, challenging goals and

receive feedback that indicates their progress toward goal achievement.

government bonds bonds issued by the U.S. Department of the Treasury.

grapevine internal information channel that transmits information from unofficial sources.

green marketing marketing strategy that promotes environmentally safe products and production methods.

grid computing linking smaller computers in a network running special software to create virtual mainframes or supercomputers.

grievance formal complaint filed by an employee or a union that management is violating some provision of a union contract.

gross domestic product (GDP) sum of all goods and services produced within a country's boundaries during a specific time period, such as a year.

guerrilla marketing innovative, low-cost marketing schemes designed to get consumers' attention in unusual ways.

hardware all tangible elements of a computer system.

health insurance category of insurance that pays for losses due to illness or injury.

high-context culture society in which communication depends not only on the message itself but also on nonverbal cues, past and present experiences, and personal relationships between the parties.

home-based businesses firms operated from the residence of the business owner.

horizontal merger combination of two or more firms in the same industry that wish to diversify, increase their customer bases, cut costs, or offer expanded product lines.

human resource management function of attracting, developing, and retaining enough qualified employees to perform the activities necessary to accomplish organizational objectives.

human resources production inputs consisting of anyone who works, including both the physical labor and the intellectual inputs contributed by workers.

human skills interpersonal skills that enable a manager to work effectively with and through people; the ability to communicate with, motivate, and lead employees to accomplish assigned activities.

hygiene factors factors that if present are essential to job satisfaction, although they cannot motivate an employee.

imports foreign goods and services purchased by domestic customers.

income statement financial record of a company's revenues, expenses, and profits over a period of time.

individual brand different brand names given to each product within a line.

inflation rising prices caused by a combination of excess consumer demand and increases in the costs of raw materials, component parts, human resources, and other factors of production.

infomercial form of broadcast direct marketing; 30-minute programs that resemble regular TV programs, but are devoted to selling goods or services.

informal communication channel messages outside formally authorized channels within an organization's hierarchy.

information knowledge gained from processing data.

information system organized method for collecting, storing, and communicating past, present, and projected information on internal operations and external intelligence.

infrastructure basic systems of communication, transportation, and energy facilities in a country.

initial public offering (IPO) sale of stock to the public for the first time.

insider trading use of material nonpublic information to make investment profits.

institutional advertising promotion of concepts, ideas, philosophies, or goodwill for industries, companies, organizations, or government entities.

insurable interest demonstration that a direct financial loss will result if some event occurs.

insurable risk requirement that a pure risk must meet for an insurer to agree to provide coverage.

insurance contract by which the insurer for a fee agrees to reimburse the insured a sum of money if a loss occurs.

integrated marketing communications (IMC) coordination of all promotional activities—media advertising, direct mail, personal selling, sales promotion, and public relations—to produce a unified customer-focused message.

integrity adhering to deeply felt ethical principles in business situations.

intensive distribution distribution strategy that involves placing a firm's products in nearly every available outlet.

International Accounting Standards Board (IASB) international organization that interprets and modifies IFRS.

International Financial Reporting Standards (IFRS) similar to GAAP; principles that encompass the conventions, rules, and procedures for determining acceptable accounting practices at a particular time; used in an increasing number of countries. The United States will adopt IFRS rules by 2016.

international law regulations that govern international commerce.

International Monetary Fund (IMF) organization created to promote trade, eliminate barriers, and make short-term loans to member nations that are unable to meet their budgets.

International Organization for Standardization (ISO) organization whose mission is to promote the development of standardized products to facilitate trade and cooperation across national borders.

intranet computer network that is similar to the Internet but limits access to authorized users.

intrapreneurship process of promoting innovation within the structure of an existing organization.

introduction section of a business plan that describes the company, the management team, and the product in detail.

inventory control management effort to balance the priority of limiting inventory costs with that of meeting customer demand.

investment-grade bond bond with a rating of BBB or above.

job enlargement job design that expands an employee's responsibilities by increasing the number and variety of tasks assigned to the worker.

job enrichment change in job duties to increase employees' authority in planning their work, deciding how it should be done, and learning new skills.

job rotation systematically moving employees from one job to another.

job sharing program management decision that allows two or more employees to divide the tasks of one job.

joint venture partnership between companies formed for a specific undertaking.

judiciary court system, or branch of government that is responsible for settling disputes by applying laws.

just-in-time (JIT) system management philosophy aimed at improving profits and return on investment by minimizing costs and eliminating waste through cutting inventory on hand.

labor union group of workers who have banded together to achieve common goals in the areas of wages, hours, and working conditions.

law standards set by government and society in the form of either legislation or custom.

law of large numbers concept that seemingly random events will follow predictable patterns if enough events are observed.

leadership ability to direct or inspire people to attain organizational goals.

leverage increasing the rate of return on funds invested by borrowing funds.

leverage ratios measures of the extent to which a company relies on borrowed funds.

leveraged buyout (LBO) transaction in which public shareholders are bought out and the firm reverts to private status.

liability claims against assets by creditors.

liability insurance a type of insurance that protects people against financial losses to others for acts for which the insured was responsible.

life insurance a type of insurance that protects people against the financial losses that occur with premature death.

lifestyle entrepreneur person who starts a business to reduce work hours and create a more relaxed lifestyle.

lifetime value of a customer revenues and intangible benefits (referrals and customer feedback) from a customer over the life of the relationship, minus the amount the company must spend to acquire and serve that customer.

limit order order that puts a ceiling or floor on a security purchase or sale.

limited-liability company (LLC) legal form of organization allowing business owners to secure the corporate advantage of limited liability while avoiding the double taxation characteristic of corporations.

line manager executive involved with the functions of production, financing, or marketing.

line organization organizational structure that establishes a direct flow of authority from the chief executive to subordinates.

line-and-staff organization structure that combines the direct flow of authority of a line organization with staff departments that support the line departments.

liquidity ratios measures of a firm's ability to meet its short-term obligations.

listening receiving a message and interpreting its intended meaning by grasping the facts and feelings it conveys.

local area network (LAN) computer network that connects machines within limited areas, such as a building or several nearby buildings.

lockout management decision to put pressure on union members by closing the firm.

logistics activities involved in controlling the flow of goods, services, and information among members of the supply chain.

low-context culture society in which communication tends to rely on explicit written and verbal messages.

macroeconomics study of a nation's overall economic issues, such as how an economy maintains and allocates resources and how a government's policies affect the standards of living of its citizens.

make, buy, or lease decision choosing whether to manufacture a needed product or component in house, purchase it from an outside supplier, or lease it.

malware any malicious software program designed to infect computer systems.

managed care plan healthcare plan in which most, if not all, of the insured's healthcare bills are paid by the insurance company; in exchange, the insured has much less say over his or her treatment.

management process of achieving organizational objectives through people and other resources.

management accountant accountant who works for a firm and provides accounting services to that firm.

management by objectives a systematic and organized approach that enables managers to focus on attainable goals and to achieve the best results based on the organization's resources.

management development program training designed to improve the skills and broaden the knowledge of current and potential executives.

management information system system designed to produce reports for managers and other professionals.

management support systems information systems that are designed to provide support for effective decision making.

manufacturer's (national) brand brand offered and promoted by a manufacturer or producer.

market order order that instructs the investor's broker to obtain the best possible price.

market penetration percentage of the market that has purchased your product.

market segmentation process of dividing a total market into several relatively homogeneous groups.

marketable securities low-risk securities with short maturities.

marketing organizational function and set of processes for creating, communicating, and delivering value to customers and for managing customer relationships in ways that benefit

marketing concept companywide consumer orientation to promote long-run success.

marketing mix blending the four elements of marketing strategy—product, distribution, promotion, and pricing—to satisfy chosen customer segments.

marketing research collecting and evaluating information to support marketing decision making.

marketing strategy section of a business plan that presents information describing the market's need for a product and how the business will satisfy it.

marketing Web site Web site whose main purpose is to increase purchases by visitors.

Maslow's hierarchy of needs theory of motivation proposed by Abraham Maslow. According to the theory, people have five levels of needs that they seek to satisfy: physiological, safety, social, esteem, and self-actualization.

mass production system for manufacturing products in large amounts through effective combinations of specialized labor, mechanization, and standardization.

materials requirement planning (MRP) computer-based production planning system by which a firm can ensure that it has needed parts and materials available at the right time and place in the correct amounts.

matrix structure project management structure that links employees from different parts of the organization to work together on specific projects.

mediation dispute resolution process that uses a third party, called a mediator, to make recommendations for settling labor–management differences.

Medicare public health insurance program for those 65 or older.

merger combination of two or more firms to form one company.

microeconomics study of small economic units, such as individual consumers, families, and businesses.

microloans Small Business Administration–guaranteed loans of up to $35,000 made to start-ups and other very small firms.

middle management second tier in the management pyramid that focuses on specific operations within the organizations.

mission statement written explanation of an organization's business intentions and aims.

missionary selling indirect selling in which specialized salespeople promote the firm's goodwill among customers, often by assisting them in product use.

mixed market economy economic system that combines characteristics of both planned and market economies in varying degrees, including the presence of both government ownership and private enterprise.

monetary policy government actions to increase or decrease the money supply and change banking requirements and interest rates to influence bankers' willingness to make loans.

money market instruments short-term debt securities issued by financial institutions, companies, and governments.

monopolistic competition market structure, like that for retailing, in which large numbers of buyers and sellers exchange relatively well-differentiated (heterogeneous) products, so each participant has some control over price.

monopoly market structure in which a single seller dominates trade in a good or service for which buyers can find no close substitutes.

morale mental attitude of employees toward their employer and jobs.

motivator factors factors that can produce high levels of motivation when they are present.

multidomestic business strategy developing and marketing products to serve different needs and tastes of separate national markets.

multinational corporation (MNC) firm with significant operations and marketing activities outside its home country.

municipal bonds bonds issued by state and local governments.

mutual fund financial intermediary that pools funds from investors by selling shares of itself and uses the funds to purchase securities.

national debt money owed by government to individuals, businesses, and government agencies who purchase Treasury bills, Treasury notes, and Treasury bonds sold to cover expenditures.

natural resources all production inputs that are useful in their natural states, including agricultural land, building sites, forests, and mineral deposits.

nearshoring outsourcing production or services to locations near a firm's home base.

negotiable instrument commercial paper that is transferable among individuals and businesses.

net worth the difference between an individual or household's assets and liabilities.

newsgroup noncommercial online forum.

nonpersonal selling promotion that includes advertising, sales promotion, direct marketing, public relations, and sponsorships—all conducted without face-to-face contact with the buyer.

nonprogrammed decision complex and unique problem or opportunity with important consequences for the organization.

nonverbal communication transmission of messages through actions and behaviors.

North American Free Trade Agreement (NAFTA) agreement among the United States, Canada, and Mexico to break down tariffs and trade restrictions.

not-for-profit corporation business-like organization such as a charitable group, social welfare group, or religious congregation that pursues objectives other than returning profit to its owners.

not-for-profit organization organization that has primary objectives such as public service rather than returning a profit to its owners.

objectives guideposts by which managers define the organization's desired performance in such areas as profitability, customer service, growth, and employee satisfaction.

odd pricing pricing method using uneven amounts, which appear less than they really are to consumers.

offshoring relocation of business processes to lower-cost locations overseas.

oligopoly market structure, like those in the airline and steel industries, in which relatively few sellers compete and high start-up costs form barriers that keep out most new competitors.

on-demand computing renting software time from application providers.

on-the-job training training method that teaches an employee to complete new tasks by performing them under the guidance of an experienced employee.

open book management practice of sharing financial information with employees and teaching them how to understand and use financial statements.

open market operations technique in which the Fed buys or sells government bonds to affect the supply of money and credit.

operational planning detailed standards that guide implementation of tactical plans.

operational support systems information systems designed to produce a variety of information on an organization's activities for both internal and external users.

order processing form of selling, mostly at the wholesale and retail levels, that involves identifying customer needs, pointing them out to customers, and completing orders.

organization structured grouping of people working together to achieve common goals.

organization chart visual representation of a firm's structure that illustrates job positions and functions.

organization marketing marketing strategy that influences consumers to accept the goals of, receive the services of, or contribute in some way to an organization.

organizing process of blending human and material resources through a formal structure of tasks and authority; arranging work, dividing tasks among employees, and coordinating them to ensure implementation of plans and accomplishment of objectives.

outsourcing using outside vendors to produce goods or fulfill services and functions that were previously handled in-house or in-country.

owners' equity funds contributed by owners plus profits not distributed to owners in the form of cash dividends.

ownership utility orderly transfer of goods and services from the seller to the buyer; also called possession utility.

pacing program company-initiated and financed program to develop new products.

paid time off (PTO) bank of time that employees can use for holidays, vacation, and sick days.

partnership form of business ownership in which the company is operated by two or more people who are co-owners by voluntary legal agreement.

patent guarantee to an inventor exclusive rights to an invention for 17 years.

penetration pricing pricing strategy that sets a low price as a major marketing tactic.

performance appraisal evaluation of an employee's job performance that compares actual results with desired outcomes.

perpetual inventory system that continuously monitors the amount and location of a company's stocks.

person marketing use of efforts designed to attract the attention, interest, and preference of a target market toward a person.

personal financial management study of the economic factors and personal decisions that affect a person's financial well-being.

personal selling interpersonal promotional process involving a seller's face-to-face presentation to a prospective buyer.

PERT (Program Evaluation and Review Technique) chart that seeks to minimize delays by coordinating all aspects of the production process.

phishing high-tech scam that uses authentic looking e-mail or pop-up ads to get unsuspecting victims to reveal personal information.

physical distribution actual movement of products from producer to consumers or business users.

picketing workers marching at a plant entrance to protest some management practice.

place marketing attempt to attract people to a particular area, such as a city, state, or nation.

place utility availability of a product in a location convenient for customers.

planned economy economic system in which strict government controls determine business ownership, profits, and resource allocation to accomplish government goals rather than those set by individual firms.

planning process of anticipating future events and conditions and determining courses of action for achieving organizational objectives.

podcast audio or video blog.

point-of-purchase (POP) advertising displays or demonstrations that promote products when and where consumers buy them, such as in retail stores.

pollution environmental damage caused by a company's products or operating processes.

pop-up ad Internet ad that pops-up in a new window; interested parties can click on the ad for more information.

positioning concept in which marketers attempt to establish their own places in the minds of customers by communicating to prospective purchasers meaningful distinctions about the attributes, price, quality, or use of a good or service.

potential sales revenue amount of revenue the business would collect if its market penetration were 100 percent.

preferred stock stock whose holders have priority over common stockholders in the payment of dividends but usually have no voting rights.

premium amount paid by the insured to the insurer to exchange for insurance coverage.

pre-roll video ad a short advertising video clip that begins automatically whenever a user visits a particular Web site.

prestige pricing establishing a relatively high price to develop and maintain an image of quality and exclusiveness.

price exchange value of a good or service.

primary market financial market in which new security issues are first sold.

private enterprise system economic system that rewards firms for their ability to identify and serve the needs and demands of customers.

private equity funds investment companies that raise funds from individuals and institutional investors and use the funds to take large stakes in a wide range of public and private companies.

private exchange secure Web site at which a company and its suppliers share all types of data related to e-business, from product design through order delivery.

private placements sale of securities to a small number of investors.

private property most basic freedom under the private enterprise system; the right to own, use, buy, sell, and bequeath land, buildings, machinery, equipment, patents, and various intangible kinds of property.

private (store) brand product that is not linked to the manufacturer, but instead carries the label of a retailer or wholesaler.

privatization recent international trend to convert government-owned and -operated companies into privately held businesses.

problem-solving team temporary combination of workers who gather to solve a specific problem and then disband.

process control system system that monitors and controls physical processes.

product bundle of physical, service, and symbolic attributes designed to satisfy buyers' wants.

product advertising nonpersonal selling of a particular good or service.

product liability responsibility of manufacturers for injuries and damages caused by their products.

product life cycle four basic stages—introduction, growth, maturity, and decline—through which a successful product progresses.

product line group of related products that are physically similar or are intended for the same market.

product mix company's assortment of product lines and individual offerings.

product placement form of promotion in which marketers pay fees to have their products showcased in movies and television shows.

production application of resources such as people and machinery to convert materials into finished goods and services.

production and operations management managing people and machinery in converting materials and resources into finished goods and services.

production control process that creates a well-defined set of procedures for coordinating people, materials, and machinery to provide maximum production efficiency.

production planning phase of production control that determines the amount of resources (including raw materials and other components) a firm needs in order to produce a certain output.

productivity relationship between the number of units produced and the number of human and other production inputs necessary to produce them.

product-related segmentation dividing consumer markets into groups based on benefits sought by buyers and usage rates.

profitability objectives firm's goal to generate enough money (its revenues) through its pricing policies to cover its expenses.

profitability ratios measures of a company's overall financial performance by evaluating its ability to generate revenues in excess of expenses.

profits rewards for businesspeople who take the risks involved to offer goods and services to customers.

programmed decision simple, common, and frequently occurring problem for which a solution has already been determined.

promotion function of informing, persuading, and influencing a purchase decision.

promotional mix combination of personal and nonpersonal selling techniques designed to achieve promotional objectives.

property and liability insurance general category of insurance that protects against losses due to a number of perils.

psychographic segmentation dividing consumer markets into groups with similar attitudes, values, and lifestyles.

public accountant accountant who provides accounting services to other organizations.

public insurance agency public agency that provides certain types of insurance coverage.

public ownership organization owned and operated by a unit or agency of government.

public relations organization's communications and relationships with its various audiences.

publicity stimulation of demand for a good, service, place, idea, person, or organization by disseminating news or obtaining favorable unpaid media presentations.

pulling strategy promotional effort by a seller to stimulate demand among final users, who will then exert pressure on the distribution channel to carry the good or service.

pure competition market structure, like that of small-scale agriculture, in which large numbers of buyers and sellers exchange homogeneous products and no single participant has a significant influence on price.

pure risk type of risk where there is only the possibility of loss.

pushing strategy promotional effort by a seller to members of the distribution channel intended to stimulate personal selling of the good or service.

quality control measuring goods and services against established quality standards.

quota limit set on the amounts of particular products that can be imported.

ratio analysis commonly used tool for measuring the financial strength of a firm.

recession cyclical economic contraction that lasts for six months or longer.

recycling reprocessing of used materials for reuse.

relationship era the business era in which firms seek ways to build long-term relationships with customers by managing every interaction.

relationship management collection of activities that build and maintain ongoing, mutually beneficial ties between a business and its customers and other parties.

relationship marketing developing and maintaining long-term, cost-effective exchange relationships with partners.

retailer channel member that sells goods and services to individuals for their own use rather than for resale.

risk uncertainty about loss or injury.

risk-return trade-off process of maximizing the wealth of the firm's shareholders by striking the optimal balance between risk and return.

robot reprogrammable machine capable of performing numerous tasks that require manipulation of materials and tools.

routing phase of production control that determines the sequence of work throughout the facility and specifies who will perform each aspect of production at what location.

rule of indemnity requirement that the insured cannot collect more than the amount of the loss and cannot collect for the same loss more than once.

S corporation modified form of the traditional corporate structure often used by firms with fewer than 100 shareholders; such businesses can elect to pay federal income taxes as partnerships while retaining the liability limitations typical of corporations.

salary compensation calculated on a periodic basis, such as weekly or monthly.

sales law law governing the sale of goods or services for money or on credit.

sales promotion nonpersonal marketing activities other than advertising, personal selling, and public relations that stimulate consumer purchasing and dealer effectiveness.

Sarbanes-Oxley Act federal legislation designed to deter and punish corporate and accounting fraud and corruption and to protect the interests of workers and shareholders through enhanced financial disclosures, criminal penalties on CEOs and CFOs who defraud investors, safeguards for whistle-blowers, and establishment of a new regulatory body for public accounting firms.

scheduling development of timetables that specify how long each operation in the production process takes and when workers should perform it.

search marketing paying search engines, such as Google, a fee to make sure that the company's listing appears toward the top of the search results.

secondary market financial market in which already issued securities are traded between investors.

Secure Sockets Layer (SSL) technology that secures a Web site by encrypting information and providing authentication.

securities financial instruments such as stocks and bonds.

seed capital initial funding needed to launch a new venture.

selective distribution distribution strategy in which a manufacturer selects only a limited number of retailers to distribute its product lines.

self-managed team work team that has the authority to decide how its members complete their daily tasks.

sell-off transaction in which assets are sold by one firm to another.

serial entrepreneur person who starts one business, runs it, and then starts and runs additional businesses in succession.

server computer that supports network applications and allows for the sharing of software, output devices, and databases by all networked computers.

set-aside program component of a government contract specifying that certain government contracts (or portions of those contracts) are restricted to small businesses and/or to women- or minority-owned companies.

sexism discrimination against members of either sex, but primarily affecting women.

sexual harassment unwelcome and inappropriate actions of a sexual nature in the workplace.

shopping product item typically purchased only after the buyer has compared competing products in competing stores.

skimming pricing pricing strategy that sets an intentionally high price relative to the prices of competing products.

skunkworks project initiated by a company employee who conceives the idea, convinces top management of its potential, and then recruits human and other resources from within the firm to turn it into a commercial project.

small business firm that is independently owned and operated, is not dominant in its field, and meets industry-specific size standards for income or number of employees.

Small Business Administration (SBA) federal agency that aids small businesses by providing management training and consulting, financial assistance, and support in securing government contracts.

Small Business Investment Company (SBIC) business licensed by the Small Business Administration to provide loans to small businesses.

social audit formal procedure that identifies and evaluates all company activities that relate to social issues such as conservation, employment practices, environmental protection, and philanthropy.

social entrepreneur person who recognizes societal problems and uses business principles to develop innovative solutions.

social responsibility business's consideration of society's well-being and consumer satisfaction, in addition to profits.

socialism planned economic system characterized by government ownership and operation of major industries.

software all the programs, routines, and computer languages that control a computer and tell it how to operate.

sole proprietorship form of business ownership in which the company is owned and operated by one person.

sovereign wealth funds government-owned investment companies

spam popular name for junk e-mail.

span of management number of subordinates a manager can supervise effectively.

specialty advertising promotional items that prominently display a firm's name, logo, or business slogan.

specialty product item that a purchaser is willing to make a special effort to obtain.

speculative (junk) bond a bond with a rating below BB.

speculative risk type of risk where the possibility of gain and loss both exist.

spin-off transaction in which divested assets form a new company.

sponsorship funding a sporting or cultural event in exchange for a direct association with the event.

spyware software that secretly gathers user information through the user's Internet connections without his or her knowledge.

staff manager executive who provides information, advice, or technical assistance to aid line managers; does not have the authority to give orders outside his or her own department or to compel line managers to take action.

stakeholders the customers, investors, employees, and public affected by or with an interest in a company.

standard of living necessities, comforts, and luxuries one seeks to obtain or to maintain.

statement of cash flows statement showing the sources and uses of cash during a period of time.

statement of owners' equity record of the change in owners' equity from the end of one fiscal period to the end of the next.

statutory law written law, including state and federal constitutions, legislative enactments, treaties of the federal government, and ordinances of local governments.

stock market (exchange) market in which common stocks are traded, such as the New York Stock Exchange.

stock options rights to buy a specified amount of company stock at a given price within a given time period.

stockholder person or organization who owns shares of stock in a corporation.

strategic alliance partnership formed to create a competitive advantage for the businesses involved; in international business, a business strategy in which a company finds a partner in the country where it wants to do business.

strategic planning process of determining the primary objectives of an organization and then acting and allocating resources to achieve those objectives.

strike temporary work stoppage by employees until a dispute is settled or a contract signed.

subcontracting international agreement that involves hiring local companies to produce, distribute, or sell goods or services in a specific country or geographical region.

subprime mortgage loan made to a borrower with a poor credit rating.

supervisory management first-line management; includes positions such as supervisor, line manager, and group leader; responsible for assigning nonmanagerial employees to specific jobs and evaluating their performance every day.

supply willingness and ability of sellers to provide goods and services.

supply chain sequence of suppliers that contribute to creating a good or service and delivering it to business users and final consumers.

supply curve graph of the amount of a product that suppliers will offer for sale at different prices; generally slopes upward to reflect larger quantities likely to be offered for sale as prices increase.

SWOT analysis method of assessing a company's internal strengths and weaknesses and its external opportunities and threats.

synergy notion that a combined firm is worth more than the two firms are individually.

tactical planning implementing the activities specified by strategic plans.

target market group of people toward whom an organization markets its goods, services, or ideas with a strategy designed to satisfy their specific needs and preferences.

tariff tax imposed on imported goods.

tax assessment by a governmental unit.

team group of employees who are committed to a common purpose, approach, and set of performance goals.

team cohesiveness extent to which team members feel attracted to the team and motivated to remain part of it.

team diversity variances or differences in ability, experience, personality, or any other factor on a team

team level average level of ability, experience, personality, or any other factor on a team.

team norm informal standard of conduct shared by team members that guides their behavior.

technical skills manager's ability to understand and use techniques, knowledge, and tools and equipment of a specific discipline or department.

technology business application of knowledge based on scientific discoveries, inventions, and innovations.

telecommuter home-based employee.

telemarketing personal selling conducted entirely by telephone, which provides a firm's marketers with a high return on their expenditures, an immediate response, and an opportunity for personalized two-way conversation.

tender offer offer made by a firm to the target firm's shareholders.

term policy pure type of life insurance policy providing only a death benefit.

test marketing introduction of a new product supported by a complete marketing campaign to a selected city or TV coverage area to examine both consumer responses to the new offering and the marketing effort used to support it.

Theory X assumption that employees dislike work and will try to avoid it.

Theory Y assumption that employees enjoy work and seek social, esteem, and self-actualization fulfillment.

Theory Z assumption that employee involvement is key to productivity and quality of work life.

time utility availability of a good or service when customers want to purchase it.

top management managers at the highest level of the management pyramid who devote most of their time to developing long-range plans for their organizations.

tort civil wrong inflicted on another person or the person's property.

trade credit credit extended by suppliers in which the buyer agrees to pay for goods and services received now at a later date.

trade promotion sales promotion geared to marketing intermediaries rather than to final consumers.

trademark brand with legal protection against another company's use, not only of the brand name but also of pictorial designs, slogans, packaging elements, and product features such as color and shape.

transaction management building and promoting products in the hope that enough customers will buy them to cover costs and earn profits.

transaction processing system system that records and processes data from business transactions.

trends consumer and business tendencies or patterns that firms can exploit to gain market share in an industry.

trial courts federal and state courts of general jurisdiction.

Trojan horse program that claims to do one thing but in reality does something else, usually something malicious.

underwriting process used by an insurance company to determine who, or what, to insure and how much to charge.

unemployment rate indicator of a nation's economic health, typically expressed as a percentage of the total workforce who are actively seeking work but are currently unemployed.

Uniform Commercial Code The basis of U.S. business law; referred to as UCC.

utility want-satisfying power of a good or service.

vendor-managed inventory company's decision to hand over its inventory control functions to suppliers.

venture capitalists business firms or groups of individuals that invest in new and growing firms in exchange for an ownership share.

vertical merger combination of two or more firms operating at different levels in the production and marketing process.

virtual team group of geographically or organizationally dispersed coworkers who use a combination of telecommunications and information technologies to accomplish an organizational task.

virus program that secretly attaches itself to other programs, changing them or destroying data.

vishing variation on phishing that involves a voice system in which the intended victim receives a voice message directing him or her to reveal personal financial information.

vision perception of marketplace needs and the methods an organization can use to satisfy them.

VoIP voice over Internet protocol; technology that uses a personal computer, special software, and a broadband connection to make and receive telephone calls over the Internet.

volume objectives pricing decisions based on market share—the percentage of a market controlled by a certain company or product.

wage compensation based on an hourly pay rate or the amount of output produced.

Web-to-store use of the Web to aid shoppers at brick-and-mortar retailers.

wheel of retailing theory of retailing in which new retailers gain a competitive foothold by offering low prices and limited services and then add services and raise prices, creating opportunities for new low-price competitors.

whistle-blowing employee's disclosure to company officials, government authorities, or the media of illegal, immoral, or unethical practices committed by an organization.

wholesaler distribution channel member that sells primarily to retailers, other wholesalers, or business users.

WiFi short for *wireless fidelity;* a wireless network that allows devices to communicate with one another through radio waves.

wiki Web page that can be edited by users.

work team relatively permanent group of employees with complementary skills who perform the day-to-day work of organizations.

World Bank organization established by industrialized nations to lend money to less developed countries.

World Trade Organization (WTO) 151-member international institution that monitors GATT agreements and mediates international trade disputes.

worm software that exploits a security hole in a network to replicate itself.

Notes

Chapter 1

1. Company Web site, http://www.deckers.com, accessed February 4, 2009; Harry Wallop, "Sales of Ugg Boots Climb Uphill as Shoppers Seek out Wooly Footwear," *The Daily Telegraph*, January 15, 2009, http://www.telegraph.co.uk; Trine Tsouderos, "Despite Exposure, Economy, Uggs Boots Keep Chugging Along," *The Buffalo News*, January 9, 2009, http://www.buffalonews.com; Yvonne Tarleton, "Uggs, Putting the Boot into Recession," *Daily Mail* (*London*), November 3, 2008, http://www.dailymail.co.uk; Claire Coulson, "Why Uggs Won't Be Feeling the Pinch," *The Sunday Telegraph* (*London*), November 2, 2008, http://www.telegraph.co.uk.

2. Mark Weinraub, "Ethanol Growth Based on Economics, Not Government," *Reuters,* January 14, 2008, http://www.reuters.com.

3. "Number of Nonprofit Organizations in the United States," National Center for Charitable Statistics, http://nccsdataweb.orban.org, accessed February 2009.

4. Paul Arnsberger, "Charities, Social Welfare, and Other Tax-Exempt Organizations," Internal Revenue Service, http://www.irs.gov, accessed February 2009.

5. Organization Web site, "About St. Jude," http://www.stjude.org, accessed February 2009.

6. Organization Web site, "Ice Storms Grip the Midwest; Red Cross Continues to Provide Shelter," http://www.redcross.org, February 2, 2009.

7. Organization Web site, "LiveStrong® Store," http://www.livestrong.org, accessed February 15, 2008.

8. Saul Hansell, "Amazon Reading Device Doesn't Need Computer," *The New York Times,* November 20, 2007, http://www.nytimes.com.

9. Anick Jesdanun, "Postal Agencies Respond to Mail Decline," *Associated Press,* February 4, 2008, http://news.yahoo.com.

10. John Sullivan, "Search Google for Top HR Practices," *Workforce Management,* November 19, 2007, http://www.workforce.com.

11. "Turning Pie in the Sky into Reality," *BusinessWeek,* January 11, 2008, http://www.businessweek.com.

12. Ina Fried, "Microsoft Office Heads to the Web," *CNET News,* September 30, 2007, http://news.cnet.com; Miguel Helft, "Moving Web-Based Software Offline," *The New York Times,* May 31, 2007, http://www.nytimes.com.

13. Frank Ahrens, "FCC Moves to Place Restrictions on Cable TV," *The Washington Post,* November 12, 2007, http://www.washingtonpost.com.

14. "Small Business Profile 2008," SBA Office of Advocacy, http://www.sba.gov, accessed February 2009.

15. Alex Markels, "Chipotle's Secret Salsa," *U.S. News & World Report,* February 18, 2008, http://www.usnews.com.

16. Company press release, "A Brief History of Foot Protection," http://www.thorlo.com, accessed September 2008.

17. Company Web site, "History," http://www.graniterock.com, accessed September 2008.

18. "How Costco Creates Fans," *Marketing Environmentalism,* January 12, 2008, http://www.virginiamiracle.com.

19. Jeff Jarvis, "Dell Learns to Listen," *BusinessWeek,* October 17, 2007, http://www.businessweek.com.

20. Jessica Mintz, "Amazon's Hot New Item: Its Data Center," *The New York Times,* February 1, 2008, http://www.nytimes.com.

21. "A Change in Climate," *The Economist,* January 17, 2008, http://www.economist.com.

22. Brad Kenney, "Green Spot: Stonyfield Farm: A Culture of Leadership," *Industry Week,* January 9, 2008, http://www.industryweek.com.

23. "Nokia Unveils 'Green' Handset Design," *CNET News,* February 13, 2008, http://news.cnet.com.

24. Alison Stein Wellner, "Nothing but Green Skies," *Inc.,* November 2007, pp. 115–120.

25. John Teresko, "Ford's Light Idea," *Industry Week,* November 1, 2007, http://www.industryweek.com.

26. Matt Richtel and John Markoff, "A Green Energy Industry Takes Root in California," *The New York Times,* February 1, 2008, http://www.nytimes.com.

27. "A Change in Climate."

28. "Engaging the Multi-Generational Workforce," *HRM Report,* http://www.hrmreport.com, accessed February 2009.

29. Deborah Gilburg, "Management Techniques for Bringing Out the Best in Generation Y," *CIO,* October 26, 2007, http://www.cio.com; Nadira A. Hira, "Attracting the Twenty Something Worker," *Fortune,* May 15, 2007, http://money.cnn.com.

30. Jarina D'Aurio, "In Defense of Gen Y Workers," *CIO,* November 20, 2007, http://www.cio.com.

31. "Working beyond Retirement," *The Boston Globe,* April 18, 2007, http://www.boston.com.

32. U.S. Census Bureau, "Resident Population by Race, Hispanic-Origin Status, and Age—Projections: 2010 and 2015," *Statistical Abstract of the United States: 2009,* http://www.census.gov.

33. Jessica Levco, "Hoofing It to the Office Passe," *Chicago Tribune,* January 6, 2008, Section 1, p. 4.

34. Barry Salzberg, "Shaping the Workforce of the Future," *BusinessWeek,* October 29, 2007, http://www.businessweek.com.

35. John Hagel and John Seely Brown, "Catching the Innovation Wave," *BusinessWeek,* January 30, 2008, http://www.businessweek.com.

36. Kimberly Palmer, "Creativity on Demand," *U.S. News & World Report,* April 30, 2007, pp. EE2–EE4.

37. Bill George, "A New Makeover for an Old Retail Face," *U.S. News & World Report,* November 19, 2007, p. 68.

38. Michael Wilson, "Flight 1549 Pilot Tells of Terror and Intense Focus," *The New York Times*, February 8, 2009, http://www.nytimes.com.

39. "America's Most Admired Companies 2008," *Fortune,* http://money.cnn.com, accessed March 7, 2008.

40. "Profits with Purpose: Herman Miller, Inc.," *Fast Company,* http://www.fastcompany.com, accessed February 20, 2009; "Herman Miller's Creative Network," *BusinessWeek,* February 15, 2008, http://www.businessweek.com; "Inside the Herman Miller Supply Chain: CEO Brian Walker Responds," *Harvard Business Review,* February 13, 2008, http://www.hbrgreen.org; Brad Kennedy, "Herman Miller: Business as Unusual," *IndustryWeek,* July 26, 2007, http://www.industryweek.com.

41. Maria Aspan, "How Sticky Is Membership on Facebook? Just Try Breaking Free," *The New York Times,* February 11, 2008, http://www.nytimes.com; "Facebook Says Hola to Spanish Amigos," *Reuters,* February 7, 2008, http://www.reuters.com; "The Face behind Facebook," *CBS News,* January 13, 2008, http://www.cbsnews.com; Amanda Natividad, "Facebook to Add more Privacy Controls, Mass Messaging: Zuckerberg on '60 Minutes,'" *Forbes,* January 10, 2008, http://www.forbes.com; Laura Locke, "The Future of Facebook," *Time,* July 17, 2007, http://www.time.com; David Kirkpatrick, "Exclusive: Facebook's New Face," *Fortune,* May 25, 2007, http://money.cnn.com; Ellen McGirt, "Hacker. Dropout. CEO," *Fast Company,* May 2007, http://www.fastcompany.com.

42. Cannondale Web site, http://www.cannondale.com, accessed February 2009; Vernon Felton, "Cannondale Sold Off," bikemag.com, March 21, 2003; "CPSC, Cannondale Corp. Recall of Bicycles with Defective Systems," U.S. Consumer Product Safety Commission, August 15, 2002, http://www.cpsc.gov.

Chapter 2

1. Company Web site, http://www.entropysurfboards.com, accessed February 6, 2009; Evan Fontaine, "Interview: Jeremy Sherwin," *Surfline San Diego,* January 8, 2009, http://www.surfline.com; "Rey Banatao," *The Craftsman Chronicle,* October 11–12, 2008, http://www.ice-ninefoamworks.com; Andy Stone, "Green Wave," *Forbes*, September 1, 2008, pp. 58–60.

2. Edward Iwata, "Businesses Grow More Socially Conscious," *USA Today Collegiate Program,* February 14, 2007, http://www.usatoday.com/educate/college.

3. Daniel Franklin, "Just Good Business," *The Economist,* January 17, 2008, http://www.economist.com.

4. Company Web site, http://www.jnj.com, accessed March 13, 2008.

5. "Target Corporate Responsibility Report Overview 2007;" John Vomhof Jr., "Target Starts Solar-Power Rollout," *Mlive.com,* April 30, 2007, http://www.mlive.com.

6. "Ethics Resource Center's National Business Ethics Survey," *Ethics Resource Center,* November 2007.

7. Daniel Franklin, "Just Good Business," *Economist,* January 17, 2008, http://www.economist.com.

8. "Ethics Resource Center's National Business Ethics Survey," *Ethics Resource Center,* 2007.

9. Michelle Kessler, "Tech Companies Caught in Web of Ethics Issues," *USA Today,* April 10, 2007, http://www.usatoday.com.

10. "Gap Vows Action After Child Labor Report," *Associated Press,* October 29, 2007, http://news.yahoo.com.

11. Thomas Fuller, "Boycott Clouds Gem Show in Myanmar," *International Herald Tribune,* November 14, 2007, http://www.iht.com.

12. Valerie Bauman, "Ethics Questions Arise as Doctors Pitch to Colleagues," *USA Today,* March 8, 2008, http://www.usatoday.com; Associated Press, "Doctors Still Taking Drug Company Freebies," *MSNBC,* April 26, 2007, http://www.smnbc.msn.com.

13. Keith J. Winstein, "MIT Admissions Dean Lied on Resume in 1979, Quits," *The Wall Street Journal,* April 27, 2007, http://online.wsj.com.

14. Mike Foster, "Avoid Employee Internet Misuse," *Progressive Distributor,* November/December 2007, http://www.progressivedistributor.com; Stephanie Armour, "Technology Makes Porn Easier to Access at Work," *USA Today,* October 17, 2007, http://www.usatoday.com; Simon Palan, "Employees Disagree Over Facebook Use and Misuse," *Australian Broadcasting Company,* September 24, 2007, http://www.abc.net.au.

15. James Sandler, "The Whistleblower's Tightrope," *Expose,* 2007, http://www.pbs.org/expose.

16. "A Dangerous Business Revisited," *Frontline,* February 5, 2008, http://www.pbs.org.

17. Company Web site, http://www.nortel.com, accessed February 20, 2009.

18. Company Web site, "2008 Ethics Awareness Training Resources," http://www.lockheedmartin.com, accessed February 20, 2009.

19. Erica Ogg, "Dell Founder Unaware of Company's Financial Shenanigans," *CNET News,* September 5, 2007, http://news.cnet.com; Tom Krazit, "Dell Accounting Probe Finds Possible Misconduct," *CNET News,* March 29, 2007, http://www.news.com.com.

20. Company Web site, http://nobisengineering.com, accessed February 2009.

21. Company Web site, http://www.boxtops4education.com, accessed February 2009.

22. "About CSPI," *Center for Science in the Public Interest,* http://www.cspinet.org, accessed February 2009.

23. Nadia Vanderhoof, "Trend in Restaurants Is Toward Healthier Trans Fat Free Food Preparation," *TC Palm,* July 22, 2007; Michael Arndt, "How KFC Went Trans-Fat Free," *BusinessWeek,* January 3, 2007, http://www.businessweek.com.

24. "Nolan Ryan Confident MLB Can Put Steroid Problem in Past," *ESPN,* March 8, 2008, http://sports.espn.go.com; "Mitchell Report: Baseball Slow to React to Players' Steroid Use," *ESPN,* December 14, 2007, http://sports.espn.go.com.

25. Steve Mufson, "Utility Fined $11.4 Million for Acid Rain," *The Washington Post,* September 21, 2007, http://www.washingtonpost.com.

26. Jennifer Hughes, "A Central Stop for All That Hazardous Waste," *The New York Times,* May 6, 2007, http://www.nytimes.com.

27. "Toyota Sees 1–2 Percent Sales Rise in U.S. in '08," *Reuters,* January 3, 2008, http://www.reuters.com.

28. Brad Kenney, "Green Spot: Setting the Green Bar High," *Industry Week,* December 31, 2007, http://www.industryweek.com.

29. Company Web site, http://www.cisco.com, accessed February 2009; David Meyer, "Cisco Keen to Be Seen as Green in China," November 2, 2007, http://news.cnet.com.

30. Marianne Lavelle, "Power Revolution," *U.S. News & World Report,* November 5, 2007, pp. 46–53.

31. Company Web site, http://www.nestle.com/SharedValueCSR, accessed February 2009.

32. U.S. Bureau of Labor Statistics, "Table 4. Quartiles and Selected Deciles of Usual Weekly Earnings of Full-Time Wage and Salary Workers by Selected Characteristics," http://www.bls.gov, accessed January 26, 2009.

33. Company Web site, http://sites.target.com, accessed February 2009.

34. Louise Kramer, "Training Local Workers Instead of Outsourcing," *The New York Times,* August 5, 2007, http://www.nytimes.com.

35. "Diversity," Coca-Cola Web site, http://www.thecoca-colacompany.com, accessed February 2009.

36. "Brand Partnerships," General Mills Web site, http://www.generalmills.com/corporate, accessed February 2009.

37. "The Good Consumer," *The Economist,* January 17, 2008, http://www.economist.com.

38. Jeffry Scott, "Peanut Corp. of America Files for Bankruptcy," *The Atlanta Journal-Constitution,* February 13, 2009, http://www.ajc.com.

39. Kate Barrett, "Airborne to Refund Consumers," *ABC News,* March 3, 2008, http://abcnews.go.com.

40. "eBay Rules and Policies Overview," *eBay,* http://pages.ebay.com/policies, accessed February 2009.

41. "Teen Workers," *U.S. Department of Labor,* http://www.osha.gov/SLTC/teenworkers/teenworkers.html, accessed February 2009.

42. Kimberly Palmer, "The New Mommy Track," *U.S. News & World Report,* September 3, 2007, pp. 40–45.

43. Ken Belson, "At IBM, a Vacation Anytime, or Maybe None," *The New York Times,* August 31, 2007, http://www.nytimes.com.

44. "Are You Discriminating Against Employees … Without Realizing It?" *Industry Week.com,* August 29, 2007, http://www.industryweek.com.

45. "Americans Love to Work—Especially after Retirement Age," *Agence France Press,* August 27, 2007, http://www.afp.com.

46. U.S. Department of Labor," *Occupational Outlook Handbook 2008–2009,* http://www.bls.gov, accessed February 2009.

47. "Sexual Harassment Charges," *EEOC,* http://www.eeoc.gov/stats/harass.html, accessed February 2009.

48. Jennifer Millman, "Stripteases, Porn, the B-Word: Isiah Thomas Is Not Alone in Sex Harassment," *Diversity Inc,* October 3, 2007, http://www.diversityinc.com.

49. Diane Carman, "Why Do Men Earn More? Just Because," *Denver Post,* April 24, 2007, http://www.denverpost.com; Ellen Simon, "Pay Gap Persists: Women Still Make Less, Study Says," *USA Today,* April 23, 2007, http://www.usatoday.com.

50. "Honda FCX," *Cars.com,* http://www.cars.com, accessed February 2009; Scott Burgess, "Honda FCX Clarity: A Glimpse at the Future," *The Detroit News,* January 30, 2008, http://info.detnews.com; Vaughan Freeman, "Impressive New Concept Fuels Honda's Green Revolution," *The London Times,* January 4, 2008, http://www.timesonline.co.uk; Tori Tellem, "Living the Hydrogen Life," *The New York Times,* December 9, 2007, http://www.nytimes.com; Norman Mayersohn, "Hydrogen Car Is Here, a Bit Ahead of its Time," *The New York Times,* December 9, 2007, http://www.nytimes.com.

51. "Why Buy Local?" *LocalHarvest,* http://www.localharvest.org, accessed February 2009; Charles Stuart Platkin, "Should I Buy Local?" *The Globe Gazette,* October 10, 2007, http://www.globegazette.com; Emily DeNitto, "Flavorful Ingredients, Grown Close to Home," *The New York Times,* October 7, 2007, http://www.nytimes.com; Kim Severson, "In Pursuit of Farm Fresh Flavor," *The New York Times,* August 19, 2007, http://www.nytimes.com; Drake Bennett, "The Localvore's Dilemma," *The Boston Globe,* July 22, 2007, http://www.boston.com.

52. Timberland Web site, http://www.timberland.com, accessed February 2009; "Timberland's 5th Annual Serv-A-Palooza Goes Global for First Time," company press release, May 30, 2002, accessed January 4, 2005; "The Timberland Company Wins Business Ethics' Corporate Social Responsibility Report's Corporate Citizenship Award," company press release, November 2, 2001, accessed January 4, 2005.

Chapter 3

1. Farhana Hossain, Amanda Cox, John McGrath, and Stephan Weitburg, "The Stimulus Plan: How to Spend $787 Billion," *The New York Times*, February 18, 2009, http://www.nytimes.com; James Oliphant, "Inside Stimulus Bill's Billions in Provisions, *Chicago Tribune*, February 15, 2009, section 1, p. 6; Jeremy Pelofsky and Richard Cowan, "House Approves Stimulus Plan; Senate Vote to Come," Reuters, February 13, 2009, http://news.yahoo.com; Annys Shin, "Economic Signs Turn from Grim to Worse," *The Washington Post*, January 30, 2009, http://www.washingtonpost.com; Jack Healy, "Steep Slide in U.S. Economy, but Not as Dire as Forecast," *The New York Times*, January 30, 2009, http://www.nytimes.com.

2. Richard Cowan and Donna Smith, "Tentative Deal Reached on Economic Package," *Reuters,* January 24, 2008, www.reuters.com; Richard Cowan and Donna Smith, "Bush, Congress Strike a Deal on Economic Plan," *Reuters,* January 24, 2008, www.reuters.com.

3. Frederick Lane, "Video Gaming Industry Shows Strong Growth in 2007," *NewsFactor Network,* January 19, 2008, http://www.newfactor.com.

4. Gary Gentile, "NBC, Fox to Launch Online Video Site," *Associated Press,* October 19, 2007, http://news.yahoo.com.

5. Clifford Krauss, "Economy and Geopolitics Decide Where Oil Goes Next," *The New York Times,* January 4, 2008, http://nytimes.com.

6. "A Wake-up Call for Coffee," *BusinessWeek,* October 22, 2007, p. 23.

7. Elizabeth M. Gillespie, "Starbucks Tests $1 Coffee, Free Refills," *Associated Press,* January 23, 2008, www.reuters.com.

8. Pallavi Gogoi, "Luxury Shoppers Shut Their Purses," *BusinessWeek,* January 14, 2008, http://www.businessweek.com.

9. Kim Severson, "California Freeze Raises U.S. Citrus Prices," *International Herald Tribune,* February 14, 2007, www.iht.com.

10. Andrew Martin, "Organic Milk Supply Expected to Surge as Farmers Pursue a Payoff," *The New York Times,* April 20, 2007, http://www.nytimes.com.

11. Jackie Farwell, "Gold and Platinum Jump to Record Highs," *Associated Press,* January 25, 2008, www.reuters.com. Stevenson Jacobs, "Gold Hits Record $900 an Ounce," *Associated Press,* January 11, 2008, www.google.com; Robert Gavin, "Pedal to Metal on Gold Jewelry Prices," *The Boston Globe,* December 11, 2007, http://www.boston.com; Javier Blas, "High Gold Prices Begin to Dent Jewelry Demand," *Financial Times,* October 16, 2007, http://www.ft.com.

12. Valerie Jones, "Fast Food Places Giving Customers Cheaper Food Options," *Houston Community Newspapers,* January 7, 2009, http://www.hconline.com.

13. Jeffrey R. Kosnett, "8 Stocks to Own in '08," *Kiplinger's Personal Finance,* January 2008, p. 44; Ben Steverman, "Cemex: Pouring it On," *BusinessWeek,* September 17, 2007, http://www.businessweek.com.

14. Steve Lohr and Miguel Helft, "Google Gets Ready to Rumble with Microsoft," *The New York Times,* December 16, 2007, http://www.nytimes.com; Michael Lev-Ram, "Office Wars: Google vs. Microsoft," *Fortune,* October 5, 2007, http://money.cnn.com.

15. Marguerite Reardon, "FCC Bans Exclusive TV Deals for Cable," *CNET News,* October 31, 2007, http://www.news.com.

16. Company Web site, http://www.aircanada.com, accessed February 2009.

17. Neil Reynolds, "U.S. Workers Leave Competition in Their Dust," *The Globe and Mail,* September 14, 2007, http://www.theglobeandmail.com.

18. "TNS Reports Record Breaking Number of Millionaires in the USA," *PR Newswire,* http://sev.prnewswire.com, accessed February 14, 2008.

19. "Statement of Philip L. Rones, Deputy Commissioner," Bureau of Labor Statistics, January 4, 2008, http://www.bls.gov.

20. World Bank Web site, http://web.worldbank.org, accessed February 2009; "Davos Discusses How to Address Climate Change, Poverty Alleviation," *Agence France Presse,* January 25, 2008, http://news.yahoo.com.

21. Martin Crutsinger, "Recession, Bailout Costs Push Deficit to Record," Associated Press, February 11, 2009, http://news.yahoo.com.

22. U.S. Treasury Department, "The Debt to the Penny and Who Holds It," http://www.treasurydirect.gov, accessed February 2009.

23. "U.S. and World Population Clocks," U.S. Census Bureau, http://www.census.gov, accessed February 2009.

24. "Fisher-Price Recalls 1 M Toys," *CNN,* August 1, 2007, http://www.cnn.com, accessed October 2008.

25. Mike Caggeso, "Coca-Cola's Big Third Quarter Highlights Its Rivalry with Pepsi," *Money Morning,* October 18, 2007, http://www.moneymorning.com, accessed October 2008.

26. Tetra Tech Web site, http://www.tetratech.com, accessed February 24, 2009; Airtricity Web site, www.aitricity.com, accessed October 2008; John Burnett, "Winds of Change Blow into Roscoe, Texas," *National Public Radio,* November 30, 2007, http://www.npr.org; John A. Sullivan and Bobette Riner, "Texas Holds Nation's First Lease Sale for Wind Tract," *Natural Gas Week,* October 8, 2007, http://www.lexisnexic.com.library.uark.edu; Liz Moucka, "Harvesting the Wind," *Texas Contractor,* September 3, 2007, http://www.acppubs.com.

27. "Music Industry Changes Coming," *The Business Journal,* January 12, 2008, http://www.biz-journal.com; David Byrne, "David Byrne's Survival Strategies for Emerging Artists—and Megastars," *Wired,* December 18, 2007, http://www.wired.com; James Montgomery, "Madonna Ditches Label, Radiohead Go Renegade: The Year the Music Industry Broke," *MTV News,* December 17, 2007, http://www.mtv.com; Greg Sandoval, "When Rockers Cut Ties from Labels," *CNET News,* November 2, 2007, http://news.cnet.com; Anders Bylund, "Record Label Defections by Major Acts a Troubling Sign for Recording Industry," *Ars Technica,* October 9, 2007, http://arstechnica.com; "A Change of Tune," *The Economist,* July 5, 2007, http://www.economist.com.

28. Josh Reid, "Burton Snowboards Establishes Learn to Ride Program," www.boarding.com, accessed January 17, 2001; "Burton Snowboards Rides the 'Net at Breakneck Speed with NaviSite," *Business Wire,* January 16, 2001; "Burton Snowboards," *Fortune,* www.fortune.com, accessed November 21, 2000; "Stowe and Burton Snowboards Work to Make Riding Easy for Beginners," press release, September 6, 2000, www.stowe.com; Portland Helmich, "Chairman of the Board," *Business People Vermont,* August 2000, www.vermontguides.com; "Snowboard Maker Finds Ideal e-Commerce Solution with Windows DNA," *Microsoft Business,* June 12, 2000, www.microsoft.com.

Chapter 4

1. "Lululemon Athletica Inc.," company profile, *BusinessWeek,* http://investing.businessweek.com, accessed February 13, 2009; company Web site, http://www.lululemon.com, accessed January 18, 2009; David Olive, "The Year of Living Dangerously," *The Star,* January 3, 2009, http://www.thestar.com; John Partridge, "Lululemon Pushing Expansion Despite Slowdown," *The Globe and Mail,* September 12, 2008, http://www.theglobeandmail.com; Karen Goldberg Goff, "Lifestyle for Sale at Lululemon," *The Washington Times,* September 3, 2008, http://www.washingtontimes.com; Melinda Peer, "Christine Day Breathes New Life into Lululemon," *Forbes,* April 3, 2008, http://forbes.com.

2. CIA *World Factbook:* "United States," https://www.cia.gov, January 24, 2008.

3. Mike Stobbe, "Against the Trend, U.S. Births Way Up," Associated Press, January 15, 2008, http://news.yahoo.com;

"How to Deal with a Falling Population," *The Economist,* July 26, 2007, http://www.economist.com.

4. CIA *World Factbook.*

5. "Wal-Mart Facts," http://www.walmartfacts.com, accessed February 2009.

6. U.S. Census Bureau, "Top Ten Countries with which the U.S. Trades," http://www.census.gov, accessed February 2009.

7. U.S. Census Bureau, *Statistical Abstract of the United States: 2008,* http://www.census.gov.

8. http://www.spiceadvice.com, accessed February 2009.

9. U.S. Census Bureau, "U.S. International Trade in Goods and Services," *Statistical Abstract of the United States, 2008,* http://www.census.gov.

10. Art Detman, "Money Sense Overseas, *CFO Asia,* October 2007, http://www.cfoasia.com; Sarah Perrin, "Overseas Careers: Where in the World?" *Accountancy Age,* May 17, 2007, http://www.accountancyage.com.

11. "SeaWorld Plans Overseas Expansion," *MSNBC,* February 29, 2008, http://www.msnbc.com.

12. Ariana Eunjung Cha, "Weak Dollar Fuels China's Buying Spree of U.S. Firms," *The Washington Post,* January 28, 2008, http://www.washingtonpost.com.

13. Bank for International Settlements, http://www.bis.org.

14. Jennifer Fishbein, "Chocolatiers Look to Asia for Growth," *BusinessWeek,* January 17, 2008, http://www.businessweek.com.

15. Gary Stroller, "Doing Business Abroad? Simple *Faux Pas* Can Sink You," *USA Today,* August 24, 2007, p. 1B.

16. Drake Bennett, "The Zero Percent Solution," *The Boston Globe,* November 4, 2007, http://www.boston.com.

17. Scott Baldauf, "Rwanda Aims to Become Africa's High-Tech Hub," *Christian Science Monitor,* October 17, 2007, http://www.csmonitor.com; Jack Ewing, "Extreme Telecom: Mobile Networks in Africa," *BusinessWeek,* September 18, 2007, http://www.businessweek.com.

18. Edward Cody, "For China's Censors, Electronic Offenders Are the New Frontier," *The Washington Post,* September 10, 2007, http://www.washingtonpost.com.

19. Organization for Economic Co-Operation and Development, "Anti-Bribery Convention," http://www.oecd.org, accessed February 4, 2008.

20. Susan Fenton, "Cracking Down on PC Software Piracy Would Create Hundreds of Thousands of Jobs Globally, a Study by IDC Claims," *Information Week,* January 22, 2008, http://www.informationweek.com; Eileen Yu, "Asia: The Steep Cost of Software Piracy," *BusinessWeek,* May 16, 2007, http://www.businessweek.com.

21. "U.S. May Take Action on EU Electronics Tariffs," *PCWorld,* January 9, 2008, http://www.pcworld.com.

22. "Administering Sugar Imports," The U.S. Department of Agriculture Foreign Agricultural Service, http://www.fas.usda.gov, accessed October 2008.

23. David Wessel and Bob Davis, "Pain from Free Trade Spurs Second Thoughts," *The Wall Street Journal,* March 28, 2007, http://online.wsj.com.

24. Sean O'Grady, "Can the Doha Trade Round Be Saved?" *BusinessWeek,* January 28, 2008, http://www.businessweek.com.

25. Kester Kenn Klomegah, "Africa: G8 Has Yet to Deliver on Aid Promises—World Bank," *Inter-Press Service,* June 8, 2007, http://www.ipsnews.net.

26. CIA *World Factbook,* "United States," https://www.cia.gov, February 24, 2009.

27. CIA *World Factbook,* "Canada," https://www.cia.gov, February 24, 2009.

28. CIA *World Factbook,* "Mexico," https://www.cia.gov, February 24, 2009.

29. CIA *World Factbook,* "European Union," https://www.cia.gov, February 24, 2009.

30. David Barboza, "Google Acquires Stake in Chinese Web Site," *The New York Times,* January 5, 2007, http://www.nytimes.com.

31. Company profile, Yahoo! Finance, http://biz.yahoo.com.

32. Company Web site, http://www.dominosbiz.com, accessed February 2009.

33. Regina Molaro, "Taste of Success," *Global License!,* April 15, 2007, http://www.licensemag.com.

34. Ann Meyer, "U.S. Exit Strategy Splits Employers," *Chicago Tribune,* October 29, 2007, Section 3, p. 2.

35. Jena McGregor, ed., "India's Competition in the Caribbean," *BusinessWeek,* December 24, 2007, p. 72.

36. Ann Meyer, "U.S. Exit Strategy Splits Employers."

37. Anand Giridharadas, "Outsourcing Works, So India Is Exporting Jobs," *The New York Times,* September 25, 2007, http://www.nytimes.com.

38. "Acer to Acquire US-Based Gateway, Inc." *Business Wire,* August 27, 2007, http://www.businesswire.com; Nandini Lakshman, "India's High-Octane Car Market," *BusinessWeek,* April 16, 2007, http://www.businessweek.com.

39. "Tyson Foods Strategically Positioned for Additional Success," *Fox Business,* February 19, 2008, http://www.foxbusiness.com.

40. Sheridan Prasso, "India's Pizza Wars," *Fortune,* October 1, 2007, pp. 61–64.

41. Company Web site, http://www.mcdonalds.com, accessed February 2009; Michael Arndt, "Knock Knock, It's Your Big Mac," *BusinessWeek,* July 23, 2007, p. 36; Clare Watson, "McDonald's to Run UK Delivery Fleet on Its Own Cooking Oil," *Food Business Review,* July 2, 2007, http://www.food-business-review.com; "McDonald's to Strengthen Home Delivery Services," *Business Line,* March 18, 2007, http://thehindubusinessline.com.

42. Leo Cendrowicz, "Lego Celebrates 50 Years of Building," *Time,* January 28, 2008, http://www.time.com; Slim Allagui, "At 50, Lego Still Going Strong Despite High-Tech Toy World," *Agence-France Presse,* January 28, 2008, http://news.yahoo.com; Jan M. Olsen, "Lego Posts Higher Sales," *USA Today,* August 29, 2007, http://www.usatoday.com; Tara Weiss, "Building Blocks for Success," *Forbes,* May 21, 2007, http://www.forbes.com.

43. ESPN Web site, http://www.international.espn.com, accessed February 2009; "ESPN Executive from Waterbury,

CT Leads High-Definition Television Venture," press release, http://www.hoovers.com; "ESPN to Be at the America's Cup," press release, February 12, 2003, http://hoovnews.hoovers.com.

End of Part 1: Launching Your Global Business and Economics Career

1. U.S. Department of Labor, "Tomorrow's Jobs," *Occupational Outlook Handbook,* 2008–2009 edition, U.S. Bureau of Labor Statistics, http://www.bls.gov.

2. U.S. Department of Labor, "Economists," *Occupational Outlook Handbook,* 2008–2009 edition, U.S. Bureau of Labor Statistics, http://www.bls.gov.

3. Adapted from Michael R. Czinkota, Ilkka A. Ronkainen, and Michael H. Moffett, "Criteria for Selecting Managers for Overseas Assignments," in *International Business,* 7th ed. (Mason, OH: SouthWestern, 2005), Table 19.2, p. 634.

4. "MBA Still Packs a Punch," January 28, 2008, *Financial Times,* http://www.ft.com.

5. Sattar Bawany, "Transition Coaching Helps Ensure Success for Global Assignments," *Today's Manager,* January 2008, accessed at Entrepreneur.com, April 14, 2008.

Chapter 5

1. Company Web site, http://www.nokia.com, accessed February 18, 2009; "Nokia Joins 8-Megapixel Phone Club with N86," *PC Magazine,* February 18, 2009, http://www.pcmag.com; Moon Ihlwan, "Samsung and LG Take Aim at Nokia," *BusinessWeek,* February 17, 2009, http://www.businessweek.com; Marin Perez, "Nokia Expands E Series of Smartphones," *InformationWeek,* February 17, 2009, http://www.information-week.com; Marin Perez, "Nokia Jumps into Application Store Game," *InformationWeek,* February 17, 2009, http://www.informationweek.com; "Nokia Eyes Apple's Success in Mobile Downloads," *InternetNews,* February 16, 2009, http://www.internetnews.com.

2. U.S. Census Bureau, "Statistics of U.S. Business," accessed March 2009, http://www.census.gov.

3. Ibid.

4. Office of Advocacy, U.S. Small Business Administration, "Frequently Asked Questions: Advocacy Small Business Statistics and Research," accessed March 2009, http://app1.sba.gov/faqs.

5. Ibid.

6. Ibid.

7. Ibid.

8. Small Business Administration, "Frequently Asked Questions (FAQs) about Small Business Size Standards," accessed March 2009, http://www.sba.gov/size.

9. Marika McElroy Cain, "Happy Green Bee Outfits Kids Organically," *nwsource,* accessed October 2008, http://www.nwsource.com; Nanette Byrnes, "Organic Growth," *BusinessWeek SmallBiz,* February/March 2007, p. 82.

10. Norm Brodsky, "How Independents Can Hold Their Ground," *Inc.,* August 2007, pp. 65–66.

11. "About Randy's Fish Market Restaurant," accessed March 2009, http://randysfishmarketrestaurant.com.

12. U.S. Department of Agriculture, *Agriculture Fact Book,* pp. 12–23, accessed October 2008, http://www.usda.gov/factbook.

13. Owen Taylor, "Holding on to Farm Life," *The Progressive Farmer,* February 2008, pp. 62–65.

14. Office of Advocacy, "Frequently Asked Questions."

15. "The Top 100 Home-Based Businesses in the Nation Revealed," Microsoft Company Web site, November 5, 2007, accessed October 2008, http://www.microsoft.com.

16. George Alexander, "Daddy's HOME!" *Black Enterprise,* October 2007, pp. 91–95.

17. Della De Lafuente, "Child's Play," *BusinessWeek SmallBiz,* June/July 2007, p. 22.

18. Office of Advocacy, "Frequently Asked Questions."

19. Small Business Administration, "Small Business Statistics," accessed March 2009, http://www.sba.gov/advo.

20. Office of Advocacy, U.S. Small Business Administration, "U.S. Receipt Size of Firm by Major Industry Group," accessed March 2009, http://www.sba.gov/advo.

21. Small Business Administration, "Welfare to Work Program," accessed March 2009, http://www.sba.gov.

22. Susan Kitchens, "Hitched to Apple," *Forbes,* January 28, 2008, p. 56.

23. David Kaplan, "Freedom Planning," Houston Chronicle, July 3, 2007, http://www.chron.com.

24. Netflix, "Fact Sheet," accessed October 2008, http://www.netflix.com.

25. "Neil Saiki," *Fortune,* January 21, 2008, p. 28.

26. Office of Advocacy, "Frequently Asked Questions."

27. Small Business Administration, Office of Advocacy, "Financing Patterns of Small Firms," accessed March 2009, http://www.sba.gov/advo.

28. "Hungry for Cash," *BusinessWeek SmallBiz,* October/November 2007, pp. 21–22.

29. U.S. Department of Labor, "As an Employer, Are You Engaged in Commerce or in an Industry or Activity Affecting Commerce?" elaws—Family and Medical Leave Act Advisor, accessed March 2009, http://www.dol.gov.

30. "Performance Stats for the SBA," May 1, 2007, accessed October 2008, http://inc.com.

31. Robb Mandelbaum, "Soldiering on to Remake the SBA," *Inc.,* October 2008, p. 21.

32. Small Business Administration, Office of Disaster Assistance, "Fact Sheet about U.S. Small Business Administration Disaster Loans," accessed March 2009, http://www.sba.gov.

33. Small Business Administration, "The Microloan Program for Entrepreneurs," accessed March 2009, http://www.sba.gov.

34. Office of Advocacy, U.S. Small Business Administration, "Financing Patterns of Small Firms," accessed March 2009, http://www.sba.gov/advo.

35. Active Capital, "Frequently Asked Questions," accessed March 2009, http://activecapital.org.

36. Small Business Administration, "Government Contracting: What We Do," accessed March 2009, http://www.sba.gov.

37. Small Business Administration, "SBA, OMB, GSA and DOD Work Together to Integrate PRO-Net and CCR Database and Simplify Contracting Process for Small Businesses," accessed March 2009, http://www.pro-net.sba.gov.

38. National Business Incubator Association, accessed February 2008, http://www.nbia.org.

39. "New UT Business Incubator Supports High-Tech Innovations," *Ceramic Industry,* August 2007, p. 9.

40. National Foundation for Women Business Owners, "Key Facts about Women-Owned Businesses," accessed March 2009, http://www.nfwbo.org.

41. Amy Barrett, "This Time It's Mine," *BusinessWeek SmallBiz,* February/March 2007, pp. 40–48.

42. National Foundation for Women Business Owners, "National Numbers," accessed March 2009, http://www.nfwbo.org.

43. "About Rebel Monkey," accessed April 2008, http://www.rebelmonkey.com; "About Skunk Studios," accessed October 2008, http://games.skunkstudios.com.

44. "About Springboard," accessed October 2008, http://www.springboardenterprises.org.

45. Ying Lowrey, "Minorities in Business: A Demographic Review of Minority Business Ownerships," Small Business Administration, accessed March 2009, http://www.sba.gov/advo.

46. "Dynamic Trends," Hispanic Trends.com, accessed February 2008, www.hispaniconline.com/trends.

47. Denene Brox, "Minority-Owned Business: The Untapped Market for Small Business Lending," *Community Banker,* May 2007, pp. 34–36.

48. Franchise Industries LLC, Statistics, accessed March 2009, http://www.franchiseindustries.com.

49. "Fastest Growing," *Entrepreneur,* accessed October 2008, http://entrepreneur.com.

50. "Top Ten Successful Franchising Sectors for the Next 20 Years," accessed October 2008, http://www.franchisegod.com.

51. "Franchise Zone," *Entrepreneur,* accessed October 2008, http://www.entrepreneur.com/franchises.

52. Ibid.

53. Adam Stone, "How to Target the Niche Market," *Lodging Hospitality,* November 2007, pp. 58–62.

54. Jenny Wiggin, "Managers Learn Their Trade at Hamburger University," *Financial Times,* January 27, 2008, p. 2.

55. "It's a Pip," *American Printer,* November 2007, p. 27.

56. Raymund Flandez, "Enterprise: New Franchise Idea," *The Wall Street Journal,* September 18, 2007, p. B4.

57. Tom Herman, "Self-Employed or Rich? IRS May Take a Look," *The Wall Street Journal,* February 3, 2008, p. 3.

58. Shelly Banjo, "Before You Tie the Knot . . . ," *The Wall Street Journal,* November 26, 2007, p. R4.

59. "The 2008 *Fortune* 500: Full List," *Fortune,* accessed November 2008, http://www.money.cnn.com.

60. Internal Revenue Service, "IRS Launches Study of S Corporation Reporting Compliance," accessed October 2008, http://www.irs.gov.

61. Mark E. Battersby, "Unlimited Possibilities with Limited Liability," *Air Conditioning, Heating and Refrigeration News,* January 7, 2008, pp. 21–22.

62. Melvin H. Daskal, "Limited Liability Companies (LLCs)," *Agency Sales,* January 2008, pp. 42–45.

63. "Shareholders Meeting: The Things that Mattered," *Retailing Today,* June 18, 2007, p. 66.

64. National Center for Employee Ownership, "Research and Statistics: A Statistical Profile of Employee Ownership," accessed March 2009, http://www.nceo.org.

65. National Center for Employee Ownership, "Largest Study Yet Shows ESOPs Improve Performance and Employee Benefits," accessed October 2008, http://www.nceo.org.

66. San Francisco Ballet Web site, accessed March 2009, http://www.sfballet.org.

67. Jon Fortt, "Got Cash?" *Fortune,* February 4, 2008, pp. 21–26.

68. Jia Lynn Yang, "Making Mergers Work," *Fortune,* November 26, 2007, p. 42.

69. Henry Maurer and Cristina Linblad, "M&A: Still Going Strong," *BusinessWeek,* January 14, 2008, p.8.

70. Katie Benner, "M&A 2008: War Chest Watch," *Fortune,* January 21, 2008, p. 24.

71. Yang, "Making Mergers Work."

72. "Tata Motors to Buy Jaguar, Land Rover, *FinancialWire,* March 26, 2008, http://www.investrend.com.

73. Jane Croft, "Lenders Plan Joint Ventures to Survive," *Financial Times,* February 11, 2008, p. 22.

74. David Fish, "Survey: Government-Owned Telecom Up 54 Percent," *IT&T News,* accessed February 2008, http://www.heartland.org.

75. "Veteran Who Inspired Little Caesars Veterans Program Opens Second Location," *PRNewswire,* accessed March 3, 2009, http://www.prnewswire.com; "Robbie Doughty and Lloyd Allard, Paducah, Kentucky," accessed October 2008, http://franchise.littlecaesars.com; Gregg Cebrzynski, "Emerging CiCi, Revitalized Little Caesars Intensify Competition in Pizza Segment with Expansion Pushes," *Nation's Restaurant News,* June 25, 2007, pp. 102–105; Dina Berta, "Chains Aim to Attract Military Vets as Franchisees," *Nation's Restaurant News,* May 21, 2007, pp. 12–14; "Little Caesars Pizza Reaches Milestone with Innovative Veterans Program," April 30, 2007, news release, http://www.littlecaesars.com; "Franchises Creating Opportunities for Veterans," *Franchising World,* January 2007, p. 104.

76. "About Us," accessed March 2009, http://www.furniturefirst.com; Karen E. Klein, "Small Retailers Band Together," *BusinessWeek SmallBiz,* October 24, 2007, http://www.businessweek.com/smallbiz; Clint Engel, "Furniture First Adds Stores, Elects New Officers, Board," *Furniture Today,* April 23, 2007, http://www.furnituretoday.com.

77. UL Web site, accessed September 8, 2006, http://www.ul.com; "Underwriters Laboratories Inc.," *Hoovers,* accessed March 2009, http://www.hoovers.com; "Underwriters Laboratories," eNotes.com, accessed October 2008, http://business.enotes.com; Mark Thornton, "The Market for Safety," accessed October 2008, http://www.westga.edu.

Chapter 6

1. Company Web site, http://www.revfoods.com, accessed February 25, 2009; "Meet Kristin Groos Richmond and Kirsten Tobey," *Net Impact*, http://www.netimpact.org, accessed February 18, 2009; Nicole Perlroth, "Revolution Foods, Inc.," *BusinessWeek*, http://investing.businessweek.com, accessed February 18, 2009; "Health Nuts," *Forbes*, February 2, 2009, p. 42; Sara Stroud, "Leading the Healthy Lunches Revolution," *San Jose Mercury News*, November 26, 2008, http://www.mercurynews.com; "Starting a Revolution," *Reuters*, March 11, 2008, http://www.reuters.com.

2. "Inc. 500: The CEOs," *Inc.* 500 Special Issue, September 1, 2007.

3. Maggie Gilmour, "Threadless: From Clicks to Bricks," *BusinessWeek*, November 26, 2007, p. 84.

4. "The iSommelier Will Take Your Order," *BusinessWeek*, February 25, 2008, p. 72; Potion Design Web site, accessed March 2009, http://www.potiondesign.com.

5. Jennifer L. Schenker, "The Rise of the Affinity Cell Phone," *BusinessWeek*, October 15, 2007, p. 84.

6. "Background on Social Entrepreneurship," The Skoll Foundation, accessed March 2009, http://www.skollfoundation.org.

7. Jessi Hempel, "The Business of Giving," *Fortune*, January 21, 2008, pp. 58–68.

8. Erland Bullvaag, Zoltan Acs, I. Elaine Allen, William D. Bygrave, and Stephen Spinelli Jr., "Global Entrepreneurship Monitor: National Entrepreneurship Assessment United States of America," Global Entrepreneurship Monitor Consortium, accessed October 2008, http://www.gemconsortium.org.

9. "America's Young Entrepreneurs: Trend Data at-a-Glance," National Association for the Self-Employed, accessed March 2009, http://www.nase.org.

10. Robert W. Fairlie, "Kauffman Index of Entrepreneurial Activity," Ewing Marion Kauffman Foundation, accessed March 2009, http://www.kauffman.org.

11. Leigh Buchanan, "How I Did It: George Naddaff," *Inc.*, February 2008, pp. 98–101.

12. Liz Lange Maternity Web site, accessed March 2009, http://www.lizlange.com; Yelena Moroz, "Maternity Fashion a New Labor of Love," *Retailing Today*, December 10, 2007, p. 11; Pallavi Gogoi, "Liz Lange's Labor of Love," *BusinessWeek Online*, accessed March 2009, http://www.businessweek.com.

13. Ramana Nanda, "Cost of External Finance and Selection into Entrepreneurship," *HBS Working Knowledge*, January 30, 2008, accessed April 2008, http://hbswk.hbs.edu.

14. Liz Welch, "Things They Can't Live Without," *Inc.*, December 2007, pp. 197–112.

15. Office of Advocacy, U.S. Small Business Administration, "Frequently Asked Questions: Advocacy Small Business Statistics and Research," accessed March 2009, http://sba.gov/.

16. Mel Zuckerman and Daniel McGinn, "How I Did It," *Inc.*, December 2007, pp. 140–142.

17. Office of Advocacy, U.S. Small Business Administration, "The Facts about Small Business," accessed March 2009, http://www.sba.gov/advo.

18. Mike Hofman, "Breaking Through," *Inc.*, February 2008, pp. 90–93; Keith R. McFarland, *The Breakthrough Company: How Everyday Companies Become Extraordinary Performers*, New York: Crown Publishing Group, 2008.

19. Leigh Buchanan, "I'll Be Back for Entrepreneurs, Retirement Doesn't Mean Forever," *Inc.*, February 2008, pp. 35–36.

20. "Cause and Effect," *Entrepreneur*, accessed March 2009, http://www.entrepreneur.com.

21. Niels Bosma, Kent Jones, Erkko Autio, and Jonathan Levie, "Global Entrepreneurial Monitor: 2007 Executive Report," accessed March 2009, http://www.gemconsortium.org.

22. Ibid.

23. "Top 50 Entrepreneurial Colleges for 2007," *Entrepreneur*, accessed October 2008, http://www.entrepreneur.com.

24. "Hinman CEOs Overview," Hinman Campus Entrepreneurship Opportunities Program, accessed February 2008, http://www.hinmanceos.umd.edu.

25. "Students in Free Enterprise," SIFE, accessed October 2008, http://www.sife.org.

26. Mark Henricks, "Honor Roll," *Entrepreneur*, accessed March 2009, http://www.entrepreneur.com.

27. Luke Pittaway and Jason Cope, "Entrepreneurship Education," *International Small Business Journal*, October 2007, p. 479.

28. George Gendron, "Forget the Elaborate Business Plan. Kids with Passion Are Our Next Generation of Entrepreneurs," *Inc.*, October 2007, pp. 87–88.

29. Steven Levy, "The Peach Fuzz Billionaires," *Newsweek*, December 24, 2007, p. 24.

30. Michael Myser, "Software That Writes Itself," *Business 2.0*, September 2007, p. 21.

31. Tennille M. Robinson, "Getting on the Franchise: FAST TRACK," *Black Enterprise*, September 2007, pp. 79–82.

32. Steven M. Sears, "A Wikipedia for Traders," *Barron's*, February 18, 2008, p. M11.

33. Thomas Pack, "Offline Readers Meet in Online Community," *Information Today*, February 2008, pp. 38–39.

34. Helen Coster, "Fanbook," *Forbes*, January 28, 2008, p. 62.

35. Sara Wilson, "Sea Potential," *Entrepreneur*, January 2008, accessed March 2009, http://www.entrepreneur.com.

36. Lawrence M. Fisher, "The Gray Entrepreneur," *Business 2.0*, January 2008, p. 34.

37. Ibid.

38. Amy S. Choi, "Course of Action," *BusinessWeek SmallBiz*, August/September 2007, p. 82.

39. Pat Regnier, "Getting Rich in America," *Money*, July 2007, p. 74.

40. Welch, "Things They Can't Live Without."

41. "Oprah Winfrey—About.com Readers' Most Admired Entrepreneur," accessed March 2009, http://entrepreneurs.about.com.

42. Jeffrey M. O'Brien," The PayPal Mafia," *Fortune*, November 26, 2007, pp. 96–106.

43. Amy Feldman, "Recessionade," *Inc.*, February 2008, pp. 19–20.

44. Jon Fine, "The Last Tycoon of Print," *BusinessWeek*, November 12, 2007, p. 120.

45. Bobbi Brown and Athena Schindelheim, "How I Did It," *Inc.*, November 2007, pp. 110–112.

46. "Inc. 500," *Inc.*, September 2007, pp. 72–75.

47. Nick Leiber, "Whippersnappers," *BusinessWeek SmallBiz*, October/November 2007, p. 23.

48. George Gendron, "The Origin of the Entrepreneurial Species," *Inc.*, February 2000, pp. 104–113.

49. Dee Gill, "When Good Deals Go Bad: How to Renegotiate a Contract," *Inc.*, November 2007, pp. 33–34.

50. Starlight Tattoo Web site, accessed March 2009, http://www.starlighttattoo.com; Max Chafkin, "King Ink," *Inc.*, November 2007, pp. 98–108.

51. "Firefly Phone," Firefly Web site, accessed March 2009, http://www.fireflymobile.com.

52. Susan Berfield, "A Thirst for Change," *BusinessWeek*, December 3, 2007, pp. SC2–SC6.

53. Oliver Ryan, "Game Boy," *Fortune*, October 29, 2007, p. 39.

54. "Inc. 500: The Companies," *Inc.* 500 Special Issue, September 1, 2007.

55. "Businessweek.com," *BusinessWeek*, January 21, 2008, p. 12.

56. Susan Greco, "A Little Goes a Long Way," *Inc.*, accessed March 2009, http://www.inc.com.

57. Steve Swanson, "Time Is Right for Starting a Business," *Business and Economic Review*, July–September, 2007, pp. 20–21.

58. Robert Janis, "Small-Business Credit Card Use on the Rise," *Black Enterprise*, April. 2007, p. 48.

59. Arden Dale, "Enterprise: Small Firms Use Credit Cards for Capital," *The Wall Street Journal*, July 24, 2007, p. B4.

60. Karl Williams, personal communication with the author, April 10, 2008; "Security Café," WABC News, New York, March 28, 2008, accessed April 2008, http://abclocal.go.com.

61. Steve Brooks, "Don't Get Trapped," *Restaurant Business*, March 2007, pp. 11–12.

62. Lee Conrad, "What Do Women (Owners) Really Want—and Need," *U. S. Banker*, January 2007, p. 38.

63. "Inc. 500: The Companies," *Inc.* 500 Special Issue, September 1, 2007.

64. Steve Hamm, "The Electric Car Acid Test," *BusinessWeek*, February 4, 2008, pp. 42–46.

65. Jeffrey M. O'Brien, "1% Inspiration, 99% Obliteration," *Fortune*, December 10, 2007, pp. 49–58.

66. "Benefits of Incubators," New York Foundation for Science, Technology and Innovation, accessed March 2009, http://www.nystar.state.ny.us/incubators/benefits.htm.

67. Clean Energy Incubator, accessed March 2009, http://www.cleanenergyincubator.com.

68. Florida Enterprise Zones, accessed March 2009, http://www.floridaenterprisezones.com.

69. Immigration Act of 1990 (IMMACT 90), accessed March 2009, http://www.labor.state.ny.us.

70. "A Culture of Innovation," 3M Web site, accessed March 2009, http://www.3M.com.

71. "Post-It: The Whole Story," 3M Web site, accessed March 2009, http://www.3M.com.

72. Kevin J. Delaney, "Start-ups Make Inroads with Google's Work Force," *The Wall Street Journal*, June 28, 2007, p. B1.

73. Matthew Kenney and Bahaudin G. Mujtaba, "Understanding Corporate Entrepreneurship and Development: A Practitioner View of Organizational Intrapreneurship," *The Journal of Applied Management and Entrepreneurship*, July 2007, pp. 73–88.

74. Carolyn Walkup, "Revived and Thriving," *Nation's Restaurant News*, January 28, 2008, pp. 122–123; Mario Villarreal and Daniel M. Rothschild, "The New Latin Quarter," *The Wall Street Journal*, August 28, 2007, p. A12; John Tozzi, "New Orleans: A Startup Laboratory," *BusinessWeek SmallBiz*, August 27, 2007, http://www.businessweek.com; Molly Reid, "Two Years after Katrina," Reports from the *Birmingham News*, August 26, 2007, http://blog.al.com/bn; "Rebirth of a New Orleans Coffee Tradition," *BusinessWeek SmallBiz*, August 24, 2007, http://www.businessweek.com; Rick Jervis, "New Online Trading Biz Helps Put Big Easy in 'Start-up Mode,'" *USA Today*, August 20, 2007, http://www.usatoday.com.

75. "The Common Good," accessed March 2009, http://www.newmansown.com; Christopher Tkaczyk, "The Business of Giving: The Star," *Fortune*, January 21, 2008, p. 62; Christopher Palmeri, "The Paul Newman of Punk Rock," *BusinessWeek SmallBiz*, September 21, 2007, http://www.businessweek.com.

76. The Geek Squad Web site, http://www.geeksquad.com, accessed October 2008; Kristin Davis, "This Geek for Hire," *Kiplinger Magazine*, December 2002, http://www.kiplinger.com.

Chapter 7

1. "Can All That Twitters Turn to Gold Amid the Gloom?" *Associated Press*, February 15, 2009, http://tech.yahoo.com; Steve Echeverria Jr., "Welcome to the Twitter Nation," *Herald Tribune*, February 5, 2009, http://www.heraldtribune.com; Renee Hopkins Callahan, "Twitter Time," *Forbes*, February 5, 2009, http://www.forbes.com; C.G. Lynch, "Twitter: The How to Get Started Guide for Businesspeople," *Computerworld*, February 3, 2009, http://www.computerworld.com; "Twitter's Tweaking Marketing," *Austin Business Journal*, January 23, 2009, http://austin.bizjournals.com; Mike Harvey, "Twitter to Hit the Big Time with Explosions in Microblogging," *TimesOnline*, January 22, 2009, http://technology.timesonline.co.uk; C.G. Lynch, "Twitter's Potential for Business Users," *CIO*, July 1, 2008, http://www.cio.com.

2. U.S. Census Bureau. "Quarterly Retail E-Commerce Sales," February 17, 2009, http://www.census.gov.

3. Sydney Jones, "Generations Online in 2009," *Pew Internet & American Life Project*, January 28, 2009, http://www.pewinternet.org.

4. U.S. Census Bureau, "E-Stats," http://www.census.gov, accessed March 2009.

5. Statistics Canada, "Electronic Commerce and Technology," http://www.statcan.ca, accessed March 2009.

6. Tom Pullar-Strecker, "E-voting Back in the Frame for 2011," *The Dominion Post* (Wellington, New Zealand), http://www.lexisnexis.com, accessed February 25, 2008.

7. Internet World Stats, "Top 20 Countries with the Highest Number of Internet Users," http://www.internetworldstats.com, accessed February 6, 2009.

8. Internet World Stats, "Half of Households in the United States Now with Broadband Internet," http://www.internetworldstats.com, accessed March 2009.

9. IBM Annual Report, http://www.ibm.com, accessed March 2009.

10. Erin Hutchins, "Maine.gov Wins Seventh National Best of the Web Award," *Business Wire*, http://www.proquest.com, accessed March 3, 2008.

11. U.S. Census Bureau, "Quarterly Retail E-Commerce Sales."

12. Fast Facts, eBay Media Center, http://news.ebay.com, accessed October 2008.

13. "AT&T Wi-Fi Coupon Online Campaign," Level 10 Design, http://www.leveltendesign.com, accessed October 2008.

14. Enid Burns, "One Quarter of Consumer Electronic Purchases Researched Online," *ClickZ News*, http://www.clickz.com, accessed March 2009.

15. "Consumers Flock to the Web to Find Savings and Deals on Holiday and Everyday Items in Soft Economy," ShopLocal Press Release, January 10, 2008, http://www.crossmediaservices.com, accessed October 2008.

16. U.S. Census Bureau, "E-Stats," accessed March 5, 2009.

17. Ibid.

18. "New Extranet to Empower Global Charity to Meet Exponential Growth Goals," Microsoft Office Customer Solution Case Study, Microsoft Corporation, http://www.microsoft.com, accessed October 2008.

19. "How Cisco IT Uses Extranets to Connect Global Partners to Cisco," Cisco IT Case Study Summary, Cisco Systems, http://www.cisco.com, accessed October 2008.

20. David Hannon, "Exchanges Are Dead, but Collaboration Is Not," *Purchasing*, http://www.purchasing.com, accessed October 2008; Cara Cannella, "Why Online Exchanges Died," *Inc.*, http://www.inc.com, accessed October 2008.

21. "Ariba Spotlight: British Airlines," Ariba, http://www.ariba.com, accessed October 2008.

22. "NC E-procurement @ Your Service," http://www2.eprocurement.ncgov.com. accessed October 2008.

23. "SAP Customer Success Story," SAP, http://sap.com/usa/, accessed October 2008.

24. U.S. Census Bureau, "Quarterly Retail E-Commerce Sales."

25. Jones, "Generations Online in 2009."

26. "About Southwest Airlines," Southwest Airlines, http://www.southwest.com, accessed October 2008.

27. "An Introduction to Walmart.com," Wal-Mart Stores, http://www.walmart.com, accessed March 2009.

28. "About Lands' End," Lands' End, http://www.landsend.com, accessed October 2008.

29. Enid Burns, "U.S. Broadband Adoption Continues to Rise," *ClickZ Network*, http://www.clickz.com, accessed March 2009.

30. Rob McGann, "Broadband: High Speed, High Spend," *ClickZ Network*, http://www.clickz.com, accessed March 2009.

31. Pew Internet & American Life Project, "Online Shopping," February 13, 2008, http://www.pewinternet.org, accessed March 2009.

32. Bob Tedeschi, "Travel Sales Still Growing, but Numbers of Customers Are Declining," *The New York Times*, http://www.nytimes.com, accessed October 2008.

33. Pew Internet and American Life Project, "Online Shopping."

34. Ibid.

35. Enid Burns, "E-Tailers Beat Offline Stores in Customer Satisfaction," *ClickZ Network*, http://www.clickz.com, accessed March 2009.

36. Tedeschi, "Travel Sales Still Growing."

37. "About Us," VeriSign, http://www.verisign.com, accessed October 2008.

38. "Welcome to the PCI Security Standards Council," PCI Security Standards Council, http://www.pcisecuritystandards.org, accessed October 2008; Pam Baker, "Practicing Safe E-Commerce," *E-Commerce Times*, February 23, 2008, http://www.ecommercetimes.com, accessed March 7, 2008.

39. Pew Internet and American Life Project, "Online Shopping."

40. Baker, "Practicing Safe E-Commerce"; "Bell Recovers Stolen Data on 3.4 Customers," *CBC News*, February 12, 2008, http://www.cbc.ca, accessed October 2008; Stephen Castle, "Today in Business," *The New York Times*, December 1, 2007, http://www.nytimes.com, accessed October 2008; Eric Dash, "Data Breach Could Affect Millions of TJX Shoppers," *The New York Times*, January 19, 2007, http://www.nytimes.com, accessed October 2008.

41. John Markoff, "Researchers Find Way to Steal Encrypted Data," *The New York Times*, February 22, 2008, http://www.nytimes.com, accessed October 2008.

42. "Annual Report," Internet Crime Complaint Center, http://www.ic3.gov, accessed October 2008.

43. "Phishing," Federal Trade Commission, http://onguardonline.gov, accessed March 2009.

44. "PayPal and eBay Partner with Yahoo! to Enhance Anti-Phishing Protection," *M2 Internet Business News*, http://www.m2.com, accessed March 7, 2008.

45. "Vishing Attacks Increase," Internet Crime Complaint Center, January 17, 2008, http://www.ic3.gov, accessed March 2009.

46. Pew Internet and American Life Project, "Online Shopping."

47. "About FeedBurner," FeedBurner.com, http://www.feedburner.com, accessed October 2008.

48. P.J. Fusco, "Five Getting-Started Blog Questions," *ClickZ Network*, January 30, 2008, http://www.clickz.com, accessed March 2009.

49. Matt Villano, "Blogging the Hand that Feeds You," *The New York Times*, http://www.lexisnexis.com, accessed March 9, 2008.

50. Jeff Jarvis, "Love the Customers Who Hate You," *BusinessWeek*, http://www.lexisnexis.com, accessed March 9, 2008.

51. Michael Learmonth, "Pre-Roll Video Ads Scare Viewers Away. Get Used to It," *Silicon Alley Insider*, January 22, 2008, http://www.alleyinsider.com, accessed October 2008.

52. Kevin Newcomb, "Pre-Roll Not the Answer for Online Video," *ClickZ Network*, http://www.clickz.com, accessed March 2009.

53. Internet World Stats, "Usage and Population Statistics," http://www.internetworldstats.com, accessed February 6, 2009.

54. Clay Chandler, "China's Web King," *Fortune*, http://www.fortune.com, accessed March 9, 2008.

55. Internet World Stats, "Internet Usage Statistics: The Big Picture," http://www.internetworldstats.com, accessed February 25, 2008.

56. Frank Smith, "Stanford Forum Unearths Big Benefits in B2B Outsourcing," Manufacturing Business Technology, ProQuest, http://www.proquest.umi.com, accessed March 9, 2008.

57. "Client Success Stories," Coremetrics, http://www.coremetrics.com, accessed October 2008.

58. Daisy Whitney, "Tracking Viewers on All Platforms," *Television Week*, http://www.lexisnexis.com, accessed March 9, 2008.

59. Steve Lohr, "Your Ad Here," *The New York Times*, http://www.lexisnexis.com, accessed March 9, 2008.

60. Company Web site, http://www.ask.com, accessed March 2009; Jennifer LeClaire, "Do Searchers Really Care about Privacy?" *NewsFactor Network*, December 12, 2007, http://www.newsfactor.com; Miguel Helft, "Ask.com Puts a Bet on Privacy," *The New York Times*, December 11, 2007, http://www.nytimes.com; Jessica Guynn, "Ask.com to Let Users Erase Queries," *Los Angeles Times*, December 11, 2007, http://www.latimes.com; Richard Waters, "Search Engines Set Hard Privacy Question by Ask," Financial Times (London), December 11, 2007, http://www.ft.com.

61. Company Web site, http://livegamer.com, accessed March 2009; Nick Wingfield, "Start-Up to Create Market for Trade of Virtual Goods," *The Wall Street Journal*, December 17, 2007, http://online.wsj.com; "Business: World of Dealcraft," *The Economist*, December 8, 2007, http://www.economist.com; Julian Dibbell, "The Life of the Chinese Gold Farmer," *The New York Times Magazine*, June 17, 2007, pp. 38–41; Dave Gilson, "Even Better than the Real Thing," *Mother Jones*, May/June 2007, http://www.motherjones.com.

62. Jim Jacoby and Carolyn Chandler, personal interview, July 20, 2006; Manifest Digital Web site, accessed October 2008, http://www.manifestdigital.com; NEC IT Guy Games Web site, accessed October 2008, http://www .necitguy.com/home.html; Wilson Baseball Web site, accessed October 2008, http://www.wilson.com/wilson/baseball/ index.jsp; "NEC's AdverGame Campaign Delivers Big Rewards," *Eyeblaster Newsletter*, accessed September 8, 2006, http://www.eyeblaster.com.

Part 2: Launching Your Entrepreneurial Career

1. Michael Ames, cited in "Is Entrepreneurship for You?" Small Business Administration, accessed October 2008, http://www.sba.gov.

2. U.S. Department of Labor, "Tomorrow's Jobs," *Occupational Outlook Handbook*, 2008–2009 edition, Bureau of Labor Statistics, accessed October 2008, http://www.bls.gov.

3. Alex Salkever, "The Furniture Company Wanted to Sell Him Its Buildings—and Close Down. Should He Buy the Company, Too?" *Inc.*, November 2007, pp. 60–65.

4. U.S. Department of Labor, "Career Guide to Industries: Management, Scientific, and Technical Consulting Services," Bureau of Labor Statistics, accessed October 2008, http://www.bls.gov.

5. U.S. Small Business Administration, "Protecting Your Ideas," accessed October 2008, http://www.sba.gov.

Chapter 8

1. Company Web site, http://www.campbellsoup.com, accessed March 2, 2009; Julie Gallagher, "Douglas Conant," *Supermarket News*, http://www.supermarketnews.com, accessed February 23, 2009; "Douglas R. Conant," *Forbes*, http://people.forbes.com, accessed February 23, 2009; Bruce Horovitz, "CEO Profile: Campbell Exec Nears Extraordinary Goal," *USA Today*, January 25, 2009, http://www.usatoday.com; Emily Bryson York, "Economy May Be Rotten, but It's Ripe for Package Food," *Advertising Age*, September 22, 2008, http://adage.com; Julie Jargon, "Campbell's Chief Looks for Splash of Innovation," *The Wall Street Journal*, May 30, 2008, http://online.wsj.com.

2. Southwest Airlines Officer Biographies, accessed March 2009, http://www.southwest.com/swamedia.

3. Peter Gumbel, "Galvanizing Gucci," *Fortune*, January 21, 2008, pp. 81–88.

4. Linda Casey, "Bagging Cookies Is a Sweet Reward," *Packaging Digest*, February 2008, pp. 32–35.

5. Jena McGregor, "The 2008 Winners," *BusinessWeek*, March 3, 2008, pp. 47–50.

6. Erin White, "Theory and Practice: Firms Step Up Training for Front-Line Managers," *The Wall Street Journal*, August 27, 2007, p. B3.

7. David Desracher, "Train to Retain," *Incentive*, September 2007, pp. 58–62.

8. Andy Serwer, "Starbucks Fix," *Fortune*, February 4, 2008, p. 14.

9. Daryl Koehn, "Code of Ethics: When in Rome, Behave as the Romans," *European Business Forum*, Winter 2007, pp. 15–26.

10. Ann Zimmerman and Mary Ellen Lloyd, "Home Depot Tries to Mollify Holders," *The Wall Street Journal*, May 25, 2007, p. B3.

11. Christopher Lawton, "Dell Treads Carefully into Selling PCs in Stores," *The Wall Street Journal*, January 3, 2008, p. B1.

12. Mike Troy, "The New Direction," *Retailing Today*, June/July 2007, p. 9.

13. Ann Zimmerman, "Wal-Mart Revamps Apparel Operations," *The Wall Street Journal*, January 31, 2008, p. 8.

14. Curtis Siegel, "Contingency Planning for All Sizes," *Futures*, February 2008, pp. 60–62.

15. David Hamilton, "Survive the Worst: Is Your Business Ready?" *Accountancy Ireland*, December 2007, p. 42.

16. Catherine Holahan, "Ebay's New Tough Love CEO," *Business Week*, February 4, 2008, p. 58.

17. George Anders, "Sears Unorthodox Tactics Encounter Stiff Winds," *The Wall Street Journal*, January 23, 2008, p. A1.

18. "Corporate Information: Company Overview," accessed March 2009, http://www.google.com.

19. "Bayer: Science for a Better Life," Bayer Web site, accessed March 2009, http://www.bayer.com.

20. "What Are Toyota's Mission and Vision Statements?" Toyota, accessed March 2009, http://www.toyota.com.

21. Starbucks Corporation Annual Report, accessed March 2009, http://www.starbucks.com; "Coffee House Tradition," Starbucks Corporation Fiscal 2007 Year in Review, accessed March 2009, http://www.starbucks.com.

22. Amy Chozick, "Toyota Shrugs Off Slow Sales in U.S. to Post Record Profit," *The Wall Street Journal,* August 4, 2007, p. A3.

23. "Toyota Plans Hybrid Versions of Every Model within Car Range," *Marketing Week,* January 10, 2008, p. 5.

24. James Dyson, "Ask James Dyson," *Inc.,* February 2008, p. 53.

25. "About Motion Theory," accessed October 2008, http://www.motiontheory.com.

26. Diane Mehta, "Loco Motion," *Fast Company,* February 2008, pp. 80–85.

27. Bill Orr, "Is Google Getting Too Good?" *ABA Banking Journal,* October 2007, pp. 69–70.

28. Stephen H. Wildstrom, "The MacBook Air: So Close and Yet . . ." *BusinessWeek,* February 11, 2008, p. 79–80; Tiernan Ray, "Our Gadget of the Week: Thin as Air," *Barron's,* February 25, 2008, p. 34.

29. Mary Ellen Lloyd, "Best Buy Strategy Pays Off as Circuit City Falters," *The Wall Street Journal,* April 5, 2007, p. C6.

30. "100 Best Corporate Citizens 2007," *CRO Magazine,* accessed October 2008, http://www.thecro.com.

31. Barney Gimbel, "A Look Inside the Top 20: Southwest Airlines," *Fortune,* March 17, 2008, p. 113.

32. "The Wisdom of the Tao: Dr. Wayne Dyer's Secret to Finding Joy," *Bottom Line Personal,* February 15, 2008, pp. 9–11.

33. Melissa Waite, "Managing Under Crisis: The Source of Atonement at JetBlue Airways," *The Business Review, Cambridge,* December 2007, pp. 187–191.

34. "Hamburger University," McDonald's Web site, accessed March 2009, http://www.mcdonalds.com.

35. "The Walt Disney Company—Culture," Disney's Web site, accessed March 2009, http://www.disney.go.com.

36. Jim Collins, "The Secret of Enduring Greatness," *Fortune,* May 5, 2008, p. 74; Jena McGregor, "The World's 25 Most Innovative Companies," *BusinessWeek,* April 28, 2008, pp. 62–63; "GE Culture," http://www.ge.com, accessed April 24, 2008.

37. Adam Lashinsky, "Back2Back Champs," *Fortune,* February 4, 2008, p. 70.

38. "Hierarchical Structure of the Catholic Church," *Jerome's Pages on the Catholic Church and Faith,* accessed October 2008, http://jerome2007.tripod.com.

39. "Products and Services," 3M Web site, accessed March 2009, http://www.3M.com.

40. Jerry Wellman, "Leadership Behaviors in Matrix Environments," *Project Management Journal,* June 2007, pp. 62–74.

41. Heather Won Tesoriero, "Merck's Vioxx Settlement Moves Ahead," *The Wall Street Journal,* March 4, 2008, p. B2; John Simons, "From Scandal to Stardom: How Merck Healed Itself," *Fortune,* February 18, 2008, pp. 94–98; "Shock to the System: Pharmaceuticals." *The Economist,* February 2, 2008, p. 71.

42. Ellen Smith, "Ticketmaster and Cablevision May Acquire 49% of AEG Live," *The Wall Street Journal,* February 29, 2008, p. C3; Paul Sloan, "Keep on Rocking in the Free World," *Fortune,* December 10, 2007, pp. 156–160; Devin Leonard, "Question Authority," *Fortune,* May 14, 2007, p. 26.

43. Jennifer Ordonez, "California Hustlin'," *Newsweek,* accessed October 2008, www.google.com; American Apparel Web site, accessed October 2008, http://www.americanapparel.net; "Living on the Edge at American Apparel," *BusinessWeek,* accessed October 2008, www.google.com; Stephen Franklin, "More Pay Americans' Way," *Chicago Tribune,* May 30, 2006, sec. 3, pp. 1, 3.

Chapter 9

1. Company Web site, http://www.netapp.com, accessed February 25, 2009; "100 Best Companies to Work for, 2009," *Fortune,* http://money.cnn.com, accessed February 24, 2009; "NetApp: Culture-Values-Leadership—#1 on the 2009 List of the 100 Best Companies to Work for," Great Places to Work Institute, http://www.greatplacetowork.com, accessed February 24, 2009; Jim Finkle, "NetApp Revenue Misses Forecasts, Shares Fall," *Forbes,* http://www.forbes.com, February 11, 2009; Robert Levering and Milton Moskowitz, "And the Winners Are . . . ," *Fortune,* February 2, 2009, p. 67.

2. Trilogy Web site, accessed March 2009, http://www.trilogy.com.

3. Shannon Klie, "Getting Employees to Come to You," *Canadian HR Reporter,* November 19, 2007, pp. 9–10.

4. Tom Granahan, "Employers Around the World Labor to Find Qualified Job Candidates," *Manufacturing.net,* accessed March 2008, http://www.manufacturing.net.

5. "Many HR Pros Find Shortage of Skilled Workers," *BLR Human Resource Management,* accessed March 2008, http://hr.blr.com.

6. "Oldest Baby Boomers Turn 60!" U.S. Census Press Releases, accessed March 2008, http://www.census.gov.

7. Sarah E. Needleman, "More Corporate Career Sites Satisfy Job Hunters' Demands," *The Wall Street Journal,* online edition, February 14, 2008.

8. Sarah E. Needleman, "Listen Up Job Hunters," *The Wall Street Journal,* online edition, February 11, 2008.

9. "AK Steel Settles EEOC Lawsuit over Racial Harassment at Pennsylvania Plant," *Financial Wire,* February 1, 2007, p. 1.

10. "On Requiring English," *The Wall Street Journal,* December 5, 2007, p. A23.

11. Ayana Dixon, "With a Smile," *Black Enterprise,* January 2008, p. 43.

12. Dan Pompei, "NFL Teams Weigh Wonderlic Tests," *Chicago Tribune,* March 23, 2008, http://www.chicagotribune.com.

13. Samantha Murphy, "Culture Conscious," *Chain Store Age,* September 2007, p. 55.

14. Anne Fisher, "Playing for Keeps," *Fortune,* January 22, 2007, p. 85.

15. "Managers Attend Boot Camp," *Air Conditioning, Heating, and Refrigeration News,* January 7, 2008, p. 6.

16. "Investment in Training and Development," Accenture, accessed March 2009, http://careers3.accenture.com.

17. Bill Roberts, "Hard Facts about Soft-Skills E-Learning," *HR Magazine,* January 2008, pp. 76–78.

18. Carol Hymowitz, "They Ponder Layoffs, But Executives Still Have Gaps in Talent," *The Wall Street Journal,* January 2008, p. B1.

19. Thomas S. Clausen, Keith T. Jones, and Jay S. Rich, "Appraising Employee Performance Evaluation Systems," *The CPA Journal,* February 2008, pp. 64–67.

20. 360 Degree Software; Halogen Software Web site, accessed March 2009, http://www.halogensoftware.com.

21. Joanne Summer, "Calibrating Consistency," *HR Magazine,* January 2008, pp. 73–75.

22. Jeffrey M. O'Brien, "A Perfect Season," *Fortune,* February 4, 2008, pp. 62–66.

23. "Employer Costs for Employee Compensation Summary," Bureau of Labor Statistics, accessed March 2009, http://www.bls.gov.

24. "Best Gyms," *Fortune,* February 4, 2008, p. 92.

25. Ben Bradley, "Chicago's Top Cop Wants Fit Officers," March 7, 2008, http://abclocal.go.com.

26. "Paid Family Leave Insurance," Employee Development Department, accessed March 2009, http://www.edd.ca.gov.

27. O'Brien, "A Perfect Season."

28. "Employer Profile: Draft New Priorities," *Employee Benefits,* March 7, 2008, p. 37.

29. "Companies Instituting Paid Time Off versus Traditional Time Off Model Claim Reduced Absenteeism," *RTO online,* accessed October 2008, http://www.rtoonline.com.

30. Paid Time Off (PTO), Banner Health Web site, accessed March 2009, http://www.bannerhealth.com.

31. Sue Shellenbarger, "What's Ahead for Volunteering, Flextime, and Working Moms," *The Wall Street Journal,* December 20, 2007, p. D1.

32. Alex Palmer, "Right on Schedule," *Incentive,* February 2008, pp. 38–40.

33. "Case Study: Macy's," *Commuter Challenge,* accessed October 2008, http://www.commuterchallenge.org.

34. Wayne J. Guglielmo, "Job Sharing: Flexibility Has a Price," *Medical Economics,* January 18, 2008, pp. 40–43.

35. "Number of Telecommuters Is Rising," *The Boston Globe,* January 15, 2008, accessed March 2008, http://www.boston.com.

36. "Case Study: Hewlett-Packard," *Commuter Challenge,* accessed October 2008, http://www.commuterchallenge.org.

37. Craig Sebastiano, "Gen Y Wants Benefits," *Benefits Canada,* December 2007, p. 7.

38. "Employer Profile: Going the Extra Mile for Staff," *Employee Benefits,* August 10, 2007, p. 34.

39. Pui-Wing Tam, "In Silicon Valley, a Flight to Safety," *The Wall Street Journal,* March 7, 2008, p. A1.

40. "HR Works to Transfer Workforce Knowledge and Skills," *HR Focus,* January 2008, pp. 51–54.

41. Erin White, "How to Keep Your Job, or Decide to Leave, if New CEO Arrives," *The Wall Street Journal,* April 24, 2007, p. B5.

42. Piers Hollier, "HR Has Crucial Role in Erasing the Pain During Challenging Times," *Personnel Today,* January 29, 2008, p. 16.

43. "What Does a Recession Mean for Human Capital Planning?" *HR Focus,* March 2008, pp. 1–4.

44. Andy Pasztor and Melanie Trottman, "Southwest Rethinks Plane Retirement, Shelves Outsource Plan," *The Wall Street Journal,* March 17, 2008. p. A2.

45. Mia Katz, "Saying "Yes" to Success: Creating the Engaged Employee," *Women in Business,* November/December 2007, pp. 26–29.

46. Robert Levering and Milton Moskowitz, "The Rankings," *Fortune,* February 4, 2008, pp. 75–94.

47. Cliff Hocker and Wendy Isom, "Working for Pennies," *Black Enterprise,* March 2008, p. 30.

48. Pampered Chef Web site, accessed March 2009, http://www.pamperedchef.com.

49. Holly Dolezalek, "Winning Ways," *Training,* February 2008, pp. 48–56.

50. "Union Members in 2007," Bureau of Labor Statistics, accessed October 2008, http://www.bls.gov.

51. Christopher Palmeri, "A Cautionary Tale for Airline Managers," *BusinessWeek,* March 17, 2008, p. 66.

52. "Major Work Stoppages in 2007," Bureau of Labor Statistics, accessed October 2008, http://www.bls.gov.

53. "Business: Down the Pens; The Hollywood Strike," *The Economist,* November 10, 2007, p. 94.

54. "Major Work Stoppages in 2007."

55. Robert J. Hughes, "Broadway Strike Ways on New York City," *The Wall Street Journal,* November 13, 2007, p. A4.

56. Elissa Elan, "NYC Restaurants Acting Quickly to Limit Losses from Broadway Strike," *Nation's Restaurant News,* December 3, 2007, pp. 4, 47.

57. Ibid.

58. Teamsters Local 830 Web site, accessed March 2008, http://phillyunions.com.

59. Bill Mongelluzzo, "Negotiations Begin on West Coast Longshore Contract," *The Journal of Commerce Online,* accessed March 2008, http://proquest.umi.com.

60. "UAW Reaches Tentative Deal with GM," MSNBC, September 26, 2007, accessed October 2008, http://www.msnbc.com.

61. "Trends in Union Membership," AFL-CIO, accessed October 2008, http://www.aflcio.org.

62. "Google Jobs," Google Web site, accessed March 2009, http://www.google.com; Adam Lashinsky, "Back2Back Champs," *Fortune,* February 4, 2008, p. 70; John Sullivan, "The Last Word," *Workforce Management,* November 19, 2007, p. 42.

63. John D. Stoll and Nicolas Brulliard, "GM Chief Wagoner Gets 33% Raise," *The Wall Street Journal,* March 7, 2008, p. B6; John D. Stoll, "GM Is Still Facing Tricky Curves," *The Wall Street Journal,* February 5, 2008, p. C3; Alex Taylor III, "Gentlemen, Start Your Turnaround," *Fortune,* January 21, 2008, pp. 70–78; "UAW Reaches Tentative Deal With GM," MSNBC, September 26, 2007, http://www.msnbc.com, accessed October 2008.

64. Replacements, Ltd. Web site, accessed October 2008, http://www.replacements.com; "Replacements, Ltd. Continues Climb in Rankings Among Top 500 U.S. Internet Retailers," *Marketing Weekly News,* June 2, 2008, p. 11; Lisa Van Der Pool, "Animal Planet," *Adweek,* June 7, 2004, p. 29.

Chapter 10

1. Company Web site, http://www.ideo.com, accessed February 27, 2009; "IDEO Innovating Product Design Team," *Smithsonian National Museum of American History*, http://invention.smithsonian.org, accessed February 27, 2009; "Finding Innovation beyond Imagination," *CME Group Magazine,* Winter

2008, http://www.cmegroup.com; Bruce Nussbaum, "IDEO's Tim Brown on Innovation in the Harvard Business Review," *BusinessWeek,* June 25, 2008, http://www.businessweek.com.

2. "About A & A," Anderson & Associates, accessed March 2009, http://www.andassoc.com.

3. "Wabtec History," Wabtec Web site, accessed March 2009, http://www.wabtec.com.

4. Christopher Palmeri, "Hot Growth: The Shock of the Old," *BusinessWeek,* June 4, 2007, p. 54.

5. "A Statistical Profile of Employer Ownership," National Center for Employee Ownership, accessed March 2009, https//www.nceo.org.

6. Ibid.

7. Fran Hawthorne, "Retirement—Lessons Learned," *Institutional Investor,* January 2008, p. 1.

8. "How to Choose an Employee Stock Plan for Your Company," National Center for Employee Ownership, accessed March 2009, http://www.nceo.org.

9. Ibid.

10. Dan Kadlec, "Consider Your Options," *Time,* March 24, 2008, p. 67.

11. "Our Core Values," Whole Foods Market, accessed March 2009, http//www.wholefoodsmarket.com.

12. Mary Brandel, "Xtreme ROI," *Computerworld,* February 11, 2008, pp. 30–33.

13. Nancy Weil, "Global Team Management: Continental Divides," *CIO,* February 1, 2008, p. 8.

14. Lynda Gratton, Andreas Voigt, and Tamara Erickson, "Bridging Faultlines in Diverse Teams," *MIT Sloan Management Review,* Summer 2007, pp. 22–29.

15. Kay Clevenger, "Improve Staff Satisfaction with Team Building Retreats," *Nursing Management,* April 2007, p. 22.

16. Stephen B. Knouse, "Building Task Cohesion to Bring Teams Together," *Quality Progress,* March 2007, pp. 49–53.

17. "Team Norms," Rutherford County PLC Website Resource 2007/2008, accessed October 2008, http://www.rcs.k12.tn.us.

18. Patricia M. Buhler, "Managing in the New Millennium," *SuperVision,* March 2007, pp. 19–21.

19. David Brandt, "Direct from the Source," *Industrial Engineer,* February 2008, pp. 26–33.

20. Neal Augenstein, "Poor Communication Contributed to Bomb Squad Delay," WTOP Radio, accessed October 2008, http://www.wtopnews.com.

21. Charlie Nordblom, "Taking Measurement a Step Further at Volvo Group," *Strategic Communication Management,* February/March 2008, pp. 20–23.

22. Patrick Barwise and Seán Meehan, "So You Think You're a Good Listener," *Harvard Business Review,* April 2008, p. 22.

23. Arianne Cohen, "Scuttling Scut Work," *Fast Company,* February 2008, pp. 42–44.

24. Don Clark and Peg Brickley, "Intel's Email Recovery Effort Is Set to Cost 'Many Millions,'" *The Wall Street Journal,* April 25, 2007, p. B11.

25. Daisy Saunders, "Create an Open Climate for Communication," *SuperVision,* January 2008, pp. 6–8.

26. Merge Gupta-Sunderji, "Working the Grapevine," *CGA Magazine,* July/August 2007, p. 14.

27. "Lost Productivity," Strategic Net Monitoring, accessed October 2008, http://www.monitoringbox.com.

28. John Boe, "How to Read Your Prospects Like a Book," *The American Salesman,* February 2008, pp. 7–10.

29. Albert Mehrabian, *Silent Messages* (Belmont, CA: Wadsworth, 1971); Albert Mehrabian, "Communication Without Words," *Psychology Today,* September 1968, pp. 53–55.

30. Andrew Ward, "PR Crisis for Yum Brands After Rat Video," *FT.com,* February 27, 2007, p. 1.

31. Toddi Gutner, "90 Days: Dealing with a PR Crisis Takes Planning and Truth," *The Wall Street Journal,* March 24, 2008.

32. Kate MacArthur, "Taco Hell: Rodent Video Signals New Era in PR Crisis," *Advertising Age,* February 26, 2007, pp. 1–2.

33. Melanie Trottman, Andy Pasztor, and Ben Casselman, "In FAA Crackdown, American Expects More Cancellations," *The Wall Street Journal,* April 10, 2008, pp. B1–B2; Justin Baer, "Once-Pristine Southwest Hit with 'Black Eye,'" *Financial Times,* April 7, 2008, p. 25; "Lawmakers Say FAA Testimony 'Misleading,'" MSNBC, accessed October 2008, http://www,msnbc.com; Melanie Trottman and Andy Pasztor, "Southwest Airlines CEO Apologizes for Lapses," *The Wall Street Journal,* March 14, 2008, p. B1; Michael Bush and Alice Z. Cuneo, "Southwest Goes South, Turns to CRM for Salvation," *Advertising Age,* March 10, 2008, pp. 3–4.

34. "Interactive Associates Partners with Leading Responsibility Expert to Help Clients Execute Profitable CSR Strategies," *CSRwire,* accessed March 2009, http://www.csrwire.com; "About Interaction Associates," accessed March 2009, http://www.interactionassociates.com; Laura Lorber, "Giving Employees a Say in Where They'll Work," *The Wall Street Journal,* January 9, 2008, http://online.wsj.com.

35. British Petroleum Web site, accessed March 2009, http://www.bp.com; Stephanie Johnson, "Meet the Elite," Massachusetts Institute of Technology, accessed September 8, 2006, http://web.mit.edu/bp-mit; "Helping BP's Controllers Stay Connected—Yet Independent," PricewaterhouseCoopers, accessed October 2008, http://www.pwcglobal .com; *The BP Magazine,* Issue 1, 2005.

Chapter 11

1. Company Web site, http://world.honda.com, accessed February 27, 2009; Jim Henry, "Flexible Manufacturing Is a Competitive Weapon for Honda," *BNET Auto Insights*, http://industry.bnet.com, accessed February 27, 2009; "Honda Enhances Flexible Manufacturing Network in North America," *Reuters*, October 13, 2008, http://www.reuters.com; Kate Linebaugh, "Honda's Flexible Plants Provide Edge," *The Wall Street Journal*, September 23, 2008, http://online.wsj.com.

2. Joel Kotkin, "Taste: Suburban Development," *The Wall Street Journal,* November 23, 2007, p. W11.

3. Toyota Motor Manufacturing Inc., accessed March 2009, http://www.toyotageorgetown.com.

4. "Volvo Cars: 2007 Company Profile," *Just – Auto,* April 2007, pp. 17–18.

5. Steve Hamm, "Radical Collaboration: Lessons from IBM's Innovation Factory," *BusinessWeek,* September 10, 2007, p. 16.

6. "A Better View: Technology Improvements Make Vision Systems Viable Production Tools," *Manufacturing Business Technology,* March 2008, p. 38.

7. John Paul Newport, "Crazy Drivers: The Clubs About to Shake Up Golf," *The Wall Street Journal,* January 6, 2007, p. P1.

8. Peter Gumbel, "BMW Drives Germany," *Time,* July 16, 2007, accessed October 2008, http://www.time.com.

9. "MAN Execs Assess State of Industry," *Printing Impressions,* January 2007, p. 8.

10. MAN Roland Company, accessed March 2009, http://www.manroland.us.com.

11. Neil Shister, "Near-sourcing," *World Trade,* January 2008, pp. 40–42.

12. Mike Pare, "Chattanooga: VW Shifts Initial Work to March," *Chattanooga Times Free Press,* January 3, 2009, http://www.timesfreepress.com; Christoph Rauwald and Stephen Power, "Volkswagen Considers Second American Plant," *The Wall Street Journal,* July 28, 2007, pA2.

13. "Layout," Reference for Business, accessed March 2009, http://www.referenceforbusiness.com.

14. John E. Enkemann Jr. and Peter G. Lynde, "Tomorrow's Factories Will Evolve in Design, Function," *Plant Engineering,* December 2007, p. 50.

15. Hope Neal, "Outsourcing Production May Be Fashionable, But Not Everyone Is Cashing in on the Trend," *Manufacturing Business Technology,* August 2007, p. 34.

16. J. Lynn Lunsford, "Boeing Delays Delivery Again," *The Wall Street Journal,* April 10, 2008, p. B3.

17. "Spend Management Supplier Solutions," Ariba, accessed October 2008, http://www.ariba.com.

18. Lynn Andriani, "Holiday Sleepers Out of Stock," *Publishers Weekly,* January 7, 2008, p. 4.

19. John Karolefski, "Solving the Out-of-Stock Dilemma," *Frozen Food Age,* December 2007, pp. 31–33.

20. William Atkinson, "Digi-Key Picks Vendor-Managed Over Consignment Inventory," *Purchasing,* November 15, 2007, p. 17.

21. David Brandt, "Saving Lives Just in Time," *Industrial Engineer,* July 2007, pp. 34–37.

22. "Madill Equipment," *CA Magazine,* January/February 2008, pp. 32–33.

23. Matthew Boyle, "Super Bucks," *Fortune,* February 4, 2008, pp. 8–9.

24. Jeff Sabatini, "Turning Japanese," Automotive manufacturing and Production, accessed March 2009, http://autofieldguide.com.

25. Carol Casper, "Sorting It All Out," *Beverage World,* January 15, 2008, pp. 55–56.

26. Elly Valas, "Basics of Benchmarking," Dealerscope, March 2008, p. 22.

27. Praveen Gupta, "Making the Quality Department Work," *Quality,* March 2008, p. 18.

28. Jonathan Schwartz, "Featured Company: Sun Microsystems," *ASQ Six Sigma Forum Magazine,* February 2008, p. 40.

29. S. Bruce Han, Shaw K. Chen, and Maling Ebrahimpour, "The Impact of ISO 9000 on TQM and Business Performance," *Journal of Business and Economic Studies,* Fall 2007, pp. 1–25.

30. Leslie Crawford, "Can Zara Style Out the Downturn?" *Financial Times,* March 31, 2008, p. 32; Cecilie Rohwedder and Keith Johnson, "Pace-Setting Zara Seeks More Speed to Fight Its Rising Cheap-Chic Rivals," *The Wall Street Journal,* February 20, 2008, p. B1; Connie Robbins Gentry, "European Fashion Stores Edge Past US Counterparts," *Chain Store Age,* December 2007, p. 100.

31. Jena McGregor, "Service with a Smile—Or a Shrug," *BusinessWeek,* March 17, 2008, p. 84; Spencer E. Ante, "Sprint's Wake-Up Call," *BusinessWeek,* March 3, 2008, pp. 54–58; Jena McGregor, "Customer Service Champs," *BusinessWeek,* March 3, 2008, p. 37.

32. Washburn Web site, accessed March 2009, http://www.washburn.com; Dan Moran, "U.S. Music Corp.'s Washburn Guitars No Strangers to Fame," *Suburban Chicago News,* accessed September 8 2006, http://www.suburban chicagonews.com; "Washburn Guitars," Answers.com, accessed October 2008, http://www.answers.com; "Disturbed's Dan Donegan Signature Series Washburn Guitar at Winter NAMM," *All About Jazz,* October 2008, http://www.allaboutjazz.com; Washburn's 2006 Winter Catalog.

Part 3 Launching Your Management Career

1. U.S. Department of Labor, "Tomorrow's Jobs," *Occupational Outlook Handbook, 2008–2009 edition,* Bureau of Labor Statistics, accessed October 2008, http://www.bls.gov.

2. U.S. Department of Labor, "Administrative Services Managers," *Occupational Outlook Handbook, 2008–2009 edition,* Bureau of Labor Statistics, accessed October 2008, http://www.bls.gov.

3. U.S. Department of Labor, "Construction Managers," *Occupational Outlook Handbook, 2008–2009 edition,* Bureau of Labor Statistics, accessed October 2008, http://www.bls.gov.

4. U.S. Department of Labor, "Food Service Managers," *Occupational Outlook Handbook, 2008–2009 edition,* Bureau of Labor Statistics, accessed October 2008, http://www.bls.gov.

5. U.S. Department of Labor, "Human Resources, Training, and Labor Relations Managers and Specialists," *Occupational Outlook Handbook, 2008–2009 edition,* Bureau of Labor Statistics, accessed October 2008, http://www.bls.gov.

6. U.S. Department of Labor, "Lodging Managers," *Occupational Outlook Handbook, 2008–2009 edition,* Bureau of Labor Statistics, accessed October 2008, http://www.bls.gov.

7. U.S. Department of Labor, "Medical and Health Services Managers," *Occupational Outlook Handbook, 2008–2009 edition,* Bureau of Labor Statistics, accessed October 2008, http://www.bls.gov.

8. U.S. Department of Labor, "Purchasing Managers, Buyers, and Purchasing Agents," *Occupational Outlook Handbook, 2008–2009 edition,* Bureau of Labor Statistics, accessed October 2008, http://www.bls.gov.

9. U.S. Department of Labor, "Industrial Production Managers," *Occupational Outlook Handbook, 2008–2009 edition,* Bureau of Labor Statistics, accessed October 2008, http://www.bls.gov.

Chapter 12

1. Company Web site, http://petshotel.com, accessed March 2, 2009; Carol Wolf, "Passion for Pets Makes PetSmart a Success," *The Seattle Times*, http://seattletimes.com, accessed March 2, 2009; Lawrence Rothman, "PetSmart: A Doggie Paradise," *Banking and Finance Crossing*, http://www.bankingandfinancecrossing.com, accessed March 2, 2009; "Hiring and Developing World Class Talent," *HR Strategy Forum*, February 11, 2009, http://www.hrstrategyforum.org; "Secret Shopper—Pet Product Reviews," *Dogtime.com*, September 23, 2008, http://blogs.dogtime.com.

2. American Marketing Association, "AMA Adopts New Definition of Marketing," MarketingPower, www.danavan.net, accessed March 2009.

3. Bruce Shreiner, "Papa John's Takes Texted Pizza Orders," *Newsweek*, November 15, 2007, www.yahoo.com; "Domino's First in Industry to Offer Mobile Order," *Yahoo! Finance*, September 27, 2007, http://www.biz.yahoo.com.

4. "iPhone Review from CNET Editors," *CNET News*, http://reviews.cnet.com, accessed October 2008; Antone Gonsalves, "Apple Profits Soar 67% on iPhone, Mac Sales," *Information Week*, October 22, 2007, http://www.informationweek.com.

5. "Facts and Figures about Charitable Organizations," *Independent Sector*, January 4, 2007, http://www.independentsector.org.

6. "Measuring Civil Society and Volunteering," Johns Hopkins University Center for Civil Society Studies, 2007 report, http://www.johnshopkinsuniversity.org.

7. "Peyton Manning's Children's Hospital," St. Vincent Health, http://www.stvincent.org, accessed March 2009; G. Bruce Knecht, "Big Players in Charity," *The Wall Street Journal*, April 28, 2007, http://online.wsj.com.

8. Teddy Kider, "Congressional Is the Draw for Woods's Invitational," *The New York Times*, July 5, 2007, http://www.nytimes.com.

9. "The Adventures of Quatchi, Miga, and Sumi Begin in Earnest," Vancouver 2010, http://www.vancouver2010.com, accessed March 2009.

10. "Tour de Cure 2008," American Diabetes Association, http://tour.diabetes.org, accessed March 2009.

11. Jumpstart, http://www.jstart.org, accessed January 5, 2008.

12. "Environmentally Conscious Entrepreneur Offers Alternative to Plastic Bags," *Colgate Scene*, January 2008, p. 28.

13. "Oprah's Angel Network Fact Sheet," Oprah.com, http://www.oprah.com, accessed March 2009.

14. *ABC News*, January 17, 2008; Kimberly Palmer, "An Rx for Women," *U.S. News & World Report*, November 1, 2007, http://www.usnews.com.

15. Mark Mullen, "U.S. Companies Adapt to Chinese Market," *The Daily Nightly (MSNBC)*, February 10, 2007, www.google.com.

16. "Toyota, Isuzu Agree to Develop Diesel Engines," *International Herald Tribune*, August 23, 2007, www.google.com.

17. Leslie Cauley, "Cellphone Users Complain about Function Fatigue," *USA Today*, February 13, 2007, http://www.usatoday.com.

18. Bruce Horovitz, "Marketers Zooming in on Your Daily Routines," *USA Today*, April 23, 2007, http://www.usatoday.com.

19. Ibid.

20. Pottery Barn Kids Web site, http://www.potterybarnkids.com, accessed October 2008.

21. "About IdeaStorm," Dell Web site, http://www.ideastorm.com, accessed October 2008.

22. Grant Gross, "Google Expands Search Appliance Functionality," *Network World*, January 4, 2007, http://www.networkworld.com.

23. Reena Jana, "Mining Virtual Worlds for Market Research," *BusinessWeek*, August 13, 2007, http://www.businessweek.com.

24. Alexandra Rankin Macgill, "Data Memo," *Pew Internet & American Life Project*, October 24, 2007, http://www.pewinternet.org.

25. Alexis Blue, "The Value of Play," *The Arizona Daily Star*, November 3, 2007, http://www.azstarnet.com.

26. Pascale Le Draoulec, "Service That'll Play in L.A.," *Los Angeles Times*, October 24, 2007, http://www.latimes.com.

27. "Can Thinking about Shopping Change the Route You Take?" *Science Daily*, October 8, 2007, http://www.sciencedaily.com.

28. U.S. Census Bureau, "Resident Population Projections by Sex and Age: 2010 to 2050," *Statistical Abstract of the United States*; http://www.census.gov.

29. Eileen P. Gunn, "Prime Time," *U.S. News & World Report*, May 14, 2007, pp. 56–58.

30. Ylan Q. Mui, "As the Kids Go Buy," *The Washington Post*, June 4, 2007, www.google.com.

31. Elaine Misonzhnik, "Back to the Future," *Retail Traffic*, November 1, 2007, www.google.com.

32. David Dodson, "Minority Groups' Share of $10 Trillion U.S. Consumer Market Is Growing Steadily," *Fortune*, July 31, 2007, http://www.terry.uga.edu.

33. "U.S. Census Reports Minority Population Tops 100 Million," *PR Newswire*, May 17. 2007, http://www.prnewswire.com.

34. Hildy Medina, "Language of the Future," *Hispanic Business*, December 2007, http://www.hispanicbusiness.com.

35. Nina Bernstein, "Immigrant Entrepreneurs Shape a New Economy," *The New York Times*, February 6, 2007, http://www.nytimes.com.

36. Company Web site, http://www.gmblogs.com, accessed March 2009.

37. John Tozzi, "They're Making Money from Your Kids," *BusinessWeek*, November 13, 2007, http://www.businessweek.com.

38. Ernest Beck, "The American Green House," *BusinessWeek*, November 6, 2007, http://www.businessweek.com.

39. "Sodexho Marriott Services," *Claritas*, www.google.com, accessed March 2009.

40. Bruce Horovitz, "Would You Like Fries with that Latte?" *USA Today*, January 9, 2008, www.google.com.

41. Jad Mouwad, "Oil Hits $100 a Barrel for the First Time," *The New York Times*, January 2, 2008, http://www.nytimes.com.

42. Company Web site, http://www.timberland.com, accessed March 2009.

43. Company Web site, http://www.marriott.com, accessed March 2009.

44. Company Web site, http://www.apple.com/ipod/nike/gear.html, accessed October 2008.

45. "Queue Buster Improves Customers' Call Centre Experience," *CRM Today,* September 2007, www.google.com.

46. Company Web site, http://www.unilever.com, "Environment & Society," accessed March 2009; "Branding Land," *The Economist,* January 7, 2008, http://www.economist.com; Eric Newman, "Study: Retailers Push Charity, Ecology to Boost Sales," *Brandweek,* November 28, 2007, http://www.brandweek.com; Pete Engardio, "Beyond the Green Corporation," *BusinessWeek,* January 29, 2007, pp. 50–64.

47. Company Web site, http://disney.go.com, accessed March 2009; Jennifer Martinez, "Daily Entertainment Break: Vanessa Hudgens Tells all About 'HSM3,'" *San Jose Mercury News,* November 30, 2007, http://www.mercurynews.com; "'High School Musical 2' Shines Light on TV Viewing Habits of Teens, Parents," *Media Buyer Planner,* September 20, 2007, http://www.mediabuyerplanner.com; "'High School Musical 2' Sets Record," *Yahoo! News,* August 20, 2007, www.google.com; "Move Over Mickey: A New Franchise at Disney," *The New York Times,* August 20, 2007, www.google.com; "'High School Musical': The Phenomenon," *ShowBuzz,* August 16, 2007, http://www.showbuzz.com.

48. WBRU Web site, www.wbru.com, accessed October 2008.

Chapter 13

1. Company Web site, http://www.buckle.com, accessed March 2, 2009; "Brief: The Buckle January Same-Store Sales," *Forbes,* February 5, 2009, http://www.forbes.com; Christopher Palmeri, "Youth Will Be Served," *BusinessWeek,* January 26–February 2, 2009, p. 20; "The Buckle, Inc., Reports December 2008 Net Sales," *StreetInsider*.com, January 8, 2009, http://www.streetinsider.com; Kristin Graham, "A Retail Play for 2009," *The Motley Fool,* December 26, 2008, http://www.fool.com; Katherine Field, "Buckle Up," *Chain Store Age,* September 2008, http://www.chainstoreage.com.

2. "Windows Vista: Learn about the Features," company Web site, http://www.microsoft.com, accessed March 2009; Matt Slagle, "PC to Leapfrog Standalone Game Consoles," *Associated Press,* April 20, 2007, http://news.yahoo.com.

3. Andrew Martin, "Makers of Sodas Try a New Pitch: They're Healthy," *The New York Times,* March 7, 2007, http://www.nytimes.com.

4. Company Web sites, http://www.generalmills.com and http://www.curves.com, accessed March 2009; Tanya Irwin, "General Mills, Curves Partner in Cereal Box Appearance Contest," *MediaPost Publications,* October 9, 2007, www.mediapost.com/publications.

5. Jill Jusko, "Failure to Launch," *Industry Week,* September 1, 2007, http://www.industryweek.com.

6. Jacqui Cheng, "Yahoo! and SanDisk Roll Out Hopeful iPod Competitor," *Ars Technica,* April 9, 2007, http://arstechnica.com.

7. Christopher Lawton, "TV Screens Grow, Prices Drop," *The Arizona Republic,* November 20, 2007, http://www.azcentral.com.

8. "Wal-Mart Picks Blu-ray over HD DVD," *CBS News,* February 15, 2008, http://www.cbsnews.com; Erica Ogg, "Blu-Ray vs. HD DVD: War without End," *CNET News,* November 27, 2007, http://www.news.com.

9. Stuart Elliott, "Old Spice Tries a Dash of Humor to Draw Young Men," *The New York Times,* January 8, 2007, http://www.nytimes.com.

10. Stefanie Olsen, "Barbie's Last Online Stand?" *CNET News,* May 18, 2007, http://www.news.com.

11. Dannon Probiotics Web site, http://www.dannonprobioticscenter.com, accessed March 2009; Carol Matlack, "How Dannon Turns Bacteria into Bucks," *BusinessWeek,* November 15, 2007, http://www.businessweek.com.

12. William Yardley, "Army Is Going Wrinkle-Free; Velcro Becomes Norm," *The New York Times,* February 5, 2007, http://www.nytimes.com.

13. Claudia H. Deutsch, "Procter & Gamble to Benefit in All But Name from Water Purifier," *International Herald Tribune,* July 23, 2007, http://www.iht.com.

14. Tom Merritt, "Top 10 Worst Products," *CNET,* www.google.com, accessed March 2009.

15. Edwin Colyer, "Can IKEA's Dominance Be Disassembled?" *Brand Channel,* May 14, 2007, http://www.brandchannel.com.

16. Elizabeth Woyke, "Flunking Brand Geography," *BusinessWeek,* June 18, 2007, p. 14.

17. Euan Rocha, "U.S. Retailers Push Packagers to Think 'Green,'" *Reuters,* September 4, 2007, http://news.yahoo.com.

18. Andrew Bridges, "FDA Considers Additional Food Labels," *Associated Press,* September 10, 2007, http://news.yahoo.com.

19. Company Web site, http://www.chiquita.com, accessed March 24, 2009; Jenn Abelson, "Yes, We Have One Banana," *The Boston Globe,* March 7, 2007, http://www.boston.com.

20. Emily Brandon, "On the Record: Reed Hastings," *U.S. News & World Report,* September 16, 2007, p. 60.

21. *Statistical Abstract of the United States,* U.S. Census Bureau, http://www.bls.gov; "Occupational Outlook Handbook," Bureau of Labor Statistics, http://www.bls.gov, both accessed October 2008.

22. Company Web site, http://www.retailadvantagegroup.com, accessed March 2009.

23. U.S. Census Bureau. "Quarterly Retail E-Commerce Sales," February 17, 2009, http://www.census.gov.

24. "From Designer Shoes to Designer Zip Codes," *ABC News,* May 25, 2007, http://abcnews.com.

25. Sarah Skidmore, "Nike Focusing on Its Niche Businesses," *Associated Press,* September 21, 2007, http://news.yahoo.com.

26. Barry Silverstein, "Trader Joe's," *Brand Channel,* February 19, 2007, http://www.brandchannel.com.

27. Christopher Palmeri, "Online Extra: The Battle to Be Top Dog," *BusinessWeek,* August 7, 2007, www.google.com.

28. Dan Daly, "Will Crossing Lure Tenants Away from the Mall?" *Rapid City Journal,* December 27, 2007, www.google.com.

29. "Starbucks Heading to TV to Increase Traffic," *Brandweek,* November 16, 2007, http://www.brandweek.com.

30. Company Web site, "About Us," http://www.easy.com, accessed March 2009.

31. Beth Negus Viveiros, "A Corny Idea," *Direct,* January 1, 2008, http://directmag.com.

32. Tom Krazit, "Best Buy Wants Macs in More of Its Stores," *CNET News,* January 9, 2008, http://www.news.com.

33. "Philadelphia Premium Outlets Opens to Shoppers," *Associated Content,* November 9, 2007, www.google.com.

34. "RFID New Roundup," *RFID Journal,* November 23, 2007, http://www.rfidjournal.com.

35. "Trucking Statistics," *Truck Info,* http://www.truckinfo.net, accessed October 2008.

36. "The North American Railroad Industry," Association of American Railroads, http://www.aar.org, accessed January 16, 2008.

37. Company Web site, http://www.blogonthecusp.com, accessed October 2008; Adam Shahbaz, "Neiman Marcus Takes over YouTube Homepage, *iMedia Connection,* September 10, 2007, http://www.imediaconnection.com; "Teens Seek Luxury Items for Back-to-School Wardrobes," *CNN,* August 1, 2007, http://www.cnn.com; Vanessa O'Connell, "Neiman Marcus Has Idea to Draw a Younger Crowd," *The Wall Street Journal,* June 17, 2007, http://online.wsj.com.

38. "Joost—Next-Generation TV," company Web site, http://www.joost.com, accessed January 31, 2008; Wayne Friedman, "Cable Customers Leaving for Internet TVs? If Price Is Right," *Media Magazine,* January 11, 2008, http://publications.mediapost.com; Elinor Mills, "Watching TV on the Laptop—and on the Cheap," *CNET News,* October 17, 2007, http://www.news.com; Brad Stone, "Do We Need an Internet TV Network?" *The New York Times,* October 1, 2007, http://bits.blogs.nytimes.com; Phil Cogar, "TV vs. The Internet: Internet Wins," *Bit-Tech.net,* August 23, 2007, http://www.bit-tech.net; Kristina Knight, "Adults Watch More TV and Movies Than Teens," *BizReport,* August 3, 2007, http://www.bizreport.com; "Would You Pay to Watch YouTube Clips on Your TV?" *eMarketer,* May 17, 2007, http://www.emarketer.com; John Blau, "Skype's New Video Venture Now Called Joost," *PC World,* January 16, 2007, www.google.com.

39. Monopoly Web site, http://www.monopoly.com, accessed March 2009; "Hasbro Inc.," *Hoover's Online,* http://www.hoovers.com, accessed October 2008.

Chapter 14

1. Company Web site, http://www.etrade.com, accessed March 16, 2009; "E*Trade Super Bowl Commercial—the Cute Baby Hook," *Ad Savvy,* http://www.adsavvy.org, accessed March 4, 2009; Charles Leroux, "E*Trade Baby Ad Puts Shankopotamus in Play," *Chicago Tribune,* February 5, 2009, http://www.chicagotribune.com; "NBC Reportedly Struggling to Sell Out Super Bowl Pregame Ads," *Sports Business Daily,* January 26, 2009, http://www.sportsbusinessdaily.com; "E*Trade Announces Super Bowl XLIII Advertisement," *Yahoo! Finance,* January 23, 2009, http://biz.yahoo.com; Rafael Grillo, "The Online Brokerage Wars: E*Trade Offers Compelling Risk/Reward," *Seeking Alpha,* May 27, 2008, http://seekingalpha.com; "Talking and Trading Baby Blows Away Star-Studded Super Bowl Competition," *Reuters,* February 4, 2008, http://www.reuters.com.

2. Louise Story, "The Campaign Is Clean, the Stunts Fairly Dirty," *The New York Times,* September 28, 2007, http://www.nytimes.com.; Louise Story, "Anywhere the Eye Can See, It's Likely to See an Ad," *The New York Times,* January 15, 2007, http://www.nytimes.com; Rachel Konrad, "Advertisers Learn to Exploit Secret Codes in Video Games," *USA Today,* January 5, 2007, http://www.usatoday.com.

3. "TV Ads for Drugs High on the Emotions But Low on Facts," *News-Medical.Net,* January 30, 2007, http://www.news-medical.net.

4. Dale Buss, "Buick Seeks to Extend Enclave's Magic—But Will It Reach?" *Edmund's Auto Observer,* January 12, 2008, http://www.autoobserver.com.

5. "McDonald's Pours on the Iced Coffees," *Money Central,* May 1, 2007, www.google.com.

6. Wayne Friedman, "Product Placement: Broadcast Up, Cable Down in '07," *Media Post Publications,* December 31, 2007, http://publications.mediapost.com.

7. "PQ Media Market Analysis Finds Global Product Placement Spending Grew 37% in 2006," *PQMedia,* March 14, 2007, http://www.pqmedia.com.

8. Greg Sandoval, "Toying with the Diet Coke and Mentos Experiment," *CNET News,* February 14, 2007, http://www.news.com.

9. Michael Fitzgerald, "Case Study: Anatomy of a Business Decision," *Inc.,* June 2007, pp. 52–55.

10. Story, "Anywhere the Eye Can See, It's Likely to See an Ad."

11. "100 Leading National Advertisers," *Advertising Age,* June 25, 2007, http://adage.com/datacenter.

12. Ibid.

13. "Foundation Fact Sheet," The Bill and Melinda Gates Foundation, http://www.gatesfoundation.org, accessed March 2009.

14. Todd Spangler, "Google: Melding TV's 'Emotion' with Web Tracking," *Multichannel News,* January 15, 2008, http://www.multichannel.com.

15. Elinor Mills, "Satellite Circuit for Google TV Ads," *CNET News,* April 3, 2007, http://www.news.com.

16. Louise Story, "Viewers Fast-Forwarding Past Ads? Not Always," *The New York Times,* February 16, 2007, http://www.nytimes.com.

17. Eric Morath, "Ads Invade Satellite Radio," *The Detroit News,* February 1, 2007, www.google.com.

18. Federal Trade Commission, "Credit Bureaus," FTC Consumer Alert, http://www.ftc.gov, accessed March 2009.

19. "Facts & Figures," Outdoor Advertising Association of America, Inc., http://www.oaaa.org, accessed October 2008.

20. Andrew Adam Newman, "Your Ad Here, on My S.U.V.? And You'll Pay?" *The New York Times,* August 27, 2007, http://www.nytimes.com.

21. Sarah Karush, "Amtrak Turns Train into Billboard," *Associated Press,* November 7, 2007, http://news.yahoo.com.

22. "Study: Online Ad Spending to Hit $50B by 2011," *Boston Business Journal,* January 18, 2008, http://www.bizjournals.com/boston; Enid Burns, "Q3 Online Ad Spend: Strong Increases, Slower Growth," *ClickZ Network,* November 12, 2007, http://www.clickz.com.

23. Dan Briody, "Puppy Power: Using a New Tool Called a Widget to Boost Your Brand," *Inc.,* November 2007, pp. 55–56; Paul Thomasch, "Advertisements in Web Videos Seen Missing Mark," *Reuters,* November 9, 2007, http://news.yahoo.com; Greg Sandoval, "New Ads Jar Some YouTube Fans," *CNET News,* August 22, 2007, http://www.news.com.

24. Dan Fost, "Viral Campaign Spreading," *San Francisco Chronicle,* June 9, 2007, www.google.com.

25. Neda Ulaby, "State-of-the-Art Ads Are Increasingly One-to-One," *NPR*, January 8, 2008, www.google.com.

26. John Manasso, "Aflac Looks to Deepen NASCAR Sponsorship," *Atlanta Business Chronicle*, October 26, 2007, http://www.bizjournals.com.

27. "Effective Infomercials," *Infomercial DRTV*, http://www.infomercialdrtv.com, accessed March 2009.

28. Fran Daniel, "Pushing Savings: With Coupon Use Down, New Approaches Are Tried," *Winston-Salem Journal*, January 18, 2008, http://www.journalnow.com.

29. Yardena Ara, "Are Mail-In Rebates Headed for Extinction?" *PC World*, February 27, 2007, http://pcworld.about.com.

30. Jessica Mintz, "Food Commercials Reach the Supermarket," *Associated Press*, January 14, 2008, http://news.yahoo.com.

31. U.S. Department of Labor, Bureau of Labor Statistics, "Employment Projections," http://www.bls.gov, accessed March 2009.

32. Mark Huber, "Life of a Salesman," *Air Space Magazine*, February–March 2007, http://www.airspacemag.com.

33. Matthew Perrone, "Drug Promotion Takes to the Web," *Associated Press*, December 4, 2007, http://news.yahoo.com.

34. Eileen Alt Powell, "Do-Not-Call Law Heads for Update," *Charleston Evening Post*, January 14, 2008, http://www.charleston.net.

35. Henry Canaday, "Carefully Composed: How to Use E-mail to Get the Best Sales Results," *Selling Power*, May 2007, pp. 44–46.

36. Michael Fitzgerald, "On Beyond PowerPoint: Presentations Get a Wake-Up Call," *Inc.*, November 2007, pp. 58–59.

37. Chris Kohler, "How Protests against Games Cause Them to Sell More Copies," *Wired*, October 30, 2007, www.google.com.

38. Susan G. Komen Race for the Cure Web site, http://cms.komen.org, accessed March 26, 2009.

39. Tracy Samantha Schmidt, "Flying the Precarious Skies," *Time*, June 11, 2007, http://www.time.com; Jeff Bailey, "JetBlue's Leader Is Giving Up Chief Executive Title," *The New York Times*, May 11, 2007, http://www.nytimes.com.

40. "Too Young to Be Old," company press release, February 8, 2007, http://www.campaignforrealbeauty.com.

41. Charles Cooper, "Perspective: Why PCs Aren't Pricey Anymore," *CNET News*, December 7, 2007, http://www.news.com.

42. Pallavi Gogoi, "How Wal-Mart's TV Prices Crushed Rivals," *BusinessWeek*, April 23, 2007, http://www.businessweek.com.

43. Lisa Anderson, "Seeking Status? It's in the Bag," *Chicago Tribune*, August 5, 2007, Section 1, pp. 1, 26.

44. Marco R. della Cava, "Web Scalping Boosts Ticket Prices and Frustration," *USA Today*, November 5, 2007, http://usatoday.com; "Brokers Snatch Joy from Hannah Montana Fans," *CNN*, October 12, 2007, http://www.cnn.com.

45. Rondolf E. Schmid, "Raising Prices Enhances Wine Sales," *Associated Press*, January 14, 2008, http://news.yahoo.com.

46. "Dollar Stores Outlook," About.com: Retail Industry, http://retailindustry.about.com, accessed March 26, 2009; Kelly Johnson, "Economic Woes Tighten Holiday Spending at Dollar Stores," *Sacramento Business Journal*, November 23, 2007, www.google.com; Steve Painter, "Bucking the Big Boys," *Arkansas Democrat-Gazette*, April 22, 2007, pp. 8–9.

47. The Project for Excellence in Journalism, "The State of the News Media 2007," http://www.stateofthenewsmedia.com, accessed March 2009; "Baby Boomers Increasingly Embrace Mobile Technology," *Marketing VOX*, September 25, 2007, http://www.marketingvox.com; Gary Levin, "Network Audiences Are Showing their Age," *USA Today*, June 27, 2007, p. 4D; "Interview with Baby Boomer Advertising Expert Chuck Nyren," *Life Two*, June 4, 2007, http://lifetwo.com, National Federation of Independent Businesses press release, "Marketing to Baby-Boomer Women," April 5, 2007, http://www.nfib.com; "Experts Predict Top Trends in Marketing to Baby Boomers in 2007," *Senior Journal*, March 6, 2007, http://seniorjournal.com.

48. FUBU Web site, http://www.fubu.com, accessed March 2009; Urban Clothing Web site, http://www.urbanclothing.net, accessed January 10, 2005 (for pricing information); "The Rumors Are True, FUBU & Snoop Dogg Set Their Sights on Hotlanta," *Business Wire*, January 23, 2003, accessed at www.google.com; "FUBU," *CNN.com*, February 2002, http://www.cnn.com/SPECIALS/2002/black.history/stories/05.fubu.

Part 4: Launching Your Marketing Career

1. U.S. Department of Labor, "Market and Survey Researchers," *Occupational Outlook Handbook*, 2008–2009, Bureau of Labor Statistics, accessed October 2008, http://www.bls.gov.

2. U.S. Department of Labor, "Advertising Sales Agents," *Occupational Outlook Handbook*, 2008–2009, Bureau of Labor Statistics, accessed October 2008, http://www.bls.gov.

3. U.S. Department of Labor, "Advertising and Public Relations Services," *Occupational Outlook Handbook*, 2008–2009, accessed October 2008, http://www.bls.gov.

4. Ibid.

Chapter 15

1. Company Web site, http://www.rim.com, accessed March 6, 2009; "BlackBerry App World Poised to Bring App Goodness to BB Users," *San Francisco Chronicle*, March 5, 2009, http://www.sfgate.com; "Gartner Sees Unstable Handset Demand until 2010," *CNNMoney*, March 3, 2009, http://money.cnn.com; Al Sacco, "RIM Wins Mobile World Congress Award for BlackBerry Storm Screen," *CIO*, February 19, 2009, http://advice.cio.com; Priya Ganalati, "BlackBerry's Storm Rages On," *Portfolio.com*, January 29, 2009, http://www.portfolio.com; Amol Sharma and Sara Silver, "Bumpy Start for BlackBerry Storm," *The Wall Street Journal*, January 26, 2009, pp. B1, B5; Bonnie Cha, "RIM BlackBerry Storm (Verizon Wireless)," *CNET*, December 12, 2008, http://reviews.cnet.com; Stephen H. Wildstrom, "RIM's Impressive BlackBerry Storm," *BusinessWeek*, October 8, 2008, http://www.businessweek.com; Bonnie Cha, "Verizon Officially Debuts RIM BlackBerry Storm," *CNET News*, October 7, 2008, http://news.cnet.com.

2. Larry Dignan, "CIO Salary Survey: 13 Millionaires; Financial Services Take Top Spots," ZDNet, www.google.com, accessed March 2009.

3. Mary Hayes Weier, "Airbus Inks Multi-Million Dollar RFID Software Contract," *Information Week*, April 10, 2008, www.google.com, accessed October 2008.

4. "A Timeline of Computer History," http://www.computerhistory.org, accessed March 2009.

5. Brian Solomon, "Smartphones Drive Growth in Handheld Sales," TMCnet, March 24, 2008, http://voipservices.tmcnet.com, accessed October 2008.

6. Cimage, "Intranet Success Story," Cimage, http://www.nova-soft.com, accessed March 2009.

7. Check Point, "Success Stories: The Equitable Bank Invests in Affordable Check Point Express," Check Point Software Technologies Ltd., http://www.checkpoint.com, accessed October 2008.

8. Toshiba, "Toshiba Strata CIX a Powerful Performance at Circle BMW," Toshiba, www.google.com, accessed October 2008.

9. Data Theft & Security News, March 25, 2008, http://datatheft.org, accessed April 17, 2008; Jaikumar Vijayan, "Vermont Ski Area Reports Hannaford-like Data Theft," *Computerworld*, April 7, 2008; Kim Zetter, "Palin E-mail Hacker Says It was Easy," WIRED Blog Network, September 18, 2008, http://blog.wired.com, accessed October 20, 2008; M. J. Stephey, "Sarah Palin's E-mail Hacked," *Time*, September 17, 2008, www.time.com, accessed October 20, 2008.

10. Data Theft & Security News.

11. Brian Krebs, "Firms Struggle Against Web Viruses; Security Companies Scramble to Combat Rise of Malicious Programs," *The Washington Post,* March 20, 2008, page D3.

12. "Symantec Report Reveals Computer Viruses Exceed One Million," *Internet Business News,* April 11, 2008.

13. "Adware Caused Most Infections in Q1 2008, According to PandaLabs; Attacks on Cell Phones Also on the Rise," *PR Newswire,* April 1, 2008.

14. "Mobile Users Do Not Take Security Precautions," *Business Wire,* March 4, 2008.

15. Mark Ferelli, "Strategies for Online Backup; Don't Wait for a Disaster—Protect Your Data Now," *Accounting Today,* February 25, 2008, p. 20.

16. Eve Tahmincioglu, "Small Business; Trying to Stay a Step Ahead of Murphy's Law," *The New York Times,* http://www.nytimes.com, accessed October 2008.

17. Dave Levinthal, "Dallas Water Billing Full of Glitches with $30 million Computer," *Dallas Morning News,* April 8, 2008; "Levi's 1Q Profit Rises 12 Percent, But Rest of Year Looks Challenging," *International Herald Tribune,* April 8, 2008; Paul McDougall, "British Airways Cancels Heathrow Flights Amid Computer Chaos," *Information Week,* March 28, 2008.

18. Bureau of Labor Statistics, "Work at Home Summary," http://www.bls.gov, accessed March 2009.

19. Richard Verrier, "Disney IT Jobs to Be Unloaded," *Los Angeles Times,* www.google.com, accessed October 2008.

20. "Hewlett-Packard Sees 'Exploding' Africa IT Growth," *Information Week,* April 22, 2008, www.google.com; Ryan Kim, "Chron 200: CEO of the Year," *San Francisco Chronicle,* April 20, 2008, www.google.com; Louise Lee, "HP's International Appeal," *BusinessWeek,* February 19, 2008, http://www.businessweek.com; Spencer Ante, "HP: A Steady Ship in Troubled Waters," *BusinessWeek,* November 20, 2007, http://www.businessweek.com.

21. Company Web site, http://www.trendmicro.com, accessed March 2009; Robert McMillan, "Trend Micro Hit by Massive Web Hack," *InfoWorld,* March 14, 2008, http://www.info-world.com; Chaniga Vorasarun, "Branding Exercise," *Forbes,* December 10, 2007, www.google.com; Catherine Holahan, "Trend Micro Zaps the Bugs," *BusinessWeek,* November 2, 2007, http://www.businessweek.com.

22. Peet's Web site, accessed March 2009, http://www.peets.com; "National Coffee Roaster Streamlines B2C Fulfillment System," FloStor, accessed October 2008, http://www.flostor.com; "Peet's Coffee & Tea, Inc.," Google Finance, accessed October 2008, http://finance.google.com; "Peet's Coffee & Tea Celebrates 40 Years of Craftsmanship," *Badgett's Coffee Journal,* accessed October 2008, http://www.aboutcoffee.net.

Chapter 16

1. Theo Francis, "New FASB Rules: Back to Square One?" *BusinessWeek*, April 2, 2009, http://www.businessweek.com; Karey Wutkowski, "U.S. Bill Would Revamp Accounting Oversight," *Reuters*, March 6, 2009, http://www.reuters.com; "House Panel Sets Hearing on Mark-to-Market Accounting," *The Washington Post*, March 5, 2009, http://voices.washingtonpost.com; Emily Chasan, "Ex-SEC Accounting Chief Refused to Nix Fair Value," *Reuters UK*, March 4, 2009, http://uk.reuters.com; Jeff Bishop, "Exec: Accounting Rule Hurting Local Banks," *Times-Herald*, February 16, 2009, http://www.times-herald.com; Allen Sloan, "Don't Blame Mark-to-Market Accounting," *The Washington Post*, October 28, 2008, http://www.washingtonpost.com; Elizabeth Williamson and Kara Scannell, "Momentum Gathers to Ease Mark-to-Market Accounting Rule," *The Wall Street Journal*, October 2, 2008, http://online.wsj.com; Alex Dumortier, "Mark-to-Market Accounting: What You Should Know," *The Motley Fool*, October 2, 2008, http://www.fool.com.

2. Bureau of Labor Statistics, *2008–09 Occupational Outlook Handbook,* http://www.bls.gov, accessed October 2008.

3. "Accounting Firms Scramble to Find Experienced CPAs," *The Wall Street Journal,* January 18, 2008, www.google.com, accessed October 2008.

4. "Tax Assistance Program Seeks Volunteers," AARP, http://www.aarp.org, accessed March 2009.

5. Ernst and Young, "Roberts Hotels Group's Michael V. Roberts and Steven C. Roberts Named Ernst & Young Entrepreneur of the Year," www.google.com, accessed October 2008.

6. Smart Pros, "Double-Digit Growth for Accounting Firms on CCH List," www.google.com, accessed October 2008.

7. Inside Public Accounting, "Top 100 Accounting Firms," www.accountingmajors.com, accessed March 2009.

8. Financial Accounting Standards Board, "Facts about FASB," http://www.fasb.org, accessed March 2009.

9. Johnson & Johnson financial statements, MSN Investor, http://moneycentral.msn.com, accessed March 30, 2008.

10. Sage Software, "Customer Success Story," http://www.sagesoftware.com, accessed March 2009.

11. Ken Bailey and Amy Kleiboeker, "Using QuickBooks to Manage Your Dairy Farm," Department of Agricultural Economics, University of Missouri, http://agebb.missouri.edu, accessed October 2008.

12. McDonald's Corporation Annual Report, http://www.mcdonalds.com/corp, accessed October 2008.

13. Floyd Norris, "U. S. Moves Toward International Accounting Rules," *New York Times*, August 28, 2008, http://www.nytimes.com, accessed October 2008.

14. PricewaterhouseCoopers, "Ten Minutes on IFRS," http://www.pwc.com, accessed March 2009; Deloitte, "IFRS in Your Pocket," http://www.iasplus.com, accessed March 2009.

15. "Lawson Software; Holland Hospital Simplifies Management of Supplies and Finances with Lawson Healthcare Applications," *Health & Medicine Week,* March 31, 2008, www.google.com; "Unified Government of Wyandotte County/Kansas City, Kansas Selects Lawson Software to Help Streamline Budgeting and Reporting," *Business Wire,* March 18, 2008, www.google.com; "New York Health Network Simplifies Budgeting with Lawson Software Implementation," *Business Wire,* May 2, 2007, www.google.com.

16. Company Web site, http://www.rsmmcgladrey.com, accessed March 2009; company Web site, McGladrey & Pullen LLP, http://www.mcgladrey.com, accessed March 2009; "RSM McGladrey, Inc.," *BusinessWeek* company profile, www.google.com, accessed October 2008; "Looming National Debt Crises Subject of RSM McGladrey Lecture at UI," press release, the University of Iowa News Services, www.google.com, accessed October 2008.

17. The Little Guys Web site, accessed March 2009, http://www.thelittleguys.com; Alan Wolf, "Consumers Cutting Back on CE Purchases This Summer," *This Week in Consumer Electronics,* accessed October 2008, http://www.twice.com; Lisa Johnston, "Study: Brand-Name Importance Drops for CE Shoppers," *This Week in Consumer Electronics,* accessed October 2008, http://www.twice.com; Alan Wolf, "Glikes to HTSA: Stay Ahead of the Curve," *This Week in Consumer Electronics,* accessed October 2008, http://www.twice.com.

Part 5: Launching Your Information Technology and Accounting Career

1. U.S. Department of Labor, "Tomorrow's Jobs," *Occupational Outlook Handbook, 2008–2009,* Bureau of Labor Statistics, accessed October 2008, http://www.bls.gov.

2. U.S. Department of Labor, "Accountants and Auditors," *Occupational Outlook Handbook, 2008–2009,* Bureau of Labor Statistics, accessed October 2008, http://www.bls.gov.

3. U.S. Department of Labor, "Computer Software Engineers," *Occupational Outlook Handbook, 2008–2009,* Bureau of Labor Statistics, accessed October 2008, http://www.bls.gov.

4. U.S. Department of Labor, "Computer and Information Systems Managers," *Occupational Outlook Handbook, 2008–2009,* Bureau of Labor Statistics, accessed October 2008, http://www.bls.gov.

Chapter 17

1. Thomas J. Slattery, "The Financial Supermarket Falls Apart, Again," *Risk & Insurance,* February 2, 2009, http://www.ris-kandinsurance.com; Andy Kessler, "The End of Citi's Financial Supermarket," *The Wall Street Journal,* January 16, 2009, http://online.wsj.com; Andrew Ross Sorkin, "Breaking Up a Must for Citi," *The New York Times,* January 15, 2009, http://www.dealbook.blogs.nytimes.com; Eric Dash, "Citigroup Plans to Split Itself Up, Taking Apart the Financial Supermarket," *The New York Times,* January 14, 2009, http://www.nytimes.com; "Long Live the Financial Supermarket," *The Wall Street Journal,* January 14, 2009, http://bw.dowjones.com; Eric Dash, "A Stormy Decade for Citi Since Travelers Merger," *The New York Times,* April 3, 2008, http://www.nytimes.com.

2. Reuters, "Oracle's $5 billion bond sale biggest since January," April 4, 2008, http://biz.yahoo.com, accessed October 2008.

3. Jay R. Ritter, "Some Factoids about the IPO Market," March 20, 2008, www.google.com, accessed October 2008.

4. New York Stock Exchange, "NYSE Statistics Archive," http://www.nyse.com, accessed October 2008.

5. New York Stock Exchange, "About the NYSE," http://www.nyse.com, accessed March 2009.

6. Federal Deposit Insurance Corporation, *Statistics on Banking,* http://www2.fdic.gov, accessed March 2009.

7. U.S. Census Bureau, *2008 Statistical Abstract of the United States,* http://www.census.gov, accessed October 2008.

8. U.S. Census Bureau, *2008 Statistical Abstract of the United States.*

9. Federal Deposit Insurance Corporation, *Statistics on Banking.*

10. Ibid.

11. National Credit Union Administration, *Credit Union Statistics,* http://www.ncua.gov, accessed October 2008.

12. Insurance Information Institute, *Financial Services Facts,* http://www.iii.org, accessed March 2009.

13. Ibid.

14. Investment Company Institute, *Mutual Fund Fact Book,* http://www.ici.org, accessed October 2008.

15. Ibid.

16. Press Release, Federal Reserve Board, April 22, 2008, http://www.federalreserve.gov, accessed October 2008.

17. Banker's Almanac, "Top 50 Banks in the World," http://www.bankersalmanac.com, accessed April 30, 2008.

18. "The Vanguard Group," *BusinessWeek,* http://investing.businessweek.com, accessed March 2009; Sue Asci, "Vanguard Edges American as Top Mutual Funds Seller," *Investment News,* February 11, 2008, http://www.investmentnews.com; David Hoffman, "Vanguard Bolsters Efforts to Woo Financial Advisers," *Investment News,* http://www.investmentnews.com.

19. Anthony Malakian, "Banks Are Failing—But It's Nothing Like the Old Days," *US Banker,* May 1, 2008, http://www.americanbanker.com; Kalen Holliday, "Counting on Community & Customers," *Community Banker,* November 2007, http://www.aba.com; Mark E. Macomber, "Building on Our Success," *Community Banker,* July 2007, http://www.aba.com; Randall S. Kroszner, "Community Banks: The Continuing Importance of Relationship Finance," Board of Governors of the Federal Reserve System, http://www.federalreserve.gov.

20. Morgan Stanley corporate Web site, www.morganstanley.com, accessed March 2009; Louise Story and Andrew Ross Sorkin, "Morgan Agrees to Revise Terms of Mitsubishi Deal," *The New*

York Times, October 13, 2008, www.nytimes.com, accessed October 15, 2008; Morgan Stanley Online investment services Web site, www.online.msdw.com, accessed October 2008; Anna Bernasek, "Papa Bear," *Fortune,* January 8, 2001, www.fortune.com.

Chapter 18

1. "Intel to Invest $7 Billion in U.S. Factory Upgrades," *Money News,* February 11, 2009, http://moneynews.newsmax.com; Franklin Paul and Janet Kornblum, "Intel to Invest $7 Billion in U.S. as Recession Deepens," *Reuters,* February 10, 2009, http://uk.reuters.com; Patrick Thibodeau, "Intel's $7 Billion 'Made in the USA' Investment," *ComputerWorld,* February 10, 2009, http://www.computerworld.com; Brian Caulfield, "Intel's Chief on His $7 Billion Bet," *Forbes,* February 10, 2009, http://www.forbes.com; Brian Forbes, "Stimulating Tech," *Forbes,* February 10, 2009, http://www.forbes.com.

2. "Executive Compensation Trends," *Equilar,* http://www.equilar.com, accessed April 2009.

3. Josh Funk, "Berkshire CFO Gets More Compensation than Buffett," *CNBC,* March 17, 2008, http://www.huffingtonpost.com, accessed October 2008.

4. Airbus for Analysts, Airbus, http://www.airbus.com, accessed October 2008.

5. Tom Reason, "Budgeting in the Real World," *CFO Magazine,* http://www.cfo.com, accessed October 2008.

6. "BMW Announces Plant Expansion in South Carolina," *Reuters,* March 10, 2008, http://findarticles.com, accessed October 2008.

7. Ibid.

8. FRED Database, St. Louis Federal Reserve Bank, http://research.stlouisfed.org, accessed October 2008.

9. Board of Governors of the Federal Reserve System, *Federal Reserve Bulletin,* http://www.federalreserve.gov, accessed October 2008.

10. Bill Vlasic, "With Warning, GM Takes Wide Cost Cuts," *The New York Times,* July 16, 2008, http://www.nytimes.com.

11. Board of Governors of the Federal Reserve System, *Federal Reserve Bulletin.*

12. U.S. Census Bureau, *2008 Statistical Abstract of the United States,* http://www.census.gov, accessed October 2008.

13. Ibid.

14. "About DFJ," Draper Fisher Jurvetson, http://www.dfj.com, accessed April 2009.

15. "Current Investment," Cerberus Capital Management, http://www.cerberuscapital.com, accessed October 2008.

16. Eric Dash and Andrew Ross Sorkin, "Citigroup Sells Abu Dhabi Fund $7.5 Billion Stake," *The New York Times,* http://www.nytimes.com, accessed October 2008.

17. "Hedge Funds Do about 60% of Bond Trading, Study Says," *The Wall Street Journal,* http://www.wsj.com, accessed May 15, 2008.

18. "Hedge Fund Assets Flows and Trend Report 2008," *Institutional Investor News,* http://www.iialternatives.com, accessed October 2008.

19. Carolyn Murphy, "Mars Grabs Wrigley for $23 Billion," *Daily Deal,* April 29, 2008.

20. "LBOs: The Long View," *Daily Deal,* January 25, 2008, http://www.thedeal.com, accessed October 2008.

21. Matthew Karnitschinig and Kevin J. Delaney, "Microsoft Sees Yahoo Being Split in New Offer," *The Wall Street Journal,* May 26, 2008, http://online.wsj.com; Jay Greene, "Microsoft–Yahoo: Desperation Sets In," *BusinessWeek,* May 20, 2008, http://www.businessweek.com; Mariko Katsumara, "Facebook Stresses Independence Amid Microsoft Talk," *Reuters UK,* May 19, 2008, http://uk.reuters.com; Stephen Taub, "Do Buybacks Boost Share Price?" *CFO,* December 17, 2007, http://www.cfo.com; Matt Marshall, "Microsoft's Ballmer: MSFT Will Acquire 20 Companies a Year," *VentureBeat,* October 18, 2007, http://venturebeat.com.

22. Phyllis Korkki, "Who Needs to Travel When There's Home?" *The New York Times,* May 19, 2008, http://www.nytimes.com; Luke Mullins, "Dissecting the Declining Dollar," *U.S. News & World Report,* March 7, 2008, http://www.usnews.com; "The Declining U.S. Dollar—An Opportunity for Manufacturers?" *Production Machining,* December 20, 2007, http://www.productionmachining.com; David Ellis, "Declining Dollar: Who Wins, Who Loses," *CNNMoney,* September 24, 2007, http://money.cnn.com.

23. CBS Video, "Employees Say a Lot about an Airline," http://www.cbsnews.com/video/; Steve Call, http://news.google.com; Southwest Airlines Annual Report, http://www.southwest.com; "Southwest Airlines Announces Fares and Flights to/from Minneapolis-St. Paul: Carrier Will Operate Eight Daily Nonstop Flights to Chicago Midway beginning in March 2009," http://www.marketwatch.com; "Even the Best Fuel Hedges Can Lead to Turbulence," http://www.thestreet.com. All Web sites accessed November 2008.

Part 6: Launching Your Finance Career

1. U.S. Department of Labor, "Tomorrow's Jobs," *Occupational Outlook Handbook, 2008–2009,* Bureau of Labor Statistics, accessed October 2008, http://www.bls.gov.

2. National Association of Colleges and Employers, "Starting Salary Offers," October 2008, accessed at http://www.career.vt.edu.

3. U.S. Department of Labor, "Financial Managers," *Occupational Outlook Handbook, 2008–2009,* Bureau of Labor Statistics, accessed October 2008, http://www.bls.gov.

Appendix A

1. Randall Stross, "For Palm, Some Tough Acts to Follow," *The New York Times,* March 22, 2009, p. BU 3; Tom Krazit, "Palm Waiting for Pre to End Revenue Slump," *CNET News,* March 3, 2009, http://news.cnet.com; Erika Morphy, "Will Apple's iPhone Patent Pre-empt the Pre?" *E-Commerce Times,* January 27, 2009, http://www.ecommercetimes.com; Sinead Carew, "Palm Investors Worry Apple May Get Touchy over Pre," *Reuters,* January 22, 2009, http://uk.reuters.com; John Paczkowski, "Apple COO: 'We Will Not Stand for Having Our IP Ripped Off,'" *Digital Daily,* January 21, 2009, http://digitaldaily.allthingsd.com.

2. Peter J. Johnson, Jr., "10 Ways to Protect Yourself from Frivolous Lawsuits," *Fox News,* July 5, 2007, http://www.foxnews.com, accessed October 22, 2008.

3. "All States Have Silly Laws," American Public Human Services Association, http://foodstamp.aphsa.org, accessed April 2009.

4. "Geographic Boundaries," U.S. Fourth Circuit Court of Appeals, http://www.ca4.uscourts.gov, accessed October 22, 2008.

5. "The Justices' Caseload," Supreme Court of the United States, http://supremecourtus.gov, accessed April 17, 2009.

6. "China's Newest Export: Lawsuits," *Fortune,* July 23, 2007, p. 48.

7. "HR 3915 Addresses Many Aspects of Predatory and Other Mortgage Lending," *Mortgage News Daily,* March 5, 2008, http://www.mortgagenewsdaily.com, accessed October 22, 2008.

8. "USA Patriot Act," The White House, http://www.whitehouse.gov, accessed October 22, 2008.

9. Kim Hart, "FCC Vote Opens Cable Competition," *The Washington Post,* October 31, 2007, http://www.washingtonpost.com, accessed October 22, 2008.

10. Jim Tankersley and Patricia Callahan, "Senate OK's Sweeping Consumer Safety Reform," *Chicago Tribune,* March 7, 2008, http://www.chicagotribune.com, accessed October 22, 2008.

11. "Renewed Legislation Improves Safety of FDA-Regulated Products," U.S. Department of Agriculture, http://www.fda.gov, accessed October 22, 2008.

12. Robert Pear, "U.S. Ruling Backs Benefit Cut at 65 in Retiree Plans," *The New York Times,* December 27, 2007, http://www.nytimes.com, accessed October 22, 2008.

13. David Kravets, "Google Unveils YouTube Copyright Filter to Mixed Reviews," *Wired,* October 15, 2007, http://www.wired.com, accessed October 22, 2008; Rob Hof, "Google to Viacom: Sorry, You're All Wrong," *BusinessWeek,* April 30, 2007, http://www.businessweek.com, accessed October 22, 2008; Jeremy W. Peters, "Viacom Sues Google over YouTube Video Clips," *The New York Times,* March 14, 2007, http://www.nytimes.com, accessed October 22, 2008.

14. Legal Information Institute, Cornell University Law School, http://www.law.cornell.edu/ucc/ucc.table.html, accessed April 7, 2009.

15. "Appeals Court Clarifies Eminent Domain Law," *United Press International,* February 25, 2008, http://www.upi.com, accessed October 22, 2008; Robyn Blumner, "Eminent Domain May Be a Bit Less Eminent," *St. Petersburg Times,* August 19, 2007, http://www.sptimes.com.

16. Brad Stone, "Settlement Lets Apple Use 'iPhone,'" *The New York Times,* February 22, 2007, http://www.nytimes.com, accessed October 22, 2008.

17. "S.1145: Patent Reform Act of 2007," GovTrack.us, http://www.govtrack.us, accessed October 22, 2008; Patrick Thimangu, "U.S. Patent Law in Flux," *Mass High Tech: The Journal of New England Technology,* February 29, 2008, http://masshightech.bizjournals.com, accessed October 22, 2008; "Justices Get Another Shot at Patent Law," *The Wall Street Journal,* January 16, 2008, http://online.wsj.com, accessed October 22, 2008.

18. Ruth David, "Scrabulous Facing Copyright Infringement Charges," *Forbes,* January 17, 2008, http://www.forbes.com, accessed October 22, 2008.

19. Eric Pfanner, "In Europe, Apple Faces Hurdles to iTunes Movie Rentals," *The New York Times,* January 21, 2008, http://www.nytimes.com, accessed October 22, 2008.

20. Maria Vogel-Short, "Pet-Food Lawsuits Are Near Settlement, Say Attorneys," *New Jersey Law Journal,* March 10, 2008, http://www.law.com, accessed October 22, 2008.

21. "The New Bankruptcy Law," *FindLaw,* January 21, 2008, http://www.bankruptcy.findlaw.com, accessed October 22, 2008.

22. Mark Hefflinger, "Chinese Music Orgs File Copyright Lawsuit against Baidu," *Digital Media Wire,* February 28, 2008, http://www.dmwmedia.com, accessed October 22, 2008; "Music Group Joins YouTube Copyright Lawsuit," *MSNBC,* August 6, 2007, http://www.msnbc.msn.com, accessed October 22, 2008.

Appendix B

1. Beatrice E. Garcia, "State Farm Wants to Drop Homeowners Insurance in Florida," *The Maimi Herald,* March 9, 2009, http://www.maimiherald.com; Terrence Stutz, "Texans Still Pay Highest Insurance Rates for Homeowner Policies," *The Dallas Morning News,* March 3, 2009, http://www.khou.com; Wayne Faulkner, "Lawmakers Join in Fight against Insurance Hikes," *Star News Online,* February 24, 2009, http://www.starnewsonline.com; "Coastal Homeowners Vow to Fight Insurance Rate Hikes," *WRAL.com,* February 17, 2009, http://www.wral.com; Jennifer LaFleur and Ed Timms, "Coverage at What Cost?" *The Dallas Morning News,* February 15, 2009, http://www.dallasnews.com; "State Farm to Stop Insuring Florida," *CNN Money,* January 27, 2009, http://cnnmoney.com; Mike Baker, "Homeowner Insurance Rates to Soar Along Coast," *News-Record,* December 19, 2008, http://www.news-record.com.

2. American Council of Life Insurers, Life Insurance Fact Book, http://www.acli.com, accessed October 22, 2008.

3. Insurance Information Institute, http://www.iii.org, accessed October 22, 2008.

4. Insurance Information Institute, Hurricane and Windstorm Deductibles, http://www.iii.org, accessed October 22, 2008.

5. Supplier Information, Wal-Mart Stores, http://walmartstores.com, accessed October 22, 2008.

Appendix C

1. "Campus Credit Card Trap Report," Truth about Credit, http://www.truthaboutcredit.org, accessed February 25, 2009; John Carlson, "Banks Give Kids Too Much Credit, in a Bad Way," *Des Moines Register,* February 13, 2008, http://www.desmoinesregister.com; Laura Hanson, "Students Note Credit Card Debt; Bill Would Ban Campus Offers," *East Valley Tribune,* February 10, 2008, http://www.eastvalleytribune.com, accessed October 22, 2008; Kimberly Palmer and Emily Brandon, "The Rush to Push Plastic; Companies Use Free Food and Facebook to Lure Students," *U.S. News & World Report,* January 28, 2008, http://www.usnews.com, accessed October 22, 2008; Shelly Banjo, "Arm Teens with Good Credit Skills," *The Wall Street Journal,* January 27, 2008, http://online.wsj.com, accessed October 22, 2008; Andy Kwalwaser, "Credit Card Debt Takes Toll on Students," *The Daily Illini,* January 24, 2008, http://www.dailyillini.com, accessed October 22, 2008.

2. *Income, Poverty, and Health Insurance Coverage in the United States*, U.S. Census Bureau, http://www.census.gov, accessed October 21, 2008.

3. *Employee Tenure*, Bureau of Labor Statistics, http://www.bls.gov, accessed February 11, 2008; "Anxious Workers," *FRBSF Economic Letter*, Federal Reserve Bank of San Francisco, http://www.frbsf.org, accessed October 21, 2008.

4. Alan Zibel, "Personal Bankruptcy Filings Rise 40%," *The Washington Post*, http://www.washingtonpost.com, accessed October 21, 2008.

5. Federal Reserve Statistical Release G-19, http://www.federalreserve.gov, accessed October 21, 2008.

6. Nellie Mae, "Undergraduate Students and Credit Cards," http://www.nelliemae.com, accessed October 21, 2008.

Appendix D

1. Company Web site, http://www.feedgranola.com, accessed April 7, 2009; "Feed Granola Snacks," *iFit & Healthy,* http://www.ifitandhealthy.com/feed-granola-snacks/, accessed October 22, 2008; Amy Palanjian, "From Ad Man to Granola Guru," *The Wall Street Journal,* March 25, 2008, http://online.wsj.com, accessed October 22, 2008; "Feed Granola Co.," in "30 Under 30," *Inc.*, October 2007, http://www.inc.com, accessed October 22, 2008; Stacy Perman, "From Home Kitchen to Whole Foods," *BusinessWeek,* September 7, 2007, http://www.businessweek.com, accessed October 22, 2008.

Appendix E

1. U.S. Census Bureau, *Statistical Abstract of the United States: 2008,* http://www.census.gov, accessed October 22, 2008.

2. Joseph Ogando, "Teaching the New Engineering Skills," *Design News,* March 17, 2008, http://www.designnews.com, accessed October 22, 2008.

3. Liz Wolgemuth and Katy Marquardt, "Career Guide 2008," *U.S. News & World Report,* March 24–31, 2008, pp. 45–52.

4. Lindsey Gerdes, "Internships: The Best Places to Start," *BusinessWeek,* November 30, 2007, http://www.businessweek.com, accessed October 22, 2008.

5. "Internships and Co-operative Education Programs," *The Princeton Review,* http://www.princetonreview.com, accessed October 22, 2008.

6. Career Explorer, http://www.careerexplorer.net/aptitude.asp, accessed April 7, 2009.

7. Company Web site, http://www.pauladeen.com, accessed April 7, 2009.

8. Kim Isaacs, "Five Resume Tips for College Students," *Monster.com,* http://www.monster.com, accessed October 22, 2008; Douglas MacMillan, "The Art of the Online Resume," *BusinessWeek,* May 7, 2007, p. 86.

9. Isaacs, "Five Resume Tips for College Students."

10. "Ten Tips for Writing Effective Cover Letters," *AllBusiness.com,* http://www.allbusiness.com, accessed April 7, 2009.

11. Douglas MacMillan, "The Art of the Online Resume," *BusinessWeek,* May 7, 2007, p. 86.

12. Carole Martin, "Ten Tips to Boost Your Interview IQ," *Monster.com,* http://career-advice.monster.com, accessed April 7, 2009.

13. Carmine Gallo, "Preparing for a Tough Job Interview," *BusinessWeek,* October 16, 2007, http://www.businessweek.com, accessed October 22, 2008.

14. "Tomorrow's Jobs," *Occupational Outlook Handbook,* U.S. Department of Labor, http://www.bls.gov, accessed October 22, 2008.

15. "Tomorrow's Jobs," *Occupational Outlook Handbook.*

16. "Tomorrow's Jobs," *Occupational Outlook Handbook.*

17. "Tomorrow's Jobs," *Occupational Outlook Handbook.*

18. Barbara Rose, "Weak Job Market Is Actually Mad for Grads," *Chicago Tribune,* March 16, 2008, section 1, pp. 1, 12.

Name Index

Subject Index

France (continued)
  euro in, 108
  Internet users in, 235
  as member of Group of Eight, 119
  mixed-market economy in, 81
  Organization for Economic Cooperation and Development Anti-Bribery Convention and, 113
  price setting in, 116
  shopping bag use in, 472
  trade in, 104
Franchisees, 160–162
Franchises/franchising
  benefits of, 161–162
  drawbacks of, 162
  explanation of, 125, 159–160
  guidelines for buying, 199
  in information technology fields, 191
  nature of agreements in, 160–161
Franchisors, 125, 160, 161
  Fraud
  credit card, 501
  accounting, 526, 529
  Internet, 228–229, A-9
  Ponzi scheme and, 25, 527
FRCA (Fair Credit Reporting Act), 397
Free credit reports, 397
Freedom of choice, 10
Free-rein leadership, 270
Free-trade area, 119
Frequency marketing, 412–413
Frictional unemployment, 87, 88
Full-function merchant wholesalers, 439
Functional résumés, A-60

G

GAAP. See Generally accepted accounting principles (GAAP)
Gadgets, 469
Games, 472–473
Gasoline
  demand for, 70, 71
  oil price swings and, 74
GDP. See Gross domestic product (GDP)
Gender, 404. See also Women
General Agreement on Tariffs and Trade (GATT), 117–118, 130, 132
Generally accepted accounting principles (GAAP), 528–530, 542, 544

General obligation bonds, 562
Geographical segmentation, 402–403, 408
Germany
  African debt relief from, 119
  Alando in, 122
  banking in, 581
  eBay in, 113
  euro in, 108
  flextime in, 299
  Internet use in, 235
  as low-context culture, 337
  as member of Group of Eight, 119
  Organization for Economic Cooperation and Development Anti-Bribery Convention and, 113
  price setting in, 116
  trade in, 104
Ghana, 123
Gifts, 40, 109
Gift barters, 76
Global business strategies, 128
Global economic crisis. See also Economic downturn/crisis
  cell phone makers and, 142
  credit-rating agencies and, 565
  oil price swings and, 74
  stimulus plan and, 67-68
Global marketplace
  absolute and comparative advantage and, 104–105
  careers in, 137–138
  challenges for, 90–91
  corruption in, 113–115
  e-business and, 217, 234–235
  entrepreneurship and, 189, 190
  expansion into, 121–127
  financial system and, 581–583
  international asset management and, 599
  Internet use in, 235
  organizations to ease trade barriers and, 117–121
  reasons to trade in, 102–105
  regulation of, 115–116
  size of, 103–104
  types of trade barriers in, 108–117
  workforce management in, 110
Gmail, 513
Goals
  explanation of, 304
  personal financial, A-35–A-36
Goal-setting theory, 307–308
Gold Bond brand, 427
Golden parachutes, 295
Goods. See also **Products**

business, 423–424
consumer, 423
Google Apps, 513
Government bonds, 562
Government-owned corporations, 172
Government regulation
  antitrust and business, A-5–A-6
  of financial markets, 579–580
  overview of, A-4–A-5
  of small businesses, 153
Gramm-Leach-Bliley Act, A-6
Grapevine, 342
Great Britain. See United Kingdom
Great Depression, 15, 67. See also Economic downturn/crisis
Great Value brand, 429
Greece
  entrepreneurship in, 190
  euro in, 108
  social and cultural differences in, 109
Greenland, Internet penetration rate in, 234, 235
Green marketing. See also Environment; Environmental issues
  explanation of, 49–50
  trends in, 18–19
Grid computing, 515
Grievances, 312
Grocery IQ app, 13
Gross domestic product (GDP)
  explanation of, 85
  in United States, 102, 103
Group of Eight (G8), 119
Growth stage, in product life cycle, 426–427
Guatemala
  CAFTA-DR and, 120
  Domino's Pizza in, 125
  Pollo Campero and, 406
Guerrilla marketing, 464–465
Guest worker visa programs, 114
Guitar Hero, 9

H

H-1B visa debate, 114
Hand-held devices, 504
Harassment, sexual, 58–59
Hard currencies, 108
Hardware, 503–504. See also Computers
Health care, rising costs of, 56
Health insurance
  employee, 296, 297
  explanation of, A-27
  health "rewards" programs and, 56

Health maintenance organizations (HMOs), A-27–A-28
Health "reward" programs, 56
Health service managers, 386
Hedge funds, 607
Hierarchy of needs (Maslow), 305
High-context cultures, 337
Hijacking, on high seas, 82
HIPAA Privacy Rule, 47
Hiring process. See Recruitment
Hispanics. See also Minorities
  as entrepreneurs, 192
  marketing to, 405
  in small businesses, 157–159
  statistics regarding, 20
HMOs. See Health maintenance organizations (HMOs)
Hobbies, A-55
Home-based businesses, 146–147
Home-based work programs, 300
Homeland Security Act, A-9
Home ownership, A-39–A-40
Homeowners' insurance, A-26
Homeowner's insurance rate hikes, A-18–A-19
Homes, recycled, 49
Honda's East Liberty facility, 355
Honduras, CAFTA-DR and, 120
Honesty, 40–41
Hong Kong
  entrepreneurship in, 190
  Internet penetration rate in, 235
  political climate in, 113
  shopping bag use in, 472
  virtual teams in, 331
Horizontal mergers, 171
Hotlines, employee, 44
Hot spots, 507
Hot Wheels, 429
How to Make Meetings Work (Straus and Doyle), 351
Hudson River, 19, 23, 213
Human factor, IDEO and, 325–326
Human resource management
  careers in, 386
Human resource management (continued)
  compensation and, 294–300
  employee motivation and, 304–310
  employee separation and, 300–304
  explanation of, 288
  labor-management relations and, 310–315
  orientation, training, and evaluation function of, 291–294
  raise requests and, 597

recruitment and selection
function of, 289–291
responsibilities of, 288–289
Human resources, 7–8
Human skills, 256
Hungary
entrepreneurship in, 190
European Union and, 120, 121
Hurricanes, homeowners insurance
rate hikes and, A-18–A-19
Hurricane Katrina
disaster loans following, 155
insurance companies and, A-18
revitalization following,
208–209
Hygiene factors, 306
Hyperinflation, 85

I

IASC. *See* **International Accounting
Standards Committee (IASC)**
Iceland
entrepreneurship in, 190
gross domestic product in, 103
Internet penetration rate in, 235
Ice storms, 6
Identity Theft and Assumption
Deterrence Act, A-9
IMC. *See* Integrated marketing
communications (IMC)
IMF. *See* International Monetary
Fund (IMF)
Immigration Act of 1990, 204
Implied warranties, A-11
Importers, 123–124
Imports. *See also* Trade
explanation of, 102
major U.S., 106–107
nontariff barriers on, 116–117
tariffs on, 116
Inbound telemarketing, 476
Income
demand and household, 71
in developing nations, 104
education level and, 50–51
in United States, A–32
Income statements, 534, 536
Incorporators, 167
Independent wholesaling intermediaries, 439–440
India
currency in, 108
direct investment in, 126
economic growth in, 90
as high-context culture, 337
industrial growth in, 71
Intel and, 591
Internet penetration rate in, 234

Internet use in, 235
multinational corporations in,
127
offshoring in, 21, 126
population in, 103
socialism in, 80
software piracy in, 116
technology products in, 127
Indirect exporting, 123
Individual branding, 433
Indonesia
political climate in, 113
population in, 103
technology products in, 127
Industrial entrepreneurs, 14–15
Industrial Revolution, 14
Inflation, 85–86
Infomercials, 470
Informal communication channel,
339, 342
Information
consumer right to, 52–53
empowerment by sharing,
326–327
explanation of, 498
Information systems. *See also* Computer networks; Computers;
Management information
systems (MISs)
for application service provider,
514
components of, 499, 500
computer-based, 499–500
databases and, 500
disaster recovery and backup
of, 512
for distributed workforce,
513–514
ethical issues affecting,
510–511
explanation of, 498, 499
management support, 502
on-demand computing,
514–515
operational support, 501–502
security issues affecting,
508–510
Information Technology Agreement
(ITA), 116
Information technology (IT). *See
also* Computer networks;
Computers
careers in, 555–556
for distributed workforce,
513–514
entrepreneurs in, 191
Informative advertising, 363, 466
Infrastructure, 111–112
Initial public offering (IPO), 566

Innovation
entrepreneurship and, 11
small businesses and, 149–150
through collaboration, 22
Insider trading, 580
Installations, 423
Institutional advertising, 465
Insurable interest, A-21–A-22
Insurable risk, A-22
Insurance
concepts related to, A-21–A-24
explanation of, A-21
personal, A-40
homeowner's insurance,
A-18–A-19, A-26
types of, A-25–A-29
Insurance companies
credit crisis of 2008 and, 578
explanation of, 574–575,
A-18–A-19
operation of, A-22
private, A-25
public, A-24–A-25
Intangible personal property, A-12
**Integrated marketing communica-
tions (IMC),** 460, 461
Integrity, 40–41
Intellectual property
explanation of, A-12–A-14
regulation of, 114, 116
Intel's nanometer technology, 591
Intensive distribution, 448
Interactivity, 217
Interest rates
for commerial loans, 571
global, 582–583
Intermittent production process, 359
Internal auditors, 527
Internal data, 399
Internal locus of control, 196–197
International accounting, 544–546
**International Accounting Standards
Board (IASB),** 546
International Accounting Standards
Committee (IASC), 544, 546
International business. *See* Global
marketplace
**International Financial Reporting
Standards (IFRS),** 546
International fiscal policy, 89
International law, A-4
explanation of, A-4
**International Monetary Fund
(IMF),** 119
**International Organization for
Standardization (ISO),** 376
International trade. *See* Trade
International unions, 310. *See also*
Labor unions

Internet. *See also* **E-business
(electronic business);** Web
sites
accounting process and, 533
advertising on, 466, 469
auctions on, 228
banks and, 573
business plan resources on, 200
cultural sensitivity on, 109
currency converters on, 108
employee training programs
on, 293
file-sharing services, A-13
focus groups using, 400
fraud on, 228–229
functions of, 230
home-based businesses and,
147
infrastructure and, 111
intellectual property violations
and, 114
legislation related to, A-8–A-9
payment systems on, 226
personal use during work, 41
privacy issues related to, 41,
227–228, A-8–A-9
recruitment via, 290, A-
56–A-57
retailing on, 441
safe online payment systems
on, 226
shopping on, 221–226
telecommuters and, 300
workplace use of, 511
Internet Service Providers (ISPs),
238
Internet penetration rate
Antigua and Barbuda, 235
Canada, 235
China, 234, 235, 242
Falkland Islands, 235
Greenland, 234, 235
India, 234
Norway, 235
Internet use
in China, 113, 122
in Europe, 128
in United States, 214, 234, 235
The Internship Bible (Princeton
Review), A-53
Internships, A-52–A-53
Interviews
job, A-61–A-64
Intranets, 506, 507
Intrapreneurship, 204–205
Intrinsic rewards, 304
Introduction, in business plan, A-47
Introduction stage, in product life
cycle, 26

Morale, 304
Mortgage pass-through securities, 563
Mortgage Reform and Anti-Predatory Lending Act of 2007, A-5
Mortgages
explanation of, 86, A-5, A-39
subprime, 563, A-40
subprime mortgage crisis and, 565, 574, 660
Motivation
equity theory and, 307
expectancy theory and, 306–307
goal setting theory and, 307–308
Herzberg's two-factor model of, 305–306
job design and, 308–309
managers' attitudes and, 309–310
Maslow's hierarchy of needs and, 305
overview of, 304
Motivator factors, 306
Motives, 304
Motor Carrier Act and Staggers Rail Act, A-6
Multidomestic business strategies, 128
Multinational corporation (MNC), 127
Municipal bonds, 562, 563
Muslims, religious beliefs of, 111
Mutual associations, A–25
Mutual funds, 575
Myanmar, 39

N

NAFTA. See North American Free Trade Agreement (NAFTA)
NAICS. See North American Industry Classification System (NAICS)
Nanometer microchips, 591
NASCAR pit crews, 325
Nasdaq stock market, 567, 569
National brand, 432
National debt, 90
National Environmental Policy Act, A-7
National Labor Relations Act of 1935 (Wagner Act), 311
National unions, 310. See also Labor unions
Native Americans, 158. See also Minorities

Natural resources, 6
Nearshoring, 21
Needs
achievement, 194
consumer, 390
Maslow's hierarchy of, 305
Negotiable instruments, A-11
Netbooks, 302, 504
Netherlands
banking in, 581
entrepreneurship in, 190
euro in, 108
European Union and, 121
gross domestic product in, 103
Internet penetration rate in, 235
multinational corporations in, 127
trade and, 104
Networking, 368
Net worth, 561, A-36
New-product development. See also Products
product introduction and, 426–427
stages in, 429–431
Newsgroups, 231
Newspapers, 467
New ventures. See also Businesses; Entrepreneurs; Entrepreneurship
business plans for, 199–200
financing for, 200–202
government support for, 203–204
ideas for, 197–199
New York Stock Exchange (NYSE), 254, 529, 546, 567–568, 581, 584
New Zealand
Internet penetration rate in, 235
online voting in, 214
trade barriers in, 108
Nicaragua, CAFTA-DR and, 120
Nigeria, 71, 103, 141
Noise, 338
Nondepository financial institutions, 574–575
Nonpersonal selling, 461
Nonprogrammed decisions, 267
Nonstore retailers, 440–442
Nontariff trade barriers, 116–117
Nontraditional students, A–65
Nonverbal communication, 339, 342–344
Norming, as team development stage, 334
North American Free Trade Agreement (NAFTA), 119–120, 130, 158, 408

North American Industry Classification System (NAICS), 408
North Carolina Beach Plan, A-19
North Korea, 80
Norway, 103, 190
Notebook computers, 503–504
Not-for-profit corporations, 169–170
Not-for-profit organizations
accounting in, 528
economic decisions by, 68
explanation of, 5–6
income statement for, 534
marketing by, 393–395, 401
Nutrition Labeling and Education Act, A-7

O

Obama's economic stimulus package, 67–68, 295
Objectives, 265
Observational studies, 400
Odd pricing, 485
Odyssey minivan, 355
Offensive listening, 339
Office, Microsoft, 302, 513
Offset agreement, 123–124
Offshoring
explanation of, 21, 126
working conditions and, 39
Off-the-job training, 292–293
Ohio, Honda's East Liberty facility in, 355
Oil, demand for, 70, 71
Oil price swings, 74
Oligopoly, 77–78
On-demand computing, 514–515
101 Dalmatians, 389
One-on-one marketing, 413
Online communities, 230–231
Online payment systems, 226
Online résumés, A-60
Online shopping. See Business-to-consumer (B2C) e-business; E-business (electronic business)
On-the-job training, 292
Open market operations, 578
Open-source XML (Extensible Markup Language) standards, 220
Operating activities, 525
Operating plans. See Financial plans
Operating system, 505
Operational planning, 260–261
Operational support systems, 501–502

Optimism, 194–195
Oral communication, 338–340
Order processing, 449, 475
Organic lunches, 181
Organization charts, 273
Organization for Economic Cooperation and Development Anti-Bribery Convention, 113
Organization marketing, 396
Organizations. See also Businesses
committee, 277
delegation in, 274–275
departmentalization in, 273–274, 276
explanation of, 272
line, 275–276
line-and-staff, 276, 277
matrix, 277–278
not-for-profit, 5–6, 68, 393–394
qualities of admired, 24
regulatory environment for, A-4–A-6
role in shaping ethical conduct, 42–44
Organizing, 257
Organizing process, steps in, 272–273
OSHA Act, A-7
Outbound telemarketing, 476
Outdoor advertising, 469
Outsourcing
of airline maintenance, 375
Boeing and, 360
disadvantages of, 368
explanation of, 21, 303–304
to small businesses, 149
Overseas divisions, 127
Over-the-counter selling, 474
Owner's equity, 536, 537
Ownership utility, 391

P

Pacific (San Francisco) Stock Exchange, 569
Pacing programs, 204, 206–207
Packaging, 435–436
Paid time off (PTO), 297, 298
Pakistan, 103,
Palm Pre, A-1, A-2
Paraguay, 119
Partnerships
explanation of, 18, 164–165
joint venture as, 171
Patents, 114, A1-A-2, A-13
Patient Journey Punch Card, 325
Pawnshops, 77, 78

International Index

Sweden
    entrepreneurship in, 190
    gross domestic product in, 103
    Internet penetration rate in, 235
    socialism in, 80
    socialist features in, 80
Switzerland
    banking in, 581
    entrepreneurship in, 190
    flextime in, 299
    gross domestic product in, 103
    as low-context culture, 337

T

Taiwan
    currency in, 108
    Gateway in, 126
Tariffs, 115
Teams, 110
Thailand
    entrepreneurship in, 189, 190
Thailand *(continued)*
    social and cultural differences
        in, 109
    technology products in, 127
Toronto Stock Exchange, 569
Trade
    balance of, 106
    contractual agreements and,
        125–127
    international accounting
        standards and, 546
    measures of, 105–108
    overview of, 102
    reasons for, 102–105
Trade barriers
    economic differences as,
        111–113
    nontariff, 116–117
    organizations to ease, 117–121
    political and legal differences
        as, 113–116

reasons for, 108, 109
    social and cultural differences
        as, 109–111
    tariffs as, 116
Trademarks, 114
Turkey
    entrepreneurship in, 190
    political climate in, 113

U

UBS AG, 581
Ugg, 3–4
United Arab Emirates
    entrepreneurship in, 190
United Kingdom
    advertising in, 116
    African debt relief from, 119
    American colonies and, 13, 14
    banking in, 581
    corporations in, 165
    countertrade in, 124
    currency in, 108
    entrepreneurship in, 189, 190
    exchange rate in, 599
    Fair Trade products in, 52
    Industrial Revolution in, 14
    Internet use in, 235
    as member of Group of
        Eight, 119
    multinational corporations
        in, 127
    Organization for Economic
        Cooperation and Develop-
        ment Anti-Bribery Convention
        and, 113
    social and cultural differences
        in, 109
    trade in, 104
    Ugg sales in, 3
United States
    African debt relief from, 119
    aging of population in, 20, 404

business history in, 12–17
CAFTA-DR and, 120
commercial banks in,
    570–571
countertrade in, 124
coupon use in, 471
demographic information for,
    404–405
e-business in, 214, 234, 235
employment rate in, 86–87
entrepreneurship in, 11,
    189, 190
exchange rate in, 107, 108
federal budget in, 90–91
gross domestic product in,
    102, 103
gross national product in, 85
interest rates in, 583
Internet penetration rate in,
    235
Internet use in, 214, 234, 235
labor unions in, 310–311,
    314, 315
as low-context culture, 337
as member of Group of
    Eight, 119
merchandise exports and import
    in, 106, 107
merchandise imports and
    exports in, 106–107
multinational corporations
    in, 127
mutual funds in, 570–571
not-for-profit organizations
    in, 5–6
Organization for Economic
    Cooperation and Develop-
    ment Anti-Bribery Convention
    and, 113
personal space in, 337
personal values in, 110–111
plastic bag use in, 472
political climate in, 113

population in, 103
software piracy in, 116
tariffs in, 116
telecommuting in, 300
television reach in, 467
trade and, 123
transportation methods in, 450
vacation time in, 110
University of Toronto, 221
Uruguay
    entrepreneurship in, 190
    MERCOSUR and, 119
Uruguay Round, 118
U.S. dollar, 107, 108, 433

V

Values, as barrier to trade,
    110–111
Venezuela, 189, 190
Vietnam
    accounting in, 545
    Intel's assembly test facility in,
        591
    software piracy in, 116
    technology products in, 127
Virtual teams, 331, 332

W

Web sites, 122
Workforce, 21
World Bank, 118–119
World Factbook (CIA), 121
**World Trade Organization
(WTO),** 118

Y

Yen, 108
Yugoslavia, former, 113
Waterford Wedgwood, 112
World Economic Forum panel, 565